Fodor's 05

GREAT BRITAIN

Where to Stay and Eat
for All Budgets

Must-See Sights
and Local Secrets

Ratings You Can Trust

Fodor's Travel Publications   New York, Toronto, London, Sydney, Auckland
www.fodors.com

FODOR'S GREAT BRITAIN 2005

Editor: Linda Cabasin

Editorial Production: David Downing
Editorial Contributors: Robert Andrews, Catherine Belonogoff, Jacqueline Brown, Nick Bruno, James Gracie, Satu Hummasti, Julius Honnor, Kate Hughes, Shona Main, Roger Thomas, Julie Tomasz, Amy Wang, Alex Wijeratna
Maps: David Lindroth *cartographer;* Bob Blake and Rebecca Baer, *map editors*
Design: Fabrizio La Rocca, *creative director;* Guido Caroti, *art director;* Melanie Marin, *senior picture editor*
Production/Manufacturing: Angela McLean
Cover Photo (Bakewell, Derbyshire): Catherine Karnow

COPYRIGHT

Copyright © 2005 by Fodors LLC

Fodor's is a registered trademark of Random House, Inc.

All rights reserved under International and Pan-American Copyright Conventions. Published in the United States by Fodor's Travel Publications, a unit of Fodors LLC, a subsidiary of Random House, Inc., and simultaneously in Canada by Random House of Canada Limited, Toronto. Distributed by Random House, Inc., New York.

No maps, illustrations, or other portions of this book may be reproduced in any form without written permission from the publisher.

ISBN 1–4000–1414–X

ISSN 0071–6405

SPECIAL SALES

This book is available for special discounts for bulk purchases for sales promotions or premiums. Special editions, including personalized covers, excerpts of existing books, and corporate imprints, can be created in large quantities for special needs. For more information, write to Special Markets/Premium Sales, 1745 Broadway, MD 6-2, New York, New York 10019, or e-mail specialmarkets@randomhouse.com.

AN IMPORTANT TIP & AN INVITATION

Although all prices, opening times, and other details in this book are based on information supplied to us at press time, changes occur all the time in the travel world, and Fodor's cannot accept responsibility for facts that become outdated or for inadvertent errors or omissions. So **always confirm information when it matters,** especially if you're making a detour to visit a specific place. Your experiences—positive and negative—matter to us. If we have missed or misstated something, **please write to us.** We follow up on all suggestions. Contact the Great Britain editor at editors@fodors.com or c/o Fodor's at 1745 Broadway, New York, New York 10019.

PRINTED IN THE UNITED STATES OF AMERICA

10 9 8 7 6 5 4 3 2 1

DESTINATION GREAT BRITAIN

Never mind whether or not you've been to Great Britain before—for the English-speaking traveler, to come here is to come *back* here. Even before you arrive, its images are imprinted on your consciousness. In London, the dome of St. Paul's is iconically familiar, as are Big Ben and the Thames. Beyond the capital, an afternoon at any stately home, whether in Yorkshire or Kent, reveals another side of Britain. The house is so splendid it must be a mirage, the gardens headily perfumed by flowers. A spot of sun emerges, and you half expect to encounter a character out of English literature. The experience is all the finer because you know that wherever you find yourself on this island, you may come upon some other grace note around the next bend. It may be an enchanted castle or a village whose clocks seem to have stopped two centuries ago, a brooding moor or a glittering loch rimmed by craggy peaks, a half-timber Tudor house or a long-distance footpath where you can tramp for miles with a view of the sea. Wherever you go, have a wonderful trip!

Tim Jarrell, Publisher

CONTENTS

On the Road with Fodor's *F7*
About This Book *F8*
What's Where *F12*
Great Itineraries *F18*
When to Go *F22*

On the Calendar *F23*
Pleasures & Pastimes *F27*
Fodor's Choice *F30*
Smart Travel Tips *F37*

1 London 1

Exploring London *5*
Where to Eat *52*
Where to Stay *67*
Nightlife & the Arts *82*

Sports & the Outdoors *90*
Shopping *92*
London A to Z *102*

2 The Southeast 110

Canterbury to Dover *114*
Rye to Glyndebourne *126*
Brighton to East Grinstead *133*

Masterpieces & Moats *147*
Southeast A to Z *156*

3 The South 159

From Winchester to
   Southampton *162*
Isle of Wight *178*
Salisbury to the New Forest *182*

Bournemouth to Lyme Regis
   195
The South A to Z *206*

4 The West Country 209

Bristol to North Devon *212*
Cornwall *229*
South Devon to Cadbury Castle
   245

The West Country A to Z *262*

5 The Thames Valley 265

Windsor & Environs *268*
To Henley & Beyond *279*
Oxford *283*

Blenheim Palace to Althorp *293*
Thames Valley A to Z *302*

6 Shakespeare Country 305

Stratford-upon-Avon *308*
Around Shakespeare Country
   321

Shakespeare Country A to Z
   329

7 Bath & the Cotswolds 332

Bath & Environs *336*
The Cotswolds *350*
Gloucester to the Forest of
   Dean *374*

Bath & the Cotswolds A to Z
   381

8 The Welsh Borders 385

Birmingham 388
From Worcester to Dudley 400

From Shrewsbury to Chester 410
Welsh Borders A to Z 421

9 Wales 424

North Wales 428
Mid-Wales 445

South Wales 454
Wales A to Z 467

10 Lancashire & the Peaks 471

Manchester 474
Liverpool 487
The Peak District 497

Lancashire & the Peaks A to Z
507

11 The Lake District 511

The Southern Lakes 516
Penrith & the Northern Lakes
533

Lake District A to Z 542

12 East Anglia 547

Cambridge 551
From Ely to Bury St. Edmunds
567
Colchester & the Suffolk Coast
575

Norwich to North Norfolk 583
Lincoln, Boston & Stamford
593
East Anglia A to Z 599

13 Yorkshire 603

West Yorkshire & Brontë
Country 607
The Yorkshire Dales 618
York 625

York Environs 633
The North Yorkshire Coast 637
The North York Moors 645
Yorkshire A to Z 649

14 The Northeast 653

Durham, Newcastle &
Environs 656
Hadrian's Wall Country 670

The Far Northeast Coast 678
The Northeast A to Z 683

15 Scotland 686

Edinburgh 692
Glasgow 715
The Borders 726

Aberdeen & Royal Deeside 732
Inverness & Loch Ness 740
Scotland A to Z 746

Understanding Great Britain 752

Great Britain at a Glance 753
The Curtain Rises on the
   Performing Arts 755
Splendid Stones & British
   Architecture 759

Books & Movies 764
Chronology 768

Index 772

Maps

Great Britain F10–F11
London 10–11
London Postal Districts 12
Where to Eat in London 54–55
Where to Stay in London 70–71
London Shopping 94–95
The Southeast 118–119
Canterbury 120
Brighton 135
The South 168–169
Winchester 170
Salisbury 183
The West Country 218–219
Plymouth 247
Exeter 257
The Thames Valley 270–271
Oxford 284
Shakespeare Country 310
Stratford-upon-Avon 312
Bath Environs 340
Bath 342
The Cotswolds 352
The Forest of Dean 375

The Welsh Borders 391
Birmingham 392
Shrewsbury 412
Wales 430–431
Cardiff 455
Lancashire & the Peaks 476
Manchester 478
Liverpool 489
The Lake District 518–519
East Anglia 552–553
Cambridge 555
Norwich 585
Lincolnshire 594
Yorkshire 608–609
York 627
The Northeast 658
Durham 660
Scotland 694–695
Edinburgh 698
Glasgow 717
The Borders 728
Aberdeen & Royal Deeside 733
Inverness & Environs 741

CloseUps

Where to See the Royals 13
Where to Refuel Around Town
   62
All Hail the Regent 136
Visiting the Treasure Houses 151
In Search of Jane Austen 172
Hardy's Dorset 200
All About Arthur 231
Bath's Georgian Architecture 344
Arts and Crafts in the
   Cotswolds 360

Cotswold Stone 370
The Venice of the North 394
The Language of Cymru 449
Stoke-on-Trent: The Potteries
   498
Poetry, Prose & the Lakes 536
Punting on the Cam 566
Whitby Jet 642
The Jarrow Crusade 670
Clans & Tartans 744

ON THE ROAD WITH FODOR'S

A trip takes you out of yourself. Concerns of life at home disappear, driven away by more immediate thoughts—about, say, what marvels will beguile the next day, or where you'll have dinner. That's where Fodor's comes in. We make sure that you know all your options, so that you don't miss something that's around the bend just because you didn't know it was there. Because the best memories of your trip might well have nothing to do with what you came to Great Britain to see, we guide you to sights large and small all over the country. You might set out to see the Tower of London, but back at home you find yourself unable to forget sharing beer and conversation at an ancient pub. With Fodor's at your side, serendipitous discoveries are never far away.

Our success in showing you every corner of Great Britain is a credit to our extraordinary writers.

Longtime contributor Robert Andrews loves warm beer and soggy moors, but hates shopping malls and the sort of weather when you're not sure if it's raining—all of which he found in abundance while updating the South, West Country, and Bath & the Cotswolds. He writes and revises other guidebooks and has also penned his own guide to Devon and Cornwall.

San Francisco–born travel writer Catherine Belonogoff moved to London in 2000. She has worked on several Fodor's guides, including *Europe*. Catherine updated London lodging and Smart Travel Tips as well as the Thames Valley, Shakespeare Country, and East Anglia, adding a wealth of new discoveries.

Writer and editor Jacqueline Brown, a London resident for more than 20 years, has found the best and the quirkiest places around the city, some of which she revealed in *Fodor's Around London with Kids*. Jacqueline also updates *Fodor's London*, and she shares her insights in the Exploring and Shopping sections of the London chapter.

Nick Bruno, a freelance writer, editor, and translator, contributes to many online and print publications. He updated portions of the Scotland chapter.

James Gracie, who updated the Edinburgh and Borders section of Scotland, has worked as a travel writer for more than a decade. His articles have appeared in the *Sunday Herald* and Scottish magazines.

Julius Honnor, who revised Sports & the Outdoors in the London chapter, lives in the city. His Fodor's territory also covered the Southeast and the Lake District. His work for other guidebooks has taken him to Italy and other places.

Writer and editor Kate Hughes spent her formative years in Yorkshire and studied classical literature in Liverpool. She enjoyed traveling the Northeast coast, but she also checked out the urban pleasures of Manchester in updating the Welsh Borders, Lancashire & the Peaks, Yorkshire, and Northeast chapters.

Shona Main, who updated the Scotland chapter, gave up law to be a journalist. She now writes about travel and culture. Her work for other guidebooks has taken her to Norway and Italy.

A former Fodor's editor and incorrigible globe-trotter, Julie Tomasz lives in London and works as a freelance writer and editor. Her enviable assignment was updating Nightlife & the Arts for London.

Always hoping to entertain—and surprise—his readers, longtime Fodor's contributor Roger Thomas spends almost every minute tracking down the latest and the best of Wales. He has to: he's editor of *A View of Wales* magazine.

A Londoner born and bred, Alex Wijeratna updated the London dining section. With his English/Sri Lankan roots, Alex knows that the real flavor of London is found in its ethnic diversity. He has written for newspapers, including the *Times*.

ABOUT THIS BOOK

The best source for travel advice is a like-minded friend who's just been where you're headed. But with or without that friend, you'll be in great shape to find your way around your destination once you learn to find your way around your Fodor's guide.

SELECTION

Our goal is to cover the best properties, sights, and activities in their category, as well as the most interesting communities to visit. We make a point of including local food-lovers' hot spots as well as neighborhood options, and we avoid all that's touristy unless it's really worth your time. You can go on the assumption that everything in this book is recommended wholeheartedly by our writers and editors. Flip to On the Road with Fodor's to learn more about who they are. It goes without saying that no property pays to be included.

RATINGS

Orange stars ★ denote sights and properties that our editors and writers consider the very best in the area covered by the entire book. These, the best of the best, are listed in the Fodor's Choice section in the front of the book. Black stars ★ highlight the sights and properties we deem Highly Recommended, the don't-miss sights within any region. In cities, sights pinpointed with numbered map bullets ❶ in the margins tend to be more important than those without bullets.

SPECIAL SPOTS

Pleasures & Pastimes and text on chapter-title pages focus on experiences that reveal the spirit of the destination. Off the Beaten Path sights may be out of the way or quirky; all are worthwhile. When the munchies hit, look for Need a Break? suggestions.

TIME IT RIGHT

Check On the Calendar up front and chapters' Timing sections for weather and crowd overviews and best days and times to visit.

SEE IT ALL

Use Fodor's exclusive Great Itineraries as a model for your trip. Either follow those that begin the book, or mix regional itineraries from several chapters. In cities, Good Walks guide you to important sights in each neighborhood; ☞ indicates the starting points of walks and itineraries in the text and on the map.

BUDGET WELL

Hotel and restaurant price categories from £ to ££££ are defined in the opening pages of each chapter—expect to find a balanced selection for every budget. For attractions, we always give standard adult admission fees; reductions are usually available for children, students, and senior citizens. Look in Discounts & Deals in Smart Travel Tips for information on destination-wide ticket schemes. Want to pay with plastic? AE, DC, MC, V following restaurant and hotel listings indicate whether American Express, Diner's Club, MasterCard, or Visa are accepted.

BASIC INFO

Smart Travel Tips lists travel essentials for the entire area covered by the book; city- and region-specific basics end each chapter. To find the best way to get around, see the transportation section; see individual modes of travel ("Car Travel," "Train Travel") for details.

ON THE MAPS	**Maps** throughout the book show you what's where and help you find your way around. Black and orange numbered bullets ❶ ❶ in the text correlate to bullets on maps.
BACKGROUND	We give background information within the chapters in the course of explaining sights as well as in **CloseUp** boxes and in **Understanding Great Britain** at the end of the book. To get in the mood, review the **Books & Movies** section. The **chronology** can be invaluable.
FIND IT FAST	Within the book, chapters are arranged in a roughly south to north direction, starting with London. Chapters are divided into small regions, within which towns are covered in geographical order; attractive routes and interesting places between towns are flagged as **En Route.** Heads at the top of each page help you find what you need.
DON'T FORGET	**Restaurants** are open for lunch and dinner daily unless we state otherwise; we mention dress only when there's a specific requirement and reservations only when they're essential or not accepted—it's always best to book ahead. **Hotels** have private baths, phones, TVs, and air-conditioning and operate on the European Plan (a.k.a. EP, meaning without meals) or, if indicated in the service information after the review, CP (Continental Plan, with Continental breakfast), BP (Breakfast Plan, with full breakfast), or MAP (Modified American Plan, with breakfast and dinner). We list facilities but not whether you'll be charged extra to use them, so when pricing accommodations, find out what's included.
SYMBOLS	

Many Listings		Hotels & Restaurants	
★	Fodor's Choice	🏨	Hotel
★	Highly recommended	🛏	Number of rooms
⊠	Physical address	♨	Facilities
✛	Directions	⏼⊘⏼	Meal plans
⬠	Mailing address	✕	Restaurant
🕾	Telephone	⌑	Reservations
🖶	Fax	🏛	Dress code
⊕	On the Web	↘	Smoking
✎	E-mail	⑄⚲	BYOB
🎟	Admission fee	✕🏨	Hotel with restaurant that warrants a visit
☉	Open/closed times		
▶	Start of walk/itinerary	**Other**	
ⓤ	Underground (tube) stations	ℭ	Family-friendly
		🛈	Contact information
⊟	Credit cards	⇨	See also
		⊠	Branch address
		☞	Take note

WHAT'S WHERE

Britain isn't large, but it contains enormous scenic diversity, from the grassy downs of the South to the fjordlike lochs and heather-covered mountains of Scotland. This section reflects the order of the chapters in this guide. London, the capital of Great Britain, is first, followed by regions south, west, and north of London, including Wales. Scotland, the farthest north, is the final region.

① London

The city of Big Ben is one of the most exciting places on the planet, with its glittering arts scene, outrageous restaurants created by superstar chefs, and stylish boutiques. Yet despite the buzz, Europe's largest metropolis remains the bastion of much that the British traditionally hold most dear. Have tea at the Savoy, stroll through Hyde Park, ogle the jewels in the Tower of London, or take in the British Museum or the Tate Modern. As you explore, the national character begins to reveal itself. Treasure troves such as Kensington Palace and Apsley House, once home to the duke of Wellington, exhibit the national fondness for heroes—after all, this was the duke who defeated Napoléon at Waterloo (and gave his name to Wellies, essential foot protection against British downpours). Sacred places such as Westminster Abbey and St. Paul's are laden with reminders of centuries of history. Landmarks such as the Globe Theatre, a copy of Shakespeare's original, recall the British way with words and gift for theater.

The trick to taming this vast metropolis is to regard it as a number of villages. They include the heraldic splendor of Westminster, the glamour of Kensington and Belgravia, the cosmopolitan charms of Soho, the ancient core of the City, and the museums and cultural centers of the South Bank. No matter which district you adopt as your home-away-from-home, London's contrasts can best be savored by strolling from one neighborhood to another. And as the time-honored ceremony of the Changing of the Guard outside Buckingham Palace proves, London's trends may come and go, but the essence of the city will endure.

② The Southeast

With fields and orchards unrolling toward the Channel coast, this compact region, including Kent, Surrey, and East and West Sussex, is filled with places that even the British consider quintessentially English: eccentric, vibrant Brighton by the sea, with the fairy-tale Royal Pavilion; the extraordinary medieval castles of Bodiam, Leeds, and Hever; Lewes, with its secret lanes and immense beech trees. The Southeast holds major icons, from Christ Church in Canterbury, the beloved cathedral made famous by the death of Archbishop Thomas à Becket and immortalized by Geoffrey Chaucer, to the white cliffs of Dover, cherished symbol of the realm. Here, too, are notable examples of that triumph of British civilization, the stately country house, often with splendid gardens that equal the treasures within: Knole, Ightham Mote, Penshurst Place, Sissinghurst. The closeness of this area to the European continent means that history has a strong presence here. The Romans, Saxons, and Normans left their mark as invaders, in sites from Hastings to

Chichester; this is where William the Conqueror landed in 1066. Castles and fortifications, from medieval to World War II vintage, line the coast. Because of the Southeast's closeness to London, you can make easy excursions and round up a delightful choice of day trips.

③ The South

If Jane Austen's countryside "sweet to the eye and mind" seems familiar, it may be because so much of British history has been played out in this area southwest of London. Thousands of years ago, stone monuments such as Avebury and Stonehenge, and earth-and-stone hill forts such as Maiden Castle, rose on the plains, and these mysterious prehistoric sites attract endless speculation. Winchester, with its imposing cathedral, was England's capital until the 11th century. Salisbury, too, has its cathedral, with its famous spire, captured in the paintings of John Constable. Stourhead and other stately homes, such as Wilton House and Longleat House, evoke the traditions of past eras. Make a pilgrimage to Jane Austen Country or travel to Dorset—immortalized by Thomas Hardy as his part-fact, part-fiction county of Wessex—to get away from the madding crowd. During Britain's seafaring heyday, the coast here was essential to both commercial and military concerns, with Portsmouth leading the way. Today the Portsmouth Historic Dockyard interprets this past, displaying a vessel from the Tudor navy and Admiral Lord Nelson's flagship, HMS *Victory*. Other destinations in the South remain highly popular, from the peaceful shores of the Isle of Wight, with its Victorian flavor, to the New Forest.

④ The West Country

The southwestern peninsula made up of the counties of Somerset, Devon, and Cornwall is one of the most beautiful places in Britain. Outside cathedral towns such as Wells and Exeter, maritime centers such as Plymouth, and tourist-laden fishing villages, however, the region can resemble an ancient ghost town. Scattered throughout the countryside are eroded castles and enigmatic prehistoric stone structures such as the Stanton Drew Circles. The brooding heaths and moors of Exmoor and Dartmoor add to this sense of separateness. To some, the area's mystery is embodied by the legend of King Arthur, who is thought to have been born in Tintagel, to have battled at Bodmin Moor, and to have been buried in Glastonbury. Begin with Bristol—gateway to the West Country and historic shipping port. You'll find that on your way down to Land's End, at the southernmost point of the peninsula, every zig and zag of the road reveals rugged moorlands, lush river valleys, and festive coastal resorts. The towns of St. Ives and Newlyn have attracted artists and writers for generations; the galleries of the Tate St. Ives celebrate this legacy. The Eden Project, with its vast conservatories, shelters more than 70,000 plants. You may have to remind yourself that you're in Britain as you gaze at the palm trees, white beaches, and turquoise waters of Cornwall. Although crowds arrive in summer, it's still a treat to explore the coastal towns and bays—if you stray far enough, you'll find countryside where the sense of isolation can be exciting.

⑤ The Thames Valley

The rose-cloaked countryside that flanks this stretch of old father Thames west and north of London has become something of a weekend destination for sophisticated urbanites. Rarefied social occasions persist: the annual meeting at Ascot, the world's most famous horse race, and the Henley Royal Regatta, rowing's toniest competition. Windsor, the largest inhabited castle in the world and home to eight successive royal houses, is a popular retreat for Queen Elizabeth. Year-round, the top magnet remains spired-and-turreted Oxford—seat of England's oldest university. Lewis Carroll invented Alice along Oxford's River Cherwell. The duke of Marlborough's Blenheim Palace, close to Oxford, epitomizes baroque splendor. Many other great houses and gardens are nearby, from Woburn Abbey to Althorp, where Diana, the late Princess of Wales, is buried. Close to London, St. Albans has a notable cathedral and reminders of the Roman past. But before you assume that these well-groomed riverbanks belong only to the titled and entitled, remember that Western Europe took a bold step toward democracy here when King John signed the Magna Carta at Runnymede in 1215.

⑥ Shakespeare Country

Admirers of Shakespeare, and even those with only a passing acquaintance with the Bard, cannot resist the lure of the countryside in which he grew up, worked, and—after a career in London—died. The center is Stratford-upon-Avon, 100 mi northwest of the capital. The man dominates this town, and Elizabethan-era sites bear witness to his days here—Shakespeare's Birthplace and Anne Hathaway's Cottage, to name two highlights. The Royal Shakespeare Theatre presents the master's works by the River Avon, and attending a play here is an experience not to be missed. Warwickshire, the ancient county of which Stratford is the southern nexus, is a gentle landscape of thatch-roof cottages, sleepy villages, and sun-dappled meadows. Heaping doses of history await: Warwick Castle, with its towers and turbulent history, has been called "medieval England in stone," and Kenilworth Castle, although in ruins, is equally evocative. The manor houses of Charlecote Park and Baddesley Clinton, and other stately piles, are additional landmarks.

⑦ Bath & the Cotswolds

Begin with the golden-stone city of Bath—where you can see, as the eminent writer Nigel Nicolson put it, "18th-century England in all its urban glory." After following in the footsteps of social organizer Beau Nash and novelist Jane Austen through Bath's splendid terraces and crescents (or taking in the pleasures of the modern Thermae Bath Spa), head northward to Regency-era Cheltenham, another spa town, to embark on a tour of the Cotswolds. In the peaceful hamlets, stone cottages, old coaching inns, tidy gardens, and tile-roof farmsteads add up to pure rural delight. The many stone churches are a legacy of the age when Cotswold wool made merchants here rich. The finest Cotswold towns include Chipping Campden, Upper Slaughter, and Bourton-on-the-Water, but let the back roads lead you to your own discoveries. Stow-on-the-Wold has antiques shops, although you can't expect bargains: these heavenly tracts are as refined as they are pastoral. Be sure to explore such beauty spots as Hidcote Manor Gardens and Owlpen, and treasure houses such as Sudeley Castle and Chastleton House. Near urban Gloucester is the sylvan Forest of Dean, ideal for hikers.

8 The Welsh Borders

Some of England's loveliest countryside rises and drops over the hills and valleys of Shropshire, Herefordshire, and Cheshire. The border with Wales stretches from the town of Chepstow on the Severn estuary in the south to the well-preserved medieval city of Chester in the north. Brooding fortresses such as Goodrich Castle loom over the landscape, a reminder that the border was not always tranquil. Herefordshire, in the south, has rich, rolling countryside and river valleys, gradually opening out to Shropshire's high hills and plateaus. Half-timber buildings line elegant avenues in Ludlow, a center of fine dining. A visit to Shrewsbury, with its churches and medieval buildings, is a bit of time travel. In the north, the gentler Cheshire plain is dairy country, dotted with small villages and market towns, full of ancient black-and-white, half-timber buildings. A highlight for some is the Black Country, named for the environmental damage, now mostly erased, from 19th-century industry. From Shrewsbury to Chester, you'll find monuments of the Industrial Revolution, including the museums at Ironbridge Gorge. Gateway to the region from the British heartland is the city of Birmingham, now undergoing a cultural renaissance.

9 Wales

On the western border of England, Wales is a country of outstanding natural beauty, with mountain scenery in its interior and long stretches of magnificent coastline. With the exception of the engaging capital, Cardiff, and Swansea, Wales's second-largest city, the country has few large urban areas. What it does have, from north to south, are pretty villages, attractive market towns, traffic-free roads, and fine countryside. Few other regions are as free of modern encroachment, and many people head for the open spaces of the three national parks: Snowdonia with its footpath-beribboned heights, Pembrokeshire Coast, and Brecon Beacons. Beyond the parks, other discoveries beckon: numerous medieval castles such as Conwy and Caernarfon, the slate caverns at Blaenau Ffestiniog, seaside resorts, restored 19th-century mining villages, the glorious Bodnant Garden, the Victorian spa of Llandrindod Wells, and steam train rides through Snowdonia and central Wales.

10 Lancashire & the Peaks

This northwest region of England witnessed the birth of the Industrial Revolution, when Manchester and Liverpool flourished as major manufacturing centers. Today Manchester is cleaning up a faded industrial landscape and polishing its Victorian treasures as the city experiences renewed cultural energy. The restored warehouses at Liverpool's Albert Dock hold shops and restaurants that interpret the port city's maritime history, and the Tate Liverpool displays cutting-edge art. Fans of the Beatles can check out Liverpool tours tracing the Beatles' earliest days and visit 20 Forthlin Road and Mendips, home of the young Paul McCartney and John Lennon, respectively. As a respite from the urban scene, escape to the emerald tranquillity of the Peak District and Derbyshire's Wye Valley—home to pretty towns such as Bakewell and three supremely regal houses: Chatsworth, Haddon Hall, and Hardwick Hall. The Peak District draws many hikers, who delight in the area's rocky outcrops.

(11) The Lake District

Bordered by Scotland and the waters of Solway Firth, Morecambe Bay, and the Irish Sea, this is a startlingly beautiful area of craggy hills, wild moorland, stone-built villages, and glittering silvery lakes—more than 100 of them. The Lake District, now a national park, has been one of the most popular tourist destinations in Britain since the beginning of the 19th century, when poets and painters—William Wordsworth, who was born and lived here, and J. M. W. Turner foremost among them—extolled the region's allure. High points of any tour of Cumbria include Wordsworth's homes at Rydal, Grasmere, and Cockermouth, John Ruskin's abode at Coniston, Beatrix Potter's tiny house near Hawkshead, and boating on Derwentwater and Windermere. Some 250 days of rain a year ensure that such noted spots as Keswick, on the shores of Derwentwater, are pleasingly verdant. Follow in the footsteps of Samuel Taylor Coleridge, John Ruskin, and Thomas De Quincey and go for a ramble. Everywhere you'll find places that inspired great poems about subjects as humble as daffodils.

(12) East Anglia

This large knob of land jutting out into the North Sea has charms that are endearing for their subtlety. Its flat, arable lands and gentle forests have been spared urbanization by the simple fact that the region is not on the way to anywhere but itself. The region's gateway is Cambridge, one of the world's leading centers of learning. Take a stroll among its medieval colleges or go punting on the River Cam. Then there are the glorious cathedrals of Ely and Norwich and time-warp towns such as 18th-century King's Lynn or medieval Lavenham, unchanged since it boomed with the wool trade five centuries ago. Some aristocratic families built magnificent houses here, including Norfolk's stunning Holkham Hall, Blickling, and Houghton Hall. Norfolk has a glorious north coast, with golden, sandy beaches and dark fir trees guarding the shore. You can go boating in the canals and fens of the reed-bordered Broads. Increasing numbers of Londoners are heading to this area not for nature, however, but for the antiques shops and gastro-pubs. In the Suffolk countryside, rich farmlands are dotted with villages of thatched, pink-washed cottages. Immortalized in paintings by Thomas Gainsborough and Constable, the sylvan countryside all around is splendid.

(13) Yorkshire

A wilder part of England in the north, the heather-covered Yorkshire Moors—notable for open spaces, wide horizons, and hills that appear to rear violently out of the plain—were inspiration for the Brontë sisters, who, in the hamlet of Haworth, wrote *Jane Eyre* and *Wuthering Heights*. The moors are linked to the contrasting landscape of the Yorkshire Dales, with their green valleys, burgeoning rivers, waterfalls, and sights such as the ruins of Bolton Priory and the castles at Skipton and Richmond. It would be almost unthinkable to journey here without paying a call on the ancient city of York—a must-see for those interested in impressive medieval monuments, including York Minster, the largest Gothic church in the country. To the north are the seaside resort of Scarborough, the cliff-lined harbor at Whitby, and the splendid sights of the North York Moors, including picture-perfect Hutton-le-Hole, the soaring, evocative ruins of Rievaulx Abbey, and Castle Howard, one of Britain's most famous treasure houses.

(14) The Northeast

The gateway to Scotland, this remote, less-populated corner of England is the climax to all that is grand and wild in the nation's footpath-crossed northerly reaches. For centuries, Northeasterners struggled to keep outsiders out. Barbarian attacks from the north were repelled by mammoth fortifications such as Hadrian's Wall, the Roman Empire's northernmost boundary. You can now walk along the wall and explore its ancient forts. On the stark, rugged Northumberland coastline, towering castles such as Bamburgh and Dunstanburgh held marauders at bay; the one at Lindisfarne, also known as Holy Island, sheltered one of England's earliest Christian communities as well. Alnwick Castle, with its resplendent interior and gardens, grew up around a Norman keep. Durham Cathedral, the stone centerpiece of one of England's most memorable medieval cities, was described as "half church of God, half castle 'gainst the Scot." Newcastle is the region's liveliest city, reinvigorated with ambitious cultural centers, but it also holds reminders of the Industrial Revolution, another force that shaped the Northeast.

(15) Scotland

North Sea to Irish Sea, Highlands to Lowlands, the landscapes of Scotland—lush woodlands, windswept moors, lochs as deep as the imagination—may take your breath away. In the southeast, Edinburgh is a gloriously dignified capital, with its castle providing spectacular views. The Old Town district displays evidence of its colorful medieval history, and the 18th-century classical buildings of the New Town are an elegant contrast. An excursion to St. Andrews is a pilgrimage for golf aficionados. To the west of the capital is Glasgow, a Victorian powerhouse whose full-fledged urban renaissance crackles with energy. The Borders area—immortalized in the tales of Sir Walter Scott—takes in the hills, moors, and farmland that stretch south from Lothian, the region crowned by Edinburgh, to England. In the north, heath-clad slopes, salmon-filled streams, and the great castles of baronial pride stand hard among the hills. To enjoy the Highlands, head for Royal Deeside, the burg that Queen Victoria made her own. Her Majesty's Balmoral—and numerous other castles—polka-dot northeast Scotland. Northward lie Inverness and shimmering Loch Ness.

Highlights of Britain
16 days

It's no wonder that many people see Great Britain as a giant patchwork quilt thickly studded with must-see sights. This roundup introduces you to the best of them. After two days doing the town in London, head out to Windsor.

WINDSOR
1 day. Windsor Castle, resplendent in its finery, is the main reason to be here, but a respite from the riches within is found in its tranquil Great Park. If you want to live like a duke for a day, head up the valley to Lord Astor's Cliveden, the Thames Valley's most spectacular hotel. ⇨ *Windsor & Environs in Chapter 5.*

SALISBURY
1 day. Visible for miles around, Salisbury Cathedral's soaring spire is one of the quintessential images of rural England, immortalized in paint by John Constable. Pay an afternoon call on either awe-inspiring Stonehenge or Stourhead, the finest garden of England's neo-classical era. ⇨ *Salisbury to the New Forest in Chapter 3.*

BATH & THE COTSWOLDS
2 days. Once upon a time Bath was *the* place to be, and this elegant, small city has never forgotten it. Its popularity today is understandable, as Bath is an immaculately preserved gem of Georgian architecture. Stop by the Roman Baths Museum to see the town's beginnings. The next day head via car or guided-tour bus to the storybook villages of the Cotswolds. Antique-shop in Stow-on-the-Wold and then feed the ducks at the brook in Lower Slaughter. ⇨ *Bath & Environs and The Cotswolds in Chapter 7.*

OXFORD
1 day. The "dreaming spires" of Oxford's weathered old buildings bear witness to the transience of countless generations of students. Tour the town's largest quad at Christ Church College, then don't miss the short trip to Blenheim Palace, England's grandest house. ⇨ *Oxford and Blenheim Palace to Althorp in Chapter 5.*

STRATFORD-UPON-AVON
1 day. If you don't chime with the Bard, skip this stop, because this is Shakespeare's town. See Shakespeare's Birthplace and Anne Hathaway's Cottage, and catch a performance at the Royal Shakespeare Theatre. ⇨ *Stratford-upon-Avon in Chapter 6.*

WORCESTER
2 days. Worcester Cathedral is a majestic sight, with one of the finest chantry chapels in the country. The town's 15th-century Commandery brings alive the days of England's Civil War. Spend your second day here roaming the spa towns of the Malvern Hills, then head north to see the half-timber houses of Shrewsbury and Chester. ⇨ *From Worcester to Dudley and From Shrewsbury to Chester in Chapter 8.*

THE LAKE DISTRICT
2 days. In the area surrounding Windermere and Kendal, explore the English lakes and mountains and do some real walking. Check out the local Wordsworth industry at Dove Cottage and Grasmere. Bring your sketch pad for your cruise on Windermere. ⇨ *The Southern Lakes in Chapter 11.*

YORK
2 days. The principal city of northern England since Roman times, York is crammed with 15th- and 16th-century buildings in varying degrees of sag, but don't miss York Minster, England's largest Gothic church, and the medieval streets of the Shambles. Save half a day for visiting Castle Howard, where baroque grandeur is the keynote. ⇨ *York and The North York Moors in Chapter 13.*

LINCOLN & CAMBRIDGE
2 days. Heading south, make a lunchtime stop at Lincoln, whose stunning Cathedral of St. Mary demands a slow wander. Bed down in Cambridge for your last stop. After touring King's College Chapel, leave an hour or two to hone your punting skills on the River Cam before heading back to London. ⇨ *Lincoln, Boston & Stamford and Cambridge in Chapter 12.*

By Public Transportation
For Windsor, take a train from either London's Waterloo or Paddington station. For Salisbury, head back to London's Clapham Junction to catch a train on the Portsmouth line. Trains leave twice hourly from Salisbury to Bath, itself connected by hourly trains to Oxford. From Oxford there are direct trains to Stratford-upon-Avon, or opt for more frequent Stagecoach bus service. For Worcester change trains at Oxford or Birmingham's New Street station, which is the place to catch trains to Windermere and Oxenholme. Take a train via either station to York (changes required). From York to Lincoln transfer at Doncaster or Retford. For Cambridge change at Doncaster or Newark and again at Peterborough. Trains leave Cambridge for London frequently.

The Literary Trail
12 days
After the Beatles, perhaps the greatest contribution that Britain has made to Western culture has been its literary achievements. The legacy of many centuries of literature has insinuated itself into every aspect of life. Many of these landscapes appear as romantic backdrops in movies, too.

LONDON

2 days. One author strongly associated with London is Charles Dickens, and Dickens House, where he wrote *Oliver Twist* and *Nicholas Nickleby*, sits appropriately in literary Bloomsbury. Dr. Johnson's House lies a short walk south of here, and Shakespeare beckons across the Thames in Southwark at the reconstruction of the Bard's Globe Theatre. ⇨ *Exploring London in Chapter 1.*

WINCHESTER & CHAWTON

1 day. Stop in the lovely old city of Winchester; Jane Austen is buried in Winchester Cathedral. Sixteen miles northeast lies Chawton and Jane Austen's House, where the atmosphere still reverberates with the tinkle of teacups lofted by the likes of Emma and the dashing Mr. Darcy. ⇨ *From Winchester to Southampton in Chapter 3.*

DORCHESTER & LYME REGIS

2 days. Thomas Hardy immortalized this region in *Far from the Madding Crowd* and other novels. The town of Dorchester was the 19th-century author's Casterbridge. The Dorset County Museum contains a re-creation of his study, and Hardy walking tours lead to Hardy's Cottage at Higher Bockhampton. To the west is Lyme Regis, a setting in John Fowles's *The French Lieutenant's Woman* and Jane Austen's *Persuasion.* ⇨ *Bournemouth to Lyme Regis in Chapter 3.*

BATH

1 day. Head north to honey-toned Bath, identified with a host of Georgian-era literati, chief among them Jane Austen, who set parts of *Northanger Abbey* and *Persuasion* here. Check out the Jane Austen Centre, look into guided theme walks, and visit the Holburne Museum, where genteel Jane promenaded in the gardens. ⇨ *Bath & Environs in Chapter 7.*

STRATFORD-UPON-AVON

2 days. Everyone visits Shakespeare's Birthplace, though you may feel closer to him at his simple tomb in Holy Trinity Church. Take in a play at the Royal Shakespeare Theatre. Escape the tour buses in town by exploring Master Will's country haunts, from Henley-in-Arden to Warwick Castle.
⇨ *Stratford-upon-Avon and Around Shakespeare Country in Chapter 6.*

THE LAKE DISTRICT

2 days. The countryside around Keswick and Windermere is the cradle of English Romanticism: its mountains and lakes attracted Wordsworth and other men and women of letters. Visit the poet's homes (Dove Cottage in Grasmere and Rydal Mount in Rydal), young William's school in Hawkshead, and his and sister Dorothy's birthplace at Cockermouth. Brantwood, the home of John Ruskin, is near Coniston and Hawkshead. Beatrix Potter lived at Hill Top, near Hawkshead. ⇨ *The Southern Lakes and Penrith & the Northern Lakes in Chapter 11.*

HAWORTH

2 days. Fans of the Brontë canon will appreciate this literary shrine. Unfortunately that can create some crowds on cobbled Main Street in summer. Still, the Brontë Parsonage Museum casts a spell, as do the paths to the moors and the Brontë Waterfall. Overnight here and head back to London the next day. ⇨ *West Yorkshire & Brontë Country in Chapter 13.*

By Public Transportation

Take the train from Waterloo station to Winchester. For Dorchester change trains at Southampton. To reach Bath from Dorchester change at Yeovil. For Stratford change at Bristol and Birmingham. Catch connections for Keswick or Windermere at Birmingham's New Street Station. From the Lake District to reach Haworth take a train for Keighley

from Windermere or Oxenholme, changing at Lancaster, sometimes at Leeds. From Keighley there are frequent Keighley and District buses, which also head to Bradford, from which frequent trains depart for London.

A Stately Homes Grand Tour
9 days

Though occasionally changing hands and even dynasties, Britain's stately homes as a rule have retained the priceless furniture and—sometimes—the wallpaper of generations past. They contain some of the finest architecture and landscape gardening in the country.

SALISBURY

2 days. Base yourself in this graceful Wiltshire town for trips to a trio of superb stately homes. Wilton House, rebuilt in 1647, contains magnificent state rooms, including the Double Cube Room with its gigantic Sir Anthony Van Dyck family portrait. In western Wiltshire, Palladian Stourhead is most loved for its parkland. Nearby Longleat House is an Italian Renaissance pile complete with safari park. ⇨ *Salisbury to the New Forest in Chapter 3.*

OXFORD

2 days. Blenheim Palace, home of the dukes of Marlborough and birthplace of Winston Churchill, is one of the most ornate baroque concoctions anywhere. Twenty miles southwest of Oxford is Kelmscott Manor, home of William Morris and an Arts and Crafts landmark. Southeast of Oxford you can visit Elizabethan Mapledurham House, model for Toad Hall in *Wind in the Willows.* ⇨ *To Henley & Beyond and Blenheim Palace to Althorp in Chapter 5.*

BROADWAY

2 days. Stay in this lovely Cotswold town to explore Sudeley Castle, home of Catherine Parr, Henry VIII's last wife. Stanway House, a short drive away, is a Jacobean manor in keeping with its setting. Nearby Snowshill Manor, a 17th-century house in pretty Snowshill, has a pretty garden; the house is closed until spring 2005. Farther west, tiny Owlpen is a Cotswold classic. ⇨ *The Cotswolds in Chapter 7.*

BAKEWELL

2 days. Within hailing distance of this town are three of England's most fabulous historic homes: one of them, Chatsworth House, displays the art treasures of the dukes of Devonshire. Medieval in style, nearby 15th-century Haddon Hall is among the most English of great houses. Hardwick Hall is an Elizabethan treasure. ⇨ *The Peak District in Chapter 10.*

YORK

1 day. Doing the tedious crawl up the M1 motorway is worthwhile so that you can see Yorkshire's spectacular Castle Howard. Twenty-five miles away are Harewood House, which has a cornucopia of Chippendale furniture, and Studley Royal, with its exquisite water gardens. Overnight in York and head back to London the next morning. ⇨ *West Yorkshire & Brontë Country, York Environs, and The North York Moors in Chapter 13.*

By Public Transportation

This tour often leads to backwaters and byways, so public transport can be sketchy. Buses can get you close to many stately homes, but a taxi is sometimes required for the last leg of the journey. From London's Waterloo Station take a train to Salisbury, then a bus to Wilton House or Warminster, for Longleat; for Stourhead, continue on the train to Gillingham. From Salisbury, change at Bath or Basingstoke for Oxford, then catch a bus to Blenheim and, for Kelmscott Manor, Faringdon. Take a train from Oxford to Moreton-in-Marsh for Broadway, then walk to Snowshill Manor; for Sudeley Castle, take a bus from Broadway to Winchcombe, then walk. Take a train back to Oxford and then up to Manchester for the connection to Buxton, then a bus to Bakewell. Take a train from Manchester to York, then a bus to Castle Howard; take a train to Leeds, then a bus over to Harewood House; for Studley Royal, take a train to Harrowgate, then a bus to Ripon. Express trains connect York with London.

WHEN TO GO

The British tourist season is year-round—with short lulls. It peaks from mid-April to mid-October, with a burst at Christmas (although many historic houses close from October to Easter). The countryside is greenest in spring, whereas in fall the northern moorlands and Scottish Highlands are at their most colorful. During July and August, when most of the British take vacations, accommodations in popular resorts and areas are in high demand and at their most expensive. The winter cultural season in London is lively, and hotel rates are lower. Museums and sights can be busy during school vacations called half-terms: these are generally the third week in October, the last week of December and first week of January, the third week of February, the last week of March, and the first week of June.

Climate

In the main, the climate in Britain is mild. Summer temperatures can reach the 90s and the atmosphere can be humid. In winter there can be heavy frost, snow, thick fog, and, of course, rain. What follows are the average daily maximum and minimum temperatures for three major cities.
Forecasts **Weather Channel** ⊕ www.weather.com.

ABERYSTWYTH (WALES)

Month	°F	°C	Month	°F	°C	Month	°F	°C
Jan.	44F	7C	May	58F	15C	Sept.	62F	16C
	36	2		45	7		51	11
Feb.	44F	7C	June	62F	16C	Oct.	56F	13C
	35	2		50	10		46	8
Mar.	49F	9C	July	64F	18C	Nov.	50F	10C
	38	4		54	12		41	5
Apr.	52F	11C	Aug.	65F	18C	Dec.	47F	8C
	41	5		54	12		38	4

EDINBURGH (SCOTLAND)

Month	°F	°C	Month	°F	°C	Month	°F	°C
Jan.	42F	6C	May	56F	14C	Sept.	60F	16C
	34	1		43	6		49	9
Feb.	43F	6C	June	62F	17C	Oct.	54F	12C
	34	1		49	9		44	7
Mar.	46F	8C	July	65F	18C	Nov.	48F	9C
	36	2		52	11		39	4
Apr.	51F	11C	Aug.	64F	18C	Dec.	44F	7C
	39	4		52	11		36	2

LONDON

Month	°F	°C	Month	°F	°C	Month	°F	°C
Jan.	43F	6C	May	62F	17C	Sept.	65F	19C
	36	2		47	8		52	11
Feb.	44F	7C	June	69F	20C	Oct.	58F	14C
	36	2		53	12		46	8
Mar.	50F	10C	July	71F	22C	Nov.	50F	10C
	38	3		56	14		42	5
Apr.	56F	13C	Aug.	71F	21C	Dec.	45F	7C
	42	6		56	13		38	4

Great Britain's top seasonal events are listed below, and any one of them could provide the stuff of lasting memories. Tickets for popular sporting events must be obtained months in advance; your travel agent may be able to help. Contact information is listed below. VisitBritain's Web site, ⊕ www.visitbritain.com, also has information about events.

Throughout 2005, special events—boat races, museum exhibitions, lectures, festivals, and more—are planned around the country to commemorate SeaBritain 2005, a celebration of the role the sea has played in the national identity of Britain. Also part of SeaBritain, the year-long Trafalgar Festival is set to examine the contributions of Admiral Lord Nelson. The Trafalgar Weekend (October 21 through October 23) marks the 200th anniversary of the Battle of Trafalgar, in which Nelson was killed during a brilliant, decisive naval victory against Napoléon's French navy. SeaBritain 2005 (⊕ www.seabritain2005.com) has the latest information.

ONGOING

Mid-Mar. & Mid-Sept.	**Chelsea Antiques Fair** is a twice-yearly fair with pre-1830 pieces for sale. ✉ *Old Town Hall, King's Rd., London SW3* ☎ *01444/482514* ⊕ *www.penman-fairs.co.uk.*
Late May–Aug.	**Glyndebourne Opera** presents high-quality performances in a lovely rural setting; booking opens in April. ✆ *Box 2624, Lewes, East Sussex BN8 5UW* ☎ *01273/815000 information, 01273/813813 box office* ⊕ *www.glyndebourne.com.*
Late May– Mid-Sept.	**Shakespeare Under the Stars** gives you the chance to see the Bard's plays at the Regent's Park Open Air Theatre. Performances are usually Monday through Saturday at 8, with matinees on Wednesday, Thursday, and Saturday. ✉ *Inner Circle, London NW1* ☎ *020/ 7486–2431* ⊕ *www.openairtheatre.org.*
Mid-July– Mid-Sept.	**Henry Wood Promenade Concerts** is a celebrated series of classical music concerts. ✉ *Royal Albert Hall, Kensington Gore, London SW7* ☎ *020/7589–8212* ⊕ *www.bbc.co.uk/proms.*

WINTER

Mid-Dec.	**Olympia International Show Jumping Championships** is London's main international equestrian competition, held in Olympia's Grand Hall. Tickets go on sale in June. ✉ *London* ☎ *0870/733–0733* ⊕ *www. olympiashowjumping.com.*
Dec. 27– Jan. 2	**Hogmanay,** an energetic, Scottish-style celebration of the new year in Edinburgh, includes candlelight processions, concerts, and fireworks. ☎ *0131/473–2000* ⊕ *www.edinburghshogmanay.org.*

Dec. 31	**New Year's Eve at Trafalgar Square** in London is a huge, freezing, sometimes drunken slosh through the fountains to celebrate the new year. Not organized by any official body, it is held in the ceremonial heart of London under an enormous Christmas tree.
Jan. 1	**London Parade**, an extravaganza with floats and marching bands, starts on the south side of Westminster Bridge around noon and finishes in Berkeley Square around 3 PM. No tickets are required. ⊠ *London* ⊕ *www.londonparade.co.uk.*
Last Sun. in Jan.	**Charles I Commemoration**, held in London on the anniversary of the monarch's execution, brings out Londoners dressed in 17th-century garb to trace Charles's last walk to the Banqueting House in Whitehall.

SPRING

Mid-Mar.	**British Antique Dealers' Association Fair** is large and prestigious, with many affordable pieces. ⊠ *Duke of York's Headquarters, King's Rd., London SW3* ☎ *020/7589–6108, 877/872–0778 in U.S.* ⊕ *www.bada-antique-fair.co.uk.*
Mid-Mar.	**Crufts Dog Show** brings together more than 8,000 championship dogs for Britain's top canine event. ⊠ *National Exhibition Centre, Birmingham* ☎ *0207/518–1012* ⊕ *www.crufts.org.uk.*
Late Mar.	**Head of the River Boat Race** offers the spectacle of 420 eight-man crews from Oxford and Cambridge universities dipping their 6,720 oars in the Thames as they race the 4¼ mi from Mortlake to Putney. The best view is from Surrey Bank above Chiswick Bridge (tube to Chiswick).
Mid-Apr.	**Flora London Marathon** runners start in Greenwich and Blackheath at 9–9:30 AM and run via the Docklands, the Tower of London, and Parliament Square to the Mall. ⊕ *www.london-marathon.co.uk.*
Apr. 21	The **Queen's Birthday** earns a showy 41-gun salute at Hyde Park in London. In June, Elizabeth II's ceremonial birthday is celebrated by Trooping the Colour.
Mid-May	**Royal Windsor Horse Show**, a major five-day show-jumping event, is attended by some members of the Royal Family. ⊠ *Show Office, Royal Mews, Windsor* ☎ *0870/121–5370* ⊕ *www.royal-windsor-horse-show.co.uk.*
Mid–Late May	The **Chelsea Flower Show**, a prestigious four-day floral extravaganza, covers 22 acres on the Royal Hospital grounds in London's Chelsea neighborhood. Tickets can sell out well in advance of the event. ⊠ *Royal Horticultural Society, Royal Hospital Rd., London SW3* ☎ *0870/906–3781* ⊕ *www.rhs.org.uk/chelsea.*
Late May	The **Hay Festival** in the Welsh border town of Hay-on-Wye gathers authors and readers from all over Britain for a weeklong celebration of the town's status as the used-book capital of the world. Ex-

pect plenty of readings of fiction, nonfiction, and poetry. ⊠ *Hay-on-Wye* ☎ *01497/821–299* ⊕ *www.hayfestival.co.uk.*

SUMMER	
Early June	**Derby Day** is the world-renowned horse-racing event, at Epsom Downs Racecourse. ⊠ *Epsom Downs, Surrey* ☎ *01372/470047* ⊕ *www.epsomderby.co.uk.*
Early June	**Grosvenor House Antiques Fair** is one of the most prestigious antiques fairs in Britain. ⊠ *Grosvenor House Hotel, Park La., London W1* ☎ *020/7399–8100* ⊕ *www.grosvenor-antiquesfair.co.uk.*
Early June	**Trooping the Colour** is Queen Elizabeth's colorful official birthday show at Horse Guards Parade, Whitehall, London. (Her actual birthday is in April.) Note that on the two previous Saturdays, there are Queen-less rehearsals—the Colonel's Review and the Major General's Review. *Write for tickets from January 1 to February 28 (enclose SASE or International Reply Coupon):* ✏ *Ticket Office, Headquarters Household Division, Horse Guards, London SW1 2AX* ☎ *020/ 7414–2479.*
Mid-June	**Royal Ascot** is the most glamorous date in British horse racing. Usually held during the third week of June, the four-day event is graced by the Queen and other celebrities. Reserve months in advance for tickets. ⊠ *Ascot Racecourse, Ascot, Berkshire* ☎ *01344/876876* ⊕ *www.ascot-authority.co.uk.*
Late June– Early July	**Wimbledon Lawn Tennis Championships** get bigger every year. Applications for the ticket lottery for the two-week tournament are available October–December of the preceding year. ✏ *All-England Lawn Tennis & Croquet Club, Church Rd., Wimbledon, London SW19 5AE* ☎ *020/8946–2244* ⊕ *www.wimbledon.org.*
Late June– Early July	**Royal Henley Regatta** attracts premier rowers from around the world on the first weekend in July. High society lines the banks of the Thames during this four-day event. ⊠ *Henley-on-Thames, Oxfordshire* ☎ *01491/572153* ⊕ *www.hrr.co.uk.*
Late June– Late July	**City of London Festival** fills the City with theater, poetry, classical music, and dance performed by international artists. ☎ *020/7377–0540* ⊕ *www.colf.org.*
Early July	**Hampton Court Palace Flower Show,** a five-day event on the grounds of the palace, nearly rivals the Chelsea Flower Show for glamour. ⊠ *Hampton Court Palace, East Molesey, Surrey* ☎ *0870/906– 3791* ⊕ *www.rhs.org.uk/hamptoncourt.*
Early–Mid-July	**Llangollen International Musical Eisteddfod** sees the little Welsh town of Llangollen overflow with music, including concerts and competitions. Participants come from more than 40 nations. ⊠ *Musical Eisteddfod Office, Llangollen* ☎ *01978/860000* ⊕ *www. international-eisteddfod.co.uk.*

Late July–early Aug.	The National Eisteddfod of Wales, a popular weeklong event, rotates annually between locations in North and South Wales. Besides musical competitions, it includes the Gorsedd ceremonies, during which writers of poetry and prose are honored. ☎ *029/2076–3777* ⊕ *www.eisteddfod.org.uk.*
Early Aug.	Cowes Regatta draws high flyers, top yachtsmen, and the occasional royal to this grand weeklong boating festival held off the Isle of Wight. ☎ *01983/295744* ⊕ *www.cowesweek.co.uk.*
Mid–Late Aug.	Edinburgh Festival Fringe, one of the world's largest theater and music festivals focusing on fringe art, takes place over three weeks, during the Edinburgh International Festival. It's a great chance to see up-and-comers. ☎ *0131/226–0026* ⊕ *www.edfringe.com.*
Mid-Aug.–Early Sept.	Edinburgh International Festival, the world's largest festival of the arts, coincides with the nighttime Edinburgh Military Tattoo. ✉ *Castlehill, EH1 2NE* ☎ *0131/473–2020 information, 0131/473–2000 tickets* ⊕ *www.eif.co.uk.*
Late Aug.	International Beatles Festival sees hundreds of Beatles tribute bands descend on Liverpool for a week to play to an international crowd of fans. ✉ *Liverpool* ☎ *0151/236–9091* ⊕ *www.visitliverpool.com.*
Late Aug.	Notting Hill Carnival, one of the liveliest street festivals in London, includes Caribbean foods, reggae music, and street parades. ✉ *Notting Hill, London* ☎ *020/8964–0544.*
FALL	
Mid-Oct.	Cheltenham Festival of Literature draws world-renowned authors, actors, and critics to the elegant, Regency-era town. ☎ *01242/227979* ⊕ *www.cheltenhamfestivals.co.uk.*
Nov. 5	Guy Fawkes Day celebrates a foiled 1605 attempt to blow up Parliament. Fireworks are held throughout London, but the place to be is the bonfire festivity on Primrose Hill near Camden Town.

PLEASURES & PASTIMES

English Gardens What is it with the English and gardens? Is it the inroads of urban and suburban living, transforming green fields into gray concrete, that have made this a nation of gardeners? Or is it the love of nature that compels this wet-weather people to attempt to colonize their own patch of it? Despite the frenzied assaults of frosts, slugs, and plentiful rain, the English will grit their teeth, retrieve their gardening forks, and get down on their knees for the sake of an immaculate floral border or weed-free shrubbery. In fact, this is no recent obsession. The Tudors were the first to produce gardens that were more than strictly utilitarian, and since then French, Italian, Dutch, and even Japanese ideas have been imported and adapted to suit the English aesthetic. As a result, a pilgrimage to an English garden is an essential part of any visit. Some superb gardens are as celebrated as the stately home they adorn. Don't think only colorful flowers: ponds exuberantly carpeted with lilies, monumental box hedges, weird topiary, conservatories with exotic plants of all kinds, and manicured swaths of lawn all play a role in the national pastime. Naturally, spring and summer are the best seasons to view these English Edens. Some places have very limited opening times, most close in winter, and some require no small effort to reach. But beware: what started as a casual jaunt may grow into an all-consuming passion, come rain or shine, whatever the weather.

The Performing Arts There's no better antidote to an overdose of history, pageantry, and assorted heaps of stones—however evocative the history and stones are—than a face-to-face encounter with another British specialty, the performing arts. After all, the past really resonates only when plugged into the present, and the arts in Britain, fueled by a seemingly bottomless well of talent, provide a direct link. Nowhere is this more true than in the dramatic arts, a field in which Britain can still claim to reign supreme. Every provincial town has its own venue, with offerings that may range from the sublime to the absurd, and there is more guarantee of consistently superb productions at the theatrical meccas of Stratford-upon-Avon and London's West End. All the same, don't dismiss the rest of the pack: you can find yourself surprised and delighted by productions in places from York to Chichester, or by a night out at the open-air cliff-top Minack Theatre, on the tip of Cornwall. For other areas of the performing arts—ballet and opera—choose from among the tried and trusted companies of London and Birmingham, though even here some of the remoter places can be quite fine. In summer, look out for festivals, which encompass everything from classical music concerts to poetry readings. These gatherings have a buzz and atmosphere that more formal events cannot match.

The Pub Experience The British could no more live without their "locals" (their neighborhood pubs) than they could forgo dinner. The pub—or public house, to give it its full title—is ingrained in the British psyche as social center, refuge, second home. Pub culture—revolving around pints, pool, darts, and sports—is still male-dominated. However, as a result of the gentrification trend that was launched in the late '80s by the major breweries (which own most pubs), transforming many ancient, smoke-stained dives into fantasy Edwardian drawing rooms, women have been entering pubs' welcoming doors in unstoppable numbers. The trend, in London and other big cities, is toward the bar, superficially identified by its cocktail list, creative paintwork, bare floorboards, and chrome fittings, and toward the gastro-pub, where a good kitchen fuels the relaxed ambience. The social function remains the same, however.

In London, some of the best pubs are Victorian-themed miniparks. Etched glass, chandeliers, wood paneling, art nouveau sculptures—all these elements make up some of the city's most distinctive interiors. Of course, many pubs in London (and throughout the country) have been modernized in dubious taste, with too much chrome, plush, and plastic. But some can be a real joy. They will often be called by the name of the local landed family—*The Bath Arms,* or *Lord Crewe's Arms,* "arms" meaning the family coat of heraldic arms on the inn sign—and very possibly they will have old beams and inglenooks, and a blazing log fire in winter. If you sit at a table in the corner, you can have privacy of a sort; but at the bar, conversation is general, and new acquaintances are quickly made. Locals congregate at lunch and in the evening—either right after work, for a sundowner pint, or right after dinner. In areas popular with walkers and hikers, such as the Lake District, people gather at pubs at the end of the day to share experiences as well as a pint. At these times, there's no easier way to meet the locals. Whichever brew you order, just remember the locals drink their beer *warm.*

Sports & the Outdoors

Britain has endless opportunities for golf, tennis, and other outdoor activities, but if you really want to savor the landscape while escaping the crowds, the country can't offer any better physical pursuit than walking. Footpaths, usually well out of sight of roads, interweave through every part of the country and give access to some of the most alluring spots. More ambitious hikers can set out on one of the long-distance trails, such as the South West Coast Path and the Cotswold Way. Obviously, you can join and leave these paths at any stage (with some planning, you can coordinate a hike's beginning or end with public transportation routes), and most local tourist offices have details of fun circular walks within one area. In all cases, take a good map as well as provisions for the worst eventualities—usually connected with sudden storms or fogs. Most of Britain's footpaths are scrupulously maintained, and liberally supplied with refreshment stops as well as bed-and-breakfasts along the way. Other outdoor pursuits include swimming or surfing from some surprisingly large, sandy beaches (expect cold water, and check on the state of the sea beforehand), relaxed cruising on the extensive network of inland waterways, and horse-back riding, for which numerous stables exist close to moors and downs.

Stately Homes

A recipe for a half day of bliss: take a generous pinch of history, blend in plenty of art and beauty, wrap it in anecdote, and serve it in the rural heart of Britain. An Englishman's home is his castle, the saying goes, but very often the reverse is true. If it's not a castle, it may be a country pad of palatial proportions, surrounded by ornamental gardens and endless vistas of parkland. Alternatively, it could be a relatively modest, bijou affair, more likely to inspire affection than awe. Indeed, the sheer diversity and ubiquity of Britain's stately homes—every county has its share—are what impel some travelers to devote whole vacations to tracking down the most remote of these historic piles. Whether predominantly Tudor, Jacobean, baroque, Georgian, or Victorian in character, each is steeped in its own idiosyncratic style, and each has volumes of tales to tell, sometimes touching on pivotal moments in the nation's history and other times (equally absorbing) illustrating the arcane routines of domestic life. Until recently, few outsiders ever came past the gates, and the houses were, in effect, private museums. In the best aristocratic tradition, prestige was reflected in the use of the finest craftspeople, architects, and gardeners from the ranks of those previously recruited to work on great religious buildings, and in the rooms full of art, decorative objects, and rich furnishings (much of this booty was acquired on extended European tours). You've glimpsed these glamorous backdrops in the movies and on television, but the reality is far better.

And a Word About Harry Potter

J. K. Rowling's five novels about Harry Potter, a young British wizard-in-training, have won the hearts of fans of all ages around the world. The release of film versions of the books—as of this writing, *Harry Potter and the Sorcerer's Stone* (in Britain, *Harry Potter and the Philosopher's Stone*), *Harry Potter and the Chamber of Secrets*, and *Harry Potter and the Prisoner of Azkaban*, with *Harry Potter and the Goblet of Fire* planned for 2005—has brought a surge of interest in the British locations used to depict Harry's adventures, from the Reptile House in the London Zoo to the train station in Goathland, North Yorkshire. VisitBritain has created a Harry Potter map, "Discovering the Magic of Britain," that describes key locations in the movies and related sights, and some tour operators (contact VisitBritain for information) have created Potter-themed tours. In this book, key sights linked with the movies are indexed together under Harry Potter sights.

FODOR'S CHOICE

The sights, restaurants, hotels, and other travel experiences on these pages are our editors' top picks—our Fodor's Choices. They're the best of their type in the area covered by the book—not to be missed and always worth your time. In the destination chapters that follow, you will find all the details.

LODGING

£££££	**Cliveden**, Thames Valley. Want to live like Lord Astor for a night? He once called this mansion home, and today lucky you can enjoy his palatial parlors and breathtaking river parterres.
£££££	**Covent Garden Hotel**, London. Relentlessly stylish, this vintage 1880 abode, a former hospital in artsy Covent Garden, shimmers with painted silks, 19th-century oils, and off-duty celebrities.
£££££	**The Dorchester**, London. Off-the-scale opulence *and* charm come with 1,500 square yards of gold leaf and 1,100 square yards of marble at this gem in the heart of Mayfair.
£££££	**Lumley Castle Hotel**, Chester-le-Street, near Durham, Northeast. Antiques and rich fabrics, dungeons and flagstone corridors—you can take yourself back to medieval times but still stay in modern luxury at this sumptuously baronial Norman castle.
£££££	**Middlethorpe Hall**, York, Yorkshire. This handsome, superbly restored 18th-century mansion looks like a Gainsborough painting come to life, with stunning grounds to match.
£££££	**One Aldwych**, London. This luxurious hotel in an Edwardian building is the ultimate in 21st-century style, and the swimming pool has underwater music.
£££££	**The Samling**, Windermere, Lake District. Sculptures dot the grounds of this refined but casual refuge above busy Windermere.
£££££	**The Scotsman**, Edinburgh, Scotland. In a previous incarnation this majestic sandstone building housed the offices of the *Scotsman* newspaper; now it's a model of chic, contemporary hotel design.
££££–£££££	**The Lowry Hotel**, Manchester, Lancashire & the Peaks. The sleekness and Italian-inspired modernity of this glass building reflect the new energy of this old industrial city.
£££–£££££	**Queensberry Hotel**, Bath, Bath & the Cotswolds. Beau Nash would feel right at home. This intimate hotel near the Circus is in three 1772 town houses built for the marquis of Queensberry.
£££–£££££	**Victoria at Holkham**, Wells-next-the-Sea, East Anglia. In the shadow of stately Holkham Hall, this exotic Eastern-inspired hideaway provides a colorful place for a peaceful rest by the seashore.

BUDGET LODGING

££	**Ambassador Hotel,** Glasgow, Scotland. Sophisticated rooms and faultless service are the trademarks of this superior hotel in a terraced town house across from the Botanic Gardens.
££	**Cardynham House,** Painswick, Bath & the Cotswolds. Laying on the luxury in a typically understated English manner, this delightful Cotswold retreat both pampers and soothes.
££	**County Hall Travel Inn Capital,** London. What this South Bank chain offering lacks in trendy decor, it makes up for with an enviable Thames-side location (no river views, though) and a low price.
££	**Express by Holiday Inn,** Liverpool, Lancashire & the Peaks. You're close to all the action and the amenities of Albert Dock and the waterfront at this up-to-date, thoughtfully decorated hotel.
££	**Ocean House,** Aldeburgh, East Anglia. You're close to the beach at this simple 19th-century B&B pleasantly filled with bric-a-brac and antiques.
££	**St. Margaret's,** London. Near the British Museum and in a quiet, dignified area of Bloomsbury, this hotel is run by a friendly and helpful Italian family. Georgian details such as cornice moldings are nice touches.
£–££	**Dairy Guest House,** York, Yorkshire. Although no one comes to this former dairy to buy milk anymore, all the period features of the Victorian house remain, as well as the peaceful courtyard full of rambling plants.
£–££	**The Old Rectory,** Boscastle, West Country. This Victorian B&B is a must for all Thomas Hardy fans—he stayed here when he was courting his future wife—but it makes an alluring stop whatever your literary tastes.
£–££	**Portobello Gold,** London. This small, funky, alternative accommodation is on Portobello Road, London's best-known antiques shopping street.
£–££	**T'Gallants,** Charlestown, West Country. Everything is ship-shape and spruce aboard this Georgian B&B within a stone's throw of the fascinating harbor of this tiny Cornwall port.
£	**Lamperts Cottage,** near Cerne Abbas, South. Thatch-roofed and wood-beamed, this rural hideaway a short drive from Dorchester makes a perfect base for jaunts around the leafy lanes of Dorset.

RESTAURANTS

£££££	**Gordon Ramsay at Claridge's,** London. Nobody does it better than this hot spot's eponymous French-inspired chef, so people book months in advance for his incomparable creations. (If you're heading to Scotland, check out his Amaryllis in Glasgow.)

£££££	**Hibiscus**, Ludlow, Welsh Borders. Who says country dining has to be traditional? The food here, from eel with pork belly to basil ice cream, is a culinary adventure.
£££££	**Le Manoir aux Quat' Saisons**, Great Milton, Thames Valley. Owner-chef Raymond Blanc's 15th-century manor house has held its position as one of Britain's most patrician restaurants for years because of the creative French cuisine.
£££££	**The Merchant House**, Ludlow, Welsh Borders. Foodies flock to this pretty town, a culinary hot spot. In a Jacobean building you can savor both the best of modern British cuisine and more eclectic fare.
££££–£££££	**Rogano**, Glasgow, Scotland. Its dramatic art deco style is the initial lure, but the oyster bar and impeccable seafood and meat dishes keep people coming back.
£££–£££££	**The Seafood Restaurant**, Padstow, West Country. Celebrity chef Rick Stein rules his gastronomic empire from this lively Cornwall fishing port, and seafood fans should make every effort to secure a reservation for an unforgettable repast.
££–£££££	**Locanda Locatelli**, London. The food at this elegant Italian restaurant is confident and polished—superb risottos, silky handmade pastas, beautiful desserts.
£££–££££	**St. John**, London. The ultra-British cooking at this converted smokehouse favors strange animal parts and can be intimidating, but rest assured: it is all delicious.
££–£££	**Drunken Duck Inn**, near Hawkshead, Lake District. Ancient and full of good cheer, this pub and restaurant has oak settles, cozy nooks, and creative modern British fare. You might start with Chesters Strong and Ugly, one of the beers brewed here.
££–£££	**Magpie Café**, Whitby, Yorkshire. All kinds of fish are treated well at this old-fashioned favorite in a glorious coastal town.
££–£££	**The Wolseley**, London. You might actually think you're in Europe at this Viennese-style café. Feast on wiener schnitzel, Hungarian goulash, and strudel, or stop by for tea and decadently rich pastries.

BUDGET RESTAURANTS

££	**The Lighthouse**, Aldeburgh, East Anglia. Look for fresh local produce and creatively prepared oysters, crabs, and other seafood at this easygoing brasserie on the coast.
£–££	**busabe eathai**, London. This Thai canteen with hardwood tables is one of Londoners' favorite cheap spots in Soho; everything from the curries to the stir-fries is delicious.

£–££	**The Eagle,** London. This superior gastro-pub, with wooden floors, a few sofas, and art on the walls, serves amazingly good-value Portuguese-Spanish food.
£–££	**Grand Café,** Oxford, Thames Valley. Try this gracious spot with columns and marble tables for coffee and dessert or excellent sandwiches and salads.
£–££	**Herbie's,** Exeter, West Country. Simple vegetarian dishes served with a smile—and exquisite organic ice cream—refresh body and spirit in this pleasant eatery near the town center.
£–££	**Kalpna,** Edinburgh, Scotland. Behind the plain exterior of this South Side eatery, extraordinary vegetarian Indian food is served.
£–££	**Milecastle Inn,** near Greenhead, Northeast. The cook has no difficulty satisfying her customers with meat pies and duck with dumplings at this sturdy 17th-century pub close to Hadrian's Wall.
£	**City Fish Bar,** Canterbury, Southeast. People line up for classic, crisply fried fish-and-chips at this popular spot in the center of town.

PARKS & GARDENS

	Bodnant Garden, near Conwy, Wales. Mountains create a magnificent backdrop for Italianate terraces, rock and rose gardens, and plant collections that include magnolias and camellias; the colors here are dramatic.
	Eden Project, near St. Austell, West Country. More than anything, it's the imaginative power of this ambitious gallery of plants that really impresses. The outsize geodesic greenhouses at its heart contain specimens from around the world.
	Hidcote Manor Gardens, Hidcote Bartrim, Bath & the Cotswolds. The individually themed "rooms" that make up these gardens in the Arts and Crafts style are a succession of delights and represent the pinnacle of horticultural art in England.
	Kew Gardens, near London. The spectacular, 300-acre Royal Botanic Gardens at Kew contains more than 30,000 species of plants, and the 19th-century greenhouses are particular treasures.
	Sissinghurst Castle Garden, Cranbrook, Southeast. Vita Sackville-West designed this intimate garden around the striking remains of an Elizabethan house; the White Garden is especially celebrated.
	Stourhead, Stourton, South. In a nation of noteworthy house-and-garden combinations, this Palladian mansion and 18th-century masterwork of naturalistic landscaping is one of the most impressive.

Stowe Landscape Gardens, near Aylesbury, Thames Valley. The greatest gardeners of the 18th century worked on this influential, 980-acre example of large-scale landscaping; artfully placed statues, arches, and temples grace the valleys and rivers.

Wisley, near Guildford, Southeast. The Royal Horticultural Society's garden splendidly blends the pretty and the practical, with innovative gardens that will inspire anyone with a green thumb.

QUINTESSENTIAL BRITAIN

Changing of the Guard, London. Adding a dash of red to the gloomiest of London days, the colorful regiments of guards march with regal pomp as the band plays.

Conwy Castle, Conwy, Wales. Built by Edward I to control the Welsh, this well-preserved fortress with eight large towers captures the spirit of the medieval age. Walk the town walls for magnificent views of the fortifications.

Durham Cathedral, Durham, Northeast. The impressive view of the cathedral perched above this small university city is matched by its stunning Norman interior; it's a metaphor for English solidity.

Edinburgh Castle, Edinburgh, Scotland. Standing proud on a hill in the Old Town, despite damage sustained in seven centuries' worth of conflicts, the castle epitomizes Scotland's fortitude and nationalism.

Houses of Parliament at sunset, London. Cross the Thames to Jubilee Gardens to see this view of the capital at its storybook best.

Punting on the river, Oxford, Thames Valley. From the river, perspectives change and Oxford becomes an idyllic landscape, complete with weeping willows on the shore and medieval spires in the background.

A ramble around Borrowdale, Lake District. South of scenic Derwentwater is this verdant valley surrounded by jagged peaks. Have a colored-pencil kit handy to capture the sublime scenery that has inspired many artists and poets.

Shakespeare at the Royal Shakespeare Theatre, Stratford-upon-Avon, Shakespeare Country. Seeing any play by the Bard performed in his hometown is an unforgettable theatrical experience.

Stonehenge early in the morning, near Amesbury, South. Crowds can detract from the magic, so arrive early to appreciate the timeless power of this ancient stone circle on the wide Salisbury plan.

Tintagel Castle, Tintagel, West Country. Despite its popularity, this fabled ruin, supposedly King Arthur's birthplace, retains its mystique. The black, forsaken remains are poised dramatically over the swirling sea.

View of Salisbury Cathedral from the town path, Salisbury, South. Dramatically poised over the town for more than 600 years, this mighty stone confection has one of the most famous profiles in the country. Constable captured the classic view of its soaring spire.

A walk along Hadrian's Wall, Northeast. There's no better way to fire up your imagination to appreciate the legacy of the Romans in Britain than a walk along this wall and a visit to its forts.

Westminster Abbey, London. The majestic abbey exudes history. Nearly all of England's monarchs have been crowned here, amid great heraldic splendor; many are buried here, too.

STATELY HOMES

Blenheim Palace, Woodstock, Thames Valley. "Magnificent" is the adjective to describe this early-18th-century house, seat of the dukes of Marlborough and England's only rival to Versailles.

Castle Howard, Coneysthorpe, Yorkshire. The masterpiece of English baroque architecture, this birthday cake of a house was used to memorable effect as Lord Marchmain's residence in TV's *Brideshead Revisited*. The landscaping is equally extravagant.

Cawdor Castle, near Nairn, Scotland. Shakespeare's Macbeth was Thane (clan chief) of Cawdor, but this 14th-century castle exudes centuries of real, not fictional, history.

Floors Castle, near Kelso, Scotland. The largest inhabited house in Scotland, this 18th-century pile has been the home of the dukes of Roxburghe since it was built. Today you can wander through glorious formal rooms as well as the billiard room.

Haddon Hall, near Bakewell, Lancashire & the Peaks. A medieval book illumination come to life, this castellated 15th-century manor bristles with slate roofs and towers and is surrounded by famous rose gardens.

Holkham Hall, Wells-next-the-Sea, East Anglia. A splendid 60-foot-tall marble entryway modeled after the Roman Baths of Diocletian and salons filled with old masters distinguish this splendid Palladian palace, near an expanse of sandy beaches and a salt marsh.

Ightham Mote, near Sevenoaks, Southeast. This 14th-century manor house with a moat and a lovely garden will transport you back to the Middle Ages.

Knole, Sevenoaks, Southeast. A vast deer park surrounds this sprawling Elizabethan mansion, which counts a remarkable set of silver furniture, impressive tapestries, and family portraits of the Sackvilles among its many highlights.

Lanhydrock, near Bodmin, West Country. It's a stunning ensemble: formal gardens, expansive parkland, and a house that presents the spectrum of life in a Victorian country home, from the kitchen to the drawing room.

Petworth House, Petworth, Southeast. Grounds landscaped by Capability Brown, superb paintings, and wood carvings by Grinling Gibbons make this one of the National Trust's treasures.

Waddesdon Manor, near Aylesbury, Thames Valley. The Rothschilds built and renovated this 19th-century French-style chateau, a treasure-packed delight in the countryside.

TOWNS & VILLAGES

Castle Combe, Bath & the Cotswolds. A stand-in Puddleby-on-the-Marsh in the Rex Harrison film *Doctor Dolittle,* this village with simple stone cottages and a graceful church has a toylike, once-upon-a-time magic.

Clovelly, West Country. The sheer prettiness of this village perched on a cliff edge above the sea will beguile the most cynical heart.

Dedham, East Anglia. Good restaurants and lodgings add to the pleasure of a visit to this tiny, picture-book town in the heart of Constable country.

Lacock, Bath & the Cotswolds. This slumbering Wiltshire village has it all (including too many summer visitors): an abbey that is now a stately home, some choice inns and tearooms, and a scattering of antiques shops.

Lavenham, East Anglia. Sweet and small, this village is chock-full of well-preserved Tudor half-timber buildings, the former homes of wool merchants and weavers.

Lower Slaughter, Bath & the Cotswolds. One of the Cotswold's "water villages," this is built around Slaughter Brook, home to a gaggle of geese, which can often be seen paddling under the footbridges.

Ludlow, Welsh Borders. Even without its unique concentration of superb restaurants, this town clustered below the ruins of a medieval castle would merit a visit for its fine medieval, Georgian, and Victorian buildings.

Portmeirion, Wales. This fantasy-Italianate village, complete with town hall, shops, and grand hotel, is quite un-Welsh but totally charming.

Whitby, Yorkshire. A ruined abbey and a striking harbor lined with cliffs combine with a rich legacy of fishing and whaling lore to enhance this scenic coastal town.

SMART TRAVEL TIPS

Finding out about your destination before you leave home means you won't squander time organizing everyday minutiae once you've arrived. You'll be more streetwise when you hit the ground as well, better prepared to explore the aspects of Great Britain that drew you here in the first place. The organizations in this section can provide information to supplement this guide; contact them for up-to-the-minute details, and consult the A to Z sections that end each chapter for facts on the various topics as they relate to different regions. Happy landings!

AIR TRAVEL

BOOKING

When you book, look for nonstop flights and remember that "direct" flights stop at least once. Try to avoid connecting flights, which require a change of plane. Two airlines may operate a connecting flight jointly, so ask whether your airline operates every segment of the trip; you may find that the carrier you prefer flies you only part of the way. To find more booking tips and to check prices and make online flight reservations, log on to www.fodors.com.

CARRIERS

British Airways is the national flag carrier and offers mostly nonstop flights from 18 U.S. cities to Heathrow and Gatwick airports outside London, along with flights to Manchester, Birmingham, and Glasgow. It offers myriad add-on options that help bring down ticket costs. In addition, it has a vast program of discount airfare-hotel packages. Britain-based Virgin Atlantic is a strong competitor in terms of packages.

Because Britain is such a small country, internal air travel is much less important than it is in the United States. For trips of less than 200 mi, the train is often quicker, with rail stations more centrally located. Flying tends to cost more, but for longer trips—for example, between London and Glasgow or Edinburgh—or where a sea crossing is involved, to places such as the Scottish islands, air travel has a considerable time advantage.

Air Travel
Airports
Airports & City Transfers to London
Bike Travel
Boat & Ferry Travel
Business Hours
Bus Travel
Cameras & Photography
Car Rental
Car Travel
The Channel Tunnel
Children in Great Britain
Computers on the Road
Consumer Protection
Cruise Travel
Customs & Duties
Disabilities & Accessibility
Discounts & Deals
Eating & Drinking
Electricity
Embassies
Emergencies
Etiquette & Behavior
Gay & Lesbian Travel
Health
Holidays
Insurance
Lodging
Mail & Shipping
Media
Money Matters
Packing
Passports & Visas
Rest Rooms
Safety
Senior-Citizen Travel
Shopping
Sports & Outdoors
Students in Great Britain
Taxes
Telephones
Time
Tipping
Tours & Packages
Train Travel
Transportation Around Great Britain
Travel Agencies
Visitor Information
Web Sites

British Airways operates shuttle services between Heathrow or Gatwick and Edinburgh, Glasgow, and Manchester. Passengers can simply turn up and get a flight (usually hourly) without booking. bmi/British Midland operates from Heathrow to Aberdeen, Belfast, Dublin, Edinburgh, Glasgow, Leeds, Manchester, and Teesside, as well as to Washington, D.C., Chicago, and major cities in eastern Canada; it also serves Chicago, Washington, D.C., and Toronto from Manchester.

Low-cost airlines such as Easyjet, bmi baby, and Ryanair offer flights within the United Kingdom as well as to cities in Ireland and continental Europe. Prices are low, but don't expect to fly into a major destination. These airlines usually use satellite cities and fly out of smaller British airports such as Stansted and Luton (both near London).

🔂 To & from Great Britain **Aer Lingus** ☎ 800/474-7424, 0845/084-4444 in London ⊕ www.aerlingus.com to Heathrow, Gatwick. **American Airlines** ☎ 800/433-7300, 020/7365-0777 in London, 1300/130-757 in Australia, 09/309-9159 in New Zealand ⊕ www.aa.com to Heathrow, Gatwick, Glasgow. **bmi/British Midland** ☎ 800/788-0555, 020/8745-7321 in London ⊕ www.flybmi.com. **British Airways** ☎ 800/247-9297, 0845/773-3377 in London, 1300/767-177 in Australia, 09/356-8690 in New Zealand ⊕ www.britishairways.com to Heathrow, Gatwick. **Continental** ☎ 800/231-0856, 0800/776464 in London, 1300/361-400 in Australia, 09/308-3350 in New Zealand ⊕ www.continentalairlines.com to Heathrow, Gatwick, Glasgow. **Delta** ☎ 800/241-4141, 0800/414767 in London, 02/9251-3211 in Australia, 09/379-3370 in New Zealand ⊕ www.delta.com to Gatwick. **Northwest Airlines** ☎ 800/447-4747, 0870/507-4074 in London, 008/221-714 in Australia ⊕ www.nwa.com to Gatwick. **United** ☎ 800/538-2929, 0845/844-4777 in London, 008/131-777 in Australia, 09/379-3800 in New Zealand ⊕ www.ual.com to Heathrow. **US Airways** ☎ 800/622-1015, 0845/600-3300 in London, 02/9959-3922 in Australia, 09/623-4294 in New Zealand ⊕ www.usairways.com to Gatwick. **Virgin Atlantic** ☎ 800/862-8621, 01293/747-747 in London, 02/9244-2747 in Australia ⊕ www.virgin-atlantic.com to Heathrow, Gatwick, Glasgow.

🔂 **Within Great Britain & to Europe** bmi baby ☎ 0870/264-2229 in London ⊕ www.bmibaby.com.

Easyjet ☎ 0870/600-0000 in London ⊕ www.easyjet.com. **Ryanair** ☎ 0870/246-0000 in London ⊕ www.ryanair.com.

CHECK-IN & BOARDING

Always **find out your carrier's check-in policy.** Plan to arrive at the airport about two hours before your scheduled departure time for domestic flights and 2½ to 3 hours before international flights. You may need to arrive earlier if you're flying from one of the busier airports or during peak air-traffic times. If you're flying to Europe from Great Britain, arrive at the airport at least two hours in advance.

To avoid delays at airport-security checkpoints, try not to wear any metal. Jewelry, belt and other buckles, steel-toe shoes, barrettes, and underwire bras are among the items that can set off detectors.

Assuming that not everyone with a ticket will show up, airlines routinely overbook planes. When everyone does, airlines ask for volunteers to give up their seats. In return, these volunteers usually get a several-hundred-dollar flight voucher, which can be used toward the purchase of another ticket, and are rebooked on the next flight out. If there are not enough volunteers, the airline must choose who will be denied boarding. The first to get bumped are passengers who checked in late and those flying on discounted tickets, so get to the gate and check in as early as possible, especially during peak periods.

Always **bring a government-issued photo I.D.** to the airport; even when it's not required, a passport is best.

CUTTING COSTS

The least expensive airfares to Great Britain are priced for round-trip travel and must usually be purchased in advance. Airlines generally allow you to change your return date for a fee; most low-fare tickets, however, are nonrefundable. It's smart to call a number of airlines and check the Internet; when you are quoted a good price, book it on the spot—the same fare may not be available the next day, or even the next hour. Always check different routings and look into using alternate airports. Also, price off-peak flights, which may be significantly less expensive than others. Travel agents, especially low-fare specialists (⇨ Discounts & Deals), are helpful.

Consolidators are another good source. They buy tickets for scheduled flights at reduced rates from the airlines, then sell them at prices that beat the best fare available directly from the airlines. (Many also offer reduced car-rental and hotel rates.) Sometimes you can even get your money back if you need to return the ticket. Carefully read the fine print detailing penalties for changes and cancellations, purchase the ticket with a credit card, and confirm your consolidator reservation with the airline.

In Britain, the best place to **search for consolidator, or so-called bucket shop, tickets** is through Cheap Flights, a Web site that pools all flights available and then directs you to a phone number or site to purchase tickets.

When you fly as a courier, you trade your checked-luggage space for a ticket deeply subsidized by a courier service. There are restrictions on when you can book and how long you can stay. Some courier companies list with membership organizations, such as the Air Courier Association and the International Association of Air Travel Couriers; these require you to become a member before you can book a flight.

If you plan to fly within Britain or Europe, **look into airline discount passes,** which you must purchase before you leave home. The Europe Pass from British Airways offers travelers a way to choose from the airline's and its partners' networks in Great Britain and Europe; prices vary. It can be hard to find pass information on Web sites: try typing the name of the pass into a search engine, or search for "pass" within the carrier's Web site.

🔁 Consolidators **AirlineConsolidator.com** ☎ 888/468-5385 ⊕ www.airlineconsolidator.com; for international tickets. **Best Fares** ☎ 800/880-1234 or 800/576-8255 ⊕ www.bestfares.com; $59.90 annual membership. **Cheap Flights** ⊕ www.cheapflights.com. **Cheap Tickets** ☎ 800/377-1000

or 800/652-4327 ⊕ www.cheaptickets.com. **Expedia** ☎ 800/397-3342 or 404/728-8787 ⊕ www.expedia.com. **Hotwire** ☎ 866/468-9473 or 920/330-9418 ⊕ www.hotwire.com. **Now Voyager Travel** ⊠ 45 W. 21st St., Suite 5A New York, NY 10010 ☎ 212/459-1616 🖷 212/243-2711 ⊕ www.nowvoyagertravel.com. **Onetravel.com** ⊕ www.onetravel.com. **Orbitz** ☎ 888/656-4546 ⊕ www.orbitz.com. **Priceline.com** ⊕ www.priceline.com. **Travelocity** ☎ 888/709-5983, 877/282-2925 in Canada, 0870/876-3876 in the U.K. ⊕ www.travelocity.com.

🔁 Courier Resources **Air Courier Association/Cheaptrips.com** ☎ 800/280-5973 or 800/282-1202 ⊕ www.aircourier.org ⊕ www.cheaptrips.com; $34 annual membership. **International Association of Air Travel Couriers** ☎ 308/632-3273 ⊕ www.courier.org; $45 annual membership.

🔁 Discount Airfares & Passes **British Airways** ☎ 800/247-9297, 0845/773-3377 in London, 1300/767-177 in Australia, 09/356-8690 in New Zealand ⊕ www.britishairways.com. **DER Travel Services** ⊠ 9501 W. Devon Ave., Rosemont, IL 60018 ☎ 800/782-2424 🖷 800/282-7474 for information, 800/860-9944 for brochures ⊕ www.der.com. **Flight-Pass,** EuropebyAir, ☎ 888/387-2479 ⊕ www.europebyair.com.

ENJOYING THE FLIGHT

State your seat preference when purchasing your ticket, and then repeat it when you confirm and when you check in. For more legroom, you can request one of the few emergency-aisle seats at check-in, if you're capable of moving obstacles comparable in weight to an airplane exit door (usually between 35 pounds and 60 pounds)—a Federal Aviation Administration requirement of passengers in these seats. Seats behind a bulkhead also offer more legroom, but they don't have underseat storage. Don't sit in the row in front of the emergency aisle or in front of a bulkhead, where seats may not recline.

Ask the airline whether a snack or meal is served on the flight. If you have dietary concerns, request special meals when booking. These can be vegetarian, low-cholesterol, or kosher, for example. It's a good idea to pack some healthful snacks and a small (plastic) bottle of water in your carry-on bag. On long flights, try to maintain a normal routine, to help fight jet lag. At night, get some sleep. By day, eat light meals, drink water (not alcohol), and **move around the cabin** to stretch your legs. For additional jet-lag tips consult *Fodor's FYI: Travel Fit & Healthy* (available at bookstores everywhere).

Smoking policies vary from carrier to carrier. Many airlines prohibit smoking on all of their flights; others allow smoking only on certain routes or certain departures. Ask your carrier about its policy.

FLYING TIMES

Flying time is about 6½ hours from New York, 7½ hours from Chicago, 9½ hours from Dallas, 10 hours from Los Angeles, and 21½ hours from Sydney.

HOW TO COMPLAIN

If your baggage goes astray or your flight goes awry, complain right away. Most carriers require that you **file a claim immediately.** The Aviation Consumer Protection Division of the Department of Transportation publishes *Fly-Rights,* which discusses airlines and consumer issues and is available online. You can also find articles and information on mytravelrights.com, the Web site of the nonprofit Consumer Travel Rights Center.

7 Airline Complaints **Aviation Consumer Protection Division** ✉ U.S. Department of Transportation, Office of Aviation Enforcement and Proceedings, C-75, Room 4107, 400 7th St. SW, Washington, DC 20590 ☎ 202/366-2220 ⊕ airconsumer.ost.dot.gov. **Federal Aviation Administration Consumer Hotline** ✉ for inquiries: FAA, 800 Independence Ave. SW, Washington, DC 20591 ☎ 800/322-7873 ⊕ www.faa.gov.

RECONFIRMING

Check the status of your flight before you leave for the airport. You can do this on your carrier's Web site, by linking to a flight-status checker (many Web booking services offer these), or by calling your carrier or travel agent. Always confirm international flights at least 72 hours ahead of the scheduled departure time.

AIRPORTS

Most international flights to London arrive at either Heathrow Airport (LHR), 15 mi west of London, or at Gatwick Airport (LGW), 27 mi south of the capital. Most flights from the United States go to Heathrow, which is divided into four terminals, with Terminals 3 and 4 handling transatlantic flights (British Airways uses Terminal 4). Gatwick is London's second gateway, serving 21 U.S. destinations. A third, newer airport, Stansted (STN), is 35 mi northeast of the city. It handles mainly European and domestic traffic, although there is a scheduled service from New York. Luton Airport (LLA), just 30 mi north of the city, serves British and European destinations. Luton is the hub for the low-cost Easyjet airline. There are fast connections from all the London airports into the capital. Manchester in northwest England is the hub for bmi/British Midland's flights from the United States. Birmingham, in the Midlands, handles mainly European and British flights as well as flights from Chicago, Denver, Newark, New York, and Orlando. Almost all international flights to Scotland arrive at Glasgow airport; at this writing Continental had service to Edinburgh from New York (⇨ Scotland A to Z *in* Chapter 15).

7 Airport Information **Birmingham Airport** ☎ 0870/733-5511 ⊕ www.bhx.com. **Heathrow Airport** ☎ 0870/000-0123 ⊕ www.baa.co.uk/heathrow. **Gatwick Airport** ☎ 0870/000-2468 ⊕ www.baa.co.uk/gatwick. **Luton Airport** ☎ 01582/405100 ⊕ www.london-luton.co.uk. **Manchester Airport** ☎ 0161/489-3000 ⊕ www.manairport.co.uk. **Stansted Airport** ☎ 0870/000-0303 ⊕ www.baa.co.uk/stansted.

DUTY-FREE SHOPPING

In July 1999, duty-free shopping allowances between Britain and other European Union member countries were abolished, although there are still numerous merchandise offers for those traveling between EU countries by boat, plane, and via the Channel Tunnel. Duty-free sales for travel outside the EU remain business as usual (⇨ Customs & Duties).

AIRPORTS & CITY TRANSFERS TO LONDON

See London A to Z *in* Chapter 1 for information on transportation between the airports and London.

BIKE TRAVEL

Bikes are banned from freeways and most divided highways or main trunk roads, but on side roads and country lanes, the bike is one of the best ways to explore Britain. The National Cycle Network, a work in progress, covers about 7,000 mi of cycling and walking routes. Some routes are in towns and parts of the countryside; for example, in the Peak District National Park, bikes can be rented by the day for use on special traffic-free trails. Cyclists can legally use public bridleways—green, unsurfaced tracks reserved for horses, walkers, and cyclists. Some former railway lines have become popular bike paths, such as the Tarka Trail in North Devon and the Camel Trail in Cornwall. Bikes, from racing to mountain, are usually available for rental, and prices vary by area, anywhere from £3–£5 an hour to £7–£20 for a full day. A deposit of £25 or more is often required. For night cycling, the law requires a full set of reflectors on the wheels and pedals, and lights at the back and front.

Sustrans (a nonprofit organization concerned with sustainable transportation) and the Cyclists' Touring Club (CTC, a national organization; ⇨ Sports & Outdoors) can provide route guides and information on cycling in Britain. For maps, the Landranger by Ordnance Survey series costs £5.99 a map and covers the country in scale 1:50,000 in more than 30 editions. Stanfords bookshop stocks the world's largest selection of maps and has a telephone and Internet ordering service. The Highway Code booklet (£1.50), available at a service station, newsstand, or bookstore, contains information for cyclists.

Call tourist information offices for lists of local rental outlets, or contact the Britain Visitor Centre. The Yellow Pages classified telephone directory lists cycle rentals.

🚲 Bike Maps & Travel Information **Cyclists' Touring Club** ✉ Cotterell House, 69 Meadrow, Godalming, GU7 3HS ☎ 0870/873-0060 ⊕ www.ctc.org.uk. **Landranger by Ordnance Survey** ✉ Order Processing, Romsey Rd., Southampton, SO16 4GU ☎ 0845/2002712 ⊕ www.ordnancesurvey.co.uk. **National Cycle Network (Sustrans)** ✉ 35 King St., Bristol, BS1 4DZ ☎ 0117/926-8893 ⊕ www.sustrans.org.uk.

Stanfords ✉ 12–14 Long Acre, London, WC2E 9LP ☎ 020/7836-1321 ⊕ www.stanfords.co.uk. 🚲 Bike Rentals **Britain Visitor Centre** ✉ 1 Regent St., London, SW1Y 4NX ☎ No phone ⊕ www. visitbritain.com. **Yellow Pages** ⊕ www.yell.co.uk.

BIKES IN FLIGHT

Most airlines accommodate bikes as luggage, provided they are dismantled and boxed; check with individual airlines about packing requirements. Some airlines sell bike boxes, which are often free at bike shops, for about $20 (bike bags can be considerably more expensive). International travelers often can substitute a bike for a piece of checked luggage at no charge; otherwise, the cost is about $100. Most U.S. and Canadian airlines charge $40–$80 each way.

BIKES ON TRAINS

Most trains allow bicycles on board for free or for up to £3 per journey. Bicycles are generally not allowed during commuter hours; folding bikes are almost always allowed, however. Check with the railway before bringing your bike.

BOAT & FERRY TRAVEL

Ferries, hovercraft, and Seacats (a kind of ferry) travel regular routes to France, Spain, Ireland, and Scandinavia. There are also numerous canal boats through the countryside and to the coast (⇨ Sports & Outdoors).

Hoverspeed provides fast travel to France and Belgium. P&O runs ferries between Belgium, Great Britain, Ireland, France, the Netherlands, and Spain. DFDS Seaways covers Denmark, Holland, Germany, Norway, Poland, and Sweden. Stena Line covers Ireland and the Netherlands.

FARES & SCHEDULES

For fares and schedules, contact ferry companies directly. Travelers checks (in pounds), cash, and major credit cards are accepted for payments. Prices vary; booking early ensures cheaper fares, but also ask about special deals. The Ferry Information Service can help with questions about routes and overviews of ferry companies. Seaview is a comprehensive on-line ferry and cruise booking portal for Great Britain and continental Europe.

Boat & Ferry Information DFDS Seaways ☎ 01255/240240 or 0870/533-3000 ⊕ www. dfdsseaways.co.uk. **Ferry Information Service** ☎ 020/7436-2449 ⊕ www.ferryinformationservice. co.uk. **Hoverspeed** ☎ 0870/240-8070 ⊕ www. hoverspeed.com. **P&O Irish Sea** ☎ 0870/242-4666 ⊕ www.poirishsea.com. **P&O North Sea** ☎ 0870/ 129-6002 ⊕ www.ponsf.com. **P&O Portsmouth** ☎ 0870/242-4999 ⊕ www.poportsmouth.com. **P&O Stena Line** ☎ 0870/600-0600 ⊕ www.posl. com. **P&O Ireland and Holland** ☎ 0870/570-7070 ⊕ www.poirishsea.com. **Seaview** ⊕ www.seaview. co.uk. **Stena Line** ☎ 0870/570-7070 ⊕ www. stenaline.co.uk.

BUSINESS HOURS

BANKS & OFFICES

Most banks are open weekdays from 9:30 until 3:30 or 4:30. Some have Thursday evening hours, and a few are open Saturday morning. Many offices are open weekdays 9:30–5:30.

GAS STATIONS

Most gas stations in central London are open seven days, 24 hours. Farther out of London or off the major roads, hours vary considerably but are usually daily 8–8.

MUSEUMS & SIGHTS

The major national museums and galleries are open daily, including lunchtime, but with shorter hours on Sunday. Regional museums are usually closed Monday and have shorter hours in winter. In London, many museums are open late one evening a week.

PHARMACIES

British pharmacies are called chemists. Independent chemist shops are generally open Monday–Saturday 9:30–5:30, although in larger cities some stay open until 10 PM; local newspapers list which pharmacies are open late. In London, the leading chain drugstore, Boots, is open until 6; the Oxford Street and Piccadilly Circus branches are open daily, and until 8 PM Thursday.

SHOPS

Usual business hours are Monday–Saturday 9–5:30; on Sunday, small grocery stores stay open all day, as do larger food markets, superstores, and shopping malls. Outside the main centers, most shops close at 1 PM once a week, often Wednesday or Thursday. In small villages, many also close for lunch. In large cities—especially London—department stores stay open late (usually until 7:30 or 8) one night a week. On national holidays, most stores are closed, and over the Christmas holidays, most restaurants are closed as well (⇨ Holidays).

BUS TRAVEL

Britain has a comprehensive bus (short-haul) and coach (long-distance) network that offers an inexpensive way of seeing the country. National Express is the major coach operator, and Victoria Coach Station in London is the hub of the National Express network, serving around 1,200 destinations within Great Britain and, via Eurolines, continental Europe. Tickets (payable by most major credit cards; reservations are advisable) and information are available from any of the company's 2,500 agents nationwide, including offices at London's Heathrow and Gatwick airport coach stations. Green Line is the next-largest national service; although it serves fewer destinations, airports and major tourist towns are covered. In Scotland, Scottish Citylink runs a similar operation.

Coach tickets can be as low as half the price of a train ticket, and buses are just as comfortable as trains. However, most bus services will double the travel time of trains. Nearly all bus services have a no-smoking policy, and both National Express and Scottish Citylink have on-board refreshments and toilets. There is only one class of service.

Double-decker buses make up many of the extensive networks of local bus services, run by private companies. Check with the local bus station or tourist information center for bus schedules. Most companies offer day or week Explorer or Rover unlimited-travel tickets, and those in popular tourist areas invariably operate special scenic tours in summer. The top deck of a stately double-decker bus is a great place from which to view the countryside.

CUTTING COSTS

National Express's Tourist Trail Pass costs £49 for 2 days of travel within a 3-day period; £85 for 5 days of travel within 30 days; £135 for 8 travel days within 30 days; £190 for 15 travel days within 30 days; and £205 for 15 travel days within 60 days. A Discount Coach Card for students, 16–25s, and over-50s, which costs £10 and is good for one year, qualifies you for 20%–30% discounts off many fares. You can buy your National Express Tourist Trail Pass in advance from the U.S.-based British Travel International travel agency. Most companies offer a discount for children under 15. Scottish Citylink offers the Smart Card for students, 16–25s, and over-50s, which costs £7 for one year and qualifies you for up to 30% off standard fares. Discount cards usually require a passport-size photo upon application. The Scottish Citylink Explorer Pass covering Scotland costs £39 for 3 consecutive days of travel; £59 for 5 consecutive days of travel out of 10; and £85 for 8 consecutive days of travel out of 16. The Explorer Pass includes discounts on some Scottish ferries as well as at independent hostels.

🚌 **Bus Information British Travel International**
🗂 Box 299, Elkton, VA 22827 ☎ 800/327-6097 ⊕ www.britishtravel.com. **Green Line** ✉ Green Line Travel Office, 4A Fountain Sq., 123–151 Buckingham Palace Rd., London, SW1 ☎ 0870 /608-7261 ⊕ www.greenline.co.uk. **National Express** ☎ 0870/ 580-8080 ⊕ www.nationalexpress.com. **Scottish Citylink** ✉ Buchanan Bus Station, Killermont St., Glasgow, G2 3NP ☎ 0870/550-5050 ⊕ www. citylink.co.uk. **Victoria Coach Station** ✉ 164 Buckingham Palace Rd., London, SW1W 9TP ☎ 020/ 7730-3466 ⊕ www.victoriacoachstation.com.

CAMERAS & PHOTOGRAPHY

Don't be surprised if you are asked to refrain from taking pictures during theater, ballet, or opera productions, and in galleries. In most museums and stately homes, you need to get permission, and you usually cannot use a flash. Locals are generally happy to feature in your photos, but it's polite to ask. There are many must-photograph sights in Britain, but London's Big Ben and the guards on horseback in Whitehall are top of the list. In the countryside, try for a thatched- or slate-roof cottage or a typical English garden. The *Kodak Guide to Shooting Great Travel Pictures* (available at bookstores everywhere) is loaded with tips.

🖼 **Photo Help Kodak Information Center** ☎ 800/ 242-2424 ⊕ www.kodak.com.

EQUIPMENT PRECAUTIONS

Don't pack film or equipment in checked luggage, where it is much more susceptible to damage. X-ray machines used to view checked luggage are extremely powerful and therefore are likely to ruin your film. Try to ask for hand inspection of film, which becomes clouded after repeated exposure to airport X-ray machines, and keep videotapes and computer disks away from metal detectors. Always keep film, tape, and computer disks out of the sun. Carry an extra supply of batteries, and be prepared to turn on your camera, camcorder, or laptop to prove to airport security personnel that the device is real.

FILM & DEVELOPING

Film is available from chemists, news dealers, and supermarkets, as well as photography stores. Kodak, followed by Agfa and Fuji, are the most common brands, and prices range from £2 to £4 for a roll of 36-exposure color print film. Chain drugstores, such as Boots or Superdrug, and supermarkets run cost-cutting deals and offer one-hour photo developing.

VIDEOS & DVDs

Remember that most video cartridges sold in Britain (marked PAL) do not interface with American video players (NTSC). The top tourist attractions that have videos also market versions specially made for the American and overseas market. If you're bringing your own video camcorder, bring a supply of cassettes as well. If you're purchasing DVDs, note that Canada and the United States use players and discs coded as Region 1, but Europe and other areas are Region 2. Don't buy DVDs in Britain unless your player is multi-region.

CAR RENTAL

Rental rates vary widely but are generally expensive, beginning at £50 ($80) a day and £200 ($320) a week for a small economy car, usually with manual transmission. Air-conditioning and unlimited mileage generally come with larger automatic transmission cars.

Major Agencies Alamo ☎ 800/522-9696 ⊕ www.alamo.com. **Avis** ☎ 800/331-1084, 800/879-2847 in Canada, 0870/606-0100 in the U.K., 02/9353-9000 in Australia, 09/526-2847 in New Zealand ⊕ www.avis.com. **Budget** ☎ 800/527-0700, 0870/156-5656 in the U.K. ⊕ www.budget.com. **Dollar** ☎ 800/800-6000, 0800/085-4578 in the U.K. ⊕ www.dollar.com. **Hertz** ☎ 800/654-3001, 800/263-0600 in Canada, 0870/844-8844 in the U.K., 02/9669-2444 in Australia, 09/256-8690 in New Zealand ⊕ www.hertz.com. **National Car Rental** ☎ 800/227-7368, 0870/600-6666 in the U.K. ⊕ www.nationalcar.com.

CUTTING COSTS

For a good deal, book through a travel agent who will shop around. Do look into wholesalers, companies that do not own fleets but rent in bulk from those that do and often offer better rates than traditional car-rental operations. Prices are best during off-peak periods. Rentals booked through wholesalers often must be paid for before you leave home.

Easy Car rents stick-shift Mercedes A-class minivans for as little as £9 ($12) a day. You must book early via the Web site. Phoning costs 60p ($1) per minute. Costs are kept low by not offering extras, by using advertising on the vehicles, and by having rental outlets in a limited number of cities: London, Birmingham, Glasgow, Liverpool, and Manchester.

Local Agencies Dimple Car Hire ✉ 19 Varley Parade, London, NW9 6RR ☎ 020/8205-1200 🖷 020/7243-4408 ⊕ www.dimple-selfdrive.co.uk. **Easy Car** ☎ 0906/333-3333, 60p per minute within the U.K. ⊕ www.easycar.com. **Enterprise** ✉ 466-480 Edgware Rd., London, W2 1EL ☎ 020/7723-4800 🖷 020/7723-4368. **Europcar** ✉ 12 Semley Pl., London, SW1W 9QL ☎ 020/259-1600 ⊕ www.europcar.com.

Wholesalers Auto Europe ☎ 207/842-2000 or 800/223-5555 🖷 207/842-2222 ⊕ www.autoeurope.com. **Destination Europe Resources** (DER) ✉ 9501 W. Devon Ave., Rosemont, IL 60018 ☎ 800/782-2424 🖷 800/282-7474 ⊕ www.der.com. **Europe by Car** ☎ 212/581-3040 or 800/223-1516 🖷 212/246-1458 ⊕ www.europebycar.com. **Kemwel** ☎ 877/820-0668 or 800/678-0678 🖷 207/842-2147 ⊕ www.kemwel.com.

INSURANCE

When driving a rented car you are generally responsible for any damage to or loss of the vehicle. Collision policies that car-rental companies sell for European rentals typically do not cover stolen vehicles. Before you rent—and purchase collision or theft coverage—see what coverage you already have under the terms of your personal auto-insurance policy and credit cards.

REQUIREMENTS & RESTRICTIONS

In Britain your own driver's license is acceptable. An International Driver's Permit is a good idea; it's available from the American or Canadian automobile association, and, in the United Kingdom, from the Automobile Association or Royal Automobile Club. These international permits, valid only in conjunction with your regular driver's license, are universally recognized, and having one in your wallet may save you a problem with the local authorities. Companies may not rent cars to people who are under 23 or over 75.

SURCHARGES

Before you pick up a car in one city and leave it in another, ask about drop-off charges or one-way service fees, which can be substantial. Also inquire about early-return policies; some rental agencies charge extra if you return the car before the time specified in your contract while others give you a refund for the days not used. To avoid a hefty refueling fee, fill the tank just before you turn in the car, but be aware that gas stations near the rental outlet may overcharge. It's almost never a deal to buy the tank of gas that's in the car when you rent it; the understanding is that you'll return it empty, but some fuel usually remains. Car seats for children usually cost about £20 extra. Adding one extra driver is usually included in the original rental price.

CAR TRAVEL

With close to 60 million inhabitants in a country about the size of California, Britain has some of the most crowded roads in the world. In London, it's best to rely on the excellent public transport network—with the city's tediously slow traffic and restrictive parking rules, a car is a proverbial noose. But away from the towns and cities, you can find miles of little-used roads and lanes where driving can be a real pleasure.

EMERGENCY SERVICES

If your car breaks down, position the red hazard triangle (which should be in the trunk) a few paces away from the rear of the car. Leave the hazard warning lights on. On major highways, emergency roadside telephone booths are positioned within walking-distance intervals. Contact your car rental company or call the Automobile Association toll-free. You can join and receive assistance from the AA on the spot, but the charge is higher—around £75—than a simple membership fee. If you are a member of the AAA (American Automobile Association) or another association, check your membership details before you travel; reciprocal agreements may give you free roadside aid.

🔃 **Ambulance, fire, police** ☎ 999. **Automobile Association** ☎ 0800/085-2721 ⊕ www.theaa.co.uk.

GASOLINE

Gasoline is called petrol in the United Kingdom and is sold by the liter. Most large stations are open 24 hours a day, seven days a week, except in rural areas, where hours can vary. Service stations generally accept all major credit cards. Service is self-serve; only in small villages are you likely to find a friendly attendant (tips aren't expected). Petrol is becoming increasingly expensive, at 80p per liter at press time. Supermarket pumps just outside the city centers frequently offer the best prices. Unleaded petrol is predominant, denoted by green stickers on fuel pumps and pump lines. Premium and super premium are the two varieties, and most cars run on regular premium.

PARKING

Parking regulations are strictly enforced. In London, meters have an insatiable hunger—£1 buys almost 15 minutes—and some will permit only a two-hour stay. Check the regulations on the meter, as most meters do not require feeding at night or on weekends. Do not park within 15 yards of an intersection. Within central London parking is permitted on single yellow lines during certain hours (check the signs on the sidewalk), usually after 6 or 7 PM and on weekends. Do not park on double yellow lines or in bus lanes. On "Red Routes"—busy roads with red lines painted in the street—you may not stop even to let out a passenger. At night, you can park in 30-mph zones, but only if you are within 25 yards of a lighted streetlight.

ROAD CONDITIONS

There's a very good network of superhighways (motorways) and divided highways (dual carriageways) throughout most of Britain, although in more remote areas, especially in parts of Wales and Scotland, where unclassified roads join village to village and are little more than glorified agricultural cart tracks, travel is noticeably slower. Motorways (with the prefix M), shown in blue on most maps and road signs, are mainly two or three lanes in each direction. Other fast major roads (with the prefix A) are shown on maps in green and red. Sections of fast dual carriageway (with black-edged, thick outlines on maps) have both traffic lights and traffic circles, and right turns are sometimes permitted. Turnoffs are often marked by highway numbers, rather than place names, so know the road numbers.

The vast network of lesser roads, for the most part old coach and turnpike roads, might make your trip take twice the time but show you twice as much. Minor roads drawn in yellow or white, the former prefixed by B, the latter unlettered and unnumbered, are the ancient lanes and byways, a superb way of discovering the real Britain. Some of these (the white roads, in the main) are pothole-filled switchbacks, littered with blind corners and barely wide enough for one car. Be prepared to reverse into a passing place if you meet an oncoming car or truck.

ROAD MAPS

You can purchase maps and atlases (Michelin is one brand) in advance from bookstores, or buy them in Britain. Good planning maps are available from Britain's Automobile Association or the Royal Automobile Club. The excellent Ordnance Survey or Collins maps, available from newsstands and bookstores in Britain, cost about £5 for a paper foldout to £7 for a spiral-bound paperback.

⚐ In the U.K. Automobile Association ☎ 0870/600-0371 ⊕ www.theaa.co.uk. **Royal Automobile Club** ☎ 0800/731-1104 ⊕ www.rac.co.uk.

RULES OF THE ROAD

Always remember to **drive on the left in Britain**; this takes a bit of getting used to, and it's much easier if you're driving a British car where the steering and mirrors are designed for U.K. conditions. Study your map before leaving the airport, and be sure to give yourself plenty of time to adjust. The use of seat belts is obligatory in the front seat and in the back seat where they exist (except for particularly old models, all cars should have both front and rear seat belts). You can still talk on a hand-held cell phone while you drive, but legislation is being considered that would ban this practice.

If you plan to drive in Britain, **pick up a copy of the official Highway Code** (£1.50) at a service station, newsstand, or bookstore. Besides driving rules and illustrations of signs and road markings, this booklet contains information for motorcyclists, cyclists, and pedestrians. For license information, *see* Car Rental.

Speed limits are complicated, and traffic police can be hard on speeders, especially in urban areas. In those areas, the limit (shown on circular red signs) is generally 30 mph, but 40 mph on some main roads. In rural areas the limit is 60 mph on ordinary roads and 70 mph on motorways. At traffic circles ("roundabouts" in Britain), circulation is clockwise, and entering motorists must yield to cars coming from their right. The use of horns is prohibited between 11:30 PM and 7 AM.

Pedestrians have the right-of-way on "zebra" crossings (black and white stripes that stretch across the street between two Belisha beacons—orange-flashing globe lights on posts). The curb on each side of the zebra crossing has zigzag markings. It is illegal to park within the zigzag area or to pass another vehicle at a zebra crossing. At other crossings, pedestrians must yield to traffic, but they do have the right-of-way over traffic turning left—if they dare.

Drunk-driving laws are strictly enforced. The legal limit is 80 milligrams of alcohol, which means roughly two units of alcohol—two glasses of wine, one pint of beer, or one glass of whisky—but these amounts vary, depending on your body weight or the amount you have eaten that day. It's far safer to avoid alcohol if you're driving.

THE CHANNEL TUNNEL

Short of flying, taking the "Chunnel" is the fastest way to cross the English Channel: 35 minutes from Folkestone to Calais, 60 minutes from motorway to motorway, or 2 hours and 35 minutes from London's Waterloo Station to Paris's Gare du Nord. Eurostar service from London to Brussels takes 2 hours and 20 minutes.

Booking Eurostar by telephone directly in Great Britain entails a £5 booking fee. Booking ahead through the Eurostar Web site usually yields the cheapest option. Low-cost airlines have given Eurostar intense competition, so train ticket prices have dropped (at this writing, to as low as $90 for a weekday round-trip).

⚐ Car Transport Eurotunnel ☎ 0870/535-3535 in the U.K., 070/223210 in Belgium, 03-21-00-61-00 in France ⊕ www.eurotunnel.com. **French Motorail/Rail Europe** ☎ 0870/241-5415 ⊕ www.raileurope.co.uk/frenchmotorail.

⚐ Passenger Service Eurostar ☎ 1233/617575 or 0870/518-6186, in the U.K. ⊕ www.eurostar.co.uk. **Rail Europe** ☎ 800/942-4866 or 800/274-8724, 0870/584-8848 U.K. inquiries and credit-card bookings ⊕ www.raileurope.com.

CHILDREN IN GREAT BRITAIN

Plan your itinerary to include places and activities that will keep your children happy, and **involve your youngsters** as you outline your trip. Many museums and major attractions offer special interactive features that appeal to kids; for example, some stately homes and castles have added children's "fun trails," where kids can play detective as they explore the property. Cinemas, concert halls, and theaters have plenty of kid-friendly entertainment, particularly during school holidays. And even the more chic restaurants are learning to welcome well-behaved children.

For information on events for kids in and around London, look for *Kids Out!,* a monthly magazine available from newsstands and bookstores. London Line, the London Tourist Board's information line, offers two options: What's On for Children and Places for Children to Go, both 60p per minute from a U.K. phone. The tourist board publishes *Where to Take Children. Fodor's Around London with Kids* (available in bookstores everywhere) can help you plan your days together.

If you are renting a car, don't forget to arrange for a car seat when you reserve. For general advice about traveling with children, consult *Fodor's FYI: Travel with Your Baby* (available in bookstores everywhere).
🚩 Local Information **London Line** ☎ 09068/663344.

FLYING

If your children are two or older, ask about children's airfares. As a general rule, infants under two not occupying a seat fly at greatly reduced fares or even for free. But if you want to guarantee a seat for an infant, you have to pay full fare. Consider flying during off-peak days and times; most airlines will grant an infant a seat without a ticket if there are available seats. When booking, confirm carry-on allowances if you're traveling with infants. In general, for babies charged 10% to 50% of the adult fare you are allowed one carry-on bag and a collapsible stroller; if the flight is full, the stroller may have to be checked or you may be limited to less.

Experts agree that it's a good idea to use safety seats aloft for children weighing less than 40 pounds. Airlines set their own policies: if you use a safety seat, U.S. carriers usually require that the child be ticketed, even if he or she is young enough to ride free, because the seats must be strapped into regular seats. And even if you pay the full adult fare for the seat, it may be worth it, especially on longer trips. Do **check your airline's policy about using safety seats during takeoff and landing.** Safety seats are not allowed everywhere in the plane, so get your seat assignments as early as possible.

When reserving, request children's meals or a freestanding bassinet (not available at all airlines) if you need them. But note that bulkhead seats, where you must sit to use the bassinet, may lack an overhead bin or storage space on the floor.

FOOD

You'll find the usual gamut of burger and fast-food chains (Burger King, McDonald's, Kentucky Fried Chicken) in Britain. Pizza chains, such as Pizza Hut and Pizza Express, are family-friendly—with foods to please parents, too; London has one on nearly every corner, and they also crop up in larger cities nationwide. Many families find that ethnic restaurants offer the best combination of moderate prices and interesting food. Almost every town has its share of Asian eateries and Italian pasta joints. If your children have a taste for spices, try Indian restaurants, which are particularly common in London and in the northern cities of Birmingham and Manchester. Most pubs and small country hotels are becoming more family oriented and have family eating rooms (although these can lack character). Unless your children's behavior is impeccable, avoid the high-class, terribly British establishments.

LODGING

Most hotels in Great Britain allow children under a certain age to stay in their parents' room at no extra charge, but others charge for them as extra adults; be sure to find out the cutoff age for children's discounts, which is usually about 12 years old.

PUBS

Most pubs tend to be child-friendly, but many have restricted hours for children. At some pubs, children between the ages of 14 and 17 can enter bar areas; children younger than 14 can be admitted, with an adult, only if the pub has a Children's Certificate. At other pubs, anyone younger than 21 is not allowed in a bar after 6 PM. The Web site www.pubs.com, which covers London pubs, sorts out restrictions and lists child-friendly pubs.

SIGHTS & ATTRACTIONS

Places that are especially appealing to children are indicated by a rubber-duckie icon (🐤) in the margin.

SUPPLIES & EQUIPMENT

You'll find everything you need for babies and children in supermarkets such as Sainsbury's and Tesco's and in the Boots and Superdrug pharmacies. American brands are widely available.

TRANSPORTATION

For air transportation, *see* Flying. On trains and buses, children between the ages of 5 and 15 pay half or reduced fares, and kids under 5 travel free. When riding in a car, children are required by law to use seat belts. Children under 5 must ride in a child seat. Many car rental companies rent car seats for younger children; ask in advance.

COMPUTERS ON THE ROAD

If you're traveling with a laptop, carry a spare battery and adapter. If you are going to use dial-up, get a telephone cord that's compatible with a British phone jack. Never plug your computer into any socket before asking about surge protection. Some hotels do not have built-in current stabilizers, and extreme electrical fluctuations and surges can short your adapter or even destroy your computer. Before connecting your computer to a phone line, you may want to test the line as well. IBM sells an invaluable pen-size modem tester that plugs into a telephone jack to check whether the line is safe to use. More hotels are upgrading their Internet services and offering ISDN and wi-fi, and in cities Internet cafés are plentiful; even coffee shops may have access points.

CONSUMER PROTECTION

Whether you're shopping for gifts or purchasing travel services, **pay with a major credit card** whenever possible, so you can cancel payment or get reimbursed if there's a problem (and you can provide documentation). If you're doing business with a particular company for the first time, contact your local Better Business Bureau and

the attorney general's offices in your state and (for U.S. businesses) the company's home state as well. Have any complaints been filed? Finally, if you're buying a package or tour, always consider travel insurance that includes default coverage (⇨ Insurance).

🎫 BBBs Council of Better Business Bureaus ✉ 4200 Wilson Blvd., Suite 800, Arlington, VA 22203 ☎ 703/276-0100 📠 703/525-8277 ⊕ www.bbb.org.

CRUISE TRAVEL

In 2004 the Cunard Line's *Queen Mary 2* replaced the *Queen Elizabeth 2* on regular crossings, April–December, between Southampton, England, and Baltimore, Boston, and New York City; arrangements can include one-way airfare. Check the travel pages of your Sunday newspaper for other cruise ships that sail to Britain, or consult a travel agent. For information about cruising waterways in Great Britain, *see* Sports & Outdoors. To learn how to plan, choose, and book a cruise-ship voyage, consult *Fodor's FYI: Plan & Enjoy Your Cruise* (available in bookstores everywhere).

🎫 Cruise Lines Cunard Line ☎ 800/728-6273 ⊕ www.cunard.com.

CUSTOMS & DUTIES

When shopping abroad, keep receipts for all purchases. Upon reentering the country, **be ready to show customs officials what you've bought.** Pack purchases together in an easily accessible place. If you think a duty is incorrect, appeal the assessment. If you object to the way your clearance was handled, note the inspector's badge number. In either case, first ask to see a supervisor. If the problem isn't resolved, write to the appropriate authorities, beginning with the port director at your point of entry.

IN AUSTRALIA

Australian residents who are 18 or older may bring home A$400 worth of souvenirs and gifts (including jewelry), 250 cigarettes or 250 grams of cigars or other tobacco products, and 1,125 ml of alcohol (including wine, beer, and spirits). Residents under 18 may bring back A$200 worth of goods. Members of the same family traveling together may pool their allowances. Prohibited items include meat products. Seeds, plants, and fruits need to be declared upon arrival.

Australian Customs Service ⬦ Regional Director, Box 8, Sydney, NSW 2001 ☎ 02/9213-2000 or 1300/363263, 02/9364-7222 or 1800/020-504 quarantine-inquiry line ⬦ 02/9213-4043 ⊕ www.customs.gov.au.

IN CANADA

Canadian residents who have been out of Canada for at least seven days may bring in C$750 worth of goods duty-free. If you've been away fewer than seven days but more than 48 hours, the duty-free allowance drops to C$200. If your trip lasts 24 to 48 hours, the allowance is C$50. You may not pool allowances with family members. Goods claimed under the C$750 exemption may follow you by mail; those claimed under the lesser exemptions must accompany you. Alcohol and tobacco products may be included in the seven-day and 48-hour exemptions but not in the 24-hour exemption. If you meet the age requirements of the province or territory through which you reenter Canada, you may bring in, duty-free, 1.5 liters of wine *or* 1.14 liters (40 imperial ounces) of liquor *or* 24 12-ounce cans or bottles of beer or ale. Also, if you meet the local age requirement for tobacco products, you may bring in, duty-free, 200 cigarettes and 50 cigars. Check ahead of time with the Canada Customs and Revenue Agency or the Department of Agriculture for policies regarding meat products, seeds, plants, and fruits.

You may send an unlimited number of gifts (only one gift per recipient, however) worth up to C$60 each duty-free to Canada. Label the package UNSOLICITED GIFT—VALUE UNDER $60. Alcohol and tobacco are excluded.

Canada Customs and Revenue Agency ⬦ 2265 St. Laurent Blvd., Ottawa, Ontario K1G 4K3 ☎ 800/461-9999 in Canada, 204/983-3500, 506/636-5064 ⊕ www.ccra.gc.ca.

IN NEW ZEALAND

All homeward-bound residents may bring back NZ$700 worth of souvenirs and gifts; passengers may not pool their allowances, and children can claim only the concession on goods intended for their own use. For those 17 or older, the duty-free allowance also includes 4.5 liters of wine or beer; one 1,125-ml bottle of spirits; and either 200 cigarettes, 250 grams of tobacco, 50 cigars, *or* a combination of the three up to 250 grams. Meat products, seeds, plants, and fruits must be declared upon arrival to the Agricultural Services Department.

New Zealand Customs ⬦ Head office: The Customhouse, 17-21 Whitmore St., Box 2218, Wellington ☎ 09/300-5399 or 0800/428-786 ⊕ www.customs.govt.nz.

IN THE U.K.

Fresh meats, plants and vegetables, controlled drugs, and firearms and ammunition may not be brought into the United Kingdom. Pets from the United States or Canada with the proper documentation may be brought into the country without quarantine under the U.K. Pet Travel Scheme (PETS). The process takes about six months to complete and involves detailed steps.

You will face no customs formalities if you enter Scotland or Wales from any other part of the United Kingdom.

HM Customs and Excise ⬦ Valiant House, 365 High Rd., Wembley, Middlesex, HA9 6AY ☎ 0208/929-0152 or 0845/010-9000 advice service ⊕ www.hmce.gov.uk. **Pet Travel Scheme** ⬦ Department for Environment, Food and Rural Affairs, Area 201, 1A Page St., London, SW1P 4PQ ☎ 0870/241-1710 ⊕ www.defra.gov.uk/animalh/quarantine/index.htm.

IN THE U.S.

U.S. residents who have been out of the country for at least 48 hours may bring home, for personal use, $800 worth of foreign goods duty-free, as long as they haven't used the $800 allowance or any part of it in the past 30 days. This exemption may include 1 liter of alcohol (for travelers 21 and older), 200 cigarettes, and 100 non-Cuban cigars. Family members from the same household who are traveling together may pool their $800 personal exemptions. For fewer than 48 hours, the duty-free allowance drops to

$200, which may include 50 cigarettes, 10 non-Cuban cigars, and 150 ml of alcohol (or 150 ml of perfume containing alcohol). The $200 allowance cannot be combined with other individuals' exemptions, and if you exceed it, the full value of all the goods will be taxed. Antiques, which U.S. Customs and Border Protection defines as objects more than 100 years old, enter duty-free, as do original works of art done entirely by hand, including paintings, drawings, and sculptures. This doesn't apply to folk art or handicrafts, which are in general dutiable.

You may also send packages home duty-free, with a limit of one parcel per addressee per day (except alcohol or tobacco products or perfume worth more than $5). You can mail up to $200 worth of goods for personal use; label the package PERSONAL USE and attach a list of its contents and their retail value. If the package contains your used personal belongings, mark it AMERICAN GOODS RETURNED to avoid paying duties. You may send up to $100 worth of goods as a gift; mark the package UNSOLICITED GIFT. Mailed items do not affect your duty-free allowance on your return.

To avoid paying duty on foreign-made high-ticket items you already own and will take on your trip, register them with Customs before you leave the country. Consider filing a Certificate of Registration for laptops, cameras, watches, and other digital devices identified with serial numbers or other permanent markings; you can keep the certificate for other trips. Otherwise, bring a sales receipt or insurance form to show that you owned the item before you left the United States.

For more about duties, restricted items, and other information about international travel, check out U.S. Customs and Border Protection's online brochure, *Know Before You Go.*

🖪 **U.S. Customs and Border Protection** ⊠ for inquiries and equipment registration, 1300 Pennsylvania Ave. NW, Washington, DC 20229 ⊕ www.cbp. gov ☎ 877/287-8667, 202/354-1000 ⊠ for complaints, Customer Satisfaction Unit, 1300 Pennsylvania Ave. NW, Room 5.2C, Washington, DC 20229.

DISABILITIES & ACCESSIBILITY

Compared with the United States, Great Britain has a ways to go in helping people with disabilities, but it is making strides in making its major cities more accessible. In London, for instance, most Underground (subway) stations have vast escalators and steps, but contact the London Transport information line for their booklet "Access to the Underground," which gives facts about elevators and ramps at individual tube stations as well as information about buses and Braille maps. The spacious, regal London Black Cabs are perfectly accommodating for people in wheelchairs, and further good news is that many London hotels have wheelchair ramps. More buses are now equipped to deal with wheelchairs, too. The London Tourist Board produces an updated newsletter, *London for All,* available from Tourist Information Centres. Note that VisitBritain and the London Tourist Board will provide lists of London hotels for people with disabilities; these hotels often post the sign H at their door to welcome such travelers.

Artsline provides information on the accessibility of arts venues (theaters and cinemas) and events. For vacation bookings and special deals on equipped hotel rooms, contact Holiday Care or Can Be Done travel agency. RADAR, or the Royal Association for Disability and Rehabilitation, has travel information and advice on accommodations throughout the British Isles and Europe. DIAL, or the Disablement Information and Advice Line, offers information on local groups in Britain that can provide advice. Tripscope covers the ground on all transport questions. Wheelchair Travel & Access Mini Buses advise on where to find converted cars to rent, including chauffeured minibuses and cars with hand controls.

🖪 **Local Resources Artsline** ⊠ 54 Chalton St., London, NW1 1HS ☎ 020/7388-2227 ⊕ www. artslineonline.com. **Can Be Done** ⊠ 7-11 Kensington High St., London, W8 5NP ☎ 020/8907-2400 ⊕ www.canbedone.co.uk. **DIAL** ☎ 01302/310123. **Holiday Care** ⊠ 7th Floor Sunley House, 4 Bedford Pk., Croydon, Surrey, CR0 2AP ☎ 0845/124-9971 ⊕ www.holidaycare.org.uk. **London Transport's Unit for Disabled Passengers** ⊠ 172 Buckingham

Palace Rd., London, SW1 9TN ☎ 020/7918-3312 🖷 020/7918-3876 ⊕ www.londontransport.co.uk. **RADAR** ✉ 12 City Forum, 250 City Rd., London, EC1V 8AF 🖷 020/7250-3222 ⊕ www.radar.org.uk. **Tripscope** ✉ The Vassall Centre, Gill Ave., Bristol, BS16 2QQ 🖷 0845/758-5641 ⊕ www.tripscope.org.uk. **Wheelchair Travel & Access Mini Buses** ✉ 1 Johnston Green, Guildford, Surrey, GU2 6XS 🖷 01483/237668 ⊕ www.wheelchair-travel.co.uk.

LODGING

The definition of accessibility may differ from hotel to hotel, so it's best to ask questions. If you have mobility problems, ask for the lowest floor on which accessible services are offered. If you have a hearing impairment, check whether the hotel has devices to alert you visually to the ring of the telephone, a knock at the door, and a fire/emergency alarm. Some hotels provide these devices without charge. Discuss your needs with hotel personnel if this equipment isn't available, so that a staff member can personally alert you in the event of an emergency. If you're bringing a guide dog, get authorization ahead of time and write down the name of the person with whom you spoke.

If you book directly through Holiday Care, rates at some hotels with special facilities for visitors with disabilities can be discounted.

RESERVATIONS

When discussing accessibility with an operator or reservations agent, ask hard questions. Are there any stairs, inside *or* out? Are there grab bars next to the toilet *and* in the shower/tub? How wide is the doorway to the room? To the bathroom? For the most extensive facilities meeting the latest legal specifications, opt for newer accommodations. If you reserve through a toll-free number, consider also calling the hotel's local number to confirm the information from the central reservations office. Get confirmation in writing when you can.

SIGHTS & ATTRACTIONS

The London Tourist Board can provide information on city attractions with accessible facilities. It is best to phone ahead to check on the details of venues around

Britain. Alternatively, you could put yourself in the hands of a tour company such as Tour Guides Ltd.; they not only tailor custom tours but also have a dynamic Blue Badge guide who is a wheelchair user. 🔼 **Local Resources Tour Guides Ltd.** ☎ 020/7495-5504 ⊕ www.tourguides.co.uk.

TRANSPORTATION

🔼 **Complaints Aviation Consumer Protection Division** (⇨ Air Travel) for airline-related problems. **Departmental Office of Civil Rights** ✉ for general inquiries, U.S. Department of Transportation, S-30, 400 7th St. SW, Room 10215, Washington, DC 20590 ☎ 202/366-4648 🖷 202/366-9371 ⊕ www.dot.gov/ost/docr/index.htm. **Disability Rights Section** ✉ NYAV, U.S. Department of Justice, Civil Rights Division, 950 Pennsylvania Ave. NW, Washington, DC 20530 🖷 ADA information line 202/514-0301, 800/514-0301, 202/514-0383 TTY, 800/514-0383 TTY ⊕ www.ada.gov. **U.S. Department of Transportation Hotline** 🖷 for disability-related air-travel problems, 800/778-4838 or 800/455-9880 TTY.

TRAVEL AGENCIES

In the United States, the Americans with Disabilities Act requires that travel firms serve the needs of all travelers. Some agencies specialize in working with people with disabilities. 🔼 **Travelers with Mobility Problems Access Adventures/B. Roberts Travel** ✉ 206 Chestnut Ridge Rd., Scottsville, NY 14624 🖷 585/889-9096 ⊕ www.brobertstravel.com ✍ dltravel@prodigy.net, run by a former physical-rehabilitation counselor. **CareVacations** ✉ No. 5, 5110-50 Ave., Leduc, Alberta, Canada, T9E 6V4 🖷 780/986-6404 or 877/478-7827 🖷 780/986-8332 ⊕ www.carevacations.com, for group tours and cruise vacations. **Flying Wheels Travel** ✉ 143 W. Bridge St., Box 382, Owatonna, MN 55060 ☎ 507/451-5005 🖷 507/451-1685 ⊕ www.flyingwheelstravel.com.

DISCOUNTS & DEALS

Be a smart shopper and compare all your options before making decisions. A plane ticket bought with a promotional coupon from travel clubs, coupon books, and direct-mail offers or purchased on the Internet may not be cheaper than the least expensive fare from a discount ticket agency. And always keep in mind that what you get is just as important as what you save.

DISCOUNT PASSES

If you plan to visit castles, gardens, and historic houses during your stay in Britain, **look into discount passes or organization memberships** that can provide significant savings. The National Trust, English Heritage, and the Historic Houses Association are involved with hundreds of properties. English Heritage's Overseas Visitors Pass costs £15 for a 7-day pass and £19 for a 14-day pass for one adult. VisitBritain's Great British Heritage Pass is £22 for 4 days, £35 for one week, £46 for 15 days, and £60 for one month. Annual membership in the National Trust (the Royal Oak Foundation is the U.S. affiliate) is $50 a year through the Royal Oak Foundation. English Heritage membership is £34, and the Historic Houses Association is £32. Most passes can be purchased online, and all offer free admission as well as a guide to the properties. The VisitBritain Web site (⇨ Visitor Information) has information about these and other discounts. Be sure to **match what the pass or membership offers against your itinerary** to see if its worthwhile. For London Pass information, *see* London A to Z *in* Chapter 1. For passes specifically for Wales and Scotland, *see* Wales A to Z *in* Chapter 9 and Scotland A to Z *in* Chapter 15.

🎫 **English Heritage** ☎ 0870/333-1181 ⊕ www.english-heritage.org.uk. **Historic Houses Association** ☎ 020/7259-5688 ⊕ www.hha.org.uk. **Royal Oak Foundation** ✉ 26 Broadway, Suite 950, New York, NY 10004 ☎ 212/480-2889 or 800/913-6565 ⊕ www.royal-oak.org.

DISCOUNT RESERVATIONS

To save money, look into discount reservations services with Web sites and toll-free numbers, which use their buying power to get a better price on hotels, airline tickets (⇨ Air Travel), even car rentals. When booking a room, always **call the hotel's local toll-free number** (if one is available) rather than the central reservations number—you'll often get a better price. Always ask about special packages or corporate rates.

When shopping for the best deal on hotels and car rentals, look for guaranteed exchange rates, which protect you against a falling dollar. With your rate locked in, you won't pay more, even if the price goes up in the local currency.

🎫 **Airline Tickets Air 4 Less** ☎ 800/AIR4LESS; low-fare specialist.
🎫 **Hotel Rooms Accommodations Express** ☎ 800/444-7666 or 800/277-1064 ⊕ www.acex.net. **Hotels.com** ☎ 800/246-8357 ⊕ www.hotels.com. **Steigenberger Reservation Service** ☎ 800/223-5652 ⊕ www.srs-worldhotels.com. **Turbotrip.com** ☎ 800/473-7829 ⊕ www.turbotrip.com.

PACKAGE DEALS

Don't confuse packages and guided tours. When you buy a package, you travel on your own, just as though you had planned the trip yourself. Fly/drive packages, which combine airfare and car rental, are often a good deal. In cities, ask the local visitor's bureau about hotel and local transportation packages that include tickets to major museum exhibits or other special events. If you **buy a rail/drive pass,** you may save on train tickets and car rentals. All Eurailpass holders get a discount on Eurostar fares through the Channel Tunnel and often receive reduced rates for buses, hotels, ferries, sightseeing cruises, and car rentals. BritRail Pass holders can purchase Eurostar tickets with their rail passes, too.

EATING & DRINKING

The stereotypical notion of British meals as parades of roast beef, overcooked vegetables, and stodgy puddings is gradually being replaced—particularly in London and other major cities—with a more contemporary picture of Britain as hot foodie territory. From trendy gastro-pubs to the see-and-be-seen dining shrines, Britain is shedding its tired image and becoming one of the most global palates on earth.

The restaurants reviewed in this book are the cream of the crop in each price category. Properties indicated by ✕🏠 are lodging establishments whose restaurants warrant a special trip. Price-category information is given in each chapter. In general, restaurant prices are high. If you're watching your budget, **seek out pubs and ethnic restaurants,** which offer excellent food at reasonable prices.

CATEGORY	COST
££££££	over £22
££££	£18–£22
£££	£13–£17
££	£7–£12
£	under £7

Prices are for a main course at dinner and are given in pounds.

CUTTING COSTS

Eating out in Britain's big cities in particular can be an expensive affair, but you can do it cheaply. Try local cafés, often called workers' cafés, where heaping plates of British comfort food (bacon sandwiches and stuffed baked potatoes, for example) are served. Fast-food outlets offer cheap meals, but choose carefully for healthy items. There are plenty of the big names in fast food, as well as smaller places selling sandwiches, fish and chips, burgers, falafel, and the like. Check out curry houses; Indian food is popular in Britain. Marks & Spencer, Sainsbury's, Waitrose, COOP, and Budgens are chain supermarkets that sell take-out food and picnic fixings.

MEALS & SPECIALTIES

Cafés serving the traditional English breakfast of eggs, bacon, beans, half a grilled tomato, and strong tea are often the cheapest—and most authentic—places for breakfast. For lighter morning fare (or for real brewed coffee), try the Continental-style sandwich bars offering croissants and other pastries.

At lunch, you can grab a sandwich between sights, pop into the local pub, or sit down in a restaurant. Dinner, too, has no set rules, but a three-course meal is standard in most mid-range or high-end restaurants. Pre- or post-theater menus, offering two or three courses for a set price, are usually a good value. Note that most pubs do not have any waitstaff and that you are expected to go to the bar, order a beverage and your meal, and inform them of your table number.

These days, especially in London, "local" could mean nearly any global flavor, but for pure Britishness, a traditional roast beef dinner still tops the list. Its typical accompaniment is Yorkshire pudding—a savory soufflé-like batter of eggs, milk, and flour oven-baked until crisp, then topped with a rich, dark gravy. Shepherd's pie, a classic pub dish, is made with diced or minced lamb and a mashed potato topping. In the pubs, you'll also find a ploughman's lunch—crusty bread, English cheese (perhaps cheddar, blue Stilton, crumbly Cheshire, or smooth red Leicester), and pickles. And of course, there's also fish-and-chips, usually made from cod or haddock deep-fried in a crispy batter and served with thick "chips"—what Americans know as French fries. Take time for afternoon tea—whether with scones (with cream and jam) or cucumber sandwiches, it's still a civilized respite.

You can eat your way around the country seeking out regional specialties. Every region has its own cheese, beer, cake, and candy—from the crumbly, sharp cheeses of the Yorkshire and Derbyshire dales to the hard cheddars of Somerset, the creamy goats' rounds in Wales, and the nutty Cornish yarg. In Devon and Cornwall, look for tooth-tingling fudge and toffee made with clotted cream.

MEALTIMES

Breakfast is generally served between 7:30 and 9 and lunch between noon and 2. Tea—often a meal in itself—is taken between 4 and 5:30, dinner or supper between 7:30 and 9:30, sometimes earlier, seldom later except in large cities. High tea, at about 6, replaces dinner in some areas like the north, where lunch is always called dinner. Sunday roasts at pubs last from 11 AM or noon to 3 or 5 PM.

Unless otherwise noted, the restaurants listed in this guide are open daily for lunch and dinner.

PAYING

Be sure that you **don't double pay a service charge.** Many restaurants exclude service charges from the printed menu (which the law obliges them to display outside), then add 10%–15% to the check, or else stamp SERVICE NOT INCLUDED along the bottom, in which case you should add the 10%–15% yourself. Just don't pay twice for service—some restaurateurs have been known to add service, but leave the total on the credit card slip blank. Larger establishments generally accept major credit cards; pubs, small cafés, or ethnic restaurants may be cash-only.

RESERVATIONS & DRESS
Reservations are always a good idea; we mention them only when they're essential or not accepted. Book as far ahead as you can, and reconfirm as soon as you arrive. (Large parties should always call ahead to check the reservations policy.) We mention dress only when men are required to wear a jacket or a jacket and tie.

WINE, BEER & SPIRITS
Traditional British beer is not the golden-colored designer stuff in fancy bottles served in trendy cafés. Although hundreds of varieties are brewed around the country, the traditional brew is known as bitter. Lighter American-style beer is called lager, and the black brew is called stout (with Guinness the major brand). Real ales, which have a natural second fermentation in the cask, have a shorter shelf life (so many are brewed locally) but special flavor. You may also find traditional "hard" cider made from pressed apples, which can pack an alcoholic punch. Generally the selection and quality is higher in a wine bar or café than in a pub. Pub hours are 11–11, with last orders called about 20 minutes before closing time, though the law may change to allow later closings. The legal drinking age is 18; unless there's a special family room or a beer garden, children are not welcome in some pubs (⇨ Children in Great Britain).

ELECTRICITY
To use electric-powered equipment purchased in the U.S. or Canada, **bring a converter and adapter.** The electrical current in Great Britain is 240 volts (in line with the rest of Europe), 50 cycles alternating current (AC); wall outlets take three-pin plugs, and shaver sockets take two round, oversize prongs. Blackouts and brownouts are rare and are usually fixed in a few hours.

If your appliances are dual-voltage, you'll need only an adapter. Don't use 110-volt

outlets marked FOR SHAVERS ONLY for high-wattage appliances such as blow-dryers. Most laptops operate equally well on 110 and 220 volts and so require only an adapter. For converters, adapters, and advice, contact the British Airways Travel Shop.

🚺 **British Airways Travel Shop** ✉ 213 Piccadilly, W1J 9HQ ☎ 0845/606-0747.

EMBASSIES
🚺 **Australia Australia House** ✉ Strand, London, WC2 ☎ 020/7379-4334 ⊕ www.australia.org.uk.
🚺 **Canada MacDonald House** ✉ 38 Grosvenor St., London, W1 ☎ 020/7258-6600 ⊕ www.canada.org.uk.
🚺 **New Zealand New Zealand House** ✉ 80 Haymarket, London, SW1 ☎ 020/7930-8422 ⊕ www.nzembassy.com.
🚺 **United States American Embassy** ✉ 24 Grosvenor Sq., London, W1 ☎ 020/7499-9000 ⊕ www.usembassy.org.uk; for passports, go to the **U.S. Passport Unit** ✉ 55 Upper Brook St., London, W1 ☎ 020/7499-9000.

EMERGENCIES
If you need to report a theft or an attack, go to the nearest police station, listed in the Yellow Pages or the local directory. For severe emergencies, dial 999 for police, fire, or ambulance. Be prepared to give the telephone number you're calling from. National Health Service hospitals give free, 24-hour treatment in Accident and Emergency sections, although delays can be an hour or more. Prescriptions are valid only if made out by doctors registered in the U.K. For additional information, *see* the A to Z sections in each chapter.

🚺 **Ambulance, fire, police** ☎ 999.

ETIQUETTE & BEHAVIOR
The traditional British reserve is starting to thaw. Particularly with the younger generations, spontaneous displays of delight or displeasure are becoming more commonplace. But in the theater, the opera, and the church, and in other traditional spots, decorum is the word. If you're visiting a family home, a simple bouquet of flowers is a welcome gift. If you're invited for a meal, bringing a bottle of wine is appropriate, if you wish, as is some candy for the children. Kissing on

greeting is still too Continental for most Brits (except among the fashion and media types, who go for two or three air kisses); a warm handshake is just fine. The British can never say please or thank you too often, and to thank a host for hospitality, either a phone call or thank-you card is always appreciated.

BUSINESS ETIQUETTE

Punctuality is of prime importance, so **call ahead if you anticipate a late arrival.** Spouses do not generally attend business dinners, unless invited. If you invite someone to dine, it's usually assumed that you will pick up the tab. However, if you are the visitor, your host may insist on paying.

GAY & LESBIAN TRAVEL

Most major cities (particularly Birmingham, Brighton, Edinburgh, Glasgow, Manchester, and London) have gay communities and social centers. In London, the main gay areas are in the center city—Soho, Old Compton Street, and west to Kensington and Earl's Court. There's a thriving social scene of clubs and cafés; for London event notices, contact Gay's the Word bookshop. The *Pink Paper,* available at libraries, large bookstores, and gay bars, *Gay Times,* and *Time Out* have comprehensive London listings. The round-the-clock London Lesbian & Gay Switchboard is a font of information on London's gay scene. VisitBritain has a brochure and Web site for gay and lesbian travelers.

⚑ Local Resources Gay Times ☎ 020/8340-8644 ⊕ www.gaytimes.co.uk. **Gay's the Word** ✉ 66 Marchmont St., London, WC1N 1AB ☎ 020/7278-7654 ⊕ www.gaystheword.co.uk. **London Lesbian & Gay Switchboard** ☎ 020/7837-7324 ⊕ www.llgs.org.uk. **VisitBritain** ☎ 800/462-2748 ⊕ www.gaybritain.org.

⚑ Gay- & Lesbian-Friendly Travel Agencies Different Roads Travel ✉ 8383 Wilshire Blvd., Suite 520, Beverly Hills, CA 90211 ☎ 323/651-5557 or 800/429-8747 (Ext. 14 for both) 🖷 323/651-5454 ✎ lgernert@tzell.com. **Kennedy Travel** ✉ 130 W. 42nd St., Suite 401, New York, NY 10036 ☎ 212/840-8659, 800/237-7433 🖷 212/730-2269 ⊕ www.kennedytravel.com. **Now, Voyager** ✉ 4406 18th St., San Francisco, CA 94114 ☎ 415/626-1169 or 800/

255-6951 🖷 415/626-8626 ⊕ www.nowvoyager.com. **Skylink Travel and Tour/Flying Dutchmen Travel** ✉ 1455 N. Dutton Ave., Suite A, Santa Rosa, CA 95401 ☎ 707/546-9888 or 800/225-5759 🖷 707/636-0951; serving lesbian travelers.

HEALTH

Great Britain enjoys high standards of health, from safe drinking water to pasteurized foods. That noted, all travelers should pack medicines to help cope with diet changes and consequent irregularity, although these are also available over the counter in British pharmacies. If you take prescription drugs, keep a supply in your carry-on luggage and make a list of all your prescriptions to keep on file at home while you are abroad. You will not be able to renew a U.S. prescription at a pharmacy in Britain. Prescriptions are accepted only if issued by a U.K.-registered physician.

In recent years, there has been concern in Great Britain and throughout Europe about Bovine Spongiform Encephalopathy (BSE), commonly known as Mad Cow Disease, a fatal illness believed to have spread to cattle through the use of feed enriched with body parts of sheep infected with a related disease. It's possible for humans to contract Creutzfeldt-Jakob Disease, an extremely rare, fatal, brain-wasting illness, by eating meat from infected cattle. Although the chance of catching the disease is extremely small, you may wish to avoid eating beef or choose beef or beef products, such as solid pieces of muscle meat (as opposed to burgers or sausages), that might have a reduced opportunity for contamination with tissues that might harbor the BSE agent. For more information, contact the Centers for Disease Control and Prevention.

⚑ Health Warnings National Centers for Disease Control and Prevention (CDC) ✉ Office of Health Communication, National Center for Infectious Diseases, Division of Quarantine, Travelers' Health, 1600 Clifton Rd. NE, Atlanta, GA 30333 ☎ 877/394-8747 international travelers' health line, 800/311-3435 other inquiries, 404/498-1600 Division of Quarantine 🖷 888/232-3299 ⊕ www.cdc.gov/travel. **World Health Organization** (WHO) ⊕ www.who.int.

HOLIDAYS
ENGLAND & WALES
Holidays are New Year's Day; Good Friday and Easter Monday; May Day (first Monday in May); spring and summer bank holidays (last Monday in May and August, respectively); Christmas Day; and Boxing Day (day after Christmas). If any of these holidays falls on a weekend, then the holiday is observed on the following Monday. During the Christmas holidays, many restaurants, as well as museums and other attractions, may close for at least a week—call to verify hours. Book hotels for Christmas travel well in advance, and check whether the hotel restaurant will be open.

SCOTLAND
Holidays are the same as in England, but Scots take the day after New Year's Day to nurse the frantic celebrations of Hogmanay, an end-of-the-year festival. Easter Monday is not a holiday.

INSURANCE
The most useful travel-insurance plan is a comprehensive policy that includes coverage for trip cancellation and interruption, default, trip delay, and medical expenses (with a waiver for preexisting conditions).

Without insurance you'll lose all or most of your money if you cancel your trip, regardless of the reason. Default insurance covers you if your tour operator, airline, or cruise line goes out of business—the chances of which have been increasing. Trip-delay covers expenses that arise because of bad weather or mechanical delays. Study the fine print when comparing policies.

If you're traveling internationally, a key component of travel insurance is coverage for medical bills incurred if you get sick on the road. Such expenses aren't generally covered by Medicare or private policies. Australian citizens need extra medical coverage when traveling abroad.

Always **buy travel policies directly from the insurance company**; if you buy them from a cruise line, airline, or tour operator that goes out of business you probably won't be covered for the agency or operator's default, a major risk. Before making any purchase, review your existing health and home-owner's policies to find what they cover away from home.

☐ Travel Insurers In the U.S.: **Access America** ✉ 2805 N. Parham Rd., Richmond, VA 23294 ☎ 800/284-8300 🖷 804/673-1491 or 800/346-9265 ⊕ www.accessamerica.com. **Travel Guard International** ✉ 1145 Clark St., Stevens Point, WI 54481 ☎ 715/345-0505 or 800/826-1300 🖷 800/955-8785 ⊕ www.travelguard.com.

☐ In the U.K.: **Association of British Insurers** ✉ 51 Gresham St., London EC2V 7HQ ☎ 020/7600-3333 🖷 020/7696-8999 ⊕ www.abi.org.uk. In Canada: **RBC Insurance** ✉ 6880 Financial Dr., Mississauga, Ontario L5N 7Y5 ☎ 800/668-4342 or 905/816-2400 🖷 905/813-4704 ⊕ www.rbcinsurance.com. In Australia: **Insurance Council of Australia** ✉ Insurance Enquiries and Complaints, Level 12, Box 561, Collins St. W, Melbourne, VIC 8007 ☎ 1300/780808 or 03/9629-4109 🖷 03/9621-2060 ⊕ www.iecltd.com.au. In New Zealand: **Insurance Council of New Zealand** ✉ Level 7, 111-115 Customhouse Quay, Box 474, Wellington ☎ 04/472-5230 🖷 04/473-3011 ⊕ www.icnz.org.nz.

LODGING
Hotels, bed-and-breakfasts, or small country houses—there's a style and price to suit most travelers. The lodgings listed are the cream of the crop in each price category. Wherever you stay, make reservations well in advance: Great Britain is popular.

Properties are assigned price categories based on a range that includes the cost of the least expensive standard double room in high season (excluding holidays) and the most expensive. Lodgings are indicated in the text by 🏨 . Properties indicated by ✕🏨 are lodging establishments whose restaurants warrant a special trip. Price-category information is given in each chapter. Unless otherwise noted, all lodgings listed have a private bathroom, air-conditioning, a room phone, and a television. For camping, see Sports & Outdoors.

We always list the facilities that are available—but we don't specify whether they cost extra: when pricing accommodations, always ask what's included and what costs extra. Throughout Britain, lodging prices often include breakfast of some kind, but this is generally not the case in London. Assume that hotels operate on the **European Plan** (EP, with no meals) unless we specify that they use the **Continental Plan** (CP, with a Continental breakfast), **Breakfast Plan** (BP, with a full breakfast), or the **Modified American Plan** (MAP, with breakfast and dinner). Meal plan symbols appear at the end of a review.

CATEGORY	LONDON	ELSEWHERE
£££££	over £250	over £160
££££	£180–£250	£120–£160
£££	£120–£180	£90–£120
££	£70–£120	£60–£90
£	under £70	under £60

Prices are for two people in a standard double room in high season, including VAT, and are given in pounds.

APARTMENT & HOUSE RENTALS

If you want a home base that's roomy enough for a family and comes with cooking facilities, consider a furnished rental. These can save you money, especially if you're traveling with a group. Home-exchange directories sometimes list rentals as well as exchanges.

Also *see* Cottages.

🔂 International Agents At Home Abroad ✒ 163 Third Ave., No. 319, New York, NY 10003 ☎ 212/421-9165 🖷 212/533-0095 ⊕ www.athomeabroadinc. com. **Hideaways International** ✉ 767 Islington St., Portsmouth, NH 03801 ☎ 603/430-4433 or 800/843-4433 🖷 603/430-4444 ⊕ www.hideaways. com, annual membership $145. **Hometours International** ✉ 1108 Scottie La., Knoxville, TN 37919 ☎ 865/690-8484 or 866/367-4668 ⊕ thor.he. net/~hometour/. **Interhome** ✉ 1990 N.E. 163rd St., Suite 110, North Miami Beach, FL 33162 ☎ 305/940-2299 or 800/882-6864 🖷 305/940-2911 ⊕ www. interhome.us. **Vacation Home Rentals Worldwide** ✉ 235 Kensington Ave., Norwood, NJ 07648 ☎ 201/767-9393 or 800/633-3284 🖷 201/767-5510 ⊕ www.vhrww.com. **Villas and Apartments Abroad** ✉ 183 Madison Ave., Suite 201, New York, NY 10016 ☎ 212/213-6435 or 800/433-3020 🖷 212/213-8252 ⊕ www.vaanyc.com. **Villas International** ✉ 4340 Redwood Hwy., Suite D309, San Rafael, CA 94903 ☎ 415/499-9490 or 800/221-2260 🖷 415/499-9491 ⊕ www.villasintl.com.

🔂 Local Agents The Apartment Service ✉ 5 Francis Grove, Wimbledon, SW19 4DT ☎ 020/8944-1444 🖷 020/8944-6744 ⊕ www. apartmentservice.com. **English Country Cottages** ✉ Stoney Bank, Earby, Barnoldswick, BB94 0AA ☎ 0870/781100 ⊕ www.english-country-cottages.

co.uk, from studio apartments to castles. **In the English Manner** ✉ Lancych Bowcath, Boncath Dyfed, SA37 0LJ ☎ 01559/371600 ⊕ www.english-manner. co.uk ✉ American agent ✉ 515 S. Figueroa St., Suite 1000, Los Angeles, CA 90071-3327 ☎ 213/629-1811 or 800/422-0799 🖷 213/629-4759, apartments and cottages.

BED & BREAKFASTS

A special British tradition, and the backbone of budget travel, bed-and-breakfasts (B&Bs) are usually in a family home; few have private bathrooms, and most offer only breakfast. Guest houses are a slightly larger, somewhat more luxurious version. Upscale B&Bs, more along the line of American B&Bs, are now appearing around the country.

Tourist Information Centres around the country can help you find a B&B. Bed & Breakfast (GB) reservation service offers rooms in a range of prices and has discounts for families and off-peak reductions. It represents tourist board–accredited places in London, across the country, and in France. Wolsey Lodges, a consortium of 200 private homes mostly in Britain, includes many luxurious country homes and some more modest houses. Guests are encouraged to dine with their hosts at least one night of their stay. For reservation services in London, *see* London A to Z *in* Chapter 1.

🔂 Reservation Services Bed & Breakfast (GB) ☎ 800/454-8704, 01491/578803 in U.K. 🖷 01491/410806 ⊕ www.bedbreak.com. **Wolsey Lodges** ✉ 9 Market Pl., Hadleigh, Ipswich, IP7 5DL ☎ 01473/822058, 01473/827500 for brochure 🖷 01473/827444 ⊕ www.wolsey-lodges.co.uk.

CAMPING

Camping and caravanning (traveling in a motor home or with a trailer) are popular, and campgrounds are well maintained. Most campgrounds have everything from a restaurant and bar to activities such as fishing, golf, sailing, swimming, and tennis. If you plan to travel between June and September, make reservations months in advance. The most popular camping areas are in Snowdonia, the Lake District, Devon, Cornwall, and the New Forest. Contact VisitBritain in the United States or the Camping and Caravanning Club for information.

The Youth Hostels Association (YHA; ⇨ Hostels) maintains a series of "camping barns"—barns converted into sleeping areas for 6 to 24 people. Facilities are basic, but barns are characterful and are operated by the farmers who own them. Prices start at £3.50 per night. Contact the Forestry Commission for campgrounds and log cabins for rent in Britain's seven forests. Prices are about £4 to £7 per night.

📱 Camping and Caravanning Club ⊠ Greenfields House, Westwood Way, Coventry, West Midlands, CV4 8JH 📞 02476/694995 ⊕ www. campingandcaravanningclub.co.uk. **Forestry Commission** ⊠ 231 Corstorphine Rd., Edinburgh, EH12 7AT, Scotland 📞 0131/334-6505 ⊕ www. forestholidays.co.uk.

COTTAGES

Houses and cottages are available for weekly rental in all areas of the country. These vary from quaint older homes to brand-new buildings in scenic surroundings. For families and large groups, they offer the best value-for-money accommodations, but because they are often in isolated locations, a car is vital. Lists of rental properties are available free of charge from VisitBritain (⇨ Visitor Information). Some National Trust properties have cottages available on the estates of stately homes. Luxury Cottages Direct deals exclusively in four- and five-star properties. You may find discounts of up to 50% on rentals during the off-season (October–March).

📱 Luxury Cottages Direct ⌂ 8 Ty Mawr Ave., Rumney, Cardiff, CF3 3AF 📞 029/2021-2491 ⊕ www.findcottages.co.uk. **National Trust** ⌂ Box 536, Melksham, Wiltshire, SN12 8SX 📞 0870/458-4422 ⊕ www.nationaltrust.org.uk/cottages. **Rural Retreats** ⊠ Retreat House, Station Rd., Blockley, Moreton-in-Marsh, Gloucestershire, GL56 9DZ 📞 01386/701177 ⊕ www.ruralretreats.co.uk.

FARMHOUSES

Farmhouses have become increasingly popular in recent years; their special appeal is the rustic, rural experience. Consider this option only if you are touring by

car. Prices are generally very reasonable. Ask VisitBritain (⇨ Visitor Information) for the booklet "Stay on a Farm" or contact Farm Stay UK.

📱 Farm Stay UK ⊠ National Agricultural Centre, Stoneleigh Park, Kenilworth, Warwickshire, CV8 2LG 📞 0247/669-6909 📠 0247/669-6630 ⊕ www. farmstayuk.co.uk.

HISTORIC BUILDINGS

Want to spend your vacation in a Gothic banqueting house, an old lighthouse, a seaside castle, or maybe in an apartment at Hampton Court Palace? Several organizations, such as the Landmark Trust, National Trust (⇨ Cottages), and Vivat Trust have specially adapted historic buildings to rent. Celtic Castles, an Internet-based booking service, represents castles in Britain and Ireland. Rural Retreats renovates historic buildings including lighthouses around Britain. Most are self-catering (meaning that they include kitchens).

📱 Celtic Castles 📞 01422/356000 ⊕ www. celticcastles.com. **Landmark Trust** ⊠ Shottesbrooke, Maidenhead, Berkshire, SL6 3SW 📞 01628/825925 ⊕ www.landmarktrust.co.uk. **Portmeirion Cottages** ⊠ Hotel Portmeirion, Gwynedd, Wales, LL48 6ET 📞 01766/770228 ⊕ www.portmeirionvillage.com. **Rural Retreats** ⊠ Retreat House, Station Rd., Blockley, Moreton-in-Marsh, Gloucestershire, GL56 9DZ 📞 01386/701177 ⊕ www.ruralretreats.co.uk. **Vivat Trust** ⊠ 70 Cowcross St., London, EC1M 6EJ 📞 020/7336-8825 ⊕ www.vivat.org.uk.

HOME EXCHANGES

If you would like to exchange your home for someone else's, join a home-exchange organization, which will send you its updated listings of available exchanges for a year and will include your own listing in at least one of them. It's up to you to make specific arrangements.

📱 Exchange Clubs HomeLink International ⌂ Box 47747, Tampa, FL 33647 📞 813/975-9825 or 800/638-3841 📠 813/910-8144 ⊕ www.homelink. org; $110 yearly for a listing, online access, and catalog; $70 without catalog. **Intervac U.S.** ⊠ 30 Corte San Fernando, Tiburon, CA 94920 📞 800/756-4663 📠 415/435-7440 ⊕ www.intervacus.com; $125 yearly for a listing, online access, and a catalog; $65 without catalog.

HOSTELS

No matter what your age, you can save on lodging costs by staying at hostels. In some 4,500 locations in more than 70 countries around the world, Hostelling International (HI), the umbrella group for a number of national youth-hostel associations, offers single-sex, dorm-style beds and, at many hostels, rooms for couples and family accommodations. Membership in any HI national hostel association, open to travelers of all ages, allows you to stay in HI-affiliated hostels at member rates; one-year membership is about $28 for adults (C$35 for a two-year minimum membership in Canada, £14 in the U.K., A$52 in Australia, and NZ$40 in New Zealand); hostels charge about $10–$30 per night. Members have priority if the hostel is full; they're also eligible for discounts around the world, even on rail and bus travel in some countries.

⧉ Organizations **Hostelling International–USA** ✉ 8401 Colesville Rd., Suite 600, Silver Spring, MD 20910 ☎ 301/495-1240 🖷 301/495-6697 ⊕ www. hiusa.org. **Hostelling International–Canada** ✉ 205 Catherine St., Suite 400, Ottawa, Ontario K2P 1C3 ☎ 613/237-7884 or 800/663-5777 🖷 613/ 237-7868 ⊕ www.hihostels.ca. **YHA England and Wales** ✉ Trevelyan House, Dimple Rd., Matlock, Derbyshire DE4 3YH, U.K. ☎ 0870/870-8808, 0870/ 770-8868, 0162/959-2600 🖷 0870/770-6127 ⊕ www.yha.org.uk. **YHA Australia** ✉ 422 Kent St., Sydney, NSW 2001 ☎ 02/9261-1111 🖷 02/9261-1969 ⊕ www.yha.com.au. **YHA New Zealand** ✉ Level 1, Moorhouse City, 166 Moorhouse Ave., Box 436, Christchurch ☎ 03/379-9970 or 0800/278-299 🖷 03/365-4476 ⊕ www.yha.org.nz.

HOTELS

Great Britain is a popular vacation destination, so be sure to **reserve hotel rooms weeks (months for London) in advance.** The country has everything from budget chain hotels to luxurious retreats in converted country houses. In many towns and cities you will find old inns that are former coaching inns, which served travelers as they journeyed around the country in horse-drawn carriages and stagecoaches. Most hotels have rooms with "en suite" bathrooms—as private bathrooms are called in Great Britain—although some

older ones may have only washbasins; in this case, showers and bathtubs (and toilets) are usually just down the hall. When you book a room in the mid-to-lower price categories, it's best to confirm your request for a room with en suite facilities. Tourist Information Centres will reserve rooms for you, usually for a small fee. A great many hotels offer special weekend and off-season bargain packages.

HOTEL GRADING SYSTEM

Hotels in England are graded from one to five stars, and guest houses, inns, and B&Bs are graded from one to five diamonds by VisitBritain in association with the Automobile Association (AA) and the Royal Automobile Association (RAC). Basically, the more stars or diamonds a property has, the more facilities it has. A property with one star or diamond has the minimum necessary for a night's sleep and won't include any extras such as minibars, a concierge, or on-site dining. At the top of the scale, five-star properties will have luxurious decor, a broad range of facilities such as a swimming pool and health club, and a highly trained staff.

In Scotland and Wales, the star system is based on quality and comfort, and properties are graded more subjectively by inspectors; they do not use a checklist of facilities. It's a fairly good reflection of lodging from campsites to palatial hotels. Five stars are for the most luxurious hotels; one star is for fair and acceptable. Hostels are graded from one to three stars.

CUTTING COSTS

Youth hostels, especially those in rural areas favored by hikers and walkers, attract all ages, and many have double rooms at excellent prices. Chains such as Premier Lodge and Travel Inn offer low rates and reliable rooms, and are usually close to major sights and cities. At this writing VisitLondon.com, London's official Web site, was offering a lowest-price guarantee on hotel rooms; the Web site has details. LondonTown.com's London Visitor Information Centre provides free maps, tourist information, and last-minute hotel bookings in the city, with savings of up to 50%. Its kiosk in Leicester Square is open daily 8 AM–11 PM. Lastminute.com offers deals on hotel rooms all over the United Kingdom. Hotel rates in major cities tend to be cheapest on weekends, while rural hotels are cheapest on weeknights. Early December and most of January have the lowest occupancy rates, so hotels offer cheaper rooms at these times.

🔢 Local Resources **Lastminute.com** ⊕ www. lastminute.com. **Premier Lodge** ☎ 0870/201–0203, 1604/824202 outside the U.K. ⊕ www. premierlodge.co.uk. **Travel Inn** ☎ 0870/242–8000, 1582/567890 outside the U.K. ⊕ www.travelinn.co. uk. **LondonTown.com's London Visitor Information Centre** ✉ Leicester Sq. ☎ 020/7292–2333 ⊕ www.londontown.com. **VisitLondon** ⊕ www. visitlondon.com

UNIVERSITY HOUSING

In larger cities and in some towns, certain universities offer their residence halls to paying vacationers between terms. The facilities available are usually compact single sleeping units that share bath facilities, and they can be rented on a nightly basis.

🔢 Universities **British Universities Accommodation Consortium** ⌖ University Park, Box 1564, Nottingham, NG7 2RD ☎ 01159/504571.

MAIL & SHIPPING

Stamps may be bought from post offices (open weekdays 9–5:30, Saturday 9–noon), from stamp machines outside post offices, and from news dealers' stores and newsstands. Mailboxes, known as post or letter boxes, are painted bright red; large tubular ones are set on the edge of sidewalks, and smaller boxes are set into post-office walls. Allow seven days for a letter to reach the United States and about 10 days to two weeks to Australia or New Zealand by air mail. Surface mail service can take up to four or five weeks. The useful Royal Mail Web site has information on everything from buying stamps to finding a post office.

🔢 **Royal Mail** ⊕ www.royalmail.com.

🔢 **London Post Offices** ✉ 17 Euston Rd., NW1 ✉ 125–131 Westminster Bridge Rd., SW1 ✉ 54 Great Portland St., W1 ✉ 43 Seymour St., Marble Arch, W1 ✉ The Science Museum, Exhibition Rd., SW7 ✉ 24 William IV St., Trafalgar Sq., WC2.

OVERNIGHT SERVICES

Contact the services listed below for information about the nearest office or package drop-off point.

🔢 Major Services **DHL** ✉ Unit 24 Mastmaker Ct., Mastmaker Rd., London, E14 9UB ☎ 0870/110–0300 ⊕ www.dhl.co.uk. **Federal Express** ✉ 27 Poland St., London, W1V 3DB ☎ 0800/123800 ⊕ www. fedex.com. **Parcelforce** ☎ 0870/850–1150 ⊕ www. parcelforce.co.uk.

POSTAL RATES

Airmail letters up to 10 grams to North America cost 47p; postcards, 42p. The same rates apply to Australia and New Zealand. Letters within Britain are 28p for first-class, 20p for second-class. Always check rates before sending mail, because they are subject to change.

RECEIVING MAIL

If you're uncertain where you'll be staying, **arrange to have your mail sent to American Express.** The service is free to cardholders and traveler's check holders; all others pay a small fee. You can also collect letters at any main or sub post office throughout Britain, so mail can reach you while you are traveling. Ask the sender to mark the envelope "Poste Restante" or "To Be Called For." The letter must be marked with the recipient's full name (as it appears on your passport), and you'll need your passport or another official form of identification for collection.

SHIPPING PARCELS

Most department stores and retail outlets can arrange to ship your goods back home. You should check your insurance for coverage of possible damage. If you want to ship goods yourself, use an overnight postal service, such as Federal Express, DHL, or Parcelforce. Shipping to North America, New Zealand, or Australia can take anywhere from overnight to a month, depending on how much you pay.

MEDIA

NEWSPAPERS & MAGAZINES

For the latest information about shops, restaurants, and art events, peruse Britain's glossy monthly magazines—*Tatler, Country Living, Harpers & Queen,*

Vogue, Wallpaper, World of Interiors, House & Garden, The Face, and *Time Out.* Many of these are available in major cities around the world. Many better newsstands around the world also carry the Sunday editions of the leading British newspapers, such as the *Times,* the *Evening Standard,* the *Independent,* and the *Guardian*; the "Arts" sections of these papers often have news of future events. In addition, London newspapers have Web sites, full of tips and reviews of the hottest eateries, most chic restaurants, and newest hotels. The British tabloids, such as the *Sun, Mirror* and *Daily Mail,* present a lively version of the news, with an emphasis on the sensational.

Scotland's major newspapers include the *Scotsman*—a conservative sheet that styles itself as the journal of record—and the moderate *Glasgow Herald,* along with the tabloid *Daily Record.* The *Sunday Post,* conservative in bent, is the leading Sunday paper; *Scotland on Sunday* competes directly with London's *Sunday Times.* The *Sunday Herald,* an offshoot of the *Glasgow Herald,* is another major title. *List,* a twice-monthly magazine with listings comparable to London's *Time Out,* covers the Glasgow and Edinburgh scenes.

RADIO & TELEVISION

The main television channels are BBC1 and BBC2 from the British Broadcasting Corporation. BBC2 is considered the more eclectic and artsy, with a higher proportion of alternative humor, drama, and documentaries. The independent channels are ITV (Independent Television), which regionalizes into many companies across the country. Channel 4 is a mixture of mainstream and off-the-wall, whereas Channel 5 has more sports and films. You'll see big-budget highbrow productions on television occasionally (most often on the BBC), but there are more mainstream soaps, both homegrown—*Brookside* and *Coronation Street* (which the Queen is rumored to watch)—and international (the Australian *Neighbors*), and the U.S. daytime talk shows such as *Oprah* and general interest shows. Cable channels (many

of which are available in hotel rooms) have increased the diet of entertainment.

Radio has seen a similar explosion for every taste, from 24-hour classical music on Classic FM (100.9 FM), and rock on Capital FM (95.8 FM) and Branson's Virgin (105.8 FM), to nostalgic on Heart (106.2 FM) and talk on Talk Radio (1053 AM)—and that's just a sample of the independents. The BBC's Radio 1 (98.8 FM) is for the young and hip; 2 (89.1 FM) for middle-of-the-roadsters; 3 (91.3 FM) for classics, jazz, and arts; 4 (93.5 FM) for news, current affairs, drama (such as *The Archers* radio soap), and documentary; 5 Live (693 AM) for sports and news with phone-ins; and BBC World Service (648 AM) for the best of the BBC.

MONEY MATTERS

A cup of coffee will run from 60p to £3, depending on where you buy it; a pint of beer is about £1 in the countryside and £2 in a city, and a ham sandwich costs £1.75–£3.50. A short taxi ride averages £6.

Prices throughout this guide are given for adults. Substantially reduced fees are almost always available for children, students, and senior citizens. For information on taxes, *see* Taxes.

ATMS

A debit card, also known as a check card, deducts funds directly from your checking account, which can help you stay within your budget. When you want to rent a car, though, you will need a credit card. Although you can usually *pay* for your car with a debit card, agencies will not allow you to *reserve* a car with a debit card.

Otherwise, the two types of plastic are virtually the same. Both credit and debit cards offer excellent, wholesale exchange rates. And both protect you against unauthorized use if the card is lost or stolen. Your liability is limited to $50, as long as you report the card missing.

Both cards will get you cash advances at ATMs worldwide if your card is properly programmed with your personal identification number (PIN). **Make sure before leaving home that your card has been** programmed for ATM use there—ATMs in Great Britain accept PINs of four or fewer digits only; if your PIN is longer, ask about changing it. If you know your PIN as a word, learn the numerical equivalent, since most Great Britain keypads show numbers only, no letters. Most ATMs are on both the Cirrus and Plus networks. ATMs are available at most main-street banks, at most large supermarkets, such as Sainsbury's and Tesco's, some tube stops in London, most rail stations, and large shops such as John Lewis or Virgin Megastore.

CREDIT CARDS

Throughout this guide, the following abbreviations are used: **AE,** American Express; **DC,** Diners Club; **MC,** MasterCard; and **V,** Visa.

The Discover card is not accepted in Britain.

🚺 **Reporting Lost Cards American Express** ☎ 01273/696933. **Diners Club** ☎ 0800/460800. **MasterCard** ☎ 0800/964767. **Visa** ☎ 0800/891725.

CURRENCY

The unit of currency in Britain is the pound sterling (£), divided into 100 pence (p). The bills (called notes in Britain) are 50, 20, 10, and 5 pounds. Scotland and the Channel Islands have their own bills, and the Channel Islands their own coins, too. The Scottish bills are accepted in the rest of Britain, but you cannot use Channel Islands currency outside the islands. Coins are £2, £1, 50p, 20p, 10p, 5p, 2p, and 1p.

CURRENCY EXCHANGE

At this writing, the exchange rate was about Australian $2.43, Canadian $2.48, New Zealand $2.83, and U.S. $1.84 to the pound (also known as quid). Britain's adoption of the European Union's currency—the euro—continues to be debated.

For the most favorable rates, **change money through banks.** Although ATM transaction fees may be higher abroad than at home, ATM rates are excellent because they're based on wholesale rates offered only by major banks. The currency exchange at Marks & Spencer department stores is also good; they usually have favorable rates and do not charge commission.

You won't do as well at exchange booths in airports or rail and bus stations, in hotels, in restaurants, or in stores. To avoid lines at airport exchange booths, **get a bit of local currency before you leave home.**

🚺 **Exchange Services International Currency Express** ✉ 427 N. Camden Dr., Suite F, Beverly Hills, CA 90210 ☎ 888/278-6628 orders 📠 310/278-6410 ⊕ www.foreignmoney.com. **Travel Ex Currency Services** ☎ 800/287-7362 orders and retail locations ⊕ www.travelex.com.

TRAVELER'S CHECKS

Do you need traveler's checks? It depends on where you're headed. If you're going to rural areas and small towns, go with cash; traveler's checks are best used in cities. Lost or stolen checks can usually be replaced within 24 hours. To ensure a speedy refund, buy your own traveler's checks—don't let someone else pay for them: irregularities like this can cause delays. The person who bought the checks should make the call to request a refund. If you plan to use traveler's checks in Britain, buy them in pounds.

PACKING

Britain can be cool, damp, and overcast, even in summer. You'll want a heavy coat for winter and a lightweight coat or warm jacket for summer. There's no time of year when a raincoat or umbrella won't come in handy. For the cities, **pack as you would for an American city:** coats and ties for expensive restaurants and nightspots, casual clothes elsewhere. Jeans are popular in Britain and are perfectly acceptable for sightseeing and informal dining. Casual blazers are popular here with men. For women, ordinary street dress is acceptable everywhere.

If you plan to stay in budget hotels, take your own soap. Many do not provide soap, and some give guests only one tiny bar per room. In your carry-on luggage, pack an extra pair of eyeglasses or contact lenses and enough of any medication you take to last a few days longer than the entire trip. You may also ask your doctor to write a spare prescription using the drug's generic name, as brand names may vary from country to country. In luggage to be checked, **never pack prescription drugs, valuables, or undeveloped film.** And don't forget to carry with you the addresses of offices that handle refunds of lost traveler's checks. Check *Fodor's How to Pack* (available at online retailers and bookstores everywhere) for more tips.

To avoid customs and security delays, carry medications in their original packaging. Don't pack any sharp objects in your carry-on luggage, including knives of any size or material, scissors, nail clippers, and corkscrews, or anything else that might arouse suspicion.

To avoid having your checked luggage chosen for hand inspection, don't cram bags full. The U.S. Transportation Security Administration suggests packing shoes on top and placing personal items you don't want touched in clear plastic bags.

CHECKING LUGGAGE

You're allowed to carry aboard one bag and one personal article, such as a purse or a laptop computer. Make sure what you carry on fits under your seat or in the overhead bin. Get to the gate early, so you can board as soon as possible, before the overhead bins fill up.

Baggage allowances vary by carrier, destination, and ticket class. On international flights, you're usually allowed to check two bags weighing up to 70 pounds (32 kilograms) each, although a few airlines allow checked bags of up to 88 pounds (40 kilograms) in first class. Some international carriers don't allow more than 66 pounds (30 kilograms) per bag in business class and 44 pounds (20 kilograms) in economy. On domestic flights, the limit is usually 50 to 70 pounds (23 to 32 kilograms) per bag. In general, carry-on bags shouldn't exceed 40 pounds (18 kilograms). Most airlines won't accept bags that weigh more than 100 pounds (45 kilograms) on domestic or international flights. Expect to pay a fee for baggage that exceeds weight limits. Check baggage restrictions with your carrier before you pack.

Airline liability for baggage is limited to $2,500 per person on flights within the United States. On international flights it amounts to $9.07 per pound or $20 per kilogram for checked baggage (roughly $640 per 70-pound bag), with a maximum of $634.90 per piece, and $400 per passenger for unchecked baggage. You can buy additional coverage at check-in for about $10 per $1,000 of coverage, but it often excludes a rather extensive list of items, shown on your airline ticket.

Before departure, itemize your bags' contents and their worth, and label the bags with your name, address, and phone number. (If you use your home address, cover it so potential thieves can't see it readily.) Include a label inside each bag and **pack a copy of your itinerary.** At check-in, make sure each bag is correctly tagged with the destination airport's three-letter code. Because some checked bags will be opened for hand inspection, the U.S. Transportation Security Administration recommends that you leave luggage unlocked or use the plastic locks offered at check-in. TSA screeners place an inspection notice inside searched bags, which are re-sealed with a special lock.

If your bag has been searched and contents are missing or damaged, file a claim with the TSA Consumer Response Center as soon as possible. If your bags arrive damaged or fail to arrive at all, file a written report with the airline before leaving the airport.

🛂 Complaints **U.S. Transportation Security Administration Contact Center** ☎ 866/289-9673 ⊕ www.tsa.gov.

PASSPORTS & VISAS

When traveling internationally, carry your passport even if you don't need one (it's always the best form of I.D.) and **make two photocopies of the data page** (one for someone at home and another for you, carried separately from your passport). If you lose your passport, promptly call the nearest embassy or consulate and the local police.

U.S. passport applications for children under age 14 require consent from both parents or legal guardians; both parents must appear together to sign the application. If only one parent appears, he or she must submit a written statement from the other parent authorizing passport issuance for the child. A parent with sole authority must present evidence of it when applying; acceptable documentation includes the child's certified birth certificate listing only the applying parent, a court order specifically permitting this parent's travel with the child, or a death certificate for the nonapplying parent. Application forms and instructions are available on the Web site of the U.S. State Department's Bureau of Consular Affairs (⊕ travel.state.gov).

ENTERING GREAT BRITAIN

U.S. and Canadian citizens need only a valid passport to enter Great Britain for stays of up to six months. Australian citizens need a passport with at least six months' validity and can stay in Britain for up to six months without a visa when on vacation. New Zealand citizens need a valid passport and can stay up to six months on vacation. Travelers should be prepared to show sufficient funds to support and accommodate themselves while in Britain and to show a return or onward ticket. Health certificates are not required.

PASSPORT OFFICES

The best time to apply for a passport or to renew is in fall and winter. Before any trip, check your passport's expiration date, and, if necessary, renew it as soon as possible.

🚹 Australian Citizens **Passports Australia** Australian Department of Foreign Affairs and Trade ☎ 131-232 ⊕ www.passports.gov.au.
🚹 Canadian Citizens **Passport Office** ✉ to mail in applications: 200 Promenade du Portage, Hull, Québec J8X 4B7 ☎ 819/994-3500 or 800/567-6868 ⊕ www.ppt.gc.ca.
🚹 New Zealand Citizens **New Zealand Passports Office** ☎ 0800/22-5050 or 04/474-8100 ⊕ www. passports.govt.nz.
🚹 U.S. Citizens **National Passport Information Center** ☎ 877/487-2778, 888/874-7793 TDD/TTY ⊕ travel.state.gov.

RESTROOMS

Public toilets are sparse in Britain. Most big cities maintain public facilities that are clean and modern. If there is an attendant,

you are expected to pay admission (usually 30p). Rail stations and department stores have public toilets that occasionally charge a small fee. Most pubs, restaurants, and even fast-food chains reserve toilets for customer use only. Hotels and museums are usually a good place to find clean, free toilets. Some upscale London establishments have attendants who expect a small tip—about £1. On the road, gas station facilities are usually clean and welcoming.

SAFETY

Great Britain has a low incidence of violent crime. However, petty crime is on the rise, and tourists can be the target. Don't wear a money belt or a waist pack, both of which peg you as a tourist. Distribute your cash and any valuables (including your credit cards and passport) between a deep front pocket, an inside jacket or vest pocket, and a hidden money pouch. Do not reach for the money pouch once you're in public.

When paying at a shop or a restaurant, **never put your wallet down or let your bag out of your hand.** When sitting on a chair in a public place, keep your purse on your lap. Always use the bag hooks in public toilet stalls instead of putting your bag on the floor where it may be snatched.

Don't wear expensive jewelry or watches, as they are easily lifted. **Store your passport in the hotel safe;** use your driver's license for identification. Don't leave anything in your car—take valuables with you and put everything else, even a coat, out of sight in your trunk.

Over the years there have been terrorist incidents in England and Northern Ireland, and although U.S. citizens are not targeted, some have been injured. Since the September 2001 attacks on the World Trade Center in New York and the Pentagon in Washington, D.C., London has become a possible target of terrorist violence. Bomb threats are taken seriously. **Don't leave any bags unattended,** as they may be viewed as a security risk and taken away by the authorities. (For U.S. State Department advisories, *see* Visitor Information.)

LOCAL SCAMS

Although scams do occur in Britain, they are not pervasive. Do, however, **watch out for pickpockets,** particularly in London and other large cities. They often work in pairs, with one distracting you in some way (asking for directions or bumping into you) while the other takes your valuables. Always take a licensed black taxi or call a car service (sometimes called minicabs) recommended by your hotel. Passengers have been robbed or overcharged by unlicensed drivers in fake cabs. Avoid using minicab services offered by drivers on the street. In most cases, they will drive an indirect route and overcharge you. When withdrawing cash from an ATM, be sure to cover the number pad with one hand while inputting your PIN. Always buy theater tickets from a reputable dealer. If you are driving in from a British port, beware of thieves posing as fake customs officials. The thieves stop travelers after they have followed them away from the port. Then they flag them down and "confiscate illegal goods."

WOMEN IN GREAT BRITAIN

Women are unlikely to be harassed, but the usual precautions apply—be vigilant if walking alone at night and avoid dimly lit or deserted areas. Avoid unlicensed minicabs.

SENIOR-CITIZEN TRAVEL

Many museums and galleries in Britain offer free admission to anyone over age 60, and stately homes and gardens may give discounts of up to 40%. To qualify for age-related discounts, mention your senior-citizen status up front when booking hotel reservations (not when checking out) and before you're seated in restaurants (not when paying the bill). Be sure to have identification on hand. When renting a car, ask about promotional car-rental discounts, which can be cheaper than senior-citizen rates.

🎓 Educational Programs **Elderhostel** ✉ 11 Ave. de Lafayette, Boston, MA 02111-1746 ☎ 877/426-8056, 978/323-4141 international callers, 877/426-2167 TTY 📠 877/426-2166 ⊕ www.elderhostel.org. **Interhostel** ✉ University of New Hampshire, 6 Garrison Ave., Durham, NH 03824 ☎ 603/862-1147 or 800/733-9753 📠 603/862-1113 ⊕ www.learn.unh.edu.

SHOPPING

Britain is a global market: Europe's best labels and fashion boutiques can be found in London and in many of the country's major cities, and several U.S. chain stores operate here as well. Department stores, including John Lewis, Selfridges, and Debenhams, have a wide range of everyday items and goods that make great gifts for the folks back home. Designer outlet malls have sprung up around the country, too. If you followed no other pursuit save shopping, you could really exercise your plastic—but the prices may well exhaust it. In any shopping excursion, seek out original designs, ethnic finds (from the many craft markets and fairs), and historical items, which you'll find in abundance, since nearly every village has at least one antiques shop. Take advantage of sales at the end of each season; the biggest are the post-Christmas sales that run through January.

KEY DESTINATIONS

London is the center of the British shopper's universe. Whatever department store, boutique, or specialty shop there is in the whole of the kingdom, you need look no farther than London's Oxford and Regent streets, Knightsbridge, and Kensington. Antiques hunters head for the capital's markets and auction rooms, particularly in the Portobello, Bermondsey, and Bond Street areas. For bespoke tailoring from top to toe, anything can be made to measure—at a price—on Savile Row and Jermyn Street. For fine china, department stores and specialty shops are fruitful hunting grounds. And for one-stop shopping for art, crafts, and beautiful clothes, head for Covent Garden.

To seek out Britain's most famous products on their home turf, you must travel beyond London. If you're seeking true tartans, Shetland sweaters, shortbread, and whisky, Edinburgh should top your shopping itinerary. For Welsh wool rugs and woolen clothing, visit Cardiff and the Welsh folk museums. In Stoke-on-Trent, you can visit museums of pottery and china and purchase these items from the many stores and outlets. The Isle of Wight in the south produces designs to rival the Venetians' Murano glass. Hay-on-Wye, on the Welsh border, is a bibliophiles' center, full of bookshops.

SMART SOUVENIRS

Shops in museums, galleries, and stately homes around the country are often good choices for interesting merchandise, such as high-quality art reproductions, stationery, and beautifully packaged foods such as jam, toffee, and tea. Bookshops and antiques stores stock a plethora of unique and interesting souvenirs. For British crafts and jewelry, the Victoria & Albert Museum shop in London is a smart choice, and for souvenirs with a historical bent, visit the British Museum shop.

WATCH OUT

For art or antiques more than 100 years old, get a Certificate of Age and Origin for customs from the Association of Art and Antique Dealers (LAPADA) or from the dealer selling the piece. Anything more than 50 years old and valued at £39,600 or more needs a certificate, too. Beware of antique items that contain anything from an endangered species, such as tortoiseshell or ivory. You need a permit from the Department of Environment, Food and Rural Affairs to take such items out of Britain.

🇫 **Association of Art and Antiques Dealers** ✉ 535 Kings Rd., London, SW10 0SZ 📞 020/7823-3511 ⊕ www.lapada.co.uk. **Department of Environment, Food and Rural Affairs** ✉ Global Wildlife Division, 2 The Square, Temple Quay, Bristol, BS1 6EH 📞 0117/372-8433.

SPORTS & OUTDOORS

In addition to the associations listed below, VisitBritain and local Tourist Information Centres can recommend places to enjoy your favorite sport.

BIKING

The national body promoting cycle touring is the Cyclists' Touring Club (CTC: £31 a year, £11 for those under 26, £19 for those over 65, and £50 for a family of more than three). Members get free advice and route information, a B&B handbook, and a magazine. The CTC and VisitBritain (⇨ Visitor Information) publish a free guide, "Britain for Cyclists." Both the CTC and BTA provide lists of travel agencies specializing in cycling vacations. Also *see* Bike Travel for further information.

🚲 **Cyclists' Touring Club** ✉ Cotterell House, 69 Meadrow, Godalming, Surrey, GU7 3HS 📞 01483/417217 or 0870/873-0060 ⊕ www.ctc.org.uk.

BOATING

Boating can be a leisurely way to explore the countryside. For boat-rental operators along Britain's several hundred miles of historic canals and waterways, from the Norfolk Broads to the Lake District, contact the Association of Pleasure Craft Operators or Waterway Holidays UK. British Waterways has maps and other information. U.K. Waterway Holidays arranges boat accommodations of all kinds, from traditional narrow boats (small, slender barges) to motorboats and sailboats.

🚤 **Association of Pleasure Craft Operators** ✉ Audley Ave., Newport, Shropshire, TF10 7BX 📞 01952/813572. **British Waterways** ✉ Customer Services, Willow Grange, Church Rd., Watford, WD17 4QA 📞 01923/201120 ⊕ www.britishwaterways.co.uk. **U.K. Waterway Holidays** ✉ 1 Port Hill, Hertford, SG14 1PJ 📞 01992/550616 ⊕ www.ukwh.freeserve.co.uk. **Waterway Holidays UK** 📞 0870/241-5956 ⊕ www.waterwayholidaysuk.com.

GOLF

Originally from Scotland, golf is a beloved pastime all over Great Britain. Some courses take advantage of spectacular natural settings, from the ocean to mountain backdrops. Most courses are reserved for club members and adhere to strict rules of protocol and dress. However, many famous courses, such as St. Andrews in Scotland, can be used by visiting golfers if they reserve well in advance. Package tours with companies such as Golf International and Owenoak International Golf Travel allow visitors into usually exclusive clubs. VisitBritain has a "Golf in Britain" map and brochure that covers 147 courses. For further information on courses, fees, and locations, try the Web sites UK Golf Guide and Golfcourses.org.

F Golf Courses ⊕ www.golfcourses.org. **Golf International** ✉ 14 E. 38th St., New York, NY 10016 ☎ 212/986–9176 or 800/833–1389 ⊕ www. golfinternational.com. **Owenoak International Golf Travel** ✉ 40 Richards Ave., Norwalk, CT 06854 ☎ 203/854–9000 or 800/426–4498 🖷 203/854–1606 ⊕ www.owenoak.com. **UK Golf Guide** ⊕ www.uk-golfguide.com.

WALKING
Walking and hiking, from the slowest ramble to a mountainside climb requiring technical equipment, are enormously popular in Britain. Chapters in this book contain information about a number of long-distance paths. The Ramblers' Association publishes a magazine and a yearbook full of resources, and a list of B&Bs within 2 mi of selected long-distance footpaths.

F **Countryside Commission** ✉ John Dower House, Crescent Pl., Cheltenham, Gloucestershire, GL50 3RA ☎ 01242/521381 ⊕ www.countryside.gov. uk and www.nationaltrail.co.uk. **Long Distance Walkers Association** ✉ Membership Secretary, 63 Yockley Close, Camberley, Surrey, GU15 1QQ ☎ 01753/866685 ⊕ www.ldwa.org.uk. **The Ramblers' Association** ✉ Camelford House, 87–90 Albert Embankment, London, SE1 7TW ☎ 020/7339–8500 ⊕ www.ramblers.org.uk.

STUDENTS IN GREAT BRITAIN
To save money, look into deals available through student-oriented travel agencies. To qualify, you'll need a bona fide student I.D. card. Members of international student groups are also eligible.

F **I.D.s & Services STA Travel** ✉ 10 Downing St., New York, NY 10014 ☎ 212/627–3111, 800/777–0112 24-hr service center 🖷 212/627–3387 ⊕ www.sta. com. **Travel Cuts** ✉ 187 College St., Toronto, Ontario M5T 1P7, Canada ☎ 800/592–2887 in the U.S., 416/979–2406 or 866/246–9762 in Canada 🖷 416/979–8167 ⊕ www.travelcuts.com.

TAXES
An airport departure tax of £20 (£10 for travel within U.K. and EU countries) per person is payable, and may be subject to more government increases; it's included in the price of your ticket.

VALUE-ADDED TAX
The British sales tax (V.A.T., Value Added Tax) is 17½%. The tax is almost always included in quoted prices in shops, hotels, and restaurants. The most common exception is at high-end hotels, where prices often exclude V.A.T. Be sure to verify whether the room price includes V.A.T.

Most travelers can **get a V.A.T. refund** by either the Retail Export or the more cumbersome Direct Export method. Refunds apply for V.A.T. only on goods being taken out of Britain, and purchases must exceed a minimum limit (check with the store—generally £50–£100). Many large stores provide V.A.T.-refund services, but only if you request them; they will handle the paperwork. For the Retail Export method, you must ask the store to complete Form V.A.T. 407 (you must have identification—passports are best), to be given to customs at your last port of departure. Have the form stamped like any customs form by customs officials when you leave the country or, if you're visiting several European Union countries, when you leave the EU. Be ready to show customs officials what you've bought (pack purchases in your carry-on luggage); budget extra time at the airport for this. After you're through passport control, take the form to a refund-service counter for an on-the-spot refund (if the retailer has an agreement with the firm running the counter; ask the store when you make your purchase), or mail it back to the store or a refund service from the airport or after you arrive home. The refund will be forwarded to you in about eight weeks, minus a service charge, either in the form of a credit to your charge card or as a British check, which American banks charge you to convert.

With the Direct Export method, the goods are mailed directly to your home; you must have a Form V.A.T. 407 certified by customs, police, or a notary public when you get home and then sent back to the store, which will refund your money. For inquiries, call the local Customs & Excise office listed in the telephone directory. Remember, V.A.T. refunds can't be processed after you arrive back home.

A commercial service also processes refunds for most shops. You receive the total refund stated on the form. Global Refund is a Europe-wide service with 210,000 affiliated stores and more than 700 refund counters—located at major airports and border crossings. Its refund form is called a Tax Free Check. The service issues refunds in the form of cash, check, or credit-card adjustment. If you don't want to wait at the refund counter, you can mail in the form instead.

V.A.T. Refunds Global Refund ⊠ 99 Main St., Suite 307, Nyack, NY 10960 ☎ 800/566-9828 🖷 845/348-1549 ⊕ www.globalrefund.com.

TELEPHONES
British Telecom runs the telephone service in Great Britain and is generally reliable.

AREA & COUNTRY CODES
The country code for Great Britain is 44. When dialing a British number from abroad, drop the initial 0 from the local area code. For example, let's say you're calling Buckingham Palace—020/7839–1377—from the United States. First, dial 011 (the international access code), then 44 (Great Britain's country code), then 20 (London's center city code—without its initial 0), then the remainder of the telephone number.

Dialing from Great Britain to back home, the country code is 1 for the United States and Canada, 61 for Australia, and 64 for New Zealand.

DIRECTORY & OPERATOR ASSISTANCE
To call the U.K. operator, dial 100; to call the international operator, dial 155. For directory inquiries (information), dial 118500; for international directory assistance, dial 118505.

INTERNATIONAL CALLS
For direct overseas dialing, dial 00, then the country code, area code, and number. For the international operator, credit card, or collect calls, dial 155. Bear in mind that hotels usually levy a hefty (up to 300%) surcharge on calls; it's better to use the pay phones in most hotel foyers or a U.S. calling card.

LOCAL CALLS
You do not need to dial the area code if you are making a call within the same area code.

LONG-DISTANCE CALLS
For long-distance calls within Britain, dial the area code (which usually begins with 01, except in London), followed by the telephone number. The area code prefix is used only when you are dialing from outside the region. In provincial areas, the dialing codes for nearby towns are often posted in the phone booth.

LONG-DISTANCE SERVICES
AT&T, MCI, and Sprint access codes make calling long-distance relatively convenient, but you may find the local access number blocked in many hotel rooms. First ask the hotel operator to connect you. If the hotel operator balks, ask for an international operator, or dial the international operator yourself. One way to improve your odds of getting connected to your long-distance carrier is to travel with more than one company's calling card (a hotel may block Sprint, for example, but not MCI). If all else fails, call from a pay phone.

Access Codes AT&T Direct In the U.K., there are AT&T access numbers to dial the U.S. using three different phone types: ☎ 0500/890011 Cable & Wireless, 0800/890011 British Telecom, 0800/013-0011 AT&T. **MCI WorldPhone** ☎ 0800/279-5088 in the U.K. for the U.S. via MCI. **Sprint International Access** ☎ 0800/890877.

PHONE CARDS
Public card phones operate with British Telecom (BT) chip cards that you can buy from post offices or newsstands. They are ideal for longer calls; are composed of units of 20p; and come in values of £3, £5, £10, and £20. To use a card phone, lift the receiver, insert your card, and dial the number. An indicator panel shows the number of units used. At the end of your call, the card will be returned. Where credit cards are taken, slide the card through, as indicated. Beware of buying cards that require you to dial a free phone number; some of these are not legitimate. It's better to get a BT card.

PUBLIC PHONES
There are three types of phones: those that accept (a) only coins, (b) only British Telecom (BT) phone cards, or (c) BT phone cards and credit cards.

The coin-operated phones are of the push-button variety; their workings vary, but there are usually instructions on each unit. Most take 10p, 20p, 50p, and £1 coins. Insert the coins *before* dialing (minimum charge is 20p). If you hear a repeated single tone after dialing, the line is busy; a continual tone means the number is unobtainable (or that you have dialed the wrong—or no—prefix). The indicator panel shows how much money is left; add more whenever you like. If there is no answer, replace the receiver and your money will be returned.

All calls are charged according to the time of day. Standard rate is weekdays 8 AM–6 PM; cheap rate is weekdays 6 PM–8 AM and all day on weekends, when it's even cheaper. A local call before 6 PM costs 15p for three minutes; this doubles to 30p for the same from a pay phone. A daytime call to the United States will cost 24p a minute on a regular phone (weekends are cheaper), 80p on a pay phone.

TIME

England sets its clocks by Greenwich Mean Time, five hours ahead of the U.S. East Coast. British summer time (GMT plus one hour) requires an additional adjustment from about the end of March to the end of October.

TIPPING

Some restaurants, bars, and most hotels add a service charge of 10%–15% to the bill. In this case, you are not obliged to tip extra. If no service charge is indicated, add 10%–15% to your total bill. Beware when signing credit-card slips that you fill in the correct total; some restaurants leave the gratuity entry empty even when they have levied a service charge. There's no need to tip at clubs (it's acceptable at posher establishments, though) unless you're being served at your table. Taxi drivers should also get 10%–15%. If you get help from a hotel concierge, a tip of £1–£2 is appropriate. You are not expected to tip theater or cinema ushers, elevator operators, or bartenders in pubs. Hairdressers and barbers should receive 10%–15%.

TOURS & PACKAGES

Because everything is prearranged on a prepackaged tour or independent vacation, you spend less time planning—and often get it all at a good price.

BOOKING WITH AN AGENT

Travel agents are excellent resources. But it's a good idea to collect brochures from several agencies, as some agents' suggestions may be influenced by relationships with tour and package firms that reward them for volume sales. If you have a special interest, find an agent with expertise in that area; the American Society of Travel Agents (ASTA; ⇨ Travel Agencies) has a database of specialists worldwide. You can log on to the group's Web site to find an ASTA travel agent in your neighborhood.

Make sure your travel agent knows the accommodations and other services of the place being recommended. Ask about the hotel's location, room size, beds, and whether it has a pool, room service, or programs for children, if you care about these. Has your agent been there in person or sent others whom you can contact?

Do some homework on your own, too: local tourism boards can provide information about lesser-known and small-niche operators, some of which may sell only direct.

BUYER BEWARE

Each year consumers are stranded or lose their money when tour operators—even large ones with excellent reputations—go out of business. So check out the operator. Ask several travel agents about its reputation, and try to **book with a company that has a consumer-protection program.** (Look for information in the company's brochure.) In the United States, members of the United States Tour Operators Association are required to set aside funds ($1 million) to help eligible customers cover payments and travel arrangements in the event that the company defaults. It's also a good idea to choose a company that participates in the American Society of Travel Agents' Tour Operator Program; ASTA will act as mediator in any disputes between you and your tour operator.

Remember that the more your package or tour includes, the better you can predict the ultimate cost of your vacation. Make sure you know exactly what is covered, and beware of hidden costs. Are taxes, tips, and transfers included? Entertainment and excursions? These can add up.

🔁 Tour-Operator Recommendations **American Society of Travel Agents** (⇨ Travel Agencies). **National Tour Association** (NTA) ⊠ 546 E. Main St., Lexington, KY 40508 ☎ 859/226–4444 or 800/682–8886 🖷 859/226–4404 ⊕ www.ntaonline.com. **United States Tour Operators Association** (USTOA) ⊠ 275 Madison Ave., Suite 2014, New York, NY 10016 ☎ 212/599–6599 🖷 212/599–6744 ⊕ www. ustoa.com.

TRAIN TRAVEL

Privatization of rail service in Britain has produced some difficulties, with more service delays and more accidents than in past years. Despite these concerns, the train system, offering service by more than two dozen companies, is extensive and helpful. Changes in the next few years will include the introduction of high-speed trains on popular routes such as London to Manchester. Ask about express or high-speed service if you plan to travel by train.

When traveling by train, **make a reservation whenever possible;** there are often discounts for early booking. Specify if you require nonsmoking or smoking; most trains have one or two carriages designated for smokers. On long-distance runs, some rail lines have buffet cars; on others, you can purchase snacks from a mobile snack cart.

Britain has some fabulously scenic rail routes, often on steam trains, which generally run from April to October. In Wales, the Vale of Rheidol Railway from Aberystwyth climbs up sheer rock faces to Devil's Bridge. In the north of England, the Settle-to-Carlisle Railway travels the Yorkshire Dales; in the west country, the West Somerset Railway's Dunster-to-Minehead route takes in glorious coastline; and in the east, the Romney Marsh-to-Dymchurch runs along the marshland, skirting the Kent coast. A tour on the Orient-Express train *Northern Belle* takes in London, York, Edinburgh,

Chester, Wales, and Bath. Steam Dreams runs steam trains on regular lines out of London stations to Bath, Canterbury, Chichester, Ely, Norwich, Portsmouth, Salisbury, and Winchester.

CLASSES

Most rail lines have a couple of first-class carriages on each train, which have superior seating and tables—but the difference in price between a first-class and standard ticket varies considerably between rail companies. Check with National Rail Enquiries for details.

CUTTING COSTS

If you plan to travel by train in Great Britain, **consider purchasing a BritRail Pass,** which gives unlimited travel over the entire British rail network and will save you money. But be aware that if you don't plan to cover many miles, you may come out ahead by buying individual tickets. You must **buy your BritRail Pass before you leave home.** They are available from most travel agents or from BritRail, DER, or Rail Europe; check their Web sites for complete details. Note that EurailPasses are not honored in Britain and that the rates listed here are subject to change.

BritRail passes come in two basic varieties. The Classic pass allows travel on consecutive days, and the FlexiPass allows a number of travel days within a set period of time. The cost (in U.S. dollars) of a BritRail Consecutive Pass adult ticket for 8 days is $269 standard and $405 first-class; for 15 days, $405 standard and $609 first-class; for 22 days, $515 and $769; and for a month, $609 and $915. The cost of a BritRail FlexiPass adult ticket for 4 days' travel in two months is $235 standard and $355 first-class; for 8 days' travel in two months, $349 standard and $519 first-class; and for 15 days' travel in two months, $525 standard and $779 first-class. Prices drop by about 25% for off-peak travel passes between October and March. Passes for students, seniors, and ages 16–25 are discounted, too.

If you want the flexibility of a car combined with the speed and comfort of the train, try BritRail/Drive (from $299 for one adult, with a $144 supplement for additional adults and $70.50 for children 5–15); this gives you a two-day BritRail FlexiPass and three vouchers valid for Hertz car rental from more than 100 locations throughout Great Britain. A six-day rail pass with seven days of car rental is also available (from $958 car and driver, with $241 adult supplement, $105 children, with a "free child per adult" deal for children under five traveling gratis). Prices listed are for compact, automatic transmission cars, with first-class seats; other options—manual transmission, larger cars, and so on—are available at different prices. If you call your travel agency or Hertz's international desk (⇨ Car Rental), the car of your choice will be waiting for you at the train station.

The Freedom of Scotland Travelpass allows unlimited standard-class travel: $139 for 4 days, $180 for 8 days, and $215 for any 12 or 15 days. The England Flexipass and Freedom of Wales pass are other options, and you can purchase a Eurostar ticket for Paris or Brussels in conjunction with a BritRail Pass.

Many travelers assume that rail passes guarantee them seats or sleeping accommodations on the trains they wish to ride. Not so. You need to **book seats ahead even if you are using a rail pass,** especially on trains that may be crowded, particularly in summer on popular routes.

There are also some discount passes for travel within regions; individual chapters in this book have information, or you can call National Rail Enquiries (⇨ Fares & Schedules).

🚹 Discount Passes **BritRail** ☎ 877/677-1066 ⊕ www.britrail.net. **DER Travel Services** ✉ 9501 W. Devon Ave., Rosemont, IL 60018 ☎ 800/782-2424 🖷 800/782-2424 for information, 800/860-9944 for brochures ⊕ www.der.com. **Rail Europe** ✉ 226 Westchester Ave., White Plains, NY 10604 ☎ 877/257-2887 ⊕ www.raileurope.com ✉ 94 Cumberland St., Toronto, Ontario M5R 1A3 ☎ 416/482-1777 or 800/361-7245 ✉ 179 Piccadilly, London, W1V 0BA ☎ 0870/584-8848.

FARES & SCHEDULES

The monthly *OAG Rail Guide* (about £6.95 and available from WH Smith

branches and most larger main line rail stations) covers all national rail services and Eurostar, including private, narrow-gauge, and steam lines, as well as special services, buses, ferries, and rail-based tourist facilities. You can find timetables of rail services in Britain and some ferry services in the *Thomas Cook European Timetable,* issued monthly and available at travel agents and some bookstores in the United States.

National Rail Enquiries provides an up-to-date railways schedule. Rail travel can be expensive: for instance, a round-trip ticket to Bath from London can cost around £60 per person at peak times. The fee reduces to around £30 at other times, so it's best to travel before or after the commuter rush (after 10 AM and before 4 PM).

🚹 Train Information **National Rail Enquiries** ☎ 0845/748-4950, 020/7278-5240 outside Britain ⊕ www.nationalrail.co.uk. **Orient-Express** ☎ 800/524-2420 ⊕ www.orient-express.com. **Royal Scotsman** ☎ 0131/555-1344 ⊕ www.royalscotsman.com. **Steam Dreams** ☎ 01483/209888 ⊕ www.steamdreams.co.uk. **UK Public Transport Information** ☎ 0870/608-2608 ⊕ www.traveline.org.uk.

PAYING

You can pay in cash, and credit cards are accepted for train fares paid both in person and by phone.

RESERVATIONS

Reserving your ticket in advance is always recommended. Even a reservation 24 hours in advance can provide a substantial discount. Look into cheap day returns if you plan to travel a round-trip in one day.

TRANSPORTATION AROUND GREAT BRITAIN

Ask any Briton about public transportation in the country and the answer will be long and woeful. Air travel within a relatively small country is best saved for the longest trips, though low-cost airlines offer some good deals. Trains can be faster and cheaper, and they go from central point to central point, so that you avoid costly transfers. The train system is extensive but probably in the worst shape, suffering from frequent delays, cancellations, over-crowding at times, and even accidents and strikes. Buses are convenient but can take up to twice as long as the train; service can be infrequent in the most rural areas.

However, most tourists are not affected by the souring of the British public transportation system. Compared with the United States, it's easy to get around by train or bus. For day trips, the train will do just fine, but for longer trips or wanderings around the countryside, a car will make the trip more flexible—and wonderfully scenic, if you choose the slower roads. Buses and cars face the rising problem of congestion, especially in and around London and on the major highways. If you avoid rush hour, you can escape much of this. If you really want to go slow, perhaps the best way is by foot or canal boat. Britain has a well-developed network of footpaths and waterways, and both offer a relaxing way of getting around with the added benefit of getting to stop and talk to locals.

TRAVEL AGENCIES

A good travel agent puts your needs first. Look for an agency that has been in business at least five years, emphasizes customer service, and has someone on staff who specializes in your destination. In addition, **make sure the agency belongs to a professional trade organization.** The American Society of Travel Agents (ASTA)—the largest and most influential in the field with more than 20,000 members in some 140 countries—maintains and enforces a strict code of ethics and will step in to help mediate any agent-client disputes involving ASTA members if necessary. ASTA (whose motto is "Without a travel agent, you're on your own") also maintains a Web site that includes a directory of agents. (If a travel agency is also acting as your tour operator, *see* Buyer Beware *in* Tours & Packages.)

🚩 Local Agent Referrals **American Society of Travel Agents (ASTA)** ✉ 1101 King St., Suite 200, Alexandria, VA 22314 ☎ 703/739-2782 or 800/965-2782 24-hr hotline 🖷 703/684-8319 ⊕ www. astanet.com. **Association of British Travel Agents** ✉ 68-71 Newman St., London W1T 3AH ☎ 020/7637-2444 🖷 020/7637-0713 ⊕ www.abta.com. As-

sociation of Canadian Travel Agencies ✉ 130 Albert St., Suite 1705, Ottawa, Ontario K1P 5G4 ☎ 613/237-3657 🖷 613/237-7052 ⊕ www.acta.ca. **Australian Federation of Travel Agents** ✉ Level 3, 309 Pitt St., Sydney, NSW 2000 ☎ 02/9264-3299 or 1300/363-416 🖷 02/9264-1085 ⊕ www.afta.com. au. **Travel Agents' Association of New Zealand** ✉ Level 5, Tourism and Travel House, 79 Boulcott St., Box 1888, Wellington 6001 ☎ 04/499-0104 🖷 04/499-0786 ⊕ www.taanz.org.nz.

VISITOR INFORMATION

Learn more about foreign destinations by checking government-issued travel advisories and country information. For a broader picture, consider information from more than one country.

The main London Visitor Centre is at Waterloo International Terminal Arrivals Hall (daily 8:30 AM–10:30 PM), with branches at Heathrow Airport (Terminals 1, 2, and 3). The Britain and London Visitor Centre (open June–October, weekdays 9:30–6:30, Saturday 9–5, Sunday 10–4; November–May, weekdays 9:30–6:30, weekends 10–4) provides details about travel, accommodations, and entertainment for the whole of Britain, but you need to visit the center in person to get information. London Line (accessible only in Britain) is VisitLondon's 24-hour phone service—it's a premium-rate (60p per minute at all times) recorded information line, with different numbers for theater, events, museums, sports, getting around, and so on.

VisitBritain has a vast amount of information, both printed and on its Web site; you can even check out information online about film locations in the Harry Potter movies and obtain a Harry Potter map.

🚩 In London **Britain and London Visitor Centre** ✉ 1 Regent St., Piccadilly Circus, SW1Y 4NX ☎ No phone ⊕ www.visitbritain.com. **London Line** ☎ 09068/663344. **London Visitor Centre** ✉ Arrivals Hall, Waterloo International Terminal, Waterloo Rd. ☎ No phone ⊕ www.visitlondon.com.
🚩 In the U.S. **VisitBritain** ✉ 551 5th Ave., 7th fl., New York, NY 10176 ☎ 212/986-2200 or 800/462-2748 ⊕ www.visitbritain.com/usa ✉ 625 N. Michigan Ave., Suite 1510, Chicago, IL 60611 ☎ 800/462-2748.

⑦ In Canada **VisitBritain** ✉ 5915 Airport Rd., Suite 120, Mississauga, Ontario, L4V 1T1 ☎ 905/405–1840 or 800/847–4885 ⊕ www.visitbritain.com/ca. **⑦** **Government Advisories U.S. Department of State** ✉ Overseas Citizens Services Office, 2100 Pennsylvania Ave. NW, 4th floor, Washington, DC 20520 ☎ 202/647–5225 interactive hotline or 888/407–4747 ⊕ www.travel.state.gov. **Consular Affairs Bureau of Canada** ☎ 800/267–6788 or 613/944–6788 ⊕ www.voyage.gc.ca. **Australian Department of Foreign Affairs and Trade** ☎ 300/139–281 travel advice, 02/6261-1299 Consular Travel Advice Faxback Service ⊕ www.dfat.gov.au. **New Zealand Ministry of Foreign Affairs and Trade** ☎ 04/439-8000 ⊕ www.mft.govt.nz.

WEB SITES

Do check out the World Wide Web when planning your trip. You'll find everything from weather forecasts to virtual tours of famous cities. Be sure to visit Fodors.com (⊕ www.fodors.com), a complete travel-planning site. You can research prices and book plane tickets, hotel rooms, rental cars, vacation packages, and more. In addition, you can post your pressing questions in the Travel Talk section. Other planning tools include a currency converter and weather reports, and there are loads of links to travel resources.

VISITOR INFORMATION

The VisitBritain Web site is at ⊕ www.visitbritain.com. Its U.S. gateway Web site, ⊕ www.visitbritain.com/usa, focuses on information most helpful to Britain-bound U.S. travelers, from practical information to money-saving deals. The official London Web site for visitors is ⊕ www.visitlondon.com. VisitLondon's site for kids, ⊕ www.kidslovelondon.com, has interactive features and virtual tours. British Information Services, part of the British Embassy in Washington, D.C., maintains ⊕ www.britainusa.com, a site loaded with practical travel information. The British government's Foreign and Commonwealth Office runs ⊕ www.i-uk.

com, with information about culture, business, and education in Britain, as well as tourism information.

SPECIAL INTERESTS

For information about SeaBritain 2005, a country-wide series of events focusing on maritime heritage (including the 200th anniversary of the battle of Trafalgar), look at ⊕ www.seabritain2005.com. Anyone planning to visit Britain's stately homes, castles, and gardens should study the Web sites of the National Trust (⊕ www.nationaltrust.org.uk), the National Trust for Scotland (⊕ www.nts.org.uk), and English Heritage (⊕ www.english-heritage.org.uk). Gardens are the subject of VisitBritain's site at ⊕ www.visitbritain.com/gardens; also check out ⊕ www.ngs.org.uk, the site of Britain's National Gardens Scheme, which organizes the opening of private gardens to the public. You can find information about more than 100 arts festivals from the British Arts Festivals Association (⊕ www.artsfestivals.co.uk), and U.K. Theatre Web (⊕ www.uktw.co.uk) covers theater around Britain. The official Web site of the British monarchy is ⊕ www.royal.gov.uk. If you're looking for smoke-free establishments, check ⊕ www.smokefreeworld.com. Other Web sites are given throughout Smart Travel Tips.

LONDON ARTS

Many travelers wonder how to find out about London events and news in advance; sometimes a box-office phone call is needed. You can start by using *Time Out*'s weekly listings— ⊕ www.timeout.co.uk—but these listings often don't extend more than a few weeks. For arts coverage and reviews, click on the daily newspaper site (⊕ www.thetimes.co.uk). Theatergoers should log on to ⊕ www.officiallondontheatre.co.uk, which provides a rundown of theater and opera events months down the road.

LONDON

GET THE BEST VIEW OF ST. PAUL'S
from the Millennium Bridge ⇨p.30

FIND THE HOTTEST SPOT TO CHILL
at Sketch in St. James's ⇨p.63

GO FOR PURE POMP AND CEREMONY
at the Changing of the Guard ⇨p.9

TAKE A THAMES-SIDE ART LESSON
at the Tate Modern gallery ⇨p.40

GRAB A SEAT IF YOU CAN
at Gordon Ramsay at Claridge's ⇨p.61

SEE FRESH TWISTS ON THE CLASSICS
at the Young Vic theater ⇨p.90

SALUTE KINGS AND POETS
at Westminster Abbey ⇨p.19

BE ABOVE IT ALL
during a ride on the London Eye ⇨p.36

Updated by
Catherine
Belonogoff,
Jacqueline
Brown, Julius
Honnor, Julie
Tomasz, Alex
Wijeratna

LONDON IS AN ANCIENT CITY whose history greets you at every turn. To gain a sense of its continuity, stand on Waterloo Bridge at sunset. To the east, the great globe of St. Paul's Cathedral glows golden in the fading sunlight as it has since the 17th century, still majestic amid the modern towers of glass and steel that hem it in. To the west stand the mock-medieval ramparts of Westminster, home to the "Mother of Parliaments," which has met here or hereabouts since the 1250s. Past them both snakes the swift, dark Thames, following the same course as when it flowed past the Roman settlement of Londinium nearly 2,000 years ago. If the city contained only its famous landmarks—the Tower of London, Big Ben, Westminster Abbey, Buckingham Palace—it would still rank as one of the world's top cities. But London is so much more.

For much of its history, innumerable epigrams and observations have been directed at London by enthusiasts and detractors. The great 18th-century author and wit Samuel Johnson said that a man who is tired of London is tired of life. Oliver Wendell Holmes said, "No person can be said to know London. The most that anyone can claim is that he knows something of it." In short, the capital of Great Britain is simply one of the most interesting cities on earth. There's no other place like it in its agglomeration of architectural sins and sudden intervention of almost rural sights, in its medley of styles, in its mixture of the green loveliness of parks and the modern gleam of neon. Thankfully, the old London of Queen Anne and Georgian architecture can still be discovered under the hasty routine of later additions.

A city that loves to be explored, London beckons with great museums, royal pageantry, and history-steeped houses. Discovering it takes a bit of work, however. Modern-day London largely reflects its medieval layout, a willfully difficult tangle of streets. This swirl of spaghetti will be totally confusing to anyone brought up on the rigidity of a grid system. Even Londoners, most of whom own a dog-eared copy of an indispensable A–Z street finder, get lost in their own city. But the bewildering street patterns will be a plus for anyone who likes to get lost in atmosphere. London is a walker's city and will repay every moment you spend exploring on foot. If you want to penetrate beyond the crust of popular knowledge, you are well advised not only to visit St. Paul's Cathedral and the Tower of London, but also to set aside some time for random wandering. Walk in the city's backstreets and mews, around Park Lane and Kensington. Pass up Buckingham Palace for Kensington Palace. Take in the National Gallery, but don't forget London's "time machine" museums, such as the 19th-century homes of Lord Frederic Leighton and Sir John Soane. Abandon the city's standard-issue chain stores to discover the gentlemen's outfitters of St. James's. In such ways you can best visualize the shape or, rather, the many shapes of Old London, a curious city that engulfed its own past for the sake of modernity but still lives and breathes the air of history.

Today, that sense of modernity is stronger than ever, as swinging-again London holds its own as one of the coolest cities in the world. Millennium fever left its trophies on the capital, with the opening of buildings and bridges and impressively revamped museums, and the city's art, style,

In a city with as many richly stocked museums and marvels as London, you risk seeing half of everything and all of nothing. You could easily spend two weeks exploring the city, but if time is limited you must plan carefully.

If you have 1 day

Touring the largest city in Britain in a day sounds like an impossible goal, but it can actually—almost—be done in a sunrise-to-sunset span. Think London 101, though many of these sights merit an extended visit. Begin at the Houses of Parliament, best viewed from Westminster Bridge. If you're lucky, you may hear Big Ben chiming. Move on to centuries-old Westminster Abbey—site of many a coronation—then tube it from the Westminster stop to Charing Cross (if you want to catch a glimpse of Her Majesty's two mounted sentries at Horse Guards Parade, bus it up to Whitehall) to arrive at Trafalgar Square for your photo op with Nelson's Column. Take in the treasures of the National Gallery; history buffs might opt instead for a flip-book-fast tour of the adjacent National Portrait Gallery, heavy on the likes of England's heroes and litterateurs. Break for lunch in the National Gallery, then take a short taxi trip to a sight dear to your heart: for connoisseurs, this might be the Wallace Collection, the Tate Britain, or the Tate Modern; for time travelers, Apsley House (the home of the duke of Wellington) or Sir John Soane's Museum; for kids, the London Dungeon or Madame Tussaud's. For a midafternoon session, choose between royal monuments. First choice: heading west from Trafalgar Square, taxi through the Admiralty Arch down the Mall to Buckingham Palace. In summer, the State Rooms are open to the public. At night, Theatreland awaits palace trekkers; try a West End play for a refreshing finale. Second choice: eastward lies the Tower of London, with the Beefeaters, the Crown Jewels, and the resident ravens. At dusk, after leaving the Tower, head across the way to the East End for a spine chiller, a Jack the Ripper guided walking tour. Or board the British Airways London Eye at twilight for an aerial view.

If you have 3 days

A breakneck first day in London has been outlined above. On your second day, begin at the British Museum, resting place of such wonders as the Rosetta Stone and the Elgin Marbles. If the idea of traipsing through "mankind's attic" doesn't grab you, head for the fun house, Sir John Soane's Museum, with interiors that transport you to Regency-era England. Here in Bloomsbury other treats beckon, such as the Charles Dickens House. For an early lunch, tube it from Russell Square to Tottenham Court Road in Soho, for dim sum in Chinatown, or the menu du jour at a cute French bistro. Next, for a dose of magisterial grandeur, hop back on the tube to arrive at the St. Paul's stop and St. Paul's Cathedral. Walk off lunch by strolling south through Blackfriars—a district full of crooked streets and minuscule cul-de-sacs—to the Thames River. After downing a pint at the Black Friar, cross Blackfriars Bridge (or take the pedestrian-only Millennium Bridge, which ends near the Tate Modern) to Southwark's riverside embankment for a splendid view of St. Paul's dome. A stone's throw away is the rebuilt Shakespeare's Globe Theatre. If you're not catching a performance at the Globe (held only in warm-weather months), tour the museum beneath the theater. Keep heading west along the river and cross Waterloo Bridge to Somerset House. Walk through the courtyard to the Strand at the foot of Covent Garden. If you want to cross the river at the modern Hungerford Bridge, walk a few minutes more and take the steps by the Royal Festival Hall, which finish on the north bank by the Savoy. Dine at one of Covent Garden's chic restaurants and then watch the street performers, called buskers, or attend a gala evening (book ahead) at the Royal Opera House.

Start your third day with Buckingham Palace's Changing of the Guard, held April–July at 11:30 daily, August–March at the same hour on alternate days. Warm up for this ceremony by viewing the treasures in the Queen's Gallery and the nearby Royal Mews. If the State Rooms of the palace are closed to viewing, head through Green Park to Apsley House, the 18th-century mansion of the Duke of Wellington. Check out the Wellington Arch on Hyde Park Corner, then wander up Park Lane into ritzy Mayfair and stroll past Grosvenor Square and Oxford Street to Manchester Square and the Wallace Collection, whose gilded interiors are stuffed with 18th-century art. For retail therapy, return south, then east to scout three great shopping destinations: Bond Street for glitz, Regent Street for savvy sophistication, and Carnaby Street for some rocker-style street gear. For an evening highlight, pick a play.

If you have **7 days**   Each section of London provides distinct clues to the city's past. Kick off day four at the South Kensington museums, a district planned by the Victorians to induce gallery gout and museum feet: the Victoria & Albert, the Natural History Museum, and the Science Museum. Art lovers gravitate to the first, whereas budding Einsteins may run for the others. Each of these cultural palaces could easily consume an entire day, so pick one. Then head over to Knightsbridge to mercantile-and-fashion giants Harrods or Harvey Nichols. Move on to Kensington Gardens, where almost everyone throws a kiss to the statue of *Peter Pan,* and to Kensington Palace, the home of royals from Queen Anne to today's Windsors, to see the State Rooms.

Day 5 dawns at the City—London's ancient core. Built up around St. Paul's, the area has numerous attractions, including Dr. Johnson's House, the Museum of London, and several Christopher Wren churches. After lunch, serious folk can tube westward over to Holborn (Chancery Lane, Temple stops) to visit the Inns of Court and the Temple, the historic foundations of legal London. Farther east lies that storybook icon, Tower Bridge, which you cross to reach the South Bank, where the London Dungeon awaits—this waxworks show is devoted to the more gory aspects of British history.

On Day 6, leave the city behind for pleasures along the Thames, at Greenwich or the storied palace and gardens of Hampton Court—don't even *consider* attempting both. Begin your last day by taking the tube to the Knightsbridge stop and heading south for a morning stroll through Belgravia; it's London at its most Edwardian. Head over to the emporiums of Sloane Street and Sloane Square and enjoy some high-style shopping. Chelsea, along King's Road, is where much of London comes to shop and stroll. Relax over lunch at a King's Road eatery, then bus over to Millbank to take in the Tate Britain's collection of paintings by J. M. W. Turner, the romantic-period artist who painted the most beautiful sunsets of any century. As dusk settles, head over to the South Bank Centre for a play in the Olivier Theatre or a concert in the Queen Elizabeth Hall. Don't fret if the performances are booked—London itself is the most wonderful free show in the world.

fashion, and dining scenes make headlines around the world. London's chefs have become superstars. Its fashion designers have conquered Paris, avant-garde artists have caused waves at the august Royal Academy of Arts, the raging after-hours scene is packed with music mavens ready to catch the Next Big Thing, and the theater continues its tradition of radical, shocking productions.

On the other hand, although the outward shapes may alter and the inner spirit may be warmer, the base-rocks of London's character and tradition remain the same. Deep down, Britons have a sense of the continuity of history. Even in the modern metropolis, some things rarely change. The British bobby is alive and well. The tall, red, double-decker buses (most in an updated model) still lumber from stop to stop, although their aesthetic match at street level, the glossy red telephone booth, has been replaced by glass and steel boxes. Teatime is still a hallowed part of the day, with, if you search hard enough, toasted crumpets honeycombed with sweet butter. Then there's that greatest living link with the past— the Royal Family. Don't let the tag of "typical tourist" stop you from enjoying the pageantry of the Windsors: the Changing of the Guard, at Buckingham Palace and at Whitehall, is one of the greatest free shows in the world.

The London you might discover may include some enthusiastic recommendations from this guide, but be prepared to be taken by surprise. The best that a great city has to offer often comes to you in unexpected ways. Armed with energy and curiosity, you can find, to quote Dr. Johnson again, "in London all that life can afford."

EXPLORING LONDON

London grew from a wooden bridge built over the Thames in the year AD 43 to its current 600 square mi and 7 million souls in haphazard fashion, meandering from its two official centers: Westminster, seat of government and royalty, to the west, and the City, site of finance and commerce, to the east. In these two areas are most of the grand buildings that have played a central role in British history: the Tower of London and St. Paul's Cathedral, Westminster Abbey and the Houses of Parliament, Buckingham Palace, and the older royal palace of St. James's. However, London's *un*official centers multiply and mutate year after year, and it would be a shame to stop only at the postcard views. Life is not lived in monuments, as the patrician patrons of the great Georgian architects understood when they commissioned the city's elegant squares and town houses. Within a few minutes' walk of Buckingham Palace, for instance, lie St. James's and Mayfair, neighboring quarters of elegant town houses built for the nobility during the 17th and early 18th centuries and now notable for shopping opportunities. Westminster Abbey's original vegetable patch (or convent garden), which became the site of London's first square, Covent Garden, is now an unmissable stop.

Hyde Park and Kensington Gardens, preserved by past kings and queens for their own hunting and relaxation, create a swath of green parkland across the city center. A walk across Hyde Park brings you to the museum district of South Kensington, with the Natural History Museum, the Science Museum, and the Victoria & Albert Museum. If the great parks such as Hyde Park are, in Lord Chatham's phrase, "the lungs of London," then the River Thames is its backbone. The fast-developing South Bank has many cultural highlights: the theaters of the South Bank Centre, the Hayward and Saatchi galleries, Tate Modern, and the reconstruction of Shakespeare's Globe theater. The London Eye observation wheel here gives stunning city views, or you can walk across the Millennium or Hungerford bridges. Farther downstream is the gorgeous 17th- and 18th-century symmetry of Greenwich, where the world's time is measured.

Westminster & Royal London

Westminster and Royal London might be called "London for Beginners." If you went no farther than these few acres, you would have seen many of the famous sights, from the Houses of Parliament, Big Ben, Westminster Abbey, and Buckingham Palace, to two of the world's greatest art collections, in the National and Tate Britain galleries. You can truly call this area Royal London, since it is bounded by the triangle of streets that make up the route that the Queen usually takes when journeying from Buckingham Palace to Westminster Abbey or to the Houses of Parliament on state occasions. The three points on this royal triangle are Trafalgar Square, Westminster, and Buckingham Palace. Naturally, in an area that regularly sees the pomp and pageantry of royal occasions, the streets are wide and the vistas long. St. James's Park lies at the heart of the triangle, which has a feeling of timeless dignity—flower beds bursting with color, long avenues of trees framing classically proportioned buildings, glimpses of pinnacles and towers over the treetops, the distant *bong!* of Big Ben counting off the hours. This is concentrated sightseeing, so pace yourself. For a large part of the year, much of Royal London is floodlighted at night, adding to the theatricality of the experience.

Numbers in the text correspond to numbers in the margin and on the London map.

a good walk

Trafalgar Square ❶ ➤, the obvious place to start, is the geographical core of London, by dint of a plaque on the corner of the Strand and Charing Cross Road from which distances on U.K. signposts are measured. After taking in the instantly identifiable **Nelson's Column** in the center (read about the area on a plaque marking its 150th anniversary), head for the **National Gallery ❷** on the north side, Britain's greatest trove of masterpieces. Detour around the corner to see the **National Portrait Gallery ❸**—a parade of the famous that can be rewarding to anyone interested in what makes the British tick. East of the National Gallery, still on Trafalgar Square, see the much-loved church of **St. Martin-in-the-Fields ❹**. Then, stepping through grand Admiralty Arch down on the southwest corner, enter the royal pink road, the Mall, with **St. James's Park** running along the south side. On your right is the **Institute of Contemporary Arts ❺**, in the great Regency architect John Nash's **Carlton House Terrace**. At the end of Pall Mall is the small, Tudor brick **St. James's Palace**. Continue along Cleveland Row by the side of the palace to see York

Museums & Marvels

A blizzard of blue plaques all over town proclaims the historical importance of structures such as Dickens House and the Handel House Museum, turning London itself into something of a living museum. High culture and low, it's all here. The National Gallery holds the richest trove of old-master paintings in Britain and the Tate Modern some of art's latest creations, whereas the London Dungeon and Madame Tussaud's take a more populist approach to history. The British Museum is a jumbo time capsule, with treasures from civilizations around the world. Sir John Soane's Museum, in contrast, is a Regency-era phantasmagoria of unusual perspectives and objets d'art. You can take your pick among stately homes such as Spencer House, Apsley House, and Hampton Court Palace; national monuments such as the Tower of London; or exquisite, specialized fare such as the French art in the Wallace Collection or the Courtauld Institute Gallery.

Pub Scene

London's pubs include some of the most gorgeous and historic interiors in the city. An integral part of the British way of life, public houses dispense beer on tap and usually a basic, inexpensive menu of sandwiches, quiche, and salads, and other snacks at lunchtime. But you don't go to a "local" for just pub grub or even the fancier fare at the increasingly popular gastro-pubs. Rather, pubs are the best place to meet the locals in their habitat. Sit at a table if you want privacy; better, help prop up the bar, where no introductions are needed, and watch that legendary British reserve fade away.

Theater

From Shakespeare to the glossiest musical, London's West End has the cream of the city's theater offerings. But you can see more in London than the offerings of Theatreland and the national companies: of the 100 or so legitimate theaters operating in the capital, only about half are officially "West End." The remainder fall under the blanket title of "Fringe," which encompasses everything from off-the-wall "physical theater" to premieres of new plays and revivals of old ones. Shakespeare supplies the backbone to the theatrical life of the city. You can see his plays in the reconstructed Globe Theatre on the banks of the Thames, 200 yards from where it stood in the 16th century. Elsewhere in London, the plays have survived being turned into musicals (from Purcell to rock); they have made the reputations of generations of famous actors (and broken not a few). Though the Bard of Bards remains a headliner, the theater scene is amazingly varied. From a West End *My Fair Lady* revival to an East End feminist staging of *Ben-Hur*, London remains a theatergoer's town.

Walking Through London

London is a great walking city because so many of its real treasures are untouted: tiny alleyways barely visible on the map, garden squares, churchyards, shop windows, sudden vistas of skyline or park. Walking is the traditional way that the capital would have been viewed centuries ago, and it's a grand way to appreciate the quirky character of the city's "villages" (now neighborhoods) and church parishes or boundaries. Some quarters that you might want to explore on foot are more richly endowed than others, such as Chelsea, Kensington, and St. James. In others, such as

Soho and parts of the City and East End, time-warped streets abut modern of-fice towers. Longer, signposted walks are easily found by the river. On the South Bank, the Millennium Mile passes the pedestrian Hungerford and Millennium bridges, with their striking architecture and views. Remember that London weather is variable, so wear comfortable, waterproof shoes and carry a fold-ing umbrella or raingear. That way, even your enthusiasm won't be dampened by the weather.

House, home of the Duke and Duchess of Kent; then turn left into Sta-ble Yard Road to **Clarence House** ❻, residence of the Prince of Wales and his sons. Head north along St. James's Street to No. 27, one of Lon-don's most spectacular mansions, **Spencer House** ❼, home of Diana's an-cestors. At the foot of the Mall is one of London's most famous sights, **Buckingham Palace** ❽, home to the monarch of the land, with the **Queen's Gallery**—showing some of Her Majesty's vast art collection—and the **Royal Mews** ❾ nearby. Turning left and left again, almost doubling back, follow the southern perimeter of St. James's Park around Birdcage Walk, passing the headquarters of the Queen's foot guard, the **Welling-ton Barracks** ❿, on your right. Cross Horse Guards Road at the eastern edge of the park, walk down Great George Street, and across Parlia-ment Square, and you come to another of the great sights of London, the **Houses of Parliament** ⓫. A mock-medieval extravaganza designed by two Victorian-era architects, it was built along the Thames and in-cludes the Clock Tower, known as Big Ben after the nickname of the bell that chimes the hour. A clockwise turn around the square brings you to historic **Westminster Abbey** ⓬. Complete the circuit and head north up Whitehall, where you can see a simple monolith in the middle of the street—the Cenotaph, designed by Edwin Lutyens in 1920 in com-memoration of the 1918 Armistice. The gated alley on your left leads to **Ten Downing Street** ⓭, where England's modest "White House" stands. Soon after that you pass **Horse Guards Parade** ⓮, setting for the Queen's birthday celebration, Trooping the Colour, with the Inigo Jones–designed neoclassical **Banqueting House** ⓯, scene of Charles I's execution, oppo-site. The control center of Sir Winston's war is back down toward West-minster on the left, deep in Foreign Office government buildings, in the **Cabinet War Rooms** ⓰. If it's art you're mad about, skip the last three sights and head down Millbank to the **Tate Britain** ⓱—the most famous museum for British painting and sculpture.

TIMING You could finish this walk of roughly 3 mi in just over an hour or spend a week's vacation on this route alone. Allow as much time as you can for the three great museums—the National Gallery and the Tate Britain require *at least* two hours each, the National Portrait Gallery one to two. Westminster Abbey can take a half day—especially in summer, when lines are long. In summer, you can get inside Buckingham Palace and Clarence House; a half-day's operation will be increased to a whole day if you see Spencer House (open Sundays only), the Royal Mews, or the Queen's Gallery. If the Changing of the Guard is a priority, make sure you time this walk correctly.

What to See

⑮ Banqueting House. Commissioned by James I, Inigo Jones (1573–1652), one of England's great architects, created this banqueting hall in 1619–22 out of an old remnant of the Tudor Palace of Whitehall. Influenced by Andrea Palladio's work, which he saw during a sojourn in Tuscany, Jones remade the palace with Palladian sophistication and purity. James I's son, Charles I, enhanced the interior by employing the Flemish painter Peter Paul Rubens to glorify his father all over the ceiling. These allegorical paintings, depicting a wise monarch being received into heaven, were the last thing Charles saw before he was beheaded on a scaffold outside in 1649. Phone or check the Web site for information about lunchtime concerts. ☒ *Whitehall, Westminster SW1* ☏ *020/7930–4179, 0870/751–5178 recorded information, 0870/751–5187 concert tickets* ⊕ *www.hrp.org.uk* ☞ *£4, includes audio guide* ☉ *Jan.–late Dec., Mon.–Sat. 10–5; may close on short notice for banquets* Ⓤ *Charing Cross, Embankment, Westminster.*

❽ Buckingham Palace. Supreme among the symbols of London—indeed of
Fodor'sChoice   Britain generally and of the Royal Family in particular—Buckingham
★   Palace tops many must-see lists, although the building itself is no masterpiece and has housed the monarch only since Victoria (1819–1901) moved here from Kensington Palace on her accession in 1837. Its great gray bulk sums up the imperious splendor of so much of the city: stately, magnificent, and ponderous. In 1824 the palace was substantially rebuilt by John Nash, that tireless architect, for George IV, that tireless spendthrift. Compared with other great London residences, it is a fairly recent affair: the Portland stone facade dates from 1913, and the interior was renovated and redecorated after World War II bombs damaged it. The palace contains some 600 rooms, including the State Ballroom and the Throne Room. These State Rooms are where much of the business of royalty is played out—investitures, state banquets, receptions. The royal apartments are in the north wing; when the Queen is in, the royal standard is raised. The State Rooms can be toured from August to early October, when the Royal Family is away. The **Changing of the Guard**—which, with all the pomp and ceremony monarchists and children adore, remains one of London's best free shows—culminates in front of the palace. Marching to live music, the **Queen's guards** proceed up the Mall from St. James's Palace to Buckingham Palace. Shortly afterward, the replacement guard approaches from Wellington Barracks via Birdcage Walk. Once the old and new guards are in the forecourt, the old guard symbolically hands over the keys to the palace. The ceremony takes place daily at 11:30 AM April–July and on alternating days August–March, but the guards sometimes cancel because of bad weather; check the signs in the forecourt, or phone. Arrive by 10:30 AM for a decent view of the panoply. ☒ *Buckingham Palace Rd., St. James's SW1* ☏ *020/7839–1377, 020/7799–2331 24-hr information, 020/7321–2233 credit-card reservations (50p booking charge)* ⊕ *www.royal.gov.uk* ☞ *£12.95; prebooking by phone required* ☉ *Early Aug.–early Oct. (confirm dates, which are subject to the Queen's mandate), daily 9:30–4:15* Ⓤ *St. James's Park, Victoria.*

TO HAMPSTEAD

Abbey
Road Studios

Regent's Park

Inner
Circle

71

King's Cross
Station

St. Pancras
Station

23

Euston
Station

BLOOMSBURY

Coram's
Fields

70

Telecom
Tower

24

22

Paddington
Station

BAYSWATER

69

Manchester
Square

SOHO

Oxford
Circus

26

25

27

U.S. Embassy

MAYFAIR

Royal
Academy

Piccadilly
Circus

20

18 19

21

2

3 4

Charing
Cross Stn.

53

Peter Pan
Statue

Hyde Park

1

5

51 52

65

Kensington
Gardens

7

6

SOUTH

66

Serpentine
Gallery

67

Green Park

St. James's
Park

14

13

16

15

11

56

54 55

County
Hall

Wat
Stati

64

63

KNIGHTSBRIDGE

8

Birdcage Walk

10

12

57

58

Lambeth Rd.

62

60

Harrods

68

9

Victoria
Station

VICTORIA

61

BELGRAVIA

CHELSEA

17

Vauxhall
Station

Kennington
Oval

Thames

*Battersea
Park*

London

KEY

Tourist information

Start of walk

Westminster & Royal London ▼

Banqueting House **15**

Buckingham Palace **8**

Cabinet War Rooms ...**16**

Clarence House **6**

Horse Guards Parade ..**14**

Houses of Parliament ..**11**

Institute of Contemporary Arts **5**

National Gallery **2**

National Portrait Gallery .**3**

Royal Mews **9**

St. Martin-in-the-Fields **4**

Spencer House **7**

Tate Britain **17**

Ten Downing St. **13**

Trafalgar Square **1**

Wellington Barracks ...**10**

Westminster Abbey ...**12**

Soho & Covent Garden ▼

Covent Garden Piazza ..**18**

London's Transport Museum **19**

Royal Opera House **20**

Somerset House **21**

Bloomsbury & Legal London ▼

British Library **23**

British Museum **22**

Dickens House **24**

Lincoln's Inn **25**

Sir John Soane's Museum **26**

Temple **27**

The City ▼

Bank of England **36**

Barbican Centre **33**

Dr. Johnson's House ...**28**

Guildhall **34**

Monument **38**

Museum of London **32**

Old Bailey **30**

St. Bride's **29**

St. Mary-le-Bow **35**

St. Paul's Cathedral ...**31**

Temple of Mithras **37**

Tower of London **39**

The South Bank ▼

British Airways London Eye **54**

Butler's Wharf **40**

The Clink **46**

Design Museum **41**

Florence Nightingale Museum **57**

Golden Hinde **47**

Hay's Galleria **43**

Hayward Gallery **52**

H.M.S. *Belfast* **42**

Imperial War Museum .**59**

Lambeth Palace **58**

London Aquarium **55**

London Dungeon **44**

OXO Tower **50**

Royal Festival Hall **53**

Royal National Theatre **51**

Saatchi Gallery **56**

Shakespeare's Globe Theatre **48**

Southwark Cathedral ..**45**

Tate Modern **49**

Kensington, Knightsbridge & Mayfair ▼

Albert Memorial **64**

Apsley House (Wellington Museum) ..**67**

Belgrave Place **68**

Kensington Palace **65**

Kensington Palace Gardens **66**

London Zoo **71**

Madame Tussaud's **70**

Natural History Museum **61**

Royal Albert Hall **63**

Science Museum **62**

Victoria & Albert Museum **60**

Wallace Collection **69**

WHERE TO SEE THE ROYALS

THE QUEEN AND THE ROYAL FAMILY attend some 400 functions a year, and if you want to know what they are doing on any given date, turn to the Court Circular printed in the major London dailies. But most people want to see the Royals in all their dazzling pomp and circumstance. For this, the best bet is the second Saturday in June, when Trooping the Colour is usually held to celebrate the Queen's official birthday. This spectacular parade begins when she leaves Buckingham Palace in her carriage and rides down the Mall to arrive at Horse Guards Parade at 11 AM exactly.

If you wish to obtain one of the 7,000 seats (no more than two per request, distributed by ballot), enclose a letter and self-addressed, stamped envelope or International Reply Coupon—January to February 28 only—to Ticket Office, Headquarters Household Division, Horse Guards, London SW1A 2AX, ☎ 020/

7414–2479. You can also just line up along the Mall with your binoculars.

Another time you can catch the Queen in all her regalia is when she and the Duke of Edinburgh ride in state to Westminster to open the Houses of Parliament. In late October or early November, the famous gilded coach is escorted by the Household Cavalry. As the Queen enters the building, the air shakes with the booming of heavy guns, and all London knows that the democratic processes have once again been renewed with all their age-old ceremony.

Should you miss seeing the Queen, or if you just want to read about the Royals, visit ⊕ www.royal.gov.uk, the official Web site of the British monarchy.

🕭 ⓰ **Cabinet War Rooms.** From this small maze of bombproof underground rooms—in the back of the hulking Foreign Office—Britain's World War II fortunes were directed. During air raids, the cabinet met here, and the Cabinet Room is still arranged as if a meeting were about to convene. In the Map Room, the Allied campaign is charted. The Prime Minister's Room holds the desk from which Winston Churchill made his morale-boosting broadcasts, and the Telephone Room has his hotline to FDR. The rest of the rooms have been preserved as they were when the last light was turned off, at the end of the war. A museum dedicated to Winston Churchill is scheduled to open here in early 2005. ⊠ *Clive Steps, King Charles St., Westminster SW1* ☎ *020/7930–6961* ⊕ *www.iwm.org.uk* 🎫 *£7* ⊙ *Apr.–Sept., daily 9:30–5:15; Oct.–Mar., daily 10–5:15* Ⓤ *Westminster.*

Carlton House Terrace. A grand example of Regency architect John Nash's genius, Carlton House Terrace was built between 1812 and 1830, under the patronage of George IV (Prince Regent until George III's death in 1820). Nash was responsible for a series of West End developments, of which the white-stucco facades and massive Corinthian columns on this street may be the most imposing. Today No. 12 houses the **Institute of Contemporary Arts,** one of Britain's leading modern-art centers. ⊠ *The Mall, St. James's W1* Ⓤ *Charing Cross, Piccadilly Circus.*

❻ Clarence House. The London home of Queen Elizabeth the Queen Mother for nearly 50 years, this Regency mansion is now the Prince of Wales's residence. It was built by John Nash for the duke of Clarence, and it has remained a royal home—the present monarch, Queen Elizabeth, lived here after her marriage. The rooms have been sensitively preserved as the Queen Mother chose, with the addition of works of art from the Royal Collection. It is less palace, and more home (for Prince Charles and his sons, William and Harry), with informal family pictures and comfortable sofas. The tour (by timed ticket entry only) is of the ground-floor rooms. ☒ *The Mall, St. James's SW1* ☏ *020/7766–7303* ⊕ *www.royal.gov.uk* 🖾 *£5* ☉ *Aug.–mid-Oct.; call for hrs and to book tickets* Ⓤ *Green Park.*

❿ Horse Guards Parade. Once the tiltyard of Whitehall Palace, where jousting tournaments were held, the Horse Guards Parade is now notable mainly for the annual Trooping the Colour ceremony, in which the Queen takes the Royal Salute, her official birthday gift, on the second Saturday in June. (Like Paddington Bear, the Queen has two birthdays; her real one is on April 21.) There's pageantry galore, and throngs of onlookers. Covering the vast expanse of the square that faces Horse Guards Road, opposite St. James's Park at one end and Whitehall at the other, the ceremony is televised. You can also attend the queenless rehearsals on the preceding two Saturdays. At the Whitehall facade of Horse Guards, the changing of two mounted sentries known as the **mounted guard** provides what may be London's most popular photo opportunity. ☒ *Whitehall, Westminster SW1* ☉ *Queen's mounted guard ceremony: Mon.–Sat. 11 AM, Sun. 10 AM* Ⓤ *Westminster.*

⓫ Houses of Parliament. Seat of Great Britain's government, the Houses of
Fodor'sChoice Parliament are, arguably, the city's most famous and photogenic sight.
★ Facing them you see, from left to right, Big Ben—keeping watch on the corner—the Houses of Parliament themselves, Westminster Hall (the oldest part of the complex), and the Victoria Tower. The most romantic view of the complex is from the opposite, south side of the river, a vista especially dramatic at night when the spires, pinnacles, and towers of the great building are floodlighted green and gold. After a catastrophic fire in 1834, these buildings arose, designed in glorious, mock-medieval style by two Victorian-era architects, Sir Charles Barry and Augustus Pugin. The Palace of Westminster, as the complex is still properly called, was established by Edward the Confessor in the 11th century. It has served as the seat of English administrative power, on and off, ever since. Now virtually the symbol of London, the 1858 **Clock Tower** designed by Pugin contains the bell known as **Big Ben** that chimes the hour (and the quarters). Weighing a mighty 13 tons, the bell takes its name from Sir Benjamin Hall, the far-from-slim Westminster building works commissioner. At the other end of Parliament is the 336-foot-high **Victoria Tower.** There are two houses, the Lords and the Commons. The visitors' gallery, known as the **Strangers' Gallery,** is open while the House of Commons sits. You need to get in line at the main St. Stephen's entrance at least an hour in advance—and even then you might not get a space—for the most popular session, the prime minister's Question Time, on Wednes-

day. Other days are easier, though you should still arrive an hour before the session starts. A complete tour of the public galleries is available to overseas visitors during the summer opening only (late July–August, mid-September–early October). Tickets can be prebooked, or you can take a chance and buy on the day from the ticket office opposite the Houses of Parliament. The **Lord Chancellor's Residence** within the Palace of Westminster is spectacular; be sure to have your name placed in advance on the waiting list for the twice-weekly tours. ⊠ *St. Stephen's Entrance, St. Margaret St., Westminster SW1* ☎ *020/7219–4272 Commons information, 020/7219–3107 Lords information, 020/7219–2184 Lord Chancellor's Residence, 0870/906–3773 for summer tours* ⊕ *www. parliament.uk* 🖾 *Free, £7 summer tours* ☉ *Commons Mon. 2:30–10, Tues. and Wed. 11:30–7:30, Thurs. 11:30–7:30, Fri. 9:30–3; Lords Mon.–Thurs. 2:30–10; Lord Chancellor's Residence Tues. and Thurs. 10:30–12:30. Closed Easter wk, 3 wks for party conference recess mid-Sept.–early Oct., and 3 wks at Christmas* Ⓤ *Westminster.*

---

need a break?

The **Wesley Café** (⊠ Storey's Gate, Westminster SW1 ☎ 020/7222–8010), a popular budget haunt, is almost opposite Westminster Abbey, in Central Hall. In the crypt of this former Methodist church, you can grab a hot or cold meal for around a fiver (£5).

---

❺ Institute of Contemporary Arts. A Regency building houses the ICA, one of Britain's leading modern-art centers and a stage for the avant-garde in theater, dance, visual art, and music since 1947. It has two cinemas, a library of video artists' works, a bookshop, a café and a hip bar, and a team of adventurous curators. ⊠ *The Mall, 12 Carlton House Terr., St. James's W1* ☎ *020/7930–3647* ⊕ *www.ica.org.uk* 🖾 *£1.50 weekdays, £2.50 weekends, additional charge for specific events* ☉ *Daily noon–7:30, later for some events* Ⓤ *Charing Cross, Piccadilly Circus.*

★ **❷ National Gallery.** Jan Van Eyck's *Arnolfini Marriage,* Leonardo da Vinci's *Virgin and Child,* Diego Velázquez's *Rokeby Venus,* John Constable's *Hay Wain . . .* you get the picture. There are approximately 2,200 other paintings in this museum, many of them among the most treasured works of art anywhere. The museum's low, gray, colonnaded, neoclassical facade fills the north side of Trafalgar Square. The National's collection includes paintings of the early Renaissance—in the modern Sainsbury Wing, designed by the U.S. architect Robert Venturi—the Flemish and Dutch masters, the Spanish school, and the English tradition (notably William Hogarth, Thomas Gainsborough, George Stubbs, and Constable).

The museum is really too overwhelming to absorb in a single viewing. The **Micro Gallery,** a computer information center in the Sainsbury Wing, might be the place to start. You can access in-depth information on any work here, choose your favorites, and print out a free personal tour map. Rounding out the top-10 list (the first four lead off above) are Paolo Uccello's *Battle of San Romano* (children love its knights on horseback), Giovanni Bellini's *Doge Leonardo Loredan* (notice the snail-shell buttons), Sandro Botticelli's *Venus and Mars,* Michelangelo Caravaggio's *Supper at Emmaus* (almost cinematically lit), J. M. W. Turner's *Fighting*

Téméraire (one of the artist's greatest sunsets), and Georges Seurat's *Bathers at Asnières*. Note that free admission encourages repeat visits: the National Gallery reveals more gems the more one explores. For a great timeout or lunch, head for the Brasserie in the Sainsbury Wing. ⊠ *Trafalgar Sq., Covent Garden WC2* ☎ *020/7747–2885* ⊕ *www.nationalgallery. org.uk* ✉ *Free, charge for special exhibitions* ⊙ *Thurs.–Tues. 10–6, Wed. 10–9; 1-hr guided tour starts at Sainsbury Wing daily at 11:30 and 2:30, and also 6:30 Wed.* Ⓤ *Charing Cross, Leicester Sq.*

★ ❸ **National Portrait Gallery.** An idiosyncratic collection that presents a potted history of Britain through its people, past and present, this museum is an essential stop for all history and literature buffs. As an art collection it is eccentric, because the subject, not the artist, is the point. Many of the faces are obscure, because the portraits outlasted their sitters' fame—not so surprising when the portraitists are such greats as Sir Joshua Reynolds, Gainsborough, Sir Thomas Lawrence, and George Romney. But the annotation is comprehensive, and the chronological layout easy to negotiate. The spacious, bright galleries are accessible via glass escalator, through which you can view the paintings as you ascend to the skylit Tudor Gallery, displaying the oldest works. Don't miss the Victorian and early-20th-century portrait galleries. At the summit, a restaurant with classy British cuisine, open beyond gallery hours, has great skyline views. A separate research center (with bookshop and café in the basement) assists those who get hooked on particular personages. ⊠ *St. Martin's Pl., Covent Garden WC2* ☎ *020/7312–2463 recorded information* ⊕ *www.npg.org.uk* ✉ *Free* ⊙ *Mon.–Wed. and weekends 10–6, Thurs. and Fri. 10–9* Ⓤ *Charing Cross, Leicester Sq.*

Nelson's Column. Centerpiece of Trafalgar Square, this famed landmark is topped with E. H. Baily's 1843 statue of Admiral Lord Horatio Nelson (1758–1805), who keeps watch from his 145-foot-high granite perch. The celebrated naval hero died at the battle of Trafalgar (hence the name of the square) during a spectacular victory against the combined French and Spanish fleets. The bas-reliefs around the base depict scenes of Nelson's life and were cast from cannons he captured. The four majestic lions, designed by the Victorian painter Sir Edwin Landseer, were added in 1867. The calling cards of generations of pigeons have been a corrosive problem for the statue; this may have been finally solved by the addition of a gel coating to it. ⊠ *Trafalgar Sq., Covent Garden WC2* Ⓤ *Charing Cross, Leicester Sq.*

Queen's Gallery. An expanded former chapel at the south side of **Buckingham Palace** displays wonderful changing selections of treasures from the Queen's vast art collection, with computer access to pictures on display and in storage. The Pennethorne Gallery is dominated by the larger-than-life portrait of Charles I (Van Dyck) in equestrian mode, which almost overshadows works by Holbein, Frans Hals, Jan Vermeer, and Rubens. These contrast starkly with the frank portrait of Queen Elizabeth II by Lucian Freud in the Nash Gallery. Between and beneath the paintings are cabinets, tables, and silverwork. The E-gallery reveals hidden details of some artworks, allowing you to open lockets and remove a sword from its scabbard. Admission is by timed ticket. ⊠ *Buckingham Palace,*

Buckingham Palace Rd., St. James's SW1 ☎ *020/7766–7301 to prebook timed tickets* ⊕ *www.royal.gov.uk* ✉ *£7.50* ☉ *Daily 10–5:30; last admission at 4:30* Ⓤ *St. James's Park, Victoria.*

☾ ❾ **Royal Mews.** Unmissable children's entertainment, this museum is the home of Her Majesty's Coronation Coach. Standing nearly next door to the Queen's Gallery, the Royal Mews were designed by Regency-era architect John Nash. Mews were falcons' quarters (the name comes from their "mewing," or feather-shedding), but horses gradually eclipsed birds of prey. Now some of the royal beasts live here alongside the bejeweled coaches. ⊠ *Buckingham Palace Rd., St. James's SW1* ☎ *020/7766–7302* ⊕ *www.royal.gov.uk* ✉ *£5.50* ☉ *Late Mar.–Oct., Sat.–Thurs. 11–4; last admission 45 mins before closing. Call to confirm hrs; Royal Mews often closes for holidays or for royal events* Ⓤ *St. James's Park, Victoria.*

St. James's Palace. With its solitary sentry posted at the gate, this surprisingly small palace of Tudor brick was once a home for many British sovereigns, including the first Elizabeth and Charles I, who spent his last night here before his execution. Today it is the working office of another Charles—the Prince of Wales. Matters to ponder as you look (you can't go in): foreign ambassadors to Britain are still accredited to the Court of St. James's even though it has rarely been a primary royal residence; and the present queen made her first speech here. ⊠ *Friary Court, St. James's SW1* ⊕ *www.royal.gov.uk* Ⓤ *Green Park.*

☾ **St. James's Park.** London's smallest, most ornamental park (and the oldest of its royal ones) makes a spectacular frame for the towers of Westminster and Victoria—especially at night, when the illuminated fountains and the skyline beyond the trees look like a floating fairyland. Its current shape more or less reflects what John Nash designed under George IV, turning the canal into a graceful lake (cemented in at a depth of 4 feet in 1855) and naturalizing the gardens. More than 17 species of birds—including swans that belong to the Queen—congregate on Duck Island at the lake's east end. In summer the deck chairs (which you must pay to use) are often crammed with lunchers being serenaded by music from the bandstands. Along the park's northern side is the grand thoroughfare known as the **Mall.** ⊠ *Entrances at the Mall, Horse Guards approach, or Birdcage Walk, St. James's SW1* ⊕ *www.royalparks.gov. uk* Ⓤ *St. James's Park, Westminster.*

☾ ❹ **St. Martin-in-the-Fields.** One of Britain's best-loved churches, St. Martin's was completed in 1726; James Gibbs's classical temple-with-spire design became a familiar pattern for churches in colonial America. The church is also a haven for music lovers, since the Academy of St. Martin-in-the-Fields, an internationally known orchestra, was founded here, and a popular program of lunchtime and evening concerts (often free) continues today. The church's fusty interior is wonderful for music making, but the wooden benches can make it hard to give your undivided attention to the music. The **London Brass-Rubbing Centre,** where you can make a souvenir knight from reproduction tomb brasses, with metallic waxes, paper, and instructions provided for about £5, is in the crypt, along with an excellent café and a bookshop. ⊠ *Trafalgar Sq.,*

Covent Garden ☎ 020/7766–1100, 020/7839–8362 *evening-concert credit-card bookings* ⊕ *www.stmartin-in-the-fields.org* ۞ *Church daily 8–8; crypt Mon.–Sat. 10–8 (brass-rubbing center until 6), Sun. noon–6; box office Mon.–Sat. 10–5, or purchase tickets on-line* Ⓤ *Charing Cross, Leicester Sq.*

❼ Spencer House. Ancestral abode of the Spencers, the family of Princess Diana, this great mansion is perhaps the finest London example of 18th-century elegance on a domestic scale. The house was built in 1766 for the first earl Spencer, heir to the first duchess of Marlborough; the family hasn't lived here since 1926. James "Athenian" Stuart decorated the gilded state rooms, including the Painted Room, the first completely neoclassical room in Europe. The most ostentatious part of the house is the florid bow window of the Palm Room: covered with stucco palm trees, it conjures up both ancient Palmyra and modern Miami Beach. Children under 10 are not admitted. ✉ *27 St. James's Pl., St. James's SW1* ☎ *020/7499–8620* ⊕ *www.spencerhouse.co.uk* 🎫 *£6* ۞ *Feb.–July and Sept.–Dec., Sun. 10:30–5:30; 1-hr guided tour leaves about every 25 mins (tickets on sale Sun. at 10:30)* Ⓤ *Green Park.*

★ ⑰ Tate Britain. This museum, funded by the sugar magnate Sir Henry Tate and opened in 1897, is a brilliant celebration of great British artists from the 16th century to the present day, with theme rooms that display key works from different eras alongside one another. Noteworthy artists include Hogarth, Gainsborough, Reynolds, and Stubbs from the 18th century, and Constable, William Blake, and the Pre-Raphaelite painters from the 19th. Rotating selections from the J. M. W. Turner Bequest, the largest collection of work by this leading British Romantic artist, are shown in the James Stirling–designed **Clore Gallery.** The **Linbury Galleries** on the lower floors present changing exhibitions. ✉ *Millbank, Westminster SW1* ☎ *020/7887–8000, 020/7887–8008 recorded information* ⊕ *www.tate. org.uk* 🎫 *Free, special exhibitions £3–£10* ۞ *Daily 10–5:50* Ⓤ *Pimlico.*

⑬ Ten Downing Street. The British version of the White House occupies three unassuming 18th-century houses. No. 10 has been the official residence of the prime minister since 1732. The cabinet office, hub of the British system of government, is on the ground floor; the prime minister's private apartment is on the top floor. The chancellor of the exchequer traditionally occupies No. 11. Downing Street is cordoned off, but you should be able to catch a glimpse of it from Whitehall. Just south of Downing Street, in the middle of Whitehall, is the **Cenotaph,** a stark white monolith designed in 1920 by Edward Lutyens to commemorate the 1918 Armistice. ✉ *Whitehall, Westminster SW1* Ⓤ *Westminster.*

▶ ❶ Trafalgar Square. Permanently alive with people—Londoners and tourists alike—and pigeons and roaring traffic, Trafalgar Square remains London's "living room." Great events, such as royal weddings, elections, and sporting triumphs, always draw crowds to the city's most famous square. It is a commanding open space—built to reflect the width and breadth of an empire that once reached to the farthest corners of the globe—with many attractions, including **Nelson's Column** and the **National Gallery.** A redesign has joined the front of the National Gallery to the rest of the square, so that buses, cars, and taxis no longer roar around the north side. The square's pigeons have also been moved on, although some remain. Celebratory occasions here peak in December, first when the lights on the gigantic Christmas tree are turned on, and then when thousands see in the New Year. The statue of Charles I, looking south toward the Banqueting House, receives a wreath on the anniversary of his execution, January 30. ⊠ *Trafalgar Sq., Covent Garden SW1* Ⓤ *Charing Cross, Leicester Sq.*

🔟 **Wellington Barracks.** These are the headquarters of the Queen's five regiments of foot guards, who protect the sovereign and patrol her palace dressed in tunics of gold-purled scarlet and tall busbies of black bearskin. The entrance to the **Guards Museum** is next to the Guards Chapel. ⊠ *Wellington Barracks, Birdcage Walk, Westminster SW1* ☎ *020/ 7414–3428 museum* ⊡ *£2* ⊙ *Daily 10–4; last admission at 3:30* Ⓤ *St. James's Park.*

⓬ **Westminster Abbey.** Nearly all of Britain's monarchs have been crowned
Fodor'sChoice here since the coronation of William the Conqueror on Christmas Day
★ 1066—and most are buried here, too. The abbey's majestic main nave is packed with memories (and, often, crowds), as it has witnessed many splendid royal events. Other than the mysterious gloom of the vast interior, the first thing that strikes most people is the proliferation of statues, tombs, and commemorative tablets. In parts, the building seems more like a stonemason's yard than a place of worship. But in its latter capacity, this landmark truly comes into its own. Although attending a service is not something to undertake purely for sightseeing reasons, it provides a glimpse of the abbey in its full majesty, with the service accompanied by music from the Westminster choristers and the organ that composer Henry Purcell once played.

The current abbey is a largely 13th- and 14th-century rebuilding of the 11th-century church founded by Edward the Confessor, with one notable addition being the 18th-century twin towers over the west entrance, designed by Sir Christopher Wren and completed by Nicholas Hawksmoor. Entering by the north door, what you see first on your left are the extravagant 18th-century monuments of statesmen in the north transept, as well as the north-transept chapels. Look up to your right to see the painted-glass rose window, the largest of its kind. At many points the view of the abbey is crowded by the many statues and screens; to your right is the mostly 19th-century choir screen (part is 13th-century), while to the left is the sacrarium, containing the medieval kings' tombs that screen the **Chapel of St. Edward** (because of its fragility the shrine is closed off, unless you take a tour with the verger—see the admission desk). Continuing to the foot of the Henry VII Chapel steps, you can still see the hot seat of power, the **Coronation Chair,** which has been graced by nearly every royal posterior. Then proceed into one of the architectural glories of Britain, the **Henry VII Chapel** (also known as the Lady Chapel), passing the huge white marble tomb of Elizabeth I, buried with her half-sister, "Bloody" Mary I. All around the chapel are magnificent sculptures of saints, philosophers, and kings, with mermaids and monsters carved on the choir-stall misericords (undersides), and exquisite fan vaulting above (binoculars will help you spot the statues high on the walls)—the last riot of medieval design in England and one of the miracles of Western architecture.

Continue to **Poets' Corner;** in 1400 Geoffrey Chaucer became the first poet to be buried here. There are memorials to William Shakespeare, William Blake, and Charles Dickens (who is also buried here). Exit the abbey by a door from the south transept. Outside the west front is an archway into the quiet, green **Dean's Yard** and the entrance to the **Cloisters.** If time allows, visit the **Chapter House,** a stunning octagonal room, adorned with 14th-century frescoes, where the King's Council met between 1257 and 1547. The **Abbey Museum** is in the **Undercroft,** which survives from Edward the Confessor's original church. The museum includes effigies made from the death masks and actual clothing of Charles II and Admiral Lord Nelson, among other fascinating relics. Adjoining these rooms, the **Little Cloister** is a quiet haven. Just beyond, the **College Garden,** under cultivation for more than 900 years, is planted with medicinal herbs. As you return to the abbey, look again at the truly awe-inspiring nave. Pause for the **Tomb of the Unknown Warrior,** an anonymous World War I martyr who lies buried here in memory of the soldiers fallen in both world wars.

Arrive early if possible, but be prepared to wait in line to tour the abbey. Photography is not permitted. ⊠ *Broad Sanctuary, Westminster SW1* ☎ *020/7222–5152* ⊕ *www.westminster-abbey.org* ✉ *Abbey and museum £6* ⊗ *Abbey Mon., Tues., Thurs., and Fri. 9:30–3:45, Wed. 9:30–6, Sat. 9–1:45 (closes 1 hr after last admission). Museum daily 10–4. Abbey closed to visitors during weekday and Sun. services* Ⓤ *Westminster.*

Soho & Covent Garden

A quadrilateral bounded by Regent Street, Coventry and Cranbourn streets, Charing Cross Road, and the eastern half of Oxford Street encloses Soho, the most entertaining part of the West End. This appellation, unlike the New York City neighborhood's similar one, is not an abbreviation of anything, but a blast from the past—derived from the shouts of "So-ho!" that royal huntsmen in Whitehall Palace's parklands were once heard to cry. One of Charles II's illegitimate sons, the duke of Monmouth, was an early resident, his dubious pedigree setting the tone for the future: for many years Soho was London's strip show–peep show–sex shop–brothel center. The mid-1980s brought legislation that granted expensive licenses to a few such establishments and closed down the rest. Today Soho remains the address of many wonderful ethnic restaurants, including those of London's Chinatown.

Eliza Doolittle's stomping grounds in George Bernard Shaw's *Pygmalion* and Alan Jay Lerner and Frederick Loewe's *My Fair Lady,* the Covent Garden Market became the Covent Garden Piazza in 1980, and it still functions as the center of a neighborhood—one that has always been alluded to as "colorful." It was originally the "convent garden" belonging to the Abbey of St. Peter at Westminster (later Westminster Abbey). Centuries of magnificence and misery, vice and mayhem, and periods of art-literary bohemia followed, until Covent Garden became London's vegetable supplier when its market building went up in the 1830s, followed by the Flower Market in 1870. When the produce moved to the Nine Elms Market in Vauxhall in 1974, the plan for a new neighborhood with the piazza and the glass-covered market halls as its focus was born; its realization is one of London's success stories.

<table>
<tr><td>

a good walk

</td><td>

Soho, being small, is easy to explore, although it's also easy to mistake one narrow, crowded street for another. Enter from the northwest corner, Oxford Circus, and head south for about 200 yards down Regent Street, turn left onto Great Marlborough Street, and head to the top of **Carnaby Street** ▶. Turn right off Broadwick Street onto Berwick (pronounced *ber*-rick) Street, famed as central London's best fruit and vegetable market. Then step through tiny Walker's Court, cross Brewer and Wardour streets, and you arrive at Soho's hip hangout, Old Compton Street. From here, Wardour, Dean, Frith, and Greek streets lead north, all of them bursting with restaurants and clubs. Either of the latter two leads north to Soho Square—its Tudor-style cottage is a perfect backdrop for a picnic—but for lunch, head one block south instead, to Shaftesbury Avenue, heart of Theatreland, across which is Chinatown's main drag, **Gerrard Street.** Below Gerrard Street is **Leicester Square,** and running along its west side is Charing Cross Road, a bibliophile's dream. Some of the best of the specialty bookshops are in little Cecil Court, running east just before Trafalgar Square. During your Soho sojourn, visit the neighborhood's wonderful rival patisseries: the old-style French Maison Bertaux at 8 Greek Street, or the busy Italian-run but French-accented Pâtisserie Valerie at 44 Old Compton Street.

</td></tr>
</table>

The easiest way to find the **Covent Garden Piazza** ⑱ is to walk down Cranbourn Street, next to Leicester Square tube, then down Long Acre, and turn right at James Street. Near here are St. Paul's—the actors' church—and **London's Transport Museum** ⑲, shops, and cafés. (If your aim is to shop, Neal Street, Floral Street, the streets around Seven Dials, and the Thomas Neal's mall all repay exploration.) At the northwest corner of the Piazza is the **Royal Opera House** ⑳. A detour down Wellington Street to the Strand brings you to **Somerset House** ㉑ and the impressionist-stocked **Courtauld Institute Gallery.**

TIMING   The distance covered here is a couple of miles, although you may well get lost, because the streets in Covent Garden and Soho are winding and chaotic. You can whiz around both neighborhoods in an hour or, if the area appeals at all, you can spend all day—for shopping, lunch, the transportation museum, and Somerset House. You might stop by Leicester Square and visit tkts, the Society of London Theatre (SOLT) half-price ticket kiosk (opens at 10 Monday–Saturday, noon Sunday), pick up tickets for later, and walk, shop, and eat in between.

What to See

▶ **Carnaby Street.** The 1960s synonym for swinging London fell into a post-party depression, re-emerging sometime during the '80s as the main drag of a public-relations invention called West Soho. Blank stares would greet anyone asking directions to such a place, but it's geographically logical, and the tangle of streets around Carnaby—Foubert's Place, Broadwick Street, Marshall Street—do cohere, at least, in type of merchandise (youth accessories, mostly, with a smattering of designer boutiques). ⊠ *Carnaby St., Soho W1* Ⓤ *Oxford Circus.*

Courtauld Institute Gallery. An 18th-century classical mansion, **Somerset House,** houses London's finest impressionist and postimpressionist collection, founded in 1931 by textile maven Samuel Courtauld. Édouard Manet's *Bar at the Folies-Bergère* is the star, with bonus baroque works thrown in. The collection has been expanded with key works by modernists, including Henri Matisse, Maurice de Vlaminck, and Raoul Dufy. The splendid rooms of Somerset House can be viewed for free, but the Gilbert Collection and Hermitage Rooms (also here) charge admission. ⊠ *The Strand, Covent Garden WC2* ☎ *020/7848–2526* ⊕ *www.courtauld.ac.uk* ✉ *£5, free Mon. 10–2 (not bank holiday Mon.); joint ticket with one other collection at Somerset House, £1 discount* ☉ *Mon.–Sat. 10–6, Sun. noon–6; last admission at 5:15* Ⓤ *Covent Garden, Holborn, Temple (closed Sun.).*

Ⓒ ⑱ **Covent Garden Piazza.** The original "convent garden" produced vegetables for the 13th-century Abbey of St. Peter at Westminster. In 1630 the duke of Bedford, having become owner, commissioned Inigo Jones to lay out a square, with **St. Paul's Church** (designed by Jones and known as the actors' church) at one end. Open-air entertainers known as buskers perform under the church's portico, where George Bernard Shaw set the first scene of *Pygmalion* (reshaped as the musical *My Fair Lady*). The fruit, flower, and vegetable market established in the 1700s flourished until 1974, when it moved south of the Thames. Since then, the area has been transformed into the Piazza, a mostly higher-class shopping mall that has a couple of cafés and beauty and gift stores. A superior crafts market, the **Apple Market,** is open daily; the less upscale **Jubilee Market** is across the cobbles in the Jubilee Hall. ⊠ *Bordered by Henrietta St., King St., Russell St., and Bedford St., Covent Garden WC2* Ⓤ *Covent Garden.*

Gerrard Street. Pedestrianized Gerrard Street, south of Shaftesbury Avenue, is the hub of London's compact Chinatown, with restaurants, dim sum houses, Chinese supermarkets, and Chinese New Year's celebrations, plus a brace of scarlet pagoda-style archways and a pair of phone booths with pictogram dialing instructions.

Leicester Square. This is the big magnet for nightlife lovers. Looking at the neon of the major movie houses, the fast-food outlets, and the disco entrances, you'd never guess the square—it's pronounced *les*-ter—was laid out around 1630. The Odeon, on the east side, is the venue for all the Royal Film Performances (members of the Royal Family, often the Queen, attend a special screening once a year), and a jaunty little statue of Charlie Chaplin in the opposite corner continues the movie theme. Shakespeare sulks in the middle, chin on hand, clearly wishing he were somewhere else. One landmark worth visiting is **tkts,** the Society of London Theatre (SOLT) ticket kiosk, on the southwest corner, which opens at 10 (noon Sunday) and sells half-price tickets for many of that evening's performances. ⊠ *Leicester Sq., Covent Garden WC2* Ⓤ *Covent Garden.*

🕐 ⑲ **London's Transport Museum.** Occupying the old Flower Market at the south-east corner of the piazza, this museum tells the story of mass transportation in the capital. For children there are lots of touch-screen interactives, old rolling stock, period smells and sounds, and, best of all, a tube-driving simulator. The shop sells the wonderful old London Transport posters, printed with the tube map. ✉ *Covent Garden Piazza, Covent Garden WC2* ☎ *020/7379–6344, 020/7565–7299 recorded info* ⊕ *www. ltmuseum.co.uk* ✑ *£5.95* ⊘ *Sat.–Thurs. 10–6, Fri. 11–6; last admission at 5:15* Ⓤ *Covent Garden.*

⑳ **Royal Opera House.** Mammoth renovations brought the fabled home of the Royal Ballet and Britain's finest opera company smartly into the 21st century. London's premier opera and ballet venue was designed in 1858 by E. M. Barry, son of Sir Charles, the architect of the House of Commons building. Without doubt, the glass-and-steel Floral Hall is the most jaw-dropping feature, and you can wander in during the day, when there may be free lunchtime concerts and events. The Amphitheatre Bar and Piazza concourse give a splendid panorama across the city. ✉ *Bow St., Covent Garden WC2* ☎ *020/7304–4000* ⊕ *www.royaloperahouse.org* Ⓤ *Covent Garden.*

★ 🕐 ㉑ **Somerset House.** This grand 18th-century pile, constructed during the reign of George III, was designed to house government offices, principally those of the navy. The gracious rooms on the south side of the building, by the river, are on view for free, including the Seamen's Waiting Hall and the Nelson Stair. The **Courtauld Institute Gallery** occupies most of the north building, facing the busy Strand. Cafés and a river terrace adjoin the property, and a footbridge leads on to Waterloo Bridge. In the vaults of the house is the **Gilbert Collection,** a museum with intricate works of silver, gold snuffboxes, and Italian mosaics. **The Hermitage Rooms** have changing exhibitions of treasures from the State Hermitage Museum in Russia. An ice-skating rink opens at Somerset House in December and January. ✉ *The Strand, Covent Garden WC2* ☎ *020/7845–4600, 020/7485–4630 Hermitage information* ⊕ *www.somerset-house.org.uk* ✑ *Somerset House free, Courtauld Institute Gallery £5, Gilbert Collection £5 (free after 4:30), Hermitage Rooms £6. Visit 2 collections, save £1; visit all 3, save £2* ⊘ *Daily 10–6; last admission at 5:15* Ⓤ *Charing Cross.*

Bloomsbury & Legal London

The character of an area of London can change visibly from one street to the next. Nowhere is this so clear as in the contrast between fun-loving Soho and intellectual Bloomsbury, a mere 100 yards to the northeast, or between arty, trendy Covent Garden and—on the other side of Kingsway—sober Holborn. Both Bloomsbury and Holborn (pronounced *hoe*-bun) are almost purely residential and should be seen by day. The first district is best known for its famous flowering of literary-arty bohemia, personified during the first three decades of the 20th century by the clique known as the Bloomsbury Group, and for the British Museum and the University of London, which dominate it now. The second sounds as exciting as, say, a center for accountants or dentists, but don't be put off—filled with ancient buildings, Holborn is more interesting and beautiful than you might suppose.

Many people head here to find the ghosts of all those great Bloomsbury figures such as Virginia Woolf, E. M. Forster, Vanessa Bell, and Lytton Strachey. Ghosts of their literary salons soon lead into the time-warp territory of interlocking alleys, gardens and cobbled courts, and town houses and halls where London's legal profession grew up. The Great Fire of 1666 razed most of the city but spared the buildings of legal London, and all of Holborn oozes history. Leading landmarks here are the Inns of Court, where the country's top solicitors and barristers have had their chambers for centuries.

a good walk

From Russell Square tube station, walk south down Southampton Row and west on Great Russell Street, passing Bloomsbury Square on the left, en route to London's biggest and most important collection of antiquities, the **British Museum** ㉒ ▶. Leaving this via the north exit leads you to Montague Place; then head left to Malet Street if you want to walk around the University of London. Head north on Gordon Street to busy Euston Road and east toward St. Pancras and the bold redbrick **British Library** ㉓. If time is short, head south through the university, veering left down Guilford Street past Coram's Fields, then right to Doughty Street and the **Dickens House** ㉔. Two streets west, parallel to Doughty Street, is Lamb's Conduit Street (whose pub, the Lamb, Dickens frequented). At the bottom of Lamb's Conduit Street you reach Theobalds Road, where you enter the first of the Inns of Court, Gray's Inn, emerging from here onto High Holborn—the noisy main route from the City to the West End and Westminster—and Hatton Garden, running north from Holborn Circus and still the center of London's diamond and jewelry trade. Pass another ghost of former trading, Staple Inn, and turn left down tiny Great Turnstile Row to reach **Lincoln's Inn** ㉕. Cross to the north side of Lincoln's Inn Fields to **Sir John Soane's Museum** ㉖. Head south and cross the Strand to the **Temple** ㉗, and pass through the elaborate stone arch to Middle Temple Lane, which you follow to the Thames.

TIMING This substantial walk of 3 to 4 mi has two distinct halves. The first half, around Bloomsbury, is not so interesting on the surface, but it includes the British Museum, where you could spend two hours—or two days. The Dickens House is also worth a stop. The second half, legal London, is a real walker's walk: most of the highlights are in the architecture, with the exception of Sir John Soane's Museum. The walk alone can be done comfortably in two hours.

What to See

㉓ **British Library.** Since 1759, the British Library had been housed in the British Museum—but space ran out in the 1990s, necessitating this grand edifice, a few blocks north of the museum, between Euston and St. Pancras stations. The collection includes 18 million volumes, and the library's treasures are on public view: the John Ritblat Gallery displays the Magna Carta, the Gutenberg Bible, Jane Austen's manuscripts, Shakespeare's First Folio, and musical manuscripts by George Frideric Handel and Sir Paul McCartney. Use the headphones to listen to some interesting snippets in a small showcase of the **National Sound Archive** (which is the world's largest collection, but not on view), such as the voice of Florence Nightingale and an extract from the Beatles' last tour interview. ✉ *96 Euston Rd., Bloomsbury NW1* ☎ *020/7412–7332* ⊕ *www.bl.uk* ✏ *Free; charge for special exhibitions* ☉ *Mon. and Wed.–Fri. 9:30–6, Tues. 9:30–8, Sat. 9:30–5, Sun. 11–5* Ⓤ *Euston or King's Cross.*

★ ☙ ☛ ㉓ **British Museum.** With a facade like a great temple, this celebrated treasure house, filled with plunder of incalculable value and beauty from around the globe, occupies a ponderous Greco-Victorian building that makes a suitably grand impression. Inside are some of the greatest relics of humankind: the Elgin Marbles, the Rosetta Stone, the Sutton Hoo Treasure—almost everything, it seems, but the Ark of the Covenant. The museum has shaken off its dust and opened new galleries, and many sections have been updated, particularly in ethnography, including the impressive **Sainsbury African Galleries.** The focal point is the **Great Court,** a brilliant techno-classical design with a vast glass roof that highlights and reveals the museum's most well-kept secret—an inner courtyard. The revered **Reading Room** has a blue-and-gold dome, ancient tomes, and computer screens. If you want to navigate the highlights of the almost 100 galleries, join at least one of the free **Eyeopener** 50-minute tours by museum guides (details at the information desk).

The collection began in 1753 and grew quickly, thanks to enthusiastic kleptomaniacs during the Napoleonic Wars—most notoriously the seventh earl of Elgin, who acquired the marbles from the Parthenon and Erechtheum in Athens during his term as British ambassador in Constantinople. Here follows a highly edited résumé (in order of encounter) of the British Museum's greatest hits: close to the entrance hall, in Room 4, is the **Rosetta Stone,** found by French soldiers in 1799, and carved in 196 BC with a decree of Ptolemy V in Egyptian hieroglyphics, demotic (a cursive script developed in Egypt), and Greek. This inscription provided the French Egyptologist Jean-François Champollion with the key to deciphering hieroglyphics. Maybe the **Elgin Marbles** ought to be back in Greece, but since these graceful sculptures are here, make a beeline for them in Room 18, west of the entrance in the Parthenon Galleries. These galleries include the spectacular remains of the Parthenon frieze that girdled the cella of Athena's temple on the Acropolis, carved around 440 BC. Also in the West Wing is one of the Seven Wonders of the Ancient World—in fragment form—in Room 21: the **Mausoleum of Halikarnassos.** The **JP Morgan Chase North American Gallery** (Room 26) has one of the largest collections of native culture outside the North American continent, going back to the earliest hunters 10,000 years ago.

Upstairs are some of the most popular galleries, especially beloved by children: Rooms 62–63, where the **Egyptian mummies** live. The Roxie Walker Galleries display even more Egyptian relics. Nearby are the glittering 4th-century **Mildenhall Treasure** and the equally splendid 8th-century Anglo-Saxon **Sutton Hoo Treasure.** A more prosaic exhibit is that of Pete Marsh, sentimentally named by the archaeologists who unearthed the **Lindow Man** from a Cheshire peat marsh; poor Pete was ritually slain in the 1st century, probably as a human sacrifice. The **Korean Gallery** (Room 67) delves into the art and archaeology of the country, including precious porcelain and colorful screens. ⊠ *Great Russell St., Bloomsbury WC1* ☎ *020/7636–1555* ⊕ *www.thebritishmuseum. ac.uk* ⊠ *Free, suggested donation £2* ☉ *Museum Sat.–Wed. 10–5:30, Thurs. and Fri. 10–8:30. Great Court Sun.–Wed. 9–6, Thurs.–Sat. 9 AM–11 PM* Ⓤ *Holborn, Russell Sq., Tottenham Court Rd.*

> **need a break?** The British Museum's **Gallery Café** gets very crowded but serves a reasonably tasty menu beneath a plaster cast of a part of the Parthenon frieze. It's open daily 10–5. The self-service café in the Great Court concourse is open Sunday–Wednesday 9–5:30 and Thursday–Saturday 9–9.

㉔ Dickens House. This is the only one of the many London houses Charles Dickens (1812–70) inhabited that's still standing. The great novelist wrote *Oliver Twist* and *Nicholas Nickleby* and finished *The Pickwick Papers* here between 1837 and 1839. The house looks exactly as it would have in Dickens's day, complete with first editions, letters, and tall clerk's desk, plus a treat for Lionel Bart fans—his score of *Oliver!* Special exhibitions give insight into the Dickens family and the author's works. During Christmas, the rooms are decorated in traditional style. ⊠ *48 Doughty St., Bloomsbury WC1* ☎ *020/7405–2127* ⊕ *www.dickensmuseum.com* ⊠ *£4* ☉ *Mon.–Sat. 10–5, Sun. 11–5; last admission at 4:30* Ⓤ *Chancery La., Russell Sq.*

◔ King's Cross Station. Known for its 120-foot-tall clock tower, this yellow-brick Italianate building with large, arched windows was constructed in 1851–52 as the London terminus for the Great Northern Railway. Harry Potter and fellow aspiring wizards took the Hogwarts Express to school from the imaginary platform 9¾ (platforms 4 and 5 were the actual shooting site) in the movies based on J. K. Rowling's popular novels. The station has put up a sign for platform 9¾; you can snap a picture there. ⊠ *Euston Rd. and York Way, Euston NW1* ☎ *0845/748–4950* Ⓤ *King's Cross.*

㉕ Lincoln's Inn. One of the oldest, best preserved, and most attractive of the Inns of Court, Lincoln's Inn offers plenty to see—from the Chancery Lane Tudor brick gatehouse to the wide-open, tree-lined, atmospheric Lincoln's Inn Fields and the 15th-century chapel remodeled by Inigo Jones in 1620. The wisteria-clad New Square is London's only complete 17th-century square. ⊠ *Chancery La., Bloomsbury WC2* ☎ *020/7405–1393* ⊠ *Free* ☉ *Gardens weekdays 7–7; chapel weekdays noon–2:30; public may also attend Sun. service at 11:30 in chapel during legal terms* Ⓤ *Chancery La.*

★ ㉖ Sir John Soane's Museum. Guaranteed to raise a smile from the most blasé traveler, this collection hardly deserves the burden of its dry name. Sir John, architect of the Bank of England, who lived here from 1790 to 1831, created one of London's most idiosyncratic and fascinating houses. Sir John owned 12, 13, and 14 Lincoln's Inn Fields, and No. 14 has been added to the museum space. Everywhere mirrors and colors play tricks with light and space, and split-level floors worthy of a fairground fun house disorient you. In a basement chamber sits the vast 1300 BC sarcophagus of Seti I, lit by a skylight two stories above. ⊠ *13 Lincoln's Inn Fields, Bloomsbury WC2* ☎ *020/7405–2107* ⊕ *www.soane.org* ✆ *Free* ⊘ *Tues.–Sat. 10–5; also 6–9 PM on 1st Tues. of every month* Ⓤ *Holborn.*

㉗ **Temple.** This is the collective name for the **Inner Temple** and **Middle Temple**, and its entrance, the point of entry into the City, is marked by a young (1880) bronze griffin, the **Temple Bar Memorial.** In the buildings opposite is an elaborate stone arch through which you pass into Middle Temple Lane, past a row of 17th-century timber-frame houses, and on into Fountain Court. If the Elizabethan **Middle Temple Hall** is open, don't miss its hammer-beam roof—among the finest in the land. ⊠ *2 Plowden Bldgs., Middle Temple La., Bloomsbury* ☎ *020/7427–4800* ⊘ *Weekdays 10–11 and (when not in use) 2–4* Ⓤ *Temple.*

The City

When people in London tell you that they work in the City, they aren't being vague: they're using the British equivalent of Wall Street. The City extends eastward from Temple Bar to the Tower of London, and north from the Thames to Chiswell Street. Despite its small size (it's known as the Square Mile), this area is the financial engine of Britain and one of the world's leading centers of trade. The City also holds two of London's most notable sights, the Tower of London and St. Paul's, one of the world's greatest cathedrals—truly, a case of the money changers encompassing the temple. The pedestrian-only Millennium Bridge connects the area with the South Bank.

Twice, the City has been nearly wiped off the face of the earth. The Great Fire of 1666 necessitated a total reconstruction, in which Sir Christopher Wren had a big hand, contributing not only his masterpiece, St. Paul's Cathedral, but 49 additional parish churches. The second wave of destruction was dealt by the German bombers of World War II. The ruins were rebuilt, but slowly, and with no overall plan, leaving the City a patchwork of the old and the new, the interesting and the flagrantly awful. Since a mere 8,000 or so people call it home, the financial center of Britain is deserted on weekends, with restaurants shuttered.

a good walk

Begin at the gateway to the City, the Temple Bar, a bronze griffin on the Strand opposite the Royal Courts of Justice. Walk east to Fleet Street and turn left on Bolt Court to Gough Square, and **Dr. Johnson's House** ㉘ ➤, passing Ye Olde Cheshire Cheese on Wine Office Court en route back to Fleet Street and the journalists' church, **St. Bride's** ㉙. At the end of Fleet Street, cross Ludgate Circus to Ludgate Hill to reach the **Old Bailey** ㉚ and the Central Criminal Courts. Continuing along Ludgate Hill, you arrive at **St. Paul's Cathedral** ㉛, Wren's masterpiece.

Retrace your steps to Newgate Street to reach London's meat market, Smithfield—where, for centuries, livestock was sold. From Smithfield Market, cross Aldersgate Street and take the right fork to London Wall, named for the Roman rampart that stood along it, with a remaining section of 2nd- to 4th-century wall at St. Alphege Garden. There's another bit outside the **Museum of London** ㉜, behind which is the **Barbican Centre** �33, an important arts venue. Back on London Wall, turn south onto Coleman Street, then right onto Masons Avenue to reach Basinghall Street and the **Guildhall** �34, then follow Milk Street south to Cheapside. Here is another symbolic center of London, the church of **St. Mary-le-Bow** �35.

Walk to the east end of Cheapside, where seven roads meet, and you face the **Bank of England** �36. Turn your back on the bank and there's the Lord Mayor's Palladian-style abode, the Mansion House, with Wren's St. Stephen Walbrook church—considered his finest effort by architectural historians—behind it, and the Royal Exchange in between Threadneedle Street and Cornhill. Now head down Queen Victoria Street, where you pass the remains of the Roman **Temple of Mithras** �37, then, after a sharp left turn onto Cannon Street, you come upon the **Monument** �38, Wren's memorial to the Great Fire of London. Just south of it is London Bridge. Turn left onto Lower Thames Street, for almost a mile's walk—passing Billingsgate, London's principal fish market for 900 years, until 1982, and the Custom House, built early in the last century—to the **Tower of London** �39, which may be the single most unmissable of London's sights. Children of all ages will be enchanted by that Thames icon, the **Tower Bridge.**

TIMING This is a marathon. Unless you want to walk all day, without a chance to do justice to London's most famous sights, the Tower of London (take the tube here) and St. Paul's Cathedral—not to mention the Museum of London, Tower Bridge, and the Barbican Centre—you should consider splitting the walk into segments. However, if you're not planning to go inside, this walk makes for a great day out, with lots of surprising vistas, river views, and history. The City is a wasteland on weekends and after dark, so choose your time accordingly.

What to See

�36 **Bank of England.** Known for the past couple of centuries as "the Old Lady of Threadneedle Street," the bank has been central to the British economy since 1694. Sir John Soane designed the neoclassical hulk in 1788, wrapping it in windowless walls (which are all that survive of his building) to project a facade of stability. The bank's history is traced in the entertaining Bank of England Museum, around the corner. ⊠ *Bartholomew La., The City EC4* 🕿 *020/7601–5545 museum* ⊕ *www. bankofengland.co.uk* 🖃 *Free* ☉ *Weekdays 10–5 and Lord Mayor's Show Day (2nd Sat. in Nov.)* Ⓤ *Bank, Monument.*

�33 **Barbican Centre.** An enormous concrete maze Londoners love to hate, the Barbican is home to the London Symphony Orchestra and its auditorium, the Guildhall School of Music and Drama, two movie theaters, a convention center, and the **Barbican Art Gallery,** which showcases modern, populist topics. The center's year-round dance, music, and theater programs, called Barbican International Theatre Events (BITE), focus on the contemporary and new but also present established companies and artists. The **Museum of London** is also part of the complex. ⊠ *Silk St., The City EC2* 🕿 *020/7638–8891 box office* ⊕ *www.*

barbican.org.uk ✉ *Barbican Centre free, gallery £5* ⊘ *Barbican Centre Mon.–Sat. 9* AM*–11* PM*, Sun. noon–11; gallery Mon.–Sat. 10–7:30, Sun. noon–7:30* Ⓤ *Barbican, Moorgate.*

▶ ㉘ **Dr. Johnson's House.** Samuel Johnson lived here between 1746 and 1759, while in the worst of health, compiling his famous *Dictionary of the English Language* in the attic. The only one of Johnson's abodes remaining today, the 17th-century house is a shrine to the man possibly more attached to London than anyone else has ever been. It includes a first edition of his dictionary among the Johnson-and-Boswell mementos. After your visit, repair around the corner in Wine Office Court to Ye Olde Cheshire Cheese pub, once Johnson's and James Boswell's favorite watering hole. ✉ *17 Gough Sq., The City EC4* ☎ *020/7353–3745* ⊕ *www. drjohnsonshouse.org* ✉ *£4* ⊘ *May–Sept., Mon.–Sat. 11–5:30; Oct.–Apr., Mon.–Sat. 11–5* Ⓤ *Blackfriars, Chancery La.*

㉞ **Guildhall.** In the symbolic nerve center of the City, the Corporation of London ceremonially elects and installs its Lord Mayor, as it has done for 800 years. The Guildhall was built in 1411, and although it failed to escape either the 1666 or 1940 flames, its core survived. The fabulous hall is a psychedelic patchwork of coats of arms and banners of the City Livery Companies. Also here is the Worshipful Company of Clockmakers' Museum in the Guildhall Library, with more than 600 timepieces; to the right of Guildhall Yard is the **Guildhall Art Gallery**, the corporation's collection of London scenes and portraits of royals and statesmen. During construction of the gallery, London's only Roman amphitheater was discovered and excavated, and you can walk among the remains. The Museum of London displays additional relics from the dig. Entry to the amphitheater is included in admission to the art gallery. ✉ *Gresham St., The City EC2* ☎ *020/7606–3030, 020/7332–1632 gallery, 020/7332–3700 recorded information* ⊕ *www.guildhall-art-gallery.org.uk* ✉ *Free, gallery and amphitheater £2.50 (free after 3:30, all day Fri., and Lord Mayor's Show Day, 2nd Sat. in Nov.)* ⊘ *Mon.–Sat. 9:30–5; Clockmakers' Museum weekdays 9:30–4:45; gallery Mon.–Sat. 10–5, Sun. noon–4* Ⓤ *Bank, Mansion House, Moorgate, St. Paul's.*

⎧ off the ⎫
⎨ beaten ⎬
⎩ path ⎭

JACK THE RIPPER'S LONDON – *Cor blimey, guv'nor, Jack the Ripper woz here!* Several organizations offer tours of "Jack's London"—the (still) mean streets of the East End, the working-class neighborhood directly to the east of the City. Here, in 1888, the Whitechapel murders traumatized Victorian London. At the haunting hour, tour groups head out to Bucks Row and other crime scenes. Even with a large group, this can be a spooky experience. Original London Walks (☎ 020/7624–3978 ⊕ www.walks.com) has frequent tours leaving at 7 PM from the Tower Hill tube stop. The Jack the Ripper Mystery Walk (☎ 020/8558–9446) departs from the Aldgate tube stop at 8 PM on Wednesday and Sunday and at 7 PM on Friday. The Blood and Tears Walk: London's Horrible Past (☎ 020/8348–9022) goes beyond Jack the Ripper, although he is the star criminal, and describes other murderers. Tours depart from the Barbican tube; phone for times.

Lloyd's of London. Architect Richard Rogers's (of Paris Pompidou Center fame) fantastical 1980s steel-and-glass medium-rise of six towers around a vast atrium, with his trademark inside-out ventilation shafts, stairwells, and gantries, is one of the most exciting modern structures in London. This fun house of a building, which contains the offices of the world-famous insurance agency, is best seen at night, when cobalt and lime spotlights make it leap out of the gray skyline. ☒ *1 Lime St., The City EC3* Ⓤ *Aldgate, Bank, Liverpool St., Monument.*

Ⓒ **Millennium Bridge.** Norman Foster and sculptor Anthony Caro designed this strikingly modern, pedestrian-only bridge of aluminum and steel. The bridge connects the City—the St. Paul's Cathedral area—with the Tate Modern art gallery. On the South Bank side, the bridge marks the middle of the **Millennium Mile**, a walkway taking in a clutch of popular sights. The city views from the bridge are breathtaking, with perhaps the best-ever view of St. Paul's. ☒ *Peters Hill to Bankside, The City, South Bank, EC4, SE1* Ⓤ *Mansion House, Blackfriars, or Southwark.*

Ⓒ ㉚ **Monument.** Commemorating the "dreadful visitation" of the Great Fire of 1666, the world's tallest isolated stone column is the work of Christopher Wren. The viewing gallery is 311 steps up the 202-foot-high structure. ☒ *Monument St., The City EC3* ☎ *020/7626–2717* ☒ *£2, £6.50 combination ticket with Tower Bridge* ☉ *Daily 10–5:40; hrs subject to change, phone before visiting* Ⓤ *Monument.*

off the
beaten
path

MUSEUM IN DOCKLANDS – This museum, in a converted quayside warehouse, focuses on the days when ships and sailors, rather than office towers, filled this part of London. Displays and interactive zones tell the story: Early Years, Water Zone, Dock Work, and Building. ☒ *No. 1 Warehouse, Hertsmere Rd., West India Quay, East End E14* ☎ *0870/444–3855* ⊕ *www.museumindocklands.org.uk* ☒ *£5 (tickets valid for 1 year)* ☉ *Daily 10–6* Ⓤ *West India Quay.*

★ Ⓒ ㉜ **Museum of London.** Anyone with the least interest in how this city evolved may adore this museum, especially its reconstructions and dioramas of the Great Fire (flickering flames! sound effects!), a 1940s air-raid shelter, a Georgian prison cell, and a Victorian street complete with stocked shops. The London Now gallery brings things up to date. World City charts one of the city's most dynamic periods, from the French Revolution to World War I, and the Medieval Gallery is a time journey to an age when London depended on the Thames. The remains unearthed at the Roman amphitheater at the Guildhall are on display. ☒ *London Wall, The City EC2* ☎ *020/7600–0807* ⊕ *www.museumoflondon.org.uk* ☒ *Free* ☉ *Mon.–Sat. 10–5:50, Sun. noon–5:50* Ⓤ *Barbican.*

㉚ **Old Bailey.** The present-day Central Criminal Court is where legendary Newgate Prison stood from the 12th century until the beginning of the 20th century. Ask the doorman which current trial is likely to prove juicy, if you're that kind of ghoul—you may catch the conviction of the next Crippen or Christie (England's most notorious wife murderers, both tried here). There are restrictions on entry (cameras, drinks, large bags, and children under 14 are not allowed), and you will be searched before you enter; call the information line first. The court has no storage facilities for items. ✉ *Newgate St., The City EC4* ☎ *020/7248–3277* ⊕ *www. cityoflondon.gov.uk/leisure_heritage* ☉ *Public Gallery weekdays 10:30–1 and 2–4:30; line forms at Newgate St. entrance* Ⓤ *St. Paul's.*

㉙ St. Bride's. One of the first of Christopher Wren's city churches, St. Bride's was one of those bomb-damaged in World War II; it was reconsecrated in 1960 after a 17-year-long restoration. From a distance, study its extraordinary steeple. Its tiered shape gave rise, legend has it, to the traditional wedding cake. ✉ *Fleet St., The City EC4* ☎ *020/7427–0133* ⊕ *www.stbrides.com* ✆ *Free* ☉ *Weekdays 8–4:30, Sat. 10–3:30, Sun. for services only 11–2; crypt closed Sun.* Ⓤ *Chancery La.*

㉟ St. Mary-le-Bow. Christopher Wren's 1673 church has one of the most famous sets of bells around—a Londoner must be born within the sound of Bow Bells to claim to be a true cockney. The origin of that idea was probably the curfew rung on the Bow Bells during the 14th century, even though "cockney" only came to mean "Londoner" three centuries later (and then the term was an insult). The Bow in the name comes from the bow-shape arches in the Norman crypt. ✉ *Cheapside, The City EC2* ☎ *020/7248–5139* ⊕ *www.stmarylebow.co.uk* ☉ *Mon.–Thurs. 6:30–5:45, Fri. 6:30–4* Ⓤ *Mansion House.*

> **need a break?** **The Place Below** (✉ Cheapside, The City EC2 ☎ 020/7329–0789) occupies St. Mary-le-Bow's crypt. The self-service vegetarian menu includes good soups and quiches. Lunches are served from 10:30 until 2:30, weekdays only, or you can stop by for breakfast and morning coffee (from 7:30), or for snacks (until 3:30).

★ ㉛ St. Paul's Cathedral. The symbolic heart of London, St. Paul's may take your breath away. The dome—the world's third largest—peeps through on the skyline from many an angle around London. The structure is Sir Christopher Wren's masterpiece, completed in 1710 after 35 years of building, and, much later, miraculously spared (mostly) by World War II bombs. Wren's first plan, known as the New Model, did not make it past the drawing board. The second, known as the Great Model, got as far as the 20-foot oak rendering you can see here before it also was rejected. The third, however, was accepted, with the fortunate coda that the architect be allowed to make changes as he saw fit. Without that, there would be no dome, since the approved design had a steeple. When you enter and see the dome from the inside, you may find that it seems smaller than you expected. You aren't imagining things; it *is* smaller, and 60 feet lower than the lead-covered outer dome. Beneath the lantern is Wren's famous epitaph, which his son composed and had set into the pavement, and which reads succinctly: *Lector, si monumentum requiris, circumspice*—"Reader, if you seek his monument, look around you." The epitaph also appears on Wren's memorial in the Crypt. Up 259 spiral steps is the **Whispering Gallery,** an acoustic phenomenon; you whisper something to the wall on one side, and a second later it transmits clearly to the other side, 107 feet away. Ascend to the **Stone Gallery,** which encircles the base of the dome. Farther up (280 feet from ground level) is the small **Golden Gallery,** around the dome's highest point. From here you can walk outside for a spectacular panorama of London. The climb up the spiraling steps can be fun for older kids.

The remains of the poet John Donne, who was dean of St. Paul's for his final 10 years (he died in 1631), are in the south choir aisle. The vivacious choir-stall carvings nearby are the work of Grinling Gibbons, as are those on the organ, which Wren designed and Handel played. Behind the high altar is the **American Memorial Chapel,** dedicated in 1958 to the 28,000 GIs stationed in the United Kingdom who lost their lives in World War II. Among the famous whose remains lie in the **Crypt** are the duke of Wellington and Admiral Lord Nelson. The Crypt also has a gift shop and a café. ⊠ *St. Paul's Churchyard, The City EC4* ☎ *020/7236–4128* ⊕ *www.stpauls.co.uk* ⊠ *£6, audio tour £3.50, guided tour £2.50* ☉ *Cathedral Mon.–Sat. 8:30–4, closed occasionally for special services; ambulatory, Crypt, and galleries Mon.–Sat. 9–5:15. Shop and Crypt Café also open Sun. 10:30–5* Ⓤ *St. Paul's.*

㊲ Temple of Mithras. Unearthed on a construction site in 1954 and taken, at first, for an early Christian church, this was a minor place of pilgrimage in Roman London. Worshipers here favored Jesus' chief rival, Mithras, the Persian god of light, during the 3rd and 4th centuries. You can see the foundations of the temple on this site. ⊠ *Temple Court, Queen Victoria St., The City EC4* Ⓤ *Bank.*

㊳ Tower Bridge. Despite its venerable appearance, this Victorian youngster dates from 1894. Constructed of steel, then clothed in Portland stone, the bridge was built in the Gothic style to complement the Tower of London next door. It's famous for the enormous bascules, the "arms" that open to allow large ships through. The **Tower Bridge Experience** exhibition is a fun tour inside the structure to discover how one of the world's most famous bridges actually works. One highlight is the glorious view from up high on the covered walkway between the turrets. Even if you don't see the exhibition, it's still fun to walk across the bridge on the regular walkway. ☎ *020/7403–3761, 020/7940–3984 for bridge-opening schedule* ⊕ *www.towerbridge.org.uk* ⊠ *£4:50, joint ticket available for the Monument* ☉ *Daily 9:30–5:30; last entry at 5* Ⓤ *Tower Hill.*

★ ㊴ Tower of London. Nowhere else does London's history come to life so vividly as in this minicity of 20 melodramatic towers stuffed to bursting with heraldry and treasure, the intimate details of lords and dukes and princes and sovereigns etched in the walls (literally, in some places), and quite a few pints of royal blood spilled on the stones. This is one of Britain's most popular sights—the Crown Jewels are here—and you can avoid lines by buying a ticket in advance on the Web site, by phone, or at any tube station; arriving before 11 can also help at busy times. The visitor center, opened in 2004, provides an introduction to the Tower. Allow at least three hours for exploring, and stroll along the battlements before you leave; from them, you get a wonderful overview of the whole Tower.

The Tower holds the royal gems because it's still one of the royal palaces, although no monarch since Henry VII has called it home. It has also housed the Royal Mint, the Public Records, the Royal Menagerie (which formed the basis of the London Zoo), and the Royal Observatory, although its most renowned and titillating function has been as a jail and place of torture and execution.

A person was mighty privileged to be beheaded in the peace and seclusion of **Tower Green** instead of before the mob at Tower Hill. In fact, only seven people were ever important enough—among them Anne Boleyn and Catherine Howard, wives two and five of Henry VIII's six; Elizabeth I's friend Robert Devereux, earl of Essex; and the nine-day queen, Lady Jane Grey, age 17. The executioner's block and ax, along with the equally famous rack, plus assorted thumbscrews, "iron maidens," and so forth, have been moved to the Royal Armouries in Leeds, Yorkshire. (Fans of this genre of heavy metal might want to pay a call on the London Dungeon attraction, just across the Thames.)

Free tours depart every half hour or so from the Middle Tower. They are conducted by the 39 Yeoman Warders, better known as Beefeaters—ex-servicemen dressed in resplendent navy-and-red (scarlet-and-gold on special occasions) Tudor outfits. Beefeaters have been guarding the Tower since Henry VII appointed them in 1485. One of them, the Yeoman Ravenmaster, is responsible for making life comfortable for the Tower ravens (six birds plus reserves)—an important duty, because if the ravens were to desert the Tower, goes the legend, the kingdom would fall. Today, the Tower takes no chances: the ravens' wings are clipped.

In prime position stands the oldest part of the Tower and the most conspicuous of its buildings, the **White Tower;** the other towers were built in the next few centuries. This central keep was begun in 1078 by William the Conqueror; Henry III (1207–72) had it whitewashed, which is where the name comes from. The spiral staircase is the only way up, and here are the **Royal Armouries,** with a collection of arms and armor. Most of the interior of the White Tower has been altered over the centuries, but the **Chapel of St. John the Evangelist,** downstairs from the armories, is a pure example of 11th-century Norman style—very rare, very simple, and very beautiful. Across the moat, **Traitors' Gate** lies to the right. Immediately opposite Traitors' Gate is the former Garden Tower, better known since about 1570 as the **Bloody Tower.** Its name comes from one of the most famous unsolved murders in history, the saga of the "little princes in the Tower." In 1483 the uncrowned boy king, Edward V, and his brother Richard were left here by their uncle, Richard of Gloucester, after the death of their father, Edward IV. They were never seen again, Gloucester was crowned Richard III, and in 1674 two little skeletons were found under the stairs to the White Tower. The obvious conclusions have always been drawn—and were, in fact, even before the skeletons were discovered. The **New Armouries** have become a restaurant.

The most famous exhibits are the **Crown Jewels,** in the Jewel House, Waterloo Block. Moving walkways on either side of the jewels hasten progress at the busiest times. You get so close to the fabled gems you feel you could polish them (there are, however, wafers of bulletproof glass), if your eyes weren't so dazzled by the sparkle of the gems, enhanced with special lighting. Before you see them, you view a short film that includes scenes from Elizabeth's 1953 coronation. Security is tight because the jewels—even though they would be impossible for thieves to sell—are *so* priceless that they're not insured. However, they are polished every January by the crown jewelers. A brief résumé of the top jewels: finest of all is the Royal Sceptre, containing the earth's largest cut diamond, the 530-carat Star of Africa. This is also known as Cullinan I, having been cut from the South African Cullinan, which weighed 20 ounces when dug up from a De Beers mine at the beginning of the 20th century. Another chip off the block, Cullinan II, lives on the Imperial State Crown (made for Queen Victoria's coronation in 1838 and adapted to hold the large diamond); Elizabeth II wore this crown at her coronation and wears it annually for the State Opening of Parliament. Another famous gem is the Koh-i-noor, or "Mountain of Light." The legendary diamond, which was supposed to bring luck to women, came from India, and was given to the Queen in 1850. You can see it, in cut-down shape, in the late Queen Mother's Crown.

The little chapel of **St. Peter ad Vincula** is the second church on the site, and it conceals the remains of some 2,000 people executed at the Tower, Anne Boleyn and Catherine Howard among them.

One of the more evocative towers is **Beauchamp Tower,** built west of Tower Green by Edward I (1272–1307). It was soon designated as a jail for the higher class of miscreant, including Lady Jane Grey, who is thought to have added her Latin graffiti to the many inscriptions carved by prisoners that you can see here.

For tickets to the Ceremony of the Keys (locking of main gates, nightly between 9:30 and 10), write well in advance to the Resident Governor and Keeper of the Jewel House (at the Queen's House, address below). Give your name, the date you wish to attend (include alternate dates), and number of people (up to seven) in your party, and enclose a self-addressed, stamped envelope. ✉ *H. M. Tower of London, Tower Hill, The City EC3N* ☎ *0870/756–6060 recorded information and advance booking* ⊕ *www.hrp.org.uk* ✉ *£13.50; joint tickets available with Kensington Palace and Hampton Court Palace* ⊘ *Mar.–Oct., Mon.–Sat. 9–5, Sun. 10–5; Nov.–Feb., Tues.–Sat. 9–4, Sun. and Mon. 10–4; Tower closes 1 hr after last admission time and all internal bldgs. close 30 mins after last admission. Free Yeoman Warder guided tours leave daily from Middle Tower (subject to weather and availability) about every 30 mins until 3:30 Mar.–Oct., 2:30 Nov.–Feb.* Ⓤ *Tower Hill.*

The South Bank

There's an old North London quip about needing a passport to cross the Thames. Visitors rarely frequented the area unless they were departing from Waterloo Station. Times have changed dramatically. The Tate Modern is the star attraction, installed in a 1930s power station, with the eye-catching Millennium Bridge linking its main door across the river to the City. At the South Bank Centre, the world's largest observation wheel, the British Airways London Eye, gives you a flight over the city.

Even from a great height, the South Bank of the Thames isn't beautiful, but this area of theaters and museums has Culture with a capital C. Following the 1976 construction of the South Bank Centre, developers and local authorities expanded the area's potential farther east, turning this district into an exciting neighborhood. The '80s brought renovations and innovations such as Hay's Galleria and Butler's Wharf. In the '90s came the OXO Tower, the London Aquarium, and the reconstruction of Shakespeare's Globe. With the new century came the massive glass, mushroomlike building designed by Norman Foster, which sits by the Thames near Tower Bridge; it is City Hall, which houses the London Assembly. Cultural options have increased with the arrival of art galleries such as the Saatchi Gallery at County Hall and the Hayward Gallery at the South Bank Centre.

It's fitting that so much of London's artistic life should once again be centered on the South Bank—in the past, Southwark was the location of theaters, taverns, and cockfighting arenas. The Globe Theatre, in which Shakespeare acted and held shares, was one of several here. In truth the Globe was as likely to stage bear-baiting as Shakespeare, but today, at the reconstructed "Wooden O," you can see only the latter. Be sure to take a walk along Bankside, the embankment along the Thames from Southwark to Blackfriars Bridge.

a good walk

Start at the south end of Tower Bridge, finding the steps on the east (left) side, which descend to the start of a pedestrians-only street, Shad Thames. You get a good view of City Hall here. Turn your back on the bridge and follow this path between cliffs of the good-as-new warehouses that now constitute **Butler's Wharf** ④ ⏵ but were once the dangerous shadowlands where Dickens kills off Bill Sikes in *Oliver Twist*. See the foodies' center, the Gastrodrome, and the **Design Museum** ④; then just before you get back to Tower Bridge, turn away from the river along Horselydown Lane, follow Tooley Street, and take the right turn at Morgan's Lane to **HMS *Belfast*** ④, or continue to **Hay's Galleria** ④ and the grisly **London Dungeon** ④. Across Borough High Street and down Cathedral Street is **Southwark Cathedral** ④. See the west wall, with rose window outline, of Winchester House, palace of the bishops of Winchester until 1626, built into it, and **The Clink** ④ next door. At the end of the cobbled alleyway is St. Mary Overie Dock, with a replica of Sir Francis Drake's ship the *Golden Hinde* ④. Nearby on New Globe Walk is **Shakespeare's Globe Theatre** ④. Continue west to reach Bankside Power Station, now the **Tate Modern** ④. The pedestrians-only Millennium Bridge crosses the Thames near here.

Ahead lies Blackfriars Bridge, which you pass beneath to join the street called Upper Ground, spending some time in the Coin Street Community Builders' fast-emerging neighborhood, which includes the **OXO Tower** ⑤ and Gabriel's Wharf, a marketplace of shops and cafés. Farther along Upper Ground, you reach the South Bank Centre, with the **Royal National Theatre** ⑤, **Hayward Gallery** ⑤, and the **Royal Festival Hall** ⑤. The **National Film Theatre** is also here. Outside the wide paths of the complex are interesting distractions—secondhand book–stalls, entertainers, and more. Walk around the curve of the river, passing another restored footbridge, this time the Hungerford, running parallel to the Charing Cross rail line, and you come to the Jubilee Gardens, with the **British Airways London Eye** �54 observation wheel. Look to the opposite bank for the postcard vista of the Houses of Parliament. Just after the London Eye, you reach the old County Hall building, which houses the **London Aquarium** �55, the surrealist museum Dalí Universe, and the **Saatchi Gallery** �56. Farther along the river, beyond the **Florence Nightingale Museum** �57, **Lambeth Palace** �58—for 800 years the London base of the archbishop of Canterbury, top man in the Church of England—stands by Lambeth Bridge. A little farther east along Lambeth Road is the **Imperial War Museum** �59.

TIMING   On a fine day, this 2- to 3-mi walk makes for a very scenic wander, since you're following the south bank of the Thames nearly all the way. Views across to the north bank include everything from St. Paul's to the Houses of Parliament, and you pass—under, over, or around—no fewer than nine bridges, from the Tower to Lambeth. Allow a full day to see the sights, or split the walk and do the west or east section. The Tate Modern, the Imperial War Museum, Shakespeare's Globe, the Design Museum, and the Aquarium each could take more than an hour, but the London Dungeon doesn't take long, unless you have kids in tow. The other museums are compact; you can choose among them en route to what may be your main event, evening theater tickets. Remember, though, that the theaters stay dark on Sundays. Dinner or a riverside drink at the OXO Tower Brasserie, Gastrodome, or the People's Palace is another idea for a big finish, or you can ride the London Eye. Public transportation is thin here, so pick a day when you're feeling energetic; there are few shortcuts.

What to See

☾ �54 **British Airways London Eye.** If you want a pigeon's-eye view of London, this is the place to get it. The highest observation wheel in the world, at 500 feet, towers over the South Bank from the Jubilee Gardens next to County Hall. For 25 minutes, passengers hover over the city in a slow-motion flight. You can book by phone or on-line, or buy tickets in advance at the Eye itself; it's very popular. ✉ *Jubilee Gardens, South Bank SE1* ☎ *0870/500–0600* ⊕ *www.ba-londoneye.com* ✑ *£11.50* ☺ *Mon.–Thurs. 9:30–8, Fri.–Sun. 9:30–9, but subject to change, so call ahead* Ⓤ *Waterloo.*

▶ ㊵ **Butler's Wharf.** An '80s development that is maturing gracefully, this wharf is full of loft-style warehouse conversions and swank buildings housing restaurants and galleries. People flock here thanks partly to London's saint of the stomach, Sir Terence Conran (also responsible for high-profile restaurants Bibendum, Mezzo, and Quaglino's). He gave the wharf his Gastrodome of four restaurants, a vintner's, a deli, and a bakery. ✉*South Bank SE1* Ⓤ *London Bridge or Tower Hill, then walk over bridge.*

㊻ **The Clink.** Giving rise to the term "the clink," which still refers to a jail, this institution was originally the prison attached to Winchester House, palace of the bishops of Winchester until 1626. It was one of the first prisons to detain women, most of whom were called "Winchester

Geese"—a euphemism meaning prostitutes. The world's oldest profession was endemic in Southwark; a museum traces the history of prostitution here and shows what the Clink was like in its 16th-century prime. ⊠ *1 Clink St., South Bank SE1* ☎ *020/7403–0900* ⊕ *www.clink.co. uk* ⊡ *£4* ⊙ *Daily 10–6; last admission 5:30* Ⓤ *London Bridge.*

④ Design Museum. This was the first museum in the world to elevate everyday design to the status of art, presenting designs in their social and cultural context. Fashion, creative technology, and architecture are explored in thematic displays, and temporary exhibitions provide an in-depth focus. Check out the very good Blueprint Café, with its own river terrace. ⊠ *28 Shad Thames, South Bank SE1* ☎ *0870/909–9009 weekdays 9–5, 0870/833–9955 recorded information* ⊕ *www.designmuseum. org* ⊡ *£6* ⊙ *Sun.–Thurs. 10–5:45, Fri. 10–9; last admission 30 min before closing* Ⓤ *London Bridge, Tower Gateway (DLR), Tower Hill.*

㊿ Florence Nightingale Museum. Here you can learn all about that most famous of health care reformers, the "Lady with the Lamp." On view are fascinating reconstructions of the barracks ward at Scutari (Turkey), where Nightingale tended soldiers during the Crimean War (1854–56) and earned her nickname, and a Victorian East End slum cottage, to show what she did to improve living conditions among the poor. The museum is in St. Thomas's Hospital. ⊠ *2 Lambeth Palace Rd., South Bank SE1* ☎ *020/ 7620–0374* ⊕ *www.florence-nightingale.co.uk* ⊡ *£5.80* ⊙ *Weekdays 10–5, weekends 10–4:30; last admission 1 hr before closing* Ⓤ *Waterloo or Westminster, then walk over the bridge.*

☙ ㊼ Golden Hinde. In the late 16th century, Sir Francis Drake circumnavigated the globe in this little galleon, or one just like it, anyway. This exact reproduction finished a 23-year, round-the-world voyage—much of it spent along American coasts, both Pacific and Atlantic—and has settled here to continue its educational mission. ⊠ *St. Mary Overie Dock, Cathedral St., South Bank SE1* ☎ *020/7403–0123* ⊕ *www.goldenhinde. co.uk* ⊡ *£3.50, £4 for prebooked guided tour* ⊙ *Apr.–Oct., daily 9:30–5:30; Nov.–Mar., daily 9:30–5; last admission 30 mins before closing; may close Christmas wk and for special events* Ⓤ *London Bridge.*

㊸ Hay's Galleria. Once known as "London's larder" because of the edibles sold here, Hay's Galleria was reborn in 1987 as a Covent Garden–esque parade of bars and restaurants, offices, and shops, all weatherproofed by an arched glass atrium roof supported by tall iron columns. Jugglers, string quartets, and crafts stalls abound. ⊠ *2 Battle Bridge La., South Bank SE1* ☎ *020/7940–7770* ⊕ *www.haysgalleria. co.uk* ⊙ *Hrs vary from shop to shop* Ⓤ *London Bridge.*

㊺ Hayward Gallery. This is the one gallery you can't miss, thanks to the multicolor neon tube sculpture topping the building, which blinks away through the night. The windowless bunker tucked behind the South Bank Centre concert halls has an extended foyer that gives more daylight and exhibit space; the highlight is an elliptical mirrored glass pavilion by New York–based artist Dan Graham. The gallery encompasses different media, crossing history and cultures, bridging the experimental and the established. One aim is to find new perspectives from which to present the well-known, from Picasso to Lichtenstein. ⊠ *South Bank Centre, Belvedere Rd., South Bank SE1* ☎ *020/7960–5226* ⊕ *www.hayward. org.uk* ✉ *Admission varies according to exhibition* ⊙ *Thurs.–Mon. 10–6, Tues. and Wed. 10–8* Ⓤ *Waterloo.*

🐚 ㊷ **HMS *Belfast*.** At 613 feet long, this is one of the largest cruisers the Royal Navy has ever had. It played a role in the D-Day landings off Normandy. An outpost of the **Imperial War Museum** is on board. ⊠ *Morgan's La., Tooley St., South Bank SE1* ☎ *020/7940–6300* ⊕ *www.iwm.org.uk* ✉ *£7* ⊙ *Mid-Mar.–Oct., daily 10–6; Nov.–mid-Mar., daily 10–5; last admission 45 mins before closing* Ⓤ *London Bridge.*

Hungerford Bridge. Actually two pedestrian bridges, this stunning suspension update on the previous footbridge provides a convenient crossing from Charing Cross to Jubilee Gardens and South Bank sights. ⊠ *Jubilee Gardens, South Bank SE1.*

🐚 ㊾ **Imperial War Museum.** This museum of 20th-century warfare does not glorify bloodshed but attempts to evoke what it was like to live through the two world wars. There's hardware—a Battle of Britain Spitfire, a German V2 rocket—but also an equal amount of war art (John Singer Sargent to Henry Moore) and interactive material. One affecting exhibit, "The Blitz Experience," provides a 10-minute taste of an air raid in a street of acrid smoke, sirens, and searchlights. There's also a Holocaust exhibition. The museum is in an elegantly colonnaded 19th-century building that was once the home of the infamous insane asylum called Bedlam. ⊠ *Lambeth Rd., South Bank SE1* ☎ *020/7416–5320* ⊕ *www.iwm. org.uk* ✉ *Free* ⊙ *Daily 10–6* Ⓤ *Lambeth N.*

㊺ **Lambeth Palace.** The London residence of the archbishop of Canterbury, the senior archbishop of the Church of England since the 13th century, is closed to the public, but you can admire the Tudor gatehouse. ⊠ *Lambeth Palace Rd., South Bank SE1* ⊕ *www.archbishopofcanterbury.org* Ⓤ *Waterloo.*

🐚 ㊋ **London Aquarium.** County Hall was the original name of this curved, colonnaded neoclassical hulk, which took 46 years (1912–58; two world wars interfered) to build. It housed London's local government, the Greater London Council, until it disbanded in 1986. The three-level aquarium is full of sharks and stingrays, educational exhibits, and exotic piscine sights. ⊠ *Westminster Bridge Rd., South Bank SE1* ☎ *020/7967–8000* ⊕ *www.londonaquarium.co.uk* ✉ *£9.75* ⊙ *Daily 10–6; last admission at 5* Ⓤ *Waterloo, or Westminster and walk over the bridge.*

🐚 ㊹ **London Dungeon.** Did you ever wonder what a disembowelment actually looks like? See it here. Preteens seem to adore this place, which, although grisly, usually has long lines. Inside, realistic waxwork people are subjected to the horrors that you hear about at the Tower of London. Tableaux depict bloody historic moments—like Anne Boleyn's decapitation—alongside the torture and ritual slaughter of more anonymous victims, all to a sound track of agonized moaning. Displays deal with the Great Fire and the Great Plague, and a whole section is devoted to Jack the Ripper. ⊠ *28–34 Tooley St., South Bank SE1* ☎ *020/7403–7221*

⊕ *www.thedungeons.com* 🖼 *£14.50* ⊘ *Mid-Apr.–mid-July, Sept. and Oct., daily 10–5:30; mid-July–Aug., daily 10–7:30; Nov.–mid-Apr., daily 10:30–5; phone to confirm hrs* Ⓤ *London Bridge.*

National Film Theatre. The NFT has the best repertory programming in London; it's also home to the British Film Institute and to international film festivals, such as the London Film Festival during November, the Gay and Lesbian Film Festival in April, and a Crime Thriller Festival. The **BFI London IMAX Cinema** (✉ 1 Charlie Chaplin Walk, South Bank SE1 ☎ 020/7902–1234) has the country's largest screen for 2D and 3D films; it's a short walk toward Waterloo Station. Films include science, history, and action titles. ✉ *South Bank Centre, South Bank SE1* ☎ *020/ 7928–3232* ⊕ *www.bfi.org.uk* 🖼 *£7.20* ⊘ *Daily 11:30 AM–8:30 PM* Ⓤ *Waterloo.*

⑤⓪ OXO Tower. Long a London landmark to the cognoscenti, this art deco tower has graduated from its former incarnations as power-generating station and warehouse into a vibrant community with artists' and designers' workshops, restaurants and cafés, and five floors of excellent low-income housing, thanks to Coin Street Community Builders. A rooftop viewing gallery adjacent to the well-regarded OXO Tower Restaurant and Brasserie provides the best river vista in town, and the first floor has a performance area. ✉ *Barge House St., South Bank SE1* ☎ *020/7401–3610* 🖼 *Free* ⊘ *Studios and shops Tues.–Sun. 11–6* Ⓤ *Blackfriars, Waterloo.*

⑤③ Royal Festival Hall. The largest auditorium of the South Bank Centre has superb acoustics and a 3,000-plus capacity. It's the oldest of the riverside blocks raised as the centerpiece of the 1951 Festival of Britain, a postwar morale-boosting exercise. The London Philharmonic resides here; symphony orchestras from around the world visit; and choral works, ballet, serious jazz and pop, and even films with live accompaniment are presented. There's a fine bookstore and the good People's Palace restaurant. An adjacent building contains two concert halls, the **Queen Elizabeth Hall** and the **Purcell Room.** ✉ *South Bank Centre, Belvedere Rd., South Bank SE1* ☎ *020/7960–4242* ⊕ *www.rfh.org.uk* Ⓤ *Waterloo.*

⑤① Royal National Theatre. Dark and low-slung, Sir Denys Lasdun's stolid 1976 building may not do much for the landscape, but the interior of the Royal National Theatre—abbreviated colloquially to the pre–royal warrant "NT"—makes up for its exterior. Three auditoriums—the Olivier, named after Sir Laurence, first artistic director of the National Theatre Company; the Lyttelton; and the Cottesloe—host ever-changing productions. The NT attracts many of the nation's top actors in addition to launching stars and star productions. ✉ *South Bank Centre, South Bank SE1* ☎ *020/7452–3000 box office, 020/7452–3400 tour availability* ⊕ *www.nationaltheatre.org.uk* 🖼 *Tour £5* ⊘ *1-hr backstage tours Mon.–Sat. at 10:15, 12:30, and 5:30* Ⓤ *Waterloo.*

⑤⑥ Saatchi Gallery. The high-profile, edgy Saatchi contemporary art collection moved to the South Bank in 2003, where it rubs shoulders with Tate Modern and the Hayward Gallery. Charles Saatchi is no stranger to newspaper headlines; in the 1980s his advertising empire "rebranded" Margaret Thatcher's Conservative Party. An astute art collector, he has made acquisitions that sometimes create news and controversy. Paula Rego, Damien Hirst, Rachel Whiteread, Janine Antoni, and Tracey Emin are exhibited here. ⊠ *County Hall, Riverside Building, Westminster Bridge Rd., South Bank SE1* ☎ *020/7823–2363* ⊕ *www. saatchi-gallery.co.uk* ✍ *£8.75* ⊙ *Sun.–Thurs. 10–8, Fri.–Sat. 10–10* Ⓤ *Waterloo, Westminster.*

★ ⏱ ㊽ **Shakespeare's Globe Theatre.** A spectacular theater, this is a replica of Shakespeare's open-roof, wood-and-thatch Globe Playhouse (built in 1599 and burned down in 1613), where most of the Bard's great plays premiered. For several decades, American actor and director Sam Wanamaker worked ceaselessly to raise funds for the theater's reconstruction, 200 yards from its original site, with authentic materials and techniques; his dream was realized in 1996. The "pit," or orchestra level, can take 500 standees—or "groundlings," to use the historical term— in front of the high stage, and 1,000 can sit in the covered wooden bays. A repertory season of three or four Shakespeare plays is presented during summer, in daylight—and sometimes rain. The audience becomes as much a part of the proceedings as the actors on stage. Throughout the year, you can tour the theater as part of the **Shakespeare's Globe Exhibition,** an adjacent museum that provides fascinating background material on both the Elizabethan theater and the construction of the modern-day Globe. If you're thrilled by the reconstruction of Shakespeare's Globe, you can get the complete picture by visiting an exhibition at its near neighbor, the **Rose Theatre,** at 56 Park Street, which was built even earlier, in 1587. ⊠ *New Globe Walk, Bankside, South Bank SE1* ☎ *020/ 7401–9919 box office, 020/7902–1500 New Shakespeare's Globe Exhibition* ⊕ *www.shakespeares-globe.org* ✍ *£8 for exhibition and tour; joint ticket available with Rose Theatre* ⊙ *Exhibition daily 10–5, plays May–Sept.; call for schedule* Ⓤ *Mansion House, then walk across Southwark Bridge; Blackfriars, then walk across Blackfriars Bridge; or Southwark, then walk down to the river.*

㊺ **Southwark Cathedral.** This cathedral (pronounced *suth*-uck) is the second-oldest Gothic church in London, next to Westminster Abbey. Look for the gaudily renovated 1408 tomb of the poet John Gower, friend of Chaucer, and for the Harvard Chapel, named after John Harvard, founder of the United States college, who was baptized here in 1608. Also buried here is Edmund Shakespeare, brother of William. ⊠ *Montague Close, South Bank SE1* ☎ *020/7367–6700* ⊕ *www.dswark.org* ✍ *Free, suggested donation £4* ⊙ *Daily 8–6* Ⓤ *London Bridge.*

★ ⏱ ㊾ **Tate Modern.** This former power station has glowered on the banks on the Thames since the 1930s, and after a dazzling renovation by Herzog de Meuron, provides a grand space for a massive collection of international modern art. The vast Turbine Hall is a dramatic entrance point. On permanent display in the galleries are classic works from 1900 to the present day, by Matisse, Picasso, Dalí, Francis Bacon, Andy Warhol, and the most-talked-about upstarts. They are arranged in themes that mix the historic with the contemporary—Landscape, Still Life, and The Nude—on different levels, reached by a moving staircase. This is a good museum for kids, who respond to the unusual space as well as the art; there are kids' programs, too. The changing exhibitions, for which there are often long lines, are always the talking point of Londoners who have their fingers on the pulse. ✉ *25 Summer St., South Bank SE1* ☎ *020/ 7887–8000* ⊕ *www.tate.org.uk* ✉ *Free; charge for special exhibitions* ⊗ *Sun.–Thurs. 10–6, Fri. and Sat. 10–10* Ⓤ *Blackfriars, Southwark.*

Kensington, Knightsbridge & Mayfair

Splendid houses with pillared porches, as well as fascinating museums, stylish squares, and glittering antiques shops, line the streets of this elegant area of the Royal Borough of Kensington. Also here is Kensington Palace (the former home of both Diana, Princess of Wales, and Queen Victoria), which put the district literally on the map back in the 17th century. To Kensington's east is one of the highest concentrations of important artifacts anywhere, the "museum mile" of South Kensington, with the rest of Kensington offering peaceful strolls and a noisy main street. Kensington first became the *Royal* Borough of Kensington (and Chelsea) when William III, who suffered terribly from the Thames mists over Whitehall, decided in 1689 to buy Nottingham House in the rural village of Kensington so that he could breathe more easily. Courtiers and functionaries and society folk soon followed where the crown led, and by the time Queen Anne was on the throne (1702–14), Kensington was overflowing. In a way, it still is, since most of its grand houses have been divided into apartments, or are serving as embassies.

Hyde Park and Kensington Gardens together form by far the biggest of central London's royal parks. It's probably been centuries since any major royal had a casual stroll here, but the parks remain the property of the Crown, and it was the Crown that saved them from being devoured by the city's late-18th-century growth spurt.

Around the borders of Hyde Park are several of London's most beautiful and posh neighborhoods. To the south of the park and a short carriage ride from Buckingham Palace is the splendidly aristocratic enclave of Belgravia. Its white-stucco buildings and grand squares—particularly Belgrave Square—are Regency-era jewels. On the eastern border of Hyde Park is Mayfair, which gives Belgravia a run for its money as London's wealthiest district. Two mansions here allow you to get a peek into the lifestyles of London's rich and famous: Apsley House, the home of the duke of Wellington, and the Wallace Collection, a mansion on Manchester Square stuffed with great art treasures.

a good walk

When you surface from the Knightsbridge tube station, you are immediately engulfed by the manic drivers, professional shoppers, and ladies-who-lunch who compose the local population. Walk west down Brompton Road, past **Harrods** ▶, to the junction of Cromwell Road and the pale, Italianate Brompton Oratory, which marks the beginning of museum territory. The **Victoria & Albert Museum** ⑳, or V&A, is at the start of Cromwell Road, followed by the **Natural History Museum** ㉑ and the **Science Museum** ㉒ behind it. Turn left to continue north up Exhibition Road, a kind of unfinished cultural main drag that was Prince Albert's conception, toward the road after which British moviemakers named their fake blood, Kensington Gore, to reach the giant, round Wedgwood china box of the **Royal Albert Hall** ⑥ and the gilded **Albert Memorial** ⑭ opposite, on the edge of **Kensington Gardens.**

Walk northwest through the park to reach **Kensington Palace** ⑥. From here you can either head west to check out some of London's current sanctuaries of the rich and famous at **Kensington Palace Gardens** ⑯ or take an extra leg of the journey to see **Leighton House** or the **Linley Sambourne House.** If opulent 19th-century interiors are not your cup of tea, head east instead to explore **Kensington Gardens.** When you cross the bridge over the Serpentine, you leave Kensington Gardens and enter **Hyde Park.** Walk to the southern perimeter and along the sand track called Rotten Row. It's still used by the Household Cavalry (the brigade that mounts the guard at the palace), who live at the Knightsbridge Barracks to the left. Then head toward the Hyde Park Corner exit of the park and discover glorious **Apsley House (Wellington Museum)** ⑰. If you decided to skip Hyde Park, tube it from Kensington High Street (and Leighton House) over to Hyde Park Corner to take in the Wellington Museum, then head south to see chic **Belgrave Place** ⑱ or north for some more palatial treats at the **Wallace Collection** ⑲. You can head northward to discover the child-pleasing sights around **Regent's Park** and the park itself: **Madame Tussaud's** ⑳ and the **London Zoo** ㉑.

TIMING This walk is at least 4 mi long, with many places to stop along the way; you need plenty of time and some money for taxis or the tube. A jaunt from Belgrave Square up to the Apsley House and on to the Wallace Collection would add another 2 mi. You could cut out much of Hyde Park without missing essential sights, and walk the whole thing in a good five hours. The best way to approach these neighborhoods is to treat Knightsbridge shopping and the South Kensington museums as separate days out, although the three vast museums may be too much to take in at once. The parks are best in the growing seasons and during fall, when the foliage is turning, although the summer roses in Regent's Park are stunning. On Sunday, the Hyde Park and Kensington Gardens railings all along the Bayswater Road are hung with mediocre art, which may slow your progress; this is prime perambulation day for locals.

What to See

off the
beaten
path

ABBEY ROAD STUDIOS – Strawberry Fields Forever. Here, outside the Abbey Road Studios, is the world's most famous zebra crossing. Immortalized on the Beatles' *Abbey Road* album of 1969, this footpath is a spot beloved by Beatlemaniacs and baby boomers. The studios (closed to the public) are where the Beatles recorded their entire output from "Love Me Do" on, including *Sgt. Pepper's Lonely Hearts Club Band* (1967). To see Fab Four sites, Original London Walks (☎ 020/7624–3978 ⊕ www.walks.com) offers two Beatles tours: "The Beatles In-My-Life Walk" and "The Beatles Magical Mystery Tour." Abbey Road is a 10-minute ride on the Jubilee tube line from central London. After you exit, head southwest three blocks down Grove End Road. ⊠ *3 Abbey Rd., Hampstead NW8 ⊕ www. abbeyroad.co.uk* Ⓤ *St. John's Wood.*

64 Albert Memorial. This gleaming, neo-Gothic shrine to Prince Albert created by George Gilbert Scott epitomizes the Victorian era. The 14-foot bronze statue of Albert looks as if it had been created yesterday, thanks to its brilliant restoration by English Heritage. Albert's grieving widow, Queen Victoria, had this elaborate confection erected on the spot where his Great Exhibition had stood a decade before his early death, from typhoid, in 1861. ⊠ *Kensington Gore, opposite Royal Albert Hall, Hyde Park, Kensington SW7* Ⓤ *Knightsbridge.*

★ **67 Apsley House (Wellington Museum).** Once known, quite simply, as Number 1, London, this was celebrated as the best address in town. Built by Robert Adam in the 1770s, the mansion was the home of the celebrated conqueror of Napoléon, the duke of Wellington, who lived here from the 1820s until his death in 1852. The great Waterloo Gallery—scene of legendary dinners—is an orgy of opulence. Not to be missed, in every sense, is the gigantic Antonio Canova statue of a nude (but fig-leafed) Bonaparte in the entry stairwell. The current duke of Wellington lives here. During certain weekends, entrance to the house is free, and there are special events and costumed guides. These include the weekend closest to June 18 (the day of the battle of Waterloo) and a weekend before Christmas. Imposing statues flank the house: opposite is the 1825 **Wellington Arch** by John Nash, with the four-horse chariot of peace as its pinnacle; it's open to the public as an exhibition area and viewing platform. On the other side of the ducal mansion, at the tip of Hyde Park, is the **Achilles** statue. Cast from captured French guns, the statue points the way to the ducal mansion with a thrusting shield. Beside the house is the 1828 archway to Hyde Park by Decimus Burton. ⊠ *Hyde Park Corner, Mayfair W1* ☎ *020/7499–5676* ⊕ *www.english-heritage.org.uk* ⊠ *£4.50 includes audio guide* ☉ *Tues.–Sun. 11–5* Ⓤ *Hyde Park Corner.*

68 Belgrave Place. One of the main arteries of Belgravia—London's swankiest neighborhood—Belgrave Place is lined with grand, imposing Regency-era mansions, now mostly embassies. Walk down this street toward Eaton Place to pass two of the area's most beautiful mews—Eaton Mews North and Eccleston Mews, both fronted by grand Westminster-white rusticated entrances right out of a 19th-century engraving. There are few places where London is so elegant. ⊠ *Belgravia* Ⓤ *Hyde Park Corner.*

Handel House Museum. The former home of composer George Frideric Handel, where he lived for more than 30 years until his death in 1759, celebrates his genius in its fine Georgian rooms. You can linger over original manuscripts (others are in the British Library) and gaze at portraits and art illustrating the times. Some of Handel's most famous pieces were created here, including *Messiah* and *Music for the Royal Fireworks.* The museum occupies No. 25 and the adjoining house, which contains exhibits on life in Georgian London. ⊠ *25 Brook St., Mayfair W1* ☎ *020/ 7495–1685* ⊕ *www.handelhouse.org* ⊠ *£4.50* ☉ *Tues., Wed., Fri., and Sat. 10–6, Thurs. 10–8, Sun. noon–6* Ⓤ *Bond St.*

☾ ☛ **Harrods.** Just in case you hadn't noticed it, this well-known shopping destination outlines its domed terra-cotta Edwardian bulk in thousands of white lights at night. Owned by Mohamed Al Fayed, whose son Dodi was killed in the car crash that also claimed Princess Diana's life in 1997, the 15-acre store has wonderful, frenetic sale weeks. Don't miss the extravagant **Food Hall,** with its art nouveau tiling. This is the department in which to acquire your green-and-gold-logo souvenir Harrods bag, since food prices are competitive. ⊠ *87–135 Brompton Rd., Knightsbridge SW1* ☎ *020/ 7730–1234* ⊕ *www.harrods.com* ⊗ *Mon.–Sat. 10–7* Ⓤ *Knightsbridge.*

☾ **Hyde Park.** Along with the smaller St. James's and Green parks to the east, Hyde Park started as Henry VIII's hunting grounds. Along its south side runs **Rotten Row,** once Henry's royal path to the hunt—the name is a corruption of *route du roi* (route of the king). It's still used by the Household Cavalry, who live at the **Knightsbridge Barracks**—a high-rise and a low, ugly, red block to the left. This brigade mounts the guard at the palace, and you can see them leave to perform this duty, in full regalia, at about 10:30, or await the return of the ex-guard about noon. Hyde Park is wonderful for strolling, watching the locals, or just relaxing by the **Serpentine,** the long body of water near its southern border. On the south side of the Serpentine, by the Lido, is the site of the **Diana Princess of Wales Memorial Fountain.** On Sunday, **Speakers' Corner,** in the park near Marble Arch, is an unmissable spectacle of vehement, sometimes comical, and always entertaining orators. ☎ *020/ 7298–2100* ⊕ *www.royalparks.gov.uk* ⊗ *Daily 5 AM–midnight* Ⓤ *Hyde Park Corner, Lancaster Gate, Marble Arch.*

☾ **Kensington Gardens.** More formal than neighboring Hyde Park, Kensington Gardens was first laid out as palace grounds. The paved Italian garden at the top of the Long Water, **The Fountains,** is a reminder of this, although **Kensington Palace** itself is the main clue to its royal status, with the early-19th-century Sunken Garden north of it. Nearby is George Frampton's beloved 1912 *Peter Pan,* a bronze of the boy who lived on an island in the Serpentine and never grew up, and whose creator, J. M. Barrie, lived at 100 Bayswater Road, not 500 yards from here. The **Round Pond** is a magnet for model-boat enthusiasts and duck feeders. The fabulous **Princess Diana Memorial Playground** has the usual play equipment and specially designed structures and areas on the theme of Barrie's Neverland. ⊕ *www.royalparks.gov.uk* ⊗ *Daily dawn–dusk* Ⓤ *Lancaster Gate, Queensway.*

★ ㉕ **Kensington Palace.** The long history of this palace has been eclipsed in the last few years by—some might say its most famous inhabitant—the late Princess Diana. Still, royals have lived here in grand style for more than 300 years, and a walk through the palace's Royal Ceremonial Dress Collection and State Apartments (with an excellent audio-guide device as your companion) puts in perspective the protocol-filled royal lifestyle of the past. When King William III decided in the late 17th century to make his palace at Kensington, 12 years of renovation to the original building were needed by Wren and Hawksmoor before the king and Queen Mary could move in. The palace continued to undergo refurbishment during the reigns of Queen Anne and George I and II. The pleasantly domestic state rooms where Queen Victoria had her ultrastrict upbringing (originally part of the King's Apartments) have been restored with items that belonged to Victoria and Prince Albert.

The State Apartments, especially the King's Apartments, reminded visitors none too subtly of the king's power. The King's Grand Staircase (the original entrance; plans are under way to make it the starting point of a visit to the rooms) is impressive, with trompe l'oeil paintings of courtiers by William Kent. As you progress from the Presence Chamber to the Privy Chamber (with its Mortlake tapestries commissioned by Charles I) to the lavish Cupola Room, keep in mind that being admitted beyond the Presence Room was a mark of status; each room is grander than the previous one. Elsewhere, look for Tintorettos and Van Dycks among the canvases in the 96-foot-long King's Gallery.

Today the Duke and Duchess of Gloucester and Prince and Princess Michael of Kent have apartments here, as did the late Princess Margaret (at the time of this writing, plans called for her apartments to open for public view before 2005).

With garments dating to the 18th century, the Royal Ceremonial Dress Collection (viewed before the State Apartments) showcases a selection of state and occasional dresses, hats, and shoes worn by Britain's Royal Family. On permanent exhibition are 14 of Princess Diana's dazzling evening gowns. Another dazzler is a regal mantua—a 6-foot-wide court dress which recalls the truth that part of the aristocratic game was to impress your fellow courtiers. ⊠ *The Broad Walk, Kensington Gardens, Kensington W8* ☎ *0870/751–5180 advance booking and information* ⊕ *www.hrp.org.uk* ✉ *£10.80; joint tickets available with Hampton Court Palace and the Tower of London* ⊙ *Mar.–Oct., daily 10–6; Nov.–Feb., daily 10–5; last admission 1 hr before closing* Ⓤ *High St. Kensington.*

need a break?

A separate building from the rest of Kensington Palace, the **Orangery** (⊠ The Broad Walk, Kensington Gardens, Kensington W8 ☎ 020/7376–0239) was built for Queen Anne in 1704–05. The setting, beneath the white-and-gold arches, is perfect for tea. Light lunches, coffee, and kids' menus are offered daily from 10 to 6.

66 **Kensington Palace Gardens.** Immediately behind Kensington Palace is Kensington Palace Gardens (called Palace Green at the south end), a wide, leafy avenue of mid-19th-century mansions that used to be one of London's most elegant addresses. Today, it's largely Embassy Row, including those of Russia and Israel. Ⓤ *High St. Kensington.*

Leighton House. The exotic richness of late-19th-century aesthetic tastes is captured in this fascinating home, once the abode of Lord Frederic Leighton (1830–96)—painter, sculptor, and president of the Royal Academy. Persian tiles and pieced woodwork lavishly line the Arab Hall. The neighborhood was one of the principal artists' colonies of Victorian London. If you are interested in 19th-century domestic architecture, wander through the surrounding streets. ⊠ *12 Holland Park Rd., Kensington W14* ☎ *020/7602–3316* ⊕ *www.rbkc.gov.uk* ✉ *£3* ⊙ *Wed.–Mon. 11–5:30* Ⓤ *High St. Kensington.*

Linley Sambourne House. Stuffed with Victorian and Edwardian antiques, fabrics, and paintings, this 1870s house was the home of Edward Linley Sambourne, who for more than 30 years was the political cartoon-ist for the satirical magazine *Punch*. It was the scene for society parties when Anne Messel lived here in the 1940s. There's a royal connection, too: her son, Antony Armstrong-Jones, married the late Princess Margaret, and their son has preserved the connection by taking the name Viscount Linley. ⊠ *18 Stafford Terr., Kensington W8* ☎ *020/7602–3316* ⊕ *www.rbkc.gov.uk* ⊗ *Guided tours by costumed actors weekends at 10, 11:15, 1, 2:15, and 3:30; call to arrange other days* Ⓤ *High St. Kensington.*

Ⓒ ❼❶ **London Zoo.** Opened in 1828 and now housing animals from all over the world, this zoo has long been a local favorite. A modernization program progresses gradually. Many traditional cages remain, but elephants have been moved to the countryside branch, Whipsnade. One modern highlight is the Web of Life, a conservation and education center. Thrills include a desert swarming with locusts, meerkats perching on termite mounds, and an otter exhibit with underwater viewing. The Reptile House is a draw for Harry Potter fans—it's where Harry, in the book and film versions of *Harry Potter and the Sorcerer's Stone*, discovers that he can converse with snakes and make magic happen. ⊠ *Regent's Park NW1* ☎ *020/7722–3333* ⊕ *www.zsl.org* 💷 *£13* ⊗ *Mar.–Oct., daily 10–5:30; Nov.–Feb., daily 10–4; last admission 1 hr before closing* Ⓤ *Camden Town, then Bus 274.*

Ⓒ ❼❶ **Madame Tussaud's.** This is nothing more, nothing less, than the world's premier exhibition of lifelike waxwork models of celebrities. Madame T. learned her craft while making death masks of French Revolution victims and in 1835 set up her first show of the famous ones near this spot. You can see everyone from Shakespeare to Benny Hill here, but top billing still goes to the murderers in the Chamber of Horrors, who stare glassy-eyed at you—one from the electric chair. Next door is the London Planetarium, which offers a special combo ticket with Tussaud's. Beat the crowds by booking online or calling in advance for timed entry tickets. ⊠ *Marylebone Rd., Regent's Park NW1* ☎ *020/7935–6861, 0870/ 400–3000 advance tickets* ⊕ *www.madame-tussauds.com* 💷 *From £14.99, combined ticket with planetarium £16.99 (prices vary by day and season); call or check Web site* ⊗ *Sept.–June, weekdays 10–5:30, weekends 9:30–5:30; July and Aug., daily 9:30–5:30. Planetarium show every 30 mins; call for 1st show time* Ⓤ *Baker St.*

★ Ⓒ ❻❶ **Natural History Museum.** When you want to heed the call of the wild, explore this fun place—enter to find Dinosaurs on the left and the Ecology Gallery on the right. Both exhibits (the former with life-size moving dinosaurs, the latter complete with moonlit "rain forest") are essential viewing in a large museum that has overhauled itself creatively. Don't miss the ambitious Earth Galleries or the Creepy Crawlies Gallery, which includes a nightmarish, super-enlarged scorpion. In the basement, hands-on activities can be experienced in Investigate, which allows you to do just that, with actual objects, from old bones to bugs. The Darwin Centre showcases all the museum's creatures great and small in their pickling jars and vats, from a tiny frog to the giant Komodo dragon lizard. Daily Explore tours leave from the museum's main information desk. ✉ *Cromwell Rd., South Kensington SW7* ☎ *020/ 7942–5000* ⊕ *www.nhm.ac.uk* ✉ *Free* ☉ *Mon.–Sat. 10–5:50, Sun. 11–5:50* Ⓤ *South Kensington.*

Notting Hill. Currently the best place to wear sunglasses, smoke Gauloises, and contemplate the latest issue of *Wallpaper,* "the Hill" is much beloved of London's celebrities and fashion set. Centered on the Portobello Road antiques market, this district is bordered to the west by Lansdowne Crescent—lined by the Hill's poshest 19th-century terraced row houses—and to the east by Chepstow Road, with Notting Hill Gate and Westbourne Grove Road marking south and north boundaries. In between, Rastafarians rub elbows with so-called "trustafarians" (wealthy urban hippies living off trust funds), and residents like fashion designer Rifat Ozbek, CNN's Christiane Amanpour, and historian Lady Antonia Fraser can be spotted at the chic shops on Westbourne Grove and in the lively bars and cafés on Kensington Park Road. There are no historic sites here, so explore just to savor the flavor. Ⓤ *Notting Hill Gate, Ladbroke Grove.*

☙ **Regent's Park.** Laid out in 1812 by John Nash for the Prince Regent (hence the name), who was crowned George IV in 1820, the park was designed to re-create the atmosphere of a grand country residence close to the center of town. A walk around the Outer Circle, taking in the white stucco terraces of grand houses facing the park, including the famous **Cumberland Terrace,** shows that it succeeds magnificently. The Inner Circle has many garden themes, the most impressive being **Queen Mary's Gardens,** a scented riot of roses in summer. From June to August, the **Regent's Park Open-Air Theatre** (☎0870/060–1811 ⊕www.openairtheatre. org) mounts Shakespeare productions. ☎ *020/7486–7905* ⊕ *www. royalparks.gov.uk* Ⓤ *Baker St. or Regent's Park.*

❻❸ **Royal Albert Hall.** This famous theater was made possible by the Victorian public, who donated funds for the domed, circular, 8,000-seat auditorium. The Albert Hall is best known for its annual July through September Henry Wood Promenade Concerts (the "Proms"), with bargain-price standing (or promenading, or sitting-on-the-floor) tickets sold on the night of the classical concerts. ✉ *Kensington Gore, Kensington SW7* ☎ *020/7589–4185* ⊕ *www.royalalberthall.com* ✉ *Admission varies according to event* Ⓤ *South Kensington.*

☙❻❷ **Science Museum.** Up-to-date, hands-on exhibits make this museum enormously popular with children and adults. Highlights include the Launch Pad gallery, the Computing Then and Now show, *Puffing Billy* (the oldest steam locomotive in the world), and the actual *Apollo 10* capsule. A must-do attraction is the spectacular **Wellcome Wing,** devoted to contemporary science, medicine, and technology, which also has a 450-seat IMAX cinema. Special exhibitions can be great, too. ✉ *Exhibition Rd., South Kensington SW7* ☎ *020/7942–4000* ⊕ *www.sciencemuseum. org.uk* ✉ *Free; charge for special exhibitions and IMAX* ☉ *Daily 10–6* Ⓤ *South Kensington.*

★ ☙❻❶ **Victoria & Albert Museum.** Recognizable by the copy of Victoria's Imperial Crown it wears on the lantern above the central cupola, this huge museum showcases the decorative arts of all disciplines, all periods, all nationalities, and all tastes. Prince Albert was responsible for the genesis of this permanent version of the 1851 Great Exhibition, and Victoria laid its foundation stone in her final public London appearance in 1899. The collections of the V&A, as it's always called, are *so* all-encompassing that confusion is a hazard; you should select a few galleries to focus on. One minute you're gazing on the Jacobean oak, 12-foot-square four-poster Great Bed of Ware (one of the V&A's most prized possessions, given that Shakespeare immortalized it in *Twelfth Night*), and the next, you're in the 20th-century end of the equally celebrated Dress Collection, coveting a Jean Muir frock. The British Galleries provide a social context for British art and design from 1500 to 1900 (from Henry VIII through Victoria), with displays such as George Gilbert Scott's model of the Albert Memorial and the first English fork ever made (1632). Throughout the galleries are interactive corners for all ages, where you can discover, design, and build things. Free one-hour tours whirl you by some of the museum's prized treasures. Head for the brick-walled restaurant for daily brunch and lunch, candlelit dinners on Wednesday, or traditional roasts on Sunday. ⊠ *Cromwell Rd., South Kensington* ☎ *020/7942–2000* ⊕ *www.vam.ac.uk* ✉ *Free* ☉ *Thurs.–Tues. 10–5:45, Wed. 10–10* Ⓤ *South Kensington.*

★ ⑥⑨ **Wallace Collection.** Assembled by four generations of marquesses of Hertford, the Wallace Collection is important, exciting, undervisited— and free. Hertford House itself, a fine late-18th-century mansion, is part of the show. The eccentric fourth marquess really built the collection, snapping up paintings by François Boucher, Jean-Honoré Fragonard, Antoine Watteau, and Nicolas Lancret for a song after the French Revolution rendered this art dangerously unfashionable. A highlight among the Gainsborough and Romney portraits is Fragonard's *The Swing*, which conjures up the 18th-century's let-them-eat-cake frivolity. Don't forget to smile back at Frans Hals's *Laughing Cavalier* in the Big Gallery. ⊠ *Hertford House, Manchester Sq., Marylebone W1* ☎ *020/7935–0687* ⊕ *www.wallacecollection.org* ✉ *Free* ☉ *Mon.–Sat. 10–5, Sun. 2–5* Ⓤ *Bond, Baker St.*

Wellington Arch. Opposite the duke of Wellington's mansion, Apsley House, this majestic stone arch dominates the busy traffic intersection that is Hyde Park Corner. Designed by John Nash in 1825, it was created as a grand entrance to the extensive grounds leading to Buckingham Palace. Atop the arch, the Angel of Peace descends on the chariot of war. The arch has a viewing platform with panoramas over the park. ⊠ *Hyde Park Corner, Mayfair SW1* ☎ *020/7930–2726* ⊕ *www.english-heritage. org.uk* ✉ *£3* ☉ *Apr.–Oct., Wed.–Sun. 10–5:30; Nov.–Apr., Wed.–Sun. 10–4* Ⓤ *Hyde Park Corner.*

Up & Down the Thames

Downstream—meaning seaward, or east—from central London, Greenwich has enough riches, especially if the maritime theme (strong in an island nation, and the focus of the year-long SeaBritain 2005 festivities) is your thing, that you should allow a very full day to see them. Upstream, the royal palaces and grand houses that dot the area were built not as town houses but as country residences with easy access to London by river; Hampton Court Palace is the best and biggest of all.

Greenwich
8 mi east of central London.

Greenwich makes an ideal day out from central London, thanks to its historic and maritime attractions. Sir Christopher Wren's Royal Naval College and Inigo Jones's Queen's House reach architectural heights; the Old Royal Observatory measures time for the entire planet; and the Greenwich Meridian divides the world in two. You can stand astride it with one foot in either hemisphere. The National Maritime Museum and the clipper ship *Cutty Sark* will appeal to seafaring types, and landlubbers can stroll the parkland that surround the buildings, the pretty 19th-century houses, and the weekend crafts and antiques markets.

Once, Greenwich was considered remote by Londoners, with only the river as a direct route. With direct transportation links in the form of the Docklands Light Railway (DLR) and the tube's Jubilee Line, getting here is easy and inexpensive. The quickest route to maritime Greenwich is the tube to Canary Wharf and the Docklands Light Rail to the Greenwich stop. However, river connections to Greenwich (you can take the tube and DLR one way and a ferry the other) make the journey memorable in itself. On the way, the boat glides past famous London sights and the ever-changing Docklands. **Ferries** (☎ 020/7987–1185 from Embankment and Tower piers, 020/7930–4097 from Westminster Pier, 020/8305–0300 from Barrier Gardens Pier) from central London to Greenwich take 30–55 minutes and leave from different piers.

☺ ***Cutty Sark.*** This romantic clipper was built in 1869, one of a multitude of similar wooden tall-masted clippers that during the 19th century plied the seven seas, trading in exotic commodities—tea, in this case. The *Cutty Sark,* the last to survive, was also the fastest, sailing the China–London route in 1871 in only 107 days. Now the photogenic vessel lies in dry dock, a museum of one kind of seafaring life—and not a comfortable kind for the 28-strong crew. The collection of figureheads is amusing, too. ⊠ *King William Walk, Greenwich SE10* ☎ *020/8858–3445* ⊕ *www. cuttysark.org.uk* 🎫 *£4.25* ☉ *Daily 10–5; last admission at 4:30* Ⓤ *DLR: Cutty Sark.*

★ ☺ **National Maritime Museum.** One of Greenwich's outstanding attractions contains everything to do with the British at sea, in the form of paintings, models, maps, globes, sextants, and uniforms (including the one Nelson died in at Trafalgar, complete with bloodstained bullet hole). Explorers such as Captain James Cook and Robert F. Scott are celebrated, along with the valuable research gleaned from their grueling voyages. Best of all, there are actual boats, including an ornately gilded royal barge. New exhibitions, such as the excellent, interactive All Hands gallery for kids, and an immense glazed roof that creates an indoor courtyard, have revitalized this museum. Don't miss the Nelson galleries. ⊠ *Romney Rd., Greenwich SE10* ☎ *020/8858–4422* ⊕ *www.nmm.ac.uk* 🎫 *Free* ☉ *Apr.–Sept., daily 10–6; Oct.–Mar., daily 10–5* Ⓤ *DLR: Greenwich.*

The old **Trafalgar Tavern** (⊠ Park Row, Greenwich SE10 ☎ 020/ 8858–2437), with views of the Thames, is a grand place to have a pint and some upscale pub grub. In warm weather, the terrace has outdoor seating overlooking the now-closed Millennium Dome.

Old Royal Observatory. Founded in 1675 by Charles II, this observatory (now a museum) was designed the same year by Christopher Wren for John Flamsteed, the first Astronomer Royal. The red ball you see on its roof has been there since 1833. It drops every day at 1 PM, and you can set your watch by it, as the sailors on the Thames always have. Everyone comes here to be photographed astride the **Prime Meridian,** a brass line laid on the cobblestones at zero degrees longitude, one side being the eastern, one the western, hemisphere. An exhibit on the solution to the problem of measuring longitude includes John Harrison's famous clocks, H1–H4. ⊠ *Greenwich Park, Greenwich SE10* ☎ *020/8312–6565* ⊕ *www.rog.nmm.ac.uk* ☜ *Free* ☉ *Apr.–Sept., daily 10–6; Oct.–Mar., daily 10–5; last admission 30 mins before closing* Ⓤ *DLR: Greenwich.*

Queen's House. The queen for whom Inigo Jones began designing the house in 1616 was James I's Anne of Denmark, but she died three years later, and it was Charles I's French wife, Henrietta Maria, who inherited the building when it was completed in 1635. Britain's first classical building to use the lessons of Italian Renaissance architecture, it is of enormous importance in the history of English architecture. Paintings of the Muses, the Virtues, and the Liberal Arts decorate the Great Hall, a perfect cube exactly 40 feet in all three directions. ⊠ *Romney Rd., Greenwich SE10* ☎ *020/8293–9618* ⊕ *www.nmm.ac.uk* ☜ *Free* ☉ *Weekends 10–5, weekdays guided visits only, departing on the hr 11–4; phone for extended hrs Apr.–Sept.* Ⓤ *DLR: Greenwich.*

Ranger's House. This handsome, early-18th-century villa, which was the Greenwich Park Ranger's official residence during the 19th century, is hung with Stuart and Jacobean portraits. The most interesting diversion, however, is the Wernher Collection, more than 650 works of medieval and Renaissance art (and splendid jewelry) with a north European flavor, amassed by millionaire Julius Wernher at the turn of the 20th century. The house stands just outside the southwest side of Greenwich Park, one of London's oldest royal parks. ⊠ *Chesterfield Walk, Blackheath, Greenwich SE10* ☎ *020/8853–0035* ⊕ *www.english-heritage.org. uk* ☜ *£5* ☉ *Apr.–Sept., Wed.–Sun. 10–6; Oct., Wed.–Sun. 10–5; Nov.–Mar., Wed.–Sun. 10–4* Ⓤ *DLR: Greenwich; no direct bus access, only to Vanbrugh Hill (east) and Blackheath Hill (west).*

Royal Naval College. Designed by Christopher Wren in 1694 as a home for ancient mariners, these buildings became a school for young ones in 1873; today the University of Greenwich uses them for classes. Between the two main blocks you can see the Queen's House, set behind the central lawns; this is one of England's most famous architectural set pieces. Wren, with the help of his assistant, Nicholas Hawksmoor, was at pains to preserve the river vista from the house, and there are few more majestic views in London than the awe-inspiring symmetry he achieved. The **Painted Hall** and the **College Chapel** are the two outstanding interiors on view here. ✉ *King William Walk, Greenwich SE10* ☎ *0800/ 389–3341 recorded information* ⊕ *www.greenwichfoundation.org.uk* 🎫 *Free, guided tours £5* ⊙ *Painted Hall and Chapel Mon.–Sat. 10–5, Sun. 12:30–5, last admission at 4:15; grounds 8–6* Ⓤ *DLR: Greenwich.*

Hampton Court Palace

★ ⊙ *20 mi southwest of central London.*

On a loop of the Thames lies Hampton Court, one of London's oldest royal palaces and more like a small town in size; you need a day to do it justice. It's actually two palaces in one—a Tudor residence and a late-17th-century baroque one—as well as a renowned garden. The magnificent Tudor brick house, with its cobbled courtyards and cavernous kitchens, was begun in 1514 by Cardinal Wolsey, the ambitious lord chancellor (roughly, prime minister) of England and archbishop of York. He wanted it to be the best palace in the land, and he succeeded so well that Henry VIII grew envious, whereupon Wolsey felt obliged to give Hampton Court to the king. Henry moved in during 1525, added a great hall and chapel, and proceeded to live much of his astonishing life here. Later, during the reign of William and Mary, Christopher Wren expanded the palace substantially, adding the graceful baroque south and east fronts that are highlights of the palace. Six themed routes, including Henry VIII's State Apartments and the King's (William III's) Apartments, help you plan your visit; special guides in period costume add to the fun. The site beside the slow-moving Thames is idyllic, with 60 acres of ornamental gardens, lakes, and ponds, including William III's Privy Garden on the palace's south side. Its parterres, sculpted turf, and clipped yews and hollies brilliantly set off Wren's addition. Other horticultural highlights are Henry VIII's Pond Garden and the enormous conical yews around the Fountain Garden. On the east side of the house, 544 lime trees were replanted in 2004 along the Long Water, a canal built during the time of Charles II. Perhaps best of all is the almost half-mile of paths in the celebrated maze, planted in 1714 and truly fiendish. Trains run here frequently from London Waterloo, with the trip taking about 30 minutes. The palace is a five-minute walk from the station. ✉ *A308, East Molesey* ☎ *0870/753–7777* ⊕ *www.hrp.org.uk* 🎫 *Palace, gardens, and maze £11.80, gardens £4, maze alone £3.50, park grounds free. Joint tickets available with Kensington Palace and the Tower of London* ⊙ *State apartments Apr.–Oct., Tues.–Sun. 9:30–6, Mon. 10:15–6; Nov.–Mar., daily 9:30–4:30; grounds daily 7–dusk* Ⓤ *National Rail, South West: Hampton Court Station from Waterloo. Tube: Richmond, then bus R68.*

Kew Gardens

Fodor's Choice *6 mi southwest of central London.*
★

Kew Gardens, or more formally the Royal Botanic Gardens at Kew, is the headquarters of the country's leading botanical institute as well as a spectacular public garden of 300 acres and more than 30,000 species of plants. The highlights of a visit to this UNESCO World Heritage Site are the two great 19th-century greenhouses filled with tropical plants, many of which have been there as long as their housing. The bold glass roofs of the ultramodern Princess of Wales Conservatory shelter no fewer than 10 climatic zones. Two 18th-century royal ladies, Queen Caroline and Princess Augusta, were responsible for the garden's founding. Kew Palace, on the grounds (not open to the public until 2006 because of renovation), was the home of George III for much of his life. ✉ *Kew Rd., Kew* ☎ *020/8332–5655* ⊕ *www.kew.org* 🎫 *£8.50* ☉ *Gardens Apr.–Oct., weekdays 9:30–6:30, weekends 9:30–7:30; Nov.–Mar., daily 9:30–4:30* Ⓤ *Kew Gardens.*

WHERE TO EAT

No longer would Somerset Maugham be justified in saying, "If you want to eat well in England, have breakfast three times a day." London is in the midst of a restaurant revolution, and its dining scene is one of the hottest around. The city has fallen head over heels in love with its restaurants—all 6,700 of them—from its vast, glamorous eateries to its tiny neighborhood joints, from pubs where young foodies find their feet to swank trendsetters where celebrity chefs launch their ego flights.

This restaurant renaissance is due to talented entrepreneurs and chefs: Sir Terence Conran, Marco Pierre White, Gordon Ramsay, Jamie Oliver, and Oliver Peyton lead the list. Read all about them, and many others, when you get here, which you can easily do by picking up any newspaper. To keep up with the onslaught, each has reviewers aplenty. Luckily, London also does a good job of catering to people more interested in satisfying their appetites without breaking the bank than in following the latest food fashions. The listings here strike a balance between these extremes and include hip-and-happening places, neighborhood spots, ethnic alternatives, and old favorites.

A caveat: many restaurants are closed on Sunday, especially for dinner; the same is true on public holidays. Over the Christmas period, the London restaurant community all but shuts down—only hotels will be prepared to feed you. When in doubt, call ahead.

Prices

London is not an inexpensive dining city, although set-price menus at lunchtime may bring even the finest establishments within reach. Fixed-price dinners are beginning to proliferate, too. Few places these days mind if you order a second appetizer instead of an entrée. Ethnic restaurants have always been a good bet here, especially the thousands of Indian restaurants. The law obliges all British restaurants to display their prices, including VAT (sales tax) outside, but watch for extras such as bread and vegetables charged separately, and service. Most restaurants add 10%–15% to the check, or else stamp SERVICE NOT INCLUDED along the bottom, in which case you should add the 10%–15% yourself. Beware of paying twice for service—restaurateurs have been known to add service, then leave the total on the credit-card slip blank, hoping for more.

WHAT IT COSTS In pounds				
££££££	**££££**	**£££**	**££**	**£**
AT DINNER over £22	£18–£22	£13–£17	£7–£12	under £7

Prices are for a main course at dinner.

Bloomsbury

FRENCH
£££–££££

✕ **Elena's L'Etoile.** London's most popular maitre d', Elena Salvoni presided for years over L'Escargot in Soho, where she made so many friends she opened her own restaurant, taking over an existing establishment. This century-old place is one of London's few remaining unreconstructed French bistros. The traditional dishes of lamb confit, salmon cakes, and crème brûlée are joined by newer treats, and most diners get a warm smile from Elena even if they're not her politician-journalist-actor regulars. ✉ *30 Charlotte St., Bloomsbury W1* ☎ *020/7636–7189* ▤ *AE, DC, MC, V* ☺ *Closed Sun. No lunch Sat.* Ⓤ *Goodge St.*

££–££££

✕ **Villandry.** Heaven for food lovers, this posh and tempting cave of wonders is crammed with fancy French pâtés, Continental cheeses, fruit tarts, biscuits, organic vegetables, and breads galore. There's a tearoom, bar, charcuterie counter, and fashionable dining room. Breakfast is served daily. ✉ *170 Great Portland St., Bloomsbury W1* ☎ *020/7631–3131* ▤ *AE, DC, MC, V* Ⓤ *Great Portland St.*

JAPANESE
£–££

✕ **Wagamama.** Londoners drain endless bowls of Japanese noodles in this big basement. It's high-tech, high-volume, and high-turnover, with a fast-moving line at the door. Choose ramen in or out of soup (topped with sliced meat) or "raw energy" vegetarian dishes and juices. This formula is so successful that the restaurant now has a clothing line. London has 16 branches; see www.wagamama.com. ✉ *4A Streatham St., Bloomsbury WC1* ☎ *020/7323–9223* ⬧ *Reservations not accepted* ▤ *AE, DC, MC, V* Ⓤ *Tottenham Court Rd.* ✉ *10A Lexington St., near Piccadilly Circus* ☎ *020/7292–0990* Ⓤ *Piccadilly Circus* ✉ *101A Wigmore St.* ☎ *020/7409–0111* Ⓤ *Bond St.*

SEAFOOD
★ **££–£££**

✕ **North Sea Fish Restaurant.** Come here and nowhere else for the national British dish of fish-and-chips—battered cod or deep-fried whitefish and thick fries with salt and vinegar. It's tricky to find: three blocks south of St. Pancras station, down Judd Street. They serve only freshly caught fish, which you can order grilled—though that defeats the purpose. You can take out or eat in. ✉ *7–8 Leigh St., Bloomsbury WC1* ☎ *020/7387–5892* ▤ *AE, DC, MC, V* ☺ *Closed Sun.* Ⓤ *Russell Sq.*

Chelsea

AMERICAN/
CASUAL
££–££££

✕ **PJ's Grill.** Enter PJ's and you've adopted the Polo Joe lifestyle—wooden floors and stained glass, a slowly revolving propeller from a 1911 Vickers Vimy flying boat, and polo memorabilia. The place is relaxed, friendly, and efficient, and the menu, which includes all-American staples from steaks to brownies, is likely to please all but vegetarians. PJ's stays open late, and the bartenders can mix anything. Weekend brunch is popular. ✉ *52 Fulham Rd., Chelsea SW3* ☎ *020/7581–0025* ▤ *AE, DC, MC, V* Ⓤ *South Kensington.*

FRENCH
★ **£££££**

✕ **Gordon Ramsay.** Ramsay whips up a storm with white beans, foie gras, scallops, and truffles. He's one of Britain's best chefs, and tables are booked months in advance. For £80, splurge on the seven-course option; for £65, wallow in a three-course dinner; or go for lunch (£35 for three courses)

Where to Eat in London

Admiralty **45**
Asia de Cuba **42**
Baltic **49**
Bertorelli's **37**
Bibendum **12**
Brasserie St. Quentin . . .**8**
Browns **24**

busabe eathai **31**
The Capital **6**
Cargo **53**
Clarke's **3**
Club Gascon **48**
The Cow **1**
E & O **2**

The Eagle **46**
Electric Brasserie **4**
Elena's L'Etoile **22**
The Enterprise **11**
fish! **55**
Food for Thought **36**
Gordon Ramsay **14**

Gordon Ramsay at
Claridge's **19**
The Ivy **39**
J Sheekey **41**
Joe Allen **40**
La Poule au Pot **15**
Le Caprice **29**
Le Gavroche **17**

Coram's Fields

OMSBURY

32

Bernard St.
Russell Square
Guilford St.

Torrington Pl.

Gower St.

Gr. Ormond St.

John St.

Gr. Ormond St.

British Museum

Theobalds Rd.

Southampton Row

Jockey's Fields

Gray's Inn Rd.

Leather Ln.

Hatton Gd.

Clerkenwell Rd.

Cowcross St.

Charterhouse St.

W. Smithfield

W. Long Ln.

47

Beech St.

Barbican Center

London Wall

Liverpool St. Station

Broad St. Station

53

Court Rd.

New Oxford St.

33

Great

High Holborn

Holborn

Kingsway

Red Lion St.

46

St. Andrew St.

Shoe Ln.

Holborn Viaduct

Newgate St.

48

THE CITY

Moorgate

Bank Of England

Bishopsgate

Soho Square

31 **34**

Charing Cross Rd.

Shaftesbury Ave.

36

Drury Ln.

Lincoln's Inn

Covent Garden

Carey St.

Fetter Ln.

Old Bailey ◆

St. Paul's

Ludgate Hill

Cheapside

Cornhill

Leadenhall St.

51

Fenchurch St.

35

39

37 **38**

Aldwych

Law Courts

Fleet St.

New Bridge St.

Queen Victoria St.

52

Cannon St. Station

Lower Thames St.

40

Bedford St.

Strand

Temple Pl.

45

Victoria Embankment

Blackfriars Br.

Blackfriars Station

Millennium Br.

Cannon St.

Southwark Br.

London Br.

Thames

Wardour St.

0

rcus

41 **42** **43**

44

Orange St.

National Gallery

Charing Cross Stn.

Northumberland Ave.

Hungerford Br.

Waterloo Rd.

49 **50**

Stamford St.

Bankside

Park St.

Summer St.

Southwark St.

Bridge Road

Southwark Br. Rd.

Blackfriars Rd.

55

London Br.

Tooley St.

54

London Bridge Station

Piccadilly

cus

Regent St.

The Mall

James's lace

Whitehall

South Bank Centre

The Cut

Union St.

St. Thomas St.

SOUTH BANK

Borough High St.

Tower Bridge Rd.

James's lace

Houses of Parliament

Westminster Br.

Waterloo Station

York Rd.

Westminster Br. Rd.

Borough Rd.

Newington Causeway

Harper Rd.

cage Walk

n

Westminster Abbey

Great Peter St.

Millbank

Lambeth Palace Rd.

St. George's Rd.

London Rd.

Elephant Rd.

New Kent Rd.

Old Kent Rd.

ØRIA

ncent quare

Horseferry Rd.

Marsham St.

Regency St.

Lambeth Br.

Lambeth Rd.

Kennington Rd.

Brook Dr.

Imperial War Museum

Walworth Rd.

xhall Br.

Tate Britain

Rd.

Albert Embankment

Kennington Ln.

Kennington Park Rd.

Nine Elms Ln.

Vauxhall Station

Kennington Oval

Kennington

| 0 | 550 yards |

| 0 | 500 meters |

Le Pont de la Tour	**54**	The Ritz	**28**
L'Escargot	**34**	Rules	**43**
Lindsay House	**35**	St. John	**47**
Locanda Locatelli	**16**	Savoy Grill	**44**
Momo	**26**	Simpson's Tavern	**51**
New Piccadilly	**30**	Sketch	**25**
Nobu	**20**	The Social	**23**
North Sea Fish Restaurant	**32**	Sweetings	**52**
Orso	**38**	Tom Aikens	**13**
OXO Tower Brasserie and Restaurant	**50**	Villandry	**21**
PJ's Grill	**10**	Wagamama	**33**
Providores	**18**	The Wolseley	**27**
Racine	**9**	Zafferano	**7**
		Zuma	**5**

for a gentler check. ⊠ 68–69 Royal Hospital Rd., Chelsea SW3 ☎ 020/ 7352–4441 ⌂ Reservations essential ▭ AE, DC, MC, V ۞ Closed weekends Ⓤ Sloane Sq.

★ **££–££££** ✕ **Racine.** There's an upscale buzz at this excellent addition to the Brompton Road dining scene. Henry Harris's smart French brasserie packs them in because he does the simple things well—and doesn't charge the earth. Classics like steak *au poivre* with béarnaise sauce or chilled cucumber and mint soup hit the spot. Desserts and wines by the glass are reasonably priced. ⊠ 239 Brompton Rd., Knightsbridge SW3 ☎ 020/ 7548–4477 ▭ AE, MC, V Ⓤ South Kensington.

The City

CONTEMPORARY ✕ **St. John.** You either love or hate Fergus Henderson's ultra-British cook-
£££–££££ ing at this converted smokehouse. His chutzpah is scary: one appetizer
Fodor'sChoice is sliced pig spleen. Entrées (venison liver and boiled egg, haddock and
★ fennel) may appear stark on the plate but always have style. Expect an all-French wine list with affordable bottles, plus malmseys and ports. Try the rice pudding with plums, or the English Eccles cakes and Lancashire cheese. ⊠ 26 St. John St., The City EC1 ☎ 020/7251–0848 ⌂ Reservations essential ▭ AE, DC, MC, V ۞ Closed Sun. No lunch Sat. Ⓤ Farringdon.

ENGLISH ✕ **Simpson's Tavern.** A bastion of English tradition, this back-alley
£–££ chophouse was founded in 1759 and only began admitting women in 1916. It's popular with stockbrokers, who come for the traditional fare: steak-and-kidney pie, liver and bacon, chops from the grill, Simpson's salmon cakes, or the house specialty, stewed cheese (melted Cheddar on toast with béchamel and Worcestershire sauce). The tavern fills up at lunch, so wander in early for a taste of the old City of London. ⊠ 38½ Cornhill, at Ball Ct., The City EC3 ☎ 020/7626–9985 ⌂ Reservations not accepted ▭ AE, DC, MC, V ۞ Closed weekends. No dinner Ⓤ Bank.

FRENCH ✕ **Club Gascon.** It's hard to find a sexier scene than this in all London.
★ Maybe it's the restrained, marble- and leather-walled interior, the per-
£££–£££££ fect service, the cut flowers, or the way the tapas-style, new French cuisine is served—on a slab of rock rather than on a plate. Foie gras runs through the menu from start to finish: feast on it steeped in 10-year-old Maury wine, and then have it for dessert with gingerbread and grapes. *Magnifique.* ⊠ 57 W. Smithfield, The City EC1 ☎ 020/ 7796–0600 ⌂ Reservations essential ▭ AE, MC, V ۞ Closed Sun. No lunch Sat. Ⓤ Barbican.

LATIN ✕ **Cargo.** This is possibly London's best venue for a combination of
£–££ music, drink, and food. Deep in the trendy east-side Hoxton district, it's a friendly restaurant—a fave with young urbanites—but also a top late-night bar with great live acts. The Latin street grub works well for groups—peri-peri chicken, quesadillas—but it's the delicious cocktails and crazy dancing that really make the scene. ⊠ Kingsland Viaduct, 83 Rivington St., Hoxton EC2 ☎ 020/7739–3440 ▭ AE, MC, V Ⓜ Old St.

ON THE MENU

The days are long gone when British cuisine was best known for shepherd's pie and fish-and-chips. Still, there's a real interest in British favorites, with standbys like bangers and mash getting modish treatments.

This thriving dining scene rests on ethnic cuisines. Thousands of Indian restaurants have long ensured that Londoners view access to a tasty tandoori as a birthright. Chinese restaurants in London's tiny Chinatown and beyond have been around

a long time, as have Greek tavernas, and there are even more Italian restaurants than Indian. Now add Thai, Malaysian, Spanish, and Japanese cuisines to those easily found in England's capital. After all this, traditional British food appears as one more exotic cuisine. If you're out for traditional fare but with a stylish twist (often less fancy prices, too), head for a gastro-pub.

MEDITERRANEAN
£–££
Fodor's Choice
★

✕ **The Eagle.** It's the gastro-pub of gastro-pubs, and it belongs in the "Restaurants" section by virtue of its amazingly good-value Portuguese-Spanish food. There are about nine dishes on the menu each day—a pasta, three vegetarian choices, and a risotto always among them. Quite a few places in London charge three times the price for similar food; the Eagle all but started the welcome trend toward pubs serving good meals. ⊠ *159 Farringdon Rd., The City EC1* ☎ *020/7837–1353* ⌔ *Reservations not accepted* ▭ *DC, MC, V* Ⓤ *Farringdon.*

SEAFOOD
££–££££

✕ **Sweetings.** Uniquely English, Sweetings (established 1830) is a time warp from the old City of London. There are many things Sweetings doesn't do: dinner, reservations, weekends, and coffee. It does, however, do seafood. It's not far from St. Paul's Cathedral, and City gents come for "luncheon." They drink tankards of Black Velvet (Guinness and champagne) and eat meals of potted shrimp, whitebait, Welsh rarebit, and roe on toast. The West Mersey oysters are good, and the desserts are English-schoolboy favorites like spotted dick (suet pudding with currants) and steamed syrup pudding. ⊠ *39 Queen Victoria St., The City EC4* ☎ *020/7248–3062* ⌔ *Reservations not accepted* ▭ *AE, MC, V* ☾ *Closed weekends. No dinner* Ⓤ *Mansion House.*

Covent Garden

AMERICAN
££–£££

✕ **Joe Allen.** Long hours (thespians flock here after the curtains fall) and a welcoming interior mean New York Joe's London branch still swings after more than two decades. The fun menu helps: roasted poblano peppers and black-bean soup are typical starters; entrées include barbecued ribs and London's only available corn muffins, or monkfish with sundried-tomato salsa. There are Yankee desserts, too, such as grilled banana bread with ice cream and hot caramel sauce. Weekend brunch here is a London institution. ⊠ *13 Exeter St., Covent Garden WC2* ☎ *020/7836–0651* ⌔ *Reservations essential* ▭ *AE, MC, V* Ⓤ *Covent Garden.*

CONTEMPORARY ✕ **The Ivy.** It's London's favorite restaurant, and thus hard to get into.
★ **££–£££££** In a wood-paneled, art deco room with blinding-white tablecloths and Howard Hodgkins paintings on the walls, the theater set dines on Caesar salad, kedgeree, salmon cakes, and baked Alaska. For star-trekking ("Don't look now, dear, but there's Ralph Fiennes") this is the prime spot in London. The weekend three-course lunch is a deal at £19.50. Try walking in off the street for a table on short notice—it's been known to work. ⊠ *1 West St., Covent Garden WC2* ☎ *020/7836–4751* ⌒ *Reservations essential* ⊟ *AE, DC, MC, V* Ⓤ *Covent Garden.*

CONTINENTAL ✕ **Savoy Grill.** Gordon Ramsay's protegé Marcus Wareing proves tri-
£££££ umphant at this bastion of establishment power dining. There's kind lighting, wood paneling, and silver-plated pillars in the classic art deco interior, and the assembled press barons, corporate executives, and politicians are exceedingly pleased with Wareing's menu. On it is pork belly, sweetbreads, an omelet Arnold Bennett (with smoked haddock and gruyère béchamel sauce), and beef Chateaubriand. Wines are excellent but pricey. ⊠ *The Strand, Covent Garden WC2* ☎ *020/7836–4343* ⌒ *Reservations essential* ⌂ *Jacket and tie* ⊟ *AE, DC, MC, V* Ⓤ *Covent Garden.*

ENGLISH ✕ **Rules.** Come, escape from the 21st century. This is probably the single
£££–££££ most beautiful dining salon in London. More than 200 years old (it opened in 1798), this gorgeous institution has welcomed everyone from Dickens to the current Prince of Wales. The menu includes fine historical dishes—try the steak-and-kidney pudding for a taste of the 18th century. The decoration is delicious: plush red banquettes and lacquered Regency yellow walls crammed with oil paintings and engravings. For a main dish, try something from the list of daily specials, which will, in season, include game from Rules's Teesdale estate. ⊠ *35 Maiden La., Covent Garden WC2* ☎ *020/7836–5314* ⊟ *AE, DC, MC, V* Ⓤ *Covent Garden.*

FRENCH ✕ **Admiralty.** It's a restaurant worthy of the courtyard setting of Somer-
£££££ set House, just off the Strand. London is rejecting fusion food, and Admiralty does fine French cuisine with simplicity and integrity. The snail ravioli in Chablis with artichokes is a classic starter, and the sea bass with saffron sauce tastes as good as it looks. Political heavy-hitters flock for the splendid cuisine, and (surely?) their hearts melt when they try the steaming hot chocolate *moelleux* (pudding). There's a lot on the menu for vegetarians. ⊠ *Somerset House, Strand, Covent Garden WC2* ☎ *020/7845–4646* ⊟ *AE, DC, MC, V* ⊘ *No dinner Sun.* Ⓤ *Charing Cross.*

ITALIAN ✕ **Bertorelli's.** Across from the stage door of the Royal Opera House,
££–£££ Bertorelli's is quietly chic. The food is tempting, and the menu is just innovative enough: typical dishes include veal Milanese and monkfish ragout with fennel, wonder beans, and Swiss chard. There's a café-bar below and a restaurant above. There are branches at 19–23 Charlotte Street and 11 Frith Street in Soho. ⊠ *44A Floral St., Covent Garden WC2* ☎ *020/7836–3969* ⊟ *AE, DC, MC, V* ⊘ *Closed Sun.* Ⓤ *Covent Garden.*

££–£££ ✕ **Orso.** It shares the same snappy staff and glitzy clientele as its sister restaurant, Joe Allen. The Tuscan menu changes daily but always includes excellent pizza and pasta dishes plus entrées based, perhaps, on grilled rabbit or roast sea bass. Food here is never boring, nor is the place itself.

Orsino, at 119 Portland Road, W11, is a stylish offshoot, serving much the same food. ✉ *27 Wellington St., Covent Garden WC2* ☎ *020/ 7240–5269* ⚫ *Reservations essential* ▤ *AE, MC, V* Ⓤ *Covent Garden.*

PAN-ASIAN
£££–£££££

✕ **Asia de Cuba.** A trendy restaurant in a trendy hotel, Asia de Cuba is the star attraction at Ian Schrager's St. Martins Lane. Philippe Starck–designed, it's bold and loud—check out the dangly light bulbs, Latin music, library books, portable TVs, and satin-clad pillars. The food is Pan-Asian fusion and you're encouraged to share. The palomino of lamb (beaten and pounded meat) is delicious, as is the beef satay with quinoa salad. It isn't cheap, but it's totally disco. ✉ *45 St. Martin's La., Covent Garden WC2* ☎ *020/7300–5588* ▤ *AE, DC, MC, V* Ⓤ *Leicester Sq.*

SEAFOOD
££–£££££

✕ **J Sheekey.** This is where the stars go as an alternative to the Ivy and Le Caprice. Sleek and discreet, in the heart of Theatreland, the popularity of this seafood haven is evidenced by the photos on the walls— Peter O'Toole, Charlie Chaplin, Noel Coward, and Peter Sellers. And sultry J Sheekey really charms: cracked tiles, lava-rock bar tops, American oak paneling. Sample the wonderful jellied eels, Dover sole, Cornish fish stew, and the famous Sheekey fish pie. The weekend fixed-price lunch is £18.50. ✉ *28–32 St. Martin's Ct., Covent Garden WC2* ☎ *020/ 7240–2565* ▤ *AE, DC, MC, V* Ⓤ *Leicester Sq.*

VEGETARIAN
£–££

✕ **Food for Thought.** Although this is a simple vegetarian restaurant with no liquor license, you almost always find a line of people down the stairs here. The menu—stir-fries, casseroles, salads, and desserts—changes daily, and each dish is freshly made. ✉ *31 Neal St., Covent Garden WC2* ☎ *020/7836–0239* ⚫ *Reservations not accepted* ▤ *No credit cards* ☉ *Closed Christmas wk* Ⓤ *Covent Garden.*

Kensington

CONTEMPORARY
£££££

✕ **Clarke's.** There's no choice on the evening menu at Sally Clarke's restaurant; her four-course, fixed-price dinners contain fresh ingredients, plainly but perfectly cooked, accompanied by home-baked breads. The flower-and-art-speckled room is similarly home-style—if home is one of the big, white, £2 million Kensington stucco town houses you see around here. ✉ *124 Kensington Church St., Notting Hill W8* ☎ *020/ 7221–9225* ⚫ *Reservations essential* ▤ *AE, DC, MC, V* ☉ *Closed Sun. and 2 wks in Aug. No lunch Sat.* Ⓤ *Notting Hill Gate.*

Knightsbridge

FRENCH
£££££

✕ **The Capital.** The clublike dining room here has a grown-up atmosphere and formal service. Chef Eric Chavot does classic, superb French cooking. Try the turbot with creamed baby leeks and mushroom ravioli. Desserts follow the same exciting route. Set-price menus at lunch (£28.50) make it somewhat more affordable. ✉ *22–24 Basil St., Knightsbridge SW3* ☎ *020/7589–5171* ⚫ *Reservations essential* ▤ *AE, DC, MC, V* Ⓤ *Knightsbridge.*

£££–£££££

✕ **Brasserie St. Quentin.** French expats and locals alike frequent this popular slice of Paris. Every inch of France is explored—queen scallops, escargots, pheasant and partridge, fillet of beef brioche, tart Tatin—in the bourgeois provincial comfort that so many London chains (Dômes, Cafés Rouges) try for but fail to achieve. ✉ *243 Brompton Rd., Knightsbridge SW3* ☎ *020/7589–8005* ▭ *AE, DC, MC, V* Ⓤ *South Kensington.*

★ **£££–££££** ✕ **La Poule au Pot.** The Chelsea set—and Americans—love this candlelit corner of France in Belgravia, complete with bare brick walls, rustic furniture, and potted red roses on the tables. Though not spectacular, the country cooking is decent. The *poule au pot* (stewed chicken) and *lapin à la moutarde* (rabbit with mustard) are strong and hearty, and there are fine classics, such as beef bourguignonne and French onion soup, to accompany the cheerful service. ✉ *231 Ebury St., Knightsbridge SW1* ☎ *020/7730–7763* ⌘ *Reservations essential* ▭ *AE, DC, MC, V* Ⓤ *Sloane Sq.*

ITALIAN ✕ **Zafferano.** Any number of Cartier-wearing Belgravians flock to Zaf-
££££–£££££ ferano, one of London's best exponents of *cucina nuova.* The fireworks are in the kitchen, and *what* fireworks: buckwheat pasta with leek and sage, lamb cutlets with hazelnut crust and white truffle polenta. The desserts are *delizioso,* especially the nougat parfait with chestnuts and the poached pears and mascarpone ice cream. ✉ *15 Lowndes St., Knightsbridge SW1* ☎ *020/7235–5800* ⌘ *Reservations essential* ▭ *AE, DC, MC, V* Ⓤ *Knightsbridge.*

JAPANESE ✕ **Zuma.** This is a wildly popular, Tokyo-style restaurant. Superbly lit
££–£££££ and designed, with polished granite and blond wood, it also includes a bar, robata grill, and sushi counter, which doesn't accept reservations. Try the fabulous spider rolls, lobster tempura, or wagyu (Japanese) beef. There's also a "sake expert" on hand to help with the 30 hot and cold sakes. ✉ *5 Raphael St., Knightsbridge SW7* ☎ *020/7584–1010* ⌘ *Reservations essential* ▭ *AE, DC, MC, V* Ⓜ *Knightsbridge.*

Marylebone

ECLECTIC ✕ **Providores.** New Zealander Peter Gordon scores a perfect 10 with his
★ **££–£££** Pacific Rim fusion food in trendy Marylebone. Have a sophisticated meal in the formal restaurant upstairs, or try out the more relaxed ground-floor Tapa Rooms—on the menu are sweet potato and miso, kangaroo filets, and roast *chioca* (a tuber similar to Jerusalem artichoke). ✉ *109 Marylebone High St., Marylebone W1* ☎ *020/7935–6175* ▭ *AE, MC, V* Ⓤ *Baker St.*

ENGLISH ✕ **The Social.** The friendliest of the new wave of hip DJ-bars springing
£ up around town, the Social offers great sounds with decent grub. The weekly DJ sessions are a knockout (you may hear anything from electronica to Latino dub salsa) and the food is English old-school comfort: bangers and mash, steak-and-Guinness pie, fish sandwiches, and beans on toast. ✉ *5 Little Portland St., Marylebone W1* ☎ *020/7636–4992* ▭ *AE, MC, V* Ⓤ *Oxford Circus.*

Mayfair

ENGLISH ✕ **Browns.** Crowd-pleasing, child-friendly English cooking is performed
££–£££ well at the former site of bespoke tailors Messrs. Cooling and Wells. The classic Browns steak-and-Guinness pie is on the menu, but king

prawns, roasted peppers, salads, burgers, and pastas predominate. ⊠ 47 *Maddox St., Mayfair W1* ☎ *020/7491–4565* ⊟ *AE, DC, MC, V* Ⓤ *Oxford Circus.*

FRENCH ✕ **Gordon Ramsay at Claridge's.** Ramsay is one of Britain's best; sit at
££££££ the chef's table inside the kitchens, and marvel at the art and intensity.
FodorśChoice Try the eight-hour roast shoulder of lamb, sea trout, or brill in red wine.
★ It's open for breakfast, bargain three-course lunches (£30), and stunning dinners for £55 and £70. Book *months* ahead, but arrive early and have a drink at Claridge's art deco bar, the sassiest cocktail lounge in town. ⊠ *Claridge's Hotel, Brook St., Mayfair W1* ☎ *020/7499–0099* ⚐ *Reservations essential* 🏚 *Jacket and tie* ⊟ *AE, MC, V* Ⓤ *Bond St.*

★ ££££££ ✕ **Le Gavroche.** Michel Roux inherited the family cooking gene and runs one of London's finest restaurants. He's a master of classic French cooking—formal, flowery, decorated. The fixed-price lunch is relatively affordable at £42 (for canapés, three courses, plus mineral water, a half-bottle of wine, coffee, and petits fours). In fact it's by far the most economical way to eat here if you don't have an expense account, which most patrons do. Book at least a week in advance. ⊠*43 Upper Brook St., Mayfair W1* ☎*020/ 7408–0881* ⚐ *Reservations essential* ⊟ *AE, DC, MC, V* ☉ *Closed Sun. and 10 days at Christmas. No lunch Sat.* Ⓤ *Marble Arch.*

ITALIAN ✕ **Locanda Locatelli.** The phones are busy at London's top Italian restau-
££–££££££ rant. Everything chef Giorgio Locatelli touches turns to gold—hence the
FodorśChoice waiting list at this elegant David Collins–designed restaurant at the
★ Churchill Inter-Continental, replete with convex mirrors, etched glass, swivel chairs, and banquettes. The food's incredibly accomplished—superb risottos, handmade pastas, beautiful desserts. Be bold: try the deep-fried calves' head or the sweetbread with artichoke and marsala sauce, and choose from the all-Italian wine list. ⊠ *8 Seymour St., Mayfair W1* ☎ *020/7935–9088* ⚐ *Reservations essential* ⊟ *AE, MC, V* ☉ *Closed Sun.* Ⓤ *Marble Arch.*

JAPANESE ✕ **Nobu.** Nobuyuki Matsuhisa wows with his new-style sashimi with a
££–££££££ Peruvian touch—he sells 300 pounds of Alaskan black cod a day. Nobu is in the Metropolitan, a hip hotel, with staff, attitude, clientele, and prices to match. Ubon (that's Nobu backwards), a sister restaurant, operates in Canary Wharf. ⊠ *Metropolitan Hotel, 19 Old Park La., Mayfair W1* ☎ *020/7447–4747* ⚐ *Reservations essential* ⊟ *AE, DC, MC, V* ☉ *No lunch weekends* Ⓤ *Hyde Park.*

Notting Hill

CONTEMPORARY ✕ **The Cow.** Not *another* Conran. A chic gastro-pub (belonging to Tom,
★ £££–££££ son of Sir Terence), the Cow has a faux-Dublin back-room bar that serves oysters, salmon cakes, and baked brill. Upstairs the chef whips up Anglo-French specialties—cod and mash is one temptation. Notting Hill-billies love the house special: a half-dozen Irish rock oysters with a pint of Guinness. ⊠ *89 Westbourne Park Rd., Notting Hill W2* ☎ *020/ 7221–0021* ⚐ *Reservations essential* ⊟ *MC, V* Ⓤ *Westbourne Park.*

★ ££–£££ ✕ **Electric Brasserie.** There's nowhere better for people-watching than the Electric on market day at Portobello. Go for the bustle of the interior,

CloseUp
WHERE TO REFUEL AROUND TOWN

WHEN YOU'RE ON THE GO or don't have time for a leisurely meal (or you just want to save some money), you might want to try a local chain restaurant or sandwich bar where you can stop for a quick bite or get some take-away, as the British call takeout fare. Although many of London's chains serve standardized, soulless fare, the ones listed below are fairly priced and committed to quality, using decent, fresh ingredients. Wagamama, a good noodle-shop chain mentioned in the Where to Eat section, has many branches.

Carluccio's Caffe: Affable TV chef Antonio Carluccio's chain of seven all-day traditional Italian cafés/bars/food shops are freshly sourced and make brilliant stops on a shopping spree.

Ed's Easy Diner: OD on made-to-order hamburgers, onion rings, and thick milk shakes at this chain of shiny, '50s-theme American diners.

New Culture Revolution: There's a lot for vegetarians at these handy north Chinese noodle, soup, and dumpling refueling stops. Don't expect much legroom, mind you.

Pizza Express: Serving utterly predictable pizzas, Pizza Express seems to be everywhere (there are 95 in London). Soho's branch has a live jazz program.

Pret a Manger: London's takeout sandwich shop supremo. There are wraps, noodles, sushi, and tea cakes.

Strada: Stop here for great pizzas baked over a wood fire, plus simple pastas and risottos. It's stylish, cheap, and packed.

YO! Sushi: The Soho one is the best of the seven branches. These futuristic, conveyor-belt sushi outlets have color-coded plates and robotic drink carts.

---

too—zinc fittings, mirrors, shared tables, and flattering lighting—and expect chunky sandwiches, steaks, salads, and seafood platters. Or just settle in at the bar with a long drink. ⊠ *191 Portobello Rd. Notting Hill W11* ☎ *020/7908–9696* ▤ *AE, DC, V* Ⓤ *Notting Hill.*

PAN-ASIAN ✕ **E&O.** If you like stars, you'll love E&O. It's one of London's most
★ **££–£££££** popular scene restaurants. E&O stands for Eastern and Oriental, and the intelligent mix of Chinese, Japanese, Vietnamese, and Thai cuisines also includes many options for vegetarians. Don't skip the Thai rare-beef salad with red *nam jhim* (bean sprouts) or the albacore sashimi. ⊠ *14 Blenheim Crescent, Notting Hill W11* ☎ *020/7229–5454* ⚘ *Reservations essential* ▤ *AE, DC, MC, V* Ⓤ *Ladbroke Grove.*

St. James's

AUSTRIAN ✕ **The Wolseley.** There's a grand mittel-Europe elegance at this instant
££–£££ classic run by Messrs. Corbin and King, two of London's top restaura-
Fodor'sChoice teurs. Right on Piccadilly and framed with black lacquerware, this Vi-
★ ennese-style café begins its long, sumptuous days with breakfast at 7 AM and stays open until midnight. On the menu, there's Nurnberger bratwurst, Wiener schnitzel, Hungarian goulash, and, for dessert, strudel

and *kaiserschmarren* (shredded pancake with stewed fruit). It's ideal for decadently rich pastries and afternoon tea. ⊠ *160 Piccadilly, St. James's W1* ☎ *020/7499–6996* ▤ *AE, DC, MC, V* Ⓤ *Green Park.*

CONTEMPORARY ✕ **Le Caprice.** Secreted behind the Ritz Hotel, Le Caprice commands the
★ **££–££££** deepest loyalty of any restaurant in London because it gets everything right: the glossy Eva Jiricna interior; the perfect service; the menu, halfway between Euro-peasant and fashion plate. This food—grilled rabbit with rosemary, San Daniele ham and figs—has no business being so good. Frequented by Joan Collins and David Bowie, Le Caprice has some of the best people-watching in town. ⊠ *Arlington House, Arlington St., St. James's SW1* ☎ *020/7629–2239* ⌁ *Reservations essential* ▤ *AE, DC, MC, V* Ⓤ *Green Park.*

CONTINENTAL ✕ **The Ritz.** This palace of marble, gilt, and trompe l'oeil would moisten
£££££ Marie Antoinette's eye. Add the view over Green Park and the Ritz's sunken garden, and it seems beside the point to eat. But the cuisine stands up to the visual onslaught, with super-rich morsels—foie gras, lobster, truffles, caviar—all served with a flourish. Englishness is wrested from Louis XVI by a daily roast from the trolley. A three-course lunch at £37 or four-course dinner at £55 make the check more bearable than the £65 you pay for the Friday and Saturday dinner-dance (a dying tradition). ⊠ *150 Piccadilly, St. James's W1* ☎ *020/7493–8181* ⌁ *Reservations essential* 🎩 *Jacket and tie* ▤ *AE, DC, MC, V* Ⓤ *Green Park.*

FRENCH ✕ **Sketch.** Dinner for two for £450? Surely some mistake! It's make or
★ **££££** break for London's most notorious event–dining experience, with French chef Pierre Gagnaire at the helm. Owner Mourad Mazouz's madcap £12 million emporium comprises the astronomical Lecture Room restaurant, disco-dining in the much cheaper Gallery, a tearoom, art space, a bookshop, and two scene bars, East and West. The Lecture Room's loony prices—main courses £40–£70—cause the outcry. Judge for yourself; it's a once-in-a-lifetime experience, and the food can be sublime. ⊠ *9 Conduit St., St. James's W1* ☎ *0870/777–4488* ⌁ *Reservations essential* ▤ *AE, DC, MC, V* ◷ *Closed Sun. (Lecture Room also closed Mon.)* Ⓤ *Oxford Circus.*

NORTH AFRICAN ✕ **Momo.** It's a hot ticket so go if you can. Mourad Mazouz—Momo
★ **££–££££** to friends—storms beau London with his Casbah-like North African restaurant off Regent Street. The seats are low and close together, and there's a resident DJ and often live North African music. Downstairs is the members-only Kemia Bar, and next door is Mô—a popular Moroccan tearoom, open to all. The menu doesn't match the excitement of the scene, but *merguez* (lamb sausages) are delicious. ⊠ *23–25 Heddon St., St. James's W1* ☎ *020/7434–4040* ⌁ *Reservations essential* ▤ *AE, DC, MC, V* Ⓤ *Piccadilly Circus.*

Soho

CAFÉS ✕ **New Piccadilly.** Nothing's changed at this eccentric family-run diner,
£ just behind Piccadilly Circus, since it opened in 1952 (not even the menu). The waiter wears whites and shouts out orders as they're received. Fifties fans love the decor—upturned lampshades, Formica tables, bench

seats, and cigarette cards on the wall—and the food's cheap and not bad, either. It ain't glam, but it's got nostalgic charm. ⊠ *8 Denman St., Soho W1* ☎ *020/7437–8530* ▤ *No credit cards* Ⓤ *Piccadilly Circus.*

CONTINENTAL
£££

✕ **L'Escargot.** It's hard not to feel glamorous at this Soho haunt that serves French food in a ground-floor, art deco salon (and also in a formal restaurant upstairs, the Picasso Room). The wine goes well with partridge and cèpes, wood-pigeon pithiviers (filled puff pastry) and chestnuts, simple grilled fish, or calves' liver. Owned by Marco Pierre White, L'Escargot is grown-up, relaxed, and reliable. ⊠ *48 Greek St., Soho W1* ☎ *020/ 7437–2679* ▤ *AE, DC, MC, V* ☺ *Closed Sun.* Ⓤ *Leicester Sq.*

IRISH
£££–££££

✕ **Lindsay House.** Richard Corrigan brings his Irish charm to Soho and fills up this 1740s Georgian town house with his large personality. He wraps rabbit and black pudding in Bayonne ham and excels with mash and Irish beef, and his white asparagus and langoustine dish can't be bettered. Petits fours with coffee will send you home oh-so-happy. ⊠ *21 Romilly St., Soho W1* ☎ *020/7439–0450* ▤ *AE, DC, MC, V* ☺ *Closed Sun.* Ⓤ *Leicester Sq.*

THAI
£–££
Fodor'sChoice
★

✕ **busabe eathai.** One of Londoners' favorite cheap spots in Soho, this superior Thai canteen is fitted with rattans, benches, hardwood tables, and paper lamp shades. It's no less seductive for its communal dining. The menu includes noodles, curries, stir-fries, rice, and sides. Try chicken with butternut squash, cuttlefish curry, or seafood vermicelli (prawns, squid, and scallops). The mantra here is *gan gin gan yuu*, which means "as you eat, so you are." It's no-smoking and there's a great second branch at 22 Store Street, W1. ⊠ *106–110 Wardour St., Soho W1* ☎ *020/7255–8686* ⚹ *Reservations not accepted* ▤ *AE, MC, V* Ⓤ *Leicester Sq.*

South Bank

CONTEMPORARY
££££–£££££

✕ **OXO Tower Brasserie and Restaurant.** London has a room with a view— and what a view it is. On the eighth floor of the OXO Tower on the South Bank, this elegant restaurant serves Euro-Asian food with the latest trendy ingredients (oxtail with purple broccoli, for instance). The ceiling slats turn from white to blue, but who notices, with St. Paul's Cathedral and the London skyline across the water? The Brasserie is cheaper than the restaurant, but both have great river views, especially in summer when tables are on the terrace. ⊠ *Barge House St., South Bank SE1* ☎ *020/7803–3888* ▤ *AE, DC, MC, V* Ⓤ *Waterloo.*

EASTERN
EUROPEAN
★ **££–£££**

✕ **Baltic.** To eat well in Southwark, perhaps before a play at the Young Vic or a visit to Tate Modern, come to this bustling vodka-party playground—a good spot for drinks at the bar or a decent East European meal in sexy surroundings. Under the same ownership as Wòdka in Kensington, Baltic serves fine blinis—with herring, smoked salmon, or caviar—and great *leniwe* (potato dumplings) and gravlax. The vodkas are fruity and eclectic: Siberian, bison grass, rowanberry, and rye and honey, to name a few. ⊠ *74 Blackfriars Rd., South Bank SE1* ☎ *020/ 7928–1111* ▤ *AE, MC, V* Ⓤ *Southwark.*

FRENCH ✕ **Le Pont de la Tour.** This is the perfect spot in summer—the outside ta-
★ **ff–fffff** bles by the Thames, just by Tower Bridge, are heavenly. Inside are a wine
merchant, bakery, deli, seafood bar, brasserie, and this diner-style restaurant, smart as the captain's table. Fish and seafood (lobster salad, Dover
sole) and meat and game (Denham-estate venison and Gressingham duck)
are prominent. Prune-and-Armagnac tart is a fine finish to a glamorous
meal. ⊠ *36D Shad Thames, Butler's Wharf, South Bank SE1* ☏ *020/*
7403–8403 ☝ *Reservations essential* ⊟ *AE, DC, MC, V* Ⓤ *Tower Hill.*

SEAFOOD ✕ **fish!** Sleek and modern, this diner sits in the shadow of Southwark
★ **ff–fff** Cathedral, near Borough Market. The fish here is fresh—and politically
correct: the langoustines are creel-caught, the cod farmed by sustainable methods, and the scallops landed by divers. There are 12 types of
fish on the menu, including swordfish, brill, skate, and turbot. ⊠ *Cathe-*
dral St., South Bank SE1 ☏ *020/7407–3803* ⊟ *AE, DC, MC, V* Ⓤ *Lon-*
don Bridge.

South Kensington

CONTEMPORARY ✕ **Bibendum.** This converted 1911 Michelin showroom, adorned with art
fff–fffff deco prints and stained glass, remains a London showpiece. Chef Matthew
Harris cooks with Euro-Brit flair. Try calves' brains, any risotto, tripe
(just as it ought to be cooked), or Pyrenean milk-fed lamb with garlic
and gravy. The £25 fixed-price lunch is money well spent. ⊠ *Michelin*
House, 81 Fulham Rd., South Kensington SW3 ☏ *020/7581–5817*
☝ *Reservations essential* ⊟ *AE, DC, MC, V* Ⓤ *South Kensington.*

ff–fff ✕ **The Enterprise.** A hot spot near Harrods and Brompton Cross, the
Enterprise is filled with decorative types who complement the striped
wallpaper, Edwardian side tables covered with baskets, vintage books
piled up in the windows, and white linen and fresh flowers. The menu
is fairly subtle—braised lamb shank with rosemary and celeriac puree—
and the heartiness of the room contributes to a fun experience. ⊠ *35*
Walton St., South Kensington SW3 ☏ *020/7584–3148* ⊟ *AE, MC, V*
Ⓤ *South Kensington.*

FRENCH ✕ **Tom Aikens.** Culinary newcomer Aikens trained under Joel Robuchon
fffff and excelled at the restaurant Pied à Terre. Now relaunched here, he loves
complicated constructions on the plate. You may be intrigued by his configurations of pig's head with pork belly, stuffed pig's trotter, and celery
root lasagna. There's a knowledgeable sommelier to help you navigate
the good wine list. ⊠ *43 Elystan St., Knightsbridge SW3* ☏ *020/7584–2003*
☝ *Reservations essential* ⊟ *AE, DC, MC, V* Ⓤ *South Kensington.*

Pubs

The city's pubs, or public houses, dispense beer, good cheer, and casual
grub in settings that range from ancient wood-beam rooms to ornate
Victorian interiors to utilitarian modern rooms. London's culinary fever
has not passed pubs by, however, and gastro-pub fever is still sweeping
the city. At many places, char-grills are being installed in the kitchen out
back, and up front the faded wallpapers are being replaced by abstract
paintings (the best of these luxe pubs are reviewed above). Some of the

following also showcase nouveau pub grub, but whether you have Moroccan chicken or the usually dismal ploughman's special, do order a pint. Note that American-style beer is called "lager" in Britain, whereas the real British brew is "bitter" (usually served warm). You can order up your choice in two sizes—pints or half pints. If this is your first taste of British beer, order a half. Some London pubs also sell "real ale," which is less gassy than bitters and, many would argue, has a better flavor. When doing a London pub crawl, remember that arcane licensing laws forbid the serving of alcohol after 11 PM (10:30 on Sunday; there are different rules for restaurants)—a circumstance you see in action at 10 minutes to 11, when the "last orders" bell triggers a stampede to the bar. However, a new law under review at the time of this writing may allow more places to serve alcohol later.

Black Friar. A step from Blackfriars tube stop, this spectacular pub has an Arts and Crafts interior that is entertainingly, satirically ecclesiastical, with inlaid mother-of-pearl, wood carvings, stained glass, and marble pillars all over the place. In spite of the finely lettered temperance tracts on view just below the reliefs of monks, fairies, and friars, there is a favorable group of beers on tap from independent brewers. ✉ *174 Queen Victoria St., The City EC4* ☎ *020/7236–5474* Ⓤ *Blackfriars.*

Dove Inn. Read the list of famous ex-regulars, from Charles II and Nell Gwyn to Ernest Hemingway, as you wait for a beer at this very popular, very comely 16th-century riverside pub by Hammersmith Bridge. If the Dove is too full, stroll upstream to the Old Ship or the Blue Anchor. ✉ *19 Upper Mall, Hammersmith W6* ☎ *020/8748–5405* Ⓤ *Hammersmith.*

George Inn. The inn overlooks a courtyard where Shakespeare's plays were once staged. The present building dates from the late 17th century and is central London's last galleried inn. Dickens was a regular, and the George is featured in *Little Dorrit*. Entertainments include Shakespeare performances, medieval jousts, and morris dancing. ✉ *77 Borough High St., South Bank SE1* ☎ *020/7407–2056* Ⓤ *London Bridge.*

Lamb & Flag. This 17th-century pub was once known as the Bucket of Blood because the upstairs room was used as a ring for bare-knuckle boxing. Now it's a trendy, friendly, and bloodless pub, serving food (lunchtime only) and real ale. It's on the edge of Covent Garden, off Garrick Street. ✉ *33 Rose St., Covent Garden WC2* ☎ *020/7497–9504* Ⓤ *Covent Garden.*

Mayflower. An atmospheric 17th-century riverside inn with exposed beams and a terrace, this is practically the very place from which the Pilgrims set sail for Plymouth Rock. The inn is licensed to sell American postage stamps. ✉ *117 Rotherhithe St., South Bank SE16* ☎ *020/7237–4088* Ⓤ *Rotherhithe.*

Museum Tavern. Across the street from the British Museum, this gloriously Victorian pub makes an ideal resting place after the rigors of the culture trail. With lots of fancy glass—etched mirrors and stained-glass panels—gilded pillars, and carvings, the heavily restored hostelry once helped Karl Marx unwind after a hard day in the Library. He could now spend his *Kapital* on any of six beers available on tap. ✉ *49 Great Russell St., Bloomsbury WC1* ☎ *020/7242–8987* Ⓤ *Tottenham Court Rd.*

Sherlock Holmes. This pub used to be known as the Northumberland Arms, and Arthur Conan Doyle popped in regularly. It figures in *The Hound of the Baskervilles,* and you can see the hound's head and plaster casts of its huge paws among other Holmes memorabilia. ✉ *10 Northumberland St., Euston WC2* ☎ *020/7930–2644* Ⓤ *Charing Cross.*

Ye Olde Cheshire Cheese. Yes, it's a tourist trap, but it's also the most historic of all London pubs (from 1667), and it deserves a visit for its sawdust-covered floors, low wood-beam ceilings, and the 14th-century crypt of Whitefriars' monastery under the cellar bar. This was the most regular of Dr. Johnson's and Dickens's *many* locals (neighborhood pubs). ✉ *145 Fleet St., The City EC4* ☎ *020/7353–6170* Ⓤ *Blackfriars.*

Afternoon Tea

In the grandest places, teatime is still a ritual, so be prepared for a dress code: Claridge's, the Ritz, and the Savoy all require jacket and tie.

Claridge's. This is the real McCoy, with liveried footmen proffering sandwiches, scones, and superior patisseries (£27, or £35) in the palatial yet genteel Foyer, to the sound of the resident "Hungarian orchestra" (actually a string quartet). ✉ *Brook St., Mayfair W1* ☎ *020/7629–8860* ▤ *AE, DC, MC, V* ⊘ *Tea daily 3–5:30* Ⓤ *Bond St.*

Fortnum & Mason. Upstairs at the Queen's grocers, three set teas are ceremoniously served: standard afternoon tea (sandwiches, scones, cakes, £18.50), old-fashioned high tea (the traditional nursery meal, adding something more robust, £20.50), and champagne tea (£26.50). ✉ *St. James's Restaurant, 4th floor, 181 Piccadilly, St. James's W1* ☎ *020/7734–8040* ▤ *AE, DC, MC, V* ⊘ *Tea Mon.–Sat. 3–5:45* Ⓤ *Green Park.*

Harrods. For sweet-toothed people, the fourth-floor Georgian Restaurant at this well-known department store has a high tea that will give you a sugar rush for a week. ✉ *Brompton Rd., Knightsbridge SW3* ☎ *020/7730–1234* ▤ *AE, DC, MC, V* ⊘ *Tea Mon.–Sat. 3:30–5:30* Ⓤ *Knightsbridge.*

The Ritz. The Ritz's huge, stagy, sometimes overly formal Palm Court has tiered cake stands, silver pots, a harpist, and Louis XVI chaises, plus a great deal of rococo glitz, all for £29. Reserve at least four weeks ahead, further for weekends. ✉ *150 Piccadilly, St. James's W1* ☎ *020/7493–8181* ▤ *AE, DC, MC, V* ⊘ *Tea daily 1:30–5:30* Ⓤ *Green Park.*

The Savoy. The glamorous Thames-side hotel does one of the most pleasant teas (£24 or £27). Its triple-tier cake stands are packed with goodies, and its tailcoated waiters are wonderfully polite. ✉ *The Strand, Covent Garden WC2* ☎ *020/7836–4343* ▤ *AE, DC, MC, V* ⊘ *Tea daily 2–6* Ⓤ *Charing Cross.*

WHERE TO STAY

Staying at one of London's grand-dame hotels is the next best thing to—some say better than—being a guest at the palace. Royally resplendent furnishings set the tone, and armies of extra-solicitous staff are stuck in the pampering mode. Even in more affordable choices, classic British style brings you a taste of home, with tea-makers and pastel wallpapers. Still not cozy enough? Borrow some door keys, and be a bed-and-breakfast guest. Happily, there is no dearth of options where friendliness out-distances luxe. The latest trends are new hotels with chic, contemporary furnishings, cookie-cutter but convenient budget chain offerings in the heart of town, and new hotels in areas far outside the West End, Kensington, and Knightsbridge.

Where you stay can affect your experience. The West End is equivalent to downtown, but there's a big difference between, say, posh Park Lane and bustling, touristy Leicester Square. Hotels in Mayfair and St. James's are central and yet distant in both mileage and sensibility from funky, youthful neighborhoods such as Notting Hill and from major tourist sights such as the Tower of London, St. Paul's Cathedral, and the Kensington museums. On the edges of the West End, Soho and Covent Garden are crammed with eateries and entertainment options. South Kensington, Kensington, Chelsea, and Knightsbridge are patrician and peaceful, which will give you a more homey feeling than anything in the West End; Belgravia is super elegant. From Bloomsbury it's a stroll to the shops and restaurants of Covent Garden, to Theatreland, and to the British Museum; Hampstead and Islington are close enough to explore easily, too. Bayswater is an affordable haven north of Hyde Park. The South Bank, with all its cultural attractions, is another option.

Reservations

Wherever you decide to stay, do reserve in advance. London is popular, and special events can fill hotels suddenly. If you arrive without a room, the **London Tourist Board Information Centres** at Heathrow, Victoria Station Forecourt, and Waterloo International Terminal can help. **London Line** (☎ 09068/663344 at 60p per minute) provides general advice 24 hours a day. The **VisitLondon Accommodation Booking Service** (☎ 020/7932–2020) is open weekdays 9–6, Saturday 10–2.

Prices

London is an expensive city, and in the £££££ category, you can often pay considerably more than £250 per room. In any event, you should confirm *exactly* what your room costs before checking in. British hotels are obliged by law to display a price chart at the reception desk; study it carefully. In January and February you can often find reduced rates, and large hotels with a business clientele have frequent weekend packages. The usual practice these days in all but the cheaper hotels is for quoted prices to cover room alone; breakfast, whether Continental or "full English," costs extra. VAT (Value Added Tax—sales tax) follows the same rule, with the most expensive hotels excluding a hefty 17.5%, whereas middle-of-the-range and budget places include it in the initial quote.

WHAT IT COSTS In pounds				
£££££	**££££**	**£££**	**££**	**£**
FOR 2 PEOPLE over £250	£180–£250	£120–£180	£70–£120	under £70

Prices are for two people in a standard double room in high season, including VAT, with no meals or, if indicated, CP (with Continental breakfast), BP (Breakfast Plan, with full breakfast), or MAP (Modified American Plan, with breakfast and dinner).

Bayswater & Notting Hill

★ **£££–££££** ▦ **Miller's Residence.** From the moment you are ushered up the winding staircase flanked by antiques and curios, you know you've entered a realm where history is paramount. Jacobean, Victorian, Georgian, and Tudor antiques create a rich lesson in bygone days. Run by Martin Miller of *Miller's Antique Price Guides* fame, this town house serves as his home, gallery, and B&B. Sip a complimentary evening cocktail in the long, candlelit drawing room with fireplace. The rooms are named for Romantic poets. ⊠ *111A Westbourne Grove, Notting Hill W2 4UW* ☎ *020/7243–1024* 🖷 *020/7243–1064* ⊕ *www.millersuk.com* ➥ *6 rooms, 2 suites* ♭ *Dining room, room service, fans, in-room data ports, some in-room faxes, lounge, dry cleaning, laundry service, concierge, Internet, meeting room; no a/c* ▤ *AE, DC, MC, V* ⦿ *CP* Ⓤ *Notting Hill Gate.*

£££–££££ ▦ **The Portobello.** This small, eccentric place—really two adjoining Victorian houses backed onto a large garden—has long been a favorite of high-style mavens in the music and design worlds. Some rooms have balconies and Victorian claw-foot bathtubs, and the round-bed suite has the *pièce de résistance* of the bath world: a Victorian "bathing machine," complete with knobs and shiny brass pipes. Access to a nearby health club with an indoor pool can be arranged. ⊠ *22 Stanley Gardens, Notting Hill W11 2NG* ☎ *020/7727–2777* 🖷 *020/7792–9641* ⊕ *www. portobello-hotel.co.uk* ➥ *24 rooms* ♭ *Restaurant, dining room, fans, in-room data ports, in-room safes, some in-room hot tubs, minibars, cable TV, in-room VCRs, bar, lounge, babysitting, dry cleaning, laundry service, concierge, Internet, business services, car rental, no-smoking rooms; no a/c in some rooms* ▤ *AE, MC, V* ⊗ *Closed 10 days at Christmas* ⦿ *CP* Ⓤ *Notting Hill Gate.*

££–£££ ▦ **Main House.** A brass lion door knocker marks the front door of the unassuming Main House. With just four rooms, it has a simple aim: to provide a good night's sleep in an interesting Victorian home. Furnished with animal hide rugs, antique furniture, Asian art, and huge beds, the rooms are uncluttered and delightfully spacious. The tiny urban terrace is a great place for stargazing or enjoying the complimentary morning paper and coffee or tea. A day rate at the local health club is available, too. ⊠ *6 Colvile Rd., Notting Hill W11 2BP* ☎ *020/7221–9691* ⊕ *www.themainhouse.com* ➥ *4 rooms* ♭ *Fans, in-room data ports, in-room VCRs, massage, bicycles, babysitting, dry cleaning, laundry service, Internet, meeting rooms, airport shuttle, parking (fee); no smoking* ▤ *MC, V* ⦿ *CP* Ⓤ *Notting Hill Gate.*

££ ▦ **The Pavilion.** This eccentric town house is the trendy address in London for fashionistas and musicians. Often used for fashion shoots, bedrooms are decorated along different themes, such as "Casablanca Nights," a Moroccan fantasy, or "Enter the Dragon," a quirky mix of East Asian styles. It's a relaxed, laid-back hotel, and the triples and family rooms are ideal for groups looking for space *and* style. ⊠ *34–36 Sussex Gardens, Bayswater W2 1UL* ☎ *020/7262–0905* 🖷 *020/7262–1324* ⊕ *www.eol.net.mt/pavilion* ➥ *30 rooms* ♭ *Room service, fans, in-room data ports, cable TV, some in-room DVD players, lounge, dry clean-*

Where to Stay in London

Aster House **9**

Astons Budget Studios **7**

The Berkeley **21**

Blakes **8**

City Inn Westminster **43**

Claridge's **24**

County Hall
Travel Inn Capital **42**

Covent Garden Hotel **37**

The Dorchester **23**

Dukes **26**

Four Seasons Hotel **14**

The Gallery **10**

The Generator **30**

Great Eastern **35**

Harlingford Hotel **32**

Hazlitt's **36**

Knightsbridge Green **19**

Knightsbridge Hotel **17**

L'Hotel **18**

The Leonard **16**

Lincoln House Hotel **15**

London Bridge Hotel **40**

Main House **1**

Malmaison **34**

Mandarin Oriental
Hyde Park **20**

The Metropolitan **22**

Milestone Hotel &
Apartments **6**

Miller's Residence **3**

myhotel bloomsbury **33**

myhotel chelsea **12**

One Aldwych **38**

The Pavilion **13**

The Pelham **11**

The Portobello **5**

Portobello Gold **2**

Premier Lodge South Bank . . .**41**

The Ritz **27**

St. Margaret's **31**

Sanderson **29**

The Savoy **39**

Tophams Belgravia **25**

22 Jermyn Street **28**

Vancouver Studios **4**

ing, laundry service, parking (fee), no-smoking rooms; no a/c ☐ *AE, D, MC, V* ❍I *CP* Ⓤ *Paddington, Edgware Rd.*

££ ▥ **Vancouver Studios.** This little hotel in a Victorian town house is perfect for those wanting a home away from home. Rooms come with kitchenettes, and you can even pre-order groceries to stock your mini-refrigerator on arrival. Each studio has daily maid service as well as room service. Some rooms have working fireplaces, and one opens onto the leafy, paved garden. ⊠ *30 Prince's Sq., Bayswater W2 4NJ* ☎ *020/7243–1270* 🖷 *020/7221–8678* ⊕ *www.vancouverstudios.co. uk* ☞ *45 studios* ⚘ *Room service, in-room data ports, kitchens, microwaves, refrigerators, dry cleaning, laundry facilities, lounge, parking (fee); no a/c* ☐ *AE, DC, MC, V* Ⓤ *Bayswater, Queensway.*

£–££ ▥ **Portobello Gold.** This no-frills B&B in the heart of the Portobello Road
Fodors**Choice** antiques area occupies the floor above the pub and restaurant of the same
★ name. TVs are mounted on the wall, and the beds—which take up almost the entire room in the doubles—convert into desks. Double rooms have their own showers and basins, but share toilets. The best of the bunch is the split-level apartment (£££) with roof terrace, small kitchen, and soothing aquarium. The restaurant serves modern British food with an emphasis on seafood and vegetarian dishes. ⊠ *95–97 Portobello Rd., Notting Hill W11 2QB* ☎ *020/7460–4910* ⊕ *www.portobellogold. com* ☞ *6 rooms, 1 apartment* ⚘ *Restaurant, room service, cable TV, bar, laundry service, Internet* ☐ *MC, V* ❍I *CP* Ⓤ *Notting Hill Gate.*

Bloomsbury, Covent Garden & Soho

£££££ ▥ **Covent Garden Hotel.** A former 1880s hospital in the midst of artsy,
Fodors**Choice** boisterous Covent Garden, this hotel is now the London home-away-
★ from-home for a mélange of off-duty celebrities, actors, and style mavens. The public salons keep even the most picky happy: with painted silks, style *anglais* ottomans, and 19th-century Romantic oils, they're perfect places to decompress over a glass of sherry from the honor bar. Stylish guest rooms showcase matching-but-mixed couture fabrics to stunning effect. ⊠ *10 Monmouth St., Covent Garden WC2H 9HB* ☎ *020/ 7806–1000, 800/553–6674 in U.S.* 🖷 *020/7806–1100* ⊕ *www.firmdale. com* ☞ *55 rooms, 3 suites* ⚘ *Restaurant, room service, in-room data ports, some in-room faxes, in-room safes, minibars, cable TV, in-room VCRs, gym, spa, cinema, library, babysitting, dry cleaning, laundry service, concierge, Internet, business services, meeting rooms, car rental* ☐ *AE, MC, V* Ⓤ *Covent Garden.*

£££££ ▥ **One Aldwych.** This hotel's understated blend of contemporary and
Fodors**Choice** classic is pure, modern luxury. Flawlessly designed inside an Edwardian
★ building, One Aldwych is coolly eclectic, with an artsy lobby, feather duvets, Italian linen sheets, and quirky touches (a TV in every bathroom, all-natural toiletries, a pool with underwater music). It's the ultimate in 21st-century style, down to the awesome health club. Suites have amenities such as a private gym, a kitchen, and a terrace. Breakfast is made with organic ingredients. ⊠ *1 Aldwych, Covent Garden WC2 4BZ* ☎ *020/7300–1000* 🖷 *020/7300–1001* ⊕ *www.onealdwych.co.uk* ☞ *93 rooms, 12 suites* ⚘ *2 restaurants, room service, in-room data ports, in-room safes, some kitchens, minibars, cable TV with movies, indoor pool,*

health club, spa, 3 bars, cinema, shop, dry cleaning, laundry service, concierge, Internet, business services, meeting rooms, parking (fee), no-smoking floors ▭ *AE, MC, V* Ⓤ *Charing Cross, Covent Garden.*

£££££ 🖻 **Sanderson.** Sister to St. Martins Lane hotel, the Sanderson urban spa sits in the revamped box that was the Sanderson fabrics headquarters. From the serene Japanese garden to the billowy cloth that separates the bathrooms from the bedrooms, this hotel is definitely walking to the beat of its own whimsical drum. The furniture is a mix of French Louis XV and industrial, and bedrooms have sleigh beds. Some might find Agua (the "holistic bath house"), the in-room massage and spa services, and the indoor–outdoor fitness classes just what the doctor ordered. Foodies can try the popular Spoon+ restaurant. ✉ *50 Berners St., Bloomsbury W1T 3NG* ☎ *020/7300–1400* 🖷 *020/7300–1401* ⊕ *www. ianschragerhotels.com* 📞 *150 rooms* ⚒ *Restaurant, room service, in-room data ports, some in-room faxes, in-room safes, minibars, cable TV, in-room VCRs, gym, sauna, spa, billiards, 2 bars, lobby lounge, shop, babysitting, dry cleaning, laundry service, concierge, Internet, business services, meeting room, parking (fee), no-smoking rooms* ▭ *AE, DC, MC, V* Ⓤ *Oxford Circus, Tottenham Court Rd.*

★ **£££££** 🖻 **The Savoy.** This grand hotel hosted Elizabeth Taylor's first honeymoon in one of its famous river-view rooms; and it poured one of Europe's first dry martinis in its equally famous American Bar, haunted by Hemingway, Fitzgerald, and Gershwin. Does it measure up to this high profile? Absolutely. The art deco rooms are especially fabulous, but all rooms are impeccably maintained, spacious, elegant, and comfortable. A room facing the Thames costs a fortune and requires an early booking, but it's worth it. Bathrooms have original fittings, with sunflower-size showerheads. Top-floor rooms are newer and less charming. ✉ *Strand, Covent Garden WC2R 0EU* ☎ *020/7836–4343* 🖷 *020/ 7240–6040* ⊕ *www.savoy-group.com* 📞 *263 rooms, 19 suites* ⚒ *3 restaurants, room service, in-room data ports, in-room fax, in-room safes, minibars, cable TV with movies, in-room VCRs, indoor pool, gym, hair salon, sauna, spa, steam room, 2 bars, lobby lounge, theater, shop, babysitting, dry cleaning, laundry service, concierge, Internet, business services, meeting rooms, parking (fee), no-smoking rooms* ▭ *AE, DC, MC, V* Ⓤ *Aldwych.*

★ **££££** 🖻 **Hazlitt's.** Three connected, early-18th-century houses, one of which was the last home of essayist William Hazlitt (1778–1830), make up this charming Soho hotel. It's a disarmingly friendly place, full of personality but devoid of elevators. Robust antiques are everywhere, floors slant and creak, and every room has a Victorian claw-foot tub in its bathroom. There are tiny sitting rooms, wooden staircases, and more restaurants within strolling distance than you could patronize in a year. This is *the* London address of visiting antiques dealers and theater and literary types. ✉ *6 Frith St., Soho W1V 5TZ* ☎ *020/7434–1771* 🖷 *020/ 7439–1524* ⊕ *www.hazlittshotel.com* 📞 *20 rooms, 3 suites* ⚒ *Room service, fans, in-room data ports, minibars, cable TV, in-room VCRs, dry cleaning, laundry service, concierge, Internet, meeting rooms, parking (fee), some pets allowed, no-smoking floors; no a/c in some rooms* ▭ *AE, DC, MC, V* Ⓤ *Tottenham Court Rd.*

★ **ffff** 🖼 **myhotel bloomsbury.** Before you arrive you are asked to fill out a preferences sheet so that your room is just as you like it. If anything should go wrong, just contact your personal assistant for help. Rooms are minimalist, with wooden floors and simple color schemes. Superior doubles are bigger and have separate sitting rooms. For the most space, book one of the two penthouse apartments in "myspace" on the top floor. From the "jinja" spa to the library stocked with CDs, books, and free beverages, myhotel's novel approach succeeds brilliantly. ⊠ *11–13 Bayley St., Bedford Sq., Bloomsbury WC1B 3HD* ☎ *020/7667–6000* 🖨 *020/7667–6001* ⊕ *www.myhotels.com* ⇆ *76 rooms* ♿ *Restaurant, room service, in-room data ports, in-room safes, cable TV with movies, gym, spa, bar, lounge, library, babysitting, concierge, Internet, business services, no-smoking floors* ▤ *AE, DC, MC, V* Ⓤ *Tottenham Court Rd.*

ff 🖼 **Harlingford Hotel.** The Harlingford is by far the sleekest and most contemporary of the Cartwright Gardens hotels. Bold color schemes and beautifully tiled bathrooms enliven this family-run establishment. The quad rooms are an excellent choice for traveling families. ⊠ *61–63 Cartwright Gardens, Bloomsbury WC1H 9EL* ☎ *020/7387–1551* 🖨 *020/7383–4616* ⊕ *www.harlingfordhotel.com* ⇆ *43 rooms* ♿ *In-room data ports, tennis court, lounge; no a/c* ▤ *AE, DC, MC, V* ⑩ *BP* Ⓤ *Russell Sq.*

ff 🖼 **St. Margaret's.** This popular hotel in a Georgian-era building near the British Museum has well-lit rooms with high ceilings. The friendly Italian family that runs the hotel is sure to welcome you by name if you stay long enough. Back rooms have garden views, and each room retains Georgian touches such as a fireplace and beautiful cornice moldings. ⊠ *26 Bedford Pl., Bloomsbury WC1B 5JL* ☎ *020/7636–4277* 🖨 *020/7323–3066* ⊕ *www.stmargaretshotel.co.uk* ⇆ *64 rooms, 12 with bath* ♿ *Dining room, fans, cable TV, lounge, babysitting, laundry service, no-smoking rooms; no a/c* ▤ *MC, V* ⑩ *BP* Ⓤ *Russell Sq.*

Fodor'sChoice
★

f 🖼 **The Generator.** Easily the grooviest youth hostel in town, this former police barracks has a friendly, funky, international clientele. The Internet café provides handy maps and leaflets. The Generator Bar has cheap drinks and a rowdy, young crowd, and the Fuel Stop cafeteria provides inexpensive meals. Rooms are designed on a prison-cell theme, complete with bunk beds and dim views. There are singles, twins, and dormitory rooms, each with a washbasin, locker, and free bed linen. ⊠ *MacNaghten House, Compton Pl. off 37 Tavistock Pl., Bloomsbury WC1H 9SE* ☎ *020/7388–7666* 🖨 *020/7388–7644* ⊕ *www.generatorhostels. com* ⇆ *215 beds* ♿ *Restaurant, fans, lobby lounge, pub, sports bar, recreation room, shop, concierge, Internet, meeting rooms, airport shuttle, travel services, parking (fee), no-smoking floors; no a/c, no room phones, no room TVs* ▤ *MC, V* ⑩ *CP* Ⓤ *Russell Sq.*

The City

fffff 🖼 **Great Eastern.** Another style coup for designer and food maven Sir Terence Conran, this hotel is a sturdy pillar of the modern establishment. Choose among the five restaurants (serving sushi, fish, brasserie fare, pub grub, and haute cuisine), visit the florist, or browse in the Ren bath-products shop. All rooms have a modern, sleek sense: some look out over Liverpool Street and Bishopsgate, while others look inward to the stained-glass dome of the Aurora restaurant or the Gallery. ✉ *Liverpool St. at Bishopsgate, The City E2M 7QN* ☎ *020/7618–5010* 🖷 *020/7618–5011* ⊕ *www.great-eastern-hotel.co.uk* 🛏 *246 rooms, 21 suites* ⚘ *5 restaurants, 12 dining rooms, room service, in-room data ports, some in-room faxes, in-room safes, minibars, cable TV with video games, in-room VCRs, gym, spa, 2 bars, pub, library, shop, babysitting, dry cleaning, laundry service, concierge, Internet, business services, meeting rooms, car rental, no-smoking rooms* ⊟ *AE, DC, MC, V* Ⓤ *Liverpool St.*

££££ ▦ **Malmaison.** Part of a small chain of trendy U.K. boutique hotels, this Clerkenwell address holds its own, with contemporary furnishings, clean lines, and black-and-white photographs of London scenes. Guest rooms have huge beds, CD systems with a library of music on demand, and up-to-the-minute style. The brasserie serves French cuisine and has a long wine list. ✉ *Charterhouse Sq., The City EC1M 6AH* ☎ *020/7012–3700* 🖷 *020/7012–3702* ⊕ *www.malmaison.com* 🛏 *95 rooms, 2 suites* ⚘ *Restaurant, room service, in-room data ports, in-room safes, minibars, cable TV, gym, bar, dry cleaning, laundry service, babysitting, concierge, meeting room, no-smoking rooms* ⊟ *AE, MC, V* ⏏⊘ *CP* Ⓤ *Barbican, Farringdon.*

Kensington & South Kensington

£££££ ▦ **Milestone Hotel & Apartments.** An intimate, luxurious experience awaits at this gorgeous pair of intricately decorated brick Victorian town houses overlooking Kensington Palace and Gardens. From offering you a drink upon arrival to preparing a post-theater midnight snack in your room, the staff is friendly and efficient. Each sumptuous room is full of antiques; many have canopied beds, and some have balconies. ✉ *1 Kensington Ct., Kensington W8 5DL* ☎ *020/7917–1000* 🖷 *020/7917–1010* ⊕ *www.milestonehotel.com* 🛏 *45 rooms, 12 suites, 6 apartments* ⚘ *2 restaurants, room service, in-room fax, in-room safes, some kitchens, minibars, cable TV with movies, in-room VCRs, gym, hot tub, sauna, bar, lounge, babysitting, dry cleaning, laundry service, concierge, Internet, business services, meeting rooms, some pets allowed (fee); no smoking* ⊟ *AE, DC, MC, V* Ⓤ *High St. Kensington.*

★ ▦ **Blakes.** Designed by owner Anouska Hempel, Blakes is another world.
££££–£££££ Each room is a fantasy—there are Chinese opium dens and bright white spaces with colonial furnishings—packed with precious Biedermeier, Murano glass, and modern pieces collected from all over. The foyer sets the tone with piles of cushions, Phileas Fogg valises and trunks, black walls, rattan, and bamboo. ✉ *33 Roland Gardens, South Kensington SW7 3PF* ☎ *020/7370–6701* 🖷 *020/7373–0442* ⊕ *www.blakeshotels. com* 🛏 *38 rooms, 11 suites* ⚘ *Restaurant, room service, in-room data ports, some in-room faxes, in-room safes, minibars, cable TV, in-room VCRs, gym, bar, babysitting, dry cleaning, laundry service, concierge, Internet, business services, meeting rooms, car rental, parking (fee); no a/c in some rooms* ⊟ *AE, DC, MC, V* Ⓤ *South Kensington.*

££££–£££££ ▦ **The Pelham.** Museum lovers flock to this sweet hotel across the street from the South Kensington tube station. The Natural History, Science, and Victoria & Albert (V&A) museums are all a short stroll away, as is King's Road. At the end of a day's sightseeing, settle down in front of the fireplace in one of the two snug drawing rooms with their honor bars. The stylish, contemporary country-house rooms have sash windows and marble bathrooms. Some top-floor rooms have sloping ceilings and casement windows. ⊠ *15 Cromwell Pl., South Kensington SW7 2LA* ☎ *020/7589–8288, 800/553–6674 in U.S.* 🖷 *020/7584–8444* ⊕ *www.firmdale.com* ↬ *47 rooms, 4 suites* ♻ *Restaurant, room service, in-room data ports, some in-room safes, minibars, cable TV with movies, in-room VCRs, bar, concierge, business services, meeting rooms, parking (fee)* ➡ *AE, MC, V* Ⓤ *South Kensington.*

£££   🖬 **Aster House.** Country-casual rooms fill this delightful guest house. The friendly owners go out of their way to make you feel at home and answer questions. The conservatory where breakfast is served is an airy, light place, and the small garden at the back has a charming pond. Note that this is a five-story building with no elevator. Rooms have tea- and coffeemakers. ⊠ *3 Sumner Pl., South Kensington SW7 3EE* ☎ *020/7581–5888* 🖷 *020/7584–4925* ⊕ *www.welcome2london.com/asterhouse* ↬ *14 rooms* ♻ *Dining room, in-room safes, cable TV, lounge, Internet; no smoking* ➡ *MC, V* ⏛ *BP* Ⓤ *South Kensington.*

£££   🖬 **The Gallery.** It's a small, Edwardian world apart from the bustling city. Across the street from its sister property, the Gainsborough, the Gallery has an Arts and Crafts–style living room with a piano, lush carpets, cozy fires, and sturdy furniture. You can check your e-mail on the computer in a sitting area with William Morris furnishings. The bedrooms are a good size for London, with solid, comfortable beds. The bathrooms have London's ubiquitous polished granite. Included in the price is a full English breakfast, which will make lunch a challenge. ⊠ *10 Queensberry Pl., South Kensington SW7 2E8* ☎ *020/7915–0000, 800/270–9206 in U.S.* 🖷 *020/7915–4400* ⊕ *www.eeh.co.uk* ↬ *34 rooms, 2 suites* ♻ *Room service, in-room data ports, some in-room faxes, in-room safes, some in-room hot tubs, some minibars, cable TV, bar, dry cleaning, laundry service, concierge, Internet, meeting rooms, airport shuttle; no a/c in some rooms* ➡ *AE, DC, MC, V* ⏛ *BP* Ⓤ *South Kensington.*

££–£££   🖬 **Astons Budget Studios.** Rooms tend toward Ikea chic at these three redbrick Victorian town houses on a residential street. The studios and apartments all have concealed kitchenettes, and the apartments (£££) have marble bathrooms and trouser presses. It's worth paying that little bit extra for the designer rooms here. ⊠ *31 Rosary Gardens, South Kensington SW7 4NH* ☎ *020/7590–6000, 800/525–2810 in U.S.* 🖷 *020/7590–6060* ⊕ *www.astons-apartments.com* ↬ *43 rooms, 12 suites* ♻ *Dining room, fans, in-room data ports, in-room safes, kitchenettes, microwaves, refrigerators, cable TV, concierge, Internet, business services, airport shuttle, car rental, parking (fee), some pets allowed, no-smoking floors; no a/c* ➡ *AE, MC, V* Ⓤ *Gloucester Rd.*

Knightsbridge, Chelsea & Belgravia

£££££   🖬 **The Berkeley.** This hotel successfully mixes the old and the new in a luxurious, modern building with a splendid penthouse swimming pool. The bedrooms either have swags of William Morris prints or are art deco. All have sitting areas, CD players, and big bathrooms with bidets. There are spectacular penthouse suites with their own conservatory terraces, and others with saunas or balconies. Dining venues include Marcus Wareing's high-class Pétrus restaurant and Gordon Ramsay's New York-style Boxwood Café. ⊠ *Wilton Pl., Belgravia SW1X 7RL* ☎ *020/7235–6000, 800/637–2869 in U.S.* 🖷 *020/7235–4330* ⊕ *www.the-berkeley.com* ⇦ *103 rooms, 55 suites* ⚭ *Restaurant, room service, in-room fax, in-room safes, some kitchens, minibars, cable TV, in-room VCRs, indoor-outdoor pool, gym, hair salon, sauna, spa, Turkish bath, bar, cinema, babysitting, dry cleaning, laundry service, concierge, Internet, business services, meeting rooms, airport shuttle, car rental, parking (fee), no-smoking floors* ⊟ *AE, DC, MC, V* Ⓤ *Knightsbridge.*

★ **£££££** 🏨 **Mandarin Oriental Hyde Park.** Stay here, and the three greats of Knightsbridge are on your doorstep—Hyde Park, Harrods, and Harvey Nichols. The Mandarin Oriental, built in 1880, is one of London's poshest places to stay. Bedrooms are traditional Victorian with hidden high-tech gadgets and luxurious touches—potted orchids, chocolates, and fruit. The service here is legendary and includes butlers on every floor. Some rooms facing the park have balconies. Shopping, spa, and theater packages are available. ⊠ *66 Knightsbridge, Knightsbridge SW1X 7LA* ☎ *020/7235–2000* 🖷 *020/7235–2001* ⊕ *www. mandarinoriental.com* ⇦ *177 rooms, 23 suites* ⚭ *2 restaurants, room service, in-room data ports, some in-room faxes, in-room safes, minibars, cable TV, in-room VCRs, gym, hot tub, sauna, spa, steam room, bar, babysitting, dry cleaning, laundry service, concierge, Internet, business services, meeting rooms, airport shuttle, car rental, parking (fee), no-smoking rooms* ⊟ *AE, DC, MC, V* Ⓤ *Knightsbridge.*

££££–£££££ 🏨 **Knightsbridge Hotel.** Just off glamorous Knightsbridge in quiet Beaufort Gardens, this chic hotel near Harrods and Harvey Nichols is well-placed for shoppers. The balconied suites and regular rooms benefit from CD players, writing desks, and large granite and oak bathrooms. The fully loaded honor bar in the drawing room is an excellent place to unwind amid African sculptures and modern art. Bedrooms offer understated, classic interiors. ⊠ *10 Beaufort Gardens, Knightsbridge SW3 1PT* ☎ *020/7584–6300, 800/553–6674 in U.S.* 🖷 *020/7584–6355* ⊕ *www. knightsbridgehotel.co.uk* ⇦ *42 rooms, 2 suites* ⚭ *Room service, in-room data ports, in-room safes, minibars, cable TV, some in-room VCRs, gym, bar, library, babysitting, dry cleaning, laundry service, concierge, Internet, meeting rooms, parking (fee)* ⊟ *AE, MC, V* Ⓤ *Knightsbridge.*

££££–£££££ 🏨 **myhotel chelsea.** This fashionable town house, part of the small myhotel chain, sends out a pre-arrival form asking guest preferences on smoking, music, and movies; likes and dislikes; and dietary requirements. Many other quirky services set this place apart—hot water bottles at bedtime, Botox specialists on call, and resident tarot card and palm readers in the bar during cocktail hour. Rooms are decorated in pinks, grays, and creams, and equipped with wide-screen TVs and other super-modern amenities. ⊠ *35 Ixworth Pl., Chelsea SW3 3QZ* ☎ *020/7225–7500* 🖷 *020/7225–7555* ⊕ *www.myhotels.com* ⇦ *45 rooms, 9 suites* ⚭ *Room service, fans, in-room safes, in-room data ports, minibars, cable TV, in-room DVD players, gym, massage, spa, bar, lounge, babysitting, laundry service, Internet, some pets allowed, no-smoking floors* ⊟ *AE, D, MC, V* Ⓤ *South Kensington.*

£££–££££ ⊡ **L'Hotel.** Rooms at this upscale B&B have an air of provincial France, with white bedcovers, pine furniture, and beige color schemes. It's like staying in a house—you're given your own front-door key, there's no elevator, and the staff leaves in the evening. Ask for a fireplace room: they're the biggest. Delicious breakfast croissants and baguettes are served in Le Metro cellar wine bar or brought to your room. You also have access to the restaurant and concierge services of the plush Capital Hotel, run by the same family, a few doors down the street. ⊠ *28 Basil St., Knightsbridge SW3 1AT* ☎ *020/7589–6286* 🖷 *020/7823–7826* ⊕ *www.lhotel.co.uk* ⥱ *11 rooms, 1 suite* ⌂ *Restaurant, fans, in-room data ports, minibars, cable TV, in-room VCRs, bar, babysitting, dry cleaning, laundry service, concierge, Internet, parking (fee); no a/c* ▤ *AE, V* ❂ *CP* Ⓤ *Knightsbridge.*

£££ ⊡ **Knightsbridge Green.** Near Harrods and Hyde Park, this modern hotel has affordable triples and quads with sofa beds that are good for families. Rooms have double-glaze windows that help muffle the sound of traffic on busy Knightsbridge. Breakfast can be delivered to your room, and there are two lounges where you can have complimentary tea or coffee. ⊠ *159 Knightsbridge, Knightsbridge SW1X 7PD* ☎ *020/7584–6274* 🖷 *020/7225–1635* ⊕ *www.thekghotel.co.uk* ⥱ *28 rooms, 12 suites* ⌂ *In-room data ports, in-room safes, cable TV, babysitting, dry cleaning, concierge, Internet; no smoking* ▤ *AE, DC, MC, V* Ⓜ *Knightsbridge.*

Mayfair, Marylebone & St. James's

★ £££££ ⊡ **Claridge's.** Stay here, and you're staying at a hotel legend (founded in 1812), with one of the world's classiest guest lists. The friendly, liveried staff is not in the least condescending, and the rooms are never less than luxurious. Enjoy a cup of tea in the lounge, or retreat to the stylish bar for cocktails—or, better, to Gordon Ramsay's inimitable restaurant. The bathrooms are spacious (with enormous showerheads), as are the bedrooms (Victorian or art deco), with bells to summon maid, waiter, or valet. The grand staircase and magnificent elevator complete with sofa and driver are equally glamorous. ⊠ *Brook St., St. James's W1A 2JQ* ☎ *020/7629–8860, 800/637–2869 in U.S.* 🖷 *020/7499–2210* ⊕ *www.claridges.co.uk* ⥱ *203 rooms* ⌂ *Restaurant, in-room data ports, in-room fax, in-room safes, some in-room hot tubs, minibars, cable TV with movies, in-room VCRs, gym, hair salon, spa, bar, lobby lounge, shop, babysitting, dry cleaning, laundry service, concierge, Internet, business services, meeting rooms, airport shuttle, car rental, parking (fee), no-smoking rooms* ▤ *AE, DC, MC, V* Ⓤ *Bond St.*

£££££ ⊡ **The Dorchester.** No other hotel this opulent manages to be quite so
Fodor'sChoice   charming. The glamour level is off the scale: 1,500 square yards of gold
★   leaf and 1,100 square yards of marble. Bedrooms (some not as spacious as you might expect) have Irish-linen sheets on canopied beds, brocades and velvets, and Italian marble and etched-glass bathrooms with Floris toiletries. Furnishings throughout are opulent English country-house style, with more than a hint of art deco, in keeping with the original 1930s building. You can take afternoon tea, drink, and pose in the catwalk-shape Promenade lounge. ⊠ *Park La., Mayfair W1A 2HJ* ☎ *020/7629–8888* 🖷 *020/7409–0114* ⊕ *www.dorchesterhotel.com* ⥱ *195 rooms, 55 suites* ⌂ *3 restau-*

rants, in-room data ports, in-room safes, minibars, cable TV with movies, in-room VCRs, gym, health club, hair salon, spa, bar, lobby lounge, night-club, shop, babysitting, dry cleaning, laundry service, concierge, Internet, business services, meeting rooms, car rental, parking (fee), no-smoking rooms ⊟ *AE, DC, MC, V* Ⓤ *Marble Arch, Hyde Park Corner.*

£££££ ▣ **Dukes.** This small, exclusive, Edwardian-style hotel with a gas lantern–lit courtyard entrance is in a discreet cul-de-sac. Overstuffed sofas, oil paintings of assorted dukes, and muted, rich colors create the perfect setting for sipping the finest dry martinis in town. The hotel's trump card is that, for such a central location, it's peaceful and quiet. The floral print- and wood-covered rooms are cozy. ⊠ *35 St. James's Pl., St. James's SW1A 1NY* ☎ *020/7491–4840, 800/381–4702 in U.S.* 🖷 *020/7493–1264* ⊕ *www.dukeshotel.co.uk* ⇝ *80 rooms, 9 suites* ⌂ *Restaurant, dining room, in-room data ports, some in-room faxes, in-room safes, minibars, cable TV, some in-room VCRs, gym, sauna, spa, steam room, bar, lobby lounge, dry cleaning, laundry service, concierge, business services, meeting rooms, parking (fee)* ⊟ *AE, DC, MC, V* Ⓤ *Green Park.*

★ £££££ ▣ **The Metropolitan.** This supertrendy hotel is one of the only addresses for visiting fashion, music, and media folk in London. Its Met bar has an exclusive guest list, and the restaurant is the famed Nobu, leased by Japanese wonder-chef Nobu Matsuhisa. The lobby is sleek and post-modern, as are the bedrooms, which have identical minimalist taupe-and-white furnishings. The best rooms overlook Hyde Park, but all have a groovy minibar hiding the latest alcoholic and health-boosting beverages. ⊠ *Old Park La., Mayfair W1K 1LB* ☎ *020/7447–1000, 800/337–4685 in U.S.* 🖷 *020/7447–1100* ⊕ *www.metropolitan.co.uk* ⇝ *137 rooms, 18 suites* ⌂ *Restaurant, room service, in-room data ports, in-room fax, in-room safes, minibars, cable TV with movies and video games, some in-room VCRs, gym, massage, bar, shop, babysitting, dry cleaning, laundry service, concierge, Internet, business services, meeting room, parking (fee), no-smoking floors* ⊟ *AE, DC, MC, V* Ⓤ *Hyde Park Corner.*

£££££ ▣ **The Ritz.** The name conjures the kind of opulence associated with swagged curtains, handwoven carpets, and the smell of cigars, polish, and fresh lilies. The only thing that has been lost is a certain vein of mon-eyed naughtiness that someone like F. Scott Fitzgerald, at least, would have banked on. The bedrooms are bastions of pastel Louis XVI style, with gilded furniture and crystal chandeliers. With a ratio of two staff members to every bedroom, you're guaranteed personal service despite the hotel's massive size. Formal dress is encouraged, and jeans are not allowed in public areas. ⊠ *150 Piccadilly, St. James's W1J 9BR* ☎ *020/7493–8181* 🖷 *020/7493–2687* ⊕ *www.theritzhotel.co.uk* ⇝ *133 rooms* ⌂ *2 restaurants, room service, in-room data ports, some in-room faxes, in-room safes, cable TV, some in-room VCRs, gym, hair salon, bar, babysit-ting, dry cleaning, laundry service, concierge, Internet, business services, meeting rooms, car rental, parking (fee), no-smoking rooms* ⊟ *AE, DC, MC, V* Ⓤ *Piccadilly Circus.*

££££–£££££ ▣ **The Leonard.** Its four 18th-century buildings make up a stunning, re-laxed, and friendly boutique hotel. Shoppers will appreciate the loca-tion, just around the corner from Oxford Street. Rooms are decorated with a judicious mix of lived-in antiques and comfortable reproductions. For more elbow room, try one of the aptly named grand suites, with their palatial sitting rooms and tall windows. The roof garden is great for warm weather, and the welcoming lobby is stocked with complimentary newspapers to read by the fire. ⊠ *15 Seymour St., Mayfair W1H 5AA* ☎ *020/7935–2010* 🖷 *020/7935–6700* ⊕ *www.theleonard.com* 🛏 *22 rooms, 21 suites* ♿ *Café, dining room, room service, in-room data ports, in-room safes, some kitchens, minibars, cable TV, in-room VCRs, gym, bar, lounge, babysitting, dry cleaning, laundry service, concierge, Internet, business services, meeting rooms, no-smoking rooms* ▭ *AE, DC, MC, V* Ⓤ *Marble Arch.*

££££ 🏨 **22 Jermyn Street.** This guest house is on a fashionable shopping street near Fortnum & Mason. Flexible room configurations, including sitting rooms that convert to bedrooms, mean families have plenty of space. In fact, the hotel rolls out the red carpet for children, providing anything from high chairs and coloring books to nannies and kids' bathrobes. For grownups, there's access to a nearby gym, complimentary newspapers, and a shoe shine. ⊠ *22 Jermyn St., St. James's SW1Y 6HL* ☎ *020/7734–2353, 800/682–7808 in U.S.* 🖷 *020/7734–0750* ⊕ *www.22jermyn.com* 🛏 *5 rooms, 13 suites* ♿ *Room service, in-room data ports, in-room safes, minibars, cable TV with movies, in-room VCRs, babysitting, dry cleaning, laundry service, concierge, Internet, business services, airport shuttle, car rental, parking (fee)* ▭ *AE, DC, MC, V* Ⓤ *Piccadilly Circus.*

££ 🏨 **Four Seasons Hotel.** This has nothing to do with the Four Seasons opposite Hyde Park; there are no stunning views over the Thames, no soundless elevators here. The hotel has, however, well-presented, Italianate bedrooms in soothing pastel colors, and is close to Regent's Park. The conservatory is a light, airy space for breakfast. ⊠ *173 Gloucester Pl., Mayfair NW1 6DX* ☎ *020/7724–3461* 🖷 *020/7402–5594* ⊕ *www.4seasonshotel.co.uk* 🛏 *28 rooms* ♿ *Room service, fans, in-room data ports, cable TV, babysitting, dry cleaning, laundry service, Internet, business services, car rental, some pets allowed, no-smoking rooms; no a/c* ▭ *AE, DC, MC, V* ⑩ *CP* Ⓤ *Baker St.*

££ 🏨 **Lincoln House Hotel.** On a fairly busy street just north of Oxford Street and Marble Arch, this family-run Georgian town house is done up with lots of wood and plaid. Rooms have a slightly dated look, but are well-equipped. Prices decrease the more days you stay. ⊠ *33 Gloucester Pl., Mayfair W1U 8HY* ☎ *020/7486–7630* 🖷 *020/7486–0166* ⊕ *www.lincoln-house-hotel.co.uk* 🛏 *24 rooms* ♿ *Cable TV, some refrigerators, lounge, babysitting, dry cleaning, laundry service, parking (fee); no a/c* ▭ *AE, DC, MC, V* ⑩ *BP* Ⓤ *Marble Arch.*

South Bank

££££ 🏨 **London Bridge Hotel.** Just steps away from the London Bridge rail and tube station, this thoroughly modern, stylish hotel is popular with business travelers. Most of the South Bank's attractions are within walking distance. Each sleek room is understated and contemporary. Three spacious two-bedroom apartments (£££££) come with kitchen, living room, and dining room. Foodies can stop at the delightful Borough Market on Friday and Saturday, just across the street, for some local London color. ⊠ *8–18 London Bridge St., South Bank SE1 9SG* ☎ *020/ 7855–2200* 🖷 *020/7855–2233* ⊕ *www.london-bridge-hotel.co.uk* ⛵ *138 rooms, 3 apartments* ⚭ *Restaurant, room service, in-room data ports, in-room safes, some kitchens, minibars, cable TV with movies, gym, sauna, bar, lobby lounge, dry cleaning, laundry service, concierge, meeting rooms, parking (fee), no-smoking floors* ▭ *AE, DC, MC, V* Ⓤ *London Bridge.*

££   🏨 **County Hall Travel Inn Capital.** Don't get too excited—this neighbor

Fodor'sChoice   of the fancy Marriott lacks the river view (it's at the back of the grand

★   former seat of local government). Still, you get an incredible value, with the standard facilities of the cookie-cutter rooms of this chain. Best of all for families on a budget are the foldout beds that let you accommodate two kids at no extra charge. *That's* a bargain. ⊠ *Belvedere Rd., South Bank SE1 7PB* ☎ *087/0238–3300* 🖷 *020/7902–1619* ⊕ *www. travelinn.co.uk* ⛵ *313 rooms* ⚭ *Restaurant, coffee shop, fans, in-room data ports, bar, business services, meeting rooms, parking (fee), no-smoking floors; no a/c* ▭ *AE, DC, MC, V* Ⓤ *Westminster.*

££   🏨 **Premier Lodge Southwark.** Practically riverside, this branch of the Premier Lodge chain has an excellent location across the cobbled road from Vinopolis. Rooms have desks, tea- and coffeemakers, and the chain's signature 6-foot-wide beds (really two zipped together). Family rooms can accommodate four people. The nautical Anchor restaurant and pub is adjacent to the hotel. ⊠ *34 Park St., South Bank SE1 9EF* ☎ *0870/990–6402* 🖷 *0870/990–6403* ⊕ *www.premierlodge.co.uk* ⛵ *56 rooms* ⚭ *In-room data ports, cable TV, parking (fee), no-smoking rooms* ▭ *AE, DC, MC, V* Ⓤ *London Bridge.*

Westminster & Victoria

££££   🏨 **City Inn Westminster.** In a rather stark steel-and-glass building steps from the Tate Britain, this modern hotel, part of a small U.K. chain, has some rooms with spectacular views of Big Ben and the London Eye. Extras like floor-to-ceiling windows, CD players, and flat screen TVs complement the sleek, contemporary, monochrome guest rooms. Cots, baby baths, and special menus are all on tap for kids. The restaurant and bar serve modern British cooking. ⊠ *30 John Islip St., Westminster SW1P 4DD* ☎ *020/7630–1000* 🖷 *020/7233–7575* ⊕ *www.cityinn.com* ⛵ *444 rooms, 16 suites* ⚭ *Restaurant, room service, minibars, in-room data ports, in-room safes, cable TV, in-room DVD players, gym, bar, lobby lounge, babysitting, dry cleaning, laundry service, concierge, Internet, business services, meeting rooms, parking (fee), no-smoking rooms* ▭ *AE, MC, V* Ⓤ *Pimlico.*

£££   🏨 **Tophams Belgravia.** Family-owned since 1937, this place extends a warm welcome—and a good value. The hotel is in five linked Georgian houses. Bedrooms, which include family and four-poster rooms, are done in English country-house florals or deep greens and reds. ⊠ *28 Ebury St., Belgravia SW1W 0LU* ☎ *020/7730–8147* 🖷 *020/7823–5966* ⊕ *www. tophams.co.uk* ⛵ *39 rooms* ⚭ *Restaurant, room service, in-room data ports, cable TV, bar, lobby lounge, babysitting, meeting room, parking (fee)* ▭ *AE, DC, MC, V* ⦿ *BP* Ⓤ *Victoria.*

NIGHTLIFE & THE ARTS

There isn't a single London nightlife or arts scene but an infinite assortment of them. As long as audiences exist for Feydeau revivals, drag queens, teenage rock bands, hit musicals, body-painted dancers, and improvised stand-up comedy, someone will find a space or stage for them in London. Admission prices are not always bargain basement, but when you consider how much a London hotel room costs, the city's arts and nightlife diversions are a bargain.

Nightlife

London is one of the party capitals of Europe. Despite draconian liquor laws and the inconvenience of tubes that stop running around midnight, Londoners still go out every night. The restrictions on late-night drinking have relaxed in the past few years, however, and are set to become even more liberal. There are already a staggering number of places with late licenses, where you can party after 11 PM, when the neighborhood pubs close their doors.

In one night, whether you're in the West End, trendier-than-thou East London, or racially diverse Brixton, you can drop into half a dozen bars and in each one find a completely unique world. Ultraswank hotel bars, wine-soaked experimental jazz clubs, and Asian-themed cocktail bars are just a few of the choices. Once 2 AM arrives, much of the bar scene moves on to the clubs, where you can dance until dawn to any kind of music.

Bars

★ **American Bar.** Festooned with club ties, signed celebrity photographs, and baseball caps, this sensational bar rakes in praise for its martinis and cocktails. ⊠ *Stafford Hotel, 16–18 St. James's Pl., St. James's SW1A* ☎ *020/7493–0111* 🏛 *Jacket required after 5* ⊙ *Weekdays 11:30 AM–11 PM, Sat. noon–3 and 5:30–11, Sun. noon–2:30 and 6:30–10:30* Ⓤ *Green Park.*

Atlantic Bar. A marble staircase descends into the glamorous art deco ballroom that is the Atlantic Bar. The original furnishings are intact, and the impeccable service, the superb cocktails, and Oliver Peyton's excellent restaurant keep pulling in the crowds. ⊠ *20 Glasshouse St., Soho W1* ☎ *020/7734–4888* ⊙ *Mon.–Sat. noon–3 AM* Ⓤ *Piccadilly Circus.*

Beach Blanket Babylon. Close to Portobello Market, this always-packed Notting Hill bar is distinguishable by its eclectic interior filled with Gaudiesque curves and snuggly corners—like a fairy-tale grotto or a medieval dungeon, visited by the gargoyles of Notre-Dame. ⊠ *45 Ledbury Rd., Notting Hill W11* ☎ *020/7229–2907* ⊙ *Mon.–Thurs. noon–midnight, Fri. and Sat. noon–1 AM, Sun. noon–10:30 PM* Ⓤ *Notting Hill Gate.*

Hoxton Square Bar & Kitchen. The rectangular concrete bar, reminiscent of an airport hangar, has long, comfortable sofas, plate-glass windows, and outdoor tables overlooking leafy Hoxton Square. The vibe is less pretentious than at neighboring bars, and creative types keep it packed. ⊠ *2–4 Hoxton Sq., Hoxton E1* ☎ *020/7613–0709* ⊙ *Mon.–Sat. 11 AM–midnight, Sun. 11–10:30* Ⓤ *Old St.*

Opium. Fashionable young things sip exotic cocktails amid trappings of the East. Amber light, delicate wooden carvings, and small alcoves dripping in velvet and gold re-create French-colonial Vietnam. The cocktails are impressive and pricey, as is the nouvelle Vietnamese cuisine. ⊠ *1 Dean St., Soho W1* ☎ *020/7287–9608* ⊙ *Weekdays 5 PM–3 AM, Sat. 7:30 PM–3 AM* Ⓤ *Tottenham Court Rd.*

Comedy

Comedy Store. At what is known as the birthplace of alternative comedy, Britain's funniest stand-ups have cut their teeth before being launched onto prime-time TV. Weekends have up-and-coming comedians performing on the same stage as established talent. Note that children under 18 are not admitted to this venue. ⊠ *1A Oxendon St., Soho SW1* ☎ *0870/060–2340* ⊠ *£12–£15* ⊙ *Shows Tues.–Thurs. and Sun. 8 PM–10:15 PM, Fri. and Sat. 8 PM–10:15 PM and midnight–2:30 AM* Ⓤ *Piccadilly Circus, Leicester Sq.*

Dance Clubs

The End. Top-name DJs, a state-of-the-art sound system, and minimalist steel-and-glass decor—clubbing doesn't get much better than this. Next door, the aka Bar (owned by the same people) is a stylish split-level Manhattan-esque cocktail bar with excellent food and a movie theater. ⊠ *18 West Central St., Holborn WC1* ☎ *020/7419–9199* ⊠ *£4–£15* ⊙ *Mon. 10 PM–3 AM, Thurs. 9 PM–4 AM, Fri. 10 PM–5 AM, Sat. 10 PM–7 AM; also some Sun.* Ⓤ *Tottenham Court Rd.*

★ **Fabric.** This sprawling subterranean club has been *the* place to be for the past few years. *Fabric Live* hosts hip-hop crews and other live acts on Fridays, and big-name international DJs play slow bass lines and cutting-edge music on Saturdays. Sunday is Polysexual Night. Arrive early to avoid a lengthy line, and don't wear a suit. ⊠ *77A Charterhouse St., East End EC1* ☎ *020/7336–8898* ⊠ *£12–£15* ⊙ *Fri. and Sun. 9:30 PM–5 AM, Sat. 10 PM–7 AM* Ⓤ *Farringdon.*

Hanover Grand. A former Masonic Hall is now an extravagant and opulent West End club, popular with a glitzy crowd. There is an elaborate sound-and-light show and a large dance floor. Glam disco and chart-bound house and garage nights attract long lines, so dress up to impress the bouncers. ⊠ *6 Hanover St., Mayfair W1* ☎ *020/7499–7977* ⊠ *£5–£15* ⊙ *Wed. 10:30 PM–3:30 AM, Thurs. and Fri. 10:30 PM–4 AM, Sat. 10:30 PM–5 AM* Ⓤ *Oxford Circus.*

Eclectic Music

The Borderline. This important small venue has a solid reputation for booking everything from metal to country and beyond. Oasis, Pearl Jam, Blur, Sheryl Crow, PJ Harvey, Jeff Buckley, and Counting Crows have played here. ⊠ *Orange Yard off Manette St., Soho W1* ☎ *020/7395–0777* ⊠ *£6–£15* ⊙ *Mon.–Sat. 7 PM–3 AM, Sun. 7 PM–midnight* Ⓤ *Tottenham Court Rd.*

Brixton Carling Academy. This legendary Brixton venue has seen it all—mods and rockers, hippies and punks. Despite a capacity of 4,000, the refurbished Victorian hall with original art deco fixtures retains a club-like charm; it has plenty of bars, and upstairs seating. ⊠ *211 Stockwell Rd., Brixton SW9* ☎ *0870/771–2000* ⊠ *£10–£30* Ⓤ *Brixton.*

★ **Union Chapel.** Excellent acoustics and sublime architecture distinguish this beautiful old chapel. The unique beauty of the space and its impressive multicultural programming has made it one of London's best musical venues. Performers have included Ravi Shankar, Björk, Beck, Beth Orton, and Bob Geldof. ✉ *Compton Terrace, Islington N1* ☎ *020/ 7226–1686 or 0870/120–1349* 📧 *Free–£25* Ⓤ *Highbury & Islington.*

Jazz

★ **Jazz Café.** A palace of high-tech cool remains an essential hangout for fans of both the mainstream end of the repertoire and hip-hop, funk, rap, and Latin fusion. Book ahead for a prime table overlooking the stage, in the balcony restaurant. ✉ *5 Parkway, Camden Town NW1* ☎ *020/ 7916–6060 or 020/7344–0044* 📧 *£10–£25* ☉ *Mon.–Thurs. 7 PM–1 AM, Fri. and Sat. 7 PM–2 AM, Sun. 7 PM–midnight* Ⓤ *Camden Town.*

Pizza Express. The capital's best-loved pizza chain is also a principal jazz club. The darkly lit Soho venue hosts top-quality international jazz acts every night except Mondays, and eight other branches also have live music. ✉ *10 Dean St., Soho W1* ☎ *020/7437–9595 or 020/7439–8722* 📧 *£12–£20* ☉ *From 11:30 AM for food; music Mon.–Thurs. and Sun. 9 PM–midnight, Fri. and Sat. 7:30 PM–midnight* Ⓤ *Tottenham Court Rd.*

Ronnie Scott's. Since the '60s, this legendary jazz club has attracted big names. It's usually crowded and hot, the food isn't great, and service is slow—but the atmosphere can't be beat, even since the sad departure of its eponymous founder and saxophonist. Reservations are recommended. ✉ *47 Frith St., Soho W1* ☎ *020/7439–0747* 📧 *£15–£25 nonmembers, £5–£15 members, annual membership £100* ☉ *Mon.–Sat. 8:30 PM–3 AM, Sun. 7:30 PM–11 PM* Ⓤ *Leicester Sq.*

Rock

Barfly Club. At one of the finest small clubs in the capital, punk, indie guitar bands, and new metal attract a nonmainstream crowd. Weekend club nights at the Club Monarch, upstairs, host DJs who rock the decks. ✉ *49 Chalk Farm Rd., Camden Town NW1* ☎ *020/7691–4244* 📧 *£5–£8* ☉ *Mon.–Thurs. 7:30–midnight, Fri. and Sat. 8–2, Sun. 7:30–11* Ⓤ *Camden Town, Chalk Farm.*

Forum. The best medium-to-big-name rock performers consistently play at this 2,000-capacity club, a converted 1920 art deco movie theater, with a balcony overlooking the dance floor. Saturday club night, "House of Fun," focuses on '70s and '80s nostalgia. ✉ *9–17 Highgate Rd., Kentish Town NW5* ☎ *020/7284–1001* 📧 *£12–£25* ☉ *Opening hours vary depending on concert schedule* Ⓤ *Kentish Town.*

The Arts

London's arts scene pushes the boundaries, whether you prefer your art classical or modern, or as a contemporary twist on a time-honored classic. Celebrity divas sing original-language librettos at the Royal Opera House, whereas the Almeida Opera focuses on radical productions of new opera and musical theater. Shakespeare's plays are brought to life at the reconstructed Globe Theatre, and challenging new writing is produced at the Royal Court.

To find out what's showing during your stay, the weekly magazine *Time Out* (it comes out every Tuesday) is an invaluable resource. The *Evening Standard,* especially the Thursday edition, also carries listings, as do the "quality" Sunday papers and the Saturday *Independent, Guardian,* and *Times.* Leaflets and fliers are found in most cinema and theater foyers, and you can pick up the free bimonthly *London Theatre Guide* leaflet from most hotels and tourist information centers.

Classical Music

It's possible to hear first-rank musicians in outstanding venues almost every day of the year. The London Symphony Orchestra is in residence at the Barbican Centre, although other top orchestras—including the Philharmonia and the Royal Philharmonic—also perform here. The Barbican also hosts chamber music concerts with such celebrated orchestras as the City of London Sinfonia. Wigmore Hall, a lovely venue for chamber music, is renowned for its recitals by up-and-coming young instrumentalists. The South Bank Centre has an impressive international music season, held in the Royal Festival Hall (one of the finest concert halls in Europe), the Queen Elizabeth Hall, and the small Purcell Room. Full houses are rare, so even at the biggest concert halls you should be able to get a ticket for £12. If you can't book in advance, arrive at the hall an hour before the performance for a chance at returns.

Lunchtime concerts take place in smaller concert halls, the big arts-center foyers, and churches. They usually cost less than £5 or are free, and will showcase string quartets, singers, jazz ensembles, or gospel choirs. St. John's in Smith Square and St. Martin-in-the-Fields are popular locations. Performances usually begin about 1 PM and last one hour.

A great British tradition of more than 110 years, the **Henry Wood Promenade Concerts** (known more commonly as the "Proms") last eight weeks, from July to September, at the Royal Albert Hall. It's renowned for its last night, a madly jingoistic display of singing "Land of Hope and Glory," Union Jack waving, and general madness. Demand for tickets is so high you must enter a lottery. For regular Proms, where the best music is heard, tickets run £4–£80, with hundreds of standing tickets for £4 available at the hall on the night of the concert. The last night is broadcast in Hyde Park on a jumbo screen, but even here a seat on the grass requires a paid ticket that can set you back around £20.

Kenwood House. Concerts are held in the grassy amphitheater in front of Kenwood House on Saturday evening from July to late August. ⊠ *Hampstead Heath, Hampstead* ☎ *020/7973–3427* Ⓤ *Golders Green, then bus 210.*

★ **Royal Albert Hall.** Built in 1871, this splendid iron-and-glass domed auditorium hosts a varied music program, including Europe's most democratic music festival, the Henry Wood Promenade Concerts—the Proms. ⊠ *Kensington Gore, Kensington SW7* ☎ *020/7589–8212* Ⓤ *South Kensington.*

St. John's in Smith Square. This baroque church behind Westminster Abbey presents chamber music, organ recitals, and orchestral concerts September through July. Free lunchtime recitals are held every two weeks or so. ⊠ *Smith Sq., Westminster W1* ☎ *020/7222–1061* Ⓤ *Westminster.*

St. Martin-in-the-Fields. Regular evening concerts and free lunchtime concerts are held in this lovely 1726 church. ⊠ *Trafalgar Sq., Covent Garden WC2* ☎ *020/7839–8362* Ⓤ *Charing Cross.*

South Bank Centre. The Royal Festival Hall hosts large-scale choral and orchestral works, the Queen Elizabeth Hall hosts chamber orchestras and A-list soloists, and the Purcell Room has chamber music and recitals. ⊠ *South Bank, SE1* ☎ *020/7960–4242* Ⓤ *Waterloo.*

★ **Wigmore Hall.** Hear chamber music and recitals in this hall with near perfect acoustics. Don't miss the midmorning Sunday concerts. ⊠ *36 Wigmore St., Marylebone W1* ☎ *020/7935–2141* Ⓤ *Bond St.*

Contemporary Art

For centuries, Britain has accumulated extraordinary collections of art in national institutions such as the National Gallery, National Portrait Gallery, the Tate, and the Victoria & Albert Museum. No less high profile is London's contemporary art scene, displayed in publicly funded exhibition spaces such as the Barbican Gallery, Hayward Gallery, Institute of Contemporary Arts, Serpentine Gallery, and Whitechapel Art Gallery. And with the arrival of the Tate Modern, London has a flagship modern art gallery. Since the early 1990s, the contemporary art scene here has exploded, and Young British Artists (YBA)—Damien Hirst, Tracey Emin, Gary Hume, Rachel Whiteread, Jake and Dinos Chapman, Sarah Lucas, Gavin Turk, Steve McQueen, and others—have made London one of the most dynamic spots for contemporary art in the world.

In addition to the trendy, Arts Council–funded scene, hundreds of other small galleries exist all over London. Check the weekly listings for details. Expect to pay around £8 for entry into touring exhibitions, but most permanent displays and commercial galleries are free.

Barbican Centre. Innovative exhibitions of 20th-century and current art and design are presented here. ⊠ *Silk St., The City EC2* ☎ *020/7638–8891* ⊠ *£5–£7* ⊙ *Mon., Tues., and Thurs.–Sat. 10–6, Wed. 10–9, Sun. noon–6* Ⓤ *Barbican.*

Hayward Gallery. This example of 1960s brutalist architecture is one of London's major venues for touring exhibitions. ⊠ *South Bank Centre, Belvedere Rd., South Bank SE1* ☎ *020/7960–5226* ⊠ *£7* ⊙ *Thurs.–Mon. 10–6, Tues. and Wed. 10–8* Ⓤ *Waterloo.*

Institute of Contemporary Arts. Visual art, contemporary drama, film, new media, literature, and photography are the focus at this center in a Regency terrace. ⊠ *Nash House, The Mall, St. James's SW1* ☎ *020/7930–3647 or 020/7930–0493* ⊠ *Weekdays £1.50, weekends £2.50* ⊙ *Daily noon–7:30* Ⓤ *Charing Cross.*

Lisson. This respected gallery represents more than 40 blue-chip artists. A new branch at 29 Bell Street features work by younger up-and-comers. ⊠ *52–54 Bell St., Marylebone NW1* ☎ *020/7724–2739* ⊠ *Free* ⊙ *Weekdays 10–6, Sat. 11–5* Ⓤ *Edgware Rd.*

Photographer's Gallery. Cutting-edge photography is the draw at this distinguished gallery. ⊠ *5 & 8 Great Newport St., Covent Garden WC2* ☎ *020/7831–1772* ⊠ *Free* ⊙ *Mon.–Sat. 11–6, Sun. noon–6* Ⓤ *Leicester Sq.*

Saatchi Gallery. This headline-grabbing gallery favors high-profile, provocative modern art. ⊠ *County Hall, South Bank SE1* ☎ *020/ 7823–2363* 🖾 *£8.50* ⊙ *Daily 10 AM–8 PM, Fri. and Sat. until 10 PM* Ⓤ *Waterloo.*

Serpentine Gallery. A tea pavilion in Kensington Gardens houses a gallery that has earned a reputation for exhibitions of modern and contemporary art. ⊠ *Kensington Gardens, South Kensington W2* ☎ *020/ 7402–6075* 🖾 *Donation* ⊙ *Daily 10–6* Ⓤ *South Kensington.*

★ **Tate Modern.** This converted power station is the largest modern art gallery in the world. ⊠ *25 Summer St., South Bank SE1* ☎ *020/7887–8008* 🖾 *Free–£8.50* ⊙ *Sun.–Thurs. 10–6, Fri. and Sat. 10–10* Ⓤ *Southwark.*

★ **Whitechapel Art Gallery.** Established in 1897, this independent East End gallery is one of London's most innovative. ⊠ *80–82 Whitechapel High St., East End E1* ☎ *020/7522–7888* 🖾 *Free* ⊙ *Tues.–Sun. 11–6, Thurs. 11–9* Ⓤ *Aldgate East.*

White Cube. Jay Joplin's influential gallery is in a 1920s light-industrial building on trendy Hoxton Square. ⊠ *48 Hoxton Sq., East End N1* ☎ *020/7930–5357* 🖾 *Free* ⊙ *Tues.–Sat. 10 AM–6 PM* Ⓤ *Old St.*

Dance

The **English National Ballet** and visiting international companies usually perform at the London Coliseum. The **Royal Ballet,** world renowned for its classical excellence, as well as innovative contemporary dance from several companies and scores of independent choreographers, can be seen at the Royal Opera House. **Royal Festival Hall** in the South Bank Centre has a fine contemporary dance program that hosts top international companies and British choreographers. **The Place** presents the most daring,
★ cutting-edge dance performances. **Sadler's Wells** hosts ballet companies and regional and international modern dance troupes. The city's biggest annual event, **Dance Umbrella** (☎ 020/8741–5881 ⊕ www.danceumbrella. co.uk), a six-week season in October and November, showcases international and British-based artists at venues across the city.

DANCE BOX **London Coliseum** (⊠ St. Martin's La., Covent Garden WC2N ☎ 020/
OFFICES 7632–8300 Ⓤ Leicester Sq.).

The Place (⊠ 17 Duke's Rd., Bloomsbury WC1 ☎ 020/7380–1268 Ⓤ Euston).

Royal Opera House (⊠ Bow St., Covent Garden WC2 ☎ 020/7304–4000 Ⓤ Covent Garden).

Sadler's Wells (⊠ Rosebery Ave., Islington EC1 ☎ 020/7863–8000 Ⓤ Angel).

South Bank Centre (⊠ Belvedere Rd., South Bank SE1 ☎ 020/7960–4242 Ⓤ Embankment, Waterloo).

Film

There are many lovely movie theaters in London and several that are committed to nonmainstream cinema, notably the National Film Theatre. Most of the major houses (Odeon Leicester Square and UCI Empire) are in the Leicester Square–Piccadilly Circus area, where tickets average £8. Mondays and matinees are often cheaper, at around £5, and crowds are smaller. Check *Time Out* or *The Guardian*'s "Guide section" (free with the paper on Saturdays) for listings.

National Film Theatre. The NFT's three theaters show more than 2,000 titles each year, including foreign films, documentaries, cult Hollywood features, and animation. The London Film Festival, held in November, is based here. ⊠ *South Bank Centre, Belvedere Rd., South Bank SE1* ☏ *020/7633–0274 information, 020/7928–3232 box office* Ⓤ *Waterloo.*

Opera

The two key players in London's opera scene are the Royal Opera (which ranks with the Metropolitan Opera in New York) and the more innovative English National Opera (ENO), which presents English-language productions at the London Coliseum. Only the Theatre Royal, Drury Lane, has a longer theatrical history than the Royal Opera House, and the current theater—the third to be built on the site since 1858—completed a monumental renovation in 1999. The new building has been well received, especially the restored Victorian auditorium and the Floral Hall foyer, which beautifully integrate with the Covent Garden Piazza.

The Royal Opera House struggles to shrug off its reputation for elitism and mismanagement. Ticket prices go up to £170. Since the renovation, it has, however, made good on its promise to be more accessible—the cheapest tickets are just £6 (for a restricted-view matinee seat). Conditions of purchase vary; call for information. Prices for ENO are generally lower, ranging from £8 to £80. ENO sells same-day balcony seats for as little as £5.

Almeida Opera and BAC Opera (at the Battersea Arts Centre) produce festivals that showcase new opera and cutting-edge music theater. During the summer months, Holland Park Opera presents the usual chestnuts in the open-air theater of leafy Holland Park.

OPERA BOX OFFICES

Almeida Theatre (⊠ Almeida St., Islington N1 ☏ 020/7359–4404 Ⓤ Angel, Highbury & Islington).
BAC Opera (⊠ Lavender Hill, Battersea SW11 ☏ 020/7223–2223 Ⓤ Clapham Junction).
English National Opera (⊠ London Coliseum, St. Martin's La., Covent Garden WC2 ☏ 020/7632–8300 Ⓤ Leicester Sq.).
Holland Park Opera (⊠ Holland Park, Kensington High St., Kensington W8 ☏ 020/7602–7856 Ⓤ Covent Garden).
★ **Royal Opera House** (⊠ Bow St., Covent Garden WC2 ☏ 020/7304–4000 Ⓤ Covent Garden).

Theater

One of the special experiences the city has to offer is great theater. London's theater scene consists, broadly, of the state-subsidized companies, the Royal National Theatre and the Royal Shakespeare Company; the commercial West End, equivalent to Broadway; and the Fringe—small, experimental companies. Another category could be added: known in the weekly listings magazine *Time Out* as Off-West End, these are shows staged at the longer-established fringe theaters. Most of the West End theaters are in the neighborhood nicknamed Theatreland, around the Strand and Shaftesbury Avenue.

The Royal Shakespeare Company and the Royal National Theatre Company often stage contemporary versions of the classics. The Almeida, Battersea Arts Centre (BAC), Donmar Warehouse, Royal Court Theatre, Soho Theatre, and the Young Vic attract famous actors and have excellent reputations for new writing and innovative theater. These are the places that shape the theater of the future, the venues where you can see an original production before it becomes a (more expensive) hit in the West End. From mid-May through mid-September you can see the Bard served up at the open-air reconstruction of Shakespeare's Globe Theatre on the South Bank.

Theatergoing isn't cheap. Tickets under £10 are a rarity; in the West End you should expect to pay from £15 for a seat in the upper balcony to at least £25 for a good one in the stalls (orchestra) or dress circle (mezzanine). However, as the vast majority of theaters have some tickets (returns and house seats) available on the night of performance, you may find some good deals at box offices as well as at tkts, the Society of London Theatre's discount ticket booth. Tickets may be booked through ticket agents, at individual theater box offices, or over the phone by credit card; be sure to inquire about any extra fees. All the larger hotels offer theater bookings, but they tack on a hefty service charge. Fringe tickets are always considerably less expensive than tickets for West End productions.

Be *very* careful of scalpers and unscrupulous ticket agents outside theaters and in the line at tkts. They will try to sell tickets at five times the price of the ticket at legitimate box offices, and you pay a stiff fine if caught buying a scalped ticket.

First Call (☎ 0870/906–3838 ⊕ www.firstcalltickets.com) sells theater tickets. **Keith Prowse** (✉ 234 W. 44th St., Suite 1000, New York, NY 10036 ☎ 212/398–0154 or 800/669–8687) can book London tickets in the U.S. **Ticketmaster** (☎ 0870/243–9000, 800/775–2525 in U.S. ⊕ www.ticketmaster.com) sells tickets to various theaters.

The **Society of London Theatre** (✉ 32 Rose St., Covent Garden, London WC2 E9E5 ☎ 020/7557–6700 ⊕ www.officiallondontheatre.co.uk) operates tkts, the half-price ticket booth (no phone) on the southwest corner of Leicester Square, and sells the best available seats to performances at nearly all major theaters. It's open Monday–Saturday 10–7, Sunday noon–3; there's a £2.50 service charge. All major credit cards are accepted. The society has good information about theatrical events.

SELECTED **Almeida.** Hollywood stars often perform at this Off-West End venue that
THEATERS premieres excellent new plays and exciting twists on the classics.
★ ✉ *Almeida St., Islington N1* ☎ *020/7359–4404* Ⓤ *Angel, Highbury & Islington.*

Barbican Centre. Barbican International Theatre Events (BITE) presents groundbreaking performance, dance, drama, and musical theater. ✉ *Silk St., The City EC2* ☎ *020/7638–8891* Ⓤ *Barbican.*

BAC. Battersea Arts Centre has an excellent reputation for producing innovative new work. Check out Scratch, a night of low-tech cabaret theater by emerging artists, and the BAC Octoberfest of innovative performance. ✉ *176 Lavender Hill, Battersea SW11* ☎ *020/7223–2223* Ⓤ *National Rail: Clapham Junction.*

★ **Donmar Warehouse.** Hollywood stars often perform in diverse and daring new works, bold interpretations of the classics, and small-scale musicals. It works both ways, too—director Sam Mendes went straight from here to directing *American Beauty.* ✉ *41 Earlham St., Covent Garden WC2* ☎ *020/7369–1732* Ⓤ *Covent Garden.*

The Old Vic. Oscar-winning American actor Kevin Spacey is the new artistic director of this grand 1818 Victorian theater, thriving again after decades of financial duress. Legends of the stage have performed here, including John Gielgud, Vivian Leigh, Peter O'Toole, Richard Burton, Judi Dench, and Laurence Olivier, who called it his favorite theater. ✉ *The Cut, Southwark SE1* ☎ *020/7928–7616* Ⓜ *Waterloo.*

Open Air Theatre. On a warm summer evening, classical theater in pastoral Regent's Park is hard to beat. Enjoy a supper before the performance and during the interval on the picnic lawn, and drinks in the spacious bar. ✉ *Inner Circle, Regent's Park NW1* ☎ *020/7486–2431* Ⓤ *Baker St., Regent's Park.*

Royal Court Theatre. Britain's undisputed epicenter of new writing, the RCT has produced gritty British and international drama since the mid-20th century. Don't miss the best deal in town: £7.50 tickets on Mondays. ✉ *Sloane Sq., Chelsea SW1* ☎ *020/7565–5000* Ⓤ *Sloane Sq.*

Royal National Theatre. The NT has three theaters: the 1,120-seat Olivier, the 890-seat Lyttelton, and the 300-seat Cottesloe. Musicals, classics, and new plays are staged. It's closed Sunday. ✉ *South Bank Centre, Belvedere Rd., South Bank SE1* ☎ *020/7452–3000* Ⓤ *Waterloo.*

Royal Shakespeare Company. The RSC schedules its high-quality productions in different West End venues; in 2004 performances took place at the Gielgud Theatre and Queen's Theatre. ☎ *0870/609–1110 reservations.*

★ **Shakespeare's Globe Theatre.** This reconstruction of the open-air playhouse for which Shakespeare wrote many of his greatest plays re-creates the 16th-century theatergoing experience. Standing room costs £5. The season runs May through September. ✉ *New Globe Walk, Bankside, South Bank SE1* ☎ *020/7401–9919* Ⓤ *Southwark, Mansion House (walk across Southwark Bridge), Blackfriars (walk across Blackfriars Bridge).*

Soho Theatre + Writers' Centre. This sleek theater is devoted to new writing and work by emerging writers. ✉ *21 Dean St., Soho W1* ☎ *020/7478–0100* Ⓤ *Tottenham Court Rd.*

Tricycle Theatre. The focus here is the best in Irish, African-Caribbean, and Asian works, as well as political drama and new plays. ✉ *269 Kilburn High Rd., Kilburn NW6 7JR* ☎ *020/7328–1000* Ⓤ *Kilburn.*

★ **Young Vic.** Big names perform in innovative productions of classic plays. No one sits more than five rows from the stage in this theater-in-the-round auditorium. The seats are unreserved; each has a perfect view. ✉ *66 The Cut, South Bank SE1* ☎ *020/7928–6363* Ⓤ *Waterloo.*

SPORTS & THE OUTDOORS

There are the Wimbledon Tennis Championships, and there's cricket, and then there's football (soccer), and that's about it for the sports fan in London, right? Wrong. London is a great city for the weekend player of almost anything. It comes into its own in summer, when the parks sprout nets and goals and painted white lines, outdoor swimming pools open, and a season of spectator events gets under way. If you feel like joining in, *Time Out* magazine, available at newsstands, is a great resource. Bring your gear, and branch out from that hotel gym.

Cricket

★ **Lord's** (⊠ St. John's Wood Rd., St. John's Wood NW8 ☎ 020/7432–1066) has been hallowed turf for worshippers of England's summer game since 1811. Tickets (by application and lottery) can be hard to procure for the five-day Test Matches (full internationals) and one-day internationals played here. Forms are sent out in early December. Standard Test Match tickets cost between £26 and £48. County matches (Middlesex plays here) can usually be seen by lining up on the day of the match.

Football

Three of London's football (soccer) clubs competing in the **Premier League** and the Football Association's FA Cup are particularly popular, though not always correspondingly successful: **Arsenal** (⊠ Highbury, Avenell Rd., Islington N5 ☎ 0870/906–3366), **Chelsea** (⊠ Stamford Bridge, Fulham Rd., Fulham SW6 ☎ 0870/300–2322), and **Tottenham Hotspur,** also known as "Spurs," (⊠ White Hart La., 748 High Rd., Tottenham N17 ☎ 0870/420–5000). Try to buy tickets in advance, and don't get too carried away by the excitement a vast football crowd can generate.

Gyms

The **Central YMCA** (⊠ 112 Great Russell St., Bloomsbury WC1 ☎ 020/7343–1700) has every facility and sport, including a great 25-meter pool and a well-equipped gym. Weekly membership is £42.50, a "one-day taster" £15. At **The Gym Covent Garden** (⊠ 30 The Piazza, Covent Garden WC2 ☎ 020/7379–0008), a very crowded but trendy and superwell-equipped central gym, the day rate is £8. The trendy yoga school **Life Centre** (⊠ 15 Edge St., Kensington W8 ☎ 020/7221–4602) specializes in the energetic Ashtanga Vinyasa yoga technique. Classes cost £9–£12.

Ice-Skating

★ ☾ It's hard to beat the skating experience at **Somerset House** (⊠ The Strand, Covent Garden WC2 ☎ 020/7845–4670). During December and January a rink is set up in the spectacular courtyard of this central London palace. Adults pay £9.50–£10.50, children £6.

Running

Green Park and St. James's Park are convenient to the Piccadilly hotels. It's about 2 mi around the two parks. Hyde Park and Kensington Gardens together supply a 4-mi perimeter route, or you can do a 2½-mi run in Hyde Park if you start at Hyde Park Corner or Marble Arch and encircle the Serpentine. Near the Park Lane hotels, Regent's Park has the Outer Circle loop, measuring about 2½ mi. **London Hash House Harriers** (☎ 020/8995–7879) organizes noncompetitive hour-long runs (£1) around interesting parts of town, with loops, shortcuts, and pubs built in. Runs start at tube stations at noon on either Saturday or Sunday during the winter, and at 7 PM on Monday during the summer.

The **Flora London Marathon** (☎ 020/7620–4117) starts at 9:30 AM on a Sunday in April, with some 30,000 athletes running from Blackheath or Greenwich to the Mall. Entry forms for the following year are available between August and October.

Swimming

☺ **Chelsea Sports Centre** (✉ Chelsea Manor St., Chelsea SW3 ☎ 020/7352–6985), with a turn-of-the-century 32-by-12-meter pool, is just off King's Road, so it's busy, especially on weekends when it's packed with kids. Each swim costs £2.80. **Oasis** (✉ 32 Endell St., Covent Garden WC2 ☎ 020/7831–1804) is just that, with a heated outdoor pool, open year-round, right in Covent Garden, and a 30-by-10-yard pool indoors. A swim costs £3.10.

Tennis

The **Wimbledon Lawn Tennis Championships,** the most prestigious of the four Grand Slam tournaments, is also one of London's most eagerly awaited annual events. To enter the lottery for show-court tickets, send a self-addressed, stamped envelope (or an international reply coupon) after August 1 and return the application form before December 31 to **All England Lawn Tennis & Croquet Club** (✑ Box 98, Church Rd., Wimbledon SW19 5AE ☎ 020/8946–2244). Alternatively, during the last-week-of-June, first-week-of-July tournament, tickets collected from early departing spectators are resold (profits go to charity). These can provide grandstand seats with plenty to see: play continues until dusk. You can also line up (start as early as possible) for tickets for the outside courts.

SHOPPING

Napoléon must have known what he was talking about when he called Britain a nation of shopkeepers. The finest emporiums are in London, still. You can shop like royalty at Her Majesty's glove maker, discover an uncommon Toby jug in a Kensington antiques shop, or find a leather-bound edition of *Wuthering Heights* on Charing Cross Road. If you have a yen to keep up with the Windsors, head for stores proclaiming they are "By Appointment" to H. M. the Queen—or to Prince Philip or the Prince of Wales. The fashion-forward crowd favors places such as Harvey Nichols or Browns of South Molton Street, whereas the most ardent fashion victims will shoot to Notting Hill, London's prime fashion location. If you have only limited time, zoom in on one or two of the West End's grand department stores, such as Harrods or Marks & Spencer, where you can find enough booty for your entire gift list. Below is a brief introduction to the major shopping areas.

CHELSEA Chelsea centers on King's Road, once synonymous with ultra-high fashion; it still harbors some designer boutiques, plus antiques and home furnishings stores.

COVENT GARDEN This something-for-everyone neighborhood has chain clothing stores and top designers, stalls selling crafts, and shops selling gifts of every type—bikes, kites, tea, herbs, beads, hats—you name it.

FULHAM Newly popular, Fulham is divided into two postal districts, SW6 (farther away from the center of town) and SW10 (which is the closer, beyond Chelsea) on the high-fashion King's Road.

KENSINGTON Kensington's main drag, Kensington High Street, houses some small, classy shops, with some larger stores at the eastern end. Try Kensington Church Street for expensive antiques, plus a little fashion.

KNIGHTSBRIDGE Knightsbridge, east of Kensington, has Harrods but also Harvey Nichols, the top clothes stop, and many expensive designers' boutiques along Sloane Street, Walton Street, and Beauchamp Place.

MARYLEBONE Behind Oxford Street lies this quiet backwater, with Marylebone High Street as its main artery. Restaurants coexisted peacefully with delis and practical stores until the arrival of designer furniture stores. Satellite streets have designer women's wear and menswear.

MAYFAIR In Mayfair are the two Bond streets, Old and New, with desirable dress designers, jewelers, and fine art. South Molton Street has high-price, high-style fashion, and the tailors of Savile Row have worldwide reputations.

NOTTING HILL Go westward from the famous Portobello Road market and explore the Ledbury Road–Westbourne Grove axis, Clarendon Cross, and Kensington Park Road for a mix of antiques and up-to-the-minute must-haves for body and lifestyle. Toward the more bohemian foot of Portobello are Ladbroke Grove and Golborne Road, where, in among the tatty stores, Portuguese cafés, and patisseries, you can bag bargains.

REGENT STREET At right angles to Oxford Street is Regent Street, with possibly London's most pleasant department store, Liberty, plus Hamleys, the capital's favorite toy store. Shops around once-famous Carnaby Street stock designer youth paraphernalia and 57 varieties of the T-shirt.

ST. JAMES'S Here the English gentleman buys everything but the suit (which is from Savile Row): handmade hats, shirts and shoes, silver shaving kits, and hip flasks. Nothing in this neighborhood is cheap, in any sense.

Department Stores

Debenhams (⊠ 334–348 Oxford St., Mayfair W1 ☎ 020/7580–3000 Ⓤ Oxford Circus) has moved up the fashion stakes with the pretty, affordable, Jasper Conran collection for women. Other creations—for men, too—by in-house designers are desirable. ★ **Harrods** (⊠ 87 Brompton Rd., Knightsbridge SW1 ☎ 020/7730–1234 Ⓤ Knightsbridge), one of the world's most famous department stores, can be forgiven its immodest motto, *Omnia, omnibus, ubique* ("everything, for everyone, everywhere"), because it has more than 230 well-stocked departments. The food halls are stunning—so are the crowds, especially during the sales that usually run during the last three weeks of January. **Harvey Nichols** (⊠ 109 Knightsbridge, Knightsbridge SW1 ☎ 020/7235–5000 Ⓤ Knightsbridge) is famed for five floors of ultimate fashion; every label any chic, well-bred London lady covets is here. There's a home furnishings department. It's also known for the restaurant, Fifth Floor. **John Lewis** (⊠ 278 Oxford St., Mayfair SW1 ☎ 020/7629–7711 Ⓤ Oxford Circus) claims

London Shopping

Paddington Station

Marylebone Rd.

Oxford Circus

Oxford St.

Manchester Square

Grosvenor Square

U.S. Embassy ◆

Berkeley Square

Royal Academy ◆

Hyde Park

Kensington Gardens

The Serpentine

Royal Albert Hall

South Kensington Museums

Belgrave Square

Cadogan Sq.

Sloane Sq.

St. James's Palace

Green Park

St. James Park

Buckingham Palace

Victoria Station

Knightsbridge

Constitution Hill

Royal Hospital Rd.

Chelsea Embankment

Cheyne Walk

0   550 yards
0   500 meters

Agnès B **7**
Antiquarius **8**
Aquascutum **43**
Asprey **30**
British Museum
Company **55**
Browns **15, 26**
Burberry **33**
Butler & Wilson **24**
Cath Kidston **2**
Cecil Court **61**
Crafts Council
Gallery Shop/
Victoria & Albert
Museum Shop **6**
The Cross **1**
Daisy & Tom **9**
David Linley
Furniture **17**
David Mellor **12**
Debenhams **27**
Dinny Hall **3**
Divertimenti **23**
Favourbrook **45**
Floris **48**
Forbidden Planet **54**
Fortnum & Mason **44**
Foyles **52**
Garrard **22**
General Trading Co. . . .**12**
Ghost **5**
Grays Antique
Market **25**
Grosvenor Prints **60**
Hamleys **38**
Harrods **14**
Harvey Nichols **16**
Hatchards **46**
Herbert Johnson **40**
HMV **29**
Jigsaw **34**
Jimmy Choo **10**
John Lewis **28**
Koh Samui **59**
Laura Ashley **36**
Les Senteurs **18**
Lesley Craze Gallery . . .**65**
Liberty **37**
London Glassblowing
Workshop **68**
London Silver Vaults . . .**64**
Lush **62**
The Map House **13**
Marks &
Spencer **21, 50**

MDC Classic Music **66**
Mr CD **49**
OXO Tower **67**
Ozwald Boateng **41**
Paul Smith **58**
Penhaligon's **63**
Ray's Jazz **52**
Selfridges **22**
Stanfords **57**
Summerill & Bishop **4**
Tea House **56**
Thomas Goode **19**
Topshop **35**
Turnbull & Asser **47**
Virgin Megastore **51**
Vivienne Westwood . . .**20**
Waterstone's **32**
Zara **42**
Zwemmer **53**

KEY

 Tourist information

as its motto "Never knowingly undersold." This traditional department store carries a good selection of dress fabrics and curtain and uphol-

★ stery materials. **Liberty** (⌧ 200 Regent St., Mayfair SW1 ☎ 020/7734–1234 Ⓤ Oxford Circus), full of nooks and crannies, is famous principally for its fabulous fabrics. It also carries Asian goods, menswear, womenswear, fragrances, soaps, and accessories. **Selfridges** (⌧ 400 Oxford St., Mayfair SW1 ☎ 020/7629–1234 Ⓤ Bond St.), London's mammoth version of Macy's, has been revamped to a modish shopping experience that caters to every lifestyle, whether cool or classic: Burberry or mountain bikes, anyone? Among the maelstrom of rails, lights, and loud music, there is still the world class food hall, a theater ticket counter, and a British Airways travel shop.

Specialty Stores

Antiques

Antiquarius (⌧ 131–145 King's Rd., Chelsea SW3 ☎ 020/7351–5353 Ⓤ Sloane Sq.), near Sloane Square, is an indoor antiques market with more than 200 stalls offering collectibles, including smaller items: art deco brooches, meerschaum pipes, silver salt cellars. It's closed Sunday. **Grays Antique Market** (⌧ 58 Davies St., Mayfair W1 ☎ 020/7629–7034 Ⓤ Bond St.) assembles dealers specializing in everything from Sheffield plates to Chippendale furniture. Bargains are not impossible, and proper pedigrees are guaranteed. It's closed Saturday (except December) and Sunday. **London Silver Vaults** (⌧ 53–64 Chancery La., Holborn WC2 ☎ 020/7242–3844 Ⓤ Chancery La.) has 36 dealers specializing in antique silver and jewelry. It's closed Saturday afternoon and Sunday.

Books, CDs & Records

BOOKS Charing Cross Road is London's "booksville," with a couple dozen antiquarian booksellers, and many mainstream bookshops, too. **Cecil Court,** off Charing Cross Road, is a pedestrian-only lane filled with specialty bookstores. **Marchpane** (⌧ 16 Cecil Ct., Covent Garden WC2 ☎ 020/7836–8661 Ⓤ Tottenham Court Rd.) stocks rare and antique illustrated children's books with many first editions, from 18th-century volumes to today's Harry Potter. **Pleasures of Past Times** (⌧ 11 Cecil Ct. , Covent Garden WC2 ☎ 020/7836–1142 Ⓤ Tottenham Court Rd.) indulges the collective nostalgia for Victoriana in its stock of modern and old books.

Tindley & Chapman (⌧ 4 Cecil Ct., Covent Garden WC2 ☎ 020/7240–2161 Ⓤ Tottenham Court Rd.), previously Bell, Book & Radmall, still offers quality antiquarian tomes and specializes in modern first editions. **Forbidden Planet** (⌧ 179 Shaftesbury Ave., Bloomsbury WC1 ☎ 020/7420–3666 Ⓤ Tottenham Court Rd.) is the place for sci-fi, fantasy, horror, and comic books. **Foyles** (⌧ 113–119 Charing Cross Rd., Soho WC2 ☎ 020/7437–5660 Ⓤ Tottenham Court Rd.) is so vast, you can find almost anything. There are two great, unique concessions:

★ the Silver Moon for women and Ray's Jazz for music. **Hatchards** (⌧ 187 Piccadilly, St. James's W1 ☎ 020/7439–9921 Ⓤ Piccadilly Circus) has a huge stock and a well-informed staff. **Stanfords** (⌧ 12–14 Long Acre, Covent Garden WC2 ☎ 020/7836–1321 Ⓤ Covent Garden) specializes in travel books and maps. **Waterstone's** (✉ 203–206 Piccadilly, St. James's W1 ☎ 020/7851–2400 Ⓤ Piccadilly Circus) is part of an admirable chain with long hours and a program of author readings and signings. Their most upscale branch is book buying as hedonistic leisure activity, with five floors, a studio cocktail lounge with a view, and a café in the basement. **Zwemmer** (✉ 72 Charing Cross Rd., Covent Garden WC2 ☎ 020/7240–1559 Ⓤ Tottenham Court Rd. ✉ 80 Charing Cross Rd., Covent Garden WC2 ☎ 020/7240–4157 Ⓤ Tottenham Court Rd.) has two locations on Charing Cross Road: No. 72 sells books on design and related fields, and No. 80 covers cinema and photography.

CDS & RECORDS London created the great music megastores that have taken over the globe, but don't forget to check out the many independents for a more eclectic selection. **HMV** (✉ 150 Oxford St., Soho W1 ☎ 020/7631–3423 Ⓤ Oxford Circus) has branches everywhere, but make a special trip to the HMV (which stands for "His Majesty's Voice") flagship store for the widest selection. There are autograph sessions and free shows, too. **MDC Classic Music** (✉ 437 Strand, Covent Garden WC2 ☎ 020/7240–2157 Ⓤ Charing Cross) has helpful staff who will guide you to the best deals on any diva. There's some jazz, too. **Mr CD** (✉ 80 Berwick St., Soho W1 ☎ 020/7439–1097 Ⓤ Oxford Circus) stocks a wide selection for all tastes

★ in a tiny shop where you must delve to find the bargains. **Ray's Jazz** (✉ 113–119 Charing Cross Rd., Soho WC2 ☎ 020/7437–5660 Ⓤ Tottenham Court Rd.) is no longer its own store, but there is no less selection here within the Foyles empire. Not only do you get to buy from a superior selection of jazz and world music, but you can hear live sessions, too, in one of the top jazz spots in the country. **Virgin Megastore** (✉ 14–16 Oxford St., Soho W1 ☎ 020/7631–1234 Ⓤ Tottenham Court Rd.), Richard Branson's pride and joy, carries music of all kinds, books, magazines, and computer games under one roof.

China & Glass

David Mellor (✉ 4 Sloane Sq., Chelsea SW1 ☎ 020/7730–4259 Ⓤ Sloane Sq.) sells practical Dartington crystal along with more unique porcelain and pottery pieces by British craftspeople. **Divertimenti** (✉ 33–34 Marylebone High St., Regent's Park W1 ☎ 020/7935–0689 Ⓤ Oxford Circus) specializes in beautiful kitchenware and French pottery from Provence. **Summerill & Bishop** (✉ 100 Portland Rd., Notting Hill W11 ☎ 020/7221–4566 Ⓤ Notting Hill Gate), a little piece of French country, supplies French embroidered linen, Portuguese and Tuscan stoneware, and designer culinary ware. **Thomas Goode** (✉ 19 S. Audley St., Mayfair W1 ☎ 020/7499–2823 Ⓤ Bond St.) stocks vast ranges of formal china and lead crystal, including English Wedgwood and Minton, and is one of the world's top shops for these items.

Clothing

Aquascutum (✉ 100 Regent St., Soho W1 ☎ 020/7675–8200 Ⓤ Piccadilly Circus) is known for its classic raincoats but also stocks expensive garments to wear underneath, for both men and women. Styles keep up with the times but are firmly on the safe side. **Burberry** (✉ 21–23 New Bond St., Mayfair W1 ☎ 020/7839–5222 Ⓤ Piccadilly Circus ✉ 165 Regent St., Soho W1 ☎ 020/7734–4060 Ⓤ Piccadilly Circus) tries to evoke English tradition, with mahogany closets and merchandise with the trademark "Burberry Check" tartan—scarves, umbrellas, short-bread tins, and those famous raincoat linings. **Daisy & Tom** (✉ 181–183 King's Rd., Chelsea SW3 ☎ 020/7352–5000 Ⓤ Sloane Sq.) is for cool kids and smart parents. On one floor are high-fashion junior clothes (Kenzo, IKKS, and Polo), shoes aplenty (for newborns to 10-year-olds), a bookshop, and a soda fountain café. **Marks & Spencer** (✉ 458 Oxford St., Mayfair W1 ☎ 020/7935–7954 Ⓤ Marble Arch ✉ 173 Oxford St., Soho ☎ 020/7437–7722 Ⓤ Tottenham Court Rd., Oxford Circus) is a major chain that's an integral part of the British way of life—sturdy, prac-tical clothes and good materials. What it *is* renowned for is underwear; the English all buy theirs here. **Topshop** (✉ 214 Oxford St., Soho W1 ☎ 020/7636–7700 Ⓤ Oxford Circus), one of the niftiest retail fashion operations for teens and women, favors top young designers. Topman is the male version of the chain.

MENSWEAR **Favourbrook** (✉ 18 Piccadilly Arcade, St. James's W1 ☎ 020/7491–2337 Ⓤ Piccadilly Circus) tailors exquisite handmade vests, jackets, ties, and cummerbunds. **Herbert Johnson** (✉ 54 St. James's St., St. James's W1 ☎ 020/7408–1174 Ⓤ Piccadilly Circus) is one of a handful of gentle-men's hatters who still know how to construct deerstalkers, bowlers, flat caps, and panamas—and Ascot-worthy hats for women, too. **Ozwald Boateng** (✉ 9 Vigo St., Mayfair W1 ☎ 020/7437–0620 Ⓤ Piccadilly Cir-cus) is one of the modern breed of bespoke tailors not on Savile Row but on the fringe. His made-to-measure suits are sought after by rock luminaries for their shock-color linings as well as great classic cuts. **Paul Smith** (✉ 40–44 Floral St., Covent Garden WC2 ☎ 020/7379–7133 Ⓤ Covent Garden) can do the job if you don't want to look outlandish but you're bored with plain pants and sober jackets. **Turnbull & Asser** (✉ 71–72 Jermyn St., St. James's W1 ☎ 020/7808–3000 Ⓤ Piccadilly Circus) is *the* custom shirtmaker. Alas, the first order must be for a min-imum of six shirts, from about £100 each. There are less expensive, still exquisite ready-to-wear shirts, too.

WOMENSWEAR **Agnès B** (✉ 111 Fulham Rd., South Kensington SW3 ☎ 020/7225–3477 Ⓤ South Kensington) has oh-so-pretty, timeless, understated French clothing. Prices are midrange and worthy for the quality. There are branches in Marylebone High Street (W1) and Heath Street, Hamp-stead (NW3); Floral Street (WC2) has elegant men's suits. **Browns** (✉ 23–27 South Molton St. , Mayfair W1 ☎ 020/7491–7833 Ⓤ Bond St. ✉ 6C Sloane St., Knightsbridge SW1 ☎ 020/7514–0040 Ⓤ Knights-bridge), the first notable store to populate the South Molton Street pedes-trian mall, seems to sprout offshoots every time you visit. Well-established designers (Donna Karan, Romeo Gigli, Jasper Con-ran) rub shoulder pads here with younger, funkier names (Dries Van Noten, Jean Paul Gaultier, Hussein Chalayan). The July and January sales are famed. **Cath Kidston** (✉ 8 Clarendon Cross, Notting Hill W11 ☎ 020/7221–4000 Ⓤ Notting Hill Gate) translates fresh ging-hams and flower-sprig cotton prints into nightclothes, bed linens, and bath wear. There are also cozy hand-knit sweaters, skirts in flouncy wools, and a children's-wear line. **Ghost** (✉ 36 Ledbury Rd., Notting

Hill W11 ☎ 020/7229–1057 Ⓤ Notting Hill Gate) presents up-to-the-minute offerings such as willowy dresses and skirts in silks, velvets, and viscose. It's also at 14 Hinde Street (W1). **Jigsaw** (✉ 126–127 New Bond St., Mayfair W1 ☎ 020/7491–4484 Ⓤ Bond St.) wins points for its reasonably priced separates, which don't sacrifice quality for fashion and suit women in their twenties to forties. **Jimmy Choo** (✉ 169 Draycott Ave., Chelsea SW3 ☎ 020/7584–6111 Ⓤ South Kensington), the name on every supermodel's and fashion editor's feet, creates exquisite, elegant shoes; nothing is less than £100.

Koh Samui (✉ 65 Monmouth St., Covent Garden WC2 ☎ 020/7240–4280 Ⓤ Covent Garden) stocks the clothing of around 40 hot young designers. Discover the next fashion wave before *Vogue* gets there. **Laura Ashley** (✉ 256–258 Regent St., Soho W1 ☎ 020/7437–9760 Ⓤ Oxford Circus) has designs from the firm founded by the late high priestess of English traditional. **Vivienne Westwood** (✉ 6 Davies St., Mayfair W1 ☎ 020/7629–3757 Ⓤ Bond St.), one of the top British designers, produces Pompadour-punk ball gowns, Lady Hamilton vest coats, and foppish getups that still represent the apex of high-style British couture. **Zara** (✉ 118 Regent St., Soho W1 ☎ 020/7534–9500 Ⓤ Piccadilly Circus) has swept Europe. The style is young and snappy, and the prices are low. Don't expect durability—these are fun pieces, for men and kids, too.

Crafts
The Crafts Council Gallery Shop/Victoria & Albert Museum Shop (✉ Cromwell Rd., South Kensington SW7 ☎ 020/7589–5070 Ⓤ South Kensington) showcases a microcosm of British crafts—jewelry, glass, ceramics, and toys. **David Linley Furniture** (✉ 60 Pimlico Rd., Chelsea SW1 ☎ 020/7730–7300 Ⓤ Sloane Sq.) is the outpost for Viscount Linley—the only gentleman in the kingdom who can call the Queen "Auntie" and one of the finest furniture designers today. The large pieces are expensive, but small desk accessories and objets d'art are available. The **Lesley Craze Gallery** (✉ 33–35 Clerkenwell Green, Clerkenwell EC1 ☎ 020/7608–0393 Ⓤ Farringdon) carries exquisite jewelry by some 100 young British designers. The adjacent Two gallery specializes in nonprecious metals and sumptuous scarves and textiles. **London Glassblowing Workshop** (✉ 7 The Leathermarket, Weston St., South Bank SE1 ☎ 020/7403–2800 Ⓤ London Bridge) showcases glassblowers and designers who make decorative and practical pieces on-site. On weekdays you can see them at work, and buy or commission your own variation. In the Leathermarket are other craftspeople, most notably a silversmith and papermaker. **OXO Tower** (✉ Bargehouse St., South Bank SE1 ☎ 020/7401–2255 Ⓤ Southwark) holds shops and studios, open Tuesday–Sunday 11–6, that sell excellent handmade goods. At Gabriel's Wharf, a few steps farther west along the river, a collection of craftspeople sell porcelain, jewelry, clothes, and more.

Gifts
The **British Museum Company** (✉ 22 Bloomsbury St., Bloomsbury WC1 ☎ 020/7637–9449 Ⓤ Tottenham Court Rd.) carries cute gift items—Egyptian scarabs in ceramic, Rosetta stone tins, and the like. You can also buy ancient pottery pieces, and the bookshop is a mine of infor-

mation. **The Cross** (⊠ 141 Portland Rd., Notting Hill W11 ☎ 020/ 7727–6760 Ⓤ Notting Hill Gate), is big with the high-style crowd, thanks to its hedonistic, beautiful things: silk scarves, brocade bags, and jew-

★ eled baubles. **Floris** (⊠ 89 Jermyn St., St. James's W1 ☎ 020/7930–2885 Ⓤ Piccadilly Circus) is one of London's most beautiful shops, with 19th-century glass and mahogany showcases filled with swan's-down

★ powder puffs, cut-glass bottles, and faux tortoiseshell combs. **Fortnum & Mason** (⊠ 181 Piccadilly, St. James's W1 ☎ 020/7734–8040 Ⓤ Piccadilly Circus), the Queen's grocer, is, paradoxically, the most egalitarian of gift stores, with plenty of luxury foods, stamped with the gold "By Appointment" crest, for less than £5. Try the teas, preserves, tins of pâté, or turtle soup. **General Trading Company** (⊠ 2 Symons St., Sloane Sq., Chelsea SW3 ☎ 020/7730–0411 Ⓤ Sloane Sq.) "does" just about every upper-class wedding gift list, but caters also to slimmer pockets with its merchandise shipped from far shores but moored securely to English taste. **Hamleys** (⊠ 188–196 Regent St., Soho W1 ☎ 0870/333– 2455 Ⓤ Oxford Circus) has six floors of toys and games for children and adults.

Les Senteurs (⊠ 71 Elizabeth St., Belgravia SW1 ☎ 020/7730–2322 Ⓤ Sloane Sq.), an intimate, unglossy gem of a perfumery, sells little-known yet timeless fragrances, such as Creed, worn by Eugenie, wife of Emperor Napoléon III. **Lush** (⊠ 11 The Piazza, Covent Garden WC2 ☎ 020/ 7240–4570 Ⓤ Covent Garden) is crammed with fresh, very wacky, handmade cosmetics. **Penhaligon's** (⊠ 41 Wellington St., Covent Garden WC2 ☎ 020/7836–2150 Ⓤ Covent Garden), established by William Penhaligon, court barber to Queen Victoria, was perfumer to Lord Rothschild and Winston Churchill. The **Tea House** (⊠ 15A Neal St., Covent Garden WC2 ☎ 020/7240–7539 Ⓤ Covent Garden) purveys everything to do with the British national drink. Dispatch your gift list here with "teaphernalia"—strainers, trivets, infusers, and such.

Jewelry

Asprey (⊠ 168–169 New Bond St., Mayfair W1 ☎ 020/7493–6767 Ⓤ Bond St.), described as the "classiest and most luxurious shop in the

★ world," offers exquisite jewelry and gifts, both antique and modern. **Butler & Wilson** (⊠ 20 South Molton St., Mayfair W1 ☎ 020/7409–2955 Ⓤ Bond St.) has irresistible retro costume jewelry and is strong on diamanté, jet, and French gilt. You can also find nostalgic gowns here. There's another branch at 189 Fulham Road, South Kensington SW3. **Dinny Hall** (⊠ 200 Westbourne Grove, Notting Hill W11 ☎ 020/7792–3913 Ⓤ Notting Hill Gate) sells simple designs in gold and silver, including dainty gold and diamond earrings or chokers with delicate curls. There's another branch at 54 Fulham Road, SW3. **Garrard** (⊠ 24 Albemarle St., Mayfair W1 ☎ 020/7758–8520 Ⓤ Bond St.), after sharing premises with Asprey, has returned to its original site; Jade Jagger is the designer employed by the company to draw in the younger market. Garrard is the royal jeweler, in charge of the upkeep of the Crown Jewels.

Prints

Besides print stores, browse around the gallery shops, such as those at the Tate Britain and Tate Modern. In the open air, try hunting around

Waterloo Bridge along the Riverside Walk Market, at St. James's Craft Market at St. James's Church in Piccadilly, and at the Apple Market near The Piazza, Covent Garden. **Grosvenor Prints** (⊠ 28 Shelton St., Covent Garden WC2 ☎ 020/7836–1979 Ⓤ Covent Garden) sells antiquarian prints, with an emphasis on views and architecture of London—and dogs. The **Map House** (⊠ 54 Beauchamp Pl., Knightsbridge SW3 ☎ 020/ 7589–4325 Ⓤ Knightsbridge) has antique maps in all price ranges, and fine reproductions of maps and prints, especially of botanical subjects and cityscapes.

Street Markets

Bermondsey is the market the dealers frequent for small antiques, which gives you an idea of its scope. The real bargains start going at 5 AM, but there'll be a few left if you arrive later. Take Bus 15 or 25 to Aldgate, then Bus 42 over Tower Bridge to Bermondsey Square; or take the tube to London Bridge and walk. ⊠ *Tower Bridge Rd., South Bank SE1* ۞ *Fri. 5 AM–noon* Ⓤ *London Bridge.*

Borough Market, a foodie's delight, carries whole-grain, organic everything, mainly from Britain but with an international flavor. ⊠ *Borough High St., South Bank SE1* ۞ *Fri. noon–6, Sat. 9–4* Ⓤ *London Bridge, Borough.*

Camden Passage is hugged by curio stores and is dripping with jewelry, silverware, and other antiques. Saturday and Wednesday are when the stalls go up; the rest of the week, only the stores are open. Bus 19 or 38 or the tube will get you there. ⊠ *Off Upper St., Islington N1* ۞ *Wed. and Sat. 8:30–3* Ⓤ *Angel.*

Covent Garden has craft stalls, jewelry designers, clothes makers, potters, and other artisans, who congregate in the undercover central area known as the Apple Market. The Jubilee Market, toward Southampton Street, is less classy (printed T-shirts and the like), but on Monday the selection of vintage collectibles is worthwhile. ⊠ *The Piazza, Covent Garden WC2* ۞ *Daily 9–5* Ⓤ *Covent Garden.*

★ **Portobello Market,** London's most famous market, still wins the prize for the all-round best. There are 1,500 antiques dealers here, so bargains are still possible. Nearer Notting Hill Gate, prices and quality are highest; the middle is where locals buy fruit and vegetables and hang out in trendy restaurants. Under the Westway elevated highway is a great flea market, and more bric-a-brac and bargains appear as you walk toward Golborne Road. Take Bus 52 or the tube here. ⊠ *Portobello Rd., Notting Hill W11* ۞ *Fruit and vegetables Mon.–Wed. and Fri. 8–5, Thurs. 8–1; antiques Fri. 8–3; food market and antiques Sat. 6–5* Ⓤ *Ladbroke Grove, Notting Hill Gate.*

Spitalfields, an old 3-acre indoor fruit market near Petticoat Lane, has turned into Trendsville, with crafts and design shops. It also has food and clothes stalls, cafés, and performance areas. On Sunday the place comes alive, with stalls selling antique clothing, handmade rugs, and cookware. The resident stores have lovely things for body and home. For refreshment, you can eat anything from tapas to Thai. ⊠ *Brushfield St., East End E1* ⊘ *Organic market Fri. and Sun. 10–5; general market weekdays 11–3, Sun. 10–5* Ⓤ *Liverpool St., Aldgate, Aldgate East.*

LONDON A TO Z

To research prices, get advice from other travelers, and book travel arrangements, visit www.fodors.com.

ADDRESSES

Central London and its surrounding districts are divided into 32 boroughs—33, counting the City of London. More useful for finding your way around, however, are the subdivisions of London into postal districts. The first one or two letters give the location: N means north, NW means northwest, etc. You won't find W2 next to W3, but the general rule is that the lower numbers, such as W1 or SW1, are closest to the city center. Abbreviated (for general location) or full (for mailing information) postal codes are given for many listings in this chapter. Neighborhood names are also provided.

AIR TRAVEL TO & FROM LONDON

For information, *see* Air Travel *in* Smart Travel Tips.

AIRPORTS & TRANSFERS

For information about Heathrow, Gatwick, and Stansted airports, *see* Airports *in* Smart Travel Tips. Airport Travel Line has information on transfers between Heathrow and Gatwick and into London by bus. However, you may be directed to some of the numbers listed below.

From Heathrow, the least-expensive route into London is by train, via the Piccadilly line of the Underground. Trains on the tube run every four to eight minutes from all four terminals; the 50-minute trip costs £3.70 one-way and connects with London's extensive tube system. The first train departs at 5:04 AM (5:47 on Sunday), and the last at 12:31 AM (11:56 PM on Sunday). The quickest way into London is the Heathrow Express, which takes just 15 minutes to and from Paddington Station (in the city center and a main hub on the Underground). One-way tickets cost £13 for standard-express class (£25 round-trip). Daily service departs every 15 minutes, from 5:07 AM Mon.–Sat., 5:13 AM Sun., to 11:33 PM Mon.–Sat., 11:17 PM Sun.

Bus service to London is available from the Heathrow Central Bus Station. Airbus A2 costs £8 one-way, £12 round-trip; travel time is about one hour and 40 minutes. Buses leave for King's Cross and Euston, with stops at Marble Arch and Russell Square, every 30 minutes 5:30 AM–9:45 PM from Terminal 4, 5:45 AM–10:08 PM from Terminal 3, but can be tedious because there are more than a dozen stops en route. National Express buses (incorporating Jetlink service) leave every 30 minutes 5:40 AM–9:35 PM to Victoria Coach Station from Heathrow Central Bus Station—connected to arrival terminals by a pedestrian underpass, and next to Heathrow Underground Station for Terminals 1–3: cost is £7 one-way.

From Gatwick, the fast, nonstop Gatwick Express train has frequent departures to Victoria Station. From 5:20 AM to 6:05 AM trains leave every 20 minutes, then at 5, 20, 35 and 50 minutes past the hour, until the last departure at 1:35 AM. The 30-minute trip costs £11 one-way, £21.50 round-trip. A frequent local train also runs all night. National Express Jetlink bus services from North and South terminals do not go to London, but to many other major cities, such as Bristol, Cambridge, and Oxford.

Stansted serves mainly European destinations. The Stansted Express train to Liverpool Street station costs £13 one-way, £21 round-trip; travel time is about 40 minutes. From 5:20 AM to 6:05 AM trains leave every 30 minutes, then every 15 minutes until 12:50 AM, with the last departure at 1:35 AM. Sunday times are delayed due to track repairs; call for details. To get from Liverpool Street to London Victoria at night when the Tube is closed, take the A7 National Express bus, which departs every 30 minutes from midnight to 4:30 AM. Airbus 6, by National Express, runs cheaper bus services to Victoria Coach Station, departing every 20 minutes; the cost is £8 one-way, £10 round-trip, and travel time is about an hour and 40 minutes.

If you are thinking of taking a taxi from Heathrow and Gatwick, remember that they can get caught in traffic; the trip from Heathrow, for example, can take more than an hour and costs about £35. From Gatwick, the taxi fare is about £75; the ride takes about an hour and 20 minutes. From Stansted, the £75 journey takes a little over an hour. Your hotel may be able to recommend a car service for airport transfers. Charges are usually about £35 to any of the airports. Add a tip of 10% to 15% to the basic fare.

You can get discounts on many tickets if you book on the Internet. The Web site for British Airports Authority has links to all the previously mentioned services, with fare details and timetables.

🚌 Taxis & Shuttles **Airbus A2** ☎ 0870/574-7777. **Airport Travel Line** ☎ 0870/574-7777. **British Airports Authority** ⊕ www.baa.co.uk. **Gatwick Express** ☎ 0870/530-1530 ⊕ www.gatwickexpress.co.uk. **Heathrow Express** ☎ 0845/600-1515 ⊕ www.heathrowexpress.co.uk. **National Express** ☎ 0870/580-8080, Airbus from Stansted, 0870/574-7777 ⊕ www.nationalexpress.com. **Stansted Express** ☎ 0845/850-0150 ⊕ www.stanstedexpress.co.uk. **Transport for London** ☎ 020/7222-1234 ⊕ www.tube.tfl.gov.uk.

BUS TRAVEL TO & FROM LONDON

Buses, or "coaches," as long-distance services are known, operate mainly from London's Victoria Coach Station to more than 1,200 major towns and cities. Buses are about half as expensive as the train, but trips can take twice as long. For information, *see* Bus Travel *in* Smart Travel Tips.

BUS TRAVEL WITHIN LONDON

In central London, Transport for London (TfL) buses are traditionally bright red double- and single-deckers, although there are now many privately owned buses of different colors. Not all buses run the full length of their route at all times, so check with the driver or conductor. On some buses you pay after finding a seat; on others you pay upon boarding. Increasingly, in central London, and on Bendy buses, which have three doors, you purchase tickets from machines at bus stops along the routes before you board. Bus stops are clearly indicated: the main stops have a red TfL symbol on a white background. When the word REQUEST is written across the sign, you must flag the bus down. Buses are a good way to see the town, but don't take one if you're in a hurry. Single fares start at 65p for short hops in the central zone.

London is divided into six concentric zones for both bus and tube fares: the more zones you cross, the higher the fare. A new flat-rate fare now applies for adults (£1) and children (40p). A Bus Saver book of single bus tickets bought in advance reduces this to 70p and 35p per trip. A One-Day Bus Pass for zones one through four is a good deal at £2.50 (a seven-day pass is £9.50) but must be bought before boarding the bus, from one of the machines at bus stops, most newsagents, or underground stations. Off-peak Day Travelcards (£4.70) allow unrestricted travel on bus *and* tube after 9:30 AM and all day on weekends and national holidays (except on N-prefixed Night Buses). Day Travelcards (peak) are more expensive (£7.30). Other options are Weekend Travelcards, for Saturday and Sunday or on any two consecutive days during public holidays (£7); Family Travelcards, which are one-day tickets for one or two adults with one to four children (£3.10 per adult, with one child; additional children cost 80p each—kids travel free on weekends and public holidays); or the Carnet, a book of 10 single Underground tickets valid for central Zone 1 (£15) to use anytime over a year—a savings of £5. Visitor Travelcards are similar to Day Travelcards but with the bonus of a booklet of money-off vouchers to major attractions (available only in the United States, for three, four, and seven days). Visitor Travelcards are available from BritRail or Rail Europe.

Traveling without a valid ticket makes you liable for an on-the-spot fine (£10 at the time of this writing), so always pay your fare before you travel. For more information, there are Transport for London Travel Information Centres at the following tube stations: Euston, Liverpool Street, Piccadilly Circus, Victoria, and Heathrow (in Terminals 1, 2, 3, and 4). Most are open in daytime only; call for hours.

Night Buses can prove helpful when traveling in London from 11 PM to 5 AM—these buses add the prefix "N" to their route numbers and don't run as frequently or operate on quite as many routes as day buses. You may have to transfer at one of the Night Bus nexuses: Victoria, Westminster, and either Piccadilly Circus or Trafalgar Square. For safety reasons, avoid sitting alone on the top deck of a Night Bus.

FARES &
SCHEDULES
BritRail ☎ 877/677-1066 ⊕ www.britrail.net. **Rail Europe** ☎ 888/274-8724 ⊕ www.raileurope.com. **Transport for London** ☎ 020/7222-1234 ⊕ www.tfl.gov.uk.

CAR TRAVEL

The major approach roads to London are motorways (six-lane highways; look for an "M" followed by a number) or "A" roads; the latter may be "dual carriageways" (divided highways), or two-lane highways. Motorways (from Heathrow, M4; from Gatwick, M23 to M25, then M3;

Stansted, M11) are usually the faster option for getting in and out of town, although rush-hour traffic is horrendous. Stay tuned to local radio stations for regular traffic updates.

The simple advice about driving in London is: don't. Because the city grew as a series of villages, there was never a central street plan, and the result is a chaotic winding mass, made no easier by the one-way street systems. If you must drive in London, remember to drive on the left and stick to the speed limit (30 mph on most city streets).

A £5 "congestion charge" is levied on all vehicles entering central London (bounded by the Inner Ring Road; street signs and "C" road markings note the area) on weekdays from 7 AM to 6:30 PM, excluding bank holidays. Pay in advance or on that day until 10 PM if you're entering the central zone. You can pay by phone, mail, or Internet, or at retail outlets (look for signs indicating how and where you can pay). There are no tollbooths; cameras monitor the area. The penalty for not paying is stiff: £80 (£40 for prompt payment). For current information, check ⊕ www.cclondon.com.

DISCOUNTS & DEALS
All national collections (such as the Natural History Museum, Science Museum, Victoria & Albert Museum) are free, a real bargain for museum goers. The London Pass, a smart card, offers entry to more than 50 top attractions, such as museums and tours on boats and buses. The charge is £23 for one day, which can be reduced to £12 per day if a weekly pass is bought. There are optional discounts on travel and restaurants for a higher daily charge. London Pass is available by phone, online, or from the Britain Visitor Centre and Tourist Information Centre branches. For other discounts, *see* Discounts & Deals *in* Smart Travel Tips.
🖪 **London Pass** ☎ 0870/242-9988 ⊕ www.londonpass.com.

EMBASSIES
For information, *see* Embassies *in* Smart Travel Tips.

EMERGENCIES
For hospitals in different areas of London that provide free 24-hour accident and emergency facilities, the following are listed: in the west of London is Charing Cross Hospital; in the city center is University College Hospital; to the north of the center is the Royal Free Hospital; and on the south bank of the city center is St. Thomas's Hospital. Bliss Chemist is open daily 9 AM–midnight. NHS Direct offers 24-hour general expert medical advice from the National Health Service. In addition, many mainstreet branches of Boots, a pharmacy chain, stay open late in rotation.
🖪 **Emergency Services** Ambulance, fire, police ☎ 999. **NHS Direct** ☎ 0845/4647.
🖪 **Hospitals** Charing Cross Hospital ⊠ Fulham Palace Rd., Hammersmith W6 ☎ 020/8846-1234. **Royal Free Hospital** ⊠ Pond St., Hampstead Hampstead, NW3 ☎ 020/7794-0500. **St. Thomas's Hospital** ⊠ Lambeth Palace Rd., South Bank SE1 ☎ 020/7928-9292. **University College Hospital** ⊠ Grafton Way, Bloomsbury WC1 ☎ 020/7387-9300.
🖪 **Late-night Pharmacies** Bliss Chemist ⊠ 5 Marble Arch, Bayswater W1 ☎ 020/7723-6116.

LODGING

Bed-and-breakfasts (rooms in private homes) or apartment rentals may
be an economical choice for your stay. A number of agencies offer
rooms and apartments in different neighborhoods. You can check out
many of the properties online before you book. Of the firms listed
below, the Bulldog Club and Uptown Reservations offer tonier accommodations; London B&B also represents some fancier homes; Primrose
Hill B&B is committed to affordable lodgings. For other suggestions,
see Lodging *in* Smart Travel Tips.

🚹 **Reservation Services Bulldog Club** ✉ 14 Dewhurst Rd., West Kensington W14 0ET
☎ 020/7371-3202 🖨 020/7371-2015 ⊕ www.bulldogclub.com. **London B&B** 🖅 Box
124859, San Diego, CA 92112 ☎ 800/872-2632 ⊕ www.londonbb.com. **Primrose Hill
B&B** ✉ 14 Edis St., Primrose Hill NW1 8LG ☎ 020/7722-6869. **Uptown Reservations**
✉ 41 Paradise Walk, Chelsea SW3 4JL ☎ 020/7351-3445 🖨 020/7351-9383.

TAXIS

Taxis are expensive, but if you're with several people, they can be a practical option. Hotels and main tourist areas have taxi ranks; you can also
hail taxis on the street. If the yellow FOR HIRE sign is lighted on top, the
taxi is available. Drivers often cruise at night with their signs unlighted,
so if you see an unlighted cab, keep your hand up. The fare structure is
both expensive and complicated, but generally fares start at £2 and increase by units of 20p (per 125–191 yards or 24.5–37.6 seconds) after a
certain initial distance, which ranges from about 250 yards (late nights)
to 381 yards (6 AM–8 PM on weekdays). Surcharges are added around Christmas and New Year's days. Tips are extra, usually 10%–15% per ride.

TOURS

In summer, narrow boats and barges cruise London's two canals, the
Grand Union and Regent's Canal. Most vessels operate on the latter,
which runs between Little Venice in the west (the nearest tube is Warwick Avenue on the Bakerloo Line) and Camden Lock (about 200 yards
north of Camden Town tube station). Jason's Trip operates one-way and
round-trip narrow-boat cruises on this route. The London Waterbus Company operates this route year-round with a stop at London Zoo: trips
run daily April–October and weekends only November–March. Canal
Cruises offers three or four cruises daily March–October on the *Jenny
Wren* and all year on the cruising restaurant *My Fair Lady* from Walker's
Quay, Camden.

Boats cruise the Thames throughout the year. Most leave from Westminster Pier, Charing Cross Pier, and Tower Pier. Downstream routes
go to the Tower of London, Greenwich, and the Thames Barrier; upstream destinations include Kew, Richmond, and Hampton Court. Depending on the destination, river trips may last from 30 minutes to four
hours. For trips downriver from Charing Cross to Greenwich Pier and
historic Greenwich, call Catamaran Cruisers or Westminster Passenger
Services (which runs the same route from Westminster Pier). Thames
Cruises goes to Greenwich and onward to the Thames Barrier. Westminster Passenger Service (Upriver) runs through summer to Kew and
Hampton Court from Westminster Pier. A Rail and River Rover ticket
combines the modern wonders of Canary Wharf and Docklands devel-

opment by Docklands Light Railway with the historic riverside by boat. Tickets are available year-round from Westminster, Tower, and Greenwich piers, and Dockland Light Railway stations. Transport for London (⇨ Bus Travel) should be able to give information on all companies.

🚤 **Canal Cruises** ☎ 020/7485-4433 ⊕ www.walkersquay.com. **Catamaran Cruisers** ☎ 020/7987-1185 ⊕ www.catamarancruisers.co.uk. **Jason's Trip** ☎ 020/7286-3428 ⊕ www.jasons.co.uk. **Rail and River Rover** ☎ 020/7363-9700 ⊕ www.tfl.gov.uk. **Thames Cruises** ☎ 020/7930-3373. **Westminster Passenger Services** ☎ 020/7930-4097. **Westminster Passenger Service (Upriver)** ☎ 020/7930-2062 ⊕ www.wpsa.co.uk.

BUS TOURS   Guided sightseeing tours provide a good introduction to the city from double-decker buses, which are open-topped in summer. Tours run daily and depart from Haymarket, Baker Street, Grosvenor Gardens, Marble Arch, and Victoria. You may board or alight at any of about 21 stops to view the sights, and then get back on the next bus. Tickets (£12) may be bought from the driver; several companies run tours. The Original London Sightseeing Tour also offers frequent daily tours and has informative staff on easily recognizable double-decker buses. Tours depart from 8:30 AM from Baker Street (Madame Tussaud's), Marble Arch (Speakers' Corner), Piccadilly (Haymarket), or Victoria (Victoria Street) around every 12 minutes (less often outside peak summer season). The Big Bus Company runs a similar operation with a Red and Blue tour. The Red is a two-hour tour with 18 stops, and the Blue, one hour with 13. Both start from Marble Arch, Speakers' Corner. Evan Evans offers good bus tours that also visit major sights just outside the city. Another reputable agency for bus tours is Frames Rickards.

Green Line, Evan Evans, and Frames Rickards offer day excursions by bus to places within easy reach of London, such as Hampton Court, Oxford, Stratford, and Bath.

🚌 **Big Bus Company** ☎ 020/7233-9533 ⊕ www.bigbustours.com. **Evan Evans** ☎ 020/7950-1777 ⊕ www.evanevans.co.uk. **Frames Rickards** ☎ 020/7837-3111, 800/992-7700 in U.S. ⊕ www.goldentours.co.uk. **Green Line** ☎ 0870/608-7261 ⊕ www.greenline.co.uk. **Original London Sightseeing Tour** ☎ 020/8877-1722 ⊕ www.theoriginaltour.com.

PRIVATE GUIDES   Black Taxi Tour of London is a personal tour by cab direct from your hotel. The price is per cab, so the fare can be shared among as many as five people. An introductory two-hour tour is £75 by day, £85 by night. You can hire a Blue Badge accredited guide for walking or driving tours.

🚖 **Black Taxi Tour of London** ☎ 020/7935-9363 ⊕ www.blacktaxitours.co.uk. **Blue Badge** ☎ 020/7495-5504 ⊕ www.blue-badge.org.uk.

WALKING TOURS   One of the best ways to get to know London is on foot. Original London Walks has theme tours devoted to the Beatles, Sherlock Holmes, Dickens, Jack the Ripper—you name it. If horror and mystery are your interest, then the City holds plenty of that, as you may discover on a Blood and Tears tour (not suitable for younger children). Tour Guides provides themed historic walks led by accredited Blue Badge guides. Peruse the leaflets at a London Tourist Information Centre for special-interest walks.

🚶 **Blood and Tears Walk** ☎ 020/8348-9022. **Original London Walks** ☎ 020/7624-3978 ⊕ www.walks.com. **Tour Guides** ☎ 020/7495-5504 ⊕ www.tourguides.co.uk.

TRAIN TRAVEL

London has 15 major train stations, each serving a different area of the country, all accessible by Underground or bus. The once-national British Rail is now private companies, under National Rail, but there is a central rail information number. For further information on train travel, *see* Train Travel *in* Smart Travel Tips.

🚹 **National Rail Enquiries** ☎ 0845/748-4950 ⊕ www.nationalrail.co.uk.

TRAVEL AGENCIES

🚹 **Local Agent Referrals American Express** ⊠ 30-31 Haymarket, St. James's SW1 ☎ 020/7484-9600 ⊠ 89 Mount St., Mayfair W1 ☎ 020/7659-0701. **Thomas Cook** ⊠ 1 Woburn Pl., Bloomsbury WC1 ☎ 020/7837-0393 ⊠ 184 Kensington High St., Kensington W8 ☎ 020/7707-2300.

UNDERGROUND TUBE TRAVEL

London's extensive Underground (tube) system has color-coded routes, clear signage, and extensive connections. Trains run out into the suburbs, and all stations are marked with the London Underground circular symbol. (In Britain, the word "subway" means "pedestrian underpass.") Trains are all one class; smoking is *not* allowed on board or in the stations. Some lines have branches (Central, District, Northern, Metropolitan, and Piccadilly), so be sure to note which branch is needed for your destination. Electronic platform signs tell you the final stop and route of the next train and how many minutes until it arrives. The zippy Docklands Light Railway runs through the Docklands with an extension to Greenwich.

FARES & London is divided into six concentric zones (ask at Underground ticket
SCHEDULES booths for a map and booklet, which give details of the ticket options), so make sure to buy a ticket for the correct zone or you may be liable for an on-the-spot fine (£10 at the time of this writing). You can buy a single or return ticket, the equivalent of a one-way and a round-trip, for travel anytime on the day of issue. Singles vary in price from £2 to £2.50. For information, including discount passes for bus and tube travel, *see* Bus Travel Within London.

Trains begin running just after 5 AM Monday–Saturday; the last services leave central London between midnight and 12:30 AM. On Sunday, trains start two hours later and finish about an hour earlier. Frequency of trains depends on the route and the time of day, but normally you should not have to wait more than 10 minutes in central areas. Travelers with disabilities should get the free leaflet "Access to the Underground."

🚹 **Transport for London** ☎ 020/7222-1234 ⊕ www.tfl.gov.uk.

VISITOR INFORMATION

The main London Tourist Information Centre at Victoria Station Forecourt is open in summer, Monday–Saturday 8–7 and Sunday 8–5; winter, Monday–Saturday 8–6 and Sunday 8:30–4; also at Heathrow Airport (Terminals 1, 2, and 3). Britain and London Visitor Centre, open weekdays 9:30–6:30, weekends 10–4, provides details about travel, accommodations, and entertainment for the whole of Britain, but you need to visit the center in person to get information. London Line is VisitLondon's 24-hour phone service—it's a premium-rate (60p per minute at all times) recorded information line, with different numbers for theater, events, museums, sports, getting around, and so on. VisitLondon, the city's tourist board, also has a helpful Web site with links to other sites.

🚩 **Britain and London Visitor Centre** ✉ 1 Regent St., Piccadilly Circus, St. James's SW1Y 4NX ☎ No phone ⊕ www.visitbritain.com. **London Line** ☎ 09068/663344 at 60p per minute. **London Tourist Information Centre** ✉ Victoria Station Forecourt, Victoria ☎ No phone. **VisitLondon** ⊕ www.visitlondon.com.

THE SOUTHEAST
CANTERBURY, DOVER, BRIGHTON, TUNBRIDGE WELLS

2

FEEL THE BREEZE ON YOUR FACE
by Dover's famous White Cliffs ⇨*p.125*

STOP AND SMELL THE ROSES
at Sissinghurst Castle Garden ⇨*p.154*

PONDER ENGLISH HISTORY IN STONE
at Canterbury Cathedral ⇨*p.115*

STEP INTO A SEASIDE XANADU
at Brighton's Royal Pavilion ⇨*p.135*

TRAWL FOR POTTERY TREASURES
along Rye's cobbled streets ⇨*p.126*

MAKE TIME STAND STILL
at medieval Ightham Mote ⇨*p.153*

GIVE A GREEN THUMB'S-UP
to the garden masters at Wisley ⇨*p.144*

HAVE A DICKENS OF A TIME
in Broadstairs ⇨*p.124*

Updated by
Julius Honnor

IN AN ERA WHEN EVERYTHING SMALL IS FASHIONABLE, from cell phones to digital cameras, the Southeast will inevitably have great appeal. Where ancient hedgerows have been allowed to stand, this is still a landscape of small-scale features and pleasant hills. Viewed from the air, the tiny fields, neatly hedged, form a patchwork quilt. On the ground, once away from the motorways and London commuter tract housing, the Southeast, including Surrey, Kent, and Sussex, East and West, reveals some of England's loveliest countryside. Gentle hills and woodlands are punctuated with farms and storybook villages rooted in history and with cathedral cities waiting to be explored. Rivers wind down to a coast that is alternately sweeping chalk cliff and seaside resort. This area, farthest from the unpredictable influences of the Atlantic, is England at its warmest. Fruit trees and even vineyards flourish in archetypal English landscapes and, often, atypical English sunshine.

Although it is one of the most densely populated areas of Britain because of its proximity to London, the Southeast includes Kent, the "Garden of England." Fields of hops and acre upon acre of orchards burst into a mass of pink and white blossoms in spring and stretch away into the distance, though even here large-scale modern farming has done much to homogenize the landscape. In the Southeast, too, are ancient Canterbury, site of the mother cathedral of England, and Dover, whose chalky white cliffs and brooding castle have become symbols of Britain. Medieval castles and a trove of superb stately homes, such as Petworth House and Knole, are found throughout the region.

Famous seaside towns and resorts dot the coasts of Sussex and Kent, the most famous being that eccentric combination of carnival and culture, Brighton, site of 19th-century England's own Xanadu, the Royal Pavilion. Also on the coast, the busy ports of Newhaven, Folkestone, Dover, and Ramsgate have served for centuries as gateways to continental Europe. The Channel Tunnel, linking Britain to France by rail, runs from near Folkestone.

Indeed, because the English Channel is at its narrowest here, a great deal of British history has been forged in the Southeast. The Romans landed in this area and stayed to rule Britain for four centuries. So did the Saxons—Sussex means "the land of the South Saxons." William ("the Conqueror") of Normandy defeated the Saxons at a battle near Hastings in 1066. Canterbury has been the seat of the Primate of All England, the Archbishop of Canterbury, since Pope Gregory the Great dispatched St. Augustine to convert the heathen hordes of Britain in 597. And long before any of these invaders, the ancient Britons blazed trails that formed the routes for today's modern highways.

Exploring the Southeast

For sightseeing purposes, the Southeast can be divided into four sections. The eastern part of the region takes in the cathedral town of Canterbury, in the heart of Kent, as well as Dover, England's Continental gateway, to the south. Another area is part of the southern coast, from Rye in the east to Lewes in the west, including historic seaside towns along the way. A third area begins in the coastal resort of Brighton and takes in Chichester, in West Sussex, and then swings north into Surrey, taking in Guildford and East Grinstead. The fourth region takes in the spa town of Royal Tunbridge Wells and western Kent, with its rich collection of stately homes, castles, and historic landmarks. Many towns can be reached by public transportation from London for a day trip. Buses, trains, and occasionally even steam trains service most major sights. To visit stately homes or quiet villages, it's wiser to rent a car.

About the Restaurants

If you're in a seaside town, look for that great British staple, fish-and-chips. Perhaps "look" isn't the word—just follow your nose. In all the coastal areas, seafood, much of it locally caught, is a specialty. You'll discover local dishes such as Sussex smokies (smoked mackerel) and some of the most succulent oysters in Britain. English vineyards, mostly in Surrey, Sussex and Kent, have seen boom years, boosted by an apparent change in climate, and sparkling wines have been some of the most successful. Look for local white wines on menus.

About the Hotels

All around the coast, resort towns stretch along beaches, their hotels standing cheek by jowl. Of the smaller hotels and guest houses, only a few remain open year-round; most do business only from mid-April to September or October. Some hotels have all-inclusive rates for a week's stay, which is cheaper than taking room and meals by the day. Prices rise in July and August, when the seaside resorts can get solidly booked, especially Brighton, a popular conference center. Places in Brighton may not take a booking for a single night in summer or on weekends.

WHAT IT COSTS In pounds				
	££££響	££££	£££	££	£
RESTAURANTS	over £22	£18–£22	£13–£17	£7–£12	under £7
HOTELS	over £160	£120–£160	£90–£120	£60–£90	under £60

Restaurant prices are for a main course at dinner. Hotel prices are for two people in a standard double room in high season, including VAT, with no meals or, if indicated, CP (with Continental breakfast), BP (Breakfast Plan, with full breakfast), or MAP (Modified American Plan, with breakfast and dinner).

Timing

Because the counties of Kent, Surrey, and Sussex offer some of the most scenic landscapes in southern England, lovers of the open air will want to get their fill of the many outdoor attractions here. Most of the privately owned castles and mansions are open only between April and September or October, so it's best to tour the Southeast in the spring, summer, or early fall. Failing that, however, the great parks surrounding the stately houses are often open all year. In Canterbury and in the seaside towns, avoid August, Sunday, and national holidays if you don't like crowds.

The relatively compact Southeast is densely packed with points of interest. Most of the essential sights are contained in and around the towns, whereas the rustic attractions such as castles, country homes, and gardens invite a more leisurely appreciation. Note that your own transportation is essential for some. You could spend several weeks here and still have more to see, but if you have only three days, confine your travels to one or two specific areas. A visit of seven days or so will allow you to explore a number of highlights as well as some of the Southeast's better-kept secrets.

2

Numbers in the text correspond to numbers in the margin and on the Southeast, Canterbury, and Brighton maps.

If you have
3 days

You could opt for the glories of historic 🏛 **Canterbury** ❶–❸ 🚩 as a first choice. Stay one night here, making a cathedral visit your priority, and spend any extra time meandering through the old streets, taking in the city's secondary sights. For your next two nights, pencil in 🏛 **Brighton** ㉚–㉛, where the Royal Pavilion is a must on any itinerary. Keeping Brighton as your base, you could spend a third day exploring **Lewes** ㉙, with its castle in a commanding position over the town and Tudor timber-frame buildings scattered along its steep lanes. Or, if you're lucky enough, you might attend a performance at the nearby Glyndebourne Opera House.

If you have
7 days

Your first two nights will be spent in the ancient city of 🏛 **Canterbury** ❶–❸ 🚩. If you're traveling east from London, stop en route and spend half a day at the dockyards at Chatham and the castle and cathedral at neighboring **Rochester** ㉟, both of which should be a great hit with children. In the morning, explore the cathedral and other sights in Canterbury, reserving the afternoon for a foray to the coast, tracing it down from **Broadstairs** ⓲, with its Dickensian associations, to **Dover** ㉒. On your third morning, head back west, veering south near Maidstone for **Leeds Castle** ㊱, whose lovely grounds vie for your attention with the castle's treasures. Farther south, **Sissinghurst Castle Garden** ㊲ is likely to convert even those who have never lifted a trowel. Overnight in 🏛 **Rye** ㉓; take in nearby **Winchelsea** ㉔ the next day; then continue west to the site of the Battle of Hastings at **Battle** ㉖, where the remains of an abbey founded by William the Conqueror mark one of the most momentous events in English history. **Hastings** ㉕ is a typical south-coast town, but Herstmonceux, 12 mi farther west, has beautiful **Herstmonceux Castle** ㉗. From here, head to 🏛 **Brighton** ㉚–㉛, which deserves a two-night stay. After a morning of ambling around the promenades of this bustling seaside town and shopping in the Lanes and North Laine area, visit nearby **Lewes** ㉙, where some advance planning may get you seats at the Glyndebourne Opera for an evening treat.

Proceeding west along the coast on your sixth morning, take in 🏛 **Arundel** ㊳ and 🏛 **Chichester** ㊴, either of which would make a wonderful place to spend the night. Arundel is dominated by Arundel Castle, whereas Chichester has a Norman cathedral in town and a Roman villa outside. For your last day, you can opt to travel north and toward London, which will bring you through 🏛 **Guildford** ㊹, a commuter town with some 18th-century remnants and, east of here, a graceful Italianate palace, **Clandon Park** 🏷. An alternative is to drive northeast back into Kent, where you can choose among the magnificent historic houses around 🅃 **Royal Tunbridge Wells** 🏷. Some of the most stirring are the medieval manor house **Penshurst Place** 🏷; **Hever Castle** 🏷, associated with two famous families, the Boleyns of the Tudor era and the Astors of the 20th century; medieval **Ightham Mote** 🏷; and **Chartwell** 🏷, home of Sir Winston Churchill for more than 40 years.

CANTERBURY TO DOVER

The ancient city of Canterbury, worldwide seat of the Church of England, shrine of Thomas à Becket, and immortalized in Geoffrey Chaucer's *Canterbury Tales,* is a prime historic center. Even in prehistoric times, this part of England was relatively well settled. Saxon settlers, Norman conquerors, and the folk who lived here in late-medieval times all left their mark—most notably in the city's magnificent cathedral, the Mother Church of England. You can make endless excursions through the countryside between Canterbury and the busy port of Dover. Here, the Kentish landscape ravishes the eye in the spring with apple blossoms. It is a county of orchards, market gardens, and round, red-roof oasthouses, used for drying hops.

Canterbury

▶ *56 mi southeast of London.*

For many people, Geoffrey Chaucer's *Canterbury Tales,* about a pilgrimage to Canterbury Cathedral, brings back memories of sleepy high school English classes. Judging from the tales, however, medieval Canterbury was as much a party for people on horses as it was a spiritual center. The height of Canterbury's popularity came in the 12th century, when thousands of pilgrims flocked here to see the shrine of the murdered Archbishop St. Thomas à Becket, making this southeastern town one of the most visited in England, if not Europe. Buildings that served as pilgrims' inns still dominate the streets of Canterbury's center.

There is evidence of prosperous society in the Canterbury area as early as the Bronze Age (around 1000 BC). An important Roman city, an Anglo-Saxon center in the Kingdom of Kent, and currently headquarters of the Anglican Church, Canterbury remains a lively place, a fact that has impressed visitors since 1388, when Chaucer wrote his stories. Today, most pilgrims come in search of history and picture-perfect moments rather than spiritual enlightenment, and magnificently medieval Canterbury, with its ancient city walls, leaning Tudor buildings, and remnants of its Roman past, obliges. The absence of cars in the center brings some tranquillity to its streets, but to see Canterbury at its best, walk around early, before the tourist buses arrive, or wait until after they depart.

Canterbury is bisected by a road running northwest, beside which lie all the major tourist sites. This road, which crosses a branch of the River

Stour in the city, begins as St. George's Street, becomes High Street, and finally turns into St. Peter's Street. On St. George's Street a lone church

❶ tower marks the site of **St. George's Church**—the rest of the building was destroyed in World War II—where playwright Christopher Marlowe was baptized in 1564.

❷ The **Canterbury Roman Museum**, including its colorful mosaic Roman pavement and a hypocaust (the Roman version of central heating), is below ground, at the level of the Roman town. Displays of excavated objects (some of which you can hold in the Touch the Past area) and computer-generated reconstructions of Roman buildings and the marketplace help re-create the past. ⊠ *Butchery La.* ☎ *01227/785575* ⊕ *www.canterbury-museums.co.uk* 🖃 *£2.80* ⊙ *June–Oct., Mon.–Sat. 10–5, Sun. 1:30–5; Nov.–May, Mon.–Sat. 10–5; last admission at 4. Closed last wk in Dec.*

❸ Mercery Lane, with its medieval-style cottages and massive, overhanging timber roofs, runs right off High Street and ends in the tiny **Butter-market**, an old dairy market square that was known in the 15th century as the Bullstake: animals were tied here for baiting before slaughter.

❹ The immense **Christchurch Gate**, built in 1517, leads into the cathedral close. As you pass through, look up at the sculpted heads of two young figures: Prince Arthur, elder brother of Henry VIII, and the young Catherine of Aragon, to whom Arthur was betrothed. After Arthur's death, Catherine married Henry. Her failure to produce a male heir after 25 years of marriage led to Henry's decision to divorce her, creating an irrevocable breach with the Roman Catholic Church and altering the course of English history.

★ ❺ **Canterbury Cathedral**, the focal point of the city, was the first of England's great Norman cathedrals. Nucleus of worldwide Anglicanism, the Cathedral Church of Christ Canterbury (its formal name) is a living textbook of medieval architecture. The building was begun in 1070, demolished, begun anew in 1096, and then systematically expanded over the next three centuries. When the original choir section burned to the ground in 1174, another replaced it, designed in the Gothic style, with tall, pointed arches. The North Choir aisle holds two windows that show Jesus in the Temple, the three kings asleep, and Lot's wife turned to a pillar of salt. The windows are among the earliest parts of the cathedral, but only 33 of the original 208 survive.

The cathedral was only a century old, and still relatively small, when Thomas à Becket, the archbishop of Canterbury, was murdered here in 1170. Becket, an uncompromising defender of ecclesiastical interests, had angered his friend Henry II, who was heard to exclaim, "Who will rid me of this troublesome priest?" Thinking they were carrying out the king's wishes, four knights burst in on Becket in one of the side chapels and killed him. Two years later Becket was canonized, and Henry II's subsequent submission to the authority of the Church and his penitence helped establish the cathedral as the undisputed center of English Christianity. Becket's tomb, destroyed by Henry VIII in 1538 as part of his campaign to reduce the power of the Church and confiscate its treasures, was one of the most extravagant shrines in Christendom. In **Trinity Chapel**, which held the shrine, you can still see a series of 13th-century stained-glass windows illustrating Becket's miracles. So hallowed was this spot that in 1376, Edward, the Black Prince, warrior son of Edward III and a national hero, was buried near it. The actual site of Becket's murder is down a flight of steps just to the left of the nave. In the corner, a second flight of steps leads down to the enormous Norman **undercroft**, or vaulted cellarage, built in the early 12th century. A row of squat pillars whose capitals dance with fantastic animals and strange monsters supports the roof.

If time permits, be sure to explore the **cloisters** and other small monastic buildings to the north of the cathedral. The 12th-century octagonal water tower is still part of the cathedral's water supply. The Norman staircase in the northwest corner of the Green Court dates from 1167 and is a unique example of the domestic architecture of the times. The cathedral is very popular, so arrive early or late in the day to avoid the worst crowds. ⊠ *Cathedral Precincts* ☎ *01227/762862* ⊕ *www.canterbury-cathedral.org* ☐ *£4.50, free for services and ½ hr before closing* ☉ *Easter–Sept., Mon.–Sat. 9–6:30, Sun. 12:30–2:30 and 4:30–5:30; Oct.–Easter, Mon.–Sat. 9–5, Sun. 12:30–2:30 and 4:30–5:30. Restricted access during services.*

need a break?   **The Custard Tart** (⊠ 35A St. Margaret's St. ☎ 01227/785178), a short walk from the cathedral, serves a great selection of freshly made sandwiches, pies, tarts, and cakes. You can take your choice upstairs to the seating area. It's not open for dinner.

❻ To vivify some of Canterbury's history, spend some time at an exhibition called **The Canterbury Tales,** an audiovisual (and occasionally olfactory) dramatization of 14th-century English life. You'll "meet" Chaucer's pilgrims at the Tabard Inn near London and view tableaus illustrating five tales. Don't be surprised if one of the figures comes to life: an actor in period costume often performs a charade as part of the scene. ⊠ *St. Margaret's St.* ☎ *01227/479227* ⊕ *www.canterburytales.org.uk* ☐ *£6.95* ☉ *Nov.–Feb., daily 10–4:30; Mar.–June, Sept. and Oct, daily 10–5; July–Aug., daily 9:30–5.*

❼ Huguenot weavers who settled here after fleeing from religious persecution in France occupied the 16th-century **Weavers' Houses,** a lopsided group of half-timber buildings. The houses are just past where St. Peter's **❽** Street crosses a branch of the River Stour. The 12th-century **Eastbridge Hospital of St. Thomas** (which would now be called a hostel) lodged pilgrims who came to pray at the tomb of Thomas à Becket. The refectory, the chapel, and the crypt are open to the public. ⊠ *25 High St.* ☎ *01227/462395* ⊕ *www.eastbridgehospital.org.uk* ☐ *£1* ☉ *Mon.–Sat. 10–5; last admission at 4:30.*

★ ❾ The medieval Poor Priests' Hospital is the site of the **Museum of Canterbury** (previously the Canterbury Heritage Museum). The exhibits provide an excellent overview of the city's history and architecture from Roman times to World War II, as well as special features on Bagpuss, the Blitz, Rupert Bear, and the mysterious death of Christopher Marlowe. Visit early in the day to avoid the crowds. ⊠ *20 Stour St.* ☎ *01227/ 452747* ⊕ *www.canterbury-museums.co.uk* ☐ *£3.10* ☉ *Jan.–May,*

Stately Homes & Castles

Britain has a rich heritage of stately homes scattered all over the nation, but this region has one of the greatest concentrations. To select the superlatives: Petworth House holds remarkable art; Chartwell was home and is permanent memorial to Sir Winston Churchill; Hever Castle was the abode of Henry VIII's second wife, Anne Boleyn, and was restored in the last century by William Waldorf Astor; Ightham Mote is perhaps the most enchanting medieval house in all Europe; Knole, one of the largest houses in Europe, is built around seven romantic courtyards; Leeds Castle, pretty as a picture, stands in the middle of a lake; Penshurst Place, dating from 1340, was once the home of poet Sir Philip Sidney, whose descendants still live there; and Sissinghurst Castle Garden won renown through the horticultural vision of author Vita Sackville-West.

Walking

Long sweeps of chalky downland—open, rolling terrain used mainly for pasture—characterize the Southeast and make walking a pleasure. Ardent walkers can explore both the North Downs Way (141 mi) and the South Downs Way (106 mi), following ancient paths along the tops of the downs. Both trails give you wide views over the countryside. The North Downs Way follows in part the ancient Pilgrim's Way to Canterbury. The South Downs Way crosses the chalk landscape of Sussex Downs, with parts of the route going through deep woodland. You can easily walk short sections of both trails. Along the way, plenty of towns and villages, mostly just off the main trail, have old inns that offer refreshment and/or accommodations. The 30-mi (north–south) Downs Link joins the two routes. Along the Kent coast, the Saxon Shore Way, 143 mi from Gravesend to Rye, passes many historic sites, including four Roman forts. Guides to these walks are available from the Southeast England Tourist Board.

Nov., and Dec., Mon.–Sat 10:30–5; June–Oct., Mon.–Sat 10:30–5, Sun. 1:30–5; last admission at 4.

 Only one of the city's seven medieval gatehouses survives, complete with twin castellated towers; it now contains the **West Gate Museum.** Inside are medieval bric-a-brac and armaments used by the city guard, as well as more contemporary weaponry. The building became a jail in the 14th century, and you can view the prison cells. Climb to the roof for a panoramic view of the city. ⊠ *St. Peter's St.* ☎ *01227/452747* ⊕ *www.canterbury-museums.co.uk* ⊠ *£1.10* ⊙ *Mon.–Sat. 11–12:30 and 1:30–3:30; last admission one hr before closing* ⊙ *Closed Christmas wk.*

 For an essential Canterbury experience, follow the circuit of the 13th- and 14th-century **medieval city walls,** built on the line of the original Roman walls. Those to the east survive intact, towering some 20 feet high and offering a sweeping view of the town. You can access these from a number of places, including Castle Street and Broad Street.

 Augustine, England's first Christian missionary, was buried in 597 at **St. Augustine's Abbey,** one of the oldest monastic sites in the country. When

The
Southeast

Thames

Hampstead
LONDON
Windsor
Hounslow
Heathrow
Airport
Richmond
Woolwich
Thames
Dartf
Egham
Staines
Merton
Sydenham
Sidcup
M3
Bromley
Beckenham
Woking
Leatherhead
Great Bookham 46
Westerham
Knole 53
A25
Clandon Park
Box Hill
M25
A25
52
54
Guildford 45
A246
47
Chartwell
Ig
M
44
Dorking
B2027
Hever Castle 51
A31
A248
Reigate
50 B2176
Farnham
NORTH DOWNS
Penshurst Place
To
A287
A3
SURREY
Gatwick
Airport
Penshurst
A264
Hartfield
A49
Milford
M23
Royal
Tunbridge Wells
Haslemere
A286
A283
Crawley
A264
East
Grinstead 48
Wadhu
THE
A286
A24
A264
Handcross
Horsham
A22
Wisborough Green
Cuckfield
Bur
WEST
Haywards Heath
A265
Midhurst
A272
SUSSEX
Uckfield
EAST
Petworth
House 43
Burgess
Hill
SUSSE
SOUTH
A285
A283
Storrington
A22
Singleton 42
DOWNS
A281
A23
Lewes
Glyndebourne
Sculpture at
Goodwood 41
B2139
Amberley
A27
29
Her
Cas
Fishbourne
Roman Palace
38
Arundel
Rodmell
Wilmington 28 A27
40 39 Chichester
A259
Hove
Eastbourne
Bognor Regis
Worthing
Brighton
30 – 37
see detail
map
A259

English Channel

Chelmsford
Maldon
Blackwater
ESSEX
Crouch
Rayleigh
Basildon
CANVEY
ISLAND
Southend-
on-Sea
Thames
Grays
North
Sea
GREAT
BRITAIN

Sheerness
Queenborough
Herne Bay
Margate
Birchington
Broadstairs **18**
Rochester **55**
Gillingham
Chatham *A2*
Whitstable
The Swale
A291
Ramsgate
A2
Faversham **17**
A299
A290
Fordwich
A28
A257
Sandwich **19**
M26
M2
A2
Harbledown **15**
14
Canterbury
1 – **13**
see detail
map
Deal
Maidstone
B2163
A251
A252
16
Chilham
A256
20
21
Walmer
Castle
Leeds **56**
Castle
A20
M20
Wye
B2068
B2065
A258
A2
Headcorn
KENT
Ashford
M20
A20
Dover **22**
A20
Channel Tunnel
Biddenden
Sissinghurst Castle **57**
Garden
Cranbrook
Folkestone
Hythe
A259
Romney Marsh
Hawkhurst
B2068
Great Dixter **59**
House and Gardens
Northiam
New Romney
Bodiam **58**
60
Castle
Rye **23**
Lydd
Winchelsea **24**
B2089
A259
Rye Bay
Battle **26**
Strait of Dover
Bexhill
25
Hastings
Pevensey
*Pevensey
Bay*

KEY
▶ Start of itinerary

0   5 miles
0   5 km

Buttermarket ..3

Canterbury
Cathedral 5

Canterbury
Roman
Museum 2

The Canterbury
Tales
Exhibition 6

Christchurch
Gate 4

Dane John
Mound 13

Eastbridge
Hospital of St.
Thomas 8

Medieval
city walls 11

Museum of
Canterbury 9

St. Augustine's
Abbey 12

St. George's
Church 1

Weavers'
Houses 7

West Gate
Museum 10

Henry VIII seized the abbey in the 16th century, he destroyed some buildings and converted others into a royal manor for his fourth wife, Anne of Cleves. A free interactive audio tour vividly puts events into context. Contemporary sculpture is placed in the grounds, and in other locations in the city, May through August. ⊠ *Longport* ☎ *01227/767345* ⊕ *www. english-heritage.org.uk* 🎫 *£3.50* ☺ *Apr.–Sept., daily 10–6; Oct., daily 10–5; Nov.–Mar., daily 10–4.*

🖐 **⑬** The **Dane John Mound,** just opposite the Canterbury East train station, was originally part of the city defenses. There is a fantastic medieval maze here.

Where to Stay & Eat

★ **££–££££** ✗ **Lloyds.** The magnificent beamed barn roof of this older building remains, but the interior—stripped wooden floor, white walls enlivened by contemporary paintings—and the cooking are definitely up-to-the-minute. A crew of young chefs creates such dishes as salad of spiced eggplant, caviar, and eggplant crisps with roasted cumin, and chicken and crayfish with braised fennel. The ice creams are homemade. ⊠ *89–90 St. Dunstan's St.* ☎ *01227/768222* ▭ *AE, MC, V.*

★ **££–£££** ✗ **The Goods Shed.** Near Canterbury West station, this vaulted wooden space with exposed brick and stone walls was a goods shed in Victorian times. In 2002 it was transformed into a farmers' market and restaurant offering the best of Kentish food—from freshly caught fish and smoked meats to local cider and bread baked on the premises. The menu varies with the availability of the local produce, and food is served at wooden tables on a raised platform. ⊠ *Station Rd. West* ☎ *01227/459153* ⊟ *MC, V* ☺ *Closed Sun. evening.*

ff–fff ╳ **Weavers.** In the Old Weavers House, one of the Weavers' Houses on the River Stour, this popular restaurant in the center of town is an ideal place to feast on Tudor atmosphere as well as generous portions. The menu lists traditional English, seafood, and pasta dishes, and a good choice of wines. ⊠ *1 St. Peter's St.* ☎ *01227/464660* ⊟ *AE, MC, V.*

f ╳ **City Fish Bar.** Long lines and lots of satisfied finger-licking attest to
Fodor's Choice the deserved popularity of this excellent fish-and-chips outlet in the cen-
★ ter of town. Everything is freshly fried, the batter crisp and the fish tasty; the fried mushrooms are also surprisingly good. It closes at 7. ⊠ *30 St. Margarets St.* ☎ *01227/760873* ⊟ *No credit cards.*

f ╳ **Tapas en las Trece.** Interesting tapas in this atmospheric small restaurant include rabbit and bacon, and lamb in orange and chili. There are also some respectable vegetarian options. The dim lighting hides the fact that this is not quite the Mediterranean. ⊠ *13 Palace St.* ☎ *01227/762637* ⊟ *MC, V.*

ff–fff ╳▥ **County Hotel.** First licensed in 1588, the year of the Spanish Armada, this hotel includes up-to-date comforts, but touches such as old wood and antiques keep the past alive. A number of more expensive specialty bedrooms are done in Tudor, Georgian, or Colonial style; others are standard modern. The bar and tea rooms are pleasantly old-fashioned, and the formal Sully's Restaurant is known for traditional English dining. ⊠ *High St., CT1 2RX* ☎ *01227/766266* 🖷 *01227/451512* ⊕ *www. macdonaldhotels.co.uk* ➳ *73 rooms* ♻ *Restaurant, coffee shop, bar, meeting rooms, some pets allowed; no a/c* ⊟ *AE, DC, MC, V* ⧦ *BP.*

ff ╳▥ **Falstaff Hotel.** This old coaching inn with a courtyard sits right outside Westgate. Some of the beamed and oak-furnished bedrooms overlook the River Stour; rooms have a mix of old features and new, and some have four-posters. Classic English fare at the restaurant includes pan-fried salmon, roast leg of lamb, and medallions of pork. The central location is a big plus: reserve well in advance. ⊠ *8 St. Dunstan's St., CT2 8AF* ☎ *01227/462138* 🖷 *01227/463525* ⊕ *www.corushotels. com* ➳ *48 rooms* ♻ *Restaurant, in-room data ports, cable TV, bar; no a/c* ⊟ *AE, DC, MC, V* ⧦ *EP.*

ff–fff ▥ **Magnolia House.** Kept in apple-pie order, this Georgian detached house is charmingly elegant, with a lovely walled garden for relaxation. Bedrooms have floral motifs and traditional furnishings; one has a four-poster. Evening meals are available from November to February by prior arrangement. ⊠ *36 St. Dunstan's Terr., CT2 8AX* ☎🖷 *01227/765121* ⊕*freespace.virgin.net/magnolia.canterbury* ➳*7 rooms* ♻*No a/c, no room phones, no kids under 12, no smoking* ⊟ *AE, DC, MC, V* ⧦ *BP.*

ff ▥ **Pointers.** This homey, redbrick Georgian hotel, built around 1740, stands within easy walking distance of the cathedral and city center; it looks down to the Westgate and overlooks the 10th-century church of St. Dunstans. Some of the simply furnished rooms are small, but you can stretch out a bit more in the sitting room. Extra window glazing ensures quiet, despite the location on a busy road. ✉ *1 London Rd., CT2 8LR* ☎ *01227/456846* 🖷 *01227/452786* ⊕ *www.pointers.hotel. dial.pipex.com* ⇨ *12 rooms* ⌂ *Dining room, bar; no a/c* ⊟ *AE, DC, MC, V* ⊗ *Closed late Dec.–mid-Feb.* ¶◉¶ *BP.*

£–££ 🏛 **Cathedral Gate Hotel.** Older even than the adjoining cathedral gateway, this hotel was built as a hostelry for pilgrims in 1438. The large beams, sloping floors, and twisting corridors are evidence of its medieval origins; the plainly furnished rooms, however, have been sympathetically modernized. The bow-window restaurant looks out over the Buttermarket. A full English breakfast costs an extra £7. ✉ *36 Burgate, CT1 2HA* ☎ *01227/464381* 🖷 *01227/462800* ⊕ *www.cathgate.co. uk* ⇨ *27 rooms* ⌂ *Restaurant, bar, some pets allowed; no a/c* ⊟ *AE, DC, MC, V* ¶◉¶ *CP.*

£ 🏛 **The White House.** Reputed to have been the house in which Queen Victoria's head coachman came to live upon retirement, The White House is a handsome Regency building on a quiet road off St Peter's Street, between the city center and Canterbury West train station. Rooms are decorated in pastel shades with an abundance of floral patterns, and great care is taken with both vegetarian and carnivorous breakfasts. ✉ *6 St Peter's Ln., CT1 2BP* ☎ *01227/761836* ⊕ *www.canterburybreaks. co.uk* ⇨ *9 rooms* ⌂ *Guest lounge* ⊟ *No credit cards* ¶◉¶ *BP.*

Nightlife & the Arts

The two-week-long, mixed-arts **Canterbury Festival** (☎ 01227/452853 ⊕ www.canterburyfestival.co.uk) is held every October. The **Gulbenkian Theatre** (✉ Giles La. ☎ 01227/769075), at the University of Kent, mounts all kinds of plays, particularly experimental works, as well as dance, music, comedy and films. The **Marlowe** (✉ St. Margaret's St. ☎ 01227/787787), named after the Elizabethan playwright, who was born in Canterbury, is a venue for touring drama and opera companies.

Shopping

Hawkin's Bazaar (✉ 34 Burgate ☎ 01227/785809) carries an exceptional selection of traditional and modern toys and games. The **National Trust Shop** (✉ 24 Burgate ☎ 01227/457120) stocks the National Trust line of household items, ideal for gifts.

Fordwich

⑭ *1½ mi east of Canterbury.*

The village of Fordwich was originally the river port for Canterbury; the Caen stone quarried in Normandy and shipped across the Channel to be used in the construction of the cathedral was brought ashore here. Don't miss England's smallest town hall, with stocks and ducking stool outside.

Harbledown

⑮ *1 mi west of Canterbury.*

Along the old Roman road to London (now A2) lies Harbledown; once a separate village, it's now part of Canterbury. The main sight here is the cluster of almshouses, built in the 11th century to house the poor.

Harbledown was customarily the spot from which pilgrims caught their first glimpse of Canterbury Cathedral.

Chilham

★ ⑯ *5 mi southwest of Canterbury.*

From this hilltop village, midway between Canterbury and Ashford on the A252 (off the A28), you can walk the last few miles of the traditional Pilgrim's Way back to Canterbury. The village square is filled with textbook examples of English rural architecture, with gabled windows beneath undulating roofs. The church dates from the 14th century.

Where to Eat

££ ✕ **White Horse.** This 15th-century inn shadowed by Chilham's church has a pleasant beer garden and provides lunchtime and evening meals superior to the usual pub grub, with many good pasta dishes. The pub used to be a vicarage, and the ghost of a 17th-century vicar is said to regularly appear in front of the large fireplace. ⊠ *The Square* ☎ *01227/ 730355* ▤ *MC, V.*

Faversham

⑰ *9 mi west of Canterbury, 11 mi northwest of Chilham.*

In Roman times, Faversham was a thriving seaport. Today the port is hidden from sight, and you could pass through this market town without knowing it was there. Still, Faversham is a must for those in search of Ye Quaint Olde Englande: the town center, with its Tudor houses grouped around the 1574 guildhall and covered market, looks like a perfect stage set.

Where to Stay & Eat

★ **£££££** ✕ **Read's.** The glorious food in this elegant restaurant is assuredly British, but with an audacious spin on old favorites. The accent falls firmly on local ingredients, many of which come from the vegetable garden (in which you are welcome to stroll). After a main course of honey-glazed breast of duck or Kentish lamb in a fresh herb crust with mini–shepherd's pie, try the "chocoholics anonymous" dessert. Prices are fixed, with three-course lunch options at £19.50 and a three-course dinner costing £42. You can overnight here in one of six spacious Georgian rooms. ⊠ *Macknade Manor, Canterbury Rd.* ☎ *01795/535344* ▤ *AE, DC, MC, V* ☾ *Closed Sun. and Mon.*

£–££ ✕ **Sun Inn.** The flagship of the Shepherd Neame Brewery chain, established in Faversham in the 17th century, this clapboard pub is even older, dating to the 1400s. The inn follows the local tradition of hanging up hops in September; they add a distinctive fragrance. A recent refurbishment has added guest rooms and a beer garden. ⊠ *10 West St.* ☎ *01795/535098* ▤ *MC, V* ☾ *No dinner.*

★ **££** ✕▣ **White Horse Inn.** Mentioned in Chaucer's *Canterbury Tales*, this 15th-century coaching inn outside Faversham on the old London-to-Dover road (now A2) retains much of its traditional character. The pale blue guest rooms have antique furniture. In addition to the friendly bar, there's an excellent restaurant in what used to be a courtroom; you might find shark steak on the list of daily specials. ⊠ *The Street, Boughton, ME13 9AX* ☏ *01227/751343* 🖷 *01227/751090* ⊕ *www.shepherd-neame.co.uk* ⮧ *13 rooms* ♨ *Restaurant, bar; no a/c* ⊟*AE, MC, V* ⦿*BP.*

Broadstairs

⑱ *25 mi east of Faversham, 17 mi east of Canterbury.*

Like other towns such as Margate and Ramsgate on this stretch of coast, Broadstairs was once the playground of vacationing Londoners. Charles Dickens spent many summers here between 1837 and 1851 and wrote glowingly of its bracing freshness. One of Dickens's favorite abodes was **Bleak House,** perched on a cliff overlooking Viking Bay, where he wrote much of *David Copperfield* and drafted *Bleak House,* after which the building was later renamed. His study and other rooms have been preserved. Displays explore local history, including the wrecks at nearby Goodwin Sands, and the cellars have exhibits about smuggling, a longtime local activity. ⊠ *Fort Rd.* ☏ *01843/862224* ⊕ *www. bleakhouse.ndo.co.uk* 🖅 *£3* ☉ *Late-Feb.–June and Sept.–mid-Dec., daily 10–6; July and Aug., daily 10–9.*

What is now the **Dickens House Museum** was originally the home of Mary Pearson Strong, on whom Dickens based the character of Betsey Trotwood, David Copperfield's aunt. There's a reconstruction of Miss Trotwood's room, a few objects which once belonged to the Dickens family, and prints and photographs commemorating Dickens's association with Broadstairs. ⊠ *2 Victoria Parade* ☏ *01843/861232* ⊕ *www. dickenshouse.co.uk* 🖅 *£1.50* ☉ *Apr.–mid-Oct., daily 2–5.*

Nightlife & the Arts

Each June, Broadstairs holds a **Dickens Festival** (☏ 01843/865265), lasting about a week, with readings, people in Dickensian costume, a Dickensian cricket match, a Victorian bathing party, and Victorian vaudeville, among other entertainments. Aficionados of the author are also drawn to another Dickens festival in Rochester.

Sandwich

⑲ *11 mi south of Broadstairs, 12 mi east of Canterbury.*

The coast near Canterbury holds three of the ancient **Cinque Ports** (pronounced sink ports), a confederacy of ports along the southeast seaboard whose heyday lasted from the 12th through the 14th centuries. These towns, originally five in number (hence *cinque,* from the Norman French)—Sandwich, Dover, Hythe, Romney, and Hastings—are rich in history and are generally less crowded than the other resorts of Kent's northeast coast.

In Saxon times Sandwich stood in a sheltered bay; it became the most important of the Cinque Ports in the Middle Ages and later England's chief naval base. From 1500 the port began to silt up, however, and the town is now 2 mi inland, though the River Stour still flows through it. The 16th-century checkerboard barbican (gatehouse) by the toll bridge is one of many medieval and Tudor buildings here; Strand Street has many half-timber structures.

Deal

㉑ *7 mi south of Sandwich, 8 mi northeast of Dover.*

The large seaside town of Deal is famous in history books as the place where Caesar's legions landed in 55 BC, and it was from here that William Penn set sail in 1682 on his first journey to the American colony he founded, Pennsylvania.

Deal Castle, erected in 1540 and intricately built to the shape of a Tudor rose, is the largest of the coastal defenses constructed by Henry VIII. A moat surrounds its gloomy passages and austere walls. The castle museum has exhibits about prehistoric, Roman, and Saxon Britain. ✉ *Victoria Rd.* ☎ *01304/372762* ⊕ *www.english-heritage.org.uk* ✍ *£3.50* ⊙ *Apr.–Sept., daily 10–6; Oct., daily 10–5; Nov.–Mar., Wed.–Sun. 10–4.*

Walmer Castle

㉑ *7 mi northeast of Dover, 1 mi south of Deal.*

Walmer Castle, one of Henry VIII's fortifications, was converted in 1730 into the official residence of the lord warden of the Cinque Ports, and it now resembles a cozy country house. Among the famous lord wardens were William Pitt the Younger; the duke of Wellington, hero of the Battle of Waterloo, who lived here from 1829 until his death here in 1852 (a small museum contains Wellington memorabilia); and Sir Winston Churchill. The Queen Mother held the post until her death in 2002. Except for when the lord warden is in residence, the drawing and dining rooms are open to the public, and attractive gardens and a grassy walk fill what was the moat. ✉ *A258* ☎ *01304/364288* ⊕ *www.english-heritage.org.uk* ✍ *£5.80* ⊙ *Apr.–Sept., daily 10–6; Oct., daily 10–5; Mar., Nov., and Dec., Wed.–Sun. 10–4; Jan. and Feb., weekends 10–4.*

Dover

㉒ *7 mi south of Walmer Castle, 78 mi east of London.*

One of the busiest passenger ports in the world, Dover has for centuries been Britain's gateway to Europe. Its chalk **White Cliffs** are a famous and inspirational sight. You may find the town disappointing; the savage bombardments of World War II and the shortsightedness of postwar developers have left their scars on the city center. Roman legacies include a lighthouse, adjoining a stout Anglo-Saxon church. The **Roman Painted House,** believed to have been a hotel, includes some well-preserved wall paintings, along with the remnants of an ingenious heating system. ✉ *New St.* ☎ *01304/203279* ✍ *£2* ⊙ *Apr.–Sept., Tues.–Sun. 10–5.*

★ ♻ Spectacular **Dover Castle,** towering high above the ramparts of the White Cliffs, was one of the mightiest medieval castles in Western Europe and served as an important strategic center over the centuries. Most of the castle, including the keep, dates to Norman times. It was begun by Henry

II in 1181 but incorporates additions from almost every succeeding century. There's a lot to see here besides the castle rooms: exhibits, many of which will appeal to kids, include the Siege of 1216, the Princess of Wales Regimental Museum, and Castle Fit for a King. You can tour the secret wartime tunnels, a medieval and Napoleonic-era system that was used as a World War II command center during the evacuation of Dunkirk in 1940. ⊠ *Castle Rd.* ☎ *01304/211067* ⊕ *www.english-heritage.org.uk* ⊠ *£8.50* ⊘ *Apr.–Sept., daily 10–6; Oct., daily 10–5; Nov.–Mar., daily 10–4.*

The Victorian cells of the **Old Town Gaol**, beneath the town hall, evoke the misery endured by convicted felons. Audiovisual gadgetry enhances the reconstructed courtroom and exercise yard. ⊠ *Biggin St.* ☎ *01304/ 202723* ⊠ *£3.50* ⊘ *June–Sept., Tues.–Sat. 10–4:30, Sun. 2–4:30; Oct.–May, Wed.–Sat. 10–4:30, Sun. 2–4:30.*

Where to Stay

★ £ 🏠 **Number One Guest House.** This popular, family-run guest house with garage parking is a great bargain. Wallpapers and porcelain collections decorate the cozy corner terrace home built in the early 19th century, and you can even have breakfast in your room. The walled garden has a fine view of the castle. ⊠ *1 Castle St., CT16 1QH* ☎ *01304/202007* 🖨 *01304/214078* ⊕ *www.number1guesthouse.co.uk* ↵ *4 rooms* ⚠ *No a/c, no room phones* 🚫 *No credit cards* ⦿ *BP.*

RYE TO GLYNDEBOURNE

From Dover, the coast road winds west through Folkestone (a genteel resort, small port, and Channel Tunnel terminal), across Romney Marsh (reclaimed from the sea and famous for its sheep and, at one time, its ruthless smugglers), to the delightful town of Rye. The region along the coast is noted for Winchelsea, the history-rich sites of Hastings and Herstmonceux, and the famous Glyndebourne Opera House festival, based outside Lewes, a town celebrated for its architectural heritage. One of the three steam railroads in the Southeast services part of the area: the Romney, Hythe, and Dymchurch Railway, a main-line service that uses locomotives one-third the regular size.

Rye

★ ㉓ *68 mi southeast of London, 34 mi southwest of Dover.*

With cobbled streets and timbered dwellings, Rye on its hill remains an artist's dream, sprinkled with such historic buildings as the Mermaid Inn, as well as the secret places that made it a smuggler's retreat. Today the former port of Rye lies nearly 2 mi inland, overlooking the Romney Marshes. The town is famous for its pottery, produced by four working potteries and shipped all over the world. The tourist office has an interesting audio tour of the town.

Rye Castle Museum, below the castle, displays watercolors and examples of Rye pottery, including 19th-century hopware decorated with hop motifs in relief. Among the exhibits on local history is an 18th-century fire

engine. ⊠ *3 East St.* ☎ *01797/226728* ⊕ *www.rye.org.uk* ⊠ *£1.90,*
£2.90 including Ypres Tower ۞ *Apr.–Oct., weekdays 2–5, Sat. 10:30–1,*
Sun. 10:30–2; last admission 30 mins before closing.

On an elevation behind Church Square, **Ypres Tower** was built as part
of the town's fortifications in 1249; it later served as a prison. The stone
chambers hold a motley collection of local items, such as smuggling bric-
a-brac and shipbuilding mementos. A topographical map of Romney
Marsh shows changes in sea level. ⊠ *Gungarden* ☎ *01797/226728*
⊠ *£1.90, £2.90 including Rye Castle* ۞ *Apr.–Oct., Thurs.–Mon.*
10:30–1 and 2–5; Nov.–Mar., weekends 10:30–3:30; last admission 30
mins before closing.

Several well-known writers have lived in **Lamb House,** an early 18th-cen-
tury structure. The most famous was the novelist Henry James, who lived
here from 1898 to 1916. E. F. Benson, one-time mayor of Rye and author of the witty *Lucia* novels (written in the 1920s and 1930s, with
some set in a town based on Rye), was a later resident. The ground-floor
rooms contain some of James's furniture and personal belongings.
⊠ *West St.* ☎ *01892/890651* ⊕ *www.nationaltrust.org.uk* ⊠ *£2.70*
۞ *Apr.–Oct., Wed. and Sat. 2–6; last admission at 5:30.*

A wonderfully nostalgic tour of the exhibits at the **Rye Treasury of Mechanical Music** treats you to tunes from music boxes, barrel organs, and
a 1920s dance organ. ⊠ *20 Cinque Ports St.* ☎ *01797/223345* ⊠ *£3*
۞ *Mar.–Oct., daily 10–5; Nov.–Feb., Wed.–Mon. 11–4.*

Where to Stay & Eat

★ **££–£££** ✕ **Landgate Bistro.** Although definitely a bistro, this restaurant in a small
shop unit near one of the ancient gateways is serious about its food. Fish
is always a good choice, or you can opt for the wild rabbit or griddle-
cooked cutlets of Gloucester Old Spot pork with sage, applesauce, and
potatoes. A fixed-price menu (about £17) is available Tuesday–Thursday. ⊠ *5–6 Landgate* ☎ *01797/222829* ▤ *DC, MC, V* ۞ *Closed Sun.*
and Mon., last wk in Dec., and 1st wk in Jan. No lunch.

★ **£££££** ✕▤ **The Mermaid.** Once the headquarters of a notorious smuggling
gang, this classic half-timber inn has served Rye for nearly six centuries. Sloping floors, oak beams, low ceilings, and a huge open hearth
in the bar testify to its age: it was rebuilt in 1420, though it dates from
1156. Rooms vary in size but are comfortable; some have four-posters.
The main restaurant allows you to soak up the period details while choosing from an extensive English menu. An adjacent bar serves pub meals,
and in summer the Tudor Tearoom offers a lovely cuppa. Be warned:
the Mermaid is *very* popular, and you must book well ahead. ⊠ *Mer-*
maid St., TN31 7EY ☎ *01797/223065* 🖨 *01797/225069* ⊕ *www.*
mermaidinn.com ⊃ *31 rooms* ↻ *Restaurant, bar, meeting room; no a/c*
▤ *AE, MC, V* ۞ *BP.*

£££ ▤ **Jeake's House.** Antiques and books fill the cozy bedrooms of this rambling 1689 house, and print fabrics and brass or mahogany beds add
charm. The snug, painted-and-paneled parlor has a wood-burning stove
for cold days. Breakfast, which might include deviled kidneys or kippers, is served in a galleried room formerly used for Quaker meetings

and as a Baptist chapel. Book well in advance. ⊠ *Mermaid St., TN31 7ET* ☎ *01797/222828* 🖨 *01797/222623* ⊕ *www.jeakeshouse.com* 🛏 *11 rooms, 10 with bath* ♤ *Bar, some pets allowed (fee); no a/c, no kids under 12* ⊟ *MC, V* ⊧⊘⊧ *BP.*

££ 🔲 **The Old Vicarage.** Roses frame the door of this bay-front Georgian house in a peaceful location close to the church (double glazing ensures that the peal of the bells does not intrude). The sunny rooms combine Victorian, Edwardian, and French furniture. You can breakfast on scrumptious homemade bread, scones, and locally produced eggs and bacon in a dining room that overlooks a walled garden. ⊠ *66 Church Sq., TN31 7HF* ☎ *01797/222119* 🖨 *01797/227466* ⊕ *www.oldvicaragerye.co.uk* 🛏 *4 rooms* ♤ *No a/c, no room phones, no kids under 8, no smoking* ⊟ *No credit cards* ⊘ *Closed last wk in Dec.* ⊧⊘⊧ *BP.*

Shopping

Of Rye's working potteries, **Cinque Ports Pottery** (⊠ The Monastery, Conduit Hill ☎ 01797/222033) is one of the best. **David Sharp Pottery** (⊠ 55 The Mint ☎ 01797/222620) specializes in the ceramic name plaques that are a feature of the town. **Rye Farmers' Market** (⊠ Strand Quay ☎ 01424/812854) has a great selection of local produce, including cheeses, fruit, cakes, and fish. **Rye Pottery** (⊠ 77 Ferry Rd. ☎ 01797/ 223363 ⊠ Wishward ☎ 01797/223038), an excellent outlet, has two locations, with its Wishward branch offering cheaper seconds.

Winchelsea

㉔ *2 mi southwest of Rye, 71 mi southeast of London.*

Like Rye, Winchelsea perches atop its own small hill amid farmland and tiny villages. One of the prettiest places to visit in the region, it has many attractive houses, some with clapboards, and a splendid (though damaged) church built in the 14th century with Caen stone from Normandy. The town was built on a grid system devised in 1283, after the sea destroyed an earlier settlement at the foot of the hill. The sea later receded, leaving the town high and dry. Some of the original town gates still stand.

Where to Stay & Eat

£–££ ✕🔲 **The New Inn.** This 18th-century hostelry in the heart of town is an excellent place to stop for a pub lunch or a bed for the night. The quiet, refurbished rooms have deep-pile carpets and pleasant views. The bar serves up juicy roasts and quaffable cask ales, and there's a warming log fire. ⊠ *German St.* ☎ *01797/226252* 🛏 *6 rooms* ♤ *Restaurant; no a/c, no room phones* ⊟ *AE, MC, V* ⊧⊘⊧ *BP.*

Hastings

㉕ *9 mi southwest of Winchelsea, 68 mi southeast of London.*

Hastings, famous as the base for the invasion led by William, duke of Normandy, in 1066, is now a large, slightly run-down seaside resort. A visit to the old town provides an interesting overview of 900 years of English maritime history. Below the East Cliff, tall wooden towers called **net shops**, unique to the town, are still used for drying fishermen's nets.

You can take the West Hill Cliff Railway from George Street precinct to the Norman **Hastings Castle,** built by William the Conqueror in 1069. All that remains are fragments of the fortifications, some ancient walls, and a number of gloomy dungeons. Nevertheless, you get an excellent view of the chalky cliffs, the coast, and the town below. "The 1066 Story" retells the Norman invasion using audiovisual technology. ⊠ *West Hill* ☎ *01424/781112* ⊕ *www.discoverhastings.co.uk/castle/* ☎ *£3.40* ☉ *Easter–Sept., daily 10–5; Oct.–Easter, daily 11–3; last admission 30 mins before closing.*

Ⓒ Waxworks and exhibits recall the history of coastal smuggling at **Smuggler's Adventure,** in a labyrinth of caves and passages a 5- or 10-minute walk above Hastings Castle. ⊠ *St. Clement Caves* ☎ *01424/422964* ⊕ *www.smugglersadventure.co.uk* ☎ *£5.95* ☉ *Easter–Sept., daily 10–5:30; Oct.–Easter, daily 11–4:30; last admission 30 mins before closing.*

Where to Stay & Eat

££–££££   ✕ **Bonaparte's.** A hands-on approach to food distinguishes this slightly haughty seafront restaurant, which has dark walls and booths for dining. Owner Bob Bone shoots his own game and buys fish fresh from the market to create dishes such as game pie in beer and wine sauce and halibut steak with crayfish tails. His inventive vegetarian choices include a Tibetan roast with buckwheat, spinach, mushrooms, and walnuts. ⊠ *64 Eversfield Pl., St. Leonards* ☎ *01424/712218* ▭ *AE, DC, MC, V* ☉ *Closed Mon. No lunch Sun.*

£   ▦ **Eagle House.** Its own attractive garden surrounds this guest house in a large Victorian building. Guest rooms and public areas have Victorian touches, and the restaurant uses fresh produce from local farms. The lodging is in St. Leonards, the western section of Hastings, within easy reach of the town center. ⊠ *12 Pevensey Rd., St. Leonards, TN38 0JZ* ☎ *01424/430535* ☎ *01424/437771* ⊕ *www.eaglehousehotel.com* ↬ *18 rooms* ☆ *Restaurant; no a/c* ▭ *AE, DC, MC, V* ❙◎❙ *BP.*

Battle

㉖ *7 mi northwest of Hastings, 61 mi southeast of London.*

Battle is the actual site of the crucial Battle of Hastings, at which, on October 14, 1066, the more disciplined forces of William of Normandy trounced King Harold's Anglo-Saxon army. Harold II was killed, and the Norman state was established with the coronation of William I—also known as William the Conqueror—in Westminster Abbey in London on Christmas Day.

The ruins of **Battle Abbey,** the great Benedictine abbey William the Conqueror erected after his victory, and the surrounding area still convey the sense of past conflict. A memorial stone marks the high altar, which stood on the spot where Harold II was killed. The abbey was destroyed in 1539 during Henry VIII's dissolution of the monasteries, but you can take the mile-long Battlefield Walk around the edge of the battlefield and see the remains of many of the domestic buildings. The **Abbot's House** (closed to the public) is now a girls' school. ⊠ *High St.* ☎ *01424/*

773792 ⊕ *www.english-heritage.org.uk* ✉ *£5* ☉ *Apr.–Sept., daily 10–6; Oct., daily 10–5; Nov.–Mar., daily 10–4.*

Where to Stay & Eat

£££–££££ ✕⌂ **Powder Mills Hotel.** On 150 acres of parkland, this Georgian house, close to Battle Abbey, adjoins the 1066 battlefield. Among the bedrooms lavishly furnished in country-house style are one used by the duke of Wellington and another supposedly haunted by a "lady in white." The seafood receives high marks at the conservatory-style Orangery Restaurant. There's a fixed-price menu at lunch and dinner. ✉ *Powdermill La., TN33 0SP* ☎ *01424/775511* 🖷 *01424/774540* ⊕ *www.grandheritage.com* ⤴ *40 rooms* ⚹ *Restaurant, cable TV, pool, fishing, meeting rooms, some pets allowed; no a/c* ⊟ *AE, DC, MC, V* ✴ *BP.*

£££ ✕⌂ **Little Hemingfold Hotel.** The surrounding 40 acres of fields and woodland, including a trout lake and a grass tennis court, provide the main enticement of this informal, early Victorian farmhouse hotel. Guest rooms, done in simple country style, are bright and serene, and there's a piano in one of the sitting rooms. The fixed-price dinner in the candlelit dining rooms uses homegrown fruit and vegetables, the menu changing daily. The hotel is 2 mi south of Battle off the A2100. ✉ *Hastings Rd., Telham, TN33 0TT* ☎ *01424/774338* 🖷 *01424/775351* ⊕ *www.littlehemingfoldhotel.co.uk* ⤴ *12 rooms* ⚹ *Restaurant, tennis court, lake, boating, fishing, croquet, bar, some pets allowed; no a/c, no kids under 7* ⊟ *AE, MC, V* ✴ *BP.*

Herstmonceux Castle

㉗ *11 mi southwest of Battle, 61 mi southeast of London.*

Back in the Edwardian era, square-shape Herstmonceux was famous as the quintessential romantic English castle, complete with moat and rose-color brick and limestone crenellations. In 1911 rich connoisseurs so completely renovated the structure that the magic nearly evaporated, but Herstmonceux remains a fabled name for castle lovers. Sir Roger Fiennes, ancestor of actor Ralph Fiennes, built it in 1444. Now housing the International Study Centre owned by Queen's University of Canada, the castle is open for guided tours only, and you can explore the gardens and grounds. There are no deluxe salons, but the interior still has some fine Elizabethan-era staircases and ceilings. ✉ *Hailsham* ☎ *01323/834444* ⊕ *www.herstmonceux-castle.com* ✉ *Castle tours £2.50, grounds £4.50* ☉ *Mid-Apr.–Sept., daily 10–6; Oct., daily 10–5; last admission 1 hr before closing.*

Where to Eat

£££–££££ ✕ **The Sundial.** This 17th-century brick farmhouse holds a popular French restaurant run by chef Vincent Rongier and his wife, Mary. The extensive, frequently changing menu lists imaginative choices: foie gras and truffles vie with smoked salmon from the Shetland Isles. The fixed-price options are a good value. ✉ *Gardner St., Herstmonceux* ☎ *01323/832217* ⊟ *DC, MC, V* ☉ *Closed Mon. No dinner Sun.*

Wilmington

②⑧ *9 mi southwest of Herstmonceux Castle, 7 mi west of Pevensey on A27.*

Wilmington has a famous landmark. High on the downs to the south of the village (signposted off A27), a 226-foot-tall white figure, known as the **Long Man of Wilmington,** is carved into the chalk; he has a staff in each hand. His age is a subject of great debate, but some researchers think he might have originated in Roman times.

Ⓒ Designed for children, **Drusilla's Park** is one of the best small zoos in England, with gardens, a miniature railroad, an adventure playground, and animals, including lemurs, meerkats, crocodiles and penguins. The zoo is 1½ mi west of Wilmington in the Cuckmere Valley. ⊠ *A27, Alfriston* ☎ *01323/874100* ⊕ *www.drusillas.co.uk* ⌖ *£9.99* ☉ *Apr.–Oct., daily 10–6; Nov.–Mar., daily 10–5; last admission 1 hr before closing.*

Where to Stay

££ ⌗ **Crossways Hotel.** This handsome, whitewashed house with two acres of gardens is near the Long Man of Wilmington, under the hills of the South Downs near the river Cuckmere. The interior is decorated in warm, upbeat colors that contrast with the antiques the owners have collected. Convenient for walking, the hotel is also only a 15-minute drive from Glyndebourne. ⊠ *Lewes Rd., BN26 5SG* ☎ *01323/482455* ☎ *01273/479575* ⊕ *www.crosswayshotel.co.uk* ⌖ *7 rooms* ⌖ *No a/c* ☰ *MC, V* ⍾ *BP.*

Lewes

★ **②⑨** *10 mi northwest of Wilmington, 8 mi northeast of Brighton, 54 mi south of London.*

The town nearest to the celebrated Glyndebourne Opera House, Lewes is so rich in architectural history that the Council for British Archaeology has named it one of the 50 most important English towns. A walk is the best way to appreciate its appealing jumble of building styles and materials—flint, stone, brick, tile—and the secret lanes (called "twittens") behind the castle, with their huge beeches. Here and there are smart antiques shops and secondhand-book dealers. Buildings of all ages, styles, and descriptions line High Street, including a timber-frame house once occupied by Thomas Paine (1737–1809), author of *The Rights of Man.*

Lewes is one of the few towns in England that still celebrate in high style Guy Fawkes Night (November 5), the anniversary of Fawkes's attempt to blow up the Houses of Parliament in 1605. It's rather like an autumnal Mardi Gras, with costumed processions and flaming tar barrels rolled down High Street.

High above the valley of the River Ouse stand the majestic ruins of **Lewes Castle,** begun in 1100. For a panoramic view of the surrounding region, climb the keep. The **Barbican House Museum** inside the castle includes the Town Model, a re-creation of Lewes in the 19th century. ⊠ *169 High St.* ☎ *01273/405730* ⊕ *www.sussexpast.co.uk* ⌖ *£4.30, £6 includes Anne of Cleves House* ☉ *Tues.–Sat. 10–5:30 or dusk, Sun., Mon., and holidays 11–5:30 or dusk; last admission 30 mins before closing.*

The 16th-century **Anne of Cleves House,** a fragile, timber-frame building, holds a notable collection of Sussex ironwork and other items of local interest, such as Sussex pottery. A famous painting of the local Guy Fawkes procession is also here. The house was part of Anne of Cleves's divorce settlement from Henry VIII, but she did not live in it. To get to the house, walk down steep, cobbled Keere Street, past lovely Grange Gardens, to Southover High Street. ⊠ *52 Southover High St.* ☎ *01273/ 474610* ⊕ *www.sussexpast.co.uk* ✉ *£2.90, £6 includes Lewes Castle* ⊙ *Mar.–Oct., Tues.–Sat. 10–5, Sun., Mon., and holidays 11–5; Nov.–Feb., Tues.–Sat. 10–5; last admission at 4.*

Of interest to serious Bloomsbury fans, **Monk's House** was the home of novelist Virginia Woolf and her husband, Leonard Woolf, who purchased it in 1919. Leonard lived here until his death in 1969. Rooms in the small cottage include Virginia's study, where she wrote a number of her books, and her bedroom. Artists Vanessa Bell (Virginia's sister) and Duncan Grant helped decorate the house. ⊠ *C7, off A27, 3 mi south of Lewes, Rodmell* ☎ *01892/890651* ⊕ *www.nationaltrust.org.uk* ✉ *£2.80* ⊙ *Apr.–Oct., Wed. and Sat. 2–5:30.*

Art and life mixed at **Charleston,** the farmhouse Vanessa Bell bought in 1916 and decorated with Duncan Grant (who resided here until 1978), painting the walls, doors, and furniture. The house became a refuge for writers and artists of the Bloomsbury Group and holds ceramics and textiles of the Omega Workshop—in which Bell and Grant participated—and paintings by Picasso and Renoir as well as by Bell and Grant. The house is seen on a guided tour, except on Sunday. ⊠ *Off A27, 7 mi east of Lewes, Firle* ☎ *01323/811265* ⊕ *www.charleston. org.uk* ✉ *£6, gardens only £2.50* ⊙ *May, June, Sept., and Oct., Wed.–Sun. 2–6; July and Aug., Wed.–Sat. 11:30–6, Sun. 2–6; last admission at 5.*

Where to Stay & Eat

£££££ ✕ **Circa.** Fascinatingly different food without pretentiousness is the attraction at this ambitious restaurant. Global fusion dishes such as six-mushroom tortellini with yam crunch and seared blue-fin tuna with yuzu (a Japanese citrus fruit) dressing are presented by helpful staff in cool but friendly modern surroundings. The marginally simpler lunch menu is a good value at £11.75 for two courses. There is live jazz or blues on the last Friday of the month. ⊠ *145 High St.* ☎ *01273/471777* ▤ *MC, V* ⊙ *Closed Sun. and Mon.*

★ ✕▦ **Horsted Place.** Perfect for outdoor activities or relaxation, this lux-
££££–£££££ urious hotel sits on 1,100 acres, a few minutes' drive from Glyndebourne. Built as a private home in 1850 with Gothic Revival elements by Augustus-Charles Pugin, it is richly furnished in country-house style and has a magnificent Victorian staircase and a Gothic library with a secret door that leads to a courtyard. The dining room, also Gothic, prepares such elegant fare as roasted quail cutlet. ⊠ *Little Horsted TN22 5TS, 2½ mi south of Uckfield, 6 mi north of Lewes* ☎ *01825/750581* 🖷 *01825/750459* ⊕ *www.horstedplace.co.uk* ⇆ *15 rooms, 5 suites* ⚹ *Restaurant, cable TV with movies, golf privileges, tennis court, cro-*

quet, library, business services, meeting rooms; no a/c ☰ *AE, DC, MC, V* ⦿ *BP.*

££££–£££££ 🏠 **Shelleys.** A 17th-century building, this hotel on the hilly main road is a traditional overnight stop for Glyndebourne operagoers. Public rooms are on the grand scale, furnished throughout with antiques, and the garden is a joy. The hotel maintains a reputation for old-fashioned, friendly service. ✉ *High St., BN7 1XS* ☎ *01273/472361* 🖷 *01273/ 483152* ⦿ *www.shelleys-hotel.com* ⇆ *19 rooms* ⚴ *Restaurant, bar, meeting rooms, some pets allowed; no a/c* ☰ *AE, DC, MC, V* ⦿ *BP.*

££ 🏠 **Berkeley House.** In a smart townhouse in one of Lewes's Georgian terraces, Berkeley House is a small but welcoming bed-and-breakfast. Rooms are spacious and homely, if somewhat beige, and full English breakfasts are made using free-range eggs from a local farmer. ✉ *2 Albion St., BN7 2ND* ☎ *01273/476057* 🖷 *01273/479575* ⦿ *www. berkeleyhousehotel.co.uk* ⇆ *3 rooms* ⚴ *No a/c* ☰ *AE, DC, MC, V* ⦿ *BP.*

Nightlife & the Arts

Glyndebourne Opera House (✉ Glyndebourne, near Lewes ☎ 01273/ 813813 ⦿ www.glyndebourne.com) is one of the world's leading opera venues. Nestled beneath the downs, Glyndebourne combines first-class productions, a state-of-the-art auditorium, and a beautiful setting. Seats are *very* expensive (£25–£140) and often difficult to acquire, but they're worth every penny to aficionados, some of whom wear evening dress and bring a hamper for a picnic in the gardens. The main season runs from the end of May to the end of August. The Glyndebourne Touring Company performs here in October, when seats are cheaper and slightly easier to obtain.

BRIGHTON TO EAST GRINSTEAD

The self-proclaimed belle of the coast, Brighton is an upbeat, friendly, old-new sprawl. It started in the 16th century as a tiny fishing village called Brighthelmstone, with a thriving herring fleet, but had no claim to fame until a certain Dr. Russell sent his patients there for its dry, bracing, crystal-clear air in the late 18th century. The prince regent, later George IV, discovered sea bathing in Brighton, and for nearly 200 years, the place prospered—deservedly so, for few British resorts have ever catered so well as Brighton to its appreciative patronage from London and the world over. Today the city is a youthful and lively mixture of carnival and culture, and it contains one of the must-sees of Britain—the mock-Asian Royal Pavilion. The city's second iconic structure, the West Pier, has been closed to the public since 1975 and is now a barely recognizable skeleton. Brighton Pier, however, remains in business. After the children have had their fill of Brighton's amusements, the surrounding area beckons with great residences, including Arundel Castle, Petworth House, and Polesden Lacey. Along the way, you'll discover the largest Roman villa in Britain, the bustling city of Guildford, and Chichester, whose cathedral is a poem in stone.

Brighton

9 mi southwest of Lewes, 54 mi south of London.

Ever since the prince regent first visited in 1783, Brighton has been England's most exciting seaside city, and today it remains as vibrant, eccentric, and cosmopolitan as ever. A rich cultural mix—Regency architecture, pleasure pier, specialty shops, sidewalk cafés, lively arts, a flourishing gay scene, and the exotic Royal Pavilion—makes the city truly unique. In decades gone by, it became known for its faded glamor. Happily, a young, bustling spirit has given a face-lift to this ever-popular resort, which shares its city status with neighboring Hove, as genteel a retreat as Brighton is abuzz.

The city owes its modern fame and fortune to the supposed healing attributes of seawater. In 1750 physician Richard Russell published a book recommending seawater treatment for glandular diseases. The fashionable world flocked to Brighton to take Dr. Russell's "cure," and sea bathing became a popular pastime. The next windfall for the town was the arrival of the prince of Wales (later George IV). "Prinny," as he was called, created the Royal Pavilion, a pleasure palace that attracted London society. The influx of visitors triggered a wave of villa-building. Fortunately, this was one of the most creative periods in the history of English architecture, and the elegant terraces of Regency houses are today among the town's greatest attractions. The coming of the railroad set the seal on Brighton's popularity: the luxurious *Brighton Belle* brought Londoners to the coast within an hour. They expected to find the same comforts they had in London, and Brighton obliged, which explains the town's remarkable assortment of restaurants, hotels, and pubs. Horse racing was, and still is, another strong attraction.

Although fast rail service to London has made Brighton an important base for commuters, the town has unashamedly set out to be a pleasure resort. The first examples of that peculiarly British institution, the amusement pier, appeared in Sussex in the 1850s, and the restored ★ ➌⓿ **Brighton Pier** (⊕ www.brightonpier.co.uk), built in 1899, follows the great tradition. Amusement piers traditionally had music halls, with a certain brand of slapstick, ribald humor, and popular theater, and they've always had games and rides. The pier's handsome ironwork is worth a look. The town museum exhibits some of the original mechanical amusements, including the celebrated flip-card device, "What the Butler Saw." The decaying ghost of a Victorian structure down the beach from Brighton Pier is the **West Pier** (☎ 01273/321499 ⊕ www.westpier.co.uk). Built in 1866, it was the more upscale of Brighton's piers and was for many the city's most recognizable landmark.

➌❶ The heart of Brighton is the **Steine** (pronounced steen), a large open area close to the seafront. This was a river mouth until the Prince of Wales had it drained in 1793. One of the houses here was the home of Mrs. Maria Fitzherbert, later the prince's wife.

The most remarkable building on the Steine, perhaps in all Britain, is unquestionably the Prince of Wales's extravagant fairy-tale palace, the

Brighton Museum and Art Gallery . . .**33**

Brighton Pier **30**

British Engineerium .**37**

The Lanes **34**

Royal Pavilion **32**

Sea Life Centre **35**

The Steine . . .**31**

Volk's Electric Railway **36**

Brighton

KEY

English Channel

🛈 *Tourist information*

★ **32** domed and pinnacled **Royal Pavilion.** Planned as a simple seaside villa and built in the fashionable classical style of 1787 by architect Henry Holland, the Pavilion was rebuilt between 1815 and 1822 by John Nash for the Prince Regent (later George IV), who favored an exotic, Eastern design with opulent Chinese interiors. When Queen Victoria came to the throne in 1837, she so disapproved of the palace that she stripped it of its furniture and planned to demolish it. Fortunately, the local council bought it from her, and today the Pavilion looks much as it did in its Regency heyday. Quantities of superb period furniture and ornaments, some given or lent by the current Royal Family, fill the interior. The two great set pieces are the **Music Room,** styled in the form of a Chinese pavilion, and the **Banqueting Room,** with its enormous flying-dragon "gasolier," or gaslight chandelier, a revolutionary invention in the early 19th century. In the kitchens, palm-tree columns support the ceilings. The upstairs bedrooms contain a selection of cruel caricatures of the prince regent, most produced during his lifetime. The gardens, too, have been restored to Regency splendor, following John Nash's naturalistic design of 1826. For an elegant time-out, repair to one of the Pavilion's bedrooms, where a tearoom serves snacks and light meals. ⊠ *Old Steine* ☏ *01273/290900* ⊕ *www.royalpavilion.org.uk* 🎟 *£5.95* ⊙ *Oct.–Mar., daily 10–5:15; Apr.–Sept., daily 9:30–5:45; last admission 45 mins before closing.*

CloseUp

ALL HAIL THE REGENT

The term "Regency" comes from the last 10 years of the reign of George III (1811–20), who was deemed unfit to rule because of advancing insanity. Real power was officially given to the prince of Wales, also known as the prince regent, who became King George IV and ruled until his death in 1830. Throughout his regency, George spent grand sums indulging his flamboyant tastes in architecture and interior decorating—while failing in affairs of state. The distinctive architecture of the Royal Pavilion is a prime, if extreme, example of the Regency style, popularized by architect John Nash (1752–1835) in the early part of the 19th century. The style is characterized by a diversity of influences—French, Greek, Italian, Persian, Japanese, Chinese, Roman, Indian—you name it. Nash was George IV's favorite architect, beloved for his interest in Indian and Asian designs and for his neoclassical designs, as evidenced in his plans for Regent's Park and its terraces in London.

🕉 The grounds of the Royal Pavilion contain the **Brighton Museum and Art Gallery,** whose buildings were designed as a stable block for the Prince Regent's horses. The museum includes especially interesting art nouveau and art deco collections. Look out for Salvador Dali's famous sofa in the shape of Mae West's lips, and pause at the Balcony Café for its bird's-eye view over the 20th-century Art and Design Gallery. ⊠ *Church St.* ☎ *01273/290900* ⊕ *www.brighton.virtualmuseum.info* ⊠ *Free* ☉ *Tues. 10–7, Wed.–Sat. 10–5, Sun. 2–5.*

🕉 **The Lanes** (⊠ bordered by West, North, East, and Prince Albert Sts.), a maze of alleys and passageways, was once the home of fishermen and their families. Closed to vehicular traffic, the area's cobbled streets are filled with interesting restaurants, boutiques, and antiques shops. Fish and seafood restaurants line the heart of the Lanes, at Market Street and Market Square.

need a break? Just south of the Lanes, and less than a five-minute walk from the Royal Pavilion, the **Mock Turtle** (⊠ 4 Pool Valley ☎ 01273/328380) is a great old-fashioned, homey café. Alongside a decent selection of teas and coffees are four types of rarebit, homemade soup, meringues, and scones. It's closed Monday.

🕙 🕉 Brighton's **Sea Life Centre,** near the Palace Pier, has a large number of sea-dwelling creatures—from sharks to sea horses—in more than 30 marine habitats. It also has a giant-turtle convalescence center. ⊠ *Marine Parade* ☎ *01273/604234* ⊕ *www.sealife.co.uk* ⊠ *£7.25.*

🕙 🕉 **Volk's Electric Railway,** built by inventor Magnus Volk in 1883, was the first public electric railroad in Britain. In summer you can take the 1¼-mi trip along Marine Parade. ⊠ *Marine Parade* ☎ *01273/292718* ⊠ *£1.20 one-way, £2.20 round-trip* ☉ *Mid-Apr.–Sept., weekdays 10:30–5, weekends 10:30–6.*

(C) (37) The **British Engineerium,** a restored Victorian pumping station, houses hundreds of steam engines, electric motors, motorcycles, and interactive children's exhibits. Note that boilers are lighted and engines set in full steam only on the first Sunday of the month and on national holidays. ⊠ *Nevill Rd., Hove* ☎ *01273/559583* www.britishengineerium.com ⊞£4 ☉ Daily 10–5; last admission at 4 ☉ Closed wk before Christmas.

Where to Stay & Eat

££££–£££££ ✗ **One Paston Place.** Bare floorboards and plenty of pictures help give the relaxed mood of a bistro to this roomy, well-established restaurant. The menu changes regularly, but you might expect pan-fried foie gras as a starter, and roast rabbit with tomato and coriander as a main dish. Prices are high, but fixed-price lunches at £16.50 and £19 are a good deal. The French cuisine makes no compromises for vegetarians. ⊠ *1 Paston Pl.* ☎ *01273/606933* ⊟ *AE, DC, MC, V* ☉ *Closed Sun. and Mon., 1st 2 wks in Jan. and 1st 2 wks in Aug.*

££–££££ ✗ **English's of Brighton.** One of the few old-fashioned seafood havens left in England is buried in the Lanes in three fisherman's cottages. It has been a restaurant for more than 150 years and a family business for more than 50. You can eat succulent oysters and other seafood dishes at the counter or take a table in the smart restaurant section. English's popularity means it's usually busy and service can sometimes be slow. ⊠ *29–31 East St.* ☎ *01273/327980* ⊟ *AE, DC, MC, V.*

£££ ✗ **The Mangerie.** At one of the Brighton and Hove area's best bring-your-own restaurants, you can turn up with a bottle of cheap (or not so cheap) wine and drink it with your meal. This small place is friendly and French, and the food (£15 for a three-course fixed-price menu) ranges from duck breast with mango sauce to deep-fried ice cream. ⊠ *Church Rd., Hove* ☎ *01273/327329* ⊟ *MC, V.*

££–£££ ✗ **Havana.** The high ceilings, dark wood, and leather furnishings of this Cuban-style restaurant, along with the sophisticated food, might make you think you're in London. Don't let that deter you, however—this place is a pleasure. Expect modern twists on British classics: the sautéed sea bream, for example, comes on a bed of braised fennel. The chic bar area is a perfect place to rest your feet at the end of the day. ⊠ *32 Duke St.* ☎ *01273/773388* ⊟ *AE, MC, V.*

★ **££** ✗ **Terre à Terre.** This inspiring vegetarian restaurant is popular, so come early for a light lunch or a more sophisticated evening meal. The Jerusalem artichoke soufflé, sumac-scented almond eggplant, and an eclectic choice of salads should satisfy most palates, and dishes have names to match their culinary inventiveness, such as Colonel Gnocchi Chowder and Jabba Jabba Beefy Tea. ⊠ *71 East St.* ☎ *01273/729051* ⊟ *AE, DC, MC, V* ☉ *No lunch Mon., in winter closed Mon. and no lunch Tues.*

£ ✗ **Nia Café.** In the interesting North Laine area, Nia has views down Trafalgar Street from its pavement tables. Besides good coffees and leaf teas, excellent café food is available all day, from simple (but freshly made) sandwiches to oak-smoked kippers with rye bread and lemon. The decor is simple, but large windows and fresh flowers add a friendly feel. It's also near the station, which is handy if you have time to kill before a train or you need to reenergize before a busy day's sightseeing. ⊠ *87–88 Trafalgar St.* ☎ *01273/671371.*

★ ££££ ✕🏠 **Blanch House.** A theatrical experience as much as a night's rest lies behind this small hotel's Georgian facade. You can take your pick from the eclectic mix of superbly executed theme rooms, from '70s-style Boogie Nights to Moroccan and rich Renaissance. Beds are queen- and king-size, and bathrooms are stylish. The hip cocktail bar (the owner is a former manager of London's Groucho Club) and sleek modern restaurant complete the picture. The restaurant's set-price lunches are a good value, and its contemporary international menu lists dishes such as smoked pancetta–wrapped scallops and pheasant with spiced pumpkin soup. ✉ *17 Atlingworth St., BN2 1PL* ☎ *01273/603504* 🖷 *01273/689813* ⊕ *www. blanchhouse.co.uk* ⇋ *9 rooms, 3 suites △ Restaurant, in-room data ports, sound systems, bar, meeting rooms; no a/c* ☰ *MC, V* ⊙ *BP.*

£££–££££ ✕🏠 **Hotel du Vin.** Brighton continues to attract trendy new hotels such as this stylish place near the seafront. Rooms are crisply modern, with pampering touches such as Egyptian linens and large "monsoon" showers. The bistro restaurant offers classic fare that makes use of local seafood, and the extensive wine list includes many good values. The wine bar will satisfy connoisseurs (special events take place throughout the year), and you can have a cigar from the cigar gallery before you play billiards. ✉ *Ship St., BN1 1AD* ☎ *01273/718588* 🖷 *01273/718599* ⊕ *www. hotelduvin.com* ⇋ *33 rooms, 3 suites △ Restaurant, billiards, wine bar, meeting rooms; no a/c* ☰ *AE, DC, MC, V.*

£££££ 🏠 **Grand Hotel.** A Brighton classic that lives up to its name, this imposing but elegant hotel built in 1864 overlooks and dominates this part of the seafront. The high-ceiling public rooms tend toward the chandelier-and-marble variety; the spacious bedrooms are traditional in style, with luxurious drapes and large bathrooms. ✉ *King's Rd., BN1 2FW* ☎ *01273/ 321188* 🖷 *01273/202694* ⊕ *www.grandbrighton.co.uk* ⇋ *200 rooms △ Restaurant, in-room data ports, cable TV with movies, indoor pool, gym, sauna, lounge, business services, meeting rooms, night club, some pets allowed (fee); no a/c in some rooms* ☰ *AE, DC, MC, V* ⊙ *BP.*

£££–£££££ 🏠 **Granville Hotel.** Three former grand residences facing the sea make up this hotel opposite the West Pier on hotel row, to the west of the Grand. Guest rooms, beautifully decorated and themed, include the pink-and-white Brighton Rock and the art deco Noel Coward rooms. Dadu, the hotel's restaurant, is downstairs. ✉ *124 King's Rd., BN1 2FA* ☎ *01273/ 326302* 🖷 *01273/728294* ⊕ *www.granvillehotel.co.uk* ⇋ *24 rooms △ Restaurant, coffee shop, bar, some pets allowed; no a/c* ☰ *AE, DC, MC, V* ⊙ *BP.*

£££–£££££ 🏠 **Nineteen.** Definitely urban in style, but on a quiet side street close to Brighton Pier, this hotel is a calm oasis of white. Original contemporary art and designer accessories set the style in the guest rooms, and beds are supported on platforms of glass bricks that filter an ocean-blue light. Massages, yoga sessions, and manicures are pampering amenities. A basement kitchen with snacks is for guests' use. ✉ *19 Broad St., BN2 1TJ* ☎ *01273/675529* 🖷 *01273/675531* ⊕ *www.hotelnineteen.co.uk* ⇋ *7 rooms △ In-room VCRs, some pets allowed; no a/c, no kids, no smoking* ☰ *MC, V* ⊙ *BP.*

★ ££–£££ 🏠 **Pelirocco.** A wonderful, vicarious, eclectic romp through pop art and rock and roll, Pelirocco is one of Britain's grooviest hotels. The imaginations of designers and pop stars have been given free rein here, and each room is different. From '70s kitsch (Lenny Beige's Love Palace) to the slickly modern (O2 Bubble Suite), Pelirocco has it all, including an upside-down fireplace and a stylish bar with a PlayStation area. Other hotels may never seem the same again. ⊠ *10 Regency Sq., BN1 2FG* ☎ *01273/327055* 🖷 *01273/733845* ⊕ *www.hotelpelirocco.co.uk* ⇗ *19 rooms, 1 suite* ⚶ *Bar, in-room data ports; no a/c* ☰ *MC, V* ¶⊙¶ *BP.*

★ **£–£££** ⟦□⟧ **The Dove.** Washes of light and an uncluttered look are the keynotes of this immaculate Regency house. Rooms at the front have enormous bay-window views across the square, and you can see the sea from the narrow balconies. There's no elevator, and the stairs to the attic rooms are steep. Breakfasts are generous. ⊠ *18 Regency Sq., BN1 2FG* ☎ *01273/779222* 🖷 *01273/746912* ⊕ *www.thedovehotel.co.uk* ⇗ *9 rooms* ⚶ *Dining room; no a/c* ☰ *AE, MC, V* ¶⊙¶ *BP.*

£–££ ⟦□⟧ **Genevieve.** This Regency guest house, near the seafront and Brighton Pier, has large, freshly decorated rooms, some with sea views. Less expensive rooms are done in pastels; some more expensive ones have enormous four-posters. All rooms have their own bathrooms, but some of these are out-side the bedrooms. Breakfast is served in the basement dining room. ⊠ *18 Madeira Pl., BN2 1TN* ☎ *01273/681653* 🖷 *01273/681653* ⊕ *www. genevievehotel.co.uk* ⇗ *11 rooms* ⚶ *No a/c* ☰ *MC, V* ¶⊙¶ *BP.*

Nightlife & the Arts

NIGHTLIFE Live music is played in clubs and bars most nights, and on weekends a lively club scene pulls in crowds from across the Southeast. Brighton resident Fatboy Slim (also known as Norman Cook) is still the UK dance scene's preeminent figure. Try the popular **Escape Club** (⊠ 10 Marine Parade ☎ 01273/606906) in an art deco building east of Brighton Pier. Specialty nights at the **Funky Buddha Lounge** (⊠ 169 Kings Rd. Arches ☎ 01273/725541) are at the forefront of Brighton's underground, with funk and acid disco blasting out to a fairly sophisticated crowd. Small, friendly and unfailingly funky, the **Jazz Place** (⊠ 10 Ship St. ☎ 01273/328439) can get a little cramped but makes up for it with plenty of cool, jazzy attitude. **The Zap** (⊠ 188–193 King's Rd. Arches ☎ 01273/202407), under the arches right on the beach, is Brighton's most well-established club, but no longer always as trendy as it once was.

THE ARTS The three-week-long **Brighton Festival** (☎ 01273/706771 ⊕ www. ★ brighton-festival.org.uk), one of England's biggest and liveliest arts fes-tivals, takes place every May in venues around town. The more than 600 events include drama, music, dance, and visual arts.

The **Brighton Dome** (⊠ New Rd. ☎ 01273/709709), just west of the Royal Pavilion, was converted from the prince regent's stables in the 1930s. It includes a theater and a concert hall that stage pantomime (a British theatrical entertainment with songs and dance) and classical and pop concerts. The **Gardner Arts Centre** (⊠ Off A27, Falmer ☎ 01273/685861), on the University of Sussex campus a few miles northeast of town, pre-sents plays, concerts, and cabaret. The Regency **Theatre Royal** (⊠ New Rd. ☎ 01273/328488), close to the Royal Pavilion, has a gem of an au-ditorium that is a favorite venue for shows on their way to or fresh from London's West End.

The **Cinematheque** (✉ 9–12 Middle St. ☎ 01273/384300 ⊕ www.cinematheque.org) screens sub-art-house oddities, obscurities and rarities. The elegant 1910 **Duke of York's Picture House** (✉ Preston Circus ☎ 01273/626261), a 10-minute walk north of the main train station, is one city option for art-house movies.

Shopping

The main shopping area to head for is **the Lanes,** especially for antiques or jewelry. It also has clothing boutiques, coffee shops, and pubs. Across North Street from the Lanes lies the **North Laine,** a network of narrow streets full of little stores, less glossy than those in the Lanes, but fun, funky, and exotic.

Colin Page (✉ 36 Duke St. ☎ 01273/325954), at the western edge of the Lanes, stocks a wealth of antiquarian and secondhand books at all prices. The **Pavilion Shop** (✉ 4–5 Pavilion Bldgs. ☎ 01273/292798), next door to the Royal Pavilion, carries well-designed toys, trinkets, books and cards—all with a loose Regency theme—and high-quality fabrics, wallpapers, and ceramics based on material in the Pavilion itself. Beautiful, if expensive, tapenades, flavored oils, soaps, candles and pots—all with an olive content or theme—fill **Oliviers and Co.** (✉ 23A East St. ☎ 01273/739840). The old-fashioned **Pecksniff's Bespoke Perfumery** (✉ 45–46 Meeting House La. ☎ 01273/723292) will mix and match ingredients to suit your wishes. **Simultane** (✉ 37 Trafalgar St. ☎ 01273/818031), a boutique in the North Laine, displays women's fashions from its own label—contemporary looks inspired by the styles of the 1940s and '50s—and clothing from other designers. An authentic taste of Marrakech can be had for very reasonable prices at **Souk Trading** (✉ 4 Little East St. ☎ 01273/776477), with superb lamps, candlesticks, pots and mirrors.

Arundel

③⑧ *23 mi west of Brighton, 60 mi south of London.*

The little hilltop town of Arundel is dominated by its great castle, the much-restored home of the dukes of Norfolk for more than 700 years, and an imposing neo-Gothic Roman Catholic cathedral—the duke is Britain's leading Catholic peer. The town itself is full of interesting old buildings, well worth a stroll.

Begun in the 11th century, vast **Arundel Castle** remains rich with the history of the Fitzalan and Howard families and with paintings by Van Dyck, Gainsborough, and Reynolds. It suffered destruction during the Civil War and was remodeled during the 18th century and the Victorian era. The keep, rising from its conical mound, is as old as the original castle, whereas the barbican and the Barons' Hall date from the 13th century. The castle interior was reconstructed in the fashionable Gothic style of the 19th century. Among the treasures on view are the rosary beads and prayer book used by Mary, Queen of Scots, in preparing for her execution. The ceremonial entrance to Arundel Castle is at the top of High Street, but you enter at the bottom, close to the parking lot. ✉ *Mill Rd.* ☎ *01903/882173* ⊕ *www.arundelcastle.org* 🎟 *£9.50, grounds only £4.50* ⊙ *Apr.–Oct., Sun.–Fri. noon–5; last admission at 4.*

Where to Stay & Eat

£–££ ✕ **Black Rabbit.** This renovated 18th-century pub is a find, and you must persevere along Mill Road to find it. Its location by the River Arun, with views of the castle and a bird sanctuary, makes it ideal for a summer lunch. There's a good selection of real ales and an all-day restaurant. ⊠ *Mill Rd., Offham* ☎ *01903/882828* ▤ *DC, MC, V.*

★ 🏰 **Amberley Castle.** The lowering of the portcullis every night at mid-
££££–£££££ night is a sure sign that you're in a genuine medieval castle, one that celebrated its 900th birthday in 2003. Across the dry moat, you'll find present-day luxury. Antiques and rich drapery furnish the individually designed bedrooms, and many have lattice windows, beamed ceilings, and curtained four-posters. You can dine in either the Queens restaurant, beneath a 12th-century barrel-vaulted ceiling, or in the presence of suits of armor in the Great Room. ⊠ *Off B2139, Amberley, BN18 8ND, 5 mi north of Arundel,* ☎ *01798/831992* 🖷 *01798/831998* ⊕ *www.amberleycastle.co.uk* ⇄ *19 rooms* ☖ *Restaurant, in-room hot tubs, in-room VCRs, putting green, tennis court, bar, meeting rooms; no a/c, no kids under 12* ▤ *AE, DC, MC, V* ❙❉❙ *CP.*

£££–£££££ 🏰 **Hilton Avisford Park.** This converted Georgian house on 89 acres of parkland began as the home of an admiral and became a hotel in the 1970s. Bedrooms are in floral or classic style, with close attention to detail. The least expensive prices do not include breakfast. The hotel is 3 mi west of Arundel off A27, on B2132. ⊠ *Yapton La., Walberton, BN18 0LS* ☎ *01243/551215* 🖷 *01243/552485* ⊕ *www.arundel.hilton. com* ⇄ *139 rooms* ☖ *Restaurant, 18-hole golf course, 2 tennis courts, indoor-outdoor pool, gym, sauna, croquet, squash, meeting rooms, helipad; no a/c* ▤ *AE, DC, MC, V* ❙❉❙ *BP.*

££££ 🏰 **Norfolk Arms Hotel.** Like the cathedral and the castle in Arundel, this 18th-century coaching inn on the main street was built by one of the dukes of Norfolk. The main body of the hotel is traditional in appearance, with narrow passages and cozy little rooms. An annex in the courtyard block holds modern rooms. ⊠ *22 High St., BN18 9AD* ☎ *01903/882101* 🖷 *01903/884275* ⊕ *www.norfolkarmshotel.com* ⇄ *34 rooms* ☖ *Restaurant, 2 bars, business services, meeting rooms, some pets allowed (fee); no a/c* ▤ *AE, DC, MC, V* ❙❉❙ *BP.*

Nightlife & the Arts

The **Arundel Festival** (☎ 01903/883690 ⊕ www.arundelfestival.co.uk) presents drama productions and classical and pop concerts in and around the castle grounds for a week in August and September.

Chichester

39 *10 mi west of Arundel, 66 mi southwest of London.*

The Romans founded Chichester, the capital city of West Sussex, on the low-lying plains between the wooded South Downs and the sea. Although it has a large cathedral and all the trappings of a commercial city, Chichester is not much bigger than many of the towns around it. The city walls and major streets follow the original Roman plan; the intersection of the four principal streets is marked by a cross dated 1501.

Norman **Chichester Cathedral,** near the corner of West and South streets, stands on Roman foundations and includes sections from later periods, such as a freestanding bell tower from the 15th century. Inside, a glass panel reveals Roman mosaics uncovered during restoration. Other treasures are the wonderful, moving Saxon limestone reliefs of the raising of Lazarus and Christ arriving in Bethany, both in the choir area, and some outstanding contemporary art, notably a stained-glass window by Marc Chagall, a colorful tapestry by John Piper, and a painting by Graham Sutherland. ✉ *West St.* ☎ *01243/782595* ⊕ *www. chichestercathedral.org.uk* ✆ *£3 suggested donation* ☉ *Easter–Sept., daily 7:30–7; Oct.–Easter, daily 7:30–6. Tours Mon.–Sat. at 11 and 2:15.*

Today Chichester is mainly Georgian, with countless 18th-century houses, and one of the best is **Pallant House,** built in 1712 as a wine merchant's mansion. At that time, its state-of-the-art design showed the latest in complicated brickwork and superb wood carving. Appropriate antiques and porcelains furnish the faithfully restored rooms. The **Pallant House Gallery** showcases a small but important collection of mainly modern British art. Admission includes entry to the **Hans Fiebusch Studio,** nearby in St. Martin's Square, with an exact re-creation of the St. John's Wood (London) studio of this exiled German artist (1898–1998) who was the last member of the so-called degenerate art group. The gallery reopens in spring 2005 after a major refurbishment and the building of a new wing. ✉ *9 N. Pallant* ☎ *01243/774557* ⊕ *www.pallant.org.uk* ✆ *£4* ☉ *Tues.–Sat. 10–5, Sun. and national holidays 12:30–5.*

Where to Stay & Eat

£££ ✕ **Comme Ça.** Its location, about a five-minute walk across the park from the Chichester Festival Theatre, makes this attractively converted pub a pleasant spot for a meal before a performance. Bunches of dried hops, suspended from the ceiling, and antique children's toys decorate the dining room. The owner, Michel Navet, is French, and his chef produces authentic French dishes. Simpler fare is served in the bar at much lower prices, and the fixed-price lunchtime menu is £15. ✉ *67 Broyle Rd.* ☎ *01243/788724* ▱ *AE, DC, MC, V* ☉ *Closed Mon. No dinner Sun. No lunch Tues.*

£££ ▥ **Ship Hotel.** Built in 1790, this architecturally interesting hotel near the Chichester Festival Theatre was originally the home of Admiral Sir George Murray, one of Admiral Nelson's right-hand men. Among the outstanding elements are the flying (partially freestanding) staircase and colonnade. The house has been carefully restored to its 18th-century elegance. Reproduction period furniture fills the pastel guest rooms, which are simpler than the public areas. Prices rise steeply during the Glorious Goodwood horse race in July. ✉ *North St., PO19 1NH* ☎ *01243/778000* 🖷 *01243/788000* ⊕ *www.shiphotel.com* ⇌ *36 rooms* ♿ *Restaurant, cable TV, bar, meeting rooms, some pets allowed; no a/c* ▱ *AE, DC, MC, V* ⋈ *BP.*

Nightlife & the Arts

The **Chichester Festival Theatre** (✉ Oaklands Park ☎ 01243/781312) presents classics and modern plays from May through September and is a venue for touring companies the rest of the year. Built in 1962, it has an international reputation and can be the evening focus for a relaxed day out of London.

Fishbourne Roman Palace

40 *½ mi west of Chichester, 66 mi southwest of London.*

Intricate mosaics and painted walls lavishly decorate many of the 100 rooms of Fishbourne Roman Palace, the largest and grandest Roman villa in Britain. Sophisticated bathing and heating systems remain, and the Roman garden, the only known example extant in northern Europe, is laid out in the style of the 1st century AD. A museum displays artifacts from the site and provides a history of the building. ⊠ *Salthill Rd., Fishbourne* ☎ *01243/785859* ⊕ *www.sussexpast.co.uk* ☎ *£5.20* ☉ *Mar.–July, Sept., and Oct., daily 10–5; Aug., daily 10–6; Nov.–mid-Dec. and Feb., daily 10–4; mid-Dec.–Jan., weekends 10–4.*

Sculpture at Goodwood

★ **41** *3 mi north of Chichester, 63 mi southwest of London.*

Twenty acres of woodland provide a backdrop for this collection of contemporary British sculpture, specially commissioned by the Hat Hill Sculpture Foundation. A third of the approximately 40 exhibits changes annually, and the pieces, sited to maximize their effect, are connected by walks through glades and green fields. A gallery displays models of new sculptures. The park is signposted on the right off A286. ⊠ *Hat Hill Copse, Goodwood* ☎ *01243/538449* ⊕ *www.sculpture.org.uk* ☎ *£10* ☉ *Easter–Oct., Thurs.–Sat. 10:30–4:30.*

Singleton

42 *5 mi north of Chichester, 59 mi south of London.*

Singleton, a secluded village, merits a stop for its excellent open-air museum. The **Weald and Downland Open Air Museum** gives sanctuary to endangered historical buildings. Among the 45 structures on 50 acres of wooded meadows are a cluster of medieval houses, a working water mill, a Tudor market hall, and an ancient blacksmith's shop. ⊠ *A286* ☎ *01243/811348* ⊕ *www.wealddown.co.uk* ☎ *£7.50* ☉ *Mar.–Oct., daily 10:30–6; Nov.–Feb., weekends 10:30–4; last admission 1 hr before closing.*

Petworth House

43 *8 mi northeast of Singleton, 12 mi northwest of Arundel, 54 mi south*
FodorsChoice *of London.*
★

One of the National Trust's greatest treasures and still the home of Lord and Lady Egremont, Petworth House stands in a scenic patch of Sussex. A 13th-century chapel is all that remains of the original manor house, and most of the current building was constructed between 1688 and 1696; the celebrated landscape architect Capability Brown (1716–83) later added a 700-acre deer park. Among the house's outstanding collection of English paintings are works by Gainsborough, Reynolds, Van Dyck, and J. M. W. Turner, the great proponent of Romanticism, who immortalized Petworth's sumptuous interiors in evocative watercolors. Other highlights include Greek and Roman sculpture and Grinling Gibbons wood carvings, such as those in the spectacular Carved Room. Six rooms in the servants' quarters, among them the old kitchen, are open to the public, and the Servants Block serves light lunches. Explore the town of Petworth, too, a jewel studded with narrow old streets and timbered houses. You can access the house off A272 and A283 (parking lots are off the latter). Between 11 and 1 visits are by guided tour only. ⊠ *Petworth* ☎ *01798/342207* ⊕ *www.nationaltrust.org.uk* 💷 *£7, gardens only £1.50* ☉ *House late Mar.–early Nov., Sat.–Wed. 11–5:30; last admission at 5. Gardens late Mar.–early Nov., Sat.–Wed. 11–6. Park daily 8–dusk.*

Guildford

④ *22 mi north of Petworth House, 28 mi southwest of London, 35 mi north of Chichester.*

Guildford, the largest town in Surrey and the county's capital, is an important commuter town, but it retains a faint 18th-century air. No other English town can claim such a brilliant succession of royal visits, from Alfred the Great down to the current queen. Gabled merchants' houses line the steep, pleasantly provincial High Street, now filled with upscale fashion and household shops. You can't miss the massive Tudor facade of the ancient Hospital of the Blessed Trinity. Displays in the **Guildford Museum,** in the old castle building, include interesting exhibits on local history and archaeology, as well as memorabilia of Charles Dodgson, better known as Lewis Carroll, the author of *Alice in Wonderland*. Dodgson spent his last years in a house on nearby Castle Hill. He was buried in the Mount Cemetery, up the hill on High Street. **Castle Arch,** all that remains of the entrance of the old castle, displays a slot for a portcullis. Beyond the arch lie the remains of the castle. ⊠ *Quarry St.* ☎ *01483/444750* ⊕ *www.guildfordmuseum.co.uk* 💷 *Free* ☉ *Mon.–Sat. 11–5.*

Guildford Cathedral, looming on its hilltop across the River Wey, is only the second Anglican cathedral to be built on a new site since the Reformation in the 1500s. It was consecrated in 1961. The redbrick exterior is severely simple, whereas the interior, with its stone and plaster, looks bright and cool. Call several weeks in advance if you want to arrange a guided tour. ⊠ *Stag Hill* ☎ *01483/565287* ⊕ *www.guildford-cathedral.org* 💷 *Donation accepted, tours £3* ☉ *Daily 8:30–5:30.*

Fodor'sChoice ★ In a nation of gardeners, **Wisley,** the Royal Horticultural Society's showpiece, is one of Britain's most popular gardens. Both an ornamental and scientific center, it claims to have greater horticultural diversity than any other garden in the world. Founded by businessman and inventor George Ferguson Wilson in 1878, Wisley has expanded to 240 innovative, colorful acres. The alpine meadow in spring, the lilies, the rose gardens, and the year-round conservatories are highlights, along with a center that sells more than 10,000 types of plants. The garden, near Woking, is 10 mi northeast of Guildford. ⊠ *A3, Woking* ☎ *01483/224234* ⊕ *www.rhs.org.uk/gardens/wisley* ✑ *£7* ☉ *Mar.–Oct., weekdays 10–6, weekends 9–6, until 9 on Wed. June and July; Nov.–Feb., weekdays 10–4:30, weekends 9–4:30.*

Where to Stay & Eat

££–££££ ✕ **Café de Paris.** An 18th-century building holds this busy, family-owned French restaurant and brasserie. The menu focuses on game and fish: try the venison in juniper berry and sloe gin sauce, bouillabaisse, or one of the couscous dishes, but leave enough room for a sorbet. The brasserie has a fine blackboard menu, and there's a prix fixe menu at lunchtime. ⊠ *35 Castle St.* ☎ *01483/534896* ⊟ *AE, MC, V.*

★ **£–££** ✕ **Rumwong.** The elegant waitresses at this Thai restaurant wear traditional long-skirted costumes, so at busy times the dining room looks like a swirling flower garden. On the incredibly long menu, the Thai name of each dish appears with a clear English description. Good choices are the fisherman's soup, a spicy mass of delicious saltwater fish in a clear broth, or *yam pla muek,* a hot salad with squid. The restaurant has opened an Asian supermarket next door. ⊠ *16–18 London Rd.* ☎ *01483/ 536092* ⊟ *MC, V* ☉ *Closed Mon.*

★ ✕▦ **Angel Posting House and Livery.** Guildford was famous for its old **££££–£££££** coaching inns, and this luxurious, 400-year-old hotel is the last of them. The courtyard, where coaches and horses clattered to a stop, still opens to the sky, and light lunches are offered here in summer. Individually designed guest rooms have attractive fabrics, reproductions of antiques, and marble-lined bathrooms; 10 are in a modern annex. There's a salon with a fireplace and minstrel's gallery, and the 13th-century stone-vaulted crypt serves as the backdrop for fine modern British food. ⊠ *91 High St., GU1 3DP* ☎ *01483/564555* ✆ *01483/533770* ⊕ *www.slh. com/angel* ➫ *21 rooms* ⚭ *Restaurant, coffee shop, in-room data ports, meeting rooms, some pets allowed; no a/c* ⊟ *AE, DC, MC, V.*

Nightlife & the Arts

The **Yvonne Arnaud Theatre** (⊠ Millbrook ☎ 01483/440000), a horse-shoe-shape building on an island in the River Wey, frequently previews West End productions; it also has a restaurant.

Clandon Park

㊺ *3 mi east of Guildford, 29 mi southwest of London.*

Venetian architect Giacomo Leoni built the grand Clandon Park for Lord Onslow in the 1730s in the graceful Palladian style. Capability Brown landscaped the park, but the real glory of the mansion is its interior, especially the magnificent two-story Marble Hall, which sometimes hosts concerts. On display are fine collections of 18th-century furniture, needlework, and porcelain, and weapons and medals fill a regimental museum on the grounds. The gardens, too, deserve a look, with a parterre, grotto, and sunken garden. ⊠ *A247, West Clandon* ☎ *01483/ 222482* ⊕ *www.nationaltrust.org.uk* ✑ *£6* ☉ *Apr.–early Nov., Tues.–Thurs. and Sun. 11–5; last admission at 4:30.*

Great Bookham

● 8 mi northeast of Guildford, 25 mi southwest of London.

Great Bookham has some fine old buildings at its core, including a 12th-century church, one of the most complete medieval buildings extant in Surrey. The town is identified with the Highbury of Jane Austen's *Emma*. The most absorbing historic attraction is **Polesden Lacey,** a Regency mansion built in 1824 by Thomas Cubitt on the site of one owned by the famed 18th-century playwright Richard Brinsley Sheridan. Edwardian society hostess Mrs. Ronald Greville lived here from 1906 to 1942 and remodeled the house substantially. Elizabeth, the late Queen Mother, and her husband, the duke of York (later George VI), stayed here in 1923 for part of their honeymoon. Polesden Lacey contains beautiful collections of furniture, paintings, porcelain, and silver. In summer, open-air theatrical performances are given on the grounds. You can also rent equipment from the house (book in advance) and take advantage of the croquet lawns. ⊠ Off A246 ☎ 01372/458203 ⊕ www.nationaltrust.org.uk ✎ £8, grounds only £5 ⊙ House late Mar.–early Nov., Wed.–Sun. 11–5; grounds daily 11–6 or dusk.

en route	As you make your way southeast to Tunbridge Wells via Dorking (about 28 mi), you'll pass **Box Hill** (⊠ A24 ☎ 01306/885502 ⊕ www.nationaltrust.org.uk), the site of the famous picnic in Jane Austen's *Emma*. It's a favorite spot for walking excursions, with lovely views of the South Downs. At the bottom of Box Hill, the Burford Bridge Hotel was where Keats wrote the last sections of *Endymion*; Admiral Nelson also stayed there when traveling down to Portsmouth, and on to fame and death at Trafalgar.

Dorking

● 6 mi south of Great Bookham, 29 mi south of London.

The southeasterly route to Royal Tunbridge Wells leads to the commuter town of Dorking, a pleasant neighborhood that has inspired the pens of many writers. The cemetery holds the remains of the writer George Meredith (1828–1909). On the wide High Street stands the White Horse Inn, or the Marquis o' Granby, as Dickens dubbed it in *The Pickwick Papers*.

Where to Eat

£££–£££££ **Burford Bridge.** Romantic historical associations abound at this beautifully sited hotel at the foot of Box Hill, next to the Mole River. Here Keats completed "Endymion," and Lord Nelson spent his last hours with Emma Hamilton before the battle of Trafalgar; Robert Louis Stevenson, Sheridan, and Wordsworth are among other past visitors. There has been an inn here since the 13th century, though the oldest parts of the existing building date from around 1600. Oak beams and antiques give a cozy feel. ⊠ Box Hill, RH5 6BX ☎ 0870/4008283 ☎ 01306/880386 ⊕ www.heritage-hotels.co.uk ➪ 57 rooms ⌂ Restaurant, outdoor pool, croquet, Internet; no a/c ▤ AE, DC, MC, V ⑩ BP.

East Grinstead

48 *15 mi southeast of Dorking, 32 mi south of London.*

The small country town of East Grinstead claims the longest continuous run of 14th-century timber-frame buildings in the country. Six miles to the east is the village of Hartfield, where A. A. Milne wrote his Winnie the Pooh stories in the 1920s. Tours of Saint Hill Manor, 2 mi southwest of town, concentrate on the five families who have occupied the house since its construction in 1795. The house was for many years the home of L. Ron Hubbard (1911–86), science fiction writer and founder of the Church of Scientology, who left his 530 published works on display in the library.

★ A well-preserved family country house dating from the 1890s and set in a beautiful hillside garden, **Standen** typifies the Arts and Crafts movement. Designed by the influential architect Philip Webb (1831–1913), it contains a wealth of William Morris carpets, wallpapers, and fabrics, and even original electric-light fittings. The house is 2 mi south of East Grinstead. ⊠ *Off B2110* ☎ *01342/323029* ⊕ *www.nationaltrust.org.uk* 🖼 *£6, garden only £3.20* ⊙ *House late Mar.–early Nov., Wed.–Sun. 11–5. Garden late Mar.–early Nov., Wed.–Sun. 11–6; early Nov.–mid-Dec., Fri.–Sun. 11–3.*

At lush **Nymans Garden,** exotic plants collected by the gardener Ludwig Messel beginning in 1885 mingle with more homely varieties. The garden reflects the tastes of three generations of the Messel family. Spring is the best time to appreciate the prolific rhododendrons and the rare Himalayan magnolias in the romantic walled garden; in summer the roses are lovely. The surrounding estate has wild flowers and woodland walks. ⊠ *B2114, Handcross, 10 mi southwest of East Grinstead* ☎ *01444/400321* ⊕ *www.nationaltrust.org.uk* 🖼 *£6.50* ⊙ *Mar.–early Nov., Wed.–Sun. 11–6 or dusk; Nov.–Feb., weekends 11–4.*

Where to Stay & Eat

★ **£££££** ✕🏨 **Gravetye Manor.** This Elizabethan stone mansion, built in 1598, stands on a hilltop site in 1,000 acres of grounds landscaped by William Robinson (1838–1935), an advocate of natural rather than formal gardens. Restored with oak paneling and ornamental plaster ceilings, it represents the epitome of the luxurious English country-house hotel; guest rooms are appropriately plush. The superb if expensive restaurant (fixed-price menu; reservations essential) favors seafood and has an excellent wine list. Two-night breaks, inclusive of meals, are better value. ⊠ *Off B2110, 5 mi south of East Grinstead, RH19 4LJ* ☎ *01342/810567* 🖷 *01342/810080* ⊕ *www.gravetyemanor.co.uk* ⇆ *18 rooms* ♿ *2 restaurants, cable TV, lake, fishing, croquet, bar, meeting rooms; no a/c, no kids under 7 except infants* ⊟ *MC, V.*

MASTERPIECES & MOATS
TUNBRIDGE WELLS TO BURWASH

One of England's greatest attractions is its many magnificent stately homes and castles. But for people with limited time, the dismaying fact is that the greatness is thinly spread, with many houses scattered across the country. Within a 15-mi radius of Tunbridge Wells, however, in that area of hills and hidden dells known as the Weald, lies a remarkable group of historic homes, castles, gardens, and monuments: Penshurst Place, Hever Castle, Chartwell, Knole, Ightham Mote, Leeds Castle, Sissinghurst Castle Garden, Bodiam Castle, Great Dixter House and Gardens, and Rudyard Kipling's Batemans.

Royal Tunbridge Wells

49 *13 mi east of East Grinstead, 39 mi southeast of London.*

Tunbridge Wells has been the butt of humorists who have made it out to be ludicrously straitlaced, but it's a pleasant town favored by many London commuters. Although the city's official name is Royal Tunbridge Wells, locals ignore the prefix "royal," which was added only in 1909, during the reign of Edward VII. The city owes its prosperity to the 17th- and 18th-century passion for spas and mineral baths, initially as medicinal treatments and later as social gathering places. In 1606 a spring of chalybeate (mineral) water was discovered here, drawing legions of royal visitors. It's still possible to drink the waters when a "dipper" (the traditional water dispenser) is in attendance, from Easter through September. Tunbridge Wells reached its zenith in the mid-18th century, when Richard "Beau" Nash presided over its social life. The buildings at the lower end of High Street are mostly 18th century, but as the street climbs the hill north, changing its name to Mount Pleasant Road, structures become more modern.

A good place to begin a visit is at the **Pantiles,** a famous promenade with colonnaded shops near the spring on one side of town, which derives its odd name from the Dutch "pan tiles" that originally paved the area. Now bordered on two sides by busy main roads, the Pantiles remains an elegant, tranquil oasis. The **Church of King Charles the Martyr** (✉ Chapel Pl.), across the road from the Pantiles, dates from 1678, when it was dedicated to Charles I, who was executed by Parliament in 1649. Its plain exterior belies its splendid interior; take special note of the beautifully plastered baroque ceiling.

Tunbridge Wells Museum and Art Gallery, at the northern end of Mount Pleasant Road, contains a fascinating jumble of local artifacts, prehistoric relics, and Victorian toys, as well as a permanent exhibition of Tunbridge Ware pieces: small, wooden items inlaid with tiny pieces of colored woods. ✉ *Civic Centre, Mount Pleasant Rd.* ☎ *01892/554171* ⊕ *www.tunbridgewells.gov.uk* ✉ *Free* ☉ *Mon.–Sat. 9:30–5, Sun. 10–4.*

off the beaten path

ALL SAINTS CHURCH – A modest building dating from the 13th and 14th centuries holds one of the glories of 20th-century church art. The church is awash with the luminous yellows and blues of 12 windows by Marc Chagall (1887–1985), commissioned as a tribute by the family of a young girl who was drowned in a sailing accident in 1963. The church is 4 mi north of Tunbridge Wells; turn off A26 before Tonbridge and continue a mile or so east along B2017. ✉ *B2017, Tudeley* ☎ *0870/744–1456* ✉ *Free* ☉ *Daily 9–6 or dusk.*

Where to Stay & Eat

£££–££££ ✕ **Gracelands Palace.** Fun elements—not least of which is owner Paul Chan's cabaret of Elvis songs—as well as the food have made this popular Chinese restaurant famous. The fixed-price menu includes Szechuan and Cantonese fare. ⊠ *3 Cumberland Walk* ☎ *01892/540754* ▭ *AE, MC, V* ⊘ *Closed Sun. No lunch Mon.*

★ **£££–££££** ✕ **Thackeray's House.** This mid-17th-century tile-hung house, once the home of Victorian novelist William Makepeace Thackeray, is now an elegant restaurant known for creative, modern French cuisine. Specialties include duck salad with toasted brioche and grilled tuna loin with sun-dried tomatoes and mille-feuille of eggplant. The lunchtime Menu du Jour is a very good value at £12.50 for three courses. ⊠ *85 London Rd.* ☎ *01892/511921* ▭ *AE, MC, V* ⊘ *Closed Mon. and last wk in Dec. No dinner Sun.*

£–£££ ✕ **Mount Edgcumbe.** On the hill above the old center of the town, this restaurant is smart but friendly, pristinely fitted out but full of old-fashioned character. A snack menu is a good accompaniment to the real ales, or you can choose from a more substantial à la carte menu with dishes such as chargrilled fillet of Scottish beef with shallot cream, and venison sausages with herb mash. ⊠ *The Common, TN4 8BX* ☎ *01892/526823* ⊜ *01892/536607* ▭ *MC, V.*

★ **£–££** ✕ **Himalayan Gurkha Restaurant.** It's not what you might expect to find in the cozy confines of Tunbridge Wells, but the Nepalese cuisine of this friendly spot seems popular with locals. Spicy mountain dishes are cooked with great care in traditional clay ovens or barbecued on flaming charcoal. There are appealing vegetarian options. ⊠ *31 Church Rd.* ☎ *01892/527834* ▭ *MC, V.*

£££–££££ ✕▥ **Hotel du Vin.** Formerly a private house, this elegant sandstone building dating from 1762 has been transformed into a chic boutique hotel with polished wood floors and luxurious armchairs and sofas. Oriental rugs give public rooms an air of warmth that is both intimate and grand, and guest rooms are modern, with pampering bathrooms. The Burgundy Bar stocks a fine selection of wines from the eponymous region of France. The contemporary menu in the bistro changes daily but is strong on creamy soups and crisp salads. ⊠ *Crescent Rd., near Mount Pleasant Rd., TN1 2LY* ☎ *01892/526455* ⊜ *01892/512044* ⊕ *www.hotelduvin.com* ⏎ *36 rooms* ⚘ *Restaurant, cable TV, billiards, 2 bars, meeting rooms; no a/c* ▭ *AE, DC, MC, V.*

£££–££££ ▥ **Spa Hotel.** The Goring family, which also runs the noted Goring Hotel in London, owns this plush hotel loaded with amenities. Carefully chosen furnishings and details help maintain the country-house flavor of the 1766 Georgian mansion, although guest rooms come with many modern extras. There are superb views from the 14-acre grounds across the town and into the Weald of Kent. The traditional English fare of the Chandelier Restaurant is popular with locals. ⊠ *Mount Ephraim, TN4 8XJ* ☎ *01892/520331* ⊜ *01892/510575* ⊕ *www.spahotel.co.uk* ⏎ *71 rooms* ⚘ *Restaurant, cable TV, tennis court, indoor pool, 2 gyms, hair salon, sauna, spa, croquet, meeting rooms, some pets allowed; no a/c in some rooms* ▭ *AE, DC, MC, V.*

££ 🏠 **Old Parsonage.** This friendly guest house, 2 mi south of Tunbridge Wells via A267, stands at the top of a quiet lane beside the village church. Built in 1820, the Georgian manor has lovely antique furniture, a dining room with oak refectory table, and a big conservatory for afternoon tea. Two pubs and a restaurant lie within a short walk of the house. ✉ *Church La., Frant, TN3 9DX* 📠📠 *01892/750773* ⊕ *www.theoldparsonagehotel.co.uk* 🛏 *3 rooms* ♿ *No a/c* ☰ *MC, V* ⦿ *BP.*

Penshurst Place

★ 🌀 *7 mi northwest of Royal Tunbridge Wells, 33 mi southeast of London.*

At the center of the hamlet of Penshurst stands one of England's finest medieval manor houses, hidden behind tall trees and walls. Although it has retained its 14th-century hall, Penshurst is mainly Elizabethan, with additions from later periods. It has been in the Sidney family since 1552, giving the house particular historical interest. The most famous Sidney is the Elizabethan poet, Sir Philip, author of *Arcadia*. The **Baron's Hall,** topped in 1341 with a chestnut roof, is the oldest and one of the grandest halls to survive from the early Middle Ages. Family portraits, furniture, tapestries, and armor help tell the story of the house. The grounds include a 10-acre walled Tudor garden, and there's a toy museum and a restaurant. Although Penshurst is basically an appendage of the Great House, the village is a delightful destination. It centers around Leicester Square, which has late-15th-century half-timber structures adorned with soaring brick chimneys. ✉ *Off B2188; from Tunbridge Wells, follow A26 and B2176* 📞 *01892/870307* ⊕ *www.penshurstplace.com* 🎟 *£7, grounds only £5.50* 🕐 *Mar., weekends noon–5:30; Apr.–Oct., daily noon–5. Grounds daily 10:30–6. Last admission 30 mins before closing.*

Where to Stay & Eat

££–££££ ✗ **Spotted Dog.** This pub first opened its doors in 1520; today, it tempts you with an inglenook fireplace, heavy beams, imaginative food, and a splendid view of Penshurst Place. ✉ *Smarts Hill* ☎ *01892/870253* ☰ *MC, V.*

£££–££££ 🏠 **Rose and Crown.** Originally a 16th-century inn, this hotel on the main street in Tonbridge (5 mi east of Penshurst, 5 mi north of Tunbridge Wells) has a distinctive portico, added later. Inside, low-beam ceilings and Jacobean woodwork make the bar and the restaurant snug and inviting. Guest rooms in the main building are traditionally furnished, whereas rooms in the newer annex are more modern in style. ✉ *125 High St., Tonbridge, TN9 1DD* ☎ *01732/357966* 📠 *01732/357194* ⊕ *www.rose-andcrownhotel.co.uk* 🛏 *50 rooms* ♿ *Restaurant, cable TV, bar, meeting rooms; no a/c* ☰ *AE, MC, V* ⦿ *BP.*

Hever Castle

★ 🌀 *3 mi west of Penshurst, 10 mi northwest of Royal Tunbridge Wells, 30 mi southeast of London.*

For some, 13th-century Hever fits the stereotype of what a castle should look like: all turrets and battlements, the whole encircled by a water lily–bound moat. For others, it's too squat in structure (and perhaps too

VISITING THE TREASURE HOUSES

CURIOSITY AS TO HOW the other half lives is undoubtedly one of the most deep-seated traits of human nature, and it's pleasing to know you can satisfy your healthy desire to snoop through stately homes, including the glorious specimens in Kent, for the payment of a small amount of conscience money. The fact that you will see some of the world's greatest treasures at the same time is a bonus.

Even the most highly developed sense of curiosity isn't enough to explain why millions of people have surged onto England's stately home trail, however. They have been urged to move by a great deal of exposure—the houses all over the country touched by Royal Family upheavals, such as Althorp, the ancestral home of Princess Diana; the numerous television serials, which have brought further fame to such spectacular houses as Castle Howard and Blenheim Palace; the continuing spate of historical movies shot on location. Here, in Kent, Penshurst Place and Knole are still the homes of the aristocratic families who built them more than half a millennium ago.

The reason owners of stately homes open them to the public is simply that they need the ready money. Spiritually rewarding as it must be to own vast tracts of countryside, paintings by Rembrandt and Gainsborough, a house designed by one of the Adam brothers, and tapestries by the mile and porcelain by the ton—it is all a dead loss as far as cash flow (and death duties) are concerned.

What you get for your entrance fee differs enormously from one house to another. In some houses you are left completely free to wander at will, soaking up the splendor. In others, you are organized into groups that proceed through the rooms like bands of prisoners behind enemy lines. Occasionally you may find that your mentor is a chatty member of the family.

A few things should be kept in mind when you're touring these treasure houses. You may be able to save money by purchasing a special pass or joining an organization such as the National Trust (⇨ Discounts & Deals in Smart Travel Tips). Many houses are unreachable except by car. Hours are always subject to abrupt change, so be sure to call the day before and inquire. Although most houses are open only from April to October, some have celebrated parks—Blenheim Palace and Chatsworth come to mind—that are utter delights and are open much of the year. The most popular houses can be extremely busy in peak summer months. You may want to plan off-season visits or arrive early in the day to avoid crowds.

The National Trust (⊕ www. nationaltrustcottages.co.uk) owns several properties that may be rented: an apartment in the servants' quarters at Standen, for example, or the garden cottage at Polesden Lacey. For posterity the Trust has also preserved some less stately homes which are now available for rent, from lighthouse-keepers' cottages to former fish processing sheds.

Many people have a top-10 list of favorite houses—Knole, Longleat, Woburn, and so on—but don't forget lesser-known neoclassical abodes and those mock-medieval Victorian piles, such as Castle Drogo in Devon, designed for Sir Julius Drewe, the founder of a chain of grocery stores. There is something keenly appropriate about the fact that the last great castle built in Britain was created for a shopkeeper. Napoléon, who echoed Adam Smith in observing that England was a nation of shopkeepers, would have approved.

renovated). Here the ill-fated Anne Boleyn, second wife of Henry VIII and mother of Elizabeth I, was courted and won by Henry, who had her beheaded in 1536. He later gave Hever to his fourth wife, Anne of Cleves. American millionaire William Waldorf Astor acquired the castle in 1903, and the Astor family owned it until 1983. Astor built a Tudor village to house his staff (it's now a hotel for corporate functions) and had the stunning gardens laid out, with Italian and Tudor plantings, a yew maze, and topiary. ⊠ *Off B2026, Hever* ☎ *01732/865224* ⊕ *www.hevercastle.co.uk* ⊠ *£8.80, grounds only £7* ⊙ *Castle Apr.–Oct., daily noon–6; Mar. and Nov., daily noon–4. Grounds Apr.–Oct., daily 11–6; Mar. and Nov., daily 11–4. Last admission 1 hr before closing.*

Chartwell

52 *9 mi north of Hever Castle, 12 mi northwest of Tunbridge Wells, 28 mi southeast of London.*

Chartwell was Sir Winston Churchill's home from 1924 until his death in 1965. The Victorian house was acquired by the National Trust, and today it appears much as it did in Churchill's lifetime, with personal memorabilia and even a half-smoked cigar in an ashtray. In the garden you can see a wall he built himself. ⊠ *Off B2026, Westerham* ☎ *01732/866368* ⊕ *www.nationaltrust.org.uk* ⊠ *£7, garden and studio only £3.50* ⊙ *Late Mar.–June and Sept.–early Nov., Wed.–Sun. 11–5; July and Aug., Tues.–Sun. 11–5. Last admission at 4:15.*

Knole

53 *8 mi east of Chartwell, 11 mi north of Royal Tunbridge Wells, 27 mi*

Fodor'sChoice *southeast of London.*
★

The town of Sevenoaks lies in London's commuter belt, a world away from the baronial air of its premier attraction, Knole, the grand home of the Sackville family since the 16th century. Begun in the 15th century and enlarged in 1603 by Thomas Sackville, Knole, with its complex of courtyards and buildings, resembles a small town. You'll need most of an afternoon to explore it thoroughly. The house is noted for its tapestries, embroidered furnishings, and the most famous set of 17th-century silver furniture to survive. Most of the salons are in the pre-baroque mode, rather dark and armorial. Paintings on display include family portraits by 18th-century artists Thomas Gainsborough and Sir Joshua Reynolds. The magnificently florid staircase was a novelty in its Elizabethan heyday. Vita Sackville-West grew up at Knole and set her novel *The Edwardians,* a witty account of life among the gilded set, here. Encompassed by a 1,000-acre deer park, the house lies in the center of Sevenoaks, opposite St. Nicholas Church. To get there from Chartwell, drive north to Westerham, then pick up A25 and head east for 8 mi. ⊠ *Off A225* ☎ *01732/450608* ⊕ *www.nationaltrust.org.uk* ⊠ *House £6, gardens £2* ⊙ *Late Mar.–early Nov., Wed.–Sun. and national holidays 11–4, last admission at 3:30; gardens May–Sept., 1st Wed. of each month 11–4, last admission at 3.*

Ightham Mote

54 *7 mi southeast of Knole, 10 mi north of Royal Tunbridge Wells, 31 mi southeast of London.*

Finding Ightham Mote requires careful navigation, but it's worth the effort to see a vision right out of the Middle Ages. To enter this outstanding example of a small manor house, you cross a stone bridge over one of the dreamiest moats in England—the absolute quintessence of medieval romanticism. This moat, however, does not relate to the "mote" in the name, which refers to the role of the house as a meeting place, or "moot." Ightham (pronounced *i*-tem) Mote's magical exterior has changed little since it was built in the 14th century, but within you'll find that it encompasses styles of several periods, Tudor to Victorian. The Great Hall is an antiquarian's delight, both comfy and grand, and the magnificent Tudor chapel, drawing room, and billiards room in the northwest quarter are highlights. Ongoing restoration may mean that parts of the house are sometimes closed. Take time to explore the 14-acre garden and the woodland walks or to eat at the restaurant. To reach the house from Sevenoaks, follow A25 east to A227 (8 mi) and follow the signs. ⊠ *Off A227, Ivy Hatch, Sevenoaks* ☎ *01732/810378* ⊕ *www.nationaltrust.org.uk* ⊠ *£6.50* ☉ *Apr.–Oct., Mon., Wed.–Fri., and Sun.: house 10:30–5:30, garden 10–5:30. Estate daily all year, dawn–dusk.*

Rochester

55 *15 mi north of Ightham Mote, 28 mi southeast of London.*

Kent is Charles Dickens country, and Dickens aficionados will want to head to Rochester, the place outside of London most closely associated with the great author. He lived for many years at Gad's Hill Place, just outside of town. You can find out all about Dickens and his connections with the town at the **Charles Dickens Centre,** with life-size models of scenes from the author's books that can amuse and horrify at the same time (parents, be warned). Opposite the center, look for the abode of Uncle Pumblechook in *Great Expectations,* one of the many buildings in High Street still "full of gables with old beams and timbers," as Dickens described them. ⊠ *Eastgate House, High St.* ☎ *01634/844176* ⊠ *£3.90* ☉ *Apr.–Sept., daily 10:30–5:30; Oct.–Mar., Wed.–Sun. 10:30–4:30.*

Rochester Castle is one of the finest surviving examples of Norman military architecture. The keep, built in the 1100s and partly based on the Roman city wall, is 125 feet high, the tallest in England. ⊠ *Boley Hill* ☎ *01634/402276* ⊕ *www.english-heritage.org.uk* ⊠ *£4* ☉ *Apr.–Sept., daily 10–6; Oct.–Mar., daily 10–4; last admission 30 mins before closing.*

In AD 604, Augustine of Canterbury ordained the first English bishop in a small cathedral on the site of **Rochester Cathedral.** The current cathedral, England's second-oldest, is rather a jumble of architectural styles. Work was started in 1077 by the Norman Bishop Gundulph, who also built the castle. The elaborate Norman west front is striking, as is the crypt. ☒ *Boley Hill* ☎ *01634/843366* 💷 *£2 donation suggested* ⊙ *Mon.–Sat. 7:30–6, Sun. 7:30–5.*

The buildings and 47 retired ships at the **Historic Dockyard** across the River Medway from Rochester constitute the world's most complete Georgian–early Victorian dockyard. The dockyard's origins go back to the time of Henry VIII, and some 400 naval ships were built here over as many years, as shown in the museum and the Wooden Walls exhibit. There's a guided tour of the submarine HMS *Ocelot,* the last warship to be built for the Royal Navy at Chatham. ☒ *Chatham* ☎ *01634/823807* ⊕ *www.chdt.org.uk* 💷 *£10* ⊙ *Feb.–Oct., daily 10–6 (or dusk if earlier).*

Where to Stay

£ 🏠 **Mrs. Thomas' Bed & Breakfast.** This small B&B in an 1851 building re-creates the atmosphere of a Dickens-era town house, complete with period furnishings and an early Victorian four-poster in one bedroom. It's a two-minute walk from the railway station. ☒ *255 High St., ME1 1HQ* ☎ *01634/842737* 🛏 *3 rooms, 1 with bath* ⚴ *No a/c* 🍴 *BP.*

Nightlife & the Arts

Rochester sponsors a **Dickens festival** (☎ 01634/306000) in late May or early June, at which thousands of people in period dress attend enactments of scenes from the author's novels. Another important Dickens festival takes place in Broadstairs (40 mi east).

Leeds Castle

★ ❺❻ *12 mi south of Rochester, 19 mi northwest of Royal Tunbridge Wells, 40 mi southeast of London.*

The bubbling River Medway runs through Maidstone, Kent's county seat, with its backdrop of chalky downs. Nearby, the fairy-tale stronghold of Leeds Castle commands two small islands on a peaceful lake. Dating to the 9th century and rebuilt by the Normans in 1119, Leeds (not to be confused with Leeds in the North of England) became a favorite home of many medieval English queens. Henry VIII liked it so much he had it converted from a fortress into a grand palace. The house (much restored) offers a fine collection of paintings and furniture, plus an unusual dog-collar museum. Other attractions include a maze, a grotto, an aviary of native and exotic birds, and woodland gardens. The castle is 5 mi east of Maidstone. ☒ *A20* ☎ *01622/765400* ⊕ *www. leedscastle.org.uk* 💷 *Mid-Mar.–Nov. £12.50, Dec.–mid-Mar. £10.50; grounds only mid-Mar.–Nov. £10, Dec.–mid-Mar. £9* ⊙ *Apr.–Oct., daily 10–5; Nov.–Mar., daily 10–3. Castle closed last Sat. in June and 1st Sat. in July.*

Sissinghurst Castle Garden

❺❼ *10 mi south of Leeds Castle, 53 mi southeast of London.*

Fodor'sChoice
★

One of the most famous gardens in the world, Sissinghurst rests deep in the Kentish countryside around the remains of a moated Tudor castle. Unpretentiously beautiful, quintessentially English, the gardens were laid out in the 1930s around the remains of a former wing of the castle by the writer Vita Sackville-West (one of the Sackvilles of Knole) and her husband, the diplomat Harold Nicolson. The grounds are at their best in June and July, when the roses are in bloom. The gardens are informal in style; the White Garden, with its white flowers and silver-gray foliage, is a classic, and the herb garden and cottage garden show Sackville-West's knowledge of plants. Children may feel restricted in the gardens, and strollers (push chairs, in Britain) are not allowed. From Leeds Castle, make your way south on B2163 and A274 through Headcorn, then follow signs. ⊠ *A262, Cranbrook* ☎ *01580/710701* ⊕ *www. nationaltrust.org.uk* ☜ *£7* ⊙ *Mar.–Nov., Mon., Tues., and Fri. 11–6:30, weekends 10–6:30; last admission at 5:30. Admission often restricted because of limited space; a timed ticket system may be in effect, usually May–July.*

Where to Stay & Eat

£ ✕ **Claris's Tea Shop.** Claris's, near Sissinghurst Castle Garden, serves traditional English teas in a half-timber room and displays attractive English crafts items. There's a garden for summer, and a gift shop stocks pottery, china, and glass. ⊠ *3 High St., Biddenden* ☎ *01580/291025* ▭ *No credit cards* ⊙ *Closed Mon. No dinner.*

★ £ 🏠 **Frogshole Oast.** This converted 18th-century rural oasthouse has three kilns that were once used for drying hops. The house retains many period features, and the rooms and sitting area have some antiques. There's a garden and a natural duck pond. ⊠ *Sissinghurst Rd., 2 mi east of Sissinghurst Castle Garden, Biddenden, TN27 8HB* ☎☎ *01580/291935* ✐ *hartley@frogsholeoast.freeserve.co.uk* ☞ *3 rooms* ⊖ *No a/c, no room TVs* ⦿| *BP.*

en route | As you leave Sissinghurst Castle Garden, continue south along A229 through Hawkhurst, a little village that was once the headquarters of a notorious gang of smugglers. Turn left onto the B2244 and left at the Curlew pub to arrive in the tiny Sussex village of Bodiam.

Bodiam Castle

★ ⟳ ⑱ *9 mi south of Cranbrook, 15 mi southeast of Royal Tunbridge Wells, 57 mi southeast of London.*

Immortalized in 1,001 travel posters, Bodiam Castle is one of Britain's most picturesque medieval strongholds, despite being virtually a shell. Built in 1385 to withstand a threatened French invasion, it was "slighted" (partly demolished) during the English Civil War of 1642–46 and has been uninhabited ever since. Nevertheless, you can climb some of the towers. Surrounded by a lovely moat and adorned with battlements and turrets, this castle seems designed to be photographed. Activities for kids are run during school holidays. ⊠ *Off B2244, Bodiam* ☎ *01580/ 830436* ⊕ *www.nationaltrust.org.uk* ☜ *£4.20* ⊙ *Mid-Feb.–Oct., daily 10–6 or dusk; Nov.–mid-Feb., weekends 10–4 or dusk; last admission 1 hr before closing.*

Great Dixter House & Gardens

59 *3 mi east of Bodiam, 18 mi southeast of Royal Tunbridge Wells, 60 mi southeast of London.*

Combining one of the largest timber-frame halls in the country with a cottage garden on a grand scale, this place will get your green fingers twitching. The house dates to 1464 and was restored in 1910 by architect Edwin Lutyens, who also designed the garden. From these beginnings, horticulturist and writer Christopher Lloyd, whose birthplace this is, has developed a series of "garden rooms" and a dazzling herbaceous Long Border. There's a nursery on site. ⊠ *Off A28, Northiam* ☎ *01797/252878* ⊕ *www.greatdixter.co.uk* ⊠ *£6.50, gardens only £5* ⊘ *Apr.–Oct., Tues.–Sun. 2–5:30; last admission at 5.*

Burwash

60 *13 mi west of Northiam, 14 mi south of Royal Tunbridge Wells, 58 mi southeast of London.*

Burwash, a pretty Sussex village, is known for its association with writer Rudyard Kipling. Close by, between Burwash Common and the River Dudwell, is the setting for *Puck of Pook's Hill,* one of Kipling's well-known children's books.

Kipling lived from 1902 to 1936 at **Bateman's,** a beautiful 17th-century house a half mile south of the village that was built for a prominent iron-master when Sussex was the center of England's iron industry. Many of the rooms, including Kipling's study, look as they did when the writer lived here, and you can also see his Rolls Royce. In the garden, a water mill still grinds flour (most Saturdays in summer at 2 PM); it's thought to be one of the oldest working water turbines. ⊠ *Off A265* ☎ *01435/ 882302* ⊕ *www.nationaltrust.org.uk* ⊠ *£5.50* ⊘ *Mar., weekends 11–4, garden only; late Mar.–late Sept., Sat.–Wed. 11–5 (house), 11–5:30 (grounds); last admission 1 hr before closing.*

Sports & the Outdoors

Bewl Water, one of England's largest reservoirs, has aquatic sports, waterside walks, bicycle rentals, and boat trips. There are also special events and an adventure playground. There's a £2.50–£5 parking fee. ⊠ *Off B2099, 5 mi north of Burwash* ☎ *01892/890661* ⊕ *www.bewl. co.uk* ⊘ *Open daily 9–sunset.*

SOUTHEAST A TO Z

To research prices, get advice from other travelers, and book travel arrangements, visit www.fodors.com.

AIRPORTS

Gatwick Airport, 27 mi south of London, has direct flights from many U.S. cities and is more convenient for this region than Heathrow. The terminal for the British Rail line is in the airport buildings, and there are connections to major towns in the region. *See* London A to Z *in* Chapter 1 for information about transfers from Gatwick to London.

🚶 **Gatwick Airport** ✉ M23, Junction 9, Crawley ☎ 0870/000–2468 ⊕ www.baa.co.uk.

BUS TRAVEL

National Express serves the region from London's Victoria Coach Station. Trips to Brighton and Canterbury take less than two hours; to Chichester, about three hours. For regional bus transport inquiries, contact Traveline. Maps and timetables are available at bus depots, train stations, local libraries, and tourist information centers.

FARES &   🚶 **National Express** ☎ 0870/580–8080 ⊕ www.nationalexpress.com. **Traveline**
SCHEDULES   ☎ 0870/608-2608 ⊕ www.traveline.org.uk.

CAR RENTAL

🚶 **Local Agencies Avis** ✉ 6A Brighton Marina, Brighton ☎ 01273/673738 ✉ Eastern Docks, Dover ☎ 01304/206265. **Hertz** ✉ 47 Trafalgar St., Brighton ☎ 01273/738227 ✉ c/o Elf Garage, Broad Oak Rd., Canterbury ☎ 01227/470864 ✉ 173-177 Snargate St., Dover ☎ 01304/207303 ✉ Guildford Railway Station, Station Approach, Guildford ☎ 01483/536677.

CAR TRAVEL

Major routes radiating outward from London to the Southeast are, from west to east, M23/A23 to Brighton (52 mi); A21, passing by Royal Tunbridge Wells to Hastings (65 mi); A20/M20 to Folkestone; and A2/M2 via Canterbury (56 mi) to Dover (71 mi).

A good link route for traveling through the region, from Hampshire across the border into Sussex and Kent, is A272 (which becomes A265). It runs through the Weald, which separates the North Downs from the more inviting South Downs. Although smaller, less busy roads forge deeper into the downs, even the main roads take you through lovely countryside and villages. The main route east from the downs to the Channel ports and resorts of Kent is A27. To get to Romney Marsh (just across the Sussex border in Kent), take A259 from Rye. Be warned that more traffic tickets are issued per traffic warden in Brighton than anywhere else in the country.

EMERGENCIES

🚶 **Ambulance, fire, police** ☎ 999. **Royal Sussex County Hospital** ✉ Eastern Rd., Brighton ☎ 01273/696955. **Canterbury Hospital** ✉ Ethelbert Rd., Canterbury ☎ 01227/766877.

TOURS

BUS TOURS   City Sightseeing's hop-on, hop-off bus tour of Brighton leaves Brighton Pier every 20–30 minutes and lasts about an hour. It operates April–October; cost is £6.50.

🚶 **City Sightseeing** ☎ 01789/294466 ⊕ www.city-sightseeing.com.

PRIVATE GUIDES   The Southeast England Tourist Board (⇨ Visitor Information) can arrange private tours with qualified Blue Badge guides. The Canterbury Guild of Guides provides guides who have a specialized knowledge of the city and its surrounding area. Tickets are available from the Information Center.

🚶 **Canterbury Guild of Guides** ✉ Arnett House, Hawks La. ☎ 01227/459779.

TRAIN TRAVEL

Connex South Eastern and Connex South Central serve the area from London's Victoria and Charing Cross (for all areas) and Waterloo (for the west). From London, the trip to Brighton takes about one hour by the fast train, and to Dover, about two hours. South West Trains runs service to Guildford. The line running west from Dover passes through Ashford, where you can change trains for Hastings and Eastbourne. There are connections from Eastbourne for Lewes, and from Brighton for Chichester. For local and regional information, call National Rail Enquiries. For a special piece of railway nostalgia, **Steam Dreams** (☎ 01483/209888 ⊕ www.steamdreams.co.uk) runs the Cathedrals Express steam train several times a summer from London Victoria to Canterbury, returning via Hove. Round-trip tickets start at £45.

CUTTING COSTS A Network Railcard costing £20, valid throughout the southern and southeastern regions for a year, entitles you and three companions to one-third off many off-peak fares.

FARES & SCHEDULES 🔳 **National Rail Enquiries** (☎ 0845/748-4950 ⊕ www.nationalrail.co.uk).

TRAVEL AGENCIES

Besides those listed below, Thomas Cook has offices in Dover, Eastbourne, Folkestone, Guildford, Hastings, Hove, Maidstone, Ramsgate, and Sevenoaks.
🔳 Local Agent Referrals **American Express** ✉ 82 North St., Brighton ☎ 01273/712900. **Thomas Cook** ✉ 58 North St., Brighton ☎ 01273/367700 ✉ 9 High St., Canterbury ☎ 01227/597800 ✉ 109 Mount Pleasant Rd., Royal Tunbridge Wells ☎ 01892/791500.

VISITOR INFORMATION

The Southeast England Tourist Board will send you useful illustrated booklets, *South East Breaks* and *Walk South East England*, and can give you information on tours and excursions. The office is open Monday–Thursday 9–5:30 and Friday 9–5. Local tourist information centers (TICs) are normally open Monday–Saturday 9:30–5:30, but hours vary seasonally; offices are listed below by town.
🔳 **Southeast England Tourist Board** ✉ The Old Brew House, 1 Warwick Park, Royal Tunbridge Wells, TN2 5TU ☎ 01892/540766 🖷 01892/511008 ⊕ www.southeastengland.uk.com. **Arundel** ✉ 61 High St., BN18 9AJ ☎ 01903/882268 ⊕ www.sussex-by-the-sea.co.uk. **Brighton** ✉ 10 Bartholomew Sq., BN1 1JS ☎ 0906/7112255 ⊕ www.visitbrighton.com. **Canterbury** ✉ 12–13 Sun St., CT1 2HX ☎ 01227/378100 ⊕ www.canterbury.co.uk. **Chichester** ✉ 29A South St., PO19 1AH ☎ 01243/775888, ⊕www.chichester.gov.uk. **Dover** ✉ The Old Town Gaol, Biggin St., CT16 1DL ☎ 01304/205108. **Guildford** ✉ 14 Tunsgate, GU1 3QT ☎ 01483/444333 ⊕ www.guildfordborough.co.uk. **Hastings** ✉ Queens Sq., Priory Meadow, TN34 1TL ☎ 01424/781111 ✉ 2 The Stade ☎ 01424/781111 ⊕www.visithastings.com. **Lewes** ✉ 187 High St., BN7 2DE ☎ 01273/483448 ⊕ www.lewes.gov.uk. **Maidstone** ✉ Town Hall, Middle Row, High St., ME14 1TF ☎ 01622/602169 ⊕ www.tour-maidstone.com. **Royal Tunbridge Wells** ✉ The Old Fish Market, The Pantiles, TN2 5TN ☎ 01892/515675 ⊕ www.visittunbridgewells.com. **Rye** ✉ The Heritage Centre, Strand Quay, TN31 7AY ☎ 01797/226696 ⊕ www.rye-tourism.co.uk.

THE SOUTH
WINCHESTER, SALISBURY & STONEHENGE

LISTEN FOR ANCIENT ECHOES
at always-mysterious Stonehenge ⇨*p.192*

HIKE PAST BEACHES AND CLIFFS
along the Dorset Coast path ⇨*p.206*

SEE ENGLAND'S TALLEST SPIRE
at soaring Salisbury Cathedral ⇨*p.182*

SNUGGLE UNDER A THATCH ROOF
at Lamperts Cottage B&B ⇨*p.202*

GO NAUTICAL OVER NELSON
at Portsmouth Historic Dockyard ⇨*p.174*

STROLL LANDSCAPING PERFECTION
at 18th-century Stourhead ⇨*p.188*

SIP A PINT BY CASTLE RUINS
at the age-old Fox pub in Corfe ⇨*p.199*

CHANNEL THE LITERARY LIFE
at Jane Austen's House in Chawton ⇨*p.171*

Updated by
Robert
Andrews

CATHEDRALS, STATELY HOMES, STONE CIRCLES—the South, made up of Hampshire, Dorset, and Wiltshire counties, holds all kinds of attractions, and not a few quiet pleasures. Two important cathedrals, Winchester and Salisbury (pronounced *sawls*-bree), are here, as are stately homes—Longleat, Stourhead, and Wilton House, among them—intriguing market towns, and hundreds of haunting prehistoric remains, two of which, Avebury and Stonehenge, should not be missed. These are but the tourist-brochure superlatives. Sooner or later, anyone spending time in these parts should rent a bike and set out to discover the back-road villages—much favored by those who migrate here from every corner of the country in search of upward mobility—*not* found in those brochures. After a drink in the village pub and a look at the cricket game on the village green, take a break at a strawberry farm, where you can lie on straw strewn between the rows and gorge yourself on sun-warmed berries, or collapse in a grassy field that has "nap time" written all over it. *This* is what summer in England is all about.

Hampshire has been called the Cinderella County because for many it is just a county to be crossed in the feverish holiday migration from London to the cliffs and coves of Devon and Cornwall in the west. To many others, Hampshire means the last sight of England from departing steamers, or a first solid acquaintance with her on stepping ashore at Southampton. The county may seem but the gateway to England, through which to pass hurriedly. Nothing could be further from the truth, for the sandwich shire holds much for the perceptive.

One of the area's many historical highlights was when Alfred the Great, teaching religion and letters, made Winchester the capital of 9th-century England and helped lay plans for Britain's first navy, sowing the seeds of the Commonwealth. This well-preserved market town is dominated by its cathedral, an imposing edifice dotted with the Gothic tombs of 15th-century bishops, who lie peacefully behind grillwork, their marble hands crossed for eternity. Winchester is a good center from which to visit quiet villages where so many of England's once great personages, from Florence Nightingale to Lord Mountbatten, lived or died. Jane Austen and her works are enduringly popular, and thanks to devoted readers and a spate of filmed versions of her classic novels, her home at Chawton has become a favored pilgrimage spot. But everywhere the unscheming hand of time has scattered over Hampshire's pretty villages, many with cottages grouped around a green.

Beyond the gentle, gardenlike landscape of Hampshire, you can explore the somewhat harsher terrain of Salisbury Plain. Two monuments, millennia apart, stand sentinel over the plain. One is the 404-foot-tall stone spire of Salisbury Cathedral, which dominates the entire Salisbury valley and has been immortalized in oil by John Constable. Not far away is the most imposing and dramatic prehistoric structure in Europe: Stonehenge. The many theories about its construction and purpose only add to its attraction, which endures despite the hordes of visitors.

Other districts have their own pleasures, and many have literary or historical associations. Turn your sights to the Dorset heathland, the countryside explored in the novels of Thomas Hardy. This district is spanned by grass-covered chalk hills—the downs—wooded valleys, and meadows through which course meandering rivers. Along the coastline are Lyme Regis, where the tides and currents strike fear into the hearts of sailors, and Cowes, on the Isle of Wight—Queen Victoria's favorite getaway—which welcomes high-flyers who enter their yachts in the famous regattas.

The South has been quietly central to England's history for well over 4,000 years, occupied successively by prehistoric man, the Celts, the Romans, the Saxons, and the modern British. History continues to be made here, even in the modern era. On D-Day, Allied forces sailed for Normandy from ports along this coast; nearly 40 years later, British forces set out to recover the Falklands.

Exploring the South

The South of England ranges from the broad plains of Wiltshire, including the Marlborough Downs, the Vale of Pewsey, and the great Salisbury Plain, to the gaudy bucket-and-spade resorts of the coast and the sedate retirement homes of the Isle of Wight. The wide-open, windblown inland county of Wiltshire offers a sharp contrast to the tame, sequestered villages of Hampshire and Dorset and the self-important bustle of Southampton and Portsmouth. You may not want to spend much time in these two ports; instead, spend your nights in the more compelling towns of Salisbury and Winchester.

This area has a number of distinctive, self-contained touring destinations. The cathedral city of Winchester makes a useful base for visiting a handful of villages before you move on to the historic ports of the coastal cities of Southampton and Portsmouth. You can end your tour on the Isle of Wight. Salisbury, with its own lovely cathedral, is another major starting point. The obvious draw outside town is Stonehenge, but you are also within reach of an equally interesting prehistoric monument, Avebury. From there, you can swing south to the cultivated woodlands of the New Forest. The southern coast of Dorset is another major area, with a couple of popular holiday resorts, Bournemouth and Weymouth, and a string of ancient sites: Corfe Castle, Maiden Castle, and Cerne Abbas. Lyme Regis, on the Devon border at the center of the wide arc of Lyme Bay, is a favorite holiday destination in this area. It provides a gateway to the World Heritage Site called the Jurassic Coast, with its fossil-rich cliffs from Swanage in the east to Exmouth in the west.

About the Restaurants
Fertile soil, well-stocked rivers, and a long coastline ensure excellent farm produce and a plentiful stock of fish throughout the South. Try fresh-grilled river trout or sea bass poached in brine, or dine like a king on the New Forest's renowned venison. Hampshire is noted for its pig farming, and you might zero in on pork products on local restaurant menus.

About the Hotels
Modern hotel chains are well represented, and in rural areas you can choose among elegant country-house hotels, traditional coaching inns

(updated to different degrees), and modest guest houses. Some seaside hotels do not accept one-night bookings in summer. If you plan to visit Cowes on the Isle of Wight during Cowes Week, the annual yachting jamboree in late July or early August, book well in advance.

	WHAT IT COSTS In pounds				
	££££class	££££	£££	££	£
RESTAURANTS	over £22	£18–£22	£13–£17	£7–£12	under £7
HOTELS	over £160	£120–£160	£90–£120	£60–£90	under £60

Restaurant prices are for a main course at dinner. Hotel prices are for two people in a standard double room in high season, including VAT, with no meals or, if indicated, CP (with Continental breakfast), BP (Breakfast Plan, with full breakfast), or MAP (Modified American Plan, with breakfast and dinner).

Timing

Make sure you don't see the cathedrals of Salisbury and Winchester on a Sunday, when your visit will be restricted, or during services, when it won't be overly appreciated by worshippers. Places such as Stonehenge and Longleat House attract plenty of people at all times; bypass such sights on weekends or public holidays. In summer, day-trippers and longer-stay tourists crowd the coastal resorts of Bournemouth and Weymouth; it may be difficult to find suitable accommodations. The Isle of Wight, too, gets its fair share of summer visitors, especially during the weeklong Cowes Regatta in late July or early August, and you may have to wait longer for the ferries. The New Forest is at its most alluring in spring and early summer (for the foaling season) and fall (for the colorful foliage), while summer can be quite busy with walkers and campers. In fall, take waterproof boots for the puddles. Wherever you go, choose smaller, less frequented stops if you're concerned about running into crowds. Otherwise, the South is one area of the country you can enjoy visiting at any time of year.

FROM WINCHESTER TO SOUTHAMPTON

From the cathedral city of Winchester, 70 mi southwest of London, you can meander southward to the coast, stopping at the bustling ports of Southampton and Portsmouth to explore their maritime heritage. From either port you can strike out for the restful shores of the Isle of Wight, vacation home of Queen Victoria and thousands of modern-day Britons.

Winchester

▶ *70 mi southwest of London, 14 mi north of Southampton.*

Winchester is among the most historic of English cities, and as you walk its graceful streets and wander its many gardens, a sense of the past envelops you. Although it is now merely the county seat of Hampshire, for more than four centuries Winchester served as England's capital. Here, in AD 827, Egbert was crowned first king of England, and his successor, Alfred the Great, held court until his death in 899. In late Saxon times the town became the home of the finest school of calligraphy and

You could spend weeks exploring the South, but you can do a good sampling of the area in less time. On a three-day visit, you can see the highlights of Winchester and Salisbury, plus Stonehenge and a stately home or two. A week-long visit allows time to see areas and sights off the beaten path—to see Avebury in addition to Stonehenge, for example—and to explore the New Forest or relax by the shore a bit.

Numbers in the text correspond to numbers in the margin and on the South, Winchester, and Salisbury maps.

3

If you have 3 days

With limited time, you may want to combine the most sights with the least amount of traveling. If you're coming from London or southeast England, 🏛 **Winchester** ①–⑧ ▶ will be your first stop. It's a quiet, solid town, conducive to walking about, with the great cathedral at its heart. Other historic sites include the Great Hall and Winchester College, one of the country's noted "public" schools. Spend a night here, then move west to another cathedral city, 🏛 **Salisbury** ㉑–㉙. Surely few cathedrals have a more beautiful setting than this town—worth a two-night stay to take in the sights and nearby **Stonehenge** ㊲. Even closer to Salisbury are **Wilton House** ㉚ and its gardens, which you can see on your way to visit the village of **Shaftesbury** ㉛, and two more country estates, **Stourhead** ㉝ and **Longleat House** ㉞. The former holds—many believe—the most beautiful garden in England; the latter marries an African game park with a famous Elizabethan house.

If you have 7 days

Spend your first day and night touring 🏛 **Winchester** ①–⑧ ▶ and nearby **Chawton** ⑩, indelibly associated with Jane Austen. The next morning, head for the south coast and **Portsmouth** ⑫ to take in its historic ships and the Royal Naval Museum. Take a ferry across to **Cowes** ⑮ on the Isle of Wight, a favorite island haven of both Queen Victoria and Charles Dickens. The former vacationed at Osborne House, an Italianate villa, whereas one of her forebears, Charles I, was the unwilling guest of the Parliamentary army during his incarceration in **Carisbrooke Castle** ⑳. Overnight in nearby 🏛 **Ryde** ⑯. Leave the Isle of Wight from Cowes, disembarking at **Southampton** ⑬, which is not particularly noteworthy but has several absorbing museums, as well as the Pilgrim Fathers' Memorial. North of town, **Romsey** ⑭ is an attractive village, with the 18th-century mansion of Broadlands lying just outside. From here, you are well placed to spend two nights in 🏛 **Salisbury** ㉑–㉙ to take in the city and nearby attractions such as Wilton House, in **Wilton**, and **Stonehenge** ㊲. From here, a short drive westward brings you to **Stourhead** ㉝ and **Longleat House** ㉞. If you have time, you could travel north to the stone circles of **Avebury** ㉟ and to **Marlborough** ㊱, said to be the burial place of Merlin. If you have already toured this area, you might swoop down instead to the leafy New Forest; **Lyndhurst** ㊳ is an excellent place to take a breather and some exercise, including riding. Heading westward, stop in at 🏛 **Bournemouth** ㊶, containing the Russell-Cotes Art Gallery and Museum, a Victorian edifice brimming with treasures, and the burial place of Mary Shelley, author of *Frankenstein*. If the seaside frivolity doesn't grab you, carry on as far as **Corfe Castle** ㊹. Farther west is the genteel resort of **Weymouth** ㊽, where you can dine on fish by the harborside. South of Weymouth lies the **Isle of Portland** ⓐ, which, together with Chesil Beach, can provide both beach fun and interest to anyone intrigued by geological phenomena. ⊞ **Dorchester** ⓐ and **Maiden Castle** ⓐ lie just north of here, and a few miles west, **Abbotsbury** ⓐ contains a famous 600-year-old swannery. Farther along Lyme Bay is the pretty port of **Lyme Regis** ⓐ.

---

manuscript illumination in Europe. After the Norman Conquest in 1066, William I ("the Conqueror") had himself crowned in London, but took the precaution of repeating the ceremony in Winchester. William also commissioned the local monastery to produce the Domesday Book, a record of the general census begun in England in 1085. The city remained the center of ecclesiastical, commercial, and political power until the 13th century. Winchester's power has long vanished, and some fast-food outlets and retail chains have moved onto High Street, but the city still preserves much of its past glory.

★ ❶ The city's greatest monument, **Winchester Cathedral,** begun in 1079 and consecrated in 1093, presents a sturdy, chunky appearance in keeping with its Norman construction, so that the Gothic lightness within is even more breathtaking. Its tower, transepts, and crypt, and the inside core of the great Perpendicular nave, reveal some of the world's best surviving examples of Norman architecture. Other features, such as the arcades, the presbytery (behind the choir, holding the high altar), and the windows, are Gothic alterations carried out between the 12th and 14th centuries. Little of the original stained glass has survived, however, thanks to Cromwell's Puritan troops, who ransacked the cathedral in the 17th century during the English Civil War, but you can still see the sumptuously illuminated 12th-century Winchester Bible in the Library and Triforium Gallery.

Among the many well-known people buried in the cathedral are William the Conqueror's son, William II ("Rufus"), mysteriously murdered in the New Forest in 1100; Izaak Walton (1593–1683), author of *The Compleat Angler,* whose memorial window in Silkestede's Chapel was paid for by "the fishermen of England and America"; and Jane Austen, whose grave lies in the north aisle of the nave. Firmly in the 20th century, Antony Gormley's evocative statue, *Sound II* (1986), looms in the crypt, as often as not standing in water (as it was designed to do), because of seasonal flooding. You can also explore the bell tower—with views as far as the Isle of Wight in fair weather—and other recesses of the building on a tour. Occasionally, special services or ceremonies may mean the cathedral is closed to visits, so telephone first to avoid disappointment. ⊠ *The Close, Cathedral Precincts* ☎ *01962/857200* ⊕ *www. winchester-cathedral.org.uk* ✉ *£3.50 donation requested; Library and Triforium Gallery £1, bell tower tour £3* ☉ *Mon.–Sat. 8:30–6, Sun. 8:30–5:30, longer for services. Free tours on the hr Mon.–Sat. 10–3, bell tower tours Wed. 2:15 and Sat. 11:30 and 2:15.*

❷ The **Close,** behind the cathedral, is an area containing neat lawns and the
❸ Deanery, Dome Alley, and Cheyney Court. **King's Gate,** on St. Swithun Street on the south side of the Close, was built in the 13th century and

is one of two gates remaining from the original city wall. **St. Swithun's Church** is built over the ancient King's Gate. The saint himself is interred in Winchester Cathedral; it is said that it rained for 40 days when his body was transferred there from the churchyard, giving rise to the legend that rain on St. Swithun's Day (July 15) means another 40 days of wet weather. (Elsewhere in England the name is spelled "Swithin.") Nearby, at 8 College Street, is the house where Jane Austen died on July 18, 1817, three days after writing a comic poem about the legend of St. Swithun's Day (copies are usually available in the cathedral).

4 **Winchester College,** one of England's oldest "public" (i.e., private) schools, was founded in 1382 by Bishop William of Wykeham, who has his own chapel in Winchester Cathedral. The school chapel is notable for its delicately vaulted ceiling. Among the original buildings still in use is Chamber Court, center of college life for six centuries. Notice the "scholars"—students holding academic scholarships—clad in their traditional gowns. ⊠ *College St.* ☎ *01962/621209* ⊕ *www. winchestercollege.org* ⊠ *£3.50* ☉ *1-hr tours Mon., Wed., Fri., and Sat. 10:45, noon, 2:15, and 3:30; Tues. and Thurs. 10:45 and noon; Sun. 2:15 and 3:30.*

5 **Great Hall,** a few blocks west of the cathedral, is all that remains of the city's Norman castle. Here the English Parliament met for the first time in 1246; Sir Walter Raleigh was tried for conspiracy against King James I and condemned to death in 1603 (although he wasn't beheaded until 1618); and Dame Alice Lisle was sentenced to death by the infamous Judge Jeffreys for sheltering fugitives, after Monmouth's Rebellion in 1685. A huge and gaudy sculpture of Victoria, carved by Sir Alfred Gilbert (responsible for *Eros* in Piccadilly Circus) to mark the queen's Golden Jubilee in 1887, dominates the floor of the Great Hall. But the hall's greatest relic hangs on its west wall: the object fondly known as King Arthur's Round Table has places for 24 knights and a portrait of Arthur bearing a remarkable resemblance to King Henry VIII. In fact, the table dates back no further than the 13th century and was repainted by order of Henry on the occasion of a visit by the Holy Roman Emperor Charles V; the real Arthur was probably a Celtic cavalry general who held off the invading Saxons after the fall of the Roman Empire in the 5th or 6th century AD. The Tudor monarchs revived the Arthurian legend for political purposes. Take time to wander through Queen Eleanor's Medieval Garden—a re-creation of a noblewoman's shady retreat. ⊠ *Castle Hill* ☎ *01962/846476* ⊠ *Free* ☉ *Apr.–Oct., daily 10–5; Nov.–Mar., weekdays 10–5, weekends 10–4.*

6 Across from the cathedral, the **City Museum** interprets Winchester's past through displays of Celtic pottery, Roman mosaics, Saxon coins, and reconstructed Victorian shop fronts. ⊠ *The Square* ☎ *01962/848269* ⊠ *Free* ☉ *Apr.–Oct., Mon.–Sat. 10–5, Sun. noon–5; Nov.–Mar., Tues.–Sat. 10–4, Sun. noon–4.*

7 **City Mill** is a working 18th-century water mill, complete with small island garden, at the east end of High Street. Part of the premises is a National Trust gift shop open year-round, and part is used as a youth hostel. ✉ *Bridge St.* ☎ *01962/870057* ⊕ *www.nationaltrust.org.uk* 🗐 *£2.20* ⊘ *Mar., weekends 11–5; Apr.–June, Sept. and Oct., Wed.–Sun. 11–5; July and Aug., daily 11–5; Nov. and Dec., daily 11–4. Call for milling schedule.*

❽ To top off a tour of Winchester, you can climb **St. Giles's Hill** for a panoramic view of the city. A walk down High Street and Broadway will bring you to the hill.

Where to Stay & Eat

£££££ ✕ **Chesil Rectory.** The timbered and gabled building may be old English—15th- or 16th-century—but the cuisine is essentially French, mixing classic recipes with local ingredients. On the set-price menu, starters such as three-cheese soufflé, and desserts, which include crème brûlée, elegantly complement such main courses as Bresse pigeon with Jerusalem artichokes and wild mushrooms from the New Forest. Service and the antique charm of the surroundings match the quality of the food. ✉ *1 Chesil St.* ☎ *01962/851555* 🖃 *AE, DC, MC, V* ⊘ *Closed Sun. and Mon. No lunch (except Sat.).*

£–££ ✕ **The Royal Oak.** Try a half pint of draft bitter or dry cider at this lively traditional pub, which claims to have Britain's oldest bar (it has a Saxon wall). The two no-smoking areas—a rarity in Britain—are in the cellar and on the upper level. Bar meals are served until 7 PM. ✉ *Royal Oak Passage, off High St.* ☎ *01962/842701* 🖃 *AE, MC, V.*

£ ✕ **Cathedral Refectory.** The bold, modern style of this self-service eatery next to the cathedral helps make it a refreshing lunch or snack stop. The menu ranges from traditional soups to Welsh rarebit and Hampshire fish pie, but do sample the local "trenchers." This thick bread was used in medieval times as a plate from which to eat meat; once soaked in the meat juices, the bread was passed down to the poor. Today the trenchers, soaked in toppings such as meat or fish, are grilled. ✉ *Inner Close* ☎ *01962/857258* 🖃 *MC, V* ⊘ *No dinner.*

£££–££££ ✕🖫 **Winchester Royal.** Formerly a bishop's house and then a Benedictine convent, this classy hotel lies within easy reach of the cathedral on a quiet side street. Bedrooms, decorated with floral fabrics and dark wood, surround a large inner garden; rooms in the main building have more period features. You can have an excellent lunch in the bar or a fuller, fixed-price meal in the Conservatory Restaurant. ✉ *St. Peter St. near High St., SO23 8BS* ☎ *01962/840840* 🖷 *01962/841582* ⊕ *www. marstonhotels.com* ↪ *75 rooms* ⚭ *Restaurant, cable TV, bar, business services, meeting rooms, some pets allowed; no a/c* 🖃 *AE, DC, MC, V* ⦿| *BP.*

£££ ✕🖫 **Hotel du Vin.** Rooms in this elegant redbrick Georgian town house are richly furnished in modern style, with Oriental rugs enhancing the polished wooden floors. Egyptian-cotton bed-linens, huge baths, and power showers make for a luxurious stay. The many eclectic wine selections in the stylish bistro complement traditional French and English fare such as game pie and Aberdeen Angus rib-eye steak with french fries. Call to arrange a private wine-tasting session. In summer, food is served in the walled garden. ✉ *14 Southgate St., SO23 9EF* ☎ *01962/841414* 🖷 *01962/842458* ⊕ *www.hotelduvin.com* ↪ *23 rooms* ⚭ *Restau-*

Ancient Sites All around Britain, prehistoric monuments dot the landscape, silent but tantalizing reminders of civilizations long vanished. Ceremonial stone circles, barrows used for burials, and Iron Age hill forts attract endless speculation about the motives and methods of their ancient builders. The South contains not only 5,000-year-old Stonehenge, one of the great treasures of Britain and, indeed, Europe, but also an abundance of other sites, some of them overlaid with reminders of other eras. At Old Sarum, near Salisbury, the earthwork ramparts of an Iron Age hill fort survive, although Romans and Normans took over the site. The evocative Avebury Stone Circles surround part of a village; nearby is the West Kennett Long Barrow, a chambered tomb. Close to Dorchester, Maiden Castle is a stone and earth hill fort with ramparts that enclose 45 acres. If all this fuels your imagination, the shop at Stonehenge sells plenty of books with plenty of theories, and the Salisbury and South Wiltshire Museum in Salisbury and the Alexander Keillor Museum in Avebury provide helpful background. Start by visiting one site, and you may find yourself rerouting your trip to seek out others.

Literary Landmarks Like a library, the South is tailor-made for browsing, thanks in part to its many literary shrines. In Dorset, Thomas Hardy country, you can get far from the madding crowd. The Victorian novelist brought immortality to the peaceful countryside and to towns such as Shaftesbury and Dorchester, which appear in a number of his works, though with different names. In addition to Hardy landmarks, Jane Austen sites and shrines abound in the South of England, including the house in which she lived, in Chawton, and her burial place in Winchester Cathedral. Lyme Regis, an important setting for Austen's *Persuasion*, was where John Fowles set his classic novel of pseudo-Victoriana, *The French Lieutenant's Woman*.

Markets The tradition of local markets is alive and well in the South, and the numerous open-air markets in towns and villages sell everything from mundane housewares to crafts and foodstuffs. Exploring a local market can provide a unique sense of place; for a complete list, ask Tourism Southeast. Among the best are Salisbury's traditional city market (Tuesday and Saturday), Kingsland Market in Southampton for bric-a-brac (Thursday), and a general country market (Wednesday) at Ringwood, near Bournemouth. At the country's biggest farmers' market, held in Winchester's Middle Brook Street on the last Sunday of the month, everything you can buy that's edible is grown, reared, baked, or caught in Hampshire or within 10 mi of its borders.

---

rant, in-room data ports, cable TV, bar, meeting rooms; no a/c ⊟ *AE, DC, MC, V.*

★ **£££** ✕⛾ **Wykeham Arms.** This old place is conveniently central, near the cathedral and the college. Bedrooms at the inn itself are cozy and furnished in pine; those across the road in the St. George annex are more elegant, with period touches. The bars, happily cluttered with prints and pewter,

The South

Bristol
Bath
Melksham
Calne
Av
Devizes
Bristol Channel
WILTSH
Trowbridge
Westbury
Wells
Frome
Shepton Mallet
Warminster
34 Longleat House
SALISBURY PLAIN
SOMERSET
33 Stourhead
Mere
Teffont Evias
Tisbury
Swallowcliffe
Sandford Orcas
31 Shaftesbury
Yeovil
32 Sherborne
Illminster
Farnham
DORSET
43 Blandford Forum
46 Cerne Abbas
42 Wimborne Minster
51 Lyme Regis
Godmanstone
Bridport
Puddletown
Tolpuddle
Poole
West Bexington
45 Dorchester
B
Lyme Bay
Abbotsbury
50
47 Maiden Castle
Portesham
Wareham
Brownsea Island
PURBECK HILLS
West Lulworth
44 Corfe Castle
Chesil Beach
48 Weymouth
Lulworth Cove
Swanage

GREAT BRITAIN

49 Isle of Portland

KEY

▶ Start of itinerary

City Mill 7

City Museum . . .6

Close 2

Great Hall 5

King's Gate/
St. Swithun's
Church 3

St. Giles's Hill . . .8

Winchester
Cathedral 1

Winchester
College 4

make use of old school desks for tables. A good wine list sets off the French and English dishes at the restaurant, which is popular with locals; call for reservations. ⊠ *75 Kingsgate St., SO23 9PE* ☎ *01962/ 853834* 🖷 *01962/854411* ✐ *wykehamarms@accommodating-inns. co.uk* ➟ *14 rooms* ⌂ *Restaurant, 2 bars, some pets allowed, no-smoking rooms; no a/c, no kids under 14* ☰ *AE, DC, MC, V* ¶◯¶ *BP.*

£££££ 🏨 **Lainston House.** Dating from 1668, this elegant country-house hotel in a 63-acre park is discreetly secluded, an obvious attraction for such eminent guests as Margaret Thatcher, who stayed here to write her memoirs. Inside, cedar and oak paneling and other restored 17th-century details adorn the public rooms. Bedrooms, many of which are beamed, are done in warm colors and rich fabrics. Ground-floor suites have the added attraction of access to the gardens, and a converted stable holds luxury rooms. The hotel is 2½ mi northwest of Winchester. ⊠ *Off B3049, Sparsholt, SO21 2LT* ☎ *01962/863588* 🖷 *01962/776672* ⊕ *www.exclusivehotels.co.uk* ➟ *41 rooms* ⌂ *Restaurant, some in-room hot tubs, 2 tennis courts, gym, croquet, meeting rooms, helipad, some pets allowed; no a/c in some rooms* ☰ *AE, DC, MC, V* ¶◯¶ *BP.*

£ 🏨 **Church Cottage.** Five minutes from High Street, this ancient and tiny bed-and-breakfast adjacent to the graveyard of St. John's Church could be in a remote village, but for the odd glimpse of the cathedral from the top windows. Accessed via a spiral staircase, the cramped but characterful accommodations are a thick-beamed double bedroom and a plainer room with twin beds; each room has a private bath, but the bath is outside the room. ⊠ *20 St. John's St., SO23 0HF* ☎ *01962/865058* ✎ *junerowlands@petuchio.freeserve.co.uk* ⌨ *2 rooms* ♢ *No a/c, no room phones, no smoking* ⊟ *No credit cards* ⏐⊖⏐ *BP.*

Shopping

A complete list of local antiques stores is available from the **Winchester Tourist Information Centre** (⊠ The Guildhall, Broadway ☎ 01962/840500). **Antique and Craft Centre** (⊠ King's Walk, off Friarsgate ☎ 023/8022–8650) sells crafts and gift items and antiques. **P&G Wells** (⊠ 11 College St. ☎ 01962/852016), the oldest bookshop in town, stocks new titles and carries a small selection of secondhand books and prints in an annex in nearby Kingsgate Street.

Britain's largest **farmers' market** (☎ 01962/845135 ⊕ www. hampshirefarmersmarkets.co.uk), held in Middle Brook Street on the last Sunday of each month, specializes in local produce and goods. Look for Dexter beef, the products of water buffalo and Manx Loughton sheep, and walking sticks made from local wood. In September the market is the focal point of Hampshire Hog Day, the hog being the symbol of Hampshire. Pig farmers from around the county sell all kinds of pig-related products.

New Alresford

❾ *8 mi northeast of Winchester, by A31 and B3046.*

New Alresford (pronounced *awls*-ford) has a pleasant village green crossed by a stream and some Georgian houses and antiques shops. The village is the starting point of the **Watercress Line,** a 10-mi railroad reserved for steam locomotives that runs to Alton. The line (named for the watercress beds formerly in the area) takes you on a nostalgic tour through reminders of 19th-century England. ⊠ *Railway Station* ☎ *01962/733810* ⊕ *www.watercressline.co.uk* ⊡ *£9* ⊖ *May–Sept., daily departures; Mar., Apr., and Oct., weekends and national holidays; call for details.*

Chawton

❿ *8 mi east of New Alresford.*

Jane Austen (1775–1817) lived the last eight years of her life in the village of Chawton; she moved to Winchester only during her final illness. The site now draws literary pilgrims. Here, in an unassuming redbrick house, Austen revised *Sense and Sensibility,* created *Pride and Prejudice,* and worked on *Emma, Persuasion,* and *Mansfield Park.* Now a museum, the rooms of **Jane Austen's House** retain the atmosphere of restricted gentility suitable to the unmarried daughter of a clergyman. In the left-hand parlor, Jane would play her piano every morning, then repair to her mahogany writing desk in the family sitting room—leaving her sister Cassandra to do the household chores ("I find composition impossible with

CloseUp

IN SEARCH OF JANE AUSTEN

A TOUR OF "JANE AUSTEN COUNTRY" in the South of England and beyond invariably leads to or enhances the experience of reading Austen's novels. Thanks to the 1990s film adaptations of Sense and Sensibility, Emma, Persuasion, and Pride and Prejudice, the great author has captured another audience eager to peer into her decorous 18th- and early-19th-century world. By visiting one or two main locales—such as Chawton and Winchester—it is possible to imagine hearing the tinkle of teacups raised by the likes of Elinor Dashwood and Mr. Darcy. Serious Janeites will want to retrace her life—starting out in the hamlet of Steventon, southwest of Basingstoke, where she spent her first 25 years, then moving on to Bath, Southampton, Chawton, and Winchester.

It is easy to see the self-contained world that is Jane Austen country—a pleasant landscape filled with intimately scaled villages—as a perfectly civilized stage on which her characters organized visits to stately homes and husband-hunting expeditions. As Austen described this terrain in Emma, "It has a sweet view—sweet to the eye and the mind. English verdure, English culture, English comfort." Entering that world, you find that its heart is not Bath, nor London, nor Winchester, but the tiny Hampshire village of Chawton. Here at a former bailiff's cottage on her brother's estate—now a museum—Austen produced three of her greatest novels, writing at the minute, pedestaled table still standing in the dining parlor. Her daily 6-mile walks often took her to Chawton Manor—her brother's regal Jacobean mansion, which opened in 2003 as Chawton House Library, a center for the study of 16th–18th-century women's literature (for a consultation, call ☎ 01420/541010 or see ⊕ www.chawton.org)—or to nearby Lyards Farm,

where her favorite niece, Anna Lefroy (thought to be the model for Emma Woodhouse), came to live in 1815. A bit farther away is Great Bookham—closely identified with the "Highbury" of Emma—and nearby lies Box Hill (to the east of A24 between Leatherhead and Dorking), the probable inspiration for the locale of the famous walking expedition that left Miss Woodhouse in tears.

Driving southwest from Chawton, take A31 for about 15 mi to Winchester, where you can visit Austen's austere grave within the cathedral; then take in No. 8 College Street, where her battle with Addison's disease ended with her death on July 18, 1817. Heading 110 mi southwest you can visit Lyme Regis, the 18th-century seaside resort on the Devon border where Austen spent the summers of 1804–05. Here, at the Cobb, the stone jetty that juts into Lyme Bay, Louisa Musgrove suffers her terrible accident when she jumps off the steps known as Granny's Teeth—a turning point in Chapter 12 of Persuasion. Northwest of Winchester by some 60 mi is Bath, the elegant setting that served as the backdrop for some of Austen's razor-sharp observations. The Jane Austen Centre in Bath explores the relationship between Bath and the writer.

"It is the only place for happiness," Austen once said of the county of Kent, some 150 mi to the east of Chawton. "Everybody is rich there." Godmersham Park, another of her brother's estates (off the A28 between Canterbury and Ashford), offered her an escape to the countryside. The magnificent redbrick mansion is privately owned, but you can take a nearby public footpath to pass the little Grecian temple where she completed Sense and Sensibility. Whether you search for Jane Austen country in Hampshire or Kent, you can revisit it again and again in its home base: English literature.

my head full of joints of mutton and doses of rhubarb," Jane wrote). In the early 19th century, the road near the house was a bustling thoroughfare, and one traveler reported that a window view proved that the Misses Austen were "looking very comfortable at breakfast." Jane was famous for working through interruptions, but one protection against the outside world was the famous door that creaked. She asked that its hinges remain unattended to because they gave her warning that someone was coming. ⊠ *Signed off the A31/A32 roundabout* ☎ *01420/83262* ⊕ *www.janeaustenmuseum.org.uk* 🎫 *£4.50* ☉ *Mar.–Nov., daily 11–4:30; Dec.–Feb., weekends 11–4:30; last admission 30 mins before closing.*

Petersfield

⑪ *10 mi south of Chawton, along B3006 and A325.*

The Georgian market town of Petersfield is in a wide valley between wooded hills and open downs. **Queen Elizabeth Country Park,** part of an Area of Outstanding Beauty in the South Downs, 4 mi south of town, has 1,400 acres of chalk hills and shady beeches with scenic hiking trails. You can climb to the top of Butser Hill (888 feet) to take in a splendid view of the coast. ⊠ *A3* ☎ *023/9259–5040* ⊕ *www.hants.gov.uk/ countryside/qecp* 🎫 *Free; car park £1, Sun. £1.50* ☉ *Park open 24 hrs; visitor center (including café and shop) Apr.–Oct., daily 10–5:30; Nov. and Dec., daily 10–dusk; Jan.–Mar., weekends 10–dusk.*

Portsmouth

⑫ *15 mi south of Petersfield, 77 mi southwest of London.*

This city has been England's naval capital and principal port of departure for centuries. Plenty of ferries still leave here for the Continent and the Isle of Wight. The harbor covers about 7 square mi, incorporating the world's first dry dock (built in 1495) and extensive defenses. The waterfront area possesses England's richest collection of maritime memorabilia, including the Royal Naval Museum and some well-preserved warships. Although much of Portsmouth is not particularly scenic, the newly developed Gunwharf Quays and the soaring Spinnaker Tower demonstrate the city's ongoing vitality.

In 2005, maritime-related events around Britain will mark the SeaBritain 2005 celebration (www.seabritain2005.com). A highlight will be the Trafalgar Festival, in honor of the 200th anniversary of Admiral Lord Nelson's final victory. Portsmouth will be the focus of many festivities through summer and fall, culminating around October 21, the date of the Battle of Trafalgar.

Portchester Castle incorporates the walls of a Roman fort built more than 1,600 years ago; these are the most complete set of Roman walls in northern Europe. In the 12th century the castle (now in ruins) was built inside the impressive fortifications. From the keep's central tower you can take in a sweeping view of the harbor and coastline. ⊠ *Off A27, near Fareham* ☎ *023/9237–8291* ⊕ *www.english-heritage.org.uk* 🎫 *£3.50* ☉ *Apr.–Sept., daily 10–6; Oct.–Mar., daily 10–4.*

★ ☾ The city's most impressive attraction, the **Portsmouth Historic Dockyard**, includes an unrivaled collection of historic ships and the comprehensive Royal Naval Museum (a great place to learn about British naval hero Admiral Lord Horatio Nelson). The dockyard's youngest ship, **HMS *Warrior 1860***, was England's first ironclad battleship. Admiral Nelson's flagship, **HMS *Victory***, has been painstakingly restored to appear as she did at the battle at Trafalgar (1805). You can inspect the cramped gun decks, visit the cabin where Nelson entertained his officers, and stand on the spot where he was mortally wounded by a French sniper. Visits aboard the *Victory* are by guided tour only and may entail a long wait. The *Mary Rose*, former flagship of the Tudor navy, which capsized and sank in the harbor in 1545, was raised in 1982. Described in the 16th century as "the flower of all the ships that ever sailed," the *Mary Rose* is now housed in a special enclosure, where water continuously sprays her timbers to prevent them from drying out and breaking up. Exhibits in the intriguing *Mary Rose* Museum display more than 1,200 artifacts from the ship. The **Royal Naval Museum** has a fine collection of painted figureheads, extensive exhibits about Nelson and the battle of Trafalgar, and galleries of paintings and mementos recalling naval history from King Alfred to the present. **Action Stations**, an interactive attraction, gives you insight into life in the modern Royal Navy through a swashbuckling movie and tests your sea legs with tasks such as piloting boats through gales. ⊠ *Historic Dockyard, Portsmouth Naval Base* ☎ *023/9286–1512* ⊕ *www.historicdockyard.co.uk* ✑ *£15.50 includes harbor tour; valid for return visits* ☉ *Apr.–Oct., daily 10–5:30; Nov.–Mar., daily 10–5; last admission 1 hr before closing.*

> [need a break?] After a slog around the Historic Dockyard you can find rest and replenishment, including seafood, at the harborside **Still & West Country House** (⊠ Bath Sq. ☎ 023/9282–1567), a pub with outdoor seating. It faces the Spice Island Inn, another pub.

Newly erected on the lively Gunwharf Quays development of shops and bars, **Spinnaker Tower** (⊠ Gunwharf Quays) provides a striking visual focus on Portsmouth's skyline. The slender structure, with the form of a mast and billowing sail, rises to a height of 541 feet. Once the tower is completed (late 2004 or early 2005), an elevator will whisk you to viewing platforms and an open deck 330 feet high, for thrilling all-round views over the harbor and up to 20 mi beyond.

In the popular **D-Day Museum**, in nearby Southsea, exhibits reconstruct the planning and logistics involved in the D-Day landings, as well as the actual invasion on June 6, 1944. The museum's centerpiece is the Overlord Embroidery ("Overlord" was the code name for the invasion), a 272-foot-long tapestry with 34 panels illustrating the history of World War II, from the Battle of Britain in 1940 to D-Day and the first days of the liberation. ⊠ *Clarence Esplanade, Southsea* ☎ *023/9282–7261* ⊕ *www.ddaymuseum.co.uk* ✑ *£5* ☉ *Apr.–Oct., daily 10–5:30; Nov.–Mar., daily 10–5; last admission 30 mins before closing.*

☾ The highlight of **Submarine World** is the tour with an ex-submariner of the World War II submarine HMS *Alliance*, from the cramped quarters to the engine room. The museum fills you in on submarine history and lets you view Portsmouth Harbour through a periscope. There are plenty of historic subs, weapons, and diving paraphernalia around the extensive site. From Portsmouth Harbour, take the ferry to Gosport and walk along Millennium Promenade past the huge sundial clock. ⊠ *Haslar Jetty Rd., Gosport* ☎ *023/9252–9217* ⊕ *www.rnsubmus.co.uk* ☞ *£4.50, £6.75 with Explosion!* ◷ *Apr.–Oct., daily 10–5:30; Nov.–Mar., daily 10–4:30.*

In a former ordnance depot near Submarine World, **Explosion!** (the name given to the Museum of Naval Firepower) gathers together a huge diversity of munitions, mines, and missiles in relating the history of armaments used at sea. The museum also tells the story of the many locals who manufactured them. Interactive technology helps create the mood of, for example, walking along the seabed in the Mines Gallery. ⊠ *Priddy's Hard, Gosport* ☎ *023/9250–5600* ⊕ *www.explosion.org.uk* ☞ *£5.50, £6.75 with Submarine Museum* ◷ *Apr.–Oct., daily 10–5.30; Nov.–Mar., Thurs. and weekends 10–4:30.*

Where to Stay & Eat

££££–£££££ ✕ **Bistro Montparnasse.** Modern paintings on terra-cotta walls add a contemporary touch to this bustling restaurant. The fixed-price menu may include prawn and lentil bisque, or roasted lamb with apple and celeriac purée. ⊠ *103 Palmerston Rd., Southsea* ☎ *023/9281–6754* ☐ *AE, MC, V* ◷ *Closed Sun. and Mon.*

££ ✕▦ **Sally Port.** This timber-frame old tavern opposite the cathedral in Old Portsmouth has subtle nautical associations, such as the top spar around which the handsome Georgian staircase is built; the 40-foot mast is said to have come from a frigate. Sloping floors and marine pictures are additional details. The street-level bar and first-floor restaurant (open Friday–Sunday) provide good light meals or fuller fare, such as sea bass, Dover sole, steaks, and lamb fillets. Rooms are comfortable and fully equipped, with private washbasins and showers; toilets are shared. ⊠ *57–58 High St., PO1 2LU* ☎ *023/9282–1860* ☐ *023/ 9282–1293* ⇥ *10 rooms without bath* ⚐ *Restaurant, bar; no a/c* ☐ *AE, DC, MC, V* ⊚ *BP.*

££ ▦ **Westfield Hall.** Portsmouth is well supplied with chain offerings, but this pleasant smaller establishment has personal service and character. It occupies two converted early 20th-century houses close to the water in the resort of Southsea. Rooms (seven of which are on the ground floor) have large bay windows and are restfully furnished in greens and creams; three sitting rooms provide a place to relax. ⊠ *65 Festing Rd., off Eastern Parade, PO4 0NQ* ☎ *023/9282–6971* ☐ *023/9287–0200* ⊕ *www. whhotel.info* ⇥ *26 rooms* ⚐ *Dining room, cable TV, no-smoking rooms; no a/c* ☐ *AE, DC, MC, V* ⊚ *BP.*

Southampton

⓭ *21 mi northwest of Portsmouth, 25 mi southwest of Salisbury, 79 mi southwest of London.*

Seafaring Saxons and Romans used Southampton's harbor, Southampton Water, as a commercial trading port for centuries, and the city thrived, becoming one of England's wealthiest. But Plymouth eventually supplanted it, and Southampton has been going downhill ever since. Still, it remains England's leading passenger port, and as the home port of Henry V's fleet bound for Agincourt, the *Mayflower,* the *Queen Mary,* and the ill-fated *Titanic,* along with countless other great ocean liners of the 20th century, Southampton has one of the richest maritime traditions in England. Much of the city center is shoddy, having been hastily rebuilt after World War II bombing, but bits of the city's history peek out from between modern buildings. The Old Town retains its medieval air, and considerable parts of Southampton's castellated walls remain. Other attractions include a good art gallery, extensive parks, and a couple of superb museums. The Southampton International Boat Show, a 10-day event in mid-September, draws huge crowds.

Incorporated in the town walls are a number of old buildings, including **God's House Tower,** originally a gunpowder factory and now an archaeology museum. Displays focus on the Roman, Saxon, and medieval periods of Southampton's history, and an interactive computer allows virtual access to the archaeological collections. ⊠ *Winkle St.* ☎ *023/8063–5904* ⊕ *www.southampton.gov.uk* ⊠ *Free* ☉ *Tues.–Fri. and Sun. 10–5, Sat. 10–4.*

Mayflower Park and the Pilgrim Fathers' Memorial (⊠ Western Esplanade) commemorate the departure of the North America–bound *Mayflower* from Southampton on August 15, 1620. (The ship was forced to stop in Plymouth for repairs.) John Alden, the hero of Longfellow's poem *The Courtship of Miles Standish,* was a native of Southampton.

The **Southampton Maritime Museum** brings together models, mementos, and items of furniture from the age of the great clippers and cruise ships, including a wealth of memorabilia relating to the *Titanic*—footage, photos, crew lists, etc. Boat buffs will relish plenty of other vital statistics dealing with the history of commercial shipping. ⊠ *Bugle St.* ☎ *023/8022–3941* ⊕ *www.southampton.gov.uk* ⊠ *Free* ☉ *Tues.–Fri. and Sun. 10–5, Sat. 10–4.*

Where to Stay & Eat

££–£££   ✕ **Langleys.** At this busy bistro convenient to Southampton's docks, dishes such as Breton fish soup and fillet steak with local shellfish share the menu with Mediterranean fare. Modern art adorns the walls, and ceiling fans keep things cool in summer. The Garden Room Cafe and Terrace makes an appealing lunchtime stop. ⊠ *10–11 Bedford Pl.* ☎ *023/8022–4551* ⊟ *MC, V* ☉ *Closed Sun. No lunch Sat.*

££–£££   ✕ **Oxford Brasserie.** This informal place gets lively in the evening, but it's calmer at lunchtime. Fresh fish is always available (the set-price menus are a particularly good value), along with French and international fare. The tiled floor and cream-color walls hung with paintings are straightforward and not gimmicky. ⊠ *33–34 Oxford St.* ☎ *023/8063–5043* ⊟ *AE, DC, MC, V* ☉ *Closed Sun. No lunch Sat.*

£££   ▦ **Dolphin Hotel.** Originally a Georgian coaching inn—although there's been an inn of some sort on this site for seven centuries—the Dolphin has seen such illustrious visitors as Queen Victoria, Lord Nelson, and Jane Austen. Many of the traditional trappings have been replaced by sleek, modern furnishings, with works of art up and down the stairs and in every bedroom, where beds have individually styled headboards and white Egyptian-cotton duvets. The Oak Bar and Bleu Restaurant serve bar snacks and full meals, respectively. ✉ *35 High St., SO14 2HN* ☎ *023/8033–9955* 🖷 *023/8033–3650* ⊕ *www.thedolphin.co.uk* ⇒ *70 rooms* ⚫ *Restaurant, bar, business services, meeting rooms, some pets allowed; no a/c* ⊟ *AE, DC, MC, V* ⦿*| BP.*

Nightlife & the Arts

The **Mayflower Theatre** (✉ Commercial Rd. ☎ 023/8071–1811) is among the larger theaters outside London; the Royal Shakespeare Company and Barnum on Ice are among the organizations that have packed the house. The **Nuffield Theatre** (☎ 023/8067–1771), on the Southampton University campus, has its own repertory company and also hosts national touring groups.

Romsey

⑭ *10 mi northwest of Southampton.*

This small town on the River Test has an authentic Norman abbey church and, in the marketplace, an iron bracket said to have been used to hang two of Cromwell's soldiers. The flint and stone house near the marketplace, known as King John's Hunting Box, dates from the 13th century. Florence Nightingale is buried under a simple stone in East Wellow churchyard in Romsey, near her former house at Embley Park.

Broadlands, outside Romsey, was the home of the late Lord Mountbatten (1900–79), uncle of Queen Elizabeth II, and is undoubtedly the grandest house in Hampshire. Ornate plaster moldings and paintings of British and Continental royalty decorate the 18th-century Palladian mansion, which also contains personal mementos that trace Lord Mountbatten's distinguished career in the navy and in India. Landscape designer Capability Brown laid out the gardens, and the wide lawns sweep down to the banks of the River Test. In 1947 the Queen and the Duke of Edinburgh spent their honeymoon here, and Prince Charles and the late Princess Diana spent a few days here after their wedding in 1981. ✉ *A3090 Romsey bypass* ☎ *01794/505010* ⊕ *www.broadlands.net* 🎫 *£7* ⊙ *July–Aug., daily 1–5:30; last tour at 4.*

Where to Stay

£££ 🏨 **Potters Heron Hotel.** An ideal place to stay if you're visiting Broadlands, this modern hotel is behind the original thatched building. Some bedrooms have floral themes and are paneled in pine, whereas others are plainer; many have balconies. Dining is in the oak-beam Potters Pub or the Garden Restaurant. ✉ *Ampfield, SO51 9ZF, 3 mi east of Romsey* ☎ *023/8026–6611* 🖷 *023/8025–1359* ⊕ *www.corushotels.com* ⇒ *54 rooms* ⚫ *Restaurant, cable TV with movies, sauna, pub, business services, meeting rooms, some pets allowed; no a/c in some rooms* ⊟ *AE, DC, MC, V.*

Sports
Hilly parkland cradles the par-68, 5,767-yard golf course of the **Dunwood Manor Country Club** (⊠ Danes Rd., Awbridge, near Romsey ☎ 01794/340549).

ISLE OF WIGHT

The Isle of Wight (pronounced white) has a special atmosphere, quite distinct from that of the mainland: it is essentially Victorian. Although the island was known to the Romans and the ill-fated Stuarts, Queen Victoria put it on the map by choosing it for the site of Osborne House. She lived here as much as she could, and ultimately she died here. Clearly she created a great vogue, because most of the domestic architecture is Victorian. The islanders are fiercely chauvinistic; like Tennyson, once an inhabitant of the island until tourist harassment drove him away, they resent vacationers somewhat. But every season the day-trippers arrive—thanks to the ferries, hovercraft, and hydrofoils that connect the Isle of Wight with Southampton, Portsmouth, Southsea, and Lymington. People come to this 23-mi-long island for its holiday resorts— Ryde, Bembridge, Ventnor, Freshwater (stay away from tacky Sandown and Shanklin)—its rich vegetation, narrow lanes, thatched cottages, curving bays, sandy beaches, and walking paths. The fabulous ocean air, to quote Tennyson, is "worth six pence a pint." All is not sea and sails, however. There is splendid driving to be done in the interior of the island, in such places as Brading Down, Ashley Down, and Mersely Down, and the occasional country house to visit, none more spectacular than Queen Vicky's own Osborne House.

Cowes

🅕 *11 mi northwest of Ryde.*

If you embark from Southampton, your ferry will cross the Solent channel and dock at Cowes (pronounced cows), a magic name in the sailing world and internationally known for the Cowes Week annual yachting festival, held in July or August. Fifty years ago, the Cowes Regatta was a supreme event, attended by imperial majesties and serene highnesses from all over the world; the world's most famous figures crowded the green lawns of the Royal Yacht Squadron. Although elegance is a thing of the past, the Cowes Regatta remains an important yachting event and is occasionally attended by that royal seaman, the Duke of Edinburgh. At the north end of High Street, on the Parade, a tablet commemorates the 1633 sailing from Cowes of two ships carrying the first English settlers of the state of Maryland.

Queen Victoria's **Osborne House,** designed by Prince Albert after a villa in the stodgiest Italian Renaissance style, holds enormous interest for anyone drawn to the domestic side of history. After Albert's death in 1861 the queen spent much of her time here, mourning her loss in relative seclusion. In this massive pile, one sees the engineer manqué in Prince Albert and his clever innovations—even central heating—as well as evidence of Victoria's desperate attempts to give her children a normal but disciplined upbringing. A carriage ride will take you to the Swiss Cottage, a superior version of a playhouse, especially built for the children. The antiques-filled state rooms have scarcely been altered since Victoria's death here in 1901. The house and grounds—which can be quite crowded during July and August—were used as a location for the 1998 movie *Mrs. Brown*. ⊠ *Off A3021, 1 mi southeast of Cowes* ☎ *01983/ 200022* ⊕ *www.english-heritage.org.uk* ✍ *£8.50, grounds only £5* ⊙ *Apr.–Oct., daily 10–5 (last admission to house at 4); phone for prebooked guided tours in winter.*

Where to Stay

£££ ⊞ **New Holmwood Hotel.** This Best Western hotel occupies an unrivaled location above the Esplanade—ideal for watching yachters in the Solent. The three sitting rooms include one with an open fire on winter evenings and one for nonsmokers, and the sun terrace and pool take full advantage of fine weather. Patterned fabrics contrast with plain walls in the guest rooms. ⊠ *Queens Rd., Egypt Point, PO31 8BW* ☎ *01983/ 292508* 🖶 *01983/295020* ⊕ *www.newholmwoodhotel.co.uk* ⇆ *26 rooms* ⌂ *Restaurant, in-room data ports, cable TV, pool, bar, meeting rooms, some pets allowed; no a/c* ▭ *AE, DC, MC, V* ⦿ *BP.*

Ryde

⑯ *11 mi southeast of Cowes.*

The town of Ryde has long been one of the Isle of Wight's most popular summer resorts, with several family attractions. After the construction of Ryde Pier in 1814, elegant (and occasionally ostentatious) town houses sprang up along the seafront and on the slopes behind, commanding fine views of the harbor. In addition to its long, sandy beach, Ryde has a large boating lake (you can rent rowboats and pedal boats) and children's playgrounds. To get here from Cowes, leave on A3021, then follow the signs on A3054.

Where to Stay & Eat

£££–£££££ ✕⊞ **Seaview Hotel.** A strong maritime flavor defines this smart hotel, a converted house dating to around 1800, in the heart of a harbor village just outside Ryde. Antiques, original watercolors, and bold fabrics furnish the guest rooms. The main attractions, however, are the restaurants, which specialize in seafood and fresh island produce. Try the hot crab ramekin, baked with cream and tarragon with a cheese topping, to start, and don't pass up desserts; floating islands (poached meringues) are a must. For a fee, guests can use the well-equipped Isle of Wight Sports Club nearby. ⊠ *High St., Seaview, PO34 5EX* ☎ *01983/612711* 🖶 *01983/613729* ⊕ *www.seaviewhotel.co.uk* ⇆ *16 rooms, 2 cottages* ⌂ *2 restaurants, in-room data ports, 2 bars, some pets allowed, no-smoking rooms* ▭ *AE, DC, MC, V* ⦿ *BP.*

£££££ ⊞ **Priory Bay Hotel.** This hotel, part of which dates to medieval times, has been sympathetically developed in country-house style. Lawns and woodlands on the 70-acre estate, as well as a beach, help make for a pampered, private sojourn. Antiques furnish the public rooms, and guest rooms are light-filled and airy. On the grounds are nine chalets, four of them with kitchens; pets are allowed in these. Modern European cuisine is served in the restaurant, and seafood, salads, and pastas are available at the Priory Oyster beach café (open July and August). ✉ *Priory Dr., Seaview, PO34 5BU* ☎ *01983/613146* 🖷 *01983/616539* ⊕ *www.priorybay.co.uk* 🛏 *16 rooms, 9 chalets* ♿ *2 restaurants, 9-hole golf course, 2 tennis courts, pool, beach, bar, business services, meeting rooms; no a/c* ⊟ *AE, DC, MC, V* ❙⊙❙ *BP.*

Brading

❼ *3 mi south of Ryde on A3055.*

In Brading, St. Mary's Church, dating from Norman times, contains monuments to the local Oglander family. Next to the Old Town Hall stands the 16th-century rectory, said to be the oldest inhabited dwelling on the island; it now holds a wax museum.

The remains of the substantial 3rd-century **Brading Roman Villa,** a mile south of Brading, include splendid mosaic floors and a well-preserved heating system. Refurbishment in 2004 has added a high-tech shelter for the mosaics, as well as a visitor center and café. ✉ *Off A3055* ☎ *01983/406223* 🎟 *£5; call to confirm* ☉ *Apr.–Oct., daily 9:30–6; Nov.–Mar., daily 10–4; call to confirm.*

Ventnor

❽ *11 mi south of Ryde.*

The south coast resorts are the sunniest and most sheltered on the Isle of Wight. Handsome Ventnor rises from such a steep slope that the ground floors of some of its houses are level with the roofs of those across the road. The lovely **Ventnor Botanic Gardens,** laid out over 22 acres, contain more than 3,500 species of trees, plants, and shrubs. The impressive greenhouse includes banana trees and a waterfall, and a pavilioned visitor center puts the subtropical and display gardens into context. ✉ *Undercliff Dr.* ☎ *01983/855397* ⊕ *www.botanic.co.uk* 🎟 *Free* ☉ *Jan. and Feb., weekends 10–4; Mar.–Oct., daily 10–6; Nov. and Dec., Tues.–Thurs. 10–3, weekends 10–4.*

Sports
James Braid, who designed the Gleneagles golf course in Scotland, helped create the challenging par-70, 5,804-yard, heathland **Shanklin and Sandown** (✉ The Fairway, Sandown ☎ 01983/403170) course.

---

en route

The coast road from Ventnor to the Needles passes the fantasy theme park **Blackgang Chine,** built in a deep chine (cleft in the cliffs) overlooking a former smugglers' landing place. Besides a film about the history of the area, attractions for ages 3–12 include Dinosaurland, Smugglersland, Cowboytown, and Water Force (a large water slide). ✉ *A3055, Ventnor* ℗ *01983/730330* ⊕ *www. blackgangchine.com* 🎟 *£7.50* ☉ *Apr.–mid-July and early Sept.–Oct., daily 10–5; mid-July–early Sept., daily 10–10; early Nov., daily 10–5.*

Alum Bay & the Needles

⑲ *19 mi northwest of Ventnor, 18 mi southwest of Cowes.*

At the western tip of the Isle of Wight is the island's most famous natural landmark, the **Needles,** a long line of jagged chalk stacks jutting out of the sea like monstrous teeth, with a lighthouse at the end. It's part of the Needles Pleasure Park, which has mostly child-oriented attractions. Adjacent is **Alum Bay,** accessed from the Needles by chairlift. Here you can catch a good view of the multicolor sand in the cliff strata or take a boat to view the lighthouse.

Dimbola Lodge was the home of Julia Margaret Cameron (1815–79), the eminent Victorian portrait photographer and friend of Lord Tennyson. The gallery in the building includes more than 60 examples of her work, as well as a bookshop and café. ⊠ *Terrace La., Freshwater Bay* ☎ *01983/756814* ⊕ *www.dimbola.co.uk* ⊠ *Gallery £4* ⊘ *Jan.–June and Sept.–Dec., Tues.–Sun. and national holidays 10–5; July and Aug., daily 10–5.*

Where to Stay

££££ ⌂ **Farringford Hotel.** For more than 40 years this splendid 18th-century house was the home of the Victorian poet laureate Alfred, Lord Tennyson. Now a gracious hotel on 33 acres of parkland, it also includes self-catering accommodations. Victorian mahogany and rich damask fabrics reign supreme in the bedrooms in the main house. ⊠ *Bedbury La., Freshwater Bay, PO40 9PE, near Alum Bay* ☎ *01983/752500* 🖷 *01983/ 756515* ⊕ *www.farringford.co.uk* ⇒ *15 rooms, 23 suites, 5 apartments, 4 cottage rooms* ⚏ *2 restaurants, 9-hole golf course, tennis court, pool, croquet, lawn bowling, some pets allowed (fee); no a/c* ⊟ *AE, DC, MC, V* ⏉ *BP.*

Sports

Overlooking the bay, the par-69, 5,725-yard **Freshwater Bay Golf Club** (⊠ Southdown Rd., Freshwater Bay ☎ 01983/752955) is on land owned by the National Trust.

Carisbrooke Castle

★ **⑳** *14 mi east of Alum Bay, 1¼ mi southwest of Newport, 5 mi south of Cowes.*

Standing above the village of Carisbrooke, this castle built by the Normans and enlarged in Elizabethan times had its moment of historical glory when King Charles I was imprisoned here during the English Civil War. Note the small window in the north curtain wall through which he tried unsuccessfully to escape. A museum holds items from his incarceration. You can stroll along the battlements and visit the well house, where donkeys draw water from a deep well. The castle is a short distance outside the Isle of Wight's modern-day capital, Newport. ⊠ *Off B3401* ☎ *01983/522107* ⊕ *www.english-heritage.org.uk* ⊠ *£5* ⊘ *Apr.–Sept., daily 10–6; Oct.–Mar., daily 10–4.*

SALISBURY TO THE NEW FOREST
STOURHEAD, AVEBURY & STONEHENGE

The roster of famous sights in this area begins in the attractive city of Salisbury, renowned for its glorious cathedral, then loops west around Salisbury Plain, up to Avebury, and back to Stonehenge. A trio of stately homes reveals the ambitions and wealth of the builders—Wilton House with its Inigo Jones–designed state rooms, Stourhead and its exquisite gardens, and the Italian Renaissance pile of Longleat. From Stonehenge you can dip south into Hampshire, to the wild, scenic expanse of the New Forest, ancient hunting preserve of William the Conqueror. Your own transportation is essential to see anything beyond Salisbury.

Salisbury

25 mi northwest of Southampton, 55 mi southeast of Bristol, 90 mi southwest of London.

The unique silhouette of Salisbury Cathedral's majestic spire signals your approach to this historic city long before you arrive. Although the cathedral is the principal interest in the town, and the Cathedral Close one of the country's most atmospheric spots (best experienced on a foggy night), Salisbury has much more to see, not least its largely unspoiled—and relatively traffic-free—old center. Here are stone shops and houses that grew up in the shadow of the great church over the centuries. You're never far from any of the three rivers that meet here, or from the bucolic water meadows that stretch out to the west of the cathedral and provide the best views of it.

Salisbury did not become important until the early 13th century, when the seat of the diocese was transferred here from Old Sarum, the original settlement 2 mi to the north, of which only ruins remain. In the 19th century, novelist Anthony Trollope based his tales of ecclesiastical life, notably *Barchester Towers*, on life here, although his fictional city of Barchester is really an amalgam of Salisbury and Winchester. The local tourist office organizes walks—of differing lengths for varying stamina—to lead you to the treasures.

❷❶ Salisbury continues to be dominated by the towering **Salisbury Cathe-**
Fodor'sChoice **dral,** a soaring hymn in stone. It is unique among cathedrals in that it
★ was conceived and built as a whole, in the amazingly short span of 38 years (1220–58). The spire, added in 1320, is the tallest in England and a miraculous feat of medieval engineering—even though the point, 404 feet above the ground, is 2½ feet off vertical. For a fictional, keenly imaginative reconstruction of the drama underlying such an achievement, read William Golding's novel *The Spire*. The excellent model of the cathedral in the north transept, the "arm" of the church to your left as you look toward the altar, shows the building about 20 years into construction, and makes clear the ambition of Salisbury's medieval builders. For all their sophistication, the height and immense weight of the great spire have always posed structural problems. In the late 17th century

High Street
Gate **24**

Long
Bridge **28**

Market
Square **26**

Mompesson
House **23**

Old Mill **29**

Poultry
Cross **25**

St. Thomas's
Church **27**

Salisbury
and South
Wiltshire
Museum **22**

Salisbury
Cathedral **21**

Sir Christopher Wren was summoned from London to strengthen the spire, and in the mid-19th century Sir George Gilbert Scott, a leading Victorian Gothicist, undertook a major program of restoration. He also initiated a clearing out of the interior and removed some less-than-sympathetic 18th-century alterations. Despite this, the interior seems spartan and a little gloomy, but check out the remarkable lancet windows and sculpted tombs of crusaders and other medieval heroes. The clock in the north aisle—probably the oldest working mechanism in Europe, if not the world—was made in 1386. You can join a free 45-minute tour of the church leaving two or more times a day, and there are also tours to the roof and spire at least once a day. The spacious **cloisters** are the largest in England, and the octagonal **Chapter House** contains a marvelous 13th-century frieze showing scenes from the Old Testament. In the Chapter House you can also see one of the four original copies of the **Magna Carta,** the charter of rights the English barons forced King John to accept in 1215; it was sent here for safekeeping in the 13th century. ⊠ *Cathedral Close* ☏ *01722/555120* ⊕ *www.salisburycathedral. org.uk* 🖃 *Cathedral £3.80 requested donation, roof tour £4, Chapter House free* ⊙ *Cathedral mid-June–Aug., Mon.–Sat. 7:15–7:15, Sun. 7:15–6:15; Sept.–mid-June, daily 7:15–6:15. Chapter House mid-June–Aug., Mon.–Sat. 9:30–6:45, Sun. noon–5:30; Sept.–Oct. and*

Mar.–mid-June, Mon.–Sat. 9:30–5:30, Sun. noon–5:30; Nov.–Feb., Mon.–Sat. 10–5:15, Sun. noon–5:30.

Salisbury's **Cathedral Close** forms probably the finest backdrop of any British cathedral, with its smooth lawns and splendid examples of architecture from many periods (except modern) creating a harmonious background. Some of the historic houses are open to the public.

㉒ Models and exhibits at the Stonehenge Gallery of the **Salisbury and South Wiltshire Museum** arm you with helpful background information for a visit to the famous stones. Also on view are collections of costumes, lace, embroidery, and Wedgwood, all dwarfed by the medieval pageant figure of St. Christopher, a 14-foot-tall, red-cloaked giant and his companion hobbyhorse, Hob Nob. ✉ *The King's House, 65 The Close* ☎ *01722/332151* ⊕ *www.salisburymuseum.org.uk* 💷 *£4* ⊙ *July and Aug., Mon.–Sat. 10–5, Sun. 2–5; Sept.–June, Mon.–Sat. 10–5.*

㉓ Elegant **Mompesson House,** on the north side of Cathedral Close, dates from 1701 and is one of Britain's most appealing Queen Anne houses. There are no treasures per se, but some fine original paneling and plasterwork, as well as a fascinating collection of 18th-century drinking glasses, are highlights. Tea and refreshments are served in a walled garden. ✉ *The Close* ☎ *01722/335659* ⊕ *www.nationaltrust.org.uk* 💷 *£4* ⊙ *Apr.–Oct., Sat.–Wed. 11–5; last admission 4:30.*

㉔ On the north side of the Cathedral Close is **High Street Gate,** one of the four castellated stone gateways built to separate the close from the rest of the city. Passing through it, you enter into the heart of the modern **㉕** town. One of Salisbury's best-known landmarks, the hexagonal **Poultry Cross** (✉ Silver St.) is the last remaining of the four original medieval market crosses, and dealers still set up their stalls beside it. One of south-**㉖** ern England's most popular markets fills **Market Square** on Tuesday and Saturday. Permission to hold an annual fair here was granted in 1221, and that right is still exercised for four days every October, when the Charter Fair takes place. A narrow side street links Poultry Cross to Market Square.

㉗ **St. Thomas's Church** contains a rare medieval doom painting of Judgment Day, the best-preserved and most complete of the few such works left in Britain. Created around 1470 and covering the chancel arch, the scenes of heaven and hell served to instill the fear of damnation into the congregation. It's best seen on a spring or summer evening when the light through the west window illuminates the details. ✉ *Silver St.* ☎ *01722/322537* 💷 *Free* ⊙ *Apr.–Oct., Mon.–Sat. 9:30–6, Sun. noon–6; Nov.–Mar., Mon.–Sat. 9:30–3:30, Sun. noon–6.*

need a break? In a lively, central location but away from traffic, **Michael Snell Tea Room** (✉ 8 St. Thomas's Sq. ☎ 01722/336037) provides relief from sightseeing fatigue in the form of lemon curd gâteaux (cake), Wiltshire cream teas, and freshly ground coffee. It's closed Sunday.

㉘ For a classic view of Salisbury, head to the **Long Bridge** and the town path. From High Street walk west to Mill Road, which leads you across

Queen Elizabeth Gardens. Cross the bridge and continue on the town path; along here you can find the very spot where John Constable set down his easel to create that 19th-century icon, *Salisbury Cathedral*, now hung in the Constable Room of London's National Gallery. Reached via a 20-minute walk southwest of the town center along the town path, **❷❾** the **Old Mill** (✉ Town Path, West Harnham), dating from the 12th-century, makes a pleasant destination. It is now a restaurant and coffee shop under the same management as the Old Mill Hotel next door.

Massive earthwork ramparts in a bare sweep of Wiltshire countryside are all that remain of the impressive Iron Age hill fort of **Old Sarum,** which was successively taken over by Romans, Saxons, and Normans (who built a castle and cathedral within the earthworks). The site was still fortified in Tudor times, though the population had mostly decamped in the 13th century for the more amenable site of New Sarum, or Salisbury. You can clamber over the huge banks and ditches and take in the bracing views over the chalk downland. ✉ *Off A345, 2 mi north of Salisbury* ☎ *01722/335398* ⊕ *www.english-heritage.org.uk* 💷 *£2.80* ☯ *Apr.–June and Sept., daily 10–5; July and Aug., daily 9–6; Oct., daily 10–4; Nov.–Mar., daily 10–3.*

Where to Stay & Eat

££ ✕**Harper's.** The cuisine at this popular second-floor restaurant overlooking Market Square mingles English and French dishes. Specialties include fillet of salmon and casserole of beef cooked in ale, and there are good-value early-bird lunches and dinners. ✉ *7 Ox Row* ☎ *01722/333118* 🖃 *AE, DC, MC, V* ☯ *Closed Sun. Oct.–May. No lunch Sun. June–Sept.*

££ ✕**Haunch of Venison.** This place opposite the Poultry Cross has been going strong for more than six centuries, and the wood-paneled restaurant brims with period details, such as the mummified hand of an 18th-century card player still clutching his cards that was found by workmen in 1903. You can choose between simple bar food or more substantial meals such as a Haunch Platter—selections of venison—and fortify yourself with any of 40-odd malt whiskys. ✉ *1 Minster St.* ☎ *01722/322024* 🖃 *MC, V* ☯ *No dinner Sun. in winter, usually Nov.–Easter.*

££ ✕**Lemon Tree.** It's just a few steps from Cathedral Close and the High Street Gate to this light, airy café-bistro. There's a good selection of snacks and full meals, from quiches to casseroles, and you can sit in the small, busy conservatory or in the garden. ✉ *90–92 Crane St.* ☎ *01722/333471* 🖃 *MC, V* ☯ *Closed Sun.*

££ ✕**LXIX Bar and Bistro.** A stone's throw from the cathedral, this convivial and relaxed bistro has a cool, modern style, making it an ideal spot for a light lunch or dinner. The menu lists everything from fish cakes and pastas to sea bass and steaks. ✉ *69 New St.* ☎ *01722/340000* 🖃 *AE, DC, MC, V* ☯ *Closed Sun. and last wk in Dec.*

★ ££££ ✕🏨 **Howard's House.** If you're after complete tranquillity, head for this early 17th-century house 10 mi west of Salisbury, set on 2 acres of grounds in the Nadder valley. French windows lead from the tidy lawns into the restaurant, which lists sophisticated contemporary fare such as roasted scallops with eggplant caviar and *sauce vierge* (a green sauce with olive oil, lemon juice, and herbs) on its set-price menus. The inviting sitting room mixes pastels and bright fabrics, and the soothing bedrooms use subtle colors. ⊠ *Off B3089, Teffont Evias, SP3 5RJ* ☎ *01722/716392* 🖷 *01722/716820* ⊕ *www.howardshousehotel.com* ⟋9 *rooms* ♿ *Restaurant, meeting rooms, some pets allowed (fee); no a/c* 🖃 *AE, DC, MC, V* ¶◯¶ *BP.*

££££   ✕🖽 **Red Lion Hotel.** A former coaching inn—parts of the building date from 1220—this centrally located hotel in the Best Western consortium makes a good base for exploring the city on foot. It's packed with old clocks and other relics from its long past. Rooms are in either modern or antique style, with an abundance of drapery and rich red, gold, and blue colors. Room 22 has a restored fireplace dating from the inn's original construction. The Vine restaurant (reservations essential) serves mainly modern British dishes such as roast pork with mustard sauce. ⊠ *Milford St., SP1 2AN* ☎ *01722/323334* 🖷 *01722/325756* ⊕ *www.theredlion.co.uk* ⟋ *51 rooms* ♿ *Restaurant, cable TV, business services, meeting rooms; no a/c* 🖃 *AE, DC, MC, V.*

££££   🖽 **White Hart.** Behind the pillared portico and imposing facade of this 17th-century hotel in the heart of Salisbury lie cozily old-fashioned yet spacious public rooms. The muted cream-and-brown color scheme complements the unhurried pace, and the functional bedrooms are grouped around the inner courtyard. ⊠ *1 St. John St., SP1 2SD* ☎ *0870/400–8125* 🖷 *01722/412761* ⊕ *www.whitehart-salisbury.co.uk* ⟋ *68 rooms* ♿ *Restaurant, bar, business services, meeting rooms, some pets allowed (fee); no a/c* 🖃 *AE, DC, MC, V* ¶◯¶ *BP.*

££   🖽 **Cricket Field House Hotel.** As the name suggests, this modernized gamekeeper's cottage overlooks a cricket ground, allowing you to puzzle over the intricacies of the game at leisure. Some rooms are in the main house and others in the pavilion annex, but all are individually furnished in soft shades. The hotel is on the main A36 road, a mile or so west of Salisbury's center. ⊠ *Wilton Rd., SP2 9NS* ☎☎ *01722/322595* ⊕ *www. cricketfieldhousehotel.co.uk* ⟋ *14 rooms* ♿ *Dining room; no a/c, no kids under 14, no smoking* 🖃 *AE, MC, V* ¶◯¶ *BP.*

£   🖽 **Wyndham Park Lodge.** This solid Victorian house in a quiet part of town (off Castle Street) provides an excellent place to rest and a good breakfast, as well as a garden. Furnishings are in keeping with the period, with antiques and elegant patterned wallpapers and drapes, and one room has its own patio. ⊠ *51 Wyndham Rd., SP1 3AB* ☎ *01722/ 416517* 🖷 *01722/328851* ⊕ *www.wyndhamparklodge.co.uk* ⟋ *4 rooms* ♿ *No a/c, no room phones, no smoking* 🖃 *MC, V* ¶◯¶ *BP.*

Nightlife & the Arts

★   The **Salisbury Festival** (⊠ 75 New St. ☎ 01722/332241 ⊕ www. salisburyfestival.co.uk), held in May and June, has outstanding classical concerts, recitals, plays, and outdoor events. The **Salisbury Playhouse** (⊠ Malthouse La. ☎ 01722/320333) presents high-caliber drama all year and is the main venue for the Salisbury Festival.

Sports

Hayball's Cycle Shop (⊠ 26–30 Winchester St. ☎ 01722/411378) rents bikes for about £10 per day or £55 per week, with a £25 cash deposit.

Shopping

Rivermead Books (✉ 30 Catherine St. ☎ 01722/325818) stocks all kinds of tax-free secondhand books, including some rare first editions. **Watsons** (✉ 8–9 Queen St. ☎ 01722/320311) specializes in Aynsley and Wedgwood bone china, Waterford and Dartington glass, Royal Doulton, and fine ornaments. The buildings, dating from 1306 and 1425, have their original windows and an oak mantelpiece.

Wilton

③⓪ *4 mi west of Salisbury.*

Five rivers—the Avon, the Bourne, the Nadder, the Wylye, and the Ebble—wind slowly from Salisbury into the rich heart of Wiltshire. Following the valley of the Nadder will lead you to the ancient town of Wilton, from which the county takes its name. A traditional market is held here every Thursday, and the Wilton Carpet Factory Shop draws people (Wilton is renowned for its carpets), but the main attraction is Wilton House.

★ The home of the 17th earl of Pembroke, **Wilton House** would be noteworthy if it contained no more than the magnificent 17th-century state rooms designed by Inigo Jones, Ben Jonson's stage designer and the architect of London's Banqueting House. John Webb rebuilt the house in neoclassical style after fire damaged the original Tudor mansion in 1647. In fine weather, the lordly expanse of sweeping lawns that surrounds the house, bisected by the River Avon and dotted with towering oaks and a gracious Palladian bridge, is a quintessential English scene. Wilton House contains the Single Cube Room (built as a perfect 30-foot cube) and one of the most extravagantly beautiful rooms in the history of interior decoration, the aptly named Double Cube Room. The name refers to its simple proportions (60 feet long by 30 feet wide and 30 feet high), evidence of Jones's classically inspired belief that beauty in architecture derives from harmony and balance. The room's headliner is the spectacular Van Dyck portrait of the Pembroke family. Adorned with gilded furniture by William Kent, the Double Cube was where Eisenhower prepared plans for the Normandy invasion; it has been used in many films, including *The Madness of King George* and Emma Thompson's adaptation of *Sense and Sensibility*. Other delights include superb old master paintings, an exhibition of 7,000 toy soldiers, and the Wareham Bears (200 dressed teddy bears). Be sure to explore the extensive gardens; children may appreciate the large playground. ✉ *Off A30* ☎ *01722/746729* ⊕ *www.wiltonhouse.co.uk* 💷 *£9.75, grounds only £4.50* ☉ *Apr.–Oct., Tues.–Sun. 10:30–5:30; last admission 4:30.*

Shaftesbury

③① *18 mi west of Wilton, 22 mi west of Salisbury.*

The old village of Shaftesbury—the model for the town of Shaston in Thomas Hardy's *Jude the Obscure*—lies on a ridge overlooking Blackmore Vale just inside the Dorset county border. From the top of **Gold Hill**, a steep, relentlessly picturesque street lined with cottages, you can catch a sweeping view of the surrounding countryside. Although Gold Hill is something of a tourist cliché (it has even appeared in TV commercials), it's still well worth visiting.

Sherborne

32 *15 mi west of Shaftesbury.*

Once granted cathedral status, until deferring to Old Sarum in 1075, this unspoiled market town is awash with medieval buildings honed from the honey-color local stone. The focal point of the winding streets is the abbey church. Also worth visiting here are the ruins of the 12th-century Old Castle and Sherborne Castle with its grounds.

The glory of **Sherborne Abbey,** a warm, "old gold" stone church, is the delicate and graceful 15th-century fan vaulting that extends the length of the soaring nave and choir. If you're lucky you might hear "Great Tom," one of the heaviest bells in the world, pealing out from the bell tower. Guided tours are offered in summer on Tuesday morning and Friday afternoon, or by prior arrangement. ⊠ *Abbey Close* ☎ *01935/812452* ⊕ *www.sherborne-abbey.fsnet.co.uk* ⊠ *Free, guided tour £2.50* ☉ *Apr.–Sept., daily 9–6; Oct.–Mar., daily 9–4.*

Sherborne Castle, built by Sir Walter Raleigh in 1594, remained his home for 10 years before it passed to the custodianship of the Digby family. The interior has been remodeled in 19th-century Gothic style, and ceilings have splendid plaster moldings. After admiring the extensive collections of Meissen and Asian porcelain, stroll around the lake and landscaped grounds, the work of Capability Brown. The house is a half mile southeast of town. ⊠ *Off A352* ☎ *01935/813182* ⊕ *www. sherbornecastle.com* ⊠ *£7, gardens only £3.50* ☉ *Apr.–Oct., Tues.–Thurs., Sun., and national holidays 11–5, Sat. 2:30–5.*

Where to Stay

£ 🏠 **The Alders.** A quiet, unspoiled village 3 mi north of Sherborne contains this B&B, an old stone house with a walled garden. The lounge has an inglenook fireplace, and the bedrooms are modern and cheerfully decorated. The house displays the owner's watercolors and sleek pottery, which you can view while tasting homemade jam during breakfast at the large farmhouse table. Nearby village pubs provide evening meals. ⊠ *Sandford Orcas, DT9 4SB* ☎ *01963/220666* 🖷 *01963/ 220106* ⊕ *www.thealdersbb.com* 🛏 *3 rooms* ⚪ *No smoking* ⊟ *No credit cards* ¶Ol *BP.*

Stourhead

33 *15 mi northeast of Sherborne, 30 mi west of Salisbury.*

Fodor's Choice
★

Close to the village of Stourton lies one of Wiltshire's most breathtaking sights—Stourhead, a country-house-and-garden combination that has few parallels for beauty anywhere in Europe. Most of Stourhead was built between 1721 and 1725 by Henry the Magnificent, the wealthy banker Henry Hoare. Many rooms in the Palladian mansion contain Chinese and French porcelain, and some have furniture by Chippendale.

The elegant library and floridly colored picture gallery were built for the cultural development of this exceedingly civilized family. Still, the house must take second place to the adjacent gardens designed by Hoare's son, Henry Hoare II, which are the most celebrated example of the English 18th-century taste for "natural" landscaping. Temples, grottoes, and bridges have been skillfully placed among colorful shrubs, trees, and flowers to make the grounds look like a three-dimensional oil painting. A walk around the artificial lake (1½ mi) reveals changing vistas that conjure up the 17th-century landscapes of Claude Lorrain and Nicolas Poussin. The best time to visit is early summer, when the massive banks of rhododendrons are in full bloom, but the gardens are beautiful at any time of year. You can get a fine view of the estate from Alfred's Tower, a 1772 folly (a structure built for picturesque effect). In summer there are occasional concerts, sometimes accompanied by fireworks and gondoliers on the lake. A restaurant and plant shop are on the grounds. From London by train, get off at Gillingham and take a five-minute cab ride to Stourton. ⊠ *Off B3092, Stourton, northwest of Mere* ☎ *01747/841152* ⊕ *www.nationaltrust.org.uk* ☑ *£9.40, house only £5.40, gardens only £5.40 (Mar.–Oct.) or £4.10 (Nov.–Feb.)* ☉ *House mid-Mar.–Oct., Fri.–Tues. 11–5 or dusk; last admission 30 mins before closing, or 4 in Oct.; gardens daily 9–7 or dusk.*

Where to Stay & Eat

£££ ✕☒ **Spread Eagle Inn.** You can't stay at Stourhead, but this popular hostelry, built at the beginning of the 19th century at the entrance to the landscaped park, is the next best thing (and guests are admitted free to the house and gardens). Bedrooms are elegant and understated, with some period features. The restaurant serves traditional English fare, from wood pigeon to prime fillet steak, and there are seafood and vegetarian choices. ⊠ *Stourton, BA12 6HQ, northwest of Mere* ☎ *01747/840587* 🖷 *01747/840954* ⊕ *www.latonahotels.co.uk* ⊅ *5 rooms* ⚬ *Restaurant, bar; no a/c* ⊟ *AE, DC, MC, V* ⧖ *BP.*

Longleat House

★ ☺ ㉞ *6 mi north of Stourhead, 19 mi south of Bath, 27 mi northwest of Salisbury.*

Home of the marquess of Bath, Longleat House is one of southern England's most famous private estates. The blocklike Italian Renaissance building was completed in 1580 (for just over £8,000, an astronomical sum at the time) and contains outstanding tapestries, paintings, porcelain, and furniture, as well as notable period features such as the Victorian kitchens, the Elizabethan minstrels' gallery, and the great hall with its massive wooden beams. Giant antlers of the extinct Irish elk decorate the walls. In 1966 the grounds of Longleat became Britain's first safari park, with giraffes, zebras, rhinos, and lions all on view. Longleat also has dollhouses, a butterfly garden, a private railroad, the world's longest hedge maze, and an adventure castle, all of which make it extremely popular, particularly in summer and during school vacations. You can easily spend a whole day here, in which case it's best to visit the house in the morning, when tours are more relaxed, and the safari park in the afternoon. Call to confirm opening hours in winter. ⊠ *Off A362, Warminster* ☎ *01985/844400* ⊕ *www.longleat.co.uk* ▭ *house and safari park £16, house £9, safari park £9* ⊙ *House Jan.–Mar., weekends and school vacations 11–3; Apr.–Sept., daily 10–5:30; Oct.–Dec., daily 11–3; guided tours only (call for times). Safari park Apr.–Oct., weekdays 10–4, weekends and school vacations 10–5. Other attractions Apr.–Oct., daily 11–5:30.*

Where to Stay & Eat

★ **£££££** ✕▣ **Bishopstrow House.** It's not often that you discover a Georgian house converted into a luxurious but refreshingly relaxed hotel that combines antiques and fine carpets with modern amenities such as whirlpool baths and CD players. There's an airy conservatory, and the lavish, chintz-filled guest rooms overlook either the grounds (27 acres) or an interior courtyard. The Mulberry restaurant creates imaginative French meals (fixed-price menus) with a penchant for the piquant. Bishopstrow House is 1½ mi out of town. ⊠ *Boreham Rd., Warminster, BA12 9HH* ☎ *01985/212312* ▭ *01985/216769* ⊕ *www.bishopstrow.co.uk* ⤤ *32 rooms* ⚑ *Restaurant, some in-room hot tubs, golf privileges, 2 tennis courts, 2 pools (1 indoor), gym, hair salon, sauna, spa, fishing, croquet, bar, piano bar, business services, meeting rooms, helipad, some pets allowed; no a/c* ▭ *AE, DC, MC, V* ⑩ *BP.*

> **en route** Four miles west of Avebury, on A4, **Cherhill Down** is a prominent hill carved with a vivid white horse and topped with a towering obelisk. It's one of a number of hillside etchings in Wiltshire, but unlike the others, this one isn't an ancient symbol—it was put there in 1780 to indicate the highest point of the downs between London and Bath. The views from the top are well worth the half-hour climb. (The best view of the horse is from A4, on the approach from Calne.)

Avebury

❸❺ *25 mi northeast of Longleat, 27 mi east of Bath, 34 mi north of Salisbury.*

The village of Avebury was built much later than the stone circles that ★ brought it fame. The **Avebury Stone Circles** are one of England's most evocative prehistoric monuments—not so famous as Stonehenge, but all the more powerful for their lack of commercial exploitation. The stones were erected around 2500 BC, some 500 years after Stonehenge was started but about 500 years before that much smaller site assumed its present form. As with Stonehenge, the purpose of this stone circle has never been ascertained, although it most likely was used for similar ritual purposes. Unlike Stonehenge, however, there are no astronomical alignments at Avebury, at least none that have survived. The main site consists of a wide, circular ditch and bank, about 1,400 feet across and well over half a mile around; it actually surrounds part of the village of Avebury. Entrances break the perimeter at roughly the four points of the compass, and inside stand the remains of three stone circles. The largest one originally had 98 stones, although only 27 remain. Many of the stones on the site were destroyed centuries ago, especially in the 17th century when they were the target of religious fanaticism. Some stones were pillaged to build the thatched cottages you see flanking the fields. You can walk around the circles at any time; early morning and early evening are recommended. Be sure to visit the nearby Alexander Keiller Museum. ⊠ *1 mi north of A4* 🕾 *No phone* ⊕ *www.english-heritage.org.uk* 🎫 *Free* ⊙ *Daily.*

In the **Alexander Keiller Museum and Barn Gallery,** finds from the Avebury area, and charts, photos, models, and home movies taken by the archaeologist Keiller himself, put the Avebury Stone Circles and the site into context. Recent revelations suggest that Keiller, responsible for the excavation of Avebury in the 1930s, may have adapted the site's layout more in the interests of presentation than authenticity. ⊠ *1 mi north of A4* 🕾 *01672/539250* ⊕ *www.english-heritage.org.uk* 🎫 *£4.20* ⊙ *Apr.–Oct., daily 10–6; Nov.–Mar., daily 10–4.*

The Avebury monument lies at the end of **Kennett Stone Avenue,** a sort of prehistoric processional way leading to Avebury. The avenue's stones were spaced 80 feet apart, but only the half mile nearest the main monument survives intact. The lost stones are marked with concrete.

Where to Eat

£–££ ✕ **Waggon and Horses.** This spot just beside the traffic circle linking A4 and A361, a two-minute drive from the Avebury site, serves excellent lunches and evening meals beside a blazing fire. Homemade dishes include beef and Stilton pie, curries, and casseroles, or you can opt for a sandwich. The thatch-roof pub, mentioned in Dickens's *Pickwick Papers,* is built of stones taken from the Avebury site. ⊠ *Beckhampton* 🕾 *01672/539418* 🖃 *AE, MC, V.*

en route   Prehistoric relics dot the entire Avebury area; be sure to stop at the **West Kennett Long Barrow,** a chambered tomb dating from about 3250 BC, 1 mi east of Avebury on A4. As you turn right at the traffic circle onto A4, **Silbury Hill** rises on your right. This man-made mound, 130 feet high, dates from about 2500 BC and is the largest of its kind in Europe. Excavations over 200 years have provided no clue as to its original purpose, but the generally accepted notion is that it was a massive burial chamber.

Marlborough

🔟 *7 mi east of Avebury, 28 mi north of Salisbury.*

The attractive town of Marlborough developed as an important staging post on the old London–Bath stagecoach route. Today it is better known for its unusually wide main street, its Georgian houses—these replaced the medieval town center, which was destroyed in a great fire in 1653—and its celebrated public school. The grounds of the school, on the west side of town, enclose a small, man-made hill called Castle Mound, or Maerl's Barrow, which gave the town its name. This was said to be the grave of Merlin, King Arthur's court wizard, but it is clearly much older than the period when the historic Arthur may have lived.

Where to Stay

££ ▦ **Ivy House.** This redbrick Georgian house on colonnaded High Street makes an excellent touring base. Public rooms are clubby, and the traditionally styled bedrooms are predominantly beige and cream, some with exposed beams or arches. Those in the Vines annex, across the street, are less expensive. A courtyard bar serves light meals, and a more formal restaurant has views overlooking the sun terrace. ⊠ *43 High St., SN8 1HJ* ☎ *01672/515333* ♨ *01672/515338* ⊕ *www.ivyhousemarlborough.co.uk* ↘ *36 rooms* ♨ *Restaurant, cable TV, bar, meeting room; no a/c* ⊟ *AE, MC, V* ⊺⊙⊺ *BP.*

Sports

Marlborough Golf Club (⊠ The Common ☎ 01672/512147), with a par-72, 6,514-yard course, has fine views down the Og Valley.

Stonehenge

③⑦ *21 mi south of Marlborough, 8 mi north of Salisbury.*

Fodor'sChoice
★

One of England's most visited and most puzzling monuments, Stonehenge is dwarfed by its lonely isolation on the wide sweep of Salisbury Plain. Sadly, the great circle of stones has been enclosed by barriers to control both the relentless throngs of tourists and, during the summer solstice, crowds of New Age druids intent on celebrating, in the monument's imposing shadows, an obscure pagan festival. But if you visit in the early morning, when the crowds have not yet arrived, or in the evening, when the sky is heavy with scudding clouds, you can experience Stonehenge as it once was: a magical, mystical, awe-inspiring place.

Stonehenge was begun about 3000 BC, enlarged between 2100 and 1900 BC, and altered yet again by 150 BC. It has been excavated and rearranged several times over the centuries. The medieval term "Stonehenge" means "hanging stones." Many of the huge stones that ringed the center were brought here from great distances. The original 80 bluestones (dolerite), which made up the two internal circles, were transported from the Preseli mountains, near Fishguard on the Atlantic coast of Wales, presumably by raft over sea and river. Next they were dragged on rollers across country—a total journey of 130 mi as the crow flies, but closer to 240 by the practical route. The labor involved in quarrying, transporting, and carving these stones is astonishing, all the more so when you realize that it was accomplished about the same time that the major pyramids of Egypt were built.

Although some of the mysteries concerning the site have been solved, the reason Stonehenge was built remains unknown. It is fairly certain that it was a religious site, and that worship here involved the cycles of the sun; the alignment of the stones to point to sunrise at midsummer and sunset in midwinter makes this clear. For some historians one thing is certain: the druids had nothing to do with the construction. The monument had already been in existence for nearly 2,000 years by the time they appeared. Most historians think Stonehenge may have been a kind of neolithic computer, with a sophisticated astronomical purpose—an observatory of sorts.

A paved path for visitors surrounds Stonehenge, so that you can't get very close to the monoliths except in one section of the site. Bring a pair of binoculars to help make out the details more clearly. It pays to walk all about the site, near and far, to get that magical Kodak shot. Romantics may want to view Stonehenge at dawn or dusk, or by a full moon. You can rent an audio tour, but in general, visitor amenities at Stonehenge are rather squalid, with no indoor seating. The grand plans to improve the site include a tunnel for a section of A303 and a new visitor center, but no completion date has been set.

Buses leave from the Salisbury bus station for Stonehenge at 11, 12, 1, and 2 (confirm times); buy an Explorer ticket on board for £6. There's no place to leave luggage, though. Other options are a taxi or an organized tour. Visitors coming by car from Marlborough should join A345 south for Stonehenge, turning west onto A303 at Amesbury. The monument stands near the junction with A344. ⊠ *Junction of A303 and A344/A360, near Amesbury* ☎ *01980/624715* ⊕ *www.english-heritage. org.uk* 🖼 *£5.20* ☉ *Mid-Mar.–May and Sept.–mid-Oct., daily 9:30–6; June–Aug., daily 9–7; mid-Oct.–mid-Mar., daily 9:30–4.*

Lyndhurst

38 *26 mi southeast of Stonehenge, 18 mi southeast of Salisbury, 9 mi west of Southampton.*

Lyndhurst is famous as the capital of the New Forest. To explore the depths of this natural wonder, take A35 out of Lyndhurst (the road continues southwest to Bournemouth). To get here from Stonehenge, head south along A360 to Salisbury, then follow A36, B3079, and continue along A337 another 4 mi or so. The New Forest **Visitor Information Centre** (⊠ High St. ☎ 023/8028–2269) in the town's main car park is open daily year-round. Fans of Lewis Carroll's *Alice in Wonderland* should note that Alice Hargreaves (*née* Liddell), the inspiration for the fictional Alice, is buried in the **churchyard at Lyndhurst.**

The **New Forest** (☎ 01590/689000 ⊕ www.thenewforest.co.uk) consists of 150 square mi of mainly open, unfenced countryside interspersed with dense woodland, a natural haven for herds of free-roaming deer, cattle, and, most famously, hardy New Forest ponies. The forest was "new" in 1079, when William the Conqueror cleared the area of farms and villages and turned it into his private hunting grounds. Although some popular spots can get crowded in summer, there are ample parking lots, picnic areas, and campgrounds. Miles of walking trails crisscross the region.

Where to Stay & Eat

★ **£££–££££** ✕🖼 **Le Poussin at Parkhill.** Originally a hunting lodge and later a school and a control center for the D-Day landings, this Georgian manor house with extensive grounds is a mile southeast of Lyndhurst. Strumming cherubs, copious flowers, and soothing prospects of parkland and the

New Forest contribute to the cosseted air. Rooms are traditionally styled but not particularly special. Many people come just for the superb restaurant, run by chef and co-proprietor Alex Aitken, whose offerings might include New Forest pork brined in beer and pot-roasted with honey and cloves. A restaurant at Brockenhurst, Simply Poussin, serves similar but less expensive fare. ☒ *Beaulieu Rd., SO43 7FZ* ☎ *023/8028–2944* 🖷 *023/8028–3268* ⊕ *www.lepoussin.co.uk* 🔄 *19 rooms* ☖ *Restaurant, bar, fishing* ▭ *AE, MC, V* ⏐◉⏐ *CP.*

Sports & the Outdoors

GOLF   You may see New Forest ponies grazing on the par-69, 5,772-yard **New Forest Golf Course** (☒ Southampton Rd. ☎ 023/8028–2752), right in the middle of the New Forest.

HORSEBACK RIDING   The New Forest was created for riding, and there's no better way to enjoy it than on horseback. You can arrange a ride at the **Forest Park Riding Stables** (☒ Rhinefield Rd., Brockenhurst ☎ 01590/623429 🗺 £19 for 1 hr). The **New Park Manor Stables** (☒ New Park, Brockenhurst ☎ 01590/ 623919 🗺 £17 for 1 hr) gives full instruction.

WALKING   The **New Forest** is more domesticated than, for example, the Forest of Dean, and the walks it provides are not much more than easy strolls. For one such walk (about 4 mi), start from Lyndhurst and head directly south for Brockenhurst, a commuter village. The path goes through woods, pastureland, and leafy river valleys—and you may even see some New Forest ponies.

Beaulieu

🟤 *7 mi southeast of Lyndhurst.*

The unspoiled village of Beaulieu (pronounced *byoo*-lee) has three major attractions in one **Beaulieu,** with a ruined abbey, a stately home, and an automobile museum, can satisfy different interests. In 1204 King John established **Beaulieu Abbey** for the Cistercian monks, who gave their new home its name, which means "beautiful place" in French. It was badly damaged during the reign of Henry VIII, leaving only the cloister, the doorway, the gatehouse, and two buildings. A well-planned exhibition in one building re-creates daily life in the monastery. **Palace House** incorporates the abbey's 14th-century gatehouse and has been the home of the Montagu family since they purchased it in 1538, after the dissolution of the monasteries. In this stately home you can see drawing rooms, dining halls, and fine family portraits. The present Lord Montagu is noted for his work in establishing the **National Motor Museum**, which traces the development of motor transport from 1895 to the present. You can see more than 250 classic cars, buses, and motorcycles. Museum attractions include a monorail, audiovisual presentations, and a trip in a 1912 London bus (weekends only in winter, excluding January). **Beaulieu Cycle Hire** (☎ 01590/611029), on the grounds of the motor museum, rents bicycles from February through October. ☒ *Off B3056* ☎ *01590/ 612345* ⊕ *www.beaulieu.co.uk* 🗺 *Abbey, Palace House, and Motor Museum £14* ⊙ *May–Sept., daily 10–6; Oct.–Apr., daily 10–5; last admission 40 mins before closing.*

Buckler's Hard

40 *2 mi south of Beaulieu.*

Among interesting places around Beaulieu is the museum village of Buckler's Hard, an almost perfectly restored 18th-century hamlet of 24 brick cottages, leading down to an old shipyard on the Beaulieu River. There's a small hotel here, too. The fascinating **Maritime Museum** tells the story of Lord Nelson's favorite ship, HMS *Agamemnon,* which was built here of New Forest oak. Exhibits and model ships trace the shipbuilding history of the town. Also part of the museum are four building interiors in the hamlet that re-create 18th-century village life. Easter through October, you can arrange to take a cruise on the Beaulieu River. ☎ *01590/616203* ⊕ *www.bucklershard.co.uk* ✉ *£5.25* ⊙ *Easter–Oct., daily 10:30–5; Nov.–Easter, daily 11–4.*

en route From Beaulieu, take any of the minor roads leading west through wide-open heathland to Lymington and pick up A337 for the popular seaside resort of Bournemouth, a journey of about 18 mi.

BOURNEMOUTH TO LYME REGIS
FAR FROM THE MADDING CROWD

"I am convinced that it is better for a writer to know a little bit of the world remarkably well than to know a great part of the world remarkably little," wrote Thomas Hardy, the immortal author of *Far from the Madding Crowd* and other classic Victorian-era novels. His "little bit" was the county of Dorset, the setting for most of his books and, today, a green and hilly area that is largely unspoiled. A visit to one of the last remaining corners of old, rural England follows the Dorset coastline, immortalized by Hardy and, more recently, by John Fowles. Places of historic interest such as Maiden Castle and the chalk-cut giant of Cerne Abbas are interspersed with the seaside resorts of Bournemouth and Weymouth, although you may find the quieter towns of Lyme Regis and the smaller villages scattered along the route closer to your ideal of rural England. Chief glory of the county is Dorchester, an ancient agricultural center with a host of historical and literary associations, and worth a prolonged visit.

Bournemouth

41 *30 mi southwest of Southampton, 30 mi south of Salisbury, 30 mi east of Dorchester.*

The beach resort of Bournemouth was founded in 1810 by Lewis Tregonwell, an ex-army officer who had taken a liking to the area when stationed there some years before. He settled near what is now the Square and planted the first pine trees in the steep little valleys—or chines—cutting through the cliffs to the famous Bournemouth sands. The scent of fir trees was said to be healing for consumption (tuberculosis) sufferers, and the town grew steadily. Gardens laid out with trees and lawns link the Square and the beach. This is an excellent spot to relax and listen to music wafting from the Pine Walk bandstand. Regular musical programs take place at the Pavilion and at the Winter Gardens (home of the Bournemouth Symphony Orchestra) nearby.

Taking the zigzag paths through the leafy public gardens, you can descend to the seafront, where Bournemouth Pier juts into the channel from the pristine sandy beach. Bournemouth has 7 mi of beaches, and the waters are said to be some of southern England's cleanest. If you're not tempted to swim, you can always saunter along the wide promenade behind the beach.

Concerts and shows are staged at the **Bournemouth International Centre** (⊠ Exeter Rd. ☎ 0870/111–3000 ⊕ www.bic.co.uk), which includes a selection of restaurants and bars, and a swimming pool. For an old-fashioned tea, try the **Cumberland Hotel** (⊠ E. Overcliffe Dr. ☎ 01202/ 290722), which serves outdoors in summer.

On the corner of Hinton Road stands **St. Peter's** parish church, easily recognizable by its 200-foot-high tower and spire. Lewis Tregonwell, founder and developer of Bournemouth, is buried in the churchyard. Here, too, is the elaborate tombstone of Mary Shelley, author of *Franken-stein* and wife of the great Romantic poet Percy Bysshe Shelley, whose heart is buried with her.

★ The **Russell-Cotes Art Gallery and Museum,** a late Victorian mansion perched on top of East Cliff, overflows with Victorian paintings and miniatures, cases of butterflies, and treasures from Asia, including an exquisite suit of Japanese armor. Members of the Russell-Cotes family, wealthy hoteliers who traveled widely, collected the items. Fine landscaped gardens, restored to their original 1921 design, surround the house. ⊠ *East Cliff* ☎ *01202/451858* ⊕ *www.russell-cotes.bournemouth.gov.uk* ▨ *Free* ☉ *Tues.–Sun. 10–5.*

Where to Stay & Eat

££–££££ ✕ **CH2.** Shiny, metallic, and elegant with wooden flooring, this busy modern restaurant specializes in steaks and mussels, served with inventive sauces such as red Thai curry and garlic and shallot. For something lighter, opt for a simple pizza. It's close to the sea and not far from the International Centre. ⊠ *37 Exeter Rd.* ☎ *01202/296296* ▤ *AE, MC, V* ☉ *Closed Sun., Mon.*

★ **£££££** ✕▨ **Chewton Glen.** Once the home of Captain Frederick Marryat, author of *The Children of the New Forest,* this early-19th-century country house on extensive grounds is now a supremely luxurious hotel, among Britain's most acclaimed—and most expensive. All the rooms are sumptuously decorated in rich fabrics, with an eye to the minutest detail, and the plush spa provides the latest treatments. Many diners consider the restaurant, the Marryat Room, and the cooking of its chef, Luke Matthews, worth a pilgrimage. The fixed-price menu concentrates on classic meat and seafood dishes enlivened with contemporary elements, and there's a choice of more than 500 wines. Chewton Glen is 12 mi east of Bournemouth. ⊠ *Christchurch Rd., New Milton, BH25 6QS*

☎ 01425/275341, 800/344–5087 in U.S. ⊠ 01425/272310, 800/398–4534 in U.S. ⊕ www.chewtonglen.com ⟿ 59 rooms ⚘ Restaurant, in-room data ports, cable TV, 9-hole golf course, 4 tennis courts, 2 pools (1 indoor), gym, spa, croquet, business services, meeting rooms, helipad; no a/c in some rooms, no kids under 6 ☰ AE, DC, MC, V ⊺◎⊺ BP.

££££ ✕⊞ **Langtry Manor Hotel.** Edward VII built this house for his mistress Lillie Langtry in 1877, and it still preserves some of its Edwardian style, even in the newer annex. Individually named rooms continue the theme. In the formal restaurant (fixed-price menu), lacy tablecloths, silver cutlery, and other details set off the dishes, which are mainly British with French trimmings and include Lillie's Meringue Swans for dessert. There's an Edwardian banquet every Saturday. Guests have access to a nearby health club. ⊠ 26 Derby Rd., East Cliff, BH1 3QB ☎ 01202/553887 ⊠ 01202/290115 ⊕ www.langtrymanor.com ⟿ 27 rooms ⚘ Restaurant, in-room data ports, meeting rooms; no a/c ☰ AE, DC, MC, V ⊺◎⊺ BP.

Nightlife & the Arts

Bournemouth holds a **Music Festival** (☎ 01202/451700) June–July, with choirs, brass bands, and orchestras, some from overseas.

Wimborne Minster

㊷ 7 mi northwest of Bournemouth.

The impressive minster of this quiet market town makes it seem like a miniature cathedral city. To get here from Bournemouth, follow the signs northwest on A341. The crenellated and pinnacled twin towers of **Wimborne Minster** present an attractive patchwork of gray and reddish-brown stone. The church's powerful Norman nave has zigzag molding interspersed with carved heads, and the Gothic chancel has tall lancet windows. Stop in to see the chained library (accessed via a spiral staircase), where valuable books have been kept on chains since 1686, and look out for the 14th-century astronomical clock on the inside wall of the west tower. ⊠ High St. ☎ 01202/884753 ⊕ www.wimborneminster.org.uk ⊠ £1.50 donation requested for church, chained library free ☉ Church Mar.–Dec., Mon.–Sat. 9:30–5:30, Sun. 2:30–5:30; Jan. and Feb., Mon.–Sat. 9:30–4, Sun. 2:30–4. Chained library Easter–Oct., Mon.–Thurs. 10:30–12:30 and 2–4, Fri. 10:30–2:30.

The **Priest's House Museum,** on the main square in a Tudor building with a garden, includes rooms furnished in period styles and a Victorian kitchen. It also has Roman and Iron Age exhibits, including a cryptic, three-faced Celtic stone head. ⊠ 23 High St. ☎ 01202/882533 ⊠ £2.70 ☉ Apr.–Nov., Mon.–Sat. 10–4:30; also open 2 wks after Christmas.

Kingston Lacy, a grand 17th-century house built for the Bankes family (who had lived in Corfe Castle), was altered in the 19th century by Sir Charles Barry, co-architect of the Houses of Parliament in London. The building holds a choice picture collection with works by Titian, Rubens, Van Dyck, and Velásquez, as well as the fabulous Spanish Room, lined with gilded leather and topped with an ornate Venetian ceiling. There's also a fine collection of Egyptian artifacts. Parkland with walking paths surrounds the house. ⊠ *B3082, 1½ mi northwest of Wimborne Min-ster* ☎ *01202/883402* ⊕ *www.nationaltrust.org.uk* ⊠ *£7.20, park and garden only £3.60* ⊘ *House late Mar.–Oct., Wed.–Sun. 11–5 (last ad-mission 4). Garden and park Feb.–late Mar., weekends 10:30–4; late Mar.–Oct., daily 10:30–6; Nov. and Dec., Fri.–Sun. 10:30–4.*

Where to Eat

££–£££ ✕ **Primizia.** This popular bistro serves dishes with French and Italian in-fluences; try the pasta and bean soup for starters, followed by carpac-cio of beef with wild mushrooms, and crème brûlée for dessert. ⊠ *26 Westborough* ☎ *01202/883518* ⊟ *MC, V* ⊘ *Closed Sun.–Mon.*

Blandford Forum

❸ *11 mi northwest of Wimborne Minster.*

Endowed with perhaps the handsomest Georgian town center in the south-west, this market town of brick and stone on the River Stour was Thomas Hardy's "Shottesford Forum." The Church of St. Peter and St. Paul, with an imposing cupola and dating from 1739, deserves a look.

Where to Stay & Eat

££–£££ ✕▣ **Museum Inn.** It's worth making the detour 9 mi northeast of Bland-ford Forum to find this characterful inn. Despite a stylish transformation, the building remains in harmony with its 17th-century beginnings, retaining its flagstone floors and inglenook fireplace. Bedrooms are rustic but smart. Good fresh fare, from tagliatelle of leeks with blue cheese and mar-joram to braised lamb casserole with shallot dumplings and eggplant, is available daily in the bar, and on weekends you can dine more formally in the Shed restaurant. ⊠ *Farnham, DT11 8DE* ☎ *01725/516261* ▣ *01725/516988* ⊕ *www.museuminn.co.uk* ▱ *8 rooms* ♦ *Restaurant, bar, some pets allowed; no a/c, no kids under 8* ⊟ *MC, V* ⦿ *BP.*

Corfe Castle

★ ❹ *20 mi south of Blandford Forum, 15 mi south of Poole, 6 mi south of Wareham.*

One of the most impressive ruins in Britain, the remains of Dorset's Corfe Castle overlook the appealing gray limestone village of Corfe. The cas-tle site guards a gap in the surrounding Purbeck Hills and has been for-tified from very early times. The present ruins are of the castle built between 1105, when the great central keep was erected, and the 1270s, when the outer walls and towers were built. It owes its ramshackle state to Cromwell's soldiers, who blew up the castle in 1646 during the Civil War after Lady Bankes led its defense during a long siege. ⊠ *A351* ☎ *01929/481294* ⊕ *www.nationaltrust.org.uk* ⊠ *£4.70* ⊘ *Mar. and Oct., daily 10–5; Apr.–Sept., daily 10–6; Nov.–Feb., daily 10–4.*

> **off the beaten path**
>
> **CLOUDS HILL –** A tiny, spartan, brick-and-tile cottage served as the retreat of T. E. Lawrence (Lawrence of Arabia) before he was killed in a motorcycle accident on the road from Bovington in 1935. The house remains very much as he left it, with photos and memorabilia

from the Middle East. It's particularly atmospheric on a gloomy day, as there's no electric light. ⊠ *Wareham, 8 mi northwest of Corfe, off B3390* ☎ *01929/405616* ⊕ *www.nationaltrust.org.uk* 🎟 *£3.10* ☉ *Apr.–Oct., Thurs.–Sun. and national holidays noon–5 or dusk.*

Where to Stay & Eat

★ **££** ✕ **The Fox.** An age-old pub, the Fox has a fine view of Corfe Castle from its flower garden. There's an ancient well in the lounge bar and more timeworn stonework in an alcove, as well as a pre-1300 fireplace. The bar cheerfully doles out soups and sandwiches, as well as steaks and curries, but things can get uncomfortably congested in summer. ⊠ *West St., Corfe* ☎ *01929/480449* ▤ *MC, V.*

£–££ 🏨 **Castle Inn.** This thatched hotel, 10 mi west of Corfe and just five minutes' walk from the sea, has a flagstone bar and other 15th-century features. Bedrooms are individually furnished, some with four-posters, and there's an extensive garden to sit in, including a rose garden. A lengthy bar menu is available daily, and on weekend evenings the good restaurant has an à la carte menu. Satisfying walks are nearby. ⊠ *Main Rd., West Lulworth, BH20 5RN* ☎ *01929/400311* 🖷 *01929/400415* ⊕ *www. thecastleinn-lulworthcove.co.uk* 🛏 *15 rooms, 12 with bath* ♿ *Restaurant, bar, some pets allowed; no a/c, no phones in some rooms* ▤ *AE, DC, MC, V* ⊺○⊺ *BP.*

Dorchester

㊺ *21 mi west of Corfe on A351 and A352, 30 mi west of Bournemouth, 43 mi southwest of Salisbury.*

In many ways Dorchester, the Casterbridge of Thomas Hardy's novel *The Mayor of Casterbridge,* is a traditional southern country town. The town owes much of its fame to its connection with Hardy, whose bronze statue looks westward from a bank on Colliton Walk. Born in a cottage in the hamlet of Higher Bockhampton, about 3 mi northeast of Dorchester, Hardy attended school in the town and was apprentice to an architect here.

Roman history and artifacts abound in Dorchester. The Romans laid out the town about AD 70, and a walk along Bowling Alley Walk, West Walk, and Colliton Walk follows the approximate line of the original Roman town walls. On the north side of Colliton Park lies an excavated Roman villa with a marvelously preserved mosaic floor.

Dorchester is also associated with Monmouth's Rebellion of 1685, when Charles II's illegitimate son, the duke of Monmouth, led a rising against his unpopular uncle, James II. The rebellion was ruthlessly put down, and the chief justice, Lord Jeffreys, arrived from London to try the rebels and sympathizers for treason. A bullying drunkard, Jeffreys was the prototypical hanging judge, and stories of his mass executions lingered for centuries throughout the South. The trials became known as the Bloody Assizes. Jeffreys's courtroom in Dorchester was in what is now the Antelope Hotel on South Street.

To appreciate the town's character, visit the Wednesday market in **Market Square,** where you can find handcrafted items and Dorset delicacies

CloseUp

HARDY'S DORSET

Among this region's proudest claims is its connection with Thomas Hardy (1840–1928), one of England's most celebrated novelists. If you read some of Hardy's novels before visiting Dorset—recreated by Hardy as his part-fact, part-fiction county of Wessex—you may well recognize some places immediately from his descriptions. The tranquil countryside surrounding Dorchester, is lovingly described in Far from the Madding Crowd, and Casterbridge, in The Mayor of Casterbridge, stands for Dorchester itself. Any pilgrimage to Hardy's Wessex begins at the author's birthplace in Higher Bockhampton, 3 mi east of Dorchester. Salisbury makes an appearance as "Melchester" in Jude the Obscure. Walk in the footsteps of Jude Fawley by climbing Shaftesbury—"Shaston"—and its steeply Gold Hill, a street lined with charming cottages. Today, many of these sights seem frozen in time, and Hardy's spirit is ever present.

such as Blue Vinney cheese (which some connoisseurs prefer to Blue Stilton). Things have changed a bit since the days when, to quote Hardy, "Bees and butterflies in the cornfields at the top of the town, who desired to get to the meads at the bottom, took no circuitous route, but flew straight down High Street . . ."

The **Dorset County Museum** contains ancient Celtic and Roman remains and a local-history gallery, but is better known for its large collection of Hardy memorabilia. ⊠ *High West St.* ☎ *01305/262735* ⊕ *www. dorsetcountymuseum.org* ⊡ *£4.20* ⊘ *May–Oct., daily 10–5; Nov.–Apr., Mon.–Sat. 10–5.*

The small thatch-and-cob **Hardy's Cottage,** where the writer was born in 1840, was built by his grandfather and is little altered since that time. From here Thomas Hardy would make his daily 6-mi walk to school in Dorchester. Among other things, you can see the desk at which the author completed *Far from the Madding Crowd.* ⊠ *½ mi south of Blandford Rd. (A35), Higher Bockhampton* ☎ *01305/262366* ⊕ *www. nationaltrust.org.uk* ⊡ *£3* ⊘ *Apr.–Oct., Thurs.–Mon. 11–5 or dusk.*

Thomas Hardy lived in **Max Gate** from 1885 until his death in 1928. An architect by profession, Hardy designed the house, in which the dining room and the light, airy drawing room are open to the public. He wrote much of his poetry here and many of his novels, including *Tess of the d'Urbervilles* and *The Mayor of Casterbridge.* ⊠ *Allington Ave., 1 mi east of Dorchester on A352* ☎ *01305/262538* ⊕ *www.nationaltrust. org.uk* ⊡ *£2.60* ⊘ *Apr.–Sept., Mon., Wed., and Sun. 2–5.*

The **Maumbury Rings** (⊠ *Maumbury Rd.*), the remains of a Roman amphitheater on the edge of town, were built on a prehistoric site that later served as a place of execution. (Hardy's *Mayor of Casterbridge* contains a vivid evocation of the Rings.) As late as 1706, a girl was burned at the stake here.

The popular **Dinosaur Museum** has life-size models, interactive displays, and a hands-on Discovery Gallery. ⊠ *Icen Way, off High East St.* ☎ *01305/269741* ⊕ *www.dinosaur-museum.org.uk* ⊠ *£6* ☉ *Apr.–Oct., daily 9:30–5:30; Nov.–Mar., daily 10–4:30.*

It's hardly what you might expect from a small county town, but the **Tutankhamun Exhibition,** in a former Catholic church, re-creates the young pharaoh's tomb and treasures in all their glory. The smells of ointments and cedarwood oil complement the displays; the same ticket admits you to the small Mummies Exhibition next door, showing the process of mummification with copies of mummies. ⊠ *High West St.* ☎ *01305/269571* ⊕ *www.tutankhamun-exhibition.co.uk* ⊠ *£5.50* ☉ *Apr.–Oct., daily 9:30–5:30; Nov.–Mar., weekdays 9:30–5, weekends 10–5; last admission 45 mins before closing.*

need a break?

Reflect on some of the region's darker history at **Judge Jeffreys** (⊠ 6 High West St. ☎ 01305/264369), where you can have coffee, cream teas, and light meals in the beamed building where Judge Jeffreys held his Bloody Assizes in 1685.

Fine 19th-century gardens complement an outstanding example of 15th-century domestic architecture at **Athelhampton House and Gardens,** 5 mi east of Dorchester and 1 mi east of Puddletown. Thomas Hardy called this place Athelhall in some of his writings, referring to the legendary King Aethelstan, who had a palace on this site. The current house includes the Great Hall, with much of its original timber roof intact, the King's Room, and the Library, with oak paneling and more than 3,000 books. The 10 acres of landscaped gardens contain water features and the Great Court with its 12 giant yew pyramids. ⊠ *A35* ☎ *01305/848363* ⊕ *www.athelhampton.co.uk* ⊠ *£7.75, gardens only £5.50* ☉ *Mar.–Oct., Sun.–Thurs. 10–5; Nov.–Feb., Sun. 10:30–dusk.*

Where to Stay & Eat

££–£££ ✕ **Potters Café-Bistro.** This café on two floors of a 17th-century cottage is just the place for a daytime break for teas, coffees, and delicious cakes and pastries, as well as sandwiches and light lunches. In the evening, the menu may list scallops and vegetarian caviar for starters, and mille-feuille of Mediterranean vegetables and duck breast with wild rice for main courses. The inglenook fireplace adds coziness in winter, and the courtyard garden is pleasant in summer. ⊠ *19 Durngate St.* ☎ *01305/260312* ☰ *MC, V* ☉ *Closed Sun. No dinner Mon.–Wed.*

★ £££ ✕ **Yalbury Cottage.** A thatch roof and inglenook fireplaces enhance the traditional appeal of this 300-year-old cottage, just 2½ mi east of Dorchester and close to Hardy's birthplace. The three-course fixed-price menu of superior modern British and European fare might include griddled fillet of beef on a Stilton mash with caramelized shallots, or pan-seared brill on a foie gras mash. Pine-furnished bedrooms are available in a discreet extension overlooking gardens or adjacent fields. ⊠ *Lower Bock-hampton, DT2 8PZ* ☎ *01305/262382* ☎ *01305/266412* ⊕ *www.s-h-systems.co.uk* ⊷ *8 rooms* ☖ *Restaurant, some pets allowed (fee); no a/c, no smoking* ☰ *MC, V* ☉ *Closed 1 wk Jan. No lunch* ⦿ *BP.*

★ **££–£££** ⊡ **Casterbridge Hotel.** Small but full of character, this Georgian building (1790) reflects its age with period furniture and elegance. Guest rooms are each individually and impeccably furnished in traditional style, and the conservatory overlooks a leafy courtyard garden. A congenial husband-and-wife team owns and runs the hotel. ⊠ *49 High East St., DT1 1HU* ☎ *01305/264043* 🖷 *01305/260884* ⊕ *www. casterbridgehotel.co.uk* ➷ *14 rooms* ⚅ *In-room data ports, bar; no a/c* ⊟ *AE, DC, MC, V* ⦿| *BP.*

The Outdoors
From April through October the **Thomas Hardy Society** (⊡ Box 1438, Dorchester DT1 1YH ☎☎ 01305/251501 ⊕ www.hardysociety.org) organizes walks that follow in the steps of Hardy's novels. Readings and discussions accompany the walks, which take most of a day.

Cerne Abbas

46 *6 mi north of Dorchester.*

The village of Cerne Abbas, worth a short exploration on foot, has some appealing Tudor houses on the road beside the church. Nearby you can also see the original village stocks. Tenth-century **Cerne Abbey** is now a ruin, with little left to see except its old gateway, although the nearby Abbey House is still in use.

Cerne Abbas's main claim to fame is the colossal and unblushingly priapic **figure of a giant,** cut in chalk on a hillside overlooking the village. The 180-foot-long giant carries a huge club and bears a striking resemblance to Hercules, although he may have originated as a tribal fertility symbol long before Roman times; authorities disagree. His outlines are formed by 2-foot-wide trenches. The present giant is thought to have been carved in the chalk about AD 1200. The best place to view the figure is from the A352 itself, where you can park in any of numerous nearby turnouts.

Where to Stay
£ ⊡ **Lamperts Cottage.** This idyllic thatch-roof B&B, about 2 mi southwest of Cerne Abbas, has a stream in front and back, so you must cross a little bridge to reach it. In summer roses cover the cottage. The house, dating from the 16th century, is extremely comfortable even though it's small; the rooms share two baths. The interior has exposed beams and fireplaces. ⊠ *10 Dorchester Rd., Sydling St. Nicholas, DT2 9NU* ☎ *01300/341659* 🖷 *01300/341699* ✉ *nickywillis@tesco.net* ➷ *3 rooms without bath* ⚅ *No a/c, no room phones, no room TVs, no kids under 8, no credit cards* ⦿| *BP.*

FodorśChoice
★

Maiden Castle

★ **47** *2 mi southwest of Dorchester.*

After Stonehenge, Maiden Castle is the most important pre-Roman archaeological site in England. It's not an actual castle but an enormous, complex hill fort of stone and earth with ramparts that enclose about 45 acres. England's mysterious prehistoric inhabitants built the fort, and many centuries later it was a Celtic stronghold. In AD 43 invading Romans, under the general (later emperor) Vespasian, stormed the fort. Finds from the site are on display in the Dorset County Museum in Dorchester. To experience an uncanny silence and sense of mystery, climb Maiden Castle early in the day (access to it is unrestricted). Leave your car at the lot at the end of Maiden Castle Way, a 1½-mi lane signposted off the A354. ⊠ *A354.*

Weymouth

48 *8 mi south of Dorchester.*

Dorset's main coastal resort, Weymouth, is known for its wide, safe, sandy beaches and its royal connections. King George III took up sea bathing here for his health in 1789, setting a trend among the wealthy and fashionable people of the day. Popularity left Weymouth with many fine buildings, including the Georgian row houses lining the esplanade. Striking historical details clamor for attention: a wall on Maiden Street, for example, holds a cannonball that was embedded in it during the Civil War. Nearby, a column commemorates the launching of United States forces from Weymouth on D-Day.

Where to Stay & Eat

££–£££ ✗ **Perry's.** A busy, family-run restaurant right by the harbor, Perry's specializes in simple dishes using the best local seafood. Try the lobster or crab, or grilled fillet of turbot with leeks, new potatoes, and shellfish sauce. Meat dishes, such as roast leg of lamb, are tasty, too. ⊠ *The Harbourside, 4 Trinity Rd.* ☎ *01305/785799* ⊟ *AE, MC, V* ⊗ *No lunch Mon. and Sat.; no dinner Sun. Sept.–Easter.*

£–££ ✗ **Old Rooms.** A fisherman's pub full of maritime clutter and low beams, this popular choice has great views over the harbor. The long menu is strongest on steaks, but pastas, curries, and pies are other choices. There's a separate dining area, or you can mix with the locals at the bar. ⊠ *7 Cove Row* ☎ *01305/771130* ⊟ *AE, MC, V.*

££ ⊞ **Streamside Hotel.** This black-and-white timbered hotel on the outskirts of town is a stone's throw from the beach and has spectacular gardens. Bedrooms are furnished in pine with white bed linens, and the restaurant—open Easter–September only—serves English fare, with steaks, smoked salmon, and different fish in season. ⊠ *29 Preston Rd., Overcombe, DT3 6PX* ☎ *01305/833121* 🖷 *01305/832043* ⤴ *11 rooms* ⅏ *Restaurant, meeting rooms, some pets allowed (fee); no a/c* ⊟ *MC, V* ⦿❘ *BP.*

Isle of Portland

49 *4 mi south of Weymouth.*

A 5-mi-long peninsula jutting south from Weymouth leads to the Isle of Portland, well known for its limestone. The peninsula is the eastern end of the unique geological curiosity known as **Chesil Beach**—a 200-yard-wide, 30-foot-high bank of pebbles that decrease in size from east to west. The beach extends for 18 mi. A powerful undertow makes swimming dangerous, and tombstones in local churchyards attest to the many shipwrecks the beach has caused.

Abbotsbury

50 *10 mi northwest of Weymouth.*

The attractive village of Abbotsbury is at the western end of Chesil Beach. A lagoon outside the village serves as the **Abbotsbury Swannery,** a famous breeding place for swans. Introduced by Benedictine monks as a source of meat in winter, the swans have remained for centuries, building new nests every year in the soft, moist pampas grass. ⊠ *New Barn Rd.* ☎ *01305/871858* ⊕ *www.abbotsbury-tourism.co.uk* ⊠ *£6.50* ۞ *Late Mar.–Sept., daily 10–6; Oct., daily 10–5; last admission 1 hr before closing.*

On the hills above Abbotsbury stands the **Hardy Monument**—dedicated not to the novelist but to Sir Thomas Masterman Hardy, Lord Nelson's flag captain at Trafalgar, to whom Nelson's dying words, "Kiss me, Hardy," were addressed. The monument is without much charm, but in clear weather you can scan the whole coastline between the Isle of Wight and Start Point in Devon. ⊠ *Black Down, Portesham* ☎ *01297/561900* ⊕*www.nationaltrust.org.uk* ⊠*£1* ۞ *Apr.–Sept., weekends 11–5. Subject to closure in bad weather.*

Where to Stay & Eat

£££ ✕☶ **Manor Hotel.** The pedigree of this honey-color hotel and restaurant goes back more than 700 years—note its flagstone floors, oak paneling, and beamed ceilings. Among the English and French dishes in which the Manor specializes are seafood and game; the fixed-price menu changes daily. Some of the rooms, which are individually decorated in pastel colors and furnished with antiques, have sea views, and Chesil Beach is a few minutes' walk away. Self-catering facilities are available. ⊠ *Beach Rd., West Bexington, DT2 9DF, 3 mi west of Abbotsbury* ☎ *01308/897785* 🖶 *01308/897035* ⊕ *www.themanorhotel.com* ➪ *13 rooms* ♿ *Restaurant, playground; no a/c* ⊟ *AE, MC, V* ⍠ *BP.*

Lyme Regis

51 *19 mi west of Abbotsbury.*

"A very strange stranger it must be, who does not see the charms of the immediate environs of Lyme, to make him wish to know it better," wrote Jane Austen in *Persuasion.* Judging from the summer crowds, most people appear to be not at all strange. The ancient, scenic town of Lyme Regis and the so-called Jurassic Coast (a World Heritage Site, including the coast from Exmouth in the west to Swanage in the east, that encompasses 185 million years of the Earth's geological history) are highlights of southwest Dorset. The crumbling seaside cliffs in this area are especially fossil rich. In 1810 a local child named Mary Anning dug out a complete ichthyosaur here (it's on display in London's Natural History Museum). Exhibits in the Philpot Museum and the Lyme Regis Marine Aquarium provide insight into local history and marine life, respectively.

Lyme Regis is famous for its curving stone breakwater, **The Cobb**, built by King Edward I in the 13th century to improve the harbor. The duke of Monmouth landed here in 1685 during his ill-fated attempt to overthrow his uncle, James II. The Cobb figured prominently in the movie *The French Lieutenant's Woman*, based on John Fowles's novel, as well as in the film version of Jane Austen's *Persuasion*. Fowles is Lyme's most famous current resident.

The lively **Philpot Museum,** in a gabled and turreted Victorian building, contains engaging items that illustrate the town's maritime and domestic history, as well as a section on local writers and a good selection of local fossils. ⊠ *Bridge St.* ☎ *01297/443370* ⊕ *www.lymeregismuseum. co.uk* 🎫 *£2* ⊙ *Apr.–Oct., Mon.–Sat. 10–5, Sun. 11–5; Nov.–Mar., weekends 10–5, Sun. 11–5.*

Ⓒ The **Dinosaurland Fossil Museum,** in a former church, displays an excellent collection of local fossils and gives the background on regional geology and how fossils develop. Although the museum is aimed at children, most people find it informative. Ask here about guided fossil-hunting walks. The **Lyme Regis Fossil Shop** on the ground floor sells books and fascinating fossils from around the world as well as copies, some fashioned into jewelry or ornaments. ⊠ *Coombe St.* ☎ *01297/ 443541* ⊕ *www.dinosaurland.co.uk* 🎫 *£4* ⊙ *July and Aug., daily 10–6; Sept.–June, daily 10–5.*

Where to Stay & Eat

£–££ ✕ **Bell Cliff Restaurant.** This friendly little place at the bottom of Lyme's main street makes a great spot for a light lunch or tea, although it can get noisy and cramped. Apart from teas and coffees, you can order seafood, including whitebait, plaice, and the chef's salmon fish cakes, or a gammon steak (a thick slice of cured ham) or nut roast. ⊠ *5–6 Broad St.* ☎ *01297/442459* ⊟ *MC, V* ⊙ *No dinner Oct.–June.*

£££–££££ ✕▥ **Alexandra.** A short walk from the Cobb, the Alexandra is a genteel, old-fashioned haven with a high, panoramic location. Informal lunches and teas are served in a sunny conservatory that overlooks an expanse of lawn. The formal restaurant has an impressive wine list to complement the fixed-price four-course dinners, with straightforward entrées such as poached salmon and roast Aylesbury duckling in orange sauce. Depending on the cost, some guest rooms have a restrained elegance and others are purely functional, although you're almost guaranteed a view over garden and sea. ⊠ *Pound St., DT7 3HZ* ☎ *01297/ 442010* 🖶 *01297/443229* ⊕ *www.hotelalexandra.co.uk* ⬖ *26 rooms* ⬧ *Restaurant, bar, some pets allowed (fee); no a/c* ⊟ *MC, V* ⊙ *Closed Jan.* �� *BP.*

£ ▥ **Coombe House.** The main stone building of this B&B tucked away on one of the oldest lanes in Lyme (dating from the 16th century) has spacious, simply decorated modern guest rooms. Across the yard is a larger studio with a kitchen. Breakfast is brought to your room. ⊠ *41 Coombe St., DT7 3PY* ☎ *01297/443849* ⊕ *www.coombe-house.co. uk* ⬖ *2 rooms, 1 studio* ⬧ *No a/c; no room phones, no smoking* ⊟ *No credit cards* ⑐ *BP.*

Sports & the Outdoors

The 72-mi **Dorset Coast Path** (✉ South West Coast Path Association, Windlestraw, Penquit, Ermington ☎ 01752/896237) runs east from Lyme Regis to Poole, bypassing Weymouth and taking in the quiet bays, shingle beaches, and low chalk cliffs of the coast. Some highlights are Golden Cap, the highest point on the South Coast; the Swannery at Abbotsbury; Chesil Beach; and Lulworth Cove (between Weymouth and Corfe Castle). Villages and isolated pubs dot the route, as do many rural B&Bs.

THE SOUTH A TO Z

To research prices, get advice from other travelers, and book travel arrangements, visit www.fodors.com.

AIRPORTS

The small international airport at Southampton is useful for flights to the Channel Islands and some European destinations.

🛪 **Southampton International Airport** ✉ M27, Junction 5 ☎ 023/8062-0021 ⊕ www.baa.co.uk.

BOAT & FERRY TRAVEL

Wightlink operates a car-ferry service between the mainland and the Isle of Wight. The crossing takes about 30 minutes from Lymington to Yarmouth; 35 minutes from Portsmouth to Fishbourne. The company also operates catamaran service between Portsmouth and Ryde (15 minutes). Red Funnel runs a car-ferry (one hour) and hydrofoil service (25 minutes) between Southampton and Cowes. Hovertravel has a hovercraft shuttle between Southsea (Portsmouth) and Ryde (10 minutes).

FARES & SCHEDULES   🛪 **Hovertravel** ☎ 01983/811000 or 023/9281-1000 ⊕ www.hovertravel.co.uk. **Red Funnel** ☎ 0870/444-8898 ⊕ www.redfunnel.co.uk. **Wightlink** ☎ 0870/582-7744 ⊕ www.wightlink.co.uk.

BUS TRAVEL

National Express buses at London's Victoria Coach Station on Buckingham Palace Road depart hourly for Bournemouth (2½ hours) and Southampton (2½ hours), and every 2 hours for Portsmouth (2 hours, 20 minutes) and Winchester (2 hours). There are three buses daily to Salisbury (about 3 hours). Solent Blue and Stagecoach Hampshire Bus operate a comprehensive service in the Southampton, New Forest, Winchester, and Bournemouth areas. Southern Vectis covers the Isle of Wight. Traveline can provide information about travel throughout the region.

CUTTING COSTS   Wilts (Wiltshire) & Dorset Bus Co. offers both one-day Explorer and seven-day Busabout tickets; ask about the Rover tickets offered by Solent Blue and Southern Vectis.

🛪 **National Express** ☎ 0870/580-8080 ⊕ www.nationalexpress.com. **Solent Blue** ☎ 023/8061-8233 ⊕ www.solentblueline.com. **Southern Vectis** ☎ 01983/532373 ⊕ www.svoc.co.uk. **Stagecoach Hampshire Bus** ☎ 0845/121-0180 ⊕ www.stagecoachbus.com. **Traveline** ☎ 0870/608-2608 ⊕ www.traveline.org.uk. **Wilts (Wiltshire) & Dorset Bus Co.** ☎ 01722/336855 ⊕ www.wdbus.co.uk.

CAR RENTAL

⑦ Local Agencies Avis ⊠ 33–39 Southcote Rd., Bournemouth ☎ 01202/296942. **Enterprise Rent-a-Car** ⊠ Train Station, Winchester ☎ 01962/844022. **Esplanade** ⊠ 9–11 George St., Ryde ☎ 01983/562322. **Europcar** ⊠ c/o Ibis Hotel, 1 West Quay Rd., Southampton ☎ 023/8033–2973. **Hertz** ⊠ Hinton Rd., Bournemouth ☎ 01202/291231 ⊠ 1 Queensway, Southampton ☎ 023/8063–8437. **Thrifty** ⊠ Brunel Rd., Churchfields Industrial Estate, Salisbury ☎ 01722/340954.

CAR TRAVEL

The South is linked to London and other major cities by a well-developed road network, which includes M3 to Winchester (59 mi from London) and Southampton (77 mi); A3 to Portsmouth (70 mi); and M27 along the coast, from the New Forest and Southampton to Portsmouth. For Salisbury, take M3 to A303, then A30. A31 and A35 connect Bournemouth to Dorchester and the rest of Dorset.

ROAD CONDITIONS Driving is easy in this area. In northeast Hampshire and in many parts of neighboring Wiltshire there are lanes overhung by trees and lined with thatched cottages and Georgian houses. Often these lanes begin near the exits of main highways. Salisbury Plain has long, straight roads surrounded by endless vistas; the challenge here is staying within the speed limit.

EMERGENCIES

⑦ Ambulance, fire, police ☎ 999. **Dorset County Hospital** ⊠ Williams Ave., Dorchester ☎ 01305/251150. **Queen Alexandra Hospital** ⊠ Southwick Hill Rd., Cosham, Portsmouth ☎ 023/9228–6000. **St. Mary's Hospital** ⊠ Parkhurst Rd., Newport, Isle of Wight ☎ 01983/524081. **Salisbury District Hospital** ⊠ Odstock Rd., Salisbury ☎ 01722/336262. **Southampton General Hospital** ⊠ Tremona Rd., Southampton ☎ 023/8077–7222.

TOURS

City Sightseeing has three daily Stonehenge tours from Salisbury, mid-May through mid-October, costing £16 (check for availability), and more frequent daily tours of Bournemouth from mid-April through early October and of Portsmouth from late May through September, both costing £6. A. S. Tours arranges day tours of Stonehenge and Avebury, year-round, in six-seater minibuses. Salisbury City Guides runs a program of daily summer (weekends in winter) walks in Salisbury. The Guild of Registered Tourist Guides maintains a directory of qualified Blue Badge guides who can arrange to meet you anywhere in the region for private tours. Local organizations such as Wessexplore can also arrange Blue Badge tours.

⑦ A. S. Tours ☎ 01980/862931. **City Sightseeing/Guide Friday** ☎ 01708/866000 ⊕ www.city-sightseeing.com. **Guild of Registered Tourist Guides** ☎ 0207/403 1115 ⊕ www.blue-badge.org.uk. **Salisbury City Guides** ☎ 01722/320349 ⊕ www.salisburycityguides.co.uk. **Wessexplore** ☎ 01722/326304 ⊕ www.dmac.co.uk/wessexplore.

TRAIN TRAVEL

South West Trains serves the South from London's Waterloo Station. Travel times average 1 hour to Winchester, 1¼ hours to Southampton, 2 hours to Bournemouth, and 2¾ hours to Weymouth. The trip to Salisbury takes 1½ hours, and Portsmouth about 2 hours. There is at least one fast train every hour on all these routes. For local information throughout the region, contact National Rail Enquiries.

CUTTING COSTS   A Network card, valid throughout the South and Southeast for a year, entitles you to one-third off particular fares.

FARES &   🚆 **National Rail Enquiries** ☎ 0845/748-4950 ⊕ www.nationalrail.co.uk. **South West**
SCHEDULES   **Trains** ☎ 0845/748-4950 ⊕ www.southwesttrains.co.uk.

TRAVEL AGENCIES
🚆 **Local Agent Referrals American Express** ✉ 99 Above Bar, Southampton ☎ 023/
8071-6801. **Thomas Cook** ✉ 7 Richmond Hill, Bournemouth ☎ 01202/452800 ✉ 18
Queen St., Salisbury ☎ 01722/313500 ✉ 9 Palmerston Rd., Southsea ☎ 023/9230-2100
✉ 30 High St., Winchester ☎ 01962/743100.

VISITOR INFORMATION
Tourism South East can field general inquiries and put you in touch with local information centers, which are normally open Monday–Saturday 9:30–5:30, with reduced hours in winter.
🚆 **Tourism South East** ✉ 40 Chamberlayne Rd., Eastleigh, SO50 5JH ☎ 023/8062-5400
🖶 023/8062-0010 ⊕ www.visitsouthernengland.com. **Avebury** ✉ Avebury Chapel, Green
St., SN8 1RE ☎ 01672/539425 ⊕ www.kennet.gov.uk. **Bournemouth** ✉ Westover Rd.,
near the bandstand, BH1 2BU ☎ 01202/451700 ⊕ www.bournemouth.co.uk. **Dorchester**
✉ 11 Antelope Walk, DT1 1BE ☎ 01305/267992 ⊕ www.westdorset.com. **Lyme Regis**
✉ Guildhall Cottage, Church St., DT7 3BS ☎ 01305/442138 ⊕ www.westdorset.com.
Lyndhurst ✉ Main Car Park, High St., SO43 7NY ☎ 023/8028-2269 ⊕ www.thenewforest.
co.uk. **Marlborough** ✉ Car Park, George La., SN8 1EE ☎ 01672/513989. **Portsmouth**
✉ The Hard, PO1 3QJ ☎ 023/9282-6722 ⊕ www.visitportsmouth.co.uk ✉ Clarence
Esplanade, Southsea, PO5 3PB ☎ 023/9282-6722. **Ryde** ✉ Western Esplanade, PO33
2LW ☎ 01983/813818 ⊕ www.islandbreaks.co.uk. **Salisbury** ✉ Fish Row, off Market
Sq., SP1 1EJ ☎ 01722/334956 ⊕ www.visitsalisbury.com. **Sherborne** ✉ 3 Tilton Ct., Digby
Rd. , DT9 3NL ☎ 01935/815341 ⊕ www.westdorset.com. **Southampton** ✉ 9 Civic Cen-
tre Rd., SO14 7FJ ☎ 023/8083-3333 ⊕ www.southampton.gov.uk. **Winchester** ✉ The
Guildhall, Broadway, SO23 9LJ ☎ 01962/840500 ⊕ www.visitwinchester.co.uk.

THE WEST COUNTRY

SOMERSET, DEVON, CORNWALL

4

FIND YOUR EDGE (AND BRITAIN'S)
at Land's End in Cornwall ⇨*p.235*

IMAGINE THE DAYS OF KING ARTHUR
by windswept Tintagel Castle ⇨*p.230*

GET HOOKED ON THE FRESHEST FISH
at the Seafood Restaurant ⇨*p.232*

ENTER A NATURAL PARADISE
at the exotic Eden Project ⇨*p.243*

GO GLORIOUSLY GOTHIC
at the cathedral in Wells ⇨*p.221*

SLEEP IN COUNTRY-HOUSE STYLE
at Gidleigh Park in Dartmoor ⇨*p.252*

DIP INTO THE ENGLISH RIVIERA
by the palm trees of Torbay ⇨*p.254*

DITCH THE DIET FOR A CREAM TEA
at Hansons in Exeter ⇨*p.258*

Updated by
Robert
Andrews

LEAFY, NARROW COUNTRY ROADS all around the Southwest lead through miles of buttercup meadows and cider apple orchards to countless mellow villages of stone and thatch and heathery heights overlooking the sea. This can be one of Britain's most relaxing regions to visit. The secret of exploring it is to ignore the main highways and just follow the signposts—or, even better, to let yourself get lost. The village names alone are music to the ears: there's Tintinhull, St. Endellion, Huish Episcopi, and Bower Hinton—just to name a few hamlets that *haven't* been covered below.

Somerset, Devon, and Cornwall are the three counties that make up the long southern peninsula known as the West Country. Each has its own distinct flavor, and each comes with a regionalism that borders on patriotism. Somerset is noted for its rolling green countryside; Devon's wild and dramatic moors—bare, boggy, upland heath dominated by heathers and gorse, with a scattering of trees—contrast with the restfulness of its many sandy beaches and coves; and Cornwall has managed to retain a touch of its old insularity, despite the annual invasion of thousands of people lured by the ocean or the English Channel.

Bristol is where you come across the first unmistakable burrs of the western brogue. Its historic port retains a strong maritime air, and Georgian architecture and a dramatic gorge create a backdrop to what has become one of Britain's most dynamic cities. You might weave south through the lovely Chew Valley on your way to the cathedral city of Wells, in Somerset. The county's lush countryside is best seen in a cloak of summer heat when its orchards give ample shade, its bees are humming, and its old stone houses and inns welcome you with a breath of coolness. Abutting the north coast are the Quantock and Mendip hills, and the heather-covered expanse of Exmoor, the setting for R. D. Blackmore's historical romance, *Lorna Doone.*

Devon, farther west, is famed for its wild moorland—especially Dartmoor, supposed home of the mysterious beast in Sir Arthur Conan Doyle's novel *The Hound of the Baskervilles,* and actual home of ponies and an assortment of strange tors, rocky outcroppings eroded into weird shapes. Devon's large coastal towns are as interesting for their cultural and historical appeal—many were smugglers' havens—as for their scenic beauty. Some propagandists of east Devon speak of the "red cliffs" of Devon in contrast to the more famous "white cliffs of Dover." Parts of south Devon, on the other hand, resemble some balmy Mediterranean shore—hence its soubriquet, the English Riviera.

Cornwall, England's southernmost county, has a mild climate, and here you are never more than 20 mi from the sea. The county has always regarded itself as separate from the rest of Britain, and the Arthurian legends really took root in Cornwall, not least at Tintagel Castle, the legendary birthplace of Arthur. High, jagged cliffs line Cornwall's Atlantic coast—the dangerous and dramatic settings that Daphne du Maurier often waxed eloquent about—and indeed pose a menace to passing ships. The south coast, Janus-like, is filled with sunny beaches, delightful coves, and popular resorts. England's last outposts, the flower-filled Isles of Scilly, claim the most hours of sunshine in the country.

Exploring the West Country

A circular tour of the West Country covers a large territory, from the bustling city of Bristol, two hours outside London, to the remote and rocky headlands of Devon and Cornwall to the west. Stark contrasts abound in this peninsula, and the farther west you travel, the more the sea becomes an overwhelming presence. On the whole, the northern coast is more rugged, the cliffs dropping dramatically to tiny coves and beaches, whereas the south coast shelters many more resorts and wider expanses of sand. The crowds gravitate to the south, but there are plenty of remote inlets and estuaries along this southern littoral, and you do not need to go far to find a degree of seclusion.

Unless you confine yourself to a few choice towns—for example, Exeter, Penzance, and Plymouth—you will be at a huge disadvantage without your own transportation. The region has a few main arteries, but you should take minor roads whenever possible, if only to see the real West Country at a leisurely pace. Rail travelers can make use of a fast service connecting Exeter, Plymouth, and Penzance, and there's also a good network of bus services.

About the Restaurants & Hotels

The more established restaurants are often completely booked on a Friday or Saturday night, so reserve well in advance; the same is true for hotels and other lodgings. Room availability can be scarce on the coasts during August. Accommodations in the West Country include national hotel chains, represented in all the region's principal centers, as well as ancient inns and ubiquitous bed-and-breakfast places. Many farmhouses also rent out rooms—offering tranquillity in rural surroundings—but these lodgings are often difficult to reach without a car. It's worth finding out about weekend and winter deals that many hotels offer.

WHAT IT COSTS In pounds				
	££££££	££££	£££	££	£
RESTAURANTS	over £22	£18–£22	£13–£17	£7–£12	under £7
HOTELS	over £160	£120–£160	£90–£120	£60–£90	under £60

Restaurant prices are for a main course at dinner. Hotel prices are for two people in a standard double room in high season, including VAT, with no meals or, if indicated, CP (with Continental breakfast), BP (Breakfast Plan, with full breakfast), or MAP (Modified American Plan, with breakfast and dinner).

Timing

In July and August, traffic chokes the roads leading into the West Country. Somehow the region absorbs all the "grockles," or tourists, and the chances of finding a remote oasis of peace and quiet are severely curtailed. The beaches heave with sunseekers, and the resort towns are either bubbling with zest or unbearably tacky, depending on your point of view. If you must visit in summer, your best option is to find a secluded hotel and make brief excursions from there. Try to avoid traveling on Saturday, when weekly rentals start and finish and the roads are jammed with vehicles; the August bank holiday (the last weekend of the month) is notorious for congested roads. Otherwise, time your visit to coincide with the beginning or end of summer. The West Country enjoys more hours of sunshine than most other parts of Britain, so you can take your chances with the weather. Fall and spring are good times to escape the crowds, although most people find the sea too cold for swimming and there is often a strong ocean breeze. Most properties that don't accept business year-round open for Easter and close in late September or October. Those that remain open have reduced hours. Winter has its own appeal: the Atlantic waves crash dramatically against the coast, and the austere Cornish cliffs are at their most spectacular.

The most notable festivals, with plenty of crowds and congestion, are Padstow's Obby Oss, a traditional celebration of the arrival of summer that takes place around May 1; Helston's Flora Day parades on May 8; the Cornish-themed, weeklong Golowan Festival in Penzance in late June; the Exeter Arts Festival in July; and the St. Ives Festival of Music and the Arts for eight days in mid-September. In addition, many West Country maritime towns host regattas over summer weekends. The best times to visit Devon are late summer and early fall, during the end-of-summer festivals, especially popular in the small towns of eastern Dartmoor.

BRISTOL TO NORTH DEVON

Starting out from Bristol, your journey takes you south to the cathedral city of Wells and continues on via Glastonbury, possibly the Avalon of Arthurian legend. Taunton, to the west, is the capital of cider country and was the focus of fierce skirmishes during the English Civil War. Proceed west along the Somerset coast into Devon, skirting the moorlands of Exmoor and tracing the northern shore via Clovelly.

Bristol

▶ ❶ *120 mi west of London, 46 mi south of Birmingham, 13 mi northwest of Bath.*

A treasure of great historic interest, Bristol can be called the "birthplace of America" with some confidence, for John Cabot and his son Sebastian sailed from the old city docks in 1497 to touch down on the North American mainland, which he claimed for the English crown. Bristol was also the home of William Penn, developer of Pennsylvania, and a haven for John Wesley, whose Methodist movement played a significant role in the history of colonial Georgia. The city had been a major center since medieval times, but in the 17th and 18th centuries it became an important port for trade with North America. Now that the city's industries no longer rely on the docks, the historic harbor along the River Avon has been largely given over to pleasure craft. Arts and entertainment complexes, museums, stores, pubs, and restaurants fill the quayside; and carnivals, speedboat races, and regattas take place here in summer.

Queen Elizabeth I called the rib-vaulted, 14th-century **Church of St. Mary Redcliffe** "the fairest in England." It was built by Bristol merchants who wanted a place in which to pray for the safe (and profitable) voyages of

The West Country requires some time to explore. Three days will provide only a sadly limited view of what Somerset and Devon have to offer, and you should avoid excessive traveling at the expense of exploring. If Cornwall in particular beckons, a four-day tour would take in many of its highlights. Even a week would not do justice to this dense region, but it would give you a chance to push on into Cornwall and get a more balanced idea of the West Country.

Numbers in the text correspond to numbers in the margin and on the West Country, Plymouth, and Exeter maps.

4

If you have 3 days

Start off from the gateway to the West, **Bristol** ❶ ►, where you should make a point of crossing the Avon Gorge before you head down the motorway to spend the best part of a day and your first night in 🏨 **Exeter** ❺❻–❻❹. The cathedral here commands the most attention, but the city has plenty more to offer, with its quayside and period architecture. The next morning, follow A30 back east, along the coast to the fishing village of **Beer** ❻❻ before heading inland to **Honiton** ❻❼, a handsome Georgian town renowned for its delicate lace, a collector's delight. Spend your second overnight in 🏨 **Glastonbury** ❹, a small town awash in Arthurian and early Christian myth. Explore the abbey here in the morning—run up to the tor if you're feeling energetic—before making the short hop to the tiny city of **Wells** ❺. Its cathedral is different from Exeter's but is equally grand.

If you have 4 days

This itinerary focuses exclusively on Cornwall. Traveling down along the North Devon coast, stop at the harbor village of **Boscastle** ❶❸ ► before steeping yourself in Arthurian legends at **Tintagel** ❶❹, ideally taking a coastal walk here. Overnight in 🏨 **Padstow** ❶❻ and dine on excellent seafood (reserve ahead). The next day, head for **St. Ives** ❶❾, popular with art lovers and beach fans, and push on to the country's westernmost tip, **Land's End** ❷❶. Stay in 🏨 **Penzance** ❷❸ for your second night; from here you can visit the island castle of **St. Michael's Mount** ❷❹. Then either follow the coast around to tour the **Lizard Peninsula** ❷❻, or head straight for Pendennis Castle in **Falmouth** ❷❼. Across the Carrick Roads estuary basin, explore the sequestered creeks of the Roseland Peninsula, spending your third night in 🏨 **St. Mawes** ❷❾, which has a fine castle. Start early the next day to visit the **Eden Project** ❸❷, a must for anyone with horticultural leanings, and then choose between two superb country piles: Victorian Lanhydrock, near **Bodmin** ❸❹, and **Cotehele House** ❹❼, a Tudor manor house.

If you have 7 days

Once out of **Bristol** ❶ ►, tour the northern coast of Somerset and Devon, making stops at **Dunster** ❻, site of a turreted and battlemented castle, and the twin towns of **Lynton** and **Lynmouth** ❽, in a narrow cleft. Any of these would make a good place to break for lunch before continuing on to your overnight destination, the cliff-top village of 🏨 **Clovelly** ❶❷. The second day, continue into Cornwall to take in **Tintagel** ❶❹, which, with or without the Arthurian associations, presents a dramatic sight perched on its black rock above the waves. Enjoy a refined seafood lunch in **Padstow** ❶❻ and make a stop in **Newquay** ❶❼ if you want to sample the more down-to-earth fish-and-chips atmosphere and generous beaches of this typical seaside resort. Pull into ⊠ **St. Ives** ⑲ for your second night; the town has a great deal to offer in the way of art and a good selection of hotels and restaurants. After taking in St. Ives the third day, set out for the very tip of the peninsula, **Land's End** ⑳, which is worth exploring on foot. Head for your next overnight, ⊠ **Penzance** ㉓. Nearby, the island fortress of **St. Michael's Mount** ㉔ is clearly visible and demands a closer inspection. Now make a brief sortie into the **Lizard Peninsula** ㉖, basing yourself in the resort of ⊠ **Falmouth** ㉗, which has plenty of accommodations as well as a brace of castles—the imposing Pendennis and its sibling across the estuary, **St. Mawes** ㉙. On your fifth day, begin by exploring seaside **Charlestown** ㉛, leaving the main part of the day for the eye-popping plant collection of the **Eden Project** ㉜, outside St. Austell. Spend the night either in ⊠ **Fowey** ㉝, still a thriving commercial and sailing port, or in ⊠ **Plymouth** ㊲–㊹. Explore Plymouth in the morning and then track north to Dartmoor, making a stop at Castle Drogo, near **Chagford** �51; spend your sixth night in ⊠ **Exeter** 56–64. Once you've soaked up the sights of this historic city, head up the M5, swinging east to see the majestic ruins of the abbey in ⊠ **Glastonbury** ❹ and the cathedral at nearby **Wells** ❸.

---

their ships. A chapel holds the arms and armor of Sir William Penn, father of the founder of Pennsylvania. The church is a five-minute walk from Temple Meads train station toward the docks. ⊠ *Redcliffe Way* ☎ *0117/ 929–1487* ⌦ *Free* ☽ *Mon.–Sat. 9–5 (until 4 in winter), Sun. 8–8.*

♻ The **British Empire and Commonwealth Museum,** in engineer Isambard Kingdom Brunel's 19th-century railway station by the modern Temple Meads train station, helps put Bristol in the context of the growth of Britain's colonial empire and the trading organization that succeeded it. It's an absorbing whirl through history and geography, with a fascinating collection of photographs, slides, and grainy film of missionaries and pith-helmeted memsahibs. Note the horned Ghanaian headwear made from cowrie shells as well as the beaver-skin hats, the demand for which fueled the Canadian beaver-pelt trade. The darker side of the story of the empire is not ignored, with space devoted to slavery, the Opium Wars, and the transportation of convicts to Australia. The interactive exhibits appeal to children. ⊠ *Station Approach, Temple Meads* ☎ *0117/ 925–4980* ⊕ *www.empiremuseum.co.uk* ⌦ *£6.50* ☽ *Daily 10–5.*

Among the Dissenters from the Church of England who found a home in Bristol were John Wesley and Charles Wesley, and in 1739 they built the **New Room,** a meeting place that became the first Methodist chapel. Its simplicity contrasts both with the style of Anglican churches and with the modern shopping center hemming it in. The rooms upstairs contain mementos of the early Methodists and material relating to their proselytizing work in Georgia. Call ahead to arrange a tour that can include **Charles Wesley's House** (a 10-minute walk away), a well-restored 18th-century town house where the Wesleys lived. ⊠ *Broadmead* ☎ *0117/*

926–4740 ⊕ *www.methodist.org.uk/new.room* 🏷 *Free, tour of New Room and house £4.50, New Room only £2.80* ⊙ *Mon.–Sat. and national holidays 10–4.*

☺ **@Bristol,** in the rebuilt Harbourside area, has three science- and nature-theme attractions with innovative exhibits. Explore@Bristol provides a "hands-on, minds-on" experience of science, and Wildwalk@Bristol includes interactive natural history exhibits and a walk through a rain forest aflutter with exotic birds and butterflies. The region's only giant-screen IMAX cinema shows mostly science-related films. Open spaces linking the sites act as a venue for live performances and multimedia activities, with shops, cafés, and restaurants nearby. ⊠ *Anchor Rd.* ☎ *0845/345–1235* ⊕ *www.at-bristol.org.uk* 🏷 *£6.50 for 1 attraction (£7.50 for Explore@Bristol), £11 or £12 for 2 attractions, £15.50 or £16.50 for 3 attractions* ⊙ *Daily 10–6.*

---

need a break?

The excellent café-restaurant upstairs at the **Watershed Media Centre** (⊠ 1 Canon's Rd. ☎ 0117/927–5100) overlooks part of the harborside. Sandwiches, salads, and hot snacks are served during the day, along with coffees and cakes; there's a bar, too.

On view in the harbor stands the **SS *Great Britain,*** the first iron ship to cross the Atlantic. Built by the great English engineer Isambard Brunel in 1843, it remained in service until the end of the century, first on the North American route and then on the Australian. Moored alongside is a replica of the *Matthew,* the tiny craft that carried John Cabot to North America in 1497. Your entry ticket also admits you to the **Maritime Heritage Centre,** which gives the lowdown on the restoration of the *Great Britain* as well as an overview of Bristol's seafaring history. Parts of the museum and ship may be closed while conservation work on the ship continues and a new museum is developed in the dockside buildings, with completion expected in 2005. ⊠ *Great Western Dockyard, Gas Ferry Rd.* ☎ *0117/926–0680* ⊕ *www.ss-great-britain.com* 🏷 *£6.25* ⊙ *Apr.–Oct., daily 10–5:30; Nov.–Mar., daily 10–4:30.*

In the Georgian suburb of Clifton—a sort of Bath in miniature—you can take in a monument to Victorian engineering, the 702-foot-long **Clifton Suspension Bridge** (⊠ Suspension Bridge Rd., Clifton), which spans the Avon Gorge. Work began on Isambard Brunel's design in 1831, but the bridge was not completed until 1864. Adjacent to the Bristol end of the bridge, the **Clifton Suspension Bridge Visitor Centre** (☎ 0117/974–4664 ⊕ www.clifton-suspension-bridge.org.uk) has an exhibition on the bridge and its construction. It is closed until summer 2005, but you can call for information about guided bridge tours.

☺ **Bristol Zoo Gardens,** along the leafy expanse of Clifton Downs, is one of the country's most famous zoos. More than 300 animal species live in 12 acres of landscaped gardens; the Seal and Penguin Coasts, with underwater viewing, are rival attractions for Gorilla Island, Bug World, Twilight World, and the walk-through aviary. ⊠ *Clifton Down* ☎ *0117/973–8951* ⊕ *www.bristolzoo.org.uk* 🏷 *£9.50* ⊙ *June–Aug., daily 9–5:30; Sept.–May, daily 9–4:30.*

<table>
<tr><td>

off the
beaten
path

</td><td>

TYNTESFIELD – The National Trust rescued this extravagant, 35-bedroom Victorian Gothic Revival mansion in 2002 and will gradually restore it. You can visit the house and gardens only if you prebook a two-hour tour (house, garden, and formal garden tours Sunday, Monday, and Wednesday; formal garden, chapel, and walled garden tours Thursday). Besides magnificent woodwork, stained glass, and original furniture and fabrics, the house contains the modern conveniences of the 1860s, such as a heated billiard table and gaslights in the garden. Accessed via a spiral staircase, the ornate chapel has remarkable mosaics and ironwork. Tyntesfield is 7 mi south of Bristol. ☒ *Wraxall* ☏ *0870/241–4500 for tours* ⊕ *www. nationaltrust.org.uk* ✍ *£10.50, gardens and chapel only £6.30* ☉ *Late Mar., Apr., Oct., and early Nov., Sun., Mon., Wed., and Thurs. 10–2; May–Sept., Sun., Mon., Wed., and Thurs. 10–3.*

</td></tr>
</table>

Where to Stay & Eat

For a notable overture to your West Country excursion, you might book a night at Thornbury Castle, 12 mi north of Bristol in Thornbury (⇨ Berkeley Castle *in* Chapter 7).

£££–££££ ✗ **Bell's Diner.** A local institution, this bistro in the Montpelier area occupies a converted corner shop and has polished wood floors and Bristol prints on its pale gray walls. The inventive Mediterranean menu changes regularly and includes organic and wild ingredients, as well as toothsome desserts such as prune and Armagnac soufflé with vanilla ice cream. Bell's is rather hidden—take A38 (Stokes Croft) north, then turn right on Ashley Road and immediately left at Picton Street, which will lead you to York Road. ☒ *1 York Rd.* ☏ *0117/924–0357* ▤ *AE, MC, V* ☉ *Closed Sun. and Dec. 24–30. No lunch Sat. and Mon.*

££–£££ ✗ **Old India.** Bristol's former stock exchange has found a new role as a fashionable Indian eatery. All the opulent trimmings have been restored, including the mahogany paneling, rich drapes, tiled staircase, and elegant statuary. It's the perfect setting for classic Indian cuisine and such innovative dishes as *niljiri korma* (chicken breast in a mild curry sauce with rose petals) and *macchi mazadaar* (salmon with mustard seeds, coconut, curry leaves, and tamarind water). The two-course lunch menu is a particularly good deal. ☒ *34 St. Nicholas St.* ☏ *0117/922–1136* ▤ *MC, V.*

£–££ ✗ **Wagamama.** Part of a chain that has expanded from London, this centrally located noodle bar is a convenient spot for nourishing chicken ramen (soup and noodles topped with grilled chicken breast) or salmon *karoke* (salmon and potato cakes in a sweet tamarind sauce). White walls and plain wooden tables and benches make a minimalist statement. Helpings are abundant, and the service is fast and courteous. ☒ *63 Queens Rd.* ☏ *0117/922–1188* ▤ *AE, DC, MC, V.*

££££ ✗▦ **Hotel du Vin.** This hip Anglo-French minichain has established an ambitious outlet in the Sugar House—six former sugar-refining warehouses—close to the docklands and the city center. Rooms are crisply contemporary in style, with CD and DVD players and huge showers, but retain many original industrial features. The restaurant's wine list is extensive—visit the cellar for a private tasting session—and the menu entices with modern but robust French flavors. A good-value, fixed-price

4

Walking

The coasts and moors of the West Country provide wonderfully varied walking. A fine 10-mi walk is a cliff-top hike along the coast from Hartland Quay, near Clovelly, down to Lower Sharpnose Point, just above Bude. Longer hikes in the bleak, unpeopled region of Dartmoor—for example, the tors south of Okehampton—are appropriate only for the most experienced walkers, though the areas around Widgery Cross, Becky Falls, and the Bovey Valley, and the short but dramatic walk along Lydford Gorge, have wide appeal. Walking on Exmoor is less rigorous and offers spectacular views over the Bristol Channel. In Cornwall, the coast around Tintagel is also splendidly scenic. If you are interested in longer "theme" walks, note the Saints Way, a 30-mi walk between Padstow and the Camel Estuary on Cornwall's north coast to Fowey on the south coast. Britain's longest national trail, the South West Coast Path, runs for 630 mi from Minehead (Somerset) to South Haven Point, near Poole (Dorset).

Water Sports

The beaches lining parts of the peninsula have made the West Country one of Britain's main family vacation destinations. Natives don't mind the water's temperature, but foreigners, many of them pampered by the warm waves of the Mediterranean, are not so eager to brave the elements. The sea—even in Cornwall, where it seems to be warmer than anywhere else in the British Isles—is not to be enjoyed in a sensuous way: it is a bracing experience that sometimes leaves you shivering and breathless. At many major resorts, flags show the limits of safe swimming. There can be strong undertows, especially on the northern coast, which has the region's best surfing beaches. Looe, on the south coast of Cornwall, is known for shark fishing, and you can rent boats for shark or mackerel fishing from harbors along the south coast. This is a good sailing area, with plenty of safe harbors, marinas, and deepwater channels, mainly at Falmouth, Plymouth Sound, and Torbay.

"rapide" lunch is offered. ✉ *Narrow Lewins Mead, BS1 2NU* ☎ *0117/ 925–5577* 🖷 *0117/925–1199* ⊕ *www.hotelduvin.com* ⇌ *40 rooms* ♨ *Restaurant, in-room data ports, cable TV, billiards, bar, meeting rooms; no a/c in some rooms* 🖃 *AE, DC, MC, V.*

£££ 🏨**Redwood Lodge Hotel.** Primarily a business hotel and health center, this makes a handy stopover for anyone touring by car—it's just off A4, close to the Clifton Suspension Bridge. Modern and attractively furnished, the hotel has a number of amenities, including 16 acres of woodland surroundings. Weekend rates are a good value. ✉ *Beggar Bush La., Failand, BS8 3TG* ☎ *0845/602–6787* 🖷 *01275/392104* ⊕ *www.corushotels.com* ⇌ *112 rooms* ♨ *2 restaurants, cable TV, tennis court, indoor-outdoor pool, gym, squash, cinema, meeting rooms; no a/c* 🖃 *AE, DC, MC, V.*

££ 🏨**Naseby House Hotel.** On a tree-lined street in the heart of elegant Clifton, this Victorian hotel is not far from Bristol's major sights. The basement holds the plushest, most expensive bedroom, with a four-poster and a French door opening onto the garden. Period pieces fill the sitting room,

The West
Country

GREAT
BRITAIN

ATLANTIC OCEAN

Bideford
Bay

Clovelly 12
Hartland Quay
A39

Lower Sharpnose
Point

Bude
Bude Bay

D E V O

B3254
A388

Boscastle 13 B3263
A39

Tintagel 14
Launceston 36
Lewdow
A30

Port Isaac 15 B3314

Padstow 16
Bolventor

Wadebridge
BODMIN
MOOR
Dozmary
Pool 35

Bodmin 34 A38
Cotehele
House
& Quay

Newquay 17
A30
A39

Perranporth 18
Eden
Project 32
Fowey 33
Looe

St. Austell

Truro 30
Charlestown 31

B3289
Portloe

St. Ives 19
Mylor Bridge
Trelissick 28

B3306
Zennor
St. Michael's
Mount
A394
Carrick Roads

Pendeen
Falmouth 27
29
St. Mawes

Penzance 23
Newlyn 22
24
A394
B3291

Land's
End 20
21
Helston 25
Gweek

Porthcurno B3315
Mousehole
GOONHILLY
DOWNS

A3083
B3293

TO ISLES OF SCILLY
Kynance
Cove
Lizard
Peninsula

GOWER
PENINSULA

Swansea

*Swansea
Bay*

WALES

Newport

M4

Cardiff

TO
LONDON

Bristol ❶

**Stanton
Drew Circles**
❷

Chew Magna

Cheddar

Wells
❸

Shepton
Mallet

Glastonbury

Pilton
❹

**Cadbury
Castle**

Bristol Channel

Bridgwater Bay

Porlock
Weir

Minehead

Dunster

Porlock
❻

❼

A39

Ilfracombe

**Lynton/
Lynmouth**
❽

EXMOOR
NATIONAL
PARK

Combe
Martin

**Braunton Burrows
Biosphere Reserve**
❿

BRENDON
HILLS

B3191

B3190

QUANTOCK HILLS

A39

A39

S O M E R S E T

A358

A361

Sedgemoor

Yeovilton
❻❾

❼⓪

A303

A359

A303

A303

Barnstaple
❾

A361

Dulverton

Taunton
❺

A358

**Montacute
House**
❻❽

Yeovil

❶❶

Bideford

Torridge

Taw

A377

Wellington

Bradford-on-Tone

A358

A303

A30

Tiverton

A361

M5

Exe

Honiton
❻❼

D O R S E T

Bridport

Exeter
❺❻ – ❻❹
see detail
map

Gittisham

A3052

A376

B3174

Okehampton
❺⓪

A30

Drewsteignton

N

A382

**Lydford
Gorge**
❹❾

DARTMOOR
NATIONAL
PARK

Chagford
❺❶

Kenton

A377

A380

Topsham
❻❺

A376

Sidmouth

Seaton

Beer
❻❻

Lyme
Regis

Lyme Bay

Tavistock

B3212

Morwellham Quay
❹❽

Budleigh Salterton

Exmouth

❹❼

❹❻

Yelverton

**Buckland
Abbey**

Buckfastleigh

Dart

Cockington

A379

Saltram
❹❺

A38

Dartington

Totnes
❺❸

Torbay
❺❺

Brixham
❺❹

Yealmpton

A379

Kingsbridge

Slapton

*Start
Bay*

Dartmouth
❺❷

Plymouth
❸❼ – ❹❹
see detail
map

English Channel

see detail
map

KEY
▶ *Start of itinerary*

0 ——————————— 20 miles

0 ——————————— 30 km

and the breakfast room is also impressive. ✉ *105 Pembroke Rd., BS8 3EF* 🖦 *0117/973–7859* ⊕ *www.nasebyhousehotel.co.uk* ⌂ *15 rooms, 14 with bath* ⚬ *Some pets allowed; no a/c* ☰ *AE, MC, V* ❡❙ *BP.*

£ 🖭 **Sunderland Guest House.** The rooms at this simple Georgian town house are small and plain, but clean and comfortable enough to ensure a tranquil night's sleep. The main advantage here is a location in a quiet Clifton lane, close to the city center. All rooms share bathrooms, but four have a shower in the room. Breakfast is self-service. ✉ *4 Sunderland Pl., BS8 1NA* 🖦 *0117/973–7249* ✎ *sunderland.gh@blueyonder. co.uk* ⌂ *10 rooms without bath* ⚬ *No a/c, no smoking* ☰ *No credit cards* ❡❙ *CP.*

Nightlife & the Arts

The **Bristol Old Vic** (✉ King St. 🖦 0117/987–7877), the country's oldest continuously working theater, dates to 1766. Performances, from classics to new works, are staged in three spaces. **St. George's** (✉ Great George St., off Park St. 🖦 0117/923–0359), a former church built in the 18th century, serves as one of the country's leading acoustic venues for classical, jazz, and world music. Lunchtime concerts are scheduled.

Sports

The **Badminton Horse Trials** (🖦 01454/218272) are held annually during four days in April or May at the duke of Beaufort's magnificent estate in Badminton, 12 mi northeast of Bristol.

en route The area south of Bristol is notable for its scenery and walks, attractive villages, and ancient stone circles. Take A38 (follow signs for the airport), then left onto B3130 and B3114 to the villages of Chew Magna and Chew Stoke. At Chew Magna note the gargoyles on the ancient church. Continue on to Chew Valley Lake, a reservoir in a drowned valley surrounded by woods that shelter 240 species of birds.

Stanton Drew Circles

➋ *6 mi south of Bristol, 10 mi west of Bath.*

Three rings, two avenues of standing stones, and a burial chamber make up the Stanton Drew Circles, one of the grandest and most mysterious monuments in Britain, dating from 3000 to 2000 BC. Excavations beneath the circles in 1997 revealed evidence of another site, from around 3000 BC, consisting of a wood henge, or timber circle. Its great size suggests that it was once as important as Stonehenge for its ceremonial functions, although little of great visual impact remains. The site lies in a field reached through a farmyard—you'll need suitable shoes to visit it. English Heritage supervises the stones, which stand on private land. Access is given at any reasonable time, and a small admission may be requested. To get here from Chew Magna, turn east on B3130; the circles are just east of the village of Stanton Drew. ✉ *B3130, Stanton Drew* 🖦 *0117/975–0700* ⊕ *www.english-heritage.org.uk.*

Wells

❸ *16 mi south of Stanton Drew Circles, 22 mi south of Bristol, 132 mi west of London.*

England's smallest cathedral city, with a population of 10,000, lies at the foot of the Mendip Hills. Although it feels more like a quiet country town than a city, Wells contains one of the masterpieces of Gothic architecture, its great cathedral—the first to be built in the Early English style. The city's name refers to the underground streams that bubble up into St. Andrew's Well within the grounds of the Bishop's Palace. Spring water has run through High Street since the 15th century. Seventeenth-century buildings surround the ancient marketplace in the city center. Wells has market days on Wednesday and Saturday.

★ The great west towers of the medieval **Cathedral Church of St. Andrew,** the oldest surviving English Gothic church, can be seen for miles. Dating from the 12th century, the cathedral derives its beauty from the perfect harmony of all of its parts, the glowing colors of its original stained-glass windows, and its peaceful setting among stately trees and majestic lawns. To appreciate the elaborate west front facade, approach the building on foot from the cathedral green, accessible from Market Place through a great medieval gate called "penniless porch" (named after the beggars who once waited here to collect alms from worshipers). The cathedral's west front is twice as wide as it is high, and some 300 statues of kings and saints adorn it. Inside, vast inverted arches were added in 1338 to stop the central tower from sinking to one side. The cathedral also has a rare medieval clock, consisting of the seated figure of a man called Jack Blandiver, who strikes a bell on the quarter hour while mounted knights circle in mock battle. Near the clock is the entrance to the Chapter House—a small wooden door opening onto a great sweep of stairs worn down on one side by the tread of pilgrims over the centuries. Free 45-minute guided tours begin at the information desk. Tours are suspended April–October during Quiet Hour between noon and 1. ⊠ *Cathedral Green* ☎ *01749/674483* ⊕ *www.wellscathedral.org.uk* ⊠ *£4.50 suggested donation* ⊙ *Apr.–Sept., daily 7–7; Oct.–Mar., daily 7–6.*

The Bishop's Eye gate leading from Market Place takes you to the magnificent, moat-ringed **Bishop's Palace,** which still contains most of the original 12th- and 13th-century residence. You can also see the ruins of a late-13th-century great hall. The hall lost its roof in the 16th century because Edward VI needed to use the lead it contained. ⊠ *Market Pl.* ☎ *01749/678691* ⊕ *www.bishopspalacewells.co.uk* ⊠ *£4* ⊙ *Apr.–Oct., weekdays 10:30–6, Sun. 1–6 (may also open Sat. 10:30–6); last admission at 5.*

To the north of the cathedral, the cobbled **Vicar's Close,** one of Europe's oldest streets, has terraces of handsome 14th-century houses with strange, tall chimneys. A tiny medieval chapel here is still in use.

off the beaten path

WOOKEY HOLE CAVES – Signs in Wells's town center direct you 2 mi north to limestone caves in the Mendip Hills that may have been the home of Iron Age people. Here, according to ancient legend, the Witch of Wookey turned to stone. You can tour the caves, including an underground lake, and visit a museum, a working paper mill, and a penny arcade full of Victorian amusement machines worked by predecimal pennies. ☎ *01749/672243* ⊕ *www.wookey.co.uk* ▧ *£8.80* ⊙ *Apr.–Oct., daily 10–5; Nov.–Mar., daily 10:30–4:30.*

Where to Stay & Eat

££££–£££££ ✕ **Ritcher's.** Both the downstairs bistro and the more traditional restaurant upstairs serve good-value two- or three-course fixed-price meals with fresh, sophisticated choices. Among the dishes are char-grilled sea bass with stir-fried vegetables and plum sauce, and pan-fried chicken breast filled with leek and chive mousse. Try the café-bar for breakfast or for creative wraps, salads, and desserts. Ritcher's is near the cathedral. ⊠ *5 Sadler St.* ☎ *01749/679085* ▤ *MC, V* ⊙ *Closed Sun. and Mon.*

££££ ✕▥ **Swan Hotel.** A former coaching inn built in the 15th century, the Swan faces the cathedral. Bedrooms, furnished with antiques, are done in subtle, restful colors; eight rooms have four-posters. The restaurant prepares traditional English roasts and fish dishes and displays costumes owned by the great Victorian actor Sir Henry Irving. ⊠ *11 Sadler St., BA5 2RX* ☎ *01749/836300* ▧ *01749/836301* ⊕ *www.Bhere.co.uk* ⇴ *50 rooms* ◊ *Restaurant, in-room data ports, bar, meeting rooms; no a/c* ▤ *AE, DC, MC, V* ⦿| *BP.*

££–£££ ✕▥ **The Crown.** This hotel has been a landmark in Wells since the Middle Ages, and in 1695 William Penn was arrested here for preaching without a license. A sense of the building's age remains, although most guest rooms (with the exception of four rooms with four-posters) are furnished in simple styles more modern than traditional and have whirlpool baths or full-body massage showers. The Penn Bar serves sandwiches, salads, and such hot dishes as steak and kidney pie. You can try the more comfortable French bistro, Anton's, for choices such as game sausages and rump of lamb. ⊠ *Market Pl., BA5 2RP* ☎ *01749/673457* ▧ *01749/679792* ⊕ *www.crownatwells.co.uk* ⇴ *15 rooms* ◊ *Restaurant, bar, some pets allowed; no a/c, no room phones* ▤ *AE, MC, V* ⦿| *BP.*

££ ✕▥ **Ancient Gate House.** The guest rooms of this restaurant run by Franco Rossi and his two sons make a convenient base. The premises, dating to 1473, incorporate the Great West Gate and are full of character. There's an ancient stone staircase, and many rooms have four-posters. You can dine well on either Italian or English dishes, made largely from local produce, in the Rugantino restaurant—scampi with white wine sauce is a specialty. ⊠ *20 Sadler St., BA5 2SE* ☎ *01749/672029* ▧ *01749/670319* ⊕ *www.ancientgatehouse.co.uk* ⇴ *9 rooms* ◊ *Restaurant, bar, some pets allowed; no a/c* ▤ *AE, MC, V* ⦿| *BP.*

Glastonbury

★ ❹ *5 mi southwest of Wells, 27 mi south of Bristol, 27 mi southwest of Bath.*

A town steeped in history, myth, and legend, Glastonbury lies in the lee of Glastonbury Tor, a grassy hill rising 520 feet above the Somerset Levels (drained marshes). In legend, Glastonbury is identified with Avalon, the paradise into which King Arthur was reborn after his death. It is also said to be the burial place of Arthur and Guinevere, his queen. According to Christian tradition, Glastonbury, the first Christian settlement in England, was where Joseph of Arimathea brought the Holy Grail, the chalice used by Jesus at the Last Supper. Partly because of these associations, the town has acquired renown as a New Age center, mixing crystal-gazers with Druids, yogis, and aging hippies, who are variously in search of Arthur, Merlin, Jesus—and even Elvis.

At the foot of **Glastonbury Tor** is **Chalice Well,** the legendary burial place of the Grail. It's a stiff climb up the tor, but your reward is the fabulous view across the Vale of Avalon. At the top stands a ruined tower, all that remains of **St. Michael's Church,** which collapsed after a landslide in 1271.

The ruins of the great **Glastonbury Abbey,** in the center of town, are on the site where, according to legend, Joseph of Arimathea built a church in the 1st century. A monastery had certainly been erected here by the 9th century, and the site drew many pilgrims. The ruins are those of the abbey completed in 1524 and destroyed in 1539, during Henry VIII's dissolution of the monasteries. A sign south of the Lady Chapel marks the sites where Arthur and Guinevere were supposedly buried. ⊠ *Magdalene St.* ☎ *01458/832267* ⊕ *www.glastonburyabbey.com* 🖃 *£4* ⊙ *Feb., daily 10–5; Mar., daily 9:30–5:30; Apr., May, and Sept., daily 9:30–6; June–Aug., daily 9–6; Oct., daily 9:30–5; Nov., daily 9:30–4:30; Dec. and Jan., daily 10–4:30; last admission 30 mins before closing.*

Ⓒ The **Somerset Rural Life Museum** occupies a Victorian farmhouse and the impressive 14th-century Abbey tithe barn. More than 90 feet in length, the barn once stored the one-tenth portion of the town's produce that was owed to the church. Exhibits illustrate 19th-century farming practices, and there's a cider-apple orchard nearby. Events designed for children take place most weekends during school holidays. A footpath from the museums leads up to the Tor, a half-mile east. ⊠ *Chilkwell St.* ☎ *01458/831197* ⊕ *www.somerset.gov.uk/museums* 🖃 *Free* ⊙ *Apr.–Oct., Tues.–Fri. 10–5, weekends 2–6; Nov.–Mar., Tues.–Sat. 10–5.*

Where to Stay

★ **£££** 🏠 **Number 3.** Winston Churchill lived in this elegant Georgian town house next to the abbey, which has log fires in the winter and a terrace and walled garden for summer relaxation. Grouped around the garden, the spacious bedrooms are individually styled, with mostly pastel color schemes, traditional furniture, and drapes behind the beds. Three rooms are in the separate Garden House, and the Blue Room overlooks the abbey ruins and, through the trees, Glastonbury Tor. Generous breakfasts might include fresh fruit salad, yogurt, and croissants. ⊠ *3 Magdalene St., BA6 9EW* ☎ *01458/832129* 🖷 *01458/834227* ⊕ *www. numberthree.co.uk* 📮 *5 rooms* ⚬ *No a/c, no smoking* ⛴〇⛴ *BP.*

£–££ 🏠 **George and Pilgrims Hotel.** Pilgrims en route to Glastonbury Abbey stayed here in the 15th century. Today the stone-front hotel is equipped with modern comforts but retains its flagstone floors, wooden beams, and antique furniture; three rooms have four-posters. Ask to see the rooms, as they come in different shapes and sizes. The better ones are spacious and furnished with antiques, others are smaller, and those in the newer part of the building lack character but are cheaper. ✉ *1 High St., BA6 9DP* ☎ *01458/831146* 🖷 *01458/832252* ⊕ *www.georgeandpilgrims. activehotels.com* ⇗ *13 rooms* ♿ *Restaurant, bar, meeting rooms, some pets allowed (fee); no a/c* ▭ *MC, V* ⑩ *BP.*

Nightlife & the Arts

Held annually a few miles away in Pilton, the **Glastonbury Festival** (☎01749/ 890470 ⊕ www.glastonburyfestivals.co.uk) is England's biggest and perhaps best rock festival. For three days over the last weekend in June, it hosts hundreds of bands—a mix of established and up-and-coming, with a few big names from the past—on five stages. Pick up an issue of *New Musical Express* for the lineup. Tickets are steep—around £110—but include entertainment, a camping area, and service facilities.

> **en route** West of Glastonbury, take A39 and A361 toward Taunton to cross the Somerset Levels, marshes that were drained by open ditches (known as "rhines") for peat digging, an industry that is now heavily restricted. The broad, marshy expanse of **Sedgemoor** is where, in 1685, the troops of James II routed those of his nephew, the duke of Monmouth, in the last battle fought on English soil; a flagstaff and memorial stones indicate the site. R. D. Blackmore's novel *Lorna Doone*, published in 1869, is set during Monmouth's Rebellion.

Taunton

❺ *22 mi southwest of Glastonbury, 50 mi southwest of Bristol, 18 mi northeast of Exeter.*

Somerset's principal town lies in the heart of cider-making country in the fertile Vale of Taunton. Two of the loveliest examples of the county's famous pinnacled and battlemented churches, St. James and St. Mary Magdalene, overlook the county cricket ground in the center of town. Taunton is most celebrated for its cider, which is the traditional beverage in these parts. Beware—it can be far more potent than beer. In the fall, some cider mills open their doors to visitors. The grounds of **Sheppys,** a farm and cider museum, have orchards and a fishpond and are always open for picnickers. There's a café (summer only) and farm shop, too. ✉ *Three Bridges, on A38 west of Taunton, Bradford-on-Tone* ☎ *01823/461233* ⊕ *www.sheppyscider.com* 🎟 *Museum £2, guided tour (2½ hrs) £4.75* ⊙ *Mid-Apr.–Christmas, Mon.–Sat. 8:30–6, Sun. 11–1; late Dec.–mid-Apr., Mon.–Sat. 8:30–6.*

Where to Stay & Eat

££–£££ ✕ **Brettons.** This small, casual spot serves light lunches, such as pastas and curries, and more substantial dinners, including monkfish wrapped in ham and pesto, pheasant with roasted pears, and vegetarian choices. It's a 10-minute walk from the center of town. ✉ *49 East Reach* ☎ *01823/256688* ▭ *MC, V* ⊙ *Closed Sun. No lunch Sat. and Mon.*

★ **£££££** ✕🖪 **The Castle.** The battlements and turrets of this 300-year-old stone building look particularly fine from April to June, when the 150-year-

ON THE MENU

FROM CIDER TO CREAM TEAS, many specialties tempt your palate in the West Country. Lamb, venison, and, in Devon and Cornwall, seafood are favored in restaurants, which have improved markedly, notably through the influence of Rick Stein's seafood-based culinary empire in Padstow, in Cornwall. In many towns the day's catch is unloaded from the harbor and transported directly to eateries. The catch varies by season, but lobster is available year-round, as is crab, stuffed into sandwiches at quayside stalls and in pubs. Seafood is celebrated at fishy frolics that include the Newlyn Fish Fair (late August) and Falmouth's Oyster Festival (early October).

Somerset is the home of Britain's most famous cheese—the ubiquitous cheddar, from the Mendip Hills village. Do try to taste real farmhouse cheddar, made in the traditional barrel shape known as a truckle. Devon's caloric cream teas consist of a pot of tea, homemade scones, and lots of thickened clotted cream and strawberry jam (clotted, or specially thickened cream, is a regional specialty and is sometimes called Devonshire cream). Cornwall's specialty is the pasty, a pastry shell filled with chopped meat, onions, and potatoes. The pasty was devised as a handy way for miners to carry their dinner to work; today's versions are pale imitations of the original.

For liquid refreshment, try scrumpy, a homemade dry cider that is refreshing but carries a surprising kick. Look out, too, for perry, similar to cider but made from pears. English wine, similar to German wine, is made in Somerset (you may see it on local menus), and in Cornwall you can find a variant of age-old mead made from local honey.

---

old wisteria covering the facade is in flower. Rooms are individually decorated with chintz and period furniture. The excellent restaurant (closed Sunday evening) has creative, daily-changing, fixed-price menus of traditional and modern British food. Specialties include scrambled duck egg and smoked eel and, for dessert, lemon curd chantilly with honeycomb ice cream. Softer on the wallet, the informal Brazz dishes up pastas, salads, and deluxe burgers and french fries. ⊠ *Castle Green, TA1 1NF* ☎ *01823/272671* 🖷 *01823/336066* ⊕ *www.the-castle-hotel.com* 🛏 *39 rooms, 5 suites* ⚒ *2 restaurants, in-room data ports, bar, meeting rooms, some pets allowed (fee); no a/c* ⊟ *AE, DC, MC, V* ⊙| *BP.*

en route   North of Taunton you can see the outlines of the **Quantock and Brendon hills.** Herds of red deer live in the beech-covered eastern Quantocks. Climb to the top of the hills for a spectacular view of the Vale of Taunton Deane and, to the north, the Bristol Channel.

Dunster

❻ *21 mi northwest of Taunton, 43 mi north of Exeter.*

Lying between the Somerset coast and the edge of Exmoor National Park, Dunster is a picture-book village with a broad main street. The eight-sided yarn-market building on High Street dates from 1589. **Dunster Castle,** a 13th-century fortress remodeled in 1868–72, dominates the village from its site on a hill. Parkland and unusual gardens surround the building, which has fine plaster ceilings and a magnificent 17th-century oak staircase. The climb to the castle from the parking lot is steep. ⊠ *Off A39* ☎ *01643/823004* ⊕ *www.nationaltrust.org.uk* 🖭 *£6.80, gardens only £3.70* ☉ *Castle late Mar.–late Oct., Sat.–Wed. 11–5; last wk Oct., Sat.–Wed. 11–4. Gardens late Mar.–late Oct., daily 10–5; late Oct.–late Mar., daily 11–4.*

Exmoor National Park

20 mi northwest of Taunton.

Less wild and forbidding than Dartmoor to its south, 267-square-mi Exmoor National Park is no less majestic for its bare heath and lofty views. The park extends right up to the coast and straddles the county border between Somerset and Devon. Although it is interwoven with cultivated farmland and pasturage, Exmoor can be desolate. Taking one of the many paths and bridleways through the bracken and heather (at its best in the fall), you might glimpse the ponies and red deer for which the region is noted, and you may well encounter a hunt at full gallop. Be careful: the proximity of the coast means that mists and squalls can descend with alarming suddenness. There are national park visitor centers at Combe Martin, County Gate, Dulverton, Dunster, and Lynmouth. *Exmoor National Park Authority,* ⊠*Exmoor House, Dulverton, TA22 9HL* ☎*01398/323665* ⊕ *www.exmoor-nationalpark.gov.uk* 🖭 *Free.*

Porlock

❼ *6 mi west of Dunster, 45 mi north of Exeter.*

Buried at the bottom of a valley, with the slopes of Exmoor all about, the small, unspoiled town of Porlock lies near "Doone Country," setting for R. D. Blackmore's swashbuckling saga *Lorna Doone.* Porlock had already achieved a place in literary history by the late 1790s, when Samuel Taylor Coleridge declared it was a "man from Porlock" who interrupted his opium trance while the poet was composing "Kubla Khan."

The small harbor in the town of **Porlock Weir** (☎ 01598/741270) is the starting point for an undemanding 2-mi walk along the coast through chestnut and walnut trees to **St. Culbone,** reputedly the smallest and most isolated church in England. Saxon in origin, it has a small Victorian spire and is lighted by candles only. It would be hard to find a more enchanting spot.

Where to Stay & Eat

££–£££ ✕⬚ **Andrews on the Weir.** Calling itself a restaurant with rooms, this waterfront Georgian hotel is pure relaxed English country house with touches of glamour. Guest rooms have print drapes and patchwork quilts. The ambitious contemporary menu takes advantage of seafood, Exmoor lamb, and duckling, and you can expect unusual desserts, such as mango *panna cotta* (egg custard) with passion fruit sauce, and excellent local cheeses. ⊠ *Porlock Weir, TA24 8PB* ☎ *01643/863300* ⌂*01643/863311* ⊕*www.andrewsontheweir.co.uk* ⬤*5 rooms* ⌂ *Restaurant, bar, some pets allowed; no a/c, no kids under 12* ⊟ *AE, DC, MC, V* ⊗ *Closed Jan.* ⍾⏐ *BP.*

⬛ **en route**   As you're heading west from Porlock to Lynton, the coast road A39 mounts **Porlock Hill,** an incline so steep that signs encourage drivers to "keep going." The views across Exmoor and north to the Bristol Channel and Wales are worth it. There's a less steep but quieter and equally scenic route up the hill on a toll road accessed from Porlock Weir.

Lynton & Lynmouth

❽ *13 mi west of Porlock, 60 mi northwest of Exeter.*

A steep hill separates this pretty pair of Devonshire villages, which are linked by a water-powered cliff railway. Lynmouth, a fishing village at the bottom of the hill, crouches below 1,000-foot-high cliffs at the mouths of the East and West Lynne rivers. To 19th-century visitors, the place evoked an Alpine scene. The grand landscape of Exmoor lies all about, with undemanding walks possible to Watersmeet or the Valley of the Rocks, two local beauty spots.

Where to Stay & Eat

£££–££££ ✕⬚ **Rising Sun.** A 14th-century inn and a row of thatched cottages make up this attractive hotel with great views over the Bristol Channel. One cottage is said to have hosted the poet Percy Bysshe Shelley during his honeymoon. In the main building, corridors and creaking staircases lead to cozy rooms decorated in stylish print or solid fabrics and furnished with new pine or older wooden pieces. The traditional restaurant (no smoking permitted) specializes in local cuisine such as Devonshire beef fillet, and there's a superb game menu December through February. ⊠ *Harbourside, Lynmouth, EX35 6EG* ☎ *01598/753223* ⌂ *01598/753480* ⊕ *www.risingsunlynmouth.co.uk* ⬤ *15 rooms, 1 cottage* ⌂ *Restaurant, in-room data ports, fishing, bar; no a/c, no kids under 7* ⊟ *AE, DC, MC, V* ⍾⏐ *BP.*

★ ££–£££ ⬚ **Shelley's Hotel.** The second of Lynmouth's two hotels that claim to be Percy Bysshe Shelley's honeymoon haunt does not have such a fine location as the Rising Sun, but it's more spacious and modern inside. Bright rooms have big windows and good views, and the service is cheerfully efficient. Shelley and his 16-year-old bride, Harriet Westbrook, apparently left without paying their bill—although the poet later mailed £20 of the £30 owed. During his nine-week sojourn in Lynmouth, Shelley found time to write his polemical *Queen Mab.* ⊠ *8 Wa-*

tersmeet Rd., Lynmouth, EX35 6EP ☎ *01598/753219* 🖷 *01598/ 753751* ⊕ *www.shelleyshotel.co.uk* ➫ *11 rooms* ♤ *Restaurant, bar, no- smoking rooms; no a/c* ➯ *MC, V* ⧌ *BP.*

Barnstaple

⑨ *21 mi southwest of Lynton, 42 mi northwest of Exeter.*

Northern Devon's largest town sits on the banks of the River Taw, with a bustling center that retains its traditional role as the region's princi- pal market. West of Barnstaple, along the Taw estuary, desolate stretches of sand dunes offer long vistas of marram grass and sea.

Off crowded High Street, you can catch the colorful scene at the tim- ber-roofed **Pannier Market,** where crafts are traded on Monday and Thursday, antiques on Wednesday, and general goods and local produce on Tuesday, Friday, and Saturday. The 33 arches of **Butchers Row,** along the Pannier Market, hold a handful of mainly identical butcher's shops, as well as other food stores. The 14th-century **St. Anne's Chapel,** between High Street and Boutport Street, became a grammar school in 1549; John Gay (1685–1732), author of *The Beggar's Opera,* was a pupil here. Over- looking the River Taw on Queen Anne's Walk, a colonnaded building built in the 18th century as a merchants' exchange holds the **Barnstaple Heritage Centre,** with exhibits on the town's history since Saxon times. ⊠ *Queen Anne's Walk* ☎ *01271/373003* 🖷 *£2.50* ☉ *Apr.–Oct., Mon.–Sat. 10–5; Nov.–Mar., weekdays 10–4:30, Sat. 10–3:30.*

Where to Stay & Eat

£–££ ✕⊡ **Royal and Fortescue Hotel.** Edward VII, who stayed here when he was prince of Wales, gave this Victorian hotel the royal part of its name. It's by the river in the center of town, but the functionally furnished rooms have no views to speak of. You can eat in the excellent bistro, 62 The Bank, which has fixed-price dinners, or in the self-service Lord Fortes- cue's. ⊠ *Boutport St., EX31 1HG* ☎ *01271/342289* 🖷 *01271/340102* ⊕ *www.royalfortescue.co.uk* ➫ *48 rooms* ♤ *2 restaurants, cable TV, bar; no a/c* ➯ *AE, DC, MC, V.*

Braunton Burrows Biosphere Reserve

⑩ *5 mi west of Barnstaple, 18 mi southwest of Lynton.*

Miles of trails run through the dunes at this sanctuary on the north side of the Taw estuary, designated a biosphere reserve by UNESCO. Bird- watching is first-class, especially in winter, and the flora is most color- ful between May and August. The reserve warden can advise you about organized walks. Talks are held in the **Countryside Centre** (⊠ Caen car park, Braunton ☉ Easter–Oct., Mon.–Sat. 10–4). ⊠ *Off B3231, 2 mi west of Braunton* ☎ *01271/812552 for warden* 🖷 *Free* ☉ *Daily 24 hrs.*

Bideford

⑪ *8 mi southwest of Barnstaple, 49 mi northwest of Exeter.*

The confluence of the rivers Taw and Torridge feeds broad Bideford Bay. Bideford lies on the Torridge, which you can cross either by the 14th-century 24-arch bridge or by the more modern structure to reach the scenic hillside and the town's elegant houses. The area was a mainstay of 16th-century shipbuilding; the sturdy vessels of Sir Francis Drake were built here. From the Norman era until the 18th century, the port was the property of the Grenville family, whose most celebrated scion was Sir Richard Grenville (circa 1541–91), commander of the seven ships that carried the first settlers to Virginia, and later a key player in the defeat of the Spanish Armada.

Clovelly

⑫ *12 mi west of Bideford, 60 mi northwest of Exeter.*

Fodor'sChoice
★
Lovely Clovelly always seems to have the sun shining on its flower-lined cottages and stepped and cobbled streets. Alas, its beauty is well known, and day-trippers can overrun the village in summer. Perched precariously among cliffs, a steep, cobbled road—tumbling down at such an angle that it's closed to cars—leads to the toylike harbor with its 14th-century quay. The climb back has been likened to the struggles of Sisyphus, but, happily, a Land Rover service (in summer) will take you to and from the parking lot at the top. You pay £3.50 to park and use the visitor center; this is the only way to enter the village if you arrive by car. People arriving by bicycle or on foot do not pay to enter. To avoid the worst crowds, visit on weekdays, preferably before or after school summer vacation. If you have to visit in summer, arrive early in the day.

Where to Stay & Eat

££££ ✕⌂ **Red Lion Hotel.** One of only two hotels in this coastal village, the 18th-century Red Lion sits right on the harbor. Guest rooms, some small, are decorated along a nautical theme; all have sea views. The climb up through Clovelly is perilously steep, but guests can bring cars via a back road to and from the hotel. The sophisticated restaurant (fixed-price menus at dinner) specializes in seafood dishes and homemade ice creams and sorbets. ⊠ *The Quay, EX39 5TF* ☎ *01237/431237* 🖷 *01237/431044* ⊕ *www.clovelly.co.uk* ⇝ *11 rooms* ⌂ *Restaurant, 2 bars; no a/c* ⊟ *AE, MC, V* ⊚| *BP.*

CORNWALL
COAST & MOOR

Cornwall stretches west into the sea, with plenty of coastline to explore. One way to discover it all is to travel southwest from Boscastle and the cliff-top ruins of Tintagel Castle, the legendary birthplace of Arthur, along the north Cornish coast to Land's End. From this westernmost tip of Britain, known for its savage land- and seascapes and panoramic views, turn northeast, stopping in the popular seaside resort of Penzance, the harbor city of Falmouth, and a string of fishing villages. Leave time to visit the Eden Project, with its large, surrealistic-looking conservatories in an abandoned clay pit, and to explore the boggy, heath-covered expanse of Bodmin Moor.

Boscastle

▶ ⑬ *15 mi north of Bodmin, 30 mi south of Clovelly.*

In tranquil Boscastle, some of the stone and slate cottages at the foot of the steep valley date from the 1300s. The town is centered around a little harbor, set snug within towering cliffs. Nearby, 2 mi up the valley of the Valency, is St. Juliot's, the "Endelstow" referred to in Thomas Hardy's *A Pair of Blue Eyes*—the young author was involved with the restoration of this church while he was working as an architect.

Where to Stay

£–££ ⚄ **The Old Rectory.** Hardy stayed here, in what is now a delightful B&B,
Fodor'sChoice while restoring St. Juliot's church, and this is where he first met his wife-
★ to-be, Emma, the rector's sister-in-law. The stone house, set in 3 acres of lush grounds, has been in the same family for five generations, and updates are mainly in Victorian style. At the rear of the building, the Old Stable has a wood-burning stove and a separate entrance. Breakfast may include organic produce from the kitchen garden. ⊠ *Off B3263, St. Juliot, Boscastle, PL35 0BT* 📠 *01840/250225* ⊕ *www. stjuliot.com* ☞ *4 rooms, 2 with bath* ⚘ *Croquet, some pets allowed (fee); no a/c, no room phones, no kids under 12, no smoking* ⊟ *MC, V* ☾ *Closed Dec.–Feb.* ۱◯۱ *BP.*

Tintagel

⑭ *5 mi southwest of Boscastle.*

The romance of Arthurian legend thrives around Tintagel's ruined castle on the coast. Ever since the somewhat unreliable 12th-century chronicler Geoffrey of Monmouth identified Tintagel as the home of Arthur, son of Uther Pendragon and Ygrayne, devotees of the legend cycle have revered the site. In the 19th century, Alfred, Lord Tennyson described Tintagel's Arthurian connection in *The Idylls of the King.* Today the village itself has more than its share of tourist junk—including Excaliburgers.

The **Old Post Office,** a 14th-century stone manor house with yard-thick walls, smoke-blackened beams, and a pleasingly undulating slate-tiled roof, has been restored to its Victorian appearance, when one room served as a post office. ⊠ *3–4 Tintagel Centre* 📞 *01840/770024* ⊕ *www.nationaltrust. org.uk* ☞ *£2.40* ☾ *Apr.–Sept., daily 11–5:30; Oct., daily 11–4.*

Fodor'sChoice Although all that remains of the ruined cliff-top **Tintagel Castle,** legendary
★ birthplace of King Arthur, is the outline of its walls, moats, and towers, it requires only a bit of imagination to conjure up a picture of Sir Lancelot and Sir Galahad riding out in search of the Holy Grail over the narrow causeway above the seething breakers. Archaeological evidence, however, suggests that the castle dates from much later—about 1150, when it was the stronghold of the earls of Cornwall. Long before that, Romans may have occupied the site. The earliest identified remains here are of Celtic (5th-century AD) origin, and these may have some connection with the legendary Arthur. Legends aside, nothing can detract from the castle ruins, dramatically set off by the wild, windswept Cornish coast, on an island joined to the mainland by a narrow isthmus. (There are also traces of a

ALL ABOUT ARTHUR

LEGENDS CONCERNING KING ARTHUR have resonated through the centuries, enthusiastically taken up by writers and poets from 7th-century Welsh and Breton troubadours to Tennyson and Mark Twain in the 19th century, and T. H. White in the 20th century. The historical Arthur was probably a Christian Celtic chieftain battling against the heathen Saxons in the 6th century, although most of the tales surrounding him have a much later setting, thanks to the vivid but somewhat fanciful chronicles of his exploits by medieval scholars. The virtuous warrior-hero of popular myth has always been treated with generous helpings of nostalgia for a golden age. For Sir Thomas Malory (circa 1408–71), author of Le Morte d'Arthur, the finest medieval prose collection of Arthurian romance, Arthur represented a lost era of chivalry and noble romance before the loosening of the traditional bonds of feudal society and the gradual collapse of the medieval social order. Places associated with Arthur and his consort Guinevere, the wizard Merlin, the knights of the Round Table, and the related legends of Tristan and Isolde (or Iseult) can be found all over Europe, but the West Country claims the closest association. (Contact VisitBritain for a King Arthur movie map with sites linked to the stories.) Arthur was said to have had his court of Camelot at Cadbury Castle and to have been buried at Glastonbury. Cornwall in particular holds the greatest concentration of Arthurian links, notably his supposed birthplace, Tintagel, and the site of his last battle, on Bodmin Moor. However tenuous the links—and, barring the odd, somewhat ambiguous inscription, there is nothing in the way of hard evidence of Arthur's existence—the Cornish have taken the Once and Future King to their hearts, and his spirit is said to reside in the now-rare bird, the Cornish chough.

Celtic monastery here.) Paths lead down to the pebble beach and a cavern known as **Merlin's Cave.** Exploring Tintagel Castle involves some arduous climbing on steep steps, but even on a summer's day, when people swarm over the battlements and a westerly Atlantic wind sweeps through Tintagel, you can feel the proximity of the distant past. ✉ *Castle Rd., ½ mi west of village* ☎ *01840/770328* ⊕ *www.english-heritage. org.uk* ✆ *£3.70* ⊙ *Apr.–mid-July and Sept., daily 10–6; mid-July–Aug., daily 10–7; Oct., daily 10–5; Nov.–Mar., daily 10–4.*

Displays in the **Arthurian Centre** provide background to the story of King Arthur. Highlights include Arthur's Stone, dated to 540 BC, and a woodland walk to the site of Arthur's "last battle." There's also a gift shop and tea garden. The center is 5 mi southeast of Tintagel Castle, on the edge of Bodmin Moor. ✉ *Slaughterbridge, Camelford* ☎ *01840/212450* ⊕ *www.arthur-online.com* ✆ *£2.50* ⊙ *Easter–Oct., daily 10–dusk.*

Port Isaac

15 *5 mi southwest of Tintagel.*

A mixture of granite, slate, and whitewashed cottages tumbles precipitously down the cliff to the tiny harbor at Port Isaac, still dedicated to the crab and lobster trade. Low tide reveals a pebbly beach and rock pools. Relatively unscathed by tourists, it makes for a peaceful and secluded stay. For an extra slice of authentic Cornwall life, the local choir sings shanties at the harborside on Friday nights in summer.

Where to Stay & Eat

££–£££ ✕🏠 **Slipway Hotel.** This 16th-century inn on the harborfront has low ceilings, exposed timbers, and steep staircases that lead to cozily furnished rooms. The split-level restaurant, held up by unusual slate pillars, serves supremely fresh fish, lobster, and crab dishes. ⊠ *Harbourfront, PL29 3RH* ☎ *01208/880264* 🖷 *01208/880408* ⊕ *www.portisaac.com* ➥ *10 rooms* ⟐ *Restaurant, bar, some pets allowed (fee); no a/c* ⊟ *MC, V* ⊗ *Closed Jan.–mid-Feb.* ¶◯∣ *BP.*

Padstow

🔟 *10 mi southwest of Port Isaac.*

At the mouth of the Camel River, this small fishing port has attracted considerable attention as a center of culinary excellence, largely because of the presence here since 1975 of pioneering seafood chef Rick Stein. He has made Padstow an essential stop on any foodie's itinerary. Stein's empire now includes two restaurants, a café, a delicatessen on South Quay (open April–October) good for food to go, a cooking school (classes fill up months in advance), a gift shop, and some elegant accommodations. However, Padstow is worth visiting even if seafood is not your favorite fare. The cries of seagulls fill its lively harbor, a string of fine beaches lies within a short ride—including some choice strands highly prized by surfers—and two scenic walking routes await: the Saints Way across the peninsula to Fowey, and the Camel Trail, a footpath and cycling path that follows the river as far as Bodmin Moor.

Where to Stay & Eat

£££–£££££ ✕🏠 **St. Petroc's Hotel and Bistro.** Rick Stein's cream-color bistro in an old house is a French-inspired take on his Seafood Restaurant—simpler, less expensive, and with more options for carnivores and vegetarians. Diners and hotel guests have use of the sunny walled garden. The well-equipped bedrooms are individually decorated with stylish modern pieces. ⊠ *4 New St., PL28 8EA* ☎ *01841/532700* 🖷 *01841/533574* ⊕ *www.rickstein.com* ➥ *10 rooms* ⟐ *Restaurant, bar, some pets allowed; no a/c* ⊟ *AE, MC, V* ⊗ *Closed 1 wk around Christmas* ¶◯∣ *BP.*

£££–£££££ ✕🏠 **The Seafood Restaurant.** Rick Stein's flagship restaurant (reservations **Fodor'sChoice** essential), just across from where the lobster boats and trawlers unload ★ their catches, has built its reputation on the freshest fish and high culinary artistry. The fixed-price dinners are the best option, and may include stir-fried mussels with black beans and grilled haddock with spring onion mash. If you don't want to move after your meal, book one of the sunny, individually designed guest rooms done in clean-lined modern or plush traditional style. ⊠ *Riverside, PL28 8BY* ☎ *01841/532700* 🖷 *01841/533574* ⊕ *www.rickstein.com* ➥ *13 rooms* ⟐ *Restaurant, minibars, some pets allowed; no a/c* ⊟ *AE, MC, V* ⊗ *Closed 1 wk around Christmas* ¶◯∣ *BP.*

£££££ 🏠 **St. Edmond's House.** The most luxurious Rick Stein venture has a so-phisticated minimalist style. Excellently equipped, the bedrooms have polished wooden floors, in-room DVD players, and French doors facing the harbor. Booking here guarantees a dinner table at the Seafood Restaurant, where breakfast is taken, but you should reserve as far ahead as possible. ✉ *St. Edmond's La., PL28 8BZ* ☎ *01841/532700* 🖶 *01841/533574* ⊕ *www.rickstein.com* ➥ *6 rooms* ⚐ *Minibars, cable TV, some pets allowed; no a/c* ⊟ *AE, MC, V* ☾ *Closed 1 wk around Christmas* ⧦⧦ *BP.*

Sports & the Outdoors

BIKING Bikes of all shapes and sizes can be rented at **Brinham's** (✉ South Quay ☎ 01841/532594), at the start of the Camel Trail.

SURFING **Harlyn Surf School** (✉ 16 Boyd Ave. ☎ 01841/533076) can arrange half- to five-day surfing courses.

WALKING The **Saints Way,** a 30-mi path between Padstow and the Camel Estuary on Cornwall's north coast to Fowey on the south coast, follows a Bronze Age trading route, later used by Celtic pilgrims to cross the peninsula. Several relics of such times can be seen along the way. Contact the tourist offices in Padstow or Fowey or the Cornwall Tourist Board for information.

Newquay

⑰ *14 mi southwest of Padstow, 30 mi southwest of Tintagel.*

The principal resort on the north Cornwall coast is a fairly large town established in 1439. It was once the center of the trade in pilchards (a small herringlike fish), and on the headland you can still see a white hut where a lookout known as a "huer" watched for pilchard schools and directed the boats to the fishing grounds. Newquay has become Britain's surfing capital, and in summer young California-dreaming devotees can pack the wide beaches.

Perranporth

⑱ *8 mi south of Newquay, 13 mi northwest of Truro.*

Past the sandy shores of Perran Bay, Perranporth is one of Cornwall's most popular seaside spots and becomes extremely crowded in high season. The swells off this 3-mi stretch of beach attract swarms of surfers, too. The best times to visit are the beginning and end of the summer. Enchanting coastal walks extend along the dunes and cliffs.

St. Ives

⑲ *20 mi southwest of Perranporth on A30, 10 mi north of Penzance.*

James McNeill Whistler came here to paint his landscapes, Daphne du Maurier and Virginia Woolf to write their novels. Today sand, sun, and superb art continue to attract thousands of vacationers to the fishing village of St. Ives, named after St. Ia, a 5th-century female Irish missionary said to have arrived on a floating leaf. The town has long played host to a well-established artists' colony, and there are plenty of craftspeople, too. Day-trippers often crowd St. Ives, so it's best to park away from the center.

The studio and garden of Dame Barbara Hepworth (1903–75), who pioneered abstract sculpture in England, are now the **Barbara Hepworth Museum and Sculpture Garden.** London's prominent Tate gallery runs the museum. The artist lived here for 26 years. ✉ *Trewyn Studio, Barnoon Hill* ☎ *01736/796226* ⊕ *www.tate.org.uk* 🖼 *£4.25, combined ticket with Tate St. Ives £7.50* ☉ *Mar.–Oct., daily 10–5:30; Nov.–Feb., Tues.–Sun. and national holidays 10–4:30.*

★　The spectacular **Tate St. Ives** displays the work of artists who lived and worked in St. Ives, mostly from 1925 to 1975, and has selections from the rich collection of the Tate in London. It occupies a modernist building—a fantasia of seaside deco-period architecture with a panoramic view of rippling turquoise ocean. The four-story gallery, at the base of a cliff fronted by Porthmeor Beach, may be the only art museum with special storage space for visitors' surfboards. The rooftop café is excellent. ✉ *Porthmeor Beach* ☎ *01736/796226* ⊕ *www.tate.org.uk* 🖼 *£4.75, combined ticket with Barbara Hepworth Museum and Sculpture Garden £7.50* ☉ *Mar.–Oct., daily 10–5:30; Nov.–Feb., Tues.–Sun. and national holidays 10–4:30.*

need a break?　One of Cornwall's oldest pubs (built in 1312), the harborfront **Sloop Inn** (✉ The Wharf ☎ 01736/796584) serves simple lunches as well as evening meals in wood-beam rooms that display the work of local artists. If the weather's good, you can eat at the tables outside.

At the **St. Ives Society of Artists Gallery,** local artists display selections of their current work for sale in the former Old Mariners' Church. The Crypt is rented out for private exhibitions. ✉ *Norway Sq.* ☎ *01736/ 795582* ⊕ *www.stivessocietyofartists.com* ☉ *Mid-Mar.–Oct., Mon.–Sat. and national holidays 10–4:30.*

Where to Stay & Eat

£££　✕**Porthminster Beach Café.** Unbeatable for its location alone—on the broad, golden sands of Porthminster Beach—this sleek modern eatery prepares imaginative lunches, teas, and evening meals you can savor while you take in the marvelous vista across the bay. Typical choices are Cornish crab soup; spicy braised lamb with tomato, saffron, and coriander; and grilled turbot on cassava chips with steamed bok choy. The sister Porthgwidden Beach Café, in the Downalong area of town, has a smaller and cheaper but equally varied menu. ✉ *Porthminster Beach* ☎ *01736/ 795352* ▭ *MC, V* ☉ *Closed Nov.–mid-March.*

££££　✕🏠 **Garrack Hotel.** A family-run, ivy-clad hotel with panoramic sea views from its hilltop location, the Garrack is relaxed and undemanding. Some rooms are furnished in traditional style; others are more modern. The excellent restaurant specializes in fresh local fish, including grilled or sautéed lobster, as well as Cornish lamb. Breads are made in-house, and the wine list features some Cornish vineyards. ✉ *Burthallan La., TR26 3AA* ☎ *01736/796199* 🖨 *01736/798955* ⊕ *www.*

garrack.com ⊐ *18 rooms* ☐ *Restaurant, in-room data ports, indoor pool, gym, sauna, bar; no a/c* ⊟ *AE, DC, MC, V* ♚ *BP.*

££–£££ ☐ **Primrose Valley Hotel.** Blending old-fashioned, Edwardian comforts and stylish modern touches, this family-friendly hotel with easygoing, young management has a fine location a few steps up from Porthminster Beach. Although it has few bedrooms, the hotel is a spacious place, with a large lounge that opens onto the veranda. Guest rooms are bright and contemporary. There's an extra charge for sea-facing rooms with balconies, and a minimum one-week stay is required in July and August. ⊠ *Porthminster Beach, TR26 2ED* ☎ *01736/794939* ⊕ *www. primroseonline.co.uk* ⊐ *9 rooms* ☐ *Dining room, bar; no a/c, no smoking* ⊟ *AE, MC, V* ♚ *BP.*

£ ☐ **Cornerways.** Everything in St. Ives seems squeezed into the tiniest of spaces, and this cottage B&B in the quiet Downalong quarter is no exception. The light, tastefully converted rooms are pleasingly simple in design, with neutral colors enlivened by a few choice pieces of modern art; some have sea views. Most rooms are named after characters in Daphne du Maurier's novels (she once stayed in one of them). Fresh local fish is offered at breakfast, and the galleries are minutes away. ⊠ *1 Bethesda Pl., TR26 1PA* ☎ *01736/796706* ✎ *cornerways@aol.com* ⊐ *6 rooms* ☐ *No a/c, no smoking* ⊟ *No credit cards* ♚ *BP.*

> **en route** The winding B3306 coastal road southwest from St. Ives passes through some of Cornwall's starkest yet most beautiful countryside. Barren hills crisscrossed by low stone walls drop abruptly to granite cliffs and wide bays. Evidence of the ancient tin-mining industry—the remains of smokestacks and pumping houses—is everywhere. Now a fascinating mining heritage center, the early-20th-century **Geevor Tin Mine** was the only mine left in the St. Just district by the 1930s. At its peak Geevor employed 400 men, but in October 1985 the collapse of the world tin market wiped Cornwall from the mining map. Make sure you have suitably sturdy footwear for the surface and underground tours. A museum, shop, and café are on the site. ⊠ *B3306, Pendeen* ☎ *01736/788662* ⊕ *www.geevor.com* ✉ *£6.50* ☉ *Apr.–Oct., Sun.–Fri. 10–5; Nov.–Mar., Sun.–Fri. 10–4; last admission 1 hr before closing.*

Land's End

★ ⑳ *10 mi southwest of St. Ives, 10 mi west of Penzance.*

The coastal road, B3306, ends at the western tip of Britain at what is, quite literally, Land's End. The sea crashes against the rocks here and lashes ships battling their way around the point. Approach from one of the coastal footpaths for the best panoramic view. Over the years, sightseers have caused some erosion of the paths, but new ones are constantly being built, and Cornish "hedges" (granite walls covered with turf) have been planted to prevent future erosion. The scenic grandeur of Land's End remains undiminished, although the point draws crowds of people from all over the world. The Land's End Hotel here is undistinguished, though the restaurant has good views. There A low-key theme park, the **Land's End Experience** (☎ 0870/458–0099), runs a poor second to nature.

Nightlife & the Arts

★ The open-air **Minack Theatre** perches high above a beach 3 mi southeast of Land's End. The slope of the cliff forms a natural amphitheater, with bench seats on the terraces and the sea as a magnificent backdrop. Different companies present plays from classic dramas to modern comedies afternoons and evenings in summer. An exhibition center tells the story of the theater's creation. ⊠ *Off B3315, Porthcurno* ☎ *01736/ 810181* 🖃 *Exhibition center £2.50, performances £5.50 and £7* ☉ *Apr.–Sept., daily 9:30–5:30; Oct.–Mar., daily 10–4. Exhibition center closed during matinees, currently May–Sept., Wed. and Fri. noon–4:30.*

Mousehole

★ ㉑ *7 mi east of Land's End, 3 mi south of Penzance.*

On B3315 between Land's End and Penzance, Mousehole (pronounced *mow*-zel, with the first syllable rhyming with "cow") merits a stop—and plenty of people do stop—to see this archetypal Cornish fishing village of tiny stone cottages. It was the home of Dolly Pentreath, supposedly the last native Cornish speaker, who died in 1777.

Newlyn

㉒ *2 mi north of Mousehole.*

Long the county's most important fishing port, Newlyn became the magnet for a popular artists' colony at the end of the 19th century. Few of the fishermen's cottages that attracted artists to the area remain, however. To see the works of the Newlyn School, drop by the Penlee House Gallery in Penzance. The Pilchard Works, a museum that is also an active factory, presents the history of Cornish pilchard fishing.

Penzance

㉓ *1½ mi north of Newlyn, 10 mi south of St. Ives.*

Superb views over Mount's Bay are one lure of this popular seaside resort. The town's isolated position has always made it vulnerable to attack from the sea. During the 16th century, Spanish raiders destroyed most of the original town, and the majority of old buildings date from as late as the 18th century. The main street is Market Jew Street, a folk mistranslation of the Cornish expression "Marghas Yow," which means "Thursday Market." Where Market Jew Street meets Causeway Head is Market House, constructed in 1837, an impressive, domed granite building that now serves as a bank.

The former main street and one of the prettiest thoroughfares in Penzance, **Chapel Street** winds down from Market House to the harbor. Its predominantly Georgian and Regency houses suddenly give way to the extraordinary **Egyptian House,** whose facade recalls ancient Egypt. Built around 1830 as a geological museum, today it houses vacation apartments. Across Chapel Street is the 17th-century **Union Hotel,** where in

1805 the death of Lord Nelson and the victory of Trafalgar were first announced from the minstrels' gallery in the assembly rooms. Near the Union Hotel on Chapel Street is one of the few remnants of old Penzance, the **Turk's Head,** an inn said to date from the 13th century.

The small collection at the **Penlee House Gallery and Museum,** in a gracious Victorian house in a park, focuses on paintings by members of the so-called Newlyn School from about 1880 to 1930. These works evoke the life of the inhabitants of Newlyn, mostly fisherfolk. The museum also covers 5,000 years of West Cornwall history through archaeology, decorative arts, costume, and photography exhibits. ⊠ *Penlee Park* ☎ *01736/363625* ⊕ *www.penleehouse.org.uk* 🎫 *£2, Sat. free* ☉ *May–Sept., Mon.–Sat. 10–5; Oct.–Apr., Mon.–Sat. 10:30–4:30; last admission ½ hr before closing.*

off the beaten path

ISLES OF SCILLY – Fondly regarded in folklore as the lost land of Lyonesse, this compact group of more than 100 islands 30 mi southwest of Land's End is equally famed for the warm summer climate and ferocious winter storms. In fair weather, you can find peace, a profusion of flowers—wild, cultivated, and subtropical—swarms of seabirds, and unspoiled beaches galore. If you have time, take the 2½-hour ferry service from Penzance; otherwise there's plane and helicopter service. These all arrive at the largest of the five inhabited islands, St. Mary's, which has the bulk of the lodgings, from palatial retreats to humble but comfortable B&Bs.

Where to Stay & Eat

£££–£££££ ✕ **Harris's.** Tucked away off Market Jew Street, the two small, elegant rooms here are a rare outpost of high-quality cuisine in Penzance. Seafood is the main event: whatever the boats bring in. Crab Florentine, grilled on a bed of spinach with cheese sauce, is usually available. Meat dishes might include grilled breast of guinea fowl stuffed with goat's cheese. ⊠ *46 New St.* ☎ *01736/364408* 🖃 *AE, MC, V* ☉ *Closed Sun., also Mon. Nov.–May, and 4 wks Nov.–Mar.*

★ **££–£££** ✕ **Admiral Benbow Inn.** One of the most famous inns in Penzance, the 15th-century Admiral Benbow was once a smugglers' pub—look for the armed figure of a smuggler on the roof. Seafaring memorabilia, a brass cannon, model ships, ropes, and figureheads fill the inn. In the restaurant area, decorated to resemble a ship's galley, you can dine on seafood or a steak-and-Guinness pie. ⊠ *46 Chapel St.* ☎ *01736/363448* 🖃 *MC, V.*

★ ✕🏠 **Abbey Hotel and Restaurant.** Owned by former model/icon Jean
£££–£££££ Shrimpton and her husband, this small, 17th-century hotel is marvelously homey. Books fill the drawing room, and antiques and chintzes decorate many of the rooms; there are also two small, comfortable apartments. You can dine in the cozy in-house restaurant, but the sleekly modern Abbey Restaurant next door (closed Sunday and Monday, no lunch Tuesday–Thursday) has garnered all the raves, with a short, intriguing menu that lists twice-baked goat's cheese soufflé, bourride of turbot, and iced apple and Calvados parfait, among other creations. ⊠ *Abbey St., TR18 4AR* ☎ *01736/366906 hotel, 01736/330680 restaurant* 🖷 *01736/*

351163 ⊕ *www.theabbeyonline.com* ⊄ *6 rooms, 2 apartments* ♿ *2 restaurants, some pets allowed; no a/c* ⊟ *AE, MC, V* ⅋OⅠ *BP.*

£–££ 📷 **Camilla House.** This flower-bedecked Georgian house stands on a road parallel to the promenade, close to the harbor. Guest rooms are cheerfully decorated; those at the front have sea views. The owners are great sources of local information and can help with ferry crossings and flights to the Isles of Scilly. Evening meals are available on request. ⊠ *12 Regent Terr., TR18 4DW* ☎🖹 *01736/363771* ⊕ *www.camillahouse-hotel.co.uk* ⊄ *8 rooms* ♿ *Dining room, in-room data ports, bar; no a/c, no room phones, no smoking* ⊟ *AE, MC, V* ⅋OⅠ *BP.*

£ 📷 **Holbein House.** A stout Victorian house with a garden, this family-run B&B west of the center of Penzance is quiet, friendly, and clean, and offers exceptionally good value. Breakfast is taken in the bedrooms, which are spacious and bright, with modern furnishings. Penlee House is a pleasant walk from here across the park. ⊠ *Alexandra Rd. , TR18 4LZ* ☎ *01736/332625* ⊄ *7 rooms* ♿ *No a/c, no room phones* ⊟ *No credit cards* ⅋OⅠ *CP.*

Sports & the Outdoors

Many ships have foundered on Cornwall's rocky coastline, resulting in an estimated 3,600 shipwrecks. The area around Land's End has some of the best diving in Europe, in part because the convergence of the Atlantic and the Gulf Stream here results in impressive visibility and unusual subtropical marine life. **Undersea Adventures** (⊠ 15A Cuxhaven Way, Long Rock Industrial Estate ☎ 01736/333040) offers courses and guided dives for beginners and experts.

St. Michael's Mount

★ ㉔ *3 mi east of Penzance on A394.*

Rising out of Mount's Bay just off the coast, this spectacular granite and slate island is one of Cornwall's greatest natural attractions. The 14th-century castle perched at the highest point—200 feet above the sea—was built on the site of a Benedictine chapel founded by Edward the Confessor. In its time, the island has served as a church (Brittany's island abbey of Mont St. Michel served as a model), a fortress, and a private residence. The castle rooms you can tour include the Chevy Chase Room—a name probably associated with the Cheviot Hills or the French word *chevaux* (horses), after the hunting frieze that decorates the walls of this former monks' refectory. The battlements also offer splendid views. Around the base of the rock are buildings from medieval to Victorian, but they appear harmonious. Fascinating gardens surround the Mount, and many kinds of plants flourish in its microclimates. To get to the island, follow the cobbled causeway from the village of Marazion or, when the tide is in during the summer, take the ferry. There are pubs and restaurants in the village, but the island also has a café and restaurant. Wear stout shoes for your visit to this site, which is unsuitable for anyone with mobility problems. ⊠ *Marazion* ☎ *01736/710507* ⊕ *www. stmichaelsmount.co.uk* 🖾 *£5.20, £1 for ferry each way* ☯ *Apr.–June, Sept., and Oct., weekdays 10:30–5:30, last admission 4:45; July and Aug., daily 10:30–5:30, last admission 4:45; Nov.–Mar., phone for hrs.*

Helston

㉕ *13 mi east of Marazion, 14 mi east of Penzance, 18 mi southwest of Truro.*

The attractive Georgian town of Helston is most famous for its annual "Furry Dance," which takes place on Floral Day, May 8 (unless the date is a Sunday or Monday, in which case it takes place on the previous Saturday). Flowers deck the whole town, and dancers weave their way in and out of the houses along a 3-mi route.

🜚 Besides the usual rides, **Flambards Theme Park** has an aircraft collection, a re-creation of a wartime street during the Blitz, and a reconstructed Victorian village. Family Saver tickets are a good deal. The park has reduced services in winter. ⊠ *Off A394, 2 mi from Helston* ☎ *01326/ 573404, 0845/601–8684 24-hr information line* ⊕ *www.flambards.co. uk* 🖾 *£9.95, £4.50 in winter* ☉ *Mid-Mar.–Oct., daily 10–5 (may close later in summer; call about possible Mon. and Fri. closings in Oct.); Nov.–mid-Mar., Sat.–Wed., 11–4. Closed 2 wks Dec.–Jan.*

Where to Stay & Eat

££–££££ ✕🖾 **Nansloe Manor.** Although near Helston's center, this peaceful 17th-century manor house gives the impression of being deep in the country, with its ½-mi driveway and 4 acres of grounds. Public areas and guest rooms are done in country-house style, with upholstered furniture and chintz fabrics. In the restaurant, the fixed-price, four-course menu favors traditional English fare. ⊠ *Meneage Rd., TR13 0SB* ☎ *01326/ 574691* 🖶 *01326/564680* ⊕ *www.nansloe-manor.co.uk* 🖘 *7 rooms* △ *Restaurant, miniature golf, croquet, bar; no a/c, no kids under 10* ▤ *AE, MC, V* ⋈ *BP.*

Lizard Peninsula

★ **㉖** *10 mi south of Helston.*

The southernmost point on mainland Britain, this peninsula is a government-designated Area of Outstanding Natural Beauty. The huge, eerily rotating dish antennae of the Goonhilly Satellite Communications Earth Station are visible from the road as it crosses Goonhilly Downs, the backbone of the peninsula. A path, close to the tip of the peninsula, plunges down 200-foot cliffs to the tiny **Kynance Cove,** with its handful of pint-size islands. The sands here are reachable only during the 2½ hours before and after low tide. The peninsula's cliffs are made of greenish serpentine rock, interspersed with granite; souvenirs of the area are carved out of the stone.

Falmouth

㉗ *7 mi northeast of Gweek, 12 mi south of Truro.*

The bustle of this resort town's fishing harbor, yachting center, and commercial port only adds to its charm. In the 18th century, Falmouth was the main mail-boat port for North America, and in Flushing, a village across the inlet, you can see the slate-covered houses built by prosperous mail-boat captains. A ferry service now links the two towns. On Custom House Quay, off Arwenack Street, is the King's Pipe, an oven in which seized contraband was burned.

🕒 Opened in 2002, the granite and oak-clad **National Maritime Museum Cornwall** by the harbor is an excellent place to come to grips with Cornish maritime heritage, weather lore, and navigational science. You can view the collection of 140 or so boats, examine the tools associated with Cornish boatbuilders, and study the prospect across to Flushing from the lighthouse-like Look-out, which is equipped with maps, telescopes, and binoculars. In the glass-fronted Tidal Zone below sea level, you come face to face with the sea itself. In summer, you can reach the museum by ferry from Falmouth's Prince of Wales Pier. ⊠ *Discovery Quay* ☎ *01326/313388* ⊕ *www.nmmc.co.uk* ⊡ *£6.50* ☉ *Daily 10–5.*

At the end of its own peninsula stands the formidable **Pendennis Castle,** built by Henry VIII in the 1540s and later improved by his daughter, Elizabeth I. You can explore the different defenses developed over the centuries. The castle has sweeping views over the English Channel and across the water known as Carrick Roads to St. Mawes Castle, designed as a companion fortress to guard the roads. Open-air plays and concerts are usually staged here in July and August. ⊠ *Pendennis Head* ☎ *01326/316594* ⊕ *www.english-heritage.org.uk* ⊡ *£4.50* ☉ *Apr.–June and Sept., daily 10–5; July and Aug., Sun.–Fri. 10–6, Sat 10–5; Oct.–Mar., daily 10–4.*

Where to Stay & Eat

££–£££ ✕ **Pandora Inn.** Four miles north of Falmouth, this thatched pub on a creek is a great retreat, with both a patio and a moored pontoon for summer dining. Maritime memorabilia and fresh flowers provide decoration, and you can eat in the bar (lunch or dinner) or in the candlelit restaurant (dinner only). The menu highlight is fresh seafood—try the creamy crab thermidor or check out the catch of the day. ⊠ *Restronguet Creek, Mylor Bridge* ☎ *01326/372678* ▤ *MC, V.*

★ ££–£££ ✕ **Seafood Bar.** Head down an alley off the quay to get to this restaurant with a fish tank for a window. Beyond the door is the very best local seafood, with such choices as thick crab soup, Helford River oysters, or scallops from Falmouth Bay. ⊠ *Quay St.* ☎ *01326/315129* ▤ *MC, V* ☉ *Closed Sun. Oct.–June, Mon. Oct.–Easter. No lunch.*

££–££££ 🏨 **St. Michael's Hotel.** Colorful subtropical gardens sweep down to the water at this seaside hotel in a long, low, white building overlooking Falmouth Bay. The public areas and guest rooms are sleek and contemporary, and the staff welcomes families. ⊠ *Stracey Rd., TR11 4NB* ☎ *01326/312707* 🖷 *01326/211772* ⊕ *www.corushotels.com* ⇌ *65 rooms* ☖ *Restaurant, indoor pool, gym, hot tub, sauna, bar, meeting rooms; no a/c* ▤ *AE, MC, V* ⦿ *BP.*

Trelissick

28 *6 mi north of Falmouth.*

Trelissick has a ferry terminal as well as colorful Trelissick Garden, owned by the National Trust. The **King Harry Ferry** (☎ 01872/862312 ⊕ www.

kingharryferry.co.uk), a chain-drawn car ferry, runs to the scenically splendid Roseland Peninsula three times hourly every day. From its decks you can see up and down the Fal, a deep, narrow river with steep, wooded banks. The river's great depth provides mooring for old ships waiting to be sold; these mammoth shapes lend a surreal touch to the riverscape.

★ Taking the King Harry Ferry, you can visit **St. Just in Roseland,** one of the most beautiful spots in the West Country. This tiny hamlet made up of stone cottage terraces and a 13th-century church is set within a subtropical garden, often abloom with magnolias and rhododendrons on a summer's day. St. Just is 9 mi south of Truro.

St. Mawes

㉙ *16 mi east of Falmouth by road, 1½ mi east by sea, 11 mi south of Truro by ferry.*

At the tip of the Roseland Peninsula is the quiet, unspoiled village of St. Mawes. The well-preserved Tudor-era **St. Mawes Castle,** outside the village, has a cloverleaf shape that makes it seemingly impregnable, yet during the Civil War, its Royalist commander surrendered without firing a shot. (In contrast, Pendennis Castle held out at this time for 23 weeks before submitting to a siege.) ⊠ *A3078* ☎ *01326/270526* ⊕ *www. english-heritage.org.uk* ✍ *£3.20* ⊙ *Apr.–June, daily 10–5; July and Aug., daily 10–6; Sept., Sun.–Fri. 10–5, Sat 10–4; Oct., daily 10–4; Nov.–Mar., Fri.–Mon. 10–4.*

Where to Stay & Eat

£££££ ✕🏨 **Lugger Hotel.** It's worth the winding drive on some of Cornwall's narrowest roads to get to this chic hideaway by the water in a tiny fishing village. Several 17th-century cottages have been transformed in an eclectic modern style with bleached Portuguese wood and subdued hues. Seafood is a good choice at the excellent restaurant (fixed-price menu), which overlooks the diminutive harbor. There's a terrace for drinks and sunbathing, and on either side of the hotel, the rugged coastline tempts you with exhilarating walks. The Lugger is 8 mi east of St. Mawes and 12 mi southeast or Truro. ⊠ *Portloe, TR2 5RD* ☎ *01872/501322* 🖷 *01872/501691* ⊕ *www.luggerhotel.com* ✍ *21 rooms* ♿ *Restaurant, spa, in-room data ports; no a/c* ▭ *AE, MC, V* ⊙ *Closed 2 wks in Jan.* ⦿ *BP.*

★ £££££ ✕🏨 **Tresanton Hotel.** It's the Cornish Riviera, Italian style: this former yachtsman's club, owned by Olga Polizzi, daughter of grand hotelier Charles Forte, makes for a luxuriously relaxed stay. Decorated in sunny whites, blues, and yellows, with terra-cotta pots on the terrace, the Tresanton seems distinctly Mediterranean, and the yacht and speedboat available in summer to guests reinforce the jet-set spirit. In the restaurant, the Italian-inspired menu includes steamed langoustine with fettuccine and pan-fried Dover sole. ⊠ *Lower Castle Rd., TR2 5DR* ☎ *01326/ 270055* 🖷 *01326/270053* ⊕ *www.tresanton.com* ✍ *27 rooms, 2 suites* ♿ *Restaurant, boating, fishing, bar, cinema, meeting rooms; no a/c* ▭ *AE, MC, V* ⦿ *BP.*

> **en route**   The shortest route from St. Mawes to Truro is via the King Harry Ferry. The longer way swings in a circle on A3078 for 19 mi through countryside where subtropical shrubs and flowers thrive. It takes you past Portloe and the 123-foot-tall church tower in Probus, which flaunts gargoyles and pierced stonework.

Truro

③⓪ *12 mi north of Falmouth, 19 mi north of St. Mawes.*

Truro is a compact, elegant Georgian city, nestled in a crook at the head of the River Truro. Although Bodmin is the county seat, Truro is Cornwall's only real city. For an overview of the Georgian house fronts, take a stroll down steep, broad Lemon Street. The 18th-century facades are of pale stone—unusual for Cornwall, where granite predominates. Like Lemon Street, Walsingham Place is a typical Georgian street, a curving, flower-lined pedestrian oasis.

Truro Cathedral, the **Cathedral Church of St. Mary,** dominates the city. Although comparatively modern (built 1880–1910), it evokes a medieval church, with an exterior in Early English Gothic style. The interior is filled with relics from the 16th-century parish church that stood on this site, part of which has been incorporated into a side chapel. An open, cobbled area called High Cross lies in front of the west porch, and the city's main shopping streets fan out from here. ⊠ *14 St. Mary's St.* ☎ *01872/276782* ⊕ *www.trurocathedral.org.uk* ⊑ *£3 suggested donation, tours £1* ⊗ *Mon.–Sat. 7:30–6, Sun. noon–4; tours Easter–Oct. at 11:30, also at 2 during school vacations.*

The **Royal Cornwall Museum,** in a Georgian building, displays some fine examples of Cornwall-inspired art, a sampling of Cornish archaeology, an absorbing hodgepodge of local history, and an extensive collection of minerals. There's a café and shop. ⊠ *River St.* ☎ *01872/272205* ⊕ *www.royalcornwallmuseum.org.uk* ⊑ *£4* ⊗ *Mon.–Sat. 10–5.*

Where to Stay & Eat

£££–££££ ✕▦ **Alverton Manor.** A former bishop's house and then a convent, this up-to-date hotel is both efficient and atmospheric, with a chapel that serves as a conference room. Guest rooms are large and have French cherrywood furniture. Quiet elegance is the keynote of the public areas, and in the Terrace restaurant (fixed-price menu), standards are kept high with the use of the best local produce in traditional and modern English recipes. ⊠ *Tregolls Rd., TR1 1ZQ* ☎ *01872/276633* 🖶 *01872/222989* ⊕ *www.connexions.co.uk/alvertonmanor* ⇗ *33 rooms* ♨ *Restaurant, cable TV, bar, meeting rooms, some pets allowed (fee); no a/c* ⊟ *AE, DC, MC, V* ⊗ *Closed 4 days over New Year* �ⓞⅼ *BP.*

Charlestown

③① *15 mi east of Truro.*

This port was built by a local merchant in 1791 to export the huge reserves of china clay from St. Austell, 1 mi to the north, and it became one of the ports from which 19th-century emigrants left for North

America. Charlestown has managed to avoid overdevelopment since its heyday in the early 1800s, preserving its Georgian harbor, which often appears in period film and television productions.

Where to Stay

£–££ ☒ **T'Gallants.** This refurbished Georgian house directly behind the har-
Fodor's Choice bor takes its name from top gallant, one of the sails of a square-rigged
★ sailing ship. Ask for a south-facing room to enjoy the tranquil morning view. The garden at the front is ideal for afternoon tea, and bag lunches are provided in summer. ☒ *6 Charlestown Rd., PL25 3NJ* ☎ *01726/ 70203* ⌗ *8 rooms* ⌂ *No a/c* ▭ *MC, V* ⍥ *CP.*

Eden Project

㉜ *3 mi northeast of Charlestown.*

Fodor's Choice
★ Spectacularly set in a former china clay pit, the Eden Project presents the world's major plant systems in microcosm. The crater contains more than 70,000 plants, many belonging to rare or endangered species, from three climate zones. Plants from the temperate zone are outdoors, and those from other zones are housed in biomes—hexagonally paneled geodesic domes—that are the largest conservatories in Britain. In one dome, olive and citrus groves mix with cacti and other plants indigenous to a warmer temperate climate. The tropical dome steams with heat, resounds to the gushing of a waterfall, and blooms with exotic flora. The emphasis is on conservation and ecology, yet without the slightest hint of moralizing. A free shuttle, the Land Train, helps the footsore, and well-informed guides provide information. An entertaining exhibition in the visitor center gives you the lowdown on the project. To avoid the biggest crowds, visit on a Friday or Saturday or early in the morning; you need at least half a day to see everything. ☒ *Bodelva, signposted off the A30, A390, and A391, St. Austell* ☎ *01726/811911* ⊕ *www. edenproject.com* ⌅ *£12* ⊙ *Apr.–Oct., daily 10–6; Nov.–Mar., daily 10–dusk; last admission 1½ hrs before closing.*

Fowey

㉝ *7 mi northeast of the Eden Project, 10 mi northeast of Charlestown.*

Nestled in the mouth of a wooded estuary, Fowey (pronounced Foy) is still very much a working china clay port as well as a focal point for the sailing fraternity. Increasingly, it's also the favored home of the rich and famous. Good and varied eating and sleeping options abound; these are most in demand during Regatta Week in mid-August and the annual Daphne du Maurier Festival in mid-May. The Bodinnick Ferry takes cars as well as foot passengers across the river for the coast road on to Looe.

Where to Stay & Eat

££ ✕ **Sam's.** You should be prepared to wait at this small and buzzing bistro with a rock 'n' roll flavor. Diners squeeze onto benches and into booths to savor dishes made with local seafood, including a majestic bouillabaisse, or just a simple "Samburger." ☒ *20 Fore St.* ☎ *01726/832273* ⌂ *Reservations not accepted* ▭ *No credit cards* ⊙ *Closed Jan.*

££££–£££££   🏨 **Fowey Hall.** A showy Victorian edifice, all turrets, castellations, and elaborate plasterwork, this friendly, relaxed hotel with 5 acres of gardens is very family centered—despite the abundance of antiques. Guest rooms are spacious, and there are great facilities for children. You can dine in the sumptuously oak-paneled Restaurant or in the less formal Palm Court, which opens onto the terrace. ⊠ *Hanson Dr., PL23 1ET* ☎ *01726/833866* 🖷 *01726/834100* ⊕ *www.foweyhall.com* 🛏 *12 rooms, 11 suites* ⚒ *2 restaurants, cable TV with movies, in-room VCRs, indoor pool, Ping-Pong, bar, baby-sitting, meeting rooms, some pets allowed (fee); no a/c* ⊟ *AE, MC, V* ⦿| *BP.*

Sports & the Outdoors

Between Easter and September, **Fowey River Canoe Expeditions** (⊠ 17 Passage St. ☎ 01726/833627) runs daily canoe trips up the tranquil River Fowey, the best way to observe the abundant wildlife.

Bodmin

③④   *12 mi north of Fowey.*

Bodmin, the county seat, was the only Cornish town recorded in the 11th-century Domesday Book, William the Conqueror's census. During World War I, the Domesday Book and the Crown Jewels were sent to Bodmin Prison for safekeeping. From the Gilbert Memorial on Beacon Hill, you can see both of Cornwall's coasts.

Fodor'sChoice   One of Cornwall's greatest country piles, **Lanhydrock,** former home of
★   the powerful, wealthy Robartes family, was originally constructed in the 17th century but was totally rebuilt after a fire in 1881. The granite exterior remains true to its original form, however, and the long picture gallery in the north wing, with its barrel-vaulted plaster ceiling depicting 24 biblical scenes, survived the devastation. A small museum in the north wing shows photographs and letters relating to the family. The house's endless pantries, sculleries, dairies, nurseries, and linen and livery cupboards bear witness to the immense amount of work involved in maintaining this lifestyle. Nine hundred acres of wooded parkland border the River Fowey, and in spring the gardens present an exquisite ensemble of magnolias, azaleas, and rhododendrons. ⊠ *3 mi southeast of Bodmin, signposted off A30, A38, and B3268* ☎ *01208/73320* ⊕ *www.nationaltrust.org.uk* 🖅 *£7.50, grounds only £4.20* ⊙ *House Apr.–Sept., Tues.–Sun. 11–5:30; Oct., Tues.–Sun. 11–5; garden daily 10–6; last admission 30 mins before closing.*

Dozmary Pool

③⑤   *10 mi northeast of Bodmin.*

For a taste of Arthurian legend, follow A30 northeast out of Bodmin across the boggy, heather-clad granite plateau of Bodmin Moor, and turn right at Bolventor to get to Dozmary Pool. A lake of considerable size rather than a pool, it was here that King Arthur's legendary magic sword, Excalibur, was supposedly returned to the Lady of the Lake after Arthur's final battle.

Where to Stay

££ ⌂ **Jamaica Inn.** This inn near the middle of Bodmin Moor was made famous by Daphne du Maurier's 1936 novel of the same name, and it makes a good base for excursions onto the moor. Originally a farmstead, Cornwall's best-known pub incorporates a reproduction of du Maurier's study and a smugglers' museum, both worth a look. The bedrooms are functional and traditional in style, and three have four-posters. ⊠ *Off A30, Bolventor, PL15 7TS* ☎ *01566/86250* 🖷 *01566/86177* ⊕ *www.jamaicainn.co.uk* 🖛 *6 rooms* ⌂ *Restaurant, bar; no a/c* ⊟ *AE, DC, MC, V* ⍟ *BP.*

Launceston

㊱ *25 mi northwest of Plymouth.*

Cornwall's ancient capital, Launceston (pronounced *larn*-ston), on the eastern side of Bodmin Moor, retains parts of its medieval walls, including the South Gate. For a superb view of the surrounding countryside, climb to the hilltop ruins of 14th-century **Launceston Castle.** ☎ *01566/772365* ⊕ *www.english-heritage.org.uk* 🖾 *£2.30* ⊙ *Apr.–Sept., daily 10–5; Oct., daily 10–4.*

Where to Stay & Eat

££££–£££££ ✕⌂ **Lewtrenchard Manor.** Paneled rooms, stone fireplaces, leaded-glass windows, and handsome gardens enhance this spacious 1620 manor house on the northwestern edge of Dartmoor. Victorian hymn writer Sabine Baring Gould is responsible for the eclectic mix of architectural styles. Prints, chintzes, and upholstered furniture create comfort in the individually decorated guest rooms. The restaurant (fixed-price menu), with its big log fire and family portraits, serves good, fresh fish caught an hour away, and is noted for exemplary presentation. ⊠ *Lewdown EX20 4PN, between Launceston and Okehampton* ☎ *01566/783222* 🖷 *01566/783332* ⊕ *www.lewtrenchard.co.uk* 🖛 *9 rooms* ⌂ *Restaurant, in-room data ports, croquet, bar, meeting rooms, some pets allowed (fee); no a/c* ⊟ *AE, DC, MC, V* ⍟ *BP.*

SOUTH DEVON TO CADBURY CASTLE
PLYMOUTH, DARTMOOR & EXETER

Just over the border from Cornwall is Plymouth, a fairly unprepossessing city but one with a historic old core and splendid harbor that recall a rich maritime heritage. North of Plymouth, you can explore the vast, boggy reaches of Dartmoor (setting for the Sherlock Holmes classic *The Hound of the Baskervilles*). Another choice is to continue east of Plymouth along Start Bay to Torbay, known as the English Riviera. Both options lead north to Exeter, Devon's county seat, an ancient city that has retained some of its medieval character despite wartime bombing. From Exeter you can meander south to Exmouth and then turn northeast to Yeovil in Somerset, reentering King Arthur Country at Cadbury Castle, the legendary Camelot.

Plymouth

48 mi southwest of Exeter, 124 mi southwest of Bristol, 240 mi southwest of London.

Devon's largest city has long been linked with England's commercial and maritime history. Although much of the city center was destroyed by air raids in World War II and has been rebuilt in an uninspiring style, there **㊲** are worthwhile sights. From the **Hoe,** a wide, grassy esplanade with crisscrossing walkways high above the city, you can take in a magnificent view of the inlets, bays, and harbors that make up Plymouth Sound. The **㊳** lighthouse **Smeaton's Tower,** transferred here at the end of the 19th century from its original site 14 mi out to sea, provides a sweeping vista over Plymouth Sound and the city as far as Dartmoor. ⊠ *Plymouth Hoe* ☎ *01752/603300* ⊕ *www.plymouthdome.info* 🎫 *£2.25, £6.50 includes Plymouth Dome* ☼ *Apr.–Oct., daily 10–4; Nov.–Mar., Tues.–Sat. 10–3.*

☾ **㊴** **Plymouth Dome,** next to Smeaton's Tower, has an exhibition that takes in exploration, battles, and the Blitz in its overview of local history; plenty of high-tech reconstructions add interest. One section covers the construction and rebuilding of Smeaton's Tower. Kids appreciate it, and it makes a great haven on a wet afternoon. ⊠ *Plymouth Hoe* ☎ *01752/ 603300* ⊕ *www.plymouthdome.info* 🎫 *£4.75, £6.50 includes Smeaton's Tower* ☼ *Apr.–Oct., daily 10–5; Nov.–Mar., Tues.–Sat. 10–4; last admission 1 hr before closing.*

㊵ The huge **Royal Citadel** was built by Charles II in 1666 and still operates as a military center. ⊠ *End of the Hoe* ☎ *0870/225–4950* ⊕ *www. english-heritage.org.uk* 🎫 *£3* ☼ *May–Sept., Tues.; 1¼-hr guided tours at 2:30.*

㊶ The **Barbican,** east of the Royal Citadel, is the oldest surviving section of Plymouth. Here, Tudor houses and warehouses rise from a maze of narrow streets leading down to the fishing docks and harbor. Many of these buildings have become antiques shops, art shops, and bookstores. **㊷** By the harbor you can visit the **Mayflower Steps,** where the Pilgrims embarked in 1620; the **Mayflower Stone** marks the exact spot.

Near the Barbican, just off the Royal Parade, the largely 18th-century **㊸** **Merchant's House** is a museum of local history. ⊠ *33 St. Andrew's St.* ☎ *01752/304774* 🎫 *£1.10* ☼ *Apr.–Sept., Tues.–Fri. 10–1 and 2–5:30, Sat. 10–1 and 2–5.*

★ ☾ **㊹** The excellent **National Marine Aquarium,** on a central harborside site, presents aqueous environments, from a freshwater stream to a seawater wave tank and a huge "shark theater." Not to be missed are the extensive collection of sea horses, part of an important breeding program, and the chance to walk under sharks in the Mediterranean tank. Try to visit at shark-feeding time, which takes place three times a week. ⊠ *Rope Walk, Coxside* ☎ *01752/600301* ⊕ *www.national-aquarium.co.uk* 🎫 *£8* ☼ *Apr.–Oct., daily 10–6; Nov.–Mar., daily 10–5; last admission 1 hr before closing.*

Barbican **41**

Hoe **37**

Mayflower
Steps **42**

Merchant's
House **43**

National
Marine
Aquarium **44**

Plymouth
Dome **39**

Royal
Citadel **40**

Smeaton's
Tower **38**

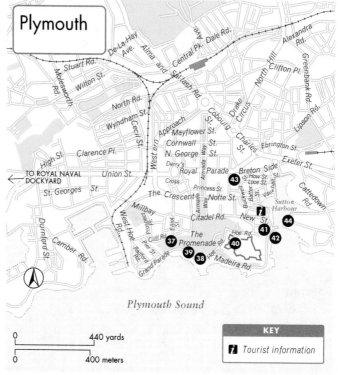

Plymouth Boat Cruises Ltd (⊠ 8 Anderton Rise, Millbrook, Torpoint ☎ 01752/822797) runs harbor and river sightseeing trips between Easter and October; boats depart every 30 minutes in peak season from Phoenix Wharf. **Tamar Cruising** (⊠ Cremyll Quay, Cremyll, Torpoint ☎ 01752/822105) has harbor cruises and longer scenic trips on the Rivers Tamar and Yealm between Easter and October. Boats leave from the Mayflower Steps and Cremyll Quay.

Where to Stay & Eat

£££££ ✕ **Tanners.** Brothers Chris and James Tanner produce their highly regarded, inventive cuisine in 15th-century Prysten House, one of the city's oldest buildings. On the eclectic, fixed-price menus are such lunch options as salad of chicken livers or roasted gilt-head bream with curried butter sauce. Evening choices include seared Cornish sea bass with tagliatelle, fennel, and vanilla sauce. One of the two lattice-windowed rooms has a well in it, and the other is hung with tapestries. The enclosed courtyard is ideal for alfresco dining. ⊠ *Finewell St.* ☎ *01752/252001* ⚑ *Reservations essential* ▤ *AE, MC, V* ✆ *Closed Sun. and Mon.*

£££–££££ ✕ **Piermaster's.** Fresh seafood landed at nearby piers, notably squid, mussels, and oysters, appears high on the menu at this Barbican eatery. The decoration is basic seafront, with a tiled floor and wooden tables. There are fixed-price menus at lunch and dinner, or you can choose individual selections. ⊠ *33 Southside St.* ☎ *01752/229345* ☰ *AE, MC, V* ⊘ *Closed Sun.*

££–££££ ⊞ **Copthorne Hotel Plymouth.** This efficient, modern chain hotel downtown delivers the expected comforts and amenities. Guest rooms are contemporary in style, with a coral, turquoise, and cream color scheme. The Burlington Restaurant has an Edwardian look, and there's also Bentley's, a no-smoking brasserie. ⊠ *Armada Way, PL1 1AR* ☎ *01752/ 224161, 0845/302–0003, 800/843–3311 in U.S.* ☎ *01752/670688* ⊕ *www.millenniumhotels.com* ⇆ *135 rooms* ⚘ *2 restaurants, cable TV with movies, indoor pool, gym, steam room, bar, business services, meeting rooms, free parking; no a/c* ☰ *AE, DC, MC, V* ⏐◯⏐ *BP.*

£ ⊞ **Bowling Green Hotel.** Friendly and unpretentious, this Victorian house overlooks Sir Francis Drake's bowling green on Plymouth Hoe. Pine pieces and floral print fabrics decorate the guest rooms. The house is convenient for shopping and sightseeing. ⊠ *9–10 Osborne Pl., Lockyer St., PL1 2PU* ☎ *01752/209090* ☎ *01752/209092* ⊕ *www.bowlinggreenhotel. com* ⇆ *12 rooms* ⚘ *Parking (fee); no a/c* ☰ *AE, MC, V* ⏐◯⏐ *BP.*

Nightlife & the Arts

Plymouth's **Theatre Royal** (⊠ Royal Parade ☎ 01752/267222) presents ballet, musicals, and plays by some of Britain's best companies.

Saltram

★ ㊺ *3½ mi east of Plymouth city center.*

A lovely 18th-century home with many of its original furnishings, Saltram was built around the remains of a late Tudor mansion. Its jewel is one of Britain's grandest neoclassical rooms, a vast, double-cube salon designed by Robert Adam and adorned with paintings by Sir Joshua Reynolds, first president of the Royal Academy of Arts, who was born nearby in 1723. The Axminster carpet was specially created for the room. Fine plasterwork adorns many rooms, and three have their original Chinese wallpaper. The house's outstanding garden includes rare trees and shrubs. Saltram appeared as Norland Park in the 1995 film *Sense and Sensibility.* There is a restaurant in the house and a cafeteria in the Coach House. ⊠ *South of A38, Plympton* ☎ *01752/333500* ⊕ *www.nationaltrust.org.uk* ⊡ *£6.60, garden only £3.30* ⊘ *House Apr.–Sept., Sat.–Thurs. noon–4:30; Oct., Sat.–Thurs. 11:30–3:30; last admission 30 mins before closing. Garden Apr.–Oct., Sat.–Thurs. 11–5; Nov.–Mar., Sat.–Thurs. 11–4.*

en route | From Plymouth, you have a choice of routes northeast to Exeter. If rugged, desolate, moorland scenery appeals to you, take A386 and B3212 northeast across Dartmoor. There is plenty to stir the imagination, no matter what the weather is.

Dartmoor National Park

10 mi north of Plymouth, 13 mi west of Exeter.

Even on a summer's day the scarred, brooding hills of this sprawling wilderness appear a likely haunt for such monsters as the hound of the

Baskervilles, and it seems entirely fitting that Sir Arthur Conan Doyle set his Sherlock Holmes thriller in this landscape. Sometimes the wet, peaty wasteland vanishes in rain and mist, although in clear weather you can see as far north as Exmoor. Much of northern Dartmoor consists of open heath and moorland, unspoiled by roads—wonderful walking and horseback-riding territory but an easy place to lose your bearings. Dartmoor's earliest inhabitants left behind stone monuments, and burial mounds, that help you envision prehistoric man roaming these pastures. Ponies, sheep, and birds are the main animals to be seen.

Several villages scattered along the borders of this 368-square-mi reserve— one-third of which is owned by Prince Charles—make useful bases for hiking excursions. Accommodations include simple inns and some elgant havens such as newly opened Bovey Castle. **Okehampton** is a main gateway, and other scenic spots include **Buckland-in-the-Moor,** a hamlet with thatched-roof cottages, **Widecombe-in-the-Moor,** whose church is known as the Cathedral of the Moor, and **Grimspound,** the Bronze Age site featured in Conan Doyle's most famous tale. Transmoor Link buses connect most of Dartmoor's towns and villages. Park information centers include the main **High Moorland Visitor Centre** in Princetown and centers in Newbridge, Postbridge, and Haytor. The park also works with tourist information centers in Ivybridge, Okehampton, Tavistock, and Totnes. ⊠ *Dartmoor National Park Authority, Parke, Haytor Rd., Bovey Tracey, Newton Abbot, TQ13 9JQ* ☎ *01626/832093* ⊕ *www.dartmoor-npa.gov.uk* ✆ *Free.*

Buckland Abbey

㊻ *8 mi north of Plymouth.*

This 13th-century Cistercian monastery became the home of Sir Francis Drake in 1581. Today it is filled with mementos of Drake and the Spanish Armada and has a restaurant. From Tavistock, take A386 south to Crapstone and then head west. ⊠ *Yelverton* ☎ *01822/853607* ⊕ *www.nationaltrust.org.uk* ✆ *£5.30, grounds only £2.90* ☉ *Mid-Feb.–Mar., Nov., and Dec., weekends 2–5; Apr.–Oct., Fri.–Wed. 10:30–5:30; last admission 45 mins before closing.*

> **off the beaten path**
>
> **GARDEN HOUSE –** Terraced around the remains of a 16th-century vicarage, this rich, naturalistic garden, developed since 1945, is vivid with wisterias cascading over ancient brick walls, azaleas, roses, and 6,000 other flowering plants, many of them rare. The 8-acre garden is a mile northeast of Buckland Abbey. ⊠ *Off A386, Buckland Monachorum, near Yelverton* ☎ *01822/854769* ⊕ *www. thegardenhouse.org.uk* ✆ *£4* ☉ *Mar.–Oct., daily 10:30–5.*

Cotehele House & Quay

★ **㊼** *4 mi west of Buckland Abbey, 15 mi north of Plymouth.*

This was formerly a busy port on the River Tamar, but it is now usually visited for the well-preserved late-medieval manor, home of the Edgcumbe family for centuries. The house has original furniture, tapestries, embroideries, and armor; there are also impressive gardens, a restored mill, and a quay museum. A limited number of visitors are allowed per day, so arrive early and be prepared to wait. Choose a bright day, because the rooms have no electric light. Shops, an arts and crafts gallery, a restaurant, and a tearoom provide other diversions. ⊠ *St. Dominick, north of Saltash, signposted off A390* ☎ *01579/352739* ⊕ *www.nationaltrust.org.uk* ⊠ *£7, gardens and mill only £4* ⊙ *House late Mar.–Sept., Sat.–Thurs. 11–5; Oct., Sat.–Thurs. 11–4:30. Mill Apr.–June and Sept., Sat.–Thurs. 1–5:30; July and Aug., daily 1–6; Oct. and Nov., Sat.–Thurs. 1–4:30. Gardens daily 10:30–dusk.*

Morwellham Quay

48 *2 mi east of Cotehele House & Quay, 5 mi southwest of Tavistock, 18 mi north of Plymouth.*

In the 19th century, Morwellham (pronounced More-wel–ham) Quay was England's main copper-exporting port, and it has been carefully restored as a working museum, with quay workers and coachmen in costume, and a copper mine open to visitors. ⚓ *Off A390, on a minor road off B3257* ☎ *01822/832766, 01822/833808 recorded information* ⊕ *www.morwellham-quay.co.uk* ⊠ *Apr.–Oct. £8.90, Nov.–Mar. £6* ⊙ *Easter–Oct., daily 10–6; Nov.–Easter, daily 10–4:30; last admission 2 hrs before closing.*

Where to Stay & Eat

★ **£££–££££** ✕🏨 **Horn of Plenty.** A "country house hotel and restaurant" is the way this establishment in a Georgian house describes itself. The restaurant (no lunch Monday) has magnificent views across the wooded, rhododendron-filled Tamar Valley. Peter Gorton's sophisticated cooking takes its inspiration from around the world; grilled sea bass with asparagus, tomato confit, and prawn sauce is a typical main course. There are three- and five-course fixed-price menus, the best value being Monday's potluck menu. A converted coach house and the main house contain sumptuously furnished guest rooms, many with balconies. ⊠ *Gulworthy PL19 8JD, 3 mi west of Tavistock on A390* ☎📠 *01822/832528* ⊕ *www.thehornofplenty.co.uk* 🛏 *9 rooms, 1 suite* 🖧 *Restaurant, in-room VCRs, meeting rooms, some pets allowed; no a/c* 🖃 *AE, MC, V* ⦿*| BP.*

Lydford Gorge

★ **49** *12 mi north of Morwellham Quay, 7 mi north of Tavistock, 9 mi east of Launceston, 24 mi north of Plymouth.*

The River Lyd has carved a spectacular 1½-mi-long chasm through the rock at Lydford Gorge, outside the village of Lydford, midway between Okehampton and Tavistock. Two paths follow the gorge past gurgling whirlpools and waterfalls with names such as the Devil's Cauldron and the White Lady. Sturdy footwear is recommended. Although the walk can be quite challenging, the paths can still get congested during busy periods. From Launceston, continue east along A30, following the signs. ⊠ *Off A386, Lydford* ☎ *01822/820320* ⊕ *www.nationaltrust.org.uk*

⊠ £4, free Nov.–Mar. ☉ Apr.–Sept., daily 10–5:30; Oct., daily 10–4; Nov.–Mar., daily 10:30–3 (walk restricted to main waterfall).

Where to Stay & Eat

£££ ✕ **Dartmoor Inn.** Locals and visitors alike make a beeline for this 16th-century pub, a good spot for snacks such as farmhouse sausages and mash or for something more substantial. You might choose a casserole of sea fish followed by a lemon and Strega (an herbal liqueur) tart. The pub is at the Lydford junction. ⊠ A386, Lydford ☎ 01822/820221 ⊟ MC, V ☉ Closed Mon. No dinner Sun.

££–£££ 🏨 **Castle Inn.** The heart of Lydford village, this 16th-century inn is next to Lydford Castle. Rose trellises frame its rosy brick facade, and the public rooms are snug, lamp-lit, and full of period clutter. Vivid colors are used in the guest rooms; one room has its own roof garden. ⊠ 1 mi off A386, Lydford EX20 4BH ☎ 01822/820241 🖷 01822/820454 ⊕ www.castleinnlydford.co.uk ➯ 8 rooms ⚘ Restaurant, bar, some pets allowed (fee); no a/c ⊟ AE, MC, V ⦿| BP.

Sports & the Outdoors

Cholwell Stables (⊠ Mary Tavy ☎ 01822/810526) has one- or two-hour or all-day horseback rides through some of Dartmoor's wilder tracts. Riders of all abilities are escorted, and equipment is provided. The stables are about 6 mi south of Lydford; call for directions.

Okehampton

🔟 8 mi northeast of Lydford Gorge, 28 mi north of Plymouth, 23 mi west of Exeter.

This town at the confluence of the Rivers East and West Okement is a good base for exploring North Dartmoor. It has numerous pubs and cottage tearooms, as well as a helpful tourist office. On the riverbank a mile southwest of the town center, the jagged ruins of the Norman **Okehampton Castle** occupy a verdant site with a picnic area and woodland walks. ☎ 01837/52844 ⊕ www.english-heritage.org.uk ⊠ £2.80 ☉ Apr.–Sept., daily 10–6.

The three floors of the informative **Museum of Dartmoor Life** contain interactive models, a working waterwheel, and photos of traditional farming methods. ⊠ 3 West St. ☎ 01837/52295 ⊕ www.museumofdartmoorlife.eclipse.co.uk ⊠ £2.50 ☉ Easter–May and Oct., Mon.–Sat. 10–4:30; June–Sept., daily 10–5; Nov.–Easter, weekdays 10–4.

Sports & the Outdoors

Skaigh Stables Farm (⊠ Skaigh La., Belstone, near Okehampton ☎ 01837/840917, 01837/840429 evenings) arranges day horseback rides and longer trips from Easter through September.

Chagford

🔟 9 mi southeast of Okehampton, 30 mi northeast of Plymouth.

Chagford was once a tin-weighing station and was an area of fierce fighting between the Roundheads and the Cavaliers during the Civil War. A

Roundhead was hanged in front of a pub on the village square. The town makes a convenient base from which to explore North Dartmoor.

The intriguing **Castle Drogo,** east of Chagford across A382, looks like a medieval fortress, complete with battlements, but construction actually took place between 1910 and 1930. Designed by Sir Edwin Lutyens for Julius Drewe, a wealthy grocer, the castle is only half finished (funds ran out). Inside, this magisterial pile combines medieval grandeur and early-20-century comforts (note the large bathrooms). Take the A30 Exeter–Okehampton road to reach the castle, which is 4 mi northeast of Chagford and 6 mi south of A30. ⊠ *Drewsteignton* ☎ *01647/433306* ⊕ *www.nationaltrust.org.uk* ☑ *£6.20, grounds only £3.15* ☉ *Castle late Mar.–Oct., Wed.–Mon. 11–5. Grounds daily 10:30–5:30 or dusk.*

Where to Stay & Eat

★ **£££££** ✕🏠 **Gidleigh Park.** One of England's foremost hotels and restaurants, lauded in poetry by Ted Hughes, occupies an enclave of landscaped gardens and streams within Dartmoor. Antiques and luxurious country-house furnishings fill the long, half-timber Tudor-style residence, and the extremely pricey contemporary French restaurant (reservations essential), directed by chef Michael Caines, has been showered with culinary awards. You may see why when you dig into the roast saddle of venison with braised chestnuts or the apple mousse with cider coulis. The locally pumped spring water is like no other. ⊠ *Gidleigh Park, TQ13 8HH* ☎ *01647/432367* 🖷 *01647/432574* ⊕ *www.gidleigh.com* ⇨ *14 rooms, 1 estate cottage* ⚇ *Restaurant, putting green, tennis court, croquet, meeting rooms, helipad, some pets allowed; no a/c* ⊟ *DC, MC, V* �t⊙l *BP.*

££ 🏠 **Easton Court.** Discerning travelers such as C. P. Snow, Margaret Mead, John Steinbeck, and Evelyn Waugh—who completed *Brideshead Revisited* here—made this their Dartmoor home-away-from-home. The Tudor thatched-roof manse has a garden and simple but elegant cottage-style rooms in an Edwardian wing; all rooms have views over the Teign Valley. ⊠ *Easton Cross, TQ13 8JL* ☎ *01647/433469* 🖷 *01647/433654* ⊕ *www.easton.co.uk* ⇨ *5 rooms* ⚇ *No a/c, no kids under 12, no smoking* ⊟ *MC, V* t⊙l *BP.*

Dartmouth

⑤② *35 mi east of Plymouth, 35 mi south of Exeter.*

An important port in the Middle Ages, Dartmouth is today a favorite haunt of yacht owners. Traces of its past include the old houses in Bayard's Cove near Lower Ferry, the 16th-century covered Butterwalk, and the two castles guarding the entrance to the River Dart. The Royal Naval College, built in 1905, dominates the town.

Where to Stay & Eat

£££ ✕ **Carved Angel Café.** Meals at this bright, light spot run the gamut from breakfasts and light lunches (a good value) to high teas (sandwiches, cakes, and scones) and fixed-price, bistro-type dinners that show Mediterranean and Thai influences. Leave room for dessert, too. Kids are made to feel especially welcome. ⊠ *7 Foss St.* ☎ *01803/834842* ▤ *MC, V* ⊘ *Closed Sun. No dinner Mon.–Thurs.*

££££–£££££ 🏛 **Royal Castle Hotel.** This hotel has truly earned the name "Royal"—several monarchs have slept here. Part of Dartmouth's historic waterfront (and consequently a hub of activity), it was built in the 17th century, reputedly of timber from wrecks of the Spanish Armada. Fireplaces and beamed ceilings are traditional features. Rooms come in different sizes and styles, but all are thoughtfully and richly furnished, with a liberal sprinkling of antiques. Number 6 has its own priest hole, a secret room used to hide Roman Catholic priests. ⊠ *11 The Quay, TQ6 9PS* ☎ *01803/833033* 🖷 *01803/835445* ⊕ *www.royalcastle.co.uk* ➳ *25 rooms ⚹ Restaurant, in-room data ports, cable TV, 2 bars, meeting rooms, some pets allowed; no a/c* ▤ *AE, MC, V* ⦿ *BP.*

> **en route** Two ferries cross the River Dart at Dartmouth; in summer, lines can be long, and you may want to try the inland route, heading west via A3122 to Halwell and then taking A381 north to Totnes.

Totnes

㊳ *9 mi northwest of Dartmouth, 28 mi southwest of Exeter.*

This busy market town preserves some of its past, particularly on summer Tuesdays and Saturdays, when most of the shopkeepers dress in Elizabethan costume. Its historic buildings include a guildhall and St. Mary's Church. You can climb up the hill in town to the ruins of **Totnes Castle**—a fine Norman motte and bailey design—for a wonderful view of Totnes and the River Dart. ☎ *01803/864406* ⊕ *www.english-heritage.org.uk* 🎟 *£2* ⊘ *Apr.–Sept., daily 10–6; Oct., daily 10–4.*

☉ Steam trains of the **South Devon Railway** run through 7 mi of the wooded Dart Valley between Totnes and Buckfastleigh, on the edge of Dartmoor. ⊠ *Littlehempston, near Totnes* ☎ *01364/642338* ⊕ *www.southdevonrailway.org* 🎟 *£8 round-trip* ⊘ *Easter–Oct., daily; call for winter times, including specials at Christmas and New Year's.*

Where to Stay & Eat

££ ✕🏛 **Cott Inn.** The exterior of this inn—a long, low, thatched building—has remained almost unchanged since 1320. Flagstone floors, thick ceiling beams, and open fireplaces are other signs of age. The snug bedrooms, tucked beneath the eaves, are furnished in modern style. Good rustic English meals are available from the restaurant, and there's a carvery with roasted meats; authentic Thai fare is available Monday–Wednesday evenings. ⊠ *Dartington TQ9 6HE, 2 mi west of Totnes on A385* ☎ *01803/863777* 🖷 *01803/866629* ⊕ *www.thecottinn.co.uk* ➳ *4 rooms ⚹ Restaurant, bar; no a/c* ▤ *MC, V* ⦿ *BP.*

Nightlife & the Arts

★ One of the foremost arts centers of the West Country, **Dartington Hall** (⊠ Dartington ☎ 01803/847070 ⊕ www.dartingtonarts.co.uk) lies 2 mi northwest of Totnes. Renovated in 1925 by the American millionaire Dorothy Elmhirst and her husband, the medieval estate was an experimental school before it evolved into an arts and education center. There are year-round concerts, film screenings, and exhibitions, usually with a contemporary slant. You can stay overnight in some rooms in the hall.

Shopping

Near Dartington Hall, a collection of stores and two restaurants inside an old cider press make up the **Dartington Cider Press Centre** (✉ Shinner Bridge, Dartington ☎ 01803/847500), which markets handmade Dartington crystal glassware, kitchenware, crafts, and toys from Devon and elsewhere. The farm shop sells fudge, ice cream, and cider, as well as local produce, and Cranks is an excellent vegetarian restaurant.

Brixham

⑤④ *10 mi southeast of Totnes by A385 and A3022.*

Brixham, at the southern point of Tor Bay, has kept much of its original charm, partly because it is still an active fishing village. Much of the catch goes straight to restaurants as far away as London. Sample fish-and-chips on the quayside, where there is a (surprisingly petite) full-scale reproduction of the vessel on which Sir Francis Drake circumnavigated the world.

Torbay

⑤⑤ *5 mi north of Brixham via A3022, 23 mi south of Exeter.*

The most important resort area in South Devon, Torbay envisions itself as the center of the "English Riviera." Since 1968, the towns of Paignton and Torquay (pronounced tor-*kee*) have been amalgamated under the common moniker of Torbay. Torquay is the supposed site of the hotel in the popular British television comedy *Fawlty Towers* and was the home of mystery writer Agatha Christie. Fans should check out the exhibition devoted to Christie at the town museum and her reconstructed study at Torre Abbey Mansion.

The town has shed its old-fashioned image in recent years, with modern hotels, luxury villas, and apartments that climb the hillsides above the harbor. Palm trees and other semitropical plants flourish in the seafront gardens. The sea is a clear and intense blue, and in summer the whole place has that unmistakable air that was once called Continental. To sun and swim, head for Anstey's Cove, a favorite spot for scuba divers, with more beaches farther along at neighboring Babbacombe.

★ For lovers of fine things, Torquay's chief attraction is the **Torre Abbey Mansion**, surrounded by parkland but close to the seafront. It was built on the site of the abbey razed in 1539, and you can still see traces of the old construction, including the Spanish Barn. The artistic riches lie within the main building: marine paintings, Victorian sculptures, Pre-Raphaelite windows, and drawings by William Blake. There's also a reconstruction of Agatha Christie's study. ✉ *King's Dr.* ☎ *01803/293593* ⊕ *www.torre-abbey.org.uk* ✆ *£3.50* ☺ *April–Oct., daily 9:30–6 (last admission at 5).*

Just outside Torbay lies the most Devonish hamlet in England, **Cockington**, which has thatched cottages, a 14th-century forge, and the square-towered Church of St. George and St. Mary. Repair to the Old Mill for a café lunch or head to the Drum Inn, designed by Sir Edwin Lutyens to be an archetypal pub. On the village outskirts lies Cockington Court— a grand estate with shops and an eatery. Although the whole has more than a touch of the faux (cottages that don't sell anything put up signs to this effect), it can be hard to resist this dreamy dollop of Devon.

Where to Stay & Eat

★ **£££** ✕ **Capers.** A place for anyone who likes enthusiasm along with the food, this small, select restaurant goes in for serious cooking. Local fish ranks high on the menu, accompanied by vegetables and herbs grown by the chef. Try sea bass with mint and spring onions, or curried crayfish risotto. ✉ *7 Lisburne Sq., Torquay* ☎ *01803/291177* ▭ *AE, MC, V* ☻ *Closed Sun. and 1 wk mid-Aug. No lunch.*

££ ✕🏠 **Mulberry House.** Healthy fare—there are cholesterol notes—is a draw at this simple but sophisticated restaurant with rooms, where dishes range from homemade tagliatelle to Brixham sole fillets to ragout of Devon lamb. (The restaurant is closed to the public, though not to overnight guests, Monday and Tuesday; call for other hours.) Eating here is like dining in someone's private home; the furnishings are light and airy, and service is personable and friendly. Upstairs, guest rooms are similarly bright and well cared for, with plants and antiques. One has a private bathroom that is adjacent to the room. ✉ *1 Scarborough Rd., Torquay TQ2 5UJ* ☎ *01803/213639* 🛏 *3 rooms* ⚭ *Restaurant; no smoking* ▭ *No credit cards.*

★ **£££££** 🏠 **The Imperial.** This is arguably Devon's most luxurious hotel, perched above the sea, overlooking Torbay. Magnificent gardens surround the property, and the interior of the 1866 hotel is, well, imperial, with chandeliers, marble floors, and the general air of a bygone world. Most of the traditionally furnished bedrooms are large and comfortable, and many have private balconies. ✉ *Park Hill Rd., Torquay, TQ1 2DG* ☎ *01803/294301* 🖶 *01803/298293* ⊕ *www.paramount-hotels.co.uk* 🛏 *153 rooms, 17 suites* ⚭ *2 restaurants, cable TV with movies, tennis court, 2 pools (1 indoor), health club, sauna, squash, business services, meeting rooms; no a/c* ▭ *AE, DC, MC, V* ⃝⃒ *BP.*

££ 🏠 **Fairmount House Hotel.** Near the village of Cockington, on the edge of Torquay, this relaxed, family-run Victorian hotel has a pleasant, south-facing garden. Guest rooms are solidly furnished; two have direct access to the garden, as does the Conservatory Bar. The dining room favors homegrown and local produce. ✉ *Herbert Rd., Chelston, Torquay, TQ2 6RW* ☎🖶 *01803/605446* ⊕ *www.fairmounthousehotel.co.uk* 🛏 *8 rooms* ⚭ *Dining room, bar, some pets allowed (fee); no a/c, no room phones* ▭ *MC, V* ⃝⃒ *BP.*

Exeter

23 mi north of Torbay, 48 mi northeast of Plymouth, 85 mi southwest of Bristol, 205 mi southwest of London.

Devon's county seat, Exeter, has been the capital of the region since the Romans established a fortress here 2,000 years ago. Little evidence of the Roman occupation exists, apart from the great city walls. Although it was heavily bombed in 1942, Exeter retains much of its medieval character, as well as examples of the gracious architecture of the 18th and 19th centuries.

56 At the heart of Exeter, the great Gothic **Cathedral of St. Peter** was begun in 1275 and completed almost a century later. Its twin towers are even older survivors of an earlier Norman cathedral. Rising from a forest of ribbed columns, the nave's 300-foot stretch of unbroken Gothic vaulting is the longest in the world. Myriad statues, tombs, and memorial plaques adorn the interior. In the minstrels' gallery, high up on the left of the nave, stands a group of carved figures singing and playing musical instruments, including bagpipes. The **Close**, a pleasant green space for relaxing on a sunny day, surrounds the cathedral. Don't miss the 400-year-old door to No. 10, the bishop of Crediton's house, ornately carved with angels' and lions' heads. ⊠ *Cathedral Close* ☎ *01392/214219* ⊕ *www.exeter-cathedral.org.uk* 🖾 *£3.50 suggested donation* ☉ *Weekdays 7:30–6:30, Sat. 7:30–5, Sun. 8–7:30. Free guided tours Apr.–Oct., weekdays at 11 and 2:30, Sat. at 11, Sun. at 4; July–Sept., Mon.–Sat. at 12:30.*

57 With its half-timber facade bearing the coat of arms of Elizabeth I, **Mol's Coffee House** (now a store), on the corner of Cathedral Close, is redolent of bygone times. It is said that Sir Francis Drake met his admirals here to plan strategy against the Spanish Armada in 1588. Opposite the **58** cathedral, the 1769 **Royal Clarence Hotel** was England's first inn to be described as a "hotel"—a designation applied by an enterprising French manager. It is named after the duchess of Clarence, who stayed here in 1827 on her way to visit her husband, the future William IV.

59 The **Guildhall,** just behind the Close, is said to be the oldest municipal building in the country still in use. The current hall, with its Renaissance portico, dates from 1330, although a guildhall has occupied this site since at least 1160. Its timber-braced roof, one of the earliest in England, dates from about 1460. ⊠ *High St.* ☎ *01392/665500* 🖾 *Free* ☉ *Weekdays 10:30–1 and 2–4, Sat. 10–noon (alternate Sat. only in winter), unless in use for a civic function.*

★ **60** Devon's **Royal Albert Memorial Museum** houses natural-history displays, a superb collection of Exeter silverware, and the work of some West Country artists. There is also an excellent international gallery and a fine archaeological section. ⊠ *Queen St.* ☎ *01392/265858* ⊕ *www.exeter.gov.uk* 🖾 *Free* ☉ *Mon.–Sat. 10–5.*

61 The **Rougemont Gardens** (⊠ Off Queen St.), behind the Royal Albert Memorial Museum, were laid out at the end of the 18th century. The land was once part of the defensive ditch of Rougemont Castle, built in 1068 by decree of William the Conqueror. The gardens contain the original Norman gatehouse and the remains of the Roman city wall, the latter forming part of the ancient castle's outer wall; nothing else remains of the castle.

62 Just off the High Street, the **Underground Passages,** which once served as conduits for fresh water, are the only medieval vaulted passages open to the public in England. They date to the mid-14th century, although many now have a Victorian veneer. An exhibition and video precede the 40-

Cathedral of
St. Peter **56**

Custom House . **63**

Guildhall **59**

Mol's Coffee
House **57**

Quay House ... **64**

Rougemont
Gardens **61**

Royal Albert
Memorial
Museum **60**

Royal Clarence
Hotel **58**

Underground
Passages **62**

minute guided tour. Many of the passages are narrow and low: be pre-pared to stoop. ⊠ *Romangate Passage* ☎ *01392/665887* ⊕ *www.exeter.gov.uk* 🎫 *June–Sept. £3.75, Oct.–May £3* ⊘ *June–Sept. and school vacations, Mon.–Sat. 10–5; Oct.–May, Tues.–Fri. noon–5, Sat. 10–5.*

㊻ Exeter's historic waterfront on the River Exe was the center of the city's medieval wool industry, and the **Custom House,** built in 1682 on The Quay, attests to the city's prosperity. Victorian warehouses flank the city's earliest surviving brick building.

> **need a break?**
>
> At **The Prospect Inn** (⊠ The Quay ☎ 01392/273152) you can contemplate the quayside comings and goings over a pint of beer or ale and a hot or cold meal. The nautical theme comes through in pictures and the ship's wheel hanging from the ceiling.

㊽ The **Quay House,** a late-17th-century stone warehouse, houses the Heritage Centre, with documents on the maritime history of the city and an audiovisual display. ⊠ *The Quay* ☎ *01392/265213* 🎫 *Free* ⊘ *Apr.–Oct., daily 10–5; Nov.–Mar., weekends 11–4.*

off the beaten path

POWDERHAM CASTLE – Seat of the earls of Devon, this notable stately home 8 mi south of Exeter is famed for its staircase hall, a soaring fantasia of white stuccowork on a turquoise background, constructed in 1739–69. Other sumptuous rooms, adorned with family portraits by Sir Godfrey Kneller and Sir Joshua Reynolds, were used in the Merchant Ivory film *Remains of the Day*. A tower built in 1400 by Sir Philip Courtenay, ancestor of the current owners, stands in the deer park. The restaurant serves traditional English fare, and there's a farm shop and plant center. ⊠ *A379, Kenton* ☎ *01626/ 890243* ⊕ *www.powderham.co.uk* ⊠ *£7.20* ☉ *Apr.–Oct., Sun.–Fri. 10–5:30.*

Where to Stay & Eat

★ **£££££** ✕ **St. Olaves.** One of the finest dining spots in the West Country, this restaurant in a Georgian house with a walled garden is part of St. Olaves Court Hotel. From the fixed-price menus, you might try saddle of venison with thyme, roasted root vegetables, and a bacon, mushroom, and lentil sauce, or wild mushroom risotto; among the desserts are blackberry mousse with an almond tuille and blackberry sorbet. The bar menu is a cheaper alternative at lunchtime. ⊠ *Mary Arches St.* ☎ *01392/217736* ▭ *MC, V.*

£–££ ✕ **Hansons.** Near the cathedral, this spot is ideal for lunch, coffee, or snacks when you're seeing the sights. You can also sample one of Devon's famous cream teas, served with jam, scones, and clotted cream. ⊠ *1 Cathedral Close* ☎ *01392/276913* ▭ *AE, DC, MC, V* ☉ *Closed Sun. No dinner.*

£–££ ✕ **Herbie's.** A mellow stop for lunch or dinner, this friendly, no-frills vegetarian restaurant is ideal for unwinding over leisurely conversation. You can snack on pita bread with hummus and cottage cheese fillings, or tackle the carrot and cashew nut loaf or spinach and mushroom lasagna. All wines and the superb ice cream are organic. ⊠ *15 North St.* ☎ *01392/ 258473* ▭ *MC, V* ☉ *Closed Sun. No dinner Mon.*

Fodor's Choice ★

£–££ ✕ **Ship Inn.** Here you can lift a tankard of stout in the very rooms where Sir Francis Drake and Sir Walter Raleigh enjoyed their ale. Drake, in fact, once wrote, "Next to mine own shippe, I do most love that old 'Shippe' in Exon." The pub dishes out casual bar fare, and the upstairs restaurant serves the usual grilled lemon sole and other English dishes. ⊠ *St. Martin's La.* ☎ *01392/272040* ▭ *MC, V* ☉ *No dinner Sat.*

★ **££££** ✕🏨 **Royal Clarence Hotel.** Master chef Michael Caines (of Gidleigh Park fame) acquired this antique hotel in a wonderful location within the Cathedral Close in 2003. The limelight now rests firmly on the ultrachic ground-floor restaurant, with its smart pinstripe upholstery and top-notch French-accented contemporary fare. A more relaxed café-bar serves coffee, snacks, and full meals throughout the day; there's live jazz some evenings. The modern style of the dining areas contrasts with the traditional approach of the rest of the hotel, which has many oak-paneled rooms (at this writing, refurbishment was planned). ⊠ *Cathedral Yard, EX1 1HB* ☎ *01392/319955* 🖷 *01392/439423* ⊕ *www.michaelcaines. com* ⇨ *56 rooms* ♿ *Restaurant, 2 bars, meeting rooms, some pets allowed (fee); no a/c* ▭ *AE, DC, MC, V.*

£££ ✕▥ **Hotel Barcelona.** Sister to the Kandinsky in Cheltenham, this hip, classy hotel occupies the old redbrick eye hospital, as the long corridors and big elevators testify. Bright, Gaudí-esque furnishings and ornaments from the 1930s to the 1960s give the rooms flair, and the aquamarine bathrooms with mosaic tiling are luxurious. You can find Spanish and other Mediterranean flavors in the pavilion-like bistro-restaurant, Café Paradiso. ⊠ *Magdalen St., EX2 4HY* ☎ *01392/281000* 🖷 *01392/ 281001* ⊕ *www.hotelbarcelona-uk.com* ➬ *46 rooms* ⚸ *Restaurant, in-room data ports, cable TV with movies, in-room VCRs, nightclub, meeting rooms, some pets allowed (fee); no a/c* ☰ *AE, DC, MC, V.*

££ ✕▥ **White Hart.** Guests have been welcomed to this inn since the 15th century, and it is said that Oliver Cromwell stabled his horses here. Beyond the lovely cobbled entrance, the main building retains all the trappings of a period inn—beams, stone walls, a central courtyard—but there are also fully modern bedrooms in one wing. The hotel has an English restaurant, a wine bar, and a more casual ale-and-port house. Try the local salmon or traditional West Country beefsteaks. ⊠ *66 South St., EX1 1EE* ☎ *01392/279897* 🖷 *01392/250159* ⊕ *www.roomattheinn. info* ➬ *55 rooms* ⚸ *Restaurant, bar, wine bar; no a/c* ☰ *AE, DC, MC, V* ⦿ *BP.*

£ ▥ **Hotel Maurice.** There's nothing fancy in this quiet hotel close by Exeter Central train station, just clean, neat, and cheerful rooms, small in size but more than adequate for a night or two. The main benefit is the location in a calm Georgian square, just a stroll away from all the sights. ⊠ *5 Bystock Terr., EX4 4HY* ☎ *01392/213079* ⊕ *www. hotelmaurice.eclipse.co.uk* ➬ *8 rooms* ⚸ *No a/c, no smoking* ☰ *MC, V* ⦿ *BP.*

Nightlife & the Arts

Among the best known of the West Country's festivals, the **Exeter Festival** (☎ 01392/265205) mixes musical and theater events each July. Some of London's best companies often stage plays at the **Northcott Theatre** (⊠ Stocker Rd. ☎ 01392/493493).

Shopping

Until 1882 Exeter was the silver-assay office for the West Country, and it's possible to find Exeter silver, particularly spoons, in some antiques and silverware stores. The earliest example of Exeter silver (now a museum piece) dates from 1218, and Victorian pieces are still sold. The Exeter assay mark is three castles. **Bruford's of Exeter** (⊠ 17 The Guildhall Centre, Queen St. ☎ 01392/254901) stocks antique jewelry and silver.

Topsham

⑥⑤ *4 mi southeast of Exeter on B3182.*

The town of Topsham is full of narrow streets and hidden courtyards. This once-bustling port remains rich in 18th-century houses and inns. Occupying a 17th-century Dutch-style merchant's house beside the river, the **Topsham Museum** includes period-furnished rooms and eclectic displays about everything from local history to wildlife; note also the memorabilia belonging to the late actress Vivien Leigh. ⊠ *25 The Strand* ☎ *01392/ 873244* 🎟 *Free* ☉ *Easter–Oct., Mon., Wed., and weekends 2–5.*

★ The 16-sided, nearly **A la Ronde,** surely one of the most unusual houses in England, was built in 1798 by two cousins inspired by the Church of San Vitale in Ravenna, Italy. Among the 18th- and 19th-century curiosities here is an elaborate display of feathers and shells. The house is 5 mi south of Topsham. ⊠ *Summer La., on A376 near Exmouth* ☎ *01395/265514* ⊕ *www.nationaltrust.org.uk* ✏ *£4.20* ⊙ *Apr.–Oct., Sun.–Thurs. 11–5:30; last admission at 5.*

> **en route**

The **Jurassic Coast** (⊕ www.swgfl.org.uk/jurassic), from Exmouth to Studland Bay in Dorset, 95 mi to the east, has been designated a World Heritage Site because of the rich geological record of ancient rocks and fossils exposed here. The reddish, grass-topped cliffs of the region are punctuated by quiet seaside resorts such as Budleigh Salterton, Sidmouth, and Seaton.

Beer

🚵 *22 mi east of Topsham, 26 mi east of Exeter, 33 mi south of Taunton.*

Beer, just outside Seaton, was once a favorite smugglers' haunt, and this fishing village has remained fairly unchanged. It was the source of the white stone used for numerous Devon churches, Exeter Cathedral, and, farther afield, Winchester Cathedral, Westminster Abbey, and the Tower of London. A tour of the **Beer Quarry Caves,** worked from Roman times until 1900, explores the impressive underground network. A small exhibition includes tools and examples of carved stone. ⊠ *Quarry La.* ☎ *01297/680282* ⊕ *www.beerquarrycaves.fsnet.co.uk* ✏ *£5* ⊙ *Easter–Sept., daily 10–5:30; Oct., daily 11–4:30; last admission 30 mins before closing.*

Honiton

🚵 *10 mi northwest of Beer on A3052/A375, 19 mi south of Taunton.*

Handsome Georgian houses line Honiton's long High Street. Modern storefronts have intruded, but the original facades remain at second-floor level. For 300 years the town was known for lace-making, and the industry was revived when Queen Victoria selected the fabric for her wedding veil in 1840. Lace has not been made here commercially since the early 20th century, but individuals keep up the craft.

After viewing the splendid collection of lace at **Allhallows Museum**—in what is claimed to be the town's oldest building—it's worth delving into the antiques shops where prized early examples are sold. ⊠ *High St.* ☎ *01404/44966* ⊕ *www.honitonmuseum.co.uk* ✏ *£2* ⊙ *Easter–Oct., weekdays 9:30–4:30, Sat. 9:30–1.*

Where to Stay & Eat

££–£££ ✕ **Dominoes.** For a satisfying lunch or dinner, try this wine bar, extravagantly decorated with murals, cherubs, and other Parisian-style frippery. You can get everything from nachos to rack of lamb. ⊠ *178 High St.* ☎ *01404/47707* ▤ *MC, V.*

££££ ✕▨ **Combe House.** Rolling parkland surrounds this luxurious Elizabethan manor house. From the imposing Great Hall, with its huge, open fireplace, to the spacious, individually decorated bedrooms, the emphasis is on country-house style that unites antiques and modern comfort. The restaurant (fixed-price menu) prepares such creations as lobster-filled ravioli and scallop risotto, and there's a wide-ranging wine list. Hotel guests can fish on a 1½-mi stretch of the River Otter and explore Gittisham, just west of Honiton, once described as "the ideal English village" by Prince Charles. ⊠ *Gittisham, EX14 3AD* ☎ *01404/540400* 🖷 *01404/46004* ⊕ *www. thishotel.com* ⌂ *14 rooms, 1 suite* ⚑ *Restaurant, fishing, meeting rooms, some pets allowed (fee); no a/c* ☰ *AE, DC, MC, V* ⱢⱢ *BP.*

Shopping
Honiton has several dozen fine antiques stores. The **Lace Shop** (⊠ 44 High St. ☎ 01404/42416) has everything needed for lace-making and examples of old and new work for sale.

Montacute House

★ ⑥⑧ *30 mi northeast of Honiton on A30 and A303, 30 mi southeast of Taunton, 44 mi south of Bristol.*

Rich with Elizabethan details, this house was built in the late 16th century of the golden limestone found in this part of Somerset and used in houses small and large throughout the area. The 189-foot-long gallery brims with Elizabethan and Jacobean portraits, most on loan from the National Portrait Gallery, and the house also contains a good collection of textiles. Pick a bright day to visit: some rooms do not have electric light. ⊠ *A3088, Yeovil, turn south off A303 at Stoke sub Hamdon* ☎ *01935/823289* ⊕ *www.nationaltrust.org.uk* 🖭 *£6.90, garden and park only £3.70 mid-Mar.–Oct., £2 Nov.–mid-Mar* ⊘ *House mid-Mar.–Oct., Wed.–Mon. 11–5; last admission at 4:30. Garden and park mid-Mar.–Oct., Wed.–Mon. 11–6 or dusk; Nov.–mid-Mar., Wed.–Sun. 11–4.*

Where to Stay & Eat
££ ✕🖼 **King's Arms.** This nicely decorated 16th-century inn was constructed with the same warm golden stone as nearby Montacute House. Much of the interior incorporates the local limestone, harmoniously integrated with details such as an engraved archway rescued from Coventry Cathedral (bombed in World War II). The pastel guest rooms are quite modern, however. The menu in the Abbey Room and Cottage restaurants lists a huge selection of dishes, but the fare is mostly British, from rib-eye steak to baked duck breast. ⊠ *Bishopston, Montacute, TA15 6UU* ☎ *01935/822513* 🖷 *01935/826549* ✉ *kingsarms@realemail.co.uk* ⌂ *15 rooms* ⚑ *2 restaurants, bar; no a/c* ☰ *AE, MC, V* ⱢⱢ *BP.*

Yeovilton

⑥⑨ *7 mi north of Yeovil.*

☾ The village of Yeovilton has a Royal Naval Air Station. The **Fleet Air Arm Museum** displays more than 50 historic aircraft, among them the Concorde 002. The spectacular "Carrier" exhibit includes a simulated helicopter ride over the ocean to an aircraft carrier and a unique re-creation of the flight deck of a working carrier, complete with 12 planes from the 1960s and '70s. ⊹ *Royal Naval Air Station Yeovilton, signposted on B3151* *at Ilchester from A303 or A37* ☎ *01935/840565* ⊕ *www.fleetairarm. com* 🖃 *£9.50* ⊙ *Apr.–Oct., daily 10–5:30; Nov.–Mar., daily 10–4:30.*

Cadbury Castle

⑳ *7 mi northeast of Yeovilton, 17 mi south of Wells.*

Cadbury Castle is said to be the site of Camelot—it's one among several contenders for the honor. Glastonbury Tor, rising dramatically in the distance across the plain, adds to the atmosphere of Arthurian romance. A legend says that every seven years the hillside opens and Arthur and his followers ride forth to water their horses at nearby Sutton Montis. Cadbury Castle is, in fact, an Iron Age fort (circa 650 BC), with grass-covered, earthen ramparts forming a green wall 300 feet above the surrounding fields. You can park off A303 and then walk about a mile, mostly uphill, to the site; the path is signposted. ⊠ *Off A303, South Cadbury.*

THE WEST COUNTRY A TO Z

To research prices, get advice from other travelers, and book travel arrangements, visit www.fodors.com.

AIRPORTS

Bristol International Airport, a few miles southwest of the city on the A38, has flights to and from destinations in Britain and Europe. Plymouth has a small airport 3 mi from town. Exeter International Airport is 5 mi east of Exeter, 2 mi from the M5 motorway. Newquay Airport, 5 mi east of town, has daily flights to London Stansted and London Gatwick. All four airports have flights to the Isles of Scilly in summer; Land's End Airport also connects daily, and British International operates helicopter flights to the islands from Penzance. Islands of Scilly Travel (⇨ Boat & Ferry Travel) runs the Skybus air service to St. Mary's from Land's End, Newquay, and, from March through September, Southampton, Bristol, and Exeter.

🚹 **Bristol International Airport** ⊠ Bridgwater Rd., Lulsgate, Bristol ☎ 0870/121-2747 ⊕ www.bristolairport.co.uk. **British International** ⊠ Penzance Airport, A30, Penzance ☎ 01736/363871 ⊕ www.scillyhelicopter.co.uk. **Exeter International Airport** ⊠ M5, Junction 29, Exeter ☎ 01392/367433 ⊕ www.exeter-airport.co.uk. **Newquay Airport** ⊠ Carloggas, Newquay ☎ 01637/860600 ⊕ www.newquayairport.com. **Plymouth City Airport** ⊠ Plymbridge Rd., Plymouth ☎ 01752/204090 ⊕ www. sutton-harbour.co.uk. **Skybus** ⊠ Land's End Airport, St. Just ☎ 0845/710-5555, 01736/334220 outside U.K. ⊕ www.ios-travel.co.uk.

BOAT & FERRY TRAVEL

Isles of Scilly Travel operates ferries from Penzance to St. Mary's at least four times weekly from late March through early November. Travel time is 2 hours and 40 minutes, and the trip can be rough.

🚹 **Isles of Scilly Travel** ☎ 0845/710-5555, 01736/334220 outside U.K. ⊕ www.ios-travel. co.uk.

BUS TRAVEL

National Express buses leave London's Victoria Coach Station for Bristol (2½ hours), Exeter (4¼ hours), Plymouth (4¾ hours), and Penzance (about 9 hours).

The bus company Stagecoach Devon covers mainly South Devon. First runs most of the services in North Devon, in Plymouth, and throughout Cornwall. Truronian operates in West Cornwall. Ask any of these companies about money-saving one-, three-, and seven-day Explorer passes good for unlimited travel. Buses serve the main towns, but it's best to have a car if you want to explore off the beaten path. For public transportation information, contact Traveline.

FARES &
SCHEDULES

🚹 **First** ☎ 01752/402060 for Plymouth, North Devon, and East Cornwall, 01209/719988 for West Cornwall ⊕ www.firstgroup.com. **National Express** ☎ 0874/580-8080 ⊕ www. nationalexpress.com. **Stagecoach Devon** ☎ 0870/608-2608 ⊕ www.stagecoachbus. com. **Traveline** ☎ 0870/608-2608 ⊕ www.traveline.org.uk. **Truronian** ☎ 01872/ 273453 ⊕ www.truronian.co.uk.

CAR RENTAL
🚹 **Local Agencies Avis** ✉ 29 Marsh Green Rd., Marsh Barton Trading Estate, Exeter ☎ 01392/259713 ✉ 20 Commercial Rd., Coxside, Plymouth ☎ 01752/221550 ✉ Tregolls Rd., Truro ☎ 01872/262226. **Enterprise Rent-a-Car** ✉ 8 Octagon St., off Union St., Plymouth ☎ 01752/601000. **Hertz** ✉ Albert Crescent, St. Philips, Bristol ☎ 0117/ 977-9777 ✉ Sutton Rd., Coxside, Plymouth ☎ 01752/207207.

CAR TRAVEL
The fastest route from London to the West Country is via the M4 and M5 motorways, bypassing Bristol (115 mi) and heading south to Exeter, in Devon (172 mi). The main roads heading west are A30—which burrows through the center of Devon and Cornwall all the way to Land's End at the tip of Cornwall—A39 (near the northern shore of the peninsula), and A38 (near the southern shore of the peninsula, south of Dartmoor and taking in Plymouth). West of Plymouth, there are few main roads, which results in heavy traffic in summer.

ROAD
CONDITIONS

Driving can be tricky, especially as you travel farther west. Most small roads are twisting country lanes flanked by high stone walls and thick hedges that severely restrict visibility.

EMERGENCIES
🚹 **Ambulance, fire, police** ☎ 999. **Derriford Hospital** ✉ Derriford, Plymouth ☎ 01752/ 777111. **Royal Cornwall Hospital (Treliske)** ✉ A390, Higher Town, Truro ☎ 01872/250000. **Royal Devon and Exeter Hospital** ✉ Wonford Rd., Exeter ☎ 01392/411611.

NATIONAL PARKS
🚹 **Dartmoor National Park Authority** ✉ Parke, Haytor Rd., Bovey Tracey, Newton Abbot, TQ13 9JQ ☎ 01626/832093 ⊕ www.dartmoor-npa.gov.uk. **Exmoor National Park Authority** ✉ Exmoor House, Dulverton, TA22 9HL ☎ 01398/323665 ⊕ www.exmoor-nationalpark.gov.uk.

OUTDOORS & SPORTS
WALKING

For information about walking in Dartmoor or Exmoor, contact the National Parks Authority (⇨ National Parks). The South West Coast Path Association has information about the 630-mi-long coastal path.
🚹 **South West Coast Path Association** ✉ Windlestraw, Penquit, Ermington, PL21 0LU ☎ 01752/896237 ⊕ www.swcp.org.uk.

TOURS

South West Tourism (⇨ Visitor Information) and local tourist information centers have lists of qualified guides. West Country Tour Guides (Blue Badge) offers walking tours around Plymouth's old town and can arrange tours throughout Devon and Cornwall.

🖪 **West Country Tourist Guides (Blue Badge)** ☎ 01726/813463 ⊕ www.luxsoft. demon.co.uk/awctg.

TRAIN TRAVEL

First Great Western and South West Trains serve the region from London's Paddington and Waterloo stations; contact National Rail Enquiries for details. Average travel time to Exeter is 2½ hours; to Plymouth, 3½ hours; and to Penzance, about 5½ hours.

CUTTING COSTS Regional Rail Rover tickets provide 8 days' unlimited travel throughout the West Country in any 15-day period, and localized Rovers cover Devon or Cornwall.

🖪 **National Rail Enquiries** ☎ 0845/748-4950 ⊕ www.nationalrail.co.uk.

TRAVEL AGENCIES

🖪 Local Agent Referrals **American Express** ⊠ 139 Armada Way, Plymouth ☎ 01752/502706. **Thomas Cook** ⊠ c/o HSBC Bank, 38 High St., Exeter ☎ 01392/425712 ⊠ 9 Old Town St., Plymouth ☎ 01752/612600.

VISITOR INFORMATION

Local tourist information centers are usually open Monday–Saturday 9:30–5:30; they are listed after the regional offices below by town.

🖪 **South West Tourism** ⊠ Woodwater Park, Pynes Hill, Exeter, EX2 5WT ☎ 0870/442-0880 🗗 0870/442-0881 ⊕ www.westcountrynow.com. **Cornwall Tourist Board** ⊠ Pydar House, Pydar St., Truro, TR1 1EA ☎ 01872/322900 🗗 01872/322895 ⊕ www. cornwalltouristboard.co.uk. **Devon Tourist Information Service** ⌗ Box 55, Barnstaple, EX32 8YR ☎ 0870/608-5531, 1392/382168 from abroad ⊕ www.discoverdevon.com. **Somerset Visitor Centre** ⊠ Sedgemoor Service Station, M5 Southbound ☎ 01934/750833 🗗 01934/750646 ⊕ www.somerset.gov.uk.

Bristol ⊠ The Annexe, Wildscreen Walk, Harbourside, BS1 5DB ☎ 0906/711-2191 at cost of 50p per min, 0845/408-0474 accommodations line ⊠ Galleries Shopping Centre, Broadmead, 🕾 no telephone ⊕ www.visitbristol.co.uk. **Exeter** ⊠ Civic Centre, Paris St., EX1 1JJ ☎ 01392/265700 ⊕ www.exeter.gov.uk. **Falmouth** ⊠ 28 Killigrew St., TR11 3PN ☎ 01326/312300 ⊕ www.go-cornwall.com. **Glastonbury** ⊠ The Tribunal, High St., BA6 9DP ☎ 01458/832954 ⊕ www.glastonburytic.co.uk. **Isles of Scilly** ⊠ Hugh St., Hugh Town, St. Mary's, TR21 0LL ☎ 01720/422536 ⊕ www.simplyscilly.co.uk. **Okehampton** ⊠ Okehampton Museum Yard, West St., EX20 1HQ ☎ 01837/53020 ⊕ www. okehamptondevon.co.uk. **Penzance** ⊠ Station Approach, TR18 2NF ☎ 01736/362207 ⊕ www.go-cornwall.com. **Plymouth** ⊠ Island House, 9 The Barbican, PL1 2LS ☎ 0870/225-4950 ⊕ www.visitplymouth.co.uk. **Princetown** ⊠ Tavistock Rd., PL20 6QF ☎ 01822/890414 ⊕ www.dartmoor-npa.gov.uk. **St. Ives** ⊠ The Guildhall, Street-an-Pol, TR26 2DS ☎ 01736/796297 ⊕ www.go-cornwall.com. **Taunton** ⊠ Paul St., TA1 3XZ ☎ 01823/336344 ⊕ www.tauntondeane.gov.uk. **Truro** ⊠ City Hall, Boscawen St., TR1 2NE ☎ 01872/274555 ⊕ www.truro.gov.uk. **Wells** ⊠ Town Hall, Market Pl., BA5 2RB ☎ 01749/672552 ⊕ www.wells-uk.com.

THE THAMES VALLEY

WINDSOR, HENLEY-ON-THAMES, OXFORD, BLENHEIM PALACE

5

GO FOR BAROQUE IN A DUKE'S DIGS
at stately Blenheim Palace ⇨*p.294*

COUNT THE DREAMING SPIRES
of Oxford's venerable colleges ⇨*p.283*

SEE THE QUEEN'S ROYAL RETREAT
at Windsor Castle ⇨*p.269*

PICK UP THE PACE
on a Thames Path hike near Marlow ⇨*p.279*

SCORE BARGAINS BY THE ARMFUL
at Bicester Village Outlet ⇨*p.293*

ROW, ROW YOUR BOAT
to watch the Henley Royal Regatta ⇨*p.282*

PLAY EDWARDIAN GRANDEE
during a stay at posh Cliveden ⇨*p.278*

DRINK TO LEWIS CARROLL AND ALICE
at the creeper-draped Trout Inn ⇨*p.289*

Updated by
Catherine
Belonogoff

THE RIVER GLIDETH AT HIS OWN SWEET WILL was how Wordsworth described the Thames in "Upon Westminster Bridge." Like other great rivers, such as the Seine and the Danube, it creates the illusion of flowing not only through the prosperous countryside of Berkshire and Oxfordshire, but through long centuries of history, too. The past seems to rise from its swiftly moving waters like an intangible mist. In London, where it's a broad, oily stream, the Thames speeds almost silently past great buildings, menacingly impressive. Higher upstream it's a busy part of the living landscape, flooding meadows in spring and fall and rippling past places holding significance not just for England but also the world. Runnymede is one of these. Here, on a riverside greensward, the Magna Carta was signed, a crucial step in the Western world's progress toward democracy.

Nearby rises the medieval bulk of Windsor Castle, home of monarchs from eight successive royal houses. Anyone who wants to understand the mystique of the British monarchy should visit Windsor, where a fraction of the current Queen's vast wealth is on display in surroundings of heraldic splendor. Farther upstream lie the quadrangles and turrets of Oxford, where generations of the ruling elite have been educated. Close by Oxford are the storybook village of Woodstock and Blenheim Palace, one of the grandest houses in all the land.

Along the River Thames, scattered throughout the unfolding landscape of trees, meadows, and hills, are numerous small villages and larger towns, some spoiled by ill-considered modern building, many still sleepily preserving their ancient charm. The railroads and superhighways carrying heavy traffic between London, the West Country, and the Midlands have turned much of this area into commuter territory, but you can easily depart from these beaten tracks to discover timeless villages whose landscapes are kept green by the river and its tributaries. The stretches of the Thames near Marlow, Henley, and Sonning-on-Thames are havens for relaxation, with rowing clubs, piers, and well-built cottages and villas. Anyone who comes to London in summer and has some time to spare would be well advised to spend it touring the Thames Valley.

Exploring the Thames Valley

An exploration of the Thames Valley can begin in the lively town of Windsor, favorite home-away-from-home of Britain's Royal Family. From there you can follow the river to Henley-on-Thames, site of the famous regatta, and then make a counterclockwise sweep west to Ewelme—the countryside immortalized by Kenneth Grahame's *The Wind in the Willows*. You can head north to Oxford next, and end with a visit to some stately homes and palaces. The area also abounds with tiny villages hidden from the major highways.

About the Restaurants

Londoners weekend here, and where they go, stellar restaurants follow. Ascot, Henley, and Woodstock claim some of Britain's best tables. Simple pub food, as well as classic French cuisine, can be enjoyed in waterside settings at many restaurants beside the Thames. Even in towns away from the river, well-heeled commuters and Oxford professors

With a car, you can see all the places outlined below on day trips from London, but it's worth staying at that perfect riverside inn or High Street hotel and settling in for a night or more. Then you can make the most of your mornings exploring the countryside. The area offers the greatest pleasure to those willing to leave the main roads to explore the smaller towns. You could spent a month exploring the Thames Valley, but three days can give you a taste of Windsor, a few towns, Blenheim Palace, and Oxford. In five days, you can spend more time in Oxford and explore additional villages and the area's stately homes and gardens.

5

Numbers in the text correspond to numbers in the margin and on the Thames Valley and Oxford maps.

If you have
3 days

Begin at 🖼 **Windsor ❶** ⮞, where royalty is the predominant note, and spend a morning visiting the castle, leaving part of the day for Eton College and Windsor Great Park. The next day, follow the river upstream, taking in the grandeur of the great Astor estate at **Cliveden ❺** and the village of **Marlow ❻**, where the pubs offer decent snacks for lunch. Head toward **Henley-on-Thames ❼**, where the Thames forms a harmonious dialogue with the medieval buildings alongside, and easy and tranquil walks beckon upstream or down. Reserve the last morning for 🖼 **Oxford ⓫–㉔**, whose scholastic air does not dampen the aesthetic and gastronomic pleasures on tap, with an afternoon visit to nearby **Woodstock ㉖**—a lovely English village—and **Blenheim Palace ㉗**, birthplace of Winston Churchill and one of the most beautiful houses in England.

If you have
5 days

Make your base at 🖼 **Windsor ❶** ⮞ for your first night. From there you can take excursions to **Ascot ❹**, for some of England's finest horse racing, and, to the north, **Cliveden ❺**. For your second night, consider staying in 🖼 **Henley-on-Thames ❼**, from which it's an easy trip to the aristocratic **Mapledurham House ❾** and a cluster of attractive Thames-side villages, such as **Sonning-on-Thames ❽** and **Dorchester-on-Thames ㉚**. Reserve the third day and night for the medieval wonders of 🖼 **Oxford ⓫–㉔**; on your fourth day head for the nearby 18th-century village of 🖼 **Woodstock ㉖**, site of magisterial **Blenheim Palace ㉗**. For the final day, swing eastward to the town of **Great Milton ㉛** for perhaps the grandest luncheon of your English trip, at Le Manoir aux Quat' Saisons. Next, pay a call on one or two of a trio of stately homes: Waddesdon Manor near **Aylesbury ㉜**, **Woburn Abbey ㉞**, or **Althorp ㉟**. An alternative is to visit Stowe landscape Gardens, near Aylesbury.

support top-flight establishments. Reservations are strongly recommended, especially on weekends.

About the Hotels

From converted country houses to refurbished Elizabethan inns, the region's accommodations are rich in history and distinctive in appeal. Many hotels cultivate traditional gardens and retain a sense of the past with impressive collections of antiques, whereas others have embraced the future with fully modern amenities. Book ahead, particularly in summer; you're competing for rooms with many Londoners in search of a getaway.

WHAT IT COSTS	In pounds			
£££££	**££££**	**£££**	**££**	**£**
RESTAURANTS over £22	£18–£22	£13–£17	£7–£12	under £7
HOTELS over £160	£120–£160	£90–£120	£60–£90	under £60

Restaurant prices are for a main course at dinner. Hotel prices are for two people in a standard double room in high season, including VAT, with no meals or, if indicated, CP (with Continental breakfast), BP (Breakfast Plan, with full breakfast), or MAP (Modified American Plan, with breakfast and dinner).

Timing

Although the verdant countryside around the Thames can be alluring year-round, the depths of winter may not be the time most conducive to appreciating its special beauty. High summer is lovely, but droves of visitors descend on popular sights in the area; avoid August and September if you can. June and July are the times for Henley's Royal Regatta and Ascot's Royal Meeting. Spring and autumn reveal the countryside at its best. Remember, however, that visiting at Eton and the Oxford colleges is much more restricted during term time. Most stately homes are open March through September or October only, and a number have very limited opening hours. Check in advance if you're planning an itinerary. Avoid any driving in the London area during afternoon rush hour, which starts an hour or two earlier than the usual 4:30 on Friday.

WINDSOR & ENVIRONS

Windsor Castle is one of the jewels of the area known as Royal Windsor, but a journey around this section of the Thames has other classic pleasures. The town of Eton holds the eponymous public school, Ascot has its famous racecourse, and Cliveden is a stately home turned into a very grand hotel. At Runnymede you can honor an early step toward democracy.

Windsor

▶ ❶ *21 mi west of London.*

Only a small part of old Windsor—the settlement that grew up around the town's famous castle in the Middle Ages—has survived. Windsor Town is not what it used to be in the time of Sir John Falstaff and the *Merry Wives of Windsor,* when it was famous for its inns, of which, in 1650, it boasted about 70. Only a handful remain, and the beer is not so strong and the wit not so rapier-sharp. The presence of sightseers can be overwhelming, but seekers of romantic history will appreciate narrow, cobbled Church Lane and Queen Charlotte Street, opposite the castle entrance. The venerable buildings of Windsor Town now house antiques shops and restaurants.

Henley Royal Regatta

During the cusp of June and July Henley hosts rowing's most elegant race, the Henley Royal Regatta. Its riverbanks become one gigantic, opulent lawn party as 500,000 visitors, including members of the Royal Family, descend en masse during the week. Each day, the racing pauses twice, at noon for luncheon and at 4 for tea (more likely a bottle of Pimm's "champers"—champagne—and some Kent strawberries with fresh Henley cream). If you're lucky enough to get a spot near the finish line, you'll swear you're back in Edwardian England.

5

Walking & Hiking

The Thames Valley is a good area for walking; it's not too hilly, and handy eateries, especially pubs, and plenty of easily accessible, comfortable lodgings dot the riverside and small towns. For long-distance walkers, the Oxfordshire Way runs 65 mi from Henley-on-Thames to Bourton-on-the-Water, on the eastern edge of the Cotswolds. The 124-mi Chiltern Way is a circular walk that passes just north of Henley. A 13-mi ramble starts in Henley, runs north through the Hambleden Valley, and returns to Henley via the Assendons, Lower and Middle. The Thames is almost completely free of car traffic along the Thames Path, a 180-mi route following the river from the London flood barrier to the river's source near Kemble, in the Cotswolds. The path follows towpaths from the outskirts of London, through Windsor, to Oxford and Lechlade. Good public transportation in the region makes it possible to start and stop easily anywhere along this route. In summer the walking is fine and no special gear is necessary, but in winter the path often floods—check before you head out.

★ **Windsor Castle,** the longtime home of England's monarchs, was built to be visible for miles around, a monumental symbol of authority. From William the Conqueror to Queen Victoria, the kings and rulers of England added towers and wings to the brooding structure, and it's now the largest inhabited castle in the world. Despite the multiplicity of hands that have gone into its design, the palace has a unity of style and character. Easily accessible from London, the castle and its surrounding town make for a rewarding day trip.

The most impressive view of Windsor Castle is from the A332 road, on the southern approach to the town. William the Conqueror began work on the castle in the 11th century, and Edward III modified and extended it in the mid-1300s. One of Edward's largest contributions was the enormous and distinctive **Round Tower.** Finally, between 1824 and 1837, George IV transformed the still essentially medieval castle into the fortified royal palace you see today. Most kings and queens of England have demonstrated their undying attachment to the castle, the only royal residence that has been in continuous use by the Royal Family since the Middle Ages.

Just outside the castle, on St. Albans Street, is the **Royal Mews,** where the royal horses are kept, with carriages, coaches, and splendid crim-

The Thames Valley

Warwick

A425

M40

A422 Lower Tysoe

Middle Tysoe

Upper Tysoe

Banbury

A43

A421

Chipping Norton

O X F O R D S H I R E *B4030*

Bic

Bourton-on-the-Water

A424

Rousham Park House & Garden 25

Weston-on-the-Green

A41

Woodstock 26

A44

A4260

A34

Blenheim Palace 27

Bladon

Burford

A40

Witney

A4095

A40

Wolvercote

Oxford
11 – 24
see detail map

Garsingt

A361

B4449

Thames

Cumnor

Kelmscott Manor 28

4095

A420

Abingdon

A4174

Dorchester-on-Thames 30

Faringdon

V A L E   O F   W H I T E   H O R S E

A338

A417

A329

A420

B4508

Uffington 29

B4507

Wantage

Swindon

L A M B O U R N
D O W N S

A34

KEY

▶ *Start of itinerary*

M4

Pangb

M4

W I L T S H I R E

B E R K S H I

Marlborough

Hungerford

Hungerford Newtown

Newbury

A4

son and gold harnesses. The **Jubilee Garden,** created in 2002, has a central stone bandstand used for concerts on summer Sunday afternoons. The garden begins at the main gates and extends to St. George's Gate on Castle Hill.

As you enter the castle, **Henry VIII's gateway** leads uphill into the wide castle precincts, where you are free to wander. Directly opposite the entrance is the exquisite **St. George's Chapel.** Here lie 10 of the kings of England, including Henry VI, Charles I, and Henry VIII (Jane Seymour is the only one of his six wives buried here). One of the noblest buildings in England, the chapel was built in the 15th- and 16th-century Perpendicular style and has elegant stained-glass windows, a high, vaulted ceiling, and intricately carved choir stalls. The colorful heraldic banners of the Knights of the Garter—the oldest British Order of Chivalry, founded by Edward III in 1348—hang in the choir. The ceremony in which the knights are installed as members of the order has been held here with much pageantry for more than five centuries. St. George's Chapel is closed to the public on Sunday.

The **North Terrace** provides especially good views across the Thames to Eton College, perhaps the most famous of Britain's exclusive "public" boys' schools. From the terrace, you enter the **State Apartments,** which are open to the public when the Queen is not in residence. (The State Apartments are sometimes closed when the Queen is in residence—usually in summer—so call to check.) Queen Elizabeth uses the castle far more than did any of her predecessors. It has become a sort of country weekend residence that allows the Royal Family a few days of informality. To see the royal abode come magnificently alive, check out the Windsor Castle **Changing of the Guard** (☎ 01753/869898), which takes place at 11 AM weekdays and Saturdays from April to the end of June and on odd-numbered days on weekdays and Saturdays from July through March. It's advisable to confirm the exact schedule. When the Queen is in town, the guard and a regimental band parade through town to the castle gate; when Her Majesty is away, a drum-and-fife band takes over.

Although a devastating fire in 1992 gutted some of the State Apartments, hardly any works of art were lost. Phenomenal repair work restored the **Grand Reception Room,** the **Green and Crimson Drawing Rooms,** and the **State and Octagonal dining rooms.** A green oak hammer-beam (a short horizontal roof beam that projects from the tops of walls for support) roof now looms magnificently over the 600-year-old **St. George's Hall,** where the Queen gives state banquets. The State Apartments contain priceless furniture, including a magnificent Louis XVI bed and Gobelin tapestries; and paintings by Canaletto, Rubens, Van Dyck, Holbein, Dürer, and del Sarto. The high points of the tour are the **Throne Room** and the **Waterloo Chamber,** where Sir Thomas Lawrence's portraits of Napoléon's victorious foes line the walls. You can also see a collection of arms and armor, much of it exotic, and an exhibition on the restoration of Windsor Castle.

☙ **Queen Mary's Doll's House,** on display to the left of the entrance to the State Apartments, is a perfect miniature Georgian palace-within-a-palace, created in 1923. Electric lights work, the doors all have keys, and there is running water. A library holds Lilliputian-size books especially written by famous authors of the 1920s. ☏ 020/7321–2233 tickets, 01753/831118 recorded information ⊕ www.royalresidences.com ▦ £12 for the Precincts, the State Apartments, the Gallery, St. George's Chapel, the Albert Memorial Chapel, and the Doll's House; £6 when the State Apartments are closed ۞ Mar.–Oct., daily 9:45–5:15, last admission at 4; Nov.–Feb., daily 9:45–4:15, last admission at 3.

Windsor Great Park, the remains of an ancient royal hunting forest, stretches for some 8 mi (about 5,000 acres) south of Windsor Castle. Much of it is open to the public and can be seen by car or on foot, including its geographical focal points, the romantic 3-mi **Long Walk,** designed by Charles II to join castle and park, and **Virginia Water,** a 2-mi-long lake. The park contains Frogmore, one of Queen Victoria's most treasured residences and still a retreat for the Royal Family. On rare occasions, however, the public is invited to **Frogmore House** (☏ 01753/869898 ⊕ www.royalresidences.com ▦ House, gardens, and mausoleum £5.20 ۞ May, selected days only [check by phone, 10–6]; Aug., selected days only [check by phone, 11–5:30]). Nearby, at the Royal Mausoleum at Frogmore, two famous royal couples are buried: inside, Victoria and Albert; outside, the Duke and Duchess of Windsor. This is open only a few days a year, with prebooked guided tours also possible on selected weekdays August–October. The main horticultural delight of Windsor Great Park, the exquisite **Savill Garden** (✉ Wick La., Englefield Green, Egham ☏ 01753/847518 ⊕ www.savillgarden.co. uk ▦ £3–£6 ۞ Mar.–Oct., daily 10–6; Nov.–Feb., daily 10–4), contains a tremendous diversity of trees and shrubs.

☺ An extensive theme park, **Legoland,** 2 mi outside Windsor, celebrates the versatile Lego building brick. Ingenious models small and large, rides and interactive activities, a lakeside picnic area, 150 acres of parkland, and restaurants allow you to make a day of it. ✉ *Winkfield Rd.* ☏ *08705/040404* ⊕ *www.legoland.co.uk* ▦ *£23* ۞ *Apr.–June and Sept.–Jan., daily 10–6; July and Aug., daily 10–7.*

Where to Stay & Eat

★ **£££££** ✕ **Fat Duck.** A creative contemporary, French-influenced sensibility prevails at this culinary star, considered one of England's best restaurants. Chef Heston Blumenthal delights in unusual taste combinations, from sardines on toast sorbet to bacon-and-egg ice cream. The fixed-price menu lists plenty of choices, such as duck cannelloni with maple syrup and foie gras with apples. Lunch, with a £23.50 fixed-price menu, is a cheaper alternative. Expect plenty of extra nibbles with your meal. Bray, which has a number of good restaurants and pubs, is 6 mi west of Windsor. ✉ *High St., Bray-on-Thames* ☏ *01628/580333* ▭ *AE, DC, MC, V* ⌥ *Reservations essential.*

£ ✕ **Two Brewers.** Two small low-ceilinged rooms make up this 17th-century pub where locals congregate. Children are not welcome, but adults will find a suitable collection of wine, espresso, and local beer, plus an excellent little menu with dishes from salmon fish cakes to chili and pasta. Reservations are essential on Sunday, when the pub serves a tra-

ditional roast. ✉ *34 Park St.* ☎ *01753/855426* ▤ *AE, DC, MC, V*
♉ *No dinner Fri.*

£££££ ✕🏨 **Oakley Court.** A romantic getaway with plenty of pampering amenities, this Victorian-era mock castle stands on landscaped grounds beside the Thames, 3 mi west of Windsor. Its bristling towers and spires
have been used in several films (including *The Rocky Horror Picture
Show*); note, however, that half the rooms are in a modern annex. The
Oakleaf restaurant serves continental cuisine in plush surroundings.
✉ *Windsor Rd. Water Oakley SL4 5UF* ☎ *01753/609988* 🖷 *01628/
637011* ⊕*www.moathousehotels.com* ➴ *106 rooms, 12 suites* ♿ *Restaurant, room service, in-room data ports, in-room safes, minibars, room
TVs with movies, 9-hole golf course, putting green, 2 tennis courts, indoor pool, gym, hot tub, sauna, spa, steam room, billiards, croquet, bar,
lobby lounge, dry cleaning, laundry service, concierge, business services, meeting rooms, no-smoking rooms; no a/c in some rooms* ▤ *AE,
DC, MC, V.*

£££££ ✕🏨 **Sir Christopher Wren's House Hotel.** A private mansion built by the
famous architect in 1676, this impressively sober house has a brick facade lightened by white columns and perfectly proportioned windows.
Wren's Bedroom, the star of the hotel, has dark wood walls and antique
furniture. The rooms, each different, are in five buildings along Thames
Street. Those in the main mansion are the most atmospheric and historic.
The riverside Strok's Restaurant has a good fixed-price Continental dinner menu and a Thames-side wooden terrace. ✉*Thames St. at Eton Bridge,
SL4 1PX* ☎*01753/861354* 🖷*01753/442490* ⊕*www.sirchristopherwren.
co.uk* ➴ *79 rooms, 5 suites, 7 apartments* ♿ *Restaurant, café, in-room
data ports, some in-room hot tubs, cable TV, some in-room VCRs, indoor-outdoor pool, gym, hair salon, outdoor hot tub, massage, sauna,
spa, steam room, bar, meeting rooms* ▤*AE, DC, MC, V* ⏐◯⏐ *BP.*

£££££ ✕🏨 **Stoke Park Club.** On a 350-acre estate 4 mi southwest of Windsor,
Stoke Park can make Windsor Castle, off in the distance, seem almost
humble in comparison. Architect James Wyatt perfected this version of
neoclassical grandeur when he built the house for the Penn family in
1791. Antiques, paintings, and original prints decorate the elegant bedrooms. The Brasserie serves traditional English cuisine. *Goldfinger* and
Bridget Jones's Diary were partly filmed here. ✉ *Park Rd., Stoke Poges
SL2 4PG* ☎ *01753/717171* 🖷 *01753/717181* ⊕ *www.stokeparkclub.
com* ➴ *21 rooms* ♿ *2 restaurants, in-room data ports, cable TV, 27-
hole golf course, 12 tennis courts, indoor pool, fitness classes, gym, hair
salon, hot tub, massage, spa, steam room, fishing, croquet, squash, 2
bars, meeting rooms* ▤ *AE, MC, V.*

£££–£££££ 🏨 **The Castle Hotel.** Past and present lie behind the Georgian facade of
this hotel, which includes a main building, built in 1528 as a coaching
inn, and a modern wing. Rooms in the older section have gently tilting
floors and flowery bedspreads; some rooms have four-poster beds.
Piano recitals take place in cozy lounges with beamed ceilings and
plush, antique furnishings—perfect for afternoon cream tea. To take advantage of lower prices, book a weekend leisure break with breakfast
or half board. ✉ *High St., SL4 ILJ* ☎ *0870/400–8300* 🖷 *01753/
830244* ⊕ *www.macdonaldhotels.co.uk* ➴ *111 rooms* ♿ *2 restau-*

rants, room service, in-room data ports, cable TV, bar, lounge, laundry service, meeting rooms, no-smoking rooms; no a/c ⊟ *AE, DC, MC, V.*

££££ 🏨 **Ye Harte & Garter Hotel.** The location couldn't be better—right across the street from Windsor Castle, with a good view of it from many rooms. Some rooms have balconies and others have whirlpool tubs. Expect a muted rose tone and floral prints in the rooms, which vary in size. The hotel has Albert's Fish and Chips shop and the stodgy Victorian Restaurant and Carvery. It also hosts amusing medieval banquets in its dungeon. ⊠ *31 High St. SL4 1PH* ☎ *01753/863426* 🖷 *01753/830527* ⊕ *www.harteandgarter.com* 🛏 *58 rooms* ⚖ *2 restaurants, some in-room hot tubs, some minibars, cable TV, bar, dry cleaning, laundry service, meeting rooms; no a/c* ⊟ *AE, DC, MC, V.*

££ 🏨 **Alma Lodge.** This friendly little bed-and-breakfast in an early Victorian town house is just one of many that can be booked through the Windsor tourist office. Ornate ceilings and ornamental fireplaces are some of the house's original features, and each well-maintained room is decorated in an uncluttered Victorian style. ⊠ *58 Alma Rd. SL4 3HA* ☎ *01753/862983* 🖷 *01753/862983* ⊕ *www.almalodge.co.uk* 🛏 *4 rooms* ⚖ *Some pets allowed; no a/c, no room phones, no smoking* ⊟ *MC, V* ⅋ *BP.*

Nightlife & the Arts

Windsor's **Theatre Royal** (⊠ Thames St. ☎ 01753/853888), where productions have been staged since 1910, is one of Britain's leading provincial theaters. It puts on plays and musicals year-round, including a pantomime for the six weeks after Christmas.

Concerts, poetry readings, and children's events highlight the two-week **Windsor Festival** (☎ 01753/714364 ⊕ www.windsorfestival.com), usually held in early September or October, with events occasionally taking place in the castle.

Sports & the Outdoors

From March through September, **John Logie Motorboats** (⊠ Barry Ave. ☎ 07774/983809) rents motorboats and row boats by the half-hour and hour.

Windsor Cycle Hire (⊠ Alexandra Gardens, Alma Rd. ☎ 01753/830220) rents bikes and in-line skates.

Shopping

Most Windsor stores are open Sunday as well as the rest of the week, particularly the antiques stores along Peascod Street, High Street, and King Edward Court. The **Windsor Royal Station shopping center** (⊠ Central Train Station ☎ 01753/797070) includes Jaeger, Pied-à-Terre, and an outpost of the quintessential London department store, Liberty.

Eton

❷ *23 mi west of London, linked by a footbridge across the Thames to Windsor.*

Some observers may find it symbolic that almost opposite Windsor Castle—which embodies the continuity of the royal tradition—stands Eton, a school that for centuries has educated many future leaders of the country. With its single main street leading from the river to the famous school, the old-fashioned town itself is a much quieter place than Windsor.

★ The splendid redbrick Tudor-style buildings of **Eton College,** founded in 1440 by King Henry VI, border the north end of High Street; signs warn drivers of "Boys Crossing." During the college semesters, the schoolboys dress in their distinctive pinstripe trousers, swallow-tailed coats, and stiff collars (top hats have not been worn by the boys since the 1940s), but don't let the dapper duds fool you. Some of the more mischievous Etonians have been known to fill visitors' heads with fantastic stories about the supposedly mythic origins of their alma mater.

The Gothic **Chapel** rivals St. George's at Windsor in size and magnificence, and is both impressively austere and intimate. Beyond the cloisters are the school's playing fields where, according to the duke of Wellington, the Battle of Waterloo was really won, since so many of his officers had learned discipline during their school days there. The **Museum of Eton Life** has displays on the school's history. You can also take a guided tour of the school and chapel. ⊠ *Main entrance Brewhouse Yard* ☎ *01753/671177* ⊕ *www.etoncollege.com* ⌑ *£3.80, £4.90 with tour* ⊙ *Mar.–mid-Apr., July, and Aug., daily 10:30–4:30; mid-Apr.–June and Sept., daily 2–4:30; guided tours mid-Mar.–Sept., daily at 2:15 and 3:15.*

Where to Stay & Eat

ff–fff ✕ **Gilbey's Bar & Restaurant.** Just over the bridge from Windsor, this restaurant sits at the center of Eton's Antiques Row and serves a fine, changing menu of inspired English fare, from salmon, ginger, and coriander fishcakes to lamb with tomato and basil mashed potatoes. Well-priced French wines are a specialty here. The conservatory is a particularly pleasant place to sit in fine weather. ⊠ *82–83 High St.* ☎ *01753/854921* ▤ *AE, DC, MC, V.*

ff ✕ **The George Inn & Eatery.** This stylish pub has stripped pine floors, wooden tables, and a menu of contemporary cuisine. You might opt for the spicy Thai beef salad or the more traditional sausage and mashed potatoes in onion gravy. The terrace is a relaxing spot for a summertime pint. ⊠ *77 High St.* ☎ *01753/861797* ▤ *AE, MC, V.*

ffff ✕▥ **Christopher Hotel.** Sister to Sir Christopher Wren's Hotel in Windsor, this former coaching inn on the main shopping street has spacious rooms in the main building as well as in the courtyard mews. All are done in traditional style, but the courtyard rooms have more privacy. The fine Renata's restaurant, serving dinner every day except Sunday, has a modern European menu. ⊠ *110 High St. SL4 6AN* ☎ *01753/852359* ⎙ *01753/830914* ⊕ *www.christopher-hotel.co.uk* ⤸ *33 rooms* ♿ *Restaurant, room service, cable TV, bar, meeting room, some pets allowed, no-smoking rooms* ▤ *AE, DC, MC, V.*

Runnymede

❸ *6 mi east of Windsor.*

A giant step in the history of democracy was taken at Runnymede on the Thames outside Egham. Here King John, under his barons' compulsion, signed the Magna Carta in 1215, affirming the individual's right to justice and liberty. On the wooded hillside, in a meadow given to the United States by Queen Elizabeth in 1965, stands a **memorial to President John F. Kennedy.** Nearby is another memorial, a classical temple in style, erected by the American Bar Association for the 750th anniversary of the signing. There is no visitor center at Runnymede, just informational plaques and a parking lot (small charge). The site is on the south side of A308; on the opposite bank of the Thames are the ruins of the 11th-century St. Mary's Priory and the 2,000-year-old Ankerwycke Yew. ⊠ *A308 Egham* ☎ *01784/432891* ⊕ *www.nationaltrust.org.uk.*

Ascot

❹ *10 mi southwest of Runnymede, 8 mi southwest of Windsor, 28 mi southwest from London.*

The town of Ascot (pronounced *as*-cut) has for centuries been famous for horse racing and for style. Queen Anne chose to have a racecourse here, and the first race meeting took place in 1711. Every third week of June (Tuesday–Friday), the titled and the gentry watch the world's finest thoroughbreds pound the turf during the **Royal Meeting,** or Royal Ascot, at **Ascot Racecourse.** The impressive show of millinery for which the Royal Meeting is also known was immortalized in Cecil Beaton's Ascot sequence in *My Fair Lady,* in which osprey feathers and black and white silk roses held high transformed Eliza Doolittle into a grand lady. Today more than a quarter of a million racegoers continue to bet, sip champagne, and be seen. The racecourse is divided into several enclosures, the Royal Enclosure being the most famous. Morning dress—meaning tailcoat, top hat, and striped pants—must be worn by gentlemen, whereas hats are de rigueur for the ladies in the Royal Enclosure. The two main public enclosures, the Grandstand and the Silver Ring, have great views and all the fun for less cash and less snobbery. Budget travelers can even try for the Ascot Heath, which costs £3. With around 100 bars and four large catering facilities, no one wants for food or drink.

The Royal Meeting may be the most chichi and the best known, but racing goes on year-round (except March) at England's largest racecourse. Diamond Day, the fourth Saturday in July, or the Ascot Festival, the last Saturday and Sunday in September, are a little more low-key. During most of the year the Royal Enclosure becomes the Members' Enclosure and seats are readily bookable, although it is always advised to phone ahead; for the Royal Meeting, book many months ahead. ⊠ *A329* ☎ *01344/622211 racecourse, 01344/876876 credit card hot line* ⊕ *www. ascot-authority.co.uk* ⊠ *Royal Ascot: grandstand and paddock £52, Silver Ring £16, Ascot Heath £3. Diamond Day and Ascot Festival: Members' Enclosure £33, grandstand and paddock £22, Silver Ring £10. All other race days: general admission £6, with special enclosures £13–£18.*

Where to Stay

£££££ ⊞ **Berystede Country House Hotel.** With its turrets and half-timbering, this Victorian-era hotel is a magnificent neo-Gothic fantasy on 9 acres of traditional British countryside. Inside, every square inch pays homage to the horsey culture of Ascot, and horse and jockey prints line the walls. Most of the rooms are pleasantly standard (in the annex); a few (in the main house) are nothing short of extraordinary. The Hyperion restaurant serves modern British cuisine. ⊠ *Bagshot Rd., SL5 9JH* ☎ *01344/ 623311* ⓑ *01344/872301* ⊕ *www.heritagehotels.co.uk* ⇨ *80 rooms, 10 suites* ⚿ *Restaurant, room service, in-room data ports, cable TV, pool, croquet, bar, lounge, library, baby-sitting, dry cleaning, laundry service, Internet, meeting rooms, some pets allowed, no-smoking rooms; no a/c* ⊟ *AE, DC, MC, V* ⦿ *BP.*

Cliveden

❺ *8 mi northwest of Windsor, 16 mi north of Ascot, 26 mi west of London.*

Deemed by Queen Victoria a "bijou of taste," this magnificent country mansion has for more than 300 years lived up to its Georgian heritage as a bastion of aesthetic delights. The house, set in 376 acres of gardens and parkland high above the River Thames, was rebuilt for the Duke of Sutherland by Sir Charles Barry in 1861; the Astors, who purchased it in 1893, made it famous. In the 1920s and '30s the Cliveden Set met here at the strongly conservative (not to say fascist) salon presided over by Nancy Astor, who—though she was an American—was the first woman to sit in Parliament, in 1919. Cliveden now belongs to the National Trust, which has leased it for use as a *very* exclusive hotel. The public can visit the spectacular grounds and formal gardens that run down to bluffs overlooking the Thames and, by timed ticket, three rooms in the west wing of the house. ⊠ *Off A404 Taplow, near Maidenhead* ☎ *01628/605069, 01494/755562 recorded information* ⊕ *www.nationaltrust.org.uk* ⓔ *Grounds £6; house additional £1* ⊙ *Grounds mid-Mar.–Oct., daily 11–6; Nov. and Dec., daily 11–4. House Apr.–Oct., Thurs. and Sun. 3–5:30. Restaurant in the Orangery mid-Mar.–Oct., Wed.–Sun. 11–5; Nov.–mid-Dec., weekends 11:30–2:30.*

Where to Stay & Eat

£££££ ✕▥ **Cliveden.** If you've ever wondered what it would feel like to be an
Fodor'sChoice Edwardian grandee, splurge for a stay at this stately home, one of
★ Britain's grandest hotels. Cliveden's opulent interior includes historic portraits such as Sargent's portrait of Nancy Astor (in the Great Hall), suits of armor, and a richly paneled staircase. The plush traditional bedrooms continue the historic note—each bears the name of someone famous who has stayed here. Since people lease many of the rooms, you may feel you're in a home rather than a hotel. Waldo's, one of three restaurants, is known for contemporary British and French cuisine. ⊠ *Off A404 near Maidenhead, Taplow SL6 0JF* ☎ *01628/668561* ⓑ *01628/661837* ⊕ *www.clivedenhouse.co.uk* ⇨ *38 rooms, 1 cottage* ⚿ *2 restaurants, room service, in-room data ports, in-room safes, cable TV with movies, in-room VCRs, 2 tennis courts, indoor-outdoor pool, gym, hair salon, outdoor hot tub, massage, sauna, spa, steam room, boating, horseback riding, squash, lounge, library, baby-sitting, dry cleaning, laundry service, meeting rooms, some pets allowed, no-smoking rooms; no a/c in some rooms* ⊟ *AE, DC, MC, V* ⦿ *BP.*

Outdoors
Cliveden Boathouse (✉ Off A404 near Maidenhead, Taplow ☎ 01628/ 668561) at Cliveden hotel has three vintage boats that ply the Thames. The champagne sunset cruise is the most affordable at £45 per person; you can rent the boats, too.

TO HENLEY & BEYOND
"WIND IN THE WILLOWS" COUNTRY

"Believe me, my young friend, there is nothing—absolutely nothing— half so much worth doing as simply messing about in boats. Simply mess- ing." You may well agree with Water Rat's opinion, voiced in Kenneth Grahame's classic 1908 children's book *The Wind in the Willows,* if you do some of your own "messing about" in this stretch of the Thames Val- ley, from Marlow to Ewelme. Boat-borne or by foot, you can discover here some of the region's most delightful scenery. On each bank are fine wooded hills, with spacious houses, greenhouses, flower beds, and neat lawns that stretch to the water's edge. It was to Pangbourne, along this stretch of the river, that Grahame retired to write his beloved book. His illustrator, E. H. Shepard, used the great house at Mapledurham as the model for Toad Hall. A Victorian boathouse, not far from Pangbourne, was immortalized in pen and ink as Rat's House. The Henley Royal Re- gatta is one of the region's most famous attractions.

Marlow

❻ *7 mi west of Cliveden, 15 mi northwest of Windsor.*

Just inside the Buckinghamshire border, Marlow overflows with Thames- side prettiness, and tourism can often overwhelm it on summer week- ends. Take particular note of its unusual suspension bridge, which William Tierney Clark, architect of the bridge linking Buda and Pest, built in the 1830s. Marlow has a number of striking old buildings, par- ticularly the stylish, privately owned Georgian houses along Peter and West streets. In 1817 the Romantic poet Percy Bysshe Shelley stayed with friends at 67 West Street and then bought **Albion House** on the same street. His second wife, Mary, completed her Gothic novel *Frankenstein* here. **Marlow Place,** on Station Road, dates from 1721 and has been lived in by several princes of Wales. Marlow hosts its own miniregatta in mid-June for one day. The town is a good base from which to join the Thames Path to Henley-on-Thames.

Swan-Upping (☎ 01628/523030), a traditional event that dates back 800 years, takes places in the third week of July. The Queen owns most of the swans on the Thames. Swan-markers in skiffs start from Sunbury- on-Thames, catching the new cygnets and marking their beaks to es- tablish ownership. The Queen's swan keeper, dressed in scarlet livery, presides over this colorful ceremony.

Where to Stay & Eat
£££££ ✕ **Vanilla Pod.** Beamed ceilings and warm, vanilla-hued walls cocoon French-inspired cuisine by chef Michael Macdonald. Some of the best

choices are the glazed chicken—embraced by layers of honey, coriander, and fennel—and the scallops with vanilla-pear puree. For dessert,
indulge in the crème caramel with orange salsa and strawberry salad.
The £14.50 fixed-price lunch menu offers a fantastic bargain, while the
seven-course *menu gourmand* for £40 is a culinary tour de force. ⊠ *31
West St.* ☎ *01628/898101* △ *Reservations essential* ⊟ *AE, MC, V.*

£££££   ✕⊡ **Compleat Angler.** Fishing aficionados might consider this luxurious,
17th-century Thames-side inn the ideal place to stay. The name comes
from Isaak Walton's 1653 masterpiece of angling advice and philosophy, which he wrote in this area. Plenty of fishy touches enhance the
chintz and floral bedrooms; most rooms and the Riverside Restaurant
(with outstanding cooking from chef Dean Timpson) have views over
the Thames. A cozy conservatory serves afternoon tea. ⊠ *Marlow
Bridge, Bisham Rd., SL7 1RG* ☎ *01628/484444* 🖷 *01628/486388*
⊕ *www.heritagehotels.co.uk* ⇆ *61 rooms, 3 suites* ⚫ *2 restaurants, room
service, minibars, cable TV with video games, fishing, 2 bars, boating,
meeting rooms, some pets allowed (fee), no-smoking rooms; no a/c*
⊟ *AE, DC, MC, V.*

Henley-on-Thames

❼ *7 mi southwest of Marlow on A4155, 8 mi north of Reading, 36 mi
west of central London.*

Henley's identity manifests itself in one word: rowing. The Henley
Royal Regatta, held in early July (in 2005, June 29 to July 3) on a long,
straight stretch of the River Thames, has made the little riverside town
famous throughout the world. Townspeople launched the Henley Regatta in 1839, initiating the Grand Challenge Cup, the most famous of
its many trophies. After 1851, when Prince Albert, Queen Victoria's consort, became its patron, it was known as the Royal Regatta. The best
amateur oarsmen from around the globe compete in crews of eight, four,
or two, or as single scullers. For many of the spectators, however, the
social side of the event is far more important and on par with Royal
Ascot and Wimbledon. Elderly oarsmen wear brightly colored blazers
and straw boater hats; businesspeople entertain wealthy clients and
everyone admires the ladies' fashions.

The town is set in a broad valley between gentle hillsides. Henley's historic buildings, including half-timber Georgian cottages and inns (as well
as one of Britain's oldest theaters, the Kenton), are all within a few minutes' walk. The river near Henley is alive with boats of every shape and
size, from luxury cabin cruisers to tiny rowboats. The 16th-century
"checkerboard" tower of **St. Mary's Church** overlooks Henley's bridge
on Hart Street. If the church's rector is about, ask permission to climb
to the top to take in the superb views up and down the river. The adjacent **Chantry House,** built in 1420, is one of England's few remaining
merchant houses from the period. Converted into a school for impoverished boys in 1604, it is an unspoiled example of the rare timber-frame
design, with upper floors jutting out. ⊠ *Hart St.* ☎ *01491/577062*
🖾 *Free* ⊙ *Church services or by appointment.*

The handsome **River & Rowing Museum** focuses not just on the history and sport of rowing but on the Thames and the town itself. One gallery interprets the Thames and its surroundings as the river flows from its source to the ocean; another explores Henley's history and the regatta. Galleries devoted to rowing display models and actual boats, from Greek triremes to lifeboats to sleek modern rowing boats. David Chipperfield's striking building, combining traditional oak and modern steel, takes full advantage of its riverside location. ⊠ *Mill Meadows* ☎ *01491/ 415600* ⊕ *www.rrm.co.uk* ⊑ *£4.95* ⊙ *Sept.–Apr., daily 10–5; May–Aug., daily 10–5:30.*

Where to Stay & Eat

££–£££ ✕ **Three Tuns Foodhouse.** What used to be a tiny pub has been redone into a delightful, antiques-filled eatery. On the menu, pan-fried scallops with saffron and fennel share space with chicken with thyme potatoes and Scottish chanterelle mushrooms. ⊠ *5 Market Pl.* ☎ *01491/573260* ⌧ *Reservations essential* ▭ *MC, V.*

££££ ✕▦ **Red Lion.** Ivy-draped and dignified, this redbrick 16th-century hotel overlooks the river and the town bridge. Guests have included King Charles I; Samuel Johnson, the 18th-century critic, poet, and lexicographer; and the duke of Marlborough, who used the hotel as a base during the building of Blenheim Palace. Rooms are furnished with antiques, and some bedrooms have river views. The restaurant serves traditional fare such as roast pheasant or beef fillet with leek and Stilton mousse; the bar has a lighter menu. ⊠ *Hart St. RG9 2AR* ☎ *01491/572161* 🖷 *01491/410039* ⊕ *www.redlionhenley.co.uk* ⤵ *26 rooms* ⌧ *Restaurant, room service, in-room data ports, cable TV, bar, lobby lounge, babysitting, dry cleaning, laundry service, Internet, meeting rooms, car rental; no a/c* ▭ *AE, MC, V.*

££££ ✕▦ **White Hart Hotel & Nettlebed Restaurant.** The focus at this modern gastro-pub with some guest rooms is delectable food, prepared with fresh, local ingredients by chef-owner Chris Barber, who spent a decade as personal chef to Prince Charles. Menu highlights are roast Cornish lobster and Orkney sirloin in Madeira sauce. With its three-course set menu and five-course tasting menu, the restaurant is more formal than the bistro, but both benefit from thoroughly professional staff. The soothing, light-filled guest rooms, done in olive green, gray, cream, and dark chocolate, are contemporary in style. ⊠ *A4130, Nettlebed RG9 5DD, 5 mi west of Henley-on-Thames* ☎ *01491/541425* 🖷 *01491/649018* ⊕ *www. whitehartnettlebed.com* ⤵ *12 rooms* ⌧ *Restaurant, room service, in-room data ports, pub, lounge, laundry service, dry cleaning, meeting rooms, no-smoking rooms; no a/c* ▭ *MC, V* ⧓ *BP.*

££££ ▦ **Thamesmead House Hotel.** Neutral tones and simple, clean-lined furnishings create restful bedrooms in this sweet but sophisticated guesthouse across the bridge from the center of Henley. The helpful staff provide a sort of concierge service and are knowledgeable about local eateries and attractions. ⊠ *Remenham La., RG9 2LR* ☎ *01491/574745* 🖷 *01491/579944* ⊕ *www.thamesmeadhousehotel.co.uk* ⤵ *6 rooms* ⌧ *In-room data ports, in-room safes, cable TV, lounge; no a/c, no kids under 10, no smoking* ▭ *AE, MC, V* ⧓ *BP.*

Nightlife & the Arts

The popular **Henley Festival** (☎ 01491/843404 ⊕ www.henley-festival. co.uk) takes place each July, during the week after the regatta. All kinds of open-air concerts and events are staged.

Sports

GOLF At **Badgemore Park** (✉ A4130 ☎ 01491/574175), a parkland 18-hole course, visitors are welcome on weekdays, and on weekends by arrangement.

ROWING **Henley Royal Regatta** (☎ 01491/572153 ⊕ www.hrr.co.uk), a series of rowing competitions that draw participants from many countries, takes place over five days at the beginning of July each year. Large tents go up, especially along both sides of the unique straight stretch of river here known as Henley Reach (1 mi, 550 yds), and every surrounding field becomes a parking lot. The most prestigious place for spectators is the Stewards' Enclosure, but admission here is by invitation only. Fortunately, there is plenty of space on the public towpath from which to watch the early stages of the races. If you want to attend, make your plans and book a room months in advance.

Sonning-on-Thames

❽ *5 mi south of Henley-on-Thames, 4 mi northeast of Reading.*

It is plausible that Sonning's reputation as the prettiest village on the Thames goes back as far as its Saxon bishops. The 18th-century bridge spanning the Thames, the Georgian houses, the ancient mill mentioned in the 11th-century Domesday Book, and the black, white, and yellow cottages make it an all-too-perfect riverside village.

Where to Stay & Eat

££££ ✕▣ **French Horn.** Elegance is the keynote of this Thames-side hotel with a lawn graced with a willow tree and calming river views. Guest rooms, some in the main building and others in cottages, are spacious. Most have sitting rooms, and the light green walls and rose-festooned fabrics are typically English. The restaurant serves inspired French cooking. ✉ *Thames St., RG4 6TN* ☎ *0118/969–2204* 🖷 *0118/944–2210* ⊕ *www.thefrenchhorn.co.uk* ⇌ *11 rooms, 10 suites* ⚭ *Restaurant, in-room data ports, some minibars, bar, lobby lounge, laundry service, meeting rooms; no a/c in some rooms* ▭ *AE, DC, MC, V* ⏏❙ *BP.*

Mapledurham House

★ ❾ *5 mi west of Sonning-on-Thames, 10 mi southwest of Henley-on-Thames.*

The section of the Thames from Caversham to Mapledurham inspired Kenneth Grahame's 1908 children's book *The Wind in the Willows*, which began as a bedtime story for Grahame's son Alastair while the Grahames were living at Pangbourne. Some of E. F. Shepard's illustrations are of specific sites along the river—none more fabled than this redbrick Elizabethan mansion, bristling with tall chimneys, mullioned windows, and battlements, which became the inspiration for Shepard's vision of Toad Hall. The Eyston family, descendants of longtime owners of the estate, still lives at Mapledurham, and the house seems warm and friendly even with all the family portraits, magnificent oak staircases, and Tudor plasterwork ceilings. Here you can see a 15th-century water mill—the last working grain mill on the Thames. On summer weekends you can reach the house in true *Wind-in-the-Willows* fashion by a **Thames River Cruises** (☎ 0118/948–1088) boat from Caversham Promenade in Reading. The boat leaves at 2 PM, and travel time is about 45 minutes. You can linger in the area at one of the 11 rental cottages around the estate (£265–£620 a week). ✉ *Mapledurham, near Reading* ☎ *0118/972–3350* ⊕ *www.mapledurham.co.uk* ☜ *House and mill £5, house only £4, grounds and mill £3* ☉ *Easter–Sept., weekends 2–5:30.*

Ewelme

➓ *12 mi north of Mapledurham House, 10 mi northwest of Henley-on-Thames off A4130.*

One of England's most unspoiled villages lies near the town of Benson, in Oxfordshire. Its picture-book almshouses, church, and school—one of the oldest in Britain—huddle close together, as they did more than 500 years ago. The church shelters the carved alabaster tomb of Alice, duchess of Suffolk, the granddaughter of medieval poet Geoffrey Chaucer. Jerome K. Jerome, author of the humorous book *Three Men in a Boat,* describing a 19th-century Thames-side vacation, is also buried here.

OXFORD

With arguably the most famous university in the world, Oxford has been a center of learning since the 12th century, with only the Sorbonne preceding it. To get the city placed in your mind's eye, say the phrase "dreaming spires" (the words are Matthew Arnold's) over and over, as all Oxford tour guides do, and think *Brideshead Revisited,* Sebastian Flyte, and Evelyn Waugh—not to mention Percy Bysshe Shelley, Oscar Wilde, and W. H. Auden. Except for the modern storefronts, the city stands as it has for hundreds of years, in part because Adolf Hitler had designs on making it his European capital and so spared it from bombings. When arriving, try to stop on one of the low hills that surround the city and look at the skyline. Stretched out in front of you is this ancient home of erudition and scholarship, where students are still required to take their exams in "sub fusc" attire (cap, gown, and white bow tie). Oxford is 55 mi northwest of London, at the junction of the Thames and Cherwell rivers. The city is bigger and more cosmopolitan than Cambridge, with two major industrial complexes on its outskirts: the Rover car factory and the Pressed Steel works. Plenty of traffic and even suburban sprawl lie beyond the hushed quadrangles, chapels, and gardens.

Exploring Oxford

Oxford University is not one unified campus but a collection of many colleges and buildings, new as well as old, scattered across the city. Undergraduates live and study at 40 colleges. Most of the grounds and magnificent dining halls and chapels are open to visitors, though the opening

Oxford

University Parks

Keble Rd.

Little Clarendon St.

Woodstock Rd.

Banbury Rd.

Keble College

Museum Rd.

㉒

South Parks Rd.

St. Cross Rd.

Mansfield College

Mansfield Rd.

St. John St.

Pusey St.

St. Giles

㉑

⑳

Wadham College

Savile Rd.

Trinity College

Jowett Walk

St. Cross Rd.

Beaumont St.

Magdalen St.

⑱

Holywell St.

Magdalen Grove

Gloucester Green

Bus Station 🛈

Broad St.

⑲

⑰ ⑯

Bodleian Library

⑬

George St.

Ship St.

Catte St.

Queen's Ln.

Longwall St.

← TO TRAIN STATION

St. Michael's St.

New Inn Hall St.

Cornmarket

Turl St.

⑮

Queen's College

High St.

Market St.

⑭

New Rd.

Market

Magpie Ln.

All Souls College

Queen St.

⑳

St. Aldate's

(The High)

Oriel College

Bear Lane

High St.

⑫

Blue Boar St.

Merton St.

⑪

Castle St.

St. Ebbe's

Main Post Office

Oriel St.

Merton College

TO MAGDALEN BRIDGE →

Norfolk St.

Pembroke St.

⑳

Dead Man's Walk

Westgate Shopping Center

Brewer St.

Corpus Cristi College

Rose Pl.

Clarks Row

Broad Walk

Thames St.

Speedwell St.

New Walk

Christ Church Meadow

Cherwell

Abingdon Rd.

Thames

Folly Bridge

Isis

KEY

🛈 *Tourist information*

🚩 *Start of walk*

0 ——— 220 yards
0 ——— 200 meters

Ashmolean Museum . . .**21**

Balliol College **18**

Carfax Tower **23**

Christ Church **24**

Magdalen College **12**

Museum of the
History of Science **17**

New College **13**

Oxford Story
Exhibition **19**

Oxford University Museum
of Natural History **22**

Radcliffe Camera **15**

Sheldonian Theatre . . .**16**

St. John's College **20**

University Church of
St. Mary the Virgin **14**

University of Oxford
Botanic Garden **11**

times (displayed at the entrance lodges) vary greatly. Some colleges are open only in the afternoons during university semesters, when the undergraduates are in residence; access is often restricted to the chapels and dining rooms (called halls) and sometimes the libraries, too, and you are requested to refrain from picnicking in the quadrangles. All are closed certain days during exams, usually from mid-April to late June, when the May Balls are held. The best way to gain access is to join a walking tour led by a Blue Badge guide. These two-hour tours leave up to five times daily from the Tourist Information Centre. As you walk through this scholastic wonderland, try to spot as many Gothic gargoyles as you can; after all, this *was* the home turf of Alice and Lewis Carroll.

The St. Clement's car park before the roundabout that leads to Magdalen Bridge is one of the only places with public parking, so pay the price if you're making a day trip.

a good walk

The most picturesque approach to a college tour is from the east, over Magdalen (pronounced *maud*-lin) Bridge. After crossing the bridge, turn left off gently curving High Street for a sojourn through the **University of Oxford Botanic Garden** ⑪ ☞ and Christ Church Meadow, or turn right into **Magdalen College** ⑫. Its quadrangle is a quiet area enclosed by ancient vaulted cloisters covered with wisteria. Almost halfway up High Street, turn right onto Queen's Lane and take in the extensive gardens and the row of gargoyles at **New College** ⑬. A little farther up High Street turn right at the 14th-century tower of the **University Church of St. Mary the Virgin** ⑭ and behold the gilded gates of All Souls College and the magnificent 17th-century dome of the **Radcliffe Camera** ⑮. The Bridge of Sighs and Bodleian Library lie straight ahead, and a left at Broad Street brings you to Christopher Wren's **Sheldonian Theatre** ⑯. Step past its iron gates and those fabulous megabusts of the Roman emperors to check out the schedule for evening concerts here. Next door to the Sheldonian is the **Museum of the History of Science** ⑰, the original site of the Ashmolean, the oldest public museum in Britain. Book lovers may want to cross the street to Blackwell's before heading down St. Giles to see **Balliol College** ⑱.

If you have time, go back to Broad Street and stop in at the **Oxford Story Exhibition** ⑲, an imaginative presentation of 800 years of Oxford life. You may want to continue north along St. Giles to a possible lunch stop, the Eagle and Child pub, where J. R. R. Tolkien often met his friends, the "Inklings." Next, check out either the lovely gardens of **St. John's College** ⑳ or the excellent **Ashmolean Museum** ㉑, on Beaumont Street. After viewing Oliver Cromwell's death mask you may be up for a spot of tea, so dip into the Randolph across the way for a reviving cuppa in its Victorian Gothic interior. If you're a natural history buff, you may want to head over to the **Oxford University Museum of Natural History** ㉒ on Parks Road. Late afternoon should lure you south, down Cornmarket, passing **Carfax Tower** ㉓, Oxford's preeminent lookout point, to St. Aldate's and **Christ Church** ㉔, Oxford's snobbiest college, with its vast Tom Quad, 800-year-old chapel, medieval dining hall, and scholarly Picture Gallery.

TIMING You can walk this route in 1½ hours, but it's easy to spend a full day here if you visit each of the key museums for an hour and take more time to absorb the scene by exploring the colleges. Be sure to note college opening hours and check in advance for special closures. If you're arriving at the train station for a day in Oxford, you might wish to start at the Ashmolean Museum and work your way backward.

What to See

㉑ Ashmolean Museum. Britain's oldest public museum contains among its priceless collections (all university-owned) many Egyptian, Greek, and Roman artifacts uncovered during archaeological expeditions conducted by the university. Michelangelo drawings, the Alfred jewels, and a Chinese gallery are some highlights. ⊠ *Beaumont St.* ☎ *01865/278000* ⊕ *www.ashmol.ox.ac.uk* ☞ *Free* ☉ *Tues.–Sat. 10–5, Sun. 2–5.*

⑱ Balliol College. The wooden doors between the inner and outer quadrangles of Balliol (founded 1263) still bear scorch marks from 1555 and 1556, when during the reign of Mary ("Bloody Mary"), Bishops Latimer and Ridley and Archbishop Cranmer were burned alive on huge pyres in Broad Street for their Protestant beliefs. A cross on the roadway marks the spot. The **Martyrs' Memorial** at St. Giles and Beaumont Street also commemorates the three men. ⊠ *Broad St. and St. Giles* ☎ *01865/277777* ⊕ *www.balliol.ox.ac.uk* ☞ *£1* ☉ *Daily 2–5.*

㉓ Carfax Tower. Passing through Carfax, where four roads meet, you can spot this tower, all that remains of **St. Martin's Church,** where Shakespeare stood as godfather for William Davenant, who himself became a playwright. Every 15 minutes, little mechanical "quarter boys" mark the passage of time on the tower front. You can climb up the dark stairwell for a good view of the town center. ⊠ *Corner of Carfax and Cornmarket* ☎ *01865/792653* ☞ *£1.20* ☉ *Apr.–Oct., daily 10–5:15; Nov.–Mar., daily 10–3:30.*

㉔ Christ Church. Built in 1546, the college of Christ Church is referred to by its members as "The House." This is the site of Oxford's largest quadrangle, Tom Quad, named after the huge bell (6¼ tons) that hangs in the gate tower and still rings 101 times at five past nine every evening in honor of the original number of Christ Church scholars. The vaulted, 800-year-old chapel in one corner has been Oxford's cathedral since the time of Henry VIII. The college's medieval dining hall contains portraits of many famous alumni, including John Wesley, William Penn, and 13 of Britain's prime ministers. (A reproduction of this room appears in the banquet scenes at Hogwarts School in the film versions of *Harry Potter and the Sorcerer's Stone* and *Harry Potter and the Chamber of Secrets.*) Lewis Carroll was a teacher of mathematics here for many years; a shop opposite the meadows on St. Aldate's sells Alice paraphernalia. ⊠ *St. Aldate's* ☎ *01865/286573* ⊕ *www.chch.ox.ac.uk* ☞ *£4* ☉ *Mon.–Sat. 9:30–5:30, Sun. 1–5:30.*

Christ Church Picture Gallery. This connoisseur's delight in Canterbury Quadrangle exhibits works by the Italian masters as well as Hals, Rubens, and Van Dyck. Drawings in the 2,000-strong collection are shown on a changing basis. ⊠ *Oriel Sq.* ☎ *01865/276172* ⊕ *www.chch.ox. ac.uk* ⊡ *£2* ⊗ *Mon.–Sat. 10:30–1 and 2–4:30, Sun. 2–4:30.*

★ ⑫ **Magdalen College.** Founded in 1458, with a handsome main quadrangle and a supremely monastic air, Magdalen is one of the richest and most impressive of Oxford's colleges. A stroll around the Deer Park and along Addison's Walk is a good way to appreciate the place. Alumni have included such diverse people as Cardinal Wolsey, Edward Gibbon, Oscar Wilde, and Dudley Moore. ⊠ *High St.* ☎ *01865/276000* ⊕ *www. magd.ox.ac.uk* ⊡ *£2* ⊗ *June–Sept., daily noon–6.*

⑰ **Museum of the History of Science.** The Ashmolean, Britain's oldest public museum, was originally housed in this 1638 building, which now holds scientific and mathematical instruments, from astrolabes to quadrants to medical equipment. You can also visit the restored 18th-century chemical laboratory in the basement. ⊠ *Broad St.* ☎ *01865/277280* ⊕ *www.mhs.ox.ac.uk* ⊡ *Free* ⊗ *Tues.–Sat. noon–4, Sun. 2–5.*

⑬ **New College.** Founded in 1379, New College has extensive gardens, partly enclosed by the medieval city wall, and an outstanding row of gargoyles. Famous alumni include actor Hugh Grant and Richard Mason, who published his international best-seller, *The Drowning People,* only months after first "coming up" to Oxford. ⊠ *Holywell St.* ☎ *01865/279555* ⊕ *www.new.ox.ac.uk* ⊡ *Easter–Sept. £2, Oct.–Easter free* ⊗ *Easter–Sept., daily 11–5; Oct.–Easter, daily 2–4.*

☾ ⑲ **Oxford Story Exhibition.** This imaginative presentation in a converted warehouse revisits 800 years of Oxford life with models, sounds, and smells. You ride through the exhibition in small cars shaped like medieval students' desks. ⊠ *6 Broad St.* ☎ *01865/728822* ⊕ *www.oxfordstory. org.uk* ⊡ *£6.75* ⊗ *July and Aug., daily 9:30–5; Sept.–June, Mon.–Sat. 10–4:30, Sun. 11–4:30.*

㉒ **Oxford University Museum of Natural History.** Eclectic collections relating to entomology, geology, mineralogy, and zoology are stored in this massive Victorian Gothic structure. Among the myriad exhibits are local dinosaur remains and the head and left foot of a dodo bird. The museum is across the street from the Rhodes House, in which hangs a portrait of former president Bill Clinton, who attended University College on High Street. ⊠ *Parks Rd.* ☎ *01865/272950, 01865/ 270949 recorded information* ⊕ *www.oum.ox.ac.uk* ⊡ *Free* ⊗ *Daily noon–5.*

★ ⑮ **Radcliffe Camera and Bodleian Library.** One of the largest domes in Britain tops Oxford's most beautiful building, built in 1737–49 by James Gibbs in Italian Baroque style. The Camera contains part of the Bodleian Library's collection, which was begun in 1602 and has grown to more than 6 million volumes, including a copy of every book ever printed in Great Britain. Although visitors are not allowed in the Camera, the general public may stop into another part of the Bodleian, the Divinity School, a superbly vaulted room dating back to 1462. In the film *Harry Potter and the Sorcerer's Stone,* some interior scenes at Hogwarts School take place in parts of the Bodleian, including the Divinity School. (For another scholarly library, medieval in vintage, check out the library at Merton College on Merton Street.) ✉ *Broad St.* ☎ *01865/277224 for information on tour* ⊕ *www.bodley.ox.ac.uk* ✍ *£3.50, extended tour £7* ⊙ *Tours of Bodleian Mar.–Oct., weekdays at 10:30, 11:30, 2, and 3; Sat. at 10:30 and 11:30; Nov.–Feb., weekdays at 2 and 3; Sat. at 10:30 and 11:30. Children under 14 not admitted. Divinity School weekdays 9–4:45, Sat. 9–12:30.*

⑯ Sheldonian Theatre. This fabulously ornate theater is where Oxford's impressive graduation ceremonies are held, conducted almost entirely in Latin. Dating to 1663, it was the first building designed by Sir Christopher Wren when he served as professor of astronomy. The D-shape theater has pillars, balconies, and an elaborately painted ceiling. Outside, stone pillars are topped by 18 massive stone heads, sculpted in the 1970s to replace originals destroyed by air pollution. ✉ *Broad St.* ☎ *01865/277299* ⊕ *www.sheldon.ox.ac.uk* ✍ *£1.50* ⊙ *Mon.–Sat. 10–12:30 and 2–4:30; mid-Nov.–Feb., closes at 3:30. Closed for 10 days at Christmas and Easter and for degree ceremonies and events.*

⑳ St. John's College. For a quiet pause, step inside St. John's (1555) to see its huge gardens, among the city's loveliest. ✉ *St. Giles* ☎ *01865/ 277300* ⊕ *www.sjc.ox.ac.uk* ⊙ *Daily 1–dusk.*

The **Eagle and Child pub** (✉ 49 St. Giles ☎ 01865/302925) is a tourist favorite not only for its good beer and snacks but for its literary history. This was the meeting place of C. S. Lewis, J. R. R. Tolkien, and their circle of literary friends, the "Inklings." The pub's narrow interior leads to a conservatory and small terrace.

⑭ University Church of St. Mary the Virgin. From the top of the church's 14th-century tower, you get a panoramic view of the city's skyline with nearly every architectural style since the 11th century. Seven hundred years' worth of funeral monuments crowd the interior, including one belonging to Amy Robsart, the wife of Robert Dudley, Elizabeth I's favorite. One pillar marks the site of Thomas Cranmer's trial under Bloody Mary for his marital machinations on behalf of Henry VIII. The Convocation House, a part of the church accessible from Radcliffe Square, serves generous portions—cafeteria style—under the room in which the charity OxFam was founded. ✉ *High St.* ☎ *01865/279111* ⊕ *www. university-church.ox.ac.uk* ✍ *Church free, tower £2* ⊙ *Sept.–June, Mon.–Sat. 9–5, Sun. noon–5; July and Aug., Mon.–Sat. 9–6, Sun. noon–6; last admission to tower 30 mins before closing.*

▶ ⑪ University of Oxford Botanic Garden. Founded in 1621 as a physic (healing) garden, this is the oldest of its kind in the British Isles. The compact but diverse garden displays 7,000 species from lilies to palms in greenhouses, a small walled garden, and special gardens (such as rock and bog gardens) outside the walled area. ✉ *Rose La.* ☎ *01865/286690* ⊕ *www.botanic-garden.ox.ac.uk* ✍ *Free* ⊙ *Garden Mar.–Sept., daily 9–5; Oct.–Feb., daily 9–4:30; greenhouse Apr.–Sept., daily 10–4:30, Oct.–Mar., daily 10–4.*

Where to Eat

The Old Bank and Old Parsonage hotels also have worthwhile restaurants.

★ **£££££** ✕ **Rosamund the Fair.** Gaze at swans and eat delicious classic cuisine with a modern twist while you glide smoothly down the Isis past Folly Bridge and the university boathouse. For £57 per person, you get dinner from a set menu plus a three-hour cruise on the lovely *Rosamund the Fair,* which seats about 20 people. Vegetarians can be accommodated if they contact the chef in advance. Dinner cruises leave at 7:30, weekend lunch cruises at 12:30. ⊠ *Castle Mill Boatyard, Cardigan St.* ☎ *01295/278690* ⚏ *Reservations essential* ⊟ *AE, MC, V* ⊗ *Closed Mon. and Jan.*

★ **£££** ✕ **Le Petit Blanc.** Raymond Blanc's sophisticated brasserie, a hipper cousin of Le Manoir aux Quat' Saisons in Great Milton, is the finest place to eat in Oxford. The changing menu always lists innovative, visually stunning adaptations of bourgeois French fare, sometimes with Mediterranean or Asian influences. Try the herb pancakes with mushrooms, Gruyère, and ham. The set menus here are a good value. ⊠ *71–72 Walton St.* ☎ *01865/510999* ⊟ *AE, DC, MC, V.*

£££ ✕ **Gee's.** With its glass and steel framework, this former florist's shop just north of the town center resembles a quintessential English conservatory. The constantly changing menu highlights French and English dishes with seasonal variations, and the place is popular with both town and gown. ⊠ *61 Banbury Rd.* ☎ *01865/553540* ⊟ *AE, MC, V* ✎ *No smoking.*

££ ✕ **Café Joe's.** For some of the best eggs Benedict in the valley, cross the Magdalen Bridge out of town, take the center fork, and continue past the café's takeout sibling, Espresso Joe, on the left. Students "living out" sip lattés and eat goat cheese salad and grilled chicken with couscous in comfortable style. ⊠ *21 Cowley Rd.* ☎ *01865/201120* ⊟ *MC, V.*

£–££ ✕ **Grand Café.** Golden-hue tiles, columns, and antique marble tables make this café both architecturally impressive and an excellent spot for a light meal or leisurely drink. The tasty menu lists sandwiches, salads, and tarts as well as perfect coffee drinks and desserts. ⊠ *84 High St.* ☎ *01865/ 204463* ⊟ *AE, MC, V.*

FodorśChoice ★

£–££ ✕ **Trout Inn.** More than a century ago, Lewis Carroll took three children on a Thames picnic. "We rowed up to Godstow, and had tea beside a haystack," he told a friend at Christ Church; "I told them the fairy tale of Alice's adventures in Wonderland." The haystacks are gone, but you can still stop at the creeper-covered Thames-side pub 2 mi north of the city center for mixed grills and baked trout. There's a corner devoted to Carroll, and a Morse bar with Morse memorabilia, as the fictional inspector often drank here. ⊠ *195 Godstow Rd., Wolvercote* ☎ *01865/ 302071* ⊟ *AE, DC, MC, V.*

Where to Stay

Oxford is pricey; for the cheapest lodging, contact the tourist information office for bed-and-breakfasts in locals' homes.

£££££   🏨 **The Randolph.** A 19th-century neo-Gothic landmark, the hotel faces both the Ashmolean and the Martyrs' Memorial. If their parents are feeling generous, undergraduates are treated to tea in the Morse Bar or dinner in the Spires Restaurant. Scenes from PBS's Inspector Morse *Mystery* series and the film *Shadowlands* were shot here. The floorboards can be *too* historic; in some rooms, squeaky ceilings can lead to sleepless nights. ✉ *Beaumont St., OX1 2LN* 🕾 *0870/400–8200* 🖷 *01865/791678* ⊕ *www.macdonald-hotels.co.uk* 🛏 *99 rooms, 10 suites* ⚭ *Restaurant, room service, fans, in-room data ports, minibars, cable TV, bar, lobby lounge, dry cleaning, laundry service, concierge, Internet, business services, meeting rooms, airport shuttle, car rental, parking (fee), some pets allowed (fee), no-smoking floors; no a/c* 🖃 *AE, DC, MC, V.*

★
££££–£££££   🏨 **Old Parsonage.** This hotel, a 17th-century gabled stone house in a small garden next to St. Giles Church, provides a dignified escape from the surrounding city center. Dark wood paneling in the lobby and the guest rooms' tasteful chintzes and marble baths are far from trendy, but memorable meals by an open fire (or in the walled garden terrace in summer) keep people coming back. The inspired international menu includes monkfish with prawn Thai curry and wild mushroom tart. Afternoon cream teas are excellent. ✉ *1 Banbury Rd., OX2 6NN* 🕾 *01865/ 310210* 🖷 *01865/311262* ⊕ *www.oxford-hotels-restaurants.co.uk* 🛏 *26 rooms, 4 suites* ⚭ *Restaurant, room service, in-room data ports, in-room safes, cable TV, bar, lobby lounge, baby-sitting, dry cleaning, laundry service, business services, car rental, free parking; no a/c* 🖃 *AE, DC, MC, V.*

££££   🏨 **Old Bank Hotel.** From its sleek lobby to the 20th-century British paintings on display and the subdued modern furnishings in the guest rooms, the former Barclay's Bank has brought some style to a city that favors the traditional. Oxford's most centrally located hotel also holds the contemporary Quod Bar and Grill, serving creative pastas and dishes such as duck confit. ✉ *92–94 High St., OX1 4BN* 🕾 *01865/799599* 🖷 *01865/799598* ⊕ *www.oxford-hotels-restaurants.co.uk* 🛏 *43 rooms* ⚭ *Restaurant, room service, in-room data ports, in-room safes, cable TV, bar, lounge, baby-sitting, dry cleaning, laundry service, meeting room, free parking, no-smoking rooms* 🖃 *AE, DC, MC, V.*

££££   🏨 **Royal Oxford Hotel.** One of Oxford's newest hotels, opened in 2002, is just a few steps from the train station, but don't let that deter you from staying here. Rooms are bright, light, and modern, with contemporary furniture—think Ikea. Tea and coffeemakers and hospitality trays of chocolates, fruit, and biscuits are welcome touches. ✉ *17 Park End St., OX1 1HR* 🕾 *01865/248431* 🖷 *01865/250049* ⊕ *www. royaloxfordhotel.co.uk* 🛏 *26 rooms* ⚭ *Restaurant, room service, in-room data ports, cable TV, dry cleaning, laundry service, business services, meeting rooms, Internet, parking (fee), no-smoking rooms; no a/c* 🖃 *AE, MC, V* ⦿ *BP.*

£££   🏨 **Bath Place Hotel.** Down a cobbled alleyway off Holywell Street stand these 17th-century weavers' cottages converted into a small hotel. A number of rooms have four-poster beds; nearly all have slanting floors and exposed beams. Some rooms have their own entrances, and others are in the main building. There's only a breakfast room, but the adjacent

Turf Tavern serves ale and bar food. ⊠ *4–5 Bath Pl., OX1 3SI* ☎ *01865/791812* 🖷 *01865/791834* ⊕ *www.bathplace.co.uk* 🖙 *14 rooms* ⌂ *Fans, minibars, bar, laundry service, free parking, some pets allowed; no a/c, no smoking* ☰ *AE, DC, MC, V* ¶⊙¶ *CP.*

££–£££ 🖫 **Victoria House Hotel.** Basic, modern rooms at a low (for Oxford) price are the draw at this no-nonsense hotel aimed at the business set. Don't expect breakfast here, but on your doorstep is a fine selection of cafés. The downstairs Mood bar attracts the trendy with its resident DJ; on weekends, clubbers use the hotel as a base. ⊠ *29 George St., OX1 2AY* ☎ *01865/727400* 🖷 *01865/727402* ⊕ *www.victoriahouse-hotel.co.uk* 🖙 *14 rooms* ⌂ *Bar; no a/c, no smoking* ☰ *AE, DC, MC, V.*

Nightlife & the Arts

Nightlife

Nightlife in Oxford centers around student life, which in turns centers around the local pubs, though you may find a few surprises, too. **Frevd** (⊠ 119 Walton St. ☎ 01865/311171), in a renovated neoclassical church, serves light meals and cocktails as well as nightly live jazz or funk. The **Kings Arms** (⊠ 40 Holywell St. ☎ 01865/242369), popular with students and fairly quiet during the day, carries excellent local brews as well as inexpensive pub grub. **Raoul's** (⊠ 32 Walton St. ☎ 01865/553732) is a trendy cocktail bar in the equally trendy Jericho neighborhood. The **Turf Tavern** (⊠ Bath Pl. ☎ 01865/243235), off Holywell Street, includes a higgledy-piggledy collection of little rooms and outdoor space good for a quiet drink and inexpensive pub food.

The Arts

FESTIVALS & CONCERTS **Choral music** at the city's churches is a calming way to spend the early evening. Drop by weekdays except Wednesday during term time at 6 PM at Christ Church, Magdalen, or New College to hear evensong.

The **Jacqueline Du Pre Music Building** (⊠ St. Hilda's College ☎ 01865/276821), endowed with the city's best acoustics, showcases rising talent at recitals. **Music at Oxford** (☎ 01865/798600), an acclaimed series of weekend classical concerts, takes place mid-September–June in such surroundings as Christ Church Cathedral and Sir Christopher Wren's Sheldonian Theatre. At the **Oxford Coffee Concerts** (⊠ Holywell Music Room, Holywell Rd. ☎ 01865/305305), a program of Sunday chamber concerts, string quartets, piano trios, and soloists present baroque and classical pieces in a venerable 1748 hall. Reasonably priced tickets are available from the Oxford Playhouse on Beaumont Street.

Blenheim Palace (☎ 01993/811091) in Woodstock is occasionally the venue for classical concerts in summer, sometimes combined with fireworks displays.

OPERA The **Garsington Opera** (⊠ Garsington ☎ 01865/361636), a well-regarded event staged in a covered outdoor auditorium, uses Garsington Manor's magical gardens as a backdrop for classic and little-known operas for a month each summer. The manor is 5 mi southeast of Oxford; you can dine in the Great Barn.

THEATERS During term time, undergraduate productions are often given in the colleges or local halls. In summer, outdoor performances may take place in quadrangles or college gardens. Look for announcement posters.

The Apollo (⊠ George St. ☏ 0870/606–3500), Oxford's main theater, stages plays, opera, ballet, pantomime, and concerts. It's the recognized second home of the Welsh National Opera and the Glyndebourne Touring Opera. **Old Fire Station** (⊠ 40 George St. ☏ 01865/794490), an alternative theater, showcases student productions, small-scale opera, and new musicals. The **Oxford Playhouse** (⊠ Beaumont St. ☏ 01865/798600) is a serious theater presenting classic and modern dramas.

Sports & the Outdoors

Biking
Bikes can be rented at **Bike Zone** (⊠ Market St. ☏ 01865/728877).

Punting
Fodor'sChoice You may choose, like many an Oxford student, to spend a summer af-
★ ternoon **punting,** while dangling your champagne bottle in the water to keep it cool. Punts—shallow-bottomed boats that are poled slowly up the river—can be rented in several places.

From mid-March through mid-October, **Cherwell Boathouse** (⊠ Bardwell Rd. ☏ 01865/515978), a punt station and restaurant a mile north of the heart of Oxford, will rent you a boat and, if you wish, someone to punt it. Rentals are £10–£12 per hour; £50–£60 per day. At the foot of **Magdalen Bridge** (⊠ High St. ☏ 01865/515978) you can rent a punt for £10 an hour, plus a £25 refundable deposit. At the St. Aldates Road end of Folly Bridge, **Salter's Steamers** (☏ 01865/243421) rents out punts and skiffs (row boats) for £10 per hour, £30 per half-day, and £50 per day. Their chauffeured punts (£35 per hour) include a bottle of wine.

Spectator Sports
At the end of May, during **Oxford's Eights Week,** men and women rowers from the university's colleges compete to be "Head of the River." Because the river is too narrow and twisting for teams of eight to race side by side, the boats set off, 13 at a time, one behind another. Each boat tries to catch and bump the one in front. Spectators can watch all the way.

Oxford University Cricket Club competes against leading county teams and, each summer, the major foreign team visiting Britain. In the middle of the sprawling University Parks—itself worthy of a walk—the club's playing field is one of the loveliest in England.

Shopping

Small shops line High Street, Cornmarket, and Queen Street, and the Clarendon and Westgate centers, which lead off them, have branches of several nationally known stores. **Alice's Shop** (⊠ 83 St. Aldate's ☏ 01865/723793) sells all manner of *Alice in Wonderland* paraphernalia. **Blackwell's** (⊠ 48–50 Broad St. ☏ 01865/792792), family-owned and -run since 1879, stocks one of the world's widest selections of books. The **Covered Market** (⊠ Off High St.) is a good place for a cheap sandwich and a leisurely browse; the smell of pastries follows you from cobbler to jeweler to cheese-monger. **Shepherd & Woodward** (⊠ 109 High St. ☎ 01865/249491), a traditional tailor, specializes in university gowns, ties, and scarves. The **University of Oxford Shop** (⊠ 106 High St. ☎ 01865/247414), run by the university, sells authorized clothing, ceramics, and tea towels, all emblazoned with university crests.

BLENHEIM PALACE TO ALTHORP

The River Thames takes on a new graciousness as it flows along the borders of Oxfordshire for 71 mi; each league it increases in size and importance. Three tributaries swell the river as it passes through the landscape: the Windrush, the Evenlode, and the Cherwell. Tucked among the hills and dales are one of England's most impressive stately homes, one of its most Edenic villages, and a former Rothschild estate. Closer to London in Hertfordshire is St. Albans, with its cathedral and Roman remains.

Rousham Park House & Garden

25 *15 mi north of Oxford.*

Wonderfully uncommercialized Rousham Park House & Garden has an expansive 18th-century English landscape park as well as the austere, gray Dormer family mansion, built in 1635. Gardener William Kent's (1685–1748) design is still preserved in the park, where there are plenty of paths, groves and meadows, and walled gardens. Longhorn cattle add an exotic—for England, anyway—touch to the rural landscape. Tickets are sold on an honesty system through a vending machine. Children under 15 are not allowed, nor are dogs. ⊠ *Rousham, near Steeple Aston* ☎ *01869/347110* ⊕ *www.rousham.org* 🏠 *House £3, garden £3* ☉ *Gardens daily 10–4:30; house Apr.–Sept., Wed. and Sun. 2–4:30.*

Shopping

Serious fashionistas and bargain hunters head for the white clapboard storefronts at **Bicester Village Outlet Shopping** (⊠ 50 Pingle Dr., off A41, Bicester ☎ 01869/323200) to scoop up European luxury brands at cut-rate prices. British highlights include Aquascutum, Burberry, Gieves & Hawkes, Waterford Wedgwood, Molton Brown, and Penhaligon's. It's like shopping at a half-price sale on London's Bond Street.

Woodstock

★ **26** *8 mi northwest of Oxford on A44.*

Handsome 17th- and 18th-century houses line the trim streets of Woodstock, which sits at the edge of the Cotswolds and is best known for nearby Blenheim Palace. In summer, tour buses clog the village's ancient streets, and the lofty halls of Blenheim echo with the clamor of voices from around the world. On a quiet fall or spring afternoon, however, Woodstock is a sublime experience: a mellowed 18th-century church and town hall mark the central square, and along its back streets you can find flower-bedecked houses and quiet lanes right out of a 19th-century etching. A public bus route runs (usually every half hour) from Oxford to Woodstock.

Where to Stay & Eat

★ **££££**   ✕🏨 **The Feathers.** Flowery, antiques-bedecked guest rooms fill a stylish hotel in the heart of town that was created from five 17th-century houses. The courtyard is a favored spot for a summertime meal, and in winter, log fires make the public rooms cozy. The seasonal menu and upscale dining room are worth the restaurant's hefty prices. You might opt for a rich risotto topped with foie gras or duck confit or seafood such as roasted sea bass. ✉ *Market St., OX20 1SX* ☏ *01993/812291* 📠*01993/813158* ⊕*www.feathers.co.uk* 🛏*22 rooms, 5 suites* ♿*Restaurant, room service, cable TV, lounge, dry cleaning, laundry service, meeting rooms; no a/c* ⊟ *AE, DC, MC, V* ⚊⚌ *BP.*

££££–£££££   🏨 **The Bear.** This is an archetypal English coaching inn, with Tudoresque wood paneling, beamed ceilings, wattle-and-daub walls, and blazing fireplaces in winter. The guest rooms, overlooking either a quiet churchyard or the town square, have plenty of carved oak; the duplex suites would make a Stuart king feel at home, thanks to their timbered loftbalconies and gargantuan four-posters. Legend has it that the Bear is where Richard Burton finally popped the question to Elizabeth Taylor. ✉ *Park St., OX20 1SZ* ☏ *0870/400–8202* 📠 *01993/813380* ⊕ *www.heritagehotels.co.uk* 🛏 *47 rooms, 6 suites* ♿ *Restaurant, room service, minibars, cable TV, bar, laundry service, meeting rooms, no-smoking rooms; no a/c* ⊟ *AE, DC, MC, V* ⚊⚌ *BP.*

££   🏨 **Blenheim Guest House & Tea Rooms.** The Cinderella of all British hotels, this small three-story guest house stands in the quiet village cul-de-sac that leads to the back gates of Blenheim Palace. Its facade still bears a Victorian-era banner that says "Views and Postcards of Blenheim," and there's a storefront tearoom. The unassuming guest rooms have modern furnishings, but the Marlborough room is unique—its bathroom offers a view of Blenheim. ✉ *17 Park St. OX20 1SJ* ☏ *01993/813814* 📠 *01993/813810* ⊕ *www.theblenheim.com* 🛏 *6 rooms* ♿ *Tea shop, laundry service; no a/c, no smoking* ⊟ *MC, V* ⚊⚌ *BP.*

Blenheim Palace

㉗ *8 mi northwest of Oxford via A44 to A4095.*

Fodor's Choice
★

So grandiose is Blenheim's masonry and so breathtaking are its articulations of splendor that some have pondered why it hasn't been named a wonder of the world. Built by Sir John Vanbrugh in the early 1700s, Blenheim was given by Queen Anne and the nation to General John Churchill, first duke of Marlborough. The exterior is mind-boggling, with its huge columns, enormous pediments, and obelisks, all exemplars of English baroque. Inside, lavishness continues in monumental extremes. In most of the opulent rooms, great family portraits look down at sumptuous furniture, tapestries illustrating important battles, and immense pieces of silver. For some, however, the most memorable room is the small, low-ceiling chamber where Winston Churchill (his father was the younger brother of the then-duke) was born in 1874; he is buried in nearby Bladon.

Sir Winston wrote that the unique beauty of Blenheim lay in its perfect adaptation of English parkland to an Italian palace. Indeed the 2,000 acres of grounds, the work of Capability Brown, 18th-century England's most gifted landscape gardener, are arguably the best example of the "cunningly natural" park in the country. Brown declared that his object at Blenheim was to "make the Thames look like a small stream compared with the winding Danube." At points he almost succeeds—the scale of these grounds must be seen to be believed. At dusk, flocks of sheep are let loose to become living mowers for the magnificent lawns. Tucked away here is the Temple of Diana, where Winston Churchill proposed to his future wife, Clementine. Blenheim's formal gardens include notable water terraces and an Italian garden with a mermaid fountain, all built in the 1920s.

The Pleasure Gardens, reached by a train that stops just outside the main entrance to the palace, contain some child-pleasers: a butterfly house, giant hedge maze, playground, and giant chess set. The fragrant herb and lavender garden is also delightful. The train runs every 30 minutes from 11 AM until 5 PM. ⊠ *Woodstock* ☎ *01993/811325* ⊕ *www. blenheimpalace.com* 🎫 *£11* 🕑 *Palace mid-Mar.–Oct., daily 10:30–4:45; park daily 9–4:45; special events, fairs, and concerts throughout year.*

en route | After taking in Blenheim Palace, stop by **Bladon,** 2 mi southeast of Woodstock on A4095 and 6 mi northwest of Oxford, to see the small, tree-lined churchyard that is the burial place of Sir Winston Churchill. His grave is all the more impressive for its simplicity.

Kelmscott Manor

28 *11 mi west of Stanton Harcourt, 20 mi southwest of Oxford.*

Behind its dignified 16th- and 17th-century exterior, limestone Kelmscott Manor was, in its Victorian heyday, a site of social unrest as well as domestic disarray. Here, artist, writer, and socialist William Morris (1834–96) launched his anti-industrial Arts and Crafts movement. At the manor his wife, Jane, openly cohabited with her lover, the painter Dante Gabriel Rossetti (1828–82), Morris's business partner. Today the house displays textiles, furniture, and ceramics by Morris and his associates. The surrounding landscape was an obvious source of Morris's inspiration. Oxford University now owns the house, a unique monument to the "Brotherhood." Morris died at Kelmscott and is buried in the local churchyard. ⊠ *Off A417, Kelmscott, Lechlade* ☎ *01367/ 252486* ⊕ *www.kelmscottmanor.co.uk* 🎫 *£7, garden £2* 🕑 *Apr.–Sept., Wed. 11–1 and 2–5; Apr.–June and Sept., 3rd Sat. 2–5; July and Aug., 1st and 3rd Sat. 2–5.*

Uffington & the Vale of the White Horse

29 *7 mi southeast of Kelmscott Manor, 18 mi southwest of Oxford, 9 mi northeast of Swindon.*

Stretching up into the foothills of the Berkshire Downs between Swindon and Oxford is a wide fertile plain known as the Vale of the White

Horse. Here, off B4507, cut into the turf of the hillside to expose the underlying chalk, is the 374-foot-long, 110-foot-high **figure of a white horse,** one of the most important of Britain's prehistoric sites. Some historians believed that the figure might have been carved to commemorate King Alfred's victory over the Danes in 871, whereas others dated it to the Iron Age, around 750 BC. More current research suggests that it is at least 1,000 years older, created at the beginning of the second millennium BC. Nearby **Dragon Hill** is equally mysterious; an unlikely legend suggests that St. George slew his dragon on Dragon Hill. **Uffington Castle,** above the horse, is a prehistoric fort. English Heritage maintains these sites. To reach the Vale of the White Horse from Oxford, follow A420, then B4508 to the village of Uffington. The 85-mi **Ridgeway National Trail** (⊕ www.nationaltrail.co.uk), which runs from south of Aylesbury to near Avebury, passes through the area.

Where to Stay

£–££ 🏠 **The Craven B&B.** Rose-filled gardens and antiques-filled rooms are among the traditional elements at this pretty thatch-roof, 17th-century cottage on the outskirts of Uffington. Bedrooms have beamed ceilings and country-cottage prints. Family photographs and the shared breakfast at the kitchen table keep the B&B convivial. Creative seasonal menus are available for dinner (guests only). ⊠ *Fernham Rd., Uffington SN7 7RD* 🕾 *01367/820449* ⊕ *thecraven.co.uk* 🛏 *6 rooms, 4 with bath* 🍴 *Dining room, lounge, laundry service; no a/c, no room phones, no room TVs, no smoking* 🖃 *MC, V* 🍴 *BP.*

Dorchester-on-Thames

㉚ *15 mi east of Uffington, 7 mi southeast of Abingdon, 9 mi southeast of Oxford.*

An important center in Saxon times, when it was the seat of a bishopric, Dorchester deserves a visit chiefly for its ancient abbey. The main street, once a leg of the Roman road to Silchester, has timber houses, thatch cottages, and ancient inns. Crossing the Thames at Day's Lock and turning left at Little Wittenham takes you on a pleasant walk past the remains of the village's Iron Age settlements. Expensive antiques shops line the High Street.

In addition to secluded cloisters and gardens, **Dorchester Abbey** has a spacious church (1170) with traceried medieval windows and a lead baptismal font. The east window was restored in 1966 by the American Friends of the Abbey in memory of Sir Winston Churchill. The abbey is a popular concert venue. ⊠ *Off A4074* 🕾 *01865/340007* ⊕ *www.dorchester-abbey.org.uk* 🖃 *Free* ⊗ *May–Sept., daily 8:30–7; Oct.–Apr., daily 8:30–dusk, except during services.*

Where to Stay

££ 🏠 **George Hotel.** Overlooking Dorchester Abbey, this 500-year-old hotel was built as a coaching inn—there's an old coach parked outside—and it retains whitewashed walls, exposed beams, and log fires. Each room has an individual style and two have four-poster beds. The modern rooms in the annex have less character. ⊠ *25 High St. OX10 7JX* 🕾 *01865/*

340404 🖷 01865/341620 🍽 17 rooms ⚘ Restaurant, room service, in-room data ports, pub, dry cleaning, laundry facilities, meeting rooms, free parking, some pets allowed, no-smoking rooms; no a/c ☰ AE, MC, V ¶⊙¶ CP.

Great Milton

③¹ 8 mi northeast of Dorchester-on-Thames, 7 mi southeast of Oxford.

With attractive thatch cottages built of local stone and a single street about a mile long with wide grass verges, this is another stop on the literary pilgrim's route. The poet John Milton, author of Paradise Lost (1667), was married in the local church, which holds an unusual collection of old musical instruments. The town is also a haunt of culinary pilgrims.

Where to Stay & Eat

££££££ ✕🖾 **Le Manoir aux Quat' Saisons.** Standards are set high at this 15th-
Fodor'sChoice century stone manor house, which has luxurious rooms in styles from
★ rococo fantasy to chic chinoiserie (most rooms have private gardens and working fireplaces, too) and one of England's finest kitchens (complete with cooking school). Chef Raymond Blanc's epicurean touch shows at every turn. Spare yourself the trouble of deciding among the innovative French creations and treat yourself to the menu gourmand—eight courses of haute cuisine for £95. A stroll through the hotel's herb and Japanese gardens is de rigueur. ✉ Church Rd., OX44 7PD ☎ 01844/278881 🖷 01844/278847 ⊕ www.manoir.com 🍽 32 rooms ⚘ Restaurant, room service, in-room data ports, in-room safes, cable TV, lounge, croquet, baby-sitting, dry cleaning, laundry service, concierge, kennel, no-smoking rooms; no a/c in some rooms ☰ AE, DC, MC, V ¶⊙¶ CP.

Aylesbury

③² 17 mi northeast of Great Milton, 22 mi east of Oxford, 46 mi northwest of London.

Aylesbury makes a good base for exploring the surrounding countryside. The area around the 13th-century St. Mary's Church is the only hint of the 17th-century town with its small Tudor lanes and cottages.

Many of the regal residences created by the Rothschild family through-
Fodor'sChoice out Europe are gone now, but **Waddesdon Manor** remains, a vision of
★ the 19th century at its most sumptuous. G. H. Destailleur built the house in the 1880s for Baron Ferdinand de Rothschild in the style of a French chateau. Furnished with Savonnerie carpets, Sèvres porcelain, furniture made by Riesener for Marie Antoinette, and numerous paintings by Rubens, Watteau, Gainsborough, and Reynolds, the mansion underwent a top-to-bottom renovation, thanks to Lord Rothschild, current head of the English branch of the family. The National Trust now owns Waddesdon Manor. The splendid Victorian gardens and the aviary deserve a look, and you can dine on English or French fare and order excellent Rothschild wines at restaurants on the grounds. ✉ Waddesdon, on the A41 near Aylesbury ☎ 01296/653226 ⊕ www.waddesdon.org.uk 🖾 House £7, grounds £4 ⊙ House Apr.–Oct., Wed.–Sun. and

bank holiday Mon. 11–4; gardens Mar.–late Dec., Wed.–Sun. and bank holiday Mon. 10–5.

Fodor's Choice   A superb example of a Georgian garden, **Stowe Landscape Gardens** was
★   created for the Temple family by the most famous gardeners of the 18th century. Capability Brown, Charles Bridgeman, and William Kent all worked on the land to create 980 acres of pleasing greenery in the valleys and meadows. More than 30 striking monuments, follies, and temples dot the landscape of lakes, rivers, and pleasant vistas. Stowe House, at its center, is now a fancy school; it's closed to the public. The gardens are about 3 mi northwest of Buckingham, which is a half mile from Aylesbury. ☒ *Stowe Ave., off 422 Buckingham–Banbury Rd., Buckingham* ☎ *01280/822850* ⊕ *www.nationaltrust.org.uk* ☒ *£5* ☼ *Mar.–Oct., Wed.–Sun. 10–5:30; Nov. and Dec., Wed.–Sun. 10–4.*

Where to Stay & Eat

££–£££   ✕🖫 **Five Arrows.** Patterned brick chimneys and purple gables decorate this Tudor-style Victorian building next to the main entrance of Waddesdon Manor. Constructed to house the manor's workers, it now holds a hotel with traditional-style bedrooms that are sweet if small. The delightful suites in the Courtyard Stables are big enough for families. A fine restaurant and pub serves inspired modern fare with a Mediterranean twist; the wine list is excellent. ☒ *High St., Waddesdon HP18 0JE* ☎ *01296/651727* 🖷 *01296/658596* ⊕ *www.waddesdon.org.uk* ➳ *9 rooms, 2 suites* ⌂ *Restaurant, bar; no a/c, no smoking* ⊟ *MC, V* � *BP.*

£££££   🖫 **The Grove.** How many high-priced retreats can the area hold? This epitome of the modern country-house hotel—a hybrid with an 18th-century manor house and a 21st-century wing—shows that there's room for one more with old-fashioned charm and contemporary style. In the manor house, luxurious touches include Victorian clawfoot bathtubs and ostrich feather–topped four-poster beds. Rooms in the modern wing are sleek, with white lacquered furniture. All rooms have plasma-screen TVs and digital radio, and some have balconies with views of the gardens. The spa is perfectly pampering. ☒ *Off Exit 19 of M25, Chandler's Cross, WD3 4TG, 14 mi east of Aylesbury* ☎ *01923/807807* 🖷 *01923/221008* ⊕ *www.thegrove.co.uk* ➳ *211 rooms, 16 suites* ⌂ *Restaurant, room service, cable TV, in-room movies, in-room DVD, in-room data ports, in-room safes, minibars, 2 tennis courts, indoor-outdoor pool, gym, hair salon, hot tub, sauna, spa, steam room, 18-hole golf course, croquet, bar, lounge, library, dry cleaning, laundry service, concierge, Internet, meeting rooms, no-smoking rooms* ⊟ *AE, D, MC, V.*

£££££   🖫 **Hartwell House.** Part Jacobean, part Georgian, this magnificent stately home provides formal luxury in the countryside. Chandeliers, valuable oil paintings, and carved ceilings adorn the marvelously ornate public areas. Bedrooms are suitably grand, and some have direct access to the gardens, including 90 acres of landscaped parkland for strolls. This is the kind of place where you must dress up for dinner. ☒ *Oxford Rd. (A418), HP17 8NL* ☎ *01296/747444* 🖷 *01296/747450* ⊕ *www. hartwell-house.com* ➳ *46 rooms* ⌂ *Restaurant, room service, in-room data ports, 2 tennis courts, indoor pool, gym, hair salon, hot tub, sauna, spa, steam room, fishing, croquet, bar, lounge, library, dry cleaning, laun-*

dry service, concierge, meeting rooms, car rental, some pets allowed, no-smoking floors; no a/c, no kids under 8 ⊟ AE, MC, V.

St. Albans

🟩 *25 mi east of Aylesbury, 27 mi northwest of London.*

St. Albans, a pleasant town on the outskirts of London, has a cathedral and a number of reminders of its long history, which extends back to the Romans. From AD 50 to 440, Verulamium was one of the largest towns in Roman Britain, and splendid Roman ruins and the Verulamium museum recall that past. The surrounding countryside gave birth to Beatrix Potter's *Peter Rabbit* and inspired George Bernard Shaw. Every Wednesday and Saturday, the Market Place comes alive with traders from all over England. St. Albans is just 20 minutes by fast train from King's Cross Station in central London. The Campaign for Real Ale (CAMRA) holds an annual beer festival here in late September.

Medieval pilgrims came from far and wide to hilltop **St. Albans Cathedral** to worship St. Alban, the Roman soldier turned Christian martyr. Construction of the impressive, mainly Norman cathedral began in the early 11th century, but the nearly 300-foot-long nave dates from 1235. The tower contains bricks from Roman buildings. ⊠ *Holywell Hill at High St.* ☎ *01727/860780* ⊕ *www.stalbanscathedral.org.uk* 🎫 *Free* ⊙ *Daily 8–5:45; guided tours weekdays 11:30 and 2:30, Sat. 11:30 and 2, Sun. 2:30.*

With exhibits on everything from Roman food to burial practices, the **Verulamium Museum,** on the site of the ancient Roman city, explores life 2,000 years ago. The re-created Roman rooms contain colorful mosaics that are some of the finest in Britain. Every second weekend of the month, "Roman soldiers" invade the museum and demonstrate the skills of the Imperial Army. ⊠ *St. Michael's St.* ☎ *01727/751810* ⊕ *www.verulamium.co.uk* 🎫 *£3.20* ⊙ *Mon.–Sat. 10–5:30, Sun. 2–5:30.*

Verulamium Park, adjacent to the Verulamium Museum, contains the usual (playground, summer wading pool, duck-filled lake) and the unusual—**Roman ruins** that include part of the Roman town hall and a hypocaust, a central heating system. The hypocaust dates to AD 200 and included one of the first heated floors in Britain. Brick columns supported the floor, and hot air from a nearby fire was drawn underneath the floor to keep bathers warm. ⊠ *St. Michael's St.* ☎ *01727/751810* ⊕ *www.verulamium.co.uk* 🎫 *Free* ⊙ *Hypocaust Mon.–Sat. 10–5:30, Sun. 2–5:30.*

Imagination can take you back to AD 130 and to a Roman stage drama as you walk around the ruins of the **Roman Theater,** one of the few in Britain. Next to the theater are the ruins of a Roman town house, shops, and a shrine. ⊠ *Bluehouse Hill* ☎ *01727/854051* 🎫 *£1.50* ⊙ *Easter–Nov., daily 10–5; Dec.–Easter, daily 10–4.*

Hatfield House, an outstanding brick mansion surrounded by formal gardens, stands as a testament to the magnificence of Jacobean architecture. Robert Cecil, earl of Salisbury, built Hatfield in 1611, and his descendants still live here. The interior, with its dark wood paneling, lush tapestries, and Tudor and Jacobean portraits, reveals much about the era. Perhaps the finest feature is the ornate Grand Staircase, with carved wooden figures on the banisters. Friday is Connoisseurs' Day; entrance is £10 and includes an extended tour and additional gardens. The **Elizabethan Banquet** (☎ 01707/262055 ⊕ www.theoldpalace.co. uk/banquets ✉ £40 ⊘ Tues., Fri., and Sat. 7:30 PM–11 PM) is a hearty five-course dinner accompanied by kitschy entertainment from King Henry VIII, Queen Elizabeth I, minstrels, and jokers. ⊠ *Hatfield, 6 mi east of St. Albans, off A1* ☎ *01707/287010* ⊕ *www.hatfield-house.co.uk* ✉ *House, gardens, and park £7.50 (£10 on Fri.), gardens £4.50, park £2* ⊘ *Easter–Sept., mansion daily noon–4, west gardens daily 11–5:30, east gardens Fri. 11–6; guided tours weekdays only.*

The Royal National Rose Society runs the **Gardens of the Rose,** which is full of the heady scents of more than 30,000 old-fashioned and modern roses. Bulbs, clematis, and other plants add interest and color through-out the season. The garden is 2 mi southeast of St. Albans. ⊠ *Chiswell Green, St. Albans* ☎ *01727/850461* ⊕ *www.roses.co.uk/harkness/rnrs/ rnrs.htm* ✉ *£4* ⊘ *Mid-Apr.–Sept., Mon.–Sat. 9–5, Sun. 10–6.*

From 1906 to his death in 1950, the famed playwright George Bernard Shaw lived in the small village of Ayot St. Lawrence. Today his small Edwardian home, **Shaw's Corner,** remains much as he left it. The most delightful curiosity is his little writing hut in the garden, which can be turned to face the sun. ⊠ *Off Hill Farm La. Ayot St. Lawrence, 9 mi northeast of St. Albans* ☎ *01438/820307, 01494/755567 recorded information* ⊕ *www.nationaltrust.org.uk* ✉ *£3.80* ⊘ *House Apr.–Nov., Wed.–Sun. 1–5; gardens Apr.–Nov., Wed.–Sun. noon–5:30.*

Where to Stay & Eat

£ ✕ **Waffle House.** Indoors or outside, you can have a great budget meal at the 16th-century Kingsbury Watermill, near the Verulamium Museum. The organic flour for the high-quality, sweet and savory Belgian waf-fles comes from Redbournbury Watermill just north of the city; daily specials add variety. In the main dining room, you can see the wheel churn the water of the River Ver. ⊠ *Kingsbury Watermill, St. Michael's St.,* ☎ *01727/853502* ▤ *AE, DC, MC, V.*

£ ✕ **Ye Olde Fighting Cocks.** Some claim this is England's oldest pub, and the octagonal building certainly looks suitably aged. The small rooms with low ceilings make a cozy stop in cold weather for a pint and sim-ple pub grub. Be prepared for crowds; this place is popular. ⊠ *Abbey Mill La.* ☎ *01727/865830* ▤ *MC, V.*

£££££ ✕▤ **St. Michael's Manor.** The Newling Ward family has owned this lux-urious 16th-century manor house in the heart of St. Albans for three gen-erations. The 5 acres of grounds, complete with a lake, add a sense of seclusion, and plush furniture helps make the antique- and painting-filled public areas inviting. The Victorian-style bedrooms are equipped with thoughtful extras like hot beverage facilities and complimentary bottled water, fruit, and cookies. The Terrace Room presents a daily set menu of fine modern British cooking, from fig and mozzarella salad with pur-ple basil to Madeira-braised beef with blood sausage. ⊠ *Fishpool St., AL3 4RY* ☎ *01727/864444* 🖷 *01727/848909* ⊕ *www.stmichaelsmanor.*

com ⮡ *22 rooms* ♿ *Restaurant, room service, cable TV, fishing, croquet, bar, lounge, dry cleaning, laundry service, baby-sitting, meeting room, no-smoking rooms; no a/c* ☐ *AE, DC, MC, V* ⊙ *BP.*

Woburn Abbey

🕐 **34** *30 mi west of St. Albans, 10 mi northeast of Aylesbury.*

Still the ancestral residence of the duke of Bedford, Woburn Abbey houses countless Grand Tour treasures and old master paintings, including 20 stunning Canalettos that practically wallpaper the crimson dining salon. Works by Gainsborough and Reynolds are also notable. The Palladian mansion contains a number of etchings by Queen Victoria, who left them behind after she stayed here. Nine species of deer roam the grounds, where an antiques center and small restaurant add to the list of attractions. **Woburn Safari Park,** a very popular drive-through experience, is home to big game from Africa and elsewhere. Jeep tours, walks with elephants, and other special packages are available. There are plenty of play areas, a boating lake with swan boats, and walkabouts with small animals such as wallabies. ✉ *Woburn* ☎ *01525/290666* ⊕ *www.woburnabbey.co. uk* 🎫 *House and deer park £8.50, safari £9, combined ticket £12; abbey grounds £2* ⊙ *Jan.–Mar. and Oct., weekends 11–4; Apr.–Sept., Mon.–Sat. 11–4, Sun. 11–5.*

Where to Stay & Eat

££££ ✕🏠 **The Inn at Woburn.** This modern hotel with traditional pine furnishings is in the center of Woburn village, a small Georgian town. Bedrooms are uncluttered and comfortable, with hot beverage makers; suites have their own entrances. Olivier's serves contemporary British cuisine, and the pub is a snug place for a pint. Ask about packages that include entrance to Woburn Abbey and Safari Park. ✉ *George St., Woburn MK17 9PX* ☎ *01525/290441* 📠 *01525/290432* ⊕ *www.theinnatwoburn. com* ⮡ *51 rooms, 7 suites* ♿ *Restaurant, room service, minibars, in-room data ports, some in-room safes, cable TV, lobby lounge, bar, dry cleaning, laundry service, meeting rooms, some pets allowed, no-smoking rooms; no a/c* ☐ *AE, DC, MC, V.*

Althorp

35 *5 mi west of Northampton, 27 mi northwest of Woburn Abbey.*

Deep in the heart of Northamptonshire sits Althorp, the ancestral home of the Spencers, the family of Diana, Princess of Wales. Here, on a tiny island within the estate park, is Diana's final resting place. Back in 1765 Horace Walpole described the setting as "one of those enchanted scenes which a thousand circumstances of history and art endear to a pensive spectator." As it turns out, Princess Diana and her siblings found the house ugly and melancholy, calling it "Deadlock Hall." What the house does have are rooms filled with Van Dycks, Reynoldses, and Rubens—all portraits of the Spencers going back 500 years—and an entry hall that architectural historian Nikolaus Pevsner called "the noblest Georgian room in the country." To these attractions, Earl Spencer has added a visitor center devoted to Diana, which includes her wedding dress, childhood memorabilia, and an exhibition on her charitable work. Tickets to Althorp must be booked in advance. On the west side of the estate park is Great Brington, the neighboring village where the church of **St. Mary the Virgin** (☉ daily noon–5) holds the Spencer family crypt; it's best reached by the designated path from Althorp. ✉ *Rugby Rd., off the A428* ☎ *01604/770107 house, 0870/167–9000 advance tickets* ⊕ *www. althorp.com* 🎟 *£11.50* ☉ *July–Sept., daily 10–5; closed Aug. 31.*

THAMES VALLEY A TO Z

To research prices, get advice from other travelers, and book travel arrangements, visit www.fodors.com.

AIR TRAVEL

The Thames Valley is convenient to major airports in London (⇨ Air Travel *in* Smart Travel Tips).

BUS TRAVEL

Traveling by bus continues to be the preferred method of transportation to the Thames Valley. Oxford's bus companies have service every 12 minutes (24 hours a day); pick-up points in London are Victoria train and bus stations, and Baker Street and Marble Arch by the Underground stops. They also offer shuttle service to Gatwick and Heathrow every half hour, and—at £9.50 for round-trip service—are considerably cheaper than the train.

The Oxford Bus Company and other local bus services, such as Stagecoach, link the towns between Oxford and Henley with services to Heathrow Airport and London. Reading Buses also connect Oxford and Reading to the airports, and First of Bracknell serves the smaller towns of Berkshire. For information about buses and other forms of public transportation, contact Traveline.

CUTTING COSTS The Oxford Bus Company offers a one-day ticket and a seven-day Freedom ticket, for unlimited bus travel within Oxford.

FARES & 🚌 **First** ☎ 01224/650100 ⊕ www.firstgroup.com. **Oxford Bus Company** ☎ 01865/
SCHEDULES 785400 ⊕ www.oxfordbus.co.uk. **National Express** ☎ 0870/580–8080 ⊕ www.
nationalexpress.com. **Reading Buses** ☎ 0118/959–4000 ⊕ www.reading-buses.co.uk.
Stagecoach Oxford Tube ☎ 01865/772250 ⊕ www.stagecoach-oxford.co.uk. **Traveline** ☎ 0870/608–2608 ⊕ www.traveline.org.uk.

CAR RENTAL

🚗 **Local Agencies A. A. Clark Self-Drive** ✉ 72–74 Arthur Rd., Windsor ☎ 01753/
800600. **Avis** ✉ 1 Abbey Rd., Oxford ☎ 01865/249000. **Europcar Interrent** ✉ BP Petrol
Station, Hartford Motors, Seacourt Tower, Botley, 4 mi north of Oxford ☎ 01865/
246373. **Hertz** ✉ City Motors Ltd., Wolvercote Roundabout, Woodstock Rd., Oxford
☎ 01865/319972.

CAR TRAVEL

The M4 and M40 radiate west from London, bringing Oxford (55 mi) and Reading (42 mi) within an hour's drive, except during rush hour. Although the roads are good, this wealthy section of the commuter belt has surprisingly heavy traffic, even on the smaller roads. Parking in towns can be a problem, too, so allow plenty of time.

EMERGENCIES

The John Radcliffe Hospital is accessible by Bus 13 from Carfax Tower in Oxford or from the A40.

🚑 **Ambulance, fire, police** ☎ 999. **John Radcliffe Hospital** ⊠ Headley Way, Oxford ☎ 01865/741166. **Princess Christian's Hospital** ⊠ 12 Clarence Rd., Windsor ☎ 01753/853121.

SPORTS & THE OUTDOORS

The Countryside Agency has been charting and preserving Thames paths for years and offers publications about them. For maps and advice, contact the National Trails Office or the Ramblers' Association. The Chiltern Conservation Board promotes walking in the Chilterns.

Cycling is perhaps the best way to see the Chilterns. Routes include the 98-mile Thames Valley Cycle Route from London to Oxford, the 200-mile Oxfordshire Cycleway around the county's countryside, and the 85-mile Ridgeway Path from Uffington that follows the Chilterns peaks; the National Trails Office has information. The 184-mile Thames Path also has plenty of cycling opportunities.

🚶 **Walking Chiltern Conservation Board** ⊠ 8 Summerleys Rd., Princes Risborough, HP27 9DT ☎ 01844/271300 ⊕ www.chilternsaonb.org. **Chiltern Way** ⊠ Chiltern Society, White Hill Centre, Chesham, HP5 1AG ☎ 01494/771250 ⊕ www.chilternsociety. org.uk. **Countryside Agency** ⊠ John Dower House, Crescent Pl., Cheltenham, GL50 3RA ☎ 01242/521381 ⊕ www.countryside.gov.uk ⊠ Dacre House, 19 Dacre St., London, SW1H 0DH ☎ 020/7340-2900. **National Trails Office** ⊠ Cultural Services, Holton, Oxford, OX33 1QQ ☎ 01865/810224 ⊕ www.nationaltrails.gov.uk. **Ramblers' Association** ⊠ Camelford House, 87–90 Albert Embankment, 2nd fl., London, SE1 7TW ☎ 020/7339-8500 ⊕ www.ramblers.org.uk. **Sustrans (Thames Valley Cycle Route)** ⊠ 35 King St., Bristol, BS1 4DZ ☎ 0117/926-8893 ⊕ www.sustrans.org.uk.

TOURS

BOAT TOURS The ideal way to see the Thames region is from the water; summertime trips range from 30 minutes to all day. Hobbs and Sons covers the Henley Reach and also rents boats. Salter Brothers runs daily steamer cruises, mid-May to mid-September from Windsor, Oxford, Abingdon, Henley, Marlow, and Reading. Thames River Cruises conducts outings from Caversham Bridge in Reading, Easter–September. French Brothers operates river trips from the Promenade, Windsor, and from Runnymede, as far as Hampton Court.

The Environment Agency's Visit Thames Web site and telephone hotline provide information about boating, fishing, and walking the Thames.

🚤 **Environment Agency Visit Thames** ☎ 0845/601-5336 ⊕ www.visitthames.com. **French Brothers** ⊠ The Promenade, Windsor ☎ 01753/851900 ⊕ www.boat-trips.co.uk. **Hobbs and Sons** ⊠ Station Rd., Henley-on-Thames ☎ 01491/572035. **Salter Brothers** ⊠ Folly Bridge, Oxford ☎ 01865/243421 ⊕ www.salterbros.co.uk. **Thames River Cruises** ⊠ Caversham Bridge, Reading ☎ 0118/948-1088.

BUS TOURS City Sightseeing runs guided, open-top bus tours of Windsor for £6 (daily mid-March–October, weekends only November–late December) and of Oxford for £9 (year-round).

🖪 **City Sightseeing** ☎ 01865/790522 ⊕ www.city-sightseeing.com.

Two-hour guided walking tours leave the Oxford Tourist Information Centre (⇨ Visitor Information) at 11 and 4 daily. Tickets (£6.50, £7.50 on Saturday) include admission to some colleges. Saturday tours include Christ Church. An Inspector Morse walking tour is offered at 1:30 on Saturdays, and ghost tours run June–September and October 31 on Friday and Saturday at 7:45 PM; cost for a theme tour is £7. The information center also sells pamphlets detailing walking tours.

Blue Badge guides provide themed walking tours (£4) of Windsor and Eton that start at the Windsor Tourist Information Centre (⇨ Visitor Information). Tours run mid-April–August on weekends at 10:30 AM. You can also purchase self-guided walking pamphlets for 50p each.

TRAIN TRAVEL

Trains to Oxford (1¼ hours) and the region depart from London's Paddington station. Ascot (½ hour) is easily accessible from London: trains leave Waterloo on the half hour. Trains to St. Albans (20 minutes) leave from Kings Cross Station. Confirm that your train is on time before going to the station—train service in this area is the busiest in all Britain. For timetables, call or log on to National Rail Enquiries. Contact Thames Trains directly for timetables and special offers, including a £50 Trio Ticket for unlimited travel on any three days within a seven-day period during summer in the Thames Valley.

🖪 **National Rail Enquiries** ☎ 0845/748–4950 ⊕ www.nationalrail.co.uk. **Thames Trains** ☎ 0800/358–3567 ⊕ www.thamestrains.co.uk.

TRAVEL AGENCIES

🖪 Local Agent Referrals **Thomas Cook** ✉ 5 Queen St., Oxford ☎ 01865/447000 ✉ 53 King Edward Ct., Windsor ☎ 01753/221400.

VISITOR INFORMATION

🖪 **Aylesbury** ✉ 8 Bourbon St., HP20 2RR ☎ 01296/330559. **Bicester** ✉ Bicester Village Outlet Shopping Centre, Pingle Dr., OX26 6WD ☎ 01869/369055. **Henley-on-Thames** ✉ King's Arms Barn, Kings Rd., RG9 2DG ☎ 01491/578034 ⊕ www.visit-henley.co.uk. **Marlow** ✉ 31 High St., SL7 1AU ☎ 01628/483597. **Oxford** ✉ 15/16 Broad St., OX1 3AS ☎ 01865/726871 ⊕ www.oxford.gov.uk. **Oxford University** ⊕ www.ox.ac.uk. **St. Albans** ✉ Town Hall, Market Pl., AL3 5DJ ☎ 01727/864511 ⊕ www.stalbans.gov.uk. **Windsor** ✉ 24 High St., SL4 1LH ☎ 01753/743900 ⊕ www.windsor.gov.uk. **Woburn** ✉ Old St. Mary's Church, Bedford St., MK17 9PJ ☎ 01525/290631. **Woodstock** ✉ Park St., Oxfordshire Museum, OX20 1SN ☎ 01993/813276.

SHAKESPEARE COUNTRY

STRATFORD-UPON-AVON & ENVIRONS

6

BRUSH UP ON THE BARD
at the Royal Shakespeare Theatre ➪ *p.320*

SIP ALE WITH THE ACTORS
at the Black Swan in Stratford ➪ *p.317*

STORM THE BATTLEMENTS
of Warwick Castle on the Avon ➪ *p.323*

EXPLORE TOWNS UNTOUCHED BY TIME
near peaceful Alderminster ➪ *p.327*

DON'T MISS THE MOAT
at medieval Baddesley Clinton ➪ *p.322*

ESCAPE THE STRATFORD BUSTLE
with a feast at the Fox & Goose ➪ *p.328*

Updated by
Catherine
Belonogoff

MUCH ADO ABOUT NOTHING? Far from it. Even if you know little about William Shakespeare, one flourish through his home territory will leave you referring to him familiarly as the Bard. Synonymous with Shakespeare, Stratford-upon-Avon has overshadowed other villages in the region with its popularity. But it was an important market town and malt-making center for more than 300 years before the Bard came along, and the surrounding area does not seem to mind the association with the Shakespeare juggernaut. Stratford has carefully preserved its ancient buildings, creating what is in many ways a perfect specimen of a four-centuries-old provincial town. It's also a home base of the Royal Shakespeare Company, where thespians pay their finest tribute to the master.

Warwickshire—the ancient county of which Stratford is the southern nexus—is a land of sleepy villages, thatch-roof cottages, and solitary farmhouses. It was the birthplace of the image of Britain that has been spread around the world by the works of Shakespeare. This is, quintessentially, the realm of the yeoman, the wooded land of Arden, the home of the prosperous tradesman and the wealthy merchant, the region where landowners still pasture deer as they have for 900 years, and the county of peace and prosperity that is the fire in the heart of what Shakespeare called "this precious stone set in the silver sea."

A rich selection of historic sites stud the verdant landscape. Three of England's most memorable abodes are here: the home of Anne Hathaway, Shakespeare's wife; Charlecote, a grand Elizabethan manor house; and Baddesley Clinton, a superb example of late medieval domestic architecture. Other treasure houses include Ragley Hall, Coughton Court, and Broughton Castle, brimming with art treasures. Also near Stratford is "medieval England in stone"—Warwick Castle, which provides a glimpse into England's turbulent history. Little wonder Henry James wrote that Warwickshire "is the core and center of the English world."

In addition to charting Shakespeare's achievements, Stratford's historic monuments give a thrilling insight into English life in late-medieval, Tudor, and Elizabethan times. Pride of place goes to the five properties administered by the Shakespeare Birthplace Trust, including Shakespeare's Birthplace. These not only give you a picture of Shakespeare as writer and man of wealth and property but also help trace the social pattern of his family, following its rise from humble beginnings to a position of eminence.

The price you pay for absorbing these scenes and treading the streets frequented by Shakespeare is the press of the thousands of others who also come to pay their respects, and the sometimes ruthless commercialization. If the hustle and bustle become too much, just take a hint from the young Shakespeare. He often turned his back on the town and followed the Avon as it wended its way through meadows and small villages. Today you, too, can wander through a landscape seemingly untouched by the brasher aspects of modern life.

Stratford-upon-Avon, the lead destination for most travelers, is ideal for day visits or as a convenient base. If you can manage only a day here, arrive early and confine your visit to two or three Shakespeare Birthplace Trust properties, a few other town sights, a pub lunch, and a walk along the river, capped off by a stroll to the cottage of Anne Hathaway. You can use the train to visit Stratford from London or other major cities; to see most sights outside the town, a car is best. A couple of nights in Shakespeare's home city allow you to savor the place without testing too severely your tolerance for crowds. With four days you can explore the rural delights of the countryside.

Numbers in the text correspond to numbers in the margin and on the Shakespeare Country and Stratford-upon-Avon maps.

If you have 2 days   **Stratford-upon-Avon ❶–❾** deserves at least a full day and a drama-packed night at the Royal Shakespeare Theatre. Five historic properties are must-sees: three are in town—**Shakespeare's Birthplace ❶**, on Henley Street, the **Nash's House and New Place ❸**, and **Hall's Croft ❻**—whereas the others—**Anne Hathaway's Cottage ❼** and **Mary Arden's House ❿**—are just a few minutes out of town. After your Stratford sojourn, spend the next day touring selected sights, including the mansions of **Baddesley Clinton ❸**, **Packwood House ⓬**, and **Charlecote Park ⓱**. In between, take in some of the villages nearby, ideal for lunch. Spend your second night back in Stratford or in one of the inns along the way.

If you have 4 days   After two days spent touring the august abodes of **Stratford-upon-Avon ❶–❾** and the Shakespeare-linked attractions of the immediate vicinity—including **Henley-in-Arden ⓫**—you will be ready for a change of scene. Dedicate your third day to visiting two or three of the stately houses within easy driving distance. Plan your route along minor roads to take in some off-the-beaten-track hamlets. Nearest of these is fetching **Welford-on-Avon ⓴**, hugging the river as it loops west from Stratford. A short distance north, on either side of the village of **Alcester ㉑**, an appealing one-horse town, lie two notable country houses, Palladian **Ragley Hall ㉒** and Elizabethan **Coughton Court ㉓**, each surrounded by inviting parkland. Head to **Warwick ⓮** for the night, devoting the next morning to exploring the town's medieval castle. Other lower-key attractions are worth an hour or two. If castles are your thing, see ruined **Kenilworth Castle ⓯**, a short drive north.

Exploring Shakespeare Country

Stratford-upon-Avon, the heart of this small region, is neighbor to a number of villages that have legends connected with the Bard, as well as architecture dating from his time. Complementing these humble hamlets, and often in the midst of them, are impressive country houses open to the public, each of which requires a half-day to explore and is easily reachable from Stratford. To the north lie two magnificent castles, Warwick and Kenilworth. Warwick has much to offer besides its castle, and it's worth a protracted jaunt.

About the Restaurants

Although Stratford has little in the way of high-class dining establishments, many reasonably priced bistros and unpretentious restaurants offer a broad international cuisine. For fancier fare, seek out one of the better hotels, whose kitchens have drawn some of the foremost chefs from London and beyond. Warwick and Kenilworth have their share of excellent eateries, ideal for a midday lunch or a more substantial evening meal, and the countryside has many old pubs.

About the Hotels

Stratford holds the highest concentration of lodgings in the area, from bed-and-breakfasts to hotels. Here you can find accommodations to fit every wallet, and for the most part they are well maintained. The best establishments are the older, centrally located ones, often with fine period architecture; national chains own most of these. Because Stratford is *so* popular with theatergoers, book ahead whenever possible. Most hotels have discounted two- and three-day packages. Outside town, some top-notch country hotels guarantee discreet but attentive service—at very fancy prices. At the other end of the scale, almost every village has a gnarled old inn with rooms at reasonable rates.

WHAT IT COSTS In pounds				
£££££	**££££**	**£££**	**££**	**£**
RESTAURANTS over £22	£18–£22	£13–£17	£7–£12	under £7
HOTELS over £160	£120–£160	£90–£120	£60–£90	under £60

Restaurant prices are for a main course at dinner. Hotel prices are for two people in a standard double room in high season, including VAT, with no meals or, if indicated, CP (with Continental breakfast), BP (Breakfast Plan, with full breakfast), or MAP (Modified American Plan, with breakfast and dinner).

Timing

In Stratford, avoid visits on weekends and school holidays, and take in the main Shakespeare shrines in the early morning to see them at their least frenetic. One high point of Stratford's calendar is the Shakespeare Birthday Celebrations, usually on the weekend nearest to April 23. If you visit during this time, make hotel reservations as early as possible. Warwick Castle, too, usually brims with visitors, and you should arrive early in the day to beat the rush. Some country properties fill up quickly on weekends, and some close in winter. Most stately homes close in winter; also check for limited summer opening days.

STRATFORD-UPON-AVON

▶ "Famous people do seem to have a habit of being born in pretty places—Mozart in Salzburg, Wordsworth in the Lake District, Hardy in Dorset, the Brontës in Yorkshire," begins Susan Hill's 1987 travel book *Shake-*

Brush Up Your Shakespeare

However Shakespeare's plays are re-shaped by directors and actors, they continue to reveal new facets of eternal truths about humanity. Stratford's Royal Shakespeare Theatre is the home of the Royal Shakespeare Company (RSC), one of the finest repertory troupes in the world and long the backbone of the country's theatrical life. The company also mounts productions in London and elsewhere, but seeing a play in Shakespeare's hometown and visiting sights associated with the playwright is an experience to treasure. The current theater has been dubbed a "factory for Shakespeare" because of its modern utilitarian aspect. No matter: "The play's the thing." Here, the Bard's plays have made the reputations of generations of actors (and broken not a few), have been staged as archaeological reconstructions and science fiction, and have seen women playing Hamlet and men playing Rosalind.

6

Walking the Countryside

The glorious, gentle countryside here, with its slow-moving rivers and sleepy villages, rewards exploration on foot. Ambitious walkers can try the 26-mi Arden Way loop that takes in Henley-in-Arden and the Forest of Arden. On the 3 mi from Stratford to Wilmcote and Mary Arden's House, you can see some ancient houses. Many of the stately homes are surrounded by parkland with scenic walks; for a leisurely stroll, the grounds of Charlecote Park, Coughton Court, and Ragley Hall are perfect. Even Stratford can be the base for easy walks along the River Avon, and the towpath bordering the Stratford-upon-Avon Canal provides a chance to escape the throng. The Stratford Tourist Information Centre has pamphlets detailing walks in and around town.

---

speare Country (now out of print). "And Stratford's charms are very evident." Under the busloads of visitors, Strat-forde—to use the old Saxon name, which means "a ford over a river"—has hung on to its original character as an English market town on the banks of the slow-flowing River Avon. It's close to Birmingham, 37 mi to the northwest, and London, 102 mi to the southeast.

Still, it is Shakespeare who counts. Born in a half-timber, early-16th-century building in the center of Stratford on April 23, 1564, Shakespeare died on April 23, 1616, his 52nd birthday, in a more imposing house at New Place. Although he spent much of his life in London as a leading figure of the theater, the world still associates him with "Shakespeare's Avon." Here, in the years between his birth and 1587, he played as a young lad, attended grammar school, and married Anne Hathaway; here he returned, as a man of prosperity. You can see his birthplace on Henley Street; his burial place in Holy Trinity Church; Anne Hathaway's Cottage; his mother's home at Wilmcote; New Place and the neighboring Nash's House, home of Shakespeare's granddaughter; and Hall's Croft, home of the physician who married the Bard's daughter. Whether or not their connections to Shakespeare are historically valid,

Shakespeare Country

TO BIRMINGHAM

12 · 13 Baddesley Clinton

11 Packwood House

Henley-in-Arden

15 Kenilworth Castle

16 Coventry

Astwood Bank

23 Coughton Court

21 Aston Cantlow · Billesley

Alcester 21

22 Ragley Hall

Mary Arden's House 10

Wilmcote

Charlecote Park 17

14 Warwick

Barford

Bidford-on-Avon

20 Welford-on-Avon

Stratford-upon-Avon 1 – 9 see detail map

Kineton

GREAT BRITAIN

19 Alderminster

Armscote

Tredington

Honington

Compton Wynyates

Banbury

VALE OF EVESHAM

Chipping Campden

Shipston-on-Stour

Brailes Broughton Castle 18

TO LONDON

0 ___ 6 miles
0 ___ 9 km

KEY

▶ Start of itinerary

these sites reveal Elizabethan England at its loveliest. Then there is the Royal Shakespeare Theatre, with its unrivaled productions.

Stratford-upon-Avon is fascinating, so take Antonio's advice (*Twelfth Night*, Act 3, scene 3) and "beguile the time, and feed your knowledge with viewing the town." By the 16th century it was already a prosperous market town with thriving guilds and industries. Characteristic half-timber houses from this era have been preserved, and they are set off by later architecture, such as the elegant Georgian storefronts on Bridge Street, with their 18th-century porticoes and arched doorways. By 1769 the town's literary preeminence was confirmed by a three-day festival commemorating Shakespeare, supported by the great actor David Garrick. Since then Stratford's flame has shone ever more brightly, yet the town is far from being a museum piece or a tourist trap. Although full of souvenir shops—every back lane seems to have been converted into a shopping mall—Stratford isn't overly strident in its search for a quick buck.

Exploring Stratford-upon-Avon

The town is easily manageable on a walking tour. Most sights cluster around Henley Street (off the roundabout as you come in on the A3400 Birmingham road), High Street, and Waterside, which skirts the public gardens through which the River Avon flows. Bridge Street and Sheep Street (parallel to Bridge) are Stratford's main thoroughfares and the site of most banks, shops, and eating places. The town's tourist office lies at Bridgefoot, between the canal and the river, next to Clopton Bridge— "a sumptuous new bridge and large of stone"—built in the 15th century by Sir Hugh Clopton, once lord mayor of London and one of Stratford's richest and most philanthropic residents.

The **Shakespeare Birthplace Trust** runs the main places of Shakespearean interest: Anne Hathaway's Cottage, Hall's Croft, Mary Arden's House, Nash's House and New Place, and Shakespeare's Birthplace. They have similar opening times, and you can buy a combination ticket to the three in-town properties or to all five properties, or pay separate entry fees if you want to visit only one or two. The trust hosts events by the Tudor Group, costumed interpreters who give demonstrations and talks about subjects such as how Tudor England celebrated Christmas. ☎ *01789/ 204016* ⊕ *www.shakespeare.org.uk* ✉ *Joint ticket to 5 properties £13; joint ticket to Shakespeare's Birthplace, Hall's Croft, and Nash's House–New Place £10.*

a good walk

To begin at the beginning, pay your respects at **Shakespeare's Birthplace ❶** ▶ on Henley Street. Elizabethan antiques and theater memorabilia are on view. Next door is the Shakespeare Centre, with its impressive library. Then head east down Henley Street to the old city center. Take High Street to the right, passing several half-timber buildings, including the magnificent, twin-gabled **Harvard House ❷**, which contains the Museum of British Pewter; at the nearby corner of Sheep Street is a stone bust of the Bard mounted on the north front of the Town Hall. Where High Street becomes Chapel Street, one block down on the left, stands the timber-and-daub **Nash's House and New Place ❸**, home of Shakespeare's granddaughter. You can count the varieties of roses in the Elizabethan knot gardens of New Place next door. On Chapel Street is the Shakespeare Hotel—its five gables make one of the longest Elizabethan facades extant. Continue south, and where Chapel Street becomes Church Street are several buildings, seen on the left, that were old when Shakespeare was young: the **Guild Chapel ❹** and the timbered **almshouses** (notice the high chimneys that carried sparks safely above what were once thatch roofs), and the **Guildhall ❺**, with Shakespeare's school. A left turn at the end of Church Street leads to Old Town and to **Hall's Croft ❻**, an impressive Tudor residence associated with the poet's daughter. Detour now, taking the footpath from Evesham Place 1 mi northwest to the country hamlet of Shottery and **Anne Hathaway's Cottage ❼**. After viewing this romantic house, stroll back to **Holy Trinity Church ❽**, by the banks of the Avon. Here is Shakespeare's tomb *and* the north aisle font where he was christened. Twilight—and your performance at the **Royal Shakespeare Theatre ❾**—may be approaching now, so head over to Southern Lane. Opt for dinner at the theater restaurant or toast the Bard at the nearby Black Swan—with an evening aperitif in its garden.

TIMING   If you don't tour the sites themselves, this walk takes two or three hours, including the walk to Anne Hathaway's Cottage. A more thorough exploration, with an hour for lunch, could last seven hours.

Stratford-
upon-Avon

Anne Hathaway's
Cottage **7**

Guild Chapel **4**

Guildhall **5**

Hall's Croft **6**

Harvard House **2**

Holy Trinity Church **8**

Nash's House
& New Place **3**

Royal
Shakespeare Theatre **9**

Shakespeare's
Birthplace **1**

What to See

Almshouses. Immediately beyond the Guildhall on Church Street is a delightful row of timber-and-daub almshouses. These were built to accommodate the poor by the Guild of the Holy Cross in the early 15th century and still serve as housing for pensioners. ⊠ *Church St.*

★ ❼ **Anne Hathaway's Cottage.** The most perfectly picturesque of the Shakespeare Trust properties, set on the western outskirts of Stratford, was the family home of the woman Shakespeare married in 1582. The "cottage," actually a substantial farmhouse, has latticed windows and a grand thatch roof; inside there is period furniture such as the rare carved-wood canopied Elizabethan bed. Set in a garden (now planted with Victorian herbs and flowers), the cottage is one of the loveliest spots in Shakespeare Country. In a nearby field the **Shakespeare Tree Garden** has 40 trees mentioned in works by the Bard, a yew maze, and sculptures with Shakespearean themes. The best way to get here is to walk, especially in late spring when the apple trees are in blossom. There are two main footpaths, one via Greenhill Street by the railroad bridge, the other leaving from Holy Trinity Church up Old Town and Chestnut Walk. ⊠ *Cottage La., Shottery* ☎ *01789/204016* ⊕ *www.shakespeare.org.uk* ⊠ *£5.20, Shakespeare Trust 5-property ticket £13* ☉ *Apr., May, Sept., and Oct., Mon.–Sat. 9:30–5, Sun. 10–5; June–Aug., Mon.–Sat. 9–5, Sun. 9:30–5; Nov.–Mar., Mon.–Sat. 10–4, Sun. 10:30–4; last entry 30 mins before closing.*

Bancroft Gardens. Between the Royal Shakespeare Theatre and Clopton Bridge lie these well-tended expanses of lawns and flower beds. The swans gliding gracefully along the river are permanent residents, coexisting with the pleasure craft on the river and the nearby canal. The centerpiece of the gardens (incidentally, Bancroft means "croft on the banks") is the **Gower Memorial statue,** designed in 1888 by Lord Gower, and adorned with bronze figures of Hamlet, Lady Macbeth, Falstaff, and Prince Hal—symbols of philosophy, tragedy, comedy, and history, respectively. ⊠ *Off Waterside.*

need a break? At **Cox's Yard Tea Shop** (⊠ Bridgefoot ☎ 01789/404600), next to Bancroft Gardens in the town center, you can sample a sweet cake and some tea or coffee for a rapid sugar and caffeine infusion before more sightseeing or a riverside walk.

↻ **Butterfly Farm.** The farm houses Europe's largest display of butterflies, a mock rain forest, and displays of spiders, caterpillars, and insects from all over the world. It's a two-minute walk past the Bridgefoot footbridge. ⊠ *Swan's Nest La.* ☎ *01789/299288* ⊕ *www.butterflyfarm.co.uk* ⊠ *£4.45* ☉ *June–Aug., daily 10–6; Sept.–May, daily 10–dusk.*

❹ **Guild Chapel.** This chapel is the noble centerpiece of Stratford's Guild buildings, including the Guildhall, the Grammar School, and the almshouses—all structures well known to Shakespeare. The ancient structure was rebuilt in the late Perpendicular style in the first half of the 15th century, thanks to the largesse of Stratford resident Hugh Clopton. The otherwise plain interior includes fragments of a remarkable medieval fresco of the Last Judgment. The chapel is currently used for occasional functions, and the bell, also given by Sir Hugh, still rings as it did to tell Shakespeare the time of day. ⊠ *Chapel La. at Church St.* ☎ *01789/293351* ⌨ *Free* ☉ *Daily 9–5.*

❺ **Guildhall.** Dating to 1416–18, the Guildhall is occupied by **King Edward's Grammar School,** which Shakespeare probably attended as a boy; it's still used as a school. On the first floor is the Guildhall proper, where traveling acting companies came to perform. Many historians believe that it was after seeing the troupe known as the Earl of Leicester's Men in 1587 that Shakespeare got the acting bug and set off for London. Upstairs is the classroom in which the Bard is reputed to have learned "little Latin and less Greek." A brass plate at its far end records the traditional position of Master Will's seat. Students use the classroom today, so visits may be made by prior arrangement only, during after-school hours or vacation time. Contact the tourist information office to schedule a visit. ⊠ *Church St.*

❻ **Hall's Croft.** One of the finest surviving Jacobean (early 17th-century) town houses, this impressive residence has a delightful walled garden. Tradition has it that Hall's Croft was the home of Shakespeare's elder daughter Susanna and her husband, Dr. John Hall, whose dispensary is on view along with the other rooms, all containing Jacobean furniture of heavy oak. ⊠ *Old Town* ☎ *01789/204016* ⊕ *www.shakespeare.org. uk* ⌨ *£3.50, Shakespeare Trust ticket for 3 in-town properties £10, 5-property ticket £13* ☉ *Nov.–Mar., daily 11–4; Apr., May, Sept., and Oct., daily 11–5; June–Aug., Mon.–Sat. 9:30–5, Sun. 10–5; last entry 30 mins before closing.*

❷ **Harvard House.** This is the grand, half-timber, 16th-century home of Katherine Rogers, mother of the John Harvard who founded Harvard University in 1636. The twin-gabled facade, dating from about 1600, is one of Stratford's glories. Note the exterior beams carved with fleurs-de-lis in relief, the sculpted human faces on the corbels, and the bear and staff (symbols of the Warwick earls) on the bracket heads. Inside, the **Museum of British Pewter** displays pewter toys, tankards, and teapots, dating from Roman times to the present. ⊠ *High St.* ☎ *01789/ 204507* ⊕ *www.shakespeare.org.uk* ⌨ *£2* ☉ *May, June, and Sept.–Nov., Fri.–Sun. 11:30–4:30; July–Aug., Thurs.–Sun. 11:30–4:30.*

❽ **Holy Trinity Church.** The fabled burial place of William Shakespeare, this 13th-century church sits on the banks of the Avon, with an avenue of lime trees framing its entrance. Shakespeare's final resting place is in the chancel, rebuilt in 1465–91 in the late Perpendicular style. He was buried here not because he was a famed poet but because he was a lay rector of Stratford, owning a portion of the township tithes. On the north wall of the sanctuary, over the altar steps, is the famous marble bust created by Gerard Jansen in 1623; along with the Droeshout engraving in the First Folio, this is one of only two known contemporary portraits of the Bard. Rigidly stylized in the Elizabethan mode, the bust offers a more human, even humorous, perspective when viewed from the side. Also in the chancel are the graves of Shakespeare's wife, Anne; his daughter Susanna; his son-in-law, John Hall; and his granddaughter's husband, Thomas Nash. Nearby, the Parish Register is displayed, containing both Shakespeare's baptismal entry (1564) and his burial notice (1616). ⊠ *Trinity St.* 🔊 *Small fee for chancel* ⊙ *Mar., Mon.–Sat. 9–5, Sun. 12:30–5; Apr.–Oct., Mon.–Sat. 8:30–6, Sun. 12:30–5; Nov.–Feb., Mon.–Sat. 9–4, Sun. 12:30–5; last admission 20 mins before closing.*

❸ **Nash's House and New Place.** This is the home of the Thomas Nash who married Shakespeare's last direct descendant, his granddaughter Elizabeth Hall. The heavily restored house has been furnished in 17th-century style, and it also contains a local museum. In the gardens (where there's an intricately laid-out Elizabethan knot garden) are the foundations of **New Place,** the house in which Shakespeare died in 1616. Built in 1483 "of brike and tymber" for a lord mayor of London, it was Stratford's grandest piece of real estate when Shakespeare bought it in 1597 for £60; tragically it was torn down in 1759. The man responsible for this, Reverend Francis Gastrell, had already shown his ire at the hordes of sightseers by cutting down a mulberry tree said to have been planted by Shakespeare himself. The townspeople were in such an uproar at Gastrell's vandalism that they stoned his house. Today what is claimed to be a descendant of the mulberry tree stands in the middle of the lawn. The **Great Garden** of New Place, beyond the knot garden, has a sculpture trail with bronze works inspired by Shakespeare's plays. ⊠ *Chapel St.* ☎ *01789/204016* ⊕ *www.shakespeare.org.uk* 🎟 *£3.50, Shakespeare Trust ticket for 3 in-town properties £10, 5-property ticket £13* ⊙ *Nov.–Mar., daily 11–4; Apr., May, Sept., and Oct., daily 11–5; June–Aug., Mon.–Sat. 9:30–5, Sun. 10–5; last entry 30 mins before closing.*

❾ **Royal Shakespeare Theatre.** The Stratford home of the Royal Shakespeare Company (RSC), amid lovely gardens along the River Avon, presents some of the finest productions of Shakespeare's plays. The company has existed since 1879, established by brewer Charles Edward Flower; its original home burned down in 1926. Six years later the current building was erected, according to a design by Elizabeth Scott, cousin of the more-famous Sir Giles Gilbert Scott, architect of Liverpool's Anglican Cathedral. Many people criticize the modern appearance of the building, calling it "a factory for Shakespeare." At the time of this writing, plans for a new theater are being hotly debated. At the rear is the **Swan Theatre,** created in the only part of the Victorian theater to survive the 1926 fire. This theater follows the lines of Shakespeare's original Globe and is one of the most exciting performing spaces in Britain. Beside the Swan is an art gallery that has theater-related exhibitions and portraits and depictions of scenes from the plays. If you want to take a tour of the theater complex, book well in advance. Farther down Southern Lane toward Holy Trinity Church is **The Other Place,** a modern auditorium for experimental productions. ⊠ *Waterside* ☎ *0870/609–1110 ticket hot line, 01789/296655 information, 01789/403405 tours* 📠 *01789/403413 box office* ⊕ *www.rsc.org.uk* 🎟 *Tour £4, gallery £1.50* ⊙ *Tour weekdays (except matinee days) 1:30 and 5:30; matinee days 5:30 and after show; Sun. noon, 1, 2, and 3. No tours when shows are being prepared. Gallery Mon.–Sat. 9:30–6:30, Sun. noon–4:30.*

▶ ❶ **Shakespeare's Birthplace.** A half-timber house typical of its time, the Bard's birthplace has been much altered and restored since Shakespeare lived here but remains a much-visited shrine. Entrance is through the **Shakespeare Centre,** the headquarters of the Shakespeare Birthplace Trust. Scholars head for the library here; lay visitors see an informative exhibition about the life and times of the Bard. Furnishings in the house reflect comfortable middle-class Elizabethan domestic life. Shakespeare's father, John, a glove maker and wool dealer, purchased the house; a reconstructed workshop shows the tools of the glover's trade. An auction notice describes the property as it was when it was offered for sale in 1847. Two widowed ladies had maintained the house in a somewhat ramshackle state, but with the approach of the tercentennial of the Bard's birth, and in response to a rumor that the building was to be purchased by P. T. Barnum and shipped across the Atlantic, the city shelled out £3,000 for the relic. It was tidied up and made the main attraction for the stream of Shakespeare devotees that was steadily growing into a torrent. You can see the signatures of earlier pilgrims cut into the windowpanes, including those of Mark Twain and Charles Dickens. ⊠ *Henley St.* ☎ *01789/204016* ⊕ *www.shakespeare.org.uk* ⊠ *£6.70, Shakespeare Trust ticket for 3 in-town properties £10, 5-property ticket £13* ⊙ *Nov.–Mar., Mon.–Sat. 10–4, Sun. 10:30–4; Apr. and May, Mon.–Sat. 10–5, Sun. 10:30–5; June–Aug., Mon.–Sat. 9–5, Sun. 9:30–5; Sept. and Oct., Mon.–Sat. 10–5, Sun. 10:30–5; last entry 30 mins before closing.*

☉ **Teddy Bear Museum.** A diversion from Shakespeareana, this museum contains hundreds of the furry creatures in all shapes and sizes from around the world, including Paddington Bear and bears previously owned by Margaret Thatcher and Tony Blair. ⊠ *19 Greenhill St.* ☎ *01789/293160* ⊕ *www.theteddybearmuseum.com* ⊠ *£2.50* ⊙ *Daily 9:30–5:30.*

Where to Eat

££££ ✕ **Quarto's.** Views of the River Avon and its resident swans enhance this attractive spot in the Royal Shakespeare Theatre, where you can dine decently before or after a play. The lounge serves pretheater canapés and champagne. The fixed-price menu is contemporary British, so expect dishes such as lamb with rosemary and goat-cheese salad. ⊠ *Royal Shakespeare Theatre, Waterside* ☎ *01789/403415* ⌁ *Reservations essential* ⊟ *AE, MC, V* ⊙ *Closed when theater is closed.*

★ **£££** ✕ **Restaurant Margaux.** One of the best places for good food in town resembles a simple, cozy bistro with its two floors, dark wood furniture, and white walls. The sophisticated menu lists quail and foie gras ravioli with baby leeks, and char-grilled tuna with crab beignet (a fritter) and saffron dressing; for dessert, try the pistachio and strawberry parfait. ⊠ *6 Union St.* ☎ *01789/269106* ⌁ *Reservations essential* ⊟ *MC, V.*

££–£££ ✕ **Lambs.** Sit downstairs in the no-smoking section to appreciate the hardwood floors and oak beams of this local epicurean favorite. The modern updates of tried-and-true dishes include roast chicken with lime butter and char-grilled sausages with leek mash. Daily specials keep the menu seasonal. The two- and three-course fixed-price menus are particularly attractive deals. ☒ *12 Sheep St.* ☎ *01789/292554* ⌖ *Reservations essential* ⊟ *AE, MC, V.*

££–£££ ✕ **Russons.** A 16th-century building holds a quaint dining room that's a favorite with theatergoers. The fare, though reasonably priced, doesn't skimp on quality. On the daily-changing menu, chalked on a blackboard, are English specialties such as roast lamb and guinea fowl. ☒ *8 Church St.* ☎ *01789/268822* ⌖ *Reservations essential* ⊟ *AE, MC, V* ⊘ *Closed Mon.*

££–£££ ✕ **The Vintner.** The imaginative, bistro-inspired menu varies each day at this café and wine bar. Shoulder of lamb is a popular main course; tapas are also popular, and a children's menu is available. To dine before curtain time, arrive early or make a reservation. The building, largely unaltered since the late 1400s, has lovely flagstone floors and oak beams. ☒ *5 Sheep St.* ☎ *01789/297259* ⊟ *AE, MC, V.*

££ ✕ **Embargo.** Leather booths and a lounge bar enhance this breezy venue for contemporary fare. Fish specials, slow-roasted lamb with garlic mashed potatoes and rosemary gravy, and tagliatelle with roast peppers, goat cheese, and pesto are good dinner choices. Crispy shredded duck with plum sauce and cucumbers in a tortilla and a steak baguette appear on the lunch menu; one late-night snack is a small coriander hamburger and chunky fries with garlic mayonnaise. ☒ *1 Shakespeare St.* ☎ *01789/262233* ⊟ *MC, V.*

££ ✕ **Opposition.** Pre- and post-theater meals are offered at this informal, family-style restaurant in a 16th-century building on the main dining street near the theater. The American and modern European dishes on the menu win praise from the locals. Try the roasted chicken breast with banana and basmati rice, wild mushroom pizza, or blood sausage salad. ☒ *13 Sheep St.* ☎ *01789/269980* ⊟ *MC, V.*

£–££ ✕ **Black Swan.** Known locally as the Dirty Duck, one of Stratford's most celebrated pubs has attracted actors since Garrick's days. Its little veranda overlooks the theaters and the river. You can sample English grill specialties as well as bar meals such as mussels and fries, Cajun chicken, or fish and chips, all while sipping a pint of lager. ☒ *Southern La.* ☎ *01789/297312* ⊟ *AE, MC, V* ⊘ *No dinner Sun.*

£–££ ✕ **1564.** The meals and snacks at this informal cafeteria below Quarto's in the theater are crowd pleasers. The river views make the simple food and hot tea seem all the more pleasant. ☒ *Royal Shakespeare Theatre, Waterside* ☎ *01789/403415* ⌖ *Reservations not accepted* ⊟ *No credit cards* ⊘ *Closed when theater is closed.*

Where to Stay

The Ettington Park Hotel and the Fox & Goose, both near Alderminster, are alternatives to hotels in town, as is Pear Tree Cottage, near Mary Arden's House in Wilmcote.

££££ ▦ **Alveston Manor.** This redbrick Elizabethan manor house surrounded by lawns and a terrace has Tudor-style rooms with four-poster beds in the main house. In the rear of the hotel are modern rooms done up in sea green and beige. Legend says the grounds were the setting for the first production of *A Midsummer Night's Dream*. The Alveston is across the river from the Royal Shakespeare Theatre. ☒ *Clopton Bridge, CV37*

7HP ☎ 08704/008181 🖶 01789/414095 ⊕ *www.macdonald-hotels. co.uk* ⌁ *110 rooms, 4 suites* ⚬ *Restaurant, room service, in-room data ports, cable TV, bar, 2 lounges, dry cleaning, laundry service, meeting rooms, free parking, some pets allowed (fee), no-smoking rooms* ▭ *AE, DC, MC, V* ⦿| *BP.*

££££ ⊡ **Menzies Welcombe Hotel & Golf Course.** With its mullioned bay windows, gables, and tall chimneys, this hotel in an 1886 neo-Jacobean-style building evokes the luxury of bygone days. You can relax in the clubby bar or the Italianate garden terrace. Public rooms such as the Great Hall, with its wood paneling, chandeliers, and marble fireplace, complement the spacious main-house guest rooms, all with period-style furnishings and some with garden views. Garden rooms in the adjacent building are comfortable but not as big. The fancy Trevelyan Restaurant (jacket and tie required) relies on a French foundation to present English cuisine. The hotel is a 10-minute drive from Stratford. ✉ *Warwick Rd., CV37 0NR* ☎ 01789/295252 🖶 01789/414666 ⊕ *www. menzies-hotels.co.uk* ⌁ *64 rooms* ⚬ *2 restaurants, room service, in-room data ports, cable TV, 18-hole golf course, tennis court, pool, gym, fishing, bar, lounge, baby-sitting, dry cleaning, laundry service, meeting rooms, car rental, free parking, no-smoking rooms; no a/c* ▭ *AE, D, MC, V* ⦿| *BP.*

★ ££££ ⊡ **Shakespeare Hotel.** Built in the 1400s, this Elizabethan town house in the heart of town is a vision right out of *The Merry Wives of Windsor,* with five gables and one of the longest black-and-white half-timber fronts in England. The comfortably modernized interiors have a touch of luxury, and Shakespeareana and old playbills adorn the public areas. Upstairs, rooms are named after the Bard's characters and leading thespians. Hewn timbers carved with rose-and-thistle patterns decorate some rooms; all have CD players. ✉ *Chapel St., CV37 6ER* ☎ *0870/ 400–8182* 🖶 *01789/415411* ⊕ *www.macdonald-hotels.co.uk* ⌁ *64 rooms, 6 suites* ⚬ *Restaurant, room service, cable TV, bar, lounge, laundry service, meeting rooms, parking (fee), some pets allowed (fee), no-smoking rooms; no a/c* ▭ *AE, DC, MC, V.*

£££–££££ ⊡ **Stratford Victoria.** Although the modern Victoria may lack the period charm of older hotels, its up-to-date facilities, spacious rooms, and ample grounds are making it a Stratford standard. Rooms, all in dark wood with burgundy and green color schemes, come in several shapes: some have four-poster beds, others accommodate four people, some are geared to business travel. ✉ *Arden St., CV37 6QQ* ☎ 01789/271000 🖶 *01789/271001* ⊕ *www.marstonhotels.com* ⌁ *102 rooms* ⚬ *Restaurant, room service, in-room data ports, cable TV, gym, hot tub, massage, bar, lounge, baby-sitting, laundry service, meeting rooms, free parking, no-smoking floors; no a/c* ▭ *AE, DC, MC, V* ⦿| *BP.*

£££ ⊡ **Caterham House.** Rooms in this 1830 building are individually decorated in early-19th-century style, with brass beds, some antiques, and knickknacks; one has a bathtub, and the rest have showers. The public areas of this B&B show discriminating taste, too. You may spot an actor or two among the guests. ✉ *58–59 Rother St., CV37 6LT* ☎ *01789/ 267309* 🖶 *01789/414836* ⌁ *10 rooms* ⚬ *Room service, bar, lounge, free parking, some pets allowed, no-smoking rooms; no a/c, no room phones, free parking* ▭ *MC, V* ⦿| *BP.*

££–£££ 🏨 **Guild Court.** This lodging overlooking Shakespeare's Birthplace is like a hotel in that the rooms have daily maid service, robes, and toiletries; but they also have kitchens with dishwashers, microwaves, and small appliances. The pleasant apartments are decorated with some antiques but are modern and basic; they can accommodate between two and six people. Guests get temporary membership at a local health club. ⊠ *3 Guild St., CV37 6QZ* ☎ *01789/293007* 📠 *01789/296301* ⊕ *www.guildcourt.co.uk* ⤵ *11 apartments* ⚙ *Fans, in-room data ports, kitchens, cable TV, some in-room VCRs, baby-sitting, dry cleaning, laundry facilities, laundry service, concierge, Internet, business services, free parking, some pets allowed; no a/c* ▤ *AE, DC, MC, V.*

££ 🏨 **Penryn House.** Traditional English prints and furnishings as well as some simple modern pieces fill this choice at the low end of the category. The friendly and helpful proprietors, Robert and Anne Dawkes, take pride in the hearty breakfast, which can accommodate vegetarians. It's an easy walk from the city center, Anne Hathaway's Cottage, and the rail station. ⊠ *126 Alcester Rd., CV37 9DP* ☎ *01789/293718* 📠 *01789/266077* ⊕ *www.penrynguesthouse.co.uk* ⤵ *7 rooms, 6 with bath* ⚙ *Laundry service, Internet, free parking; no a/c, no smoking* ▤ *MC, V* ⏹ *BP.*

££ 🏨 **Sequoia House Hotel.** The two Victorian houses that make up this B&B are a good budget option close to the heart of Stratford. The extensive gardens surrounding the property are delightful, and the antique-filled lounge is a quiet place to relax. ⊠ *51-53 Shipston Rd., CV37 7LN* ☎ *01789/268852* 📠 *01789/414559* ⊕ *www.stratford-upon-avon.co. uk/sequoia.htm* ⤵ *24 rooms* ⚙ *Bar, lounge, free parking; no a/c, no smoking* ▤ *AE, DC, MC, V* ⏹ *BP.*

££ 🏨 **Stratheden Hotel.** One advantage of this family-run budget choice is its location in the center of town. Wall-to-wall carpeting and flowery bedspreads decorate the simple rooms; one has a canopy bed previously owned by Victorian novelist Marie Corelli. The spacious rooms have either a shower or tub, and all have coffeemakers. Garret rooms are smaller but charming. ⊠ *5 Chapel St., CV37 6EP* ☎ *01789/297119* ⤵ *9 rooms* ⚙ *Baby-sitting, parking (fee), no-smoking rooms; no a/c* ▤ *MC, V* ⏹ *BP.*

££ 🏨 **Victoria Spa Lodge.** This grand B&B lies 1½ mi outside town, within view of the Stratford Canal. The clematis-draped building dates from 1837; you can see Queen Victoria's coat of arms in two of its gables. Victoria herself stayed here before ascending the throne. Dark-wood and plain white furnishings tastefully decorate the lounge–breakfast room and spacious guest rooms. ⊠ *Bishopton La., Bishopton, CV37 9QY* ☎ *01789/267985* 📠 *01789/204728* ⊕ *www.stratford-upon-avon.co. uk/victoriaspa.htm* ⤵ *7 rooms* ⚙ *Free parking; no a/c, no room phones, no smoking* ▤ *MC, V* ⏹ *BP.*

★ £ 🏨 **Heron Lodge.** Just a half-mile outside of Stratford town centre, this B&B combines budget accommodation in a family home with luxurious service. Rooms are individually decorated, and the conservatory is perfect for an afternoon cup of tea. Owners Chris and Bob Heaps are serious about breakfast, serving pancakes made from a family recipe; locally sourced ingredients—from tea to jam and sausages—appear on the menu. You can also get a top-quality English breakfast. ⊠ *260 Al-*

cester Rd., CV37 9JQ ☎ *01789/299169* ⊕ *www.heronlodge.com* ⇥ *5 rooms* ⚮ *Lounge, free parking; no a/c, no kids under 5, no smoking* ☰ *AE, MC, V* ⦿ *BP.*

Nightlife & the Arts

Festivals

The **Stratford-upon-Avon Shakespeare Birthday Celebrations** (✉ Shakespeare Centre, Henley St., Stratford-upon-Avon, CV37 6QW ☎ 01789/415536 ⊕ www.shakespeare.org.uk) take place on and around the weekend closest to April 23 (unless Easter occurs during that time). The events, spread over four days, include a formal reception, lectures, free concerts, processions, and a special performance of a play. For tickets for the three-course birthday luncheon in the marquee on the Avon Paddock, write the Shakespeare Birthday Celebrations secretary at the address above, call, or check the Web site.

The **Mop Fair**, dating from medieval times, takes place on or around October 12, traditionally the time when laborers and apprentices from the surrounding area came to seek work. The fair still attracts entertainers and fairground amusements and includes a ceremony attended by local dignitaries, the whole in essence little changed from the past.

Theater

Fodor'sChoice The **Royal Shakespeare Theatre** (✉ Waterside, Stratford-upon-Avon, ★ CV37 6BB ☎ 0870/609–1110 ticket hot line, 01789/296655 general information ☐ 01789/403413 ⊕ www.rsc.org.uk) usually puts on five of Shakespeare's plays in a season that runs from November into October. In September and October, visiting companies perform opera, ballet, and musicals. The Swan Theatre, at the rear, stages plays by Shakespeare contemporaries such as Christopher Marlowe and Ben Jonson. In the Other Place, the RSC performs some of its most adventurous work. Prices usually are £7 to £45. Book ahead, as seats go fast, but day of performance (two per person to personal callers only) and returned tickets are often available. You can book tickets from London with **Ticketmaster** (☎ 0870/534–4444 ⊕ www.ticketmaster.co.uk), operating 24 hours a day. You can book tickets in the United States (a 20% surcharge applies) with **Keith Prowse** (☎ 212/398–1430 or 800/669–8687 ⊕ www.keithprowse.com).

Sports & the Outdoors

Avon Cruises (✉ The Boatyard, Swan's Nest La. ☎☎ 01789/267073) rents boats and provides half-hour river excursions; the company can arrange longer trips from Easter to October. **Bancroft Cruises** (✉ Moathouse, Bridgefoot ☎ 01789/269669) runs half-hourly excursions on the river. Hour-long trips farther afield can also be scheduled.

Shopping

Stratford-upon-Avon's bustling shopping district sells plenty of tourist junk. That said, established shops specializing in silver, jewelry, and china sell some high-quality items. There's an open market (great for bargains) every Friday in the Market Place at Greenhill and Meer streets. **Antique Arms & Armour** (⊠ Poet's Arbour, Sheep St. ☏ 01789/293453) sells antique swords, sabers, and armor. The **Antique Market** (⊠ Ely St.) contains 50 stalls of jewelry, silver, linens, porcelain, and memorabilia. **B&W Thornton** (⊠ 23 Henley St. ☏01789/269405), above Shakespeare's Birthplace, stocks Moorcroft pottery and glass. **Chaucer Head Bookshop** (⊠ 21 Chapel St. ☏ 01789/415691) is the best of Stratford's many secondhand bookshops. The **Shakespeare Bookshop** (⊠ 39 Henley St. ☏01789/201820), run by the Shakespeare Birthplace, carries Elizabethan plays, Tudor history books, children's books, and Bard paraphernalia.

AROUND SHAKESPEARE COUNTRY

Although the section of Warwickshire known as Shakespeare Country is, in reality, no more than a continuation of that familiar Midlands scene of green fields, slow-moving, mirrorlike rivers, quiet villages, and time-burnished halls, castles, and churches, it becomes an area apart through its role as the homeland of England's greatest dramatist. Warwick and Kenilworth castles are highlights here.

Mary Arden's House

🐾 ❿ *3 mi northwest of Stratford, 8 mi southwest of Warwick.*

This bucolic site in tiny Wilmcote captured attention in 2000 because a Tudor farmhouse here, considered to have been the home of Shakespeare's mother (and so named), was proved to have been the home of Adam Palmer instead. That farmhouse has been renamed Palmer's Farm. However, research showed that Mary Arden lived in a house on the adjoining Glebe Farm; this farm has assumed the name Mary Arden's House. The Tudor farmhouse and farm form the **Shakespeare Countryside Museum,** with crafts exhibits, a café, and a garden of trees mentioned in the plays. Rare breeds of poultry, longhorn cows, and Cotswold sheep live on the grounds, and there are demonstrations of farming techniques from the last 400 years. A small falcon and owl exhibit is here, too. ⊠ Off A3400, Wilmcote ☏ 01789/204016, 01789/293455 *information on special events* ⊕ *www.shakespeare.org.uk* 🎟 *£5.70, Shakespeare Trust 5-property ticket £13* ⊗ *Nov.–Mar., Mon.–Sat. 10–4, Sun. 10:30–4; Sept., Oct., Apr., and May, Mon.–Sat. 10–5, Sun. 10:30–5; June–Aug., Mon.–Sat. 9:30–5, Sun. 10–5; last entry 30 mins before closing.*

Where to Stay

★ £ 🏠 **Pear Tree Cottage.** This lovely guest house, just around the corner from Mary Arden's House, occupies a 16th-century cottage that retains its beamed ceilings and flagstone floors despite updating and expansion over the ages. The small garden provides an ideal place to relax. Rooms, individually decorated in a flowery country style, have coffeemakers and some antique furnishings, and guests have access to the kitchen and the living room. Scholars will be interested to know that Shakespeare's parents owned Pear Tree Cottage in the late 1500s. ⊠ *7 Church Rd., Wilmcote, CV37 9UX* ☏ *01789/205889* 🖷 *01789/262862* ⊕ *www.*

peartreecot.co.uk 🖙 *5 rooms, 1 apartment* ♨ *Some in-room VCRs, lounge; no a/c, no kids under 3, no smoking* ⊟ *No credit cards* ⊘ *Closed Jan.* ⦿ *BP.*

> **en route** | From Wilmcote, continue west for 1½ mi on minor roads to reach **Aston Cantlow.** Shakespeare's parents, Mary Arden and John Shakespeare, were wed at the church here. Stop for lunch or dinner at the relaxed **King's Head** (⊠ Bearley Rd., Aston Cantlow ☎ 01789/488242) for creative pub food and good wine; reserve in advance.

Henley-in-Arden

⓫ *6 mi north of Mary Arden's House, 8 mi northwest of Stratford.*

A brief drive out of Stratford on the A3400 will take you under the Stratford-upon-Avon Canal aqueduct to pretty Henley-in-Arden, whose wide main street is an architectural pageant of many periods. You are now in the area of what was once the Forest of Arden, where Shakespeare set one of his greatest comedies, *As You Like It.* Among the buildings to look out for are the former Guildhall, dating from the 15th century, and the White Swan pub, built in the early 1600s.

Packwood House

⓬ *5 mi north of Henley-in-Arden, 12 mi north of Stratford-upon-Avon.*

Packwood House draws garden enthusiasts to its re-created 17th-century gardens, highlighted by a remarkable topiary Tudor garden in which yew trees depict Jesus' Sermon on the Mount. The house combines red-brick and half-timbering, and its tall chimneys are also typically Tudor. Although the interiors are a 20th-century version of Tudor architecture, the collections of period furniture and textiles are good. ⊠ *Off B4439, near Hockley Heath* ☎ *01564/783294* ⊕ *www.nationaltrust.org.uk* 🎟 *£5.60, garden only £2.80, combined ticket with Baddesley Clinton £9* ⊘ *House Mar.–Oct., Wed.–Sun. noon–4:30. Garden Mar., Apr., and Oct., Wed.–Sun. 11–4:30; May–Sept., Wed.–Sun. 11–5:30.*

Baddesley Clinton

★ **⓭** *2 mi east of Packwood House, 15 mi north of Stratford-upon-Avon.*

"As you approach Baddesley Clinton, it stands before you as the perfect late medieval manor house. The entrance side of grey stone, the small, creeper-clad Queen Anne brick bridge across the moat, the gateway with a porch higher than the roof and embattled—it could not be better." So wrote the eminent architectural historian Sir Nikolaus Pevsner, and the house lives up to his fervent praise. Set off a winding back road, the moated manor retains its great fireplaces, 17th-century paneling, and priest holes (secret chambers for Roman Catholic priests, who were persecuted at times throughout the 16th and 17th centuries). The café is an idyllic spot for tea and cakes. Admission to the house is by timed ticket. ⊠ *Rising La., off A4141 near Chadwick End* ☎ *01564/783294* ⊕ *www.nationaltrust.org.uk* 🎟 *£6.20, garden only £3.10, combined ticket with*

Packwood House £9 ⊙ *House Mar., Apr., and Oct., Wed.–Sun. 1:30–5; May–Sept., Wed.–Sun. 1:30–5:30. Garden Mar., Apr., and Oct., Wed.–Sun. noon–5; May–Sept., Wed.–Sun. noon–5:30; Nov.–mid-Dec., Wed.–Sun. noon–4:30.*

Warwick

⓮ *7½ mi southeast of Baddesley Clinton, 4 mi south of Kenilworth, 9 mi northeast of Stratford-upon-Avon.*

Most famous for Warwick Castle—that vision out of the feudal ages—Warwick (pronounced *wa*-rick) is an interesting architectural mix of Georgian redbrick and Elizabethan half-timbering. Much of the town center has been spoiled by unattractive postwar development, but look for the

★ 15th-century half-timber **Lord Leycester Hospital,** which has been a home—offering "hospitality"—for old soldiers since the earl of Leicester dedicated it to that purpose in 1571. Within the complex are a chapel and a fine courtyard, complete with a wattle-and-daub balcony and 500-year-old gardens. ⊠ *High St.* ☎ *01926/491422* 🎫 *£3.20* ⊙ *Apr.–Sept., Tues.–Sun. 10–5; Oct.–Mar., Tues.–Sun. 10–4.*

Crowded with gilded, carved, and painted tombs, the **Beauchamp Chapel** of the **Collegiate Church of St. Mary** is the essence of late-medieval and Tudor chivalry—although it was built (1443–64) to honor the somewhat-less-than-chivalrous Richard Beauchamp, who consigned Joan of Arc to the flames. Colored bosses (projecting blocks), fan tracery, and flying ribs distinguish the chapel, which holds many monuments to the Beauchamps (several of whom became earl of Warwick), including Richard Beauchamp's impressive effigy in bronze and the alabaster table tomb of Thomas Beauchamp and his wife. Robert Dudley, earl of Leicester, adviser and favorite of Elizabeth I, is also buried here. There's a brass-rubbing center, and you can climb the tower in summer. ⊠ *Church St., Old Sq.* ☎ *01926/403940* ⊕ *www.saintmaryschurch.co.uk* 🎫 *Free* ⊙ *Apr.–Oct., daily 10–6; Nov.–Mar., daily 10–4:30.*

★ ☺ The vast bulk of **Warwick Castle** rests on a cliff overlooking the Avon—"the fairest monument of ancient and chivalrous splendor which yet remains uninjured by time," to use the words of Sir Walter Scott. Two soaring towers mark the castle: the 147-foot-high Caesar's Tower, built in 1356, and the 128-foot-high Guy's Tower, built in 1380. The towers bristle with battlements, and their irregular forms allowed defenders to shoot from numerous points. The castle's most powerful commander was Richard Neville, earl of Warwick, known during the Wars of the Roses as the Kingmaker. He was killed in battle near London in 1471 by the army of Edward IV, whom he had just deposed in favor of Henry VI. Warwick Castle's monumental walls now enclose one of the best collections of medieval armor and weapons in Europe, as well as historic furnishings and paintings by Peter Paul Rubens, Anthony Van Dyck, and other old masters. Twelve rooms are devoted to an imaginative Madame Tussaud's wax exhibition, "A Royal Weekend Party—1898" (the Tussaud's Group owns the castle). Another exhibit displays the sights and sounds of a great medieval household as it prepares for an important battle. The year chosen is 1471, when the earl of Warwick was killed.

At the Mill and Engine House, you can see the turning water-mill and the engines used to generate electricity early in the 20th century. Below the castle, along the Avon, strutting peacocks patrol 60 acres of grounds elegantly landscaped by Capability Brown in the 18th century. Banquets (extra charge) and special events, including festivals and tournaments, take place throughout the year. A restaurant in the cellars serves lunch. Head to the bridge across the river to get the best view of the castle. ⊠ *Castle La.* ☎ *01926/495421, 0870/442–2000 recorded information* ⊕ *www.warwick-castle.co.uk* ⊠ *Nov.–Mar. £11.50 (£14.50 during school vacations and Dec. holidays), Apr.–Oct. £12.95* ⊙ *Apr.–July, and Sept., daily 10–6; Aug., weekdays 10–6, weekends 10–7; Oct.–Mar., daily 10–5.*

> **need a break?** After a vigorous walk around the ramparts at Warwick Castle, you can drop by the cream, crimson, and golden vaulted, 14th-century **Undercroft** (☎ 01926/495421) for a refreshing spot of tea or a hot meal from the cafeteria.

☺ The half-timber Oken's House, near the castle entrance, houses the **Warwickshire Doll Museum** and its large collection of antique dolls, toys, and games. ⊠ *Castle St.* ☎ *01926/495546* ⊠ *£1* ⊙ *Easter–Oct., Mon.–Sat. 10–5, Sun. 11–5; Nov.–Easter, Sat. 10–dusk.*

☺ Kids as well as adults appreciate **St. John's House,** a Jacobean building on the site of a medieval hospital; beautiful gardens surround it. Inside are period costumes and scenes of domestic life, as well as a Victorian schoolroom. ⊠ *Smith St.* ☎ *01926/412132* ⊠ *Free* ⊙ *May–Sept., Tues.–Sat. 10–5, Sun. 2:30–5; Oct.–Apr., Tues.–Sat. 10–5.*

Where to Stay & Eat

£££ ✕ **Findon's.** The imaginative menu at this posh Georgian town-house restaurant takes its inspiration from Asia and Europe as well as England. Among the delicious choices are Gressingham duck with blackberry and green peppercorn sauce, and scallops with apple couscous, creamed sweet potatoes, and lime broth. The terrace is a lovely spot to dine in summer. For the best deal, try the fixed-price menus. ⊠ *7 Old Sq.* ☎ *01926/ 411755* ⊟ *MC, V* ⊙ *Closed Sun.*

££ ⌸ **Lord Leycester Hotel.** Built in 1726, this manor house with an appealing central location became a hotel in 1925, and signs of age and history abound. The small, comfortably furnished rooms and even smaller bathrooms with showers are not to everyone's taste. ⊠ *17 Jury St., CV34 4EJ* ☎ *01926/491481* 🖷 *01926/491561* ⊕ *www.lord-leycester.co.uk* ⇥ *49 rooms* ⚫ *2 restaurants, room service, some in-room data ports, room TVs with movies, bar, lounge, baby-sitting, laundry service, meeting rooms, free parking, some pets allowed (fee), no-smoking rooms; no a/c* ⊟ *AE, DC, MC, V* ⭐ *BP.*

££ ⌸ **Rose and Crown.** Stripped pine floorboards, red walls, big wooden tables, and solidly good food and drink set the tone at this contemporary pub with rooms on the town's main square. The menu, chalked on a blackboard, caters to vegetarians too. Bedrooms are simple but clean and modern. All in all, this is a decent value for a pint and some chips or a moderately priced room. ⊠ *30 Market Pl., CV34 4SH* ☎ *01926/ 411117* ⊕ *www.peachpubs.com* ⤶ *5 rooms* ⚬ *Restaurant, in-room data ports, meeting rooms; no a/c, no smoking* ▤ MC, V ⎁ CP.

Kenilworth Castle

⑮ *5 mi north of Warwick.*

The sprawling red ruins of Kenilworth Castle loom over the somewhat nondescript village of Kenilworth and have commanding views of the countryside. Begun in 1120, this castle remained one of the most formidable fortresses in England until it was dismantled by Oliver Cromwell after the Civil War in the mid-17th century. Still intact are its keep (central tower), with 20-foot-thick walls; its great hall; and its curtain walls, the low outer walls forming the castle's first line of defense. Here the earl of Leicester, one of Elizabeth I's favorites, entertained her four times, most notably in 1575 with 19 days of sumptuous feasting and revelry. Sir Walter Scott's novel *Kenilworth* (1821) presented tales about the earl and Elizabeth, adding to the fascination with the castle. ⊠ *Off A452, Kenilworth* ☎ *01926/852078* ⊕ *www.english-heritage. org.uk* ⛶ *£4.80* ⊗ *Apr.–Sept., daily 10–6; Oct., daily 10–5; Nov.–Mar., daily 10–4.*

Where to Eat

££££–£££££ ✕ **Restaurant Bosquet.** This Victorian town-house restaurant serves fixed-price menus cooked by the French *patron*, with regularly changing à la carte selections. Try the veal or venison with wild mushrooms, and don't pass up the delicious desserts. Bosquet is mainly a dinner spot, although lunch is available by prior reservation. There's no fixed-price menu on Saturday. ⊠ *97A Warwick Rd.* ☎ *01926/852463* ▤ *AE, MC, V* ⊗ *Closed Sun., 3 wks in Aug., last wk in Dec. No dinner Mon.*

££££–£££££ ✕ **Simpson's.** The French fixed-price lunch and dinner menus here are a great way to splurge on Kenilworth's finest dining. Crisp white tablecloths and unobtrusive staff make for an elegant experience. Terrine of ham with foie gras and roast sea bass with caramelized endive are among the excellent dishes. ⊠ *101 Warwick Rd.* ☎ *01926/864567* ▤ *AE, DC, MC, V* ⊗ *Closed Sun., last 2 wks in Aug. No lunch Sat.*

£–££ ✕ **Clarendon Arms.** A location close to Kenilworth Castle helps make this pub a good spot for lunch. You can order fine home-cooked food at the small bar downstairs. A larger, slightly pricier restaurant upstairs serves complete meals, from English roasts to more international fare. ⊠ *44 Castle Hill* ☎ *01926/852017* ▤ *AE, DC, MC, V.*

Coventry

⑯ *7 mi northeast of Warwick, 16 mi northeast of Stratford-upon-Avon.*

Coventry thrived in medieval times as a center for the cloth and dyeing industries; in the 19th century it became an industrial powerhouse, but its fortunes have fallen since then. The Germans bombed the city heavily in 1940, and many people decry the postwar architecture, with the notable exception of the rebuilt cathedral. Coventry is where a naked

Lady Godiva allegedly rode through the streets to protest high taxes and where the first British automobiles were manufactured (the Coventry Transport Museum displays British cars and motorcycles).

The modern bulk of **Coventry Cathedral,** designed by Sir Basil Spence and dedicated in 1962, stands beside the ruins of the blitzed St. Michael's, a powerful symbol of rebirth and reconciliation. Outside the sandstone building is Sir Jacob Epstein's *St. Michael Defeating the Devil*; the modern artworks inside include Graham Sutherland's stunning 70-foot-high tapestry, *Christ in Glory*. The undercroft holds a visitor center that shows a film about the cathedral; there's also a charred cross wired together from timbers from the bombed building. ⊠ *Priory Row* ☎ *024/ 7622–1200* ⊕ *www.coventrycathedral.org* ✉ *Suggested cathedral donation £3, visitor center £2* ☉ *Sept.–Mar., daily 9–6; Jun.–Aug., daily 9–5:30, services permitting.*

Charlecote Park

⑰ *13 mi south of Coventry, 6 mi south of Warwick.*

This celebrated house in the village of Hampton Lucy was built in 1572 by Sir Thomas Lucy to entertain Queen Elizabeth (the house is shaped like the letter "E"). According to tradition, Shakespeare was caught poaching deer here soon after his marriage and was forced to flee to London. Years later he supposedly retaliated by portraying Sir Thomas Lucy in *Henry IV Part 2* and the *Merry Wives of Windsor* as the foolish Justice Shallow. Some historians doubt the reference, but the Bard does mention the "dozen white luces"—which figure in the Lucy coat of arms—and Shallow does tax Falstaff with killing his deer. The brick house was renovated in neo-Elizabethan style by the Lucy family during the mid-19th century; a carved ebony bed is one of the spectacular pieces of furniture. The Tudor gatehouse is unchanged since Shakespeare's day, and a collection of carriages, a Victorian kitchen, and a small brewery occupy the outbuildings. Indulge in a game of croquet near the quirky, Victorian-era summer hut, or explore the deer park landscaped by Capability Brown. ⊠ *B4086, off A429, Hampton Lucy* ☎ *01789/470277* ⊕ *www. nationaltrust.org.uk* ✉ *£6.40, grounds only £3* ☉ *House Mar.–Nov., Fri.–Sun. noon–5. Gardens Mar.–Oct., Fri.–Tues. 11–6; Nov.–mid-Dec., weekends 11–4.*

---

en route | **Compton Verney,** a neoclassical country mansion remodeled in the 1760s by Robert Adam, has been converted to an art gallery with more than 800 works. The collections are intriguingly different: British folk art and portraits, textiles, Chinese pottery and bronzes, southern Italian art from 1600 to 1800, and German art from 1450 to 1600. ⊠ *Off B4086, near Kineton* ☎ *01926/645500* ⊕ *www. comptonverney.org.uk* ✉ *£6* ☉ *Mid-Mar.–Oct., daily 10–5.*

Broughton Castle

18 *14 mi southeast of Charlecote Park, 18 mi southeast of Stratford-upon-Avon.*

Once owned by the great chancellor and patron William of Wykeham, this impressive moated mansion passed to Lord and Lady Saye and Sele in 1451 and has been occupied by their family ever since. Parts of the building date to around 1300, and it was remodeled in Tudor times. The inside is rich with fireplaces, plasterwork, and exquisite furniture. High points include the Great Chamber, the chapel, and a fine collection of Chinese wallpapers. The house appeared in a few scenes in the movie *Shakespeare in Love* as the home of Viola de Lesseps. Joseph Fiennes, who played Shakespeare, is the present baron's third cousin. ⊠ *B4035, Broughton* ☎ *01295/276070* ⊕ *www.broughtoncastle.demon.co.uk* 🎫 *£5.50* ⊗ *Mid-May–June and early–mid-Sept., Wed. and Sun. 2–5; July and Aug., Wed., Thurs., and Sun. 2–5; national holiday Mon. 2–5.*

> **off the beaten path**
>
> **COMPTON WYNYATES –** This perfect example of Tudor domestic architecture, notable for its timber roof and radiant rose hue, was constructed between 1480 and 1520 of bricks dismantled from a castle given to the family by Henry VIII. Compton Wynyates is 11 mi southeast of Stratford, near Upper Tysoe, but is best reached by turning north from Brailes off the Shipston–Banbury B4035. Today it is the private residence of the marquess of Northampton and should be viewed from the hillside roads that surround its tiny valley.

Alderminster

19 *5 mi south of Stratford-upon-Avon on A3400.*

Alderminster is one of the most interesting of the so-called "Stour villages"—those places so characteristic of Shakespeare Country, strung along the winding route of the River Stour south of Stratford. The main street holds an unusual row of old stone cottages, and the church has a Norman nave and a tower dating from the 13th century. Although the interior of the church has been much restored, it's worth a peek for the carved faces between the arches and the old altar stone.

Other Stour villages include Honington, Shipston-on-Stour, and Tredington. A village green anchors Honington, where a lovely five-arched bridge crosses the river. Shipston, the largest of the group, is an old sheep-market town, its handsome batch of Georgian houses formerly owned by wealthy wool merchants. Tredington, an exquisite nutshell of a village, has an old stone church.

Where to Stay & Eat

★ ✕🛏 **Ettington Park Hotel.** This luxurious Victorian Gothic mansion with **££££–£££££** a modern wing, built on land owned by the Shirley family since the 12th century, is an ideal retreat for Stratford theatergoers who don't want to cope with the crowds. Some of the individually decorated rooms have four-poster beds; you can also choose the unusual Kingmaker and Shakespeare suites. The oak-paneled restaurant (fixed-price menu) has extremely good contemporary food. For a break, take tea or a whisky in the antique-filled public rooms that have views of the 40-acre grounds, which contain a ruined church. ⊠ *Off A3400, Alderminster CV37 8BU* ☎ *01789/450123* 🖶 *01789/450472* ⊕ *www.handpicked.co.uk/ ettingtonpark* 🗗 *37 rooms, 11 suites* ⚹ *Restaurant, room service, in-room data ports, cable TV, 2 tennis courts, indoor pool, gym, hot tub, sauna, spa, croquet, fishing, bar, library, lounge, baby-sitting, dry cleaning, laundry service, meeting rooms, helipad; no a/c* ⊟ *AE, DC, MC, V* ⏁ *BP.*

★ **£££** ✕⛶ **Fox & Goose.** A quirky style and fabulous, fresh food make this place in the wee, unspoiled village of Armscote, just 8 mi south of Stratford, more than just a pub with rooms. Everything is in place for relaxation: Victorian clawfoot tubs with candles, a CD player, and a satisfying English breakfast served until noon. Rooms are themed around Clue (Cluedo in England) characters: Colonel Mustard's room is yellow, and Miss Scarlet's Boudoir is red and dimly lit. The dining room serves a daily-changing menu of modern British pub food such as Thai chicken or pork with fruit. ⊠ *Armscote, CV37 8DD* ☎🖶 *01608/682293* ⊕ *www.aboveaverage.co.uk* 🗗 *4 rooms* ⚹ *Pub, meeting room; no a/c, no room phones* ⊟ *MC, V* ⏁ *BP.*

Welford-on-Avon

⑳ *8 mi northwest of Alderminster, 4 mi southwest of Stratford-upon-Avon.*

Welford, off B439, is most famous for its May Day revelry, when Morris dancers wearing costumes and bells perform around the maypole on the green. To reach the maypole, go straight through town to High Street. The partly Norman church, reached by taking a right at the Bell Inn, has what is said to be the oldest lych-gate in the county. Close by the church are timber and whitewashed thatched cottages. The river path here provides plenty of opportunity for walking in the area.

£ ✕ **Bell Inn.** This quiet spot has a flagstone public bar with an open fire, and a conservatory and garden in which to enjoy the generous portions of casual food. ⊠ *High St.,* ☎ *01789/750353* ⊟ *MC, V.*

Alcester

㉑ *8 mi northwest of Welford, 8 mi west of Stratford-upon-Avon.*

The small market town of Alcester (pronounced *al*-ster) holds a cluster of ancient buildings and timber-frame Tudor houses. Search out the narrow **Butter Street,** off High Street, site of the 17th-century Churchill House, and on Malt Mill Lane (off Church Street) the **Old Malt House,** dating from 1500.

Where to Stay & Eat

£££££ ✕⛶ **Billesley Manor.** Cozy public rooms with fireplaces and antiques and 11 acres of grounds with a topiary garden enhance this 16th-century manor house. The bedrooms retain period features and are decorated in traditional country style with floral prints or in a more modern style; some have four-poster beds. The stunning wine list matches the wood-paneled restaurant's excellent food, which includes pan-fried Dover sole and chicken breast stuffed with Brie and apricots. ⊠ *Off A46, Billesley, near Alcester, B49 6NF* ☎ *01789/279955* 🖷 *01789/764145* ⊕ *www. billesleymanor.co.uk* ⟿ *69 rooms, 2 suites* ⟐ *Restaurant, room service, in-room data ports, cable TV, indoor pool, spa, gym, sauna, croquet, tennis court, baby-sitting, dry cleaning, laundry service, meeting rooms, no-smoking rooms; no a/c* ⊟ *AE, D, MC, V* ⎸○⎸ *BP*.

Ragley Hall

㉒ *2 mi southwest of Alcester.*

A Palladian-style mansion with more than 100 rooms, Ragley Hall was begun in 1680 and worked on by some of the country's most outstanding architects, including James Wyatt. Inside are architectural and decorative treasures as well as magnificent views of the parkland laid out by Capability Brown in the 1750s. The Great Hall has fine baroque plasterwork by James Gibb, and there are portraits by Joshua Reynolds and Dutch masters, among others, as well as some striking 20th-century murals by Graham Rust. This is the ancestral home of the marquesses of Hertford, the third of whom figured in Thackeray's *Vanity Fair* and the fourth of whom collected many of the treasures in London's Wallace Collection. An adventure playground and picnic area let kids blow off extra energy. ⊠ *Off A435 and A46* ☎ *01789/762090* ⊕ *www. ragleyhall.com* ⊠ *£7.50, park and gardens only £6* ○ *House Apr.–Sept., Thurs.–Sun. 11–6; park Apr.–Sept., daily 11–6; last admission 4:30.*

Coughton Court

㉓ *2 mi north of Alcester, 8 mi northwest of Stratford*

Coughton Court, a grand Elizabethan manor house, is the home of the Catholic Throckmorton family, as it has been since 1409. The impressive gatehouse, the centerpiece of a half-timber courtyard, contains a fine fan-vaulted ceiling and memorabilia, including the dress worn by Mary, Queen of Scots at her execution. There are children's clothes and a Gunpowder Plot exhibition, and you can wander in the formal gardens and along a river and lake. ⊠ *A435* ☎ *01789/400777* ⊕ *www. coughtoncourt.co.uk* ⊠ *£9.45, gardens only £6.95* ○ *House mid-Mar.–June and Sept., Wed.–Sun. 11:30–5; July and Aug., Tues.–Sun. 11:30–5; Oct., weekends 11:30–5.*

SHAKESPEARE COUNTRY A TO Z

To research prices, get advice from other travelers, and book travel arrangements, visit www.fodors.com.

AIR TRAVEL

Warwickshire is convenient to major airports in London (⇨ Airports *in* Smart Travel Tips) and Birmingham (⇨ Airports *in* Smart Travel Tips).

BOAT & FERRY TRAVEL

For information about the Stratford towpath and canal, contact British Waterways.

🚹 **British Waterways** 🕾 01564/784634 ⊕ www.britishwaterways.co.uk.

BUS TRAVEL

National Express serves the region from London's Victoria Coach Station with eight buses daily to the Stratford region. Flightlink buses run from London's Heathrow and Gatwick airports to Warwick, and Stagecoach serves local routes throughout the Stratford, Birmingham, and Coventry areas.

FARES & SCHEDULES 🚹 **Flightlink** 🕾 0870/580-8080 ⊕ www.nationalexpress.com. **National Express** 🕾 0870/580-8080 ⊕ www.nationalexpress.com. **Stagecoach** 🕾 01788/535555 or 0845/600-1314 ⊕ www.stagecoachbus.com.

CAR RENTAL

Open Road Classic Car Hire rents sports cars.

🚹 **Local Agencies Hertz** ⊠ Rail Station, Stratford-upon-Avon 🕾 01789/298827 ⊕ www.hertz.co.uk. **Open Road Classic Car Hire** ⊠ Stratford-upon-Avon 🕾 01926/624891 ⊕ www.theopenroad.co.uk.

CAR TRAVEL

Stratford lies about 100 mi northwest of London; take M40 to Junction 15. The town is 37 mi southeast of Birmingham by A435 and A46 or by M40 to Junction 15. Main roads provide easy access between towns, but one pleasure of this rural area is exploring the smaller "B" roads, which lead deep into the countryside.

EMERGENCIES

🚹 **Ambulance, fire, police** 🕾 999. **Stratford-upon-Avon Hospital** ⊠ Arden St., Stratford-upon-Avon 🕾 01789/205831. **Warwick Hospital** ⊠ Lakin Rd., Warwick 🕾 01926/495321.

TOURS

The Heart of England Tourist Board (⇨ Visitor Information) arranges tours throughout the region. City Sightseeing runs guided tours of Stratford (£8.50), Coventry (£5.50), and trips to Warwick Castle from Stratford (£19.50). The tours don't include admission to the Stratford sights (most of which are within walking distance in town), so some people find the tour isn't the best value. The two-hour Shakespeare's Life in Stratford walk (£6), led by actors, begins at 10:30 AM on Saturday October–March, Thursday and Saturday April–September, and Thursday, Saturday, and Sunday July–September.

🚹 **City Sightseeing** 🕾 01789/294466 ⊕ www.city-sightseeing.com. **Shakespeare's Life in Stratford Walk** 🕾 01789/403405.

TRAIN TRAVEL

Thames Trains and Virgin Trains serve the area. Four direct trains (two in the morning and two in the afternoon) from London's Paddington Station take two hours to reach Stratford; these avoid a change at Leamington Spa. Two direct trains return from Stratford each evening. On winter Sundays there are no direct trains. The fastest route is by train *and* bus using the Shakespeare Connection Road & Rail Link from Euston Station to Coventry, then a City Sightseeing bus (⇨ Tours).

The Shakespeare Connection trip takes two hours, and there are four departures on weekdays—the three that would allow you to catch an evening performance in Stratford are at 9:15 AM, 10:45 AM, and 4:55 PM; Saturday departures are at 9:05 AM, 10:35 AM, and 5:05 PM; the Sunday departure is at 9:45 AM. There's a train to London after performances, usually at 11:15 PM. Schedules can change, so call to confirm times. National Rail Enquiries has further information.

DISCOUNTS & DEALS A seven-day Heart of England Rover ticket is valid for unlimited travel within the region; contact National Rail Enquiries for purchasing information. The Shakespeare Country Explorer Pass from Thames Trains offers one-day (£25) or three-day (£30) tickets for rail travel to and from London once and unlimited travel within Shakespeare Country, plus discounts at area sights.

FARES & SCHEDULES **National Rail Enquiries** ☎ 0845/748–4950 ⊕ www.nationalrail.co.uk. **Thames Trains** ☎ 01789/293127 ⊕ www.thamestrains.com. **Virgin Trains** ☎ 0845/722–2333 ⊕ www.virgin.co.uk/trains.

TRAVEL AGENCIES
Local Agent Referrals American Express ✉ c/o Tourist Information Centre, Bridgefoot, Stratford-upon-Avon ☎ 01789/415856. **Thomas Cook** ✉ c/o Midland Bank, 13 Chapel St., Stratford-upon-Avon ☎ 01789/294688.

VISITOR INFORMATION
Tourist information centers are normally open Monday–Saturday 9:30–5:30, but times vary according to season.
Heart of England Tourist Board ✉ Larkhill Rd., Worcester, WR5 2EZ ☎ 01905/761100 📠 01905/763450 ⊕ www.visitheartofengland.com. **Shakespeare Country** ⊕ www.shakespeare-country.co.uk. **Coventry** ✉ Bayley La., CV1 5RN ☎ 024/7622–7264 ⊕ www.coventry.org. **Kenilworth** ✉ Kenilworth Library, 11 Smalley Pl., CV8 1QG ☎ 01926/852595. **Stratford-upon-Avon** ✉ Bridgefoot, CV37 6GW ☎ 0870/160–7930 ⊕ www.stratford-upon-avon.co.uk. **Warwick** ✉ Court House, Jury St., CV34 4EW ☎ 01926/492212 ⊕ www.warwick-uk.co.uk.

BATH & THE COTSWOLDS

WITH GLOUCESTER & THE FOREST OF DEAN

7

STROLL THE PRETTIEST STREETSCAPE
in toylike Castle Combe ⇨*p.348*

EAVESDROP ON THE 18TH CENTURY
at No. 1 Royal Crescent in Bath ⇨*p.341*

DISCOVER THE ART OF LIVING
at stylish Cardynham House hotel ⇨*p.372*

UNWIND AT GLORIOUS GARDENS
from Sudeley Castle to Sezincote ⇨*p.339*

SNAP UP ANTIQUES AND CURIOS
in golden-hued Stow-on-the-Wold ⇨*p.363*

GET UP TO SNUFF OVER WHISKIES
at the Falkland Arms pub ⇨*p.362*

COMMUNE WITH NATURE
at Westonbirt Arboretum ⇨*p.374*

TAKE A DIP INTO THE PAST
at the Roman Baths ⇨*p.343*

Updated by
Robert
Andrews

THE ROLLING UPLANDS OF THE COTSWOLD HILLS represent the quintessence of rural England, as immortalized in countless books, paintings, and films. This blissfully unspoiled region occupies much of the county of Gloucestershire, in west-central England, with slices of neighboring Oxfordshire, Worcestershire, and Somerset. Together these make up a sweep of land stretching from Shakespeare Country in the north almost as far as the Bristol Channel in the south. The area is edged by a trio of historic towns that have absorbed, rather than compromised, the flavor of the Cotswolds: Bath, among the most alluring small cities in Europe, offering up "18th-century England in all its urban glory," to use a phrase of writer Nigel Nicolson; Regency-era Cheltenham—like Bath, a spa town adorned with remarkably elegant architecture; and Gloucester, which holds one of England's outstanding medieval cathedrals and gives access to the ancient Forest of Dean, on the western edge of the area.

Bath rightly boasts of being the best-planned town in England. Although the city was founded by the Romans when they discovered here the only true hot springs in England, its popularity during the 17th and 18th centuries ensured its aesthetic immortality. Bath's fashionable period luckily coincided with one of Britain's most creative architectural eras, producing a quite remarkable urban phenomenon—money available to create virtually an entire town of stylish buildings. The city powers have been wise enough to make sure that Bath is kept spruce and welcoming. In the past, Thomas Gainsborough, Lord Nelson, and Queen Victoria traveled here to sip the waters, which Charles Dickens described as tasting like "warm flatirons." Today some people come to walk in the footsteps of Jane Austen and take tea and scones with clotted cream. Others come to bathe in the hot spring water in an up-to-the-minute spa complex that incorporates the restored 18th-century baths.

North of Bath are the Cotswolds—a region that more than one writer has called the very soul of England. Is it the sun, or the soil? The pretty-as-a-picture villages with the perfectly clipped hedges? The mellow, centuries-old, stone-built cottages festooned with honeysuckle? Whatever the reason, this idyllic region, which from medieval times grew prosperous on the wool trade, remains a vision of rural England. Here are time-defying churches, sleepy hamlets, and ancient farmsteads so sequestered that they seem to offer everyone the thrill of personal discovery. Hidden in sheltered valleys are fabled abodes—Sudeley Castle, Stanway House, and Snowshill Manor (closed until spring 2005, though the grounds are open) among them. The Cotswolds can hardly claim to be undiscovered, but, happily, the area's poetic appeal has a way of surviving the tour buses, crowds, and antiques shops that sometimes pierce its timeless tranquillity. Here you can taste the glories of the old English village—its tile or thatched roofs, low-ceiling rooms, and gardens meticulously built on a gentle slope; its atmosphere is as thick as honey, and equally as sweet.

Exploring Bath & the Cotswolds

The region's major points of interest—Bath, the Cotswold Hills, and the Gloucester–Cheltenham axis—are one way to organize your explorations. Bath, in the southwestern corner of this area, is a good place to start; it can also be visited on a day out from London. The Cotswold Hills cover some of southern England's most beautiful terrain, with which the characteristic stone cottages throughout the area are in perfect harmony. To the west of the Cotswolds lie the cities of Gloucester and Cheltenham, a former spa town; beyond them, between the River Severn and the border of Wales, is the Forest of Dean. The road from Gloucester to Bath takes you by the castle at Berkeley.

About the Restaurants

Good restaurants dot the region, thanks to a steady flow of fine chefs seeking to cater to wealthy locals and waves of demanding visitors. Restaurants have never had a problem with a fresh food supply: excellent regional produce, salmon from the Rivers Severn and Wye, local lamb and pork, venison from the Forest of Dean, and pheasant, partridge, quail, and grouse in season. Also look for Gloucestershire Old Spot pork, bacon, and sausage on area menus.

About the Hotels

While staying at a Cotswold inn during the spring of 1776, the immortal Dr. Samuel Johnson uttered his noted panegyric on English hostelries: "There is no private house in which people can enjoy themselves so well as at a capital tavern." The hotels of this region still aim to please, and they are among Britain's most highly rated—from bed-and-breakfasts in village homes and farmhouses to luxurious country-house hotels. Many hotels present themselves as deeply traditional rural retreats, but some have opted for a sleeker, fresher style, with boldly contemporary or minimalist furnishings. Because the region is so popular, book ahead whenever possible, especially if you want to visit Bath during the two weeks in May and June when Bath International Music Festival hits town, or Cheltenham in mid-March when the National Hunt Festival takes place. Brace yourself for some high prices. B&Bs are a cheaper alternative to the fancier hotels, and most hotels offer two- and three-day packages. Keep in mind when making reservations that hotels can front on heavily trafficked roads; ask for quiet rooms.

WHAT IT COSTS In pounds				
	£££££	££££	£££	££	£
RESTAURANTS	over £22	£18–£22	£13–£17	£7–£12	under £7
HOTELS	over £160	£120–£160	£90–£120	£60–£90	under £60

Restaurant prices are for a main course at dinner. Hotel prices are for two people in a standard double room in high season, including VAT, with no meals or, if indicated, CP (with Continental breakfast), BP (Breakfast Plan, with full breakfast), or MAP (Modified American Plan, with breakfast and dinner).

Timing

This area contains some of Britain's most popular destinations, and you would do well to avoid weekends in the busier areas of the Cotswolds. During the week, even in summer, you may hardly see a soul in the more remote spots. Bath is particularly congested in summer, when students

7

You can get a taste of Bath and the Cotswolds in three days, and a weeklong visit will give you plenty of time to wander this relatively small region. Bath is a useful place to start or finish, not far off the M4 motorway on the A46. The cities of Gloucester and Cheltenham also hold many attractions. Once you are outside the towns, the Cotswold Hills should be relished on a slow schedule, to allow you time to smell the roses and appreciate the moon-daisies.

Numbers in the text correspond to numbers in the margin and on the Bath Environs, Bath, the Cotswolds, and the Forest of Dean maps.

If you have 3 days

A day in ☒ **Bath** ❶–❶ ☛ will enable you to tour the Roman Baths, followed by a whirl around Bath Abbey. In the afternoon, stroll along the river or canal, view the ceramics and silverware in the Holburne Museum, and then cross town to the Royal Crescent for a promenade. Spend the night here, heading out early for **Cheltenham** ❶, whose Regency architecture and fashionable shops will occupy a morning. After lunch, drive northeast on B4632 through **Winchcombe** ❶, near which are historic **Sudeley Castle** ❶ and treasure-filled **Snowshill Manor** ❷, both with gardens worth a look. A stop in **Broadway** ❷ will allow you to sample its prettiness, or you can press on to that Cotswold showpiece, ☒ **Chipping Campden** ❷. Now head south on the A429 through the classic Cotswold villages of **Moreton-in-Marsh** ❷ and **Stow-on-the-Wold** ❷, where cottage pubs are sandwiched between antiques shops. Nearby, don't miss the smaller places such as ☒ **Lower and Upper Slaughter** ❷. For your final afternoon, head westward on A436 to **Gloucester** ❸, with its restored docks and the National Waterways Museum.

If you have 7 days

Two days in ☒ **Bath** ❶–❶ ☛ will give you time to explore this Georgian treasure, even browsing its antiques shops and sampling the services of the Thermae Bath Spa. Outside Bath, make sure you see **Castle Combe** ❶, "the prettiest village in England," or **Lacock** ❶. On your third day, head north to swank ☒ **Cheltenham** ❶ and walk its Regency-era terraces and promenades. Overnight there, then start out on a circuit of the best of the Cotswold villages and countryside; Cheltenham's tourist office has useful information. Driving north out of Cheltenham, take a look at **Winchcombe** ❶ and explore the impressive grounds of **Sudeley Castle** ❶ and **Stanway House** ❶ (the latter has limited hours). Nearby **Snowshill Manor** ❷, in an unspoiled village, has a terraced garden. The popular Cotswold center of **Broadway** ❷ lies a couple of miles to the north, on A44.

Spend your fourth night in that Cotswold gem, ☒ **Chipping Campden** ❷, from which it is an easy drive to the rare shrubs and "garden rooms" of **Hidcote Manor Garden** ❷. From here, head south, through a pair of Cotswold towns, **Moreton-in-Marsh** ❷ and **Stow-on-the-Wold** ❷, both deserving a leisurely wander. Four miles east of these towns, Jacobean Chastleton House is something of a time warp, or you might ramble around the ancient Rollright Stones, a few miles farther east. South of Stow, kids may enjoy the museum attractions of **Bourton-on-the-Water** ❷ and **Northleach** ❷. **Chedworth Roman Villa** ❸ recalls the area's importance in Roman times—nearby **Cirencester** ❷ was Corinium, an important provincial capital. Pick a rural retreat for your fifth night, perhaps in the country around 🏨 **Lower and Upper Slaughter** ㉗. In the morning, an outing eastward might take in idyllic **Bibury** ㉚ and the wool town of **Burford** ㉙. Driving west from Cirencester on A417, make your farewells to the Cotswolds in the model village of **Owlpen** ㉟, immaculate **Painswick** ㉞, and the market town of **Tetbury** ㊱. 🏙 **Gloucester** ㊲ presents an urban contrast to the rustic tone of your last few days. Spend your final day either south of here, exploring medieval **Berkeley Castle** ㊸ and the celebrated **Slimbridge Wildfowl & Wetland Trust** ㊷, or else west, toward the Wye Valley and Wales, to take a gentle hike through the ancient Forest of Dean, with an overnight in 🏨 **Coleford** ㊶. Visit the Dean Heritage Center at Soudley and then put on your walking shoes. If you have children along, the nearby Clearwell Caves can be special fun.

---

flock to its language schools. On the other hand, Gloucester and Cheltenham are workday places that can absorb many tour buses comfortably; Cheltenham does, however, get full at festival time and during race meetings. Note that the private properties of Hidcote Manor, Snowshill Manor, and Sudeley Castle close in winter. Hidcote Manor Garden is at its best in spring and fall, Bowood Gardens in May.

BATH & ENVIRONS

Anyone who listens to the local speech of Bath will note the inflections that herald the closeness of England's West Country. The city, however, has strong links with the Cotswold Hills stretching north, and the Georgian architecture and mellow stone that are such a feature of Bath recall the stone mansions and cottages of that region. In the hinterland of the county of Somerset, the gentle, green countryside harbors country pubs.

Bath

★ ▶ *13 mi southeast of Bristol, 115 mi west of London.*

"I really believe I shall always be talking of Bath . . . I do like it so very much. Oh! who can ever be tired of Bath," wrote Jane Austen in *Northanger Abbey,* and today thousands of people heartily agree with the great 19th-century author. One of the delights of staying in this city, a UNESCO World Heritage Site, is being surrounded by magnificent 18th-century architecture, a lasting reminder of the vanished world described by Austen. In the 19th century Bath lost its fashionable luster and slid into a refined gentility that is still palpable. Although the 20th century saw some slight harm from World War II bombing and slightly more from urban renewal, the damage was halted before it could ruin the city's Georgian elegance. This doesn't mean that Bath is a museum. It is lively and interesting, with good dining and shopping, excellent art galleries and museums, and theater, music, and other performances throughout the year.

The Romans put Bath on the map in the 1st century, when they built a temple here, in honor of the goddess Minerva, and a sophisticated network of baths to make full use of the mineral springs that gush from the earth at a constant temperature of 116°F (46.5°C). Visits by Queen

Anne in 1702 and 1703 brought attention to the town, and soon 18th-century "people of quality" took it to heart. Bath became the most fashionable spa in Britain. The architect John Wood created a harmonious city, building graceful terraces (row houses), crescents (curving rows of houses), and villas of the same golden local limestone used by the Romans. His son, called John Wood the Younger, also designed notable buildings in the city. Assembly rooms, theaters, and pleasure gardens were built to entertain the rich and titled when they weren't busy attending the parties of Beau Nash (the city's master of ceremonies and chief social organizer, who helped increase Bath's popularity) and having their portraits painted by Gainsborough.

Today it's once again possible to relive the experience of the Romans and Georgians. You can bathe in the hot springs and sample the therapeutic and aesthetic treatments at the Thermae Bath Spa, a much-delayed venture scheduled to open by early 2005.

a good walk

Start in the traffic-free Abbey Churchyard, at the heart of Bath, and the **Roman Baths** ❶ ► to see the impressive remains of the bath complex. The lively piazza is dominated by **Bath Abbey** ❷, whose facade—itself packed with detail—invites further investigations within. Off Abbey Churchyard, where buskers (strolling musicians) perform, tiny alleys lead to little squares of stores, galleries, and eating places. Walk up Stall and Union streets toward Milsom Street, and you encounter alleyways with fascinating shops. Work your way east to Bridge Street and the graceful, Italianate **Pulteney Bridge** ❸, a shop-lined masterpiece over the River Avon. South of here, the Grand Parade looks out over flower-filled gardens. Stroll over the bridge to Great Pulteney Street, a broad thoroughfare that leads to the **Holburne Museum** ❹, Bath's finest collection of crafted objects. Cross back over the bridge, and head up Broad Street and its extension, Lansdown Road. Turn left onto Julian Road for insight into the industrial side of Bath at the **Museum of Bath at Work** ❺. From here, cross the road to Russell Street; turn right on Bennett Street and visit the **Museum of East Asian Art** ❻, with exquisite objets d'art from 5000 BC to the present day. On the opposite side of the road lies the **Museum of Costume and Assembly Rooms** ❼. The neoclassical Assembly Rooms were the 18th-century hub of elegant society, and the Museum of Costume provides an overview of some weird and wonderful apparel from the past. From here, it's a short hop to Gay Street and the **Jane Austen Centre** ❽, on a street where the author lived in the early 1800s. Returning north on Gay Street, you can study the **Circus** ❾, an architectural tour de force compared by some to an inverted Colosseum. The graceful arc of Bath's most dazzling terrace, the Royal Crescent, embraces a swath of green lawns at one end of Brock Street. Stop in at **Number 1 Royal Crescent** ❿, a perfectly preserved example of Georgian domestic architecture. Return to the Circus and walk south down Gay Street, which brings you past **Queen Square,** with its obelisk, to **Theatre Royal** ⓫, one of the country's most impressive dramatic venues. Wander east from here back to the Roman Baths, opposite which you can relieve tired limbs in a hot spring bath at the **Thermae Bath Spa** ⓬ (set to open in fall 2004). Alternatively, head for the abbey and tea shops, including Sally Lunn's, for liquid refreshment of another kind.

TIMING Allow a full day to see everything, with frequent tea stops; save two hours for the Roman Baths. On Sunday many shops close, and Bath Abbey is more difficult to visit. Without any stops, the walk takes only about 1½ hours, but in summer the sheer volume of sightseers may hamper your progress.

What to See

American Museum and Gardens. A Greek Revival (19th-century) mansion in a majestic setting on a hill southeast of the city holds the first museum of American decorative arts to be established outside the United States. Some galleries are furnished rooms (bedrooms, parlors, and a morning room), and others contain objects—in silver, pewter, and glass, for example—dating from the 17th to 19th centuries. Several rooms are devoted to folk art, Native American culture, and quilts. The parkland includes a reproduction of George Washington's garden at Mount Vernon. ✉ *Warminster Rd. (A36), Claverton Down, 2½ mi southeast of Bath* ☎ *01225/460503* ⊕ *www.americanmuseum.org* 🏛 *Museum, special exhibitions, and grounds £6.50, special exhibitions and grounds £4* ⊙ *Late Mar.–July and Sept.–early Nov., Tues.–Sun. 2–5; Aug., daily 2–5; also national holiday Mon. and preceding Sun. 11–5.*

❷ **Bath Abbey.** Dominating Bath's center, this 15th-century edifice of golden, glowing stone has a splendid west front, with carved figures of angels ascending ladders on either side. Notice, too, the miter, olive tree, and crown motif, a play on the name of the current building's founder, Bishop Oliver King. More than 50 stained-glass windows fill about 80% of the building's wall space, giving the interior an impression of lightness. The abbey was built in the Perpendicular (English late-Gothic) style on the site of a Saxon abbey, and the nave and side aisles contain superb fan-vaulted ceilings. Visit the **Heritage Vaults,** accessible from outside the building (the entrance is in the abbey's south wall, off Abbey Churchyard), to see an audiovisual presentation of the abbey's history and a reconstruction of the Norman cathedral that preceded it. ✉ *Abbey Churchyard* ☎ *01225/422462* ⊕ *www.bathabbey.org* 🏛 *Abbey £2.50 donation, Heritage Vaults £2.50* ⊙ *Abbey Easter–Oct., Mon.–Sat. 9–6; Nov.–Easter, Mon.–Sat. 9–4:30; call for Sun. hrs. Heritage Vaults Mon.–Sat. 10–4.*

need a break?

The quiet courtyard of two adjacent cafés, the **Café René and Café Parisien** (✉ 2 Shires Yard, off Broad St. ☎ 01225/447147) is handy for coffee and a croissant or a lunchtime baguette.

Building of Bath Museum. This absorbing museum in the Georgian Gothic–style Countess of Huntingdon's Chapel is an essential stop on any exploration of Bath, particularly for fans of Georgian architecture. It explains and illustrates the evolution of the city, with examples of everything from window design and wrought-iron railings to marquetry and other interior ornamentation. ✉ *The Paragon* ☎ *01225/333895* ⊕ *www.bath-preservation-trust.org.uk* 🏛 *£4* ⊙ *Mid-Feb.–Nov., Tues.–Sun. 10:30–5.*

Antiques & Markets

The antiques shops here are, it is sometimes whispered, "temporary" storerooms for the great families of the region, filled with tole-ware, treen, faience firedogs, toby jugs, and silhouettes, plus country furniture, Edwardiana, and ravishing 17th- to 19th-century furniture. The center of antiquing, with more than 30 dealers, is Stow-on-the-Wold. Other towns that have a number of antiques shops are Burford, Cirencester, Tetbury, and Moreton-in-Marsh. The Cotswolds have few of those "anything in this tray for £5" shops, however. For information about dealers and special events, contact the Cotswold Antique Dealers' Association. As across England, many towns in the region have market days, when you can purchase local produce, crafts, and items such as clothes, books, and toys. Head for Moreton-in-Marsh on Tuesday, Tetbury on Wednesday, and Cirencester on Monday and Friday.

Country Walks

Short walks thread the glorious, gentle countryside around the historic towns of the region, and tourist information centers often carry maps for theme walks. If you want to branch out on your own, but not get lost, track the rivers on which many towns are built. Easy-to-follow, scenic towpaths usually run along the water. However, rivers wind, and you may find yourself walking for much longer than you intended. The Cotswold Way, stretching about 100 mi between Bath and Chipping Campden, traces the ridge marking the edge of the Cotswolds and the Severn Valley and has incomparable views. The densely wooded Forest of Dean is quite special for walking, with interesting villages and monastic ruins. Many of its public footpaths are signposted, as are most of the Forestry Commission trails. There are easy walks out of Newland, around New Fancy (great view) and Mallards Pike Lake, and a slightly longer one (three hours), which takes in Wench Ford, Danby Lodge, and Blackpool Bridge. The area has picnic grounds, car parking, and, hidden away, old pubs where you can wet your whistle.

Glorious Gardens

Perhaps it's the sheer beauty of this area that has inspired the creation of so many superb gardens in a medley of styles. Here, as elsewhere in Britain, gardens often complement a stately home and deserve as close a look as the house. When you visit Sudeley Castle, the home of Catherine Parr (Henry VIII's last wife), for example, take time to explore the 19th-century Queen's Garden, beloved for its roses. Admirers of the naturalistic landscaping of Capability Brown can see a notable example of his large-scale work in the 2,000-acre park at Bowood House & Gardens; the spectacular Rhododendron Walks here are a later, 19th-century creation. In contrast, the 18th-century Painswick Rococo Garden, with its Gothic screen and other intriguing structures, has a pleasant intimacy. The Arts and Crafts movement in Britain transformed not only interior design but also the world of gardening; at Hidcote Manor Garden, a much-visited masterpiece of the style, hedges and walls set off vistas and surround distinct themed garden rooms. Britain wouldn't be Britain without a touch of eccentricity, and in this region the garden at the Indian-style manor of Sezincote, with its temple to a Hindu god, supplies a satisfying blend of the stately and the exotic.

★ **❾ Circus.** John Wood designed the masterful Circus, a circle of curving, perfectly proportioned Georgian houses interrupted just three times for intersecting streets. Wood died shortly after work on the Circus began; his son, the younger John Wood, completed the project. Notice the carved acorns atop the houses: Wood nurtured the myth that Prince Bladud founded Bath, ostensibly with the help of an errant pig rooting for acorns (this is one of a number of variations of Bladud's story), and the architect adopted the acorn motif in a number of places. A garden fills the center of the Circus.

★ **❹ Holburne Museum.** This elegant 18th-century building houses a small but superb collection of 17th- and 18th-century decorative arts, ceramics, and silverware. Highlights include paintings by Gainsborough (*The Byam Family,* on indefinite loan) and George Stubbs (*Reverend Carter Thelwall and Family*), and Rachmaninoff's Steinway piano. It also displays temporary exhibitions on historical themes. In its original incarnation as the Sydney Hotel, the house was one of the pivots of Bath's high society, which came to perambulate in the pleasure gardens (Sydney Gardens) that still lie behind it. One visitor was Jane Austen, whose main Bath residence was No. 4 Sydney Place, a brief stroll across the road from the museum. ⊠ *Great Pulteney St.* ☎ *01225/466669* ⊕ *www.bath.ac.uk/holburne* ⊠ £4 ☉ *Feb.–mid-Dec., Tues.–Sat. 10–5, Sun. 2:30–5:30.*

⑧ Jane Austen Centre. This cozy Georgian-house-turned-museum, a few doors up from where Jane Austen lived in 1805 (one of several addresses she had in Bath at different times), examines the influence of the city on her writings. *Northanger Abbey* and *Persuasion* are both set in the city. Displays give a pictorial introduction, and the digitally enlarged panorama of Bath in 1800 by Robert Havell helps put Austen's world in context. Jane Austen walking tours leave from the Abbey Churchyard daily at 1:30 in July and August and on weekends from September through June. ⊠ *40 Gay St.* ☏ *01225/443000* ⊕ *www.janeausten.co.uk* ☏ *£4.65, tours £4.50; combined ticket £7.35* ☉ *Mon.–Sat. 10–5:30, Sun. 10:30–5:30.*

⑤ Museum of Bath at Work. The core of this industrial-history collection, which gives a novel perspective on the city, is a complete engineering works and fizzy drinks factory, relocated to this building. It once belonged to Bath entrepreneur Jonathan Bowler, who started his many businesses in 1872. The tour includes all the original clanking machinery and also offers glimpses into Bath's stone industry and cabinetmaking. ⊠ *Julian Rd.* ☏ *01225/318348* ⊕ *www.bath-at-work.org.uk* ☏ *£3.50* ☉ *Apr.–Oct., daily 10–4; Nov.–Mar., weekends 10–4.*

★ ⑦ Museum of Costume and Assembly Rooms. In its role as the **Assembly Rooms,** this neoclassical building was the leading center for social life in 18th-century Bath, with a schedule of dress balls, concerts, and choral nights. Jane Austen came here often, and it was here, in the Ballroom, that Catherine Morland had her first, disappointing encounter with Bath's beau monde in *Northanger Abbey;* the Octagon Room was the setting for an important encounter between Anne Elliot and Captain Wentworth in *Persuasion.* Built by John Wood the Younger in 1771, the building was badly damaged by wartime bombing in 1942 but was faithfully restored. Today the Assembly Rooms house the entertaining **Museum of Costume,** displaying costumes from Elizabethan times up to the present. Throughout the year, concerts of Vivaldi, Bach, and other classical composers are given in the Ballroom, just as they were in bygone days. ⊠ *Bennett St.* ☏ *01225/477789* ⊕ *www.museumofcostume.co.uk* ☏ *£6; combined ticket with Roman Baths, valid 7 days, £12* ☉ *Mar.–Oct., daily 11–6; Nov.–Feb., daily 11–5; last admission 1 hr before closing.*

⑥ Museum of East Asian Art. Intimate galleries on three floors finely display ancient and modern pieces from China, Japan, Korea, and Southeast Asia. Highlights are graphic 19th-century watercolors depicting the Chinese idea of hell, Chinese ivory figures, and Japanese lacquerware. ⊠ *12 Bennett St.* ☏ *01225/464640* ☏ *£3.50* ☉ *Tues.–Sat. 10–5, Sun. noon–5.*

★ ⑩ Number 1 Royal Crescent. The majestic arc of the Royal Crescent, much used as a film location, is the crowning glory of Palladian architecture in Bath. The work of John Wood the Younger, these 30 houses fronted by 114 columns were laid out between 1767 and 1774. A house in the center is now the Royal Crescent Hotel. On the corner of Brock Street and the Royal Crescent, Number 1 Royal Crescent has been turned into a museum and furnished as it might have been at the turn of the 19th century. The museum crystallizes a view of the English class system—upstairs all is elegance, and downstairs is a kitchen display. ☏ *01225/*

Bath

KEY

Tourist information

Start of walk

TO
THE AMERICAN MUSEUM
AND PRIOR PARK

Bath Abbey **2**

The Circus **9**

Holburne Museum **4**

Jane Austen Centre **8**

Museum of
Bath at Work **5**

Museum of Costume and
Assembly Rooms **7**

Museum of
East Asian Art **6**

Number 1
Royal Crescent **10**

Pulteney Bridge **3**

Roman Baths/
Pump Room **1**

Theatre Royal **11**

Thermae Bath Spa **12**

428126 ⊕ *www.bath-preservation-trust.org.uk* ⌑ £4 ⊘ *Mid-Feb.–Oct.,*
Tues.–Sun. and national holidays 10:30–5; Nov., Tues.–Sun. 10:30–4;
last admission 30 mins before closing.

Prior Park. A vision to warm Jane Austen's heart, Bath's grandest house
lies a mile or so southeast of the center, with splendid views over the Georgian townscape. Built around 1738 by John Wood the Elder of honey-
color limestone, the Palladian mansion was the home of local businessman
(he owned a stone quarry) and philanthropist Ralph Allen (1693–1764),
whose guests included such luminaries as poet Alexander Pope and novelists Henry Fielding and Samuel Richardson. Today it is a Roman Catholic
school and the interior is not open to the public, but you may wander
through the beautiful grounds, designed by Capability Brown and em-
bellished with a Palladian bridge and lake. There is no parking lot here
or in the vicinity: unless you relish the uphill trudge, take a taxi or use the
frequent bus service (Nos. 2 or 4 from the center). ⊠ *Ralph Allen Dr.*
☎ *01225/833422* ⊕ *www.nationaltrust.org.uk* £4, £1 discount if arriving by public transportation ⊘ Feb.–Nov., Wed.–Mon. 11–5:30 or dusk;
Dec. and Jan., Fri.–Sun. 11–dusk; last admission 1 hr before closing.

❸ **Pulteney Bridge.** Florence's Ponte Vecchio inspired this 18th-century
span, one of the most famous landmarks in the city and the only work
of Robert Adam in Bath. It's unique in Great Britain because shops line
both sides of the bridge.

Queen Square. Houses and the Francis Hotel surround the garden in the
center of this small, peaceful square. An obelisk designed by the older
John Wood and financed by Beau Nash celebrates the 1738 visit of Frederick, Prince of Wales.

★ ▶ ❶ **Roman Baths.** The hot springs have drawn people here since prehistoric
times, so it's most appropriate to begin an exploration of Bath at this
excellent museum on the site of the ancient city's temple complex and
primary "watering hole." Here the Roman patricians would gather to
immerse themselves, drink the mineral waters, and socialize. With the
departure of the Romans, the baths fell into disuse and were partially
covered. When bathing again became fashionable, the site was reopened;
the magnificent Georgian building now standing was erected at the end
of the 18th century. During the following century, almost the entire Roman
bath complex was rediscovered and excavated, and the museum displays
relics of the temple once dedicated to Sulis Minerva. Exhibits include a
mustachioed, Celtic-influenced Gorgon's head, fragments of colorful curses
invoked by the Romans against some of their neighbors, and information about Roman bathing practices. The **Great Bath** is now roofless,
and the statuary and pillars belong to the 19th century, but much remains from the original complex, and the steaming, somewhat murky
waters are undeniably evocative. On August evenings, you can take torch-
lighted tours of the baths.

Adjacent to the Roman bath complex is the famed **Pump Room,** built
1792–96, a rendezvous place for members of 18th-century and 19th-
century Bath society, who liked to check on the new arrivals to the city.
Here Catherine Morland and Mrs. Allen "paraded up and down for an

CloseUp
BATH'S GEORGIAN ARCHITECTURE

Bath wouldn't be Bath without its distinctive 18th-century Georgian architecture, much of which was conceived by John Wood the Elder (1704–54), an antiquarian and architect obsessed. Wood saw Bath as a city destined for almost mythic greatness along the lines of Winchester and Glastonbury. Arriving in Bath in 1727, he sought an architectural style that would do justice to his concept, and found it in the Palladian style, made popular in Britain by Inigo Jones. For building material, he looked no further than the local golden limestone. Influenced by nearby ancient stone circles as well as round Roman temples, Wood broke from convention in his design for Bath's Circus, a circle of houses broken only three times for intersecting streets. After the death of Wood the Elder, John Wood the Younger (1728–82) carried out his father's plans for the Royal Crescent, an obtuse crescent of 30 interconnected houses. Today you can stop in at No. 1 Royal Crescent for a look at one of these homes—it's like eavesdropping on the 18th century.

hour, looking at everybody and speaking to no one," to quote from Jane Austen's *Northanger Abbey*. Today you can eat on the premises—or you can simply, for a small fee, taste the fairly vile mineral water. ⊠ *Abbey Churchyard* ☎ *01225/477785* ⊕ *www.romanbaths.co.uk* ✍ *Pump Room free, Roman Baths £9 with audio guide; combined ticket with Museum of Costume and Assembly Rooms (valid 7 days) £12* ☉ *Mar.–June, Sept., and Oct., daily 9–6; July and Aug., daily 9 AM–10 PM; Nov.–Feb., daily 9:30–5:30; last admission 1 hr before closing.*

⑪ Theatre Royal. George Dance the Younger designed this magnificent auditorium, which opened in 1805 and was restored in 1982 as a vision in damson plush, raspberry-striped silk, and gold grisaille. ⊠ *Saw Close* ☎ *01225/448844* ⊕ *www.theatreroyal.org.uk* ✍ *Tour £3* ☉ *Tours 1st Sat. of month at 11 and following Wed at noon; call to confirm.*

⑫ Thermae Bath Spa. The only place in Britain where you can bathe in natural hot spring water, and in an open-air rooftop location as well, this state-of-the-art complex designed by Nicholas Grimshaw consists of a Bath-stone building surrounded by a glass curtain wall. Set to open (after several delays) in early 2005 in the heart of the city, the spa has four luxurious floors offering the latest spa treatments and therapies. Close by, the Cross Bath and the Hot Bath, two 18th-century thermal baths, have been brought back into use for bathing and treatments; there's also a café and shop. You can book in advance or call on the day. ⊠ *Hot Bath St.* ☎ *01225/477051* ⊕ *www.thermaebathspa.com* ✍ *£19 for 2 hrs, £29 for 4 hrs, £45 all day; extra charges for treatments* ☉ *Daily 9 AM–10 PM.*

William Herschel Museum. In this modest Bath town house, using a handmade telescope of his own devising, William Herschel (1738–1822) identified the planet Uranus. This small museum devoted to his studies and discoveries contains examples of his telescopes, the workshop where he cast his speculum metal mirrors, musical instruments of his time (Herschel came to Bath from his native Hannover as a musician, and was organist at Bath's Octagon Chapel), and the tiny garden where the discovery of Uranus was made. ☒ *19 New King St.* ☏ *01225/311342* ⊕ *www.bath-preservation-trust.org.uk* ☑ *£3.50* ⊙ *Mid-Jan.–mid-Dec., Mon., Tues., Thurs., and Fri. 1–5, weekends 11–5; last admission at 4:30.*

Where to Stay & Eat

££££ ✕**Moody Goose.** At this restaurant serving sophisticated modern English fare, you descend the stairs to a room with comfy sofas before you enter the creamy, vaulted dining area, highlighted by a green slate floor and French watercolors on the walls. Expect carefully crafted dishes such as turbot with roasted cod and samphire grass; cheeses are served with sultana bread and poached figs. Pretheater meals are a good value. ☒ *7A Kingsmead Sq.* ☏ *01225/466688* ▭ *AE, DC, MC, V* ⊙ *Closed Sun. and 2 wks in Jan.*

£££–££££ ✕**Popjoy's Restaurant.** The former home of Richard "Beau" Nash—the dictator of fashion for mid-18th-century society in Bath—and his mistress Juliana Popjoy provides an elegant choice for a fine, English-style, pre- or post-theater dinner. You can dine on the ground floor or in the lovely Georgian drawing room upstairs. The dishes, such as seared loin of lamb with roast garlic and Madeira sauce, show eclectic international touches. ☒ *Beau Nash House, Saw Close* ☏ *01225/460494* ▭ *AE, DC, MC, V* ⊙ *Closed Sun.*

£££ ✕**Number 5 Bistro.** An ideal spot for a light lunch, this airy bistro, decorated with plants and framed posters, is just over Pulteney Bridge from the center of town. The menu changes frequently but includes soups and such dishes as foie gras served with toasted brioche, and grilled rib of beef. You can bring your own wine on Monday and Tuesday, and Wednesday is devoted to fish. ☒ *5 Argyle St.* ☏ *01225/444499* ▭ *AE, MC, V.*

££–£££ ✕**Eastern Eye.** A magnificent domed Georgian ceiling graces the dining room of one of the country's finest Indian restaurants. Besides many Balti (meat and vegetables cooked in a wok in a style developed by Kashmiri immigrants), tandoori, and *tikka* (marinated meat cooked in a tandoor) dishes, the menu lists specialties such as king prawn masala. If the choice confounds you, opt for a fixed-price meal or one of the chef's recommendations: chicken *jalfrazi* is hot, whereas *moglai* chicken in a cashew, coconut, and sultana sauce is milder. ☒ *8A Quiet St.* ☏ *01225/422323* ▭ *AE, MC, V.*

££–£££ ✕**Retro.** Pull up an old church chair at this bustling, bohemian spot and tuck into contemporary fare such as roast lamb with a pistachio and herb crust and baked-cherry-and-chocolate cheesecake. It's also a great place for a light snack at lunchtime, when club sandwiches and good vegetarian choices are on offer, and there's a Retro-To-Go next door. ☒ *18 York St.* ☏ *01225/339347* ▭ *AE, MC, V* ⊙ *Closed Mon.*

££ ✕**Pump Room.** The 18th-century Pump Room, next to the Roman Baths, serves morning coffee, lunches of steak sandwiches or chicken and lamb dishes, and afternoon tea, often to music by a string trio. Do sample the English cheese board and homemade Bath biscuits. The Terrace Restaurant has views over the Baths and is also open occasionally for dinner (there are fixed-price menus, and reservations are essential). Be prepared to wait in line for a table during the day. ⊠ *Abbey Churchyard* ☎ *01225/444477* ☰ *AE, DC, MC, V* ⊘ *No dinner except during Aug., Dec., and festivals.*

££ ✕ **Sally Lunn's.** This popular spot near Bath Abbey occupies the oldest house in Bath, dating to 1482. It's famous for the Sally Lunn bun (served here since 1680), actually a light, semisweet bread. You can choose from more than 40 sweet and savory toppings to accompany your bun, or turn it into a meal with such dishes as trencher pork (served with bread that holds the juices) with sherry and brandy sauce. Daytime diners can view the small kitchen museum in the cellar (free, 30p for nondining visitors). ⊠ *4 North Parade Passage* ☎ *01225/461634* ☰ *MC, V* ⊘ *No dinner Dec. and Jan.*

£–££ ✕ **Tilleys Bistro.** The meat and vegetarian menus of this intimate, bow-windowed eatery present an alluring selection of hot and cold dishes in appetizer-size portions. Typical choices include Somerset mushrooms with smoked ham and cheddar cheese, and lamb's kidneys in a port and cream sauce. Pretheater meals are available from 6:30. ⊠ *3 North Parade Passage* ☎ *01225/484200* ☰ *MC, V* ⊘ *Closed Sun.*

£ ✕ **The Old Green Tree.** Friendly and unspoiled, this oak-paneled pub is an option for a pint and spot of lunch. You can pick soup, salad, and rolls, or a hearty bangers and mash; specials are chalked up on the blackboard. ⊠ *12 Green St.* ☎ *01225/448259* ☰ *No credit cards.*

★ £££££ ✕▥ **Royal Crescent Hotel.** At the heart of the monumental Royal Crescent, this lavishly converted house is an architectural treasure, with prices to match. The furnishings are consistent with the building's period elegance, and a Palladian villa in the garden provides extra lodging. If some bedrooms are on the small side, there are ample luxuries to compensate. The hotel's superb Pimpernel's restaurant has won consistent praise for modern British fare. ⊠ *16 Royal Crescent, BA1 2LS* ☎ *01225/823333, 888/295–4710 in U.S.* ☒ *01225/339401, 888/295–4711 in U.S.* ⊕ *www.royalcrescent.co.uk* ⬎ *29 rooms, 16 suites* ⌂ *Restaurant, in-room data ports, cable TV, indoor pool, gym, sauna, spa, croquet, bar, meeting rooms, free parking, some pets allowed* ☰ *AE, DC, MC, V* ⦿| *BP.*

£££–£££££ ✕▥ **Queensberry Hotel.** Intimate and elegant, this hotel in a residential street near the Circus occupies three 1772 town houses built by John Wood the Younger for the marquis of Queensberry. Renovations have preserved the Regency stucco ceilings and cornices and original marble tile on the fireplaces, and each room is decorated in rich but restful tones. Downstairs, the Olive Tree restaurant serves top-notch English and Mediterranean dishes. ⊠ *Russell St., BA1 2QF* ☎ *01225/447928* ☒ *01225/446065* ⊕ *www.bathqueensberry.co.uk* ⬎ *29 rooms* ⌂ *Restaurant, some in-room data ports, bar, meeting rooms, free parking; no a/c* ☰ *AE, MC, V.*

FodorśChoice
★

££–££££ ✕▥ **Duke's Hotel.** Refurbishment of this Palladian-style mansion has revealed the true Georgian grandeur of its rooms. Elegant bedrooms (no smoking allowed) are individually decorated in English-, French-, or Italian-inspired style, and some have elaborate plasterwork or large windows facing the street. The informal Fitzroy's restaurant serves the best of contemporary British fare, such as char-grilled minute steak with watercress and butter. This hotel in the heart of town overlooks Bath's rugby and cricket ground. ⊠ *Great Pulteney St., BA2 4DN* ☎ *01225/787960* ☒ *01225/787961* ⊕ *www.dukesbath.co.uk* ⬎ *12 rooms, 5 suites*

♿ *Restaurant, cable TV, bar, meeting rooms, parking (fee), some pets allowed; no a/c* = *AE, DC, MC, V* ❋| *BP.*

£££££ ▣ **Bath Spa Hotel.** Its 7 acres of well-kept grounds (complete with grotto) give this splendid golden stone hotel, a converted Georgian mansion, a feeling of seclusion, although you're just a 10-minute walk from the heart of bustling Bath. The formal public areas have comfortable sofas and armchairs; many rooms are in wings matching the style of the original building. Guest rooms are modern and neutral in hue, with pampering touches in the large marble bathrooms. ⊞ *Sydney Rd., BA2 6JF* ✆ *0870/400–8222 or 01225/444424* = *01225/444006* ◉ *www.bathspahotel.com* ↬ *97 rooms, 5 suites* ♿ *2 restaurants, in-room data ports, cable TV, tennis court, indoor pool, gym, sauna, spa, croquet, bar, meeting rooms, free parking, some pets allowed (fee); no a/c* = *AE, DC, MC, V* ❋| *BP.*

£££–££££ ▣ **Paradise House.** Don't be put off by the 10-minute uphill walk from the center of Bath—you'll be rewarded by a wonderful prospect of the city from the upper stories of this Georgian guest house. Cool pastels and traditional furnishings decorate the rooms attractively, and there are open fires in winter and a lush garden for spring and summer. Rooms 3 and 5 have the best views. If the full English breakfast is too daunting, indulge in coffee and croissants in bed. ⊞ *88 Holloway, BA2 4PX* ✆ *01225/317723* = *01225/482005* ◉ *www.paradise-house.co.uk* ↬ *11 rooms* ♿ *Some in-room data ports, croquet, bar, free parking; no a/c, no smoking* = *AE, DC, MC, V* ☁ *Closed last wk in Dec.* ❋| *BP.*

£££ ▣ **Harington's Hotel.** It's rare to find a compact hotel in the cobblestoned heart of Bath, and this informal lodging converted from a group of Georgian town houses fits the bill nicely. The surprisingly quiet bedrooms aren't spacious, there are no views from the windows, and the parking facilities can be tricky to find, but these minuses are outweighed by the polite but friendly service and the convenience and pleasure of finding yourself in the midst of smart shops and good pubs and restaurants. The bar serves hot and cold snacks all day. Note that this three-story building has no elevator. ⊞ *Queen St., BA1 1HE* ✆ *01225/461728* = *01225/444804* ◉ *www.haringtonshotel.co.uk* ↬ *13 rooms* ♿ *Cable TV, bar, parking (fee), no-smoking rooms; no a/c* = *AE, DC, MC, V* ❋| *BP.*

££–£££ ▣ **Cranleigh.** In a quiet location on the hill high above the city center, this Victorian guest house has wonderful views from the back of the building. Rooms are richly decorated, and large breakfasts—pancakes with maple syrup, kippers, eggs with smoked haddock, and vegetarian options—are served in the dining room, which overlooks the garden. ⊞ *159 Newbridge Hill, BA1 3PX* ✆ *01225/310197* = *01225/423143* ◉ *www.cranleighguesthouse.com* ↬ *8 rooms* ♿ *Free parking; no a/c, no kids under 5, no smoking* = *AE, MC, V* ❋| *BP.*

£ ▣ **Albany Guest House.** Homey and friendly, this Edwardian house, close to Victoria Park and the center of town, has simply furnished rooms with a floral motif. The pale-blue-and-yellow attic room is the largest and best. Homemade vegetarian sausages are an option at breakfast. ⊞ *24 Crescent Gardens, BA1 2 NB* ✆ *01225/313339* ◉ *www.albanybath.co.uk* ↬ *4 rooms, 2 with bath* ♿ *Free parking; no a/c, no room phones, no kids under 7, no smoking* = *No credit cards* ❋| *BP.*

Nightlife & the Arts

FESTIVALS
★
The **Bath International Music Festival** (⊠ Bath Festivals Box Office, 2 Church St., Abbey Green ☎ 01225/463362 ⊕ www.bathfestivals.org. uk), held for two weeks in May and June, presents concerts (classical, jazz, and world music), dance performances, and exhibitions in and around Bath, many in the Assembly Rooms and Bath Abbey.

The weeklong **Bath Literature Festival** (⊠ Bath Festivals Box Office, 2 Church St., Abbey Green ☎ 01225/463362 ⊕ www.bathfestivals.org. uk) in early March features readings and talks by writers, mostly in the 18th-century Guildhall on High Street.

The **Jane Austen Festival** (☎ 01225/463362 ⊕ www.janeaustenfestival. co.uk) celebrates the great writer with films, plays, walks, and talks during a week in late September.

THEATER
The **Theatre Royal** (⊠ Box Office, Saw Close ☎ 01225/448844), a Regency playhouse, has a year-round program that often includes pre- or post-London tours. You have to reserve the best seats well in advance, but you can line up for same-day standby seats or standing room. Check the location—sight lines can be poor.

Sports & the Outdoors

To explore the River Avon by rented punt or canoe, head for the **Bath Boating Station** (⊠ Forester Rd. ☎ 01225/312900), behind the Holburne Museum. It's open April–September.

The par-71, 18-hole golf course at **Sham Castle** (⊠ North Rd. ☎ 01225/463834), 1 mi southeast of town, is one of the West's finest courses, on high ground with splendid views.

Shopping

Bath has excellent small, family-run, and specialty shops. The shopping district centers on Stall and Union streets (modern stores), Milsom Street (traditional stores), and Walcott Street (arts and crafts). Leading off these main streets are alleyways and passages lined with galleries and antiques shops. **Bartlett Street Antique Centre** (⊠ Bartlett St. ☎ 01225/466689) has more than 100 showcases and stands selling every kind of antique imaginable, including vintage clothing, linens, and furniture. **Beaux Arts Ceramics** (⊠ 12–13 York St. ☎ 01225/464850) carries the work of prominent potters and holds eight solo exhibitions a year. **Margaret's Buildings** (⊠ Halfway between the Circus and Royal Crescent) is a lane with gift shops and several stores selling secondhand and antiquarian books. The **Paragon Antiques Market** (⊠ 3 Bladud Bldgs., The Paragon ☎ 01225/463715), open Wednesday 6:30 AM–3 PM, is a wonderful place to browse; 50 dealers have stalls here, and there's a restaurant.

Castle Combe

⓭ *12 mi northeast of Bath, 5 mi northwest of Chippenham.*

Fodor'sChoice
★
This Wiltshire village lived a sleepy existence until 1962, when it was voted the Prettiest Village in England—without any of its inhabitants knowing that it had even been a contender. The village's magic is that it's so toylike, so delightfully all-of-a-piece: you can see almost the

whole town at one glance from any one position. It consists of little more than a brook, a pack bridge, a street (which is called the Street) of simple stone cottages, a market cross from the 13th century, and the Perpendicular-style church of St. Andrew. The grandest house in the village (actually, on its outskirts) is the Upper Manor House, built in the 15th century by Sir John Fastolf; it was Dr. Dolittle's house in the 1967 Rex Harrison film and is now the Manor House Hotel.

Where to Stay & Eat

★ ✕🏨 **Manor House Hotel.** The partly 14th-century manor house, outside
££££–£££££ the village in a 23-acre park, is a baronial swirl of solid chimney stacks, carvings, and columns. Inside, a stone frieze depicts characters from Shakespeare's Falstaff plays, to commemorate the fact that Sir John Fastolf, thought to be the model for the character, was lord of this manor. Antiques abound and bedrooms have lavish bathrooms; some rooms are in mews cottages. The Bybrook restaurant serves imaginative fixed-price meals—try the loin of lamb with artichoke relish. ⊠ *Castle Combe, SN14 7HR* ☎ *01249/782206* 📠 *01249/782159* ⊕ *www.exclusivehotels.co. uk* 📮 *48 rooms* ⌂ *Restaurant, in-room data ports, 18-hole golf course, tennis court, pool, bar, meeting rooms, helipad; no a/c* 🖃 *AE, MC, V.*

Lacock

⑭ *3 mi south of Chippenham, 8 mi southeast of Castle Combe.*

Fodor'sChoice
★
This lovely Wiltshire village is the victim of its own charm, its unspoiled gabled and stone-tiled cottages drawing tour buses aplenty. Left to its own devices, however, Lacock slips back into its profound slumber, the mellow stone and brick buildings little changed in 500 years. There are a few antiques shops, the handsome church of St. Cyriac (built with money earned in the wool trade), a 14th-century tithe barn, and a scattering of pubs that serve bar meals in atmospheric surroundings.

Well-preserved **Lacock Abbey** reflects the fate of many religious establishments in England—a spiritual center became a home. The abbey, at the town's center, was founded in the 13th century and closed down during the dissolution of the monasteries in 1539, when its new owner, Sir William Sharington, demolished the church and converted the cloisters, sacristy, chapter house, and monastic quarters into a private dwelling. His last descendant, Mathilda Talbot, donated the property as well as Lacock itself to the National Trust in the 1940s. The abbey's grounds are also worth a wander, with a Victorian woodland garden and an 18th-century summer house. Harry Potter fans, take note: Lacock Abbey was used for some scenes at Hogwarts School in the film *Harry Potter and the Sorcerer's Stone.* The **Fox Talbot Museum** (☎ 01249/730459 ⊘ Mid-Mar.–Oct., Wed.–Mon. 1–5:30; Nov.–mid-Mar., weekends 1–5:30), in a 16th-century barn at the gates of Lacock Abbey, illustrates the early history of photography with works by pioneers in the field and also exhibits contemporary artists. The museum commemorates the work of William Henry Fox Talbot (1800–77), who developed the first photographic negative at Lacock Abbey, showing an oriel window in his family home. Look for a copy of this (the original is in Bradford's National Museum of Photography, Film, and Television) and other results of Fox

Talbot's experiments in the 1830s. ✉ *Just east of A350* ☎ *01249/730227* ⊕ *www.nationaltrust.org.uk* ✐ *Abbey, museum, gardens, and cloisters £7; abbey, garden, and cloisters £5.60; museum, gardens, and cloisters £4.40* ⊙ *Abbey Apr.–Oct., Wed.–Mon. 1–5:30; gardens and cloisters Mar.–Oct., daily 11–5:30; last admission 30 mins before closing.*

Where to Stay & Eat

£££–££££ ✕⊡ **At the Sign of the Angel.** An inn since the 15th century, this building measures up to expectations of comfortable antiquity—polished floors, gleaming silver, antiques, and cottage-style bedrooms (one room contains a bed that belonged to famous Victorian engineer Isambard Kingdom Brunel). The restaurant is known for its Stilton and walnut paté, roasts, casseroles, and desserts such as meringues with clotted cream and fresh strawberries. ✉ *6 Church St., SN15 2LB* ☎ *01249/730230* 🖷 *01249/730527* ⊕ *www.lacock.co.uk* ⇆ *10 rooms* ⟁ *Restaurant, some in-room data ports, meeting rooms, some pets allowed; no a/c* ▤ *AE, MC, V* ⊙ *Closed last wk of Dec.* ¶⊙¶ *BP.*

Bowood House & Gardens

⟳ ⑮ *3 mi southeast of Chippenham, 3 mi east of Lacock.*

Dating to the mid-18th century, beautifully proportioned Bowood House sits in graceful parkland designed by Capability Brown. The family home of the marquess of Lansdowne owes its present appearance to Charles Cockerell, architect of the Ashmolean Museum at Oxford, and to Robert Adam, who was responsible for the south front, the orangery, and the splendid library and sculpture gallery. One room served as the laboratory where Joseph Priestley discovered oxygen gas in 1774. Among the treasures are Lord Byron's Albanian dress, much booty from India, and a dazzling collection of jewelry. The landscaped gardens, complete with Doric temple on the lake and waterfall in the woods, are at their finest in spring, when acres of rhododendrons are in flower. There's also an adventure playground for children. ✉ *South of A4, Calne* ☎ *01249/812102* ⊕ *www.bowood.org* 🖷 *£6.40, rhododendron walks £3.60 (£2.60 if combined with visit to house and gardens)* ⊙ *House and gardens Apr.–Oct., daily 11–5:30; rhododendron walks late Apr.–early June, daily 11–6.*

THE COTSWOLDS

The Thames rises among the limestone Cotswold Hills, and a more delightful cradle could not be imagined for that historic river. The Cotswolds are among the best-preserved rural districts of England, and the quiet but lovely grays and ambers of the stone buildings here are truly unsurpassed. Much has been written about the area's towns, which age has mellowed rather than withered, but on closer inspection, the architecture of the villages differs little from that of villages elsewhere in England. Their distinction lies instead in the character of their surroundings: the valleys are deep and rolling, and cozy hamlets appear to drip in foliage from church tower to garden gate. Beyond the town limits, you may often discover the "high wild hills and rough uneven ways" that Shakespeare wrote about.

Over the centuries, quarries of honey-color stone have yielded building blocks for many Cotswold houses and churches and have transformed little towns into realms of gold. Nowhere else in Britain does that superb combination of church tower and gabled manor house shine so brightly, nowhere else are the hedges so perfectly clipped, nor the churchyards so peaceful. There's an elusive spirit about the Cotswolds, so make Chipping Campden, Moreton-in-Marsh, or Stow-on-the-Wold your headquarters for a few days, and wander for a while, going through this valley and along that byroad. Then ask yourself what the area is all about. Its secret seems shared by two things—sheep and stone. The combination is not as strange as it may sound. These were once the great sheep-rearing areas of England, and during the peak of prosperity in the Middle Ages, Cotswold wool was in demand the world over. This made the local merchants rich, but many gave back to the Cotswolds by restoring old churches (the famous "wool churches" of the region) or building rows of almshouses, of limestone now seasoned to a glorious golden-gray.

Begin with Cheltenham—a gateway to the Cotswolds, but slightly outside the boundaries—then move on to the beauty spots in and around Winchcombe. Next are Sudeley Castle, Stanway House, and Snowshill Manor, among the most impressive houses of the region; the oversold village of Broadway, which has many rivals for beauty hereabouts; Chipping Campden—the Cotswold cognoscenti's favorite; and Hidcote Manor, one of the most spectacular gardens in England. Then circle back south, down through Moreton-in-Marsh, Stow-on-the-Wold, Upper Slaughter, Lower Slaughter, Bourton-on-the-Water, and end with Bibury, Tetbury, and Owlpen. This is definitely a region where it pays to go off the beaten track to take a look at that village among the trees. Many nooks and villages snuggled deep into dells can be rendered invisible by coverings of ivy. Like four-leaf clovers, their discovery must come serendipitously.

Cheltenham

⓰ *50 mi north of Bath, 13 mi east of Gloucester, 99 mi west of London.*

Although Cheltenham has acquired a reputation as snooty—and it's undeniable that the population is generally well-heeled and conservative—it's also vibrant and cosmopolitan. The town has excellent restaurants and bars, fashionable stores, and a thriving cultural life. Its primary claim to renown, however, is its architecture, rivaling Bath's in its Georgian elegance, with wide, tree-lined streets, crescents, and terraces with row houses, balconies, and iron railings. Like Bath, Cheltenham owes part of its fame to mineral springs. By 1740 the first spa was built, and after a visit from George III and Queen Charlotte in 1788, the town dedicated itself to idleness and enjoyment. "A polka, parson-worshipping place"—in the words of resident Lord Tennyson—Cheltenham gained its reputation for snobbishness when stiff-collared Raj majordomos returned from India to find that the springs—the only purely natural al-

The Cotswolds

GREAT BRITAIN

Stratford

Avon

A34

A46

Stratford-upon-Avon

Kineton

B4089

A46

B439

A429

Stour

A34

Fosse Way

Hidcote Manor Garden
23

Charingworth

B4035

Shipston-on-Stour

Evesham

VALE OF EVESHAM

Chipping Campden
22

Broadway

A44

A435

Paxford

A3400

21

Buckland

B4632

Avon

B4081

A44

Moreton-in-Marsh
24

Rollright Stones

Snowshill Manor
20

A424

A429

Chastleton House

Chipping Norton

Stanway House
19

Greet

B4077

A44

Winchcombe
17

18

Upper Swell

Stow-on-the-Wold
25

A436

Sudeley Castle

Lower Swell

Brockhampton

Upper Slaughter
27

A435

B4632

COTSWOLD HILLS

Lower Slaughter

26

Bourton-on-the-Water

A424

A361

Cheltenham
16

Compton Abdale

Fosse Way

Great Rissington

Windrush

Chedworth Roman Villa

Northleach
28

A40

Burford
29

31

Yanworth

A361

TO OXFORD →

Cowley

Chedworth

Coln

B4425

Leach

A429

30

Bibury

Barnsley

B4425

Coln St. Aldwyns

Cirencester
32

For Painswick, Stroud, Owlpen, and Tetbury, see Forest of Dean map

0   6 miles

0   9 km

kaline waters in England—were the most effective cure for their "tropical ailments."

Great Regency architectural set pieces—Lansdown Crescent, Pittville Spa, and the Lower Assembly Rooms, among them—were built solely to adorn the town. The Rotunda building (1826) at the top of Montpellier Walk—now a bank—contains the spa's original "pump room," in which the mineral waters were on draft. More than 30 statues adorn the storefronts of Montpellier Walk. Wander past Imperial Square, with its ironwork balconies, past the ornate Neptune's Fountain, and along the Promenade. In spring and summer, lush flower gardens enhance the town's buildings. Parts of the town may look like something out of a Gilbert and Sullivan stage set, but Cheltenham is the site of two of England's most progressive arts festivals—the Cheltenham Festival of Literature and the town's music festival—as well as a jazz fest.

From the 1880s onward, Cheltenham was at the forefront of the Arts and Crafts movement, and the **Cheltenham Art Gallery and Museum** contains fine displays of William Morris textiles, furniture by Charles Voysey, and simple wood and metal pieces by Ernest Gimson. Decorative arts, such as Chinese ceramics, are well represented, and British artists, including Stanley Spencer and Vanessa Bell, make their mark in the art gallery. Other exhibits focus on local archaeology and history; one is devoted to Edward Wilson, who traveled with Robert Scott to the Antarctic on Scott's ill-fated 1912 expedition. ⊠ *Clarence St.* ☎ *01242/237431* ⊕ *www.cheltenhammuseum.org.uk* 🖾 *Free* ☉ *Mon.–Sat. 10–5:20, Sun. 2–4.*

The grandest of the spa buildings remaining in town, the **Pittville Pump Room** is set amid parkland, a 20-minute walk from the town center. The classic Regency structure, built in the late 1820s, now serves mainly as a concert hall but still offers its musty mineral waters to the strong of stomach. ⊠ *East Approach Dr., Pittville* ☎ *01242/523852* 🖾 *Free* ☉ *Wed.–Mon. 10–4.*

Where to Stay & Eat

★
££££–£££££
✕ **Le Champignon Sauvage.** The relatively short menu at this well-established restaurant is perfectly balanced, and the contemporary French cooking is superb. Relax in a room with warm yellow walls and modern art as you indulge in dishes such as pork fillet with black pudding and stuffed cabbage, followed by hot fig tart. You can choose among many cheeses as well. Fixed-price menus at lunch and dinner help keep the cost down. ⊠ *24 Suffolk Rd.* ☎ *01242/573449* ▤ *AE, DC, MC, V* ☉ *Closed Sun., Mon., 3 wks in June, and 10 days in Dec. and Jan.*

£££–££££
✕ **The Daffodil.** Brasserie cuisine is the focus of this former cinema that preserves the heyday of 1930s elegance. Admire the art deco trappings, sip an aperitif in the Circle Bar, and then sweep down the staircase to watch the chefs at work "on stage." Among the delightful dishes are breast of guinea fowl with mushroom risotto and hazelnut mousse with chocolate truffle. There's live jazz on Mondays, when a special jazz menu is offered. ⊠ *18–20 Suffolk Parade* ☎ *01242/700055* ▤ *AE, MC, V* ☉ *Closed Sun.*

££–£££   ✕ **Le Petit Blanc.** In the same building as Queen's Hotel, this offshoot of renowned chef Raymond Blanc's Manoir aux Quat' Saisons in Great Milton offers French provincial cooking in contemporary surroundings that harmonize well with the good-size Regency windows. The impressive menu takes in everything from herb pancakes with mushrooms, gruyère cheese, ham, and kirsch sauce to beef bourguignonne. Among the lip-smacking desserts is an exquisite vacherin: iced meringue, vanilla ice cream, and black currant sorbet. ⊠ *The Promenade* ☎ *01242/ 266800* ⊟ *AE, DC, MC, V.*

££–£££   ✕ **Montpellier Wine Bar.** An ideal place for a light snack or a fuller evening meal, this busy, informal wine bar on two stories (downstairs for nonsmokers) in Cheltenham's fashionable shopping district serves tapas, pastas, salads, and dishes such as lemon-and-honey-glazed goose breast. Get in early for fast service. ⊠ *Bayshill Lodge, Montpellier St.* ☎ *01242/527774* ⊟ *AE, MC, V.*

£–££   ✕ **Boogaloos.** Choose between the brightly colored, vibrant rooms upstairs or the sofa seating in the relaxed basement for lunches of salads, baked potatoes, or more substantial fare such as shredded lamb with Thai noodles. Leave room for the homemade cakes and puddings. ⊠ *16 Regent St.* ☎ *01242/702259* ⊟ *MC, V* ☻ *No dinner.*

£££££   🏨 **Cowley Manor.** Good-bye, floral prints: this Georgian mansion on 55 acres brings luxury country-house hotels into the 21st century by using modern fabrics and furniture but keeping the comfort level high enough to soothe a chic clientele. Witty sculptures complement lime-green sofas with purple pillows, bedrooms are brightly colored, and bathrooms are suitably trendy, with glass walls and large showers. Half the rooms are in the house; the rest fill a transformed stable. The spa, set into the ground, looks like a work of art. Cowley Manor is 5 mi south of Cheltenham. ⊠ *Cowley, GL53 9NL* ☎ *01242/870900* 🖷 *01242/870901* ⊕ *www. cowleymanor.com* 🛏 *30 rooms* ⟁ *Dining room, 2 pools (1 indoor), gym, sauna, spa, steam room* ⊟ *MC, V* ‖◯‖ *CP.*

££££–£££££   ✕🏨 **Queen's Hotel.** Overlooking Imperial Gardens from the center of the Promenade, this hotel in a classic Regency building has welcomed people to Cheltenham since 1838. Public areas and rooms leading off the stunning inner stairway are traditionally British (and rather old-fashioned) in style, and every bedroom is individually decorated. ⊠ *The Promenade, GL50 1NN* ☎ *0870/400–8107* 🖷 *01242/224145* ⊕ *www. macdonaldhotels.co.uk* 🛏 *73 rooms* ⟁ *Restaurant, in-room data ports, cable TV, bar, some pets allowed (fee); no a/c in some rooms* ⊟ *AE, DC, MC, V* ‖◯‖ *BP.*

£££   🏨 **Hotel Kandinsky.** A fashionably cool style that doesn't stint on the comfort factor makes a stay in this Georgian hotel a memorable experience at a fairly sensible price. Colorful rugs, huge potted plants, and the occasional touch of eccentricity offset the antiques in the guest rooms and clubby public rooms. A Mediterranean-style bistro and a hip basement nightclub are on the premises, and guests have access to a nearby pool and gym. ⊠ *Bayshill Rd., GL50 3AS* ☎ *01242/527788* 🖷 *01242/ 226412* ⊕ *www.aliashotels.com* 🛏 *48 rooms* ⟁ *Restaurant, in-room data ports, cable TV, in-room VCRs, bar, nightclub, meeting rooms; no a/c* ⊟ *AE, DC, MC, V.*

ff ⊞ **Abbey Hotel.** Relaxed and family-run, this hotel in a quiet terrace near the center of town offers great value. Bedrooms are simple but stylish, decorated in subtle tones, and the breakfast area overlooks the well-stocked garden. ⊠ *14–16 Bath Parade, GL53 7HN* ☎ *01242/516053* 🖷 *01242/ 513034* ⊕ *www.abbeyhotel-cheltenham.com* ⤳ *12 rooms* ♧ *Bar; no a/c* ⊟ *AE, MC, V* ⧗⧉ *BP.*

★ **ff** ⊞ **Lypiatt House.** This splendid Victorian house—only a short walk from central Cheltenham—is an excellent B&B with attentive service. The bedrooms are spacious and have chic bathrooms. The restful drawing room is done in deep pink, and the conservatory makes a good place for a drink. ⊠ *Lypiatt Rd., GL50 2QW* ☎ *01242/224994* 🖷 *01242/224996* ⊕ *www.lypiatt.co.uk* ⤳ *10 rooms* ♧ *In-room data ports, bar; no a/c* ⊟ *AE, MC, V* ⧗⧉ *BP.*

Nightlife & the Arts

The late-19th-century **Everyman Theatre** (⊠ Regent St. ☎ 01242/572573) is an intimate venue for opera, dance, concerts, and plays.

★ For information on festivals, contact the **Festival Office** (⊠ Town Hall, Imperial Sq., Cheltenham, GL50 1QA ☎ 01242/227979 ⊕ www. cheltenhamfestivals.co.uk). The town's **Festival of Literature** in October brings together world-renowned authors, actors, and critics. There's a smaller Spring Weekend literature festival in early April. Cheltenham's famous **International Festival of Music,** during the first half of July, highlights new compositions, often conducted by the composers, together with classical pieces. The **International Jazz Festival,** held over five days in April and May, presents noted musicians.

Sports

Important steeplechase races take place at **Cheltenham Racecourse** (⊠ Prestbury Park ☎ 01242/513014), north of the town center; the Gold Cup awards crown the last day of the National Hunt Festival in mid-March.

The hilltop golf course at **Cleeve Hill** (⊠ B4632 ☎ 01242/672592), 3 mi north of Cheltenham, has great views. The par-72 course is 6,448 yards. Book at least a week ahead to play on weekends.

Shopping

A stroll along Montpellier Walk and then along the flower-bedecked Promenade brings you to high-quality stores. A bubble-blowing Wishing Fish Clock, designed by Kit Williams, dominates the Regent Arcade, a modern shopping area behind the Promenade. General markets are held every Sunday at the racecourse and every Thursday morning off Lower High Street, and an indoor antiques market is open Monday–Saturday at 54 Suffolk Road.

Cavendish House (⊠ 32–48 The Promenade ☎ 01242/521300) is a high-quality department store with designer fashions. **Early Bird** (⊠ 5 Suffolk Rd. ☎ 01242/233507) displays antiques, faux antiques, and enticing bric-a-brac. **Laura Ashley** (⊠ 92 The Promenade ☎ 01242/236948) sells products in its distinctive, Arts-and-Crafts-influenced style, including clothes, handbags, and gift items. **Martin** (⊠ 19 The Promenade ☎ 01242/ 522821) carries a good stock of modern jewelry.

Winchcombe

⑰ *7 mi northeast of Cheltenham.*

The sleepy, unspoiled village of Winchcombe, once the capital of the Anglo-Saxon kingdom of Mercia, has some attractive half-timber and stone houses, as well as a clutch of appealing old inns serving food. Almost 40 outlandish gargoyles adorn the mid-15th-century Perpendicular-style **St. Peter's Church,** a typical Cotswold wool church.

A bracing 2-mi walk south of Winchcombe on the Cotswold Way leads to the hilltop site of **Belas Knap,** a neolithic long barrow, or submerged ★ burial chamber, above **Humblebee Wood.** There's not much to see of the site itself, but you hike next to and through one of the most enchanting natural domains in England, with views stretching over to Sudeley Castle. If you have a car, take the scenic Humblebee Wood road down to the villages of Sevenhampton and Brockhampton.

A mile outside Winchcombe, at Greet, you can board a steam-hauled ☾ train of the **Gloucestershire and Warwickshire Railway,** which chugs its way along a 13-mi stretch at the foot of the Cotswolds between Toddington Station and Cheltenham Racecourse. ☎ *01242/621405* ⊕ *www.gwsr. plc.uk* ☒ *£9 round-trip* ☉ *Mid-Mar.–Dec., weekends 10:30–5; daily during school holidays and some of Dec.*

Where to Stay & Eat

££–£££ ✕▥ **Wesley House.** Beams and stone walls distinguish this 15th-century half-timber building, a restaurant with a few bedrooms. The red-carpeted dining room makes a fine backdrop for superior Mediterranean-style food; fixed-price menus include nettle and pea soup, breast of Delande duck with cherry and kirsch sauce, and chocolate blinis with brown-bread ice cream. Upstairs, the smallish rooms have twisted beams and sloping ceilings. You may smoke only in the bar. ⊠ *High St., GL54 5LJ* ☎ *01242/602366* ▤ *01242/609046* ⊕ *www.wesleyhouse.co.uk* ⇗ *5 rooms* ⚬ *Restaurant, in-room VCRs, bar; no a/c* ▤ *AE, MC, V* ⊚ *BP.*

Sudeley Castle

★ **⑱** *1 mi southeast of Winchcombe, 9 mi northeast of Cheltenham.*

One of the grand showpieces of the Cotswolds, Sudeley Castle was the home and burial place of Catherine Parr (1512–48), Henry VIII's sixth and last wife, who outlived him by one year. Here Catherine undertook, in her later years, the education of the ill-fated Lady Jane Grey and the future queen, Princess Elizabeth—Sudeley, for good reason, has been called a woman's castle. The term "castle," however, is misleading, for it looks more like a Tudor-era palace, with a peaceful air that belies its turbulent history. During the 17th century, Charles I took refuge here, causing Oliver Cromwell's army to besiege the castle, leaving it in ruins until the Dent-Brocklehurst family stepped in with a 19th-century renovation. Inside are Tudor and Civil War artifacts, as well as paintings by Van Dyck, Rubens, Turner, and Reynolds. The romantic grounds include the Queen's Garden, with its spectacular roses; a Tudor knot garden; and settings for outdoor Shakespeare performances, concerts, and other events in summer. Accommodations in 14 cottages on the grounds are booked by the week in summer, but these are available for two-night stays (or longer) in winter. ⊠ *Off B4632, Winchcombe* ☎ *01242/ 604357* ⊕ *www.sudeleycastle.co.uk* ☞ *£6.85, gardens and exhibitions only £5.50* ⊗ *Castle Apr.–late Oct., daily 11–5; gardens, grounds, plant center, and shop early Mar.–late Oct., daily 10:30–5:30.*

Stanway House

★ ⓳ *5 mi northeast of Sudeley Castle, 11 mi northeast of Cheltenham.*

This perfect Cotswold manor of glowing limestone in the small village of Stanway dates from the Jacobean era. Its triple-gabled gatehouse is a Cotswold landmark, and towering windows dominate the house's Great Hall. Divided by mullions and transoms into 60 panes, these windows are "so mellowed by time"—to quote Lady Cynthia Asquith (a former chatelaine)—"that whenever the sun shines through their amber and green glass, the effect is of a vast honeycomb." They illuminate a 22-foot-long shuffleboard table from 1620 and an 18th-century bouncing exercise machine. The other well-worn rooms are adorned with family portraits, tattered tapestries, vintage armchairs, and, at times, Lord Neidpath himself, the current owner. On the grounds is a cricket pavilion built by J. M. Barrie, author of *Peter Pan*, who leased the house. To get to Stanway, take B4632 north of Winchcombe, turning right at B4077. ⊠ *Stanway* ☎ *01386/584469* ☞ *£4* ⊗ *July and Aug., Tues. and Thurs. 2–5; other times by appointment only for groups of at least 20.*

Snowshill Manor

★ ♺ ⓴ *4 mi northeast of Sudeley Castle, 3 mi south of Broadway, 13 mi northeast of Cheltenham.*

Snowshill is one of the most unspoiled of all Cotswold villages. Snuggled beneath Oat Hill, with little room for expansion, the hamlet is centered around an old burial ground, the 19th-century St. Barnabas Church, and Snowshill Manor, a splendid 17th-century house that brims with the collections of Charles Paget Wade, gathered between 1919 and 1956. Over the door of the house is Wade's family motto, *Nequid pereat* ("Let nothing perish"). The rooms are bursting with Tibetan scrolls, spinners' tools, ship models, Persian lamps, and bric-a-brac. The Green Room displays 26 suits of Japanese samurai armor. Children love the place. Outside, an imaginative terraced garden provides an exquisite frame for the house. Note that the house is closed for renovations, such as the addition of a lighting system more in keeping with Wade's original wishes (he favored candlelight), until around Easter 2005. ⊠ *Off A44 Snowshill* ☎ *01386/852410, call to confirm opening* ⊕ *www. nationaltrust.org.uk* ☞ *£6.60, garden only £3.90* ⊗ *Mid-Mar.–Oct., Wed.–Sun. 11–5:30.*

Broadway

㉑ *3 mi north of Snowshill Manor, 17 mi northeast of Cheltenham.*

The Cotswold town to end all Cotswold towns, Broadway has become a favorite of day-trippers. William Morris first discovered the delights of this village, and J. M. Barrie, Vaughan Williams, and Edward Elgar soon followed. Today some people avoid Broadway in summer, when it's clogged with cars and buses. Named for its handsome, wide main street, the village includes the renowned Lygon Arms and numerous antiques shops, tea parlors, and boutiques. Step off onto Broadway's back roads and alleys and you can discover any number of honey-color houses and colorful gardens.

Among the attractions of **Broadway Tower Country Park,** on the outskirts of town, is its tower, an 18th-century "folly" built by the sixth earl of Coventry and later used by William Morris as a retreat. Exhibits describe the tower's intriguing past, and the view from the top takes in more than 13 counties. Peaceful countryside surrounds you on the nature trails and picnic grounds. ⊠ *Off A44* ☎ *01386/852390* 🎫 *Park free, tower £3.50* ⊙ *Tower Apr.–Oct., daily 10:30–5; Nov.–Mar., weekends 11–4:30.*

☽ If you're a nostalgia buff or love cuddly toys, you may find **Broadway Dolls and Bears** irresistible. Gathered together are "every bear that ever there was," animated snow, circus, and fairground scenes, and dolls and toys. Check out the shop and hospital. ⊠ *76 High St.* ☎ *01386/858323* 🎫 *£2.50* ⊙ *Feb.–May, Tues.–Sun. 1–4; June–Dec., Tues.–Sun. 10–5.*

Where to Stay & Eat

★ **£££££** ✕🏨 **Buckland Manor.** As an alternative to the razzmatazz of Broadway, you can splurge at this exceptional hotel 2 mi away in the idyllic hamlet of Buckland. The land was valued at £9 in the 11th-century Domesday Book, and the sprawling stone building dates back to Jacobean times. Public areas and guest rooms are plushly comfortable, with old pictures, fine rugs, and antiques everywhere. The gardens are well groomed and tranquil. In the baronial and expensive restaurant (jacket and tie required), you choose from a menu of contemporary fare from local sources. ⊠ *Off B4632, Buckland, WR12 7LY* ☎ *01386/852626* 🖷 *01386/ 853557* ⊕ *www.bucklandmanor.com* 🛏 *13 rooms* ♿ *Restaurant, cable TV, tennis court, putting green, pool, croquet, bar; no a/c, no kids under 12* 🖃 *AE, DC, MC, V* ¶◯¶ *BP.*

★ ✕🏨 **Dormy House Hotel.** Guest rooms in this converted 17th-century farm-
££££–£££££ house overlook the Vale of Evesham from high on the Cotswolds ridge, one of the region's most celebrated vistas. Luxury rules at this establishment, where you can relax by a fireplace or in one of the bars. Traditional pieces and a mixture of brass and carved bedsteads furnish the beamed bedrooms. Noted in the region, the restaurant has a superlative wine list and specializes in contemporary fare such as lemon sole with salmon and chive mousse. A more economical eating option is the beamed Barn Owl bar. The hotel is 2 mi north of Broadway. ⊠ *Willersey Hill, WR12 7LF* ☎ *01386/852711* 🖷 *01386/858636* ⊕ *www. dormyhouse.co.uk* 🛏 *48 rooms* ♿ *Restaurant, café, putting green,*

gym, sauna, steam room, croquet, 3 bars, meeting rooms, some pets allowed (fee); no a/c ⊟ *AE, DC, MC, V* ◉ *BP.*

££££–£££££ ✕▣ **Lygon Arms.** Here is modern luxury in perfect symbiosis with old-fashioned charm. In business since 1532, the inn has a multigabled facade and mullioned windows dating to 1620. Inside, look for antiques-bedecked parlors, fireplaces, 18th-century paneling, and rooms that once sheltered Charles I and Oliver Cromwell. Behind the house are more modern (and less expensive) bedrooms and 3 acres of formal gardens. One restaurant, the Great Hall, complete with a minstrel's gallery, focuses on creative adaptations of traditional dishes; it's under the direction of noted chef Martin Blunos. ⊠ *High St., WR12 7DU* ☎ *01386/852255* 🖷 *01386/858611* ⊕ *www.thelygonarms.co.uk* ⇔ *69 rooms* ⚡ *2 restaurants, in-room data ports, cable TV, in-room VCRs, tennis court, indoor pool, sauna, spa, steam room, croquet, bar, business services, meeting rooms, helipad, some pets allowed (fee); no a/c in some rooms* ⊟ *AE, DC, MC, V* ◉ *BP.*

££££ ▣ **Mill Hay House.** If the rose garden, trout-filled pond, and pet sheep at this 18th-century Queen Anne house aren't appealing enough, then the stone-flagged floors, leather sofas, and grandfather clocks should satisfy. There are only three beautiful, pastel bedrooms at this B&B, so booking ahead is essential. It's a mile from Broadway on the Snowshill road. ⊠ *Snowshill Rd., WR12 7JS* ☎ *01386/852498* 🖷 *01386/858038* ⊕ *www.broadway-cotswolds.co.uk* ⇔ *2 rooms, 1 suite* ⚡ *In-room safes, kitchenettes, no-smoking rooms; no a/c, no kids under 12* ⊟ *MC, V* ◉ *BP.*

Chipping Campden

㉒ *4 mi east of Broadway, 18 mi northeast of Cheltenham.*

Undoubtedly one of the most beautiful towns in the area, Chipping Campden is the Cotswolds in a microcosm—it has St. James, the region's most impressive church; frozen-in-time streets; a silk mill that was once the center of the Guild of Handicrafts; and pleasant (and not touristy) shops. One of the area's most seductive settings unfolds before you as you travel on B4081 through sublime English countryside and happen upon the town, tucked in a slight valley.

The soaring pinnacled tower of **St. James,** a prime example of a Cotswold wool church (rebuilt in the 15th century), announces the town from a distance; it's worth stepping inside to see the lofty nave. It recalls the old saying, which became popular because of the vast numbers of houses of worship in the Cotswolds, "As sure as God's in Gloucestershire." Nearby, on Church Street, is an important row of almshouses dating from King James I's reign. ⊠ *Church St.* ☎ *01386/841366* ⊕ *www.stjameschurchcampden.co.uk* 🖃 *£1 donation suggested* ◷ *Mar.–Oct., Mon.–Sat. 10–5, Sun. 2–6; Feb. and Nov., Mon.–Sat. 11–4, Sun. 2–4; Dec. and Jan., Mon.–Sat. 11–3, Sun. 2–4.*

The broad High Street, lined with stone houses and shops, follows a picturesque curve; in the center, on Market Street, is the **Market Hall,** a gabled Jacobean structure built by Sir Baptiste Hycks in 1627 "for the sale of local produce."

CloseUp
ARTS AND CRAFTS IN THE COTSWOLDS

HE ARTS AND CRAFTS MOVEMENT flourished throughout Britain in the late 19th and early 20th centuries, but the Cotswolds are most closely associated with it. The godfather of the movement was designer William Morris (1834–96), whose home for the last 25 years of his life, Kelmscott Manor in Gloucestershire, became the headquarters of the school. A lecture by Morris, "The Beauty of Life," delivered in Birmingham in 1880, included the injunction that became the guiding principle of the movement: "Have nothing in your houses which you do not know to be useful or believe to be beautiful."

Driven by the belief that the spirit of medieval arts and crafts was being degraded and destroyed by the mass production and aggressive capitalism of the Victorian era, and aided by a dedicated core of artisans, Morris revolutionized the art of house design and decoration. His work with textiles was particularly influential.

Many of Morris's followers were influenced by the Cotswold countryside, such as the designer and architect Charles Robert Ashbee, who transferred his Guild of Handicrafts from London to Chipping Campden in 1902. The village holds a permanent exhibition of pieces by the original group and those who followed in their wake. Their work can also be seen at Cheltenham's Art Gallery and Museum, and, in its original context, at Rodmarton Manor outside Tetbury (which Ashbee declared the finest application of the movement's ideals), and at Owlpen Manor. (Farther afield, Standen, near East Grinstead, and Blackwell, in the Lake District, are notable Arts and Crafts houses.) To see the Arts and Crafts ethic applied to horticulture, visit Hidcote Manor Garden, near Chipping Campden.

In 1902 the Guild of Handicrafts took over the **Silk Mill,** and Arts and Crafts evangelist Charles Robert Ashbee (1863–1942) brought 150 acolytes here from London, including 50 guildsmen, to revive and practice such skills as cabinetmaking and bookbinding. The operation folded in 1920, but the refurbished building houses an exhibition and workshops, including those of a silversmith, sculptor, and printmaker. ⊠ *Sheep St.* ⊠ *Free* ☉ *Weekdays 9–5, Sat. 9–1.*

Where to Stay & Eat

£££££ ✕⊡ **Charingworth Manor.** Views of the Cotswold countryside are limitless from this 14th-century manor-house hotel a short distance outside town. Mullioned windows and oak beams enhance the sofa-filled sitting room, and bedrooms are decorated with English floral fabrics and antique and period furniture. T. S. Eliot, a frequent guest in the 1930s, used to enjoy walking the 50 acres of grounds. The restaurant (fixed-price menu), with its low-beamed ceilings, is attractive but somewhat expensive, and serves traditional fare such as roast beef and Yorkshire pudding. The hotel is 3 mi east of Chipping Campden. ⊠ *Charingworth, GL55 6NS* ☏ *01386/593555* 🖶 *01386/593353* ⊕ *www.englishrosehotels.com* ⇴ *23 rooms, 3 suites* ⚭ *Restaurant, in-room safes,* *cable TV, tennis court, indoor pool, sauna, steam room, billiards, cro-quet, meeting rooms; no a/c* ⊟ *AE, DC, MC, V* ¶◎¶ *BP.*

££ ✕▦ **Churchill Arms.** This small country pub, a mile southeast of Chipping Campden, makes for an intimate stay. Plain wooden tables and benches, sepia prints, a flagstone floor, and a roaring fire provide the backdrop for excellent food. Daily specials—steamed lemon sole filled with salmon and chive mousse, and pot-roasted partridge with parsnips and red wine, for example—appear on the blackboard. Upstairs bedrooms aren't large but are nicely furnished with antiques; two are in a new wing. ✉ *Off B4035, Paxford, GL55 6XH* ☎ *01386/594000* 🖷 *01386/594005* ⊕ *www.thechurchillarms.com* ⤳ *4 rooms* △ *Restaurant, in-room data ports, in-room VCRs, no-smoking rooms; no a/c* ⊟ *MC, V* ¶◎¶ *BP.*

££££ ▦ **Noel Arms Hotel.** Dating to the 14th century, the town's oldest inn was built in the heart of town to accommodate foreign wool traders. The building retains its exposed beams and stonework, even though it has been enlarged. The bedrooms—some in the 14th-century portion—are full of reds and golds and dark oak furniture. ✉ *High St., GL55 6AT* ☎ *01386/840317* 🖷 *01386/841136* ⊕ *www.cotswold-inns-hotels.co.uk* ⤳ *26 rooms* △ *Restaurant, bar, meeting rooms, some pets allowed; no a/c* ⊟ *AE, DC, MC, V* ¶◎¶ *BP.*

Shopping

For all embroidery needs, head for the **Campden Needlecraft Centre** (✉ High St. ☎ 01386/840583), one of the leading specialty needlecraft shops in the country. At **D. T. Hart** (✉ The Silk Mill, Sheep St. ☎ 01386/841100), descendants of an original member of the Guild of Handicrafts specialize in making silver items. **Martin Gotrel** (✉ Camperdene House, High St. ☎ 01386/841360) crafts fine traditional and contemporary jewelry.

Hidcote Manor Garden

㉓
Fodor'sChoice
★

4 mi northeast of Chipping Campden, 9 mi south of Stratford-upon-Avon.

Laid out around a Cotswold manor house, Hidcote Manor Garden is arguably the most interesting and attractive large garden in Britain, with correspondingly large crowds at the height of the season. A horticulturist from the United States, Major Lawrence Johnstone, created the garden in 1907 in the Arts and Crafts style. Johnstone was an imaginative gardener and widely traveled plantsman who brought back specimens from all over the world. The formal part of the garden is arranged in "rooms" without roofs, separated by hedges, often with fine topiary work and walls. The White Garden was probably the forerunner of the popular white gardens at Sissinghurst and Glyndebourne. ✉ *Hidcote Bartrim* ☎ *01386/438333* ⊕ *www.nationaltrust.org.uk* 🎫 *£5.90* ☉ *Apr.–Sept., Mon.–Wed. and weekends 10:30–6; Oct., Mon.–Wed. and weekends 10:30–5; last admission 1 hr before closing.*

Hidcote Manor Garden borders the hamlet of **Hidcote Bartrim**, which fills another storybook Cotswold dell. A handful of thatched stone houses, a duck pond, and a well make up the center of this cul-de-sac; less than a mile away are the equally idyllic hamlet of Hidcote Boyce and a 17th-century manor, Hidcote House.

Moreton-in-Marsh

㉔ *13 mi south of Hidcote Manor Garden, 18 mi northeast of Cheltenham, 5 mi north of Stow-on-the-Wold.*

In Moreton-in-Marsh, the houses have been built not around a central square but along a street wide enough to accommodate a market (held every Tuesday). The village has fine views across the hills. One local landmark is St. David's Church, which has a tower of honey-gold ashlar. The town also possesses one of the last remaining curfew towers, dated 1633; curfew dates to the time of the Norman Conquest, when a bell was rung to "cover-fire" for the night against any invaders. From Chipping Campden, take B4081 south, then A44 south and east to reach Moreton-in-Marsh.

It comes as somewhat of an architectural surprise to see the blue onion domes and miniature minarets of **Sezincote,** a mellow stone house tucked into a valley near Moreton-in-Marsh. Created in the early 19th century, the house and estate were the vision of Sir Charles Cockerell, who made a fortune in the East India Company. He employed his architect brother, Samuel Pepys Cockerell, to "Indianize" the residence, which Samuel did with a mixture of Hindu and Muslim motifs. Note the peacock-tail arches surrounding the windows of the first floor. The exotic garden, Hindu temple folly, and Indian-style bridge have appealed to visitors ever since the future George IV came to the estate in 1807 (and was inspired to create that Xanadu of Brighton, the Royal Pavilion). If you come in spring, a glorious display of aconites and snowdrops greets you. Note that children are allowed indoors only at the owners' discretion. ⊠ *Off A44* ☎ *01386/700444* 🖃 *House and grounds £5, grounds £3.50* ⊘ *House May–July and Sept., Thurs. and Fri. 2:30–6; grounds Jan.–Nov., Thurs. and Fri. and national holidays 2–6 or dusk.*

---

off the beaten path

ROLLRIGHT STONES – A reminder of the ancient civilizations of Britain can be seen about 8 mi east of Moreton, where three stone groups occupy a high position on the Wolds. The site has none of the grandeur of Stonehenge and Avebury but is almost as important. Legend gives the stones, dating from before 1500 BC, the names of the King's Men, the King Stone, and the Whispering Knights. ⊠ *Minor road off A3400* ⊕ *www.english-heritage.org.uk* 🖃 *Free; property owner may charge small fee to see King's Men* ⊘ *Daily sunrise–sunset.*

Where to Stay & Eat

★ **££–£££**   ✕🏠 **Falkland Arms.** It's worth detouring a bit for this supremely appealing pub on the village green at Great Tew (12 mi east of Moreton), where you can still buy snuff and smoke a clay pipe. The bar has impressive malt whiskies, and mugs and jugs hangs from the beams. The small restaurant (no dinner Sunday) chalks up a traditional but creative menu. A spiral stone staircase leads to the bedrooms, which have brass bedsteads or four-posters, and snowy white bedcovers. Reservations are essential for both staying and eating here. From Moreton, take A44 to Chipping Norton, then A361 to B4022. ⊠ *Great Tew, OX7 4DB* ☎ *01608/683653* ⊕ *www.falklandarms.org.uk* ⤳ *6 rooms* ⚙ *Restaurant, bar, no-smoking rooms; no a/c, no room phones, no kids under 14* ▤ *AE, MC, V* ⦿| *BP.*

££ ✕⊡ **Bell Inn.** The coach house of this 18th-century hostelry holds spacious guest rooms, still with the original beams, and furnished with period pieces, deep carpets, and comfy sofas. The pub has a flower-filled courtyard and garden and prepares such dishes as grilled trout and venison sausages. In summer you can join in the obscure Cotswold game of Aunt Sally, which involves hitting a moving target with something akin to a rolling pin. ⊠ *High St., GL56 0AE* ☎ *01608/651688* ☎ *01608/652195* ⊕ *www.bellinncotswold.com* ⤳ *5 rooms* ⚙ *Restaurant, bar, some pets allowed; no a/c, no room phones* ▤ *MC, V* ⦿| *BP.*

££££–£££££ ⊡ **Manor House Hotel.** Secret passages and a priest's hole testify to the age of this 16th-century building, set back from the main thoroughfare. Wing chairs and chintz-covered sofas and drapes adorn the public rooms. Bedrooms, revealing original stonework, mix stylish modern furnishings and fabrics with antiques. The restaurant serves traditional English dishes. ⊠ *High St., GL56 0LJ* ☎ *01608/650501* ☎ *01608/651481* ⊕ *www.cotswold-inns-hotels.co.uk* ⤳ *38 rooms* ⚙ *Restaurant, indoor pool; no a/c* ▤ *AE, DC, MC, V* ⦿| *BP.*

Stow-on-the-Wold

㉕ *5 mi south of Moreton-in-Marsh, 15 mi east of Cheltenham.*

At an elevation of 800 feet, Stow is the highest town in the Cotswolds—"Stow-on-the-Wold, where the wind blows cold" is the age-old saying. Built around a wide square, Stow's imposing golden stone houses have been discreetly converted into a good number of high-quality antiques stores. The Square, as it is known, has a fascinating history. In the 18th century, Daniel Defoe wrote that more than 20,000 sheep could be sold here on a busy day; such was the press of livestock that sheep runs, known as "tures," were used to control the sheep, and these narrow streets still run off the main square. Also look for St. Edward's Church and the Kings Arms Old Posting House, its wide entrance still seeming to wait for the stagecoaches that used to stop here on their way to Cheltenham. As well as being a lure for the antiques hunter, Stow is a convenient base: eight main Cotswolds roads intersect here, but all—happily—bypass the town center.

★ **Chastleton House,** one of the most complete Jacobean properties in Britain, opts for a beguilingly lived-in appearance, taking advantage of almost 400 years' worth of furniture and trappings accumulated by many generations of the single family that owned it until 1991. The house was built between 1605 and 1612 for William Jones, a wealthy wool merchant, and has an appealing authenticity: cobwebs and bric-a-brac are strewn around, wood and pewter are unpolished, upholstery uncleaned. The top floor is a glorious, barrel-vaulted long gallery, and throughout the house you can see exquisite plasterwork, paneling, and tapestries. The ornamental gardens include England's first croquet lawn (the rules of croquet were codified here in 1865) and rotund topiaries. Chastleton is 6 mi northeast of Stow, signposted off A436 between Stow and A44. ✉ *Off A436, Moreton-in-Marsh* ☎ *01494/755585 booking line Tues.–Fri. 10–4, 01494/755560 for recorded information* ⊕ *www. nationaltrust.org.uk* ✍ *£5.80* ◷ *Apr.–Sept., Wed.–Sat. 1–4; Oct., Wed.–Sat. 1–3; admission is by timed ticket, for which prebooking is advised.*

Where to Stay & Eat

£ ✕ **Queen's Head.** An excellent stopping-off spot for lunch, this pub has a courtyard out back that's perfect for a summer afternoon. The bench in front, under a climbing rose, makes a relaxing spot for imbibing outdoor refreshment. Expect fairly standard pub grub, including ploughman's lunches, sandwiches, sausage and mash, steak pies, and vegetarian options such as spinach lasagna.Even if food isn't being served, you can get a drink. ✉ *The Square* ☎ *01451/830563* ▱ *AE, MC, V* ◷ *No dinner Sun. and Mon. Nov.–Feb.*

£££–££££ ✕▥ **Royalist Hotel.** Certified as the oldest inn in the country (AD 947), this hostelry is jammed with interesting features—witches' marks on the beams, a tunnel to the church across the road—and the owners have stylishly integrated designer bedrooms and a restaurant (closed Sunday and Monday). If the fixed-price, brasserie-style menu doesn't appeal, opt for pub grub in the adjacent Eagle and Child. ✉ *Digbeth St., GL54 1BN* ☎ *01451/830670* ⊠ *01451/870048* ⊕ *www.theroyalisthotel.co. uk* ⇨ *12 rooms, 1 suite* ⚘ *Restaurant, in-room data ports, 2 bars, pub, meeting rooms, no-smoking rooms; no a/c* ▱ *AE, MC, V* ⎅⎅ *CP.*

Shopping

Stow-on-the-Wold is the leading center for antiques stores in the Cotswolds, with more than 30 dealers centered around The Square, Sheep Street, and Church Street. **Duncan Baggott Antiques** (✉ Woolcomber House, Sheep St. ☎ 01451/830662) displays fine old English furniture, portraits and landscape paintings, and garden statuary and ornaments. A visit to **Huntington Antiques** (✉ Church St. ☎ 01451/830842) is like a step back into the 16th and 17th centuries; the store is replete with refectory tables, carved wooden reliefs, and Renaissance furniture. **Roger Lamb Antiques** (✉ The Square ☎ 01451/831371) specializes in objets d'art and small pieces of furniture from the Georgian and Regency periods, with Regency "faux bamboo," tea caddies, and antique needlework the particular fortes.

Bourton-on-the-Water

㉖ *4 mi southwest of Stow-on-the-Wold, 12 mi northeast of Cheltenham.*

Bourton-on-the-Water, off A429 on the eastern edge of the Cotswold Hills, is deservedly famous as a classic Cotswold village. The little River Windrush runs through Bourton, crossed by low stone bridges. This village makes a good touring base, but in summer it can be overcrowded. A stroll through Bourton takes you past stone cottages, many converted to small stores and coffee shops.

ⓒ An old mill, now the **Cotswold Motor Museum and Toy Collection,** contains more than 30 vintage motor vehicles and a collection of old advertising signs (supposedly the largest in Europe), as well as two caravans (trailers) from the 1920s, ancient bicycles, and children's toys. ⊠ *Sherborne St.* ☎ *01451/821255* ⊠ *£2.95* ⊘ *Mid-Feb.–Oct., daily 10–6.*

ⓒ The **Model Railway Exhibition** displays more than 40 British and Continental trains running on 500 square feet of scenic layout. There are plenty of trains, models, and toys to buy in the shop. ⊠ *Box Bush, High St.* ☎ *01451/820686* ⊕ *www.bourtonmodelrailway.co.uk* ⊠ *£1.90* ⊘ *Apr.–Sept., daily 11–5; Oct.–Mar., weekends 11–5 (limited opening in Jan.; call ahead).*

An outdoor reproduction of Bourton, the **Model Village** was built in 1937 to a scale of one-ninth. ⊠ *Old New Inn,* ☎ *01451/820467* ⊠ *£2.75* ⊘ *Apr.–Oct., daily 9–5:45; Nov.–Mar., daily 10–3:45.*

Where to Stay

£££ 🏨 **The Old Manse.** Built in 1748 for the local Baptist pastor, this stone hotel is only steps away from the River Windrush. The smallish bedrooms are decorated in creams and browns; one has a four-poster and a whirlpool bath, another a French sleigh bed. Traditional English fare with a contemporary touch is served in the restaurant. There's a garden at the rear and a riverside patio. ⊠ *Victoria St., GL54 2BX* ☎ *01451/ 820082* 🖷 *01451/810381* ⊕ *www.oldmansehotel.com* ⬳ *15 rooms* ⌂ *Restaurant, bar, meeting rooms; no a/c* ⊟ *AE, MC, V* |⊙| *BP.*

£ 🏨 **Rooftrees.** If you go in for frills, flounces, and leprechauns, then this old Cotswold stone house, a 10-minute walk from the center of the village, is the place for you. Ornaments abound within, and hanging baskets and garden gnomes decorate the outside. The amiable Irish hosts dish up substantial breakfasts. ⊠ *Rissington Rd., GL54 2DX* ☎ *01451/ 821943* 🖷 *01451/810614* ⬳ *3 rooms* ⌂ *No a/c, no room phones, no smoking* ⊟ *MC, V* |⊙| *BP.*

Shopping

The **Cotswold Perfumery** carries many perfumes that are manufactured here. While deciding what to buy, visit the Exhibition of Perfumery and the Perfumed Garden. Perfume bottles and jewelry are also on sale. ⊠ *Victoria St.* ☎ *01451/820698* ⊠ *Exhibition £2* ⊘ *Mon.–Sat. 9:30–5, Sun. 10:30–5.*

Lower & Upper Slaughter

㉗ *2 mi north of Bourton-on-the-Water, 15 mi east of Cheltenham.*

Fodor's Choice
★

To see the quieter, more typical Cotswold villages, seek out the evocatively named Lower Slaughter and Upper Slaughter (the names have nothing to do with mass murder, but come from the Saxon word *sloh,* which means "a marshy place"). Lower Slaughter is one of the "water villages," with Slaughter Brook running down the center road of the town. Little stone footbridges cross the brook, and the town's resident gaggle of geese can often be seen paddling through the sparkling water. Connecting the two Slaughters is Warden's Way, a mile-long pathway that begins in Upper Slaughter at the town-center parking lot and passes stone houses, green meadows, ancient trees, and a 19th-century corn mill with a waterwheel and brick chimney. Warden's Way continues south to Bourton-on-the-Water. Lower and Upper Swell are two other quiet towns to explore in the area.

Where to Stay & Eat

£££££ ✕⌨ **Lords of the Manor Hotel.** A fishing stream threads the rolling fields that surround this rambling 17th-century manor house with Victorian additions. It offers comfort and a warm welcome in a quintessential Cotswold village, with a choice of bedrooms in the main house or more modern ones in the converted granary and barn. Country-house chintzes and antiques set the style throughout, including in the acclaimed restaurant, which has a creative British-French menu that might list tartlet of quail and wild mushrooms or a slow-roasted fillet of Charolais beef with horseradish mashed potatoes. ⊠ *Upper Slaughter, GL54 2JD* ☎ *01451/ 820243, 800/872–4564 in U.S.* 🖷 *01451/820696* ⊕ *www. lordsofthemanor.com* ⇄ *27 rooms* ⚴ *Restaurant, fishing, croquet, bar, business services, meeting rooms; no a/c* ▤ *AE, DC, MC, V* ⍟ *BP.*

££££ ✕⌨ **Washbourne Court.** This fine 17th-century stone building, amid 4 acres of verdant grounds beside the River Wye, has flagstone floors, beams, and open fires. The bedrooms in the main building are done in a weathered country style, whereas rooms in the converted barn and cottages are more modern. Choices in the restaurant might include Cotswold lamb with rosemary purée or peppered cutlet of venison with braised red cabbage. ⊠ *Lower Slaughter, GL54 2HS* ☎ *01451/822143* 🖷 *01451/ 821045* ⊕ *www.washbournecourt.co.uk* ⇄ *24 rooms, 4 suites* ⚴ *Restaurant, tennis court; no a/c* ▤ *AE, DC, MC, V* ⍟ *BP.*

Northleach

28 *7 mi southwest of Lower and Upper Slaughter, 14 mi southeast of Cheltenham.*

Just off the Fosse Way (and bypassed by the busy A40), Northleach has remained one of the least spoiled of Cotswold towns. Trim cottages, many with traditional stone-tile roofs, line the streets that converge on the spacious central square. By the 13th century, Northleach had acquired substantial wealth thanks to the wool trade. The wool of the local Cotswold Lion sheep (so-called because of their thick, manelike fleeces) was praised above all other by weavers in Flanders, to whom it was exported. The 15th-century church of **St. Peter and St. Paul,** with its soaring, slender pillars and clerestory windows, contains notable memorial brasses, monuments to the merchants who endowed the church; each merchant has a wool sack and sheep at his feet. ⊠ *Mill End* ☎ *01451/ 860314* ✉ *Free, donations accepted* ☉ *Apr.–Oct., daily 8–6; Nov.–Mar., daily 8–dusk.*

At **Keith Harding's World of Mechanical Music,** the diverting tour explores pianolas, music boxes, and other mechanical instruments from times past, which you can hear played. You can even listen to the maestros Grieg, Paderewski, Rachmaninoff, and Gershwin on piano rolls. The shop stocks antique and modern music boxes and more. ⊠ *The Oak House,*

High St. ☎ *01451/860181* ⊕ *www.mechanicalmusic.co.uk* 🎫 *£5* ⊙ *Daily 10–6; last tour at 5.*

Where to Stay & Eat

££ ✕🏠 **Wheatsheaf Inn.** This elegantly remodeled traditional pub has stylish, uncluttered bedrooms in mainly neutral tones, as well as a highly regarded restaurant specializing in modern British fare. On the dinner menu you might find mussels in creamy garlic sauce or duck breast with braised red cabbage; breakfast includes fresh fruit salad and yogurt. The staff is youthful and friendly. ⊠ *West End, GL54 3EZ* ☎ *01451/ 860244* 🖨 *01451/861037* ⊕ *www.wheatsheafatnorthleach.com* 📞 *8 rooms* ⚹ *Restaurant, bar, some pets allowed; no a/c* 🖃 *MC, V* ⊺⊙⊺ *BP.*

Burford

29 *9 mi east of Northleach, 18 mi north of Swindon, 18 mi west of Oxford.*

Burford's broad main street leads steeply down to a narrow bridge across the River Windrush. The village served as a stagecoach stop for centuries and has many historic inns; it is now a popular stop for tour buses and seekers of antiques. Hidden away at the end of a lane at the bottom of High Street is the splendid parish church of **St. John,** its interior a warren of arches, chapels, and shrines. The church was remodeled in the 15th century from Norman beginnings. Among the many monuments is one dedicated to Henry VIII's barber, Edmund Harman, that shows four Amazonian Indians; it's said to be the first depiction of native people from the Americas in Britain. Look also for the elaborate Tanfield monument and its poignant widow's epitaph. ⊠ *Church Green* ☎ *01993/822275* 🎫 *Free, donations accepted* ⊙ *Apr.–Oct., daily 9–5; Nov.–Mar., daily 9–4.*

Where to Stay & Eat

£££££ ✕🏠 **Bay Tree.** This atmospheric inn, set away from Burford's bustle, occupies a 16th-century stone house visited in its prime by both Elizabeth I and James I. Flagstones, beams, and antiques enhance the public areas, and cheerful print and floral fabrics decorate the bedrooms; try for a room in the main house. A confirmed reservation requires a nonrefundable deposit. The restaurant overlooks the garden and has a fixed-price menu that might include such dishes as peppered ribeye steak and panfried sea bass. ⊠ *Sheep St., OX18 4LW* ☎ *01993/822791* 🖨 *01993/ 823008* ⊕ *www.cotswold-inns-hotels.co.uk* 📞 *21 rooms* ⚹ *Restaurant, bar, meeting rooms; no a/c* 🖃 *AE, DC, MC, V* ⊺⊙⊺ *BP.*

££–£££ ✕🏠 **The Angel.** Contemporary dishes you might see at the farmhouse-style tables of this informal brasserie (closed Sunday evening and Monday) in a 16th-century former coaching inn include bream with warm potato salad and saffron sauce, and venison with caramel peaches. Upstairs, the delightful guest rooms are furnished in different styles: Indian in deep reds and oranges, French with wooden sleigh bed, or cool-blue contemporary Italian. ⊠ *14 Witney St., OX18 4SN* ☎ *01993/822714* 🖨 *01993/822069* ⊕ *www.theangel-uk.com* 📞 *3 rooms* ⚹ *Restaurant; no a/c, no kids under 9* 🖃 *MC, V* ⊙ *Closed last 2 wks of Jan. and 1st wk of Feb.* ⊺⊙⊺ *BP.*

Bibury

③ *10 mi southwest of Burford, 6 mi northeast of Cirencester, 15 mi north of Swindon.*

The tiny town of Bibury, on B4425, sits idyllically beside the little River Coln; it was famed Arts and Crafts designer William Morris's choice for Britain's most beautiful village. Fine old cottages, a river meadow, and the church of St. Mary's are some of the delights here. **Arlington Row** is a famously pretty group of 17th-century weavers' cottages made of stone. On a site recorded in the 11th-century Domesday Book stands **Arlington Mill,** a huge 17th-century working corn mill that contains examples of agricultural implements and machinery from the Victorian era, as well as country exhibits. ☎ *01285/740368* ☜ *£1* ☉ *Daily 8–6.*

Where to Stay & Eat

££££–£££££ ✕❑ **Swan Hotel.** Chandeliers and displays of plates and glassware adorn this mid-17th-century coaching inn on the banks of the River Coln. Guest rooms, all different though most are traditional in style, come with splendid modern bathrooms—Room 3's is dramatically tiled in black and white. The formal Signet restaurant (open evenings and Sunday lunch) has fixed-price or à la carte menus with such dishes as grilled local trout, or you can dine in the cheaper Jankowski's Brasserie (open lunchtime and Friday and Saturday evenings). ⊠ *Bibury, GL7 5NW* ☎ *01285/740695* 🖷 *01285/740473* ⊕ *www.swanhotel.co.uk* ⇔ *18 rooms* ⌂ *2 restaurants, some in-room data ports, some in-room hot tubs, fishing, bar, meeting rooms, no-smoking rooms; no a/c* ☲ *AE, DC, MC, V* ⧦ *BP.*

££££ ✕❑ **New Inn.** A hop-bedecked bar leads you to the restaurant in this ancient coaching inn, 2 mi southeast of Bibury in an attractive village. The frequently changing fixed-price menu might include wild mushroom and shallot soup to start, followed by roast salmon. The bedrooms are of the floral-wallpaper-and-chintz variety. ⊠ *Off B4425, Coln St. Aldwyns, GL7 5AN* ☎ *01285/750651* 🖷 *01285/750657* ⊕ *www.new-inn.co.uk* ⇔ *11 rooms* ⌂ *Restaurant, bar, meeting rooms, some pets allowed (fee); no a/c, no kids under 10* ☲ *AE, MC, V* ⧦ *BP.*

Chedworth Roman Villa

★ **③** *6 mi northwest of Bibury, 9 mi north of Cirencester, 10 mi southeast of Cheltenham.*

The well-preserved remains of one of the largest Roman villas in England sit in a wooded valley on the eastern fringe of the Cotswolds. Thirty-two rooms, including two complete bath suites, have been identified, and there are some colorful mosaics. The visitor center and museum give a detailed picture of Roman life in Britain. From Bibury, go across A429 to Yanworth and Chedworth, where signs indicate the way; the villa is also signposted from A40. ⊠ *Yanworth* ☎ *01242/890256* ⊕ *www.nationaltrust.org.uk* ☜ *£4.10* ☉ *Apr.–late Oct., Tues.–Sun. and national holidays 10–5; Mar. and late Oct.–mid-Nov., Tues.–Sun. 11–4.*

Cirencester

32 *9 mi south of Chedworth, 14 mi southeast of Cheltenham.*

Cirencester (pronounced sirensester) has been a hub of the Cotswolds since Roman times, when it was called Corinium; the town was second only to Londinium (London) in importance. It lay at the intersection of two major Roman roads, the Fosse Way and Ermin Street (today A429 and A417). In the Middle Ages, Cirencester grew rich on wool, which funded its 15th-century parish church. Today this old market town is the area's largest, with a population of 19,000. It preserves many mellow stone buildings dating mainly from the 17th and 18th centuries, and bow-fronted shops that still have one foot in the past.

At the top of Market Place is the magnificent Gothic parish church of **St. John the Baptist,** known as the cathedral of the "woolgothic" style. Its elaborate, three-tiered, three-bayed south porch, the largest in England, once served as the town hall. The chantry chapels and many coats of arms bear witness to the importance of the wool merchants, benefactors of the church. A rare example of a 15th-century wineglass pulpit sits in the nave. ☒ *Market Pl.* ☏ *01285/659317* ☒ *Free, donations accepted* ☉ *Mon.–Sat. 9:30–4:45, Sun. 2:15–5:45.*

Not much of the Roman town remains visible, but the **Corinium Museum** displays an outstanding collection of Roman artifacts, including mosaic pavements, as well as full-scale reconstructions of local Roman interiors. Galleries, opened in fall 2004, explore the town's history in Roman and Anglo-Saxon times and in the 18th century; they include plenty of hands-on exhibits. ☒ *Park St.* ☏ *01285/655611* ⊕ *www.cotswold. gov.uk* ☒ *£3.50* ☉ *Mon.–Sat. 10–5, Sun. 2–5.*

Where to Stay & Eat

£££££ ✕🏠 **Barnsley House.** The former home of the late garden designer Rosemary Verey has been discreetly modernized and converted into a topnotch, pricey retreat. None of the charm of the Georgian, honey-and-cream Cotswold house has been jettisoned, and the gardens continue to be an attraction. The main focus, though, is on exquisite dining (no children under 12) with a strong Italian and Mediterranean influence, as in the classic *vincisgrassi*—baked pasta with Parma ham, porcini mushrooms, and truffles. Rooms are spacious and stylishly modern, with wellstocked minibars; bathrooms are positively extravagant, each with its own TV and CD player. ☒ *B4425, Barnsley, GL7 5EE, 4 mi northeast of Cirencester* ☏ *01285/740000* ☒ *01285/740900* ⊕ *www. barnsleyhouse.com* ⇆ *9 rooms* ♿ *Restaurant, minibars, in-room data ports, in-room DVDs, bar; no a/c* ▤ *AE, MC, V* ⊙ *BP.*

££–£££ ✕🏠 **Wild Duck Inn.** This family-run Elizabethan inn 3 mi south of Cirencester has richly decorated guest rooms with print fabrics and dark wood furniture. The mellow, deep-red dining room has an abundance of beams and oil portraits, and the menu is strong on fresh fish and such meat dishes as griddled chicken breast and honey-roasted duck. Make room reservations well in advance, as the inn is popular. ☒ *Ewen, GL7 6BY* ☏ *01285/770310* ☒ *01285/770924* ⊕ *www.thewildduckinn.co. uk* ⇆ *9 rooms* ♿ *Restaurant; no a/c* ▤ *AE, MC, V* ⊙ *CP.*

COTSWOLD STONE

F THERE'S ONE FEATURE of the Cotswold landscape that sums up its special flavor, it's the oolitic limestone that is the area's primary building material. This stone can be seen in everything from drystone walls (whose total length in the region is said to equal or exceed that of the Great Wall of China) to snug cottages and manor houses. Even roof tiles are fashioned from the stone, contributing to a harmonious ensemble despite the different ages of the buildings.

Malleable when first quarried, and gradually hardening with age, the stone lends itself to every use. During the late-medieval heyday of the great churches funded by wool merchants, it was used to brilliant effect in the mullions, gargoyles, and other intricate decorations on ecclesiastical buildings. Some area quarries are still active, producing stone that is used mainly for restoration and repair purposes. The varying colors of the stone are caused by impurities in the rock. They include the honey hues of the northern reaches of the Cotswolds, and modulate to a more golden tone in the central area, with a paler hue in and around Bath.

Writer and commentator J. B. Priestley, however, wrote of Cotswold stone that "the truth is that it has no color that can be described. Even when the sun is obscured and the light is cold, these walls are still faintly warm and luminous, as if they knew the trick of keeping the lost sunlight of centuries glimmering about them." Walk or drive around Cotswold villages and towns for even a day, and you will know what he meant.

£ ▦ **Ivy House.** Ivy clings to this stone Victorian house, close to the center of town, that offers excellent value. The simple bedrooms have pastel colors and pine furniture. The owners are friendly, and cyclists and walkers are welcomed. ⊠ *2 Victoria Rd., GL7 1EN* ☎ *01285/656626* ⊕ *www.ivyhousecotswolds.com* ➽ *4 rooms* ⚲ *No a/c, no room phones, no smoking* ▭ *MC, V* ⦿❘ *BP.*

Nightlife & the Arts

The **Brewery Arts Centre** (⊠ Brewery Ct. ☎ 01285/657181, 01285/655522 box office) has studios for more than a dozen artists and craftspeople, as well as a shop that sells their work. The center also includes a theater, exhibition space, and a café.

Sports & the Outdoors

You can indulge in water sports such as waterskiing and windsurfing at the **Cotswold Water Park,** 3 mi south of Cirencester. This group of 130 lakes covers 40 square mi and has multiple entrances. There's swimming June–September; the park also draws wildlife enthusiasts, walkers, cyclists, and horseback riders. You pay individual charges for the activities April–October. ⊠ *Keynes Country Park, off B4696, Shorncote*

☎ 01285/861459 ⊕ www.waterpark.org ⌷ £6 parking Apr.–Oct., £1 parking Nov.–Mar. ⊙ Daily 9 AM–9 PM.

Shopping

The **Corn Hall** (⊠ Market Pl.) is the venue for a Friday antiques market and a crafts market on Saturday (unless it's the fifth Saturday in the month). Every Monday and Friday, Cirencester's central **Market Place** is packed with stalls selling a motley assortment of goods, mainly household items but some local produce and crafts, too. **Rankine Taylor Antiques** (⊠ 34 Dollar St. ☎ 01285/652529) concentrates on 17th- and 18th-century furniture, silver, pottery, and glass. **William H. Stokes** (⊠ 6–8 Dollar St. ☎ 01285/653907) specializes in oak furniture from the 16th and 17th centuries.

Painswick

➌➌ 16 mi northwest of Cirencester, 8 mi southwest of Cheltenham, 5 mi south of Gloucester.

This old Cotswold wool town has become a chocolate-box picture of quaintness, attracting plenty of day-trippers and tour buses. But come during the week and you can discover the place in relative tranquility. The huddled gray stone houses and inns date from as early as the 14th century and include a notable group from the Georgian era. The churchyard is renowned for its 99 yew trees (legend has it that the devil prevents the 100th from growing) planted in 1792. Painswick's annual Clypping Ceremony, on the first Sunday after September 19, has nothing to do with topiary—the name derives from the Anglo-Saxon word "clyppan," meaning "encircle." Children with garlands make a ring around the church as traditional hymns are sung. Another good time to visit is the town's Victorian Market Day in early July.

The **Painswick Rococo Garden,** ½ mi north of town, has survived from the exuberant rococo period of English garden design (1720–60). After 50 years in its original form, the 6-acre garden became overgrown with woodland. Beginning in 1984, after the rediscovery of a 1748 painting of the garden by Thomas Robins, the garden was restored. Now you can view the original architectural structures—such as the vaguely Gothic Eagle House and Exedra—and asymmetrical vistas. There's also a restaurant and a shop. ⊠ B4073 ☎ 01452/813204 ⊕ www.rococogarden.co.uk ⌷ £4 ⊙ Mid-Jan.–Oct., daily 11–6 or dusk (last admission at 5).

Where to Stay & Eat

££££ ✕🏨 **Painswick Hotel.** Unstuffy and friendly, this family-run hotel occupies a Georgian mansion behind Painswick's church. Beautiful fabrics and deep, vibrant colors enhance the spacious and individually designed rooms, some of which have antique four-posters and balconies. The seasonal menu blends the traditional with the more exotic—saddle of venison with chestnuts and celeriac fondant, for example. A two-night minimum stay is required on weekends. ⊠ Kemps La., GL6 6YB ☎ 01452/812160 ⊟ 01452/814059 ⊕ www.painswickhotel.com ⇌ 19 rooms ⌂ Restaurant, meeting rooms; no a/c ⊟ AE, MC, V ⏐⊙⏐ BP.

££   ✗▥ **Cardynham House.** The Cotswolds are really about the art of liv-
FodorśChoice ing, as this 16th-century former wool merchant's house demonstrates.
★   The stylish retreat, which retains its beamed ceilings, Jacobean staircase, and Elizabethan fireplace, has four-poster beds in all rooms and creative theme rooms such as the Medieval Garden, Dovecote, and Arabian Nights. One far more expensive room has a private pool. Downstairs, the March Hare dining room (closed Sunday and Monday) serves delicious Thai food (fixed-price menu), such as red snapper curry with coconut and lime leaves. ⊠ *The Cross, GL6 6XX* ☎ *01452/814006, 01452/813452 restaurant* 🖷 *01452/812321* ⊕ *www.cardynham.co.uk* 🖙 *9 rooms* ⌂ *Restaurant; no a/c* ═ *AE, MC, V* �267 *BP.*

Stroud

❹ *3 mi south of Painswick, 12 mi west of Cirencester.*

Very much a contrast to the well-heeled, antiques-infused settlements of the Cotswolds, Stroud is a hardworking town with little time for pretensions. For centuries the wool trade dominated the economy. At one time 150 mills operated along the River Frome (pronounced froom), and the town was particularly associated with the famous Stroudwater Scarlet, used for military uniforms. Now the one mill that remains produces the green baize cloth used on snooker tables and felt for tennis balls. Stroud has become noted for its support of ecological issues.

★ ☽   Stroud's main attraction is the excellent **Museum in the Park,** which explores the history of the town and the surrounding countryside. Among the theme exhibits are "Clean, Fit, and Tidy" and "Fire and Theft"; objects displayed include medieval watering cans, 18th-century paintings showing the hanging out of Stroudwater Scarlet cloth on the hillside, eelskin gaiters from the 19th century, and the world's first lawn mower (1830). A fascinating video describes farming in the 1940s. The museum is ½ mi from the town center. ⊠ *Stratford Park, junction of A4171 and A46* ☎ *01453/763394* ⊕ *www.stroud.gov.uk* ⊡ *Free* ☉ *Apr.–Sept., Tues.–Fri. 10–5, weekends 11–5; Oct.–Mar., Tues.–Fri. 10–4, weekends 11–4:30.*

Where to Eat

£–££   ✗ **Mills Café.** This busy café, tucked away in a courtyard off the High Street in the center of town, is the best spot in Stroud for baguettes, homemade soups, and scrumptious cakes, as well as more substantial lunches. ⊠ *Withey's Yard* ☎ *01453/752222* ═ *MC, V* ☉ *Closed Sun. No dinner.*

Owlpen

★ **❺** *6 mi southwest of Stroud, 13 mi west of Cirencester.*

Prince Charles described the beauty spot of Owlpen, an off-the-beaten-path hamlet, as "the epitome of the English village." First settled in Saxon days as Olla's Pen (meaning "valley"), the village centers on a church, a Tudor manor house, and pearl-gray stone cottages, all set against a hillside. A graceful grouping of tithe barns, garden buildings, and grist mills softens the seignorial bearing of the manor house.

The triple-gabled stone **Owlpen Manor** was built between 1450 and 1616, but was restored in the 1920s by local Arts and Crafts artisans, who also created some of the furnishings. Today Nicholas and Karin Mander live here with their family. Inside are oak chests fashioned by William Morris, family portraits, Georgian doorcases, painted cloths from the Tudor and Stuart eras, and Queen Margaret's Room, said to be haunted by the spirit of Margaret of Anjou, wife of Henry VI, who visited here during the Wars of the Roses. You can also explore the terraced garden with its yew topiary, the envy of gardening masters such as Gertrude Jekyll. The Cyder Press restaurant opens at noon. Several cottages have been converted into guest accommodations, available for two-night or longer rentals. ⊠ *Off B4066, near Uley* ☎ *01453/860261* ⊕ *www.owlpen.com* ▢ *£4.80, gardens only £2.80* ☉ *Apr.–Sept., Tues.–Sun. and national holidays 2–5.*

Tetbury

36 *6 mi southeast of Owlpen, 8 mi southwest of Cirencester, 12 mi south of Painswick.*

With Prince Charles and Princess Anne both nearby neighbors, Tetbury claims right royal connections. Indeed, the soaring spire of the church that presides over this Elizabethan market town is within sight of Highgrove House, the Prince of Wales's abode. In the center of the village, look for the eye-catching, white-painted stone **Market House** on Market Square, dating from 1655 and built up on rows of Tuscan pillars. An antiques market is held here on Wednesday. The **Church of St. Mary** (⊠ Church St. ☎ 01666/502333), in 18th-century neo-Gothic style, has a spacious galleried interior with pews.

need a break? **Two Toads** (⊠ 19 Church St. ☎ 01666/503696) is a peaceful place for coffee, light lunches, and cream teas. Be sure to try the delicious pastries. The small courtyard garden is open in fine weather.

Tall gate piers and spreading trees frame the family-owned **Chavenage,** a gray Cotswold-stone Elizabethan manor house. The tour includes a room with fine tapestries, where Cromwell lodged during the Civil War, and a main hall with minstrels' gallery. ✛ *2 mi northwest of Tetbury between B4104 and A4135* ☎ *01666/502329* ⊕ *www.chavenage.com* ▢ *£4* ☉ *May–Sept., Thurs., Sun., and national holidays 2–5.*

One of the last English country houses to be constructed using traditional methods and materials, **Rodmarton Manor** (built 1909–29) is furnished with specially commissioned pieces in the Arts and Crafts style. Ernest Barnsley, a follower of William Morris, worked on the house. The notable gardens—wild, winter, sunken, and white—are divided into "rooms" bounded by hedges of holly, beech, and yew. The manor is 5 mi northeast of Tetbury. ⊠ *Off A433, Rodmarton* ☎ *01285/841253* ⊕ *www.rodmarton-manor.co.uk* ▢ *£7, garden only £4* ☉ *May–Aug., Wed., Sat., and national holidays 2–5; garden also open June and July, Mon. 2–5.*

★ The 600-acre **Westonbirt Arboretum**, 3 mi southwest of Tetbury, contains one of the most extensive collections of trees and shrubs in Europe. The best times to come for color are in late spring, when the rhododendrons, azaleas, and magnolias are blooming, and in fall, when the maples come into their own. There's a gift shop, café, and restaurant. ⊠ *Off A433* ☎ *01666/880220* ⊕ *www.forestry.gov.uk* 🖼 *£7.50 June–mid-Sept., £6 Apr., May, mid-Sept.–Oct., £5 Jan.–Mar., Nov., and Dec.* ☉ *Daily 10–8 or dusk.*

Where to Stay & Eat

★ £££ ✕ **Trouble House.** Simple but wonderfully tasty dishes are created at this relaxed, whitewashed pub with wooden floors, a beamed ceiling, and fireplaces for cool days. Your order from the bar might be slow-cooked leg of lamb with bean and tomato stew, or sea bass with lobster minestrone. The pub is 2 mi northeast of Tetbury on the Cirencester road. ⊠ *A433* ☎ *01666/502206* ⊟ *AE, MC, V* ☉ *No dinner Sun. in winter. Closed Mon.*

£££££ ✕🖼 **Calcot Manor.** Comfortable country-house furnishings with lots of greens and burgundies fill the main house and converted sandstone barns and stables of this family-friendly establishment with a luxurious spa. Guest rooms are airy and spacious; family suites have bunk beds in a separate room and refrigerators. The formal Conservatory restaurant prepares dishes such as roast rack of Cotswold lamb with garlic-and-parsley crust, and the Gumstool Inn provides farmhouse-style fare; dinner is included in the price on weekends. The hotel is 3 mi west of town. ⊠ *A4135, GL8 8YJ* ☎ *01666/890391* 🖼 *01666/890394* ⊕ *www.calcotmanor.co.uk* 🖼 *24 rooms, 4 suites* ⚫ *2 restaurants, tennis court, pool, gym, hair salon, spa, croquet, 2 bars, meeting rooms; no a/c* ⊟ *AE, DC, MC, V* 🍽 *BP.*

Shopping

Many of Tetbury's more than 20 antiques shops line Long Street. You're bound to find something from the 40-odd dealers at the **Antiques Emporium** (⊠ Old Chapel, Long St. ☎ 01666/505281), a cornucopia of treasures from kitchenware to miniatures, jewelry, and glass. **Day Antiques** (⊠ 5 New Church St. ☎ 01666/502413) specializes in oak furniture and early pottery, metalware, and treen. **Townsend and Bateson** (⊠ 51A Long St. ☎ 01666/505083) displays decorative wares and some furniture.

GLOUCESTER TO THE FOREST OF DEAN

West of the Cotswolds a rather urbanized axis connects Gloucester with Cheltenham. Despite their proximity on either side of the M5 motorway, the towns are very different; the down-to-earth Gloucester, built around docks connected to the River Severn, contrasts with the gentrified spa town of Cheltenham. North of Gloucester lies the riverside town of Tewkesbury with its imposing abbey; to the south, easily accessible from M5, stands battlemented Berkeley Castle. Southwest of Gloucester, the low-lying Forest of Dean (officially the Royal Forest of Dean), once a private hunting ground of kings, is now a recreation area for the public, with some of the most beautiful woodlands in the country.

Gloucester

㊲ *13 mi southwest of Cheltenham, 56 mi south of Birmingham, 105 mi west of London.*

Although much of the ancient heritage of this county seat has been lost to nondescript modern stores and offices, Gloucester has a number of worthwhile sights, most notably its cathedral. The historic **Gloucester Docks**, a short walk from the cathedral along the canal, still function but now cater mainly to pleasure craft. The vast Victorian warehouses have been restored, and shops and cafés added, reviving the area. One warehouse is now the Antiques Centre, and others hold good museums. **Walking tours** around the docks start at the Mariners' Church in the center of the docks. ☏ *01452/396572* ✉ *£2.50 tours* ⊙ *Tours mid-June–mid-Sept., Sun. at 11.*

★ Magnificent **Gloucester Cathedral,** with its soaring, elegant exterior, was originally a Norman abbey church, consecrated in 1100. Reflecting different periods, the cathedral mirrors perfectly the slow growth of ecclesiastical taste and the development of the Perpendicular style. The interior has largely been spared the sterilizing attentions of modern architects and is almost completely Norman, with the massive pillars of the nave left untouched since their completion. The fan-vaulted roof of the 14th-century cloisters is the finest in Europe, and the cloisters enclose a peaceful garden (used in the filming of *Harry Potter and the Sorcerer's Stone* for some Hogwarts School scenes). The Whispering Gallery has a permanent exhibition devoted to the splendid, 14th-century stained glass of the Great East Window, and tours of the tower (269 steps up) are available. ⊠ *Westgate St.* ☎ *01452/528095* ⊕ *www.gloucestercathedral.org. uk* ⊠ *£3 donation requested, exhibition £2, tower tours £2.50* ⊙ *Daily 8–6, except during services and special events. Tower tours Apr.–Oct., Wed.–Fri. 2:30, Sat. 2 and 3, and national holidays 1:30 and 2:30.*

The **Gloucester Folk Museum,** opposite the cathedral, fills a row of fine Tudor and Jacobean half-timber houses. Exhibits on local crafts and domestic life illustrate the history of Gloucester and the surrounding areas. It's open only during school vacations; call to check. ⊠ *99–103 Westgate St.* ☎ *01452/526467* ⊕ *www.gloucester.gov.uk* ⊠ *Free* ⊙ *1 wk mid-Feb., 2 wks around Easter, 1 wk June, late July–early Sept., 1 wk Oct., daily 10–5.*

The **National Waterways Museum,** in a converted Victorian warehouse, contains examples of canal houseboats, including gaily painted "canal ware"—ornaments and utensils found on barges. Exhibits interpret the role of canals in the 18th and 19th centuries, and you can try your foot at "walking the wall"—the boatmen's way of propelling barges through tunnels with their feet. ⊠ *Llanthony Warehouse, Llanthony Rd., Gloucester Docks* ☎ *01452/318200* ⊕ *www.nwm.org.uk* ⊠ *£5* ⊙ *Daily 10–5.*

The **Soldiers of Gloucestershire Museum** examines the lives and service of Gloucestershire soldiers, and the effect of military service on their wives and families. All the accoutrements of military life since 1694 are here— medals, uniforms, and souvenirs—as well as a taped sound track of firing from World War I trenches. ⊠ *Gloucester Docks, Commercial Rd.* ☎ *01452/522682* ⊕ *www.glosters.org.uk* ⊠ *£4.25* ⊙ *June–Sept., daily 10–5; Oct.–May, Tues.–Sun. and national holidays 10–5.*

need a break? While you're at the docks, drop in at **Foster's** (⊠ Kimberley Warehouse, Gloucester Docks ☎ 01452/300990), a pub, wine bar, and brasserie, where you can sit on sofas or in a glassed-in, plant-filled atrium right on the quayside. Hot and cold drinks, snacks, and full meals are available.

A Georgian mansion holds **Nature in Art,** a museum dedicated to works of art inspired by nature. Exhibits are mainly contemporary, with selections by Picasso, Henry Moore, and the wildlife artist David Shepherd, but also include a Byzantine mosaic and 19th-century Asian ivory. From February through November you can watch artists at work. The museum is 2 mi north of Gloucester. ⊠ *Wallsworth Hall, A38, Twigworth* ☎ *01452/731422* ⊕ *www.nature-in-art.org.uk* ⊠ *£3.60* ⊙ *Tues.–Sun. and national holidays 10–5.*

Where to Stay & Eat

££–£££ ✗ **Cellars Restaurant.** An informal, brick-vaulted room in the basement of an 18th-century building in the center of town is the backdrop for imaginative British dishes with Mediterranean influences, such as chicken breast filled with ricotta, spring onions, and Parma ham. Fixed-price menus are available, but not on Friday evening or Saturday. You can have a predinner drink in the conservatory wine bar. ✉ *Longsmith St.* ☎ *01452/419966* ▭ *MC, V* ⊗ *Closed Sun. and Mon.*

££–£££ ✗ **The New Inn.** This rambling coaching inn is a few steps down from the Cross—the historic heart of the old city where Northgate, Westgate, Southgate, and Eastgate streets meet. The galleried courtyard, overgrown with creepers, adds to the impression of great age. There's an extensive carvery menu (a buffet of roasted meats, carved to order) and plenty of vegetarian choices. ✉ *16 Northgate St.* ☎ *01452/522177* ▭ *AE, MC, V* ⊗ *Closed Sun.*

££–£££ ▥ **Hatherley Manor.** On 37 acres of grounds 2 mi north of Gloucester, this 17th-century redbrick house is fairly quiet, unless a conference is going on—which happens frequently. Guest rooms are spacious and restful, furnished in modern style, but the public rooms have retained their beams and low ceilings. ✉ *Down Hatherley La., GL2 9QA* ☎ *01452/730217* 🖷 *01452/731032* ⊕ *www.countrytown-hotels.co.uk* ⤵ *52 rooms* ⟂ *Restaurant, croquet, bar, meeting rooms, helipad; no a/c* ▭ *AE, DC, MC, V* ⌾❙ *BP.*

£ ▥ **Ashleworth Court.** Built of limestone, this medieval house is part of a working farm on the tranquil banks of the River Severn, with a bird blind close by. All the spacious rooms have antique pieces, but make the bedroom with the Jacobean four-poster your first choice. There are several good food pubs nearby. This B&B is 6 mi north of Gloucester. ✉ *Ashleworth, GL19 4JA* ☎ *01452/700241* 🖷 *01452/700411* ⊕ *http://members.farmline.com/chamberlayne* ⤵ *3 rooms without bath* ⟂ *No a/c, no room phones, no room TVs, no smoking* ▭ *No credit cards* ⌾❙ *BP.*

The Outdoors

From the pier outside the National Waterways Museum, boats leave for a 45-minute tour of the Gloucester Docks or all-day cruises that head as far north as Tewkesbury or south to the Severn Estuary at Sharpness. Tours take place between Easter and October: contact the **National Waterways Museum** (☎ 01452/318200) for dates and prices.

Shopping

The locals say it's best to look in Cheltenham and buy in Gloucester, where prices are lower. The more than 100 dealers in the **Antiques Centre** (✉ 1 Severn Rd. ☎ 01452/529716) offer some good buys on items—clocks, silver, china, military collectibles, and more—in a five-floor Victorian warehouse by the Gloucester Docks. The **Beatrix Potter Gift Shop** (✉ 9 College Ct. ☎ 01452/422856), next to the Cathedral Gate, is in the house that served as a model for the tailor's house in Potter's story *The Tailor of Gloucester.* The shop sells Potter-related items and also has a small museum.

Tewkesbury

38 *12 mi northeast of Gloucester.*

Tewkesbury is an ancient town of black-and-white half-timber buildings, as well as some fine Georgian ones, on the River Avon. The stonework in the Norman **Tewkesbury Abbey** has much in common with that of Gloucester Cathedral, but this church was built in the Romanesque (12th-century) and Decorated Gothic (14th-century) styles. Its exterior makes an impressive sight, with the largest Norman tower in the world—148 feet high and 46 feet square—and the 65-foot-high arch of the west front. Fourteen stout Norman pillars and myriad gilded bosses on the roof of the nave and choir (best viewed through a mirror on wheels) grace the beautifully kept interior. ⊠ *Church St.* ☎ *01684/ 850959* ⊕ *www.tewkesburyabbey.org.uk* ✉ *Requested donation £2, tours £2* ⊙ *Daily 8–6; tours Apr.–Oct., daily at 11 and 2:15.*

Where to Stay

££££ 🏨 **Royal Hop Pole.** One of the most famous old English inns, the half-timber Hop Pole is mentioned in Charles Dickens's *The Pickwick Papers.* The rooms at the rear have wood beams and views of the gardens running down to the river, where there is private mooring for boats. ⊠ *Church St., GL20 5RT* ☎ *01684/293236* 🖷 *01684/296680* 🛏 *29 rooms* ♿ *Restaurant, bar, meeting rooms, some pets allowed; no a/c* ▭ *AE, DC, MC, V* 🍽 *BP.*

£ 🏨 **Abbey Antiques B&B.** If you have yearned to wake up in an antiques shop, this may be your best option. This three-story Georgian town house, just across from the abbey, has two gorgeously furnished, antiques-filled rooms above the Aladdin's cave of a shop and one apartment on the top floor. Wooden floorboards, patchwork quilts, and fresh flowers in the house (and free-range hens in the garden) make for a fun, informal stay. ⊠ *61 Church St., GL20 5RZ* 🖷 *01684/298145* 🛏 *2 rooms, 1 apartment* ♿ *No a/c, no room phones* ▭ *No credit cards* 🍽 *BP.*

Soudley

39 *27 mi southwest of Tewkesbury, 15 mi west of Gloucester.*

★ Soudley has a museum that provides a useful introduction to the surrounding forest. The ancient **Forest of Dean** (⊕ www.forestofdean.gov. uk) covers much of the valley between the Rivers Severn and Wye. Although the primordial forest has long since been cut down and replanted, the landscape here remains one of strange beauty, hiding in its folds and under its hills deposits of iron, silver, and coal that have been mined for thousands of years. Of the original forest established in 1016 by King Canute, 27,000 acres are preserved by the Forestry Commission. It's still a source of timber, but parking lots and picnic grounds have been created and eight nature trails marked. For a driving tour of the forest, head to Littledean, where SCENIC DRIVE signs direct you through the best of the forest. To get to Littledean from Soudley, backtrack north on B4227, and turn east on A4151.

The **Dean Heritage Centre,** in a restored mill building in a wooded valley on the forest's eastern edge, tells the history of the forest, with reconstructions of a mine and a miner's cottage, a waterwheel, and a "beam engine" (a primitive steam engine used to pump water from flooded coal mines). Other galleries in the building show art with local themes as well as furniture, ornaments, and the like made from local oak. Also within the grounds is a smallholding (a small farm), with a couple of resident pigs. Craftspeople work in the outbuildings. ⊠ *B4227, near Cinderford* ☎ *01594/822170* ⊕ *www.deanheritagemuseum.com* 💷 *£4.50* ⊘ *Apr.–Oct., daily 10–5:30; Nov.–Mar., daily 10–4.*

Cinderford

40 *1 mi west of Littledean, 14 mi southwest of Gloucester.*

In Cinderford, a hiking trail links sculptures around Speech House, the medieval verderer's court in the forest's center, and now a restaurant and inn. The verderer was responsible for the enforcement of the forest laws. It was usually a capital offense to kill game or cut wood without authorization.

Where to Stay & Eat

£££ ✕🏨 **Speech House.** Dating from 1676, this former royal hunting lodge retains its satisfyingly creaky floors and low-beamed ceilings. Rooms are traditionally furnished with striped and print fabrics; some have four-posters. The wood-paneled Verderer's Court still functions four times a year, but at any other time the courtroom is a restaurant (fixed-price or à la carte menus) serving country platters that might include the local Gloucestershire Old Spot pork and treacle tart. Although the postal address for Speech House is the town of Coleford, it is outside the village of Cinderford. ⊠ *B4226, Coleford, GL16 7EL* ☎ *01594/822607* 🖨*01594/823658* ⊕*www.thespeechhouse.co.uk* 🛏*40 rooms* ⅏ *Restaurant, golf privileges, gym, spa, bar, meeting rooms, some pets allowed (fee); no a/c* ⊟ *AE, DC, MC, V* ⦿❘ *BP.*

Coleford

41 *4 mi west of Cinderford, 10 mi south of Ross-on-Wye.*

The area around Coleford is a maze of weathered and moss-covered rocks, huge ferns, and ancient yew trees—a shady haven on a summer's day. The **tourist information center** (☎ 01594/812388 ⊕ www.forestofdean. gov.uk) at Coleford (drive west from Cinderford on A4151, and then west again on B4226 and B4028) has details of picnic grounds, nature and sculpture trails, and tours of the forest.

🍂 A visit to the workings in the spectacular **Clearwell Caves,** 1½ mi south of Coleford, provides insight into the region's mining for iron and coal, which went on continuously from Roman times to 1945. Ocher (for paint pigments and cosmetics) is still mined here. ⊠ *Off B4228* ☎ *01594/ 832535* ⊕ *www.clearwellcaves.com* 💷 *£4, £5 Christmas Fantasy displays* ⊘ *Mid-Feb.–Oct., daily 10–5; Nov. and Jan., weekends and school holidays 10–4; Dec., Christmas Fantasy daily 10–5.*

Where to Stay & Eat

££–£££ ✕⊡ **Tudor Farmhouse.** Despite its name, parts of this former farmhouse date to the 13th century. Polished oak staircases, mullioned windows, and a huge stone fireplace in the sitting room imbue the place with antique calm. Most of the traditionally decorated bedrooms are in a converted barn, and three have four-poster beds. The restaurant serves good-quality fare using seasonal ingredients in such dishes as fresh spinach and apple soup and smoked duck salad. ⊠ *High St., Clearwell GL16 8JS, near Coleford* ☎ *01594/833046* 🖷 *01594/837093* ⊕ *www. tudorfarmhousehotel.co.uk* ➫ *22 rooms* ⚭ *Restaurant, some pets allowed; no a/c* ⊟ *AE, DC, MC, V* ⧖⧘ *BP.*

££–£££ ✕⊡ **Wyndham Arms Hotel.** This old-fashioned village inn, just a hundred yards from Clearwell Castle, has comfortable accommodation, a bar with fine wines and ales, and a restaurant that can rustle up sophisticated English cuisine. Try the Tintern cheese soufflé, venison stew, or pan-fried pork medallions, followed by old-fashioned bread-and-butter pudding. Bedrooms, fairly plain but well-equipped, are in the main building, where there's a suite with a beamed ceiling, or in an annex. ⊠ *The Cross, Clearwell GL16 8JT* ☎ *01594/833666* 🖷 *01594/836450* ⊕ *www.thewyndhamhotel.co. uk* ➫ *17 rooms, 1 suite* ⚭ *Restarant, bar; no a/c* ⊟ *MC, V.*

Slimbridge Wildfowl & Wetlands Trust

㊷ *38 mi east of Coleford (via Severn Bridge to the south), 12 mi south of Gloucester, 20 mi northeast of Bristol.*

On the banks of the River Severn, this 73-acre site encompasses rich marshland that harbors Britain's largest collection of wildfowl. Thousands of swans, ducks, and geese come to winter here; spring and early summer are the times to see cygnets, ducklings, and goslings. Trails with blinds (called "hides" in Britain) thread the preserve. The flashy visitor center has an observation tower, cinema, gift shop, and restaurant; a gallery of wildlife art presents changing exhibitions. The preserve is outside the village of Slimbridge (head west and across the little swing bridge over the Sharpness Canal). ☎ *01453/890333* ⊕ *www.wwt.org.uk* ⧖ *£6.75* ☉ *Apr.–Oct., daily 9:30–5; Nov.–Mar., daily 9:30–4.*

Berkeley Castle

★ **㊸** *4 mi southwest of Slimbridge, 17 mi southwest of Gloucester, 21 mi north of Bristol.*

Berkeley Castle, in the sleepy village of Berkeley (pronounced *bark*-ley), is perfectly preserved, down to its medieval turrets. It witnessed the gruesome murder of King Edward II in 1327—the cell in which it occurred can still be seen. Edward was deposed by his French consort, Queen Isabella, and her paramour, the earl of Mortimer. They then connived at his imprisonment and subsequent death. Roger De Berkeley, a Norman knight, began work on the castle in 1153, and it has remained in the family ever since. Magnificent furniture, tapestries, and pictures fill the state apartments, but even the ancient buttery and kitchen are interesting. The surrounding meadows, now the setting for pleasant Elizabethan gardens, were once flooded to make a formidable moat. ⊠ *Off*

A38, Berkeley ☎ *01453/810332* ⊕ *www.berkeley-castle.com* 💳 *£7, gardens only £4* ⊗ *Apr.–Sept., Tues.–Sat. and national holidays 11–4, Sun. 2–5; Oct., Sun. 2–5.*

Where to Stay & Eat

★ ×🖾 **Thornbury Castle.** An impressive castle-hotel, Thornbury has every-
££££–£££££ thing a genuine 16th-century Tudor castle needs: huge fireplaces, antiques, paintings, and mullioned windows, to say nothing of a large garden.
There's also plenty of history: Henry VIII, Anne Boleyn, and Mary
Tudor spent time here. The standards of comfort are famous, and the
pampering touches in the plushly decorated bedrooms include luxurious bathrooms. People come from all over to dine on sophisticated fare
such as roast fallow deer loin served on roast celeriac, and pan-fried red
mullet with new potatoes and onion marmalade. The hotel is 12 mi north
of Bristol. ⊠ *Castle St., off A38, Thornbury, BS35 1HH* ☎ *01454/281182*
🖨 *01454/416188* ⊕ *www.thornburycastle.co.uk* 🛏 *25 rooms* ⚬ *Restaurant, archery, croquet, lounge, business services, meeting rooms, some
pets allowed (fee); no a/c* ⊟ *AE, DC, MC, V* ⏐⊙⏐ *BP.*

££ 🖾 **Drakestone House.** This lovely, reasonably priced Cotswold Arts and
Crafts house 3 mi east of Berkeley has wooden floors and beamed and
plasterwork ceilings. Fine antiques and period furniture complement the
architecture. ⊠ *Off B4060, Stinchcombe, Dursley, GL11 6AS*
🖨🖨 *01453/542140* ⊕ *www.a1tourism.com/uk/cotswol1.html* 🛏 *3
rooms* ⚬ *No a/c, no room phones, no room TVs, no smoking* ⊟ *No
credit cards* ⊗ *Closed Dec. and Jan.* ⏐⊙⏐ *BP.*

BATH & THE COTSWOLDS A TO Z

*To research prices, get advice from other travelers, and book travel ar-
rangements, visit www.fodors.com.*

AIRPORTS

This area is not far from London; Bristol and Birmingham have the closest regional airports. Bristol's airport is 8 mi south of the city.
🚹 **Birmingham International Airport** ⊠ A45, off Junction 6 of M42 ☎ 0870/733-5511
⊕ www.bhx.co.uk. **Bristol International Airport** ⊠ Bridgwater Rd., Lulsgate ☎ 0870/
121-2747 ⊕ www.bristolairport.co.uk.

BUS TRAVEL

National Express serves the region from London's Victoria Coach Station. First covers the area around Bath. Stagecoach, Castleways, and Pulhams operate in the Gloucestershire and Cotswolds region. For all bus
inquiries, call Traveline. Although you can get around the Cotswolds
by bus, service between some towns can be extremely limited, perhaps
only twice a week.

Some bus routes to major Cotswold destinations are as follows (when
not stated otherwise, routes are serviced by National Express buses and
depart from London's Victoria Coach Station). Bourton-on-the-Water:
take Pulhams buses from Cheltenham or Stow-on-the-Wold. Broadway:
from Cheltenham, four Castleways coaches daily serve the town Monday–Saturday, and four Stagecoach coaches serve the town on Sunday.

Burford (A40 turnout): Swanbrook buses leave from Cheltenham three times daily Monday–Saturday, once on Sunday; from London, change at Oxford. Cheltenham and Cirencester: buses leave London hourly. Moreton-in-Marsh: buses depart eight times daily from London, changing at Cirencester. Painswick: Stagecoach buses run from Cheltenham (hourly Monday–Saturday, three buses on Sunday). Stow-on-the-Wold: Pulhams buses run 6 times daily (not Sunday in winter) from Moreton-in-Marsh. Winchcombe: from Cheltenham, 11 Castleways buses leave daily Monday–Saturday, and 4 Stagecoach buses leave on Sunday.

FARES &
SCHEDULES

Castleways ☎ 01242/602949 ⊕ www.castleways.co.uk. **First** ☎ 0845/606-4446 ⊕ www.firstbadgerline.co.uk. **National Express** ☎ 0870/580-8080 ⊕ www.nationalexpress.com. **Pulhams** ☎ 01451/820369. **Stagecoach** ☎ 01242/224853 ⊕ www.stagecoachbus.com. **Swanbrook** ☎ 01452/712386 ⊕ www.swanbrook.co.uk. **Traveline** ☎ 0870/608-2608 ⊕ www.traveline.org.uk.

CAR RENTAL

Local Agencies Avis ✉ Unit 7, Chancel Close Trading Estate, Eastern Ave., Gloucester ☎ 01452/380356. **Budget** ✉ 1 Shannon Point, Oakfield Close, Tewkesbury ☎ 01684/854960. **Ford Rental** ✉ Hayden Rd., off Tewkesbury Rd., Cheltenham ☎ 01242/229937. **Hertz** ✉ Bath Spa Railway Station, Dorchester St., Bath ☎ 01225/442911.

CAR TRAVEL

M4 is the main route west from London to Bath and southern Gloucestershire. From Exit 18, take A46 south to Bath. From Exit 20, take M5 north to Gloucester (25 mi), Cheltenham, and Tewkesbury; from Exit 15, take A419 to A429 north to the Cotswolds. From London, you can also take M40 and A40 to the Cotswolds. Driving the scenic roads of the Cotswold Hills can be one of the real joys of a British vacation.

Parking in Bath is restricted within the city, and any car illegally parked is likely to be ticketed. Fees for towed cars can be hundreds of pounds. Public parking lots in the historic area fill up early, but the Park and Ride lots on the outskirts of town provide shuttle service into the center. A car can be an encumbrance in Cheltenham and Gloucester; garage your car or leave it at your hotel and forgo the stress of finding parking spaces and negotiating one-way streets.

EMERGENCIES

Ambulance, fire, police ☎ 999. **Cheltenham General Hospital** ✉ Sandford Rd. ☎ 01242/222222. **Gloucester Royal Hospital** ✉ Great Western Rd. ☎ 01452/528555. **Royal United Hospital** ✉ Combe Park, Bath ☎ 01225/428331.

SHOPPING

For information about dealers and special events, contact the Cotswold Antique Dealers' Association.

Cotswold Antique Dealers' Association (CADA) ✉ Broadwell House, Sheep St., Stow-on-the-Wold, GL54 1JS ☎ 01451/810407 ⊕ www.cotswolds-antiques-art.com.

SPORTS & THE OUTDOORS

For information on hiking the Cotswold Way, contact the National Trail Office or town tourist centers. For information on hiking in the Forest of Dean, contact the Forestry Commission.

🚶 Hiking **Forestry Commission** ✉ Bank House, Bank St., Coleford, GL16 8BA ☎ 01594/
833057 🌐 www.forestry.gov.uk. **National Trail Office** ✉ The Malt House, Standish, Stonehouse, GL10 3DL ☎ 01453/827004 🌐 www.nationaltrail.co.uk.

TOURS

Based in Oxford, Cotswold Roaming is a stylish outfit offering tours of
the Cotswolds (Tuesday and Saturday) and excursions to Bath and Castle Combe (Wednesday and Saturday) in small vehicles. The full-day tour
of the Cotswolds takes in Bourton-on-the-Water, Upper Slaughter and
Lower Slaughter, Chipping Campden, Sudeley Castle, and Stow-on-
the-Wold. Half-day tours are also offered. The pickup point is next to
the Playhouse Theatre in Beaumont Street, Oxford.

Between mid-June and mid-September, Gloucester Civic Trust organizes tours of the city (Monday–Saturday at 11 from the tourist office)
and docks (Sunday at 11 from the Mariners' Church), or by appointment at other times. City Sightseeing runs 45-minute guided tours of
Bath year-round and half-day tours from Stratford-upon-Avon into the
Cotswolds from Easter through October.

🚌 **City Sightseeing** ☎ 01789/299123 in Stratford, 01225/330444 in Bath 🌐 www.city-
sightseeing.com. **Cotswold Roaming** ☎ 01865/308300 🌐 www.oxfordcity.co.uk/
cotswold-roaming. **Gloucester Civic Trust** ☎ 01452/501666.

TRAIN TRAVEL

First Great Western, Wales and West, Virgin, Central, and Thames
trains serve the region from London's Paddington Station, or, less frequently, from Euston. Travel time from Paddington to Bath is about 90
minutes. Most trains to Cheltenham (2 hours) and Gloucester (1¼
hours) involve a change at Swindon. A three-day or seven-day Heart of
England Rover ticket is valid for unlimited travel within the region.

Some pointers for reaching central Cotswold destinations by train follow. Broadway: train to Moreton-in-Marsh or Evesham, then bus or taxi
locally to reach the town. Burford: train to Oxford, then bus from the
Taylor Institute. Cirencester: train from London Paddington to Kemble
(4 mi from town). Bourton-on-the-Water, Chipping Campden, and
Stow-on-the-Wold: train to Moreton-in-Marsh, then local bus lines
(some have minimal schedules). Moreton-in-Marsh is serviced by train
from London Paddington daily. Local tourist offices have details.

FARES &
SCHEDULES
🚆 **National Rail Enquiries** ☎ 0845/748-4950 🌐 www.nationalrail.co.uk.

TRAVEL AGENCIES

🏢 Local Agent Referrals **Thomas Cook** ✉ 20 New Bond St., Bath ☎ 01225/492000
✉ 159 High St., Cheltenham ☎ 01242/847900 ✉ 24 Eastgate St., Gloucester ☎ 01452/
368000.

VISITOR INFORMATION

The Heart of England Tourist Board is open Monday–Thursday 9–5:30,
Friday 9–5. South West Tourism has information on Bath. Local tourist
information centers are normally open Monday–Saturday 9:30–5:30,
but times vary according to season. Note that Cirencester's and Stroud's
Web sites cover the whole of the Cotswolds.

🗗 **Gloucestershire Cotswolds** ⊕ www.glos-cotswolds.com. **Heart of England Tourist Board** ✉ Larkhill Rd., Worcester, WR5 2EZ ☎ 01905/761100 🖶 01905/763450 ⊕ www.visitheartofengland.com. **South West Tourism** ✉ Woodwater Park, Pynes Hill, Exeter, EX2 5WT ☎ 0870/442-0880 🖶 0870/442-0881 ⊕ www.westcountrynow.com. **Bath** ✉ Abbey Chambers, Abbey Church Yard, BA1 1LY ☎ 0906/711-2000 ⊕ www.visitbath.co.uk. **Bourton-on-the-Water** ✉ Victoria St., GL54 2BU ☎ 01451/820211. **Broadway** ✉ 1 Cotswold Ct., WR12 7AA ☎ 01386/852937 ⊕ www.broadway-cotswolds.co.uk. **Burford** ✉ The Brewery, Sheep St., OX18 4LP ☎ 01993/823558 ⊕ www.oxfordshirecotswolds.co.uk. **Cheltenham** ✉ 77 Promenade, GL50 1PP ☎ 01242/522878 ⊕ www.visitcheltenham.com. **Chipping Campden** ✉ The Old Police Station, High St., GL55 6HB ☎ 01386/841206. **Cirencester** ✉ Corn Hall, Market Pl., GL7 2NW ☎ 01285/654180 ⊕ www.cotswold.gov.uk. **Gloucester** ✉ 28 Southgate St., GL1 2DP ☎ 01452/396572 ⊕ www.gloucester.gov.uk/tourism. **Moreton-in-Marsh** ✉ High St., GL56 0AZ ☎ 01608/650881 ⊕ www.moreton-in-marsh.co.uk. **Painswick** ✉ The Library, Stroud Rd., GL6 6UT ☎ 01452/813552. **Stow-on-the-Wold** ✉ Hollis House, The Square, GL54 1AF ☎ 01451/831082. **Stroud** ✉ Subscription Rooms, George St., GL5 1AE ☎ 01453/760960 ⊕ www.visitthecotswolds.org.uk. **Tetbury** ✉ 33 Church St., GL8 8JG ☎ 01666/503552 ⊕ www.tetbury.org.uk. **Tewkesbury** ✉ 64 Barton St., GL20 5PX ☎ 01684/295027 ⊕ www.visitcotswoldsandsevernvale.gov.uk.

THE WELSH BORDERS

BIRMINGHAM, WORCESTER, HEREFORD, SHREWSBURY, CHESTER

BROADEN YOUR PERSPECTIVE
atop Chester's medieval walls ⇨*p.419*

GET A PRE-RAPHAELITE GLOW
in the Birmingham Museum ⇨*p.393*

WALK FLOWER-DECKED STREETS
in romantic Shrewsbury ⇨*p.411*

SCOOP UP BARGAINS ON FINE CHINA
at the Royal Worcester Factory ⇨*p.401*

BITE INTO MODERN BRITISH FARE
in Ludlow, a culinary hot spot ⇨*p.417*

WATCH COWS AND SHEEP COMPETE
at the Three Counties Show ⇨*p.403*

TOUR A MANOR BY CANDLELIGHT
at pristine, 17th-century Hellens ⇨*p.405*

SEE TOWNS THAT CHANGED THE WORLD
at Ironbridge Gorge ⇨*p.415*

Updated by
Kate Hughes

SOME OF ENGLAND'S PRETTIEST COUNTRYSIDE lies along the 108-mi border with the principality of Wales, which stretches from the town of Chepstow on the Severn estuary in the south to the city of Chester in the north. Much of the land along this border, in the counties of Herefordshire, Shropshire, and southern Cheshire, is remote and tranquil. But today's rural peace belies a turbulent past. Relations between the English and the Welsh have seldom been easy, and from earliest times the English have felt it necessary to keep the "troublesome" Welsh firmly on the other side of the border. The 177-mi Offa's Dyke Path, a National Trail that runs near the border (two-thirds is in Wales), follows part of the 8th-century earthen wall built by King Offa as protection against Welsh raiders. A string of medieval castles also bears witness to this history. Many are romantic ruins; some are brooding fortresses. Built to control the countryside and repel invaders, they still radiate a sense of mystery and menace.

For the last 500 years or so, the people of this border country have enjoyed a peaceful existence, with little to disturb the traditional patterns of country life. In the 18th century, however, one small corner of Shropshire heralded the tumultuous birth of the Industrial Revolution. Here, in a wooded stretch of the Severn Gorge, the coke blast furnace was invented and the first iron bridge was erected (1779).

The ramifications of that technological leap led to the growth of Britain's second-largest city, Birmingham, the capital of the Midlands. Birmingham has transcended its reputation as one of the country's least attractive cities, and its active artistic life draws people who appreciate what remains of its historic civic architecture, some of the most fascinating anywhere.

Herefordshire, in the south, is a county of rich, rolling countryside and river valleys, gradually opening out in the high hills and plateaus of Shropshire. North of the Shropshire hills, the gentler Cheshire plain stretches toward the great industrial cities of Liverpool and Manchester. This is dairy country, dotted with small villages and market towns, many rich in the 13th- and 14th-century black-and-white, half-timber buildings typical of northwestern England. These are the legacy of a forested countryside, where wood was easier to come by than stone. (The Victorians, however, are responsible for the more recent fashion of painting these structures black and white.) In the market towns of Chester and Shrewsbury, the more elaborately decorated half-timber buildings are monuments to wealth, dating mostly from the early Jacobean period at the beginning of the 17th century. More half-timbered structures are found in the archetypal Borders town of Ludlow, nestled in the lee of its majestic ruined castle.

Exploring the Welsh Borders

The main gateway to the region is bustling Birmingham, now one of the best places in England for the performing arts, having redeemed itself from its reputation as a post–World War II urban disaster zone. The city of Worcester is renowned for its proud cathedral and fine bone china. To the south and west, along the lovely Malvern Hills, lie the peaceful

Although the region's main towns—Worcester, Hereford, Shrewsbury, and Chester— distill the essence of the surrounding countryside, there's much in between that should not be neglected. It would be easy to base yourself in one of these towns, but you might do better to lodge in some of the smaller centers, or in one of the remoter country inns, to absorb the full flavor of the borderlands. In three days you can take in the highlights of a couple of major centers and visit some smaller towns. A week gives you a chance to explore Birmingham and some major towns, along with more scenic stops.

8

Numbers in the text correspond to numbers in the margin and on the Welsh Borders, Birmingham, and Shrewsbury maps.

If you have 3 days

The city of ⊞ **Worcester** ⑭ ▶ makes a convenient entry to the Welsh Borders. Spend your first night here, making sure you see the majestic cathedral and the Commandery, devoted to the 17th-century tussle between Cavaliers and Roundheads. Take a whirl around the Royal Worcester Porcelain Factory and the adjacent museum. On your second day, take A443 northwest, making a stop at the evocative ruins of **Witley Court** ㉓, a good place for a picnic; or opt for a pub meal in the nearby village. Keep on the same road as far as **Ludlow** ㊶, stopping to view its magnificent castle and its Tudor, Jacobean, and Georgian buildings. Make a reservation if you want to have lunch at one of its noted restaurants. Next, head south for ⊞ **Hereford** ㉔, with its stout Norman cathedral and numerous reminders of the city's importance as a market town. See the most interesting sights in the morning, and spend the afternoon exploring **Ross-on-Wye** ⑳, nearby **Goodrich** ㉑, dramatically poised over the River Wye, and the beauty spot of **Symond's Yat** ㉒.

If you have 7 days

Devote at least a day to ⊞ **Birmingham** ❶–⑬ ▶, and don't miss the Barber Institute of Fine Arts and the Birmingham Museum and Art Gallery. After an overnight stay, head south to Worcester and the Malvern Hills, dropping in along the way at Hellens, a 13th-century manor house (opening hours are limited, so check) just outside **Much Marcle** ⑲. You could take a lunch break at the generously timbered village of **Ledbury** ⑱ before continuing on toward the Wye Valley, where the nearby ruins of the castle at **Goodrich** ㉑ and **Symond's Yat** ㉒ provide good excuses to stop traveling and stretch your legs. A night in ⊞ **Hereford** ㉔ will allow you to absorb the flavor of this old market town before heading up to **Ludlow** ㊶ for lunch and a couple of hours' ramble around the castle and its surrounding streets. Spend the next two nights in ⊞ **Worcester** ⑭, taking in the Malverns and, to the north, the quiet riverside town of **Bewdley** ㉖, with its Georgian architecture. From here you can take a trip on the Severn Valley Railway, an old-style steam train. One of the main stops is **Bridgnorth** ㊵, occupying a sandstone ridge high above the Severn, and within a short distance of **Ironbridge Gorge** ㊴, the crucible of the Industrial Revolution. You can stay near Ironbridge or visit it on a day's excursion from ⊞ **Shrewsbury** ㉙– ㊱. Outside Shrewsbury lies **Attingham Park** ㊲, an 18th-century mansion with a deer park designed by Humphrey Repton. Your last overnight— entailing a sizable journey northward—can be spent in ⊞ **Chester** ㊷, famous for its black-and-white buildings and worthy of a day's sightseeing.

spa town of Great Malvern and the prosperous agricultural city of Hereford. Northward is Bewdley, a terminus of the Severn Valley Railway, and beyond, the West Midlands—birthplace of modern British industry.

The city of Shrewsbury is near the banks of the River Severn and a cluster of Ironbridge museums interpreting the region's industrial heritage. To its south lies Ludlow, an architectural and culinary jewel; at the northwestern edge of the region is the ancient city of Chester.

About the Hotels

Birmingham has splendid international restaurants but is probably most famous for its Asian eateries, the best of which are off the main roads. If you plan to dine in one of Ludlow's noted restaurants, you must book up to three months ahead for dinner (lunch is a better bet).

About the Restaurants

The Welsh Borders are full of ancient inns and venerable Regency-style houses converted into hotels. Although some of these can be pricey, bargains can be found. You may have to put up with asthmatic plumbing and creaking beams that masquerade as period charm, but it's usually worth the savings. Birmingham's hotels, geared to the convention crowd, are mostly bland and impersonal, but smart; weekend rates may be up to 50% less than they would be during the week.

WHAT IT COSTS In pounds				
£££££	**££££**	**£££**	**££**	**£**
RESTAURANTS over £22	£18–£22	£13–£17	£7–£12	under £7
HOTELS over £160	£120–£160	£90–£120	£60–£90	under £60

Restaurant prices are for a main course at dinner. Hotel prices are for two people in a standard double room in high season, including VAT, with no meals or, if indicated, CP (with Continental breakfast), BP (Breakfast Plan, with full breakfast), or MAP (Modified American Plan, with breakfast and dinner).

Timing

Most attractions are open and the countryside is most appealing in the warmer weather between April and September. The official and fringe festivals take place at Malvern at the end of May, the open-air performances at Ludlow Castle at the end of June, and the Shrewsbury International Music Festival in June and July. The Three Choirs Festival, rotating among Hereford, Gloucester, and Worcester (in 2005), takes place in mid-August (early booking is essential for the best seats). Most rural sights have limited opening hours in winter. Even in the towns, the majority of attractions close at 5, which leaves several hours of dark and often chilly winter evenings to fill. Be on the road early to catch the best light. In winter's favor are the creeping mists shrouding the valleys, and the warm hearths at inns and hotels.

BIRMINGHAM

The dynamic cultural life of Birmingham—the result of the museums, art galleries, theater, ballet, and symphony that thrive here—comes as

History in Stone and Wood

In the serene countryside, history can seem remote, but you can see its legacy all around in buildings that have survived the years. Among these are castles, ruined or intact, that recall the centuries when English-Welsh relations were tense. Brooding, medieval Goodrich and Ludlow castes evoke this period. (Eastnor Castle, in contrast, is a Norman-style extravaganza built by wealthy Victorians who admired the past.) Throughout the Welsh Borders, towns such as Chester, Shrewsbury, and Ludlow have half-timber buildings from medieval times to the Jacobean era; the more elaborate are monuments to wealth. Later on, the area witnessed the birth of the Industrial Revolution, which changed workers' lives as well as the landscape. The Black Country Living Museum contains structures that were part of everyday life in the 19th century, from a general store to a Methodist chapel. Ironbridge Gorge, once a site of industry, has museums that explain the production of iron and steel, a Victorian town, and the 1779 Iron Bridge itself, symbol of a revolution that transformed Britain and the world.

Walking

The Malvern Hills in the southern part of this region have climbs and walks of varying length and difficulty. The best places to start are Great Malvern and Ledbury. The Elgar Route extends for 45 mi and touches on Malvern and Worcester as it threads through the Malverns. The hilltop views across the countryside are spectacular—isolated hills rise up from the fairly flat plain, providing vistas for many miles around. The area around Ross-on-Wye has ideal walks with scenic river views. In Shropshire, Wenlock Edge and the uplands of Long Mynd south of Much Wenlock are popular places to walk.

---

a refreshing surprise. The city's appeal, thanks to heavy industry and German bombing during World War II, may be less than instantly evident, but treasures and historic civic architecture remain. Birmingham has become something of a monument to late-20th-century civic architecture—for better or worse. Mercifully, city officials have adopted a policy of humanizing the areas that their immediate predecessors did so much to ruin, and creative redevelopment and public art have made some areas more attractive. The redeveloped Bullring shopping center, part of which has a striking, curving facade of 15,000 aluminum disks, is one recent creation that has won praise.

Birmingham, with a metropolitan area population of 2.6 million, lies 25 mi north of Stratford and 120 mi northwest of London. "Brum," as it's known, is one of the country's most ethnically diverse urban areas, with nearly a third of its residents from minority groups. The city first flourished in the boom years of the 19th century's Industrial Revolution. Its inventive, hardworking citizens accumulated enormous wealth, and at one time the city had some of the finest Victorian buildings in the country (it still has some of the most ravishingly beautiful Pre-Raphaelite paintings, on view in the Birmingham Museum and Art

Gallery). The remaining architectural treasures can be best reached on foot or by public transportation; it's advisable to avoid negotiating the city's convoluted road network. Much of Birmingham is now pedestrian-friendly, the downtown shopping area transformed into pedestrian arcades and buses-only streets. You can also explore along restored canals and canal towpaths. If you are driving, note that Birmingham's inner ring road twists right through the city center.

Exploring Birmingham

Most of Birmingham's sights form a tight-knit group and can be easily explored on a pleasant walk in the mostly pedestrianized center. You can also reach the Jewellery Quarter by public transport, which is the best means for arriving at the Barber Institute and Cadbury World, the only two city sites away from the center. The tourist information center has information on a Tolkien Trail, with six sites in or near the city that are linked to writer J. R. R. Tolkien, who spent 16 of his early years here.

a good tour

Start from the **International Convention Centre** ❶ ⌐, where a tourist desk can equip you with information for your explorations. Cross the canal by the footbridge over to Brindleyplace, full of shops and offices in architecturally interesting new buildings. From the aptly named Water's Edge, cut across Central Square, with its fountains, to the ornate redbrick **Ikon Gallery** ❷—a good coffee stop—to find out what's new in British contemporary art. Retracing your steps over the canal bridge and through the convention center will bring you to **Symphony Hall** ❸. You can see its plush wooden and chrome interior if there's no rehearsal in progress. Entering **Centenary Square** ❹, you face the **Birmingham Repertory Theatre** ❺ and, farther down, the imposing **Hall of Memory** ❻. Centenary Way leads through the shopping arcade past the library into Chamberlain Square, where the magnificent **Birmingham Museum and Art Gallery** ❼ invites a couple of hours' lingering. South of the museum is the classical **Town Hall** ❽, behind which Victoria Square spreads out, with its modern fountains and statues. From here, your route leaves the pedestrianized area and continues northeast through the bustle of Colmore Row to the Georgian **Birmingham Cathedral** ❾, distinguished by its domed tower. Continue north past Snow Hill Station to St. Chad's Circus, where the lofty twin towers of **St. Chad's Roman Catholic Cathedral** ❿ rear incongruously above the busy intersection. Taking the metro from Snow Hill Station a couple of stops to the **Jewellery Quarter** ⓫ would save you the 10-minute walk, but you'd miss some striking examples of 19th-century redbrick and terra-cotta industrial architecture. The fascinating **Museum of the Jewellery Quarter** ⓬ explores the history of the neighborhood. After perusing this and the surrounding area, a short train ride or walk will take you back to the center. For the tour's grand finale, the **Barber Institute of Fine Arts** ⓭—one of the country's most absorbing collections of European art—you must drive or take a taxi or train (from New Street Station).

TIMING   Allow a full day to visit all the sights, which gives you time to linger in the Jewellery Quarter and browse the art museums; allow a half day if

The Welsh Borders

WALES

Liverpool
Widnes
Tatton Park
Styal
Ellesmere Port
Knutsford
Flint
Connah's Quay
42 **Chester**
Jodrell Bank
Crewe
Kidsgrove
Stoke-on-Trent
Wrexham
Nantwich
Whitchurch
Newcastle-under-Lyme
Barlaston
Oswestry
Wem
Market Drayton
Newport
Stafford
Milford
Shrewsbury
29 – **36**
see detail map
The Wrekin
Telford
Cannock
TO LICHFIELD
Attingham Park **37**
Wroxeter
Much Wenlock **38**
Dorrington
Cardington
Longville
39 **Ironbridge Gorge**
Wolverhampton
Stiperstones
LONG MYND
Church Stretton
WENLOCK EDGE
Bridgnorth **40**
Dudley **28**
Craven Arms
Severn Valley Railway
Stourbridge
27
Kidderminster
Ludlow **41**
Bewdley **26**
Bromsgrove
Birmingham
1 – **13**
see detail map
Abberley
25 **Witley Court**
◆ **Avoncroft**
Redditch
Kington
Leominster
Knightwick
Lower Broadheath
16
Droitwich
14 **Worcester**
Bromyard
MALVERN HILLS
17 **Great Malvern**
15 **Pershore**
Hay-on-Wye
Hereford **24**
Ledbury **18**
Malvern Wells
Evesham
Abbey Dore
Grafton
Much Marcle **19**
Tewkesbury
23 **Kilpeck**
Ross-on-Wye
20
WALES
21 **Goodrich**
22
Symond's Yat
Cheltenham
Gloucester

KEY
► Start of itinerary

0 ___ 10 miles
0 ___ 15 km

GREAT BRITAIN

Birmingham

KEY
- Pedestrian roads
- Rail lines
- **i** Tourist information
- ▶ Start of tour

Barber Institute of
Fine Arts **13**

Birmingham Cathedral
(St. Philip's) **9**

Birmingham Museum
and Art Gallery **7**

Birmingham
Repertory Theatre **5**

Centenary Square **4**

Hall of Memory **6**

Ikon Gallery **2**

International
Convention Centre **1**

Jewellery Quarter **11**

Museum of the
Jewellery Quarter **12**

St. Chad's Roman
Catholic Cathedral **10**

Symphony Hall **3**

Town Hall **8**

you intend to confine your walk to the city center. On Sunday some sights have limited opening hours, and the Jewellery Quarter shops are closed.

What to See

off the
beaten
path

AVONCROFT MUSEUM OF HISTORIC BUILDINGS – You can see the architecture typical of the Midlands in microcosm at this 15-acre open-air museum, which has rescued more than 25 structures from destruction. Alongside the half-timber buildings are Victorian chimneys, a collection of phone boxes, and a working windmill. The year-round program of activities and events includes battle reenactments and medieval fairs. Avoncroft is 17 mi southwest of Birmingham. ⊠ *Stokeheath, Bromsgrove* ☎ *01527/831363* ⊕ *www. avoncroft.org.uk* 🎫 *£5.50* ⊙ *Mar., Tues.–Thurs. and weekends 10:30–4; Apr.–June, Sept., and Oct., Tues.–Fri. 10:30–4:30, weekends 10:30–5; July and Aug., weekdays 10:30–5, weekends 10:30–5:30; Nov., weekends 10:30–4.*

★ ⑬ **Barber Institute of Fine Art.** Part of the University of Birmingham, the museum has a small but astounding collection of European paintings, prints, drawings, and sculpture, including works by Bellini, Canaletto, Guardi, Poussin, Murillo, Gainsborough, Turner, Whistler, Renoir, Monet, and van Gogh. To get here, take Cross City Line train from New Street Station south to University Station, or Bus 61, 62, or 63 from the city center. ⊠ *Off Edgbaston Park Rd. near East Gate, Edgbaston* ☎ *0121/414–7333* ⊕ *www.barber.org.uk* 🎫 *Free* ⊙ *Mon.–Sat. 10–5, Sun. noon–5.*

⑨ **Birmingham Cathedral.** The early 18th-century cathedral of St. Philip, a few blocks from Victoria Square, contains some lovely plasterwork in its elegant, gilded Georgian interior. The stained-glass windows behind the altar, designed by the Pre-Raphaelite Edward Burne-Jones (1833–98) and executed by William Morris (1834–96), seem to glow with a garnet hue. ⊠ *Colmore Row, City Centre* ☎ *0121/262–1840* ⊙ *Weekdays 7 AM–7 PM, weekends 9–5* 🎫 *Donation suggested.*

★ ⑦ **Birmingham Museum and Art Gallery.** Vast and impressive, this museum holds a magnificent collection of Victorian art and is known internationally for its works by the Pre-Raphaelites. All the big names are here, including William Holman Hunt, John Everett Millais, and Dante Gabriel Rossetti—reflecting the enormous wealth of 19th-century Birmingham and the aesthetic taste of its industrialists. Galleries of metalwork, silver, and ceramics also reveal some of the city's history, and selections of contemporary art are displayed. ⊠ *Chamberlain Sq., City Centre* ☎ *0121/303–2834* ⊕ *www.bmag.org.uk* 🎫 *Free* ⊙ *Mon.–Thurs. and Sat. 10–5, Fri. 10:30–5, Sun. 12:30–5.*

⑤ **Birmingham Repertory Theatre.** Set to one side of Centenary Square is the home of one of England's oldest and most esteemed theater companies. The Birmingham Rep—as it's always called—has an excellent cafeteria–restaurant in its foyer, behind sweeping windows that allow for a great view over the square. ⊠ *Centenary Sq., Broad St., City Centre* ☎ *0121/236–4455* ⊕ *www.birmingham-rep.co.uk.*

CloseUp

THE VENICE OF THE NORTH

It may come as a surprise that Birmingham has more canals in its center than Venice: its eight canals include 34 mi of waterways. The city is at the heart of a system of restored waterways built during the Industrial Revolution to connect inland factories to rivers and seaports—by 1840 the canals extended more than 4,000 mi throughout the British Isles. These canals, which carried 9 million tons of cargo a year in the late 19th century and helped make the city an industrial powerhouse, have undergone extensive cleanup and renovation, and are now a tourist attraction in their own right.

A walk along a canal near the Gas Street Basin will bring you to modern developments such as Brindleyplace and to pubs, shops, and cafés, and you can see the city from an attractive new perspective. Contact any city tourist office for maps of pleasant walks along the towpaths and for details about canal cruises on colorfully painted barges.

Cadbury World. The village of Bournville (4 mi south of the city center) contains this museum devoted to—what else?—chocolate. In 1879 the Quaker Cadbury brothers moved the family business to this "factory in a garden" from the less than healthy conditions of the city; they also constructed a model village for the factory workers. The museum traces the history of the cocoa bean and the Cadbury dynasty, and you walk through a rain forest along the way. You can watch (and smell) specialties being made in the factory, enjoy free samples, and then stock up from the cut-price shop. The restaurant has specialty chocolate cakes as well as lunches. ⊠ Off A38 (take train from New St. to Bournville Train Station), Bournville ☎ 0121/451–4159 ⊕ www. cadburyworld.co.uk ⊠ £9 ⊙ Mid-Feb.–Oct., daily; mid-Jan.–mid-Feb., Nov. and Dec., Tues.–Thurs. and weekends; times vary; reservations advised, and essential at busy times.

❹ **Centenary Square.** Just outside the International Convention Centre and near the Birmingham Repertory Theatre and Symphony Hall, the square is at the heart of the city's cultural life. Pavement bricks of different shades form a pattern like a Persian carpet. The creamy sculpture in the center of the square, Forward, shows a group of people (and a factory) and represents the city's progressive outlook.

❻ **Hall of Memory.** The octagonal war memorial, neoclassical in style, was built in the 1920s in remembrance of those who fell during World War I. It also honors those who died in World War II. Inside, there's a book containing their names and the poppies laid on Armistice Day. ⊠ Centenary Sq., City Centre ⊠ Free ⊙ Mon.–Sat. 10–4.

❷ **Ikon Gallery.** This gallery, converted from a Victorian Gothic–style school, serves as the city's main venue for exhibitions of contemporary art from Britain and abroad. The bright, white interior is divided into comparatively small display areas, making the shows easily digestible.

✉ *1 Oozells Sq., Brindleyplace, City Centre* ☎ *0121/248–0708* ⊕ *www.ikon-gallery.co.uk* ✑ *Free* ☉ *Tues.–Sun. and national holidays 11–6.*

▶ ❶ **International Convention Centre.** A network of blue struts and gleaming air ducts dominates the main atrium of the high-tech convention center, although indoor trees soften the effect. The **information center** here is useful, but the office at The Rotunda in New Street is more fully stocked. ✉ *Broad St., City Centre* ☎ *0121/200–2000* ⊕ *www.necgroup.co.uk* ☉ *Daily 7 AM–11:30 PM.*

> **need a break?**
>
> The balcony of the redbrick **Malt House** (✉ 75 King Edward's Rd. ☎ 0121/633–4171) is just the place to linger over a drink as you watch canal life go by. Former president Bill Clinton had a beer here during the G8 Summit in 1998.

⓫ **Jewellery Quarter.** For more than two centuries, jewelers have worked in the district of Hockley, northwest of the city center; today more than 200 manufacturing jewelers and 50 silversmiths continue the tradition, producing a third of the jewelry made in Britain. (This is a great place to shop for jewelry, too.) The city has its own Assay Office, which hallmarks 13 million items each year with the anchor symbol denoting Birmingham origin. The ornate green and gilded Chamberlain Clock marks the center of the district. ✉ *Hockley* ⊕ *www.the-quarter.com.*

> **off the beaten path**
>
> **LICHFIELD CATHEDRAL** – It's worth a detour (14 mi northeast of Birmingham on A38) to explore the only English cathedral with three spires. The current sandstone building, beautifully sited by a tree-fringed pool, dates mainly from the 12th and 13th centuries, and the Lady Chapel glows with some fine 16th-century stained glass from the Cistercian abbey of Herkenrode, near Liège, in Belgium. Half-timber houses surround the peaceful grounds, and the town itself has attractive Georgian buildings as well as the birthplace museum of lexicographer Dr. Samuel Johnson. ✉ *19A The Close, Lichfield* ☎ *01543/306100* ⊕ *www.lichfield-cathedral.org* ✑ *Suggested donation £3* ☉ *Daily 7:30–6:15; closes Sun. at 5 in winter.*

⓬ **Museum of the Jewellery Quarter.** The museum is built around the workshops of Smith & Pepper, a firm that operated here for more than 80 years until 1981; little has changed since the early 1900s. The factory tour and exhibits explain the history of the neighborhood and the jeweler's craft, and you can watch jewelry being made. ✉ *75–79 Vyse St., Hockley* ☎ *0121/554–3598* ⊕ *www.bmag.org.uk* ✑ *Free* ☉ *Weekdays 10–4, Sat. 11–5; last admission 1 hr before closing.*

ℭ **National Sea Life Centre.** As far from the sea as you can get in Britain, this imaginatively landscaped aquarium allows a glimpse into Davey Jones's locker. An underwater tunnel lets you view sharks and stingrays up close, and there are displays of oceanic and freshwater marine life. Children will gravitate to the touch pools and other interactive activities. ✉ *The Water's Edge, Brindleyplace, City Centre* ☎ *0121/643–6777* ⊕ *www.sealife.co.uk* ✑ *£8.95* ☉ *Mid-Feb.–Oct., daily 10–5; Nov.–mid-Feb., weekdays 10–4, weekends 10–5.*

⑩ St. Chad's Roman Catholic Cathedral. Dating from 1841, this redbrick pile was the first Roman Catholic cathedral to be built in England after the Reformation. A. W. N. Pugin, leading architect of the Gothic revival, designed St. Chad's, which basically consists of one lofty room—the nave—divided by soaring slender pillars and decorated in red, blue, and gold. Many furnishings are 15th-century. ⊠ *Queensway, City Centre* ☎ *0121/230–6208* 🖃 *Free* ☉ *Daily 8–6:30.*

❸ Symphony Hall. Attending a concert here is sufficient reason to visit Birmingham. The internationally recognized City of Birmingham Symphony Orchestra won awards for its recordings under its former conductor, Sir Simon Rattle (who occasionally guest conducts). Symphony Hall occupies the same building as the International Convention Centre. ⊠ *Broad St., City Centre* ☎ *0121/780–3333* ⊕ *www.necgroup.co.uk.*

☾ Thinktank. This interactive museum in the state-of-the-art Millennium Point center allows you to explore science and the history of Birmingham over four floors of galleries. You can walk into the giant boiler of a steam engine, explore deep space, program a robot to play the drums, and even perform a hip operation. ⊠ *Curzon St., Digbeth* ☎ *0121/202–2222* ⊕ *www.thinktank.ac* 🖃 *£6.95* ☉ *Daily 10–5; last admission at 4.*

❽ Town Hall. Classical columns surround this mid-19th-century performance hall, a copy of the Temple of Castor and Pollux in Rome. The former home of the symphony orchestra heard the premieres of Mendelssohn's *Elijah* and Elgar's *Dream of Gerontius*. The hall is due to reopen in October 2006 after a lengthy refurbishment. Locals have affectionately dubbed the statue of a woman in the prominent fountain outside the building "the floozie in the Jacuzzi." ⊠ *Victoria Sq., City Centre.*

Where to Eat

££££–£££££
★
✕ **Paris.** Star chef Patrick McDonald has created an enclave of sophistication in the trendy Mailbox shopping center. Chocolate-color walls, oil paintings, and slinky leather chairs complement superb French-influenced food. Main dishes such as seafood fricassee with bouillabaisse or pigeon with shallots and Madeira jus, and desserts such as hot passion fruit soufflé, do not disappoint. The gourmand menu is £55. Reservations are essential on weekends. ⊠ *The Mailbox, 109–111 Wharfside St., City Centre* ☎ *0121/632–1488* 🖃 *AE, MC, V* ☉ *Closed Sun. and Mon.*

££–£££
✕ **Café Lazeez.** This spacious, warmly decorated new wave Indian restaurant in a shopping center blends the traditional with the contemporary taste for lighter, less oily dishes. Try the Peshawari naan bread as an accompaniment to prawns with saffron rice and coconut sauce or herbed breast of chicken. ⊠ *The Mailbox, 116 Wharfside St., City Centre* ☎ *0121/643–7979* 🖃 *AE, MC, V.*

★ ££–£££
✕ **Le Petit Blanc.** An outpost of noted chef Raymond Blanc (of Le Manoir aux Quat' Saisons, near Oxford), this brasserie provides a contemporary showcase of gleaming metal, light wood, and plate glass for the excellent regional French menu. The deep-fried goat's cheese with mustard dressing is one of the fine starters; you might follow up with pan-fried

cod fillet with butter beans and fennel. ⊠ *9 Brindleyplace, City Centre* ☎ *0121/633–7333* ⊟ *AE, DC, MC, V.*

££–£££ ✕ **Shimla Pinks.** Birmingham has some of Britain's finest Indian restaurants, and this is one upbeat choice—the name refers to the "bright young things" of India's upper classes. Both the decoration and the cooking are a mix of modern and traditional, and waiters are elegantly turbaned. Try the Assamese *jalfrezi,* pieces of meat with coriander leaves and red peppers, or *rogan josh* made from fresh tomatoes, paprika, and chili. The Sunday evening buffet is abundant. ⊠ *214 Broad St., City Centre* ☎ *0121/633–0366* ⊟ *AE, MC, V.*

££ ✕ **Henry's.** This popular, traditional Cantonese restaurant in the Jewellery Quarter is a haven for lunch during a shopping spree. The menu lists more than 180 dishes; there's also a good-value fixed-price menu and a Sunday buffet. ⊠ *27 St. Paul's Sq., City Centre* ☎ *0121/200–1136* ⊟ *AE, DC, MC, V.*

££ ✕ **Thai Edge.** The elegant, contemporary Asian design will draw you into this restaurant. Dishes such as *gang keow waan* (green curry cooked in coconut milk with eggplant, lime leaves, and basil) are excellent. You can eat all you want for £13 at the Sunday lunch buffet. ⊠ *7 Oozells Sq., City Centre* ☎ *0121/643–3993* ⊟ *AE, DC, MC, V.*

£–££ ✕ **Brass House.** The city's first foundry is now a useful central place for full meals or bar snacks. Look for such traditional favorites as steak, roast ham and parsley sauce, and even the humble "chip buttie" (a sandwich filled with french fries). The pastel, marbled glass lights on the bar are an attraction in their own right. ⊠ *44 Broad St., City Centre* ☎ *0121/633–3383* ⊟ *AE, MC, V.*

Where to Stay

£££–£££££ ▦ **Birmingham Marriott Hotel.** Once a group of offices, this elegant building from the early 20th century now contains a luxurious hotel. The interior is rich with dark wood and chandeliers; the spacious bedrooms offer all the latest comforts. Note the Egyptian theme in the health club. The West 12 restaurant serves fine contemporary cuisine. On weekends, a full breakfast is included. ⊠ *12 Hagley Rd., Five Ways, B16 8SJ* ☎ *0121/452–1144, 800/228–9290 in U.S.* ⊟ *0121/456–3442* ⊕ *www.marriott.com* ⌂ *104 rooms, 4 suites* ⌂ *Restaurant, in-room data ports, cable TV with movies, pool, health club, spa, meeting rooms, parking (fee), some pets allowed* ⊟ *AE, DC, MC, V* �Ⓘ *BP.*

£££–£££££ ▦ **Burlington Hotel.** Wood paneling, marble, and classical columns abound at this traditional hotel, and rooms are individually decorated in a conservative style with dark woods and print fabrics. At the sumptuous Berlioz restaurant, English dishes such as liver with onion tart share menu space with classic French-influenced dishes. On weekends, a full breakfast is included. ⊠ *Burlington Arcade, 126 New St., City Centre, B2 4JQ* ☎ *0121/643–9191* ⊟ *0121/628–5005* ⊕ *www.burlingtonhotel.com* ⌂ *112 rooms* ⌂ *Restaurant, in-room data ports, cable TV with movies, gym, sauna, business services, meeting rooms, parking (fee), some pets allowed; no a/c* ⊟ *AE, DC, MC, V* Ⓘ *BP.*

★ ▦ **New Hall.** A tree-lined drive leads through 26 acres of gardens and **£££–£££££** open land to this moated 12th-century manor-house-turned-country-hotel. The public rooms reflect the house's long history with touches such as the 16th-century oak paneling and Flemish glass, 18th-century chandeliers, and a stone fireplace from the 17th century. Guest rooms, most in a more modern section, are done in English country style with print fabrics and marble-tile baths. At the elegant formal restaurant, you can indulge in sophisticated English and French cuisine. The hotel is 7 mi northeast of the city center. ⊠ *Walmley Rd., Sutton Coldfield, Birmingham, B76 1QX* ☎ *0121/378–2442, 800/847–4358 in U.S.* 🖷 *0121/378–4637* ⊕ *www.thistlehotels.com* ⚲ *60 rooms* ⚬ *Restaurant, some in-room data ports, cable TV with movies, 9-hole golf course, tennis court, pool, gym, hot tub, sauna, spa, croquet, bar, meeting rooms, free parking, some pets allowed; no a/c in some rooms* ☰ *AE, DC, MC, V* ⦿ *BP.*

£££–££££ 🏨 **Hotel du Vin & Bistro.** A Victorian eye hospital, right in the city center, received a makeover from this *très* hip mini-chain but retains details such as the ironwork double stairway and marble columns. Beyond the imposing redbrick exterior is an inner courtyard with a fountain and garden. Bedrooms are sleek and contemporary, with huge, fluffy towels and white linens. The bistro dining room is redolent of fin-de-siècle Paris, and in the Bubble Lounge you can drown in more than 50 varieties of champagne. ⊠ *25 Church St., City Centre, B3 2NR* ☎ *0121/200–0600* 🖷 *0121/236–0889* ⊕ *www.hotelduvin. com* ⚲ *66 rooms* ⚬ *Restaurant, in-room data ports, cable TV, gym, sauna, spa, steam room, bar, meeting rooms, parking (fee); no a/c* ☰ *AE, DC, MC, V.*

££–££££ 🏨 **City Inn.** This bustling, absolutely up-to-the-minute hotel in the canalside piazza, near the waterside nightlife scene, represents an excellent value. The crisp, modern bedrooms and bathrooms, though on the small side, are beautifully equipped; white and gray, with a splash of red, set off the light-wood furniture. Breakfast is included in the price on weekends. ⊠ *1 Brunswick Sq., Brindleyplace, City Centre, B1 2HW* ☎ *0121/643–1003* 🖷 *0121/643–1005* ⊕ *www.cityinn.com* ⚲ *238 rooms* ⚬ *Restaurant, in-room data ports, cable TV with movies, gym, meeting rooms, parking (fee)* ☰ *AE, DC, MC, V.*

££ 🏨 **Copperfield House Hotel.** In a quiet location a few minutes' drive from Cadbury World, this family-run hotel, a converted Victorian house with secluded lawns and simple guest rooms, is nevertheless convenient to the bustle of the city center 2 mi away. The restaurant serves good English cooking, including delicious desserts. ⊠ *60 Upland Rd., Selly Park, Birmingham, B29 7JS* ☎ *0121/472–8344* 🖷 *0121/415–5655* ⊕ *www.copperfieldhousehotel.co.uk* ⚲ *17 rooms* ⚬ *Restaurant, bar, free parking, some pets allowed (fee); no a/c* ☰ *AE, MC, V* ⦿ *BP.*

£–££ 🏨 **Fountain Court.** A five-minute drive from the city center, this cheerful family-run hotel is in a leafy, well-heeled neighborhood. Bedrooms are modern and bright, and the more traditional public rooms have patterned carpets and dark-wood furniture. ⊠ *339–343 Hagley Rd., Edgbaston, B17 8NH* ☎ *0121/429–1754* 🖷 *0121/429–1209* ⊕ *www. fountain-court.net* ⚲ *23 rooms* ⚬ *Restaurant, bar; no a/c* ☰ *AE, DC, MC, V* ⦿ *BP.*

Nightlife & the Arts

Nightlife

The city's thriving nightlife scene is concentrated around Broad and Hurst streets, as well as the Brindleyplace and Mailbox areas. **The Bar** (⊠ The Church, 55 Broad St., City Centre ☎ 0121/632–5501), converted from a church, has turned from God to Mammon. It's a bar in the early evening and later plays commercial dance music for the over-21s. **Mechu** (⊠ 59 Summer Row, City Centre ☎ 0121/212–1661), a chic drinking, dining, and dancing venue, has a roof garden. At **52°** North (⊠ Arcadian, Hurst St., City Centre ☎ 0121/622–5250), the bar specializes in classic and contemporary cocktails and mixes 14 types of martinis.

The Arts

Birmingham's performing arts companies are well regarded throughout the country. Catch a performance if you can.

BALLET   The **Birmingham Royal Ballet** (⊠ Hurst St., City Centre ☎ 0870/730–1234), the second company of the Royal Ballet, is based at the Hippodrome Theatre, which also hosts visiting companies such as the Welsh National Opera.

CONCERTS   The **City of Birmingham Symphony Orchestra** (⊠ International Conven-
★   tion Centre, Broad St., City Centre ☎ 0121/780–3333) performs regularly in Symphony Hall, also a venue for visiting artists.

THEATER   The **Alexandra Theatre** (⊠ Station St., City Centre ☎ 0870/607–7533) welcomes touring companies on their way to or from London's West End. The **Birmingham Repertory Theatre** (⊠ Centenary Sq., Broad St., City Centre ☎ 0121/236–4455), founded in 1913, is equally at home with modern or classical work.

Sports & the Outdoors

Boating

Birmingham's canals provide a novel perspective on the city. You can take an hour ride on a canal barge from **Sherborne Wharf** (⊠ Sherborne St., City Centre ☎ 0121/455–6163). Trips leave daily mid-April through October at 11:30, 1, 2:30, and 4, and on weekends throughout the rest of the year, departing from the International Convention Centre Quayside.

Cricket

To watch first-class cricket at one of the country's most hallowed venues, head for **Warwickshire County Cricket Club** (⊠ County Ground, Edgbaston ☎ 0121/446–5506). Tickets for test matches sell out six months ahead, but those at county level are not so sought after.

Shopping

The glass-roofed **Bullring** (⊠ between New St. and High St., City Centre ☎ 0121/632–1500) has three floors of retail therapy, including two department stores, Debenhams and the stunningly curved Selfridges, which is covered with aluminum disks. The development has been seen as another step in the city's regeneration. The **Jewellery Quarter** (⊠ Hockley ☎ 0121/554–3598) has more than 100 shops that sell and repair gold

and silver handcrafted jewelry, clocks, and watches. The Museum of the Jewellery Quarter sells a selection of contemporary work and provides information on artisans and retail outlets. **The Mailbox** (⊠ 150 Wharf-side St., City Centre ☎ 0121/632–1000), once a Royal Mail sorting office, entices with trendy shops and designer outlets such as Harvey Nichols and Armani, restaurants, and hotels, including Malmaison.

FROM WORCESTER TO DUDLEY

In the arc of towns to the west of Birmingham and the cluster of places around the banks of the River Wye, history and tradition rub up against deepest rural England. The cathedral towns of Worcester and Hereford make great bases to soak up the bucolic flavor of the Malverns and Elgar country, or to view the spectacular swing of the Wye at Symond's Yat. En route, there's a taste of Georgian architecture at Pershore and Bewdley, and reminders of the old industrial Midlands at Stourbridge and Dudley.

Worcester

▶ **⑭** *27 mi southwest of Birmingham, 118 mi northwest of London.*

Worcester (pronounced *wuss*-ter), on the River Severn in the center of Worcestershire, is an ancient place proud of its history, and in particular, of its nickname, "the Faithful City," bestowed on the town for steadfast allegiance to the crown during the English Civil War. In that conflict between king and Parliament, two major battles were waged here. The second one, the decisive Battle of Worcester of 1651, resulted in the exile of the future Charles II. Since the mid-18th century the town's name has become synonymous with the fine bone china produced here. Despite unfortunate "modernization" in the 1960s, some of medieval Worcester remains. This ancient section forms a convenient and pleasant walking route around the great cathedral. Worcester's mainly pedestrianized High Street runs through the center of town, from the cathedral to Foregate Street train station.

★ There are few more quintessentially English sights than that of **Worcester Cathedral,** its towers overlooking the green expanse of the county cricket ground, and its majestic image reflected in the swift-flowing—and frequently flooding—waters of the River Severn. A cathedral has stood on this site since 680, and much of what remains dates from the 13th and 14th centuries. Notable exceptions are the Norman crypt (built in the 1080s), the largest in England, and the ambulatory, a cloister built around the east end. The most important tomb in the cathedral is that of King John (1167–1216), one of the country's least-admired monarchs, who alienated his barons and subjects through bad administration and heavy taxation and in 1215 was forced to sign the Magna Carta, the great charter of liberty. The cathedral's most beautiful decoration is in the vaulted **chantry chapel of Prince Arthur,** Henry VII's elder son, whose body was brought to Worcester after his death at Ludlow in 1502. The wealthy endowed chantry chapels to enable priests to celebrate masses there for the souls of the deceased. ⊠ *College Yard at High St.* ☎ *01905/28854* ⊕ *www.cofe-worcester.org.uk* ⊠ *Suggested donation £3* ☉ *Daily 8–6.*

At the **Royal Worcester Porcelain Factory,** you can browse in the show-rooms or rummage in the seconds and clearance shops; the January and July sales have especially good bargains. Tours of the factory take you through the process of making bone china figurines. (Note that children under 11 aren't admitted on tours.) The **Museum of Worcester Porcelain** displays the world's largest collection of Worcester porcelain, bone china, and earthenware, representing work from the start of manufacturing in 1751 to the present. The factory lies south of Worcester Cathedral (follow Severn Street). ⊠ *Severn St.* ☎ *01905/21247* ⊕ *www. royal-worcester.co.uk* ᠌ *Visitor center £2.75; museum £3.95; 1-hr tour of factory £5.45; tour, museum, and visitor center £9:30; prebooked 2-hr Connoisseur Tours £18* ☉ *Mon.–Sat. 9–5:30, Sun. 11–5; tours Mon.–Thurs. 10:30–2:30.*

Now an enthralling museum focusing on the Civil War, the **Commandery** occupies a cluster of 15th-century half-timber buildings that were built as a poorhouse and later became the headquarters of the Royalist troops during the Battle of Worcester. The museum presents a colorful audiovisual presentation about the war in the magnificent, oak-beam Great Hall. The Commandery is across the road from the porcelain factory, minutes from the cathedral. ⊠ *Sidbury* ☎ *01905/361821* ⊕ *www. worcestercitymuseums.org.uk* ᠌ *£3.95* ☉ *Mon.–Sat. 10–5, Sun. 1:30–5.*

The wood-paneled rooms in the black-and-white **Greyfriars** building, a merchant's house that dates to the 15th century, contain fine period textiles and furniture. The parlor has some rare Georgian hunting wallpaper. Admission is by timed ticket. ⊠ *Friar St.* ☎ *01905/722349* ⊕ *www. nationaltrust.org.uk* ᠌ *£3.20* ☉ *Mar.–June and Sept.–Dec., Wed.–Sat. 1–5; July and Aug., Wed.–Sun. 1–5.*

Also the location of the tourist information office, the **Guildhall,** set back behind ornate iron railings, has an 18th-century facade with gilded statues of Queen Anne, Charles I, and Charles II. Note the carving of Cromwell's head pinned up by the ears. In the Assembly Room, impressive patrician portraits hang under a painted ceiling; you can admire them while having tea and buns. ⊠ *High St.* ☎ *01905/723471* ᠌ *Free* ☉ *Weekdays 8:30–4:30, Sat. 8:30–4.*

Where to Stay & Eat

★ **£££££** ✕ **Brown's.** A former grain mill contains this light, airy riverside restaurant. The fixed-price menu and daily specialties revolve around simple, well-prepared dishes. You might try poussin (a young chicken) with noodles or duck with plum and ginger sauce; finish up with rice pudding and poached rhubarb or caramelized banana cake. ⊠ *24 Quay St.* ☎ *01905/26263* ▭ *AE, MC, V* ☉ *Closed Mon. No lunch Sat., no dinner Sun.*

££–£££ ✕ **King Charles II Restaurant.** A half-timber house in which Charles II hid after the Battle of Worcester is now an oak-paneled, silver-service restaurant that exudes friendliness. The cuisine is mainly French and Italian, but traditional English selections such as beef Wellington and fish dishes including Dover sole meunière also appear on the menu. ⊠ *29 New St.* ☎ *01905/22449* ▭ *AE, DC, MC, V* ☉ *Closed Sun.*

£££ ▦ **Diglis House Hotel.** English artist John Constable was a frequent visitor to this idyllically sited 18th-century house overlooking terraced gardens and the river. Service is discreet but friendly, and furnishings are uncluttered and elegant. Choose between views over the garden or river when you dine. ⊠ *Severn St., WR1 2NF* ☎ *01905/353518* 🖷 *01905/ 767772* ⊕ *www.diglishousehotel.co.uk* ⤵ *29 rooms* ♤ *2 restaurants, bar, meeting rooms; no a/c* ☰ *AE, MC, V* ⑩ *BP.*

££ ▦ **Ye Olde Talbot Hotel.** The Olde Talbot was originally a courtroom belonging to the cathedral, which stands close by. Modern extensions supplement the 16th-century core of the building. The spacious bedrooms have double-glazed windows and are done in blue, red, and orange tones with patterned fabrics. ⊠ *Friar St., WR1 2NA* ☎ *01905/23573* 🖷 *01905/ 612760* ⊕ *www.yeoldetalbot.co.uk* ⤵ *27 rooms* ♤ *Restaurant, cable TV, in-room data ports, some pets allowed; no a/c* ☰ *AE, DC, MC, V* ⑩ *BP.*

Nightlife & the Arts

Huntingdon Hall (⊠ Crowngate ☎ 01905/611427), a refurbished Methodist chapel founded in 1773, puts on a varied program of music and poetry recitals year-round. The original pews are—thankfully—provided with cushions.

In 2005, Worcester and Worcester Cathedral will host the **Three Choirs Festival** (☎ 01905/616200 ⊕ www.3choirs.org), which rotates with Gloucester and Hereford. It takes place over one week in mid-August and concentrates on British music and large-scale choral works.

Sports & the Outdoors

BOATING In Worcester you can easily rent boats or take short cruises on the Severn. **Bickerline River Trips** (⊠ South Quay near the cathedral ☎ 01905/ 831639 or 0775/375–7424) runs 45-minute excursions on a small passenger boat daily on the hour, March through October.

HORSE RACING You can have a day at the races at **Worcester Racecourse** (⊠ Pitchcroft ☎ 0870/220–2772), attractively set on the banks of the River Severn. Admission prices start at £5.

Shopping

Bygones (⊠ Dean's Way ☎ 01905/25388 ⊠ 55 Sidbury ☎ 01905/ 23132) sells antiques, items of fine craftsmanship, and small gifts in silver, glass, and porcelain. **G. R. Pratley** (⊠ The Shambles ☎ 01905/ 22678) has tables piled high with fine china, such as Royal Worcester, Wedgwood, and Spode; it's closed Thursday afternoon. Many shoppers will first head for the emporium at the **Royal Worcester Porcelain Factory** (⊠ Severn St. ☎ 01905/23221), where, among other merchandise, you can buy seconds.

Pershore

🖲 *8 mi southeast of Worcester.*

In the fruitful Vale of Evesham sits the peaceful, unspoiled market town of Pershore. This is plum and asparagus country; trees are loaded down with blossoms in spring, and May sees the asparagus harvest. Georgian buildings with elegant facades flank the town's wide streets.

The nave of **Pershore Abbey** did not survive the dissolution of the monasteries, but the beautiful chancel and crossing have been preserved. The choir has a rare plowshare vault (so called because the curved panels resemble the blade of a plowshare) with soaring ribs that culminate in 41 carved bosses; no two are the same. Architect George Gilbert Scott opened up the fine lantern tower in the 1860s to reveal the internal tracery. He replaced the old bell-ringing chamber with a suspended platform that seems to float in space. ✉ *Church Row* ☎ *01386/552071* ⊕ *www.pershoreabbey.fsnet.co.uk* ✇ *Free* ☉ *Apr.–Oct., daily 9–5; Nov.–Mar., daily 9–4.*

Where to Stay

£££ ⌂ **Evesham Hotel.** Definitely family-centered and upbeat, this modernized Georgian house-turned-lodging stocks an abundance of toys, games, and teddy bears for all ages; there's even a rubber duck in the bathrooms. For more sophistication, opt for one of the theme rooms: the Aquarium has its own fish tank, and the Egyptian room sarcophagi and an impressive bed. The 2 acres of gardens make a peaceful refuge, though the hotel is close to town. Evesham is 6 mi southeast of Pershore. ✉ *Cooper's La., off Waterside, Evesham WR11 1DA* ☎ *01386/765566* 📠 *01386/765443* ⊕ *www.eveshamhotel.com* ⇨ *40 rooms* ⌂ *Restaurant, bar, indoor pool, meeting rooms, some pets allowed; no a/c* ▤ *AE, D, MC, V* ⦿ *BP.*

Lower Broadheath

⑯ *10 mi northwest of Pershore, 2 mi west of Worcester.*

Southwest of Worcester lie the Malvern Hills, their long, low, purple profiles rising starkly from the surrounding plain. These hills inspired much of the music of Sir Edward Elgar (1857–1934), as well as his remark that "there is music in the air, music all around us." The village of Lower Broadheath is on the B4204.

The **Elgar Birthplace Museum,** in a peaceful little garden, is the tiny brick cottage in which the composer was born. The house contains personal memorabilia, and the Elgar Centre exhibits photographs, musical scores, and letters. ✉ *Crown East La.* ☎ *01905/333224* ⊕ *www.elgar.org* ✇ *£4.50* ☉ *Feb.–Dec., daily 11–4:15.*

Great Malvern

⑰ *9 mi south of Lower Broadheath, 7 mi south of Worcester.*

Great Malvern, off the A449, is a Victorian spa town whose architecture has changed little since the mid-1800s. Exceptionally pure spring water is still bottled here and exported worldwide—the Queen never travels without a supply. Great Malvern is known both as an educational center and as a place for old folks' homes. The town also has a Winter Gardens complex with a theater, cinema, and gardens. During three days in mid-June, the agricultural **Three Counties Show** (☎ 01684/584900 ⊕ www.threecounties.co.uk) showcases rare animal breeds, equestrian events, competitions for the best cows, pigs, and sheep, and plenty of food.

CloseUp

ON THE MENU

Outside Birmingham, this area is all rich farming country where, for centuries, the orchards have produced succulent fruit, especially apples and plums. Hereford cider, for example, is popular because it tastes much sweeter than the cider brewed farther south in Devon. The meat and milk products, which come from the local black-and-white breed of cattle, are second to none. Cheshire cheese, one of the country's oldest cheeses, is noted for its rich, crumbly texture; blue-veined

Shropshire cheese is more unusual and worth trying. In May the sheltered Vale of Evesham is the center for the asparagus crop. Ludlow produces a formidable assortment of local meat products and is noted for its sausages.

Despite the natural bounty, formal dining establishments are few and far between in this rural area, with the notable exception of Ludlow, which has a group of superb restaurants.

The **Priory,** a solidly built early Norman Benedictine abbey with later Per-pendicular elements, dominates the steep streets downtown. Vertical lines of airy tracery and fine 15th-century glass decorate the building. ✉ *En-trance opposite church* ☎ *01684/561020* ⊕ *www.greatmalvernpriory.org. uk* ✍ *Free* ☉ *Apr.–Oct., daily 9–6:30; Nov.–Mar., daily 9–4:30.*

Where to Stay & Eat

£££–£££££ ✕⌂ **Cottage in the Wood.** This family-run hotel sits on shady grounds high up the side of the Malvern Hills, with splendid views of the coun-tryside. Country-house furnishings in the three buildings include floral prints and white bedspreads; rooms with a view are equipped with binoculars. The mirrored restaurant, which has the best of the panorama, serves modern English fare such as cumin-roasted salmon with saffron potatoes. You can choose from more than 600 wines, among them many local vintages. ✉ *Holywell Rd., WR14 4LG* ☎ *01684/575859* 🖶 *01684/560662* ⊕ *www.cottageinthewood.co.uk* ➫ *20 rooms* ♨ *Restaurant, in-room data ports, bar, Internet, meeting rooms, some pets allowed; no a/c* ⊟ *AE, MC, V* ❙⊙❙ *BP.*

£–££ ⌂ **Sidney House.** In addition to having stunning views, this dignified early-19th-century hotel, run by a friendly husband-and-wife team, is near the town center. Rooms, done in pastel hues, are furnished with stripped pine and period pieces. On a clear afternoon you can sit on the terrace and gaze out over the Vale of Evesham to the Cotswolds. ✉ *40 Worcester Rd., WR14 4AA* 🖶🖶 *01684/574994* ⊕ *www.sidneyhouse.co.uk* ➫ *8 rooms* ♨ *In-ternet, some pets allowed; no a/c, no room phones* ⊟ *AE, DC, MC, V* ❙⊙❙ *BP.*

Nightlife & the Arts

Malvern has historical connections with Sir Edward Elgar as well as with George Bernard Shaw, who premiered many of his plays here. The October **Malvern Festival** (☎ 01684/892277 or 01684/892289), origi-nally devoted to the works of Elgar and Shaw, also presents new music and drama.

Ledbury

18 *10 mi southwest of Great Malvern on A449.*

Among the black-and-white half-timber buildings that make up the market town of Ledbury, take special note of two late-16th-century ones: the Feathers Hotel and the Talbot Inn. Almost hidden behind the 17th-century market house, cobbled Church Lane, crowded with medieval half-timber buildings, leads to St. Michael's Church. The **Old Grammar School**, a heritage center in an old school, traces the history of local industries. It also has displays on two literary celebrities linked to the area, John Masefield and Elizabeth Barrett Browning. ⊠ *Church La.* ☎ *01531/ 636147* ☜ *Free* ☉ *Apr.–Oct., daily 10:30–4:30.*

★ Completed in 1820, **Eastnor Castle**, a turreted, stone, Norman Revival extravaganza on the eastern outskirts of Ledbury, includes some magnificent, ornate, neo-Gothic salons designed by 19th-century architect Augustus Pugin. The Hervey-Bathurst family has restored other grand rooms, all full of lush tapestries, gilded paintings, Regency chandeliers, and Auntie's old armchairs, to the height of *le style anglais*, making Eastnor a must-see for lovers of English interior decoration. ⊠ *A438* ☎ *01531/ 633160* ⊕ *www.eastnorcastle.com* ☜ *House and grounds £6.50, grounds only £4.50* ☉ *July and Aug., Sun.–Fri. 11–5; mid-Apr.–June and Sept., Sun. and national holidays 11–5; last admission 30 mins before closing.*

Where to Stay & Eat

£££–££££ ✕☒ **Feathers Hotel.** You can't miss the striking black-and-white facade of this central hostelry, which dates from the 16th century. The interior has a satisfyingly antique flavor, with creaking staircases and ancient floorboards, and some rooms have four-posters. The hop-bedecked Fuggles Brasserie (so named after a variety of hop) serves plenty of fresh fish, as well as lighter meals. If you're indulging, try the Herefordshire duck or beef. ⊠ *High St., HR8 1DS* ☎ *01531/635266* ☐ *01531/ 638955* ⊕ *www.feathers-ledbury.co.uk* ☜ *19 rooms* ☖ *Restaurant, cable TV, indoor pool, health club, bar, Internet, meeting rooms, some pets allowed; no a/c* ▭ *AE, DC, MC, V* ☖ *BP.*

Much Marcle

19 *4 mi southwest of Ledbury.*

Much Marcle is one of the English villages still holding the ancient annual ceremony of "wassailing"—beating the apple trees to make them fruitful in the coming year. The ritual takes place on Twelfth Night, January 6. Effigies and tombs richly endow the beautiful 13th-century church here, notably the exquisitely carved tomb of Blanche, Lady Grandison. If you have a detailed map and plenty of time, wander around the area and discover tiny villages down sleepy lanes overhung by high hedges.

Just outside Much Marcle lies the beautiful 17th-century manor of **Hellens**, still in singularly authentic and pristine condition. Part of the house dates from the 13th century and contains fine old-master paintings. The gloom and dust are part of the experience; candles illuminate the house, and central heating has been scorned. ✉ ½ *mi east of Much Marcle* ☎ *01531/660504* ⊕ *www.hellensmanor.com* 🎫 *£5* ⊙ *Apr.–Sept., Wed. and weekends 2–5; tours at 2, 3, and 4.*

Ross-on-Wye

❷ *6 mi southwest of Much Marcle.*

Perched high above the River Wye, Ross-on-Wye seems oblivious to modern-day intrusions and remains at heart a small market town. Its steep streets come alive on Thursday and Saturday—market days—but they're always a happy hunting ground for antiques.

Where to Stay

£££–££££ 🏨 **Chase Hotel.** The public areas in this well-renovated Georgian-style country-house hotel on 11 acres of grounds retain some original elements. Bedrooms in the main house are simply and comfortably furnished in pastels and print fabrics, and those in the newer wing are more modern. ✉ *Gloucester Rd., HR9 5LH* ☎ *01989/763161* 📠 *01989/768330* ⊕ *www.chasehotel. co.uk* 🛏 *36 rooms* ⚒ *Restaurant, in-room data ports, in-room VCRs, cable TV, gym, Internet, meeting rooms; no a/c* ⊟ *AE, DC, MC, V* ⊠| *BP.*

Goodrich

㉑ *3 mi south of Ross-on-Wye on B4234, 3 mi north of Symond's Yat on B4229.*

The ruins of a castle that resembles a fortress from the Rhineland dominate the village of Goodrich. Looming dramatically over the River Wye crossing at Kerne Bridge, **Goodrich Castle** from the south looks picturesque amid the green fields, but you quickly see its grimmer face from the battlements on its north side. Dating from the late 12th century, the red sandstone castle is surrounded by a deep moat carved out of solid rock, from which its walls appear to soar upward. Built to repel Welsh raiders, Goodrich was destroyed in the 17th century during the Civil War. ✉ *Off A40* ☎ *01600/890538* ⊕ *www.english-heritage.org.uk* 🎫 *£3.70* ⊙ *Mar.–May, daily 10–5; June–Aug., daily 10–6; Sept. and Oct., daily 10–5; Nov.–Feb., Thurs.–Sun. 10–4.*

Symond's Yat

㉒ *3 mi south of Goodrich, 6 mi south of Ross-on-Wye.*

Outside the village of Symond's Yat ("gate"), the 473-foot-high Yat Rock commands superb views of the River Wye as it winds through a narrow gorge and swings around in a great 5-mi loop.

Kilpeck

㉓ *15 mi northwest of Goodrich, 7 mi southwest of Hereford.*

Tucked away on a minor road off the A465, the tiny hamlet of Kilpeck is blessed with one of the best-preserved Norman churches in Britain. Much of the village, along with the remains of a castle and the church, is protected as a Scheduled Ancient Monument. The red sandstone **Kilpeck church,** completed in the mid-12th century, is lavishly decorated inside and out with sculpted carving exceptional for a country church. The carvings depict all manner of subjects, including animals. Some showed scenes so scandalously frank that high-minded Victorians removed them. (One or two ribald ones remain, however, so look carefully.) Don't miss the gargoyle rainwater spouts, either. ☎ *01981/ 570315* 🖾 *Donations accepted* ⊘ *Daily 9–dusk.*

Hereford

㉔ *7 mi northeast of Kilpeck, 56 mi southwest of Birmingham, 31 mi northwest of Gloucester, 54 mi northeast of Cardiff.*

A busy country town, Hereford is the center of a wealthy agricultural area known for its cider, fruit, and cattle—the white-faced Hereford breed has spread across the world. It's also an important cathedral city, and the massive Norman building towers proudly over the River Wye. Before 1066, Hereford was the capital of the Anglo-Saxon kingdom of Mercia and, earlier still, the site of Roman, Celtic, and Iron Age settlements. Today people come primarily to see the cathedral but quickly discover the charms of a town that has changed slowly but unobtrusively with the passing centuries.

Built of local red sandstone with a large central tower, **Hereford Cathedral** retains some fine 11th-century Norman carvings but suffered considerable "restoration" in the 19th century. Inside, its greatest glories include a 12th-century chair, one of the earliest pieces of furniture in the country and reputedly used by King Stephen, and some fine misericords (the elaborately carved undersides of choristers' seats). The cathedral's brass-rubbing center has copies of memorial brasses from around Britain; it's open in summer or by appointment. ✉ *Cathedral Close* ☎ *01432/374200, 01432/374202 for brass-rubbing center hrs* ⊕ *www. herefordcathedral.co.uk* 🖾 *Suggested donation £2, tours £2.50* ⊘ *Mon.–Sat. 7:30–6:30, Sun. 8–4:30; tours Apr.–Oct., daily 11 and 2.*

★ The **Mappa Mundi and Chained Library Exhibition,** an extraordinary double attraction, includes the more than 20-square-foot parchment Mappa Mundi. Hereford's own picture of the medieval world shows the Earth as flat, with Jerusalem at its center. It's now thought that the map was originally the central section of an altarpiece dating from 1290. The chained library contains some 1,500 books, among them an 8th-century copy of the Four Gospels. Chained libraries, in which books were attached to cupboards to discourage theft, are extremely rare: they date from medieval times, when books were as precious as gold. ✉ *Cathedral Close* ☎ *01432/374200* ⊕ *www.herefordcathedral.co.uk* 🖾 *£4.50* ⊘ *Apr.–Sept., Mon.–Sat. 10–5, Sun. 11–4; Oct.–Mar., Mon.–Sat. 11–4; last admission 45 mins before closing.*

The half-timber **Old House** is a fine example of domestic Jacobean architecture, furnished in 17th-century style on three floors. You can see a kitchen and hall, among other rooms. ✉ *High Town* ☎ *01432/ 260694* 🖾 *Free* ⊘ *Apr.–Sept., Tues.–Sat. 10–5, Sun. and national holidays 10–4; Oct.–Mar., Tues.–Sat. 10–5.*

The 13th-century **All Saints Church,** on the west side of High Town, contains superb canopied choir stalls and misericords, as well as an unusual Queen Anne reredos in the south chapel. There's also an excellent coffee bar and restaurant.

A farm cider house and a cooper's workshop have been re-created at the **Cider Museum,** where you can tour ancient cider cellars with huge oak vats. Cider brandy (applejack) is made here, and the museum sells its own brand, along with other cider items. ⊠ *Pomona Pl. at Whitecross Rd.* ☎ *01432/354207* ⊕ *www.cidermuseum.co.uk* ⊠ *£3* ☉ *Apr.–Oct., daily 10–5; Nov.–Mar., Tues.–Sun. 11–3.*

Where to Stay & Eat

★ £ ✕ **Café @ All Saints.** The west end and gallery of this community-minded church are given over to a coffee bar and restaurant, giving you a rare opportunity to indulge body and spirit at one sitting. The imaginative vegetarian menu is worth every penny, but for something lighter, try the tasty sandwiches, salads, cakes, and local ice creams. ⊠ *High St.* ☎ *01432/370415* ⊟ *MC, V* ☉ *Closed Sun. No dinner.*

£££££ ✕▥ **Castle House.** These conjoined Georgian villas next to the moat (all that remains of Hereford Castle) offer luxury and a warm welcome. Delicate plasterwork graces the public areas. The spacious rooms vary in style, with yellow, gold, and cream the preferred colors; each bedroom contains a decanter of cider brandy. The restaurant specializes in French fare with an Asian accent. ⊠ *Castle St., HR1 2NW* ☎ *01432/356321* 🖷 *01432/365909* ⊕ *www.castlehse.co.uk* ↪ *15 rooms* ♿ *Restaurant, in-room data ports, refrigerators, cable TV, in-room VCRs, bar, Internet, business services, meeting rooms, some pets allowed; no a/c in some rooms* ⊟ *AE, DC, MC, V* ▥ *CP.*

£ ▥ **Grafton Villa Farm.** Warm period rooms with antiques and rich furnishings fill this peaceful, early-18th-century farmhouse 2 mi south of the city. For breakfast, choose between scrambled eggs provided by the resident hens or local bacon and sausages. ⊠ *Off A49, Grafton, HR2 8ED* ☎ *01432/268689* ⊕ *www.graftonvilla.co.uk* ↪ *3 rooms* ♿ *No a/c, no room phones, no smoking* ⊟ *No credit cards.*

Shopping

Hereford has a different market each day—food, clothing, livestock—on New Market Street.

The stores in **Capuchin Yard** (⊠ Off 29 Church St.) display crafts, including handmade shoes and knitwear; other outlets sell books, posters, and watercolors. For high-quality foods, head for the **Left Bank Village** (⊠ Bridge St. ☎ 01432/34900) development and browse the delicatessen, patisserie, ice cream parlor, and wine shop.

Witley Court

❷ *27 mi northeast of Hereford, 10 mi northwest of Worcester.*

The romantic shell of Witley Court conjures up the Victorian heyday of the imposing stately home—a huge Italianate pile—that stood here before it was ravaged by fire in 1937. In contrast to this ruin, the tiny baroque parish church on the grounds is perfectly preserved. Note its parapet with balustrades, and the small golden dome over its cupola. Inside are 10 colored windows, a ceiling painted by Antonio Bellucci, and the ornate case of an organ once used by Handel. Witley Court's glorious gardens are being restored, and the enormous Perseus and Andromeda and the Flora fountains send their jets skyward. The Jerwood sculpture park contains works by Elizabeth Frink and Antony Gormley, among others. The house is little less than a mile outside Great Witley. ⊠ *A443, Great Witley* ☎ *01299/896636* ⊕ *www.english-heritage.org.uk* ⊠ *£4.90* ⊙ *Apr.–Sept., daily 10–6; Oct., daily 10–5; Nov.–Mar., Wed.–Sun. 10–4.*

Where to Stay & Eat

££££–£££££ ✕⊡ **Elms Hotel.** Formal gardens and 10 acres of grounds surround this ivy-clad Queen Anne mansion, now a luxurious, traditional country-house hotel 16 mi northeast of Worcester and near Great Witley. Gilbert White, a pupil of Sir Christopher Wren, designed the house, and public areas retain their original ornate plasterwork. All rooms are individually decorated in warm colors and include antiques. The restaurant creates imaginative contemporary fare using organic produce and vegetables from the garden. ⊠ *Stockton Rd., Abberley, WR6 6AT* ☎ *01299/896666* 🖨 *01299/896804* ⊕ *www.slh.com* 🛏 *21 rooms* ⚹ *Restaurant, in-room data ports, tennis court, croquet, Internet, meeting rooms, helipad; no a/c* ⊟ *AE, DC, MC, V* ⱺ *BP.*

Bewdley

㉖ *8 mi north of Great Witley, 14 mi north of Worcester, 3 mi west of Kidderminster.*

In Bewdley, an exceptionally attractive Severn Valley town, many tall, narrow-front Georgian buildings are clustered around the river bridge. The 18th-century butchers' market, the **Shambles,** now holds a museum of local history, trades, and crafts, with exhibits and demonstrations of rope-making and clay-pipe-making. Craftspeople working in wood, glass, and felt occupy the nearby workshops. ⊠ *Load St.* ☎ *01299/ 403573* ⊠ *Free* ⊙ *Apr.–Sept., daily 10–4:30; Oct., daily 11–4.*

ⵒ Bewdley is a southern terminus of the **Severn Valley Railway,** a steam railroad running 16 mi north along the river to Bridgnorth. It stops at a handful of sleepy stations where time has apparently stood still since the age of steam. You can get off at any of these stations, picnic by the river, and walk to the next station to get a train back. ⊠ *Railway Station* ☎ *01299/403816* ⊕ *www.svr.co.uk* ⊠ *£10.80 round-trip* ⊙ *Mid-May–Sept., trains run daily; Oct.–mid-May, weekends only.*

Stourbridge

㉗ *8 mi northeast of Bewdley via A451, 11 mi west of Birmingham.*

Stourbridge is the home of Britain's crystal glass industry, and although the industry is in decline, exquisite glassware is still being produced. A number of shops sell "factory seconds" bargains.

The **Stourport Steamer Co.** has short river trips, or you can take longer journeys as far as Worcester on Wednesday from the last week in July through August. ✉ *Riverside Walk* ☎ *01299/871177 or 0786/046–8792* ⊕ *www.riverboathire.co.uk* 🎫 *£3.50–£9* ⊙ *Mar.–mid-July and Sept., Sun.; mid-July–Aug., daily.*

Shopping

The **Crystal Glass Centre** (✉ Churton House, Audnam ☎ 01384/354400), a mile north of Stourbridge on the A491 Wolverhampton road, stocks ★ international glassware and local products; it's open daily. The **Stuart Crystal Visitor Centre and Factory Shop** (✉ Bridge St., Wordsley ☎ 01384/ 261777), open daily, carries a good selection of gift items.

Dudley

🟢 *6 mi northeast of Stourbridge, 8 mi west of central Birmingham.*

It was in Dudley, in the 17th century, that coal was first used for smelting iron. The town subsequently became known as the capital of the Black Country, a term that arose from the air pollution caused by iron-★ ⏱ works foundries and coal mining. The **Black Country Living Museum,** established to interpret the area's industrial heritage, consists of an entire village reconstructed of disused buildings from around the region. Among the exhibits on 26 acres are a chain-maker's house and workshop, with demonstrations of chain-making; a small trap works that made animal traps; a druggist and general store, where costumed women describe life in a poor industrial community in the 19th century; a Methodist chapel; the Bottle & Glass pub; Stables restaurant, serving such traditional delicacies as faggots and peas (a fried pork-liver dish); and a coal mine and wharf. The reconstructed brick-and-terra-cotta Rolfe Street Baths building (brought here from Smethwick) gives an overview of the Black Country. You can also ride on a barge (extra charge) through a tunnel to experience the canal travel of yesteryear. ✉ *Tipton Rd.* ☎ *0121/ 557–9643* ⊕ *www.bclm.co.uk* 🎫 *£9.95, barge trip £3.95* ⊙ *Mar.–Oct., daily 10–5; Nov.–Feb., Wed.–Sun. 10–4.*

At the **New Royal Brierley Experience,** next to the Black Country Living Museum, you can witness the making of glass (all by hand) on a factory tour, view documents and pieces from the Brierley company's 300 years of history, and browse through samples in the shop. ✉ *Tipton Rd.* ☎ *0121/530–5600* 🎫 *£2* ⊙ *Weekdays 9–5:30, Sat. 9–5, Sun. 10–4; self-guided factory tours finish at 3.*

FROM SHREWSBURY TO CHESTER
SKIRTING THE "BLACK COUNTRY"

The "peak" of this region—in terms of height—is the Wrekin, a hill geologists claim to be the oldest in the land, and a hill A. E. Housman and others have invested with some of their poetic charm. From its isolated summit you can gaze on a peaceful rural scene, quite different from most people's preconceptions of the industrial Midlands. Ironbridge, several miles from the Wrekin, has two identities, as a place as well as a thing. The thing itself is the first bridge to be made of iron, erected between

1777 and 1779. Now taken over by the Ironbridge Gorge Museum Trust, the bridge is the centerpiece of a vast Industrial Revolution museum complex. The place is the 6-mi stretch of the Ironbridge Gorge, once an awesome scene of mining and charcoal-burning that reeked with smoke and the stench of sulfur. Ironworks forges and coal-mining created the pollution that gave this region west of Birmingham its name—the Black Country—during the mid-19th century. The stretch has been transformed into a scene of idyllic beauty, scars grassed over, woodland filling the gaps left by tree-felling. Within easy reach of Ironbridge, rural Shropshire spreads invitingly, with towns long famed as beauty spots, such as Bridgnorth and Ludlow. Around this area are two important cities of the Welsh Border region: Shrewsbury and Chester, both famous for their medieval heritage and their wealth of half-timber buildings.

Shrewsbury

47 mi northwest of Dudley, 55 mi north of Hereford, 46 mi south of Chester, 48 mi northwest of Birmingham.

One of England's most important medieval towns, Shrewsbury (usually pronounced *shrose*-bury), the county seat of Shropshire, lies within a great horseshoe loop of the Severn. It has numerous 16th-century half-timber buildings—many built by well-to-do wool merchants—plus elegant ones from later periods. Today the town retains a romantic air (indeed, there are many bridal shops, along with churches), and it can be a lovely experience to stroll the Shrewsbury "shuts." These narrow alleys overhung with timbered gables lead off the central market square, which was designed to be closed off at night to protect local residents. The town is especially proud of its flower displays: in summer, filled window boxes and hanging baskets make a vivid contrast to the black-and-white buildings.

Walking is an ideal way to see Shrewsbury, and traffic has been banned on some of the most historic streets. A good starting point for a walking tour is the small square between Fish Street and Butcher Row. These streets are little changed since medieval times, when some of them took their names from the principal trades carried on there, but Peacock Alley, Gullet Passage, and Grope Lane clearly got their names from somewhere else. The stone spire of **St. Mary's church** (⊠ off Castle St.), built around 1200, is one of the three tallest in England. The church merits a visit for its superb stained glass, collected from continental churches by a Victorian vicar, and its Victorian encaustic tiles. ⊠ *St. Mary's St.* ☎ *01743/ 357006* 🔄 *Donations welcome* ☉ *Weekdays 10–5, Sat. 10–4.*

❸⓪ **St. Alkmund's,** prominent on the Shrewsbury skyline, is worth seeing for its stained glass. It was built in 1795 on the site of a much earlier church. ⊠ *St. Alkmund's Pl., off Fish St.* ☉ *Apr.–Oct., Mon.–Sat. 10–5; Nov.–Mar., Mon.–Sat. 10–2.*

❸① Bear Steps is a cluster of restored half-timber buildings that link Fish Street with Market Square; the most notable building is the massive **Ireland's Mansion,** built in 1575 with elaborate Jacobean timbering and richly decorated with quatrefoils. It's not open to the public.

Ireland's
Mansion **31**

Quarry Park . .**33**

St. Alkmund's .**30**

St. Chad **34**

St. Mary's **29**

Shrewsbury
Abbey **36**

Shrewsbury
Castle **35**

Shrewsbury
Museum and
Art Gallery . . .**32**

Shrewsbury

0 — 440 yards
0 — 400 meters

KEY
🛈 *Tourist information*

need a break?

The timbered lace-curtained room and—if the weather is right—the courtyard at **Poppy's Tea Rooms** (⊠ Milk St., off Wyle Cop ☏ 01743/232307) make a pleasant stop for coffee, teas, and some satisfying snacks. It's closed Sunday.

③ A magnificent 16th-century timber-frame warehouse and a brick-and-stone mansion built in 1618 house the **Shrewsbury Museum and Art Gallery,** with collections of antique clothing and Shropshire pottery and ceramics, as well as Roman finds (such as a unique silver mirror from nearby Wroxeter) and items of local history. A reconstructed 17th-century bedroom has oak, holly, and walnut paneling and a four-poster bed. Changing exhibits display contemporary art. ⊠ *Barker St.* ☏ *01743/ 361196* ⊕ *www.shrewsburymuseums.com* ☞ *Free* ☉ *Apr.–Sept., Tues.–Sat. 10–5, Sun. and Mon. 10–4; Oct.–Mar., Tues.–Sat. 10–4.*

③ Below Swan Hill, the manicured lawn of **Quarry Park** slopes down to the river. In a sheltered corner is the **Dingle,** a colorful garden with floral displays. To reach the park from the center of town, head for Welsh Bridge and stroll along the riverbank, or walk up Claremont Hill.

③ On a hilltop west of the town center, the church of **St. Chad,** designed by George Steuart, the architect of Attingham Park, is one of England's most original ecclesiastical buildings. Completed in 1792, the round Georgian church is surmounted by a tower that is in turn square, octagonal, and circular—and finally topped by a dome. When being built, it provoked riots among townsfolk averse to its radical style. The interior has a fine Venetian east window and a brass Arts and Crafts pulpit. ⊠ *St. Chad's Terrace* ☎ *01743/365478* 🖃 *Free* ☉ *Apr.–Oct., daily 8–5; Nov.–Mar., daily 8–1.*

③⑤ Guarding the northern approaches to the town, **Shrewsbury Castle** rises up over the River Severn at the bottom of Pride Hill. Originally Norman, it was dismantled during the Civil War and later rebuilt by Thomas Telford, the distinguished Scottish engineer who designed many notable buildings and bridges at the beginning of the 19th century. The castle holds the **Shropshire Regimental Museum.** ⊠ *Shrewsbury Castle, Castle Gates* ☎ *01743/358516* ⊕ *www.shrewsburymuseums.com* 🖃 *£2* ☉ *Mid-Feb.–Mar. and Oct.–Dec., Wed.–Sat. 10–4; Apr. and May, Tues.–Sat. 10–5; June–Sept., Tues.–Sat. 10–5, Sun. and Mon. 10–4. Castle grounds daily 10–4.*

③⑥ **Shrewsbury Abbey,** now unbecomingly surrounded by busy roads, was founded in 1083 and later became a powerful Benedictine monastery. The abbey church has survived many vicissitudes, including the dissolution of the monasteries, and retains a good 14th-century west window above a Norman doorway. The abbey figures in the whodunits by Ellis Peters that feature Brother Cadfael; the novels provide an excellent idea of local life in the Middle Ages. To reach the abbey from the center of town, cross the river by the English Bridge. ⊠ *Abbey Church, Abbey Foregate* ☎ *01743/232723* ⊕ *www.shrewsburyabbey.com* 🖃 *Suggested donation £2* ☉ *Apr.–Oct., daily 9:30–4:30; Nov.–Mar., daily 10:30–3.*

Where to Stay & Eat

£££££ ✕ **Country Friends.** An attractive black-and-white building, 5 mi south of Shrewsbury by the A49, houses this light and airy restaurant overlooking a garden and pond. Typical dishes on the set-price menu include potato cake with smoked salmon, pancetta, and horseradish, and guinea fowl with wild mushroom risotto. The restaurant also has a simple double bedroom available (dinner, bed, and breakfast package for two comes to £135). ⊠ *Dorrington* ☎ *01743/718707* 🖃 *MC, V* ☉ *Closed Sun.–Tues., 2 wks mid-July, mid-wk in Oct.*

£££ ✕ **Draper's Hall.** The dark wood paneling, antique furniture, and warm, intimate lighting of this 16th-century hall make it a distinctive dining spot for contemporary cuisine. You might start with a salad of beetroot leaves, wild mushrooms, and Parmesan flakes, and follow up with ostrich with goat's cheese and red pepper; leave room for desserts such as caramelized pineapple with honeycomb ice cream. There are also plenty of cheeses and salad choices. ⊠ *10 St. Mary's Pl.* ☎ *01743/344679* 🖃 *AE, MC, V* ☉ *Closed Mon.*

£–££ ✕ **The Armoury.** This smartly converted warehouse, whose arched windows overlook the river, is well stocked with books, prints, and curiosities, as well as good food, wines, and real ales. Among the appetizers is leek and blue cheese tart. Braised lamb with rosemary is a popular main course, and you can try marmalade bread-and-butter pudding for dessert. ✉ *Victoria Quay* ☎ *01743/340525* ☰ *AE, MC, V.*

££££ 🏨 **Albright Hussey Hotel.** Lovely gardens surround this Tudor manor house, originally the home of the Hussey family, which dates back to 1524 and combines black-and-white half-timbering with a later (1560) redbrick-and-stone extension. Beams, oak paneling, four-poster beds, and antiques enhance rooms in the original building; those in the extension are plainer. The hotel is 2½ mi north of Shrewsbury on A5228. ✉ *Ellesmere Rd., SY4 3AF* ☎ *01939/290571* 🖷 *01939/291143* ⊕ *www.albrighthussey. co.uk* ⟿ *22 rooms, 4 suites* ♿ *Restaurant, 2 bars, meeting rooms, some pets allowed (fee); no a/c, no kids under 3* ☰ *AE, DC, MC, V* �🍽 *BP.*

££–£££ 🏨 **The Lion Hotel.** Parts of this once-renowned coaching inn in the heart of town date to the 14th century; today the hotel envelops you in the 17th century–style luxury for which it became famous. Rooms are small and traditionally furnished, but the glorious lounge, with its high ceiling, oil paintings, and enormous carved-stone fireplace, truly sets the Lion apart. Add to this the magnificent Adam Ballroom, and you can see the appeal for former guests such as Charles Dickens, Benjamin Disraeli, and King William IV. Breakfast is included in the price on weekends. ✉ *Wyle Cop, SY1 1UY* ☎ *01743/353107* 🖷 *01743/352744* ⊕ *www.regalhotels.co.uk/thelion* ⟿ *59 rooms* ♿ *Restaurant, some in-room data ports, cable TV, bar, lounge, business services, meeting rooms; no a/c* ☰ *AE, DC, MC, V.*

££ 🏨 **Sandford House.** The hospitable Richards family runs this late-Georgian bed-and-breakfast close to the river and the town center. Original decorative plasterwork is still much in evidence; modern pine furnishes the bedrooms. Room 5 is seven-sided, with a beautiful molded ceiling. ✉ *St. Julian Friars, SY1 1XL* ☎ *01743/343829* ⊕ *www.sandfordhouse. co.uk* ⟿ *18 rooms* ♿ *Some pets allowed; no a/c, no room phones, no smoking* ☰ *AE, MC, V* �🍽 *BP.*

Nightlife & the Arts

During the **Shrewsbury International Music Festival** (☎ 01606/872633), in June and July, the town vibrates to traditional and not-so-traditional music by groups from Europe and North America.

Shopping

The Parade (✉ St. Mary's Pl. ☎ 01743/343178), just behind St. Mary's church, is a shopping mall created from the neoclassical former Royal Infirmary, built in 1830. One of the most appealing malls in England, it has attractive boutiques, apartments upstairs, a restaurant, and a terrace overlooking the river.

Attingham Park

③⑦ *4 mi southeast of Shrewsbury.*

Built in 1785 by George Steuart (architect of the church of St. Chad in Shrewsbury) for the first Lord Berwick, this elegant stone mansion has a three-story portico, with a pediment carried on four tall columns. The building overlooks a sweep of parkland, including a deer park landscaped by Humphrey Repton (1752–1818), and there are lovely walks by the river and in the deer park. Inside the house are painted ceilings and delicate plasterwork, a fine picture gallery designed by John Nash (1752–1835), and a collection of 19th-century Neapolitan furniture. ⊠ *B4380, off A5, Atcham* ☎ *01743/708162* ⊕ *www.nationaltrust.org. uk* ⊡ *£5.50, park and grounds only £2.70* ☉ *House mid-Mar.–Oct., Fri.–Tues. noon–5, national holidays 11–5; last admission 1 hr before closing. Park and grounds Mar.–Oct., daily 10–8; Nov.–Feb., daily 10–5.*

en route Continuing southeast on B4380, you can see, rising on the left, the **Wrekin,** a strange, wooded, conical, extinct volcano that is 1,335 feet high. The walk to the summit, which has panoramic views of the area, is about 5 mi. A few miles farther on, you enter the wooded gorge of the River Severn.

Much Wenlock

38 *8 mi southeast of Attingham Park, 12 mi southeast of Shrewsbury.*

Much Wenlock, a town on A458, is full of half-timber buildings, including a 16th-century guildhall. The romantic ruins of Norman **Wenlock Priory** are in an attractive garden full of topiary. ⊠ *High St.* ☎ *01952/727466* ⊕ *www.english-heritage.org.uk* ⊡ *£3* ☉ *Apr., May, Sept., and Oct., Thurs.–Mon. 10–5; June–Aug., daily 10–6; Nov.–Mar., Wed.–Sun. 10–4.*

Sports & the Outdoors

The high escarpment of **Wenlock Edge** runs southwest from Much Wenlock and provides a splendid view. This is hiking country, and if a healthful walk sounds inviting, turn off B4371 through Church Stretton into Cardingmill Valley, or to the wide heather uplands on top of Long Mynd. You can park and set off on foot.

Ironbridge Gorge

★ **39** *15 mi east of Shrewsbury, 28 mi northwest of Birmingham.*

Ironbridge Gorge is the name given to a group of villages south of Telford that were crucial in ushering in the Industrial Revolution. The Shropshire coalfields were of enormous importance to the development of the coke-smelting process, which helped make producing anything in iron much easier. The nine component sections of the **Ironbridge Gorge Museum,** spread over 6 square mi, preserve and interpret the area's fascinating industrial history. There's no public transport between them, so you need your own vehicle. Allow at least a full day to appreciate all the major sights and to perhaps take a stroll around the famous iron bridge or hunt for Coalport china in the stores clustered near it. The best starting point is the **Museum of the Gorge,** which has a good selection of literature and an audiovisual show on the gorge's history. In nearby Coalbrookdale, the **Museum of Iron** explains the production of iron and steel. You can see the original blast furnace built by Abraham Darby, who developed the original coke process in 1709. Adjacent to this, the interactive **Enginuity** exhibition is a hands-on, feet-on exploration of engineering, offering the opportunity to pull a locomotive, control a boiler, and even "fly" a magnetic carpet. From here, drive the few miles along the river until the arches of the **Iron Bridge** come into view; it was designed by T. F. Pritchard, smelted by Darby, and erected between 1777 and 1779. This infinitely graceful arch spanning the River Severn can best be seen—and photographed or painted—from the towpath, a riverside walk edged with wildflowers and dense shrubs. The tollhouse on the far side houses an exhibition on the bridge's history and restoration.

A mile farther along the river is the old factory and the **Coalport China Museum** (the china is now made in Stoke-on-Trent). Exhibits show some of the factory's most beautiful wares, and craftspeople give demonstrations. Above Coalport is **Blists Hill Victorian Town**, where you can see old mines, furnaces, and a wrought-iron works. But the main draw is the re-creation of the "town" itself, with its doctor's office, sweet-smelling bakery, grocer's, candle-maker's, sawmill, printing shop, and candy store. At the entrance you can change some money for specially minted pennies, which you can use to make purchases from the shops. Shopkeepers, the bank manager, and the doctor's wife are on hand in period dress to give you advice or information. Craft demonstrations are scheduled in summer. ⊠ *B4380, Ironbridge, Telford* ☎ *01952/ 884391* ⊕ *www.ironbridge.org.uk* ✉ *Ticket to all sights £13.25* ⊙ *Apr.–Oct., daily 10–5; Nov.–Mar., Sat.–Wed. 10–4.*

Where to Stay & Eat

£ ✕ **New Inn.** This Victorian building was moved from Walsall, 22 mi away, so that it could be part of the Blists Hill Victorian Town. It's a fully functioning pub, with gas lamps, sawdust on the floor, and traditional ales served from the cask. For an inexpensive meal, you can try a ploughman's lunch, a pasty from the antique-style bakery, or a pork pie from the butcher's store next door. ⊠ *Blists Hill Victorian Town* ☎ *01952/ 601010* ⊟ *MC, V.*

££££ ✕▩ **Clarion Hotel at Madeley Court, Telford.** Guest rooms in this restored 16th-century stone manor house, once the home of Abraham Darby, are rich in antiques and period furnishings. Modern rooms are available as well. The Priory Restaurant occupies the original Great Hall and serves contemporary British food; the brasserie is a less expensive option (both have fixed-price menus). The garden has a rare example of an Elizabethan stone cube sundial. ⊠ *Castlefields Way, Madeley, Telford, TF7 5DW* ☎ *01952/680068* 🖷 *01952/684275* ⊕ *www.choicehotelseurope.com* ➲ *47 rooms* ♿ *Restaurant, some in-room data ports, cable TV, bar, Internet, meeting rooms, some pets allowed; no a/c* ⊟ *AE, DC, MC, V* ⦿ *BP.*

★ ££ ▩ **Library House.** At one point the village's library, this small guest house on the hillside near the Ironbridge museums (and only a few steps from the bridge itself) has kept its attractive Victorian style while allowing for modern-day luxuries—a video library, for instance. Service is warm without being obtrusive; a glass of wine awaits you on arrival. ⊠ *11 Severn Bank, Ironbridge, Telford, TF8 7AN* ☎ *01952/432299* 🖷 *01952/ 433967* ⊕ *www.libraryhouse.com* ➲ *4 rooms* ♿ *Cable TV, in-room*

VCRs, some pets allowed; no a/c, no room phones, no kids under 10, no smoking ⊟ *No credit cards* ⊘ *Closed 1st 3 wks in Jan.* ⏍ *BP.*

Bridgnorth

④ *9 mi south of Ironbridge, 22 mi southeast of Shrewsbury, 25 mi west of Birmingham.*

Perching perilously on a high sandstone ridge on the banks of the Severn, the attractive market town of Bridgnorth has two distinct parts, High Town and Low Town, connected by a winding road, flights of steep steps, and—best of all—a cliff railroad. Even the tower of the Norman castle seems to suffer from vertigo, having a 17° list (three times the angle of the Leaning Tower of Pisa). Severn Valley Railway trains, which originate in Bewdley or Kidderminster, terminate here.

Ludlow

④ *29 mi south of Shrewsbury, 24 mi north of Hereford.*

Fodor'sChoice
★

Pretty Ludlow has medieval, Georgian, and Victorian buildings and a finer display of black-and-white half-timber buildings than even Shrewsbury. The great Church of St. Lawrence on College Street dominates the center, its extravagant size a testimony to the town's prosperous wool trade. Cross the River Teme and climb Whitcliff for the most spectacular view. The town is also a perfect example of how small rural places (the population is around 10,000) can become culinary hot spots, in this case from the buzz generated by a cluster of outstanding restaurants. The **Ludlow and the Marches Food Festival** (☎ 01584/861586 ⊕ www. foodfestival.co.uk) takes place over a weekend in mid-September and consists of demonstrations, competitions, and tastings (including local sausages, ale, and cider).

Dating from 1085, the massive, ruined, red sandstone **Ludlow Castle** dwarfs the town; it served as a vital stronghold for centuries and was the seat of the Marcher Lords who ruled "the Marches," the local name for the border region. The two sons of Edward IV—the little princes of the Tower of London—spent time here before being dispatched to London and their death in 1483. The earl of Powys owns the castle. Follow the terraced walk around the castle for a lovely view of the countryside. ⊠ *Castle Sq.* ☎ *01584/873355* ⊕ *www.ludlowcastle.com* 🏷 *£3.50* ⊘ *Jan., weekends 10–4; Feb., Mar., and Oct.–Dec., daily 10–4; Apr.–July and Sept., daily 10–5; Aug., daily 10–7; last admission 30 mins before closing.*

off the beaten path

STOKESAY CASTLE – This 13th-century fortified manor house built by a wealthy merchant is arguably the finest of its kind in England. Inside the main hall, the wooden cruck roof and timber staircase (a rare survival) demonstrate state-of-the-art building methods of the day. Outside, the cottage-style garden creates a bewitching backdrop for the magnificent Jacobean timber-frame gatehouse. ⊠ *Craven Arms, off the A49 Shrewsbury road, 7 mi northwest of Ludlow* ☎ *01588/672544* ⊕ *www.english-heritage.org.uk* 🏷 *£4.50* ⊘ *Apr., May, Sept., and Oct., Thurs.–Mon. 10–5; June–Aug., daily 10–6; Nov.–Mar., Fri.–Sun. 10–4.*

Where to Stay & Eat

££££ ✕ **Hibiscus.** French chef Claude Bosi creates dishes with panache: step
Fodor'sChoice into the two small rooms (one stone-walled, the other oak-paneled) of
★ this 17th-century building and feast on creations such as pan-fried foie
gras with licorice, pear, and lemon, or eel with pork belly and pineapple purée on the changing (fixed-price) menu. The adventurous may opt
for the puy lentil (a tiny black lentil), butternut squash, or basil ice cream.
Book well ahead. ⊠ *17 Corve St.* ☎ *01584/872325* ⌖ *Reservations
essential* ▤ *MC, V* ☺ *Closed Sun. and Mon, 1st 2 wks in Jan. and last
2 weeks in July. No lunch Tues.*

£££££ ✕ **The Merchant House.** Tucked away in the northern end of town, this
Fodor'sChoice black-and-white Jacobean building could be mistaken for a private ter-
★ raced house. Service at the small restaurant is not fussy, and the superb
daily-changing set menu reflects the eclectic preferences of chef Shaun
Hill, relying on organic products where possible. Typical dishes include
sea bass with saffron and pepper sauce, and Muscat creme caramel with
prunes. ⊠ *Lower Corve St.* ☎ *01584/875438* ⌖ *Reservations essential* ▤ *MC, V* ☺ *Closed Sun., Mon., 1 wk in late Dec., and 1 wk in
spring. No lunch Tues.–Thurs.*

££££–£££££ ✕▥ **Dinham Hall.** A converted merchant's town house dating from
1792, this hotel near Ludlow Castle formerly served as a boys' dormitory for the local grammar school. The owners have successfully integrated modern comforts—including comfortable furniture and print
fabrics—with the original historic elements. The deep-pink dining room
serves creative fixed-price meals, with choices such as breast of duck
with red cabbage or seared brill on oyster mushrooms with butternut
squash risotto. ⊠ *Off Market Sq., SY8 1EJ* ☎ *01584/876464* 🖷 *01584/
876019* ⊕ *www.dinhamhall.co.uk* 🛏 *15 rooms* ⌂ *Restaurant, meeting rooms, some pets allowed (fee); no a/c* ▤ *AE, DC, MC, V* ⧈ *BP.*

★ ✕▥ **Mr. Underhill's.** Occupying a converted mill building beneath the cas-
£££–£££££ tle, this secluded restaurant with rooms looks onto the wooded River
Teme. Both restaurant (closed Tuesday; reservations essential) and rooms
are informal, with plenty of pictures, and the bright bedrooms are furnished in natural fabrics. The superb, modern-British, fixed-price menu,
customized when you book, uses only fresh seasonal ingredients. Dinner could be *pavé* (a cold mousse) of brill with cardamom and wild lime
sauce or local venison with red wine and chocolate, followed by rhubarb
crumble and ginger ice cream. Book well ahead. ⊠ *Dinham Weir, SY8
1EH* ☎ *01584/874431* ⊕ *www.mr-underhills.co.uk* 🛏 *7 rooms*
⌂ *Restaurant; no a/c, no smoking* ▤ *MC, V* ⧈ *BP.*

£££–££££ ▥ **The Feathers.** Even if you're not staying here, you can't help but admire the extravagant half-timber facade of this building, described by
the architectural historian Nicholas Pevsner as "that prodigy of timber-
framed houses." The interior is equally impressive—dripping with ornate plaster ceilings, carved oak, paneling, beams, and creaking floors.
Some guest rooms are done in modern style, but others preserve the antique look. ⊠ *The Bull Ring, SY8 1AA* ☎ *01584/875261* 🖷 *01584/
876030* ⊕ *www.feathersatludlow.co.uk* 🛏 *40 rooms* ⌂ *Restaurant,
cable TV with movies, Internet, meeting rooms, some pets allowed
(fee); no a/c* ▤ *AE, DC, MC, V* ⧈ *BP.*

££ 🏠 **Hen and Chickens.** Creaking floors and sloping ceilings abound in this 18th-century former pub. Bedrooms are simply furnished, bathrooms are sizable, and on the breakfast table are home-produced eggs and preserves, as well as the famous local sausages. ⊠ *103 Old St., SY8 1NU* ☎ *01584/874318* ⊕ *www.hen-and-chickens.co.uk* 🛏 *4 rooms* ⚬ *No a/c, no room phones, no kids under 10, no smoking* ═ *MC, V* ❘◯❘ *BP.*

Nightlife & the Arts

The two-week **Ludlow Festival** (☎ 01584/872150 ⊕ www.ludlowfestival. co.uk), starting in late June, includes Shakespeare performed near the ruined castle and opera, ballet, and concerts around town.

Chester

㊷ *75 mi north of Ludlow, 46 mi north of Shrewsbury.*

Cheshire is mainly a land of well-kept farms, supporting their herds of cattle, but numerous places here are steeped in history. Villages contain many fine examples of the black-and-white "magpie" type of architecture more often associated with areas to the east. The thriving center of the region is Chester, a city similar in some ways to Shrewsbury, though it has many more black-and-white half-timber buildings (some of which were built in Georgian and Victorian times), and its medieval walls still stand. Chester has been a prominent city since the late 1st century AD, when the Roman Empire expanded north to the banks of the River Dee. The original Roman town plan is still evident: the principal streets, Eastgate, Northgate, Watergate, and Bridge Street, lead out from the Cross—the site of the central area of the Roman fortress—to the four city gates, and the partly excavated remains of what is thought to have been the country's largest Roman amphitheater lie to the south of Chester's medieval castle. Since Roman times, seagoing vessels have sailed up the estuary of the Dee and anchored under the walls of Chester. The port enjoyed its most prosperous period during the 12th and 13th centuries.

History seems more tangible in Chester than in many other ancient cities. Much medieval architecture remains in the compact town center, and modern buildings have not been allowed to intrude. A negative result of this perfection is that Chester has become a favorite bus-tour destination, with gift shops, noise, and crowds.

★ Chester's unique **Rows**, which originated in the 12th and 13th centuries, are essentially double rows of stores, one at street level and the other on the second floor with galleries overlooking the street. The Rows line the junction of the four streets in the old town. They have medieval crypts below them, and some reveal Roman foundations.

The city **walls**, accessible from several points, provide splendid views of the city and its surroundings. The whole circuit is 2 mi, but if your time is short, climb the steps at Newgate and walk along toward Eastgate to see the great ornamental **Eastgate Clock**, erected to commemorate Queen Victoria's Diamond Jubilee in 1897. Lots of small shops near this part of the walls sell old books, old postcards, antiques, and jewelry. Where the **Bridge of Sighs** (named after the enclosed bridge in Venice that it closely resembles) crosses the canal, descend to street level and walk up Northgate Street into Market Square.

Tradition has it that a church of some sort stood on the site of what is now **Chester Cathedral** in Roman times, but records indicate construction around AD 900. The earliest work traceable today, mainly in the north transept, is that of the 11th-century Benedictine abbey. After Henry VIII dissolved the monasteries in the 16th century, the abbey church became the cathedral church of the new diocese of Chester. The choir stalls reveal figures of people and dragons, and above is a gilded and colorful vaulted ceiling. In the small inner garden, a striking modern bronze statue depicts the woman of Samaria offering water to Jesus. ⊠ *St. Werburgh St., off Market Sq.* ☎ *01244/500958* ⊕ *www.chestercathedral. org.uk* ⊠ *Suggested donation £3, or audio guide £3* ⊙ *Daily 8–6.*

Chester Castle, overlooking the River Dee, lost its moats and battlements at the end of the 18th century to make way for the classical-style civil and criminal courts, jail, and barracks. The castle houses the **Cheshire Military Museum,** exhibiting uniforms, memorabilia, and some fine silver. ⊠ *Castle St.* ☎ *01244/327617* ⊠ *£2* ⊙ *Daily 10–4:30.*

⟳ Beautiful grounds and natural enclosures make the 80-acre **Chester Zoo** one of Britain's most popular zoos, as well as the largest. Highlights include Chimpanzee Island, the jaguar enclosure, and the Islands in Danger tropical habitat. Baby animals are often on display, thanks to the zoo's emphasis on breeding and conservation, and there's a regular feeding program. There are 11 mi of paths, and you can use the waterbus boats or the overhead train to tour the grounds. ⊠ *A41, 2 mi north of Chester* ☎ *01244/380280* ⊕ *www.chesterzoo.org* ⊠ *£12, bus £1.60, train £2* ⊙ *Daily 10–dusk.*

Where to Stay & Eat

££–£££   ✕ **Brasserie 10/16.** Flooded with natural light from a wall of windows, this brasserie has clean, elegant lines. The Mediterranean fare is well presented, too, ranging from sea bass with pesto mash and beef with Stilton cheese to numerous salad options. To complete your meal, indulge yourself with the orange and mango ripple cheesecake. ⊠ *Brookdale Pl.* ☎ *01244/322288* ⊟ *AE, MC, V.*

££–£££   ✕ **Francs.** Beyond the black-and-white half-timber exterior of this French eatery is an intimate dining area, with rustic basketwork on the walls and bentwood chairs. The menu lists choices such as bouillabaisse and Moroccan spiced chicken; vegetarians might consider the hazelnut pâté and mushrooms in puff pastry. Fixed-price meals are a great value. ⊠ *14 Cuppin St.* ☎ *01244/317952* ⊟ *MC, V.*

£££££   ✕⊡ **Chester Grosvenor Hotel.** At this deluxe traditional hotel in a Tudor-style building downtown, handmade Italian furniture and French silk furnishings complement the typically English architecture. Floris toiletries, three telephones, CD players, and a luxury spa are among the pampering amenities. The splendid Arkle Restaurant (named after a celebrated racehorse; closed Monday and Sunday evening and first three weeks in January) has marble and stone walls, solid mahogany tables, and gleaming silver; there's a set-price dinner as well as a daily gastronomic menu.

The wine cellar has more than 600 bins. Good, hearty food is served in the brasserie. ☒ *Eastgate St., CH1 1LT* ☏ *01244/324024, 800/525– 4800 from U.S.* 🖷 *01244/313246* ⊕ *www.chestergrosvenor.co.uk* ↩ *80 rooms* ♿ *2 restaurants, in-room data ports, cable TV, health club, spa, Internet, business services, meeting rooms, no-smoking rooms* ▭ *AE, DC, MC, V* ⦿ *BP.*

★   ✕▦ **Chester Crabwall Manor.** Eleven acres of farm and parkland surround
££££–£££££   this dramatic, castellated, part-Tudor, part-neo-Gothic mansion, a good place to pamper yourself. The hotel has elegant, subtle furnishings in floral chintzes, a wonderful stone staircase, and sumptuously large bedrooms, all with a breakfast table and a sofa or pair of armchairs. At dinner, try such fine English fare as loin of venison or saddle of rabbit. ☒ *A540, Parkgate Rd., Mollington, CH1 6NE* ☏ *01244/851666* 🖷 *01244/851400* ⊕ *www.marstonhotels.com* ↩ *48 rooms* ♿ *Restaurant, cable TV, indoor pool, health club, spa, meeting rooms, no-smoking rooms; no a/c* ▭ *AE, DC, MC, V* ⦿ *BP.*

££–£££   ▦ **Redland Hotel.** If you revel in flamboyant Victorian architecture and decoration, then this villa's original wood paneling, ornamental ceilings, colorful period furnishings, and fascinating collection of *objets* should appeal. Some bedrooms have classy four-poster beds, and all have individual character. Breakfasts match the house for quality. The hotel is a mile west of the center of Chester on A5104. ☒ *64 Hough Green, CH4 8JY* ☏ *01244/671024* 🖷 *01244/681309* ⊕ *www.redlandhotel.co.uk* ↩ *13 rooms* ♿ *Sauna, bar; no a/c* ▭ *AE, DC, MC, V* ⦿ *BP.*

£–££   ▦ **Ye Olde King's Head.** Creaky stairs and passageways lead through this centrally located black-and-white 17th-century inn to well-equipped guest rooms. Lattice windows and oak beams evoke the past, and the rich fabrics and thick green carpeting provide present-day comfort. ☒ *48–50 Lower Bridge St., CH1 1RS* ☏ *01244/324855* 🖷 *01244/315693* ↩ *8 rooms* ♿ *Restaurant, cable TV, bar; no a/c* ▭ *MC, V* ⦿ *BP.*

£   ▦ **Grove Villa.** The location of this family-run B&B, a 19th-century house on the banks of the River Dee, enhances its appeal. Add antique furniture and a sense of calm, and you are guaranteed a soothing stay. ☒ *18 The Groves, CH1 1SD* ☏ *01244/349713* ✉ *Grove.Villa@tesco.net* ↩ *3 rooms* ♿ *No a/c, no room phones, no smoking* ▭ *No credit cards* ⦿ *BP.*

Shopping

Chester has an **indoor market** in the Forum, near the Town Hall, every day except Sunday. **Adam's Antiques** (☒ 65 Watergate Row ☏ 01244/ 319421) specializes in items from the 18th and 19th centuries. **Bookland** (☒ 12 Bridge St. ☏ 01244/347323), in an ancient building with a converted 14th-century crypt, stocks travel and general-interest books.

WELSH BORDERS A TO Z

To research prices, get advice from other travelers, and book travel arrangements, visit www.fodors.com.

AIRPORTS

Birmingham International Airport, 6 mi east of the city center, is the country's second-busiest airport, with connections to all of Britain's major cities. Bus 900 runs to the city center every 20 minutes; a taxi will cost you around £16.

🚩 **Birmingham International Airport** ✉ A45, off Junction 6 of M42 ☎ 0870/733-5511 ⊕ www.bhx.co.uk.

BUS TRAVEL

National Express serves the region from London's Victoria Coach Station. Average travel time to Birmingham is 2¾ hours; to Chester is 5½ hours; to Hereford, and Shrewsbury, 4¼ hours; and to Worcester, 4 hours. Flightlink operates services from London's Heathrow (2¾ hours) and Gatwick (4¼ hours) airports to Birmingham.

Traveline fields all public transport inquiries. You can also contact local companies individually. For information about bus services and Rover tickets for the Birmingham area, contact the Centro Hotline. For Worcester, Hereford, Chester, and surrounding areas, contact First.

FARES & SCHEDULES 🚩 **Centro Hotline** ☎ 0121/200-2700 ⊕ www.centro.org.uk. **First (for Chester)** ☎ 01244/381515 ⊕ www.firstgroup.com. **First (for Worcester and Hereford)** ☎ 01905/763888 ⊕ www.firstgroup.com. **Flightlink** ☎ 0870/580-8080 ⊕ www.nationalexpress.com. **National Express** ☎ 0870/580-8080 ⊕ www.nationalexpress.com. **Traveline** ☎ 0870/608-2608 ⊕ www.traveline.org.uk.

CAR RENTAL

🚩 **Local Agencies Alamo National Car Rental** ✉ 18-20 Bristol St., Birmingham ☎ 0121/622-6131 ✉ Cathedral Service Station, Bromwich Rd., Worcester ☎ 01905/420699. **Avis** ✉ 17 Horsefair, Birmingham ☎ 0121/632-4361 ✉ 128 Brook St., Chester ☎ 01244/311463. **Hertz** ✉ Auto Travel Ltd., Abley House, Trafford St., Chester ☎ 01244/374705. **Practical Car and Van Rental** ✉ 6B Heathfield Rd., Stourport-on-Severn, between Birmingham and Worcester ☎ 01299/879191 ⊕ www.practical.co.uk.

CAR TRAVEL

To reach Birmingham (120 mi), Shrewsbury (150 mi), and Chester (180 mi) from London, take M40 and keep on it until it becomes M42, or else take M1/M6. M4 and then M5 from London take you to Worcester and Hereford in just under 3 hours. A prettier but slower route to Worcester and vicinity is M40 to Oxford and then A44, which skirts the Cotswolds.

ROAD CONDITIONS Driving can be difficult in the western reaches of this region—especially in the hills and valleys west of Hereford, where steep, twisting roads often narrow down into mere trackways. Winter travel here can be particularly grueling.

EMERGENCIES

🚩 **Ambulance, fire, police** ☎ 999. **Birmingham Heartlands Hospital** ✉ Bordesley Green E, Birmingham ☎ 0121/424-2000. **Countess of Chester Hospital** ✉ Liverpool Rd., Chester ☎ 01244/365000.

SPORTS & OUTDOORS

HIKING & WALKING For information on hiking the Malvern Hills, contact the Malvern Tourist Office or the Ross-on-Wye Tourist Office (⇨ Visitor Information).

TOURS

Local tourist offices can recommend day or half-day tours of the region and will have the names of registered Blue Badge guides. From June to

September, City Sightseeing operates tours of Birmingham and Chester in open-top buses. Walking tours of Shrewsbury depart from the tourist office (⇨ Visitor Information) daily at 2:30 from May through September and on Saturdays the rest of the year. Home James runs day trips and longer themed tours of the Shropshire area throughout the year.

City Sightseeing ⊠ Avenue Farm Rd., Stratford-upon-Avon ☎ 01789/299123 ⊕ www.city-sightseeing.com. **Home James** ⊘ Box 1, Shrewsbury SY1 1AA ☎ 01743/242424 ⊕ www.homejames.uk.com.

TRAIN TRAVEL

From London, Great Western and Arriva trains serve the region from Paddington Station, and Virgin, Central, and Silverlink Trains leave from Euston (call National Rail Enquiries for all schedules and information). Average travel times are Paddington to Hereford (with a change at Newport), 3 hours; to Worcester, 2¼ hours; Euston to Birmingham, 2 hours; Euston to Shrewsbury, with a change at Wolverhampton or Birmingham, 3 hours, or to Chester, with a change at Crewe, 2¾ hours. A direct local service links Hereford and Shrewsbury (1 hour), with a change at Crewe for Chester.

CUTTING COSTS   West Midlands Day Ranger tickets (£13.20) and three- and seven-day Heart of England Rover tickets (£51.50 and £67.50) allow unlimited travel.

FARES &   **National Rail Enquiries** ☎ 0845/748–4950 ⊕ www.nationalrail.co.uk.
SCHEDULES

TRAVEL AGENCIES

Local Agent Referrals American Express ⊠ Bank House, 8 Cherry St., Birmingham ☎ 0121/644-5555. **Thomas Cook** ⊠ 99 New St., Birmingham ☎ 0121/255-2600 ⊠ 10 Bridge St., Chester ☎ 01244/583500 ⊠ 4 St. Peter's St., Hereford ☎ 01432/422500 ⊠ 36-37 Pride Hill, Shrewsbury ☎ 01743/842000 ⊠ 26 High St., Worcester ☎ 01905/871200.

VISITOR INFORMATION

The Heart of England Tourist Board is open Monday–Thursday 9–5:30, Friday 9–5. Local tourist information centers are usually open Monday–Saturday 9:30–5:30.

Heart of England Tourist Board ⊠ Larkhill Rd., Worcester, WR5 2EZ ☎ 01905/763436 🖷 01905/763450 ⊕ www.visitheartofengland.com. **Birmingham** ⊠ The Rotunda, New St., B2 2EA ☎ 0121/202-5099, 0121/202-5005 accommodations, 0121/202-5050 weekends and short breaks ⊕ www.beinbirmigham.com ⊠ International Convention Centre, Broad St.,, B1 2EA. **Chester** ⊠ Town Hall, Northgate St., CH1 2HJ ⊠ Vicar's La.,, CH1 1QX ☎ 01244/402111 ⊕ www.chestertourism.com. **Great Malvern Tourist Office** ⊠ 21 Church St., WR14 2AA ☎ 01684/892289 ⊕ www.malvernhills.gov.uk. **Hereford** ⊠ 1 King St., HR4 9BW ☎ 01432/268430 ⊕ www.visitherefordshire.co.uk. **Ludlow** ⊠ Castle St., SY8 1AS ☎ 01584/875053 ⊕ www.ludlow.org.uk. **Much Wenlock** ⊠ The Museum, The Square, TF13 6HR ☎ 01952/727679. **Ross-on-Wye** ⊠ Swan House, Edde Cross St., HR9 7BZ ☎ 01989/562768 ⊕ www.visitherefordshire.co.uk. **Shrewsbury** ⊠ The Music Hall, The Square, SY1 1LH ☎ 01743/281200 ⊕ www.shropshiretourism.info. **Worcester** ⊠ The Guildhall, High St., WR1 2EY ☎ 01905/726311 ⊕ www.visitworcester.com.

WALES

9

LEARN ALL ABOUT THE CULTURE
at the Museum of Welsh Life ⇨*p.456*

CLIMB CASTLE TOWERS
in the walled town of Conwy ⇨*p.441*

HOP ABOARD STEAM TRAINS
for nostalgic mountain rides ⇨*p.429*

COMPARE COMPETING CHOIRS
at the International Eisteddfod ⇨*p.433*

IMAGINE ITALY IN WALES
at Portmeirion, a fantasy village ⇨*p.435*

BROWSE A BOOK LOVER'S PARADISE
in tiny Hay-on-Wye ⇨*p.446*

SCORE A PRIME SLICE OF BEACH
on the golden sands of Tenby ⇨*p.464*

RECHARGE AT A COUNTRY RETREAT
such as elegant Ynyshir Hall ⇨*p.451*

Updated by
Roger Thomas

WALES, KNOWN AS THE LAND OF SONG, is also a land of mountain and flood, where wild peaks challenge the sky and waterfalls thunder down steep, rocky chasms. It is a land of gray-stone castles, ruined abbeys, male-voice choirs, and a handful of cities. Pockets of the southeast and northeast were heavily industrialized in the 19th century, largely with mining and steelmaking, but long stretches of the coast and the mountainous interior remain areas of unmarred beauty. Small, self-contained Wales has three national parks (Snowdonia, including Snowdon, highest mountain in England and Wales; the Brecon Beacons; and the Pembrokeshire Coast) and five official Areas of Outstanding Natural Beauty (the Wye Valley, Gower Peninsula, Llŷn Peninsula, Isle of Anglesey, and Clwydian Range), as well as large tracts of unspoiled moor and mountain in mid-Wales, the least-traveled part of the country. Riches of other sorts fill the country: medieval castles, seaside resorts, traditional market towns, the glorious Bodnant Garden, the stately houses of Powis and Plas Newydd, steam-powered trains running through Snowdonia and central Wales, and the cosmopolitan capital of Cardiff.

The 1941 film *How Green Was My Valley* depicted Wales as an industrial cauldron filled with coal mines. Although mining did take place in Wales, the picture was not accurate then and is certainly not accurate now, when the country has only one fully operational mine. One of the great glories of visiting Wales is the drive through beautiful countryside from south to north without passing through any large towns. On such a drive, it's easy to believe that Wales has a population of about 2.9 million but is home to 5.5 million sheep, which fill the valleys and hillsides. The country's 750 mi of coast consists mainly of sandy beaches, grassy headlands, cliffs, and estuaries.

The Welsh are a Celtic race. When, toward the middle of the first millennium AD, the Anglo-Saxons spread through Britain, they pushed the indigenous Celts farther back into their Welsh mountain strongholds. (In fact, "Wales" comes from the Saxon word "Weallas," which means "strangers," the name impertinently given by the new arrivals to the natives.) The Welsh, however, have always called themselves "Y Cymry," the companions. Not until the English king Edward I (1272–1307) waged a brutal campaign to conquer Wales was English supremacy established. Welsh hopes were finally crushed with the death in battle of Llywelyn ap Gruffudd, last native prince of Wales, in 1282.

Today Wales has achieved a measure of independence from its English neighbor. In a 1999 referendum, a narrow majority of the Welsh people voted for partial devolution for the country. Elections were held and the Welsh Assembly was born. Unlike the Scottish Parliament, the Welsh Assembly has no law-making powers, but it does have significant administrative responsibilities and considerable control over Welsh affairs. The Welsh Assembly expects to be installed in its new building on Cardiff Bay by fall 2005.

The Welsh language continues to flourish. Although spoken by only a fifth of the population, it has a high profile within the country. Welsh-language schools are popular, there is a Welsh TV channel, and road signs are bilingual. Ironically, although in the 15th and 16th centuries the Tudor kings Henry VII and Henry VIII continued England's domination of the Welsh, principally by attempting to abolish the language, another Tudor monarch, Elizabeth I, ensured its survival by authorizing a Welsh translation of the Bible in 1588. Many older people say they owe their knowledge of Welsh to the Bible. You may see (and hear) Welsh throughout your travels, but everyone in Wales speaks English, too.

Exploring Wales

Wales has three main regions: south, mid, and north. The south is the most varied, for its boundaries include everything from Wales's capital city to unspoiled coastline, grassy mountains, and wooded valleys. Mid-Wales is pure countryside, fringed on its western shores by the great arc of Cardigan Bay. North Wales is a mixture of high, rocky mountains, popular sandy beaches, and coastal hideaways.

About the Restaurants

Today even many rural pubs are more interested in offering meals than serving pints of beer, so do consider these as a dining option. Don't overlook hotel restaurants in Wales; many, particularly those in country inns or hotels, are excellent.

About the Hotels

A 19th-century dictum, "I sleeps where I dines," still holds true in Wales, where good hotels and good restaurants often go together. Castles, country mansions, and even small railway stations are being transformed into interesting hotels and restaurants. Cozy traditional inns with low, beamed ceilings, wood paneling, and fireplaces remain Wales's pride, but they tend to be off the beaten track. A car is necessary if you want to stay at these inns; the same is true for farmhouse accommodations. Cardiff and Swansea have some large chain hotels, and, for luxury, Wales has a good choice of country-house hotels. An added attraction is that prices are generally lower than they are for equivalent properties in the Cotswolds, Scotland, or southeast England. A service charge may be added to the room cost; ask if it's included.

	WHAT IT COSTS In pounds sterling				
	£££££	**££££**	**£££**	**££**	**£**
RESTAURANTS	over £22	£18–£22	£13–£17	£7–£12	under £7
HOTELS	over £160	£120–£160	£90–£120	£60–£90	under £60

Restaurant prices are for a main course at dinner. Hotel prices are for two people in a standard double room in high season, including VAT, with no meals or, if indicated, CP (with Continental breakfast), BP (Breakfast Plan, with full breakfast), or MAP (Modified American Plan, with breakfast and dinner).

Timing

The weather in Wales, as in the rest of Britain, is a lottery. It can be warm in the spring and cool in the summer, or dry in May and wet in August. Come prepared for rain or shine. Generally speaking, southwest Wales enjoys a milder climate than elsewhere in Britain, thanks to the moderating effects of the sea. Spring and autumn can be good times to visit

Although less than 200 mi from south to north, Wales is packed with scenic variety and a daunting number of places to visit. Many people make the mistake of thinking that they can see Wales in a day or so, but that's time only to scratch the surface.

Numbers in the text correspond to numbers in the margin and on the Wales and Cardiff maps.

9

If you have
3 days

Start in **Cardiff** ㉒–㉙ ➤, Wales's capital city, and spend at least a half day here before you drive through the Brecon Beacons National Park to ⛰ **Llandrindod Wells** ⑯, a Victorian spa town. On day two, drive via Rhayader and the Elan Valley, Wales's "Lake District," to **Aberystwyth** ⑰; then travel along the north coast of Cardigan Bay to ⛰ **Porthmadog** ⑤ (accommodations are also in nearby Harlech and Portmeirion). For your final day, drive via **Blaenau Ffestiniog** ④ through the Snowdonia National Park to **Betws-y-Coed** ⑥ and, if possible, drop by to see the castle and town walls in **Conwy** ⑩ before leaving Wales via the A55 route to England.

If you have
9 days

Travel to ⛰ **Cardiff** ㉒–㉙ ➤ for a full day's visit and overnight stop, making sure to stop at the Museum of Welsh Life, at St. Fagans. On day two, drive via **Swansea** ㉝ to ⛰ **Tenby** ㉟, a resort at the southern gateway to the Pembrokeshire Coast National Park. Day three is taken up by a tour of this wild and beautiful seashore. Drive to ⛰ **St. David's** ㊲ in the far west to visit the cathedral built on a religious site founded by Wales's patron saint in the 6th century. You can walk a stretch of the coast path or explore **Fishguard** ㊳. Day four is taken up by more coastline on the way to **Cardigan** ㊴, and then a tour along the Vale of Teifi through Cilgerran to Drefach Felindre to explore the Museum of the Welsh Woolen Industry. Continue on to ⛰ **Aberystwyth** ⑰ and overnight there. From Aberystwyth, drive along the Cardigan Bay coast via **Machynlleth** ⑱ to **Dolgellau** ⑲, then head inland through the southern section of the Snowdonia National Park to lakeside ⛰ **Bala** ③.

You see more mountains on day six on the way from Bala to **Blaenau Ffestiniog** ④, where you can visit the caverns that gave this town its past reputation as the "slate capital of North Wales." From here, follow the Vale of Ffestiniog west to **Porthmadog** ⑤; stop at Portmeirion, a mock-Italian village. Continue north to ⛰ **Caernarfon** ⑧ and its medieval castle. Day 7 takes you to the Isle of Anglesey and **Beaumaris** ⑨ for a brief visit, then back along the coast of mainland North Wales via **Conwy** ⑩ to the Victorian seaside resort of ⛰ **Llandudno** ⑪. (On this leg, you might replace the trip to Anglesey with a short detour inland from Caernarfon to **Llanberis** ⑦ and Llanberis Pass in the heart of Snowdonia.) Borderland Wales is the theme of the next day, the route passing through **Denbigh** ⑫, **Ruthin** ⑬, **Llangollen** ②, **Chirk** ①, and **Welshpool** ㉑ on the way to ⛰ **Llandrindod Wells** ⑯. On your last day, visit **Hay-on-Wye** ⑭, the "town of books," then drive on through the mountains to **Brecon** ㉜ in the Brecon Beacons National Park. From here, follow the Vale of Usk through **Crickhowell** ㉛ and **Abergavenny** ㉚ before leaving Wales along the M4 motorway.

Wales (spring may arrive very early in Pembrokeshire, in the southwest). These seasons can be surprisingly dry and sunny, and you have the added advantage of quiet surroundings. That noted, crowds are rarely a problem, except in the main tourist centers, even in the height of summer. Book ahead for major festivals such as the literary Hay Festival, Brecon Jazz, Abergavenny Food Festival, and Llangollen's International Musical Eisteddfod.

NORTH WALES
IN THE REALM OF SNOWDONIA

The north is the region in which Wales masses all its savage splendor and fierce beauty. Dominating its southwestern corner is Snowdon, at 3,560 feet the highest peak in England and Wales. It is impossible to describe the magnificence of the view from the mountain on a clear day: to the northwest the Menai Strait, Anglesey, and beyond to the Irish Sea; to the south the mountains of Merionethshire, Harlech Castle, and the Cadair Idris mountain range; and all around towering masses of wild and barren rock. If you ascend the peak by the Snowdon Mountain Railway from Llanberis, telephone from the terminus to ascertain whether Snowdon is free from mist. You lose much if you arrive when clouds, as often happens, encircle the monster's brow.

The peak gives its name to **Snowdonia National Park,** which extends southward all the way to Machynlleth in mid-Wales. The park consists of 840 square mi of rocky mountains, valleys clothed in oak woods, moorlands, lakes, and rivers, all with one thing in common: natural beauty, and, to a lesser extent, solitude. As in other British national parks, much of the land is privately owned, so inside the park are towns, villages, and farms. The park has become a popular climbing center, and some fear that Snowdon itself is becoming worn away by the boots of too many walkers.

Along the sandy, north-facing coast, a string of seaside resorts has attracted people for well over a century. Llandudno, the dignified "Queen of the North Wales coast," was built in Victorian times as a seaside watering hole. Nearby Conwy, with its medieval castle and town walls, also deserves a look. If you prefer away-from-it-all seashore, there are two official Areas of Outstanding Beauty: the Isle of Anglesey (connected by bridge to mainland Wales), and the Llŷn Peninsula, dotted with quieter small resorts and coastal villages. Portmeirion, a mock-Italianate village, is a quite different kind of escape.

Chirk & the Ceiriog Valley

❶ *22 mi southwest of Chester, 60 mi southwest of Manchester.*

Chirk, poised on the border between England and Wales, is a handy gateway to the Ceiriog Valley, a narrowing vale that penetrates the silent, green foothills of the lofty Berwyn Mountains. The impressive medieval fortress of **Chirk Castle,** completed in its original form in 1310, has evolved into a grand home, with interiors furnished in 16th- to 19th-

9

Castles In this land of castles, more than 400 fortresses provide an inexhaustible supply of inspiration for any lover of history. These ancient strongholds, some of which were built by Edward I in the 13th century during his struggles with the rebellious Welsh, punctuate the landscape from south (Caerphilly) to north (Harlech, Beaumaris, Conwy), and include romantic ruins as well as well-preserved fortresses still rising to their original imperious height. To make the most of any castle visit, buy a guidebook or take a tour so that you can best appreciate the remains of a distant era. The great North Wales castles, such as Caernarfon, are nearly intact and particularly famous; four are World Heritage Sites. But for many people, a lasting memory of Wales is the sight of weather-beaten ruins crowning hilltops or guarding mountain passes deep in the lush countryside.

Steam Railways Wales is the best place in Britain for narrow-gauge steam railways, many of which wind through extraordinary landscapes. The Great Little Trains of Wales operate in spring, summer, and fall through the mountains of Snowdonia and central Wales (there are also a few lines in South Wales). The ride is just part of the interest; a good deal of history is associated with the old trains and train stations, some of which served industry before they became attractions for visitors. The Ffestiniog Railway, which links two British Rail lines at the old slate town of Blaenau Ffestiniog and Porthmadog, climbs the mountainside in Snowdonia National Park around an ascending loop. Snowdonia also has Britain's only alpine-style steam rack railway, the Snowdon Mountain Railway, where little sloping boiler engines on rack-and-pinion track push their trains 3,000 feet up from Llanberis to the summit of Snowdon.

Walking An army of bipeds descends on Wales every year for wonderful walking and hiking. Long-distance paths include the Pembrokeshire Coast Path (which runs all along the spectacular shores of southwest Wales), the south–north Offa's Dyke Path, based on the border between England and Wales established by King Offa in the 8th century, and the Glyndŵr Way, a 128-mi-long highland route that traverses mid-Wales from the border town of Knighton via Machynlleth to Welshpool. Signposted footpaths in Wales's forested areas are short and easy to follow. Dedicated enthusiasts might prefer the challenging wide-open spaces of the Brecon Beacons National Park or the mountains of Snowdonia.

---

century styles. The castle stands amid beautiful formal gardens and 18th-century parkland. ⊠ *Off B4500* ☎ *01691/777701* ⊕ *www.nationaltrust. org.uk* 🎫 *£6, garden only £3.80* ☽ *Castle Apr.–Oct., Wed.–Sun. noon–5; garden Apr.–Oct., Wed.–Sun. 11–6.*

West of Chirk is the **Vale of Ceiriog,** nicknamed Little Switzerland. Take B4500 west 6 mi through the lovely valley to the village of Glyn Ceiriog, at the foothills of the remote Berwyn Mountains. The area attracts pony trekkers, walkers, and anglers.

Wales

Bristol Channel

Month of the Severn

KEY

▶ *Start of itinerary*

GREAT BRITAIN

20 miles
30 km

Where to Stay & Eat

££–£££ ✕⊞ **Golden Pheasant.** Antiques and Victorian-style fabrics furnish this well-kept 18th-century hotel east of the village of Glyn Ceiriog. You can have a drink in the bar with its fireplace, slate floor, wooden booths, and beamed ceiling, or relax in deep-cushioned comfort in the lounge, which overlooks the countryside. There's a three-course, fixed-price menu in the restaurant, as well as a bar menu. Specialties include Ceiriog trout and game pie. ⊠ *Off B4500, Glyn Ceiriog, LL20 7BB, near Chirk* ☎ *01691/718281* ⊕ *www.goldenpheasanthotel.co.uk* ☎ *01691/718479* ➦ *19 rooms* ⊘ *Restaurant, bar, lounge, some pets allowed (fee); no a/c* ⊟ *DC, MC, V* ⫯◯⫯ *BP.*

£–££ ⊞ **Bron Heulog.** Carefully restored in period style as a guest house, this former Victorian doctor's office has 2 acres of gardens with resident donkeys. Fireplaces, high ceilings, and an oak staircase are original elements of the large stone house. Rooms have showers. ⊠ *Waterfall Rd., off B4396, Llanrhaeadr ym Mochnant, SY10 0JX* ☎ *01691/780521* ⊕ *www. kraines.enta.net* ➦ *4 rooms* ⊘ *No-smoking rooms; no a/c, no room phones* ⊟ *MC, V* ⫯◯⫯ *BP.*

---

en route | The peat-brown water of **Pistyll Rhaeadr,** the highest waterfall in Wales, thunders down a 290-foot double cascade. To get here, take B4500 southwest from Glyn Ceiriog, and then its unnumbered continuation, to reach Llanrhaeadr ym Mochnant, in the peaceful Tanat Valley. Here, in 1588, the Bible was translated into Welsh, thus ensuring the survival of the language. Turn northwest and go 4 mi up the road to the waterfall.

Llangollen

❷ *5 mi northwest of Chirk, 23 mi southwest of Chester.*

Llangollen's setting in a deep valley carved by the River Dee gives it a typically Welsh appearance. The bridge over the Dee, a 14th-century stone structure, is named in a traditional Welsh folk song as one of the "Seven Wonders of Wales." In July the popular International Musical Eisteddfod brings crowds to town. For a particularly scenic drive in this area, head for the Horseshoe Pass.

Plas Newydd (not to be confused with the grand estate on the Isle of Anglesey with the same name) was the home from 1778 to 1828 of Lady Eleanor Butler and Sarah Ponsonby, the eccentric Ladies of Llangollen, who set up a then-scandalous single-sex household, collected curios and magnificent wood carvings, and made it into a tourist attraction even during their lifetimes. Among their celebrated guests were William Wordsworth, Sir Walter Scott, and the duke of Wellington. The terraced gardens have original features such as a font from an abbey. ⊠ *Hill St.* ☎ *01978/861314* ☎ *01824/708258* ⊕ *www.borderlands.co.uk/plas-newydd* ⊡ *£3* ⊘ *Apr.–Oct., daily 10–5.*

From the **canal wharf** (☎ *01978/860702*) you can take a horse-drawn boat or a narrow boat (a slender barge) along the Llangollen Canal to ⟳ the largest navigable aqueduct in the world at Pontcysyllte. The **Llan-**

gollen Railway, a restored standard-gauge steam line, runs for a few miles along the scenic Dee Valley. The terminus is near the town's bridge. ☎ 01978/860979, 01978/860951 *recorded information* ⊕ *www. llangollen-railway.co.uk* ☜ *£10 round-trip* ☉ *Apr.–Oct., daily 10–5; Nov.–Mar., weekends, limited service.*

Where to Stay

£ ⊞ **Oakmere.** This sandstone Victorian residence with landscaped grounds, only a few minutes' walk from Llangollen center, succeeds in preserving its period flavor. Special features include tile or polished pine floors, 19th-century furniture in walnut and mahogany, a conservatory, and spacious, high-ceiling bedrooms. There are excellent views of the valley and mountains. ⊠ *Regent St., LL20 8HS* ☎ *01978/861126* ⊕ *www. oakmere.llangollen.co.uk* ☜ *6 rooms* ⚒ *Tennis court, lounge; no a/c, no room phones, no smoking* ☰ *No credit cards* ⑩ *BP.*

Nightlife & the Arts

★ The six-day **International Musical Eisteddfod** (☎ 01978/862000 ⊕ www. international-eisteddfod.co.uk), held in early July, brings together amateur choirs and dancers—more than 12,000 participants in all—from all corners of the globe for a large, colorful arts festival. The tradition of the *eisteddfod,* held throughout Wales, goes back to the 12th century. Originally gatherings of bards, the *eisteddfodau* of today are more like competitions or festivals.

Sports & the Outdoors

There are easy walks along the banks of the River Dee or along part of the **Offa's Dyke Path** (⊕ www.offasdyke.demon.co.uk), which passes through hills, river valleys, and lowlands. This 177-mi-long National Trail follows the line of an ancient earthen wall, still surviving in parts, which was built along the border with England in the 8th century by King Offa of Mercia to keep out Welsh raiders.

Bala

❸ *18 mi southwest of Llangollen.*

The staunchly Welsh town of Bala makes a good base for exploring the eastern and southern sections of Snowdonia National Park as well as the gentler landscapes of borderland Wales. It stands at the head of Llyn Tegid (Bala Lake), at 4 mi long the largest natural lake in Wales. This is a good place for kayaking and windsurfing. The scenic, narrow-gauge **Bala Lake Railway** (☎ 01678/540666 ⊕ www.bala-lake-railway. co.uk), one of the Great Little Trains of Wales, runs along the southern shore of Bala Lake.

★ To experience Wales at its wildest, you can drive over **Bwlch y Groes** (Pass of the Cross), the highest road in Wales, whose sweeping panoramas are breathtaking. To get here, take the narrow road south from Bala through Cwm Hirnant and over the mountain to Lake Vyrnwy. Turn right at the lake and drive for a mile on B4393 before heading west on the mountain road.

Where to Stay & Eat

★ ╳▦ **Lake Vyrnwy Hotel.** Awesome views of mountain-ringed Lake Vyrnwy
££££–£££££ are just one asset of this country mansion within a 24,000-acre estate. For the ultimate sporting holiday, you can fish, bird-watch, play tennis, or take long hikes. Sailboats are also available. Leather chairs, log fires, and antiques add luxury, and the bedrooms are full of pampering touches. The sophisticated contemporary cuisine (three-course fixed-price menu only) includes trout, pheasant, and duck from the reserve; marinated partridge with saffron vegetables and a casserole of monkfish and scallops are typical dishes. ⊠ *Off B4393, Llanwddyn, SY10 0LY* ☎ *01691/ 870692* 📠 *01691/870259* ⊕ *www.lakevyrnwy.com* ⇗ *35 rooms* ⚲ *Restaurant, tennis court, boating, fishing, bicycles, meeting rooms, some pets allowed (fee), kennel; no a/c* ➾ *AE, DC, MC, V* ⦿⟊ *BP.*

££ ▦ **Cyfie Farm.** This refurbished, ivy-clad 17th-century farmhouse in a tranquil area close to Lake Vyrnwy has oak beams and log fireplaces. The luxurious suites, in converted barns and stables, possess all the sophistication of those in a top hotel. ⊠ *Off B4393, Llanfihangel-yng-Ngwynfa, SY22 5JE, near Llanfyllin* ☎ *01691/648451* ⊕ *www.wales. little-places.co.uk* ⇗ *3 suites* ⚲ *Lounge, no-smoking rooms; no a/c, no room phones* ➾ *No credit cards* ⦿⟊ *BP.*

Blaenau Ffestiniog

❹ *22 mi northwest of Bala, 10 mi southwest of Betws-y-Coed.*

Most of the world's roofing tiles used to come from this former "slate capital of North Wales," and commercial quarrying continues here. On the hillsides around the town is the evidence of decades of mining. The enterprises that attract attention nowadays, however, remain the old slate mines, which opened to the public in the 1970s. The Ffestiniog Railway, which begins in Porthmadog, ends in the town, near the caverns.

At the **Llechwedd Slate Caverns,** you can take two trips: a tram ride through floodlighted tunnels where Victorian working conditions have been re-created, and a ride on Britain's deepest underground railway to a mine where you can walk by an eerie underground lake. Either tour gives a good idea of the difficult working conditions the miners endured. On the surface of this popular site are a re-created Victorian village, old workshops, and slate-splitting demonstrations. ⊠ *Off A470* ☎ *01766/ 830306* ⊕ *www.llechwedd-slate-caverns.co.uk* ⌲ *Tour £8.25, surface free* ☉ *Mar.–Sept., daily 10–5:15; Oct.–Feb., daily 10–4:15.*

Porthmadog

❺ *12 mi southwest of Blaenau Ffestiniog, 16 mi south of Caernarfon.*

The little seaside town of Porthmadog, built as a harbor to export slate from Blaenau Ffestiniog, stands at the gateway to Llŷn, an unspoiled peninsula of beaches, wildflowers, and country lanes. Its location between Snowdonia and Llŷn, as well as the good beaches nearby and the many attractions around town, makes it a lively place in summer. A mile-long embankment known as the Cob (the small toll charge goes to charity) serves as the eastern approach to Porthmadog.

The oldest of the Welsh narrow-gauge lines (founded in the early 19th century to carry slate), the **Ffestiniog Railway** runs from a quayside terminus along the Cob and continues through a wooded vale into the mountains. Its northern terminus is Blaenau Ffestiniog, where you can visit the slate caverns. ☎ *01766/516000* ⊕ *www.festrail.co.uk* 🎫 *£14 round-trip* ⊙ *Apr.–Nov., daily, plus limited winter service.*

Fodor'sChoice
★
One not-to-be-missed site in North Wales is **Portmeirion,** a tiny fantasy-Italianate village on a private peninsula surrounded by hills, which is said to be loosely modeled after Portofino. Begun in 1926 by architect Clough Williams-Ellis (1883–1978), the village has a hotel, restaurant, town hall, shops (selling books, gifts, and Portmeirion pottery), rental cottages, and woodland walks; beaches are nearby. Williams-Ellis called it his "light-opera approach to architecture," and the result is magical as well as genuinely inspirational, though distinctly un-Welsh. Royalty, political figures, artists, and other celebrities have stayed here, and the cult 1967 TV series *The Prisoner* was filmed here. Portmeirion is a short trip east of Porthmadog over the Cob. ⊠ *Off A496* ☎ *01766/770228* ⊕ *www.portmeirion-village.com* 🎫 *£5.70* ⊙ *Daily 9:30–5:30.*

North of Porthmadog is **Tremadog,** a handsome village that was the birthplace of T. E. Lawrence (1888–1935), better known as Lawrence of Arabia. In the Victorian seaside resort of **Criccieth,** a few miles west of Porthmadog on A497, a medieval castle with sweeping views crowns the headland. David Lloyd George, the prime minister of Britain from 1916 to 1922, grew up in Wales and lived here; a small museum in his childhood home honors him.

★
A wealth of legend, poetry, and song is conjured up by the 13th-century **Harlech Castle,** built by Edward I to help subdue the Welsh; it's now a UNESCO World Heritage Site. The castle, on a rocky promontory, dominates the little coastal town of Harlech, 12 mi south of Porthmadog. Its mighty ruins, visible for miles and commanding wide views, are as dramatic as its history (though you have to imagine the sea, which has since receded, edging the castle site). Harlech was occupied by Owain Glyndŵr from 1404 to 1408 during his revolt against the English. The inspiring music of Ceiriog's song *Men of Harlech* reflects the heroic defense of this castle in 1468 by Dafydd ap Eynion, who, summoned to surrender, replied: "I held a castle in France until every old woman in Wales heard of it, and I will hold a castle in Wales until every old woman in France hears of it!" Later in the 15th century the Lancastrians survived an eight-year siege during the Wars of the Roses here, and it was the last Welsh stronghold to fall in the 17th-century Civil War. ⊠ *Off B4573* ☎ *01766/780552* ⊕ *www.cadw.wales.gov.uk* 🎫 *£3* ⊙ *Apr., May, and Oct., daily 9:30–5; June–Sept., daily 9:30–6; Nov.–Mar., Mon.–Sat. 9:30–4, Sun. 11–4.*

off the beaten path

NANT GWRTHEYRN – This is a worthwhile stop—for awesome scenery on Caernarfon Bay as well as cultural information—if you're exploring the Llŷn Peninsula. A former village for granite-quarry workers on the peninsula's cliff-lined northern coast serves as the Welsh Language and Heritage Centre, offering Welsh-language classes and cultural courses (in Welsh). The chapel is a tourist information center and has modest historical exhibits, and a café serves good sandwiches and snacks. You leave your car in a lot and walk (20–30 min; 40 min for the steep uphill walk back) to the village. ⊠ *Off B4417, Llithfaen* ☎ *01758/750334* ⊕ *www.nantgwr. com* ☒ *Free* ☉ *June–Sept., daily 11–5:30; Oct.–May, Thurs.–Mon. 11–5.*

Where to Stay & Eat

★ **£££££** ✕ Hotel Maes-y-Neuadd. Eight acres of gardens and parkland create a glorious setting for this luxurious country hotel in a manor house dating from the 14th century. Walls of local granite, oak-beam ceilings, and an inglenook fireplace add character; the updated bedrooms have different shapes and details but use prints and pastel fabrics. The restaurant's three-course, fixed-price menu of Welsh, English, and French specialties uses local ingredients, including vegetables grown on the property, fish, and cheeses. The hotel is 3½ mi northeast of Harlech. ⊠ *Off B4573, Talsarnau, LL47 6YA* ☎ *01766/780200 or 800/635–3602* ☐ *01766/780211* ⊕ *www.neuadd.com* ⇆ *16 rooms* ⚘ *Restaurant, meeting room, some pets allowed (fee), no-smoking rooms; no a/c* ▭ *AE, DC, MC, V* ◯ *BP.*

★ **£££££** ✕ Hotel Portmeirion. One of the most elegant and unusual places to stay in Wales is also supremely relaxing. Clough Williams-Ellis built his Italianate fantasy village around this waterside Victorian mansion with a library, mirror room, and curved, colonnaded dining room. The pleasantly old-fashioned guest rooms have up-to-the-minute amenities. Accommodation is also available in cottage suites around the village and in chic, minimalistic suites in Castell Deudraeth, a castellated 19th-century house. The restaurant, which serves breakfast and has a fixed-price dinner menu, highlights local foods with a sophisticated contemporary style. ⊠ *Off A496, Portmeirion, LL48 6ET* ☎ *01766/77000* ☐ *01766/ 771331* ⊕ *www.portmeirion.com* ⇆ *14 rooms in main hotel, 26 rooms in cottages, 11 suites in Castell Deudraeth* ⚘ *Restaurant, cable TV, inroom VCRs, tennis court, pool, meeting rooms, some pets allowed (fee), no-smoking rooms; no a/c* ▭ *AE, DC, MC, V* ◯ *BP.*

★ **££** ✕ Castle Cottage. Close to Harlech's mighty castle, this friendly "restaurant with rooms" is a wonderful find. The emphasis is on the exceptional cuisine of chef-proprietor Glyn Roberts, who uses ingredients from salmon to Welsh lamb to create imaginative, beautifully presented contemporary dishes. There's a fixed-price dinner menu (no lunch). The annex, a former 16th-century pub, contains four spacious modern rooms, and the main building has cozy rooms with cottage-style furnishings. ⊠ *Near B4573, Harlech, LL46 2YL* ☎ *01766/780479* ☐ *01766/781251* ⊕ *www.castlecottageharlech.co.uk* ⇆ *9 rooms, 4 with bath* ⚘ *Restaurant, no-smoking rooms; no a/c* ▭ *MC, V* ◯ *BP.*

£ ✕ Yr Hen Fecws. The name of this welcoming stone restaurant and B&B near the quayside means "the old bakehouse." Bold modern colors blend with traditional furnishings at the bistro-style restaurant (dinner only), which serves dishes such as fresh wild bass with ratatouille and pesto. Bedrooms have exposed slate walls, dark wood furniture, and cheerful bed coverings. ⊠ *16 Lombard St., LL49 9AP* ☎ *01766/514625*

⊕ *www.henfecws.com* ⤴ *7 rooms* ⌂ *Restaurant; no a/c, no smoking*
🖃 *MC, V* ⍩ *BP.*

Sports

Below Harlech Castle, on an expanse of land from which the sea has
receded over the centuries, are the links of **Royal St. David's** (⊠ Harlech
☏ 01766/780361), one of Wales's best golf courses. Booking in advance
is essential.

Betws-y-Coed

❻ *25 mi northeast of Porthmadog, 19 mi south of Llandudno.*

The rivers Llugwy and Conwy meet at Betws-y-Coed, a popular resort
village set among wooded hills with excellent views of Snowdonia. Busy
in summer, the village has a good selection of hotels and crafts shops.
The chief landmark here is the ornate iron Waterloo Bridge (1815) over
the Conwy, designed by Thomas Telford (1757–1834), and the magnificent
Bodnant Garden south of the town of Conwy makes a delightful excursion. On the western (A5) approach to Betws-y-Coed are the **Swallow Falls** (small admission charge), a famous North Wales beauty spot
where the River Llugwy tumbles down through a wooded chasm.

Where to Stay & Eat

££–£££ ✕ **Ty Gwyn.** The restaurant in this 17th-century coaching inn overlooking Waterloo Bridge on the outskirts of Betws-y-Coed is a delight
for lovers of antiques, old beams, and uneven floors. Fresh local produce is used, and there are good-value bar meals and a full à la carte
menu. Wild pheasant terrine and jumbo prawns sautéed with fresh garlic and chili butter are good choices on the contemporary menu. ⊠ *A5*
☏ *01690/710383* 🖃 *MC, V.*

££££ ✕⍩ **Tan-y-Foel Country House.** Hidden away on a wooded hillside outside Betws-y-Coed, this quiet, contemporary hideaway has views over
the Conwy Valley and Snowdonia mountain range. The vibrant hues of
the stylish interior provide a striking contrast with the traditional dark
stone exterior, and many bedrooms have four-posters. Chef-owner Janet
Pitman, a Master Chef of Great Britain, prepares exquisite food (fixed-
price menu) with French influences. ⊠ *Off A5, Capel Garmon, LL26
0RE* ☏ *01690/710507* 🖷 *01690/710681* ⊕ *www.tyfhotel.co.uk* ⤴ *6
rooms* ⌂ *Restaurant, lounge; no a/c, no kids under 7, no smoking*
🖃 *MC, V* ⍩ *BP.*

££ ⍩ **Pengwern Country House.** In Victorian times, this stone-and-slate
country house on two acres of woodland was an artists' colony. Today
the polished slate floors, beamed bedrooms, and traditional furnishings
reflect the house's original charm. You can expect a warm welcome and
good food (guests can arrange dinner here). The house is about a mile
south of Betws-y-Coed. ⊠ *A5, Allt Dinas, LL24 0HF* ⊕ *www.
snowdoniaaccommodation.com* 🖷🖷 *01690/710480* ⤴ *3 rooms* ⌂ *Dining room, lounge; no a/c, no smoking* 🖃 *MC, V* ⍩ *BP.*

£ ⍩ **Aberconwy House.** This Victorian bed-and-breakfast, with its garden
and flower-covered, terraced patio, has panoramic views over Betws-y-
Coed and Snowdonia. Built in 1850, the house retains original features
such as marble fireplaces, but has large, new windows to make the most

of the setting. The modern bedrooms are a good value for the price, and the proprietors are extremely hospitable. ⊠ *Off A470, Lôn Muriau, LL24 OHD* ☎ *01690/710202* 🖷 *01690/710800* ⊕ *www.aberconwy-house. co.uk* ⇘ *8 rooms* ⚭ *Lounge; no a/c, no smoking* ▤ *MC, V* ⦿ *BP.*

Llanberis

❼ *17 mi west of Betws-y-Coed, 7 mi southeast of Caernarfon.*

Llanberis, like Betws-y-Coed, is a focal point for people visiting the Snowdonia National Park. The town stands beside twin lakes at the foot of the rocky **Llanberis Pass,** which cuts through the highest mountains in the park and is lined with slabs popular with rock climbers. There are hiking trails from the top of the pass, but the going can be rough for the inexperienced. Ask local advice before starting any ramble. At the Pen-y-Gwryd Hotel just beyond the summit of the pass, Lord Hunt and his team planned their successful ascent of Everest in 1953.

★ ⚭ Llanberis's most famous attraction is the rack-and-pinion **Snowdon Mountain Railway,** with some of its track at a gradient of 1 in 5; the train terminates within 70 feet of the 3,560-foot-high summit. Snowdon, *Yr Wyddfa* in Welsh, is the highest peak south of Scotland and lies within the 840-square-mi national park. From May through September, weather permitting, trains go all the way to the summit; on a clear day, you can see as far as the Wicklow Mountains in Ireland, about 90 mi away. In 1998 the National Trust bought the mountain, ensuring its long-term protection. ☎ *0870/458–0033* ⊕ *www.snowdonrailway.co.uk* 🖰 *£20 maximum round-trip fare* ⊙ *Mar.–Oct., daily; schedule depends on customer demand.*

On Lake Padarn in the Padarn Country Park, the old Dinorwig slate quarry serves as the **Welsh Slate Museum,** dedicated to what was an important industry here: Welsh slate roofed many a building. The museum has quarry workshops and slate-splitting demonstrations, as well as restored worker housing, all of which convey the development of the industry and the challenges faced by those who worked in it. The narrow-gauge Llanberis Lake Railway runs from here. ⊠ *A4086* ☎ *01286/870630* ⊕ *www.nmgw.ac.uk* 🖰 *Free* ⊙ *Easter–Oct., daily 10–5; Nov.–Easter, Sun.–Fri. 10–4.*

Caernarfon

❽ *7 mi northwest of Llanberis, 26 mi southwest of Llandudno.*

The town of Caernarfon, which has a historic pedigree as a walled medieval settlement, has nothing to rival the considerable splendor of its castle and, in fact, is now overrun with tourist buses. Still, don't miss the garrison church of St. Mary, built into the city walls.

★ Standing like a warning finger, the grim, majestic mass of **Caernarfon Castle,** "that most magnificent badge of our subjection," wrote Thomas Pennant (1726–98), looms over the waters of the River Seiont. It's a UNESCO World Heritage Site. Numerous bloody encounters were witnessed by these sullen walls, erected by Edward I in 1283 as a symbol of his

London, tastefully delivered.

Experience London in a style that surpasses all your expectations. British Airways' custom holidays combine the unrivaled standards of service of our two premium cabins, FIRST and Club World, with the elegance of London's finest hotels. To book your luxury vacation and for special offers visit ba.com/londoninstyle

Arrive a tourist.
Leave a poet.

*Journey to a land where wonders from every era paint
a masterpiece of spectacular settings. Wales.*

*Here you'll find over 6,000 years of history to explore,
and an adventure around every corner. Glide across the sky
in a hot air balloon, take a boat trip along the picturesque coast,
or rumble through winding hills on an authentic steam train.
Or wander on your own through magnificent gardens,
sandy beaches, and local taverns waiting to be explored.*

*Whichever direction your heart takes you, Wales has a path that
can lead you there. A path that begins only two hours from London.*

WALES CYMRU
Go a Little Further.

Visit www.travelwales.org/fodors for more information and travel offers.

determination to subdue the Welsh. The castle's towers, unlike those of Edward I's other castles, are polygonal and patterned with bands of different-colored stone. In 1284 the monarch thought of a scheme to steal the Welsh throne. Knowing that the Welsh chieftains would accept no foreign prince, Edward promised to designate a ruler who could speak no word of English. He sent his queen, Eleanor of Castile, who was expecting a child, to Caernarfon, and in this cold stone fortress the queen gave birth to a son. Edward presented the infant to the assembled chieftains as their prince "who spoke no English, had been born on Welsh soil, and whose first words would be spoken in Welsh." The ruse worked, and on that day was created the first prince of Wales of English lineage. This tradition still holds: in July 1969, Elizabeth II presented Prince Charles to the people of Wales as their prince from this castle. In the Queen's Tower, a museum charts the history of the local regiment, the Royal Welsh Fusiliers. ⊠ *Castle Hill* ☎ *01286/677617* ⊕ *www.caernarfon.com* ✆ *£4.50* ☉ *Apr., May, and Oct., daily 9:30–5; June–Sept., daily 9:30–6; Nov.–Mar., Mon.–Sat. 9:30–4, Sun. 11–4.*

Outside Caernarfon, the **Segontium Roman Museum** tells the story of the Roman presence in Wales; it includes material from one of Britain's most famous Roman forts. The extensive excavation site of the fort is here, too. ⊠ *Beddgelert Rd. (A4085)* ☎ *01286/675625* ⊕ *www.nmgw.ac.uk/ srm* ✆ *Free* ☉ *Tues.–Sun. 12.30–4.30, national holiday Mondays 12:30–4:30.*

You can take a workshop tour and short trip on a coal-fired steam locomotive at the **Welsh Highland Railway–Rheilffordd Eryri**, a narrow-gauge line that operates on the route of an abandoned railway. The terminus is on the quay near Caernarfon Castle. ⊠ *St. Helens Rd.* ☎ *01766/516073* ⊕ *www.festrail.co.uk* ✆ *£14 round-trip* ☉ *Apr.–Oct., daily 10–4; Nov.–Mar., limited weekend service.*

Where to Stay & Eat

££–£££ ✕⊡ **Ty'n Rhos.** This immaculate farmhouse between Snowdonia and the sea provides comfortable yet elegant accommodation in rooms with print fabrics and upholstered furniture. The antiques-filled lounge and the dining room have views across the fields to the Isle of Anglesey. Innovative cooking (guests only) takes advantage of the best local ingredients; try the fish of the day, the homemade cheeses and yogurt, or the Welsh breakfast, which includes local oysters. ⊠ *Off B4366, Llanddeiniolen, LL55 3AE* ☎ *01248/670489* 🖷 *01248/670079* ⊕ *www.tynrhos.co. uk* ⟿ *9 rooms* ⟳ *Dining room, in-room data ports, croquet, lounge, meeting rooms, no-smoking rooms; no a/c* ▤ *AE, MC, V* ⟦◎⟧ *BP.*

££–££££ ⊡ **Meifod Country House.** Former home of the high sheriff of Camarthen, this opulent Victorian house has polished tiled floors, wood-burning fireplaces, and bedrooms with features such as Victorian claw-foot baths and chandeliers. The atmosphere is luxurious but unpretentious, and the food (guests only) is good. The house stands in lush grounds less than 2 mi south of Caernarfon, making it a convenient base for exploring Snowdonia. ⊠ *Off A487, Bontnewydd, LL55 2TY* ☎ *01286/673351* 🖷 *01286/6713256* ⊕ *www.meifodcountryhouse.co.uk* ⟿ *5 rooms* ⟳ *Dining room; no a/c, no smoking* ▤ *MC, V* ⟦◎⟧ *BP.*

The Outdoors

Caernarfon Airparc operates Pleasure Flights in light aircraft over Snowdon, Anglesey, and Caernarfon; flights are 10–25 minutes. "Hands-on" flying lessons are offered daily (1-hour lesson £139), and there's an aviation museum (£4.50). ⊠ *Dinas Dinlle Beach Rd.* ☏ *01286/830800* 🖙 *£29–£69 per seat* ⊙ *Daily 9–5.*

Beaumaris

❾ *13 mi northeast of Caernarfon.*

Elegant Beaumaris is on the Isle of Anglesey, the largest island directly off the shore of Wales and England. It's linked to the mainland by the Britannia road and rail bridge and by Thomas Telford's remarkable chain suspension bridge, built in 1826 over the dividing Menai Strait. Though its name means "beautiful marsh," Beaumaris has become a town of pretty cottages, Georgian terraces, and bright shops. The nearest mainline train station is in Bangor, about 6 mi away on the mainland; a regular bus service operates between the station and Beaumaris. Ferries and catamarans to Ireland leave from Holyhead, on the western side of the island.

The town dates from 1295, when Edward I commenced work on impressive **Beaumaris Castle**, the last and largest link in an "iron ring" of fortifications around North Wales built to contain the Welsh. Guarding the western approach to the Menai Strait, the unfinished castle (a World Heritage Site) is solid and symmetrical, with concentric lines of fortification, arrow slits, and a moat: a superb example of medieval defensive planning. ⊠ *Castle St.* ☏ *01248/810361* ⊕ *www.cadw.wales. gov.uk* 🖙 *£3* ⊙ *Apr., May, and Oct., daily 9:30–5; June–Sept., daily 9:30–6; Nov.–Mar., Mon.–Sat. 9:30–4, Sun. 11–4.*

Opposite Beaumaris Castle is the **courthouse** (☏ 01248/811691), built in 1614. A plaque depicts one view of the legal profession: two farmers pull a cow, one by the horns, one by the tail, while a lawyer sits in the middle milking. The **Museum of Childhood Memories** is an Aladdin's cave of music boxes, magic lanterns (early optical projectors), trains, cars, toy soldiers, rocking horses, and mechanical savings banks. ⊠ *1 Castle St.* ☏ *01248/712498* 🖙 *£3.25* ⊙ *Mar.–Oct. and Dec., Mon.–Sat. 10:30–5, Sun. noon–5; Nov., Tues.–Sat. 10:30–5, Sun. noon–5.*

On Castle Street, the **Tudor Rose**, a house dating from 1400, is an excellent example of Tudor timberwork. To learn about the grim life of a Victorian prisoner, head to the old **gaol**, built in 1829 by Joseph Hansom (1803–1882), who was also the designer of the Hansom cab. ⊠ *Steeple La.* ☏ *01248/810921* 🖙 *£3* ⊙ *May–Sept., daily 10:30–5.*

The 14th-century **Church of St. Mary and St. Nicholas,** opposite the gaol in Steeple Lane, houses the stone coffin of Princess Joan, daughter of King John (1167–1216) and wife of Welsh leader Llewelyn the Great.

off the beaten path

PLAS NEWYDD – Some historians rate the mansion of Plas Newydd on the Isle of Anglesey the finest house in Wales. Remodeled in the 18th century by James Wyatt (1747–1813) for the marquesses of Anglesey (who still live here), it stands on the Menai Strait about 7 mi southwest of Beaumaris (don't confuse it with the Plas Newydd at Llangollen). The interior has some fine 18th-century Gothic Revival decorations. In 1936–40 the society artist Rex Whistler (1905–44) painted the mural in the dining room. A military museum commemorates the Battle of Waterloo, where the first marquess, Wellington's cavalry commander, lost his leg. The woodland walk, arboretum, and garden are worth exploring, and you can ask about boat trips on the strait that leave from the property. The views of Snowdonia across the strait are magnificent. ⊠ *Off A4080, southwest of the Britannia Bridge, Llanfairpwll* ☎ *01248/714795* ⊕ *www.nationaltrust.org.uk* ⊠ *£5* ⊙ *Apr.–Oct., Sat.–Wed. noon–5; last admission ½ hr before closing.*

Nightlife & the Arts

The **Beaumaris Festival** (☎ 01248/811203) takes place annually late May–early June. The whole town is used as a site for special concerts, dance performances, and plays.

Where to Stay & Eat

£££ ✕▥ **Ye Olde Bull's Head.** Originally a coaching inn built in 1472, this place is small and filled with history, and rooms are comfortably modern if not large. Samuel Johnson and Charles Dickens both stayed here. Eat in the stylish brasserie or the excellent oak-beam dining room (reservations essential), dating from 1617. Contemporary specialties on the fixed-price dinner menu include warm salad of pigeon breast with hazelnut oil, and the local widgeon (wild duck); seafood dishes win praise, too. ⊠ *Castle St., LL58 8AP* ☎ *01248/810329* 🖷 *01248/811294* ⊕ *www.bullsheadinn.co.uk* ⇖ *13 rooms* ⚭ *Restaurant, bar; no a/c* 🖃 *AE, MC, V* ⎮⚬⎮ *BP.*

Conwy

★ ❿ *23 mi east of Beaumaris, 48 mi northwest of Chester.*

The still-authentic medieval town of Conwy grew up around its castle on the west bank of the River Conwy. A ring of ancient but well-preserved walls, built in the 13th century to protect the English merchants who lived here, enclose the old town and add to the strong sense of history. It's well worth strolling the streets and walking on top of sections of the wall, which has 21 towers. Your reward on the walls is impressive views across the huddled rooftops of the town to the castle on the estuary, with mountains in the distance.

FodorśChoice Of all Edward I's fortresses, **Conwy Castle,** a mighty, many-turreted ★ stronghold built between 1283 and 1287, preserves most convincingly the spirit of medieval times. Along with Conwy's town walls, the castle is a UNESCO World Heritage Site. The eight large round towers and tall curtain wall, set on a rocky promontory, provide sweeping views of the area and the town walls. Although the castle is roofless (and floor-

ON THE MENU

Talented chefs making use of the country's bountiful resources have put Wales firmly on the culinary map. Welsh Black beef and succulent Welsh lamb are world-renowned, and the supply of fish and seafood (including mussels and oysters) from coasts and rivers is excellent. Organic products are available to restaurants and the public from specialized companies, farm shops, and farmers' markets. Tŷ Nant Welsh spring water graces restaurant tables worldwide, and wines, such as Cariad, have won medals at French wine festivals; there's even a Welsh whisky. Cheese making has undergone a remarkable revival. You can try traditionally named cheeses such as Llanboidy and Caws Cenarth or an extra-mature cheddar called Black Bomber. Contemporary cuisine has the buzz, but traditional dishes are worth seeking out. Cawl, for example, is a nourishing broth of lamb and vegetables, and laverbread is a distinctive-tasting pureed seaweed that's usually fried with eggs and bacon. For information on quality Welsh food, check out the Web site Wales—the True Taste (⊕ www.walesthetruetaste.com).

less in places), you can read the signs, take a tour, or buy a guidebook to help you visualize the Great Hall and other chambers. Narrow stairs lead into towers such as the Chapel Tower. Conwy Castle can be approached on foot by a dramatic suspension bridge completed in 1825; engineer Thomas Telford designed the bridge with turrets to blend in with the fortress's presence. ⊠ Castle Sq. ☎ 01492/592358 ⊕ www.cadw.wales.gov.uk ⊡ £3.50 ⊗ Apr., May, and Oct., daily 9:30–5; June–Sept., daily 9:30–6; Nov.–Mar., Mon.–Sat. 9:30–4, Sun. 11–4.

What is said to be the **smallest house in Britain** (⊠ Lower Gate St. ☎ 01492/593484) is furnished in mid-Victorian Welsh style. The house, which is 6 feet wide and 10 feet high, was reputedly last occupied in 1900 by a fisherman who was more than 6 feet tall.

Plas Mawr, a jewel in the heart of Conwy, is the best-preserved Elizabethan town house in Britain. Built in 1576 by Robert Wynn (who later became both a member of Parliament and sheriff of Caernarfonshire), this richly decorated house with its ornamental plasterwork gives a unique insight into the lives of the Tudor gentry and their servants. ⊠ High St. ☎ 01492/580167 ⊡ £4.50 ⊗ Apr.–Oct., Tues.–Sun. 10–6.

Built in the 14th century, **Aberconwy House** is the only surviving medieval merchant's house in Conwy. Each room in the restored building reflects different eras of its long history. ⊠ Castle St. ☎ 01492/592246 ⊡ £2.40 ⊗ Apr.–Oct., Wed.–Mon. 11–5.

Fodor'sChoice
★

With a reputation as the finest garden in Wales, **Bodnant Garden** remains a pilgrimage spot for horticulturists from around the world. Laid out in 1875, the 87 acres are particularly famed for rhododendrons, camellias, magnolias, and a laburnum arch that in May forms a huge tunnel of golden blooms. The mountains of Snowdonia form a magnificent backdrop to the Italianate terraces, rock and rose gardens, and pinetum. The gardens are about 5 mi south of Conwy, in the Vale of Conwy. ⊠ Off

A470, Tal-y-Cafn ☎ *01492/650460* ⊕ *www.nationaltrust.org.uk*
🎟 *£5.50* ⊙ *Mid-Mar.–Oct., daily 10–5.*

Where to Stay & Eat

£££–££££ ✕⬚ **Castle Hotel.** Sitting snugly within Conwy's medieval walls, this former coaching inn has wooden beams, old fireplaces, and plenty of antiques. Illustrious former guests include William Wordsworth, Samuel Johnson, and Charlotte Brontë. The individually decorated bedrooms are smallish but plushly luxurious, with elaborate modern bathrooms. Shakespeare's restaurant, decorated with Victorian paintings of scenes from the Bard's plays, serves excellent modern British cuisine, such as poached salmon rolled in soft herbs on a creamy Conwy crab risotto. Don't miss the local mussels if they're on the menu. A bar menu is also available. ⊠ *High St., LL32 8DB* ☎ *01492/582800* 🖷 *01492/582300* ⊕ *www.castlewales.co.uk* ⇆ *28 rooms* ⚘ *Restaurant, bar, lounge, meeting rooms, some pets allowed (fee), no-smoking rooms; no a/c* ⊟ *AE, MC, V* ⧖❗ *BP.*

Llandudno

⓫ *3 mi north of Conwy, 50 mi northwest of Chester.*

This appealingly old-fashioned North Wales seaside resort has a wealth of well-preserved Victorian architecture and an ornate amusement pier with entertainments, shops, and places to eat. Attractively painted hotels line the wide promenade (Llandudno has the largest choice of lodging in Wales). The shopping streets behind also look the part, thanks to their original canopied walkways. Llandudno has little in the way of garish arcades, preferring to stick to its faithful cable car that climbs, San Francisco–style, to the summit of the Great Orme headland above the resort. There's also an aerial cable car to the top, as well as a large, dry ski slope (with an artificial surface you can ski on year-round) and toboggan run.

Llandudno was the summer home of the family of Dr. Liddell, the Oxford don and father of the immortal Alice, inspiration for Lewis Carroll's *Alice's Adventures in Wonderland.* The book's Walrus and the Carpenter may be based on two rocks on Llandudno's West Shore near the Liddell home, which Alice possibly described to Carroll. The Alice in Wonderland connection is explored in the **Alice in Wonderland Centre,** where Alice's adventures come to life in displays of the best-known scenes from the book. Alice merchandise is for sale, too. ⊠ *3–4 Trinity Sq.* ☎ *01492/860082* ⊕ *www.wonderland.co.uk* 🎟 *£3* ⊙ *Easter–Oct., daily 10–5; Nov.–Easter, Mon.–Sat. 10–5.*

The prehistoric **Great Orme Mines** are at the summit of the Great Orme (*orme,* a Norse word, means "sea monster"), with its views of the coast and mountains of Snowdonia. Copper was first mined here in the Bronze Age, and you can tour the ancient underground workings. ⊠ *Great Orme* ☎ *01492/870447* ⊕ *www.greatormemines.info* 🎟 *£4.80* ⊙ *Feb.–Oct., daily 10–5.*

Where to Stay & Eat

★ **£££££** ✕⊠ **Bodysgallen Hall.** Antiques, comfortable chairs by cheery fires, pictures, and polished wood distinguish one of Wales's most luxurious country-house hotels. The part 17th-, part 18th-century building is set in walled gardens 2 mi out of town. Bedrooms in the house combine elegance and practicality; seekers of privacy may prefer the cottage suites scattered around the estate and parkland. The outstanding restaurant (three-course, fixed-price menu at dinner) uses local ingredients in creative ways, such as beef with a wild mushroom pancake or partridge with pan-fried foie gras. ⊠ *Off A470, LL30 1RS* ☎ *01492/584466* 🖷 *01492/582519* ⊕ *www.bodysgallen.com* ➴ *19 rooms, 16 cottage suites* ⚌ *Restaurant, tennis court, indoor pool, gym, sauna, spa, croquet, meeting rooms, some pets allowed, no-smoking rooms; no a/c in some rooms, no kids under 8* ⊟ *MC, V* ⍓⊨ *BP.*

£££–£££££ ✕⊠ **St. Tudno Hotel.** From the outside, one of Britain's best small seaside hotels blends unobtrusively with its neighbors, but the interior contains richly decorated and opulently furnished guest rooms and public areas with plenty of print fabrics and chintz. The fine contemporary cuisine includes dishes such as soup of local seafood and saddle of hare with spicy cabbage. ⊠ *Promenade, LL30 2LP* ☎ *01492/874411* 🖷 *01492/860407* ⊕ *www.st-tudno.co.uk* ➴ *19 rooms* ⚌ *Restaurant, in-room data ports, in-room VCRs, indoor pool, bar, some pets allowed (fee), no-smoking rooms; no a/c in some rooms* ⊟ *AE, DC, MC, V* ⍓⊨ *BP.*

£–££ ⊠ **Bryn Derwen Hotel.** Many hoteliers at British seaside resorts have not upgraded their accommodations and food, but this immaculate Victorian hotel exemplifies how it should be done. Fresh flowers, plush period furnishings in the public areas, and soothing, warm-hued bedrooms show the owners' attention to detail. Bryn Derwen offers truly excellent value for the price. ⊠ *34 Abbey Rd., LL30 2EE* ⊕ *www.bryn-derwen-hotel.co.uk* ☎☎ *01492/876804* ➴ *10 rooms* ⚌ *Dining room, lounge; no a/c, no smoking* ⊟ *MC, V* ⍓⊨ *BP.*

⬭ **en route** Inland from Rhyl, **Bodelwyddan Castle,** between Abergele and St. Asaph, is the Welsh home of London's National Portrait Gallery. Gardens, including a maze, aviary, and woodland walks, surround the Victorian castle. Galleries display Regency and Victorian portraits by artists such as John Singer Sargent, Thomas Lawrence, G. F. Watts, Dante Gabriel Rossetti, and Edwin Landseer. There are also hands-on galleries of Victorian amusements and inventions. ⊠ *Off A55, Bodelwyddan* ☎ *01745/584060* ⊕ *www.bodelwyddan-castle. co.uk* 🖾 *£4.50, grounds only £1.50* ⊙ *Apr.–Oct., daily 10:30–5; Nov.–Mar., Tues.–Thurs. and weekends 10:30–4.*

Denbigh

⓬ *25 mi southeast of Llandudno.*

This market town (market day is Wednesday) was much admired by Dr. Samuel Johnson (1709–84). A walk along the riverbank at Lawnt (a village just south of Denbigh), which he loved, brings you to a monumental urn placed in his honor. Not that it pleased him: "It looks like an intention to bury me alive," thundered the great lexicographer.

Denbigh Castle, begun in 1282 as one of Edward I's ring of castles built to control the Welsh, is known as "the hollow crown" because it is not much more than a shell—though an impressive one—set on high ground, dominating the town. H. M. Stanley (1841–1904), the intrepid 19th-century journalist and explorer who found Dr. Livingstone in Africa, was born in a cottage below the castle. ☎ 029/2050–0200 ⊕ *www.cadw. wales.gov.uk* ☒ *£2.50* ☉ *Apr.–Sept., weekdays 10–5:30, weekends 9:30–5:30.*

Ruthin

⑬ *8 mi southeast of Denbigh, 23 mi west of Chester.*

Once a stronghold of Welsh hero Owain Glyndŵr (circa 1354–1416), Ruthin is a delightful market town with elegant shops, good inns, and a fascinating architectural mix of medieval, Tudor, and Georgian buildings. The town also hosts medieval-style banquets and has a crafts complex with displays of the artisans' creations. The 17th-century **Myddleton Arms** in the town square has seven Dutch-style dormer windows, known as the "eyes of Ruthin," set into its red-tiled roof. You can tour **Ruthin Gaol,** where from 1654 to 1916 thousands of prisoners were incarcerated, and learn about conditions over the centuries. ☒ *Clwyd St.* ☎ *01824/708250* ⊕ *www.ruthingaol.co.uk* ☒ *£3* ☉ *Apr.–Oct., daily 10–5; Nov.–Mar., Tues.–Sun. 10–5.*

Where to Stay

£ ⊞ **Eyarth Old Railway Station.** This Victorian railway station 2 mi south of Ruthin has been converted into an outstanding B&B. The modern bedrooms are spacious, with large windows looking out over the Vale of Clwyd. ☒ *Off A525, Llanfair Dyffryn Clwyd, LL15 2EE* ☎ *01824/ 703643* 🖷 *01824/707464* ⊕ *www.eyarthstation.co.uk* 🛏 *6 rooms* ♿ *Pool, bar; no a/c* ⊟ *MC, V* ⊙| *BP.*

MID-WALES
THE HISTORIC HEARTLAND

Traditional market towns and country villages, small seaside resorts, quiet roads, and rolling landscapes filled with sheep farms, forests, and lakes make up mid-Wales, the country's green and rural heart. Because this is Wales's quietest vacation region, lodgings are scattered thinly. Outside of one or two large centers, Aberystwyth and Llandrindod Wells, accommodations are mainly country inns, small hotels, and farmhouses. This area also has some splendid country-house hotels. Although green is the predominant color here, the landscape differs around the region. The borderlands are gentle and undulating, rising to the west into high wild mountains. Farther north, around Dolgellau, mountainous scenery becomes even more pronounced in the southern section of the Snowdonia National Park. Mountains meet the sea along Cardigan Bay, a long coastline of headlands, peaceful sandy beaches, and beautiful estuaries that has long been a refuge from the crowd. In the 19th century, Tennyson, Darwin, Shelley, and Ruskin came to this area to work and relax; today, thousands more come to delight in the numerous antiquarian bookstores of Hay-on-Wye.

Hay-on-Wye

★ ⑭ *57 mi north of Cardiff, 25 mi north of Abergavenny.*

Bookshops and a mostly ruined castle dominate this town on the border of Wales and England. Hay is a lively place, especially on Sunday, when the rest of central Wales seems to be closed down. In 1961 Richard Booth established a small secondhand and antiquarian bookshop here. Other booksellers got in on the act, and bookshops now fill several houses, a movie theater, shops, and a pub. At last count, there were about 40, all in a town of only 1,300 inhabitants. It's now the largest secondhand bookselling center in the world, and priceless 14th-century manuscripts rub spines with "job lots" selling for a few pounds. Hay also has antiques and crafts centers. Things buzz in early summer during the

★ 10-day **Hay Festival** (☎ 0870/990–1299 ⊕ www.hayfestival.com), a celebration of literature that attracts famous writers from all over the world.

> **need a break?**
>
> After some hard browsing, take stop off at **The Granary** (⊠ Broad St. ☎ 01497/820790), a wood-beamed former grain store by the clock tower. The chalkboard menu changes regularly; look for superb homemade soups, lamb and spinach curry, and flavorful cheese and garlic toasties (toasted sandwiches).

Where to Stay & Eat

££ ✕☒ **Old Black Lion.** A 17th-century coaching inn close to Hay's center is ideal for a lunch break while you're ransacking the bookshops, or for an overnight stay in one of its country-style rooms. The oak-beamed bar serves food, and the breakfasts are especially good. The restaurant's sophisticated cooking has an international flavor and emphasizes local meats and produce. ⊠ *Lion St., HR3 5AD* ☎ *01497/820841* 🖷 *01497/ 822960* ⊕ *www.oldblacklion.co.uk* 🛏 *10 rooms* ♨ *Restaurant, bar, lounge, no-smoking rooms; no a/c, no kids under 5* ═ *MC, V* ⭧ *BP.*

Shopping

Boz Books (⊠ 13A Castle St. ☎ 01497/821277) specializes in 19th-century novels, including first editions of Dickens. A former movie theater houses the town's largest book outpost, the **Hay Cinema Bookshop** (⊠ Castle St. ☎ 01497/820071), which stocks 200,000 volumes on subjects from art to zoology at prices from 50 pence to £5,000.

Builth Wells

⑮ *20 mi northwest of Hay-on-Wye, 60 mi north of Cardiff.*

Builth Wells, a farming town and former spa on the banks of the River Wye, hosts Wales's biggest rural gathering. The countryside around Builth and its neighbor, Llandrindod Wells, varies considerably. Some of the land is soft and rich, with green hills and lush valleys, but close by are the wildernesses of Mynydd Eppynt and the foothills of the Cambrian Mountains, the lofty "backbone of Wales."

★ The annual **Royal Welsh Agricultural Show** (☎ 01982/553683 ⊕ www. rwas.co.uk), held in late July, is not only Wales's prime gathering of farming folk but also a colorful countryside jamboree that attracts huge crowds.

Where to Stay & Eat

★ £££££ ✕⌂ **Lake Country House.** This is the place to go for total Victorian country elegance and tranquillity. Its 50 acres of sloping lawns and lush rhododendrons also contain a trout-filled lake. Comfortable and quiet, the hotel has first-class service and excellent contemporary cuisine (fixed-price dinner menu) such as salmon with char-grilled eggplant and spicy couscous. Period furniture and fine fabrics decorate the large bedrooms; some have four-poster beds. The hotel is in a peaceful former spa town about 8 mi southwest of Builth. ⊠ *Llangammarch Wells, LD4 4BS* ☎ *01591/620202* 🖷 *01591/620457* ⊕ *www.lakecountryhouse.co.uk* ⌂ *18 rooms ⌂ Restaurant, 9-hole golf course, putting green, tennis court, fishing, billiards, croquet, bar, no-smoking rooms; no a/c* ▭ *AE, DC, MC, V* ⎰○⎱ *BP.*

Llandrindod Wells

⑯ *7 mi north of Builth Wells, 67 mi north of Cardiff.*

Also known as Llandod, the old spa town of Llandrindod Wells preserves its original Victorian layout and look, with fussy turrets, cupolas, loggias, and balustrades, and greenery everywhere. On a branch-line rail route and with good bus service, Llandrindod makes a useful base for exploring the region, and the town itself is easily explored on foot. Cross over to South Crescent, passing the Glen Usk Hotel with its wrought-iron balustrade and the Victorian bandstand in the gardens opposite, and you soon reach Middleton Street, another Victorian thoroughfare. From there, head to Rock Park and the path that leads to the Pump Room. On the other side of town, the lake, with its boathouse, café, and gift shop, has wooded hills on one side and a broad common on the other.

The **Radnorshire Museum,** in Memorial Gardens, presents the spa's development from Roman times and explains some Victorian "cures" in gruesome detail. ☎ *01597/824513* 🖃 *£1* ☉ *Apr.–Oct., Tues.–Sat. 10–5, Sun. 1–5; Nov.–Mar., Tues.–Fri. 10–4, Sat. 10–1.*

The **Pump Room** (⊠ Rock Park Spa ☎ 01597/822997), where visitors would "take the waters," serves tea and refreshments and one type of the many waters that used to be on tap.

During the town's **Victorian Festival** (☎ 01597/823441 ⊕ www. victorianfestival.co.uk), in late August, shop assistants, hotel staff, and anyone else who cares to join in wear period costume and enjoy "old-style" entertainment.

Where to Stay

£ ⌂ **Brynhir Farm.** You get a warm welcome at this immaculate, cream-washed farmhouse tucked into the hills on a 200-acre sheep and cattle farm. Country-style furnishings enhance the rooms. ⊠ *Chapel Rd., Howey, LD1 5PB* ☎☎ *01597/822425* ⊕ *www.brynhir.farm.btinternet. co.uk* ⟗ *5 rooms* ⌂ *Dining room; no a/c, no room phones, no smoking* ☰ *MC, V* ¹⊖¹ *BP.*

£ ▦ **Guidfa House.** Friendly hosts Tony and Anne Millan run this stylish Georgian guest house with a welcoming log fire and bright, individually furnished bedrooms. Cordon Bleu–trained Anne prepares dinners (for guests only) from fresh local produce; the guinea fowl with apple brandy and mushroom sauce is delicious. All in all, this is an ideal base from which to explore the countryside. ⊠ *Crossgates, near Llandrindod Wells, LD1 6RF* ☎ *01597/851241* ▦ *01597/851875* ⊕ *www.guidfa-house.co.uk* ⟗ *6 rooms* ⌂ *Dining room; no a/c, no room phones, no kids under 10* ☰ *MC, V* ¹⊖¹ *BP.*

en route
From Llandrindod, take A4081/A470 to Rhayader, a good pony-trekking center and gateway town for the **Elan Valley,** Wales's Lake District. This 7-mi chain of lakes, winding between gray-green hills, was created in the 1890s by a system of dams designed to supply water to Birmingham, 73 mi to the east. From the Elan Valley, you can follow the narrow Cwmystwyth mountain road west to **Devil's Bridge,** a famous (and popular) beauty spot where three bridges set one on top of the other span a chasm over the raging River Mynach, before continuing on to Aberystwyth. (You can also take the steam-operated Vale of Rheidol Railway to this site from Aberystwyth.)

Aberystwyth

❶⑦ *41 mi northwest of Llandrindod Wells via A44, 118 mi northwest of Cardiff.*

Aberystwyth makes the best of several worlds as a seaside resort (complete with promenade and amusement pier) and a long-established university town that is home to the impressive National Library of Wales. It also has a small harbor and is a major shopping center for mid-Wales. More than 5,000 students expand the full-time population of 12,000. The town, midway along Cardigan Bay, came to prominence as a Victorian watering hole thanks to a curving beach set beneath a prominent headland. Aberystwyth is a good gateway for exploring mid-Wales: few towns in Wales present such varied scenery within their immediate neighborhood, from the Devil's Bridge to the green Rheidol Valley.

The massive, neoclassical **National Library of Wales,** on a hill amid the buildings of the modern University of Wales, Aberystwyth, houses notable Welsh and other Celtic literary works among its more than 4.5 million printed volumes. Besides books and manuscripts, this self-described national treasure house has enormous archives of maps, photographs, films, and sound recordings. Material doesn't circulate, but the public can do research; many people pursue genealogical history here (there's a family history center). The gallery has art shows (works may be for sale, too), and changing exhibitions highlight Welsh and other subjects. Films and concerts are presented in the auditorium. ⊠ *Off*

THE LANGUAGE OF CYMRU

Welsh, the native language of Wales (Cymru, in Welsh), is revered in the country, but it was not legally recognized in Britain until the 1960s. Today Welsh schoolchildren under 16 are required to take classes to learn the language, and Welsh is surviving more successfully than its Celtic cousin, Breton, which is spoken in northwestern France. Welsh may look daunting to pronounce, but it is a phonetic language; pronunciation is fairly easy once the alphabet is learned. Remember that "dd" is sounded like "th" in they, "f" sounds like "v" in save, and "ff" is the equivalent of the English "f" in forest. The "ll" sound has no English equivalent; the closest match is the "cl" sound in "close."

Terms that crop up frequently in Welsh are bach or fach (small), craig or graig (rock), cwm (valley), dyffryn (valley), eglwys (church), glyn (glen), llyn (lake), mawr or fawr (great, big), mynydd or fynydd (mountain, moorland), pentre (village, homestead), plas (hall, mansion), and pont or bont (bridge).

Penglais Rd. ☎ *01970/632800* ⊕ *www.llgc.org.uk* ✉ *Free* ☉ *Weekdays 9:30–6, Sat. 9:30–5.*

The **Ceredigion Museum,** in a flamboyant 1905 Edwardian theater, has fine collections related to folk history. Highlights include a reconstructed mud-walled cottage from 1850, exhibits from the building's music-hall past, and items illustrating the region's seafaring, lead mining, and farming history. ✉ *Terrace Rd.* ☎ *01970/633088* ⊕ *www.ceredigion. gov.uk/coliseum/* ✉ *Free* ☉ *Mon.–Sat. 10–5.*

The **castle,** at the southern end of the bay near the New Promenade, was built in 1277 and rebuilt in 1282 by Edward I. It was one of several strongholds to fall, in 1404, to the Welsh leader Owain Glyndŵr. Today it is a romantic ruin on a headland separating the north shore from the harbor shore.

At the northern end of the beach promenade, a zigzag cliff path–nature trail at **Constitution Hill** leads to a view from the hilltop. An enjoyable ☺ way to reach the summit of Constitution Hill is by the **Aberystwyth Cliff Railway,** the longest electric cliff railway in Britain. Opened in 1896, it has been refurbished without diminishing its Victorian look. ☎ *01970/ 617642* ✉ *£2.50 round-trip* ☉ *Mid-Mar.–June and Oct., daily 10–5; July–Sept., daily 10–6.*

At the 430-foot summit of Constitution Hill is the **Great Aberystwyth Camera Obscura** (☎ 01970/617642), a free modern version of a Victorian amusement: a massive 14-inch lens gives a bird's-eye view of more than 1,000 square mi of sea and scenery, including the whole of Cardigan Bay and 26 Welsh mountain peaks.

At Aberystwyth Station you can hop on the narrow-gauge, steam-op-☺ erated **Vale of Rheidol Railway** for an hour ride to the **Devil's Bridge,** where the rivers Rheidol and Mynach meet in a series of spectacular falls. Clamped between two rocky cliffs where a torrent of water pours unceasingly, this bridge well deserves its name—*Pont y Gwr Drwg*, or Bridge of the Evil One. There are actually three bridges (the oldest is 800 years old), and the walk down to the lowest bridge, "the devil's," is magnificent but strictly for the surefooted. ⊠ *Alexandra St.* ☎ *01970/625819* ⊕ *www.rheidolrailway.co.uk* 🎫 *£11.50 round-trip* ☉ *Easter–Oct.; call for schedule.*

off the beaten path

LLANERCHAERON – This uniquely preserved late-18th-century Welsh gentry estate in the Aeron Valley, 17 mi south of Aberystwyth, near Aberaeron, is a superb example of the early work of John Nash (1752–1835). Nash was the leading architect of the Regency and the designer of Brighton's Royal Pavilion. The estate survived with few changes until the present; it is a self-contained world with stables, barns, and a dairy and brewery. The walled gardens are spectacular. ⊠ *Off A482, Ciliau Aeron* ☎ *01545/570200* ⊕ *www.nationaltrust. org.uk* 🎫 *£5* ☉ *Apr.–Oct., Wed.–Sun. 11:30–4:30; parkland open year-round in daylight.*

Where to Stay & Eat

££ ✕ **Gannets.** A simple, good-value bistro, Gannets specializes in hearty roasts and pies produced from locally supplied meat, fish, and game. Organically grown vegetables and a good French house wine are further draws for a university crowd. ⊠ *7 St. James's Sq.* ☎ *01970/617164* ⊟ *MC, V* ☉ *Closed Sun., Tues.*

££££ ✕🏨 **Conrah Country Hotel.** Part of the appeal of this Edwardian country-house hotel on 20 acres of grounds is its air of seclusion, even though it's just 3 mi south of Aberystwyth. Traditional country furnishings and antiques decorate the house, and fresh flowers fill each room. The restaurant is known for its imaginative British cuisine making use of local fish and meat. There's a three-course prix-fixe menu at dinner. ⊠ *A487, Chancery, SY23 4DF* ☎ *01970/617941* 🖨 *01970/624546* ⊕ *www. conrah.co.uk* 🛏 *17 rooms* ♿ *Restaurant, indoor pool, sauna, croquet; no a/c, no kids under 5* ⊟ *AE, DC, MC, V* ⦿*l BP.*

££–£££ ✕🏨 **Harbourmaster Hotel.** A drive south on the coast road from Aberystwyth brings you to Aberaeron and the delights of this early 19th-century Georgian-style building, right on the harbor among a cluster of colorfully painted structures. Modern design and strong colors dominate the public areas and bedrooms, which have wonderful harbor views. The brasserie produces sophisticated fare such as roasted parsnip soup and Thai monkfish red curry; you can also choose superb Welsh lamb and beef. ⊠ *Quay Parade, Aberaeron, SA46 OBT, 15 mi south of Aberystwyth* ☎ *01545/570755* ⊕ *www.harbour-master.com* 🛏 *7 rooms* ♿ *Restaurant, bar, some pets allowed (fee); no a/c* ⊟*MC, V* ⦿*l BP.*

££ ✕🏨 **Four Seasons.** This family-run hotel in the town center (no relation to the famous chain) is relaxed and friendly. The spacious rooms are simply decorated, with plenty of print fabrics. The restaurant serves à la carte and three-course prix-fixe menus at dinner; roast saddle of Welsh lamb is a specialty. ⊠ *50–54 Portland St., SY23 2DX* ☎ *01970/ 612120* 🖨 *01970/627458* ⊕ *www.fourseasonshotel.uk.com* 🛏 *16 rooms* ♿ *Restaurant; no a/c* ⊟ *AE, MC, V* ⦿*l BP.*

Machynlleth

⑱ *18 mi northeast of Aberystwyth.*

Machynlleth, at the head of the beautiful Dovey Estuary, does not look like a typical Welsh country town. Its long and wide main street (Heol Maengwyn), lined with a mixed style of buildings from sober gray stone to well-proportioned Georgian, creates an atypical sense of openness and space. Machynlleth's busiest day is Wednesday, when the stalls of market traders fill the main street.

At the **Owain Glyndŵr Centre,** a small exhibition celebrates Wales's last native leader, who established a Welsh parliament at Machynlleth in the early 15th century. ✉ *End of Heol Maengwyn* ☎ *01654/702827* 💷 *Free* ⊙ *Easter–Sept., Mon.–Sat. 10–5.*

In a former chapel that's now a cultural and performing arts center is the **Y Tabernacl Museum of Modern Art,** a superb gallery with permanent displays, including works by noted contemporary Welsh artist Kyffin Williams. Changing exhibitions highlight other contemporary artists. ✉ *Heol Penrallt* ☎ *01654/703355* ⊕ *www.momawales.org.uk* 💷 *Free* ⊙ *Mon.–Sat. 10–4.*

Early Welsh history is the main theme at **Celtica,** an imaginative exhibition center in the large parkland behind the shops and pubs. Interpretive displays re-create Wales's past, including village life and Celtic beliefs. ☎ *01654/702702* ⊕ *www.celtica.wales.com* 💷 *£4.95* ⊙ *Daily 10–6; last entry to main exhibition 4:40.*

☉ At the unique **Centre for Alternative Technology,** in an abandoned slate quarry in the forested hills just north of Machynlleth, a water-balanced cliff railway transports you to a futuristic, educational village equipped with all things green: alternative energy sources (solar roofs, wood-chip boilers), organic gardens, and a vegetarian café. Interactive displays present practical ideas about renewable resources, and the store is full of inspirational books and eco-friendly products. ✉ *Off A487* ☎ *01654/ 702400* ⊕ *www.cat.org.uk* 💷 *£7.20* ⊙ *Daily 9–6.*

Where to Stay & Eat

★ **£££££** ✕🔲 **Ynyshir Hall.** Idyllic gardens and grounds surround this supremely luxurious country retreat in a white-painted Georgian mansion near a wildlife reserve. Inside, the place glows: owner Rob Reen, an artist, displays his vibrant-hued work around the house. He and his wife, Joan, have decorated all surfaces in jewel-like tones. Antiques and Welsh pottery fill the public areas; the pampering guest rooms, named after artists (Hogarth, Matisse, Goya), have antique beds. The outstanding contemporary cuisine in the candlelit restaurant (fixed-price dinner menu) uses local favorites, from wild salmon and venison to farmhouse cheeses. ✉ *Off A487, Eglwysfach SY20 8TA, southwest of Machynlleth* ☎ *01654/ 781209 or 800/777–6536* 🖷 *01654/781366* ⊕ *www.ynyshir-hall.co.uk* 🛏 *10 rooms* ₺ *Restaurant; no a/c, no kids under 9, no smoking* ⊟ *AE, DC, MC, V* ⦿ *BP.*

££ ✕🔲 **Penhelig Arms.** The delightful little sailing center of Aberdovey is perched at the mouth of the Dovey Estuary, west of Machynlleth. This immaculate harborside inn has a terrace overlooking the harbor and bay, and most rooms have wonderful sea views. Meet the locals in the wood-paneled Fisherman's Bar and dine in style in the fine restaurant (three-course, fixed-price dinner menu), where local seafood is a specialty. ✉ *A493, Aberdovey, LL35 0LT* ☎ *01654/767215* 🖷 *01654/767690* ⊕ *www.penheligarms.com* 🛏 *14 rooms* ⚭ *Restaurant, bar; no a/c* ▤ *MC, V* ⦿⦿ *BP.*

Outdoors

The 128-mi **Glyndŵr's Way** (✉ Tourist Office, Heol Maengwyn ☎ 01654/702401 ⊕ www.glyndwrsway.org.uk) walking route passes through Machynlleth before it turns east to climb above the Dovey with wonderful views north to Cadair Idris.

Dolgellau

⑲ *16 mi north of Machynlleth, 34 mi north of Aberystwyth.*

A solidly Welsh town with dark stone buildings and old coaching inns made of the local gray dolerite and slate, Dolgellau (pronounced dol-*geth*-lee) thrived with the wool trade until the mid-19th century. (Sheep are still auctioned here, but they're valued for meat rather than wool.) Prosperity left striking architecture, with buildings of different eras side by side on crooked streets that are a pre-Norman legacy. The town trail booklet, sold in the tourist office on Eldon Square, tells the story. Dolgellau, in a valley, has long been a popular base for people eager to walk and explore the surrounding countryside. Look down the streets or above the buildings, and you'll see mountains rise up in the distance—a lovely sight.

The town became the center of the Welsh gold trade in the 19th century, when high-quality gold was discovered locally. A nugget of Dolgellau gold is used to make royal wedding rings. You can still try your luck and pan for gold in the Mawddach.

The **Museum of the Quakers,** in the town square, commemorates the area's strong links with the Quaker movement and the Quakers' emigration to the American colonies. ✉ *Eldon Sq.* ☎ *01341/422888* 🖾 *Free* ☾ *Easter–Oct., daily 10–6; Nov.–Easter, Thurs.–Mon. 10–5.*

To the south of Dolgellau rises the menacing bulk of **Cadair Idris** (2,927 feet); the name means "the Chair of Idris," though no one is completely sure who Idris was—probably a warrior bard. It is said that anyone sleeping for a night on a certain part of the mountain will awaken either a poet or a madman, or not at all.

Barmouth

⑳ *10 mi west of Dolgellau.*

Barmouth, on the northern mouth of the Mawddach Estuary, is one of the few places along the Welsh coast that can be described as a full-fledged seaside resort, although it's now a bit tired. It has a 2-mi-long promenade, wide expanses of golden beach, and facilities for sea, river, and mountain lake fishing. To appreciate the splendid location, walk along the footpath beside the railway bridge that crosses the mouth of the estuary: the bay stretches out on one side, and on the other are rugged, looming mountains and the river.

The arrival of the railroad in the 19th century made Barmouth a popular vacation spot. Alfred, Lord Tennyson was inspired to write *Crossing the Bar* by the spectacle of the Mawddach rushing to meet the sea. Charles Darwin worked on *The Origin of Species* and *The Descent of Man* in a house by the shore. Essayist and art critic John Ruskin was a frequent visitor and was trustee of the St. George's cottages built in 1871 by the Guild of St. George (Ruskin's organization, dedicated to founding agrarian communities) in 1871. Ruskin loved the walk from Barmouth up the river to Dolgellau.

Where to Stay

££ ⊞ **Llwyndu Farmhouse.** This restored 17th-century farmhouse, with its inglenook fireplace, mullioned windows, exposed stone walls, and ancient beams, stands on a hillside with fine views over Cardigan Bay. The country-style rooms in the house and in the adjoining converted barn have modern conveniences as well as some of the charming quirks of age. Guests can dine on traditional and contemporary dishes from Welsh rabbit to stir-fried duck with plum and ginger sauce. ⊠ *A496, Llanaber, LL42 1RR, 1 mi north of Barmouth* ☎ *01341/280144* 🖨 *01341/281236* ⊕ *www.llwyndu-farmhouse.co.uk* ⟿ *7 rooms* ⟡ *Dining room, lounge; no a/c, no smoking* ➾ *MC, V* ⎮⚬⎮ *BP.*

Welshpool

㉑ *48 mi east of Barmouth, 19 mi west of Shrewsbury.*

The border town of Welshpool, "Trallwng" in Welsh, is famous as the home of Powis Castle, one of mid-Wales's greatest treasures, but it also has an appealing town center.

★ Continuously occupied since the 13th century, **Powis Castle** is one of the most opulent residential castles in Britain, with gardens that are equally renowned. Its battlements rear high on a hilltop, and Italian- and French-influenced terraced gardens surround the castle. Below gigantic yew hedges, the grounds fall steeply down to wide lawns and neat Elizabethan gardens. The interior contains many treasures: Greek vases; paintings by Thomas Gainsborough, Joshua Reynolds, and George Romney, among others; superb furniture, including a 16th-century Italian table inlaid with marble; and the **Clive of India Museum,** with a good collection of Indian art. The tearoom is excellent. A timed-ticket system may be in effect on busy days. ⊠ *Off A483* ☎ *01938/551920* ⊕ *www. nationaltrust.org.uk* 🗗 *£8.40, gardens only £5.80* ⊙ *Castle and museum late Mar.–Sept., Thurs.–Mon. 1–5; Oct., Thurs.–Mon. 1–4. Gardens late Mar.–Oct., Thurs.–Mon. 11–6.*

The excellent **Powysland Museum,** in a converted warehouse on the banks of the Montgomery Canal, focuses on local history from the Stone Age to Victorian times. ⊠ *Canal Wharf* ☎☎ *01938/554656* 🗗 *£1* ⊙ *May–Sept., Mon., Tues., Thurs., and Fri. 11–1 and 2–5, weekends 10–1 and 2–5; Oct.–Apr., Mon., Tues., Thurs., and Fri. 11–1 and 2–5, Sat. 2–5.*

SOUTH WALES
FROM CARDIFF TO CARDIGAN

The most diverse of Wales's three regions, the south covers not only the immediate region around Cardiff and the border of Wales and England, but also the southwest as far as the rugged coastline of Pembrokeshire. The very different natures of its two national parks reveals South Wales's scenic variety. The Brecon Beacons park, a short drive north of Cardiff, is an area of high, grassy mountains, lakes, and craggy limestone gorges. In contrast, the Pembrokeshire Coast National Park holds one of Europe's finest stretches of coastal natural beauty, with mile after mile of spectacular sea cliffs, beaches, headlands, and coves. Other pieces of the complicated South Wales jigsaw include traditional farmlands, cosmopolitan urban areas, rolling border country, wooded vales, and the former industrial valleys where coal was mined in huge quantities during the 19th and early-20th centuries.

Cardiff

▶ *20 mi west of the Second Severn Bridge, which carries the M4 motorway across the Severn Estuary into Wales.*

Financially, industrially, and commercially Cardiff, with a population of 306,000, is the most important city in Wales, but those attributes, some might point out, are not exactly exciting for visitors. Cardiff is on the upswing, though, in part because of the presence of the Welsh Assembly. Once you get to know Wales's capital, there is much to delight the eye, including the handsome Civic Centre, magnificent parklands, and a castle with abundant Victorian verve. A regeneration project has transformed the city's docklands, once a coal-exporting industrial hub. As part of this, a dam across the Taff and Ely rivers created a freshwater lake edged by 8 mi of prime waterfront. Known as Cardiff Bay, this area of promenades, shops, restaurants, and attractions has become very popular. In 2005, look for special events and festivals as the city celebrates its 50th anniversary as the capital of Wales and its centenary as a city.

True to the Welsh tradition of vocal excellence, Cardiff is home base for Britain's most adventurous opera company, the acclaimed Welsh National Opera. Cardiff is also the sporting center of Wales and the Welsh capital of rugby football. To hear crowds singing their support for the Welsh team is a stirring experience.

★ ㉒ **Cardiff Castle** in Bute Park, one section of the city's hundreds of acres of parkland, is an unusual historic site, with Roman, Norman, and Victorian associations. Parts of the walls are Roman, the solid keep is Norman, and the whole complex was restored and transformed into a Victorian ego flight by the third marquess of Bute. He employed William Burges (1827–81), an architect obsessed by the Gothic period, and Burges transformed the castle into an extravaganza of medieval color and careful craftsmanship. It is the perfect expression of the anything-

Cardiff Bay . . .**26**
Cardiff
Castle **22**
Castell Coch . .**29**
Llandaff **27**
Millennium
Stadium **25**
Museum of
Welsh Life . . .**28**
National Museum
and Gallery . .**23**
St. David's
Centre **24**

goes Victorian spirit, and a reflection of the fortune made by the marquess in Cardiff's booming docklands. ⊠ *Bute Park* ☎ *029/2087–8100* ⊕ *www.cardiffcastle.com* ⊠ *Grounds and guided tour of castle £6, grounds only £3* ⊙ *Mar.–Oct., daily 9:30–6; Nov.–Feb., daily 9:30–4; call for tour times.*

 need a break?

Celtic Cauldron (⊠ 47–49 Castle Arcade ☎ 029/2038–7185), in the Victorian shopping arcade opposite Cardiff Castle, serves snacks and filling dishes with a Welsh flavor. Try the cawl, a lamb and root-vegetable stew, and the Glamorgan sausages. It's closed for dinner.

The **Civic Centre,** two blocks north and east of Cardiff Castle, is a well-designed complex of tree-lined avenues and Edwardian civic buildings with white Portland stone facades; Cathays Park is in the center. A proud Welsh dragon sits atop the domed City Hall, and inside the building the Marble Hall contains statues of Welsh heroes, including St. David, Henry Tudor, and Owain Glyndwr (although he razed Cardiff in 1404). Neo-classical law courts and elegant university campus buildings are also here. ⊠ *Bordered by North Road on the west and Park Place on the east.*

★ ㉓ The **National Museum and Gallery,** next to City Hall in the Civic Centre, tells the story of Wales through its plants, rocks, archaeology, art, and industry. Its fine collection of modern European art includes a large selection of impressionist and postimpressionist works. The interactive Glanely Gallery lets children explore artifacts from the collections and work on other projects. Allow at least half a day at the museum, and don't miss *La Parisienne* by Renoir. ⊠ *Cathays Park* ☎ *029/2039–7951* ⊕ *www.nmgw.ac.uk* 🖾 *Free* ☉ *Tues.–Sun. 10–5.*

㉔ Around **St. David's Centre,** south of the Civic Centre, are the shopping and business areas of Cardiff. A large, modern shopping mall holds **St. David's Hall,** one of Europe's best concert halls, with outstanding acoustics. People come here for classical music, jazz, rock, ballet, and even snooker championships. Nearby is the **Cardiff International Arena,** a multipurpose center for exhibitions, concerts, and conferences.

㉕ The modern, 72,000-seat **Millennium Stadium** stands beside the River Taff on the site of the famous Cardiff Arms Park, the spiritual home of Welsh rugby. The stadium's retractable roof enables it to be used for concerts and special events throughout the year, as well as for rugby. On a one-hour tour you can walk the players' tunnel and see the Royal Box, dressing rooms, pitch, and broadcasting suite. ⊠ *Entrance Gate 3, Westgate St.* ☎ *029/2082–2228* ⊕ *www.cardiff-stadium.co.uk* 🖾 *£5* ☉ *Call for times.*

Panoramic bay views, promenades, shops, restaurants, and museums make
㉖ **Cardiff Bay,** the revitalized dockland 1 mi south of the city center, worth a visit. The **Cardiff Bay Visitor Centre,** a futuristic building known locally as "the Tube" (because of its distinctive shape), tells the story of the transformation of the bay area. An imposing Victorian building, the **Pierhead,** contains a lively exhibition about the workings and values of the National Assembly. Overlooking the bay is the timber Norwegian seamen's church where Roald Dahl (noted author whose children's books include *Matilda* and *Charlie and the Chocolate Factory*) was baptized. It's now known as **The Norwegian Church Arts Centre** and houses a performance space, a gallery, and a café. You can take a bus or taxi to get to the area from the city center.

🖑 **Techniquest,** a large science-discovery center on the waterfront, has 160 interactive exhibits, a planetarium, and a science theater. ⊠ *Stuart St., Cardiff Bay* ☎ *029/2047–5475* ⊕ *www.techniquest.org* 🖾 *£6.75* ☉ *Weekdays 9:30–4:30, weekends 10:30–5.*

㉗ In **Llandaff,** a suburb that retains its village feeling, you can visit **Llandaff Cathedral,** which was repaired after serious bomb damage in World War II. The cathedral includes the work of a number of Pre-Raphaelites as well as *Christ in Majesty,* a 15-foot-tall aluminum figure by sculptor Jacob Epstein (1880–1959). To get here from Cardiff, cross the River Taff and follow Cathedral Road for about 2 mi.

★ 🖑 ㉘ On 100 acres of parklands and gardens, the excellent, open-air **Museum of Welsh Life** has farmhouses, cottages, shops, a school, chapels, St. Fagans castle (a 16th-century manor house), and terraced houses that celebrate Wales's rich rural culture and show the evolution of building styles. All but two of the structures were brought here from places around Wales. Galleries display clothing and articles from daily life. There are farming demonstrations and special events that highlight ancient rural festivals. The museum is accessible from Junction 33 on the M4. ☒ *St. Fagans* ☎ *029/2057–3500* ⊕ *www.nmgw.ac.uk* ☒ *Free* ☉ *Daily 10–5.*

★ ㉙ Perched on a hillside, **Castell Coch**, the Red Castle, is a turreted Victorian vision. It was built (on the site of a medieval stronghold) in the 1870s, about the time that Ludwig II of Bavaria was creating his fairy-tale castles, and it could almost be one of them. The castle was another collaboration of the third marquess of Bute and William Burges, builders of Cardiff Castle. Here Burges created everything—architecture, furnishings, carvings, murals—in a remarkable exercise in Victorian-Gothic whimsy. ☒ *A470, Tongwynlais, 4 mi north of Cardiff* ☎ *029/2081–0101* ⊕ *www.cadw.wales.gov.uk* ☒ *£3* ☉ *Apr., May, and Oct., daily 9:30–5; June–Sept., daily 9:30–6; Nov.–Mar., Mon.–Sat. 9:30–4, Sun. 11–4.*

The largest (with more than 30 acres of grounds) and one of the most impressive fortresses in Wales, **Caerphilly Castle** was remarkable at the time of its 13th-century construction by an Anglo-Norman lord. The concentric fortification contained inner and outer defenses. A moat surrounds the castle, but Caerphilly is no longer on guard; some walls have toppled and others lean haphazardly. Exhibits in the gatehouse trace its turbulent history. The castle is 7 mi north of Cardiff. ☒ *Access off A470–A468, Caerphilly* ☎ *029/2088–3143* ⊕ *www.cadw.wales.gov.uk* ☒ *£2.50* ☉ *Apr., May, and Oct., daily 9:30–5; June–Sept., daily 9:30–6; Nov.–Mar., Mon.–Sat. 9:30–4, Sun. 11–4.*

off the
beaten
path

TINTERN ABBEY – When Wordsworth penned "Lines Written a Few Miles Above Tintern Abbey," he had no idea of all the people who would flock to Tintern to gaze at the abbey's substantial ruins. Remote and hauntingly beautiful as the site is, Tintern's appeal is diminished in summer because of crowds, so visit early or late in the day to best appreciate the complex stonework and tracery of the Gothic church. The abbey, 5 mi north of Chepstow and 30 mi northeast of Cardiff, is on the lush banks of the River Wye. ☒ *A466, Tintern* ☎ *01291/689251* ⊕ *www.cadw.wales.gov.uk* ☒ *£2.50* ☉ *Apr., May, and Oct., daily 9:30–5; June–Sept., daily 9:30–6; Nov.–Mar., Mon.–Sat. 9:30–4, Sun. 11–4.*

Where to Stay & Eat

★ **£££££** ✕ **Le Gallois.** Its minimalist furnishings and varied menu help make this sophisticated restaurant, close to Sophia Gardens, one of the city's most popular. The cooking is European in style and takes advantage of local ingredients. Try the loin of venison with poached pear, celeriac and truffle purée, claret sauce, and chocolate oil. A good-value fixed-price menu is available at lunch, and there's a fixed-price dinner menu, too (you choose the number of courses). ☒ *8 Romilly Crescent* ☎ *029/2034–1264* ▤ *AE, MC, V* ☉ *Closed Sun. and Mon.*

££–£££ ✕ **Armless Dragon.** It's worth the five-minute drive from the city center to eat at this comfortable restaurant with a contemporary menu that changes daily. Dishes such as Monmouthshire woodland pork with smoked bacon and creamed leeks are created from seasonal, locally sourced ingredients. There are always good vegetarian options. ☒ *97*

Wyverne Rd. ☎ 029/2038–2357 ▤ MC, V ⊘ Closed Sun. and Mon.

££ ✕ **Giovanni's.** This popular, family-run Italian restaurant in the city center is known for its friendliness rather than the originality of its fare. Pastas and pizzas are among the choices. ✉ 38 The Hayes ☎ 029/2022–0077 ▤ MC, V.

£–££ ✕ **Harry Ramsden's.** You can dine on the (reputedly) world's most famous fish-and-chips in a chandeliered, 200-seat dining room with wonderful views across Cardiff Bay. If you like live music with your meal, call to ask for dates of opera and sing-along evenings. ✉ Landsea House, Stuart St. ☎ 029/2046–3334 ▤ AE, DC, MC, V.

★ £££££ ▦ **St. David's Hotel and Spa.** Natural light from a glass atrium floods this stylish, up-to-the-minute luxury hotel along the waterfront. Every room, done in soothing neutral tones with sleek modern furniture, has a private balcony and views over Cardiff Bay. You can indulge in a relaxing hydrotherapy spa treatment or feast at the Tides restaurant, under the guidance of noted London chef Marco Pierre White, which specializes in modern French fare. ✉ Havannah St., CF10 6SD ☎ 029/2045–4045 🖷 029/2048–7056 ⊕ www.roccofortehotels.com ⇌ 132 rooms ♿ Restaurant, in-room data ports, cable TV, indoor pool, gym, spa, business services, meeting rooms, no-smoking rooms ▤ AE, DC, MC, V ⊠ BP.

£–££ ▦ **Big Sleep Hotel.** Actor John Malkovich is a shareholder in this converted 1960s office tower that cleverly combines chic minimalism with good-value prices. Bright blue-and-white fabrics and white or beige Formica furniture add cheer. The city center location is convenient, but avoid the noisier rooms that overlook the nearby railroad tracks. ✉ Bute Terr., CF10 2FE ☎ 029/2063–6363 🖷 029/2063–6364 ⊕ www. thebigsleephotel.com ⇌ 81 rooms ♿ In-room data ports, cable TV, bar, no-smoking rooms; no a/c ▤ AE, DC, MC, V ⊠ CP.

£–££ ▦ **Llanerch Vineyard.** The pine-furnished, country-style rooms in the farmhouse and converted outbuildings of this Vale of Glamorgan vineyard are only 15 minutes from Cardiff center, but you are deep in the green countryside here. You can walk in the surrounding vineyard and woodlands and arrange your own personal Welsh wine tasting. Take Junction 34 off M4 and follow the brown signs. ✉ Hensol, Pendoylan, CF72 8GG ☎ 01443/225877 🖷 01443/225546 ⊕ www.llanerch-vineyard. co.uk ⇌ 11 rooms ♿ No a/c, no smoking ▤ MC, V ⊠ BP.

£–££ ▦ **Town House.** Cosmopolitan in style, this immaculate guest house near the city center (shops and castle are a short walk away) is well known as Cardiff's best B&B. The elegant Victorian building retains many original features and has neat, well-equipped bedrooms. You can have traditional British or American breakfasts in the formal dining room. ✉ 70 Cathedral Rd., CF1 9LL ☎ 029/2023–9399 🖷 029/2022–3214 ⊕ www.thetownhousecardiff.co.uk ⇌ 8 rooms ♿ Lounge; no a/c, no smoking ▤ MC, V ⊠ BP.

Nightlife & the Arts

NIGHTLIFE Cardiff's clubs and pubs support a lively nighttime scene. **Café Jazz** (✉ 21 St. Mary St. ☎ 029/2038–7026) presents live jazz five nights a week and has TV screens in the bar and restaurant so you can view the on-stage action. **Clwb Ifor Bach** (✉ Womanby St. ☎ 029/2023–2199), a distinctively Welsh club (its name means Little Ivor's Club), has three floors of eclectic music, from funk to folk to rock.

THE ARTS The big theaters present a full program of entertainment: drama and comedy, pop and the classics. The huge **Cardiff International Arena** (⊠ Mary Ann St. ☎ 029/2022–4488) showcases artists who can draw huge crowds, from Aled Jones to Bob Dylan. **St. David's Hall** (⊠ The Hayes ☎ 029/2087–8444), a popular venue, presents the Welsh Proms in July, attracting major international orchestras and soloists, and every two years hosts the prestigious Cardiff Singer of the World competition. It also stages rock, pop, jazz, and folk events.

New Theatre (⊠ Park Pl. ☎ 029/2087–8889), a refurbished Edwardian playhouse, presents big names, including the Royal Shakespeare Company, the National Theatre, and the Northern Ballet.

Wales has one of Britain's four major opera companies, the outstanding **Welsh National Opera** (⊠ Wales Millennium Centre, Cardiff Bay ☎ 029/2046–4666 for performances). The company spends most of its time touring Wales and England.

The new **Wales Millennium Centre,** a huge arts complex with a golden steel roof and slate walls, contains a 1,900-seat auditorium, dance and recording studios, and an orchestral hall. At this writing, the home base of seven leading Welsh cultural organizations, including the Welsh National Opera Company and the Dance Company of Wales, is scheduled to open in November 2004. ⊠ *Cardiff Bay* ☎ *029/2040–2000 (number may change)* ⊕ *www.wmc.org.uk.*

Sports
Celtic Manor (⊠ Coldra Woods, Newport ☎ 01633/410295), 12 mi northeast of Cardiff via A48, is Wales's most prestigious golf course. It will host the Ryder Cup in 2010.

Shopping
Interesting canopied Victorian and Edwardian shopping arcades, lined with specialty stores, weave in and out of the city's modern shopping complexes. The **Cardiff Antiques Centre** (⊠ Royal Arcade ☎ 029/2039–8891), in an 1856 arcade, is a good place to buy antique jewelry. Cardiff's traditional **covered market** (⊠ The Hayes) sells tempting fresh foods beneath its Victorian glass canopy. **Welsh Royal Crystal** (⊠ 21–25 Castle Arcade ☎ 029/2066–4422) specializes in handmade Welsh crystal—vases, glasses, decanters, and more—in traditional designs.

Abergavenny

③⓪ *28 mi north of Cardiff.*

The market town of Abergavenny, near Brecon Beacons National Park, is a popular base for walkers and hikers. The popular **Abergavenny Food Festival** (☎ 01873/851643 general information, 01873/850805 tickets ⊕ www.abergavennyfoodfestival.co.uk), held over a weekend in September, has lectures, discussions, cooking demonstrations, classes, and a large food market. It's another sign of the growing interest in regional Welsh food.

Ruined **Abergavenny Castle,** built early in the 11th century, has a good local museum. The castle witnessed a tragic event on Christmas in 1176: the Norman knight William de Braose invited the neighboring Welsh chieftains to a feast and, in a crude attempt to gain control of the area, had them all slaughtered as they sat at dinner. Afterward, the Welsh attacked and virtually demolished the castle. Most of what now remains dates from the 13th and 14th centuries. The castle's 19th-century hunting lodge houses the museum, with exhibits about area history from the Iron Age to the present. The re-creation of a Victorian Welsh farmhouse kitchen includes old utensils and butter molds. ⊠ *Castle Museum, Castle St.* ☎ *01873/854282* 🖃 *Free* ☉ *Mar.–Oct., Mon.–Sat. 11–1 and 2–5, Sun. 2–5; Nov.–Feb., Mon.–Sat. 11–1 and 2–4.*

West of Abergavenny lie the valleys—the Rhondda is the most famous—so well described by Richard Llewellyn in his 1939 novel *How Green Was My Valley* (the basis for the 1941 film). The slag heaps of the coal mines are green now, thanks to land reclamation schemes. The area southwest of Abergavenny, around the former iron- and coal-mining town of Blaenavon, has been named a World Heritage Site by UNESCO; it provides a fascinating glimpse into Wales's industrial past. (Blaenavon is also in the early stages of development as a "book town" on the model of Hay-on-Wye.) At the **Big Pit Mining Museum,** ex-miners take you underground on a tour of an authentic coal mine for a look at the hard life of the South Wales miner. You can also see the pithead baths and workshops. ⊠ *Off A4043, Blaenavon* ☎ *01495/790311* ⊕ *www.nmgw. ac.uk* 🖃 *Free* ☉ *Feb.–Nov., daily 9:30–5; underground tours 10–3:30.*

The **Blaenavon Ironworks,** dating from1789, trace the entire process of iron production in that era. Well-preserved blast furnaces, a water-balance lift used to transport materials to higher ground, and a terraced row of workers' cottages show how the business operated. ⊠ *A4043, Blaenavon* ☎ *01495/792615* ⊕ *www.cadw.wales.gov.uk* 🖃 *£2* ☉ *Apr.–Oct., daily 9:30–4:30.*

The **Community Heritage and Cordell Museum,** in the Old Town Hall, has the desk, typewriter, reference books, and manuscript fragments of writer Alexander Cordell (1914–97). He put the town of Blaenavon on the world map with his novel *Rape of the Fair Country,* about the industrial transformation of South Wales. There is information on Cordell's life and work as well as an impressive display of the front covers of his books. ⊠ *Lion St., Blaenavon* ☎ *01495/792615* ⊕ *www.cordellcountry. org* 🖃 *£1* ☉ *Phone for hrs.*

Where to Stay & Eat

££–£££ ✕ **Clytha Arms.** A converted house on the banks of the River Usk near Abergavenny serves imaginative modern food in a relaxed setting. You can eat very cheaply in the bar (try the real ales) or pay a little more in the restaurant. ⊠ *Off B4598, Clytha* ☎ *01873/840206* 🖃 *AE, MC, V* ☉ *Closed Mon.*

££££ ✕🖾 **Allt-yr-Ynys Country House Hotel.** This 16th-century manor house in the foothills of the Black Mountains provides a winning blend of ancient charm and present-day comfort. Stone-tiled roofs, Jacobean oak paneling, decorative plasterwork ceilings, and exposed beams recall the past, while the comfortable public areas, pool, and hot tub pamper modern tastes. Most of the spacious, modern bedrooms are in converted stables and outbuildings, with views over mountains and woodland. The restaurant has a reputation for excellent modern British fare; try the braised Welsh lamb with rosemary and red-currant sauce. ⊠ *Off A465, Walterstone, HR2 ODU, 5 mi north of Abergavenny* ☏ *01873/890307* 🖷 *01873/890539* ⊕ *www.allthotel.co.uk* 🛏 *21 rooms* ⚴ *Restaurant, indoor pool, hot tub, sauna, bar, lounge, no-smoking rooms, some pets allowed (fee); no a/c* ▭ *AE, MC, V* ⑪ *BP.*

Crickhowell

③① *5 mi northwest of Abergavenny.*

If you take A40 northwest out of Abergavenny, you pass Sugar Loaf mountain and come to Crickhowell, a pretty town on the banks of the River Usk with little shops, an ancient bridge, and a ruined castle. **Tretower Court,** 3 mi northwest of Crickhowell, is a splendid example of a fortified medieval manor house. Nearby, and part of the same site, are the ruins of a cylindrical Norman castle. ⊠ *A479* ☏ *01874/730279* ⊕ *www.cadw.wales.gov.uk* 🖾 *£2.50* ⊙ *Mar.–late Oct., daily 9:30–5.*

Where to Stay & Eat

££ ✕🖽 **Bear Hotel.** In the middle of town, this white-painted coaching inn with good food is full of character. The bar, decorated with memorabilia from the days when stagecoaches stopped here, has a log fire in winter. Rooms in the hotel or in a modern addition in the former stable yard vary widely (some are fairly small); the most luxurious have four-poster beds and antiques. The Bear serves creative contemporary cuisine—excellent-value bar food and restaurant offerings such as scallops with Parma ham and venison on creamed spinach. ⊠ *A40, NP8 1BW* ☏ *01873/810408* 🖷 *01873/811696* ⊕ *www.bearhotel.co.uk* 🛏 *34 rooms* ⚴ *Restaurant, bar; no a/c* ▭ *AE, MC, V* ⑪ *BP.*

££ ✕🖽 **Ty Croeso Hotel.** A hillside location with views over the Usk Valley adds to the appeal of this hotel (its name means "House of Welcome") in a stone-wall, early-19th-century building. It has comfortable rooms with print fabrics, a lounge with a log fire, and imaginative food with a Welsh emphasis, such as Welsh beef flamed in whisky. ⊠ *The Dardy, off B4558, NP8 1PU* ☏🖷 *01873/810573* ⊕ *www.wiz.to/tycroeso* 🛏 *8 rooms* ⚴ *Restaurant, bar, lounge; no a/c* ▭ *AE, MC, V* ⑪ *BP.*

Brecon

③② *19 mi northwest of Abergavenny, 41 mi north of Cardiff.*

Brecon, a historic market town of narrow passageways, Georgian buildings, and pleasant riverside walks, is also the gateway to the Brecon Beacons National Park. It's particularly appealing on market days (Tuesday and Friday). You may want to purchase a hand-carved wooden love spoon similar to those on display in the Brecknock Museum.

Cavernous **Brecon Cathedral** (☏ 01874/623857 ⊕ www.breconcathedral. org.uk), with a heritage center that traces its history, stands on the hill above the middle of town. In the colonnaded Shire Hall built in 1842 is the **Brecknock Museum** (✉ Captain's Walk ☎ 01874/624121), with its items from rural life, art exhibits, superb collection of carved love spoons, and perfectly preserved 19th-century assize court. The rural Welsh custom of giving a hand-carved wooden spoon to one's beloved dates from the mid-17th century. Shops all over Wales sell the spoons as souvenirs. The military exhibits in the **South Wales Borderers' Museum** (✉ The Watton, off the Bulwark ☎ 01874/613310 ⊕ www.rrw.org.uk) span centuries of conflict; some relate to battles in which this regiment participated. The Zulu Room recalls the Borderers' defense of Rorke's Drift in the Anglo-Zulu war of 1879, an action dramatized in the 1964 film *Zulu,* starring Michael Caine.

South of Brecon, the skyline fills with mountains, and wild, windswept uplands stretch to the horizon in the Brecon Beacons National Park. The **Brecon Beacons National Park Visitor Centre** on Mynydd Illtyd, a high, grassy stretch of upland west of A470, is an excellent source of information for attractions and activities within this 519-square-mi park of hills and open moorlands. It also gives wonderful panoramic views across to Peny-fan, at 2,907 feet the highest peak in South Wales. If you plan to explore Wales's high country on foot, come well equipped. Mist and rain can quickly descend, and the Beacons' summits are exposed to high winds. ✉ *Off A470, Libanus, Brecon, LD3 8ER, 5½ mi southwest of Brecon* ☎ *01874/623366* ⊕ *www.breconbeacons.org* ▣ *Free; fee for parking* ☉ *Daily 9:30–5; until 4:30 Nov.–Mar.*

Where to Stay & Eat

£ ✕ **Brecon Beacons National Park Visitor Centre Tearoom and Restaurant.** The spectacular view across the Beacons and high-quality homemade dishes make this a very popular spot. The parsnip and apple soup and the Welsh Black beef pie are among the good choices. You can indulge in a cream tea or fresh-baked cake, or just have coffee and enjoy the view. ✉ *Off A470, Libanus, Brecon* ☎ *01874/624979* ⊕ *www.breconbeacons.org* ▭ *MC, V* ☉ *Daily 10–4.30* ☉ *No dinner.*

£££ ✕▥ **Felin Fach Griffin.** Old and new blend perfectly in this modern country-style inn with old wood floors, leather sofas, and terra-cotta–color stone walls hung with bright prints and photographs. Some bedrooms have four-posters. The excellent menu makes use of fresh local produce. Try the roast partridge with celeriac mash or the salmon fillet with fennel confit. ✉*A470, Felin Fach, LD3 0UB, east of Brecon* ☎*01874/620111* 🖷 *01874/620120* ⊕ *www.eatdrinksleep.ltd.uk* 🛏*7 rooms* ♿ *Restaurant, no-smoking rooms; no a/c, no room TVs* ▭ *MC, V* ♦|*BP.*

£–££ ▥ **Cantre Selyf.** Spacious and exquisitely restored, this elegant 17th-century town house with a large garden is close to the center of Brecon. It offers welcoming hosts and tranquillity, as well as rooms with beamed ceilings, Georgian fireplaces, and cast-iron beds. ✉ *5 Lion St., LD3 7AU* ☎*01874/622904* 🖷*01874/622315* ⊕*www.cantreselyf.co.uk* 🛏*3 rooms* ♿ *No a/c, no room phones, no smoking* ▭ *No credit cards* ♦|*BP.*

Nightlife & the Arts

Theatr Brycheiniog (✉ Canal Wharf ☎ 01874/611622), on the canal, is the town's impressive venue for the arts. It also has a gallery and waterfront bistro.

Each summer, the town hosts **Brecon Jazz** (☎ 01874/625557 ⊕ www. breconjazz.co.uk), an international jazz festival that attracts top performers.

Shopping

Crickhowell Adventure Gear (⊠ Ship St. ☎ 01874/611586), which also has smaller shops in Crickhowell and Abergavenny, sells outdoor gear such as clothes and climbing equipment.

Swansea

㉝ *36 mi southwest of Brecon, 40 mi west of Cardiff.*

Swansea, the birthplace of poet Dylan Thomas (1914–53), marks the end of the industrial region of South Wales. Despite some undistinguished postwar architecture, Wales's second-largest city (population 224,000) has a number of appealing sights, including the waterfront pedestrian Sail Bridge, which has a 300-foot-high mast. Swansea was extensively bombed during World War II, and its old dockland has been transformed into the splendid **Maritime Quarter,** a modern marina with attractive housing and shops and a seafront that commands views across the sweep of Swansea Bay. The **National Waterfront Museum,** dedicated to interpreting Welsh industrial and maritime history, is scheduled to open here in mid-2005.

Founded in 1841, the **Swansea Museum** contains a quirky and eclectic collection that includes an Egyptian mummy, china, local archaeological exhibits, and the intriguing Cabinet of Curiosity, which holds artifacts from Swansea's past. The museum is close to the Maritime Quarter. ⊠ *Victoria Rd.* ☎ *01792/653763* ⌸ *Free* ☉ *Tues.–Sun. 10–4:45.*

The **Dylan Thomas Centre,** on the banks of the Tawe close to the Maritime Quarter, is the National Literature Centre for Wales. The center houses a permanent Dylan Thomas exhibition and hosts literary events such as the annual Dylan Thomas Festival (usually the last week in July and first two weeks of August). The Wales Tourist Board has a leaflet for a Dylan Thomas Trail around South Wales for those interested in following in the poet's footsteps. ⊠ *Somerset Pl.* ☎ *01792/463980* ⊕ *www.dylanthomas.org* ⌸ *Free* ☉ *Tues.–Sun. 10:30–5.*

Swansea's modern shopping center is nothing special, but the **covered market,** part of Quadrant Shopping Centre, is the best fresh-foods market in Wales. You can buy cockles from the Penclawdd beds on the nearby Gower Peninsula, and laverbread, that unique Welsh delicacy made from seaweed, which is usually served with bacon and eggs.

The **Egypt Centre** displays a substantial collection of ancient Egyptian artifacts, such as bead necklaces from the time of Tutankhamen and the beautiful painted coffin of a Theban musician. ⊠ *Taliesin Centre, University of Wales Swansea, Singleton Park* ☎ *01792/295960* ⊕ *www. swansea.ac.uk/egypt* ⌸ *Free* ☉ *Tues.–Sat. 10–4.*

★ The 14-mi-long **Gower Peninsula,** only minutes away from Swansea's center, was the first part of Britain to be declared an area of Outstanding Natural Beauty. Its shores are a succession of sheltered sandy bays and awesome headlands. Actress Catherine Zeta-Jones was born here, in the Victorian seaside resort of Mumbles. For the area's most breathtaking views, head to Rhossili on its western tip.

Where to Stay & Eat

££–££££ ✕ **La Braseria.** This lively, welcoming spot resembles a Spanish restaurant, with its flamenco music, oak barrels, and whitewashed walls. Among the house specialties are sea bass in rock salt, roast suckling pig, and pheasant (in season). There's a good choice of 140 Spanish and French wines. ⊠ *28 Wind St.* ☎ *01792/469683* ⊟ *AE, MC, V* ☉ *Closed Sun.*

★ ✕⊡ **Fairyhill.** Luxuriously furnished public rooms, spacious bedrooms,
££££–£££££ and 24 acres of wooded grounds make this 18th-century country house in the western part of the scenic Gower Peninsula a restful retreat. The hotel is renowned for sophisticated cuisine and a well-chosen wine list; try the Welsh Black beef with beer batter onions or the leek and mushroom strudel. There's a fixed-price dinner menu. ⊠ *Off B4295, Reynoldston, SA3 1BS, 11 mi southwest of Swansea* ☎ *01792/390139* 🖷 *01792/ 391358* ⊕ *www.fairyhill.net* ↩ *8 rooms* ☖ *Restaurant, massage, croquet, helipad; no a/c, no kids* ⊟ *AE, MC, V* ⭕ *BP.*

National Botanic Garden of Wales

★ ㉞ *20 mi northwest of Swansea, 60 mi northwest of Cardiff.*

The first modern botanic garden in Britain, opened in 2000, celebrates conservation and education. It's based at Middleton Park, a 568-acre 18th-century estate with seven lakes, cascades, water features, and a Japanese garden. The garden's centerpiece is the Norman Foster–designed Great Glass House, the largest single-span greenhouse in the world, which blends into the curving landforms of the Tywi Valley. The interior landscape includes a 40-foot-deep ravine, 10,000 plants from all the Mediterranean climates of the world, and an interactive educational area called the Bioverse. The garden is signposted off the main road between Swansea and Carmarthen. Its management is changing, but the garden plans to remain open; call in advance to check. ⊠ *Off A48 or B4310, Llanarthne* ☎ *01558/668768* ⊕ *www.gardenofwales.org.uk* ⊠ *£6.95* ☉ *Apr.–Oct., daily 9–5:30; Nov.–Mar., daily 10–3.*

Tenby

㉟ *53 mi west of Swansea.*

Pastel-color Georgian houses cluster around a harbor in this seaside resort, where two golden sandy beaches stretch below the hotel-lined cliff-top. Medieval Tenby's ancient town walls still stand, enclosing narrow streets and passageways full of shops, inns, and places to eat. From the harbor you can take a boat trip to Caldey Island and visit the monastery, where monks make perfume.

The ruins of a castle stand on a headland overlooking the sea, close to the informative **Tenby Museum** (⊠ Castle Hill ☎ 01834/842809), which recalls the town's maritime history and its growth as a fashionable resort. The late-15th-century **Tudor Merchant's House** (⊠ Quay Hill ☎ 01834/

842279 ⊕ www.nationaltrust.org.uk), in town, shows how a prosperous trader would have lived in the Tenby of old.

Where to Stay

££££ 🏨 **Penally Abbey.** Overlooking the sea close to town, this is a fine base for exploring Pembrokeshire. The dignified 18th-century house, built on the site of a former abbey, is full of period details, and most bedrooms have four-poster beds. The hotel is relaxed rather than stuffy, but service is first-class. ⊠ *Off A4139, Penally SA70 7PY, 2 mi west of Tenby* ☎ *01834/843033* 🖨 *01834/844714* ⊕ *www.penally-abbey.com* 🛏 *12 rooms* ♻ *Restaurant, indoor pool, billiards; no a/c* ⊟ *AE, MC, V* 🍴 *BP.*

Pembroke

36 *13 mi west of Tenby, 13 mi south of Haverfordwest.*

In Pembroke you are entering the heart of Pembrokeshire, one of the most curious regions of Wales. All around are English names such as Deeplake, New Hedges, and Rudbaxton. Locals more often than not don't seem to understand Welsh, and South Pembrokeshire is even known as "Little England beyond Wales." History is responsible: in the 11th century, the English conquered this region with the aid of the Normans, and the English and Normans intermarried and set about building castles.

One of the most magnificent Norman fortresses is massive **Pembroke Castle,** dating from 1190. Its walls remain stout, its gatehouse mighty, and the enormous cylindrical keep proved so impregnable to cannon fire in the Civil War that Cromwell's men had to starve out its Royalist defenders. You can climb the towers and walk the walls for fine views. This was the birthplace, in 1457, of Henry Tudor, who seized the throne of Britain as Henry VII in 1485, and whose son Henry VIII united Wales and England in 1536. ☎ *01646/681510* ⊕ *www.pembrokecastle. co.uk* 🎫 *£3* 🕑 *Apr.–Sept., daily 9:30–6; Oct. and Mar., daily 10–5; Nov.–Feb., daily 10–4.*

St. David's

37 *25 mi northwest of Pembroke, 16 mi west of Fishguard.*

This tiny village holds what has been described as the holiest ground in Great Britain, the Cathedral of St. David and the shrine of the patron saint of Wales, who founded a monastic community here in the 6th century. The entire area around St. David's, steeped in sanctity and history, was a place of pilgrimage for many centuries, two journeys to St. David's equaling (in spiritual value) one to Rome. Here, on the savagely beautiful coastline, edged by the Pembrokeshire Coast Path—Pembrokeshire at its unspoiled best—you can almost recapture the feeling of those days nearly 1,500 years ago, when this shrine was very nearly the sole outpost of Christianity in the British Isles.

Unlike any other cathedral, the venerable 12th-century **St. David's Cathedral** (⊕ www.stdavidscathedral.org.uk) does not seek to dominate the surrounding countryside with its enormous mass; it is in a vast hollow.

You must climb down 39 steps (called locally the Thirty-Nine Articles) to enter the cathedral. Its location helped protect the church from Viking raiders by hiding it from the view of invaders who came by sea. From the outside, St. David's has a simple austerity that harmonizes with the desolate countryside, but the interior more than compensates for this external severity. Treasures include the fan vaulting in Bishop Vaughan's Chapel, the intricate carving on the choir stalls, and the oaken roof over the nave. Across the brook are the ruins of the medieval **Bishop's Palace** ☎ *01437/720517* ⊕ *www.cadw.wales.gov.uk* ✉ *£2.50* ☉ *Nov.–Mar., Mon.–Sat. 9:30–4, Sun. 11–4; Apr.–Oct., daily 9:30–5.*

Where to Stay & Eat

££–££££   ✕ **Morgan's Brasserie.** One choice sounds more delicious than the next at this classic bistro in the heart of town, which has an inventive menu based on local and organic ingredients. A blackboard lists daily specials, including Pembrokeshire-caught fish. Try the Welsh spring lamb, the Porthgain lobster with risotto, or grilled Dover sole with Penclawdd cockles. ✉ *20 Nun St.* ☎ *01437/720508* ▤ *MC, V.*

££££–£££££   ✕▨ **Warpool Court Hotel.** Overlooking a stunning stretch of coastline, this hotel sits on a bluff above St. Non's Bay, near a ruined chapel. Many rooms have sea views; decorative tiles adorn public areas and some bedrooms. The building dates from the 1860s, when it housed St. David's Cathedral Choir School. The well-equipped hotel offers contemporary cuisine (four-course, fixed-price menu at dinner), with fish, including home-smoked salmon, as a specialty; the dining room overlooks the water. ✉ *Off Goat St., SA62 6BN* ☎ *01437/720300* ▤ *01437/720676* ⊕ *www. warpoolcourthotel.com* ⤳ *25 rooms* ⚫ *Restaurant, in-room data ports, tennis court, pool, gym, sauna, lounge; no a/c* ▤ *AE, MC, V* ⦿ *BP.*

Fishguard

㊳ *16 mi northeast of St. David's, 26 mi north of Pembroke.*

Fishguard is a town of three parts. The ferry terminal at Goodwick across the sheltered waters of Fishguard Bay sees activity throughout the year as boats sail to Rosslare across the Irish Sea. Fishguard's main town stands on high ground just south of Goodwick, separating the modern port from its old harbor in the Lower Town, where gabled cottages are grouped around the quayside. The Lower Town was the setting for the 1973 film of Dylan Thomas's play *Under Milkwood,* which starred Elizabeth Taylor and Welsh actor Richard Burton.

Cardigan & the Teifi Valley

㊴ *18 mi northeast of Fishguard.*

The pretty little market town of Cardigan, with its ancient bridge, was the scene of a never-allowed-to-be-forgotten victory by the Welsh over the Norman army in 1136. The town is near the mouth of the Teifi, a river that runs through a wooded valley with traditional market towns and villages. The valley also contains reminders of the area's once-flourishing woolen industry. Wales's first eisteddfod, or folk festival, took place in Cardigan in the 12th century. The eisteddfod tradition, based on the Welsh language and culture, remains strong in Wales, and events large and small are held here (mainly in summer months).

Cilgerran, a village a few miles south of Cardigan, has the dramatic ruins of 13th-century **Cilgerran Castle**, which stands above a deep, wooded gorge where the River Teifi flows. ⊠ *Off A478* ☎ *01239/615136* ⊕ *www. cadw.wales.gov.uk* ☜ *£2.50* ⊙ *Apr.–late Oct., daily 9:30–6:30; late Oct.–Mar., daily 9:30–4.*

off the beaten path

MUSEUM OF THE WELSH WOOLEN INDUSTRY – Working exhibits and displays at this museum in what was once Wales's most important wool-producing area trace the evolution of the industry. The National Textile Collection is showcased. There are also crafts workshops and a woolen mill that produces reproduction fabrics. A shop sells the best of Welsh textiles. The museum is east of Cenarth, a few miles past Newcastle Emlyn. ⊠ *Off A484, Drefach Felindre* ☎ *01559/370929* ⊕ *www.nmgw.ac.uk* ☜ *Free* ⊙ *Apr.–Sept., daily 10–5; Oct.–Mar., Tues.–Sat. 10–5.*

Where to Stay

£££ 🖼 **Penbontbren Farm Hotel.** This hotel in the peaceful countryside began life as a farm. The one-time barns now serve as cozy, country-style bedrooms and as a high-ceilinged restaurant with exposed stone walls. There's also a small but fascinating farm museum. ⊠ *Off A487, Glynarthen, SA44 6PE, 9 mi northeast of Cardigan* ☎ *01239/810248* 🖨 *01239/811129* ⊕ *www.penbontbren.com* ⤴ *10 rooms* ⚶ *Restaurant, billiards, some pets allowed; no a/c* ⊟ *AE, MC, V* �+©+ *BP.*

WALES A TO Z

To research prices, get advice from other travelers, and book travel arrangements, visit www.fodors.com.

AIR TRAVEL

London's Heathrow and Gatwick airports, with their excellent door-to-door motorway links with Wales, are convenient gateways (⇨ Airports *in* Smart Travel Tips). Manchester Airport, which offers many international flights, is an excellent gateway for North Wales, with a journey time to the Welsh border, via M56, of less than an hour. Cardiff International Airport, a 19-mi drive from the center of Cardiff, has direct international flights to European destinations, connecting services worldwide via Amsterdam, and flights within the British Isles to London Stansted, Manchester, Newcastle, Glasgow, Edinburgh, Aberdeen, Cork, and Dublin. A bus service runs from the airport to Cardiff's central train and bus stations.

AIRPORTS

🇫 **Cardiff International Airport** ⊠ A4226, Rhoose ☎ 01446/711111 ⊕ www.cial.co.uk. **Manchester Airport** ⊠ Near Junctions 5 and 6 of M56 ☎ 0161/489–3000 ⊕ www. manairport.co.uk.

BUS TRAVEL

Although the overall pattern is a little fragmented, most parts of Wales are accessible by bus. National Express serves Wales from London's Victoria Coach Station and also direct from London's Heathrow and Gatwick airports. It also has routes into Wales from many major towns and cities in England and Scotland. Average travel times from London to Wales are 3½ hours to Cardiff, 4 hours to Swansea, 5½ hours to Aberystwyth, and 4½ hours to Llandudno.

The country's network of regional buses makes travel around Wales quite easy; Traveline Cymru has information on all bus services. Wales's three national parks run summer bus services. The Snowdon Sherpa runs into and around Snowdonia and links with main rail and bus services. The Pembrokeshire Coastal Bus Service operates in the Pembrokeshire Coast National Park, and the Beacons Bus serves the Brecon Beacons National Park.

FARES & SCHEDULES
🚌 **Beacons Bus** ☎ 01874/624437 ⊕ www.breconbeacons.org. **National Express** ☎ 0870/580-8080 ⊕ www.nationalexpress.co.uk. **Pembrokeshire Coastal Bus Service** ☎ 01437/764636 ⊕ www.pembrokeshiregreenways.co.uk. **Snowdon Sherpa** ☎ 01766/770274 ⊕ www.snowdonia.org.uk. **Traveline Cymru** ☎ 0870/608-2608 ⊕ www.traveline-cymru.org.uk.

CAR RENTAL

🚗 Local Agencies **Avis** ✉ 14-22 Tudor St., Cardiff ☎ 029/2034-2111. **Budget Rent-a-Car** ✉ 281 Penarth Rd., Cardiff ☎ 029/2072-7499. **Europcar** ✉ Cardiff International Airport, A4226, Arrivals Hall, Rhoose ☎ 01446/711924. **Hertz** ✉ Cardiff International Airport, Cardiff ☎ 01466/711722. **National Car Rental** ✉ 10 Dominions Way Industrial Estate, Newport Rd., Cardiff ☎ 029/2049-6256.

CAR TRAVEL

Take the M4 from London for Cardiff (151 mi), Swansea (190 mi), and South Wales. Aberystwyth (211 mi from London) and Llandrindod Wells (204 mi) in mid-Wales are well served by major roads. The A40 is also an important route through central and South Wales. From London, M1/M6 is the most direct route to North Wales. A55, the coast road from Chester in England, goes through Bangor. Mid-Wales is reached by the M54, which links with the M6/M5/M1.

ROAD CONDITIONS
Distances in miles may not be great in Wales, but getting around takes time because there are few major highways. There is no single fast route from north to south (the mountains have discouraged that); A470 is good and scenic, and A487 runs along or near most of the coastline. Many smaller mountain roads are winding and difficult to maneuver, but they have magnificent views.

CONSULATES & EMBASSIES

🏛 Canadian Consulate ✉ Wales Airport Hotel, Port Rd., Rhoose, near Cardiff ☎ 01446/719172.
🏛 American Embassy **Welsh Affairs Office** ✉ Temple Ct., Cathedral Rd., Cardiff ☎ 029/2078-6633 ⊕ www.usembassy.org.uk/wales.

DISCOUNTS & DEALS

The Cadw/Welsh Historic Monuments Explorer Pass is good for unlimited admission to most of Wales's historic sites. The seven-day pass costs £15.50 (single adult), £26 (two adults), or £32 (family ticket); the three-day pass costs £9.50, £16.50, and £23, respectively. Passes are available at any site covered by the Cadw program. All national museums and galleries in Wales are free.

🚪 **Cadw/Welsh Historic Monuments** ✉ Crown Building, Cathays Park, Cardiff, CF1 3NQ ☎ 029/2050-0200 ⊕ www.cadw.wales.gov.uk. **National Museums and Galleries of Wales** ⊕ www.nmgw.ac.uk.

EMERGENCIES

🚪 **Ambulance, fire, police** ☎ 999. **Bronglais Hospital** ✉ Caradog Rd., Aberystwyth ☎ 01970/623131. **Morriston Hospital** ✉ Heol Maes Eglwys, Cwm Rhydyceirw, Swansea ☎ 01792/702222. **University Hospital of Wales** ✉ Heath Park, Cardiff ☎ 029/2074-7747.

NATIONAL PARKS

🚪 **Brecon Beacons National Park** ✉ Plas-y-Ffynnon, Cambrian Way, Brecon, LD3 7HP ☎ 01874/624437 ⊕ www.breconbeacons.org. **Pembrokeshire Coast National Park** ✉ Wynch La., Haverfordwest, SA61 1PY ☎ 01437/764636 ⊕ www.pembrokeshirecoast. org.uk. **Snowdonia National Park** ✉ Penrhyndeudraeth, LL48 6LF ☎ 01766/770274 ⊕ www.snowdonia.org.uk.

SIGHTSEEING GUIDES

If you are interested in a personal guide, contact the Wales Official Tourist Guide Association. WOTGA uses only guides recognized by the Wales Tourist Board and will create tailor-made tours. You can book a driver-guide or someone to accompany you as you drive.

🚪 **Wales Official Tourist Guide Association** ☎ 01633/774796 ⊕ www.walestourguides. com.

SPORTS & OUTDOORS

Hiking and walking are the most popular outdoor activities in Wales, and several organizations provide information.

🚪 **Offa's Dyke Centre** ✉ West St., Knighton, LD7 1EN ☎ 01547/528753 ⊕ www. offasdyke.demon.co.uk. **Ramblers' Association in Wales** ✉ Ty'r Cerddwyr, High St., Gresford, Wrexham, LL12 8PT ☎ 01978/855148 ⊕ www.ramblers.org.uk.

TOURS

BUS TOURS   A good way to see Wales is by local tour bus; in summer there's a large choice of day and half-day excursions to most parts of the country. In major resorts and cities you should ask for details at a tourist information center or bus station.

TRAIN TRAVEL

Travel time on the fast InterCity rail service from London's Paddington Station is about two hours to Cardiff and three hours to Swansea. Fast InterCity trains also run between London's Euston Station and North Wales. Average travel times from Euston are 3¾ hours to Llandudno in North Wales (some direct trains, otherwise change at Crewe), and about 5 hours to Aberystwyth in mid-Wales (change at Birmingham).

Regional train service covers South Wales, western Wales, central Wales, the Conwy Valley, and the North Wales coast on many scenic routes, such as the Cambrian Coast Railway, running 70 mi between Aberystwyth and Pwllheli, and the Heart of Wales line, linking Swansea and Craven Arms, near Shrewsbury, 95 mi northeast.

Wales's many scenic steam railways, including the Great Little Trains of Wales and the Snowdon Mountain Railway, have lovely views of the countryside.

CUTTING COSTS   For travel within Wales, ask about money-saving, unlimited-travel tickets (such as Freedom of Wales Flexi Pass, North and Mid Wales Rover, and the South Wales Flexi Rover), which include the use of bus services. Wanderer tickets are available from participating railways for unlimited travel on the Great Little Trains of Wales: a nine-day ticket is £55.

FARES &
SCHEDULES   🚃 **Flexi Pass information** ☎ 0845/712-4625 ⊕ www.walesflexipass.co.uk. **Great Little Trains of Wales** ✉ Tallyllyn Railway, Wharf Station, Tywyn, LL36 9EY ☎ 01654/710472 ⊕ www.greatlittletrainsofwales.co.uk. **National Rail Enquiries** ☎ 0845/748-4950 ⊕ www.nationalrail.co.uk. **Regional & Intercity Railways** ☎ 0845/748-4950 ⊕ www.thetrainline.com. **Snowdon Mountain Railway** ✉ Llanberis, Caernarfon, LL55 4TY ☎ 01286/870223 ⊕ www.snowdonrailway.co.uk.

TRAVEL AGENCIES
🚃 Local Agent Referrals **American Express** ✉ 3 Queen St., Cardiff ☎ 0870/600-1060. **Thomas Cook** ✉ 16 Queen St., Cardiff ☎ 029/2042-2500 ✉ 3 Union St., Swansea ☎ 01792/332000.

VISITOR INFORMATION
The Wales Tourist Board's Visit Wales Centre provides information and handles reservations; accommodations can also be booked online. Tourist information centers are normally open Monday through Saturday 10–5:30 and limited hours on Sunday, but vary by season.

🚃 **Visit Wales Centre** ⌀ Box 113, Bangor, LL54 4WW ☎ 08701/211251 ⊕ www.visitwales.com. **Aberystwyth** ✉ Terrace Rd. ☎ 01970/612125. **Betws-y-Coed** ✉ Royal Oak Stables ☎ 01690/710426. **Caernarfon** ✉ Oriel Pendeitsh, opposite castle entrance ☎ 01286/672232. **Cardiff** national and city information ✉ 16 Wood St., Central Station ☎ 029/2022-7281 ⊕ www.visitcardiff.info. **Llandrindod Wells** ✉ Old Town Hall ☎ 01597/822600. **Llandudno** ✉ 1–2 Chapel St. ☎ 01492/876413. **Llanfair Pwllgwyngyll** ✉ Station Site, Isle of Anglesey ☎ 01248/713177. **Llangollen** ✉ Y Chapell, Castle St. ☎ 01978/860828. **Machynlleth** ✉ Owain Glyndŵr Centre ☎ 01654/702401. **Ruthin** ✉ Craft Centre, Park Rd. ☎ 01824/703992. **Swansea** ✉ Plymouth St. ☎ 01792/468321 ⊕ www.visitswanseabay.com. **Tenby** ✉ The Croft ☎ 01834/842402. **Welshpool** ✉ Vicarage Garden, Church St. ☎ 01938/552043.

LANCASHIRE & THE PEAKS

MANCHESTER, LIVERPOOL & THE PEAK DISTRICT

10

SING "YEAH, YEAH, YEAH!"
at the Beatles Story in Liverpool ⇨*p.490*

DISCOVER ENGLAND'S WILDER SIDE
on a moorland hike near Edale ⇨*p.506*

TUNE INTO THE DUCAL LIFESTYLE
with a day at Chatsworth House ⇨*p.504*

TAKE THE TOWN BY STORM
in Manchester's bars and clubs ⇨*p.485*

INDULGE YOUR SWEETEST TOOTH
with creamy Bakewell pudding ⇨*p.502*

MUSE OVER MARITIME GLORY
at Albert Dock's warehouse-museums ⇨*p.490*

POP INTO A PLAY IN THE PEAKS
at the Buxton Opera House ⇨*p.501*

CHECK OUT THE REIGNING PASSION
at a football match in Manchester ⇨*p.486*

Updated by
Kate Hughes

FOR THOSE LOOKING FOR THE POSTCARD ENGLAND of little villages and churches, the northwest region of England might not appear at the top of their sightseeing list. After all, the Industrial Revolution thrived nowhere more strongly than the major cities here, including Manchester and Liverpool. Manchester today bustles with redevelopment and youthful culture, and Liverpool will be the European Union's Capital of Culture in 2008; but 200 years of smokestack industry, which abated only in the 1980s, have taken a toll on the east Lancashire landscape. The region does have some lovely scenery inland, in Derbyshire (pronounced "Darbyshire")—notably the spectacular Peak District, a huge, unspoiled national park at the southern end of the Pennines range. In and around this area are Victorian-era spas such as Buxton, pretty towns such as Bakewell, and magnificent stately houses such as Chatsworth, Hardwick Hall, and Haddon Hall.

The areas around Manchester and Liverpool are Britain's equivalent of the Rust Belt, a once-proud bastion of heavy industry and blue-collar values. These cities were the economic engines that propelled Britain in the 18th and 19th centuries. By the mid-18th century, the Lancashire cotton industry had become firmly established in Manchester and enjoyed a special relationship with the port of Liverpool, to the west. Here, at the massive docks, cotton was imported from the United States and sent to the Lancashire mills; the finished cotton goods were delivered to Liverpool for export to the rest of the world. Both cities suffered a marked decline during the second half of the 20th century, and today are reestablishing themselves as centers of musical and sporting excellence. Since 1962, the Manchester United, Everton, and Liverpool football (soccer in the United States) clubs have won everything worth winning in Britain and Europe, and in 2002 Manchester hosted the Commonwealth Games. The Beatles launched the Merseysound of the '60s; contemporary Manchester groups often ride both British and U.S. airwaves. On the classical side of music, Manchester is also the home of Britain's oldest leading orchestra, the Hallé (founded in 1857)—just one legacy of 19th-century industrialists' investments in culture.

The Peak District is a wilder part of England, a region of crags that rear violently out of the plain. The Pennines, a line of hills that begins in the Peak District and runs as far north as Scotland, are sometimes called the "backbone of England." In this landscape of rocky outcrops and vaulting meadowland, you'll see nothing for miles but sheep, drystone walls (without mortar), and farms, interrupted—spectacularly—by 19th-century villages and treasure houses. The delight of the Peak District is being able to ramble for days in rugged countryside but still enjoy civilization at its finest.

Exploring Lancashire & the Peak District

Manchester lies at the heart of a tangle of motorways in the northwest of England, about half an hour across the Pennines from Yorkshire. The city spreads west toward the coast and the mouth of the River Mersey, where Liverpool is still centered on its port. For the Northwest's most

10

Greater Manchester and Merseyside form one of the most built-up areas in Britain, but motorway access between the two is fast. One of the main towns of the Peak District, Buxton, could be visited on a day trip from Manchester if you wanted to base yourself in that city. But the Peaks deserve more than just a short drive around the principal sights, and a week's hiking tour here could be constructed easily. If you have only a few days, you might stay in Manchester overnight and then take in several of the area's stately homes. If you have a week, you can spend more time in the Peak District as well as explore Manchester and a bit of Liverpool.

Numbers in the text correspond to numbers in the margin and on the Lancashire and the Peaks, Manchester, and Liverpool maps.

If you have
3 days

Base yourself in 🖾 **Manchester** ❶–❶❷ ⌐ for your first night, which will give you a chance to see the central sights on your first day and take in a concert or a club that night. On the next day, journey to the green Derbyshire Wye Valley to visit two of England's most magnificent stately homes, **Haddon Hall** ❷❽ and **Chatsworth House** ❸❶. Spend your second night in nearby 🖾 **Bakewell** ❷❼ or **Buxton** ❷❻. If you're traveling when these houses are closed for the season, visit 🖾 **Liverpool** ❶❸–❷❹ instead for an overnight stay. Enjoy a lunch on the Albert Dock and spend the afternoon in the museums and attractions of this dockside center.

If you have
7 days

It's wisest to split your time between city and national park. Start by exploring 🖾 **Buxton** ❷❻ ⌐; you can overnight there or in 🖾 **Bakewell** ❷❼. Visit **Haddon Hall** ❷❽ and **Chatsworth House** ❸❶, both among the top stately homes in Britain, returning to Bakewell for the night. On the morning of your third day, move on to **Matlock** ❷❾ and its river, and take a cable-car ride to the Heights of Abraham, or visit **Hardwick Hall** ❸❶, which sums up the late Elizabethan era, before aiming for **Castleton** ❸❷ and its splendid caverns. If you want to do any walking around the isolated village of **Edale** ❸❸, spend the third night back in 🖾 **Buxton** ❷❻ (or in Edale itself), making an early start on the day. After walking on the moors, you can take a short drive to 🖾 **Manchester** ❶–❶❷, where a two-night stay will let you see the best of that city. Move on to enjoy your last night in 🖾 **Liverpool** ❶❸–❷❹.

dramatic scenery—indeed, its only real geological feature of interest—you must travel to the Peak District, a craggy national park less than an hour's drive southeast of Manchester. England at its most grand and ducal can be seen in the Derbyshire valley of the River Wye: majestic 18th-century Chatsworth; Haddon Hall, an enchanting Tudor and Jacobean structure; and Hardwick Hall, the glory of the late Elizabethan age.

About the Restaurants

Dining options in Manchester and Liverpool vary from smart café-bars offering modern British and Continental fare to ethnic restaurants. Manchester has one of Britain's biggest Chinatowns, and locals also set great store in the 40-odd Asian restaurants along Wilmslow Road in

Rusholme, a mile south of the city center, where you can savor Bangladeshi, Pakistani, and Indian food.

One local dish that has survived is Bakewell pudding (*never* called "tart" in these regions, as its imitations are elsewhere in England). The recipe for this treat was allegedly discovered in the 19th century when a cook spilled a rich cake mixture over jam tarts. Served with custard or cream, the pudding is the joy of Bakewell. Another local creation is the hearty Lancashire hot pot, a casserole of lamb (including kidneys), potatoes, onions, and carrots.

About the Hotels

If your trip centers on the cities of the Northwest, you may want to base yourself in Manchester (which has a better choice of accommodations) and make Liverpool a day trip. Because the larger city-center hotels in both cities rely on businesspeople during the week, they often markedly reduce their rates on weekends. Smaller hotels and guest houses abound in nearby suburbs, many just a short bus ride from downtown. The Manchester Visitor Centre operates a room-booking service; you can stop by in person or reserve over the phone with a credit card for a fee. The Peak District has inns, bed-and-breakfasts, and hotels, as well as a network of youth hostels. Local tourist offices have details; reserve well in advance for Easter and summer.

WHAT IT COSTS In pounds				
£££££	**££££**	**£££**	**££**	**£**
RESTAURANTS over £22	£18–£22	£13–£17	£7–£12	under £7
HOTELS over £160	£120–£160	£90–£120	£60–£90	under £60

Restaurant prices are for a main course at dinner. Hotel prices are for two people in a standard double room in high season, including VAT, with no meals or, if indicated, CP (with Continental breakfast), BP (Breakfast Plan, with full breakfast), or MAP (Modified American Plan, with breakfast and dinner).

Timing

Manchester has a reputation as one of the wettest cities in Britain, and visiting in summer won't guarantee fine weather. Nevertheless, the nature of many sights and cultural activities here and in Liverpool means that wet or cold weather shouldn't spoil a visit. Summer is the optimum time to see the Peak District, especially because early summer sees traditional festivities in many villages. The *only* time to see the great houses of the Derbyshire Wye valley and vicinity—Chatsworth, Haddon Hall, and Hardwick Hall—is from spring through fall.

MANCHESTER

▶ Manchester's center hums with the energy of cutting-edge popular music and a swank café-bar culture. Since the late 1980s, events as different as the damage to the city center caused by an IRA bomb in 1996 and the 2002 Commonwealth Games have fueled massive redevelopment in a formerly grim industrial landscape. Canals have been tidied up, cot-

10

Beatlemania

Yeah, yeah, yeah! For baby boomers in particular, Liverpool exerts a powerful lure as the birthplace of the Beatles. John, Paul, George, and Pete Best (Ringo arrived a bit later) set up shop at the Cavern in 1961, and the Liverpool Sound soon conquered the world. Today fans can follow in the footsteps of the Fab Four at the Beatles Story, an exhibition at Liverpool's Albert Dock. Many city sites linked with John and Paul have been bulldozed, including Strawberry Field orphanage (a modern structure replaced it), but others, such as the childhood homes of John and Paul (now maintained by the National Trust), have survived. The faithful celebrate the Beatles' enduring appeal at the annual International Beatle Week, usually held the last week in August when what seems to be the entire city takes time out to dance, attend John and Yoko fancy-dress parties, and listen to Beatle bands from around the world.

Well Dressing

Unique to the Peak District is the custom of well dressing, when certain wells or springs are decorated with elaborate pictures made of flowers. Frames up to four feet wide and six feet high, covered with a base of puddled clay, are filled with a colorful mosaic of seeds, grasses, berries, and moss as well as flowers and flower petals, a process that involves a team of workers and takes about a week to complete. Although the designs usually incorporate religious themes such as biblical stories, they are a Christian veneer over an ancient pagan celebration of the water's life-giving powers. The well dressing and blessing ceremony, usually accompanied by a brass band, heralds the start of several days of festivities. Of the 70 or so towns and villages that continue this summertime tradition, Tissington (May), south of Matlock; Bakewell (early July); and, near Chatsworth, Eyam (late August) are among the most popular.

---

ton mills serve as loft apartments, and contemporary architecture has transformed the skyline. In 2004 Britain's tallest sculpture, *B of the Bang*, took its place beside Manchester City Stadium. Bridgewater Hall and the Lowry, as well as the Imperial War Museum North, are outstanding cultural facilities. Sure, it still rains here, but the rain-soaked streets are part of the city's charm, in a bleak northern kind of way.

For most of its existence Manchester, which has a population of 2.6 million and is Britain's third-largest city, has been a thriving and prosperous place. The Romans built a fort here in AD 79 and named it Mamucium, but the city that stands today—with the elegant Town Hall, Royal Exchange, Midland Hotel, the waterways, and railway—is a product of the Industrial Revolution. Manchester's spectacular rise from a small town to the world's cotton capital (with the nickname Cottonopolis) in only 100 years began with the first steam-powered cotton mill, built in 1783. Dredging made the rivers Irwell and Mersey navigable to ship coal to the factories. The world's first passenger railway opened in 1830, and construction of the Manchester Ship Canal in 1894 provided the infrastructure for Manchester to dominate the industrial world.

Lancashire
& the Peaks

TO THE LAKE DISTRICT

TO DOUGLAS

GREAT BRITAIN

LANCASHIRE

CHESHIRE

WALES

Southport
Preston
Burnley
Blackburn
Bradford
Huddersfield
Holmfirth
Woodhead
Oldham
Glossop
Bolton
Wigan
Stockport
Hayfield
Wilmslow
Macclesfield
Little Moreton Hall
Buxton
Bakewell
Crewe
Kidgrove
Leek
Matlock
Matlock Bath
Ashbourne
Stoke-on-Trent
Newcastle-under-Lyme
Nantwich
Whitchurch
Wrexham
Chester
Connah's Quay
Flint
Birkenhead
Kirkby
Widnes
Warrington
Edale
Castleton
Eyam
Chatsworth House
Baslow
Haddon Hall
Hardwick Hall

Manchester ❶ – ⓬ see detail map
Liverpool ⓭ – ㉔ see detail map

Edale ㉝ ㉜ **Castleton**
Chatsworth House ㉛
Bakewell ㉖ ㉗ ㉘
Haddon Hall
Matlock ㉙
Hardwick Hall ㉚

㉕

KEY
▶ Start of itinerary

0   10 miles
0   16 km

A few people acquired great wealth, but factory hands worked under appalling conditions. Working-class discontent came to a head in 1819 in the Peterloo Massacre, when soldiers killed 11 workers at a protest meeting. The conditions under which factory hands worked were later recorded by Friedrich Engels (coauthor with Karl Marx of the *Communist Manifesto*), who managed a cotton mill in the city. More formal political opposition to the government emerged in the shape of the Chartist movement (which campaigned for universal suffrage) and the Anti-Corn Law League (which opposed trade tariffs), forerunners of the British trade unions. From Victorian times until the 1960s, daily life for the average Mancunian was so oppressive that it bred the desire to escape, a yearning that is still traceable in the popular culture of the city.

It's impossible to talk about Manchester without mentioning music and football. Out of poverty and unemployment came the brash sounds of punk and the indie record labels. The band New Order produced a unique Mancunian sound that mixed live instruments with digital sound. The now-defunct Haçienda Club marketed New Order to the world, and Manchester became the clubbing capital of England. Joy Division, Morrissey, Stone Roses, Happy Mondays, and Oasis rose to the top of the charts. The triumphant reign of the Manchester United football club, which now faces new challenges because of the departure of team captain David Beckham, has kept many eyes on Manchester.

Exploring Manchester

Manchester is compact enough that you can easily walk across the city center in 40 minutes. The walk below starts at the Town Hall, winds through historic Castlefield, and continues back through the heart of the shopping district to Manchester Cathedral.

a good
walk

Begin in Albert Square at the Albert Memorial, built in 1862 with a Gothic-style canopy and spire covering a statue of the Prince Consort. Exit by Lloyd Street, which separates the two parts of the **Town Hall ❶ ▶**, a neo-Gothic structure that reflects the economic power of 19th-century Manchester. Turning right at the end of the street will bring you to the Manchester Visitor Centre, a good place to equip yourself with information. Retrace your steps a few yards onto Princess Street, and turn left at Mosley Street, which brings you in front of the neoclassical **Manchester Art Gallery ❷**, where you could spend a couple of hours. Go back to the visitor center and continue to St. Peter's Square and the **Central Library ❸**. Take a peek inside at the glass-domed reading room, inspired by the Pantheon, on the first floor. The Edwardian building on the south side of St. Peter's Square is the Crowne Plaza Manchester—The Midland, a hotel built in 1903.

Continue south on Lower Mosley Street to the G-Mex, a Victorian train shed reconfigured into an exhibition center. Cross Lower Mosley Street to arrive at the striking Bridgewater Hall, where the Hallé Orchestra performs. From Bridgewater Hall, continue down Lower Mosley Street to Whitworth Street West. Turn right and pass Deansgate Locks, a group of trendy bars converted from railway arches, which are the gateway to Castlefield. Turn right on Deansgate and left onto Liverpool Road, and walk several blocks to **Castlefield Urban Heritage Park ❹**, the heart of Manchester's industrial boom.

Liverpool Station, a passenger railway station, is now part of the sprawling **Museum of Science and Industry ❺**, off Liverpool Road, which explores the city's industrial heritage. From the museum, walk north on Lower Byrom Street, turn right onto Quay Street, and go past the Opera House to Deansgate, where you turn left. Continue five blocks until you reach **John Rylands Library ❻**, a red neo-Gothic building on your left. Turn left in front of the library onto Wood Street and follow it to Bridge Street to visit the **PumpHouse: People's History Museum ❼**, which presents Manchester's history from a worker's perspective. Turn right, outside the Pump-House, and follow Bridge Street to Deansgate. Turn left on Deansgate, right on King Street, left on Cross Street, and left again on St. Ann Street to proceed to **St. Ann's Church ❽**, Manchester's oldest surviving classical building. Exit the church and walk north in a direct line through St. Ann's Square to the **Royal Exchange ❾**, the old cotton market.

From St. Ann's Square walk north past Marks & Spencer, and up Cathedral Street to Exchange Square in the heart of the city's Millennium Quarter. The Triangle, a shopping mall inside the historic facade of the Corn

Manchester

KEY

Ⓜ Metrolink station

🛈 Tourist information

▶ Start of walk

Castlefield Urban
Heritage Park **4**

Central Library **3**

John Rylands Library **6**

Manchester Art Gallery . . .**2**

Manchester
Cathedral **10**

Museum of Science
and Industry **5**

PumpHouse: People's
History Museum **7**

Royal Exchange **9**

St. Ann's Church **8**

Town Hall **1**

Urbis **11**

Whitworth Art Gallery . . .**12**

Exchange, is on your left, and the Printworks on your right. **Manchester Cathedral** ⑩ sits majestically in the postmodern core of Manchester. To the north of the cathedral, on Fennel Street, is **Urbis** ⑪, a high-tech exploration of city life. If you want to visit the **Whitworth Art Gallery** ⑫ at the University of Manchester, catch any bus with a number in the 40s (except 47) on Oxford Road.

TIMING Although you can complete the walk without stopping in about an hour, you must budget your time carefully at the sights if you want to see everything in a day. Be sure to save three hours for Castlefield (two of these for the Museum of Science and Industry) and an hour each for the PumpHouse and Manchester Art Gallery. Although many museums are open Sunday, the city will be emptier and some sights are closed.

What to See

❹ **Castlefield Urban Heritage Park.** Site of an early Roman fort, the district of Castlefield was later the center of the city's industrial boom, which resulted in the building of Britain's first modern canal in 1764 and the world's first railway station in 1830. What had become an urban wasteland has been beautifully restored into an urban park with canal-side walks, landscaped open spaces, and refurbished warehouses. The 7-acre site contains the reconstructed gate to the Roman fort of Mamucium, the buildings of the **Museum of Science and Industry,** and several of the city's hippest bars and restaurants. ⊠ *Off Liverpool Rd., Castlefield.*

❸ **Central Library.** The circular exterior of the city's main library, topped by a line of Doric columns and a massive Corinthian portico facing St. Peter's Square, is a major focus for Manchester's most prestigious civic quarter. Erected in 1930, it was at one time the biggest municipal library in the world; the vast, glass-topped social sciences reading room on the 1st floor is worth seeing. The **Library Theatre** is part of the complex. ⊠ *St. Peter's Sq., City Centre* ☎ *0161/234–1900* ⊕ *www.manchester. gov.uk* ☉ *Mon.–Thurs. 10–8, Fri.–Sat. 10–5.*

Imperial War Museum North. The thought-provoking exhibits in this striking, aluminum-clad building, which architect Daniel Libeskind describes as representing three shards of an exploded globe, present the reasons for war and show its effects on society. Three Big Picture audiovisual shows envelop you in the sights and sounds of conflicts from 1914 to the present, and a rotating storage system allows you to select trays of objects to view, including exhibits from the 2003 war in Iraq. A 100-foot viewing platform gives a bird's-eye view of the city. The museum is on the banks of the Manchester Ship Canal in Salford Quays, across the footbridge from the Lowry. ⊠ *Trafford Wharf Rd., Salford Quays* ☎ *0161/836–4000* ⊕ *www.iwm.org.uk* ☎ *Free* ☉ *Daily 10–6.*

❻ **John Rylands Library.** Now owned by the University of Manchester, this Gothic Revival masterpiece designed by Alfred Waterhouse was built by Enriqueta Augustina Rylands as a memorial to her husband, a cotton magnate. Constructed of red sandstone in the 1890s, the library resembles a cathedral. A staircase leads to the reading room, with ornate plaster carvings, a soaring nave, and paneled reading alcoves. The library is due to reopen late in 2005 after a lengthy restoration. ⊠ *150*

Deansgate, City Centre ☎ *0161/834–5343 for 2005 reopening* ⊕ *www. rylibweb.man.ac.uk.*

The Lowry. This impressive arts center in the heart of Manchester's waterways occupies a dramatic modern building with a steel-gray exterior that reflects the light. L. S. Lowry (1887–1976) was a local artist, and one of the few who painted the industrial landscape. Galleries showcase Lowry's and other contemporary artists' work. The theater, Britain's largest outside London, presents an impressive lineup of touring companies. The nearest Metrolink tram stop is Harbour City, a 10-minute walk from the Lowry. ⊠ *Pier 8, Salford Quays* ☎ *0161/876–2000* ⊕ *www.thelowry.com* ⊠ *Free; prices vary for theater tickets and exhibitions; tours £2.50* ☉ *Building 10 AM–last performance; galleries, daily 11–5 or 7:30, depending on performances; tours daily 11:30, 1, and 2:30.*

★ ❷ **Manchester Art Gallery.** Beyond its impressive classical portico, this splendid museum does full justice to its fine collections. Outstanding are the Pre-Raphaelite paintings (exemplified by Ford Madox Brown's masterpiece *Work*), Turner watercolors, Dutch masters, and 20th-century British works. The Manchester Gallery illustrates the city's contribution to art, and the Craft and Design Gallery shows off decorative art from ceramics and glass to metalwork and furniture. ⊠ *Mosely St., City Centre* ☎ *0161/235–8888* ⊕ *www.manchestergalleries.org.uk* ⊠ *Free* ☉ *Tues.–Sun. and national holidays 10–5.*

❿ **Manchester Cathedral.** The city's cathedral, set beside the River Irwell and originally a medieval parish church dating in part from the 15th century, is unusually broad for its length and has the widest medieval nave in Britain. Inside, angels with gilded instruments look down from the roof of the nave, and misericords in the early-16th-century choir stalls reveal intriguing carvings. Note the fine sculpted tomb brass of Warden Huntingdon, who died in 1458, and the octagonal chapter house dating from 1485. ⊠ *Victoria St., Millennium Quarter* ☎ *0161/833– 2220* ⊠ *Free* ☉ *Weekdays 7:45–5:30, Sat. 7:45–4:30, Sun. 8:45–7:30.*

★ ☙ ❺ **Museum of Science and Industry.** The museum's five buildings, one of which is the world's oldest passenger rail station (1830), hold marvelous collections relating to the city's industrial past and present. You can walk through a reconstructed Victorian sewer, be blasted by the heat and noise of working steam engines, and see cotton looms whirring in action. The Air and Space Gallery fills a graceful cast-iron-and-glass building, constructed as a market hall in 1877. Allow at least half a day to visit all the sites. ⊠ *Liverpool Rd., main entrance on Lower Byrom Rd., Castlefield* ☎ *0161/832–2244* ⊕ *www.msim.org.uk* ⊠ *Free, charges vary for special exhibitions* ☉ *Daily 10–5.*

☙ ❼ **PumpHouse: People's History Museum.** Not everyone in 19th-century Manchester owned a cotton mill or made a fortune on the trading floor. One of the city's more thought-provoking museums recounts powerfully the struggles of working people in the city since the Industrial Revolution. The museum tells the story of the 1819 Peterloo Massacre and has an unrivaled collection of trade-union banners, tools, toys, utensils, and photographs, all illustrating the working lives and pastimes of the city's people. ⊠ *Bridge St., City Centre* ☎ *0161/839–6061* ⊕ *www. peopleshistorymuseum.org.uk* ☜ *£1, free Fri.* ⊙ *Tues.–Sun. 11–4:30.*

The brick-vaulted, waterside **Mark Addy pub** (⊠ Stanley St., off Bridge St., City Centre ☎ 0161/832–4080) is a good spot to have a relaxing drink and sample an excellent spread of pâtés and cheeses. The pub is named for the 19th-century boatman who rescued more than 50 people from the River Irwell.

❾ Royal Exchange. Throughout its commercial heyday, this was the city's most important building—the cotton market. Built with Victorian panache in 1874, the existing structure accommodated 7,000 traders. The building was refurbished and the giant glass-dome roof restored after damage by the 1996 IRA bombing. Visit to see the lunar module–inspired Royal Exchange Theatre, to have a drink in the café, or to browse in the craft and clothes outlets in the arcade. ⊠ *St. Ann's Sq., City Centre* ☎ *0161/834–3731* ⊕ *www.royalexchange.co.uk.*

❽ St. Ann's Church. Built in 1712 and sometimes wrongly attributed to Christopher Wren, St. Ann's is Manchester's oldest surviving classical building. The church contains *The Descent from the Cross,* a painting by Annibale Carracci (1561–1609). The verger is usually on hand to show you around. ⊠ *St. Ann's Sq., City Centre* ☎ *0161/834–0239* ☜ *Free, donations welcome* ⊙ *Daily 9:45–4:45.*

▶ ❶ Town Hall. Manchester's exuberant Town Hall, with its imposing 280-foot-tall clock tower, speaks volumes about the city's 19th-century sense of self-importance. Alfred Waterhouse designed the Victorian Gothic building (1867–76); extensions were added just before World War II. Over the main entrance is a statue of Roman general Agricola, who founded Mamucium in AD 79. Above him are Henry III, Elizabeth I, and St. George, the patron saint of England. Murals of the city's history, painted between 1852 and 1865 by the Pre-Raphaelite Ford Madox Brown, decorate the Great Hall, with its hammer-beam roof. Guided tours (twice a month) include the murals, but ask at the front desk: if the rooms aren't being used, you may be allowed to wander in. ⊠ *Albert Sq., public entrance on Lloyd St., City Centre* ☎ *0161/234–5000* ☜ *Free; guided tours £4* ⊙ *Mon.–Sat. 9–4:30; not always open to public access; see the tourist office in Town Hall Extension for tour information.*

⓫ Urbis. A high-tech museum in this striking glass-skinned triangle of a building dissects the modern urban condition with a vengeance, though with mixed success. A glass elevator takes you to the 4th floor, from which you can explore three interactive galleries that focus mainly on Manchester. The 1st floor hosts changing exhibitions. ⊠ *Cathedral Gardens, Millennium Quarter* ☎ *0161/907–9099* ⊕ *www.urbis.org.uk* ☜ *Free; temporary exhibitions £5* ⊙ *Daily 10–6; last admission 1½ hrs before closing.*

⓬ Whitworth Art Gallery. This University of Manchester–run art museum has strong collections of British watercolors, old-master drawings, and Postimpressionist works, as well as wallpapers. Captivating rooms full of textiles—Coptic and Peruvian fabrics, Spanish and Italian vestments, tribal rugs, and contemporary weaving—are just what you might expect in a city built on textile manufacture. There's a bistro and a good gift shop. ✉ *Oxford Rd., University Quarter* ☎ *0161/275–7450* ⊕ *www.whitworth.man.ac.uk* ✑ *Free* ☉ *Mon.–Sat. 10–5, Sun. 2–5.*

Where to Eat

Marco Pierre White's River Room at the Lowry Hotel is another excellent dining choice. The city's dining scene is lively, and the annual Manchester Food & Drink Festival, held the first two weeks of October, showcases the city's chefs and regional products with demonstrations and special events.

★ ✕ **Juniper.** Chef Paul Kitchings aims to surprise and delight with his innovative combinations of ingredients: duck with Christmas pudding, curried cod with kipper sauce, piccalilli (a spiced relish) in fudge, and Earl Grey tea in crème brûlée, to name but a few. The fixed-price menus (£55–£95) offer up to 12 bite- and small-size dishes. Gilt mirrors and large paintings decorate the restaurant's mint-green walls, and service is professional but friendly. Altrincham, 8 mi from Manchester, is easily accessible by train. ✉ *21 The Downs, Altrincham* ☎ *0161/929–4008* ⚑ *Reservations essential* ⊟ *AE, D, MC, V* ☉ *Closed Mon. and 2 weeks mid-Feb., 2 weeks early fall, 1 week late Dec.*

£££–£££££

£££ ✕ **Stock.** The Edwardian building that houses this buzzy Italian restaurant was once the city's stock exchange—hence its name and grand domed setting. Chef Enzo Mauro emphasizes the flavors of southern Italy on a menu that might list linguine with fresh sardines or steak in tomato, garlic, and oregano sauce; you can accompany this with a fine-quality wine. Bonuses are a good-value lunch deal, jazz on Fridays, and occasional opera nights. ✉ *4 Norfolk St., City Centre* ☎ *0161/839–6644* ⊟ *AE, D, MC, V* ☉ *Closed Sun.*

££–£££ ✕ **Le Petit Blanc.** Famed chef Raymond Blanc's upscale Manchester brasserie is faithful to its Parisian role models. Conversation buzzes in the relaxed yet elegant surroundings of the mostly white room. The menu combines the best traditions of French bourgeois cuisine with Asian and Mediterranean accents. Try the herb pancakes or hot smoked salmon with beetroot, followed by iced meringue and black currant sorbet. ✉ *55 King St., City Centre* ☎ *0161/832–1000* ⊟ *AE, DC, MC, V.*

££–£££ ✕ **Livebait.** An offshoot of the London-based restaurant serves fresh fish from around the world in an old building across from Albert Square. Tall windows, bottle-green-and-white decoration, and a black-and-white tile floor add fresh style. Among the many good choices are Whitby crab, char-grilled tuna, or traditional cockles and mussels. Dine early for the fixed-price pretheater menu or try the excellent-value lunches. ✉ *22 Lloyd St., City Centre* ☎ *0161/817–4110* ⊟ *AE, DC, MC, V.*

££–£££ ✕ **Pacific.** Designed around feng shui principles, this split-level concept restaurant fuses old and new Asian culture. The lower floor is China, the upper Thailand; each has a separate kitchen and chef. In China you can sample dim sum and à la carte dishes, with classic favorites as well as unusual delicacies such as sun-dried abalone and primrose shark's fin. Thailand has authentic regional cooking and ingredients. ✉ *58–60 George St., City Centre* ☎ *0161/228–6668* ⊟ *AE, DC, MC, V.*

★ **££–£££** ✕ **Simply Heathcote's.** Lancastrian chef Paul Heathcote earned his reputation as the "cook of the North" for his original, modern food. A diverse clientele that includes pretheater and football crowds packs the massive, minimalist dining room. Some signature dishes are poached breast of Goosnargh chicken with lentils, calves' liver with bubble and squeak (cabbage and mashed potatoes, fried), and, for dessert, pear and almond tart. ✉ *Jackson's Row, City Centre* ☎ *0161/835–3536* ▭ *AE, DC, MC, V.*

£–£££ ✕ **Mr. Thomas's Chophouse.** The city's oldest restaurant (1872) dishes out good old British favorites such as steak and kidney pudding, Cheshire gammon (ham), and corned beef hash. This hearty food is served in a clubby, Victorian-style room with a black-and-white-checked floor, brown ceilings, and wrought-iron screens. The wine list is exceptional. ✉ *52 Cross St., City Centre* ☎ *0161/832–2245* ▭ *AE, DC, MC, V.*

★ **££** ✕ **Yang Sing.** One of Manchester's best Chinese restaurants, this place is popular with Chinese families, which is always a good sign. The menu of Cantonese dishes is huge, the dim sum are legendary, and there's plenty for those of adventurous spirit—ox tripe with black bean sauce, for example. Vegetarians won't be disappointed, either. ✉ *34 Princess St., City Centre* ☎ *0161/236–2200* ▭ *AE, MC, V.*

£–££ ✕ **Lal Halweli.** One of Rusholme's string of Indian restaurants, this bright and spacious establishment specializes in Nepalese offerings such as chicken sultani (with orange, pineapple, and chilies) and stir-fried Balti dishes from Pakistan, as well as tandooris and other Indian staples. ✉ *68–72 Wilmslow Rd., Rusholme* ☎ *0161/248–9700* ▭ *AE, MC, V.*

Where to Stay

££££–£££££
FodorsChoice
★
🏨 **The Lowry Hotel.** The strikingly modern, ergonomic Italian design of this glass edifice exudes luxury and spaciousness. The clean-lined public and guest rooms are washed in soothing neutral tones, enlivened by brilliant red splashes of furniture; marble bathrooms and walk-in closets enhance the bedrooms. Celebrity chef Marco Pierre White oversees the French-inspired menu of the elegant River Room restaurant. The hotel fronts the River Irwell across from the landmark Trinity Bridge designed by Santiago Calatrava. ✉ *50 Dearman's Place, City Centre, M3 5LH* ☎ *0161/827–4000, 800/223–6800 in U.S.* 🖷 *0161/827–4001* ⊕ *www.roccofortehotels.com* ⇆ *157 rooms, 7 suites* ↺ *Restaurant, in-room data ports, cable TV with movies, in-room VCRs, indoor pool, health club, hair salon, sauna, spa, steam room, bar, business services, meeting rooms, parking (fee), no-smoking floors* ▭ *AE, DC, MC, V* ⏺ *BP.*

£££–£££££ 🏨 **Crowne Plaza Manchester—The Midland.** The Edwardian splendor of the hotel's public rooms—including a grand lobby in which high tea is served—evokes the days when the Midland was Manchester's railroad station hotel. Guest rooms are comfortable but unremarkable, with modern amenities but none of the period flair of the public areas. ✉ *Peter St., City Centre, M60 2DS* ☎ *0161/236–3333* 🖷 *0161/932–4100* ⊕ *www.manchester-themidland.crowneplaza.com* ⇆ *303 rooms, 7 suites* ↺ *3 restaurants, in-room data ports, cable TV with movies, in-room VCRs, indoor pool, health club, hair salon, sauna, 2 bars, lounge,* *business services, meeting rooms, parking (fee), some pets allowed; no a/c* ▤ *AE, DC, MC, V* ⏺◍ *BP.*

££££ ⊡ **Malmaison Hotel.** Part of a stylish, chic minichain, this is the kind of place that's popular with British pop stars. The striking contemporary design, inside an Edwardian facade, includes good-size, individually designed rooms decorated in dramatic red, black, and cream. Traditional French cuisine is the focus in the Brasserie. The Malmaison is a few minutes' walk from Piccadilly Station, Chinatown, and Canal Street. ✉ *Piccadilly, City Centre, M1 3AQ* ☎ *0161/278–1000* 🖷 *0161/278–1002* ⏺*www.malmaison.com* ⇲*167 rooms* ♨ *Restaurant, in-room data ports, health club, sauna, spa, steam room, bar, business services, meeting rooms, no-smoking floors; no a/c* ▤ *AE, DC, MC, V.*

£££–££££ ⊡ **Etrop Grange.** A gracious Georgian mansion with a modern addition, this true gem takes you back in time, even though you're just minutes from the airport rather than out in the country. Fireplaces, chandeliers, tapestry curtains, comfortable sofas, and antiques give a sense of luxurious warmth. Bedrooms are individually furnished, some with antique-style bathtubs. The Coach House Restaurant is known for good British cuisine. ✉ *Thorley La., Manchester Airport, M90 4EG* ☎ *0161/499–0500* 🖷 *0161/499–0790* ⏺ *www.corushotels.com/etropgrange* ⇲ *64 rooms* ♨ *Restaurant, in-room data ports, cable TV, bar, business services, meeting rooms, airport shuttle, parking (fee), some pets allowed, no-smoking floor; no a/c* ▤ *AE, DC, MC, V.*

£££–££££ ⊡ **Rossetti.** The girders, parquet flooring, and tiles of this converted Victorian textile warehouse (which used to supply floral print dresses to Queen Elizabeth II) are still here, but the feather-soft beds, Molteni furniture, and funky lights are right up to date and determinedly cool. Each floor has a help-yourself breakfast bar, the café-restaurant dishes up Neapolitan pizzas, and a glitzy nightclub occupies the basement. ✉ *107 Piccadilly, City Centre, M1 2DB* ☎ *0161/247–7744* 🖷 *0161/247–7747* ⏺ *www.aliasrossetti.com* ⇲ *56 rooms, 5 suites* ♨ *Restaurant, in-room data ports, in-room VCRs, bar, nightclub, meeting rooms, parking (fee); no a/c* ▤ *AE, DC, MC, V* ⏺◍ *CP.*

££ ⊡ **Castlefield Hotel.** This popular modern redbrick hotel sits near the water's edge in the Castlefield Basin. Public rooms are cheery and traditional, with patterned carpets and plain furnishings; subdued tones help make the bedrooms restful. The leisure facilities and free breakfast make this a good value. ✉ *Liverpool Rd., Castlefield, M3 4JR* ☎ *0161/832–7073* 🖷*0161/837–3534* ⏺*www.castlefield-hotel.co.uk* ⇲*48 rooms* ♨ *Restaurant, in-room data ports, cable TV, indoor pool, health club, sauna, bar, meeting rooms, parking (fee); no a/c* ▤ *AE, DC, MC, V* ⏺◍ *BP.*

££ ⊡ **Jurys Inn.** A good-value outpost of the Irish-based chain, Jurys has a sleek wooden lobby and contemporary design that's light and attractive. Guest rooms are spacious, and you can use a nearby health club. The location is excellent—next to Bridgewater Hall and close to shopping on King Street and the café-bar scenes on Whitworth Street and in Castlefield. ✉ *56 Great Bridgewater St., Peter's Fields, M1 5LE* ☎ *0161/953–8888* 🖷 *0161/953–9090* ⏺ *www.jurysdoyle.com* ⇲ *265 rooms* ♨ *Restaurant, in-room data ports, cable TV, bar, business services, meeting rooms, parking (fee), no-smoking floors* ▤ *AE, DC, MC, V.*

£ ⭐ **The Ox.** Friendly and relaxed, this gastro-pub with rooms is a real find. Guest rooms are furnished in light wood, with patterned fabrics and subdued colors, and the buzz-filled restaurant, decorated with local artwork, serves modern British cuisine. Guest ales are on tap, complemented by a good selection of wines. ✉ *71 Liverpool Rd., Castlefield, M3 4NO* ☎ *0161/839–7740* 🖷 *0161/839–7760* ⊕ *www.theox.co.uk* ⌔ *9 rooms* ⚭ *Restaurant, bar; no a/c* ▭ *MC, V.*

Nightlife & the Arts

Manchester vies with London as Britain's capital of youth culture but has vibrant nightlife and entertainment options for all ages. For event listings, buy the twice-monthly *City Life* magazine.

Nightlife

CAFÉ-BARS & PUBS **Barça** (✉ 8–9 Catalan Sq., Castlefield ☎ 0161/839–7099) is a hip canalside bar-restaurant that has won architectural awards. **Dry Bar** (✉ 28–30 Oldham St., Northern Quarter ☎ 0161/236–9840), the original café-bar in town, is still full of young people drinking and dancing. The cavernous **Dukes 92** (✉ 14 Castle St., Castlefield ☎ 0161/839–8646) is a café-bar named after the number of the lock on the Rochdale Canal by which it's situated. **Revolution** (✉ Arch 7, Whitworth St. W, Peter's Fields ☎ 0161/839–7569), in trendy Deansgate Locks, is a vodka bar. If you're over 21, **Tiger Tiger** (✉ 5–6 The Printworks, City Centre ☎ 0161/385–8080) is the place to go for a relaxed meal and to drink or dance.

The **Gay Village,** which came to television in the British series *Queer as Folk,* has a dozen stylish bars and cafés along the Rochdale Canal; Canal Street is its heart. The area is not only the center of the gay scene but also the nightlife center for the young and trendy. The café-bar **Manto** (✉ 46 Canal St., Gay Village ☎ 0161/236–2667) draws a chic, mostly gay crowd to its split-level, postindustrial interior.

★ **The Britons Protection** (✉ 50 Great Bridgewater St., Peter's Fields ☎ 0161/236–5895) stands out as a relaxed pub, with stained glass and cozy back rooms, a Peterloo Massacre mural, high-quality cask ales, and more than 160 whiskies and bourbons. **Peveril of the Peak** (✉ 127 Great Bridgewater St., Peter's Fields ☎ 0161/236–6364), a nifty Victorian pub with a green-tile exterior, draws a crush of locals to its tiny rooms. **Sinclair's Oyster Bar** (✉ 2 Cathedral Gates, Millennium Quarter ☎ 0161/834–0430), a half-timber pub built in the 17th century, sells fresh oyster dishes.

DANCE CLUBS **Ascension** (✉ 46–50 Oldham St., City Centre ☎ 0161/228–3300) hosts live music and big name DJs, dishing out everything from house, funk, and hip hop to classic sounds. **Industry** (✉ 112–116 Princess St., City Centre ☎ 0161/228–2966), a large club on three floors, concentrates on drum and bass, funk, and R&B music.

LIVE MUSIC **Band on the Wall** (✉ 25 Swan St., Northern Quarter ☎ 0161/832–6625) is a cozy room with a formidable reputation for live music—from world fusion to folk, jazz, and rock—and club nights. **Manchester Apollo** (✉ Stockport Rd., Ardwick Green ☎ 0161/242–2560) showcases acts for all musical tastes. Major rock and pop stars appear at the **Manchester Evening**

News Arena (⊠ 21 Hunt's Bank, Hunt's Bank ☎ 0161/930–8000 or 0870/190–8000). **The Roadhouse** (⊠ 8 Newton St., City Centre ☎ 0161/ 237–9789), an intimate band venue, also hosts funk and hip-hop nights.

The Arts

FILM The city's major center for contemporary cinema and the visual arts, the **Cornerhouse** (⊠ 70 Oxford St., City Centre ☎ 0161/200–1500) has three movie screens plus galleries, a bookshop, a trendy bar, and a café. **The Filmworks** (⊠ The Printworks, Exchange Sq., Millennium Quarter ☎ 0870/010–2030) is a state-of-the-art 20-screen complex with an IMAX 3-D screen.

PERFORMING Dramatically modern **Bridgewater Hall** (⊠ Lower Mosley St., Peter's
ARTS VENUES Fields ☎ 0161/907–9000) has concerts by Manchester's renowned
★ Hallé Orchestra and hosts both classical music and a varied light-entertainment program. **The Lowry** (⊠ Pier 8, Salford Quays ☎ 0161/ 876–2000) contains two theaters and presents everything from musicals to dance and performance poetry. The **Opera House** (⊠ Quay St., City Centre ☎ 0870/401–6000) is a venue for West End musicals, opera, and classical ballet. The **Palace Theatre** (⊠ Oxford St., City Centre ☎ 0870/401–6000) presents large touring shows—major plays, ballet, and opera. **Royal Northern College of Music** (⊠ 124 Oxford Rd., University Quarter ☎ 0161/907–5555) hosts classical and contemporary music concerts, jazz, and opera.

THEATRE **Green Room** (⊠ 54–56 Whitworth St. W, City Centre ☎ 0161/615– 0500) is an alternative space for theater, poetry, dance, and performance art. **Library Theatre** (⊠ St. Peter's Sq., City Centre ☎ 0161/236– 7110) in the Central Library stages classical drama, Shakespeare, chamber musicals, and new work from local playwrights. **Royal Exchange Theatre** (⊠ St. Ann's Sq., City Centre ☎ 0161/833–9833) serves as the city's main venue for innovative contemporary theater.

Sports & the Outdoors

The **Manchester Aquatics Centre** (⊠ Oxford Rd., University Quarter ☎ 0161/ 275–9450) has two 50-meter pools, as well as separate diving and leisure pools. The public can swim here as well as watch competitions. The **Manchester Velodrome** (⊠ 1 Stuart St., SportCity ☎ 0161/223–2244) hosts regular cycling, gymnastics, badminton, and basketball events.

Football

Football (soccer in the United States) is *the* reigning passion in Manchester. Locals support the perennially unsuccessful local club, Manchester City, and glory seekers come from afar to root for Manchester United, based in neighboring Trafford. Matches for both clubs are usually sold out months in advance, but touts (scalpers, legal here) do business outside the grounds. **Manchester City** (⊠ Rowsley St., SportCity ☎ 0161/ 828–1200) plays at the City of Manchester Stadium. At the **Manchester City Experience** (⊠ Rowsley St., SportCity ☎ 0870/442–8000), you can see club memorabilia, visit the players' changing rooms, and go down the tunnel to pitch side. Excluding match days, there are four tours Monday through Saturday and two on Sunday; admission is £7.50.

Manchester United (⊠ Sir Matt Busby Way, Trafford Wharf ☎ 0161/868–8000) has home matches at Old Trafford. You can take a trip to the Theatre of Dreams at the **Manchester United Museum and Tour** (⊠ Sir Matt Busby Way, Trafford Wharf ☎ 0870/442–1994), which tells the history of the football club. The tour (not available on match days) also takes you behind the scenes, into the changing rooms and players' lounge, and down the tunnel. It's open daily 9:30–5; admission for the museum and tour is £9, museum only £5.50.

Shopping

Afflecks Palace (⊠ 52 Church St., Northern Quarter ☎ 0161/834–2039) attracts Mancunian youth with four floors of bohemian glam, ethnic crafts and jewelry, and innovative gift ideas. **Barton Arcade** (⊠ 51–63 Deansgate, City Centre ☎ 0161/839–3172) has specialty shopping inside a lovely Victorian arcade. **Chinatown**—surrounded by Portland Street, Mosley Street, Princess Street, and Charlotte Street—is at its liveliest on Sunday, when traders from all over the country stock up from the supermarkets and stalls.

Harvey Nichols (⊠ 21 New Cathedral St., City Centre ☎ 0161/828–8888), an outpost of London's chic luxury department store, is packed with designer goods and has an excellent 2nd-floor restaurant and brasserie. The **Lowry Designer Outlet** (⊠ Salford Quays ☎ 0161/848–1832), with 80 stores, has good discounts on top brands at stores such as Nike and Karen Millen. The **Manchester Craft and Design Centre** (⊠ 17 Oak St., Northern Quarter ☎ 0161/832–4274) houses 16 workshop–cum–retail outlets where you can see craftspeople at work. The world's largest **Marks & Spencer** (⊠ 7 Market St., City Centre ☎ 0161/831–7341) department store offers its own brand of fashion and has an excellent food department. **Oldham Street,** in the Northern Quarter, is littered with urban hip-hop boutiques and music shops. The **Royal Exchange Shopping Centre and Arcade** (⊠ St. Ann's Sq., City Centre ☎ 0161/834–3731) has three floors of restaurants and specialty shops, with antiques, Belgian chocolates, teddy bears, and more, inside the former cotton market. **The Triangle** (⊠ Millennium Quarter ☎ 0161/834–8961), a stylish mall in the Victorian Corn Exchange, has more than 30 stores, including independent designer shops.

LIVERPOOL

A city lined with one of the most famous waterfronts in England, celebrated around the world as the birthplace of the Beatles, and still the place to catch that "Ferry 'Cross the Mersey," Liverpool has nonetheless suffered acute decline over the past few decades. New developments, however, such as the Tate Liverpool and the refurbishment of the adjacent Albert Dock, have spurred a reverse in the city's fortunes. The naming of Liverpool as the European Union's Capital of Culture for 2008 has accelerated plans for what the city hopes will be a reinvention of itself as a center for culture and innovation. Themed events will take place each year before 2008; in 2005, look for activities celebrating the Year of the Sea. Check out ⊕ www.liverpoolculture.com for the latest information.

Liverpool, on the east bank of the Mersey River estuary, at the point where it merges with the Irish Sea, developed from the 17th century through the slave trade. It became Britain's leading port for ferrying Africans to North America and for handling cargoes of sugar, tobacco, rum, and cotton, which began to dominate the local economy after the abolition of the slave trade in 1807. Because of its proximity to Ireland, the city was also the first port of call for those fleeing famine, poverty, and persecution in that country. Liverpool was often the last British port of call for thousands of mostly Jewish refugees fleeing the pogroms in Eastern Europe.

Many of the best-known liner companies were based in Liverpool, including Cunard and White Star, whose best-known vessel, the *Titanic,* was registered in Liverpool. The city was dealt an economic blow in 1894 with the opening of the Manchester Ship Canal, which allowed traders to bypass Liverpool and head to Lancashire's other major city, 35 mi east. Liverpool's economy never recovered, and decline gradually set in. Wartime bombing in the 1940s devastated the city's infrastructure, and rebuilding was in a modern style unsympathetic to the existing architecture. The postwar growth of air travel curtailed the services of the oceangoing liners, and a few years later Britain's entry into the European Common Market saw more trade move from the west coast to the east.

As economic decline set in, Liverpool produced its most famous export—the Beatles. The group was one of hundreds that copied the rock 'n' roll they heard from visiting American GIs and merchant seamen in the late 1950s, and one of many that played local venues such as the Cavern (demolished but since rebuilt nearby). All four Beatles were born in Liverpool, but the group's success dates from the time they left for London. Nevertheless, the city has milked the group's Liverpool connections for all they are worth, with a multitude of local attractions such as Paul McCartney's and John Lennon's childhood homes.

Despite the roughness and shabbiness of parts of the city, a surprising number of people visit Liverpool to tour the Beatles sites, view the paintings in the renowned art galleries, and learn about the city's industrial and maritime heritage at the impressive Albert Dock area.

Exploring Liverpool

Liverpool has a fairly compact center, and you can see many city highlights on foot. This walk includes some civic landmarks and museums, some key Beatles sights, and the Albert Dock and its maritime heritage sights.

A Good Walk

Begin, as many people do, at Lime Street and **Lime Street Station** ⓭ ⌐, which is not just the famous railway station but also the city's grandest Classical Revival building, **St. George's Hall** ⓮. To the north lies William Brown Street, a showcase boulevard of municipal buildings, in-

Albert Dock ...**19**

Anglican
Cathedral **23**

The Beatles
Story **21**

Lime Street
Station **13**

Merseyside
Maritime
Museum **18**

Metropolitan
Cathedral
of Christ
the King **24**

Museum of
Liverpool Life ..**22**

Pier Head **17**

Royal Liver
Building **16**

St. George's
Hall **14**

Tate
Liverpool **20**

Walker Art
Gallery **15**

Liverpool

KEY

i Tourist information

► Start of walk

0   440 yards

0   400 meters

cluding the outstanding **Walker Art Gallery** 🕒. A left turn at the end of
William Brown Street leads into Whitechapel, a street of dowdy-look-
ing stores. However, Nos. 12–14 were once the NEMS (North End Music
Stores) record shop owned by Brian Epstein. In 1961 when a teenager
asked for a record by Tony Sheridan and the Beat Brothers, Epstein could-
n't find it in his catalog. He discovered that the backing band was the
Beatles, a local group. The Beatles were playing daily at a nearby club,
the Cavern, so he made the short journey—as you can do now—down
Whitechapel, turning right at Stanley Street and left onto **Mathew Street**
to get to the Cavern at No. 10. The rest is, as they say, history.

The western end of Mathew Street leads into North John Street, and a
right turn brings you out at Dale Street, overlooked (to your left) by the
looming mass of the **Royal Liver Building** 🕒, part of Liverpool's famous
waterfront skyline. Equally renowned is the palazzolike Cunard Building to the south, once the head office of the famous Cunard Steamship
Company. Ferries from **Pier Head** 🕒, near the Royal Liver Building,
travel across the wide Mersey estuary to the Wirral Peninsula. A riverside walk connects with the museum area that includes the **Merseyside
Maritime Museum** 🕒 and **Albert Dock** 🕒, 19th-century brick warehouses
that have been redeveloped into boutiques, restaurants, offices, a hotel,

and **Tate Liverpool** ⑳. The complex also includes the **Beatles Story** ㉑, detailing the story of the city's best-known sons, and the **Museum of Liverpool Life** ㉒.

From Albert Dock it's a reasonably short walk back to the city center. For a longer walk that takes in the city's two cathedrals, head southeast along Duke Street and Upper Duke Street toward the Gothic-inspired **Anglican Cathedral** ㉓. Hope Street, which runs along the eastern side of the cathedral, links the latter with its Roman Catholic counterpart to the north, the modernistic **Metropolitan Cathedral of Christ the King** ㉔, and includes some romantic Georgian properties such as Gambier Terrace (John Lennon lived at No. 3) and the College of Art where Lennon studied. From the Catholic cathedral, it's a five-minute walk northwest back to Lime Street Station.

TIMING   You can do this walk in an hour without stopping, but you need a full day to visit all the museums and churches. Remember that 20 Forthlin Road and Mendips, the childhood homes of Paul McCartney and John Lennon, are in Liverpool but lie outside the center city.

What to See

★ ⑲   **Albert Dock.** To understand the city's prosperous maritime past, head straight for waterfront Albert Dock, 7 acres of restored warehouses built in 1846. Named after Queen Victoria's consort, Prince Albert, the dock provided storage for silk, tea, and tobacco from the Far East until it was closed in 1972. Rescued by the Merseyside Development Corporation, the fine colonnaded brick warehouse buildings are England's largest heritage attraction, containing the **Merseyside Maritime Museum, Museum of Liverpool Life, Tate Liverpool,** and the **Beatles Story.** When weather allows, sit at an outdoor café overlooking the dock or take a boat trip through the docks and onto the river. Albert Dock is part of the larger area known as **Liverpool's Historic Waterfront.** ⊠ *Tourist Information Centre, Merseyside Maritime Museum, Waterfront* ☎ *0151/478–4599* ⊕ *www.albertdock.com* ⊗ *Information center, daily 10–5.*

㉓   **Anglican Cathedral.** The largest church in northern Britain overlooks the city and the River Mersey. Built of local sandstone, the Gothic-style cathedral was begun in 1903 by architect Giles Gilbert Scott; it was finally finished in 1978. Take a look at the grand interior, view the exhibit of Victorian embroidery, climb the 331-foot-tall tower, and stop at the visitor center. A refectory serves light meals and coffee. ⊠ *St. James's Mount, City Centre* ☎ *0151/709–6271* ⊕ *www.liverpoolcathedral.org.uk* 🖘 *£3 suggested donation, tower and embroidery exhibition £3.25* ⊗ *Daily 8–6. Tower Mar.–Sept., Mon.–Sat. 11–4:30; Oct.–Feb., Mon.–Sat. 11–3:30.*

> **need a break?**   **Prohibition** (⊠ 1A Bold St., City Centre ☎ 0151/707–2333) used to be a library and a gentleman's club. Now you can sink into a huge sofa for coffee or cocktails beneath the grand domed ceiling.

㉑   **Beatles Story.** You can follow in the footsteps of the Fab Four at one of the more popular attractions in the Albert Dock complex. It has an entertaining series of scenes re-created from their career, as well as the glasses

John Lennon wore when he composed "Imagine." The same owners manage **Fingerprints of Elvis** (⊠ 17–19 The Colonnades, Albert Dock, Waterfront ☎ 0151/709–1790 ⊕ www.fingerprintsofelvis.com 🎫 £4.95 ⊙ Daily 10–6), which explores Elvis Presley's life and displays some of his guitars and stage outfits. ⊠ *Britannia Vaults, Albert Dock, Waterfront* ☎*0151/709–1963* ⊕*www.beatlesstory.com* 🎫*£7.95* ⊙ *Mar.–Oct., daily 10–6; Nov.–Feb., daily 10–5; last admission 1 hr before closing.*

► ⑬ **Lime Street Station.** Perhaps the most imposing expression of the city's former industrial might is this railway station, whose cast-iron train shed was the world's largest in the mid-19th century. The opening scene in the film *A Hard Day's Night,* which shows the Beatles on a railway station platform, supposedly Lime Street, was filmed in Marylebone Station, London. ⊠ *Lime St., City Centre.*

Liverpool's Historic Waterfront. Liverpool's famous waterside sights include the Royal Liver and Cunard buildings, Pier Head (ferries leave for river trips), and the Albert Dock complex. Also here are the Merseyside Maritime Museum, Museum of Liverpool Life, Tate Liverpool, and the Beatles Story. A shuttle bus (every 20 minutes) runs to the waterfront from the Queen Square bus station, a couple of minutes' walk from Lime Street Station.

Mathew Street. It was at the Cavern on this street that Brian Epstein, who became the Beatles' manager, first heard the group in 1961. The Cavern had opened at No. 10 as a jazz venue in 1957, but beat groups, of whom the Beatles were clearly the most talented, had taken it over. Epstein became their manager a few months after first visiting the club, and within two years the group was the most talked-about phenomenon in music. The Cavern club fell on hard times in the early '70s and was demolished in 1973; it was rebuilt a few yards from the original site. At No. 31, check out the Beatles Shop.

Mendips. The august National Trust (overseers of such landmarks as Blenheim Palace) also maintains the 1930s middle-class, semidetached house that was the home of John Lennon from 1946 to 1963 and is now a must-see for Beatles pilgrims. After his parents separated, John joined his aunt Mimi here; she gave him his first guitar but banished him to play on the porch, saying, "The guitar's all very well, John, but you'll never make a living out of it." The house can be seen only on a tour, for which you must prebook a seat on the minibus that connects the site with Albert Dock (mornings) or Speke Hall (afternoons). ⊠ *251 Menlove Ave., Woolton* ☎ *0870/900–0256* ⊕ *www.spekehall.org.uk/ mendips.htm* 🎫 *£12 includes 20 Forthlin Rd. and Speke Hall gardens* ⊙ *Apr.–Oct., Wed.–Sun. and national holidays; 4 departures a day (call for times).*

♻ ⑱ **Merseyside Maritime Museum.** Part of the Albert Dock complex, the museum tells the story of the port of Liverpool by way of models, paintings, and original boats and equipment spread across five floors; it also has a gallery on the Battle of the Atlantic and Liverpool's role during World War II. In summer full-size vessels are on display. The Transatlantic Slavery exhibition, on the human misery engendered by the slave trade, is especially compelling. ⊠ *Albert Dock, Waterfront* ☎ *0151/478–4499* ⊕ *www.liverpoolmuseums.org.uk* ▣ *Free* ⊙ *Daily 10–5; last admission 4.*

㉔ Metropolitan Cathedral of Christ the King. This Roman Catholic cathedral consecrated in 1967 is a modernistic, funnel-like structure of concrete, stone, and mosaic, topped with a glass lantern. Long, narrow blue-glass windows separate chapels, each with modern works of art. An earlier design by classically inspired architect Edwin Lutyens was abandoned when World War II began (the current design is by Frederick Gibberd), but the crypt shows some of Lutyens's work. ⊠ *Mount Pleasant, City Centre* ☎ *0151/709–9222* ⊕ *www.liverpool-rc-cathedral.org.uk* ▣ *Donations welcome* ⊙ *Mon.–Sat. 8–6, Sun. 8–5.*

㉒ Museum of Liverpool Life. Discover what makes "Scousers" (as locals are known) tick. The museum, in a former Boat Hall, takes a somewhat off-beat look at the city's history and culture. Special displays on Mersey-side culture focus on matters as diverse as the city's changing trades after the decline of shipping, local sporting prowess, and arts and literature in Liverpool. ⊠ *Albert Dock, Waterfront* ☎ *0151/478–4080* ⊕ *www. liverpoolmuseums.org.uk* ▣ *Free* ⊙ *Daily 10–5; last admission 4.*

⑰ Pier Head. Here you can take a ferry across the River Mersey from Pier-head to Birkenhead and back. Boats leave regularly and offer fine views of the city—a journey celebrated in "Ferry 'Cross the Mersey," Gerry and the Pacemakers' 1964 hit song. It was from Pier Head that 9 million British, Irish, and other European emigrants set sail between 1830 and 1930 for new lives in the United States, Canada, Australia, and Africa. ⊠ *Pier Head Ferry Terminal, Mersey Ferries, Waterfront* ☎ *0151/330–1444* ⊕ *www.merseyferries.co.uk* ▣ *£2.05 round-trip, cruises £4.65* ⊙ *Ferries every 30 mins weekdays 7:45–9:15 AM and 4:15–6:45 PM; cruises hourly 10–3 weekdays and 10–6 weekends.*

⑯ Royal Liver Building. Best seen from the ferry, the 322-foot-tall Royal Liver (pronounced "lie-ver") Building with its twin towers is topped by two 18-foot-high copper birds. They represent the mythical Liver Birds, the town symbol; local legend has it that if they fly away, Liverpool will cease to exist. For decades Liverpudlians looked to the Royal Liver Society for assistance—it was originally a burial club to which families paid contributions to ensure a decent send-off. ⊠ *Water St., Waterfront.*

⑭ St. George's Hall. Built between 1839 and 1847, St. George's Hall is among the world's best Greek Revival buildings. When Queen Victoria visited Liverpool in 1851, she declared it "worthy of ancient Athens." Today the hall serves as a home for music festivals, concerts, and fairs. Refurbishment will be underway for most of 2005; call for information. ⊠ *Lime St., City Centre* ☎ *0151/707–2391* ⊕ *www.stgeorgeshall.com* ▣ *Free, different charges for events.*

Speke Hall and Gardens. This black-and-white mansion only 6 mi from downtown Liverpool is one of the best examples of half-timbering in Britain. Built around a cobbled courtyard, the earliest part, the great hall, dates to 1490; an elaborate western bay with a vast chimneypiece was added in 1560. The house, owned by the National Trust, was heavily restored in the 19th century, though a Tudor priest hole and Jacobean plasterwork remain intact. Speke Hall is on the east side of the airport; the Airportxpress 500 bus drops you a pleasant 10-minute walk away. ☒ *The Walk, Speke* ☎ *0151/427–7231* ⊕ *www.spekehall.org.uk* ▣ *£6, gardens only £3* ⊙ *House Apr.–Oct., Wed.–Sun. and national holidays 1–5:30; Nov.–mid-Dec., weekends 1–4:30. Gardens daily 11–5:30 or dusk. Last admission 30 mins before closing.*

㉔ Tate Liverpool. An offshoot of the London-based art galleries of the same name, the Liverpool museum, a handsome conversion of existing Albert Dock warehouses, was designed in the 1990s by the late James Stirling, one of Britain's leading 20th-century architects. Galleries display changing exhibits of challenging modern art. The excellent shop sells art books, prints, and posters, and there's a children's art-play area and a fashionable dockside café-restaurant. ☒ *The Colonnades, Albert Dock, Waterfront* ☎ *0151/702–7400* ⊕ *www.tate.org.uk* ▣ *Free, charge for special exhibitions* ⊙ *Tues.–Sun. and national holidays 10–5:50.*

20 Forthlin Road. Paul McCartney lived with his family in this modest 1950s council house (a building rented from the local government), with its period-authentic windows, doors, and hedges, from 1955 to 1963; now it's a shrine for fans. A number of the Beatles' songs, including "Love Me Do" and "When I'm Sixty-Four," were written here. The house is viewable only on a tour, for which you must prebook a seat on the minibus that connects the site with Albert Dock (mornings) or Speke Hall (afternoons). ☒ *20 Forthlin Rd., Allerton* ☎ *0870/900–0256* ⊕ *www.spekehall. org.uk* ▣ *£12 includes Mendips and Speke Hall gardens* ⊙ *Apr.–Oct., Wed.–Sun. and national holidays; 4 departures a day (call for times).*

★ ⑮ Walker Art Gallery. With a superb display of British art and some superb Italian and Flemish works, the Walker maintains its position as one of the best British art collections outside London. Particularly notable are the unrivaled collection of paintings by 18th-century Liverpudlian equestrian artist George Stubbs, and works by J. M. W. Turner, John Constable, Sir Edwin Henry Landseer, and the Pre-Raphaelites. Modern British artists are included, too—on display is one of David Hockney's typically Californian pool scenes. Other excellent exhibits showcase china, silver, and furniture that once adorned the mansions of Liverpool's industrial barons. The Tea Room holds center stage in the airy museum lobby. ☒ *William Brown St., City Centre* ☎ *0151/478–4199* ⊕ *www. liverpoolmuseums.org.uk* ▣ *Free* ⊙ *Mon.–Sat. 10–5, Sun. noon–5.*

Where to Eat

£–££££ ✕ **60 Hope Street.** The combination of a ground-floor restaurant and a cheaper basement café-bar make this a popular choice for any budget. A light, polished wood floor and blue-and-cream walls help create the uncluttered backdrop for dishes that reflect a Mediterranean clime, but found only on British shores is the deep-fried jam sandwich with condensed milk ice cream, one of the imaginative desserts. ☒ *60 Hope St.,*

City Centre ☎ *0151/707–6060* ⊟ *MC, V* ⊘ *Closed Sun. No lunch Sat. in restaurant.*

££–£££ ✕ **Blue Bar and Grill.** Expect to rub shoulders with local celebrities in this sophisticated modern restaurant and bar on the waterfront. The focal point is the beautiful Venetian crystal chandelier, a counterpoint to the original open brickwork, chunky furnishings, and plasma screens. Downstairs you can sample tapas, dim sum, and bruschetta; the fare in the upstairs gallery includes a large selection of meat and fish steaks, accompanied by different sauces. ⊠ *Edward Pavilion, Albert Dock, Waterfront* ☎ *0151/709–7097* ⊟ *AE, MC, V.*

££–£££ ✕ **Chung Ku.** Liverpool has a strong Chinese presence, and here you can sample Asian cuisine with a superb Merseyside view. Panoramic windows wrap around both levels of this stunning, ultramodern restaurant. Choose from 70 kinds of dim sum, or try one of the sizzling platters or something from the extensive seafood selection. ⊠ *2 Columbus Quay, Riverside Dr., Waterfront* ☎ *0151/726–8191* ⊟ *AE, MC, V.*

££–£££ ✕ **Simply Heathcote's.** This chic contemporary restaurant, an outpost of chef Paul Heathcote's expanding empire, has a curved glass front, cherrywood furnishings, and a granite floor. The menu has a local accent— black pudding, Goosnargh duckling, bread and butter pudding—along with dishes from warmer climes. Vegetarians are well served, too. The restaurant is opposite the Royal Liver and Cunard buildings. ⊠ *25 The Strand, Waterfront* ☎ *0151/236–3536* ⊟ *AE, DC, MC, V.*

£–££ ✕ **Tabac.** The warm decor and chilled-out music of this long, thin café-bar at the top of Bold Street attracts a cosmopolitan crowd. It's good for breakfasts (with home-baked bread), cocktails, sandwiches, and salads, as well as daily specials such as ragout of chicken, herby meatballs, and vegetarian options. ⊠ *126 Bold St., City Centre* ☎ *0151/709– 9502* ⊟ *MC, V.*

£–££ ✕ **Tate Café.** The Tate Liverpool's café-bar is a winner for daytime sustenance. There are dockside seats for warm summer days, and you can choose among the open sandwiches and salads, as well as more substantial meat and fish dishes. ⊠ *The Colonnades, Albert Dock, Waterfront* ☎ *0151/702–7580* ⊟ *MC, V* ⊘ *Closed Mon. No dinner.*

Where to Stay

Hotel options are expanding because of the naming of the city as the European Union's Capital of Culture in 2008. At this writing the Alias and Malmaison chains, among others, were considering plans to build hotels.

£££–£££££ ▦ **Hope Street Hotel.** Liverpool's new boutique hotel, a converted carriage warehouse built in the style of a Venetian palazzo, puts the emphasis on traditional, natural materials and retains the exposed brickwork and cast-iron columns from the 1860s. A stunning oak staircase runs the height of the building, and huge windows flood the simple, elegant bedrooms with light. The restaurant concentrates on local and seasonal produce, used in such dishes as roast mushrooms with spinach and Parmesan stuffing and grilled loin of venison. Note that the hotel was being completed at the time of this writing. ⊠ *40 Hope St., City Centre, L1*

9DA ☎ 0151/709–3000 🖷 0151/709–2454 ⊕ www.hopestreethotel. co.uk ⇘ 41 rooms, 7 suites ⚘ Restaurant, brasserie, in-room data ports, cable TV, 2 bars, business services, meeting rooms, free parking; no a/c ▤ AE, D, MC, V.

£££–££££ 🏨 **Liverpool Moat House.** Some may find this uncompromisingly modern hotel unattractive from the outside, but it lies in landscaped grounds near the River Mersey and Albert Dock, which means that many of the main city sights are at your doorstep. Bedrooms, done in cool, soothing colors, are handsome and spacious; most have two large beds. ⊠ Paradise St., City Centre, L1 8JD ☎ 0151/471–9988 🖷 0151/709– 2706 ⊕ www.moathousehotels.com ⇘ 263 rooms, 2 suites ⚘ 2 restaurants, in-room data ports, cable TV with movies, indoor pool, gym, sauna, bar, business services, meeting rooms, parking (fee), some pets allowed, no-smoking rooms ▤ AE, DC, MC, V ⎪⎢⎪ BP.

£££ 🏨 **Feathers Hotel.** One of a terrace of Georgian brick houses, this smart and efficient hotel close to both the city's cathedrals doesn't stint on decoration. Swags and drapes adorn the public rooms, and bedrooms have modern pine pieces and patterned fabrics in red, blue, and yellow. You can eat your fill at the buffet breakfast and sip a drink at night in the Beatles-themed bar. The hotel is priced at the low end of the category. ⊠ 119–125 Mount Pleasant, City Centre, L3 6DX ☎ 0151/709–9655 🖷 0151/709–3838 ⊕ www.feathers.uk.com ⇘ 75 rooms ⚘ Restaurant, cable TV, bar, meeting rooms, parking (fee); no a/c ▤ AE, MC, V ⎪⎢⎪ BP.

£££ 🏨 **Liverpool Marriott Hotel.** The presence of this modern city-center hotel is indicative of Liverpool's rise from the economic ashes. Guest rooms have cherry furniture and are decorated in rich gold and burgundy hues. The unbeatable location is a minute from Lime Street Station and the Walker Art Gallery. Breakfast is included in the cost on weekends. ⊠ 1 Queen Sq., City Centre, L1 1RH ☎ 0151/476–8000 🖷 0151/474–5000 ⊕ www.marriott.com ⇘ 143 rooms, 3 suites ⚘ Restaurant, in-room data ports, cable TV with movies, indoor pool, gym, sauna, bar, business services, meeting rooms, parking (fee) ▤ AE, DC, MC, V.

££–£££ 🏨 **Royal Hotel.** The Royal occupies an 1815 building that overlooks the Marine Gardens and the Mersey estuary, with views of the Wirral Peninsula and North Wales in the distance. The hotel retains much of its original character, with its grand proportions, fireplaces, plasterwork, and maritime features. Bedrooms are modern, done predominantly in prints and cream and red; some have four-posters and whirlpool baths. The hotel is a 10-minute drive from the city center. ⊠ Marine Terr., Waterloo, L22 5PR ☎ 0151/928–2332 🖷 0151/949–0320 ⊕ www.liverpoolroyalhotel.co.uk ⇘ 25 rooms ⚘ Restaurant, in-room data ports, cable TV, bar, meeting rooms, free parking; no a/c ▤ AE, DC, MC, V ⎪⎢⎪ BP.

££ 🏨 **Express by Holiday Inn.** The best central accommodation in terms of value, location, and style is this offering in the upper part of the Britannia Pavilion, in a converted warehouse in the heart of the waterfront district. Management is friendly and helpful, and the rich red-and-blue decor and thick carpeting reflect the style of the chain. Guest rooms are cool in tone; try for one with views of the dock. ⊠ Britannia Pavilion, Albert Dock, Waterfront, L3 4AD ☎ 0151/709–1133 or 0800/434040 🖷 0151/709–1144 ⊕ www.hiexpress.co.uk ⇘ 135 rooms ⚘ Restau-

Fodor'sChoice ★

rant, cable TV with movies, bar, meeting room, free parking; no a/c ⊟ *AE, MC, V* ⎢○⎢ *BP.*

£ 🏠 **Liverpool Youth Hostel.** This hostel just a few minutes' walk from Albert Dock really should change its name, because it offers modest hotel standards for bargain prices. The smart rooms (for two, four, or six people) are fully carpeted, with private bathrooms and heated towel rails. Guests must be members of the Youth Hostels Association; you can join on the spot (£14), but it's advisable to book well in advance. ⊠ *Chalenor St., Waterfront, L1 8EE* ☎ *0151/709–8888* 🖶 *0151/709–0417* ⊕ *www. yha.org.uk* ↝ *106 beds* ⟡ *Cafeteria, recreation room, laundry facilities; no a/c, no room TVs* ⊟ *MC, V* ⎢○⎢ *BP.*

Nightlife & the Arts

Nightlife

Baby Cream (⊠ Atlantic Pavilion, Albert Dock, Waterfront ☎ 0151/707–1004), one of the city's newer bars, is a place where you can burn your own CDs, listen to weekend DJs, and pamper yourself in the glitzy black powder room. **Blue Bar** (⊠ Edward Pavilion, Albert Dock, Waterfront ☎ 0151/709–7097), typical of the bars at the Albert Dock, attracts a funky, young professional crowd with its late hours, grill, and dockside seating. The **Cavern Club** (⊠ 8–10 Mathew St., City Centre ☎ 0871/222–1957) draws many on the Beatles trail, who don't realize it's not the original spot—that was demolished years ago. The **Cavern Pub** (⊠ 5 Mathew St., City Centre ☎ 0151/236–4041) merits a stop for nostalgia's sake; here are recorded the names of the groups and artists who
★ played in the Cavern Club between 1957 and 1973. The **Philharmonic** (⊠ 36 Hope St., City Centre ☎ 0151/707–2837), nicest of the city-center pubs and opposite the Philharmonic Hall, is a Victorian-era extravaganza (complete with ornate toilets) decorated in colorful marble, with comfortable bar rooms and good food. **Ye Cracke** (⊠ 13 Rice St., off Hope St., City Centre ☎ 0151/709–4171), one of the city's oldest pubs, was much visited by John Lennon in the 1960s; it has five cozy bars.

The Arts

The well-regarded Royal Liverpool Philharmonic Orchestra plays its
★ concert season at **Philharmonic Hall** (⊠ Hope St., City Centre ☎ 0151/709–3789).

Everyman Theatre (⊠ 5–9 Hope St., City Centre ☎ 0151/709–4776) focuses on works of all kinds by British playwrights as well as experimental productions from around the world. The **Liverpool Empire** (⊠ Lime St., City Centre ☎ 0870/606–3536) presents major ballet, opera, drama, and musical performances. **Royal Court Theatre** (⊠ 1 Roe St., City Centre ☎ 0151/709–4321), an art deco building, is one of the city's most appealing sites for pop and rock concerts and stand-up comedy.

Sports & the Outdoors

Football

Football (soccer in the United States) matches are played on weekends and, increasingly, weekdays. Ticket prices vary, but the cheapest seats start at about £20. Tourist offices can give you match schedules and directions to the grounds. **Liverpool** (☎ 0870/220–2345), one of England's top clubs, plays at Anfield, 2 mi north of the city center. **Everton** (☎ 0151/330–2300, 0870/7383–7866 booking line), once a major force but now in a seemingly perpetual rebuilding phase, plays at Goodison Park, about ½ mi north of Anfield.

Horse Racing

★ Britain's most famous horse race, the Grand National steeplechase, has been run at Liverpool's **Aintree Racecourse** (✉ Ormskirk Rd., Aintree ☎ 0151/523–2600) almost every year since 1839. The race is held in March or April. Admission on race days is £15 (for Grand National, £14–£70). The **Grand National Experience** (☎ 0151/522–2921 ☑ £7 ⏱ late May–mid-Oct., Tues.–Fri. 11 and 2) includes a tour of the racecourse, admission to the visitor center, and a ride on the race simulator; advance booking is required.

Shopping

★ The **Beatles Shop** (✉ 31 Mathew St., City Centre ☎ 0151/236–8066) may stock the mop-top knickknack of your dreams. **Circa 1900** (✉ 11–13 Holts Arcade, India Buildings, Water St., City Centre ☎ 0151/236–1282) specializes in authentic art nouveau and art deco pieces, from ceramics and glass to furniture. The **Stanley Dock Sunday Market** (✉ Great Howard St. and Regent Rd., City Centre) has more than 400 stalls operating each Sunday, selling bric-a-brac, clothes, and toys from 9 to 4. The **Walker Art Gallery** (✉ William Brown St., City Centre ☎ 0151/478–4199) has a small lobby shop with high-quality glassware, ceramics, and jewelry by local designers.

THE PEAK DISTRICT
BUXTON, BAKEWELL, HADDON HALL, CHATSWORTH

Heading southeast, away from the urban congestion of Manchester and Liverpool, it's not far to the southernmost contortions of the Pennine Hills. Here, about an hour from Manchester, sheltered in a great natural bowl, is the spa town of Buxton: at an elevation of more than 1,000 feet, it's the second-highest town in England. Buxton makes a convenient base for exploring the 540 square mi of the Peak District, Britain's oldest—and, some say, most beautiful—national park. "Peak" is perhaps misleading; despite being a hilly area, it contains only long, flat-top rises that don't reach much higher than 2,000 feet. Yet a trip around destinations such as Bakewell, Matlock, Castleton, and Edale, and the grand estates of Chatsworth House, Haddon Hall, and Hardwick Hall involves negotiating fairly perilous country roads, each of which repays the effort with enchanting views. Outdoor activities are popular in the Peaks, particularly caving (or "potholing"), walking, and hiking. Bring all-weather clothing and waterproof shoes.

CloseUp
STOKE-ON-TRENT: THE POTTERIES

The area known as the Potteries, about 55 mi southeast of Liverpool, is the center of Britain's ceramic industry and still the largest clayware producer in the world. The novels of Arnold Bennett (1867–1931), including Anna of the Five Towns, realistically describe life in the area as an "architecture of ovens and chimneys" with an atmosphere "as black as mud." There are, in fact, six towns, now administered as "the city of Stoke-on-Trent." The thousands of plump, bottle-shape kilns that once dominated the landscape are gone, but Wedgwood, Minton, Royal Doulton, Spode, Coalport, and other famous names carry on, as do many small workshops and outlets.

The most famous manufacturer, Josiah Wedgwood, established his pottery works at Etruria, near Burslem, in 1759 and created the cream-color ware (creamware) which so pleased Queen Charlotte that in 1762 she appointed him royal supplier of dinnerware. Perhaps Wedgwood's best-known innovation was his blue jasperware, decorated with white cameo figures by the British artist John Flaxman. Four museums evocatively portray the industrial and social history of this area, and the many factory shops sell all kinds of china.

Ceramica occupies an ornate former town hall and uses displays, videos, and interactive technology to explore the area's history, the process of creating china, and some noted companies. In Bizarreland (the name comes from Clarice Cliff's art deco designs), kids can dig for relics from the past and take a virtual ride over the Potteries. A shop sells wares from local manufacturers. ⊠ Market Pl., Burslem ☎ 01782/832001 ⊕ www.ceramicauk.com ⊠ £3.50 ⊙ Mon.–Sat. 9:30–5, Sun. 10:30–4:30.

The **Gladstone Pottery Museum,** the city's only remaining Victorian pottery factory, contains examples of the old ovens, surrounded by original workshops where you can watch the traditional skills of throwing, casting, and decorating. The Flushed with Pride galleries tell the story of the toilet from the 1840s onward with many splendidly decorative examples. ⊠ Uttoxeter Rd., Longton ☎ 01782/319232 ⊕ www.stoke.gov.uk/museums ⊠ £4.95 ⊙ Daily 10–5; last admission 4.

The modern **Potteries Museum and Art Gallery** has a 5,000-piece ceramic collection of international repute and is recognized worldwide for its unique Staffordshire pottery. Other excellent galleries are devoted to the fine arts and Arnold Bennett memorabilia. ⊠ Bethesda St., Hanley ☎ 01782/232323 ⊕ www.stoke.gov.uk/museums ⊠ Free ⊙ Mar.–Oct., Mon.–Sat. 10–5, Sun. 2–5; Nov.–Feb., Mon.–Sat. 10–4, Sun. 1–4.

At the **Wedgwood Visitor Centre** you can learn about the history of Wedgwood, watch all stages of pottery production (including traditional skills and the latest technologies), and even try your hand at throwing a pot. After visiting the audio-guided exhibition area, shop in the "firsts" and "seconds" stores. ⊠ Off A5035, Barlaston ☎ 01782/204218 ⊕ www.thewedgwoodstory.com ⊠ £7.25 ⊙ Weekdays 9–5, weekends 10–5.

Little Moreton Hall

★ ❷ *20 mi southwest of Buxton, 45 mi southeast of Liverpool.*

The epitome of "magpie" black-and-white half-timber buildings, this house, in the words of Olive Cook's *The English Country House,* "exaggerates and exalts the typical and humble medieval timber-framed dwelling, making of it a bizarre, unforgettable phenomenon." Covered with zigzags, crosses, and lozenge shapes crafted of timber and daub, the house was built by the Moreton family between 1450 and 1580. The long gallery and Tudor-era wall paintings are spectacular. Little Moreton Hall lies to the west of the Peak District; to get here from Liverpool, take the M6 to the A534 east to Congleton. ⊠ *A34, Congleton* ☎ *01260/272018* ⊕ *www.nationaltrust.org.uk* ⊲ *£5 Mar.–Nov., Dec. free* ⊘ *Late Mar.–Oct., Wed.–Sun. and national holidays 11:30–5; Nov., weekends 11:30–4; early–mid-Dec., ground floor only, weekends 11:30–4.*

Buxton

⊳ ❷ *20 mi northeast of Little Moreton Hall, 25 mi southeast of Manchester.*

The Romans arrived in AD 79 and named Buxton *Aquae Arnemetiae,* loosely translated as "Waters of the Goddess of the Grove," suggesting they considered this area in the Derbyshire hills special. The mineral springs, which emerge from 3,500 to 5,000 feet below ground at a constant 82°F, were believed to cure assorted ailments; in the 18th century the town became established as a popular spa, a minor rival to Bath. You can still drink water from the ancient St. Anne's Well, and it's also bottled and sold throughout Britain.

Buxton's spa days left a notable legacy of 18th- and 19th-century buildings, parks, and open spaces that give the town an air of faded grandeur. A good place to start exploring is the **Crescent** on the northwest side of the Slopes park (the town hall is on the opposite side); almost all out-of-town roads lead toward this central green. The three former hotels that make up the Georgian-era Crescent, with its arches, Doric colonnades, and 378 windows, were built in 1780 by fashionable architect John Carr for the fifth duke of Devonshire (of nearby Chatsworth House). The thermal baths at the end of the Crescent now house a shopping center. The Crescent buildings themselves are closed to the public, except for the tourist information center.

The **Devonshire Royal Hospital,** behind the Crescent, also by John Carr, was originally a stable with room for 110 horses. In 1859 the circular area for exercising horses was covered with a massive 156-foot-wide slate-color dome and incorporated into the hospital. Today the University of Derby has taken over the building.

The **Buxton Museum** contains a collection of Blue John stone, a semiprecious mineral found only in the Peak District. It also displays local archaeological finds, including a few pieces from Roman times, and there's a small art gallery. The museum is on the eastern side of the Slopes.

⊠ *Terrace Rd.* ☎ *01298/24658* ⊠ *Free* ☉ *Tues.–Fri. 9:30–5:30, Sat. 9:30–5, Sun. and national holidays (Apr.–Sept. only) 10:30–5.*

The **Pavilion** (⊠ Pavilion Gardens ☎ 01298/23114), with its ornate iron-and-glass roof, was originally a concert hall and ballroom. Erected in the 1870s, it remains a lively place, with a conservatory, several bars, a cafeteria, and a restaurant, surrounded by 25 acres of gardens. The Pavilion is adjacent to the Crescent and the Slopes on the west.

Buxton Opera House (⊠ Water St. ☎ 0845/127–2190), built in 1903, is one of the most architecturally exuberant structures in town. Its marble bulk, bedecked with carved cupids, is even more impressive inside— so impressive it may be worth buying a ticket to a concert. Otherwise, tours of the interior (£2.50) are conducted most Saturdays at 11 AM.

The Peak District's extraordinary geology is revealed close to Buxton at **Poole's Cavern,** a large limestone cave far beneath the 100 wooded acres of Buxton Country Park. Named after a legendary 15th-century robber, the cave was inhabited in prehistoric times and contains, in addition to the standard stalactites and stalagmites, the source of the River Wye, which flows through Buxton. ⊠ *Green La.* ☎ *01298/26978* ⊕ *www.poolescavern.co.uk* ⊠ *£5.50 including tour; park and visitor center free* ☉ *Mar.–Oct., daily 10–5.*

Where to Stay & Eat

£££ ✕⊞ **Old Hall.** Friendly and central, this hotel in a refurbished 16th-century building overlooks the Opera House. The individually decorated rooms are furnished in a mixture of period and modern styles. One room, Mary's Bower, in the oldest section, retains its original ceiling moldings. The Cockerel Bar is popular with theatergoers who stoke up on hearty dishes or salads and *panini* (Italian sandwiches); there's a more formal restaurant as well. ⊠ *The Square, SK17 6BD* ☎ *01298/22841* 🖷 *01298/ 72437* ⊕ *www.oldhallhotelbuxton.co.uk* ↝ *38 rooms* ⚬ *Restaurant, bar, meeting rooms, some pets allowed; no a/c* ☰ *AE, DC, MC, V* ⦿ *BP.*

££££ ⊞ **The Palace.** A Victorian pile on a grand scale, the Palace dates from the halcyon days of the spa and sits on 5 acres overlooking the town center and surrounding hills. The interior reveals a sweeping staircase, marble columns, and chandeliers, but the rooms are disappointingly modern in style, with furnishings in orange and brown. ⊠ *Palace Rd., SK17 6AG* ☎ *01298/22001* 🖷 *01298/72131* ⊕ *www.paramount-hotels.co. uk* ↝ *118 rooms, 4 suites* ⚬ *Restaurant, cable TV with movies, indoor pool, gym, hair salon, sauna, bar, business services, meeting rooms, some pets allowed (fee); no a/c* ☰ *AE, DC, MC, V* ⦿ *BP.*

★ ££ ⊞ **Buxton's Victorian Guesthouse.** One of a terrace (a group of row houses) built by the duke of Devonshire in 1860, this beautifully and imaginatively decorated house stands a stone's throw away from the Opera House. The Oriental dining room has a dragon mural, and the bedrooms have intriguing themes such as Victorian Craftsman. Victorian and Edwardian antiques and prints furnish all the rooms. ⊠ *3A Broad Walk, SK17 6JE* ☎ *01298/78759* 🖷 *01298/74732* ⊕ *www.buxtonvictorian. co.uk* ↝ *7 rooms, 1 suite* ⚬ *Some in-room data ports; no a/c, no kids under 4, no smoking* ☰ *No credit cards* ⦿ *BP.*

££ ⊞ **Lakenham Guest House.** This large Victorian structure retains many pleasant reminders of that period. Potted plants proliferate, as do antiques,
and the Victorian-style bedrooms have excellent views; the house overlooks Pavilion Gardens. ⊠ *11 Burlington Rd., SK17 9AL* ☎ *01298/79209*
⊕ *www.lakenhambuxton.co.uk* ⚓ *6 rooms* ⚐ *Refrigerators, cable TV;
no a/c, no room phones, no kids under 10* ⊟ *No credit cards* ⦿ *BP.*

£ ⊞ **Stoneridge.** Built of stone, this Edwardian B&B close to the Opera
House has been carefully and richly restored in sympathetic style. Modern pieces furnish the bedrooms. There's a complimentary glass of
sherry in the evening, and kippers and croissants for breakfast. ⊠ *9 Park
Rd., SK17 6SG* ☎ *01298/26120* ⊕ *www.stoneridge.co.uk* ⚓ *4 rooms*
⚐ *Some pets allowed; no a/c, no room phones, no kids under 10, no
smoking* ⊟ *No credit cards* ⊙ *Closed Jan.* ⦿ *BP.*

Nightlife & the Arts

★ **Buxton Opera House** (⊠ Water St. ☎ 0845/127–2190) presents excellent
theater, ballet, and jazz performances year-round; it also hosts an amateur drama festival in summer.

Buxton's renowned **Festival of Music and the Arts** (⊠ Festival Office,
The Square ☎ 01298/70395 ⊕ www.buxtonfestival.co.uk), held during the second half of July and early August each year, includes high-
quality opera, drama, classical concerts, jazz, recitals, and lectures,
many of them at the Buxton Opera House.

Shopping

Buxton has many kinds of stores, especially around Spring Gardens, the
main shopping street. Stores in the beautifully tiled **Cavendish Arcade**
(⊠ The Crescent), on the site of the old thermal baths, sell antiques, jewelry, fashions, and leather goods in stylish surroundings. A **market** is held
in Buxton every Tuesday and Saturday.

en route As you head southeast from Buxton on the A6, you pass through the
spectacular valleys of Ashwood Dale, Wyedale, and Monsal Dale
before reaching Bakewell.

Bakewell

🟊 *12 mi southeast of Buxton.*

Here, a medieval bridge crosses the winding River Wye in five graceful
arches, and the 9th-century Saxon cross that stands outside the parish
church reveals the town's great age. Narrow streets and houses built out
of the local gray-brown stone also make Bakewell extremely appealing.
Ceaseless traffic through the streets can take the shine off—though
there's respite down on the quiet riverside paths. The crowds are really
substantial on market day (Monday), attended by area farmers; a similarly popular traditional agricultural show takes place the first week
of August. For a self-guided hour-long stroll, pick up a map at the
tourist office, where the town trail begins. A museum in the office explains the terrain of the Peak District, with samples of the limestone and
grit stone that compose the landscape.

Bakewell is the source of Bakewell pudding, said to have been created inadvertently when, sometime in the 19th century, a cook at the town's Rutland Arms Hotel dropped some rich cake mixture over jam tarts. Every local bakery and tearoom claims an original recipe—it's easy to spend a gustatory afternoon tasting rival puddings.

Where to Stay & Eat

£–££ ✗ **The Old Original Bakewell Pudding Shop.** Given the plethora of local rivals, it takes a bold establishment to claim its Bakewell puddings as "original," but there's certainly nothing wrong with those served here, eaten hot with custard or cream. The oak-beam dining room also turns out commendable main courses of Yorkshireman (batter pudding with meat and vegetables) and steak and stout pie. ⊠ *The Square* ☎ *01629/ 812193* ⊟ *MC, V* ☉ *Closes 6 PM winter, 7 PM summer.*

★ ✗🖾 **Fischer's.** This stately Edwardian manor house run by the Fischer **££££–£££££** family sits on the edge of the Chatsworth estate. Rooms in the main house have fancy plasterwork ceilings, antique pine furniture, and muted colors; those in the garden annex show a more contemporary style. The formal restaurant has two options: a more expensive full menu (not available for lunch Monday) or Max's menu (for dinner on weekdays), which concentrates on lighter bistro fare. Fish often comes with fresh pastas and delicate sauces; duck, lamb, and game receive similar care. Sunday dinner is for guests only. ⊠ *Baslow Hall, Calver Rd., Baslow, DE45 1RR* ☎ *01246/583259* 🖷 *01246/583818* ⊕ *www.fischers-baslowhall.co.uk* ⇆ *11 rooms* ☖ *Restaurant, some in-room data ports, bar, meeting rooms; no a/c, no kids under 10* ⊟ *AE, DC, MC, V* 🍽 *CP.*

Haddon Hall

㉘ *2 mi southeast of Bakewell.*

Fodor'sChoice
★
Stately house scholar Hugo Montgomery-Massingberd has called Haddon Hall, a romantic, storybook medieval manor set along the River Wye, "the *beau idéal* of the English country house." Unlike other trophy homes that are marble Palladian monuments to the grand tour, Haddon Hall remains quintessentially English in appearance, bristling with crenellations and stepped roofs and landscaped with rose gardens. The house, built mainly in the 14th century, is famous as the setting (perhaps apocryphal) for the shocking 16th-century elopement of Dorothy Vernon and Sir John Manners during a banquet; the tale became a popular Victorian-era love story. (Dorothy and Sir John are buried side by side in Bakewell's parish church.) Constructed by generations of the Vernon family in the Middle Ages, Haddon Hall passed into the ownership of the dukes of Rutland. After the dukes moved their county seat to nearby Belvoir Castle, little changed in the house for hundreds of years. In the early 20th century, however, the ninth duke undertook a superlative restoration. The wider world saw the hall to impressive effect in Franco Zeffirelli's 1996 film *Jane Eyre*; part of the 1999 *Elizabeth*, starring Cate Blanchett, was also filmed here. The virtually unfurnished house has fine plasterwork and wooden paneling, and still holds some treasures, including an impressive selection of tapestries, and a famous 1932 painting of Haddon Hall by Rex Whistler. This painting shows the ninth duke

and his son gazing at the house from a nearby hillside vantage point. ⊠ *A6* ☎ *01629/812855* ⊕ *www.haddonhall.co.uk* 🖾 *£7.25, parking £1* ☉ *Apr.–Sept., daily 10:30–5; Oct., Thurs.–Sun. 10:30–4:30; last admission 30 mins before closing.*

Matlock

㉙ *5 mi south of Haddon Hall, 8 mi southeast of Bakewell.*

In the heart of the Derbyshire Dales, Matlock and its near neighbor Matlock Bath are former spa towns compressed into a narrow gorge on the River Derwent. Some surviving Regency buildings in Matlock testify to its former importance, although it's less impressive an ensemble than that presented by Buxton. The surroundings, however, are particularly beautiful. The **Matlock River Illuminations,** a flotilla of lighted boats shimmering after dark along the still waters of the river, takes place on weekends late August–late October.

At Matlock Bath, 2 mi south of Matlock, river and valley views unfold from the curving line of buildings that makes up the village. Aside from riverside strolls, the major attraction is the cable-car ride across the River Derwent that takes you to the wooded **Heights of Abraham Country Park and Caverns** on the crags above, with a visitor center and café. The all-inclusive ticket allows access to the woodland walks and nature trails of the 60-acre park, as well as entry to a cavern and a guided descent into an old lead mine, where 16th-century workers toiled by candlelight. ⊠ *A6, Matlock Bath* ☎ *01629/582365* ⊕ *www.heights-of-abraham. co.uk* 🖾 *£8.50* ☉ *Cable car and visitor center mid-Feb.–late Feb., daily 10–4:30; Mar., weekends 10–4:30; Apr.–Oct., daily 10–5.*

Where to Stay & Eat

★ ✕⊞ **Riber Hall.** Awash with romantic resonance, this partly Elizabethan, **£££–£££££** partly Jacobean manor-house hotel perches above the town. Antiques and four-poster beds decorate the half-timber bedrooms; some bathrooms have whirlpool tubs. The garden is especially lovely. The restaurant (fixed-price menu) serves imaginative dishes inspired by modern French cuisine; one choice might be roasted monkfish with haricot beans and Parma ham. There's a daily vegetarian menu. ⊠ *Off A615, DE4 5JU* ☎ *01629/582795* 🖷 *01629/580475* ⊕ *www.riber-hall.co.uk* ⇦ *14 rooms* ♿ *Restaurant, tennis court, bar, business services, meeting rooms, some pets allowed; no a/c* 🖃 *AE, DC, MC, V* 🍽 *BP.*

Sports & the Outdoors

One of the major trails in the Peak District, **High Peak Trail,** runs for 17 mi from Cromford (south of Matlock Bath) to Dowlow, following the route of an old railroad. For information, guidebooks, guide services, and maps, contact any Peak District National Park Office.

Hardwick Hall

★ ㉚ *10 mi east of Matlock.*

Few houses in England evoke the late Elizabethan era as vividly as this beautiful stone mansion and all its treasures. The facade glitters with myriad windows, making it easy to see why the house came to be known as "Hardwick Hall, more glass than wall." Choose a sunny day to see the rooms at their best; electric lighting is limited. The vast state apartments of the Long Gallery and High Great Chamber well befit their original chatelaine, Bess of Hardwick. By marrying a succession of four rich husbands, she had become second only to Elizabeth in her wealth when work on this house began. She took possession in 1597, and four years later made an inventory of the important rooms and their contents—furniture, tapestries, and embroideries. The wonder is that these items still remain here, very much as she left them. Unique patchwork hangings, probably made from clerical copes and altar frontals taken from monasteries and abbeys, grace the entrance hall, and superb 16th- and 17th-century tapestries cover the walls of the main staircase and 1st-floor High Great Chamber. The collection of Elizabethan embroideries—table carpets, cushions, bed hangings, and pillowcases—is second to none. There are also fine examples of plasterwork, painted friezes, and ornamental chimneypieces. Outside, you can visit the attractive walled gardens. Access is signposted from Junction 29 of the M1 motorway. ☒ *Doe Lea, Chesterfield* ☎ *01246/850430* ⊕ *www.nationaltrust.org. uk* ☜£6.80, gardens only £3.70 ⊙ *House Apr.–Oct., Wed., Thurs., weekends, and national holidays 12:30–4:30; gardens Apr.–Oct., Wed.–Sun. and national holidays 11–5:30.*

Chatsworth House

★ ⊙ ③ *13 mi northwest of Hardwick Hall, 4 mi northeast of Bakewell.*

Glorious parkland leads to Chatsworth House, ancestral home of the dukes of Devonshire and one of England's greatest country houses. The vast expanse of greenery, grazed by deer and sheep, sets off the Palladian-style elegance of "the Palace of the Peak." Originally an Elizabethan house, Chatsworth was conceived on a grand, even monumental, scale. It was altered over several generations starting in 1686, and the architecture now has a decidedly hodgepodge look, though the Palladian facade remains splendid. The house is surrounded by woods, elaborate, colorful gardens, greenhouses, rock gardens, and the most famous water cascade in the kingdom—all designed by two great landscape artists, Capability Brown and, in the 19th century, Joseph Paxton, an engineer as well as a brilliant gardener. Perennially popular with children, the farmyard area has milking demonstrations at 3, and an adventure playground. Plan on at least a half day to explore the grounds; avoid going on Sunday, when the place is very crowded. A brass band plays on Sunday afternoons in July and August.

Although death duties have taken a toll on the interior grandeur, with duke after duke forced to sell off treasures to keep the place going, there is more than enough to look at. Inside are intricate carvings, Van Dyck portraits, superb furniture, and a few fabulous rooms, including the Sculpture Gallery, the library, and the Blue Drawing Room, where you can see two of the most famous portraits in Britain, Sir Joshua Reynolds's *Georgiana, Duchess of Devonshire, and Her Baby,* and John Singer Sargent's enormous *Acheson Sisters.* The magnificent condition of much of the furnishings and decorations is owing to the dowager duchess's supervision of an ongoing program of repair and restoration. ⊠ *Off B6012, Bakewell* ☎ *01246/582204* ⊕ *www.chatsworth-house.co.uk* ▨ *House, gardens, and Scots rooms £10.50; house and gardens £9; gardens only £5.50; farmyard and adventure playground £4; parking £1.50* ⊙ *Mid-Mar.–mid-Dec., house daily 11–5:30, gardens daily 11–6, farmyard and adventure playground daily 10:30–5:30; last admission 1 hr before closing.*

Where to Eat

£–££ ✕ **Devonshire Arms.** Inside this stone 18th-century coaching inn, which counts Charles Dickens as one of its many visitors, are antique settles, flagstone floors, and great homemade fare. Typical dishes include deviled whitebait, duck and fig terrine, and beef and horseradish suet pudding. Friday is fresh fish day, and on Sunday you can sample a Victorian breakfast (book ahead), which comes with Buck's Fizz—champagne and orange juice—and newspapers. The inn is 2 mi south of Chatsworth. ⊠ *B6012, Beeley* ☎ *01629/733259* ▭ *AE, MC, V.*

Castleton

③② *10 mi northwest of Chatsworth, 9 mi northeast of Buxton.*

The area around Castleton, in Hope Valley, contains the most famous manifestations of the peculiar geology of the Peak District. A number of caves and mines are open to the public, including some former lead mines and Blue John mines (amethystine spar; the unusual name is a local corruption of the French *bleu-jaune*). The limestone caverns attract people from far and wide, which means that Castleton shows a certain commercialization and tends to be crowded in summer. The town has a long pedigree and was probably established by Henry II, in the mid-12th century.

It was Henry II who in 1176 added the square tower to the Norman **Peveril Castle,** whose ruins occupy a dramatic crag above the town. The castle has superb views—from here you can clearly see a curving section of the medieval defensive earthworks still visible in the town center below. Peveril Castle is protected on its west side by a 230-foot-deep gorge formed by a collapsed cave. ⊠ *Market Pl., A1687* ☎ *01433/620613* ⊕ *www.english-heritage.org.uk* ▨ *£2.50* ⊙ *Apr., Sept., and Oct., daily 10–5; May–July, daily 10–6; Aug., daily 10–7; Nov.–Mar., daily 10–4.*

Caves riddle the entire town and the surrounding area, and in the massive **Peak Cavern**—reputedly Derbyshire's largest natural cave—rope-making has been done on a great ropewalk for more than 400 years. You can also see the remains of a prehistoric village that has been excavated here. ☎ *01433/620285* ⊕ *www.devilsarse.com* ▨ *£5.50* ⊙ *Apr.–Oct., daily 10–5; Nov.–Mar., weekends 10–5; last tour at 4.*

The area's most exciting cavern by far is **Speedwell Cavern,** where 105 slippery steps lead down to old lead-mine tunnels, blasted out by 19th-century miners. Here you transfer to a small boat for the claustrophobic ¼-mi chug through an illuminated access tunnel to the cavern itself.

At this point you're 600 feet underground, in the deepest public-access cave in Britain, with views farther down to the so-called Bottomless Pit, a water-filled cavern into which the miners dumped their blasted limestone debris. A shop on-site sells items made of the Blue John mineral. Speedwell Cavern is at the bottom of Winnats Pass, 1 mi west of Castleton. ⊠ *Winnats Pass* ☎ *01433/620512* ⊕ *www.speedwellcavern.co.uk* 🎫 *£6* ۞ *Apr.–Oct., daily 9:30–5:30; Nov.–Mar., daily 10–5; last tour 45 mins before closing.*

Where to Stay

££ 🏠 **Underleigh House.** Peaceful is the word for the location of this creeper-clad cottage and barn at the end of a lane in lovely walking country. The big lounge has an inglenook fireplace, and the flagstone entrance hall has one big table for breakfasts (expect local specialties such as oatcakes and black pudding). There are plenty of games for rainy days, and lots of books, sweets, and flowers in the tidy modern bedrooms. Hope is 1 mi east of Castleton on A617. ⊠ *Off Edale Rd., Hope, S33 6RF* ☎ *01433/621372* 🖨 *01433/621324* ⊕ *www.underleighhouse.co.uk* 🛏 *6 rooms* ♨ *Some pets allowed; no a/c, no kids under 12, no smoking* ▭ *MC, V* ۞❘ *BP.*

£ 🏠 **Bargate Cottage.** This cottage dating to 1650, at the top of Market Place opposite the church, is one of Castleton's B&B treasures. The kindly owners scatter rag dolls and teddy bears with abandon, and the cutesy oak-beam rooms incorporate the necessary facilities. Breakfast is served at one table, with plenty of bonhomie and hiking advice on tap. ⊠ *Market Pl., S33 8WQ* ☎ *01433/620201* 🖨 *01433/621739* ⊕ *www.bargatecottage.co.uk* 🛏 *4 rooms* ♨ *No a/c, no kids under 12, no smoking* ▭ *No credit cards* ۞❘ *BP.*

> **en route** Heading northwest to Edale, the most spectacular driving route is over **Winnats Pass,** through a narrow, boulder-strewn valley. Beyond are the tops of Mam Tor (where there's a lookout point) and the hamlet of Barber Booth, after which you run into Edale.

Edale

③③ *5 mi north of Castleton.*

At Edale, you're truly in the Peak District wilds. This sleepy, straggling village, in the shadow of Mam Tor and Lose Hill and the moorlands of the high plateau known as Kinder Scout (2,088 feet), lies among some of the most breathtaking scenery in Derbyshire. Britain can show little wilder scenery than Kinder Scout, with its ragged edges of grit stone and its seemingly interminable leagues of heather and peat. Late summer brings a covering of reddish purple as the heather flowers, but the time to really appreciate the somber beauties of Kinder and its neighbors is in late autumn or early winter, when the clouds hang low and every gully seems to accentuate the brooding spirit of the moor.

The **Old Nag's Head** (☎01433/670291) at the top of the village has marked the official start of the Pennine Way since 1965. Call in at the Hiker's

Bar, sit by the fire, and tuck into hearty bar meals and warming hot toddies. On Mondays and Tuesdays in winter, when this pub is closed, the Ramblers' Inn, at the other end of the village, is open.

In the village, the Edale **National Park Information Centre** has maps, guides, and information on all the walks in the area. There's limited accommodation in the village (all B&B-style), but the information center can provide a list of possibilities or point you toward the local youth hostel. ☎ *01433/670207* ⊕ *www.peakdistrict.org* ☉ *Jan.–Oct., daily 9–1 and 2–5:30; Nov.–Dec., weekends 9–1 and 2–5.*

Sports & the Outdoors
An extremely popular walking center, Edale is the starting point of the 250-mi-long **Pennine Way** (⊕ www.nationaltrail.co.uk), which crosses Kinder Scout. If you plan to attempt this, seek local advice first, because bad weather can make the walk treacherous. However, several much shorter routes into the Edale Valley, like the 8-mi route west to Hayfield, give you a taste of dramatic scenery.

LANCASHIRE & THE PEAKS A TO Z

To research prices, get advice from other travelers, and book travel arrangements, visit www.fodors.com.

AIRPORTS
Manchester Airport, about 10 mi south of the city, is the third-largest airport in the country. About 100 airlines serve 175 international and United Kingdom destinations. M56 north leads directly into Manchester via the A5103. Frequent trains run from Manchester Airport to Piccadilly Railway Station (25 minutes); buses go to Piccadilly Gardens Bus Station (55 minutes). A taxi from the airport to Manchester city center costs between £12 and £15. For more details, call the Greater Manchester Passenger Transport Executive (GMPTE) information line.

Liverpool John Lennon Airport, about 8 mi southeast of the city at Speke, covers inland and European destinations. There's bus service to the city center every 30 minutes; contact Airportxpress 500.

🚌**Airportxpress 500** ☎0151/236-7676 ⊕www.merseytravel.gov.uk. **GMPTE information line** ☎ 0161/228-7811 ⊕ www.gmpte.com. **Liverpool John Lennon Airport** ✉ Off A561, Speke ☎0870/750-8484 ⊕www.liverpooljohnlennonairport.com. **Manchester Airport** ✉ near Junctions 5 and 6 of M56 ☎ 0161/489-3000 ⊕ www.manairport.co.uk.

BIKING
Special Peak District National Park Hire Centres rent bikes of all descriptions for around £12 per day. The service is restricted to April–October except for Parsley Hay, which opens on weekends in winter (excluding December and January). The most accessible centers are listed below; contact a Peak District National Park Information Centre for more information.

🚲 Bike Rentals **Peak District National Park Hire Centres** ✉ Hayfield ☎ 01663/746222 ✉ Parsley Hay ☎ 01298/84493 ✉ Middleton Top ☎ 01629/823204 ⊕ www.peakdistrict.org.

BUS TRAVEL

National Express serves the region from London's Victoria Coach Station. Average travel time to Manchester or Liverpool is five hours. To reach Matlock, Bakewell, and Buxton you can take a bus from London to Derby and change to the TransPeak bus service, though you might find it more convenient to travel first to Manchester.

Chorlton Street Coach Station, a few hundred yards west of Piccadilly Railway Station in Manchester's city center, is the main bus station for regional and long-distance buses. Most local buses leave from Piccadilly Gardens Bus Station, the hub of the urban bus network. Metroshuttle operates two free circular routes around the city center; service runs daily every 5 to 10 minutes from 7 AM to 7 PM.

In Liverpool, regional and long-distance National Express coaches use the Norton Street Coach Station, and local and cross-river buses depart from Sir Thomas Street, Queen Square, and Paradise Street.

The TransPeak service between Manchester and Derby stops at Buxton and major Peak District destinations, with departures every two hours from Manchester's Chorlton Street Bus Station. Wayfarer tickets are available for 24-hour weekdays (£7) or 48-hour weekends (£10).

FARES &
SCHEDULES
  For Manchester bus information, call the GMPTE information line (⇨ Airports). For timetables and local bus (and train and ferry) service in Liverpool, call the Mersey Travel Line. For local bus information in Buxton and the Peak District, call Traveline. The *Peak District Timetable* (60p) covers all local public transportation services and is available at area tourist offices.

🚩 **Mersey Travel Line** ☎ 0151/236-7676 ⊕ www.merseytravel.gov.uk. **National Express** ☎ 0870/580-8080 ⊕ www.nationalexpress.com. **Traveline** ☎ 0870/608-2608 ⊕ www.traveline.org.uk.

CAR RENTAL

🚩 **Local Agencies Avis** ✉ 1 Ducie St., City Centre, Manchester ☎ 0161/236-6716, 0161/934-2300 airport ✉ 113 Mulberry St., City Centre, Liverpool ☎ 0151/709-4737. **Europcar** ✉ 79-85 Liverpool St., Salford Quays, Manchester ☎ 0161/236-0311, 0161/436-2200 airport ✉ 8 Brownlow Hill, City Centre, Liverpool ☎ 0151/709-3337, 0151/448-1652 airport. **Hertz** ✉ 31 Aytoun St., City Centre, Manchester ☎ 0161/236-2747, 0161/437-8208 airport ✉ 141 Vauxhall Rd., City Centre, Liverpool ☎ 0151/227-2222, 0151/486-7444 airport.

CAR TRAVEL

To reach Manchester from London, take M1 north to M6, leaving M6 at Exit 21a and joining M62 east, which becomes M602 as it enters Greater Manchester. M60 is the ring road around Manchester. Liverpool is reached by leaving M6 at the same junction, Exit 21a, and following M62 west into the city. Travel time to Manchester or Liverpool from London is 3–3½ hours. Expect heavy traffic out of London on weekends to all destinations in the Northwest. The M6 toll road, Britain's first toll motorway (£2), which runs between exits 4 and 11a of the M6, provides a speedier alternative to the M6.

Driving from London to the Peak District, stay on M1 until you reach Exit 29, then head west via A617/A619/A6 to Buxton. From Manchester, take A6 southeast via Stockport to Buxton, about an hour's drive.

ROAD CONDITIONS Roads within the region are generally very good. In Manchester and Liverpool, try to sightsee on foot—leave your car at your hotel to avoid parking problems in the city centers. In the Peak District, park in signposted parking lots whenever possible and expect heavy summer traffic. In winter, know the weather forecast; moorland roads can quickly become impassable.

CONSULATES
🚩 Australian Consulate ⊠ Century House, 11 St. Peter's Sq., 1st Floor, City Centre, Manchester ☎ 0161/237-9440.

EMERGENCIES
🚩 Ambulance, fire, police ☎ 999. Royal Liverpool University Hospital ⊠ Prescot St., City Centre, Liverpool ☎ 0151/706-2000. Manchester Royal Infirmary & Royal Eye Hospital ⊠ Oxford Rd., University Quarter, Manchester ☎ 0161/276-1234.

NATIONAL PARK
The Peak District National Park head office is in Bakewell. There are also regional offices.
🚩 Peak District National Park head office ⊠ Baslow Rd., Bakewell, DE45 1AE ☎ 01629/816200 ⊕ www.peakdistrict.org. Bakewell ☎ 01629/813227. Castleton ☎ 01433/620679. Edale ☎ 01433/670207.

TOURS
BOAT TOURS City Centre Cruises in Manchester offers a three-hour Sunday lunch round-trip on a barge to the Manchester Ship Canal.
🚩 City Centre Cruises ☎ 0161/902-0222 ⊕ www.citycentrecruises.co.uk.

BUS TOURS Cavern City Tours has a Beatles Magical Mystery Tour of Liverpool, departing from the Beatles Story, Albert Dock, daily at noon and 2:30 (May–October) or 2:30 (November–April), with additional tours on weekends and during school vacations. The two-hour bus tour (£12) runs past Penny Lane, Strawberry Field, and other mop-top landmarks.

A novel way to travel Liverpool is by YellowDuckmarines, amphibious vehicles left over from World War II. Tours run from February to Christmas (£9.95) and leave from Albert Dock.

Tourist offices in Manchester and Liverpool can book you on short city coach tours that cover the main sights.
🚩 Cavern City Tours ⊠ Mathew St., City Centre Liverpool ☎ 0151/236-9091 ⊕ www.cavern-liverpool.co.uk. YellowDuckmarines ☎ 0151/708-7799 ⊕ www.theyellowduckmarine.co.uk.

WALKING TOURS In Manchester and Liverpool, Blue Badge Guides can arrange dozens of different tours.
🚩 Blue Badge Guides, Liverpool ☎ 0151/237-3925. Blue Badge Guides, Manchester ☎ 0161/440-0277.

TRAIN TRAVEL

Virgin Trains serves the region from London's Euston Station. Direct service to Manchester and Liverpool takes approximately three hours. To reach Buxton from London, take the Manchester train and switch at Stockport.

There are trains between Manchester's Piccadilly Station and Liverpool's Lime Street every half hour during the day; the trip takes approximately 50 minutes. Local service—one train an hour—from Manchester to Buxton takes one hour. Call National Rail Enquiries for timetable information.

🚹 **National Rail Enquiries** ☎ 0845/748-4950 ⊕ www.nationalrail.co.uk. **Virgin Trains** ☎ 0845/722-2333 ⊕ www.virgintrains.co.uk.

TRAM TRAVEL

In Manchester, Metrolink electric tram service runs through the city center and out to the suburbs. The Eccles extension has stops for the Lowry (Harbour City) and for the Manchester United Stadium (Old Trafford).

🚹 **Metrolink** ☎ 0161/205-2000 ⊕ www.metrolink.co.uk.

TRAVEL AGENCIES

🚹 Local Agent Referrals **American Express** ⊠ 54 Lord St., Liverpool ☎ 0151/702-4505 ⊠ 10-12 St. Mary's Gate, Manchester ☎ 0161/833-7301. **Thomas Cook** ⊠ 55 Lord St., Liverpool ☎ 0151/552-1400 ⊠ 23 Market St., Manchester ☎ 0161/910-8787.

VISITOR INFORMATION

General information about the region is available from the North West Tourist Board, the Heart of England Tourist Board (for Derbyshire and the Peak District), and from the Manchester Visitor Centre. Local tourist information offices are listed below by town.

🚹 Tourist Information **Heart of England Tourist Board** ⊠ Larkhill Rd., Worcester, WR5 2EZ ☎ 01905/761100 ⊕ www.visitheartofengland.com. **North West Tourist Board** ⊠ Swan House, Swan Meadow Rd., Wigan Pier, Wigan, WN3 5BB ☎ 0845/600-6040 ⊕ www.visitnorthwest.com. **Bakewell** ⊠ Old Market Hall, Bridge St., DE45 1DS ☎ 01629/813227 ⊕ www.visitpeakdistrict.com. **Buxton** ⊠ The Crescent, SK17 6BQ ☎ 01298/25106. **Liverpool** ⊠ Queen Sq., City Centre, L1 1RG ☎ 0151/709-8111, 0845/601-1125 accommodations ⊠ Merseyside Maritime Museum, Albert Dock, L3 4AQ ☎ 0151/478-4599 ⊕ www.visitliverpool.com. **Manchester Visitor Centre** ⊠ Town Hall Extension, Lloyd St., City Centre, M60 2LA ☎ 0161/234-3157 ⊕ www.manchester.gov.uk/visitorcentre ⊠ International Arrivals Hall, Manchester Airport Terminal 1 ☎ 0161/436-3344 ⊠ International Arrivals Hall, Manchester Airport Terminal 2 ☎ 0161/489-6412. **Matlock** ⊠ Crown Sq., DE4 3AT ☎ 01629/583388. **Matlock Bath** ⊠ The Pavilion, DE4 3NR ☎ 01629/55082 ⊕ www.derbyshiredales.gov.uk. **Stoke-on-Trent** ⊠ Quadrant Rd., ST1 1RZ ☎ 01782/236000 ⊕ www.visitstoke.co.uk.

THE LAKE DISTRICT

WINDERMERE, GRASMERE, KENDAL, KESWICK

LET NATURE BE YOUR TEACHER
on hikes from Kendal to Keswick ⇨ *p.515*

SET SAIL ON THE TRANQUIL WATERS
of mountain-ringed Windermere ⇨ *p.522*

LOOK FOR WORDSWORTH'S DAFFODILS
near Aira Force waterfall ⇨ *p.535*

REWARD YOURSELF WITH REAL ALE
at the cozy Drunken Duck Inn ⇨ *p.532*

PULL OUT YOUR COLORED PENCILS
to capture Borrowdale's beauty ⇨ *p.540*

NIBBLE TREATS FROM A SECRET RECIPE
at the Grasmere Gingerbread Shop ⇨ *p.529*

FOLLOW A PINE-FRINGED PATH
for perfect views of Derwentwater ⇨ *p.537*

MAKE TOPIARIES THE TOPIC
at Elizabethan Levens Hall ⇨ *p.517*

Updated by
Julius Honnor

LET NATURE BE YOUR TEACHER . . ." Wordsworth's ideal comes true in this region of jagged mountains, waterfalls, wooded valleys, and stone-built villages. The poets Wordsworth and Coleridge, and other English men and women of letters, found the Lake District an inspiring setting for their work, and visitors have followed ever since. In 1951 the Lake District National Park was created here from parts of Cumberland, Westmorland, and Lancashire. No mountains in Britain are finer in outline or give a greater impression of majesty; deeper and bluer lakes can be found, but none that fit so readily into the surrounding scene.

Perhaps it is only natural that an area so blessed with natural beauty should have become linked with so many prominent figures in English literature. It all may have started on April 15, 1802, when William Wordsworth and his sister, Dorothy, were walking in the woods of Gowbarrow Park just above Aira Force, and Dorothy noted in her journal that she had never seen "daffodils so beautiful." Two years later Wordsworth was inspired by his sister's words to write one of the best-known lyric poems in English, "I Wandered Lonely as a Cloud." In turn, other English Romantic poets came to the region and were inspired by its beauty. Besides Wordsworth, literary figures who made their homes in the Lake District include Samuel Taylor Coleridge, Thomas De Quincey, Robert Southey, John Ruskin, Matthew Arnold, and later, Hugh Walpole, and the children's writers Arthur Ransome and Beatrix Potter.

The Lake District is a contour map come to life, a stunning natural park beloved by outdoor enthusiasts. It covers an area of approximately 885 square mi and holds 16 major lakes and countless smaller stretches of water. You can cross it by car in about an hour, though that would be a shame. The mountains are not high by international standards—Scafell Pike, England's highest peak, is only 3,210 feet above sea level—but they can be tricky to climb, especially in inclement weather. In spring, many of the higher summits remain snowcapped long after the weather below has turned mild.

This area can be one of Britain's most appealing reservoirs of calm, although its calm is shattered in summer. A lakeside town, however appealing it may otherwise be, loses its charm when cars and tour buses clog its narrow streets. Similarly, the walks and hiking trails that crisscross the region seem less inviting when you share them with a crowd that churns the grass into a quagmire. Despite the challenges of popularity, the Lake District has managed tourism in a manner that retains the character of both the villages and the natural environment.

Some basic terminology will help here: if someone gives you directions to walk along the "beck" to the "force" and then climb the "fell" to the "tarn," you've just been told to hike along the stream or river (beck) to the waterfall (force) before climbing the hill or mountain (fell) to reach a small mountain lake (tarn). Moreover, town or place names in the Lake District can also refer to the lake on which the town or place stands. Windermere village is on the lake of that name, for example. And to

You could spend months tramping the hills, valleys, and fells of the Lake District, or, in three days, you could drive through the major towns and villages. The key is not to do too much in too short a time. In three days, you might pick one area—the southern lakes, for example—and spend time walking, taking a boat out on the water, and relaxing at the inns. With five days, you can stay the night in towns in both southern and northern Lakeland. If you are traveling by public transportation, many places will be off-limits.

Numbers in the text correspond to numbers in the margin and on the Lake District map.

11

If you have 3 days

If you must tour both south and north lakes together in a short time, start in **Kendal ❶** ➤. After you've looked around the market town, move on to 🖾 **Windermere and Bowness-on-Windermere ❷**, where you spend the first night. You can take a boat trip on the lake that afternoon up to **Ambleside ❹**. Next day, cross Windermere by ferry, and drive through **Hawkshead ❾** and **Coniston ❽** to rural **Elterwater ❼**, where you can have lunch in one of the fine walkers' inns thereabouts. Spend the afternoon in **Grasmere ❻** and nearby **Rydal ❺** touring the sites associated with William Wordsworth, such as Rydal Mount and Dove Cottage. Your second night is in 🖾 **Keswick ❸**, and on the third day, you can loop around Derwentwater through **Borrowdale ❹** and isolated Seatoller to **Cockermouth ❺**, Wordsworth's birthplace. From there it's an easy drive east to the market town of **Penrith ❿** and the M6 motorway, or north to Carlisle.

If you have 5 days

Kendal ❶ ➤, in the southern part of the Lake District, marks the starting point, followed by a drive to 🖾 **Windermere and Bowness-on-Windermere ❷** and a cruise on the lake that afternoon up to **Ambleside ❹**. The next morning you can mosey around the shops and museums in Bowness before venturing on to the **Lake District National Park Visitor Centre at Brockhole ❸**. In the afternoon, cross Windermere by ferry, stopping in **Hawkshead ❾** and **Coniston ❽**, before ending up at 🖾 **Elterwater ❼**. This is a splendid place to spend the night in peaceful rural surroundings, and you can take in one of the local walks the next morning. Lunch and your overnight can be in 🖾 **Grasmere ❻**, just a short distance away, giving you plenty of opportunity to explore that lovely village. From Grasmere, 🖾 **Keswick ❸** is the next overnight stop, allowing you to make a day trip into the gorgeous Borrowdale Valley and perhaps take a boat trip on Derwentwater. On the final day, you can see **Cockermouth ❺** and **Penrith ❿**.

---

confuse matters, locals would never say Lake Windermere but just Windermere, since "mere" means "lake" in Old English.

Off-season visits can be a real treat. All those little inns and bed-and-breakfasts that turn away crowds in summer are eager for business the rest of the year (and their rates drop accordingly). It's not an easy task to avail yourself of a succession of sunny days in the Lake District—some malicious statisticians allot to it about 250 rainy days a year—

but when the sun breaks through and brightens the surfaces of the lakes, it is an away-from-it-all place to remember.

Exploring the Lake District

The Lake District is in northwest England, north of the industrial belt along the River Mersey that stretches from Liverpool to Manchester, and south of Scotland. The major gateway from the south is Kendal, and from the north, Penrith. Both are on the M6 motorway. Main-line trains stop at Oxenholme, near Kendal, with a branch linking Oxenholme to Kendal and Windermere. The Lake District National Park breaks into two reasonably distinct sections. The southern lakes and valleys contain the park's most popular destinations, incorporating the largest body of water, Windermere, as well as most of what are considered the quintessential Lakeland towns and villages: Kendal, Bowness, Ambleside, Grasmere, Elterwater, Coniston, and Hawkshead. To the north, the landscape opens out across the bleaker fells to reveal challenging (and spectacular) walking country. Here, in the northern lakes, south of Keswick and Cockermouth, you have the best chance to get away from the crowds.

About the Restaurants & Hotels

Some of the area's better restaurants are at hotels. If you are not a guest but want to dine at the hotel, be sure to make reservations in advance. Also inquire if you want to eat in a particular room at the restaurant; guests may have priority.

If the front hall has a row of muddy boots, you've probably made the right choice for a hostelry. At the best of these hotels, people eat heartily and loll about in front of fires in the evenings, sharing an almost religious dedication to the mountains. Your choices include everything from small country inns to grand lakeside hotels; many hotels offer the option of paying a higher price that includes dinner as well as breakfast. The regional mainstay is the bed-and-breakfast, from the house on Main Street renting out one room to farmhouses with an entire wing to spare. Most country hotels and B&Bs gladly cater to hikers and can provide on-the-spot information. The Lake District's more than 25 youth hostels, including mountain huts and lakeside mansions, are open to anyone who purchases a membership or has a membership card from their home country's hostel association. Wherever you stay, book well in advance for summer visits, especially those in late July and August. In winter many accommodations close for a month or two. On weekends and in summer, it may be hard to find places willing to take bookings for a single night.

WHAT IT COSTS In pounds				
£££££	**££££**	**£££**	**££**	**£**
RESTAURANTS over £22	£18–£22	£13–£17	£7–£12	under £7
HOTELS over £160	£120–£160	£90–£120	£60–£90	under £60

Restaurant prices are for a main course at dinner. Hotel prices are for two people in a standard double room in high season, including VAT, with no meals or, if indicated, CP (with Continental breakfast), BP (Breakfast Plan, with full breakfast), or MAP (Modified American Plan, with breakfast and dinner).

11

Festivals & Folk Sports

With everything from rushbearing to Westmorland wrestling to traditional music, the Lake District hosts some of Britain's most unusual country festivals. Major festivals include the Cockermouth and Keswick carnivals (June), Ambleside rushbearing (August) and sports (July), Grasmere rushbearing (August) and sports (August), and Kendal Folk Festival (August), but some sort of event or festival happens somewhere during most weeks throughout the year. Rushbearing dates back to medieval times, when rushes covered church floors; today processions of flower-bedecked children and adults bring rushes to churches in a number of villages. Folk sports, often the highlights at local festivals, include Cumberland and Westmorland wrestling, in which the opponents must maintain a grip around each other's body. Fell running, a sort of cross-country run where the route goes roughly straight up and down a mountain, is also popular. A calendar of events is available at tourist information centers or on the Cumbria Tourist Board Web site.

Walking

Some people view this area in an almost mystical way, with walking a quasi-spiritual experience. Whatever your motivation, the Lake District is rugged and spectacular, and to see it at its best you must get out of the car and walk. You can choose gentle rambles near the most popular towns and villages or challenging hikes and climbs up some of England's most impressive peaks. Information boards at parking lots throughout the region point out the possibilities. British mountaineering began in the Lake District, with its notable hikes: the famous Old Man of Coniston, the Langdale Pikes, Scafell Pike, Skiddaw, and Helvellyn are all popular, though these require experience, energy, and proper hiking boots and clothing. The Cumbria Way (70 mi) crosses the Lake District, starting at the market town of Ulverston and finishing at Carlisle. The Coast-to-Coast Walk (190 mi) runs from St. Bees on the Irish Sea through the Lake District and across the Yorkshire Dales and the North York Moors; it ends at Robin Hood's Bay at the edge of the North Sea in Yorkshire. Guidebooks to these and other Lakeland walks are available in local bookstores—don't miss Alfred Wainwright's classic guides. For short walks, consult the tourist information centers: those at Ambleside, Cockermouth, Grasmere, Kendal, Keswick, and Windermere provide maps and advice. The other main sources of information are the Lake District National Park information centers. Several climbing organizations offer guided hikes as well as technical rock climbing.

Timing

The Lake District is one of the rainiest areas in Britain, but June, July, and August hold the best hope of fine weather and are the time for all the major festivals. You will, however, be sharing the roads, hotels, trails, and lakes with thousands of other people. If you must travel at this time, turn up early at popular museums and attractions, and expect to work to find parking space. April and May, as well as September and October, are appealing alternatives. Later and earlier in the year there will be even more space and freedom, but many attractions close, and snow on high ground precludes serious walking without heavy-duty equipment.

THE SOUTHERN LAKES
KENDAL, WINDERMERE, GRASMERE & CONISTON

Among the many attractions here are the small resort towns clustered around Windermere, England's largest lake, and the area's hideaway valleys, rugged walking centers, and monuments rich in literary associations. This is the easiest part of the Lake District to reach, with Kendal, the largest town, just a short distance from the M6 motorway. An obvious route from Kendal takes in Windermere, the natural touring center for the whole area, before moving north through Ambleside and Rydal Water to Grasmere. Some of the loveliest Lakeland scenery is to be found by then turning south, through Elterwater, Hawkshead, and Coniston. From Coniston, it's a simple drive south to the coast or east back to Windermere.

Kendal

▶ ❶ *70 mi north of Manchester.*

The southern gateway to the Lake District is the "Auld Gray Town" of Kendal. The town's motto, Wool Is My Bread, refers to its importance as a textile center in northern England before the Industrial Revolution. It was known for manufacturing woolen cloth, especially Kendal Green, which archers favored. Away from the busy main road are quiet courtyards and winding medieval streets known locally as "ginnels." Wool merchants used these for easy access to the River Kent. Nearby hills frame Kendal's gray stone houses and provide some delightful walks; you can also explore the ruins of Kendal Castle. Pack a slab of Kendal mint cake, the local peppermint candy that all British walkers and climbers swear by to provide them with energy. It's on sale in town gift shops.

One of the region's finest art galleries, **Abbot Hall,** occupies a Georgian mansion built in 1759. The collection includes works by Victorian artist and critic John Ruskin, who lived near Coniston, and by 18th-century portrait painter George Romney, who worked (and died) in Kendal. The gallery also displays 18th-century furniture, watercolors of the region, and 20th-century art. There's an excellent café. Abbot Hall is on the River Kent, next to the parish church; the Museum of Lakeland Life is on the same site. ⊠ *Off Highgate* ☎ *01539/722464* ⊕ *www.abbothall. org.uk* ▣ *£4.75, £6.50 combined ticket with Museum of Lakeland Life* ☯ *Apr.–Oct., Mon.–Sat. 10:30–5; mid-Jan.–Mar., Nov., and Dec., Mon.–Sat. 10:30–4.*

The **Museum of Lakeland Life,** in the former stable block of Abbot Hall, documents Cumbrian life over the past 300 years through excellent exhibits on blacksmithing, wheel-wrighting, farming, weaving, printing, local architecture and interiors, and regional customs. A room is devoted to the curious life of Arthur Ransome (1884–1967), author of the *Swal-*

lows and Amazons series of children's books, set in Coniston. ☒ *Off Highgate* ☎ *01539/722464* ⊕ *www.lakelandmuseum.org.uk* ☒ *£3.50, £6.50 combined ticket with Abbot Hall* ☉ *Apr.–Oct., Mon.–Sat. 10:30–5; mid-Jan.–Mar., Nov., and Dec., Mon.–Sat. 10:30–4.*

The **Kendal Museum** focuses on natural history and archaeology and details splendidly the flora and fauna of the Lake District. It also has displays on the region's great fell walker, Alfred Wainwright (1907–91). His multivolume, handwritten Lake District walking guides are famous; they are sold in local book and gift shops. The interactive Kendal Castle display charts the town's history from prehistoric times into the 21st century. The museum is at the northern end of town, close to the train station. ☒ *Station Rd.* ☎ *01539/721374* ⊕ *www.kendalmuseum.org. uk* ☒ *£3.50* ☉ *Apr.–Oct., Mon.–Sat. 10:30–5; Nov., Dec., and mid-Feb.–Mar., Mon.–Sat. 10:30–4.*

Sizergh Castle, one of the Lake District's finest fortified houses, has a 58-foot-tall defensive peel tower that dates from 1340, when Scottish raids were feared. It has been the home of the Strickland family for more than 760 years. Expanded in Elizabethan times, the castle includes outstanding oak-paneled interiors with intricately carved chimneypieces and oak furniture, such as the Inlaid Chamber. The estate has a rock garden and an ancient woodland with many kinds of butterflies. Sizergh is 3½ mi south of Kendal. ☒ *Off A591, Sizergh* ☎ *015395/60070* ⊕ *www. nationaltrust.org.uk* ☒ *£5.50, gardens only £3* ☉ *Apr.–Oct., Sun.–Thurs.; house 1:30–5:30, gardens 12:30–5:30.*

★ **Levens Hall,** a handsome Elizabethan house and the home of the Bagot family, is famous for its topiary garden, probably the most distinctive in the world. Laid out in 1694, the garden retains its original design, and the yew and beech hedges, cut into amazingly complex shapes that resemble enormous chess pieces, rise among a profusion of flowers. The house contains a stunning medieval hall with oak paneling, ornate plasterwork, Jacobean furniture, and Cordova goat leather wallpaper. Levens Hall is 4 mi south of Kendal. ☒ *Off A590, Levens* ☎ *015395/60321* ⊕ *www.levenshall.co.uk* ☒ *£7.50, gardens only £5.80* ☉ *Mid-Apr.–mid-Oct., Sun.–Thurs.; house noon–5, gardens 10–5, last admission 4:30.*

Where to Stay & Eat

The Brewery Arts Centre is another good dining option in Kendal.

££–£££ ✕ **The Moon.** This bistro-style establishment, decorated in pale blues and whites, has won a good local reputation with high-quality dishes on a menu that changes monthly. There's always a strong selection of vegetarian fare, and the sometimes adventurous cooking shows Mediterranean and Asian flourishes, such as wild mushrooms flamed in Madeira, and fish kebabs marinated in chilies, lime, and coriander. ☒ *129 Highgate* ☎ *01539/729254* ☱ *MC, V* ☉ *Closed Mon. No lunch.*

£ ✕ **1657 Chocolate House.** Chocolate rules at this old spot serving 38 chocolate drinks and 25 chocolate desserts. You can choose among 300 kinds of chocolates in the shop, too. Aztec Experience hot chocolate blends five spices; the milk chocolate truffle cake is scrumptious. Servers in period costumes also deliver traditional English fare such as Welsh rarebit

The Lake District

and ploughman's lunch. Credit cards are accepted for amounts more than £10. ⊠ *54 Branthwaite Brow, Finkle St.* ☎ *01539/740702* ▤ *MC, V* ⊘ *No dinner.*

£ ✕ **Waterside Wholefoods Café.** In summer, grab one of the outdoor picnic tables overlooking the River Kent and order from the vegetarian menu of savory soups, quiches, pizzas, pâtés, nut loafs, salads, and delicious cakes and scones. For the full Lakeland experience, stay at Lakeland Natural, the café's inexpensive guest house. ⊠ *2 Kent View, Waterside* ☎ *01539/729743* ▤ *MC, V* ⊘ *Closed Sun. No dinner.*

££ ✕▦ **Punch Bowl Inn.** Inspired food and a few simply decorated bedrooms draw people to this former 17th-century coaching inn, hidden along a country road in the Lyth Valley. The pub has log fires, minstrel galleries above the main room, and black-painted timbers. Modern British menus are delivered with panache: fresh fish, local lamb, warming soups, and rich desserts all hit the spot. Book well in advance. ⊠ *Off A5074, Crosthwaite LA8 8HR, 5 mi west of Kendal* ☎ *015395/68237* 🖷 *015395/ 68875* ⊕ *www.punchbowl.fsnet.co.uk* ⌁ *3 rooms* ⌂ *Pub; no a/c, no room phones* ▤ *MC, V* ⑩ *BP.*

££ ▦ **Beech House Hotel.** Old-fashioned qualities (this is a town house in a quiet conservation area) combine with modern luxuries (heated floors in bathrooms) in this comfortable option. Rooms are individually designed but share a common homeyness. A full English breakfast includes local smoked bacon, honey-glazed sausages, and pancakes. ⊠ *40 Greenside, LA9 4LD* ☎ *01539/720385* 🖷 *01539/724082* ⊕ *www.beechhouse-kendal.co.uk* ⌁ *5 rooms* ⌂ *Minibars; no a/c* ▤ *MC, V* ⑩ *BP.*

£ ▦ **Highgate Hotel.** Dating to 1768, this striking, black-and-white-painted town house in the center of Kendal is a small, family-run hotel near the arts center and several good restaurants. Rooms are simply but cozily decorated, with pine furniture, patterned fabrics, and plain white walls. ⊠ *128 Highgate, LA9 4HE* 🖷🖷 *01539/724229* ⊕ *www.highgatehotel. co.uk* ⌁ *5 rooms* ⌂ *Lounge; no a/c* ▤ *AE, MC, V* ⑩ *BP.*

Nightlife & the Arts

The **Brewery Arts Centre,** a sophisticated contemporary complex in a converted brewery, includes an art gallery, theater, cinemas, and workshop spaces. The Green Room, overlooking lovely gardens, serves lunch and dinner, and Vats Bar offers pizza and ales, lagers, and wines. In November, the Mountain Film Festival presents productions aimed at climbers and walkers. ⊠ *Highgate* ☎ *01539/725133* 🎟 *Free, except for special exhibitions* ⊘ *Mon.–Sat. 9 AM–11 PM.*

Shopping

Kendal has a pleasant mix of chain names, factory outlet stores, specialty shops, and traditional markets. The most interesting stores are tucked away in the quiet lanes and courtyards around Market Place, Finkle Street, and Stramongate. There's been a **market** in Kendal since 1189, and outdoor market stalls still line the center of town along Stramongate and Market Place every Wednesday and Saturday.

Henry Roberts Bookshop (⊠ 7 Stramongate ☎ 01539/720425), in Kendal's oldest house (a 16th-century cottage), stocks a superb selection of regional books. **K Village Outlet Centre** (⊠ Lound Rd., Junction 36 of M6

☎ 01539/732363) sells brand names at discounted prices; the best deals are at the popular K Shoes Factory. The **Kentdale Rambler** (✉ 34 Market Pl. ☎ 01539/729188) is the best local store for walking boots and equipment, maps, and guides, including Wainwright's illustrated guides. **Peter Hall & Son** (✉ Danes Rd., Staveley ☎ 01539/821633), a woodcraft workshop 4 mi north of Kendal along A591, sells ornamental bowls and attractive wood gifts.

Windermere & Bowness-on-Windermere

② *10 mi northwest of Kendal.*

For a natural touring base for the southern half of the Lake District, you don't need to look much farther than Windermere. The resort became popular in the Victorian era when the arrival of the railway made the remote and rugged area accessible. Wordsworth and Ruskin opposed the railway, fearing an influx of tourists would ruin the tranquil place. Sure enough, the railway terminus in 1847 brought with it Victorian day-trippers, and the original hamlet of Birthwaite was subsumed by the new town of Windermere, named after the lake. The day-trippers keep coming and the town has continued to flourish, despite being a mile or so from the water; the development now spreads to envelop the slate-gray lakeside village of Bowness-on-Windermere. Bowness is the more attractive, but they are so close it matters little where you stay. Bus 599, leaving every 20 minutes in summer (hourly the rest of the year) from outside Windermere train station, links the two.

The **Windermere Steamboat Centre** houses the world's finest collection of Victorian and Edwardian steam- and motor-powered yachts and launches. Displays about Windermere's nautical history include the famous names of motorboat racing on the lake. The *Dolly,* built around 1850, is one of the two oldest mechanically powered boats in the world. Among the many other vessels on view are Beatrix Potter's rowing boat and Arthur Ransome's sailing dinghy. For an additional £5, you can take a boat ride on Windermere in an antique vessel—if the weather is good. ✉ *Rayrigg Rd., Bowness-on-Windermere* ☎ *015394/45565* ⊕ *www.steamboat.co.uk* ⊡ *£3.50* ۞ *Mid-Mar.–early Nov., daily 10–5.*

۞ **The World of Beatrix Potter** interprets the author's tales with three-dimensional scenes of Peter Rabbit raiding Mr. McGregor's garden, Mrs. Tiggy-Winkle in her kitchen, and more. There are also Beatrix Potter souvenirs and a tearoom. For less commercialism, though, visit Potter's former home at Hill Top and the Beatrix Potter Gallery in Hawkshead. ✉ *The Old Laundry, Crag Brow, Bowness-on-Windermere* ☎ *015394/88444* ⊕ *www.hop-skip-jump.com* ⊡ *£3.90* ۞ *Easter–Sept., daily 10–5:30; Oct.–Easter, daily 10–4:30.*

In 1900, architect H. M. Baillie Scott (1865–45) designed **Blackwell,** a notable Arts and Crafts house full of carved paneling and delicate plasterwork. Lakeland birds, flowers, and trees are artfully integrated into the stained glass, stonework, friezes, and wrought iron. Now exquisitely restored, the house showcases exhibits of works from different periods that embody Arts and Crafts ideals. Peruse the bookshop or relax in the

Tea Room overlooking Windermere. ⊠ *B5360, Windermere* ☎ *015394/ 46139* ⊕ *www.blackwell.org.uk* 🖃 *£4.75* ☉ *Apr.–Oct., daily 10–5; Nov.–late-Dec. and mid-Feb.–Mar., daily 10–4.*

★ No sights in Windermere or Bowness compete with that of **Windermere** itself. At 11 mi long, 1½ mi wide, and 200 feet deep, the lake is England's largest and stretches from Newby Bridge almost to Ambleside, filling a rocky gorge between steep, thickly wooded hills. The cold waters are superb for fishing, especially for Windermere char, a rare lake trout. In summer, steamers and pleasure craft travel the lake, and a trip across the island-studded waters, particularly the round-trip from Bowness to Ambleside or down to Lakeside, is wonderful. Although the lake's marinas and piers have some charm, you can bypass the busier stretches of shoreline (in summer they can be packed solid) by walking beyond the boathouses. Here, from among the pine trees, is a fine view across the lake. The **car ferry,** which also carries pedestrians, crosses from Ferry Nab on the Bowness side to reach Far Sawrey and the road to Hawkshead. ☎ *0860/813427* 🖃 *Car ferry £2 cars, 40p foot passengers* ☉ *Ferries every 30 mins Mon.–Sat. 6:50 AM–9:50 PM, Sun. 9:10 AM–9:50 PM; winter 'til 8:50 PM.*

★ ☾ The excellent **Aquarium of the Lakes,** right on the quayside at the southern end of Windermere, has informative wildlife and waterside exhibits. The highlight is an underwater tunnel walk along a re-created lake bed. You can take a boat to Lakeside from the town of Windermere or drive here. ⊠ *C5062, Lakeside* ☎ *015394/30153* ⊕ *www.aquariumofthelakes. co.uk* 🖃 *£5.95* ☉ *Apr.–Oct., daily 9–6; Nov.–Mar., daily 9–5.*

☾ The **Lakeside & Haverthwaite Railway Company** runs vintage steam trains on the 4-mi branch line between Lakeside and Haverthwaite along the lake's southern tip. Departures coincide with ferry arrivals from Windermere. ☎ *015395/31594* ⊕ *http://ukhrail.uel.ac.uk/lhr.html* 🖃 *£4.50* ☉ *Late Mar. and May–late Oct., daily 10:30–6; Apr., weekends 10:30–6.*

> **off the beaten path**

ORREST HEAD – To escape the traffic and have a memorable view of Windermere, set out on foot and follow the signs near the Windermere Hotel (across from the train station) to Orrest Head. The shady, uphill path winds through Elleray Wood, and after a 20-minute hike you arrive at a rocky little summit (784 feet) with a panoramic view that encompasses the Yorkshire fells, Morecambe Bay, and Troutbeck Valley.

Where to Stay & Eat

★ **££–££££** ✕ **Porthole Eating House.** Superb French, Italian, and traditional English dishes have been served in this intimate, whitewashed 17th-century house for more than 30 years. Delicacies on the changing menu may include chargrilled partridge with pine nut and rosemary butter sauce, and risotto of wild Lakeland mushrooms and horseradish. The wine cellar stocks more than 350 vintages, or you can try a glass of Taglag, the excellent local beer. Petits fours are served with coffee. The patio is ideal for alfresco dining. ⊠ *3 Ash St., Bowness-on-Windermere* ☎ *015394/42793* ▭ *AE, DC, MC, V* ☉ *Closed Tues. No lunch Mon., Wed., and Sat.*

£££ ✗ **Jerichos.** You can watch your meal being prepared in this stylish restaurant with an open kitchen. Savory choices from the modern British menu include pan-seared duck and roast loin of suckling pig. The spiced minced lamb on baked eggplant and plum tomatoes is especially good. ⊠ *Birch St., Windermere* ☎ *015394/42522* ▤ *MC, V* ☉ *Closed Mon. No lunch.*

££–£££ ✗ **Kwela's.** Good pan-African cuisine sets this restaurant apart from some of the more traditional eateries in the center of Windermere. The changing menu lists inventive dishes such as char-grilled ostrich steak carved over thyme-scented *mielie* (corn) meal topped with gooseberry jam. Culinary influences stretch from Moroccan (*tagines,* or stews) to South African (*bobotie*—minced meat with curry). The decor is sophisticated but refreshingly minimalist, with square wooden tables and natural colors. ⊠ *4 High St., Windermere* ☎ *015394/44954* 🖷 *015394/44192* ▤ *MC, V.*

£££££ ✗🖾 **Miller Howe.** The sumptuous guest rooms in this luxurious Edwardian country-house hotel come with canopy-draped beds and binoculars that allow you to study the dazzling view across Windermere. You can relax in sitting rooms filled with fine antiques and paintings, and have afternoon tea in the conservatory. The modern British fixed-price menu lists sophisticated fare such as warm rabbit salad with apple chutney. Guests have access to a health club, and the hotel arranges activities from archery to pony trekking. ⊠ *Rayrigg Rd., Bowness-on-Windermere, LA23 1EY* ☎ *015394/42536* 🖷 *015394/45664* ⊕ *www.millerhowe.com* ⪤ *12 rooms, 3 suites in cottage* ⚴ *Restaurant, croquet, piano, Internet, airport shuttle, helipad, some pets allowed; no a/c, no kids under 8* ▤ *AE, MC, V* ⦿ *MAP.*

£££££ ✗🖾 **The Samling.** On its own sculpture-dotted 67 acres above Windermere, this place oozes exclusivity from every carefully fashioned corner. Wordsworth used to come here to pay his rent. Today the hotel is favored by the rich and famous, but it avoids the snobbishness sometimes found in such establishments. Furnishings are traditional and tasteful but not fussy, service is a good mix of professional and friendly, and the lake views are fantastic. The restaurant specializes in sophisticated fare such as char-grilled lamb with sweetbreads and herb risotto; it's open to nonguests for dinner, afternoon tea, and Sunday lunch. ⊠ *Ambleside Rd., Windermere, LA23 1LR* ☎ *015394/31922* ⊕ *www.thesamling.com* ⪤ *10 suites* ⚴ *Restaurant; no a/c* ▤ *AE, MC, V* ⦿ *BP.*

Fodor's Choice
★

££££–£££££ ✗🖾 **Gilpin Lodge.** Hidden in 20 acres of tranquil grounds, this rambling country-house hotel, in a converted 1901 house with two modern wings, pampers its guests in a low-key way. The plush but understated public rooms are furnished with sofas and rugs, warmed by log fires, and scattered with books and magazines. Bedrooms embody contemporary rustic chic with wooden furniture and antiques; all have sitting areas. The restaurant (reservations essential) is superb; local products such as smoked trout, homemade sausages, lamb, and wild mushrooms abound. You can use a nearby health club, and the hotel helps arrange sports activities. ⊠ *Crook Rd., off B5284, Bowness-on-Windermere, LA23 3NE* ☎ *015394/88818* 🖷 *015394/88058* ⊕ *www.gilpin-lodge.co.uk* ⪤ *14 rooms* ⚴ *Restaurant, room service, in-room safes, minibars, pond, croquet, 2 lounges, no-smoking rooms; no a/c, no kids under 7* ▤ *AE, DC, MC, V* ⦿ *BP.*

££–£££ ✕⌂ **The Queen's Head Hotel.** Popular with locals, this 17th-century inn north of Windermere is renowned for its innovative twist on pub food such as pan-fried pork with Cajun spices and for real ales (fermented twice in the cask) served from an Elizabethan four-poster bed. The intimate dining rooms have oak beams, flagged floors, and roaring log fires. Guest rooms are basic (seven have four-posters) but offer splendid views and good value. ⊠ *A592, Troutbeck, LA23 1PW* ☏ *015394/32174* 🖷 *015394/31938* ⊕ *www.queensheadhotel.com* ⤶ *15 rooms* ⟁ *Restaurant, no-smoking rooms; no a/c, no room phones* ▭ *MC, V* ¶⊙¶ *BP.*

£££–£££££ ⌂ **Langdale Chase.** Built in the 19th century and tastefully refurbished, this estate recalls the grandeur of the past with its baronial entrance hall, old-master paintings, oak-paneled lounge, and mosaic floors. But there's genuine comfort here, too, in the pleasing conservatory and terrace. Many guest rooms, done in traditional style with pastels, have views of Windermere; six are in an annex by the lake. The five acres of landscaped gardens are ideal for a stroll. ⊠ *Ambleside Rd. near A591, Windermere, LA23 1LW* ☏ *015394/32201* 🖷 *015394/32604* ⊕ *www.langdalechase. co.uk* ⤶ *27 rooms* ⟁ *Restaurant, miniature golf, lake, boating, croquet, bar, Internet, business services, some pets allowed; no a/c* ▭ *AE, DC, MC, V* ¶⊙¶ *BP.*

££ ⌂ **Boston House.** Built for railway executives in 1849, this attractive Victorian house is one of Windermere's oldest buildings. It's a five-minute walk from the train station, where the friendly owners will collect you on request. One of the casual, country-style bedrooms has a four-poster. ⊠ *The Terrace, Windermere, LA23 1AJ* ☏ *015394/43654* ⊕ *www. bostonhouse.co.uk* ⤶ *5 rooms* ⟁ *No a/c, no kids under 13, no smoking* ▭ *MC, V* ¶⊙¶ *BP.*

£ ⌂ **Brendan Chase.** On a quiet side road in the heart of Windermere, this comfortable Victorian guest house is close to restaurants and the bus and train stations. The common rooms are pleasantly decorated and have fresh flowers, and the owner is welcoming. Guest rooms, airy and spacious, have some antiques; for the most comfort, book ahead for a room with private shower. At the cheaper end of the scale, there are dorm rooms with four or six beds. ⊠ *1–3 College Rd., Windermere, LA23 1BU* ☏🖷 *015394/45638* ⤶ *8 rooms, 3 with bath* ⟁ *Some pets allowed, no-smoking rooms; no a/c, no room phones* ▭ *No credit cards* ¶⊙¶ *BP.*

Sports & the Outdoors

Windermere Lake Holidays Afloat (⊠ Gilly's Landing, Glebe Rd., Bowness-on-Windermere ☏ 015394/43415) rents boats, from small sailboats to large cabin cruisers.

Shopping

The best selection of shops is at the Bowness end of Windermere, on Lake Road and around Queen's Square: clothing stores, crafts shops, and souvenir stores of all kinds. At **Lakeland Jewellers** (⊠ Crag Brow, Bowness-on-Windermere ☏ 015394/42992), the local experts set semiprecious stones in necklaces and brooches. The **Lakeland Sheepskin and Leather Centre** (⊠ Lake Rd., Bowness-on-Windermere ☏ 015394/44466), which also has branches in Ambleside and Keswick, stocks moderately priced leather and sheepskin goods.

Lake District National Park Visitor Centre at Brockhole

✿ ❸ *3 mi northwest of Windermere.*

Brockhole, a lakeside 19th-century mansion with terraced gardens sloping down to the water, serves as the park's official visitor center and has exhibits about the local ecology, flora, and fauna. The gardens are at their best in spring, when floods of daffodils cover the lawns and azaleas burst into bloom. Among the park activities are lectures, guided walks, and demonstrations of traditional Lakeland crafts such as drystone wall building. Some programs are geared toward children, who will also appreciate the adventure playground here; check for special events on summer weekends. The bookstore carries hiking guides and maps, and you can picnic here or eat at the café-restaurant. Bus 555/556 goes to the center from the Windermere train station. **Windermere Lake Cruises** (☎ 015394/43360) runs a ferry service to the center from Ambleside. ✉ *A591, Ambleside Rd., Windermere* ☎ *015394/46601* ⊕ *www.lakedistrict.gov.uk* ✉ *Free; parking £3 half day, £4 full day* ☉ *Easter–Oct., daily 10–5; early–mid-Nov., weekends 10–5.*

Ambleside

❹ *4 mi north of Lake District National Park Visitor Centre at Brockhole.*

Unlike Kendal and Windermere, Ambleside seems almost part of the hills and fells. Its buildings, mainly of local stone and many built in the traditional style that forgoes the use of mortar in the outer walls, blend perfectly into their setting. The small town sits at the northern end of Windermere, making it a popular center for Lake District excursions. It has a better choice of restaurants than Windermere or Bowness, and the numerous outdoor shops are handy for fell walkers. The town does, however, suffer from overcrowding in high season. Wednesday, when the local market takes place, is particularly busy.

Bridge House, a tiny 17th-century stone cottage, perches on an arched stone bridge that spans Stone Beck. This much-photographed building holds a National Trust shop and information center. ✉ *Rydal Rd.* ☎ *015394/35599* ✉ *Free* ☉ *Easter–Oct., daily 10–5.*

need a break?

The **Apple Pie Eating House and Bakery** (✉ Rydal Rd. ☎ 015394/ 33679) is a good place to gather the strength for a walk or to relax after one. The hearty, homemade soups, meat pies, and baked goods are delicious. There are tables and chairs, but most people line up for takeout sandwiches and sugar replenishment.

The **Armitt Museum,** a fine local-history gallery and library, explores Ambleside's past and its surroundings through the eyes of local people such as William Wordsworth, Thomas De Quincey, Robert Southey, John Ruskin, and Beatrix Potter. You can study Beatrix Potter's natural-history watercolors or watch a Victorian lantern slide show. ✉ *Rydal Rd.* ☎ *015394/31212* ⊕ *www.armitt.com* ✉ *£3* ☉ *Daily 10–5.*

Where to Stay & Eat

★ **££–££££** ✕ **Glass House.** The most stylish restaurant in town occupies a converted medieval mill with waterwheel, adjacent to Adrian Sankey's Ambleside Glass Works. Inventiveness is the key in the open plan and use of plate glass, as well as in the kitchen. Modern British cuisine comes with a Mediterranean twist in dishes such as spinach, potato, and mozzarella pie, and pan-fried scallops with lemon, parsley, and butter. You can have an elegant dinner or just sip a cappuccino in the courtyard. Note that only "well-behaved, seated-at-all-times" children are welcome. ⊠ *Rydal Rd.* ☎ *015394/32137* ⚖ *Reservations essential* ⊟ *MC, V* ⊗ *Closed Tues. and Jan.*

★ **££–££££** ✕ **Lucy's on a Plate.** This friendly bistro is the perfect spot to relax, whether with a tofu and ginger burger for lunch, a gluten-free chocolate almond torte for afternoon tea, or grilled char for dinner by candlelight. The exquisite food shows influences from around the globe in dishes such as Thai ostrich plate and Louisiana mussel chowder. A shop sells Cumbrian foods: sticky toffee pudding, farm cheeses, Cumberland sausage, jams, chutneys, biscuits. ⊠ *Church St.* ☎ *015394/31191* ⊟ *MC, V.*

£–££ ✕ **Lucy 4.** You can order wine by the glass and dance to salsa music in this wine bar and bistro that caters to an upbeat crowd. Nibbling is the way to eat, with mostly Mediterranean-influenced tapas such as goat cheese bruschetta, Moroccan couscous salad, and skewered shrimp. The same owner runs Lucy's on a Plate; the name, in case you didn't guess, is a pun on "Lucifer." ⊠ *2 St. Mary's La.* ☎ *015394/34666* ⊟ *MC, V* ⊗ *Closed Tues. and Wed. No lunch.*

★ **££** ⊡ **The Old Vicarage.** A quiet edge of Ambleside's old center is the peaceful setting for this excellent-value B&B in a large Victorian former vicarage. Rooms are furnished in traditional English country style, with floral and print fabrics and dark wood furniture; some are well-equipped for families. A log fire, great breakfasts, and a warm welcome help make this a good deal even without the pool. Guests have access to a nearby health club. ⊠ *Vicarage Rd., LA22 9DH* ☎ *015394/33364* ⊠ *015394/ 34734* ⊕ *www.oldvicarageambleside.co.uk* ↬ *10 rooms* ⚖ *In-room VCRs, indoor pool, sauna, lounge, piano; no a/c* ⊟ *MC, V* ⍟ *BP.*

£ ⊡ **3 Cambridge Villas.** Ambleside has many inexpensive B&Bs, but it's hard to find a more welcoming spot than this lofty Victorian house right in the center, with hosts who know a thing or two about local walks. Although space is at a premium, the rooms are pleasantly decorated with prints and wood furniture. The sitting room has plenty of books. ⊠ *Church St., LA22 9DL* ☎ *015394/32307* ✉ *cambridgevillas3@aol. com* ↬ *7 rooms, 4 with bath* ⚖ *No a/c, no room phones, no smoking* ⊟ *No credit cards* ⍟ *BP.*

Sports & the Outdoors

The many fine walks in the vicinity include local routes north to Rydal Mount or southeast over Wansfell to Troutbeck. Each walk will take up to a half day, there and back. Ferries from Bowness-on-Windermere dock at Ambleside's harbor, called Waterhead; you can rent rowboats here for an hour or two.

Biketreks (⊠ 2 Milans Park ☎ 015394/31245) is a good source for bike rentals.

ON THE MENU

In Cumbria, which encompasses the Lake District, food is more than fuel for hiking. The area has earned a reputation for good country food using Herdwick lamb, beef, and game, as well as fish from the freshwater streams and lakes, such as salmon, Windermere char, and Borrowdale and Ullswater trout. Sold in one long strip, the thick pork-and-herb Cumberland sausage is another specialty. Local breads, cakes, pastries, and scones are scrumptious. Brown sugar, molasses, nutmeg, cinnamon, ginger, and rum—favorite ingredients in traditional cakes—were imported from the West Indies in exchange for wool and are integral to the cakes' flavor. Lyth Valley damsons (a kind of plum) have a nutty taste used in everything from beverages and desserts to cheese. Grasmere gingerbread is baked from a secret recipe, and Kendal mint cake (a candy marketed as survival food) has a home in many hikers' backpacks.

Rydal

5 *1 mi northwest of Ambleside.*

The village of Rydal, on the small glacial lake called Rydal Water, is rich with Wordsworthian associations. One famous beauty spot linked with the poet is **Dora's Field,** below Rydal Mount next to the church of St. Mary's (where you can still see the poet's pew). In spring the field is awash in yellow daffodils, planted by William Wordsworth and his wife in memory of their beloved daughter Dora, who died in 1847.

If there's one poet associated with the Lake District, it is Wordsworth, who made his home at **Rydal Mount** from 1813 until his death. Wordsworth and his family moved to these grand surroundings when he was nearing the height of his career, and his descendants still live here, surrounded by his furniture, books, and portraits. You can see the study in which he worked, the family dining room, and the 4½-acre garden, laid out by the poet himself, that gave him so much pleasure. Surrounding Rydal Mount and the areas around Dove Cottage and Grasmere are many footpaths where Wordsworth wandered. His favorite can be found on the hill past White Moss Common and the River Rothay. Spend an hour or two walking them and you may understand why the great poet composed most of his verse in the open air. ⊠ *A591* ☎ *015394/ 33002* ⊕ *www.rydalmount.co.uk* ☑ *£4.50, £garden only 2* ⊙ *Mar.–Oct., daily 9:30–5; Nov.–Feb., Wed.–Mon. 10–4. Closed 3 wks in Jan.*

Grasmere

6 *3 mi north of Rydal, 4 mi northwest of Ambleside.*

Lovely Grasmere, on a tiny, wood-fringed lake, is made up of crooked lanes in which Westmorland slate–built cottages hold shops, cafés, and galleries. The village is a focal point for literary and landscape associations because this area was the adopted heartland of the Romantic poets, notably Wordsworth and Coleridge. The Vale of Grasmere has changed over the years, but many features Wordsworth wrote about are still visible. Wordsworth lived on the town's outskirts for almost 50 years and described the area as "the loveliest spot that man hath ever known." The poet walked the hills with his guests, who included the authors Ralph Waldo Emerson and Nathaniel Hawthorne. Wordsworth, his wife Mary, his sister Dorothy, and his daughter Dora are buried in the churchyard of **St. Oswald's.** As you leave the churchyard, stop at the Gingerbread Shop, in a tiny cottage.

★ William Wordsworth lived in **Dove Cottage** from 1799 to 1808, a prolific and happy time for the poet. During this time he wrote some of his most famous works, including "Ode: Intimations of Immortality" and *The Prelude;* he was also married here. Built in the early 17th century as an inn, this tiny house is beautifully preserved, with an oak-paneled hall and floors of Westmorland slate. It first opened to the public in 1891 and remains as it was when Wordsworth lived here with his sister, Dorothy, and wife, Mary. Bedrooms and living areas contain much of Wordsworth's furniture and many personal belongings. Coleridge was a frequent visitor, as was Thomas De Quincey, best known for his 1822 autobiographical masterpiece *Confessions of an Opium Eater*—he moved in after the Wordsworths left. Your ticket includes admission to the **Wordsworth Museum,** which documents the poet's life and the literary contributions of Wordsworth and the Lake Poets. Besides seeing the poet's original manuscripts, you can hear his poems read aloud on headphones. Books, manuscripts, and artwork capture the spirit of the Romantic movement. The **Jerwood Centre,** set to open late in 2004, will house 50,000 letters and manuscripts. Afternoon tea is served at **Dove Cottage Tea Room and Restaurant.** ✉ *A591, 1 mi south of Grasmere* ☎ *015394/35544* ⊕ *www.wordsworth.org.uk* ✆ *£5.95* ☽ *Mid-Feb.–mid-Jan., daily 9:30–5:30.*

need a break?

The small, stone-built **Jumble Room Café** (✉ Langdale Rd. ☎ 015394/35188), which dates to the 18th century and was Grasmere's first shop, is a friendly, fashionable, and colorful place for a smoked salmon and dill tartlet and other sophisticated snacks, or soup such as broccoli and Stilton.

Where to Stay & Eat

£–££ ╳ **Baldry's.** This cheerful café, traditional but without too many frills, serves excellent coffee and homemade snacks. The friendly owners offer delicious scones, cakes, pies, tarts, salads, and six kinds of rarebit. For a Cumbrian treat, try the sticky gingerbread with rum butter and ginger ice cream. ✉ *Red Lion Sq.* ☎ *015394/35301* ▤ *MC, V* ☽ *No dinner.*

★ ╳▦ **White Moss House.** Wordsworth purchased this comfortable house, **££££–£££££** built in 1730 to overlook Rydal Water, for his son, Willie, whose family lived here until the 1930s. Pristine public areas and bedrooms are decorated with prints and traditional pieces such as the grandfather clock at the bottom of the stairs. The current hosts, the Dixons, lavish attention on guests, but the highlight of a stay is the renowned restaurant.

The menu changes daily, but the five courses of contemporary English cuisine always include a soup, local meat and fish, and a choice of British cheeses. ⊠ *A591, Rydal Water, LA22 9SE* ☎ *015394/35295* 🖷 *015394/35516* ⊕ *www.whitemoss.com* 🔊 *7 rooms, 1 suite* ♿ *Restaurant, fishing, lounge; no a/c* ➡ *MC, V* ⊘ *Closed Dec. and Jan.* �1O1 *MAP.*

£ 🖫 **Banerigg House.** You don't have to spend a fortune to find appealing lakeside lodgings in Grasmere. This early 20th-century family house, ¾ mi south of the village, has well-appointed rooms, most with lake views. It's walker-friendly, too, which means you get local advice from the owners, drying facilities for wet days, and a roaring fire when needed. ⊠ *Lake Rd., LA22 9PW* ☎ *015394/35204* 🔊 *6 rooms, 5 with bath* ♿ *No a/c, no room phones, no room TVs, no smoking* ➡ *No credit cards* �1O1 *BP.*

Sports & the Outdoors

The most panoramic views of lake and village are from the south, from the bare slopes of Loughrigg Terrace, reached along a signposted track on the western side of the lake. It's less than an hour's walk there, though your stroll can be extended by continuing around Rydal Water, passing Rydal Mount and Dove Cottage before returning to Grasmere, a 4-mi (three-hour) walk in total.

Shopping

The smells wafting across the churchyard draw many people to the **Grasmere Gingerbread Shop** (⊠ Church Cottage ☎ 015394/35428). Since 1854 Sarah Nelson's gingerbread has been sold from this cramped 17th-century cottage, which was once the village school. The delicious treats, still made from a secret recipe, are available in attractive tins for the journey home or to eat right away. **The Stables** (⊠ College St. ☎ 015394/35453 ⊘ Closed Dec.–Easter except by appointment) antiques shop is a little Aladdin's cave piled with great books, bottles, silver candlesticks, lamps and prints.

Elterwater

❼ *2½ mi south of Grasmere, 4 mi west of Ambleside.*

The delightful village of Elterwater, at the eastern end of the Great Langdale Valley on B5343, is a good stop for hikers. It's barely more than a cluster of houses around a village green, but from here you can choose from a selection of excellent circular walks.

Where to Stay & Eat

★ ££ ✕🖫 **Britannia Inn.** At this family-owned, 500-year-old lodging in the heart of superb walking country, antiques, comfortable chairs, and prints and oil paintings furnish the cozy, beamed public rooms. Bedrooms are more modern in style, and two cottages with kitchens can be rented by the week. You can relax with a bar meal and Cumbrian ale on the terrace while taking in the village green and the rolling scenery beyond. The hearty food is popular with locals, as are the many ales and whiskys. A nearby health club is available to guests. ⊠ *B5343, LA22 9HP* ☎ *015394/37210* 🖷 *015394/37311* ⊕ *www.britinn.co.uk* 🔊 *13 rooms, 9 with bath, 2 cottages* ♿ *Restaurant, bar, lounge, some pets allowed; no a/c* ➡ *MC, V* �1O1 *BP.*

★ ££ ⊞ **Old Dungeon Ghyll Hotel.** There's no more comforting stop after a day outdoors than the Hiker's Bar of this hotel at the head of the Great Langdale Valley. The stone floor and wooden beams echo to the clatter of hikers' boots, and the roaring stove rapidly dries out wet walking gear. The old inn has provided hospitality for more than 300 years; guest rooms are done in traditional Lakeland style with patterned carpets, wallpaper, and flowered bed linens. You can choose to include dinner in the rate. ⊠ *Off B5343, Great Langdale, LA22 9JY* ☎ *015394/37272* ⊕ *www.odg.co.uk* ⤳ *13 rooms, 8 with bath* ⚲ *Restaurant, bar, lounge; no a/c, no room phones, no room TVs* ▭ *AE, MC, V* ⦿ *BP.*

Sports & the Outdoors

There are access points to Langdale Fell from several places along B5343, the main road; look for information boards at local parking places. You can also stroll up the river valley or embark on more energetic hikes to Stickle Tarn or to one of the summits of the Langdale Pikes.

Coniston

❽ *5 mi south of Elterwater.*

This small lake resort and boating center attracts climbers with the peak known as the **Old Man of Coniston** (2,635 feet); it also has sites related to John Ruskin. **Coniston Water,** the lake on which Coniston stands, came to prominence in the 1930s when Arthur Ransome made it the setting for *Swallows and Amazons,* one of a series of novels about a group of children and their adventures in the Lake District. The lake is about 5 mi long, a tempting stretch that drew boat and car racer Donald Campbell here in 1959 to set a water speed record of 260 mph. He was killed when trying to beat it in 1967. His body and the wreckage of *Bluebird K7* were retrieved from the lake in 2001. Campbell is buried in St. Andrew's church in Coniston, and a stone seat in the village commemorates him.

The **Ruskin Museum** holds manuscripts, personal items, and watercolors by John Ruskin that illuminate his thinking and influence. Good local-interest exhibits focus on Donald Campbell, copper mining, geology, lace, and more; a drystone wall shows construction techniques. ⊠ *Yewdale Rd.* ☎ *015394/41164* ⊕ *www.ruskinmuseum.com* ☒ *£3.50* ⊘ *Mid-Mar.–mid-Nov., daily 10–5:30; mid-Nov.–mid-Mar., Wed.–Sun. 10:30–3:30.*

★ **Brantwood,** on the eastern shore of Coniston Water, was the cherished home of John Ruskin (1819–1900), the noted Victorian artist, writer, critic, and social reformer, after 1872. The rambling, white, 18th-century house (with Victorian alterations) is on a 250-acre estate that stretches high above the lake. Here, alongside mementos such as his mahogany desk and the bath chair he used in later life, is a collection of Ruskin's own paintings, drawings, and books. Also on display is much of the art—he was a great connoisseur—that Ruskin collected, not least superb drawings by the landscape painter J. M. W. Turner (1775–1851). A video on Ruskin's life shows the lasting influence of his thoughts. Ruskin himself laid out the extensive grounds and their woodland walks. It's an easy drive to Brantwood from Coniston, but it's pleasant to travel here by ferry across the lake, via either the Coniston Launch or the *Gondola,* a 19th-century steam yacht. Both depart from Coniston Pier. ⊠ *Off B5285* ☎ *015394/41396* ⊕ *www.brantwood.org.uk* 🎫 *£5.50, gardens only £3.75* ⊘ *Mid-Mar.–mid-Nov., daily 11–5:30; mid-Nov.–mid-Mar., Wed.–Sun. 11–4:30.*

Where to Stay & Eat

£–££ ✕ **Brantwood's Jumping Jenny's.** This Pre-Raphaelite–style tearoom, named after Ruskin's beloved boat, has an open log fire and mountain views. It serves morning coffee, lunch (soup, pastas, sandwiches, and salads), and afternoon tea with tasty homemade cakes. ⊠ *Off B5285* ☎ *015394/41715* ☰ *MC, V* ⊘ *Closed Mon. and Tues. mid-Nov.–mid-Mar. No dinner.*

★ ££ ✕🖬 **Sun Hotel.** Standing at the foot of the Old Man of Coniston, this country-house hotel was built at the turn of the 20th century alongside the 16th-century coaching inn that still serves as a pub. The simply furnished guest rooms and conservatory restaurant have exceptional mountain views. The ancient pub, with flagstone walls and floors and exposed beams, fills up most nights with a mix of locals and climbers. Savory pies are the specialty; there are also five real ales and 36 wines. ⊠ *LA21 8HQ* ☎ *015394/41248* 🖷 *015394/41219* ⊕ *www.thesunconiston.com* 🛏 *10 rooms, 9 with bath* ⚲ *Restaurant, pub, some pets allowed, no-smoking rooms; no a/c* ☰ *MC, V* ⏧ *BP.*

★ £ 🖬 **Beech Tree Guest House.** This Victorian stone house with friendly owners and a garden is within walking distance of the town center. The individually furnished rooms, some of which look out over an ancient beech tree, are done in a country theme, and breakfast is hearty and vegetarian. There's a TV in the sitting room. ⊠ *Yewdale Rd., LA21 8DX* ☎ *015394/413717* 🛏 *8 rooms, 4 with bath* ⚲ *Some pets allowed; no a/c, no room TVs, no smoking* ☰ *MC, V* ⏧ *BP.*

Sports & the Outdoors

Steep tracks lead up from the village to the Old Man of Coniston. The trail starts near the Sun Hotel and goes past an old copper mine to the peak, which you can reach in about two hours. Experienced hikers include the peak in a seven-hour circular walk from the village, also taking in the dramatic heights and ridges of Swirl How and Wetherlam.

Coniston Boating Centre (⊠ Lake Rd. ☎ 015394/41366) at the lake rents out launches, canoes, and wooden rowboats. A picnic area and café are near the center.

Hawkshead

❾ *3 mi east of Coniston.*

In the Vale of Esthwaite, this small market town, with a pleasing hodge-podge of tiny squares, cobbled lanes, and whitewashed houses, is perhaps the Lake District's most picturesque village. There's a good deal more history here than in most local villages, however. The Hawkshead Courthouse, just outside town, was built by the monks of Furness Abbey in the 15th century. Hawkshead lay within the monastic domain and later derived much wealth from the wool trade, which flourished here in the 17th and 18th centuries. As a thriving market center, it could afford to maintain the **Hawkshead Grammar School,** at which

William Wordsworth was a pupil from 1779 to 1787; he carved his name on a desk inside, now on display. A house in the village (Ann Tyson's House) claims the honor of providing the young William with lodgings. The twin draws of Wordsworth and Beatrix Potter—apart from her home, Hill Top, there's also a Potter gallery—conspire to make Hawkshead overcrowded throughout the year.

The **Beatrix Potter Gallery,** in the solicitor's offices formerly used by Potter's husband, displays an annually changing selection of the artist-writer's original watercolors and drawings, as well as information on her interests as a naturalist. Potter was a conservationist and an early supporter of the National Trust. Admission is by timed ticket. ⌂ *Main St.* ☎ *015394/36355* ⊕ *www.nationaltrust.org.uk* ⎙ *£3* ⊙ *Late Mar.–Oct., Sat.–Wed. 10:30–4:30.*

☺ **Hill Top** was the home of children's author and illustrator Beatrix Potter (1866–1943), most famous for her *Peter Rabbit* stories. The house looks much the same as when Potter bequeathed it to the National Trust, and fans will recognize details such as the porch and garden gate, old kitchen range, Victorian dollhouse, and 17th-century four-poster, which were depicted in the book illustrations. Admission to this often-crowded spot is by timed ticket; you can book in advance. Try to avoid visiting on summer weekends and during school vacations. Hill Top lies 2 mi south of Hawkshead by car, though you can also approach via the car ferry from Bowness-on-Windermere. ⌂ *Off B5285, Near Sawrey* ☎ *015394/36269* ⊕ *www.nationaltrust.org.uk* ⎙ *£4.50, gardens free Thurs. and Fri.* ⊙ *House Easter–Oct., Sat.–Wed. 10:30–4.30; gardens and shop Easter–Oct., daily 11–4.*

Two miles northwest of the village (follow signs on B5285) is one of the Lake District's most celebrated beauty spots, **Tarn Hows,** a tree-lined lake. Scenic overlooks let you drink it all in, or you can take an hour to putter along the paths. A free National Trust bus runs here from Hawkshead and Coniston (Easter–October, Sunday only).

Where to Stay & Eat

£££–£££££ ✕⌂ **Drunken Duck Inn.** After four centuries, this friendly old coaching
Fodor'sChoice inn remains a fine place for food and lodging. Nestle into the cozy bar
★ with oak settles and fireplaces and order a real ale from the Duck's Barnsgate Brewery. The restaurant's intimate rooms have dark wood furniture and deep orange walls with cartoons and hunting prints; venison marinated in cocoa with polenta and figs is typical of the modern British fare. Bedrooms, bright and contemporary, make use of natural materials and have wonderful views of the Langdale Pikes. The price includes afternoon tea and breakfast. The inn is 2½ mi from Ambleside and Hawkshead. ⌂ *Off B5286, Barngates, LA22 ONG* ☎ *015394/36347* ⎙ *015394/36781* ⊕ *www.drunkenduckinn.co.uk* ⇆ *16 rooms* ⚴ *Restaurant, pub, no-smoking rooms; no a/c* ▭ *AE, MC, V* ¶⎮ *BP.*

Sports & the Outdoors

Grizedale Mountain Bikes (⌂ Old Hall Car Park, Grizedale Forest Park Centre ☎ 01229/860369 ⊕ www.grizedalemountainbikes.co.uk) rents bicycles.

PENRITH & THE NORTHERN LAKES

The scenery of the northern lakes is considerably more dramatic—some would say bleaker—than much of the landscape to the south, a change that becomes apparent on your way north from Kendal to Penrith. Your easiest approach is a 30-mi drive on the A6 that takes you through the wild and desolate Shap Fells. One of the most notorious moorland crossings in the country, the fells rise to a height of 1,304 feet. Even in summer it's a lonely place to be, and in winter snows the road can be dangerous. From Penrith the road leads to Ullswater, possibly the grandest of all the lakes; then there's a steady route west past Keswick, south through the marvelous Borrowdale Valley, and on to Cockermouth and Bassenthwaite.

Penrith

⑩ *30 mi north of Kendal.*

The red-sandstone town of Penrith was the capital of Cumbria, part of the Scottish kingdom of Strathclyde in the 9th and 10th centuries. It was rather neglected after the Normans arrived, and the Scots sacked it on several occasions. Penrith has been a thriving market town for centuries; the market still takes place on Tuesday, and it continues to have good shopping.

The tourist information center, in the Penrith Museum, has information about the historic town trail, which takes you through narrow byways to the plague stone on King Street, where food was left for the stricken, to St. Andrew's churchyard and its 1,000-year-old "hog back" tombstones (stones carved as stylized "houses of the dead"), and finally to the ruins of Penrith Castle.

The evocative remains of the 14th-century redbrick **Penrith Castle** stand high above a steep, now-dry moat. Home of the maligned Richard, duke of Gloucester (later Richard III), who was responsible for keeping peace along the border, it was one of England's first lines of defense against the Scots. By the Civil War the castle was in ruins, and the townsfolk used some of the fallen stones to build their houses. The ruins stand across from the town's train station. ⊠ *Off Castlegate* ☎ *No phone* ⊕ *www.english-heritage.org.uk* ⊡ *Free* ⊘ *June–Sept., daily 7:30 AM–9 PM; Oct.–May, daily 7:30–4:30.*

The **Penrith Museum,** in a 16th-century building that served as a school from 1670 to the 1970s, contains displays on the history of the Eden Valley, including Roman pottery and a medieval cauldron. The Penrith Tourist Information Centre is here. ⊠ *Robinson's School, Middlegate* ☎ *01768/212228* ⊡ *Free* ⊘ *Apr.–Oct., Mon.–Sat. 10–4, Sun. 1–4:45; Nov.–Mar., Mon.–Sat. 10–4.*

☾ Rheged, the name of the Celtic kingdom of Cumbria that stretched from Strathclyde in Scotland to Lancashire, is the theme of this grass-covered visitor center that looks like a Cumbrian hill from the outside. Its cen-

534
    The Lake District

terpiece, a large-format cinema, shows the somewhat historically dubious *Rheged—The Movie,* which explores the region's past, introducing Celtic warriors, Scottish raiders, and Arthurian legends; the aerial scenes of lakes and mountains are awesome. The National Mountaineering Exhibition celebrates Everest and mountaineering heroes. Shops showcase Cumbrian produce and crafts, and the Reivers restaurant has mountain views. Rheged is 2 mi southwest of Penrith and 1 mi west of Junction 40 on the M6. ⊠ *A66* ☎ *01768/868000* ⊕ *www.rheged.com* 🖭 *Free, movie £5.50* ⊙ *Daily 10–6.*

Where to Stay & Eat

★ £ ✕🖭 **Queen's Head Inn.** Once owned by the Wordsworths, this 1719 inn is a true gem. Now the home of a brewery, the traditional pub and restaurant is often packed with locals sampling Tirril beers as well as guest ales on tap, malt whiskys, and rare domestic and imported wines. Sophisticated meals use local produce such as farmhouse cheeses and Ullswater trout, but may include more exotic dishes, such as ostrich flambéed with cherry brandy. Rambling hallways lead to small, pleasant rooms with plaid bedspreads and simple wood furniture. The inn is 2½ mi south of Penrith. ⊠ *B5320, Tirril, CA10 2JF* ☎ *01768/863219* 🖷 *01768/863243* ⊕ *www.queensheadinn.co.uk* 🖙 *7 rooms* ⚴ *Restaurant, pub; no a/c, no room phones* 🖃 *AE, MC, V* ⏐⊙⏐ *BP.*

££–£££ 🖭 **The George.** This large, rambling coaching inn in the center of Penrith has been hosting people for more than 300 years. The lounges are full of wood paneling, antiques, copper and brass fixtures, old paintings, and comfortable chairs. You can stay overnight in one of the modernized rooms, decorated in traditional style, and use the local gym and pool. ⊠ *Devonshire St., CA11 7SH* ☎ *01768/862696* 🖷 *01768/868223* ⊕ *www.georgehotelpenrith.co.uk* 🖙 *34 rooms, 1 suite* ⚴ *Restaurant, cable TV, bar, lobby lounge, Internet, business services, meeting rooms, some pets allowed (fee); no a/c* 🖃 *AE, MC, V* ⏐⊙⏐ *BP.*

Shopping

Penrith is a diverting place to shop, with its narrow streets, alleyways, and arcades chockablock with family-run specialty shops. Major shopping areas include Devonish Arcade, with its brand-name stores; the pedestrian-only Angel Lane and Little Dockray; and Angel Square. The stalls of the outdoor **market** line Dockray, Corn Market, and Market Square every Tuesday and sell excellent local produce and original crafts.

James & John Graham of Penrith Ltd. (⊠ Market Sq. ☎ 01768/862281), trading from this site since 1793, has a great bakery and a delicatessen that specializes in cheese and local products. **The Saddlers** (⊠ 15 Little Dockray ☎ 01768/862363) carries fine riding gear, leather items, walking sticks, gifts, and travel goods. **The Toffee Shop** (⊠ 7 Brunswick Rd. ☎ 01768/862008) is where the Queen buys her toffee; it may also have the best fudge in England. **Wetheriggs Country Pottery** (⊠ Clifton Dykes ☎ 01768/892733), 2 mi south of Penrith on the A6, sells handmade earthenware and stoneware from Britain's only remaining steam-powered pottery.

Dalemain

⑪ *3 mi southwest of Penrith.*

Home of the Hasell family since 1679, Dalemain began with a 12th-century peel tower, built to protect the occupants from raiding Scots, and is now a delightful hodgepodge of architectural styles. An imposing Georgian facade of local pink sandstone encompasses a medieval hall and extensions from the 16th through the 18th centuries. Inside are a magnificent oak staircase, furniture dating from the mid-17th century, a Chinese drawing room, a 16th-century fretwork room with intricate plasterwork, and many fine paintings, including masterpieces by Van Dyck. The gardens are also worth a look. Dalemain is 3 mi west of Junction 40 of the M6. ⊠ *A592, Penrith* ☎ *01768/486450* ⊕ *www.dalemain. com* ☞ *£5.50, gardens only £3.50* ⊗ *House late Mar.–mid-Oct., Sun.–Thurs. 11–4; gardens Apr.–Oct., Sun.–Thurs. 10:30–5.*

Ullswater

⑫ *3 mi southwest of Dalemain, 6 mi southwest of Penrith.*

Hemmed in by towering hills, Ullswater, the region's second-largest lake, draws outdoor types. Some of the finest views are from the A592 as it sticks to the lake's western shore, through the adjacent hamlets of **Glenridding** and **Patterdale** at the southern end. Lakeside strolls, teashops, and rowboat rental all help provide the usual Lakeland experience. Steamers leave Glenridding's pier for **Pooley Bridge,** offering a pleasant tour along the lake.

At **Aira Force** (⊠ Off A592, 5 mi north of Patterdale), a spectacular series of waterfalls pounds through a wooded ravine to feed into Ullswater. From the parking lot (£2–£4 fee, depending on how long you stay), it's a 20-minute walk to the falls. Bring sturdy shoes in wet weather. Just above Aira Force in the woods of Gowbarrow Park is the spot where, in 1802, William Wordsworth's sister, Dorothy, observed daffodils that, as she wrote, " . . . tossed and reeled and danced and seemed as if they verily laughed with the wind that blew upon them." Two years later Wordsworth transformed his sister's words into the famous poem "I Wandered Lonely as a Cloud." And two centuries later, national park wardens patrol Gowbarrow Park in season to prevent tourists from picking the few remaining daffodils.

★ West of Ullswater's southern end, the brooding presence of **Helvellyn** (3,118 feet), one of the Lake District's most formidable mountains, recalls the region's fundamental character. It's an arduous climb to the top, especially via the challenging ridge known as Striding Edge, and the ascent shouldn't be attempted in poor weather or by inexperienced hikers. Signposted paths to the peak run from the road between Glenridding and Patterdale and pass by **Red Tarn,** at 2,356 feet the highest small mountain lake in the region.

Where to Stay & Eat

★ **£££££** ✕⊡ **Sharrow Bay.** Sublime views and exceptional service and cuisine add distinction to this country-house hotel on the shores of Ullswater. Sa-

CloseUp
POETRY, PROSE & THE LAKES

THE LAKE DISTRICT'S BEAUTY has whetted the creativity of many a famous poet and artist. Here's a quick rundown of some of the writers inspired by the area's vistas.

William Wordsworth (1770–1850), one of the first English Romantics, redefined poetry by replacing the mannered style of his forerunners with a more conversational style. Many of his greatest works, such as The Prelude, draw directly from his experiences in the Lake District, where he spent the first 20 and last 50 years of his life. Wordsworth and his work had an enormous effect on Coleridge, Keats, Shelley, Byron, and countless other writers.

John Ruskin (1819–1900), writer, art critic, and early conservationist, was an impassioned champion of new ways of seeing. He defended contemporary artists such as William Turner and the Pre-Raphaelites. His five-volume masterwork, Modern Painters, changed the role of the art critic from that of approver or naysayer to that of interpreter.

Thomas De Quincey (1785–1859) wrote essays whose impressionistic style influenced many 19th-century writers, including Poe and Baudelaire. His most famous work, Confessions of an English Opium Eater (1822), is an imaginative memoir of his young life, which indeed included opium addiction. He settled in Grasmere in 1809.

Beatrix Potter (1866–1943) never had a formal education; instead, she spent her childhood studying nature. Her love of the outdoors, and Lakeland scenery in particular, influenced her delightfully illustrated children's books, including The Tale of Jemima Puddle-Duck and Squirrel Nutkin. Potter also became a noted conservationist who donated land to the National Trust.

lons with oil paintings and fringed lamp shades represent classic Lakeland style. The bedrooms are plushly opulent, although those in the Edwardian Gatehouse and in the Bank House, an Elizabethan farmhouse about 1½ mi away, are somewhat simpler. Your sophisticated dinner (reservations essential, fixed-price menu; request the lake-view dining room) might include roast salmon on scallop risotto or venison with sweet potato confit. Stop by for afternoon tea (£16). ✉ Howtown Rd., Pooley Bridge, CA10 2LZ ☎ 017684/86301 🖶 017684/86349 ⊕ www.sharrow-bay. com ⇨ 19 rooms, 7 suites ♻ 2 restaurants, 2 lounges, Internet, business services, some pets allowed, no-smoking rooms; no a/c in some rooms, no kids under 13 ⊟ MC, V ☉ Closed Dec.–mid-Feb. ¶Ol MAP.

££££ 🏠 **Inn on the Lake.** The freshly decorated interior of this inn is as appealing as its spectacular location looking out over Ullswater. The lawns extend to the water's edge, and at the Ramblers Bar on the grounds you can share a pint and some mountain stories with the locals. Rooms, some with lake or mountain views, are furnished in traditional style, and there's a pleasant conservatory. ✉ Glenridding, CA11 0PE ☎ 017684/82444 🖶 017684/82303 www.innonthelakeullswater.co.uk ⇨ 46 rooms ♻ Restaurant, cable TV, 2 bars, some pets allowed (fee); no a/c, no smoking ⊟ MC, V ¶Ol BP.

Keswick

🔞 *14 mi west of Ullswater.*

The great mountains of Skiddaw and Blencathra brood over the gray slate houses of Keswick (pronounced *kezz*-ick), on the scenic shores of Derwentwater. The town is a natural base for exploring the rounded, heather-clad Skiddaw range to the north, and the hidden valleys of Borrowdale and Buttermere (the latter reached by stunning Honister Pass) take you into the rugged heart of the Lake District. Nearby, five beautiful lakes are set among the three highest mountain ranges in England.

Although tourists pack its cobbled, narrow streets, Keswick doesn't have quite the Victorian charm of Windermere or Ambleside, or the specialty shops of Penrith. It is, however, the best spot in the Lake District to purchase mountaineering gear and outdoor clothing. There are also many hotels, guest houses, restaurants, and pubs, but the best places are a few miles away in the surrounding countryside.

Because traffic congestion can be horrendous in summer, and parking is difficult in the higher valleys, you may want to leave your car behind. The open-top Borrowdale bus service between Keswick and Seatoller runs frequently, and the Honister Rambler minibus is perfect for walkers aiming for the high fells of the central lakes; it makes many stops from Keswick to Buttermere. The Keswick Launch service on Derwentwater links to many walks as well as the Borrowdale bus service.

The handsome 19th-century **Moot Hall** (⊠ Market Pl. ☎ 017687/72645) has served as both the town hall and the local prison. Now it houses the main **tourist information center** for the region.

Exhibits at the **Keswick Museum and Art Gallery** in Fitz Park include letters by Wordsworth, Southey, and Walpole, a local geological and natural history collection, and watercolor paintings. ⊠ *Station Rd.* ☎ *017687/73263* 🎟 *£1* ⊗ *Easter–Oct., Tues. and Wed. 10–4, Thurs. 11–7, and by appointment.*

☯ Borrowdale's long connection with graphite is celebrated at the **Cumberland Pencil Museum.** Legend has it that shepherds found graphite on Seathwaite Fell after a storm uprooted trees in the 16th century. The Derwent company still makes pencils here, and the museum contains the world's longest one, as well as displays about graphite mining and pencil making. ⊠ *Southey Works* ☎ *017687/73626* ⊕ *www.pencils.co. uk* 🎟 *£2.50* ⊗ *Daily 9:30–4.*

★ To understand why **Derwentwater** is considered one of England's finest lakes, take a short walk from Keswick's town center to the lakeshore and follow the **Friar's Crag** path, about a 15-minute level walk from the center. This pine-tree-fringed peninsula is a favorite vantage point, with its view of the lake, the surrounding ring of mountains, and many tiny islands. Ahead, crags line the **Jaws of Borrowdale** and overhang a dramatic mountain ravine—a scene that looks as if it emerged from a Romantic painting or poem. For the best lake views, take a wooden-launch cruise with **Keswick-on-Derwentwater Launch Co.** (☎ 017687/72263 ⊕ www.

keswick-launch.co.uk) around Derwentwater. Between late March and November, cruises set off every hour in each direction from a dock at the lakeshore; there is also a limited winter timetable. You can also rent a rowboat here. Buy a "hop-on, hop-off" explorer ticket and take advantage of the seven landing stages around the lake that provide access to hiking trails, such as the two-hour climb up and down Cat Bells, a celebrated lookout point on the western shore of Derwentwater.

A Neolithic monument about 100 feet in diameter, the **Castlerigg Stone Circle** (⊠ Off A66, 4 mi east of Keswick) lies in a brooding natural hollow called St. John's Vale, ringed by peaks and ranged by sheep. The 38 stones aren't large, but the site makes them particularly impressive. Wordsworth described them as "a dismal cirque of Druid stones upon a forlorn moor." A clearly marked route leads to a 200-foot-long path through a pasture. You can visit during daylight hours, no charge.

Where to Stay & Eat

££–£££ ✕ **Luca's.** The River Greta runs beside this stylish Italian bistro-restaurant, which is somewhat isolated at the north end of town. Choose from a great selection of pastas, risottos, and wood-fired pizzas, as well as traditional Italian dishes with veal, steak, poultry, or fish. The sauces and daily specials are imaginative. ⊠ *Greta Bridge, High Hill* ☎ *017687/ 74621* ▤ *MC, V* ☉ *Closed Mon., and Jan. and Feb. Sun.–Wed.*

★ **£–££** ✕ **Square Orange Cafe.** A mix of hip young locals and wind-blown walkers gathers here for excellent teas, cordials, and some serious hot chocolate. Music is laid-back, the walls have real paintings and photos, and there are games, good pizzas, and pints of local beer for long rainy days or cold winter nights. ⊠ *20 St. Johns St.* ☎ *017687/73888* ▤ *No credit cards.*

£ ✕ **Lakeland Pedlar.** This colorful, cheerful café and bike shop serves inspired vegetarian and vegan cuisine: hearty breakfast burritos, Tex-Mex and Mediterranean food, and fun pizzas such as the Switchback, with sun-dried tomatoes, peppers, and crumbled blue cheese. You can also check out the fresh juices, real espresso, and the best baked goods in town. Admire the fells from the outdoor tables or order takeout and hit the trail. ⊠ *Henderson's Yard, Bell Close* ☎ *017687/74492* ▤ *MC, V* ☉ *Closed Wed. No dinner Sept.–June.*

£££ ✕▦ **Highfield Hotel.** Slightly austere-looking and stubbornly old-fashioned, this smart, family-run Victorian hotel overlooks the lawns of Hope Park and has rooms with great character, including turret rooms and a former chapel that holds a four-poster. The balconies of the common areas have superb valley views. The restaurant's inventive, daily-changing menu takes advantage of local ingredients in dishes such as roast lamb with minted red currant jelly and pan-fried salmon with grilled eggplant and tomatoes. ⊠ *The Heads, CA12 5ER* ☎ *017687/72508* ⊟*017687/72508* ⊕*www.highfieldkeswick.co.uk* ➔*19 rooms* ♿ *Restaurant, bar, no-smoking rooms; no a/c, no room phones, no kids under 8* ▤ *AE, MC, V* ☉ *Closed mid-Nov.–Jan.* ⦿| *MAP.*

£–££ ✕▦ **Morrel's.** One of the town's better eating places is in this pleasant, good-value hotel. Red walls, wood floors, and abundant wine bottles add coziness, and the relaxed kitchen prepares innovative cuisine: a trout and roast pepper tart accompanies the roast cod, and the peppered tuna steak is served on lemongrass. The simple but delightful bedrooms are done in cheerful prints and pastels; rooms on the top floor have great views of the fells. ⊠ *34 Lake Rd., CA12 5DQ* ☎ *017687/72666* 🖷 *017687/74879* ⊕ *www.morrels.co.uk* ➥ *15 rooms* ♿ *Restaurant, bar, some pets allowed; no a/c, no room phones* ☰ *MC, V* ⑩ *BP.*

★ **£–££** 🖾 **Howe Keld.** Those in the know bypass the rows of cookie-cutter B&Bs and head here for a bit of budget TLC. The Fisher family puts you at ease in their comfortable, pretty town house–hotel. High-quality breakfasts are the big event; vegetarians do very well here with fresh home-baked bread and pancakes, but there are also traditional, meaty Cumbrian fry-ups. Evening meals (on request) are a good value. ⊠ *5–7 The Heads, CA12 5ES* ☎ *017687/72417* ⊕ *www.howekeld.co.uk* ➥ *15 rooms, 14 with bath* ♿ *Dining room, lounge, some pets allowed, no-smoking rooms; no a/c, no room phones* ☰ *No credit cards* ☉ *Closed Jan.* ⑩ *BP.*

Nightlife & the Arts

The **Keswick Film Club** (☎ 017687/72398) has an excellent festival in February and a program of international and classic films, screened at the Alhambra Cinema on St. John's Street and at the Theatre by the Lake. The popular **Keswick Jazz Festival** (☎ 017687/74411), held each May, consists of four days of music and events. Reservations are taken before Christmas.

The resident company at the **Theatre by the Lake** (⊠ Lake Rd. ☎ 017687/74411) presents classic and contemporary productions year-round. Touring music, opera, and dance companies also perform. The Keswick Music Society season runs from September through January, and the Words on the Water literary festival takes place in October.

Sports & the Outdoors

BIKING **Keswick Mountain Bike Centre** (⊠ Southey Hill ☎ 017687/75202) rents bikes and provides information on trails; it also stocks accessories and clothing. Guided tours can be arranged with advance notice.

FISHING Permits for fishing in Derwentwater and Bassenthwaite are available at **Field & Stream** (⊠ 79 Main St. ☎ 017687/74396).

WATER SPORTS **Derwentwater Marina** (⊠ Portinscale ☎ 017687/72912) offers boat rentals and instruction in canoeing, sailing, windsurfing, and rowing.

Shopping

Keswick has a good choice of bookstores, crafts shops, and wool-clothing stores tucked away in its cobbled streets, as well as excellent outdoor shops. Keswick's **market** is held Saturday.

Bryson's of Keswick (⊠ 42 Main St. ☎ 017687/71222) makes more than 250 varieties of baked goods daily and is renowned for hot savory pies and ice cream. You can also sample these goodies in the tearoom. **George Fisher** (⊠ 2 Borrowdale Rd. ☎ 017687/72178), the area's largest outdoor equipment store, sells sportswear, travel books, and maps. Daily weather information is posted in the window. **Needle Sports** (⊠ 56 Main St. ☎ 017687/72227) supplies equipment for mountaineering and for rock and ice climbing. The **Viridian Gallery** (✉ 13 St. John St. ☎ 017687/71328), a local artists' co-op, presents the paintings, prints, and ceramics of a half-dozen Cumbrian artists.

en route

The finest route from Keswick, B5289 south, runs along the eastern edge of Derwentwater, past turnoffs to natural attractions such as Ashness Bridge, the idyllic tarn of Watendlath, the Lodore Falls (best in wet weather), and the precariously balanced Bowder Stone. Farther south is the tiny village of **Grange,** a walking center at the head of Borrowdale, where there's a riverside café.

Borrowdale

14 *7 mi south of Keswick.*

Fodor's Choice ★

South of Keswick and its lake lies the valley of Borrowdale, whose varied landscape of green valley floor and surrounding crags has long been considered one of the region's most magnificent treasures. **Rosthwaite,** a tranquil farming village, and **Seatoller,** the southernmost settlement, are the two main centers (both are accessible by bus from Keswick), though they are little more than a cluster of aged buildings surrounded by glorious countryside. The **Lake District National Park Information Centre** has displays on the area, books accommodations, and sells maps and guides. ✉ *Dalehead Base, Seatoller Barn, Seatoller* ☎ *017687/77294* ⊕ *www.lake-district.gov.uk* ☉ *Late Mar.–early Nov., daily 10–5.*

The steep **Borrowdale Fells** rise up dramatically behind Seatoller. Get out and walk whenever inspiration strikes. England's highest mountain, the 3,210-foot **Scafell Pike** (pronounced *scar*-fell) is visible from Seatoller. One route up the mountain, for experienced walkers, is from the hamlet of Seathwaite, a mile south of Seatoller.

Where to Stay & Eat

£–££ ✕ **Yew Tree Restaurant.** Two 17th-century miners' cottages make up this intimate restaurant at the foot of Honister Pass. A low-beam ceiling, open fireplace, and excellent bar serving local Hesket Newmarket Brewery beers add appeal. The menu focuses on regional ingredients: Ullswater trout, Derwentwater pike, Herdwick burgers (known as "herdy burgers"), and wonderful Cumbrian cheeses and sausages. ✉ *B5289, Seatoller* ☎ *017687/77634* ▤ *MC, V* ☉ *Closed Mon. and 3 wks in Jan.*

££££ ▦ **Hazel Bank Country House.** Hikers and others appreciate the comforts of this stately, carefully restored Victorian home, which retains original elements such as the stained-glass windows. Immaculate, spacious bedrooms are done in a faux-Victorian theme, and some have four-posters and window seats. All rooms, including the sitting area, have splendid views across manicured lawns to the Borrowdale Valley and the central Lakeland peaks. Dinner (guests only) focuses on local ingredients prepared with modern British flair. ✉ *Off B5289, Rosthwaite, CA12 5XB* ☎ *017687/77248* 🖷 *017687/77373* ⊕ *www.hazelbankhotel.co.uk* ⤢ *8 rooms* ♿ *Dining room, lounge, Internet, business services; no a/c, no kids under 10, no smoking* ▤ *MC, V* ⦿ *MAP.*

> **en route** Beyond Seatoller, B5289 turns westward through **Honister Pass** (1,176 feet) and Buttermere Fell. It's a superb drive along one of the most dramatic of the region's roads, which is lined with huge boulders and at times channels through soaring rock canyons. The road sweeps down from the pass to the village of Buttermere, sandwiched between Buttermere (the lake) and Crummock Water at the foot of high, craggy fells.

Cockermouth

⑮ *14 mi northwest of Seatoller.*

This village at the confluence of the Rivers Derwent and Cocker has the briskness of a busy market town and a maze of narrow streets that are a delight to wander. There's no public access to the ruined 14th-century castle, but the outdoor market, held each Monday, retains its traditions.

Cockermouth was the birthplace of William Wordsworth (and his sister, Dorothy), whose childhood home, **Wordsworth House,** is a handsome 18th-century Georgian town house. Some of the poet's furniture and personal items are on display, and you can explore the terraced garden that inspired his childhood poetry, such as "To a Butterfly." The **Old Kitchen Tea Room** makes traditional Cumbrian cakes and is the perfect spot for afternoon tea. Incidentally, Wordsworth's father is buried in the All Saints' churchyard, and the church has a stained-glass window in memory of the poet. ⊠ *Main St.* ☎ *01900/824805* ⊕ *www.wordsworthhouse.org.uk* ⊡ *£4.50* ⊗ *Mar.–Sept., Mon.–Sat. 11–4:30; last admission at 4.*

Castlegate House Gallery displays and sells an outstanding collection of works by Cumbrian artists. Eight exhibitions a year focus on paintings, sculpture, glass, ceramics, and jewelry. ⊠ *Castlegate* ☎ *01900/822149* ⊕ *www.castlegatehouse.co.uk* ⊡ *£3* ⊗ *Mar.–Dec., Mon.–Wed., Fri., and Sat. 10:30–5, Sun. 2–5.*

The **Cumberland Toy and Model Museum** exhibits mainly British toys from 1900 to the present. Two buildings contain good model train collections, the re-creation of a 1930s toy shop, and dolls and dollhouses. There's a play area for younger children. ⊠ *Banks Ct. and Market Pl.* ☎ *01900/827606* ⊕ *www.toymuseum.co.uk* ⊡ *£3* ⊗ *Feb. and Nov., daily 10–4; Mar.–Oct., daily 10–5; Dec. and Jan., call for times.*

Where to Stay & Eat

★ **££** ✕ **Quince & Medlar.** Sophisticated vegetarian cuisine served by candlelight is the specialty at this wood-paneled Georgian town house. Choose from at least six main courses, such as couscous-crusted eggplant and poached pear filled with cheese pâté; all come with seasonal vegetables. Desserts are delicious, especially the pineapple tartlet and chocolate truffle terrine. ⊠ *13 Castlegate* ☎ *01900/823579* ▤ *MC, V* ⊗ *Closed Sun. and Mon. No lunch.*

££ ▦ **Allerdale Court Hotel.** At this 17th-century coaching inn, which may have been home to famous mutineer Fletcher Christian, original oak beams provide a touch of old-fashioned charm, although the furnishings are mostly modern. The rooms with four-posters verge on the regal. Pickwick's restaurant serves English fare, from Lakeland pheasant to char-grilled halibut, and Oscar's specializes in grills, pizzas, and Italian dishes. ⊠ *20 Market Pl., CA13 9NQ* ☎ *01900/823654* 🖷 *01900/823033* ⊕ *www.allerdalecourthotel.co.uk* ➳ *28 rooms* ⟑ *2 restaurants, in-room data ports, bar, some pets allowed; no a/c* ▭ *MC, V* ⦿ *BP.*

Bassenthwaite

⑯ *6 mi east of Cockermouth, 4 mi north of Keswick.*

The small village of Bassenthwaite, at the northern end of Bassenthwaite Lake, is one of the most beautiful in the Lake District. The lake itself is the only body of water called a lake in the Lake District; the others are known as "meres" or "waters." Bird-watchers know this less-frequented lake well because of the many species of migratory birds found here. The shoreline habitat is the best-preserved in the national park—in part because most of it is privately owned, and also because motorboats are not allowed. Posh accommodations and good restaurants dot the area, and popular walks include the climb up Skiddaw (3,054 feet), which, on a clear day, has panoramic views of the Lake District, Pennines, Scotland, and the Isle of Man from its summit.

Where to Stay & Eat

★ **£££–££££** ✕🖬 **The Pheasant.** You won't find better service than at this traditional 17th-century coaching inn, which exudes English coziness without the usual Lakeland fussiness. Settle into a sofa by an open fire in the elegant sitting room, painted in subdued tones of butter yellow and sage green. The tasteful, modern bedrooms overlook 60 acres of forest, and a wood-beamed restaurant serves superb English fare such as venison with mushrooms and shallots, as well as a fine afternoon tea with cakes and scones. Varnished walls, oak settles, and hunting prints set the mood in the popular bar. The Pheasant is halfway between Cockermouth and Keswick. ⊠ *Off A66, Bassenthwaite Lake, CA13 9YE* ☎ *017687/76234* 🖷 *017687/76002* ⊕ *www.the-pheasant.co.uk* ➳ *16 rooms, 2 suites* ⟑ *Restaurant, bar, 3 lounges, Internet, business services, some pets allowed; no a/c, no room TVs* ▭ *MC, V* ⦿ *BP.*

LAKE DISTRICT A TO Z

To research prices, get advice from other travelers, and book travel arrangements, visit www.fodors.com.

AIRPORTS

Manchester Airport has its own rail station with direct service to Carlisle, Windermere, and Barrow-in-Furness. Manchester is 70 mi from the southern part of the Lake District.

🖪 **Manchester Airport** ⊠ Near Junctions 5 and 6 of M56 ☎ 0161/489-3000 ⊕ www.manairport.co.uk.

BIKE TRAVEL

Cycling along the numerous bicycle paths and quiet forest roads in Cumbria is pleasurable and safe. The Cumbria Cycle Way circles the county, and for local excursions guided bike tours are often available, starting at about £25 per day. Contact local tourist offices or bike rental places for details on cycle routes.

BOAT & FERRY TRAVEL

Keswick-on-Derwentwater Launch Company conducts cruises on vintage motor launches around Derwentwater, leaving from Keswick. Coniston Launch connects Coniston with Ruskin's home at Brantwood, offering hourly service for most of the year (service is reduced in winter) on its wooden *Ruskin* and *Ransome* launches. Steam Yacht *Gondola* runs the National Trust's luxurious Victorian steam yacht between Coniston, Brantwood, and Park-a-Moor at the south end of Coniston Water, daily from April through October. Ullswater Steamers sends its oil-burning, 19th-century steamers the length of Ullswater between Glenridding and Pooley Bridge. The service operates 363 days a year, and its Web site suggests walks that tie in with sailings. Windermere Lake Cruises employs modern launches and vintage cruisers year-round between Ambleside, Bowness, Brockhole, and Lakeside. Ticket prices vary; a Freedom of the Lake ticket (£10) gives unlimited travel on any of the ferries for 24 hours.

FARES & SCHEDULES **Coniston Launch** ☎ 015394/36216 ⊕ www.conistonlaunch.co.uk. **Keswick-on-Derwentwater Launch Co.** ☎ 017687/72263 ⊕ www.keswick-launch.co.uk. **Steam Yacht Gondola** ☎ 015394/41288 ⊕ www.nationaltrust.org.uk. **Ullswater Steamers** ☎ 017684/82229 ⊕ www.ullswater-steamers.co.uk. **Windermere Lake Cruises** ☎ 015395/31188 ⊕ www.windermere-lakecruises.co.uk.

BUS TRAVEL

Traveline handles public transportation inquiries. National Express serves the region from London's Victoria Coach Station and from Manchester's Chorlton Street Station. Average travel time to Kendal is just over 7 hours from London; to Windermere, 7½ hours; and to Keswick, 8¼ hours. From Manchester there's one bus a day to Windermere (3½ hours); it stops in Ambleside, Grasmere, and Keswick. There's direct bus service to the Lake District from Carlisle, Lancaster, and York.

Stagecoach in Cumbria provides local service between Lakeland towns and through the valleys and high passes. Contact Traveline for an up-to-date timetable. A one-day Explorer Ticket (£6) is available on the bus and valid on all routes. Service between main tourist centers is fairly frequent on weekdays, but much reduced on weekends and bank holidays. Don't count on reaching the more remote parts of the area by bus. Off-the-beaten-track touring requires a car or strong legs.

CUTTING COSTS The YHA Shuttle Bus operates a door-to-door service for guests at eight popular hostels in the Lakes (Easter through October only). Get on and off where you like for £2 a journey, or send your luggage ahead to the next hostel if you want to walk unencumbered. The trip from Windermere station to the Windermere or Ambleside hostel is free.

🚌 **YHA Shuttle Bus** ✉ Ambleside Youth Hostel, Waterhead ☎ 015394/32304.

🚌 **National Express** ☎ 0870/580-8080 ⊕ www.nationalexpress.com. **Traveline** ☎ 0870/608-2608 ⊕ www.traveline.org.uk.

CAR RENTAL

🚗 **Local Agencies Avis** ✉ Station Rd., Kendal ☎ 01539/733582. **Interental Ltd** ✉ Brant Cell Garage, Kendal Rd., Bowness-on-Windermere ☎ 015394/44408. **Keswick Motor Company** ✉ Lake Rd., Keswick ☎ 017687/72064.

CAR TRAVEL

To reach the Lake District from London, take M1 north to M6, getting off either at Junction 36 and joining A590/A591 west (around the Kendal bypass to Windermere) or at Junction 40, joining A66 direct to Keswick and the northern lakes region. Travel time to Kendal is about four hours, to Keswick five to six hours. Expect heavy traffic out of London on weekends to all destinations in the Northwest; construction work also often slows progress on M6.

ROAD
CONDITIONS
Roads within the region are generally very good, although many minor routes and mountain passes can be both steep and narrow. Warning signs are normally posted if snow has made a road impassable; always listen to local weather forecasts in winter before heading out. In July and August and during the long public holiday weekends, expect heavy traffic. The Lake District has plenty of parking lots, which should be used to avoid blocking narrow lanes.

EMERGENCIES

🚑 **Ambulance, fire, police** ☎ 999. **Keswick Cottage Hospital** ✉ Croswaithe Rd., Keswick ☎ 017687/72012. **Penrith New Hospital** ✉ Bridge La., Penrith ☎ 017687/245300. **Westmorland General Hospital** ✉ Burton Rd., Kendal ☎ 01539/732288.

NATIONAL PARKS

The Lake District National Park head office (and main visitor center) is at Brockhole, north of Windermere. There are also helpful regional national park information centers.

🏞 **Lake District National Park** ✉ Brockhole, A591, Ambleside Rd., Windermere ☎ 015394/46601 ⊕ www.lake-district.gov.uk. **Bowness Bay** ✉ Glebe Rd., Bowness-on-Windermere ☎ 015394/42895. **Coniston** ✉ Ruskin Ave. ☎ 015394/41533. **Glenridding** ✉ Beckside Car Park ☎ 017684/82414. **Grasmere** ✉ Red Bank Rd. ☎ 015394/35245. **Hawkshead** ✉ Main Car Park ☎ 015394/36525. **Keswick** ✉ Moot Hall, Main St. ☎ 017687/72645. **Pooley Bridge** ✉ Finkle St. ☎ 017684/86530. **Seatoller** ✉ B5289 ☎ 017687/77294. **Waterhead** ✉ Waterhead, Ambleside ☎ 015394/32729.

TOURS

BUS TOURS
Mountain Goat Holidays, Lakes Supertours, and Park Tours & Travel provide minibus sightseeing tours with skilled local guides. Half- and full-day tours, which really get off the beaten track, depart from Bowness, Windermere, Ambleside, and Grasmere.

🚌 **Lakes Supertours** ✉ 1 High St., Windermere ☎ 015394/42751 ⊕ www.lakes-supertours.co.uk. **Mountain Goat Holidays** ✉ Victoria St., Windermere ☎ 015394/45161 ⊕ www.lakes-pages.co.uk/goatmain.html. **Park Tours & Travel** ✉ The Lodge, Burnside Park, Windermere ☎ 015394/48600 ⊕ www.parktours.co.uk.

WALKING TOURS You can find walks from gentle, literary-oriented strolls to challenging ridge hikes. The Lake District National Park (⇨ National Parks) or the Cumbria Tourist Board in Windermere (⇨ Visitor Information) can put you in touch with qualified guides. Blue Badge Guides can provide experts on the area. English Lakeland Ramblers organizes single-base and inn-to-inn guided tours of the Lake District from May through October. Go Higher will take you on the more challenging routes and provides technical gear and courses on mountaineering skills.

🔢 **Blue Badge Guides** ☎ 020/7403-1115 ⊕ www.blue-badge.org.uk. **English Lakeland Ramblers** ✉ 18 Stuyvesant Oval, #1A, New York, NY 10009 ☎ 01229/587382, 212/505-1020 or 800/724-8801 in U.S. ⊕ www.ramblers.com. **Go Higher** ✉ High Dyon Side, Distington ☎ 01946/830476 ⊕ www.gohigher.co.uk.

TRAIN TRAVEL

For schedule information, call National Rail Enquiries. Two train companies serve the region from London's Euston Station: take a Virgin or First North Western train bound for Carlisle, Edinburgh, or Glasgow and change at Oxenholme for the branch line service to Kendal and Windermere. Average travel time to Windermere (including the change) is 4½ hours. If you're heading for Keswick, you can either take the train to Windermere and continue from there by Stagecoach bus (Bus 555/556; 70 minutes), or stay on the main London–Carlisle train to Penrith Station (four hours), from which Stagecoach buses (Bus X5) also run to Keswick (45 minutes). Direct trains from Manchester depart for Windermere five times daily (travel time two hours). First North Western runs a local service from Windermere and Barrow-in-Furness to Manchester Airport.

Train connections are good around the edges of the Lake District, especially on the Oxenholme–Kendal–Windermere line and the Furness and West Cumbria branch line from Lancaster to Grange-over-Sands, Ulverston, Barrow, and Ravenglass. However, these services aren't useful for getting around the central Lakeland region (you must take the bus or drive), and they are reduced, or nonexistent, on Sunday.

FARES & 🔢 **First North Western** ☎ 08456/001159 ⊕ www.firstnorthwestern.co.uk. **National**
SCHEDULES **Rail Enquiries** ☎ 0845/748-4950 ⊕ www.nationalrail.co.uk. **Virgin Trains** ☎ 0845/722-2333 ⊕ www.virgintrains.co.uk.

TRAVEL AGENCIES

🔢 **Local Agent Referrals Gates Travel** ✉ 9 Library Rd., Kendal ☎ 01539/720148 ✉ Ruskin House, Market Pl., Ambleside ☎ 01539/433200.

VISITOR INFORMATION

Cumbria Tourist Board is open Monday–Thursday 9:30–5:30 and Friday 9:30–5.

🔢 **Cumbria Tourist Board** ✉ Ashleigh, Holly Rd., Windermere, LA23 2AQ ☎ 015394/44444 ⊕ www.golakes.co.uk. **Youth Hostel Association England and Wales** ✉ Trevelyan House, Matlock, Derbyshire, DE4 3YH ☎ 0870/870-8808 ⊕ www.yha.org.uk. **Ambleside** ✉ Central Bldgs., Market Cross, Rydal Rd. ☎ 015394/32582. **Cockermouth** ✉ The Town Hall, Market St. ☎ 01900/822634. **Coniston** ✉ Ruskin Ave. ☎ 015394/41533. **Gras-**

mere ⊠ Red Bank Rd. ☎ 015394/35245. **Hawkshead** ⊠ Main Car Park ☎ 015394/36525. **Kendal** ⊠ Town Hall, Highgate ☎ 01539/725758. **Keswick** ⊠ Moot Hall, Market Sq. ☎ 017687/72645. **Penrith** ⊠ Penrith Museum, Middlegate ☎ 01768/867466. **Ullswater** ⊠ Main Car Park, Glenridding ☎ 017684/82414. **Windermere** ⊠ The Gateway Centre, Victoria St. ☎ 015394/46499.

EAST ANGLIA

CAMBRIDGE, BURY ST. EDMUNDS, NORWICH, LINCOLN

12

FLOAT IN A PUNT ON THE RIVER CAM
for the best view of Cambridge ⇨ p.566

THRILL TO MUSIC BY THE SEA
at the Aldeburgh Festival ⇨ p.582

SEE BRITAIN'S MOST SPLENDID ROOM
in Palladian Holkham Hall ⇨ p.590

FEEL THE SAND BETWEEN YOUR TOES
on a beach walk near Wells ⇨ p.589

RECAPTURE TUDOR TIMES
in small, sweet Lavenham village ⇨ p.571

EXPLORE GENTLE HILLS AND FIELDS
around picture-perfect Dedham ⇨ p.577

PREVIEW HEAVEN AND HELL
on Burghley House's ceilings ⇨ p.595

LET YOUR SPIRITS SOAR
at towering Ely Cathedral ⇨ p.567

Updated by
Catherine
Belonogoff

ONE OF THOSE BEAUTIFUL ENGLISH INCONSISTENCIES, East Anglia has no spectacular mountains or rivers to disturb the storied, quiet land, full of rural delights such as tulip fields, flint churches, and thatched-roof cottages. Occupying an area of southeastern England that juts, knoblike, into the North Sea, its counties of Essex, Norfolk, Suffolk, Lincolnshire, and Cambridgeshire are a bit cut off from the central routes and pulse of Britain. People from London once called the region "silly Suffolk" and referred to the citizens of Norfolk county as "Norfolk Dumplings." In modern times, when life for many is busy and stressful, these terms strike an almost complimentary note.

This area has also been home to some of Britain's greatest thinkers, artists, and poets. John Milton, Francis Bacon, Sir Isaac Newton, Lord Byron, William Thackeray, and Alfred, Lord Tennyson were educated at Cambridge University, one of the world's most important centers of learning and arguably the world's most attractive university town. Here, Oliver Cromwell groomed his Roundhead troops, and Tom Paine, the man who wrote "These are the times that try men's souls," developed his revolutionary ideas. Here, John Constable painted *The Hay Wain*, along with luscious landscapes of the Stour Valley, and Thomas Gainsborough achieved eminence as England's most elegant portraitist. If East Anglia has remained rural to a large extent, its harvest of legendary minds has been just as impressive as its agricultural crops.

Despite its easy access from London, East Anglia remains relatively unfamiliar to visitors, with the notable exception of Cambridge and, to a lesser degree, North Norfolk, where the unspoiled villages have become fashionable. It was a region of major importance in ancient times, as evidenced by the Roman settlements at Colchester and Lincoln; and during the medieval era, when trade in wool with the Netherlands made East Anglian towns strong and independent. But with the lack of main thoroughfares and canals, the Industrial Revolution mercifully passed East Anglia by.

As a result of being a historical backwater, the region is enormously rich in quiet villages, presided over by ancient churches, tiny settlements in the midst of otherwise deserted fenland (lowlands), and manor houses surrounded by moats. Few parts of Britain can claim so many stately churches and half-timber houses. The towns are more like large villages; even the largest city, Norwich, has a population of only about 130,000.

If you find the region's mostly quiet, flat spaces dull, you need travel only a few miles to reach the bright lights: four splendid stately houses—Holkham Hall, Blickling Hall, Houghton Hall, and Her Majesty's own Sandringham. There are incomparable cathedrals, at Ely and Lincoln particularly, and the "finest flower of Gothic in Europe," King's College Chapel in Cambridge. These are the superlatives of East Anglia. But half the attraction of the region lies in its subtle landscapes, where the beauties of rural England appear at their enduring best. To rush in search of one or two highlights is to miss these qualities, which only leisurely journeys along the byways can reveal.

12

East Anglia's reputation for being flat and featureless is mostly undeserved. But although the lowland marsh country in the west, the fens, may yield more vegetables than it does tourist attractions, you need more than a few days to soak up the medieval atmosphere of Norfolk, Suffolk, and the unspoiled coastal villages—including time to linger in a pub over a pint of locally brewed beer. On a three-day trip, it's best to concentrate on one area, probably Cambridge and its surroundings, rather than try to cover the distances separating major sights and towns. A stay of eight days would enable you to explore more highlights and to match your step to the area's slow pace; take time to follow some of the tiny country lanes.

Numbers in the text correspond to numbers in the margin and on the East Anglia, Cambridge, Norwich, and Lincolnshire maps.

If you have 3 days

🖼 **Cambridge ❶–❶ ⬥** is easy to visit even as a day trip from London—too easy, some say, to judge by the huge number of visitors year-round. It's also the best base from which to explore a bit of East Anglia. Explore some of the ancient university buildings, stroll along the Backs, or punt down the River Cam to Grantchester. The next day, head for **Ely ❶** and spend a few hours exploring the medieval town and its majestic cathedral before moving on to **Bury St. Edmunds ❷**, a town with graceful Georgian streets. Spend the third day exploring the medieval Suffolk wool towns of **Sudbury ❶**, **Long Melford ❷**, and **Lavenham ❷** before returning to Cambridge.

If you have 8 days

Start from 🖼 **Cambridge ❶–❶ ⬥** and take in the medieval sights on your first day. Spend the night and then head out to **Saffron Walden ❶** and northeast, overnighting in 🖼 **Bury St. Edmunds ❷**. Explore the town the next day, making time to visit the Abbey Ruins and Botanical Gardens, and then head south through **Long Melford ❷**, **Lavenham ❷**, and **Sudbury ❶** (with a quick stopover to see Gainsborough's House) to 🖼 **Colchester ❷**, the traditional base for exploring Constable Country. The next day, head for Constable's **Dedham ❷**, then take the B1084 to 🖼 **Orford ❷**, a tiny village with a Norman church and castle and traditional smokehouses for preparing fish. Spend the next day exploring Sutton Hoo near 🖼 **Woodbridge ❷** or 🖼 **Aldeburgh ❷**; you may also want to visit **Southwold ❷**, a seaside town where time seems to have stood still. Travel to 🖼 **Norwich ❷–❸** and visit its cathedral and medieval alleys. The extensive journey northwest to 🖼 **Lincoln ❹**, where you can spend your sixth night, takes you through flat fenland. En route, you can visit **King's Lynn ❹** or detour north toward the coast to visit one or two spectacular stately homes, such as **Blickling Hall ❸**, Holkham Hall in **Wells-next-the-Sea ❹**, **Sandringham House ❹**, and **Houghton Hall ❹**. Lincoln is worthy of a day's exploration: on the way back to Cambridge the next day, opt to stop either at **Ely ❶**, to see its great cathedral, or at **Stamford ❹** to visit Burghley House, an Elizabethan extravaganza.

Exploring East Anglia

For purposes of sightseeing, East Anglia can be divided into distinct areas: the central area surrounding the ancient university city of Cambridge and including the towns of inland Suffolk; the southeast, taking in the ancient Roman town of Colchester and sweeping upward along the Suffolk Heritage Coast; and the northeast, with the region's capital, Norwich, the waterways of Broadland, and the beaches and salt marshes of the North Norfolk coast. North of Cambridge, the fenland city of Ely has a magnificent cathedral rising out of the flatlands. Farther north, in Lincolnshire, are the city of Lincoln, landmarked by its tall, fluted cathedral towers, and the historic ports of King's Lynn and Boston, which flank the shallow bay known as the Wash.

About the Restaurants

In summer the coast gets so packed with people that reservations are essential at restaurants. Getting something to eat at other than regular mealtime hours is not always possible in small towns; look for cafés if you want a mid-morning or after-lunch snack.

About the Hotels

Few hotels in East Anglia have more than 100 rooms, so even the biggest hostelries offer friendly, personal service. In addition, few English regions have quite so many centuries-old, half-timber inns with rooms full of roaring fires and cozy bars. Cambridge has relatively few hotels downtown, and these tend to be rather overpriced. Bed-and-breakfasts are a cheaper alternative. It's always busy in Cambridge and along the coast in summer, so reserve well in advance.

WHAT IT COSTS In pounds				
	£££££	££££	£££	££	£
RESTAURANTS	over £22	£18–£22	£13–£17	£7–£12	under £7
HOTELS	over £160	£120–£160	£90–£120	£60–£90	under £60

Restaurant prices are for a main course at dinner. Hotel prices are for two people in a standard double room in high season, including VAT, with no meals or, if indicated, CP (with Continental breakfast), BP (Breakfast Plan, with full breakfast), or MAP (Modified American Plan, with breakfast and dinner).

Timing

Summer and late spring are the best times to visit. Avoid late fall and winter, as the weather can be cold, windy, and rainy. If you want to escape crowds, stay away from the popular Norfolk Broads in late July and August. The May Bumps, intercollegiate boat races, are, confusingly, held the first week of June in Cambridge. During the summer "long vac," Cambridge is empty of its students, its life and soul. To see the city in full swing, visit from October through June, although in summer there are enjoyable festivals, notably the Strawberry Fair (mid-June), and the Folk Festival and Arts Festival (both July). The world-famous Aldeburgh Festival of music and the arts, started in 1948 by Benjamin Britten, takes

Biking There's a good reason why Cambridge instantly conjures up the image of the undergraduate hurtling along the streets on a bicycle with academic gown flowing behind. It's an ideal city to traverse by bike, and everyone seems to do so. The same can be said for the entire region. "Very flat, Norfolk," Noël Coward's remark, is something of an overstatement; nonetheless, many of the flat coastal areas of East Anglia, although sometimes windswept, are perfect for cycling. A network of cycle routes and bike rental centers provides a good means of getting around the towpaths and backwaters of the Norfolk Broads, and there's good biking in North Norfolk.

12

The Landscape For many people, the joy of East Anglia is its very separateness, its desolate landscapes and isolated beaches. Of these, the fens (marshy lowlands) of northern Cambridgeshire and the Broads (expanded rivers) of Norfolk are the most dramatic—or depressing, depending on your mood. The water in the marshes and dikes reflects the arching sky, whose cloud-scapes are ever-changing, stretching toward seemingly infinite horizons. The sunsets are to be treasured. The fens resemble areas of Holland across the North Sea, and, indeed, work on much of the drainage system here was carried out by Dutch engineers beginning in the 17th century. In both Norfolk and Suffolk, the reed-bordered Broads make a gentle landscape of canals and lakes that are ideal for boating and are alive with birds and animals. The Suffolk Heritage Coast includes 40 mi of unspoiled coastline, with marshes, beaches, and broads. A compelling landscape emerges on the North Norfolk coast, where the sweeping expanses of sand beaches (good for walking, despite the wind) are backed by thin swathes of pine forest.

Walking East Anglia is a walker's dream. The long-distance footpath known as the Peddar's Way follows the line of a pre-Roman road, running from near Thetford through heathland, pine forests, and arable fields, and on through rolling chalk lands to the Norfolk coast near Hunstanton. The Norfolk Coastal Path then continues eastward along the coast, joining at Cromer with the delightfully varied Weaver's Way, which passes through medieval weaving villages and deeply rural parts of the Norfolk Broads on its 56-mi route from Cromer to Great Yarmouth. Birders or anyone interested in birds should carry binoculars and a bird identification book, as both of these routes have abundant avian life—both local and migratory.

place in June. King's Lynn and Norwich have renowned music and arts festivals, in July and October, respectively.

CAMBRIDGE

▶ If you want to think about Cambridge, think Rupert Brooke, the short-lived World War I–era poet ("There is some corner of a foreign field/ That is forever England"), a Cambridgeshire lad, who called his county

East Anglia

"The shire for Men who Understand." Think William Wordsworth and Thackeray, Byron and Tennyson, E. M. Forster and C. S. Lewis; and see *Chariots of Fire,* the 1981 film version of the true story of Harold Abrahams, a Cambridge graduate who shone in the 1924 Olympic Games. The exquisite King's College choir defines the Christmas season for an entire nation, when the *Festival of Nine Lessons and Carols* is broadcast live on Christmas Eve.

With the spires of its university buildings framed by towering trees and expansive meadows, its medieval streets and passages enhanced by gardens and riverbanks, the city of Cambridge is among the loveliest in England. Situated on a bend of the River Cam, 54 mi north of London, and 63 mi southwest of Norwich, this is also one of the most ancient cities in Britain, its foundation lost in the mists of time. This is no mere cliché, for the mists that rise from the surrounding water meadows bedevil Cambridge. Certainly the city predates the Roman occupation of Britain. There's similar confusion about when the university was founded. Its origins may lie with masters from Oxford who brought pupils to Cambridge in 1209 to escape Oxford's town-versus-gown troubles. Another story attributes its founding to impoverished students from Oxford, who came in search of eels—a cheap source of nourishment.

Keep in mind there is no recognizable campus: the scattered colleges *are* the university. The town reveals itself only slowly, filled with tiny gardens, ancient courtyards, imposing classic buildings, alleyways that lead past medieval churches, and wisteria-hung facades. Perhaps the best views are from the Backs, the green parkland that extends along the River Cam behind several colleges. Here you feel the essence of Cambridge. Resulting from the larger size of the colleges and from the lack of industrialization in the city center, this broad, sweeping openness is just what distinguishes Cambridge from Oxford.

For centuries the University of Cambridge has been among the greatest universities, rivaled in Britain only by Oxford; since the time of its most famous scientific alumnus, Sir Isaac Newton, it has outshone Oxford in the natural sciences. The university has taken advantage of its scientific prestige, pooling its research facilities with high-tech industries. As a result, the city is surrounded by IT companies and has been dubbed "Silicon Fen" in comparison to California's Silicon Valley. The prosperity brought by these businesses has enlivened the city.

Exploring Cambridge

Exploring the city means, in large part, exploring the university. Each of the 25 oldest colleges is built around a series of courts, or quadrangles, whose velvety lawns are the envy of many a gardener. Since students and fellows (faculty) live and work in these courts, access is sometimes restricted, and at *all* times you are requested to refrain from picnicking in the quadrangles. Visitors are not normally allowed into college buildings other than chapels, dining halls, and some libraries; some colleges charge admission for certain buildings. The university's Web site, ⊕ www.cam.ac.uk, has information about the colleges and other institutions associated with it. Public visiting hours vary from col-

Cambridge

Christ's College **5**

Emmanuel College **4**

Fitzwilliam Museum **15**

Jesus College **7**

Kettle's Yard **9**

King's College Chapel . . . **12**

Magdalene College **8**

Museum of Archaeology
and Anthropology **3**

Pembroke College **2**

Peterhouse College **1**

Queens' College **14**

St. John's College **10**

Sidney Sussex College . . . **6**

Trinity College **11**

Trinity Hall College **13**

University
Botanic Gardens **16**

lege to college, depending on the time of year, and it's best to call or to check with the city tourist office. Colleges close to visitors during the main exam time, late May to mid-June. Term time (when classes are in session) means roughly October to December, January to March, and April to June; summer term, or vacation, runs from July to September.

When the colleges are open, the best way to gain access is to join a walking tour led by an official Blue Badge guide—many areas are off-limits unless you do. The two-hour tours leave up to five times daily from the city tourist office. The other traditional view of the colleges is gained from a punt—the boats propelled by pole on the River Cam.

a good walk

Start at **Peterhouse College ❶** ▶, the granddaddy of them all, founded by the bishop of Ely in 1281. One of the colleges closest to the train station, it lies on one side of Trumpington Street and stands across the way from **Pembroke College ❷**—the "College of Poets," as graduates have included Edmund Spenser and Thomas Gray—where you can gain a glimpse of the 17th-century work of architect Christopher Wren in the college's chapel. From the Arts, head over to the Sciences. Walk up to Pembroke Street, turn right, and continue on Downing Street for the engaging **Museum of Archaeology and Anthropology ❸**. At the end of Downing Street you face **Emmanuel College ❹**, and more of Wren's work. You then turn left up the shopping arteries of St. Andrew's Street and Sidney Street, passing the often overlooked **Christ's College ❺**, with fine buildings from different periods. Continue along St. Andrew's Street and Sidney Street to **Sidney Sussex College ❻**—look for the portrait of Oliver Cromwell in the Hall—before turning right down Jesus Lane for one of the prettiest of all colleges, **Jesus College ❼**. Note the Chapter House entrance and the chapel's Pre-Raphaelite stained glass.

Head farther north up Sidney Street and Bridge Street to Magdalene Bridge, where you're likely to see punts on the River Cam. By the river, quiet **Magdalene College ❽** flanks busy Magdalene Street—one of the glories of Cambridge is how quickly you can move from frantic, modern England to the seclusion of scholarly academe. A little farther north on the other side, museums beckon: the art displays in **Kettle's Yard ❾** and the city-related exhibits of the **Folk Museum.** Heading south, back into the city center, cross back over the river and down St. John's Street, past **St. John's ❿** and **Trinity ⓫** colleges. In St. John's you can view the Bridge of Sighs, modeled after its Venetian namesake. Trinity is Sir Isaac Newton's college, and outside the Great Gate stands an apple tree said to be a descendant of the one whose falling fruit caused Newton to formulate the laws of gravity. Ahead lies Cambridge's most famous sight, the soaring, late-Gothic **King's College Chapel ⓬**. King's College itself faces King's Parade, where students bustle in and out of coffee shops; you can climb the tower of **Great St. Mary's,** the university's main church, for a glorious city view. Behind King's, the city's Backs—its riverside gardens and meadows—make their presence felt at **Trinity Hall ⓭** and **Queens' ⓮** colleges, both of which will lure you off the beaten path. Silver Street Bridge, by Queens', is another traditional spot to hire a chauffeured punt. To complete the circuit, regain King's Parade and walk south, down to where it becomes Trumpington Street. Call in at the Church of Little

St. Mary and pause at the monument to the Washington family on the wall to your left just inside the door. You then pass Peterhouse, where you started. Just beyond, the **Fitzwilliam** ⑮ is Cambridge's finest museum, with superb art and classical collections, or you can recuperate in the **University Botanic Gardens** ⑯, at least 10 minutes beyond, off Trumpington Street on Bateman Street. Ah, academia!

TIMING You can walk this route in two hours, but it's easy to spend a full day here if you visit the museums and explore some of the colleges. Note that many museums are closed Monday. It's possible to tour the colleges and grounds much of the year except during exams in May and June, but call the Cambridge Tourist Information Centre or the specific college to check in advance; opening hours can be complicated.

What to See

off the beaten path

CHILFORD HALL – One of the area's premier wineries, producing white and pink wines, offers tours of the vineyard and wine-making process. The gift shop and café have a good selection of local products, from jam to wine. ⊠ *Off B1052, Linton, 12 mi east of Cambridge* ☎ *01223/895600* ⊕ *www.chilfordhall.co.uk* ⊠ *Free* ⊙ *Mar.–Oct., daily 11–5:30; Nov.–mid-Dec., daily 11–4.*

❺ **Christ's College.** To see the way a college has grown over the centuries you could not do better than visit here. The main gateway bears the enormous coat of arms of its patroness, Lady Margaret Beaufort, mother of Henry VII, who established the institution in 1505. It leads into a fine courtyard, with the chapel framed by an ancient magnolia. In the dining hall hang portraits of John Milton and Charles Darwin, two of the college's more famous students. Admitted in 1625 at age 16, Milton resided in a first-floor room on the first stair on the north side of the first court. You next walk past a fellows' building credited to Inigo Jones, to the spacious garden (once the haunt of Milton), and finally to a modern zigguratlike confection. ⊠ *St. Andrew's St.* ☎ *01223/334900* ⊕ *www.christs.cam.ac.uk* ⊙ *Term time, except exam period, daily 9:30–4:30; July–Sept., daily 9:30–noon.*

❹ **Emmanuel College.** The master hand of architect Christopher Wren (1632–1723) is evident throughout much of Cambridge, particularly at Emmanuel, built on the site of a Dominican friary, where he designed the chapel and colonnade. A stained-glass window in the chapel has a likeness of John Harvard, founder of Harvard University, who studied here. The college, founded in 1584, was an early center of Puritan learning; a number of the Pilgrims were Emmanuel alumni, and they remembered their alma mater in naming Cambridge, Massachusetts. ⊠ *St. Andrew's St.* ☎ *01223/334200* ⊕ *www.emma.cam.ac.uk* ⊙ *Daily 9–6, except exam period.*

★ ⑮ **Fitzwilliam Museum.** In a classical revival building renowned for its grand Corinthian portico, the Fitzwilliam, founded by the seventh viscount Fitzwilliam of Merrion in 1816, has one of Britain's most outstanding collections of art (including paintings by Constable, Gainsborough, the Pre-Raphaelites, and the French impressionists) and antiquities. The opulent interior displays its treasures to marvelous effect, with the Egyptian section in the lower gallery particularly noteworthy. Exhibits range from rare sculptures dating to the Chinese Han dynasty of the 3rd century BC, to inch-high figurines and burial goods, to mummies, painted coffins, and stone inscriptions. Besides its archaeological collections, the Fitzwilliam contains a large display of English Staffordshire and other pottery, as well as a fascinating room full of armor and muskets. ⊠ *Trumpington St.* ☎ *01223/332900* ⊕ *www.fitzmuseum.cam.ac.uk* ☞ *Free* ⊙ *Tues.–Sat. 10–5, Sun. 2:15–5; guided tours Sun. at 2:45.*

Folk Museum. In a city where "gown" often dominates "town," this museum adjacent to Kettle's Yard redresses the balance a little. In the former 16th-century White Horse Inn, Cambridgeshire's folk history is brought to life in eight rooms that display crafts, toys, trade utensils, paintings, and domestic paraphernalia in glorious profusion. ⊠ *2–3 Castle St.* ☎ *01223/355159* ⊕ *www.folkmuseum.org.uk* ☞ *£2.50* ⊙ *Apr.–Sept., Mon.–Sat. 10:30–5, Sun. 2–5; Oct.–Mar., Tues.–Sat. 10:30–5, Sun. 2–5.*

off the beaten path

GRANTCHESTER – This little village 2 mi up the river is a delightful 2-mi walk or bicycle ride from the center of Cambridge along a signposted riverside path through college playing-fields and the Grantchester Meadows. It was put on the map by its famous son, Rupert Brooke, whose line "Stands the church clock at ten to three? And is there honey still for tea?" is from his poem *The Old Vicarage, Grantchester.* You also can reach the village enjoyably, if challengingly, by punting upstream along the Cam.

Great St. Mary's. Known as the "university church," Great St. Mary's has its origins in the 11th century, although the current building dates from 1478. The main reason to visit is to climb the 113-foot tower, which has a superb view over the colleges and the colorful marketplace. ⊠ *Market Hill, King's Parade* ☎ *01223/741716* ⊕ *www.ely.anglican. org* ☞ *Free, tower £2* ⊙ *Mon.–Sat. 9:30–5:30, Sun. noon–5:30.*

off the beaten path

IMPERIAL WAR MUSEUM DUXFORD – The buildings and grounds of this former airfield, now Europe's leading aviation museum, house a remarkable collection of 180 aircraft from Europe and the United States. You can trace technological developments as well as military history through the exhibits. The **Land Warfare Hall** holds tanks and other military vehicles. The **American Air Museum,** in a striking Norman Foster–designed building, contains American combat aircraft. It honors the 30,000 Americans who were killed in action flying from Britain during World War II; Duxford itself was the headquarters of the 78th Fighter Group. Check in advance for air shows (extra charge). The museum is 10 mi south of Cambridge, and a shuttle bus runs throughout the day from Cambridge's Crowne Plaza hotel to the Cambridge train station and Duxford. ⊠ *A505, Duxford* ☎ *01223/835000* ⊕ *www.iwm.org.uk* ☞ *£10* ⊙ *Mid-Mar.–Oct., daily 10–6; Nov.–mid-Mar., daily 10–4.*

7 Jesus College. Unique in Cambridge, the spacious grounds of Jesus College incorporate cloisters, a remnant of the nunnery of St. Radegund, which existed on the site before the college was founded in 1496. Cloister Court exudes a quiet medieval charm, an attribute evident in the adjacent chapel, another part of the nunnery. Victorian restoration of the building includes some Pre-Raphaelite stained-glass windows and ceiling designs by William Morris. ⊠ *Jesus La.* ☎ *01223/339339* ⊕ *www.jesus.cam.ac.uk* ⊙ *Daily 8–7, except exam period.*

9 Kettle's Yard. Originally a private house owned by a former curator of London's Tate galleries, Kettle's Yard contains a fine collection of 20th-century art, sculpture, furniture, and decorative arts, including works by Henry Moore, Barbara Hepworth, and Henri Gaudier-Brzeska. One gallery shows changing exhibitions of modern art and crafts, and weekly concerts (term time only) and lectures attract an eclectic mix of enthusiasts. ⊠ *Castle St.* ☎ *01223/352124* ⊕ *www.kettlesyard.co.uk* ▭ *Free* ⊙ *House Mar.–Aug., Tues.–Sun. 1:30–4:30; Sept.–Feb., Tues.–Sun. 2–4. Gallery Tues.–Sun. 11:30–5.*

★ 12 King's College Chapel. It seems almost impossible to single out one building in Cambridge from the many that are masterpieces, but King's College Chapel is perhaps the supreme architectural work in the city. Based on Sainte Chapelle, the 13th-century private royal chapel in Paris, it was constructed toward the end of the 15th century. Henry VI, the king after whom the college is named, oversaw the work. This was the last period before the classical architecture of the ancient Greeks and Romans, then being rediscovered by the Italians, began to make its influence felt in northern Europe. King's College Chapel is thus the final, perhaps most glorious flowering of Perpendicular Gothic in Britain. From the outside, the most prominent features are the expanses of glass, the massive flying buttresses, and the fingerlike spires that line the length of the building. Inside, the most obvious impression is of great space—the chapel has been described as "the noblest barn in Europe"—and of light flooding in from its huge windows. The brilliantly colored bosses (carved panels at the intersections of the roof ribs) are particularly intense, although hard to see without binoculars. An exhibition in the chantries, or side chapels, explains more about the chapel's construction. Behind the altar is *The Adoration of the Magi,* an enormous and typically lively painting by Peter Paul Rubens, painted for a convent in Louvain. Every Christmas Eve, a festival of carols sung by the chapel's famous choir is broadcast worldwide from here. Past students of King's College include the novelist E. M. Forster, the economist John Maynard Keynes, and the World War I poet Rupert Brooke. ⊠ *King's Parade* ☎ *01223/331100 college, 01223/331155 chapel* ⊕ *www.kings.cam.ac.uk* ▭ *Chapel £3.50* ⊙ *Oct.–June, weekdays 9:30–3:30, Sat. 9:30–3:15, Sun. 1:15–2:15; July–Sept., Mon.–Sat. 9:30–4:30, Sun. 1:15–2:15 and 5–5:30. Times may vary; phone in advance.*

8 Magdalene College. Across Magdalene (pronounced *maud*-lin) Bridge, a cast-iron 1820 structure, lies the only one of the older colleges to be sited across the river. Magdalene Street itself is narrow and traffic-heavy, but there's relative calm inside the redbrick courts. It was a hostel for Benedictine monks for more than 100 years before the college was founded in 1542. In the second court, the college's **Pepys Library** (☎ 01223/332187 ☉ Mid-Apr.–Aug., Mon.–Sat. 11:30–12:30 and 2:30–3:30; Oct.–mid-Mar., Mon.–Sat. 2:30–3:30)—labeled *Bibliotecha Pepysiana*—contains the books and desk of the famed 17th-century diarist Samuel Pepys. ⊠ *Magdalene St.* ☎ *01223/332100* ⊕ *www.magd. cam.ac.uk* 🎫 *Free* ☉ *Daily 9–6, except exam period.*

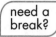

The 600-year-old **Pickerel Inn** (⊠ 30 Magdalene St. ☎ 01223/355068), one of the city's oldest pubs, makes for a good stop for a soothing afternoon pint of real ale or lager and a wee snack of greasy chips. Watch for the low beams.

❸ Museum of Archaeology and Anthropology. The university maintains some fine museums in its research halls on Downing Street—the wonder is that they are not better known to visitors. Geological collections at the Sedgwick Museum and the exhibits at the Zoological Museum are typically extensive, but be sure to see the Museum of Archaeology and Anthropology, which houses a superb collection of ethnographic objects brought back by early explorers, including members of Captain Cook's pioneering voyages to the Pacific. ⊠ *Downing St.* ☎ *01223/333516* ⊕ *museum-server.archanth.cam.ac.uk* 🎫 *Free* ☉ *Sept.–May, Tues.–Sat. 2–4:30; June–Aug., Tues.–Fri. 10–4:30, Sat. 2–4:30.*

❷ Pembroke College. Established in 1347, Pembroke has some buildings dating from the 14th century in its first court. On the south side, Christopher Wren's chapel—his first major commission, completed in 1665—looks like a distinctly modern intrusion. You can walk through the college, around a delightful garden, and past the fellows' bowling green. Outside the library you can't miss the resplendent, toga-clad statue of the precocious William Pitt the Younger; he came up to Pembroke at age 15 and was appointed prime minister of Great Britain in 1783, when he was just 24. ⊠ *Trumpington St.* ☎ *01223/338100* ⊕ *www.pem.cam. ac.uk* ☉ *Daily 9–dusk, except exam period.*

► ❶ Peterhouse College. The bishop of Ely founded Cambridge's oldest college in 1281. Parts of the dining hall date from 1290, although the hall is most notable for powerful, 19th-century stained glass by William Morris and his contemporaries. The adjacent church of Little St. Mary's served as the college chapel until 1632, when the current late-Gothic chapel was built. ⊠ *Trumpington St.* ☎ *01223/338200* ⊕ *www.pet.cam.ac. uk* ☉ *Daily 9–5, except exam period.*

⓮ Queens' College. One of the most eye-catching colleges is Queens', named after the consorts of Henry VI and Edward IV. Founded in 1448, the college is tucked away on Queens' Lane, next to the wide lawns that lead down from King's College to the Backs. The secluded "cloister court" looks untouched since its completion in the 1540s. Queens' masterpiece is the **Mathematical Bridge** (best seen from the Silver Street road bridge), an arched wooden structure that was originally held together without fastenings. The current bridge (1902) is securely bolted. ⊠ *Queens' La.*

☎ *01223/335511* ⊕ *www.quns.cam.ac.uk* ✉ *£1* ☉ *Apr.–Oct., daily 10–4:30; Nov.–Mar., daily 10–4, except exam period.*

🔟 **St. John's College.** Two mythical beasts called "yales," with the bodies of antelopes and heads of goats, hold up the coat of arms and guard the gateway of Cambridge's second-largest college. St. John's was founded in 1511 by Henry VII's mother, Lady Margaret Beaufort. Its structures lie on two sites: from the main entrance, walk to the left through the ancient courts—with their turrets, sculpted windows, and clock towers—to where a famous copy of the Bridge of Sighs in Venice reaches across the Cam to the mock-Gothic New Court (1825), nicknamed "the wedding cake." If you walk through until you reach the riverbank, you can stroll along the Backs and frame photographs of the elegant bridge (and less-than-elegant New Court buildings). ✉ *St. John's St.* ☎ *01223/338600* ⊕ *www.joh.cam.ac.uk* ✉ *£1.75* ☉ *Apr.–Oct., weekdays 10–5, Sat. 9:30–5, except exam period.*

6️⃣ **Sidney Sussex College.** Passing largely unnoticed on busy Sidney Street, Sidney Sussex is smaller than many colleges, yet it has interesting 17th- and 18th-century buildings, most of which were sadly given mock-Gothic "improvements" in 1832. Oliver Cromwell was a student here in 1616; the Hall contains his portrait, and his head has been buried in a secret location in the chapel since 1960. Cromwell charged his painter to include "all these roughnesses, pimples, and warts." ✉ *Sidney St.* ☎ *01223/338800* ⊕ *www.sid.cam.ac.uk* ☉ *Daily 9–5, except exam period.*

1️⃣1️⃣ **Trinity College.** Founded in 1546 by Henry VIII, Trinity replaced a 14th-century educational foundation and is the largest college in either Cambridge or Oxford, with nearly 700 undergraduates. Many of the buildings match its size, not least its 17th-century "great court." Here the massive gatehouse holds a giant clock that strikes each hour with high and low notes. The college's greatest masterpiece is Christopher Wren's library, colonnaded and seemingly constructed with as much light as stone, with wood carving by the 17th-century master Grinling Gibbons. Alumni include Sir Isaac Newton, William Thackeray, and Lords George Byron, Alfred Tennyson, and Thomas Macaulay. Prince Charles was an undergraduate here in the late 1960s. ✉ *St. John's St.* ☎ *01223/338400* ⊕ *www.trin.cam.ac.uk* ✉ *Mar.–Oct. £2, free rest of year* ☉ *College Mar.–Oct., daily 10–5, except exam period; library weekdays noon–2, Sat. in term time 10:30–12:30; hall and chapel open but hrs vary.*

1️⃣3️⃣ **Trinity Hall College.** The green parkland of the Backs is best appreciated from Trinity College's 14th-century neighbor, Trinity Hall, where you can sit on a wall by the river and watch students in punts maneuver under the ancient ornamental bridges of Clare and King's. Access to the river is down Trinity Lane, off Trinity Street. The **Senate House** (✉ King's Parade), which stands between Clare College and Trinity Hall, is not part of a particular college. A classical building of the 1720s, it's used for graduation ceremonies and other university events. The public can't enter, but if the gate is open you can wander into the court and grounds. ✉ *Trinity La.* ☎ *01223/332500* ⊕ *www.trinhall.cam.ac.uk* ☉ *Daily 9:15–noon and 2–5:30, except exam period and summer term.*

ON THE MENU

FARMLAND AND THE RIVERS *and sea provide ample bounty for the table in East Anglia. Look for area specialties, such as duckling,* Norfolk black turkey, hare, and partridge, *on menus around the region. In Norwich, there's no escaping the hot, bright Coleman's mustard, which is perfect smeared on some sausage and mash.*

Among the culinary treats from the sea is samphire, a delicious kind of seaweed that grows in the salt marshes along the North Norfolk and Suffolk coasts. The long coastline also provides tasty Cromer crabs and Yarmouth bloaters (a kind of smoked herring), whereas the Essex coast near Colchester has been producing oysters since Roman times. Brancaster and Stiffkey mussels, Sheringham lobster, and Thornham oysters are all seafood highlights worth indulging in while visiting North Norfolk. Eel, a delicacy in the Fens, is served smoked or jellied. Maldon

sea salt is another famous, high-quality local product. When you're traveling the coast, sample fresh fish and chips on the Suffolk coast, especially in Aldeburgh, where local creations have gained national recognition.

For liquid refreshment, Adnams, Greene King, and Tolly Cobbold are major ale producers, and a pint of Suffolk cider is usually a good accompaniment to the local food. There's an equally venerable tradition in wine making in the region. The Romans first introduced vines to Britain, and they took especially well here. Today East Anglia has more than 40 vineyards. If you want to try a bottle (dry whites are best), check wine lists in local restaurants or make a visit to Chilford Hall just outside of Cambridge for a tasting and a winery tour.

---

⑯ **University Botanic Gardens.** Laid out in 1846, these gardens contain, besides rare specimens, conservatories and a rock garden. They are a five-minute walk from the Fitzwilliam Museum. ⊠ *Cory Lodge, Bateman St.* ☎ *01223/336265* ⊕ *www.botanic.cam.ac.uk* ⊠ *£2.50 Mar.–Oct. and weekends Nov.–Feb., free weekdays Nov.–Feb.* ☉ *Nov.–Jan., daily 10–4; Feb. and Oct., daily 10–5; Mar.–Sept., daily 10–6.*

Where to Eat

★ **£££–££££** ✕ **Midsummer House.** An elegant restaurant beside the River Cam, the gray-brick Midsummer House has a comfortable conservatory. Set menus for lunch and dinner list robust yet sophisticated French and Mediterranean dishes. Choices might include tender roast spring lamb or seared sea scallops, adorned with inventively presented vegetables. ⊠ *Midsummer Common* ☎ *01223/369299* ⌖ *Reservations essential* ▭ *AE, MC, V* ☉ *Closed Mon. No lunch Sat., no dinner Sun.*

££–£££ ✕ **Loch Fyne Oyster Restaurant.** Part of a Scottish chain that harvests oysters and runs seafood restaurants, this airy, casual place across the street from the Fitzwilliam Museum is open for breakfast, lunch, and dinner. The deservedly popular oysters and other seafood—mussels, salmon, tuna, and more—are fresh and well prepared. Some good bets are the dauntingly large seafood platters. ✉ *37 Trumpington St.* ☎ *01223/362433* 🍴 *AE, MC, V.*

££–£££ ✕ **Three Horseshoes.** This early-19th-century pub-restaurant in a thatched cottage has additional dining space in the conservatory. The tempting, beautifully presented dishes focus on modern British cuisine. Some fashionable culinary accoutrements—sun-dried tomatoes, polenta, and olives—accompany char-grilled meats or roast fish. It's 3 mi west of Cambridge, about a 10-minute taxi ride. ✉ *High St., Madingley* ☎ *01954/ 210221* 🍴 *MC, V.*

££ ✕ **River Bar & Kitchen.** Fashionable and stylish, this riverside eatery designed by Terence Conran focuses on contemporary food with the occasional Eastern influence, such as spicy lamb samosas with mint and cucumber dip, wonton prawns, and tuna on Mediterranean vegetables. At lunch, choose among the creative sandwiches. ✉ *Quayside, off Bridge St.* ☎ *01223/307030* ⬧ *Reservations essential* 🍴 *AE, MC, V.*

££ ✕ **Vaults.** Whitewashed walls and slate floors lend a sleek, contemporary twist to the cellars that make up this basement restaurant. The zinc bar, with its red sofas, is perfect for lounging with a cocktail. On the menu is updated traditional fare such as grilled sea bass with salsa, lamb shank with parsnip broth, and chocolate and star anise mousse cake. On Sunday, there's a brunch with live blues. ✉ *14A Trinity St.* ☎ *01223/ 506090* ⬧ *Reservations essential* 🍴 *AE, MC, V.*

£–££ ✕ **Copper Kettle.** Over the years, students have come to love this coffee shop, where they discuss work, life, and love over frothy coffees, sticky buns, and sandwiches. It's never going to win any gastronomic awards, but for a slice of real university life (and a fine view of King's College) it can't be beat. Closing time is 5:30 PM. ✉ *King's Parade* ☎ *01223/ 365068* 🍴 *No credit cards* ☉ *No dinner.*

£ ✕ **Dojo Noodle Bar.** Many highlights of Asian cuisine are represented at this trendy spot near the river. If the different kinds of wheat, rice, or mung bean noodles aren't your thing, try a rice dish or pot stickers, tempura prawns, or chicken yakitori. ✉ *2 Millers Yard, Mill La., off Trumpington St.* ☎ *01223/363471* 🍴 *AE, MC, V.*

Where to Stay

There aren't many hotels downtown. For more (and cheaper) options, consider one of the numerous guest houses on the arterial roads and in the suburbs. These start at £18–£25 per person per night and can be booked through the tourist information center.

£££££ 🏨 **Crowne Plaza.** In the middle of historic Cambridge, this late-20th-century building doesn't mesh well with its older neighbors but does provide the high standard of accommodation you expect from this chain, as well as a top-notch location. Modern amenities such as a writing desk and trouser press enhance the colorful, contemporary rooms. ✉ *Downing St., CB2 3DT* ☎ *01223/464466* 🖷 *01223/464440* ⊕ *www.cambridge. crowneplaza.com* ⬧ *198 rooms* ⬧ *Restaurant, room service, in-room data ports, in-room safes, minibars, cable TV with movies, gym, sauna, bar, lobby lounge, pub, baby-sitting, dry cleaning, laundry service, con-*

cierge, business services, Internet, meeting rooms, parking (fee), no-smoking rooms ▭ *AE, DC, MC, V.*

£££££ ▥ **De Vere University Arms Hotel.** Elegant and sympathetically modernized, the 19th-century De Vere is a top choice in the city center. Space is at a premium in central Cambridge, and it shows here: the traditionally furnished guest rooms are comfortable but not overly large. Many rooms have views of Parker's Piece, the green backing the hotel, although you pay slightly more for these; Parker's Bar also overlooks the green. The central lounge provides a comfortable place for afternoon tea by the fireplace. Guests can use a health club 2 mi away. ⊠ *Regent St., CB2 1AD* ☎ *01223/351241* 🖷 *01223/315256* ⊕ *www.devere.com* ⤶ *116 rooms, 1 suite* ◊ *Restaurant, room service, in-room data ports, cable TV with movies, 2 bars, lounge, business services, meeting rooms, parking (fee), some pets allowed (fee)* ▭ *AE, DC, MC, V.*

£££££ ▥ **Garden Moat House Hotel.** Set among the colleges in 3 acres of private grounds, this modern hotel makes the most of its peaceful riverside location. The gardens, bar, and conservatories all overlook the Cam, as do most rooms. Request a river view when you reserve, because some rooms at the rear of the L-shape hotel have less desirable views. As with many chain hotels, the service and standards are high, but the architecture and furnishings are not particularly special. Ask about lower leisure (vacation) rates, which include breakfast. ⊠ *Granta Pl. and Mill La., CB2 1RT* ☎ *01223/259988* 🖷 *01223/316605* ⊕ *www. moathousehotels.com* ⤶ *117 rooms* ◊ *Restaurant, room service, minibars, cable TV, indoor pool, sauna, steam room, bar, lounge, Internet, business services, meeting rooms, parking (fee), no-smoking rooms; no a/c in some rooms* ▭ *AE, DC, MC, V.*

££££ ▥ **Hotel Felix.** This contemporary hotel, less than a mile from the city center, has spacious bedrooms with clean-lined, stylish modern furnishings in neutral solid colors. The main part of the building is a converted Victorian mansion; today it contains some bedrooms as well as the sophisticated Graffiti restaurant and bar, serving Mediterranean food. ⊠ *Whitehouse La., Huntingdon Rd., CB3 0LX* ☎ *01223/277977* 🖷 *01223/277973* ⊕ *www.hotelfelix.co.uk* ⤶ *52 rooms* ◊ *Restaurant, room service, in-room data ports, in-room safes, cable TV with movies, lounge, baby-sitting, dry cleaning, laundry service, meeting rooms, no-smoking rooms, free parking, some pets allowed* ▭ *AE, DC, MC, V* ⦿ *CP.*

££££ ▥ **Meadowcroft Hotel.** This redbrick Victorian house, with its pastel-hued bedrooms and the stylish Brackenhurst Restaurant, is a pleasant 1-mi walk from the center of Cambridge. English antiques and print fabrics furnish the rooms, which overlook a garden. The hotel offers (extra charge) a horse-drawn carriage ride around Cambridge or nearby Grantchester that includes afternoon tea and croquet. ⊠ *16 Trumpington Rd., CB2 2EX* ☎ *01223/346120* 🖷 *01223/346138* ⊕ *www.meadowcrofthotel. co.uk* ⤶ *12 rooms* ◊ *Restaurant, room service, in-room data ports, cable TV, bicycles, croquet, bar, lounge, meeting room, free parking, some pets allowed; no a/c, no smoking* ▭ *AE, MC, V* ⦿ *BP.*

£££ ▥ **Arundel House Hotel.** Elegantly proportioned, this Victorian hotel made up of now-connected town houses has a fine location overlooking the River Cam, with Jesus Green in the background. The comfortable bedrooms, modern in style, have locally made mahogany furniture. Rattan chairs, trailing plants, and a patio garden add a certain cachet to meals and afternoon teas in the Victorian-style conservatory. The special weekend rates are an excellent value. ⊠ *53 Chesterton Rd., CB4 3AN* ☎ *01223/367701* 🖷 *01223/367721* ⊕ *www.arundelhousehotels. co.uk* ⤴ *102 rooms* ⟋ *2 restaurants, bar, lounge, meeting rooms, free parking, no-smoking rooms; no a/c* ⊟ *AE, DC, MC, V* ⍾ *CP.*

££ 🖳 **Ashley Hotel.** Sister to the Arundel House Hotel, this pleasant smaller establishment near the center of Cambridge was converted from a private home. Rooms are decent, and you can take advantage of the nearby facilities of Arundel House. ⊠ *74 Chesterton Rd., CB4 1ER* ☎ *01223/ 350059* 🖷 *01223/350900* ⊕ *www.arundelhousehotels.co.uk* ⤴ *16 rooms* ⟋ *Free parking; no a/c, no smoking* ⊟ *AE, DC, MC, V* ⍾ *BP.*

£ 🖳 **Sleeperz.** A low-key budget option, this hostelry right outside the train station has small bedrooms with natural wood floors, white walls, and futon beds. Most double rooms have bunk beds. The sparsely furnished accommodations are recommended only for those who want a cheap, clean place to sleep. ⊠ *Station Rd., CB1 2TZ* ☎ *01223/304050* 🖷 *01223/357286* ⊕ *www.sleeperz.com* ⤴ *25 rooms* ⟋ *Free parking; no a/c, no room phones, no smoking* ⊟ *MC, V* ⍾ *CP.*

Nightlife & the Arts

Nightlife

The city's pubs provide the mainstay of Cambridge's nightlife, particularly when students are in town. The **Eagle** (⊠ Bene't St. ☎ 01223/ 505020), first among equals, is a 16th-century coaching inn with several bars and a cobbled courtyard that's lost none of its old-time character. It's extremely busy on weekends. **Fort St. George** (⊠ Midsummer Common ☎ 01223/354327), which overlooks the university boathouses, gets the honors for riverside views. The **Free Press** (⊠ Prospect Row ☎ 01223/368337) is that rare beast, a nonsmoking pub, and all the better for it, attracting a fresh-faced student rowing clientele.

The Arts

Cambridge supports its own symphony orchestra, and regular musical events are held in many colleges, especially those with large chapels. **King's College Chapel** (☎ 01223/331447) has evensong services Tuesday–Saturday at 5:30, Sunday at 3:30. The **Corn Exchange** (⊠ Wheeler St. ☎ 01223/357851), beautifully restored, presents concerts (classical and rock), stand-up comedy, musicals, opera, and ballet.

The **ADC Theatre** (⊠ Park St. ☎ 01223/503333) hosts mainly student and fringe theater productions, including the famous Cambridge Footlights revue, training ground for much comic talent since the 1970s. The **Arts Theatre** (⊠ 6 St. Edward's Passage ☎ 01223/5033333), the city's main repertory theater, was built by economist John Maynard Keynes in 1936 and supports a full program of theater, concerts, and events. It also has a good ground-floor bar and two restaurants, including the conservatory-style Roof Garden.

CloseUp

PUNTING ON THE CAM

To punt is to maneuver a flat-bottomed, wooden, gondolalike boat—in this case, through the shallow River Cam along the verdant Backs behind the colleges of the University of Cambridge. One benefit of this popular activity is that you get a better view of the ivy-covered walls from the water than from the front. Mastery of the sport lies in your ability to control a 15-foot pole, used to propel the punt. Collect a bottle of wine, some food, and a few friends, and you may find yourself saying

things such as, "It doesn't get any better than this." One piece of advice: if your pole gets stuck, let go. You can use the smaller paddle to go back and retrieve it.

The lazier-at-heart may prefer chauffeured punting, with food supplied. Students from Cambridge may do the work, and you get a fairly informative spiel on the colleges. For a romantic evening trip, there are illuminated punts.

The **Cambridge Folk Festival** (☎ 01223/357851 ⊕ www.cam-folkfest.co. uk), spread over a late July weekend at Cherry Hinton Hall, attracts major international folk singers and groups. Camping is available on the park grounds—reservations are essential.

Sports & the Outdoors

Biking

It's fun to explore Cambridge by bike. **Geoff's Bike Hire** (✉ 65 Devonshire Rd. ☎ 01223/365629), a short walk from the railroad station, charges from £8 per day and £15 per week, or £5 for up to three hours. Advance reservations are essential in July and August. Geoff's also runs guided cycle tours of Cambridge.

Punting

You can rent punts at several places, notably at Silver Street Bridge–Mill Lane, at Magdalene Bridge, and from outside the Rat and Parrot pub on Thompson's Lane on Jesus Green. Hourly rental costs about £14 (and requires a deposit of £70). Chauffeured punting on the River Cam is also possible at most rental places. Around £5 per head is the usual rate, and your chauffeur will likely be a Cambridge student. **Scudamore's Punting Co.** (✉ Mill La. and Quayside ☎ 01223/359750) rents chauffeured and self-drive punts.

Shopping

Cambridge is a main shopping area for a wide region, and it has all the usual chain stores, many in the Grafton Centre and Lion's Yard shopping precincts. More interesting are the specialty shops found among the colleges in the center of Cambridge, especially in and around Rose Crescent and King's Parade. Bookshops, including antiquarian stores, are Cambridge's pride and joy.

All Saints Garden Art & Craft Market (✉ Trinity St.) displays the wares of local artists outdoors. **Ryder & Amies** (✉ 22 King's Parade ☎ 01223/350371) carries official university wear and even straw boaters.

The **Bookshop** (✉ 24 Magdalene St. ☎ 01223/362457) is the best local secondhand bookshop. The **Cambridge University Press bookshop** (✉ 1 Trinity St. ☎01223/333333) stands on the oldest bookstore site in Britain, with books sold here since the 16th century. **G. David** (✉ 3 and 16 St. Edward's Passage ☎ 01223/354619), near the Arts Theatre, sells antiquarian books. The **Haunted Bookshop** (✉ 9 St. Edward's Passage ☎ 01223/312913) carries a great selection of old, illustrated books and British classics. **Heffer's** (✉ 20 Trinity St. ☎ 01223/568568 ✉ children's branch 30 Trinity St. ☎ 01223/568551), one of the world's biggest bookstores, stocks many rare and imported books.

FROM ELY TO BURY ST. EDMUNDS

This central area of towns and villages within easy reach of Cambridge is testament to the amazing changeability of the English landscape. The town of Ely is set in an eerie landscape of flat, empty, and apparently endless fenland, or marsh. Only a few miles south and east into Suffolk, however, all this changes to pastoral landscapes of—if not rolling, then gently undulating—hills, clusters of villages, and towns whose prettiness is easier to appreciate.

Ely

⑰ *16 mi north of Cambridge.*

Ely is the "capital" of the fens, the center of what used to be a separate county called the Isle of Ely (literally "island of eels"). Until the land was drained in the 17th century, Ely was surrounded by treacherous marshland, which inhabitants crossed wearing stilts. Today Wicken Fen, a nature reserve 9 mi southeast of town (off A1123), preserves the sole remaining example of fenland in an undrained state. Enveloped by fields of wheat, sugar beets, and carrots, Ely is a small, dense town dominated by its cathedral. The shopping area and market square lie to the north and lead down to the riverside, and the medieval buildings of the cathedral grounds and the King's School (which trains cathedral choristers) spread out to the south and west. Ely's most famous resident was Oliver Cromwell, whose house is now a museum.

★ Known affectionately as the Ship of the Fens, **Ely Cathedral** can be seen for miles, towering above the flat landscape on one of the few ridges in the fens. In 1083 the Normans began work on the cathedral, which stands on the site of a Benedictine monastery founded by the Anglo-Saxon princess Etheldreda in 673. In the center of the cathedral you see a marvel of medieval construction—the unique octagonal **Lantern Tower,** a sort of stained-glass skylight of colossal proportions, built to replace the central tower after it collapsed in 1322. The cathedral is also notable for its 248-foot-long **nave,** with its simple Norman arches and Victorian painted ceiling. Much of the decorative carving of the 14th-century **Lady Chapel** was defaced during the Reformation (mostly by knocking off the heads of the statuary), but enough delicate tracery remains to show its original beauty. The fan-vaulted, carved ceiling remains intact, as it was too high for the iconoclasts to reach. The cathedral's south triforium gallery houses a wonderful **Stained Glass Museum** (☎ 01353/660347 ⊕ www. sgm.abelgratis.com ☜ £3.50 ☉ May–Oct., weekdays 10:30–5, Sat. 10:30–5:30, Sun. noon–6; Nov.–Apr., weekdays and Sat. 10:30–5, Sun. noon–4:30), with exhibits up a flight of 41 steps. Exhibits trace the history of stained glass from medieval to modern times, with examples from all periods. ⊠ *The Gallery* ☎ *01353/667735* ⊕ *www.cathedral.ely. anglican.org* ☜ *£4.80, free on Sun.* ☉ *May–Sept., daily 7–7; Oct.–Apr., Mon.–Sat. 7:30–6, Sun. 7:30–5.*

Oliver Cromwell's House, the half-timber medieval building that was the home of Cromwell and his family, stands in the shadows of Ely Cathedral. During the 10 years he lived here, from 1636, Cromwell was leading the rebellious Roundheads in their eventually victorious struggle against King Charles I. The house contains an exhibit on its former occupant and audiovisual presentations about Cromwell and about the draining of the local fens. It's also the site of Ely's tourist information center. ⊠ *29 St. Mary's St.* ☎ *01353/662062* ☜ *£2.50* ☉ *Apr.–Sept., daily 10–6; Oct.–Mar., Mon.–Sat. 10–5.*

Where to Stay & Eat

£££ ✕ **Old Fire Engine House.** Scrubbed pine tables fill the main dining room of this restaurant in a converted fire station near the cathedral. Another room, used only for overflow, has an open fireplace and a polished wood floor, and also serves as an art gallery. Among the English dishes are traditional fenland recipes such as pike baked in white wine, as well as eel pie and game in season. ⊠ *25 St. Mary's St.* ☎ *01353/662582* ⊟ *MC, V* ☉ *Closed 2 wks at Christmas. No dinner Sun.*

££–£££ ✕ **Dominique's.** This delightful little delicatessen with stripped pine floors serves lunch in a nonsmoking environment. Choose from quiches, salads, cakes, and lovely cheeses. You can take your food out or eat in the dining room. ⊠ *8 St. Mary's St.* ☎ *01353/665011* ⊟ *MC, V* ☉ *No dinner.*

££ ▣ **Cathedral House.** Run by Jenny and Robin Farndale, this Georgian house makes a pleasant overnight stop in Ely. The cozy bedrooms have antique furniture and coffeemakers, and an oriel window and handsome staircase are original features. ⊠ *17 St. Mary's St., CB7 4ER* ☎ *01353/ 662124* ⊕ *www.cathedralhouse.co.uk* ⇋ *3 rooms, 1 cottage* ⚘ *No a/c, no smoking* ⊟ *No credit cards* ⫯⦿⫯ *BP.*

Saffron Walden

⓲ *30 mi south of Ely, 14 mi south of Cambridge.*

Best known for its many typically East Anglian timber-frame buildings, this town owes its name to the saffron crocus fields that used to be cultivated in medieval times and processed for their dye. The common at the east end of town has a 17th-century circular earth maze, created from space left among the crocus beds. Some buildings have elaborate pargeting (decorative plasterwork), especially the walls of the former Sun Inn on Church Street, which was used by Cromwell during his campaigns.

★ Palatial **Audley End House and Gardens,** a mile or so west of Saffron Walden, is a famous example of Jacobean (early-17th-century) architecture. It was once owned by Charles II, who bought it as a convenient place to break his journey on the way to the Newmarket races. Remodeled in the 18th and 19th centuries, it shows the architectural skill of Sir John Vanbrugh, Robert Adam, and Rebecca Biagio as well as original Jacobean work in the magnificent Great Hall. You can also walk around the park, landscaped by Capability Brown in the 18th century, and the fine Victorian gardens. ⊠ *B1383* ☏ *01799/522842* ⊕ *www.english-heritage. org.uk* ᗌ *£8, park only £4* ⏱ *Apr.–Sept., Wed.–Sun., park 11–6, house noon–5; Oct., park weekends 11–5, house weekends11–4.*

Where to Stay

£ ⊞ **Archway Guesthouse.** What must be one of Britain's quirkiest B&Bs embraces the early era of rock 'n' roll by packing its public rooms with rock memorabilia and toys from the 1950s and '60s. Bedrooms are tasteful, homey, and uncluttered, and hosts Flora and Haydn Miles are personable. ⊠ *Church St., CB10 1JW* ☏ *01799/501500* ☏ *01799/506003* ✍ *archwayguesthouse@ntlworld.com* ⤴ *7 rooms* ⚲ *No a/c, no smoking* ⊟ *No credit cards* ⏋⏉ *BP.*

> **en route**   **Hedingham Castle,** between Saffron Walden and Sudbury, has a wonderful 12th-century Norman keep (main tower), built on a hill by Aubrey de Vere and designed by the archbishop of Canterbury. The highlight of the 110-foot-tall keep is the Banqueting Hall, which can be viewed from the minstrels' gallery. In summer the age of knighthood is re-created through jousting tournaments and medieval festivals. ⊠ *B1058, Castle Hedingham* ☏ *01787/460261* ⊕ *www. hedinghamcastle.co.uk* ᗌ *£4, special events £5–£8 additional* ⏱ *Easter–Oct., daily 11–4.*

Sudbury

⑲ *23 mi east of Saffron Walden, 16 mi south of Bury St. Edmunds, 14 mi northwest of Colchester.*

An early silk-weaving industry (still in existence, on a smaller scale) as well as the wool trade brought prosperity to Sudbury, which has three fine Perpendicular Gothic churches and some half-timber houses. Today this town of 20,000 is the largest in this part of the Stour Valley. The Stour River was once navigable to the sea, and quays filled the town. Sudbury was Charles Dickens's model for the fictional Eatanswill, where Mr. Pickwick stands for Parliament. Thomas Gainsborough, one of the greatest English portrait and landscape painters, was born here in 1727; a **statue of Gainsborough** holding his palette stands on Market Hill.

The birthplace and family home of Thomas Gainsborough (1727–88), **Gainsborough's House,** is now a museum containing paintings and drawings by the artist (and reproductions of other works of his) and his contemporaries, as well as an arts center with exhibitions. Although it presents a Georgian facade, with touches of the 18th-century neo-Gothic style, the building is essentially Tudor. The walled garden behind the house has a mulberry tree planted in 1620. ✉ *46 Gainsborough St.* ☎ *01787/372958* ⊕ *www.gainsborough.org* ✇ *£3.50* ☉ *Mon.–Sat. 10–5, Sun 2–5.*

Where to Eat

££–£££   ✕ **Red Onion.** A former motor factory turned trendy bistro serves fixed-price lunch and dinner menus of inspired English comfort food. Try the fresh fish and soups. ✉ *57 Ballingdon St.* ☎ *01787/376777* ⊟ *MC, V.*

£–££   🏠 **Old Bull Hotel.** Comfortable chairs and some antiques furnish this 16th-century coaching inn. The homely guest rooms have period touches such as oak-beam ceilings. The small patio serves as a place for a pint in fine weather. ✉ *Church St., Ballingdon, CO10 2BL* ☎ *01787/374120* 🖷 *01787/379044* ⊕ *www.theoldbullhotel.co.uk* ⇝ *10 rooms* ☍ *Restaurant, in-room data ports, bar, lobby, lounge, meeting room, free parking, some pets allowed (fee); no a/c* ⊟ *AE, MC, V* ⦿ *BP.*

Long Melford

⓴ *2 mi north of Sudbury, 14 mi south of Bury St. Edmunds.*

It's easy to see how this village got its name, especially if you walk the full length of its 2-mi-long main street, which gradually broadens to include green squares and trees and finally opens into the large triangular green on the hill. Long Melford grew rich on its wool trade in the 15th century, and the town's buildings are an appealing mix, mostly Tudor half-timber or Georgian. Many house antiques shops. Utility poles are banned to preserve the ancient look, although the parked cars down both sides of the street make this a fruitless exercise. Away from the main road, Long Melford returns to its resolutely late-medieval roots.

The largely 15th-century **Holy Trinity Church,** founded by the rich clothiers of Long Melford, stands on a hill at the north end of the village. Close up, the delicate flint flush-work (shaped flints set into a pattern) and huge Perpendicular Gothic windows that take up most of the church's walls have great impact, especially because the nave is 150 feet long. Much of the superb original stained glass remains, notably the Lily Crucifix window. The Lady Chapel has an unusual interior cloister. ✉ *Main St.* ☎ *01787/310845* ⊕ *www.stedmundsbury.anglican.org/ longmelford* ☉ *Daily 10–4.*

Melford Hall, distinguished from the outside by its turrets and topiaries, is an Elizabethan house with its original banqueting hall, a fair number of 18th-century additions, and pleasant gardens. Much of the porcelain and other fine pieces here come from the *Santissima Trinidad,* a ship loaded with gifts from the emperor of China and bound for Spain that was captured by one of the house's owners in the 18th century. Children's writer Beatrix Potter, who was related to the owners, visited the house often; there's a small collection of Potter memorabilia. ✉ *Off A134* ☎ *01787/880286* ⊕ *www.nationaltrust.co.uk* ✇ *£4.50* ☉ *Apr. and Oct., weekends 2–5:30; May–Sept., Wed.–Sun. 2–5:30.*

☺ A wide moat surrounds **Kentwell Hall,** a fine redbrick Tudor manor house with tall chimneys and domed turrets. Built between 1520 and

1550, it was heavily restored inside after a fire in the early 19th century. On some weekends from mid-April through September, costumed "servants" and "farmworkers" perform reenactments of Tudor life or life during World War II with great panache and detail. There's also an organic farm with rare-breed farm animals. The house is a half mile north of Long Melford Green. ⊠ *Off A134* ☎ *01787/310207* ⊕ *www. kentwell.co.uk* ⊑ *£6.75, £7–£12 during special events* ⊙ *Apr.–June, Sun. and Tues.–Thurs. noon–5; July–Aug., daily noon—5; Sept., Sun., Wed., and Thurs. noon–5, Oct., Sun. noon–5.*

Where to Stay & Eat

££££ ✕▥ **The Bull.** The public rooms of the Bull—stone-flagged floors, bowed oak beams, and heavy antique furniture—show its long history. Throughout, the half-timber Elizabethan building is a joy, and whether you eat in the restaurant or the bar with its huge fireplace, service is efficient and careful. Traditional roasts and a game casserole mix on the menu with modern flavors, such as mullet in a Thai curry sauce. Creature comforts and pleasant bathrooms offset the smallish size of the bedrooms, which retain their original character. The price is at the low end of the category. ⊠ *Hall St., CO10 9JG* ☎ *01787/378494* 🖷 *01787/880307* ⊕ *www.oldenglish.co.uk* ⇆ *23 rooms, 2 suites* ⚑ *Restaurant, bar, lounge, meeting rooms, some pets allowed, no-smoking rooms; no a/c* ⊟ *AE, DC, MC, V* ⦿ *BP.*

Lavenham

㉑ *4 mi northeast of Long Melford, 10 mi south of Bury St. Edmunds.*

Fodor'sChoice
★

Virtually unchanged since the height of its wealth in the 15th and 16th centuries, Lavenham is one of the most perfectly preserved examples of a Tudor village in England. The weavers' and wool merchants' houses occupy not just one show street but most of the town. The houses are timber-frame in black oak, the main posts looking as if they could last another 400 years. The town has many examples of typical Suffolk pink buildings, in hues from pale pink to apricot. The timber-frame **Guildhall of Corpus Christi** (1529), the most spectacular building in Lavenham, dominates Market Place, a square with barely a foot in the present. The guildhall is open as a museum of the medieval wool trade. ⊠ *Market Pl.* ☎ *01787/247646* ⊕ *www.nationaltrust.org.uk* ⊑ *£3.50* ⊙ *Mar. and Nov., weekends 11–4; Apr., Wed.–Sun. 11–5; May–Oct., daily 11–5.*

The timber-frame **Little Hall,** a former wool merchant's house, shows the building's progress from its creation in the 14th century to its subsequent "modernization" through the 17th century. ⊠ *Market Pl.* ☎ *01787/ 247179* ⊑ *£1.50* ⊙ *Easter–Oct., Wed., Thurs., and weekends 2–5:30.*

A splendid Elizabethan building, the **Swan Hotel** (⊠ High St.) had a long history as a coaching inn, and in World War II it served as the special pub for the U.S. Air Force's 48th Bomber Group, whose memorabilia cover the walls of the bar. The hotel incorporates the former **Wool Hall,** torn down in 1913 but reassembled at the request of Princess Louise, sister of George V. In 1962, it was joined to the neighboring Swan.

The grand 15th-century Perpendicular **Church of St. Peter and St. Paul** (⊠ Church St.), set apart from the village on a hill, was built with wool money by cloth merchant Thomas Spring between 1480 and 1520. The height of its tower (141 feet) was meant to surpass those of the neighboring churches—and perhaps to impress rival towns. The rest of the church is perfectly proportioned, with intricate woodcarving.

Where to Stay & Eat

££ ✕ **The Angel.** Modern British cuisine is the draw at this popular spot overlooking Lavenham's picture-book main square. The specialty of the house—home-smoked fish—earns rave reviews. You can also just sit a spell at the scrubbed pine tables to enjoy one of the local beers on tap. Eight guest rooms are available, for about £75. ⊠ *Market Sq.* ☎ *01787/ 247388* ⊟ *AE, MC, V* �'⚐ *Reservations essential.*

£ ✕ **Gallery 48.** You can shop in the front gallery for locally made jewelry and arts and crafts before you retire to the back room for morning coffee, a vegetarian lunch (noon–2:30), or afternoon cake. The staff is cheerful and the mood relaxed and artsy. ⊠ *High St.* ☎ *01787/248542* ⊟ *MC, V* ⊘ *No dinner.*

££–£££ ✕▦ **Great House.** The town's finest "restaurant with rooms" occupies a 15th-century building on the medieval market square. Run by Régis and Martine Crépy, the dining room (reservations essential) has a fixed-price menu of European fare with a distinctly French touch. From the fireplace and wood floors of the restaurant to the walled courtyard garden, dining is a pleasure. The spacious bedrooms have sloping floors, beamed ceilings, and antique furnishings. ⊠ *Market Pl., CO10 9QZ* ☎ *01787/247431* 🖷 *01787/248007* ⊕ *www.greathouse.co.uk* ➹ *5 rooms* ⚐ *Restaurant, bar, lounge, baby-sitting, Internet, some pets allowed, no-smoking rooms; no a/c* ⊟ *AE, MC, V* ⊘ *Closed Jan.* ⎮◯⎮ *BP.*

££££ ▦ **Swan Hotel.** This half-timber 14th-century lodging has aging timbers, rambling public rooms, and open fires. Along corridors so low that cushions are strategically placed on beams, most of the individually styled bedrooms have rich oak cabinets, original wood paneling, and CD players. Bathrooms have been fashioned around ancient timbers and hidden rooms. The restaurant, which has its own minstrels' gallery, serves traditional English cuisine. Full-board and weekend packages can be good deals. ⊠ *High St., CO10 9QA* ☎ *01787/247477* 🖷 *01787/248286* ⊕ *www.heritage-hotels.com* ➹ *49 rooms, 2 suites* ⚐ *Restaurant, in-room data ports, cable TV, minibars, 2 bars, baby-sitting, meeting room, some pets allowed (fee); no a/c* ⊟ *AE, DC, MC, V.*

★ £££–££££ ▦ **Lavenham Priory.** You can immerse yourself in Lavenham's Tudor history at this luxurious B&B in a sprawling house that dates in part to the 13th century. The beamed great hall, sitting room (with TV and VCR), and 3 acres of gardens are great places to relax, and a walled herb garden is the scene for evening drinks in warm weather. Prints and wood furnishings fill the bedrooms; each has oak floors and ancient timbered ceilings, and some have four-posters. Reserve well in advance. ⊠ *Water St., CO10 9RW* ☎ *01787/247404* 🖷 *01787/248472* ⊕ *www. lavenhampriory.co.uk* ➹ *5 rooms, 1 suite* ⚐ *Lounge; no a/c, no room phones, no kids under 10, no smoking* ⊟ *MC, V* ⎮◯⎮ *BP.*

Bury St. Edmunds

★ ㉒ *10 mi north of Lavenham, 28 mi east of Cambridge.*

Bury St. Edmunds owes its name, and indeed its existence, to Edmund, the last king of East Anglia and medieval patron saint of England, who was hacked to death by marauding Danes in 869. He was subsequently canonized, and his shrine attracted pilgrims, settlement, and commerce. In the 11th century the erection of a great Norman abbey (now only ruins) confirmed the town's importance as a religious center. Robert Adam designed the town hall in 1774. The Georgian streetscape helps make the town one of the area's prettiest, and the nearby Greene King Westgate Brewery adds the smell of sweet hops to the air.

A walk along **Angel Hill** is a journey through the history of Bury St. Edmunds. Along one side, the Abbey Gate, cathedral, Norman Gate Tower, and St. Mary's church make up a continuous display of medieval architecture. Elegant Georgian houses line Angel Hill on the side opposite St. Mary's Church; these include the **Athenaeum,** an 18th-century social and cultural meeting place, which has a fine Adam-style ballroom. The splendid **Angel Hotel** (✉ 3 Angel Hill) is the scene of Sam Weller's meeting with Job Trotter in Dickens's *Pickwick Papers.* Dickens stayed here while he was giving readings at the Athenaeum.

Originally three churches stood within the walls of the Abbey of St. Edmunds, but only two have survived, including **St. Mary's,** built in the 15th century. It has a blue-and-gold embossed "wagon" (barrel-shape) roof over the choir. Mary Tudor, Henry VIII's sister and queen of France, is buried here. ✉ *Angel Hill at Honey Hill* ☎ *01284/706668* ☉ *Daily 10–3; call to confirm.*

St. Edmundsbury Cathedral dates from the 15th century, but the brilliant paint on its ceiling and the stained-glass windows gleaming like jewels are the result of 19th-century restoration by the architect Sir Gilbert Scott. Don't miss the memorial (near the altar) to an event in 1214, when the barons of England gathered here to take an oath to force King John to grant the Magna Carta. The cathedral's original Abbey Gate was destroyed in a riot, and it was rebuilt in the 14th century with defense in mind—you can see the arrow slits. After your visit, stop by the Refectory, a modest café filled with locals. ✉ *Angel Hill* ☎ *01284/754933* ⊕ *www.stedscathedral.co.uk* ✉ *Free, suggested donation £3* ☉ *June–Aug., daily 7:30–6; Sept.–May, daily 7:30–7.*

The **Abbey Ruins and Botanical Gardens** are all that remain of the Abbey of Bury St. Edmunds, which fell during Henry VIII's dissolution of the monasteries. The Benedictine abbey's enormous scale is evident in the surviving Norman Gate Tower on Angel Hill; besides this, only the fortified Abbot's Bridge over the River Lark and a few ruins remain. There are explanatory plaques amid the ruins, which are now the site of the Abbey Botanical Gardens, with roses, elegant hedges, and rare trees, including a Chinese tree of heaven planted in the 1830s. The **Bury St. Edmunds Tourist Information Centre** (✉ 6 Angel Hill ☎ 01284/764667 ☉ Easter–Oct., Mon.–Sat. 9:30–5:30, Sun. 10–3; Nov.–Easter, weekdays 10–4, Sat. 10-1) has a leaflet about the ruins and can arrange a guided tour. ✉ *Angel Hill* 🎟 *Free* ⊙ *Weekdays 7:30 AM–½ hr before dusk, weekends 9 AM–dusk.*

Manor House Museum, a Georgian mansion, contains excellent art collections: paintings, furniture, costumes, and ceramics from the 17th through the 20th centuries. The clocks and watches in the horological collection are extraordinary. ✉ *Honey Hill* 🕾 *01284/757072* ⊕ *www.stedmundsbury.gov.uk* 🎟 *£2.50* ⊙ *Wed.–Sun. 11–4.*

The 12th-century **Moyse's Hall,** probably the oldest building in East Anglia, is a rare surviving example of a Norman house. The rooms hold local history and archaeological collections. One macabre display relates to the Red Barn murder, a case that gained notoriety in a 19th-century theatrical melodrama, *Maria Marten, or the Murder in the Red Barn;* Maria Marten's murderer was executed in Bury St. Edmunds in 1828. ✉ *Cornhill* 🕾 *01284/706183* ⊕ *www.stedmundsbury.gov.uk* 🎟 *£2.50* ⊙ *Weekdays 10:30–4:30, weekends 11–5.*

Pop in for a pint of the local Greene King ale at **The Nutshell** (✉ Skinner St. 🕾 01905/764867), Britain's smallest pub, measuring just 16 feet by 7½ feet.

off the beaten path

ICKWORTH HOUSE – The creation of the eccentric Frederick Hervey, 4th earl of Bristol and bishop of Derry, this unusual 18th-century home was owned by the Hervey family until the 1960s. Inspired by his travels, Hervey wanted an Italianate palace and gardens to match. Today the two wings around a striking central rotunda contain a hotel (east wing) and paintings by William Hogarth, Titian, Diego Velázquez, and Gainsborough (west wing). Behind the house, the rose gardens and vineyards spread out to reach 1,800 acres of woods. A stroll over the hills to see grazing sheep and woodland deer gives the best vistas of the house, which is 7 mi southwest of Bury St. Edmunds. ✉ *Off A143, Horringer* 🕾 *01284/735270* ⊕ *www.nationaltrust.org.uk* 🎟 *£6.40, gardens and park £2.95* ⊙ *House mid-Mar–Sept., Fri.–Tues. 1–5; Oct., Fri.–Tues. 1–4:30. Garden mid-Mar.–Oct., daily 10–5; Nov.–mid-Dec., weekdays 10–4; Jan–mid-Mar., daily 10–4. Park daily 7–7.*

Where to Stay & Eat

££–£££ ✕ **Maison Bleue.** This French restaurant specializes in locally caught seafood and serves some meat dishes, too. The seafood depends on the day's catch, but mussels and grilled fillets of local trout and salmon are always available, as are cheeses imported from Paris. ✉ *30 Churchgate St.* 🕾 *01284/760623* ⌖ *Reservations essential* ⊟ *AE, DC, V* ⊙ *Closed Sun., Mon., and Jan.*

£ ✕ **Harriet's Café Tearooms.** In an elegant dining room, Harriet's brings back the tearooms of yesteryear. You can munch on a savory sandwich or have a full cream tea while listening to hits from the 1940s. ✉ *57 Cornhill* 🕾 *01284/756256* ⊟ *MC, V* ⊙ *No dinner.*

★ ✕🖥 **Ickworth Hotel.** You can live like nobility in the east wing of the Italianate Ickworth House, 7 mi southwest of Bury St. Edmunds; the rest of
££££–£££££

the house is a National Trust property worth visiting. Unlike many other stately home hotels, this one has no dress code, and children are catered to with a day-care room (for kids under 6) and a game center. The splendid public rooms have stylish 1950s and '60s furniture and striking modern art. This look extends to most bedrooms, though some still have period furnishings; all are luxe. Adults can dine in the more formal Frederick's restaurant, and the casual Café Inferno serves pizza. ⊠ *Off A143, Horringer, IP29 5QE* ☎ *01284/735350* 🖷 *01284/736300* ⊕ *www. luxuryfamilyhotels.com* 🗗 *27 rooms, 11 apartments* ♿ *2 restaurants, room service, in-room data ports, some kitchens, cable TV, tennis court, indoor pool, massage, spa, bicycles, croquet, horseback riding, lounge, baby-sitting, dry cleaning, laundry service, meeting rooms, some pets allowed, no-smoking rooms; no a/c* ☐ *AE, DC, MC, V* ⏏❶ *BP.*

£££–££££ ✕🖭 **Angel Hotel.** This spruced-up former coaching inn in the heart of town has spacious, well-furnished rooms. Several have four-posters, and the Charles Dickens Room, where the author stayed, is done in perfect 19th-century English style (the bed is a bit small, however). Morning coffee and afternoon tea are served in the cozy lobby with fireplace. Dine on English fare in the Abbeygate Restaurant overlooking the abbey's main gate, or try brasserie-style dishes in the more informal Vaults, in the cellar. ⊠ *3 Angel Hill, IP33 1LT* ☎ *01284/753926* 🖷 *01284/ 750092* ⊕ *www.theangel.co.uk* 🗗 *66 rooms* ♿ *2 restaurants, in-room data ports, cable TV with movies, bar, business services, meeting rooms, no-smoking rooms; no a/c in some rooms* ☐ *AE, DC, MC, V* ⏏❶ *BP.*

££–£££ 🖭 **Ounce House.** Small and friendly, this Victorian B&B a three-minute walk from the abbey ruins has a great deal of charm. Print fabrics and wooden furniture furnish the stylish guest rooms. You can unwind in the antiques-filled drawing room and library, where you can have a drink from the honor bar. The house is close to Bury's restaurants. ⊠ *Northgate St., IP33 1HP* ☎ *01284/761779* 🖷 *01284/768315* ⊕ *www. ouncehouse.co.uk* 🗗 *4 rooms* ♿ *In-room data ports, bar, lounge; no a/c, no smoking* ☐ *MC, V* ⏏❶ *BP.*

Nightlife & the Arts

The **Theatre Royal,** which presents touring shows, was built in 1819 and is a perfect example of Regency theater design. Guided tours (£2.50) can be booked at the box office. ⊠ *Westgate St.* ☎ *01284/769505* ☉ *Apr.–Oct., guided tours Tues. and Thurs. 11:30 and 2:30, Sat. 11:30, except during rehearsals.*

COLCHESTER & THE SUFFOLK COAST

Colchester is the oldest town on record in England, dating back to the Iron Age, and the reminders of its long history are well worth visiting. The town also serves as the traditional base for exploring Constable Country, that quintessentially English rural landscape on the borders of Suffolk and Essex made famous by the early-19th-century painter John Constable. This area runs north and west of Colchester along the valley of the River Stour. The 40-mi Suffolk Heritage Coast, which wanders northward from Felixstowe up to Kessingland, is one of the most unspoiled shorelines in the country.

Colchester

㉓ *59 mi northeast of London, 51 mi southeast of Cambridge, 68 mi south of Norwich.*

Evidence of Colchester's four centuries of Roman history is visible everywhere in this ancient town. The Roman walls still stand, together with a Norman castle, a Victorian town hall, and Dutch-style houses built by refugee weavers from the Low Countries in the late 16th century. Archaeological research indicates a settlement at the head of the Colne estuary at least as early as 1100 BC. Two thousand years ago it was the domain of Cunobelin (Shakespeare's Cymbeline), who was king of the Catuvellauni. On Cunobelin's death, the Romans invaded in AD 43. The emperor Claudius made it the first Roman colony in Britain, renaming the town *Colonia Victricensis,* the Colony of Victory. (Colchester had to wait another millennium, however, before it received its royal charter in 1189 from King Richard I.) The settlement was burned during the failed revolt in AD 60 by Boudicca, queen of the Iceni, who had knives on her chariot wheels. The Romans relocated their administrative center to Londinium (now London) after the revolt but maintained a military presence. The English Civil War saw further conflict in Colchester, as the city endured a three-month siege in 1648 before the Royalist forces surrendered. Colchester has always had a strategic importance and still has a military base; a tattoo (military spectacle) is held in even-numbered years.

Colchester was important enough for the Romans to build massive fortifications around it, and the **Roman Walls,** dating largely from the reign of Emperor Vespasian (AD 69–79, can still be seen, especially along Balkerne Hill (to the west of the town center), with its splendid Balkerne Gate (most of the foundations lie beneath the neighboring Hole-in-the-Wall pub). On Maidenburgh Street, near the castle, the remains of a **Roman amphitheater** have been discovered. The curve of the foundations is outlined in the paving stones of the roadway, and parts of the walls and floor have been exposed and preserved in a building, where they can be viewed through a window.

The castle built by William the Conqueror in about 1076 is today the
Ⓒ superb **Colchester Castle Museum.** All that remains is the keep, the largest the Normans built. The castle was constructed over the foundations of the huge Roman Temple of Claudius, and in the vaults you can descend through 1,000 years of history. The museum contains an ever-growing collection of prehistoric and Roman remains. ⊠ *Castle Park* ☎ *01206/ 282939* ⊕ *www.colchestermuseums.org.uk* 🎫 *£4.50, guided tours £1.60* ⊙ *Mon.–Sat. 10–5, Sun. 11–5.*

Ⓒ The interactive **Hollytrees Museum,** in a Georgian mansion near the castle, tells the story of the daily lives of local people through objects. There are chances to create a silhouette portrait or play with Victorian toys. ⊠ *Castle Park* ☎ *01206/282940* ⊕ *www.colchestermuseums.org.uk* 🎫 *Free* ⊙ *Mon.–Sat. 10–5, Sun. 11–5.*

Halfway down the broad High Street, which follows the line of the main Roman road, the splendid Edwardian **Town Hall** stands on the site of the original Moot (assembly) Hall. On its tower you can see four figures representing Colchester's main industries: fisheries, agriculture, the military, and engineering. The narrow medieval streets behind the Town Hall, off High Street, are called the **Dutch Quarter** because weavers—refugees from the Low Countries—settled here in the 16th century, when Colchester was the center of a thriving cloth trade.

Tymperleys Clock Museum, off Sir Isaac's Walk, displays a unique collection of beautiful, Colchester-made clocks in the surviving wing of an Elizabethan house. It also exhibits part of the Bernard Mason Collection, which consists of 217 clocks made in Colchester. ⊠ *Trinity St.* ☏ *01206/282943* ⊕ *www.colchestermuseums.org.uk* ⊡ *Free* ⊙ *June–Oct., Tues.–Sat. 10–1 and 2–5.*

Where to Stay & Eat

££–£££ ✕**Warehouse Brasserie.** Colchester's most popular eating place has a pastel green and rich red split-level dining room with wooden tables and large wall mirrors. This cheerful interior contrasts with a fairly anonymous exterior and location: it's tucked away in a converted warehouse, down a cul-de-sac off St. John's Street. The fixed-price lunch and dinner menu mixes brasserie favorites with classic English dishes. ⊠ *12 Chapel St. N* ☏ *01206/765656* ⊟ *MC, V* ⊙ *No dinner Sun. and Mon.*

£££–££££ ✕⊡ **George Hotel.** This 500-year-old inn in the heart of downtown added a modern extension but has kept plenty of age-old charm. Many rooms incorporate original oak beams and are comfortably furnished in traditional style. The George Bar also retains its ancient beams, and in the cellar a section of Roman pavement and a 16th-century wall painting are on display. The Brasserie restaurant has a good à la carte menu and is popular for afternoon tea or an evening pint. ⊠ *116 High St., CO1 1TD* ☏ *01206/578494* ⊟ *01206/761732* ⊕ *www.bestwestern. com* ⇨ *48 rooms* ⚐ *Restaurant, cable TV, bar, no-smoking rooms; no a/c in some rooms* ⊟ *AE, DC, MC, V.*

Dedham

❷❹ 8 mi northeast of Colchester, off A12 on B1029.

Fodor'sChoice
★

Dedham is the heart of Constable Country. Here, gentle hills and the cornfields of Dedham Vale, set under the district's delicate, pale skies, inspired John Constable (1776–1837) to paint some of his most celebrated canvases. He went to school in Dedham, a tiny, picture-book kind of place that consists of a single street, a church, and a few timber-frame and brick houses.

Two miles northeast of Dedham, off A12, the Constable trail continues in **East Bergholt,** where Constable was born in 1776. Only the stables remain of the house that was his birthplace. As well as many other views of East Bergholt, Constable painted its village church, **St. Mary's,** where his parents lie buried. It has one unusual feature—a freestanding wooden bell house in place of a tower.

From Dedham, on the banks of the River Stour, you can rent a rowboat, which (if you're fit enough) is an idyllic way to travel the 2 mi downriver to **Flatford Mill,** in East Bergholt, one of the two water mills owned by Constable's father, and the subject of his most famous painting, *The Hay Wain* (1821). Near Flatford Mill is the 16th-century **Willy Lott's House** (not open to the public), which is instantly recognizable from *The Hay Wain*. The National Trust owns Flatford Mill and the houses around it, including the thatched 16th-century **Bridge Cottage,** on the north bank of the Stour, which has a display about Constable's life. ⊠ *Off B1070, East Bergholt* ☎ *01206/298260* ⊕ *www.nationaltrust.org.uk* ⊠ *Free, guided tours or audio tour £2* ☉ *Jan. and Feb., weekends 11–3:30; Mar. and Apr., Wed.–Sun. 11–5:30; May–Sept., daily 10–5:30; Oct., daily 11–4:30; Nov. and Dec., Wed.–Sun. 11–3:30. Guided tours Apr.–Oct. on days open, at 11, 1, and 2:30.*

Where to Stay & Eat

★ ✕ **Le Talbooth.** A longtime favorite, this sophisticated restaurant in a Tudor
£££–£££££ house idyllically set beside the River Stour has a floodlighted terrace where drinks are served in summer. Inside, original beams, leaded-glass windows, and a brick fireplace add to the sense of age. The superb English fare at lunch and dinner may include venison with wild mushroom ravioli or cod on roasted artichokes with curry oil. ⊠ *Gun Hill* ☎ *01206/ 323150* ⚲ *Reservations essential* ⚱ *Jacket and tie* ⊟ *AE, MC, V* ☉ *No dinner Sun. Nov.–Mar.*

££ ✕ **Marlborough Head.** Fine lunches, from fisherman's pie to duck, are served at this early-18th-century pub opposite Constable's school. It gets busy during summer, so arrive early to ensure a table. ⊠ *Mill La.* ☎ *01206/323250* ⊟ *AE, MC, V.*

£££ ✕⊡ **Milsoms.** Owned by the Milsoms of Maison Talbooth fame, this sweet little hotel in a Victorian house reflects their high standards while providing a more modern style. Room decoration is understated but maintains the warmth of the countryside. The soothing, split-level restaurant specializes in updated versions of classic British fare such as baked mussels or chicken livers, and the relaxed bar is perfect for a cuppa. In warm weather, sit by the pond in the garden. ⊠ *Stratford Rd., CO7 6HW* ☎ *01206/322795* ⚱ *01206/323689* ⊕ *www.talbooth.com* ⟿ *14 rooms* ⚬ *Restaurant, room service, minibars, cable TV, bar, lounge, dry cleaning, laundry service, meeting rooms, no-smoking rooms; no a/c* ⊟ *AE, DC, MC, V.*

£££££ ⊡ **Maison Talbooth.** Constable painted the rich meadowlands in which this luxurious Victorian country-house hotel is set. Period antiques, print fabrics, and upholstered furniture decorate each of the elegant, spacious rooms. Guests are encouraged to eat in Le Talbooth restaurant, a short walk or free ride down the lane and owned by the same management. Continental breakfast is served in your bedroom. ⊠ *Stratford Rd., CO7 6HP* ☎ *01206/322367* ⚱ *01206/322752* ⊕ *www.talbooth.com* ⟿ *10 rooms* ⚬ *Room service, some in-room hot tubs, minibars, cable TV, croquet, lounge; no a/c* ⊟ *AE, MC, V* ⏅⏺ *CP.*

Woodbridge

㉕ *18 mi northeast of Dedham.*

One of the first good ports of call on the Suffolk Heritage Coast, Woodbridge, off A12, is a pleasant town whose upper reaches center on a fine old market square with two great pubs, the Bull and the King's Head. Antiques shops fill the surrounding streets, but Woodbridge is at its best around its old quayside. Boatbuilding has been carried out here since the 16th century—although these days pleasure-craft are built, rather than working vessels. The most prominent building is a white clapboard mill, which dates from the 18th century and is powered by the tides.

The visitor center at **Sutton Hoo** helps interpret one of Britain's most significant Anglo-Saxon archaeological sites. In 1938, a local archaeologist excavated three 7th-century burial mounds associated with King Raedwald of East Anglia. Traces of a buried ship were the most unique find; many artifacts uncovered are now in the British Museum in London. Later excavations revealed that this was the site of other burials, some royal. A replica of the 40-oar, 90-foot-long ship stands in the visitor center, which has displays about Anglo-Saxon society and artifacts on loan from the British Museum. Trails around the 245-acre site explore the area along the River Deben. Sutton Hoo is 2 mi east of Woodbridge. ⊠ *B1083* 🕾 *01394/389700* ⊕ *www.nationaltrust.org.uk* 🎫 *£4* ☉ *Mid-Mar.–May and Oct., Wed.–Sun. 10–5; June–Sept., daily 10–5; Nov.–Feb., weekends 10–4.*

off the beaten path

FRAMLINGHAM CASTLE – From the outside, this moated castle looks much as it would have in the 12th century. Upon entering, you'll notice that the keep is missing. (Nearby Orford Castle has an intact keep but no battlements.) An audio tour, included in the admission, leads you on a walk around the curtain wall, with its 13 towers. Most of the chimneys along the wall are fake; they were additions meant to give the impression to passersby that this was a great Tudor mansion. The open-air concerts and reenactments held in the summer are worth seeking out. ⊠ *B1119* 🕾 *01728/724189* ⊕ *www.english-heritage.org.uk* 🎫 *£4* ☉ *Apr.–Sept., daily 10–6; Oct., daily 10–5; Nov.–Mar., daily 10–4.*

Where to Stay

★ **££££** 🏨 **Seckford Hall.** This magnificent Tudor manor house recalls the days of yore with its wood-paneled walls, oak beams, fireplaces, and impressive antiques, including a 16th-century half-tester bed. The landscaped grounds are perfect for a stroll to admire the roses or the duck-filled lake. The main restaurant specializes in local lobster. ⊠ *Off A12, IP13 6NU* 🕾 *01394/385678* 🖷 *01394/380610* ⊕ *www.seckford.co.uk* 📠 *32 rooms* ⌂ *2 restaurants, room service, cable TV, golf privileges, indoor pool, gym, hair salon, hot tub, bar, lounge, laundry service, meeting rooms, some pets allowed (fee); no a/c* ⊟ *AE, DC, MC, V* ⊠ *BP.*

Orford

❷❻ *10 mi east of Woodbridge, 35 mi northeast of Colchester.*

Part of the Suffolk Heritage Coast, a 40-mi stretch that runs from Felixstowe northward to Kessingland, the ancient town of Orford is a beautiful example of the coast's many Areas of Special Scientific Interest. There are numerous beaches, marshes, and broads, with an abundance of wildflowers and birds. You can reach other areas on minor roads running east off A12 north of Ipswich.

Small and squat, **Orford Castle** surveys the flatlands from atop a green mound favored by picnickers in summer. Its splendid triple-tower keep was built in 1160 as a coastal defense. Climb it for a view over what was once a thriving medieval port; the 6-mi shingle (coarse gravel) bank of Orford Ness eventually cut off direct access to the sea. ⊠ *B1084* ☎ *01394/450472* ⊕ *www.english-heritage.org.uk* ✉ *£4* ⊙ *Apr.–Sept., daily 10–6; Oct., daily 10–5; Nov.–Mar., Wed.–Sun. 10–1 and 2–4.*

Just a boat ride beyond Orford Quay lies mysterious **Orford Ness,** Europe's biggest vegetated shingle (large gravel) spit. A 5-mi-long path takes you through beaches and salt marshes to see migrating and native birds and to discover the secret past of the spit—from 1913 until the mid-1980s, it served as a military site. If you'd rather sit than walk, book a seat on the tractor-drawn trailer tour that runs on the first Saturday of the month from July through September. ⊠ *Orford Quay* ☎ *01394/ 450057* ⊕ *www.nationaltrust.org.uk* ✉ *£5.70 including ferry crossing* ⊙ *Mid-Apr.–June and Oct., Sat. 10–2; July–Sept., Tues.–Sat. 10–2; last ferry at 5.*

Where to Stay & Eat

££ ✕ **Butley-Orford Oysterage.** What started as a little café that sold oysters and cups of tea has become a large, bustling, no-nonsense restaurant. It still specializes in oysters and smoked salmon, as well as smoked seafood platters and seasonal fish dishes. The actual smoking takes place in the adjacent smokehouse, and products are for sale in a shop around the corner. ⊠ *Market Hill* ☎ *01394/450277* ⊟ *MC, V* ⊙ *No dinner Sun.–Thurs. Nov.–Mar.*

★ ££–££££ ✕▦ **Crown and Castle.** Artsy, laid-back, and genuinely friendly, this contemporary hotel in an 18th-century building near Orford Castle is a little gem. Many rooms have bathrooms with sunflower-size showerheads; it's best to ask for one of these. The garden rooms are spacious. The Trinity Bistro, run by food writer Ruth Watson, focuses on modern British fare, including plenty of fresh fish and local Butley oysters. In warm weather, the outdoor terrace is a great place for grandstand views of Orford Castle. ⊠ *Market Hill, IP12 2LJ* ☎ *01394/450205* 🖶 *01394/ 450176* ⊕ *www.crownandcastle.co.uk* ⤶ *18 rooms* ⚑ *Restaurant, in-room VCRs, bar, lobby lounge, some pets allowed, no-smoking rooms; no a/c* ⊟ *AE, DC, MC, V* ⎢◯⎥ *BP.*

Aldeburgh

㉗ *20 mi north of Orford, 41 mi northeast of Colchester.*

Aldeburgh (pronounced owl-barrow) is a quiet seaside resort, except in June, when the town fills up with people attending the noted Aldeburgh Festival. Its beach is backed by a promenade lined with candy-color dwellings. Twentieth-century composer Benjamin Britten lived here for some time—he was born in the busy seaside resort of Lowestoft, 30 mi to the north. Britten grew interested in the story of Aldeburgh's native son, the poet George Crabbe (1754–1832), and turned his life story into the celebrated modern opera *Peter Grimes,* a piece that perfectly captures the atmosphere of the Suffolk coast.

The **Elizabethan Moot Hall,** built of flint and timber, stood in the center of a thriving 16th-century town when first erected. Now it's just a few steps from the beach, a mute witness to the erosive powers of the North Sea. ⊠ *Market Cross, Sea Front* 🎫 *£1* ⊙ *Easter–May and Oct., weekends 2:30–5; June and Sept., daily 2:30–5; July and Aug., daily 10:30–12:30 and 2:30–5.*

off the
beaten
path

THORPENESS – Two miles north of Aldeburgh lies this almost bizarrely perfect—but perfectly fake—Tudor village, as well as the whimsical **House in the Clouds,** created to disguise a water pump in the local golf course. The whole village was built as a resort in the early 20th century. The white globe that you see farther up the coast is the Sizewell B nuclear power station.

Where to Stay & Eat

££–£££ ✕ **152aldeburgh.** The Mediterranean influences the cooking at this restaurant and brasserie where seafood is the prime attraction. Bright colors, wood floors, and candlelight create a relaxed backdrop for dishes such as baked cod in herb butter, seafood risottos, and grilled duck breast. For picnic fixings or culinary souvenirs, stop by the adjacent delicatessen, which sells quiches, terrines, cold cuts, and cheeses. ⊠ *152 High St.* ☎ *01728/454152* 🗏 *MC, V.*

££
Fodor'sChoice
★

✕ **The Lighthouse.** An excellent value, this low-key brasserie relies exclusively on locally grown produce and also focuses on seafood, including oysters and Cromer crabs. All the dishes are simply but imaginatively cooked, usually with an interesting sauce that might just as easily be Asian as English. Desserts, such as the creamy bread-and-butter pudding, are particularly good. ⊠ *77 High St.* ☎ *01728/453377* 🗏 *MC, V.*

££££ 🏨 **Brudenell.** The best rooms at this bright, stylish contemporary seaside hotel face the water. Its restaurant serves fresh, uncomplicated seafood dishes. In keeping with the new trend at resort properties, the accommodating staff here is informal, helping guests feel more relaxed. The White Lion hotel, dating to 1563, is the Brudenell's historic sister property. ⊠ *Market Cross Pl., IP15 5BJ* ☎ *01728/452071* 🗏 *01728/454082* ⊕ *www.brudenellhotel.co.uk* 📑 *42 rooms* 🗏 *Restaurant, room service, in-room data ports, cable TV, bar, lounge, some pets allowed (fee); no a/c, no smoking* 🗏 *AE, MC, V* ⧖| *BP.*

£££–££££ 🏨 **Wentworth Hotel.** The Pritt family has owned and managed the Wentworth since 1920, and their caring attention shows. Huge chairs fill the public rooms on the ground floor and are a great place to sip coffee and watch people stroll by. The bedrooms are done in pastel fabrics and seem somewhat dated; sea-view rooms, which are worth the extra cost, come equipped with binoculars. All rooms have a copy of the whimsical children's favorite *Orlando the Marmalade Cat,* by Kathleen Hale, which is set in "Owlbarrow." ⊠ *Wentworth Rd., IP15 5BD* ☎ *01728/452312* 🗏 *01728/454343* ⊕ *www.wentworth-aldeburgh.com* 📑 *37 rooms, 35 with bath* 🗏 *Restaurant, room service, in-room data ports, cable TV,* bar, lobby lounge, meeting rooms, some pets allowed; no a/c, no smoking ⊟ MC, V ⌐◎| BP.

££ 🎬 **Ocean House.** Juliet and Phil Brereton are your hosts at this 1860s
Fodor'sChoice house near the beach, which is an outstanding deal for the price. An-
★ tiques and bric-a-brac decorate the public areas and bedrooms, and the
two rooms with bath have views of the sea. Breakfast is hearty and home-
cooked. ⊠ 25 Crag Path, IP15 5BS ☎ 01728/452094 ⌐◎ 6 rooms, 2
with bath ⌂ Ping-Pong, lounge, piano; no a/c, no smoking ⊟ No credit
cards ⌐◎| BP.

Nightlife & the Arts

East Anglia's most important arts festival, and one of the best known
★ in Great Britain, is the **Aldeburgh Festival,** held during two June weeks
in the small village of Snape, 5 mi west of Aldeburgh, at the Snape Maltings Concert Hall. Founded by Benjamin Britten, the festival concentrates on music but includes related exhibitions, poetry readings, and
even walks. ⊠ High St., Aldeburgh, IP15 5AX ☎ 01728/687100,
01728/453543 box office ⊕ www.aldeburgh.co.uk.

It's well worth a stop to take in the peaceful River Alde location of **Snape
Maltings** cultural center and pause for a drink at the tea shop or a meal
at the Plough & Sail pub. You can also browse in the art galleries and
crafts shops that are part of the center. Snape Maltings has special
events year-round, such as the two-day Aldeburgh Folk Festival, held
each July to celebrate traditional English folk music, and the Britten Festival in October. One-hour river cruises leave from Snape Bridge during high tide. Tickets cost £5 per person. ⊠ Snape, near Saxmundham
☎ 01728/688305 ⊕ www.snapemaltings.co.uk ⊙ Daily 10–5.

Southwold

㉘ 15 mi north of Aldeburgh, 32 mi southeast of Norwich.

This seaside town is an idyllic place to spend a day. Old-fashioned beach
huts painted in bright colors huddle together against the wind on the shingle beach, which is lined with small pebbles, and up in the town center
a pleasing ensemble of old houses faces the main street and surrounds
the central green. The handsome Church of St. Edmund dates to the 15th
century. There aren't many "sights," but the whole town gives you the
sensation of being transported back in time. George Orwell's parents lived
at 3 Queen Street during the 1930s. The **Southwold Museum** displays works
of local archaeology, natural history, and pictures of the 17th-century Battle of Sole Bay. It's in a Dutch-gabled cottage, a style typical of Southwold's domestic architecture. ⊠ Victoria St. ☎ 01502/722375 ⊕ www.
southwoldmuseum.org ⌐ Free ⊙ Easter–July, Sept., and Oct., daily
2–4; Aug., daily 10:30–noon and 2–4.

off the
beaten
path
WALBERSWICK – For many years this tranquil little village, on
B1387, was the haunt of arty types (including, during 1914–15, the
Scottish art nouveau architect Charles Rennie Mackintosh). The
village is separated from Southwold by the mouth of the River Blyth,
over which there's a footbridge (about 1 mi inland), but no main

road bridge. On summer weekends, a boatman ferries foot passengers in a rowboat every few minutes. ✉ *Ferry £1* ⊙ *Ferry May–Sept., weekends 9–12:30 and 2–5.*

Where to Stay & Eat

£££–££££ ✕⌂ **Swan Hotel.** This 17th-century inn has spacious public rooms and decent-size bedrooms decorated in traditional English-country style. Seventeen secluded, quiet garden rooms are set around the old bowling green. The restaurant's dishes are mainly traditional English fare, accompanied by an excellent wine list. Children under 5 are not allowed in the dining room after 7 PM. ⊠ *Market Pl., IP18 6EG* ☎ *01502/722186* 🖷 *01502/724800* ⊕ *www.adnams.co.uk* ⌁ *43 rooms, 41 with bath* ⌂ *Restaurant, croquet, bar, meeting rooms, some pets allowed; no a/c* ⊟ *AE, DC, MC, V* ⏐⊙⏐ *BP.*

£££ ✕⌂ **Crown Hotel.** Like the nearby Swan, the Crown is owned by the old family firm of Adnams brewery, the major employer in Southwold. Bedrooms are suitably small for a 17th-century building, but the antique furniture and friendly staff compensate. The maritime-theme Back Bar or the eclectic brasserie and wine bar provide a cozy place to dine. Seafood dishes are excellent, from pan-fried John Dory to smoked haddock. Children under 5 are not allowed in the restaurant after 7 PM. ⊠ *90 High St., IP18 6DP* ☎ *01502/722275* 🖷 *01502/727263* ⊕ *www.adnams.co. uk* ⌁ *14 rooms, 11 with bath* ⌂ *Restaurant, bar, meeting rooms; no a/c in some rooms* ⊟ *AE, DC, MC, V* ⏐⊙⏐ *BP.*

NORWICH TO NORTH NORFOLK

Norwich, unofficial capital of East Anglia and the heart of the eastern and northern part of East Anglia's "bump," is dominated by the 15th-century spire of its impressive cathedral. Norfolk's continuing isolation from the rest of the country, and its unspoiled landscape and architecture—bypassed by the Industrial Revolution—have proved to be a draw. Many of the flint-knapped (decorated with broken flint) houses in North Norfolk's villages are now weekend or holiday homes. Windmills, churches, and waterways are the area's chief defining characteristics. A few miles inland from the Norfolk coast, the Broads begin, a name that caused much comment among GIs during World War II. In fact, these Broads form a national park, a network of shallow, reed-bordered lakes, many linked by wide rivers. Boating and fishing are great lures; rent a boat for a day or a week and the waterside pubs, churches, villages, and nature reserves all fall within easy reach.

Norwich

63 mi northeast of Cambridge.

It used to be said that Norwich had a pub for each day of the week and a church for each week of the year. Although this is no longer true, both institutions are still much in evidence in this pleasant city of about 130,000. Established by the Saxons because of its prime trading position on the rivers Yare and Wensum, the town has its heart in the triangle between the two waterways, dominated by the castle and cathedral (two of the city's main attractions). The inner beltway follows the line of the old city wall, much of which is still visible. It's worth driving around after dark to see the older buildings, which, thanks to floodlighting, stand out from their newer neighbors. By the time of the Norman Conquest, Norwich was one of the largest towns in England, although much was destroyed by the Normans to create a new town with grand buildings.

You can see the old flint buildings as you walk down the medieval streets, alleyways, and narrow passageways. Despite its concessions to modernity—some industrial sites and many shopping centers—the town remains accessible, historic, and engaging. The University of East Anglia brings a cosmopolitan touch, including a lively arts scene, to an otherwise remote urban area. Norwich makes a good base from which to explore the Norfolk Broads and the coast.

★ ❷⓰ **Norwich Cathedral,** the grandest example of Norman architecture in Norwich, has the second-largest monastic cloisters in Britain (Salisbury's are bigger). Although its spire, at 315 feet tall (also second only to Salisbury's), is visible from everywhere in the city, you cannot see the building itself until you pass through St. Ethelbert's Gate. The cathedral was begun in 1096 by Herbert de Losinga, who had come from Normandy in 1091 to be its first bishop; his splendid tomb is by the high altar. Distinctly Norman elements are the plain west front and dramatic crossing tower, with its austere, geometrical decoration. The remarkable length of the nave is immediately impressive; the similarly striking height of the vaulted ceiling makes it a strain to study the delightful colored bosses, which illustrate Bible stories with great vigor and detail. Binoculars can help. The grave of Norfolk-born nurse Edith Cavell, the British World War I heroine shot by the Germans in 1915, is at the east end of the cathedral. ⊠ 62 *The Close* ☎ *01603/764385* ⊕ *www.cathedral.org.uk* ⊡ *Free* ♡ *Mid-May–mid-Sept., daily 7:30–7; mid-Sept.–mid-May, daily 7:30–6; free guided tours Mon.–Sat. 10:45, 11:30, and 2:15.*

The Cathedral **Close** (grounds) is one of the most idyllic places in Norwich; past the mixture of medieval and Georgian houses, a path leads ❸⓿ down to the ancient water gate, **Pulls Ferry.**

🜩 ❸⓵ The decorated stone facing of **Norwich Castle,** now a museum on the hill in the center of the city, makes it look like a children's book illustration of a castle. The castle is Norman (1130), but a stone keep replaced the original wooden bailey (wall) on the castle mound. The thick walls and other defenses attest to its military function. For most of its history the castle was a prison, and executions took place here well into the 19th century. Today it houses three museum zones—Natural History, Castle and Archaeology, and Art and Exhibitions. Dioramas in Natural History show Norfolk plants and wildlife, and excellent interactive displays in Castle and Archaeology explore topics from ancient Egypt to life in Norman times. You can even try out a copy of Queen Boudicca's chariot to relive her attack on Roman Colchester. Art and Exhibitions includes a gallery devoted to the Norwich School of painters who, like

City Hall **33**

Elm Hill **36**

Norwich
Castle **31**

Norwich
Cathedral **29**

Origins **32**

Pulls Ferry **30**

Sainsbury Centre
for the
Visual Arts **38**

St. Peter
Hungate **37**

St. Peter
Mancroft **34**

Tombland **35**

the Suffolk artist John Constable, focused on the everyday Norfolk landscape and seascape. This museum also holds glass, ceramics, and the world's largest teapot collection. Daily tours explore the castle's battlements or dungeons. ⊠ *Castle Meadow* ☎ *01603/493625* ⊕ *www. norfolk.gov.uk/tourism/museums* ⊠ *Entire museum £5, Castle and Archaeology £3, Art and Exhibitions £3, guided tours of the battlements or dungeons £1.20* ⊙ *Weekdays 10–4, Sat. 10–5, Sun. 2–5.*

🖐 **32** On three floors of the modern **Forum, Origins** provides an introduction to Norwich and the surrounding area via a 90-minute interactive tour. The museum delves back 2,000 years to show how the area's inhabitants and landscape have changed over time—from the Vikings and Romans to the U.S. servicemen and servicewomen who were here during World War II. You can drain a three-dimensional map of the fens, try the Norfolk dialect, and watch a film about the region on a wraparound screen. The shop stocks lots of made-in-Norfolk souvenirs, and the Forum also houses the Norwich Library, a tourist information center, a few places to eat, and an atrium space for entertainment. ⊠ *Between N. Theatre and Bethel Sts.* ☎ *01603/727920* ⊕ *www.theforumnorfolk. com* ⊠ *£4.95* ⊙ *Apr.–Sept., Mon.–Sat. 10–6, Sun. 10:30–4:30; Oct.–Mar., Mon.–Sat. 10–5:30, Sun. 10–4:30.*

With its blanket of brightly striped awnings, the **Market Place,** west of Norwich Castle, has been the heart of the city for 900 years. The large open-air market is closed Sunday. Bronze Norwich lions guard the

33 steps of the imposing—if severe—early-20th-century **City Hall** (⊠ St. Peter St.), which overlooks the Market Place. The elaborate church tower of

34 15th-century **St. Peter Mancroft** (⊠ Bethel St.) rises next to the Market Place. Narrow lanes and alleys that used to be the main streets of me-

35 dieval Norwich lead away from the market and end at **Tombland** by the cathedral. Neither a graveyard nor a plague pit, Tombland was the site

36 of the Anglo-Saxon trading place, now a busy thoroughfare. **Elm Hill,** off Tombland, is a cobbled and pleasing mixture of Tudor and Geor-

37 gian houses that hold gift shops and tearooms. **St. Peter Hungate,** at the top end of Elm Hill, is a 15th-century former church that displays church art and furnishings.

need a break? Part of an arts complex where you can buy locally made creations, the spacious **King of Hearts Café** (⊠ 7–15 Fye Bridge St. ☎ 01603/ 620805) attracts the local art crowd with its excellent snacks and drinks. Everything from cakes to hot lunch fare is served.

38 The **Sainsbury Centre for the Visual Arts,** a modern, hangarlike building designed by Norman Foster on the University of East Anglia campus, holds the private art collection of the Sainsbury family, owners of a supermarket chain. It includes a remarkable quantity of tribal art and 20th-century works, especially art nouveau, and has pieces by Pablo Picasso and Alberto Giacometti. The university was designed in the 1960s by Denys Lasdun, who used its site on the slopes of the River Yare to give a dramatic, stepped-pyramid effect. Buses 4, 5, 26, and 27 run from Norwich Castle Meadow to the university. ⊠ *Earlham Rd.* ☎ *01603/593199* ⊕ *www.uea.ac.uk* 🎫 *£2* ☉ *Tues. and Thurs.–Sun. 11–5, Wed. 11–8.*

Where to Stay & Eat

★ **£££–££££** ✕ **Adlard's Restaurant.** Wine enthusiast and chef David Adlard runs this relaxed contemporary restaurant with pine floors and white walls. Beautifully presented dishes such as roast turbot with crushed potatoes, shallots, and velouté sauce show his ability to bring classical French cooking up to date. Desserts such as prune soufflé with Earl Grey ice cream compete against excellent cheeses. Choose from a small à la carte menu or one of the set menus for lunch or dinner. ⊠ *79 Upper St. Giles St.* ☎ *01603/633522* ▱ *AE, DC, MC, V* ☉ *Closed Sun. and 1 wk after Christmas. No dinner Mon.*

££–£££ ✕ **St. Benedict's.** This brasserie presents excellent, robust English dishes in tandem with more daring creations. Crispy duck might be paired with creamy mashed potatoes and caramelized apple or a tartlet of smoked chicken and artichoke. ⊠ *9 St. Benedict's St.* ☎ *01603/765377* ▱ *AE, DC, MC, V* ☉ *Closed Sun., Mon., and 1 wk at Christmas.*

£–££ ✕ **Adam and Eve.** Said to be Norwich's oldest pub, this place dates back to 1249. From noon until 7, the kitchen serves such pub staples as beef and ale pie or Irish stew from the short but solid bar menu. Greene King and Adnams beer are available. ⊠ *Bishopsgate* ☎ *01603/667423* 🗎 *AE, MC, V.*

£ ✕ **Tree House.** Inventive global cuisine such as tofu in coconut-lime sauce, hearty salads, and tasty sweets are the specialties at this co-op vegetarian restaurant. The menu indicates sugar- and gluten-free dishes. ⊠ *14 Dove St.* ☎ *01603/763258* 🗎 *No credit cards.*

££££ 🏨 **Dunston Hall Hotel & Country Club.** Gables and tall chimneys give this redbrick mansion built in 1859 an Elizabethan look, and extensive modern additions have transformed a country house into a luxurious retreat. The peaceful landscaped gardens and woodland are ideal for relaxing after a day's sightseeing. If you seek a sense of the past, ask for a four-poster bedroom or one of the small attic bedrooms with original low beamed ceilings. The hotel is 4 mi southwest of the city center. ⊠ *Ipswich Rd., NR14 8PQ* ☎ *01508/470444* 🖨 *01508/471499* ⊕ *www. devereonline.co.uk* ⇆ *127 rooms, 3 suites* ⚲ *3 restaurants, room service, in-room data ports, cable TV, driving range, 18-hole golf course, putting green, 2 tennis courts, indoor pool, gym, hot tub, sauna, steam room, billiards, baby-sitting, dry cleaning, laundry service, concierge, meeting rooms, no-smoking rooms; no a/c* 🗎 *AE, DC, MC, V* ❖❖ *BP.*

££ 🏨 **Beeches Hotel.** Three handsome early Victorian houses in the Victorian Gardens make up this family-run hotel. The Governor's House has some rooms with terraces, and the Beeches House has a modern extension. All rooms are simply but pleasantly furnished, and several look out over the gardens and their ornate Gothic fountain and Italianate terrace. The hotel is about a mile west of the city center. ⊠ *2–6 Earlham Rd., NR2 3DB* ☎ *01603/621167* 🖨 *01603/620151* ⊕ *www.beeches.co.uk* ⇆ *36 rooms* ⚲ *Restaurant, room service, cable TV, bar, dry cleaning, laundry service; no a/c, no kids under 12, no smoking* 🗎 *AE, DC, MC, V* ❖❖ *BP.*

Nightlife & the Arts

Cinema City (⊠ St. Andrew's St. ☎ 01603/622047), Norwich's venue for art films, is in a 16th-century building with a café-bar. The **King of Hearts** (⊠ Fye Bridge St. ☎ 01603/766129), a restored medieval merchant's house, serves as a small arts center that presents chamber concerts, recitals, and poetry readings. **Norwich Arts Centre** (⊠ St. Benedict's St. ☎ 01603/660352) has an eclectic program of live music, dance, and stand-up comedy as well as a good café with free Internet access.

The **Maddermarket Theatre** (⊠ St. John's Alley ☎ 01603/620917), patterned after Elizabethan theaters, has been the base of the Norwich Players, an amateur repertory company, since 1911. The theater closes in August. **Norwich Playhouse** (⊠ Gun Wharf, St. George's St. ☎ 01603/598598), a professional repertory group, performs everything from Shakespeare to world premieres of new plays; it also runs a bookshop. Norwich's biggest and best-known theater, the **Theatre Royal** (⊠ Theatre St. ☎ 01603/630000), hosts touring companies staging musicals, ballet, opera, and plays.

Sports & the Outdoors

Traffic on the River Yare is now mostly for pleasure rather than commerce, and a summer trip with **City Boats** gives a fresh perspective on

Norwich. Longer trips are available down the Rivers Wensum and Yare to the nearer Broads. ⊠ *Elm Hill, Pulls Ferry, Station, Whitlingham Park, and Griffin Lane quays* ☎ *01603/701701* ⊠ *£4.50–£10* ⊙ *Tours at 10:15, 11, 12:30, 1:30, 3.*

Touring by car isn't really an option if you want to see something of the **Norfolk Broads** (⊕ www.broads-authority.gov.uk) , because much of this area of shallow lakes linked by wide rivers is inaccessible by road. On a boating holiday, you can cruise with your own launch through 150 mi of waterways. **Broads Tours** (☎ 01603/782207 Wroxham, 01692/670711 Potter Heigham), based at the quaysides in Wroxham, 7 mi northeast of Norwich, and Potter Heigham, 15 mi northeast of Norwich, offers day cruises in the Broads as well as half-day and full-day launch rental (lessons included). Major operators such as **Hoseasons** (☎ 01502/502588 or 0870/543–4434) rent boats by the week. The *Norada, Olive,* and *Hathor* are historic wherry yachts (sailing barges), and all may be chartered from the **Wherry Yacht Centre** (☎ 01603/782470) for luxurious cruises for up to 12 people.

Explore the Norfolk Broads by bicycle with **Broadland Cycle Hire** (⊠ The Rhond, Hoverton ☎ 01603/783096), 8 mi northeast of Norwich. Rentals (£9 per day) are available from Easter through October. The company can recommend routes 7 to 20 mi from their base.

Shopping

The medieval lanes of Norwich, around Elm Hill and Tombland, contain the best antiques, book, and crafts stores. The **Mustard Shop** (⊠ 15 Royal Arcade ☎ 01603/627889) pays homage to Colman's Mustard, a company founded in Norwich in the early 19th century; it sells collectibles and more than 15 varieties of mustard. The **Norwich Antiques Centre** (⊠ 14 Tombland ☎ 01603/619129), opposite the cathedral, is an old house crammed full of shops. **Norwich Market** (⊠ Market Pl., Gentleman's Walk ☎ 01603/212414), the city's main outdoor market, is open daily; it sells everything from jewelry to clothes and food and gives a taste of everyday Norwich life.

Blickling Hall

★ ㊴ *15 mi north of Norwich.*

Behind the wrought-iron entrance gate to Blickling Hall, two mighty yew hedges form an imposing allée, creating a magnificent frame for this perfectly symmetrical, Jacobean masterpiece. The redbrick mansion has towers and chimneys, baroque Dutch gables, and, in the center, a three-story timber clock tower. The grounds include a formal flower garden and parkland with woods that conceal a temple, an orangery, and a pyramid. Blickling belonged to a succession of historic figures, including Sir John Fastolf, the model for Shakespeare's Falstaff; Anne Boleyn's family, who owned it until Anne was executed by her husband, Henry VIII; and finally, Lord Lothian, an ambassador to the United States. The Long Gallery (127 feet) has an intricate plasterwork ceiling with Jacobean emblems, and the superb 17th-century staircase is worth examining. Most of the interior is handsome but somewhat austere, although a sumptuous tapestry of Peter the Great at the Battle of Poltawa hangs in its own room. Next to the main entrance is the Buckinghamshire Arms, a pub. ✉ *B1354, Blickling* ☎ *01263/738030* ⊕ *www.nationaltrust.org.uk* 🎫 *£7, gardens only £4* ⊙ *House Apr.–Sept., Wed.–Sun. 1–5; Oct.–Nov., Wed.–Sun. 1–4. Gardens Jan.–Mar., weekends 11–4; Apr.–July, Sept., and Oct., Wed.–Sun. 10:15–5:15; Aug., Tues.–Sun. 10:15–5:15; Nov.–late Dec., Thurs.–Sun. 11–4.*

Blakeney

40 *15 mi northeast of Blickling Hall, 27 mi northeast of Norwich.*

The Norfolk coast begins to feel wild and remote near Blakeney, 15 mi west of Cromer. Driving along the coast road from Cromer, you pass marshes, sandbanks, and coves, as well as a string of villages. Blakeney is one of the most appealing, with harbors used for small fishing boats and yachts. Once a bustling port town exporting corn and salt, it enjoys a quiet existence today, and a reputation for excellent wildlife viewing at Blakeney Point.

Blakeney Point, a thousand acres of grassy dunes, is home to nesting terns and about 500 common and gray seals. You can walk 3½ mi from Cley Beach to get here, but a boat trip from Blakeney or Morston quay is fun and educational. **Bishop's Boats** (✉ Old Lifeboat House ☎01263/740753 ⊕ www.norfolksealtrips.co.uk) runs one- or two-hour trips daily from Morston quay and Blakeney harbor for £5.50 per person. **Temples Seal Trips** (✉ Morston Quay, Morston ☎ 01263/740791) has hour-long trips daily from the quay for £5 per person. ✉ *A149* ☎ *01263/740480 Apr.–Sept., 01263/740241 Oct.–Mar.* ⊕*www.nationaltrust.org.uk* 🎫*Free.*

Where to Stay & Eat

££ ✕🍴 **White Horse at Blakeney.** Fine food is the draw at this former coaching inn. Mussels, crabs, and fish appear on the menu, along with pub classics such as steak and ale pie and Whitby scampi and chips. The restaurant (reservations essential) opens at 7 PM every day except Monday. A few of the pleasant, simply furnished rooms have sea views that are worth paying extra for. ✉ *4 High St., NR25 7TE* ☎ *01263/740574* 🖷 *01263/741303* ⊕*www.blakeneywhitehorse.co.uk* 🛏*9 rooms, 1 suite* ⚘ *Restaurant, lounge, pub, Internet; no a/c* ▬*MC, V* ⊙ *Closed 2 wks in Jan.* ❗│*BP.*

Wells-next-the-Sea

41 *10 mi west of Blakeney, 37 mi northwest of Norwich.*

A quiet base from which to explore, the harbor town of Wells-next-the-Sea and the nearby coastline remain untouched, with many excellent places for bird-watching and walking on the sandy beaches of Holkham Bay, near Holkham Hall. Today the town is a mile from the sea, but in Tudor times, when it was closer to the ocean, it served as one of the main ports of East Anglia. The remains of a medieval priory and two holy wells point to the town's past as a major pilgrimage destination in the Middle Ages. Along the nearby beach, a narrow-gauge steam train makes the short journey to Walsingham in summer.

Fodor's Choice
★
The Palladian **Holkham Hall,** one of the most splendid mansions in Britain, is the seat of the Coke family, the earls of Leicester. In the late 18th century, Thomas Coke went on the fashionable grand tour of the Continent, returning with art treasures and determined to build a house according to the new Italian ideas. Centered by a grand staircase and modeled after the Baths of Diocletian, the entryway, the 60-foot-tall Marble Hall (mostly alabaster, in fact), may be the most spectacular room in Britain. Beyond this hall lie salons brilliant with gold and alabaster, each filled with works from Coke's collection of masterpieces, including paintings by Gainsborough, Sir Anthony Van Dyck, Peter Paul Rubens, Raphael, and other old masters. Surrounding this transplant from neoclassical Italy is extensive parkland landscaped by Capability Brown in 1762. The **Bygones Museum,** in the stable block, has more than 5,000 items, from gramophones to fire engines. ⊠ *Off A149* ☎ *01328/710227* ⊕ *www.holkham.co.uk* ✍ *Hall £6.50, museum £5, combined ticket £10* ☉ *June–Sept., Thurs.–Mon. 1–5, national holiday Mon. 11:30–5.*

Where to Stay & Eat

★
£££–£££££
✕🏠 **Hoste Arms.** Paul Whittome and his wife have turned a 17th-century former coaching inn into a small hotel and destination gastro-pub. The menu lists such delights as Cromer crab, Burnham Creek oysters, and North Sea mussels, and the light sauces are more Asian than European. Though the food is trendy, the hotel's style is generally traditional, with prints in the bedrooms, walled gardens, beamed ceilings, and log fires; the six modern rooms in the Zulu Wing are the exception. For less expensive accommodation try the nearby sister property, the Railway Inn, which has six small rooms with fewer amenities. Burnham Market is a lovely town 6 mi west of Wells. ⊠ *The Green, B1155, Burnham Market, PE31 8HD* ☎ *03128/738777* 🖷 *01328/730103* ⊕ *www.hostearms.co.uk* ✍ *36 rooms* ♨ *3 restaurants, bar, Internet, meeting rooms, some pets allowed (fee); no a/c* ▭ *AE, DC, MC, V* ⑩ *BP.*

£££–£££££
Fodor's Choice
★
✕🏠 **Victoria at Holkham.** A colorful, whimsical hideaway, the Victoria is adjacent to Holkham Hall and owned by the current earl of Leicester. Guest rooms and public areas mix Victorian, colonial, and local themes, all with a touch of Asia. The ornately carved dark-wood furniture was handmade in India for the hotel. In the restaurant you can try game dishes and local seafood such as Cromer crabs, Brancaster mussels, and fresh eels. The dune-backed Holkham Beach (where the ending beach scene from *Shakespeare in Love* was filmed) is only a few minutes' walk away. ⊠ *A149, NR23 1AB* ☎ *01328/711008* 🖷 *01328/ 711009* ⊕ *www.holkham.co.uk/victoria* ✍ *11 rooms* ♨ *Restaurant, room service, in-room data ports, cable TV, bar, Internet; no a/c in some rooms* ▭ *AE, DC, MC, V* ⑩ *CP.*

££–££££
✕🏠 **Crown Hotel.** Overlooking an expanse of green known as the Buttlands, the Crown contains stylish, bright guest rooms done with minimalist flair. The wonderful restaurant serves local delights, with an occasional nod to Asia: flash-fried squid; bacon and black pudding; steamed North Sea cod with ginger, lemongrass, and lime; and apple and walnut pudding with clotted cream. The bar offers less expensive but no less innovative fare. ⊠ *The Buttlands, Wells-next-the-Sea NR23*

1EX ☎ *01328/710209* 🖷 *01328/711432* ⊕ *www.thecrownhotelwells. co.uk* ⏴⏵ *9 rooms, 2 suites ☖ Restaurant, in-room data ports, some in-room VCRs, bar, lounge, baby-sitting, meeting rooms; no a/c ▭ MC, V ⏏⏍ BP.*

Sports & the Outdoors

On Yer Bike Cycle Hire (✉ The Laurels, Nutwood Farm, Wighton ☎ 01328/820719) will deliver and collect bikes; rentals are £10 per day, and advance reservations are required.

Sandringham House

❹❷ *15 mi southwest of Wells-next-the-Sea, 8 mi northeast of King's Lynn, 43 mi northwest of Norwich.*

Sandringham House, not far from the old-fashioned but still popular seaside resort of Hunstanton, is one of the Queen's residences—it's where the Royal Family spends Christmas, as well as other vacations. The huge, redbrick Victorian mansion was clearly designed for enormous country-house parties, with a ballroom, billiard room, and bowling alley, as well as a shooting lodge on the grounds—no wonder George V wrote fondly of "dear old Sandringham." The house and gardens close when the Queen is in residence, but the woodlands, nature walks, and museum of royal memorabilia (in the old stables) remain open, as does the church, medieval but in heavy Victorian disguise. ✉ *Sandringham* ☎ *01553/772675* ⊕ *www.sandringhamestate.co.uk* 🎫 *House, gardens, and museum £6.50, gardens and museum £4.50* ☉ *Apr.–mid-July, Aug., and Sept., daily 11–5; Oct., daily 11–3.*

Houghton Hall

❹❸ *8 mi east of Sandringham, 35 mi northwest of Norwich.*

This grand Palladian pile, built by British prime minister Sir Robert Walpole in the 1720s, has been carefully restored by its current owner, the seventh marquess of Cholmondeley. The double-height Stone Hall and the sumptuous state rooms, perfect for gatherings of the powerful, reveal designer William Kent's preference for gilt, plush fabrics, stucco, and elaborate carvings. The Common Parlour, one of the original family rooms, is elegant but far simpler. New landscaping, including a 5-acre walled garden, is also part of the picture. ✉ *Off A148, near Harpley* ☎ *01485/528569* ⊕ *www.houghtonhall.com* 🎫 *£6.50, park and grounds only £4* ☉ *May–Sept., Wed., Thurs., Sun., and bank holiday Mon. 2–5:30; grounds open at 1; last admission at 5.*

King's Lynn

❹❹ *12 mi southwest of Houghton Hall, 40 mi northwest of Norwich.*

As Bishop's Lynn, the town thrived as a port on the River Ouse, growing prosperous in the 15th century through the wool trade and other kinds of trade with the continent; a Flemish influence is apparent in the church brasses and the style of the town squares. When Bishop's Lynn became royal property, the name was changed to King's Lynn. Although part of the old center was torn down and rebuilt in the mid-20th century, enough remains of its Georgian town houses, guildhalls, and ancient quayside warehouses (including the 15th-century Hanseatic Warehouse on St. Margaret's Lane) that this is still one of the most English of English towns.

The 15th-century **Trinity Guildhall,** with its striking, checkered-stone front, contains some civic treasures in the **Regalia Rooms,** in the guildhall undercroft. A recorded audio tour calls attention to such items as the unique silver-and-enamel 14th-century chalice known as King John's Cup. You enter the rooms through the adjacent **Old Gaol House,** site of the town police station until 1954, whose cells form part of an engaging law-and-order museum. The Guildhall itself is now the Civic Hall of the Borough Council and is not generally open to the public, although you can visit it during the King's Lynn Festival in July and on occasional guided tours in summer. ⊠ *Saturday Market Pl.* ☎ *01533/774297* 🖃 *£2.40* ☉ *Apr.–Oct., daily 10–5; Nov.–Mar., Fri.–Tues. 10–5.*

St. George's Guildhall, the largest surviving medieval guildhall in England, forms part of the **King's Lynn Arts Centre,** an arts and theater complex administered by the National Trust, and the focal point for the annual King's Lynn Festival. There's also a gallery, and the center has a crafts fair every December. The **Crofters Coffee House** (☎ 01553/773134), in the guildhall undercroft, is a budget choice for breakfast, lunch, or afternoon tea. ⊠ *27–29 King St.* ☎ *01553/765565, 01553/764864 box office* ⊕ *www.kingslynnarts.org.uk* 🖃 *Free* ☉ *Tues.–Sat. 10–5.*

off the
beaten
path

CASTLE RISING – Giant defensive earthworks surround this impressive 12th-century stone castle, which is 4 mi northeast of King's Lynn. The 120-foot-high walls, sadly lacking a roof after all these centuries, contain some well-preserved sections, especially the chapel and the kitchen. Owned by the Howard family since 1544, the castle has been used as a hunting lodge and royal residence and is a fine example of a domestic keep. ⊠ *A149* ☎ *01553/631330* ⊕ *www.castlerising.co.uk* 🖃 *£3.75* ☉ *Apr.–Nov., daily 10–6 or dusk; Nov.–Mar., Wed.–Sun. 10–4.*

Where to Stay & Eat

£££–££££ ✕ **Riverside Restaurant.** Part of the King's Lynn Arts Centre, this restaurant reflects the style of the original 15th-century warehouse, with its gnarled oak beams and redbrick walls. Lunches might include local mussels or fresh salmon; dinner is more elaborate, perhaps stuffed Portobello mushrooms followed by halibut steak or venison. When the weather allows, there are tables outside, overlooking the river. ⊠ *27 King St.* ☎ *01553/773134* 🖃 *MC, V* ☉ *Closed Sun.*

£££££ ✕🖫 **Congham Hall.** Parkland surrounds this lovely Georgian manor house, 6 mi east of King's Lynn. Neutral colors and traditional print fabrics keep the bedrooms light and airy. Food is taken seriously here—the hotel grows the herbs and vegetables used in the kitchen, smokes its own fish, and collects honey. Cromer crab, Norfolk pheasant, and King's Lynn shrimp all appear on the menu. ⊠ *A148, Grimston, PE32*

1AH ☎ 01485/600250 🖷 01485/601191 ⊕ *www.conghamhallhotel. co.uk* ⤶ *12 rooms, 2 suites ὐ Restaurant, lounge, baby-sitting, meeting rooms, helipad, some pets allowed, kennel, no-smoking rooms; no a/c* ▭ *AE, DC, MC, V* ⑪ *BP.*

£££ 🗔 **Duke's Head.** The location couldn't be better: wake up on Tuesday morning and the front rooms at the pink-washed Duke's Head have prime views of the market below in full swing. In the oldest, 17th-century part of the hotel, where age bows the main staircase, no two guest rooms are alike. The floorboards may be creaky, but each room has comfortable beds and relaxing armchairs. You can indulge in a cream tea in the lounge. ⊠ *Tuesday Market Pl., PE30 1JS* ☎ *01533/774996* 🖷 *01553/ 763556* ⊕ *www.regalhotels.co.uk* ⤶ *71 rooms ὐ 2 restaurants, some in-room data ports, room TVs with movies, 2 bars, lounge, some pets allowed, no-smoking rooms; no a/c* ▭ *AE, DC, MC, V* ⑪ *BP.*

££ 🗔 **Tudor Rose.** Dating back to the 16th and 17th centuries, this small hotel, right off Tuesday Market Place, makes an appealing budget choice. Exposed oak beams and sloping floors in the restaurant and the simply furnished rooms recall the building's age. The restaurant serves pub food with world flavors, such as Mediterranean lamb and Mexican chili. ⊠ *St. Nicholas Pl., PE30 1LR* ☎ *01553/762824* 🖷 *01553/ 764894* ⊕ *www.tudorrose-hotel.co.uk* ⤶ *13 rooms, 11 with bath ὐ Restaurant, room service, in-room data ports, bar, lounge, no-smoking rooms; no a/c* ▭ *AE, DC, MC, V* ⑪ *BP.*

Nightlife & the Arts

St. George's Guildhall is the venue for much of the **King's Lynn Festival** (☎ 01553/767557 ⊕ www.kl-festival.freeserve.co.uk), which takes place in July and encompasses concerts, exhibitions, theater, dance, films, literary events, and children's programs. The **Corn Exchange** (⊠ Tuesday Market Pl. ☎ 01553/764864), a splendidly revamped 19th-century building, hosts concerts, theater, comedy, and crafts events.

LINCOLN, BOSTON & STAMFORD

The fens of northern Cambridgeshire pass imperceptibly into the three divisions of Lincolnshire: Holland, Kesteven, and Lindsey are all parts of the great county, divided administratively. Holland borders the Isle of Ely and the delightfully named Soke of Peterborough. This marshland spreads far and wide south of the Wash, the place names of the district almost reflecting the squelch of mud the inhabitants of pre-drainage times must have encountered. The chief attractions are two towns: Lincoln, with its magnificent cathedral, and Stamford, to the southwest. En route to Lincoln is Peterborough, with its medieval cathedral.

The countryside around Lincoln, especially the Lincolnshire Wolds (chalk hills) to the northeast, consists of hills and copses, with drystone (unmortared) walls dividing well-tended fields. The unspoiled rural area of the Wolds, strikingly evoked in Tennyson's poetry, is particularly worth a visit, whereas the long coastline with its miles of sandy beaches and its North Sea air has all the usual, if occasionally tacky, seaside facilities for families. Tulips are the pride and joy of south Lincolnshire, drawing thousands from all parts of Britain to view the Holland and Kesteven bulb fields in springtime.

Peterborough

45 *22 mi southwest of King's Lynn, 38 mi north of Cambridge.*

Peterborough's main attraction, the cathedral, is best seen on a day trip from Cambridge. Much of the pedestrianized city center is marred by the commercial shopping center, the Queensgate.

The third building to rise on the site, **Peterborough Cathedral** was begun in 1118, and its history reflects some key events in English history. The first church was founded in 655 by Peada, a nobleman from the early English kingdom of Mercia in central Britain. It was destroyed by the Danes in 870 and reconstructed in 972, only to be burned down again, this time by mistake, in 1116. The next incarnation, consecrated in 1238 after 120 years of building, still towers over Peterborough. It has seen its fair share of strife, including occupation by Cromwell's forces, who fired muskets into the ceiling and broke most of the statues, stained-glass windows, choir stalls, and high altar. Although the cathedral has been left with few monuments, the result is a startlingly spacious interior into which light streams through the clear glass.

Three soaring arches, each 85 feet high, mark the outstanding west front. In the peaks of their gables are the figures of St. Peter, St. Paul, and St. Andrew (the cathedral is consecrated to these saints), and high inside the north arch is a modern figure of Queen Elizabeth II. Inside, the nave ceiling, dating from 1220, is one of the most significant examples of Romanesque painting in Europe—note the monsters as well as figures of saints, bishops, and kings. Henry VIII buried Catherine of Aragon, his first wife, here after her death (by natural causes) in 1536. In 1541 he conferred cathedral status on the abbey, and over the tomb of his first, most pious wife now hangs the standard of Henry VIII, given by Elizabeth II. The last addition to the cathedral is the New Building, built between 1496 and 1508. The exquisite vaulting here is probably by the architect John Wastell, who created the famous fan vaulting in King's College Chapel, Cambridge. An exhibit in the north transept depicts the life of the cathedral throughout its long history.

In the Deanery gardens (seen by tour only), 18th- and 19th-century buildings surround an early Victorian garden. Tout Hill, the remains of a Norman fortification, is in the gardens. ⊠ *Little Prior's Gate, 12A Minster Precinct* ☎ *01733/560964* ⊕ *www.peterborough-cathedral.org.uk* ⊠ *Donation requested; tour £3, tower £4, garden £3* ⊙ *Daily 8:30–5:15, garden tour Wed. and Sat. 10:45 and 1:45.*

The **Peterborough Museum and Art Gallery** explores the history of Peterborough from the Jurassic period to the modern day, including both natural and social history. The art gallery displays contemporary art and crafts. The 1816 building, a short walk from the cathedral, was originally a town house. ⊠ *Priestgate* ☎ *01733/752451* ⊕ *www. peterboroughheritage.org.uk* ⊠ *Free* ⊙ *Tues.–Fri. noon–5; Sat. 10–5, Sun. noon–4.*

Stamford

🏵 *14 mi northwest of Peterborough, 47 mi northwest of Cambridge.*

Serene Stamford, on a hillside overlooking the River Welland, has a well-preserved center, in part because in 1967 it was designated England's first conservation area. This unspoiled town, which grew rich in the medieval wool and cloth trades, is a delightful place to stroll and study the harmonious mixture of Georgian and medieval architecture.

★ **Burghley House,** an architectural masterpiece that many consider the largest and grandest house of the first Elizabethan age, is celebrated for its roof-scape bristling with pepper-pot chimneys and slate-roof towers. It was built between 1565 and 1587 to the design of William Cecil, first Baron Burghley, when he was Elizabeth I's high treasurer; his descendants still occupy the house. The interior was remodeled in the late 17th century with treasures from Europe. The house contains 18 of the most sumptuous state rooms in England, with carvings by Grinling Gibbons and ceiling paintings by Antonio Verrio (including the dramatic Heaven Room and the Hell Staircase), as well as innumerable paintings and priceless porcelain. There's an 80-minute guided tour of the house on weekdays, or you can tour at your own pace on weekends.

In the 18th century Capability Brown landscaped the grounds, creating the lake, the Lion Bridge, and the Gothic Revival Orangery, where you can have tea or lunch. A recent chatelain, the sixth marquess of Exeter, was one of the Olympic runners whose life story inspired the 1981 film *Chariots of Fire*. The house is a mile southeast of Stamford. ⊠ *Off A1* ☎ *01780/752451* ⊕ *www.burghley.co.uk* 🎫 *£7.80* ⊙ *Apr.–Oct., daily 11–4:30.*

Lincoln

★ 🚗 *93 mi northwest of Cambridge, 97 mi northwest of Norwich, 53 mi north of Stamford.*

Celts, Romans, and Danes all had important settlements here, but it was the Normans who gave Lincoln its medieval stature after William the Conqueror founded Lincoln Castle as a stronghold in 1068. Four years later William appointed Bishop Remigius to run the huge diocese stretching from the Humber to the Thames, resulting in the construction of Lincoln Cathedral, the third largest in England after York Minster and St. Paul's. Since medieval times Lincoln's status has declined. However, its somewhat remote location (there are no major motorways or railways nearby) has helped preserve its traditional character.

In the city center you can walk under the 15th-century Stonebow arch on the site of an old Roman gate. Beyond the arch is the Guildhall, which houses the city's civic regalia. The River Witham flows unobtrusively under the incongruously named High Bridge, a low, vaulted Norman bridge topped by timber-frame houses from the 16th century. West of High Bridge, the river opens out into Brayford Pool, busy with river traffic and, less attractively, road traffic. Here you can rent different kinds of boats. From April through September cruisers tour the River Witham, showing you the city from the water (contact the Lincoln tourist office).

The cathedral is set on the aptly named Steep Hill; to its south, narrow medieval streets cling to the hillside and invite exploration. Jew's House, on the Strait, dating from the early 12th century, is one of several well-preserved domestic buildings in this area.

Lincoln's crowning glory, the great **Cathedral of St. Mary,** was for hundreds of years the tallest building in Europe, but this magnificent medieval building is now among the least known of European cathedrals. The Norman bishop Remigius began work in 1072. The Romanesque church he built was irremediably damaged, first by fire, then by earthquake (in 1185), but you can still see parts of the ancient structure at the west front. The next great phase of building, initiated by Bishop Hugh of Avalon, is mainly 13th century in character. The unique west front, topped by two strikingly tall towers, gives tremendous breadth to the entrance. It is best seen from the 14th-century Exchequer Gate arch in front of the cathedral, or from the castle battlements beyond.

Inside, a breathtaking impression of space and unity belies the many centuries of building and rebuilding. The stained-glass window at the north end of the transept, known as the Dean's Eye, is one of the earliest (13th-century) traceried windows, whereas its opposite number at the south end shows a 14th-century sophistication in its interlaced designs. St. Hugh's Choir, in front of the altar, and the Angel Choir at the east end behind it have ceilings with "crazy vaulting," so called because of the irregular pattern. Look for the Lincoln Imp upon the pillar nearest St. Hugh's shrine; an angel turned this creature to stone, according to legend. Look even farther up (use binoculars or a telephoto lens) to see the 30 angels who are playing musical instruments and who give this part of the cathedral its name. Through a door on the north side is the chapter house, a 10-sided building that sometimes housed the medieval Parliament of England during the reigns of Edward I and Edward II. The chapter house is connected to the 13th-century cloister, notable for its amusing ceiling bosses. The cathedral library, a restrained building by Christopher Wren, was built onto the north side of the cloisters after the original library collapsed. Tours of the cathedral roof are fascinating. ⊠ *Minster Yard* ☎ *01522/544544* ⊕ *www. lincolncathedral.com* ▣ *£4* ⊘ *June–Aug., Mon.–Sat. 7:15 AM–8 PM, Sun. 7:15–6; Sept.–May, Mon.–Sat. 7:15–6, Sun. 7:15–5. Guided tours Oct.–Feb., daily at 11 and 2; Mar.–Sept., daily at 11, 1, and 3; roof tours weekdays at 2, Sat. 11 and 2.*

need a break? Whether you just need a warming cuppa or seek a more filling, savory meat pie or a sweet dessert, stop by **Browns Pie Shop** (⊠ 33 Steep Hill, ☎ 01522/527330), a little restaurant that serves food until 10 PM.

The **Minster Yard,** which surrounds the cathedral on three sides, contains buildings of different periods, including graceful examples of Georgian architecture. A statue of Alfred, Lord Tennyson, who was born in Lincolnshire, stands on the green near the chapter house. The **Medieval Bishop's Palace,** on the south side of Minster Yard, has a garden and exhibits about the former administrative center of the diocese. ⊠ *Minster Yard* ☎ *01522/ 527468* ⊕ *www.english-heritage.org.uk* ▣ *£3.20* ⊘ *Apr.–Sept., daily 10–6; Oct., daily 10–5; Nov.–Mar., weekends 10–4.*

Ⓒ **Lincoln Castle,** facing the cathedral across Exchequer Gate, was built on two great mounds by William the Conqueror in 1068, incorporating part of the remains of Roman garrison walls. The castle was a military base until the 17th century, after which it operated as a prison. In the extraordinary prison chapel you can see the cagelike stalls in which Victorian convicts listened to sermons. One of the four surviving copies of the Magna Carta, signed by King John at Runnymede in 1215, is on display in the same building. ⊠ *Castle Hill* ☎ *01522/511068* ▣ *£3.50* ⊘ *Apr.–Oct., Mon.–Sat. 9:30–5:30, Sun. 11–5:30; Nov.–Mar., Mon.–Sat. 9:30–4, Sun. 11–4.*

The **Usher Gallery** has an interesting collection of watches and clocks donated by its benefactor, James Ward Usher, a jeweler who invented the legend of the Lincoln Imp. The gallery also contains memorabilia

connected with the poet Tennyson. ⊠ *Lindum Rd.* ☎ *01522/527980*
🖾 *£2, free on Fri.* ☉ *Tues.–Sat. 10–5:30, Sun. 2:30–5.*

Where to Stay & Eat

£££££ ✗ **Jew's House.** Antique tables and oil paintings enhance this intimate restaurant in one of Lincoln's oldest buildings, a rare survivor of 12th-century Norman domestic architecture that was originally the home of a Jewish merchant. The cosmopolitan fixed-price menu of Continental specialties changes daily, and the restaurant is renowned for its fresh fish and rich desserts, all homemade. ⊠ *15 The Strait* ☎ *01522/524851* ▭ *AE, DC, MC, V* ☉ *Closed Sun. and Mon.*

£–££ ✗ **Wig and Mitre.** This interesting downtown pub-café-restaurant stays open from 8 AM until 11 PM, with everything from breakfast to full evening meals. Produce comes from the local markets, and dishes may include spiced lamb, herbed fish cakes, or a full English breakfast. ⊠ *30 Steep Hill* ☎ *01522/535190* ▭ *AE, DC, MC, V.*

★ **£££–££££** 🏨 **White Hart.** Lincoln's most elegant lodging is luxuriously furnished with a wealth of antiques, among them some fine clocks and china. The establishment has been a hotel for 600 years, reflecting a volume of experience. Bedrooms are individually decorated in traditional style; many are outfitted with antiques, and hardwoods such as walnut and mahogany abound. Rates that include breakfast and dinner are a particularly good deal here. ⊠ *Bailgate, LN1 3AR* ☎ *01522/526222* 🖶 *01522/531798* ⊕ *www.heritage-hotels.com* 🛏 *36 rooms, 12 suites* ⚘ *Restaurant, room service, some in-room data ports, bar, lounge, baby-sitting, dry cleaning, laundry service, meeting rooms, some pets allowed (fee), no-smoking rooms; no a/c* ▭ *AE, DC, MC, V* ❢◯❢ *BP.*

£££ 🏨 **D'Isney Place Hotel.** This pleasant small hotel occupies a converted town house near the cathedral. If you like privacy, it's ideal: there's no lounge or other communal space. A cooked breakfast served on Minton china is delivered to your room. For a bit more style, choose one of the deluxe rooms with whirlpool baths. The pleasant garden includes a piece of the old city wall. ⊠ *Eastgate, LN2 4AA* ☎ *01522/538881* 🖶 *01522/511321* ⊕ *www.disneyplacehotel.co.uk* 🛏 *17 rooms* ⚘ *Room service, some in-room hot tubs, baby-sitting, dry cleaning, laundry service, some pets allowed (fee), no-smoking rooms; no a/c* ▭ *AE, DC, MC, V* ❢◯❢ *BP.*

Nightlife & the Arts

The **Theatre Royal** (⊠ Clasketgate ☎ 01522/525555), a fine Victorian theater, previews shows before their London runs and hosts touring productions. Concerts are occasionally given on Sunday.

Shopping

Chain stores fill the Bailgate Mall and High Street. The best stores, however, are on Bailgate, Steep Hill, and the medieval streets leading directly down from the cathedral and castle. **Cobb Hall Craft Centre** (⊠ St. Paul's La., off Bailgate), a small mall of crafts shops and workshops, sells clocks, candles, and ornaments. **David Hansord** (⊠ Castle Hill ☎ 01522/530044) specializes in antiques, especially scientific instruments. Steep Hill has good bookstores, antiques shops, and crafts and art galleries, including **Harding House Galleries** (⊠ Steep Hill ☎ 01522/523537).

Boston

48 *31 mi southeast of Lincoln.*

This town on the River Witham prospered during the Middle Ages because of the wool trade with Flanders, and revived in the late 18th century after the fens were drained. It was from Boston that, in 1630, a group of Puritans including John Winthrop (the first governor of the Massachusetts Bay colony) set sail across the Atlantic in search of religious freedom. They soon founded the Massachusetts city of the same name. Among this group was poet Anne Bradstreet. The town's leading landmark is the Boston Stump, the lantern tower of the 14th-century **Church of St. Botolph** (✉ 1 Wormgate ☎ 01205/362992). With a height of 288 feet, the tower can be seen for 20 mi from both land and sea; it once housed a light that not only guided ships coming to the old port but also directed wayfarers crossing the treacherous marsh. Today it's also a directional beacon for aircraft.

The 15th-century guildhall, now the **Guildhall Museum,** contains the courtroom where the Pilgrims were tried and the cells where they were held. ✉ *St. Mary's Guildhall, South St.* ☎ *01205/365954* ⊕ *www. boston.gov.uk* ☉ *Closed during most of 2005 for renovation; call for opening information.*

Among the reminders of Boston's transatlantic links is the early-18th-century **Fydell House,** next to the guildhall, now an adult education center. A room is set aside to welcome visitors from the United States. ✉*South St.* ☎ *01205/351520* ☒ *Free* ☉ *Call to arrange a visit.*

EAST ANGLIA A TO Z

To research prices, get advice from other travelers, and book travel arrangements, visit www.fodors.com.

AIRPORTS

Norwich International Airport serves domestic and European destinations. For information about Stansted Airport in Essex, north of London, *see* Airports *in* Smart Travel Tips.

🛈 **Norwich International Airport** ✉ A140, Norwich ☎ 01603/428700 ⊕ www. norwichinternational.com.

BIKE & MOPED TRAVEL

The Broads Authority (⇨ Visitor Information) maintains a network of cycle paths and bike rental centers throughout the Broads. Rentals are £10 per day, and each rental center can provide local maps and route advice. All centers are within 30–40 minutes' drive of Norwich.

BUS TRAVEL

National Express serves the region from London's Victoria Coach Station. Average travel times: 2½ hours to Bury St. Edmunds, 2 hours to Cambridge, 2 hours to Colchester, 4 hours to Lincoln, and 3 hours to Norwich. Information about local bus service for Norfolk and parts of the surrounding counties is available from the Norfolk Bus Information

Centre. First buses serve parts of the region. Cambridgeshire's largest bus company is Stagecoach Cambus. Traveline can answer public transportation questions.

A Ranger ticket (available on the bus) from First gives a day's unlimited travel on the whole network for £5.50; a family pass for two parents and two children costs £11. Stagecoach Cambus sells Megarider tickets (£5) for seven days' travel within Cambridge.

☎ **First** 🖀 01603/760076 ⊕ www.firstgroup.com. **National Express** 🖀 0870/580-8080 ⊕ www.nationalexpress.com. **Norfolk Bus Information Centre** 🖀 0845/300-6116. **Stagecoach Cambus** 🖀 01223/423554 ⊕ www.stagecoachbus.com/cambridge. **Traveline** 🖀 0870/608-2608 ⊕ www.traveline.org.uk.

CAR RENTAL

☎ **Local Agencies Avis** ✉ 245 Mill Rd., Cambridge 🖀 01223/212551 ✉ Ermine petrol station, Riseholm Rd., Lincoln 🖀 01522/511200 ✉ Norwich Airport, Cromer Rd., Norwich 🖀 01603/416719. **Budget** ✉ 303-305 Newmarket Rd., Cambridge 🖀 0541/565656 ✉ Greetwell Rd., Lincoln 🖀 01522/513600. **Europcar** ✉ Outer Circle Rd., Lincoln 🖀 01522/511144. **Grand Touring Club** ✉ The Model Farm, Rattlesden, Bury St. Edmunds 🖀 01449/737774. **Hertz** ✉ Station Building, Station Approach, Cambridge 🖀 01223/309842 ✉ 372 Hythe Station Rd., Colchester 🖀 01206/799400 ✉ Norwich International Airport, Cromer Rd., Norwich 🖀 01603/404010.

CAR TRAVEL

From London, Cambridge (54 mi) is off M11. At Exit 9, M11 connects with A11 to Norwich (114 mi); A14 off A11 goes to Bury St. Edmunds. A12 from London goes through east Suffolk via Colchester and Ipswich. For Lincoln (131 mi), take A1 via Huntingdon, Peterborough, and Grantham to A46 at Newark-on-Trent. A more scenic alternative is to leave A1 at Grantham and take A607 to Lincoln.

East Anglia has few fast main roads. The principal routes are those mentioned above. Once off the A roads, traveling within the region often means taking country lanes that have many twists and turns.

EMERGENCIES

☎ **Ambulance, fire, police** 🖀 999. **Addenbrooke's Hospital** ✉ Hill's Rd., Cambridge 🖀 01223/245151. **Norfolk and Norwich Hospital** ✉ Brunswick Rd., Norwich 🖀 01603/286286.

TOURS

City Sightseeing operates open-top bus tours of Cambridge—the Backs, the colleges, the Imperial War Museum in Duxford, and the Grafton shopping center. Tours start from Cambridge train station but can be picked up at marked bus stops throughout the city. Buy tickets from the driver, the City Sightseeing office at Cambridge train station, or the Cambridge Tourist Information Centre for £8. Tours run mid-April–September, every 15 minutes, and October–mid-April, every 30 minutes. From July to the first week of September, hour-long tours run through Colchester daily from 10 to 6 for £5. Tours depart from the castle hourly. Hour-long tours of Lincoln depart from Minster Yard at the cathedral with various pick-up points. Tours run from 10 to 3 on weekends from mid-April until mid-May, and daily mid-May–August. Tickets cost £6.50. The 45-minute Norwich tour starts at St. Peter's Street outside City Hall, with several pick-up points. Tours (£6) run May–November and leave on the hour from 10 to 4.

🚩 **City Sightseeing** ✉ Cambridge train station ☎ 01708/866000 ⊕ www.city-sightseeing.com ✉ Colchester Castle ☎ 01708/866000 ✉ Lincoln Cathedral, Minster Yard ☎ 01522/522255 ✉ St Peter's St., Norwich ☎ 01263/587005.

WALKING TOURS Qualified guides for walking tours of the major towns, including Bury St. Edmunds, Cambridge, Ely, Colchester, Norwich, and Lincoln, can be booked through the respective tourist offices (⇨ Visitor Information). Those in Cambridge are particularly popular; book well in advance for tours (£8) that depart at 1:30 year-round and more frequently in summer. Ninety-minute audio tours of Lavenham are available for rental from the Lavenham Pharmacy on High Street for £3.

TRAIN TRAVEL

The entire region is served by trains from London's Liverpool Street station; in addition, there are trains to Cambridge, Ely, Lincoln, and Peterborough from King's Cross Station. Full information on trains to East Anglia is available from National Rail Enquiries. Average travel times are one hour to Colchester, 50–90 minutes to Cambridge, almost two hours and 50 minutes to Norwich, and two hours to Lincoln.

CUTTING COSTS A one-day Rover ticket, available from any station in either Norfolk or Suffolk for £9, lets you disembark to explore any of the little towns en route. Seven-day Regional Rover tickets for unlimited travel in the Anglia Railways region are also available.

FARES & **🚩 National Rail Enquiries** ☎ 0845/748–4950 ⊕ www.nationalrail.co.uk.
SCHEDULES

TRAVEL AGENCIES

🚩 Local Agent Referrals **American Express** ✉ 25 Sidney St., Cambridge ☎ 01223/345201. **Thomas Cook** ✉ 8 St. Andrews St., Cambridge ☎ 01223/543140 ✉ Grafton Centre, Cambridge ☎ 01223/543040 ✉ 4 Cornhill Pavement, Lincoln ☎ 01522/346400 ✉ 15 St. Stephens St., Norwich ☎ 01603/241200.

VISITOR INFORMATION

🚩 **East of England Tourist Board** ✉ Toppesfield Hall, Market Pl., Hadleigh, IP7 5DN ☎ 01473/822922 🖶 01473/823063 ⊕ www.eastofenglandtouristboard.com. **Broads Authority** ✉ 18 Colegate, Norwich, NR3 1BQ ☎ 01603/610734 ⊕ www.broads-authority. gov.uk. **Aldeburgh** ✉ 152 High St., IP15 5AQ ☎ 01728/453637 ⊕ www.suffolkcoastal. gov.uk. **Boston** ✉ Market Pl. ☎ 01205/356656 ⊕ www.boston.gov.uk. **Bury St. Edmunds** ✉ 6 Angel Hill ☎ 01284/763233 ⊕ www.stedmundsbury.gov.uk. **Cambridge** ✉ Wheeler St., CB2 3QB ☎ 01223/457577 ⊕ www.tourismcambridge.com. **Cambridge University** ⊕ www.cam.ac.uk. **Colchester** ✉ 1 Queen St. ☎ 01206/282920 ⊕ www. colchester.gov.uk. **Ely** ✉ Oliver Cromwell's House, 29 St. Mary's St., CB7 4HF ☎ 01353/662062 ⊕ www.ely.org.uk. **King's Lynn** ✉ The Custom House, Purfleet Quay, PE30 1HP ☎ 01553/763044 ⊕ www.west-norfolk.gov.uk. **Lavenham** ✉ Lady St. ☎ 01787/248207 ⊕ www.babergh-south-suffolk.gov.uk. **Lincoln** ✉ 9 Castle Hill ☎ 01522/873213 ⊕ www. lincoln.gov.uk. **Norwich** ✉ Forum, between N. Theatre and Bethel Sts. ☎ 01603/

666071 ⊕ www.norwich.gov.uk. **Peterborough** ⊠ 3 Minster Precints, PE1 1XS ☎ 01733/452336 ⊕ www.peterborough.gov.uk. **Saffron Walden** ⊠ 1 Market Pl., Market Sq. ☎ 01799/510444 ⊕ www.uttlesford.gov.uk. **Southwold** ⊠ 69 High St. ☎ 01502/724729. **Stamford** ⊠ Stamford Arts Centre, St. Marys St. ☎ 01780/755611. **Sudbury** ⊠ Town Hall, Market Hill ☎ 01787/881320 ⊕ www.babergh-south-suffolk.gov.uk. **Woodbridge** ⊠ Station Buildings ☎ 01394/382240 ⊕ www.suffolkcoastal.gov.uk. **Wells-next-the-Sea** ⊠ Staithe St., NR23 1AN ☎ 01328/710885.

YORKSHIRE
LEEDS, BRADFORD, HAWORTH, YORK, WHITBY, CASTLE HOWARD

13

LIGHTEN UP UNDER STAINED GLASS
in dazzling York Minster ⇨*p.629*

TREK RUGGED MOORLAND
on the Brontë trail in Haworth ⇨*p.616*

OPT FOR OPULENCE
at flamboyant Castle Howard ⇨*p.648*

SHOOT A CROSSBOW
at the Royal Armouries in Leeds ⇨*p.611*

FIND DRAMA IN THE DALES
on hikes around rural Malham ⇨*p.621*

COOL OFF AT THE BEACH
near rugged Robin Hood's Bay ⇨*p.640*

SEE MAJESTY IN THE RUINS
of graceful Bolton Priory ⇨*p.619*

LICK YOUR FINGERS
after Magpie Café's fish & chips ⇨*p.643*

Updated by
Kate Hughes

YORKSHIRE IS ANOTHER COUNTRY, say the locals, and a few days spent exploring this largest of English regions could well convince you they're right. The famous sights, such as the Minster at York, the moorland haunts of the Brontës near Haworth, the ruined monasteries and stately homes, are justifiably popular but provide only half the picture. Nowhere else in England have industry and the natural world collided with such significant effect, offsetting brisk manufacturing towns with untamed scenery. Author J. B. Priestley, in his *English Journey* of 1933, noted that "Industrial Man and Nature sing a rum sort of duet" in Yorkshire, a duet still played out in the hills above Priestley's native Bradford, or in Leeds, or atop the blustery moors.

Yorkshire remains an intensely rural region. The most rugged of its landscapes are the Yorkshire Moors, a vast area of lonely moorland that helped inspire Emily Brontë's 1847 *Wuthering Heights* (and if ever a work of fiction grew out of the landscape in which its author lived, it was surely this). Brilliant at times with spring flowers and heather, the moors can change dangerously, often within a few minutes, to stormy weather, when you're lucky to see as far as the next cloud-swept ridge. Between the bleak areas of moorland and the rocky Pennine hills lie lush, green valleys known as the Yorkshire Dales, where the high rainfall produces luxuriant vegetation, swift rivers, sparkling streams, and waterfalls. The villages here, immortalized through the books of the late veterinarian Alf Wight (1916–95), who wrote under the name James Herriot, are among the most utterly peaceful in England, although many burst into life as summer walking bases.

There's also a gritty, urban aspect to Yorkshire, whose towns have changed the course of British history. Leeds and Bradford, two of Britain's major industrial centers, are now being gradually rejuvenated after the decline of their industrial bases. More aesthetically pleasing is the northern, walled city of York, dominated by the towers of its minster—for some, the most noble cathedral in Britain. Settled by Romans and Vikings, York was once England's most important northern city, and it is arguably the best-preserved medieval town in the country. Beyond York, more marvels await: Castle Howard and the ruined monastic remains of Rievaulx Abbey, Whitby Abbey, and Fountains Abbey are some of the most impressive sights in Britain.

Yorkshire has historically been split into three divisions or "ridings" (from an old Norse word meaning "third"), and although the county ceased to be run as one administrative entity in 1974, natives still treat Yorkshire as one homogenous unit and tend to ignore the divisions into North, South, and West Yorkshire. York, Haworth—the center of Brontë Country—or the seaside resorts of Scarborough and Whitby make the best touring bases. Those with limited time could visit York as a day trip from London; the fastest trains take just two hours. Proper exploration of the region, especially of the moors and dales, requires time and effort, well rewarded whether you're out to see untamed natural beauty or great medieval art.

You could drive across Yorkshire in less than a day (as many do, on the way to Scotland), but you would have little time to spend anywhere. Three days allows a night in York, followed by a night in rural Yorkshire. However, only with five to seven days does a satisfying itinerary begin to take shape: you could stop longer in York and visit the coast, as well as get off the beaten track to seek out the abbeys, castles, and old moorland villages. You still must move quickly, though, if you want to see the regions of Yorkshire in a week.

Numbers in the text correspond to numbers in the margin and on the Yorkshire and York maps.

If you have
3 days

Start in ⊞ **York** ⑬– ㉕ ➤, quintessential city of Yorkshire, where, if you arrive early enough in the day, you can fit in several of the main medieval city sites, such as York Minster and the Shambles. Then take a bus tour leaving shortly before noon out to spectacular **Castle Howard** ㊶. Return to York about 4:30 in the afternoon and repair to Betty's tearooms; in the evening you might go on a walking tour. Next morning, continue to see York sights and then travel to Leeds to pick up a bus to ⊞ **Haworth** ④ for a Brontë pilgrimage. (If you have a car, you can detour to make a quick visit to stunning **Studley Royal and Fountains Abbey** ㉘.) Spend your final day in Haworth. Don't forget to hike over the moors from Top Withins ("Wuthering Heights") to the Hardcastle Crags valley. Return to Leeds.

If you have
7 days

Starting in ⊞ **Leeds** ① ➤, head for **Bradford** ③ and its museums, and make time for a curry lunch on Morley Street before spending the afternoon at the nearby model 19th-century factory community of Saltaire. It's just a short drive to ⊞ **Haworth** ④ for an overnight stop in Brontë Country; see the sights in the morning. After this, meander up through the Yorkshire Dales, via **Skipton** ⑥ and **Malham** ⑧ before stopping for the night in ⊞ **Grassington** ⑦. The next day, soak up more remote scenery as you tour the northern dales, Wensleydale and Swaledale, before hitting the main roads and heading south, via **Studley Royal and Fountains Abbey** ㉘, to the spa town of ⊞ **Harrogate** ㉖. After all this driving, you have only a short journey to York the following day. Stay in ⊞ **York** ⑬– ㉕ for two nights, and then early on the morning of departure, aim for **Helmsley** ㊴ with a sightseeing stop at either **Rievaulx Abbey** ㊵ or **Castle Howard** ㊶ before driving across the moors to **Hutton-le-Hole** ㊳, **Danby** ㊲, and on to ⊞ **Whitby** ㉟ for your overnight stop. The next day, return to York along the coast via **Robin Hood's Bay** ㉞ and **Scarborough** ㉝.

Exploring Yorkshire

Yorkshire is the largest English region to explore (its fiercely proud inhabitants would say the only English region *worth* exploring). You need to plan carefully before launching on a tour around its different areas. The industrial heartland is West Yorkshire, where the cities of Leeds and Bradford were at the forefront of both the late-medieval wool trade and the 19th-century Industrial Revolution. What the tourist office likes to call Brontë Country—basically Haworth, home of the Brontë family—is just to the northwest, and northward spread the hills, valleys, and villages of the Yorkshire Dales, stomping ground of the late James Herriot, the much-loved writer. In the center of the region, York deserves special attention, as do its environs, from the spa town of Harrogate to magnificent Fountains Abbey.

Moving east to the coast, Yorkshire reveals itself to be a seaside holiday destination, although never one that will win prizes for summerlike weather. But fine beaches and a fascinating history await you in the resort of Scarborough, the former whaling port of Whitby, Robin Hood's Bay—a cliff-top, one-time smuggler's haunt—and the traditional fishing village of Staithes. Finally, you can strike inland to the North York Moors National Park. Isolated stone villages, moorland walks, Rievaulx Abbey, and elegant Castle Howard are all within easy reach.

About the Restaurants & Hotels

Yorkshire has some fine restaurants, but pubs are often the best (and in small villages, the only) places to find good, hearty meals for a gentle sum.

For a high price, you can stay at the stately home of Lady Mary Wortley Montagu and at other luxury hotels, or, to get a real flavor of northern hospitality and cuisine, you can look for farmhouse bed-and-breakfasts. If you're traveling by public transportation, many proprietors of places on the outskirts of town will pick you up at the train station or bus depot. Rooms fill quickly at seaside resorts in July and August, and some places in the dales and moors close in winter. Always call ahead. Hikers and budgeteers love the region's youth hostels, from those in the dales and moorland villages to budget bases in York and Scarborough. Even more basic accommodation is available in camping barns (rural bunkhouses) in the Yorkshire Dales. Tourist offices have reservation numbers and details on these popular budget options.

WHAT IT COSTS In pounds				
£££££	**££££**	**£££**	**££**	**£**
RESTAURANTS over £22	£18–£22	£13–£17	£7–£12	under £7
HOTELS over £160	£120–£160	£90–£120	£60–£90	under £60

Restaurant prices are for a main course at dinner. Hotel prices are for two people in a standard double room in high season, including VAT, with no meals or, if indicated, CP (with Continental breakfast), BP (Breakfast Plan, with full breakfast), or MAP (Modified American Plan, with breakfast and dinner).

Timing

Summer is undoubtedly the best time to visit Yorkshire, especially the coastal areas and moors, when there are regattas and festivals. However, you can expect resorts and walking centers to be overcrowded; book accommodations well in advance. York's city center will also be packed shoulder to shoulder with visitors. York Minster makes a splendid focal point for the prestigious York Early Music Festival, which takes place

Hiking & Walking

The green dales, the changeable moors, the rugged North Sea coast: Yorkshire's landscapes are glorious to explore on foot. Some of Britain's finest long-distance footpaths cut through the region, but even a brief walk can give you a sharper appreciation for the countryside. Afterward, stop at a pub and reward yourself with a pint and perhaps the comradeship of other walkers. Short trails and longer paths crisscross the Yorkshire Dales National Park. The North York Moors National Park has long, empty swaths of land for tramping, and craggy cliff walks follow the dramatic coastline. Leading trails include the Cleveland Way (108 mi), from Helmsley to Filey; the hard-going Lyke-Wake Walk (40 mi), from Osmotherley to Ravenscar; and the eastern section of the Coast-to-Coast Walk (190 mi), which starts or finishes in Robin Hood's Bay. The Dales Way (80 mi) connects Leeds and Bradford with the Lake District. Perhaps the greatest of all English walks, the Pennine Way, which runs from the Peak District to Scotland, passes through the Yorkshire Dales.

13

The Monastic Past

The wealth of richly decorated and appointed monastic buildings here is a testament to the monks of medieval Yorkshire, who became some of the richest in Europe by virtue of the international wool trade that they conducted from their vast religious estates in the north. The buildings lie mostly in romantic ruins, a result of the dissolution of the monasteries during the 16th century, part of Henry VIII's struggle with the Catholic church. At places such as Fountains, Rievaulx, and Whitby abbeys, you can learn about the religious and business worlds of the great monasteries. The ruins of Bolton Abbey, praised by 19th-century art critic John Ruskin, are also memorable. Thanks to the countless poems written about these ruins by Victorian poets, and the paintings of them by celebrated 19th-century artists such as J. M. W. Turner, these sites became world famous for their powerful evocation of life in the Middle Ages.

---

in early July. Spring and fall bring their own rewards: less crowded attractions and crisp, clear days, although with an increased risk of rain and fog. Winter is hard to call: with glistening snow and bright days, the coast, moors, and dales are beautiful, but storms and blizzards set in quickly, moorland roads become impassable, and villages can be cut off. During winter, stick to York and the main towns if you must keep to a timetable.

WEST YORKSHIRE & BRONTË COUNTRY

Even before the Industrial Revolution, the towns in the hills and river valleys of West Yorkshire were important commercial centers, whose trade in wool made prodigious fortunes for local merchants and religious foundations. It's still a region synonymous with wool production, and a large number of "mill shops" sell high-quality knitting wool, sweaters, and woven wool for skirts or suits at factory prices. After in-

dustrialization, the towns took to new trades such as textiles, chemicals, and engineering, which transformed the urban scene, leaving many places today rather unattractive at first sight. However, restoration of once-glorious Victorian architecture and the regeneration of inner-city areas is having a beneficial effect, and relief is always close at hand in the region's rural and moorland surroundings.

In the gaunt hills north of the Calder Valley and south of the River Aire is the district immortalized by the writings of the Brontë sisters. Haworth, an otherwise gray West Yorkshire village, might have passed unobserved but for the magnetism of the family that lived in the old parsonage, now the museum of the Brontë Society. Every summer, thousands toil up the steep main street to visit the hilltop church and the museum, where all too often Brontë enthusiasm stops. To understand the real spirit of the Brontës it is necessary to go farther afield to the moors and the ruined farm of Top Withins, which legend, but not fact, refers to as Wuthering Heights.

Leeds, easily reached from the west by the trans-Pennine M62 and from the south by the M1, provides an obvious starting point and has its own appeal, including its glass-roofed Victorian shopping arcades and redeveloped downtown. Traditional wool towns to the south, such as Wakefield, Huddersfield, and Halifax, have a modicum of interest, and the Magna museum at Rotherham draws long lines for its thrilling exploration of steel. But the main thrust of any visit to West Yorkshire is to the west of Leeds, where Bradford and Brontë Country, around Haworth, really begin to repay investigation.

Leeds

▶ ❶ *43 mi northeast of Manchester, 25 mi southwest of York.*

Since 1990, what was formerly an industrial city in severe decline has become an example of urban regeneration. Leeds, with a population of more than 400,000, has a reputation as one of the greenest cities in Europe, although its unkempt industrial outskirts and congested traffic make this difficult to believe at first approach. Besides its parks, Leeds has long green routes that radiate from the city center. Urban heritage projects and redevelopment such as Millennium Square, and trend-setting restaurants and café-bars with outdoor seating have sprouted up all over the city. It's not quite the Mediterranean, but there's a tangible vitality in the air these days.

Leeds had a head start on most comparable cities because its wealthy 19th-century days left a fine architectural bequest. The city is well known for its superb Victorian shopping arcades, but the Georgian squares and streets of the West End are just as notable. Tucked away among the streets are old pubs and yards that date from the 14th century. One of the finest Victorian public buildings in Britain, the classical **Town Hall** (✉ The Headrow ☎ 0113/247–8384 ⊕ www.leeds.gov. uk), built in 1853, sits prominently in the city center. Town Hall is the masterpiece of local architect Cuthbert Broderick. Today it is a venue for concerts and special events.

City Art Gallery, opposite Town Hall, showcases a fine collection of painting and sculpture, with particularly strong showings of 20th-century and contemporary British art, including works by Walter Sickert, L. S. Lowry, Stanley Spencer, and Leeds artist Atkinson Grimshaw. The **Craft Centre and Design Gallery,** also in the museum, exhibits fine contemporary crafts. Adjoining the gallery is the **Henry Moore Institute,** named for the famous British sculptor, who was a student at Leeds College of Art. The institute displays temporary exhibitions of modern sculpture. The City Art Gallery has several examples of Moore's work, and you can study his *Reclining Woman* on the steps outside the gallery. ⊠ *The Headrow* ☎ *0113/247–8248* ⊕ *www.leeds.gov.uk/artgallery* ⊠ *Free* ⊙ *Mon.–Tues. and Thurs.–Sat. 10–5, Wed. 10–8, Sun. 1–5.*

need a break? Step down to the cozy, book-lined **New Conservatory** (⊠ The Albions, Albion Place, off Briggate ☎ 0133/246–1853) for *ciabattas* (a flavorful Italian bread, with various fillings), wraps, and other sandwiches. You can also sit and relax with a cup of tea or coffee.

Even the squeamish won't balk at the fun exhibits in the **Thackray Medical Museum,** which present as much social as medical history. Interactive displays help you take a trip back to the slums of the 1840s, discover the realities of surgery without anesthetics, and explore the experience of having a baby in Victorian times or today. In another exhibit, Sherlock Bones guides you around the human body. The museum is a mile east of the center and accessible by Buses 4, 4C, 42, 49, and 50. ⊠ *Beckett St.* ☎ *0113/244–4343* ⊕ *www.thackraymuseum.org* ⊠ *£4.90, parking £1* ⊙ *Daily 10–5; last admission 3.*

The River Aire, an important trading route in Leeds's early days, has been revitalized after being affected by industrial pollution. **Granary Wharf,** in the Canal Basin, reached via the Dark Arches where the River Aire flows under City Station, has design and crafts shops, music events, boat trips, and a regular festival market. **The Calls,** east of Granary Wharf by the river, has converted redbrick warehouses with smart bars, cafés, and restaurants that enliven the cobbled streets and quayside.

Much of the vast, legendary arms and armor collection from the Tower of London fills the **Royal Armouries,** which occupies a redeveloped 13-acre dockland site, a 15-minute walk from the city center. Five theme galleries—War, Tournament, Self-Defense, Hunting, and Arms and Armor of the Orient—trace the history of weaponry. The state-of-the-art building is stunningly designed: expect a full-size elephant in armor, warriors on horseback, and floor-to-ceiling tents, as well as spirited interactive displays and live demonstrations. Shoot a crossbow, direct operations on a battlefield, experience a Wild West gunfight or an Elizabethan joust—it's your choice. ⊠ *Armouries Dr., off M1 or M621* ☎ *0113/220–1999* ⊕ *www.armouries.org.uk* ⊠ *Free* ⊙ *Daily 10–5.*

The Leeds City Council uses **Temple Newsam,** a huge Elizabethan and Jacobean building that was altered in the 18th century, to display its rich collections of furniture, paintings, and ceramics. The house was the birthplace in 1545 of Lord Darnley, the doomed husband of Mary, Queen of Scots. Surrounding the house is a large public park with walled rose gardens, greenhouses, and miles of woodland walks, all originally laid out by Capability Brown in 1762, as well as a home farm. Temple Newsam is 4 mi east of Leeds on A63; buses leave from Leeds Central Bus Station every 30 minutes and stop at the Irwin Arms, a 10-minute walk from the site. ⊠ *Off Selby Rd.* ☎ *0113/264–7321* ⊕ *www.leeds. gov.uk* ⊡ *House £3, farm £3, joint ticket £5; park free* ☉ *Apr.–Oct., Tues.–Sun. and national holidays 10:30–5; Nov.–Mar., Tues.–Sun. 10:30–4. Last admission 45 min before closing.*

off the beaten path

MAGNA – A 45-minute drive south from Leeds to Rotherham brings you squarely in view of Yorkshire's industrial past. The scale of the former steelworks that houses Magna, a high-tech science museum, is impressive, but the power of the Big Melt show really hits the spot. Smoke, flames, and sparking electricity bring one of the original six arc furnaces roaring to life in a sound-and-light show. In summer former steel workers act as guides; a permanent exhibit explores the world of the people who worked in the industry. Four pavilions engagingly illustrate the elements of fire, earth, air, and water, used in the production of steel. ⊠ *Junction 33 or 34 off M1, Sheffield Rd., Rotherham* ☎ *01709/720002* ⊕ *www.visitmagna.co.uk* ⊡ *£9* ☉ *Daily 10–5.*

Where to Stay & Eat

£££££ ✕ **Pool Court at 42.** Elegant and tranquil, this restaurant in the revitalized warehouse district by the river is typical of the fashionable spots becoming popular with northern food-fanciers. Good choices on the cosmopolitan contemporary menu include fish, such as griddle-cooked scallops and fresh salmon, and expertly cooked game. There are several set-price options. The adjacent, associated Brasserie Forty 4 (££) is less formal and less expensive. ⊠ *42–44 The Calls* ☎ *0113/244–4242, 0113/234–3232 Brasserie Forty 4* ⊟ *AE, DC, MC, V* ☉ *Closed Sun. No lunch Sat.*

££–£££ ✕ **Fourth Floor Restaurant.** If the Harvey Nichols department store has been a roaring success, it's partly because of the lure of its swank Fourth Floor eatery, a standout for both food and dramatic, high-tech design. The well-crafted modern British menu changes several times a week, but is sure to have stylish takes on dishes such as pigeon breast with baby vegetables, char-grilled rib-eye steak, and the freshest lemon sole. On summer days, the terrace comes into its own. ⊠ *Harvey Nichols, 107–111 Briggate* ☎ *0113/204–8000* ⊟ *AE, DC, MC, V* ☉ *No dinner Sun.–Wed.*

£–££ ✕ **Whitelocks.** The city's oldest pub (1715), tucked away in an alley in the city center, recommends itself for traditional Yorkshire pudding and gravy, homemade pies, and real ale. The long, narrow bar has all the trappings of the Victorian era—stained glass, etched mirrors, copper-topped tables, and red plush banquettes. Service is brisk and friendly. ⊠ *Turks Head Yard, off Briggate* ☎ *0113/245–3950* ⊟ *AE, MC, V.*

★ ££££ ✕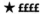 **Malmaison.** Passengers who used this building in its days as a tram and bus garage could hardly have envisaged its rebirth as an immaculately chic hotel exuding contemporary class and comfort. Guest rooms have color themes of subtle tones—plum, charcoal, yellow ocher—and are beautifully furnished with clean-lined modern pieces. The dark-paneled brasserie concentrates on French food with a Mediterranean twist. ⊠ *Sovereign Quay, LS1 1DQ* ☎ *0113/398–1000* 🖷 *0113/398–1002* ⊕ *www.malmaison.com* ↘ *100 rooms* ♿ *Restaurant, in-room data ports, cable TV, gym, spa, bar, meeting rooms* ▭ *AE, DC, MC, V.*

££££–£££££ 🛏 **42 The Calls.** Taking an old grain mill in a once-dilapidated waterfront area and converting it into a high-tech, high-comfort hotel took some nerve, but the venture has paid off. Each room shows individual flair but retains such original elements as warehouse skylights, exposed beams, and brickwork. Facilities are up-to-the-minute, including in-room CD players; some rooms even come with fishing rods (bring your own bait). ⊠ *42 The Calls, LS2 7EW* ☎ *0113/244–0099* 🖷 *0113/234–4100* ⊕ *www.42thecalls.co.uk* ↘ *41 rooms* ♿ *2 restaurants, in-room data ports, cable TV with movies, bar, meeting rooms, some pets allowed; no a/c* ▭ *AE, DC, MC, V.*

£££–££££ 🛏 **Quebecs.** The grand Leeds and County Liberal Club may have changed its identity when it became a boutique hotel, but the building has lost none of its Victorian verve. The sweeping oak staircase, lit by tall stained-glass windows, leads up to classy bedrooms of different shapes and sizes, all sympathetically decorated in muted colors. The paneled Oak Room, an unusual circular design, is a must for a drink. Lower weekend rates include breakfast. ⊠ *9 Quebec St., LS1 2HA* ☎ *0113/244–8989* 🖷 *0113/244–9090* ⊕ *www.etontownhouse.com* ↘ *45 rooms, 6 suites* ♿ *In-room data ports, in-room safes, minibars, cable TV, bar, lounge, meeting rooms* ▭ *AE, DC, MC, V.*

££ 🛏 **Aragon Hotel.** If you prefer to escape the rush of the city, one option is this late-19th-century gabled house (built by a well-to-do mill owner) with a large garden, a couple of miles from the center. Pine pieces furnish the colorful bedrooms. The hotel is on the A61 Harrogate road but set back from it. ⊠ *250 Stainbeck La., LS7 2PS* ☎ *0113/275–9306* 🖷 *0113/275–7166* ⊕ *www.aragonhotel.co.uk* ↘ *12 rooms* ♿ *Bar; no a/c, no smoking* ▭ *AE, DC, MC, V* ⊙ *BP.*

Nightlife & the Arts

NIGHTLIFE At fashionable café-bars all over Leeds, you can grab a bite or sip cappuccino or designer beer until late into the night. There's no shortage of clubs, either; Leeds has one of the best party scenes outside London. **The Atrium** (⊠ 6–9 The Grand Arcade ☎ 0113/242–6116) is the place ★ for deep soul and funk. **Bar Norman** (⊠ Call La. ☎ 0113/234–3988) has won the local in-crowd with its weird and wonderful design, including curved walls; there's music, too. **Cuban Heels** (⊠ The Arches, 28 Assembly St. ☎ 0113/234–6115) kicks out salsa sounds most nights. **Tiger Tiger** (⊠ The Light, 117 Albion St. ☎ 0113/236–6999) has dancing to classic disco Thursday–Saturday, or you can sip cocktails in the classy Kaz Bar; it attracts the over-25 set.

THE ARTS Opera North, a leading provincial opera company, has its home in ★ Leeds at the **Grand Theatre** (⊠ 46 New Briggate ☎ 0113/222–6222); the opulent gold-and-plush auditorium is modeled on that of La Scala.

Opera North also plays for free each summer on the grounds at Temple Newsam.

The Victorian **Town Hall** (⊠ The Headrow ☎ 0113/224–3801) hosts an international concert season (October–May) that attracts top performers and conductors. In September it is the site of the prestigious Leeds International Piano Competition.

The ultramodern **West Yorkshire Playhouse** (⊠ Playhouse Sq., Quarry Hill ☎ 0113/213–7700) was built on the slope of an old quarry. Its adaptable staging makes it eminently suitable for new and classic productions as well as touring shows.

Shopping

For ethnic clothes, gifts, jewelry, and accessories, visit the shops inside the old **Corn Exchange** (⊠ Call La. ☎ 0113/234–0363). **Harvey Nichols** (⊠ 107–111 Briggate ☎ 0113/204–8888), the department store regarded as the crucible of chic, contains an abundance of fashion and a great café-restaurant. The city has some excellent markets, notably **Kirkgate Market** (⊠ 34 George St. ☎ 0113/214–5162), an Edwardian beauty that's the largest in the north of England. Specialty stores and designer ★ boutiques fill the Victorian shopping arcades; the glistening **Victoria Quarter** (⊠ Briggate ☎ 0113/245–5333), with its 70 stores, epitomizes fin-de-siècle style and 21st-century chic.

Harewood House

★ ❷ *7 mi north of Leeds.*

The home of the earl of Harewood, a cousin of the Queen, Harewood House (pronounced *har*-wood) is a spectacular neoclassical mansion, built in 1759 by John Carr of York. Highlights include Robert Adam interiors, important paintings and ceramics, and a large, ravishingly beautiful collection of Chippendale furniture (Chippendale was born in nearby Otley), notably the magnificent State Bed. The Old Kitchen and Below Stairs exhibition illustrate life from the servants' point of view. Capability Brown designed the handsome grounds, and Charles Barry created a notable Italian garden with fountains in the 1840s. Also here are a bird garden with 120 rare and endangered species, an adventure playground, and a butterfly house. ⊠ A61, Harewood ☎ 0113/288–6331 ⊕ *www.harewood.org* ☜ *£10, bird garden and grounds only £7.25; prices are £1 higher on Sun.* ⊘ *House mid-Mar.–mid-Nov., daily 10–5, last admission 4. Old Kitchen mid-Mar.–mid-Nov., daily noon–4. Bird garden and grounds mid-Feb.–mid-Nov., daily 10–6; mid-Nov.–mid-Dec., weekends 10–4; last admission 1 hr before dusk.*

Bradford

❸ *17 mi southwest of Harewood House, 10 mi west of Leeds, 32 mi northeast of Manchester.*

Bradford was once one of the greatest wool towns in Europe, and it had excelled at that trade since the 16th century. Even as late as the 1960s, wool accounted for a substantial part of its economy, but as with all the West Yorkshire textile towns, recession and competition from new markets hit hard. Bradford tries hard to be likeable today, and although much of its grandeur has gone, the center still holds the odd Victorian building from its period of greatest prosperity: St. George's Hall on Bridge Street (1851) and the Wool Exchange on Market Street (1864) are two fine examples.

★ ☺ Most people come to Bradford for the museums, particularly the renowned **National Museum of Photography, Film, and Television,** which traces the history of photographic media. It's a huge and hugely entertaining place, with interactive models, machines, and related ephemera spread out over five galleries, and encompassing the world's first negative, up-to-the-minute digital imaging, and all stages between. The Insight: Collections and Research Centre allows you to view material from the museum's holdings. The museum's popularity with children means you should come early or late in the day if you want to see the displays in peace. Allow time, too, for a screening at the museum's 50-by 60-foot IMAX screen. The associated Pictureville cinema has a full repertory program. ⊠ *Pictureville, Prince's Way* ☎ *01274/202030 or 0870/701–0200* ⊕ *www.nmpft.org.uk* ⊠ *Museum free, IMAX movie £5.95, Pictureville screenings £5* ☉ *Tues.–Sun. and bank holidays 10–6.*

☺ The **Industrial Museum and Horses at Work,** in a former spinning mill 3 mi northeast of the town center, outlines Bradford's history as a wool-producing town. Exhibits include workers' dwellings dating from the 1870s and a mill owner's house from the 19th century. Children love riding in the Shire horse-drawn tram. Moorside Road is off A658 Harrogate Road; you can also take Bus 645, 646, or 613 from the city center. ⊠ *Moorside Mills, Moorside Rd.* ☎ *01274/435900* ⊕ *www.visitbradford. com* ⊠ *Free* ☉ *Tues.–Sat. and national holidays 10–5, Sun. noon–5.*

★ A UNESCO World Heritage Site, the former model factory community of **Saltaire** was built by textile magnate Sir Titus Salt in the mid-19th century. It exemplifies the enduring trait of philanthropy among certain Victorian industrialists, who erected modern terraced housing for their workers and furnished them with libraries, parks, hospitals, and schools. Saltaire, fashioned in Italianate style, has been remarkably preserved, its former mills and houses turned into shops, restaurants, and galleries. Salt's Mill, built in 1853, resembles a palazzo and was the largest factory in the world when it was built. Today it holds an art gallery and crafts and furniture shops. One-hour guided tours (£3) depart every Saturday at 2 PM and Sunday at 11 AM and 2 PM from the **tourist information center** (⊠ 2 Victoria Rd., Saltaire ☎ 01274/774993 ⊕ www. saltaire.yorks.com/touristinfo). The **1853 Gallery** (⊠ Salt's Mill, Victoria Rd. ☎ 01274/531163 ⊠ Free ☉ Daily 10–6) holds a remarkable, permanent, retrospective exhibition of 400 works by Bradford-born artist David Hockney. There are two restaurants on site. Saltaire is 4 mi north of Bradford, and there are regular bus and train services. Drivers should take A650 to Shipley and follow the signs.

Where to Stay & Eat

£ ✕ **Kashmir.** Some of Bradford's finest curry houses line Morley Street, two minutes from the National Museum of Photography, Film, and Television. The Kashmir is one of the best, a simple, no-frills place dishing out authentically spiced food at extremely low prices. ✉ *27 Morley St.* ☎ *01274/726513* 🖃 *AE, DC, MC, V.*

£ ✕▣ **Beeties.** In the center of a well-preserved former model factory village, this onetime storage house and fish shop provides intimate accommodation away from downtown Bradford. Top-floor bedrooms are pleasantly furnished with pine pieces and colorful bedspreads. Below are a vibrant tapas bar and a more formal restaurant that focuses on fine Mediterranean-style food such as roast sea bass, and lamb with puy lentils. ✉ *7 Victoria Rd., Saltaire, BD18 3LA* ☎ *01274/595988* 🖨 *01274/582118* ⊕ *www.beeties.co.uk* ➳ *5 rooms* ♨ *Restaurant, tapas bar, meeting rooms, no-smoking rooms; no a/c, no kids under 10* 🖃 *MC, V* ❙◯❙ *BP.*

Haworth: Heart of Brontë Country

❹ *10 mi northwest of Bradford, 5 mi southwest of Keighley.*

At first glance there's not much that makes the village of Haworth (pronounced *how*-weth) in West Yorkshire special. It's an old, stone-built spot on the edge of the Yorkshire Moors, superficially much like many other craggy Yorkshire settlements. But Haworth's particular claim to fame makes it probably the most celebrated literary spot in Britain after Stratford-upon-Avon. It was here, in the middle of the 19th century, that the three Brontë sisters—Emily (author of *Wuthering Heights,* 1847), Charlotte (*Jane Eyre,* 1847), and Anne (*The Tenant of Wildfell Hall,* 1848)—lived. This unlikely trio, daughters of the local vicar, were responsible for some of the most romantic novels ever written. "My sister Emily loved the moors," wrote Charlotte. "Flowers brighter than the rose bloomed in the blackest of the heath for her; out of a sullen hollow in a livid hillside her mind could make an Eden. She found in the bleak solitude many and dear delights; and not the least and best loved was liberty." Today, thousands journey to the straggling village, which lives a little too readily off its associations: summer visitors occasionally threaten to overwhelm the place entirely.

You can get to the region by taking a train to Leeds Station or a bus to Leeds's National Express Coach Station. To reach Haworth by bus or train, buy a Metro Day Rover for bus and rail, and take the Metro train from Leeds to Keighley. There are about three hourly. From Keighley, take the Keighley & Worth Valley Railway for the trip to Haworth, or Keighley and District Bus 663, 664, or 665 (one leaves every 20 minutes). From Bradford buses run every 10 minutes to Keighley.

The town's **information center** has information about accommodations, maps, and books on the Brontës, and inexpensive leaflets to help you find your way to such outlying *Wuthering Heights* sites as Ponden Hall (Thrushcross Grange) and Ponden Kirk (Penistone Crag). ✉ *2–4 West La.* ☎ *01535/642329* ⊙ *Daily 9:30–5.*

Haworth's steep, cobbled **Main Street** has changed little in outward appearance since the early 19th century, but today acts as a funnel for most of the people who crowd into the points of interest: the **Black Bull** pub, where the reprobate Branwell, the Brontës' only brother, drank himself into an early grave; the **post office** from which Charlotte, Emily, and Anne sent their manuscripts to their London publishers; and the **church,** with its gloomy graveyard (Charlotte and Emily are buried inside the church; Anne is buried in Scarborough).

★ The **Brontë Parsonage Museum,** in the somber Georgian house in which the sisters grew up, displays original furniture (some bought by Charlotte after the success of *Jane Eyre*), portraits, and books. The Brontës first came here in 1820, when the Reverend Patrick Brontë was appointed to the local church, but tragedy soon struck—his wife, Maria, and their two eldest children died within five years (done in, some scholars assert, by water wells tainted by seepage from the neighboring graveyard, a malady that inflicted a high toll on Haworth at this time). The museum contains enchanting mementos of the four surviving children, including Charlotte's wedding bonnet and the sisters' spidery, youthful graffiti on the nursery wall. Branwell painted several of the portraits on display. ⊠ *Church St.* ☏ *01535/642323* ⊕ *www.bronte.info* ⊠ *£4.80* ⊙ *Apr.–Sept., daily 10–5:30; Oct.–Dec., Feb., and Mar., daily 11–5; last admission 30 mins before closing.*

If you know and love the Brontës' works, you may well want to walk an hour or so along a field path, a lane, and a moorland track to the **Brontë Waterfall,** described in Emily's and Charlotte's poems and letters. **Top Withins,** the remains of a bleak hilltop farm 3 mi from Haworth, is often taken to be the main inspiration for Heathcliff's gloomy mansion, Wuthering Heights. Despite the bald statement on a nearby plaque, it probably isn't. There and back from Haworth is a two-hour walk. Better still is to cross the watershed to Wycollar, over the Lancashire border, or make the fine walk from Withins to the Hardcastle Crags valley. Wherever you go, wear sturdy shoes and protective clothing: if you've read *Wuthering Heights,* you have a fairly good idea of what weather can be like on the Yorkshire Moors.

☺ Haworth is on the **Keighley & Worth Valley Railway,** a gorgeous 5-mi-long branch line along which steam engines run between Keighley (3 mi north of Haworth) and Oxenhope. Kids like it even more on special days when there are family fairs en route. The **Museum of Rail Travel** (⊠ *£1* ⊙ *daily 11–4*), at Ingrow along the line, exhibits handsome vintage train cars. ⊠ *Railway Station, Keighley* ☏ *01535/645214, 01535/647777 for 24-hr information* ⊕ *www.kwvr.co.uk* ⊠ *£7 round-trip, £10 Day Rover ticket* ⊙ *Sept.–June, weekends; July–Aug., daily; call for schedules and special events.*

Where to Stay & Eat

££ ✕⊡ **Weavers.** Book well in advance to secure a room in this establishment converted from a number of old cottages in a fine village location. Weavers operates mainly as a restaurant, but the few chintz-filled rooms have antique French beds. Downstairs, the restaurant (closed Sunday night and Monday) serves traditional, organic Yorkshire fare, including smoked haddock soup and lamb with redcurrant gravy, with home-baked bread. ⊠ *15 West La., BD22 8DU* ☏ *01535/643822* 🖶 *01535/*

644832 ⊕ *www.weaversmallhotel.co.uk* ⇌ *3 rooms* ⚬ *Restaurant, bar; no a/c* ▭ *AE, DC, MC, V* ☺ *Closed 1 wk at Christmas and 1 wk in summer* ⫣ *BP.*

£ ✕⫠ **Aitches.** This intimate 19th-century stone house is close to the Brontë Parsonage on Haworth's main street. The guest rooms are modern, with pine pieces and colorful quilts and drapes. A fixed-price meal in the elegant small restaurant (closed Sunday and Monday; open to nonguests on Friday and Saturday only) might include pork cutlet with Stilton crumble followed by a traditional bread-and-butter pudding and marmalade ice cream. ⊠ *11 West La., BD22 8DU* ☎ *01535/ 642501* ⊕ *www.aitches.co.uk* ⇌ *5 rooms* ⚬ *Restaurant; no a/c, no room phones, no smoking* ▭ *MC, V* ⫣ *BP.*

££ ⫠ **Old Registry.** The lovely themed guest rooms—Memories Room, Blue Heaven, Cherub Corner, and so on—in this creeper-covered Victorian house at the lower end of the main street are all individually decorated and equipped with CD players. One room has lavender-scented pillows, another has tapestry hangings, and there's an unusual three-poster bed in the attic room. All have large bathrooms. ⊠ *2–4 Main St., BD22 8DA* ☎⫟ *01535/646503* ⊕ *www.oldregistry.com* ⇌ *8 rooms* ⚬ *Some pets allowed; no a/c, no room phones, no smoking* ▭ *MC, V* ⫣ *BP.*

££ ⫠ **Old White Lion Hotel.** Next door to the church where Patrick Brontë preached stands this former coaching inn, one of the more welcoming hostelries in Haworth. Antique touches and modern conveniences mix happily in the simple rooms; public areas have wood beams and paneling. ⊠ *6 West La., BD22 8DU* ☎ *01535/642313* ⫟ *01535/646222* ⊕ *www.oldwhitelionhotel.com* ⇌ *14 rooms* ⚬ *Restaurant, cable TV, bar, meeting rooms; no a/c* ▭ *AE, DC, MC, V* ⫣ *BP.*

THE YORKSHIRE DALES

With some of the fairest scenery in England, the Yorkshire Dales stand in complete and startling contrast to the industrial towns of West Yorkshire. These meandering river valleys fall south and east from the hills known as the Pennines and, beyond Skipton, present an almost wholly rural aspect. Most, but not all, of the dales take their names from the rivers that run through them, and the scenery is quintessentially English: a ruined priory here, a narrow country road there, a babbling river, drystone walls made without mortar, and stone moorland hamlets (which were the settings for James Herriot's books). Some of the limestone outcroppings and caves can be explored safely even by those not used to visiting such places. Villages here fit snugly into little pockets, looking as though they, like the Pennines, have been here from eternity. In places such as Bolton Priory, the monastic ruins that enchanted Wordsworth and Ruskin, loveliness of setting goes hand in hand with architectural beauty.

The Yorkshire Dales contain prime walking country, and all the villages covered in this section have access to a network of paths and trails; they also have accommodations and hiking services. Wharfedale, one of the longest of the dales, is easily accessible from Bradford. A convenient driving route would take in Bolton Priory, the castle at Skipton, and rural Grassington, Malham, and Kettlewell before moving farther north to see the towns of Askrigg and Hawes in Wensleydale and the glories of Swaledale. You might finish up at the market town of Richmond, where Henry VII had his family seat.

Bolton Priory

★ ❺ *12 mi north of Haworth, 18 mi north of Bradford, 24 mi northwest of Leeds.*

Some of the loveliest Wharfedale scenery comes into view around Bolton Priory, the ruins of an Augustinian priory, which sits on a grassy embankment inside a great curve of the River Wharfe. The priory is just a short walk or drive from the village of Bolton Abbey. You can wander through the 13th-century ruins or visit the priory church, which is still the local parish church. The duke of Devonshire owns the Bolton Abbey estate, including the ruins. Among the famous visitors enchanted by Bolton Priory were William Wordsworth (who described "Bolton's mouldering Priory" in his poem "The White Doe of Rylstone"); J. M. W. Turner, the 19th-century artist, who painted it; and John Ruskin, the Victorian art critic, who rated it the most beautiful of all the English ruins he had seen.

Close to Bolton Priory, surrounded by romantic woodland scenery, the River Wharfe plunges between a narrow chasm in the rocks (called the Strid) before reaching **Barden Tower,** a medieval hunting lodge. This lodge, where Henry, Lord Clifford, carried out his studies in alchemy in the late 15th century, is now a ruin and can be visited just as easily as Bolton Priory, in whose grounds it stands. You can ride the scenic 4-mi **Embsay & Bolton Abbey Steam Railway** (☎ 01756/710614, 01756/795189 recorded timetable), which has a station in Bolton Abbey. ✉ *Off B6160* ☎ *01756/718009* ⊕ *www.boltonabbey.com* ✑ *Free, parking £4* ☉ *Daily dawn–dusk.*

Where to Stay & Eat

★ ££££ ✕🏨 **Devonshire Arms.** Originally an 18th-century coaching inn, and still belonging to the dukes of Devonshire, this luxurious country-house hotel is near the River Wharfe, within easy walking distance of Bolton Abbey. Portraits of dukes hang on the walls, and bedrooms are tastefully decorated by the dowager duchess of Devonshire with antiques and family memorabilia. The Burlington restaurant (no-smoking) has a fixed-price menu of superb traditional fare that uses game and fish from the estate and homegrown herbs and vegetables. The brasserie serves more modest (and modestly priced) fare. ✉ *Bolton Abbey, Skipton, BD23 6AJ* ☎ *01756/710441* 🖷 *01756/710564* ⊕ *www.devonshirehotels.co. uk* 🛏 *39 rooms, 2 suites* ♨ *2 restaurants, in-room data ports, tennis court, pool, health club, sauna, fishing, 2 bars, meeting rooms, some pets allowed; no a/c* ☰ *AE, DC, MC, V* ❑ *BP.*

Skipton

❻ *6 mi west of Bolton Abbey, 12 mi north of Haworth, 22 mi west of Harrogate.*

Skipton in Airedale, capital of the limestone district of Craven, is a typical Dales market town with as many farmers as visitors milling in the

CloseUp

ON THE MENU

Exploring Yorkshire, with its fresh air and hilltop walks, positively encourages hearty appetites. Happily, locally produced meat (especially lamb) and vegetables are excellent; roast beef dinners come with Yorkshire pudding, the famous popoverlike batter traditionally cooked under the meat and served with gravy. In the days when meat was a real luxury, it was offered as a first course in hopes of filling you up. Coastal fish are a treat with freshly fried chips (thick french fries); cod or haddock is the main local catch, although sole, crab, and lobster have their seasons and should be tried.

Look for freshly baked bread, homemade cakes, and curd tarts–pastry shells filled with baked milk curds and currants, at their best in Yorkshire tearooms. Be sure to sample locally made Wensleydale cheese, which has a delicate flavor and honeyed aftertaste.

streets. There are markets Monday, Wednesday, Friday, and Saturday, and shops selling local produce predominate.

★ **Skipton Castle,** built by the Normans in 1090 and unaltered since the Civil War (17th century), is the town's most prominent attraction and one of the best preserved of English medieval castles, remarkably complete in its appearance. After the Battle of Marston Moor during the Civil War, it remained the only Royalist stronghold in the north of England. In the central courtyard, a yew tree, planted 300 years ago by Lady Anne Clifford, still flourishes. The castle is at the top of busy High Street. ⊠ *High St.* ☎ *01756/792442* ⊕ *www.skiptoncastle.co.uk* 🎟 *£5* ۞ *Mar.–Sept., Mon.–Sat. 10–6, Sun. noon–6; Oct.–Feb., Mon.–Sat. 10–4, Sun. noon–4.*

Where to Stay & Eat

££££　✕🖼 **Angel Inn.** Diners at the Angel regularly clog the hidden-away hamlet of Hetton with their vehicles, such is the attraction of this locally renowned eatery. Fish is a specialty at the restaurant (reservations essential; fixed-price menu; no dinner Sunday) and the more modestly priced bar-brasserie; fillet of sea bass or halibut with an herb crust might appear on either menu. The ancient stone barn across the road has freshly renovated, well-equipped guest rooms in unfussy country styles, from rustic to French. The inn is 5 mi north of Skipton. ⊠ *Off B6265, Hetton* ☎ *01756/730263* 🖨 *01756/730363* ⊕ *www.angelhetton.co.uk* 🛏 *5 rooms* ᕖ *Restaurant, bar; no a/c* 🖃 *AE, DC, MC, V* ❃ *BP.*

Grassington

★ ❼ *10 mi north of Skipton, 14 mi northwest of Ilkley, 25 mi west of Ripon.*

A small, stone village built around an ancient cobbled marketplace, Grassington makes a good base for exploring Upper Wharfedale. The Dales Way footpath passes through the village, and there's a good mix of guest houses, stores, pubs, and cafés. In summer, facilities become overwhelmed by day-trippers and walkers. There are plenty of local walks, however, and if you're prepared to make a day of it, you can soon leave the crowds behind. The **National Park Centre** has guidebooks, maps, and bus schedules to help you enjoy a day in the Yorkshire Dales National Park. ⊠ *Colvend, Hebdon Rd.* ☎ *01756/752774* ⊕ *www.yorkshiredales. org.uk* ⊙ *Apr.–Oct., daily 10–5; Nov.–Mar., Wed. and Fri.–Sun. 10–4.*

Where to Stay & Eat

£ ✕ **Devonshire Hotel.** This traditional Dales inn makes a comfortable and refined rural dining spot, with a fine assortment of upholstered chairs in the oak-paneled and candlelit dining room. Local lamb and dishes such as fish hot pot (stew with vegetables) and gammon (cured ham) steak appear on the menu alongside stir-frys and curries. ⊠ *Main St.* ☎ *01756/752525* ⊟ *MC, V.*

££ 🏨 **Ashfield House.** Three converted 17th-century stone cottages, once the homes of Grassington lead miners, make up this well-run small hotel off the main street. Expect a cheery welcome on arrival, simple bedrooms with pine furniture and white walls, a cozy brick-and-beam sitting room, and a walled garden. It's worth asking ahead for the deliciously hearty set dinner (£18). ⊠ *Summers Fold, BD23 5AE* ☎☎ *01756/ 752584* ⊕ *www.ashfieldhouse.co.uk* ⊅ *7 rooms* ⚖ *Dining room, Internet; no a/c, no room phones, no kids under 5, no smoking* ⊟ *MC, V* ⊙| *BP.*

££ 🏨 **Grassington Lodge** Light and airy, this Victorian house has made the most of its original features by expert and uncluttered decoration. Bedrooms have beautiful quilts; the top-floor room has the biggest bed. A roaring log fire in the sitting room takes the edge off cold days. ⊠ *8 Wood La., BD23 5LU* ☎☎ *01756/752518* ⊕ *www.grassingtonlodge. co.uk* ⊅ *7 rooms* ⚖ *No a/c, no room phones, no kids under 12, no smoking* ⊟ *No credit cards* ⊙ *Call ahead in winter* ⊙| *BP.*

Malham

★ ❽ *10 mi west of Grassington, 12 mi northwest of Skipton.*

Avid hikers descend in droves on Malham in summer to tour some of Britain's most remarkable limestone formations, Malham Cove and Gordale Scar among them. The tiny hamlet has a population of about 200, yet is visited by a half million people a year. (Come before June or after August to avoid the worst crowds.) It's a rugged and romantic spot, whatever the weather, with intensely rural surroundings described glowingly in poems by Wordsworth and W. H. Auden, painted by Turner, and photographed by David Hockney—proof indeed of Malham's aesthetic potency. To get here from Grassington, take B6265 south 2 mi through Cracoe, then branch west onto the minor road past Hetton and Calton; Malham is also northwest of Skipton, off A65.

Maps and displays at Malham's **National Park Centre** will give you ideas of what to do locally and in Yorkshire Dales National Park. You can get a list of local B&B and pub accommodations, too; they are relatively plentiful, but highly sought after in summer. ☎ *01729/830363* ⊕ *www. yorkshiredales.org.uk* ⊙ *Apr.–Oct., daily 10–5; Nov.–Mar., Fri.–Sun. 10–4.*

Where to Stay
£–££ ☞ **Lister Arms Hotel.** Right on the village green, this stone-built 17th-century hotel, once a coaching inn, has bright bedrooms that are simply but stylishly furnished, favoring white and warm reds. The inglenook bar is well-known for its beers—Dutch and Belgian as well as traditional Yorkshire—and there's a wide range of food available. ⊠ *Malham, BD23 4DB* ☎ *01729/830330* ☒ *01729/830725* ⊕ *www.listerarms. co.uk* 🛏 *9 rooms* ♨ *Restaurant, bar; no a/c* ☰ *AE, DC, MC, V* �☯ *BP.*

Sports & the Outdoors
Malham's three main destinations—Malham Cove, Gordale Scar, and Malham Tarn—can be seen on a circular walk of 8 mi that takes most people four to five hours. Those with less time should cut out the tarn: a circular walk from the village to Malham Cove and Gordale Scar can be completed in just over two hours. **Malham Cove,** a huge, 300-foot-high natural rock amphitheater, is a mile north of the village and provides the easiest local walk, although following the path *up* to the top
★ is a brutal climb, rewarded by magnificent views. At **Gordale Scar,** a deep natural chasm between overhanging limestone cliffs, the white waters of a moorland stream plunge 300 feet. It's a mile northeast of Malham by a lovely riverside path. A walk of more than 3 mi leads north from Malham to **Malham Tarn,** an attractive lake in windswept isolation. There's a nature reserve on the west bank and an easy-to-follow trail on the east bank.

> en route   North of Malham, a dramatic moorland drive follows the minor road that skirts Malham Tarn to **Arncliffe** in Littondale. In Littondale, a superb village inn, the **Falcon** (☎ 01756/770205) revives flagging spirits and provides accommodations Easter–October. In winter this road may be impassable: always check local weather forecasts. At Arncliffe, follow the signs southeast for B6160 and then turn north for Kettlewell.

Kettlewell

❾ *6 mi north of Grassington, 8 mi northeast of Malham.*

A babbling river runs through the heart of Kettlewell, the main settlement in Upper Wharfedale and a fine base for a couple of days' exploration of the local hills and valleys, with their stone-flagged pubs, riverside walks, and narrow pack bridges (built for horses and donkeys carrying sacks) constructed from rubble. The Dales Way hiking path passes through the quiet, gray-stone village, and drivers will easily be able to visit Malham and Grassington from here, returning for a peaceful night away from the crowds. This area was used to wonderful scenic effect in the filming of *Calendar Girls*; Kettlewell is called Knapely. The movie is about Yorkshire women who pose for an almost-nude calendar to raise money for charity.

Where to Stay & Eat
££ ✕☞ **Blue Bell Inn.** Horse brasses, tankards hanging from the rafters, ornamental plates, and high-back settles decorate this 17th-century coach-

ing inn. Guest rooms are simply furnished with colorfully striped quilts. The reasonably priced menu includes Dales lamb chops, grilled Wharfedale trout, and plenty for vegetarians. ✉ *BD23 5QX* ☎ *01756/760230* ⊕ *www.bluebellinn.co.uk* ⇨ *9 rooms* ⚭ *Restaurant, bar, no-smoking rooms; no a/c, no room phones* ▭ *MC* ❍❘ *BP.*

en route

From Kettlewell, it's just 4 mi north along B6160 to **Buckden,** the last village in Wharfedale. A minor road leads to the riverside hamlet of Hubberholme. Its stone chapel and ancient George Inn were favorites of Yorkshire-born author J. B. Priestley, who is buried in the churchyard. Back on B6160, you can go north through Kidstone Pass to Aysgarth in Wensleydale, where the River Ure plummets over a series of waterfalls.

Askrigg

🔟 *16 mi north of Kettlewell, 25 mi north of Malham.*

Askrigg would be just another typical Wensleydale village were it not for its association with the James Herriot TV series *All Creatures Great and Small,* which was filmed in and around it in the 1970s and 1980s. The tourist board pushes "Herriot Country" hard, but although Askrigg—dubbed "Darrowby" in the program—is a pleasing village, there's not much else to keep you here, apart from walks to a couple of local waterfalls. The **King's Arms Hotel** (✉ Market Pl. ☎ 01969/650817), a wood-paneled, 18th-century coaching inn, was rechristened the Drover's Arms for its appearance in episodes of the Herriot TV series. The atmospheric building has nook-and-cranny rooms, good local beer, and two restaurants.

Hawes

🔟 *5 mi west of Askrigg.*

The best time to visit Hawes, reputedly the highest market town in England, is on Tuesday when farmers and locals crowd into town for the weekly market. Hawes is brisk and businesslike at other times, too, since it retains some of Wensleydale's more traditional industries, not least its cheese making. Crumbly, white Wensleydale cheese has been made in the valley for centuries, and it is sold in local stores. Give yourself time to wander the cobbled side streets, some of which are filled with antiques shops and tearooms.

The **Wensleydale Creamery Visitor Centre,** in a working dairy farm, includes a museum that tells the story of Wensleydale cheese. A viewing gallery enables you to watch production (best seen between 10 and 2), and then you can repair to the shop to taste the cheeses. Besides the regular Wensleydale cheese, you can try it smoked, with ginger, or with apple pie. A restaurant is on site. ✉ *Gayle La.* ☎ *01969/667664* ⊕ *www. wensleydale.co.uk/centre.htm* 🎫 *Museum £2* ⊙ *Apr.–Oct., daily 9–5:30; Nov.–Mar., daily 9:30–4:30.*

The Yorkshire Dales National Park Information Centre in the old train station contains the **Dales Countryside Museum,** which gives a picture of

Dales life in past centuries. A traditional rope-making shop here also welcomes visitors. ⊠ *Station Yard* ☎ *01969/667450* ⊕ *www. yorkshiredales.org.uk* ⊠ *Museum £3* ⊗ *Daily 10–5.*

en route From Hawes, the most direct route to **Swaledale** is north by minor road over the Buttertubs Pass, a 7-mi run to Muker, a lovely village that hosts the annual Swaledale show in September. Many people regard Swaledale as the finest of all the Yorkshire Dales. From Muker, B6270 and A6108 run down the valley to Richmond.

Richmond

⑫ *22 mi northeast of Hawes, 25 mi northwest of Ripon.*

Richmond tucks itself into a curve above the foaming River Swale, with a network of narrow Georgian streets and terraces opening onto the country's largest cobbled marketplace. Despite appearances, it would be a mistake to date the town to the 18th century. The Normans swept in during the late 11th century, determined to subdue the local population and establish their rule in the north. This they did by building a mighty castle, around which the town grew, and throughout the Middle Ages Richmond was effectively a garrison town.

The immense keep of Norman **Richmond Castle** towers above the river, providing excellent views over the surroundings. Built around 1071 by Alan Rufus, first earl of Richmond, it was used as a prison for William the Lion of Scotland 100 years later. The castle is one of the best-preserved monuments of this era, retaining its curtain wall and chapel, and a great hall that has been partially restored to its medieval splendor; even the 14th-century graffiti remains. There's a heritage garden, and a path along the river leads to the ruins of golden-stone Easby Abbey. One historical note: when Henry Tudor (son of Edmund Tudor, earl of Richmond) became Henry VII in 1485, he began calling his palace in Shene, southwest London, Richmond (Palace), after his family seat in Richmond. The name gradually became used to describe that area of London. ☎ *01748/822493* ⊕ *www.english-heritage.org.uk* ⊠ *£3.50* ⊗ *Apr.–Sept., daily 10–6; Oct., daily 10–5; Nov.–Mar., daily 10–4.*

The tiny Georgian **Theatre Royal,** a pretty jewel box built in 1788, retains many original features, such as the wooden seating from the days of the 18th-century Shakespearean actor David Garrick. The museum holds scenery dating from 1836. ⊠ *Friars Wynd* ☎ *01748/823710, 01748/ 825252 box office* ⊕ *www.georgiantheatreroyal.co.uk* ⊠ *Museum £2.50 suggested donation* ⊗ *Museum mid-Feb.–Dec., Mon.–Sat. 10–5.*

Where to Stay & Eat

££–£££ ✕ **Frenchgate Café.** Blue wicker chairs and yellow walls capture a bit of the bright Mediterranean at this bistro-style café, just below the main cobbled square. Panache and care guide the contemporary cooking; try one of the pastas, such as penne with smoked salmon, or lamb with rosemary sauce. Cappuccino, scones, and snacks are available. ⊠ *29 Frenchgate* ☎ *01748/824949* ▭ *AE, MC, V.*

££ 🏨 **Frenchgate Hotel.** This three-story Georgian town house on a quiet cobbled street has a secluded walled garden for summer days and a bright and welcoming interior, furnished with some flair. Public rooms hark back to the 17th century, but the decorative mice (symbol of local craftsman Mousey Thompson) hidden in the woodwork are more recent. Spacious bedrooms favor prints and stripes. ✉ *59–61 Frenchgate, DL10 7AE* ☎ *01748/822087* 🖷 *01748/823596* ⊕ *www.frenchgatehotel.com* 🛏 *11 rooms ♿ Restaurant, bar; no a/c* ☰ *MC, V* ⦿❙ *BP.*

YORK

⦿ It would be unthinkable to visit North Yorkshire without going first to the historic cathedral city of York, and not just because its central location makes it a practical place to start. Named "Eboracum" in Latin, York was the military capital of Roman Britain, and traces of Roman garrison buildings survive throughout the city. The Vikings also claimed York as their capital and left bountiful evidence of their tenure, and in Norman times the foundations of York Minster, the largest medieval cathedral in England, were laid. During the great industrial age, which caused so much havoc in many northern towns and cities, York was a forgotten backwater—hence the survival of so much medieval and 18th-century architecture. That's not to say that the city exists in a time vacuum: the stores that have taken over the heart of the old city can sometimes make the place seem more like an extension of London's Oxford Street than one of the great historical survivals of Europe. The Shambles, a medieval street built between 1350 and 1450, has been particularly altered by shops and boutiques.

York is 48 mi southeast of Richmond, 25 mi northeast of Leeds, and 82 mi south of Newcastle. By far the most attractive city in the region, it is one of the most popular short-stay destinations in Britain and only two hours by fast train from London on a good day.

Exploring York

After the fall of the Roman Empire in the 5th century, a Saxon town grew up over the ruins of the Roman fort at York. On Christmas Eve, AD 627, the Northumbrian king Edwin introduced Christianity to the area by being baptized in a little wooden church here. The city grew in importance during the 9th century, after the Viking conquerors of northern and eastern England made York, which they called "Jorvik," their English capital. Many of the city's street names are suffixed with the word "-gate" (Goodramgate, Micklegate, for example). "Gate" was the Viking word for "street."

The old city center of York is a compact, dense web of narrow streets and tiny alleys, "snickleways," in which congestion is so bad that automobile traffic has been banned around the minster. It's a fine city for walking, though, provided you have a map. Try to avoid visiting in July and August, when crowds choke the narrow streets and cause long lines at the popular museums. April, May, and October are far better; April is also the time to see the embankments beneath the city walls filled with the pale gold ripple of daffodils. You can get a good overview of York by strolling along these walls. For a different perspective, walk beside the River Ouse, which cuts a sizable swath through the city and in summer is full of pleasure craft.

York's city center may be compact, but you need an early start and plenty of stamina to see everything. You can't miss your starting point: the towers of **York Minster** ⑬ ► are visible from virtually anywhere on the encircling **city walls** ⑭, so once you've got your bearings, make for Duncombe Place and the main entrance to England's largest Gothic church. After you've ogled the interior, take a few steps northward to the **Treasurer's House** ⑮ and its surprising interior. Next, head down either Low Petergate or Goodramgate to the famed **Shambles** ⑯, now a crowded shopping street. At the southern end of the Shambles, you can walk to Fossgate to visit the **Merchant Adventurers' Hall** ⑰, with its medieval timber-frame hall. Retrace your steps on Fossgate and turn left on Coppergate, and you're in one of York's oldest areas, where objects from Viking times were first discovered; the entertaining **Jorvik** ⑱ has all the details. From Coppergate, Castlegate runs south, passing the former church of St. Mary's and that connoisseur's delight, the elegant Georgian-era **Fairfax House** ⑲ before ending at the historic mound of **Clifford's Tower** ⑳. The **Castle Museum** ㉑, a collection of ephemera, costumes, and vintage machinery, marks the southernmost extent of your explorations.

From the Castle Museum, it's a 20-minute stroll back through the city center, up to the **Guildhall** ㉒ on St. Helen's Square—you can refuel in Betty's famous tearoom—and nearby **Stonegate** ㉓, another historic shopping street. Doing the walk this way, you've saved two splendid museum collections, both on the outskirts of the historic kernel, until last. From St. Helen's Square it's an easy walk up Lendal and across the main road to the archaeological exhibits of the **Yorkshire Museum** ㉔. Enjoy a stroll through the museum's gardens, then make your way to Lendal Bridge and cross the River Ouse onto Station Road. Taking a right on Leeman Road brings you to the **National Railway Museum** ㉕.

TIMING   The walk itself takes about an hour, but you need a long day (and perhaps a second, depending on your interests) if you want to spend time at the sights. Try to avoid weekends, when crowds can be intense.

What to See

★ ㉑ **Castle Museum.** A former 18th-century debtors' prison, this museum of everyday items presents detailed exhibitions and re-creations, including a Victorian street complete with crafts shops and a working water mill, as well as notable domestic, costume, and arms and armor displays. One treasure is the Coppergate Helmet, a 1,200-year-old Anglo-Saxon helmet discovered during excavations of the city; it's one of only three such objects found. You can also visit the cell where Dick Turpin, the 18th-century highwayman and folk hero, spent the night before his execution. ⊠ *Clifford St.* ☎ *01904/687687* ⊕ *www.yorkcastlemuseum.org. uk* ⊠ *£6* ☉ *Daily 9:30–5.*

⑭ **City walls.** York's almost 3 mi of ancient stone walls are among the longest and best preserved in England. A walk on the narrow paved path along

York

Castle Museum **21**

City Walls **14**

Clifford's Tower **20**

Fairfax House **19**

Guildhall **22**

Jorvik **18**

Merchant
Adventurers' Hall **17**

National Railway
Museum **25**

The Shambles **16**

Stonegate **23**

Treasurer's House **15**

York Minster **13**

Yorkshire Museum **24**

KEY

𝑖 Tourist information

▶ Start of walk

the top leads you through 1,900 years of history, from the time the earthen ramparts were raised by the Romans and York's Viking kings to repel raiders, to their fortification by the Normans, to their current landscaping by the city council. The path crosses over York's distinctive fortified gates or "bars": the portcullis on Monk's Bar on Goodramgate is still in working order, and Walmgate Bar in the east is the only gate in England with an intact barbican. Bootham Bar in Exhibition Square was the defensive bastion for the north road, and Micklegate Bar, in the city's southwest corner, was traditionally the monarch's entrance. To access the path and the lookout towers, find a staircase at one of the breaks in the walls. ⊕ *www.york.gov.uk/walls* ✇ *Free* ⊙ *Daily 8 AM–dusk.*

❷⓪ **Clifford's Tower.** Dating from the early 14th century, this forbidding stone tower stands on the mound originally erected for the keep of York Castle. You can climb to the top. In 1190, a wooden predecessor of this tower was the scene of one of the worst instances of anti-Semitism in medieval Europe. Of the 150 Jews who sought sanctuary in the castle from a mob, some committed suicide and others surrendered and were massacred. ✉ *Tower St.* ☎ *01904/646940* ✇ *£2.50* ⊙ *Apr.–Oct., daily 10–6; Nov.–Mar., daily 10–4.*

★ ❶⑨ **Fairfax House.** One of the most elegant Georgian town houses in England, Fairfax House is a masterpiece of rococo decoration. Now a museum of decorative arts, this often overlooked treasure was designed by John Carr of York and built in 1762. A distinguished collection of Georgian furniture fills the house. The marble dining room and the grand salon, all crystal chandeliers and flaming crimson silk walls, rival anything found at Castle Howard, the famous stately home northeast of York. ✉ *Castlegate* ☎ *01904/655543* ⊕ *www.fairfaxhouse.co.uk* ✇ *£4.50* ⊙ *Mid-Feb.–Dec., Mon.–Thurs. and Sat. 11–5, Sun. 1:30–5; last admission 4:30; Fri., guided tours 11 and 2.*

❷② **Guildhall.** The mid-15th-century guildhall, by the River Ouse, was a meeting place for the city's powerful guilds. It was also used for pageants and mystery plays (medieval dramas based on biblical stories and the lives of saints). Restoration after the damage done by World War II bombing has given it something of its erstwhile glory, although 14 Victorian stained-glass windows were lost—only one, at the west end, remains. The guildhall is behind the 18th-century Mansion House; you can visit it when no function is in progress. ✉ *St. Helen's Sq.* ☎ *01904/613161* ✇ *Free* ⊙ *May–Oct., weekdays 9–5, Sat. 10–5, Sun. 2–5; Nov.–Apr., weekdays 9–5.*

Sink into a leather armchair in the informal **Ha!Ha! Bar and Canteen** (✉ 13–17 New St., off Davygate ☎ 01904/655868) for a tasty Mediterranean brunch and nibbles. Liquid refreshments include cappuccino as well as cocktails.

★ ☾ ❶⑧ **Jorvik.** On an authentic Viking site, this exhibition re-creates a Viking city of the 10th century, with careful attention to detail. Its time capsules whisk you through the streets to experience the sights, sounds, and smells of Viking England, and excellent displays, using high-tech wizardry, reveal the breadth of the Viking culture and social system. The Fearsome Craftsmen exhibition explores a different craft each month and has activities that let you try your hand at it. ✉ *Coppergate* ☎ *01904/643211, 01904/543403 advance booking* ⊕ *www.vikingjorvik. com* 🖭 *£7.20* ☉ *Apr.–Oct., daily 10–5; Nov.–Mar., daily 10–4.*

⓱ Merchant Adventurers' Hall. Built between 1357 and 1368 and owned by one of the city's richest medieval guilds (its members dealt in wool and lead, which were traded far and wide), this is the largest half-timber hall in York and one of the finest in Europe. Portraits, silver, and furniture are on display. A riverfront garden lies behind the hall. On most Saturdays, antiques fairs are held inside the building. ✉ *Fossgate* ☎ *01904/ 654818* ⊕ *www.theyorkcompany.co.uk* 🖭 *£2* ☉ *Apr.–Sept., Mon.–Thurs. 9–5, Fri. and Sat. 9–3:30, Sun. noon–4; Oct.–Mar., Mon.–Sat. 9–3:30.*

★ ☾ ㉕ National Railway Museum. At this train-spotters' delight, which began as a northern outpost of the Science Museum in London, Britain's national collection of locomotives forms part of the world's largest train museum. Among the exhibits are gleaming giants of the steam era, including *Mallard,* holder of the world speed record for a steam engine (126 mph). Passenger cars used by Queen Victoria are on display, as well as the only Japanese bullet train to be seen outside Japan. You can clamber aboard some of the trains, and an interactive exhibit explores working life onboard a mail train. ✉ *Leeman Rd.* ☎ *01904/621261, 01904/ 686286 information line* ⊕ *www.nrm.org.uk* 🖭 *Free* ☉ *Daily 10–6.*

⓰ The Shambles. Ah, that this street had remained as picturesque as its name. York's best-preserved medieval street has several half-timber stores and houses with overhangs so massive you could almost reach across the street from one second-floor window to another. It's a little too cute for its own good these days, with its crafts and souvenir shops—a far cry, certainly, from the days when the Shambles was the city's meat market. Still, aim your camera at rooftop level and see if you can catch York Minster soaring over it all.

㉓ Stonegate. This narrow, pedestrian-only street of Tudor and 18th-century storefronts and courtyards retains considerable charm. It has been in daily use for almost 2,000 years, since first being paved in Roman times. A passage just off Stonegate, at 52A, leads to a 12th-century Norman stone house, one of the few remaining in England.

⓯ Treasurer's House. Surprises await you as you step inside this large 17th-century house, the home from 1897 to 1930 of industrialist Frank Green. With a fine eye for texture, decoration, and pattern, Green created a series of period rooms—including a medieval great hall—as a showcase for his collection of antique furniture. Delft tiles decorate the kitchen, copies of medieval stenciling cover the vibrant Red Room, and 17th-century stumpwork adorns the Tapestry Room. ✉ *Minster Yard* ☎ *01904/624247* ⊕ *www.nationaltrust.org.uk* 🖭 *£4.50* ☉ *Apr.–Oct., Sat.–Thurs. 11–5; last admission 30 mins before closing.*

★ ☞ ⓭ York Minster. Focal point of the city, this vast cathedral is the largest Gothic church in England and attracts almost as many visitors as London's Westminster Abbey. Inside, the effect created by its soaring pillars, lofty vaulted ceilings, and dazzling stained-glass windows—glowing with deep wine reds and cobalt blues, they are bested only by those in Chartres Cathedral in France—is almost too overpowering. The central towers are 184 feet high, and the church is 534 feet long, 249 feet across its transepts, and 90 feet from floor to roof. The structure is so high, it's best to come with binoculars if you wish to study the stained glass. Mere statistics, however, cannot convey the scale of the building. Its soaring columns; the ornamentation of its 14th-century nave; the east window, one of the greatest pieces of medieval glazing in the world; the north transept's **Five Sisters** windows, five tall lancets of frosted 13th-century glass; the enormous choir screen portraying somewhat whimsical images of every king of England from William the Conqueror to Henry VI; the imposing tracery of the **Rose Window** (just one of the minster's 128 stained-glass windows), commemorating the marriage of Henry VII and Elizabeth of York in 1486 (the event that ended the Wars of the Roses and began the Tudor dynasty)—all contribute to its cold, crushing splendor. Don't miss the exquisite 13th-century **Chapter House** and the **Undercroft, Treasury, and Crypt.** After exploring the interior, you might take the 275 winding steps to the roof of the great **Central Tower** (strictly for those with a head for heights), not only for the close-up view of the cathedral's detailed carving but for a panorama of York and the surrounding moors. ⊠ *Duncombe Pl.* ☎ *01904/557216* ⊕ *www.yorkminster.org* ☞ *Minster £4.50, Undercroft, Treasury, and Crypt £2.50, Central Tower £2.50* ☉ *Minster and Chapter House Mon.–Sat. 9–4:45 and 5:30–6:30, Sun. noon–3:45 and 4:30–6:30. Undercroft, Treasury, and Crypt Apr.–Oct., Mon.–Sat. 9–5:30, Sun. noon–5:30; Nov.–Mar., Mon.–Sat. 9–5, Sun. noon–5. Central Tower Apr.–Oct., Mon.–Sat. 9–5:30, Sun. noon–5:30; Nov.–Mar., Mon.–Sat. 9–5, Sun. noon–5.*

㉔ **Yorkshire Museum.** The natural and archaeological history of the county, including material on the Roman, Anglo-Saxon, and Viking aspects of York, is the focus of this museum. Also on display in the solid, Doric-style building is the 15th-century Middleham Jewel, a pendant gleaming with a large sapphire. Outdoors in the botanical gardens, amid the ruins of St. Mary's Abbey, the city's cycle of medieval mystery plays is performed (next scheduled for 2010, but check with the visitor center). The museum lies just outside the walled city, through Bootham Bar, one of York's old gates. ⊠ *Museum Gardens, Museum St.* ☎ *01904/551805* ⊕ *www.yorkshiremuseum.org.uk* ☞ *£4* ☉ *Daily 10–5.*

Where to Eat

£££–££££   ✕ **Blue Bicycle.** There can't be many restaurants that have the distinction of occupying a former brothel, but this is one of them. You can dine downstairs in the walled booths (where the beds were) or stay above ground in a lively room with wooden furnishings and warm orange walls. The menu concentrates on fish, such as spiced monkfish or roasted salmon escalope; among the excellent desserts, sticky toffee pudding and ice creams are good bets. ⊠ *34 Fossgate* ☎ *01904/673990* ▭ *MC, V.*

★ **££–££££** ✕ **Melton's.** Once a private house, this unpretentious but excellent restaurant has local art on the walls and an open kitchen. The seasonal menus continue to be highly imaginative, a legacy of chef Michael Hjort's stint at the Roux brothers' establishments in London. Highlights are modern English and European fare, such as home-cured pork with glazed apples, and roast chicken with wild mushroom risotto. Melton's is 10 minutes from York Minster. ⊠ *7 Scarcroft Rd.* ☎ *01904/634341* ⩍ *Reservations essential* ▤ *MC, V* ☽ *Closed Sun., 3 wks at Christmas, and 1 wk in Aug. No lunch Mon.*

££ ✕ **Café Concerto.** Music ephemera decorate this relaxed, intimate bistro in sight of York Minster, which prepares virtually any style of food you care to name, from Caribbean to Continental. You might choose the Cuban spiced chicken with sweet potatoes, and then savor a piece of homemade cake and a cappuccino. ⊠ *21 High Petergate* ☎ *01904/ 610478* ▤ *No credit cards.*

★ **£–££** ✕ **Betty's.** At the opposite end of Stonegate from the minster, this York institution since 1912 is arranged elegantly across two large floors in a beautiful art nouveau building. Best known for its teas served with mouthwatering cakes (try the "fat rascal," a bun bursting with cherries and nuts), Betty's also offers light meals and a splendid selection of exotic coffees. ⊠ *6–8 St. Helen's Sq.* ☎ *01904/659142* ▤ *MC, V.*

£ ✕ **Golden Slipper.** Although it's only a stone's throw from the busy minster, this warm and cozy place with book-lined walls resembles a country pub. Besides good homemade pies—try the pork, apple, and sage—there are stuffed baked potatoes and hot and cold sandwiches, all served until 7 PM, or 5 PM on weekends. ⊠ *20 Goodramgate* ☎ *01904/ 651235* ▤ *MC, V.*

£ ✕ **Spurriergate Centre.** Churches are not just for prayers, as this deconsecrated 15th-century church proves. Resurrected as a cafeteria by a community organization, St. Michael's is a favorite spot for travelers and mothers with strollers to refuel spiritually as well as gastronomically. You may end up eating bean and cabbage hot pot on the spot where John Wesley prayed in 1768. Don't pass up the cream scones. ⊠ *Spurriergate* ☎ *01904/629393* ☽ *Closed Sun. No dinner.*

Where to Stay

£££££ 🏠 **Middlethorpe Hall.** This splendidly restored 18th-century mansion, about
Fodor'sChoice   1½ mi from the city center, was the sometime home of the traveler and
★   diarist Lady Mary Wortley Montagu (1689–1762). Antiques, paintings, and fresh flowers fill the traditionally decorated rooms, some in cottage-style accommodations around an 18th-century courtyard. The extensive grounds include a lake and a 17th-century dovecote. The Anglo-French menu of the wood-paneled restaurant, worth a trip even if you're not staying here, changes seasonally but always has more than a hint of luxury—like the hotel itself. ⊠ *Bishopthorpe Rd., YO23 2GB* ☎ *01904/641241* 🖷 *01904/620176* ⊕ *www.middlethorpe.com* ⇨ *23 rooms, 8 suites* ⩍ *Restaurant, in-room data ports, indoor pool, health club, sauna, spa, croquet, bar, Internet, meeting rooms, free parking; no a/c, no kids under 8* ▤ *MC, V.*

£££–££££   🏨 **Dean Court Hotel.** The clergy of York Minster, just across the way, once found accommodations at this large Victorian house. It now has traditionally furnished rooms with plenty of print fabrics, plump sofas, and fine views overlooking the minster. The restaurant serves good English cuisine, including a hearty Yorkshire breakfast. ⊠ *Duncombe Pl., YO1 7EF* ☎ *01904/625082* 🖷 *01904/620305* ⊕ *www.deancourt-york.co.uk* 🛏 *39 rooms* ☺ *Restaurant, coffee shop, in-room data ports, cable TV, bar, meeting rooms, parking (fee); no a/c* ⊟ *AE, DC, MC, V* ⫧ *BP.*

£££–££££   🏨 **Judge's Lodgings.** This Georgian mansion provided rooms for justices when they traveled up north from London's Inns of Court. Past the elegant gates and front yard, you mount an imposing staircase. Beyond the lovely, somewhat shabby-genteel lobby is the main salon—a delightful, cozy cocoon of pastels, overstuffed chairs, and gilded mirrors. Upstairs, the furnishings continue in the same style. ⊠ *9 Lendal, YO1 2AQ* ☎ *01904/638733* 🖷 *01904/679947* ⊕ *www.judges-lodging.co.uk* 🛏 *14 rooms* ☺ *Restaurant, cable TV, bar, meeting rooms, free parking; no a/c* ⊟ *AE, DC, MC, V* ⫧ *BP.*

£££–££££   🏨 **One3two.** Reflecting a trend in some British hotels, this small Georgian town house manages to be plushly contemporary without sacrificing its period features. Decorated with rich solid colors, the bedrooms are fitted with either modern or period pieces; the marble bathrooms have walk-in showers and deep bathtubs. You can take breakfast in the elegant, pumpkin-hue dining-room, or have a champagne hamper delivered to your room. ⊠ *132 The Mount, YO24 1AS* ☎ *01904/600060* 🖷 *01904/676132* ⊕ *www.one3two.co.uk* 🛏 *5 rooms* ☺ *In-room data ports; no a/c, no smoking* ⊟ *AE, DC, MC, V* ⫧ *BP.*

££–£££   🏨 **The Hazelwood.** Only 400 yards from York Minster, this tall Victorian town house stands in a peaceful cul-de-sac, away from the noise of traffic. Reds and golds dominate bedrooms furnished with rich fabrics and handsome traditional wood pieces. Service is friendly and informal, and the memorable breakfasts include black pudding, Danish pastries, and vegetarian sausages. ⊠ *24–25 Portland St., YO31 7EH* ☎ *01904/626548* 🖷 *01904/628032* ⊕ *www.thehazelwoodyork.com* 🛏 *14 rooms* ☺ *Free parking; no a/c, no room phones, no kids under 8, no smoking* ⊟ *MC, V* ⫧ *BP.*

£–££   🏨 **Abbey Guest House.** This terraced guest house, formerly an artisan's home, is a 10-minute walk from the train station and town center. Although small, it's clean and friendly, with a garden by the River Ouse and ducks waddling about outside. Bedrooms, some with four-posters, are individually furnished. ⊠ *14 Earlsborough Terr., Marygate, YO3 7BQ* ☎ *01904/627782* 🖷 *01904/671743* ⊕ *www.bedandbreakfastyork.co.uk* 🛏 *7 rooms, 2 with bath* ☺ *Internet, free parking; no a/c, no room phones, no smoking* ⊟ *MC, V* ⫧ *BP.*

£–££
FodorśChoice
★   🏨 **Dairy Guest House.** Victorian stained glass, pine woodwork, and intricate plaster cornices are original features of this former dairy 200 yards from the city walls. Bedrooms, done in pleasant pastels, come with books and games, and the imaginative breakfasts can accommodate vegetarians and vegans. The flower-filled internal courtyard is lovely. ⊠ *3 Scarcroft Rd., YO23 1ND* ☎ *01904/639367* ⊕ *www.dairyguesthouse.*

co.uk ⇝ *5 rooms, 3 with bath* ⚄ *Some pets allowed; no a/c, no room phones, no smoking* ⊟ *No credit cards* ⍾⍿ *BP.*

£–££ ⊡ **Eastons.** Two Victorian houses knocked into one, this guest house successfully retains a rich sense of the era. Dark colors enhance the marble fireplaces, wood paneling, tiling, antique furniture, and big sofas, and the affable hosts are welcoming. Breakfast is substantial. It's easy to find parking on the street, which is just south of the city center, 300 yards from the city walls. ⊠ *90 Bishopthorpe Rd., YO31 1JS* ☎ *01904/ 626646* 🖶 *01904/626165* ⇝ *10 rooms* ⚄ *No a/c, no room phones, no kids under 5, no smoking* ⊟ *No credit cards* ⍾⍿ *BP.*

Nightlife & the Arts

Nightlife

York is full of historic pubs where you can while away an hour over a pint. The **Black Swan** (⊠ Peasholme Green ☎ 01904/686911) is the city's oldest pub, a 16th-century gathering place of great character. The **Judge's Lodgings** (⊠ 9 Lendal ☎ 01904/638733) has a cellar bar in which the old vaults provide a convivial drinking hole.

Festivals

York's annual **Bonfire Night** celebrations on November 5 have an added piquancy because the notorious 16th-century conspirator Guy Fawkes was a native of the city. The event commemorates Fawkes's failure to blow up the Houses of Parliament, and his effigy is burned atop every fire. The tourist office has the locations of the best fires and fireworks.

The **Viking Festival** (⊠ Jorvik, Coppergate ☎ 01904/543402 ⊕ www. vikingjorvik.com) takes place each February. The celebrations, including a parade and long-ship regatta, end with the Jorvik Viking Combat reenactment, when Norsemen confront their Anglo-Saxon enemies.

The Arts

The **Early Music Festival** (☎ 01904/658338 festival office, 01904/621756 Tourist Information Centre ⊕ www.ncem.co.uk) is held each summer.

York Theatre Royal (⊠ St. Leonard's Pl. ☎ 01904/623568) is a lively professional theater in a lovely 18th-century building. Besides plays, it presents music, poetry reading, and art exhibitions.

Shopping

The new and secondhand bookstores around Petergate, Stonegate, and the Shambles are excellent. The **Minster Gate Bookshop** (⊠ 8 Minster Gate ★ ☎ 01904/621812) sells secondhand books, old maps, and prints. **Mulberry Hall** (⊠ Stonegate ☎ 01904/620736) is a sales center for all the famous names in fine bone china and crystal. It also has a neat café. The **York Antiques Centre** (⊠ 2 Lendal ☎ 01904/641445) has 25 shops selling antiques, bric-a-brac, books, and jewelry.

YORK ENVIRONS

West and north of York, a number of sights make easy, appealing day trips from the city: the spa town of Harrogate, the castle in Knaresborough, the ruins of Fountain Abbey, the market town of Ripon and nearby Newby Hall, and Thirsk, with its James Herriot connection. If you're heading northwest from York to Harrogate, you might take the less direct B1224 across Marston Moor, where, in 1644, Oliver Cromwell won a decisive victory over the Royalists during the Civil War. A few miles beyond, at Wetherby, you can cut northwest along the A661 to Harrogate.

Harrogate

26 *21 mi west of York, 11 mi south of Ripon, 16 mi north of Leeds.*

During the Regency and early Victorian periods, it became fashionable for the noble and wealthy to retire to a spa to "take the waters" for relaxation. Nowhere else in Yorkshire did this trend reach such grand heights as in Harrogate, an elegant town that flourished during the 19th century. When the spas no longer drew crowds, Harrogate shed its old image to become a modern business center and built a huge complex that today attracts international conventions. It has been tactfully located so as not to spoil the town's landscape of poised Regency row houses, pleasant walkways, and sweeping green spaces. Of Harrogate's parks, the most appealing is the one in the town center, known as **The Stray,** a 200-acre reach of grassland that is a riot of color in spring. The **Valley Gardens,** southwest of the town center, include a boating lake, tennis courts, and a little café.

You can still drink the evil-smelling (and nasty-tasting) spa waters at the **Royal Pump Room Museum,** in the octagonal structure built in 1842 over the original sulfur well that brought great prosperity to the town. The museum displays all the equipment of spa days gone by, as well as some fine 19th-century china and bicycles. ⊠ *Crown Pl.* ☎ *01423/556188* ⊕ *www.harrogate.gov.uk* ✑ *£2.50* ☉ *Apr.–Oct., Mon.–Sat. 10–5, Sun. 2–5; Nov.–Mar., Mon.–Sat. 10–4, Sun. 2–4.*

In the **Turkish Baths** (1897), you can take a bath or a sauna in the exotic, tiled rooms; allow two hours or so for the full treatment. ⊠ *Parliament St.* ☎ *01423/556746* ⊕ *www.harrogate.gov.uk* ✑ *£10.50 per bath and sauna session, massages additional* ☉ *Daily; call for schedules.*

Where to Stay & Eat

£ ✕ **Betty's.** The celebrated Yorkshire tearoom began life in Harrogate in the 1920s, when Swiss restaurateur Frederic Belmont brought his Alpine specialties to England. The elegant surroundings have changed little since then, and the same scrumptious cakes and pastries, and traditional English meals, are on offer every day until 9 PM. A pianist plays nightly. ⊠ *1 Parliament St.* ☎ *01423/502746* ▭ *MC, V.*

£££–££££ ✕⊡ **Balmoral Hotel.** Luxurious contemporary and antique furniture, patterned wallpapers, and colorful ornaments and posters fill this mock-Tudor edifice, a Victorian creation. Ten pastel-hue bedrooms have four-poster beds, all frilled and draped. The lively Villu Toots restaurant, known for its cocktail creations, reverts to a minimalist style; the cooking is inventive and the contemporary menu eclectic, from ravioli of quail breasts to fillet steak with watercress purée. Guests have access to a nearby health club. Prices rise during conventions. ⊠ *Franklin Mt., HG1 5EJ* ☎ *01423/*

508208 🖨 *01423/530652* ⊕ *www.balmoralhotel.co.uk* ⤴ *20 rooms,*
1 suite ☖ *Restaurant, bar, meeting rooms, some pets allowed; no a/c*
⊟ *AE, DC, MC, V* ⦿⧌ *BP.*

£££ ✕⌧ **Hotel du Vin.** Tired of chintz? This hip hotel chain has taken over
a row of eight Georgian houses for its latest offering, using stripped wood
floors, clubby leather armchairs, and a purple baize billiard table to set
the tone. Bedrooms, clean-lined and modern, are done in soothing beige
and cream tones, with Egyptian linens and pampering bathrooms. The
bar is a serious place to drink, and the popular bistro has plenty of fish
as well as imaginative vegetarian choices. ⊠ *Prospect Pl., HG1 1LB*
🖀 *01423/856800* 🖨 *01423/856801* ⊕ *www.hotelduvin.com* ⤴ *35*
rooms, 8 suites ☖ *Restaurant, in-room data ports, in-room safes, cable*
TV, gym, bar, meeting rooms; no a/c ⊟ *AE, DC, MC, V.*

Nightlife & the Arts

★ Harrogate's annual **International Festival** (🖀 01423/562303 ⊕ www.
harrogate-festival.org.uk) of ballet, music, contemporary dance, film,
comedy, street theater, and more takes place during two weeks at the
end of July and beginning of August.

Knaresborough

㉗ *3 mi northeast of Harrogate, 17 mi west of York.*

A steep, rocky gorge along the River Nidd contains the photogenic old
town of Knaresborough. Central attractions include its river, lively with
pleasure boats; a little marketplace; and a medieval castle, now not much
more than the keep where Richard II was imprisoned in 1399. **Mother
Shipton's Cave**, in a park amid tree-lined riverside walks, is said to be the
birthplace of the 16th-century prophetess. Events supposedly foretold by
her include the defeat of the Spanish Armada and the Great Fire of London. It's just a short walk south of Knaresborough's town center. ⊠ *Proph-
esy House, High Bridge* 🖀 *01423/864600* ⊕ *www.mothershipton.co.uk*
⛶ *£4.95* ⊙ *Mar.–Oct., daily 10–5:30; last admission 4:45.*

Studley Royal & Fountains Abbey

★ **㉘** *9 mi northwest of Knaresborough, 4 mi southwest of Ripon.*

The 18th-century water garden and deer park Studley Royal and the
ruins of medieval Fountains Abbey blend a neoclassical vision of an ordered universe with the glories of English Gothic architecture. Lakes,
ponds, and spectacular water terraces adorn the gardens, and waterfalls
splash around classical temples, statues, and a grotto. The surrounding
deer park and woods present long vistas toward the tower of Ripon Cathedral, some 3 mi north. The majestic ruins of Fountains Abbey, with its
own tower and soaring 13th-century arches, make a striking picture on
the banks of the River Skell. Founded in 1132 but not completed until
the early 1500s, the abbey still possesses many of its original buildings,
making it one of the best places in England to learn about medieval monastic life. In this isolated valley, the Cistercian community went about its
business: the "White Monks," named for the color of their habits,
began a day of silence and prayer with vespers at 2:30 AM, and the lay

brothers oversaw operations at the abbey's sheep farms (wool was a large and profitable business). Of the surviving buildings, the lay brothers' echoing refectory and dormitory impresses most; the Perpendicular Gothic tower was an early 16th-century addition, erected by Abbot Huby, most eminent of the abbey's leaders. Fountains Mill, with sections dating back to 1140, displays reconstructed mill machinery and has exhibits on 800 years of industrial activity on the site. The entire 822-acre complex is a World Heritage Site, and 17th-century Fountains Hall (partially built with stones from the abbey) has an exhibition and video display; you can easily spend a day here. ⊠ *Off B6265* ☎ *01765/608888* ⊕ *www.fountainsabbey.org.uk* ⊠ *£5.50* ⊙ *Apr.–Sept., daily 10–7; Oct., Feb., and Mar., daily 10–5; Nov.–Jan., Sat.–Thurs. 10–dusk; last admission 1 hr before closing. Free guided tours of abbey and gardens Apr.–Oct., daily at 11, 2:30, and 3:30; water garden tour Apr.–Oct., daily at 2.*

Ripon

㉙ *4 mi northeast of Fountains Abbey, 11 mi north of Harrogate, 24 mi northwest of York.*

Ripon was thriving as early as the 9th century as an important market center. A relatively small church has been designated a cathedral since the mid-19th century, which makes Ripon, with only about 15,000 inhabitants, technically a city. Market day, Thursday, is probably the best day to stop by. Successive churches here were destroyed by the Vikings and the Normans, and the current **Ripon Cathedral,** dating from the 12th and 13th centuries, is notable for its finely carved choir stalls. The Saxon crypt, now an empty series of chambers, housed sacred relics. ⊠ *Minster Rd.* ☎ *01765/602072* ⊕ *www.riponcathedral.org.uk* ⊠ *£3 donation requested* ⊙ *Daily 8–5.*

Where to Stay

£££–£££££   🏨 **Swinton Park.** The Cunliffe-Lister family operates part of its ancestral castle—a stately pile rebuilt in the 18th and 19th centuries with turret and battlements—as an upscale country-house hotel. Two hundred acres of parkland near Yorkshire Dales National Park guarantee seclusion and abundant outdoor pursuits. The plushly furnished public rooms give you room to relax, and the traditionally decorated bedrooms vary widely in size and price. Chef-author Rosemary Shrager has a cooking school on the grounds. Masham is 8 mi north of Ripon and 35 mi north of Leeds and York. ⊠ *Off the A1, Masham, HG4 4JH* ☎ *01765/680900* 🖷 *01765/680901* ⊕ *www.swintonpark.com* 🛏 *26 rooms, 4 suites* ⌂ *Restaurant, cable TV, gym, hot tub, fishing, mountain bikes, croquet, horseback riding, meeting rooms, some pets allowed (fee); no a/c* ⊟ *AE, DC, MC, V* ¶⊙¶ *BP.*

Newby Hall

🌣 **㉚** *5 mi southeast of Ripon.*

An early 18th-century house redecorated later in the same century by Robert Adam for his patron William Weddell, Newby Hall contains some of the finest interior decorative art of its period in Western Europe, with an abundance of ornamental plasterwork and Chippendale furniture. Particularly notable are the domed Sculpture Hall, with its Roman sculptures, and the Tapestry Hall, with its priceless Gobelin tapestries; both are Adam designs. The 25 acres of gardens are justifiably famous; a double herbaceous border, which runs down to the river, separates garden "rooms," each flowering during a different season. A miniature railroad, playground, and pedal boats amuse kids. ⊠ *Skelton-on-Ure* ☎ *01423/322583* ⊕ *www.newbyhall.co.uk* ✎ *£7.80, gardens only £6.30* ⊙ *Apr.–Sept., Tues.–Sun. and national holidays, house noon–5, grounds 11–5:30; last admission 30 mins before closing.*

Thirsk

③ *15 mi north of Newby Hall, 23 mi north of York.*

This small market town on the western edge of the moors was a thriving place on the main east–west route from the dales to the coast. Lovely Georgian houses abound, and the cobbled medieval Market Place is handsome; Saturday and Monday are market days. Today Thirsk is best known as the place where veterinarian Alf Wight (who wrote about his experiences under the name James Herriot) had his practice. The popular **World of James Herriot,** in the author's actual office, re-creates the operating room and the living spaces of the 1940s and 1950s; it also displays veterinary artifacts. Plenty of Herriot mementos add appeal. ⊠ *23 Kirkgate* ☎ *01845/524234* ⊕ *www.worldofjamesherriot.org* ✎ *£4.85* ⊙ *Oct.–Mar., daily 11–4; Apr.–Sept., daily 10–6; last admission 1 hr before closing.*

THE NORTH YORKSHIRE COAST

Except during the hottest summers, the North Yorkshire coast isn't the warmest place for a beach vacation. That said, there's plenty to make you glad you came, not least the good sandy beaches, rocky coves, and villages, such as Robin Hood's Bay, Whitby, and Staithes, which seem to capture imaginations at first sight. Most coastal towns still support an active fishing industry, and every harbor offers fishing and leisure trips throughout summer. The North Sea beaches are usually fine for swimming, although the water is cold. Beaches at Scarborough, Whitby, and Filey have patrolled areas: swim between the red-and-yellow flags, and don't swim when a red flag is flying. Major towns also have indoor swimming pools.

The coast is about an hour's drive away from York. Starting at Bridlington, it's a simple matter to follow the main road north to Scarborough (A165), and on to Robin Hood's Bay and Whitby (A171).

Bridlington

③ *41 mi east of York.*

A fishing port with an ancient harbor, Bridlington makes a fine introduction to the North Yorkshire coast, with its wide arc of sand that's typical of the beach resorts in the region. Boat trips through the harbor and up the coast depart frequently in summer, or you can simply join the milling crowds that promenade up and down the seafront, eating fish-and-chips, browsing at the gift shops and stalls, and frequenting the rides at the small amusement park. At **Flamborough Head** a huge bank of chalk cliffs juts out into the North Sea.

A coastal path over the cliff tops ends at **Bempton Cliffs,** one of England's finest seabird reserves, with a colony of 7,000 puffins that nest on the 400-foot-high cliffs between March and August. The reserve, off B1229, is open at all times, and displays at the nearby visitor center provide orientation. Rent binoculars for a closer view of the puffins, shags, kittiwakes, gannets, guillemots, and razorbills that make the cliffs their home. ⊠ *Visitor Centre, Cliff La., Bempton* ☎ *01262/851179* ⊕ *www. rspb.org.uk* ⊡ *Free, parking £3 Mar.–Sept.* ☉ *Visitor center Mar.–Oct., daily 10–5; Nov.–Feb., daily 9:30–4.*

> **off the beaten path**
>
> **BEVERLEY –** A 20-mi drive southwest from Bridlington through the wolds and flatlands of the East Riding brings you to the unspoiled market town of Beverley, well worth exploring for its old streets, timbered houses, and Georgian terraces. Of the city's 350 buildings of architectural or historical merit, the standout is **Beverley Minster** (⊠ Minster Yard South ☎ 01482/868540 ⊕ www.beverleyminster. co.uk ⊡ £2 suggested donation ☉ daily 9–dusk). Architecturally equal to many cathedrals, this glorious Gothic church is regarded as Yorkshire's finest, its transepts and pinnacled towers rising golden above the town.

Where to Eat

£–££ ✕ **Jerome's.** Wrought iron decorates this seafront café-restaurant, which keeps up with these multicultural times with a selection of good-value meals from around Europe. Popular options are the Greek salad, the chef's roast, and the specialty ice creams (26 varieties). ⊠ *The Floral Pavilion, Royal Prince's Parade* ☎ *01262/671881* ⊟ *AE, DC, MC, V.*

£–££ ✕ **Seabirds.** Didn't see many seabirds on your visit to Bempton Cliffs? This village pub has a case full of them. On the menu are plenty of fish dishes, such as local crab and haddock with Mornay sauce, steaks, and imaginative vegetarian choices. Stoke up on the Yorkshire pudding and onion gravy, but be prepared to extend your waistband. ⊠ *Tower St., Flamborough* ☎ *01262/850242* ⊟ *MC, V.*

Scarborough

㉝ *17 mi north of Bridlington, 34 mi northeast of York.*

Candy floss (cotton candy) and rock candy, Victorian architecture, a sweep of cliffs above a sandy bay, and a rocky promontory capped by a ruined castle are some of the elements that make Scarborough a classic English seaside resort. A chance discovery in the early 17th century of a mineral spring on the foreshore led to the establishment of a spa, whose users not only soaked themselves in seawater but also drank it. By the late 18th century, when sea bathing came into vogue, no beaches were busier than Scarborough's, with its "bathing machines," wheeled cabins drawn by donkeys or horses into the surf and anchored there. Scarborough's initial prosperity dates from this period, as evidenced in the city's handsome Regency and early Victorian residences and hotels.

The contrast between the two faces of Scarborough makes the town all the more appealing. Its older, more genteel side in the southern half of town consists of carefully laid-out crescents and squares and cliff-top walks and gardens with views across Cayton Bay. The northern side is a riot of ice cream stands, cafés, stores selling "rock" (luridly colored hard candy), crab hawkers, and bingo halls. But enough survives of the huddle of streets, alleyways, and red-roof cottages around the harbor to give an idea of what the town was like before the resort days.

Paths link the harbor with the substantial ruins of **Scarborough Castle** on the promontory; dating from Norman times, it is built on the site of a Roman signal station and near a former Viking settlement. The castle has spectacular views across the North Bay, the beaches, and the shore gardens. ✉ *Castle Rd.* ☎ *01723/372451* ⊕ *www.english-heritage.org. uk* ✇ *£3.20* ☉ *Apr.–Sept., daily 10–6; Oct.–Mar., daily 10–4.*

Scarborough's little medieval church of **St. Mary** (✉ Castle Rd. ☎ 01723/ 500541) contains the grave of Anne, the youngest Brontë sister, who died of tuberculosis in 1849. She was taken to Scarborough from Haworth in a final, desperate effort to save her life by exposing her to the sea air. The church is near the castle on the way into town.

Wood End was the vacation home of 20th-century writers Edith, Osbert, and Sacheverell Sitwell, and the west wing houses a library of their works as well as paintings. The rest of the early Victorian house, set in delightful grounds, holds the collections of the **Museum of Natural History.** ✉ *The Crescent* ☎ *01723/367326* ✇ *£2.50 includes admission to Rotunda Museum* ☉ *June–Sept., Tues.–Sun. 10–5; Oct.–May, Wed. and weekends 11–4.*

The **Rotunda Museum,** an extraordinary circular building, was constructed in 1829 for William Smith of the Scarborough Philosophical Society to display his geological collection; it now contains important archaeological and local history collections. ✉ *Vernon Rd.* ☎ *01723/ 374839* ✇ *£2.50 includes admission to Wood End* ☉ *June–Sept., Tues.–Sun. 10–5; Oct.–May, Tues., Sat., and Sun. 11–4.*

☺ Recognizable by its white pyramids, **Scarborough Sea Life Centre** is the best of the cheerful area attractions that appeal to kids. Marine life and environmental matters are presented in an entertaining way, with different marine habitats combined under one roof. ✉ *Scalby Mills, North Bay* ☎ *01723/376125* ⊕ *www.sealife.co.uk* ✇ *£6.95* ☉ *Mar.–Oct., daily 10–6; Nov.–Feb., daily 10–4; last admission 1 hr before closing.*

Where to Stay & Eat

££–£££ ✕ **Lanterna Restaurant.** A lack of pretension and a high standard of cuisine make this Italian restaurant a good choice. The classic dishes are all represented, among them tender veal cooked with ham and cheese, but opt for seasonal specials using fresh vegetables and fish—and white

truffles (September to February). ⊠ *33 Queen St.* ☎ *01723/363616*
☰ *DC, MC, V* ⊘ *Closed Sun. and 2 wks late Oct. No lunch.*

£   ✕ **The Golden Grid.** Everyone has to have fish-and-chips at least once in
Scarborough, and this harborfront spot is a classic of its kind. Choose
an upstairs window table and tuck into freshly fried cod or haddock,
although big spenders (and those flying in the face of British seaside tradition) could also opt for grilled turbot or one of a host of other daily
specials. ⊠ *4 Sandside* ☎ *01723/360922* ☰ *MC, V* ⊘ *No dinner weekdays in winter.*

£££–££££   ▦ **The Crown.** The centerpiece of Scarborough's Regency Esplanade, this
19th-century hotel overlooks South Bay and the castle headland. Built
to accommodate fashionable visitors to Scarborough Spa, it has been
considerably refurbished; rooms are modern and done in muted colors.
Rates drop for some two-night stays. ⊠ *The Esplanade, YO11 2AG*
☎ *01723/373491* ⎙ *01723/362271* ⊕ *www.scarboroughhotel.com*
⇌ *84 rooms* ⚸ *2 restaurants, pool, health club, 2 bars, meeting rooms,
some pets allowed; no a/c* ☰ *AE, DC, MC, V* ⓌⒷⓅ *BP.*

£–££   ▦ **Interludes.** "Theatrical" is the word to describe this Georgian town
house on a steep hillside in the old town behind the harbor. Dedicated
to the theme of the performing arts, the compact rooms are full of bills,
posters, and the owners' theater photography. Antique and reproduction furniture, polished oak, and drapes create a traditional English look.
Consider the "theatre breaks"—accommodation and tickets for productions at the town's Stephen Joseph Theatre. ⊠ *32 Princess St.,
YO11 1QR* ☎ *01723/360513* ⊕ *www.interludeshotel.co.uk* ⇌ *5
rooms* ⚸ *Dining room; no a/c, no room phones, no kids under 16, no
smoking* ☰ *MC, V* ⓌⒷⓅ *BP.*

Nightlife & the Arts

Scarborough has an internationally known native son in contemporary
★   playwright Alan Ayckbourn. The **Stephen Joseph Theatre** (⊠ Westborough ☎ 01723/370541), which premieres his plays, incorporates two
stages, a cinema, a restaurant, and a bar. Stop at the theater for a program, or contact the tourist office for box office details.

Robin Hood's Bay

★ ㉞   *15 mi northwest of Scarborough.*

Many people's favorite coastal stop is at Robin Hood's Bay, a tiny fishing village squeezed into a ravine near where a stream courses over the
cliffs. Tiny, crazily scattered houses and shops fringe the perilously
steep, narrow roads. The name is curious, because there is no connection with the famous English medieval outlaw. The village didn't even
come into being until the late 15th century, after which it thrived in a
small way as a fishing port and smuggling center. Contraband was
passed up the stream bed beneath the cottages, linked to one another
by secret passages, often with customs officers in hot pursuit.

★   It would be hard to find a **beach** anywhere in the British Isles that offers the variety and interest of the one at Robin Hood Bay. The tide rushes
in quickly, so take care. Provided the tide is out, you can stroll for a cou-

ple of hours south from Robin Hood's Bay, along a rough stone shore full of rock pools, inlets, and sandy strands. A few stretches of sand are suitable for sunbathers. To the south, at the curiously named **Boggle Hole,** a ravine nestles an old water mill, now a youth hostel. Farther south is **Ravenscar,** a Victorian village that never took off and now consists of little more than a hotel, which can be reached by a hazardous but exhilarating path up the cliff. The walk back, along the cliff-top path, is less tricky but no less energetic.

Where to Stay & Eat

£–££ ✕ **Bay Hotel.** The village's most favored pub is this friendly Victorian retreat, perfectly positioned at the bottom of the village, on a rocky outcrop lapped by the sea. The bar is festooned with oak and brass; in winter, a roaring fire warms all comers. Whitby scampi and chestnut and butter-bean casserole are often on the menu. ⊠ *The Dock* ☎ *01947/ 880278* ▤ *MC, V.*

££££ ⊞ **Raven Hall Hotel.** This superb Georgian hotel with landscaped grounds offers unrivaled coastal views from the headland of Ravenscar, 3 mi southeast of Robin Hood's Bay. All rooms have faux-medieval beds, and you should try your utmost to secure a room with a bay view. The hotel is known for its good sports facilities; the bar marks the traditional end of the punishing, long-distance Lyke-Wake Walk, so on occasion you may share the lounge with exhausted walkers. It's worth checking dinner and bed-and-breakfast deals year-round. ⊠ *Ravenscar, YO13 0ET* ☎ *01723/870353* ⊕ *www.ravenhall.co.uk* ↩ *53 rooms* ⚇ *Restaurant, 9-hole golf course, 2 tennis courts, indoor pool, hair salon, sauna, croquet, bar, recreation room, Internet, meeting rooms; no a/c* ▤ *AE, MC, V* ⅩⓄⅠ *BP.*

Sports & the Outdoors

Several superb long-distance walks start at, finish in, or run through Robin Hood's Bay. The coastal **Cleveland Way** (⊕ www.clevelandway. gov.uk) runs north (to Whitby) and south (to Scarborough). The village marks one end of the 190-mi **Coast-to-Coast Walk;** the other is at St. Bees Head on the Irish Sea. Walkers finish at the Bay Hotel, above the harbor. The trans-moor **Lyke-Wake Walk** (⊕ www.lykewakewalk. co.uk) finishes 3 mi away at Ravenscar. **Wellington Lodge** (⊠ Staintondale ☎ 01723/871234 ⊕ www.llamatreks.co.uk), 3 mi south of Ravenscar, schedules llama treks along the moors or the coast; you walk, and the llamas carry your lunch.

Whitby

㉟ *7 mi northwest of Robin Hood's Bay, 20 mi northeast of Pickering.*

Fodor'sChoice
★

A scenic glory steeped in fishing and whaling lore, Whitby can claim to be the most splendid town on the English coast. It's set around a harbor of great natural beauty, formed by the River Esk as it comes down a long glenlike ravine cut through the moors. Above it, on either side, red-roof buildings rise tier upon tier. Fine Georgian houses line some of the central streets on the west side of the river, known as West Cliff. Across the swing bridge in the old town (part of the area known as East Cliff),

CloseUp

WHITBY JET

Whitby is known for its jet, a very hard, black form of natural carbon, found in thin seams along the coast and worked into jewelry and ornaments. Known since prehistoric times and sometimes used to ward off the evil eye, it reached the peak of its popularity in the mid-19th century when 1,400 men and boys, supplied by 200 miners, made a good living in jewelry workshops all over the town. The queen of Bavaria was impressed enough to order a chain more than 4 feet long.

On the death of her husband, Albert, in 1861, Queen Victoria introduced jet into court circles and set the fashion for mourning memorabilia.

You can see fine examples in the Whitby Museum on St. Hilda's Terrace and in the shop displays in the old town along Church Street and parallel to Sandgate. If you buy a piece, keep it shiny with baby oil.

---

cobbled Church Street is packed in summer with people exploring adjacent alleys, enclosed courtyards, and gift shops.

On top of the cliff are the gaunt ruins of Whitby Abbey, a sight that inspired Bram Stoker when he came here to write *Dracula*. Whitby is a small, laid-back resort, but it was an important religious center as far back as the 7th century, when Whitby Abbey was first founded, and it later came to prominence as a whaling port. The first ships sailed from here for Greenland in the mid-18th century, captained by local men such as William Scoresby, inventor of the crow's nest, to whom Herman Melville paid tribute in his novel *Moby Dick*. At much the same time as whaling made Whitby rich, its shipbuilding made it famous: Captain James Cook (1728–79), explorer and navigator, sailed on his first ship out of the town in 1747, and all four of his subsequent discovery vessels were built in Whitby.

Climbing the 199 steps from the end of Church Street leads to the rather eccentrically designed church of **St. Mary,** with its ship's-deck roof, triple-decker pulpit, and enclosed galleries. The church dates from the 12th century, although almost everything you see today is the (often less-than-happy) result of 19th- and 20th-century renovations. The spooky, weather-beaten churchyard, filled with the crooked old gravestones of ancient mariners, has superb views of the sea and the town. It was here that Bram Stoker's Dracula claimed Lucy as his victim. In the tall grass at the back is the grave of master mariner William Scoresby. ⊠ *Church La., East Cliff* ☎ *01947/603421* ✉ *Free, donation suggested* ☉ *Apr.–Oct., Mon.–Sat 10–5, Sun 1–5; Nov.–Mar., Mon.–Sat. 11–3, Sun. 1–3.*

The tumbledown but romantic ruins of **Whitby Abbey,** set high on the East Cliff, are visible from almost everywhere in town. St. Hilda founded the abbey in AD 657, and Caedmon (died circa 670), the first identifiable poet of the English language, was a monk here. An engraved cross of dubious provenance, which bears his name, stands at the top of the 199 steps near the church of St. Mary. Sacked by the Vikings in the 9th century, the monastery was refounded in the 11th century and enlarged in the 13th century, from which point these ruins date. The visitor center includes exhibits on the lives of St. Hilda and Bram Stoker, artifacts from the site, and interactive displays on the medieval abbey and monastic life. ⊠ *Abbey La., East Cliff* ☏ *01947/603568* ⊕ *www.english-heritage.org.uk* ⊠ *£3.80* ⊙ *Apr.–Sept., daily 10–6; Oct., daily 10–5; Nov.–Mar., daily 10–4.*

Filled with revealing exhibits relating to the man and explorer, the **Captain Cook Memorial Museum** is tucked into the period rooms of the 18th-century house belonging to shipowner John Walker, where the young James Cook lived as an apprentice from 1746 to 1749. On display are mementos of Cook's epic expeditions, including maps, diaries, and drawings, as well as some tracing the privations of his wife and family, left behind to cope with life, loss, and bereavement. Captain Cook is remembered in several places around town, most notably by his bronze statue on top of the West Cliff, near the pair of arched whalebones. ⊠ *Grape La.* ☏ *01947/601900* ⊕ *www.cookmuseumwhitby.co.uk* ⊠ *£3* ⊙ *Apr.–Oct., daily 9:45–5; Mar., weekends 11–3.*

Worth a stop, the **Whitby Museum** has fascinatingly eclectic collections that deal with local geology, natural history, and archaeology as well as with the maritime pursuits of Whitby townspeople, from whaling in the Arctic to trading in Asia. Look for more material about Captain Cook and displays about Whitby jet. ⊠ *St. Hilda's La., Pannett Park* ☏ *01947/602908* ⊕ *www.durain.demon.co.uk* ⊠ *£3* ⊙ *May–Sept., Mon.–Sat. 9:30–5:30, Sun. 2–5; Oct.–Apr., Tues. 10–1, Wed.–Sat. 10–4, Sun. 2–4.*

off the
beaten
path

GOATHLAND – This moorland village, 8 mi southwest of Whitby, attracts walkers and people who want to see the fictional Aidensfield of the British TV series *Heartbeat*. Its cute 1865 train station served as Hogsmeade Station for students arriving at the school of wizardry in *Harry Potter and the Sorcerer's Stone*. The 18-mi **North Yorkshire Moors Railway** (⊠ Pickering Station, Park St., Pickering ☏ 01751/472508, 01751/473535 recorded information ⊕ www.northyorkshiremoorsrailway.com ⊠ £12.50 round-trip ⊙ Late Mar.–early Nov., daily; early Nov.–Feb., some weekends and holiday periods), between Grosmont and Pickering, passes through neat towns and moorland scenery. Steam-powered trains (like the one that takes Harry Potter to Hogwarts School) provide a great outing.

Where to Stay & Eat

££–£££
Fodor's Choice
★

✕ **Magpie Café.** Whitby is full of fish-and-chip places, but no place serves it with more style than this large, busy, old-fashioned restaurant with a well-stocked menu that includes hake along with the perennial plaice, cod, and haddock. Many regulars would argue that the Magpie's nonfish dishes (especially its meat salads) offer even better value. The food and service are worth the wait. ⊠ *14 Pier Rd.* ☏ *01947/602058* ⌲ *Reservations not accepted* ⊟ *MC, V* ☉ *Closed Jan.*

★ **££** ✕⊞ **White Horse and Griffin.** When looking for the perfect inn, you want an old building with character, a roaring fire, and food to thrill. This 18th-century establishment, in which Charles Dickens once slept and railway pioneer George Stephenson lectured, fills the bill. The tidy rooms, done in an uncluttered traditional style, are warmly decorated in muted colors, and downstairs the cozy bistro-bar serves a fine, changing menu with locally caught fish and game in season. Dinner might be roast Whitby cod or crab and salmon tartlet, followed by mocha and almond tart or cheeses and homemade chutney. ⊠ *Church St., YO22 4BH* ☏ *01947/604857* ⊕ *www.whitehorseandgriffin.co.uk* ⇋ *12 rooms* ⌂ *Restaurant, bar, meeting rooms, some pets allowed; no a/c, no room phones, no smoking (in bedrooms)* ⊟ *MC, V* ❥⊘ *BP.*

£–££ ✕⊞ **Shepherd's Purse.** This splendid little complex in the cobbled old town consists of boutique-style guest rooms, a vegetarian restaurant that looks as if it has been inserted into a junk shop, and dress and health-food stores. There are two less-expensive bedrooms above the stores and others in the galleried courtyard at the back. Although small, many rooms have four-poster or brass bedsteads; floors are wooden, the furniture is country style, and the top two rooms even have little balconies. ⊠ *95 Church St., YO22 4BH* ☏ *01947/820228* ⊕ *www.shepherds-purse. co.uk* ⇋ *9 rooms, 5 with bath* ⌂ *Restaurant, meeting rooms, some pets allowed; no a/c, no room phones* ⊟ *MC, V.*

£££–££££ ⊞ **Dunsley Hall Hotel.** Built as the home of a shipping magnate, this family-run Victorian country-house hotel has four acres of gardens and grounds. Stained- and leaded-glass windows and plenty of wood paneling complement rich carpets, rocking chairs, and leather armchairs. Bedrooms are spacious and restful, the only intrusion into the peace being the occasional screech of a peacock. The hotel is 4 mi west of Whitby. ⊠ *Dunsley, YO21 3TL* ☏ *01947/893437* ☐ *01947/893505* ⊕ *www. dunsleyhall.com* ⇋ *18 rooms* ⌂ *Restaurant, putting green, tennis court, indoor pool, gym, sauna, croquet, bar, meeting rooms; no a/c* ⊟ *AE, MC, V* ❥⊘ *BP.*

Nightlife & the Arts

The **Whitby Regatta** (⊕ www.whitbyregatta.co.uk), held in August, is a three-day jamboree of boat races, fair rides, lifeboat rescue displays, parades, and music. Music (but also traditional dance and storytelling) pre-
★ dominates during **Whitby Folk Week,** usually held the week before the late-August bank holiday, when pubs, pavements, and halls become venues for more than 1,000 traditional folk events by performers from all over the country.

Staithes

🗙 *9 mi northwest of Whitby.*

There's little in the way of specific sights to see in Staithes, but over the years many travelers have been seduced by the town's stepped alleys and courtyards. These, and the surrounding coastal cliffs, were captured on canvas by many members of the so-called Staithes School of artists, who were prominent in the earlier part of the 20th century. Tourists are a vital part of the local economy these days, and they include many in wet suits, who know Staithes to have some of Britain's best surfing.

Staithes's few houses huddle below the rocky, seagull-studded outcrop of Cowbar Nab, on either side of the beck (stream). Having survived storm and flood, they present a hoary, weather-beaten aspect, but not all were so lucky. The Cod and Lobster Inn, at the harbor, is in its third incarnation, and the drygoods shop in which James Cook had his first apprenticeship before moving to Whitby fell into the sea entirely in 1745. The house known as Cook's Cottage, near the pub, is supposedly built out of the salvaged remains of the original building.

Staithes's former Methodist Chapel, imaginatively converted into the **Captain Cook and Staithes Heritage Centre,** includes a life-size mid-18th-century street scene of the kind Cook would have recognized. The shop in which the young adventurer worked was re-created, alongside a fisherman's warehouse and museum displays relating to local industries and that coastal pastime, smuggling. ⊠ *High St.* ☎ *01947/841454* ✉ *£2.75* ☽ *Jan., weekends 10–5; Feb.–Dec., daily 10–5.*

Where to Stay & Eat

★ **££** ✕🏠 **Endeavour.** This well-known restaurant, in a rather higgledy-piggledy old house on the main street, has a few guest rooms done in stripped pine and solid colors. Menus include locally caught fish and change seasonally, but dishes often come with Mediterranean or Asian flourishes; soups, salmon, and lobster are strong points. Have a drink in the tiny bar before you dine. The restaurant is closed Sunday and Monday (except national holidays), and January; call ahead in winter. ⊠ *1 High St., TS13 5BH* ☎ *01947/840825* ⊕ *www.endeavour-restaurant.co.uk* ➥ *3 rooms* ⚫ *Restaurant, bar, some pets allowed; no a/c, no smoking* ▤ *MC, V* *BP.*

THE NORTH YORK MOORS

The North York Moors are a dramatic swath of high moorland starting 25 mi north of the city of York and stretching east to the coast and west to the Cleveland Hills. Once covered in forest, of which a few pockets survive, the landscape changed with the introduction of sheep at the monastic foundations of Rievaulx and Whitby in medieval times. The evidence is clear for all to see today: heather-covered hills that, in late summer and early fall, are a rich blaze of crimson and purple, and a series of isolated, medieval standing stones that once acted as signposts on the paths between the abbeys. For more than four decades the area has been designated a national park, to protect the moors and grassy valleys that shelter brownstone villages and hamlets. Minor roads and tracks crisscross the moors in all directions, and there's no single, obvious route through the region. Perhaps the most rewarding approach is west from the coast at Whitby, along the Esk Valley to Danby, which is also accessible on the Esk Valley branch train line between Middlesbrough and Whitby. From Danby, minor roads run south over the high moors reaching Hutton-le-Hole, beyond which main roads lead to interesting towns on the moors' edge, such as Helmsley. Completing the route in this direction leaves you with an easy side trip to Castle Howard before returning to nearby York.

Danby

37 *15 mi west of Whitby.*

The straggling old stone village of Danby nestles in a green valley, just a short walk from the tops of the nearby moors. It's been settled since Viking times—Danby means "village where the Danes lived"—and these days it bumbles along contentedly in a semitouristed way. There's a pub, and a bakery with a tearoom, and if you bring hiking boots with you, within 10 minutes you can be above the village looking down, surrounded by nothing but isolated moorland. To get here from Whitby, take A171 west and turn south for Danby after 12 mi, after which it's a 3-mi drive over Danby Low Moor to the village.

In a converted country house on the eastern outskirts of Danby, the North York Moors National Park's **Moors Centre** has exhibitions, displays, and plenty of information. A tearoom and a garden front with picnic tables are other amenities. The summer Moorsbus operates from the center for the 30-minute journey south to Hutton-le-Hole. ⊠ *Danby Lodge* ☎ *01439/772737* ⊕ *www.northyorkmoors-npa.gov.uk* ✆ *Free; parking £1.50* ☉ *Jan. and Feb., weekends 11–4; Mar., Nov., and Dec., daily 11–4; Apr.–Oct., daily 10–5.*

need a break?
The cozy little **Stonehouse Bakery & Tea Shop** (⊠ 3 Briar Hill ☎ 01287/660006) serves excellent sandwiches on sun-dried-tomato or olive bread, herbal teas, local honey, and a fine peanut brittle. It's closed Sunday.

Where to Stay

£ 🏠 **Stonebeck Gate Farm.** There are sweeping moorland views from this homey family farm, set at the head of the dale. Floral fabrics decorate the bedrooms, and downstairs are big sofas, welcoming fires, a big oak dresser, and hunting pictures. Home-baked bread and freshly laid eggs form part of the communal breakfast, and the country fare at dinner (£15) uses the farm's produce. Stonebeck Gate is 3 mi south of Danby. ⊠ *Little Fryup Dale, YO21 2NS* ☎ *01287/660363* 🖷 *01287/660363* 🛏 *3 rooms* ⚘ *Dining room, cable TV, some pets allowed; no a/c, no room phones, no room TVs, no smoking* ⊟ *No credit cards* ⧉ *BP.*

en route
From Danby take the road due west for 2 mi to Castleton, and then turn south over the top of the moors toward Hutton-le-Hole. The narrow road offers magnificent views over North York Moors National Park, especially at the old stone **Ralph Cross** (5 mi), which marks the park's highest point. Drive carefully: sheep-dodging is something of a necessary art in these parts.

Hutton-le-Hole

★ **38** *13 mi south of Danby.*

Even after seeing the varied splendors of villages throughout North York Moors National Park, it's difficult not to think that Hutton-le-Hole is the pick of the bunch. It's almost too pastoral to be true: a tiny hamlet, based around a wide village green, with sheep wandering about and a stream babbling in the background. The surroundings are equally attractive, and in summer, the local parking lots fill quickly as people arrive to take to the nearby hills for a day's walking.

The excellent 3-acre, open-air **Ryedale Folk Museum** interprets life in the Dales from prehistory onward through craft demonstrations and 13 historic buildings, including a medieval kiln, 16th-century cottages, a 19th-century blacksmith's shop, and an early photographer's studio. ☎ *01751/ 417367* ⊕ *www.ryedalefolkmuseum.co.uk* ✆ *£3.50* ◷ *Early Mar.–Oct., daily 10–5:30; last admission 4:30.*

Helmsley

39 *8 mi southwest of Hutton-le-Hole, 27 mi north of York.*

The market town of Helmsley, well known as a hiking center, is attractive enough in itself for a day trip and has a castle (partly ruined during the Civil War) and a traditional country marketplace surrounded by fine old inns, cafés, and stores. Market day is Friday.

Where to Stay

£££–££££ ☒ **Black Swan.** A splendid, relaxing base, this ivy-covered property sits on the edge of the market square. The building is a hybrid—part 16th-century coaching inn, part Georgian house. Cozy rooms overlook either the square or the fine walled garden at the back. The restaurant serves traditional British and local dishes; an open fire keeps things warm in winter. ☒ *Market Pl., YO6 5BJ* ☎ *01439/770466, 888/892–0038 in the U.S.* 🖷 *01439/770174* ⊕ *www.heritage-hotels.com* ➴ *45 rooms* ⚘ *Restaurant, cable TV, croquet, bar, meeting rooms, some pets allowed; no a/c* ⊟ *AE, DC, MC, V* ⊠ *BP.*

Sports & the Outdoors

The town, on the southern edge of the moors, is the starting point of the **Cleveland Way** (⊕ www.clevelandway.gov.uk), the long-distance moor-and-coastal footpath. Boots are donned at the old cross in the market square; it's 50 mi or so across the moors to the coast and then a similar distance south to Filey along the cliff tops. The footpath is 108 mi long, which most people aim to complete in nine days. The trail passes close to Rievaulx Abbey, a few miles outside the town. A leaflet from the tourist information center indicates the route.

Rievaulx Abbey

★ **40** *2 mi northwest of Helmsley.*

One of the most graceful of all medieval English seats of learning, Rievaulx (pronounced ree-*voh*) Abbey occupies a dramatic setting on the River Rye. The wealth of this Cistercian foundation, which dates from 1132, came from the wool trade, and the extensive surviving ruins (as well as exhibits in the museum here) give some indication of the thriving trade with Europe in which the medieval monks engaged. Rising from the landscaped grounds are elegant Gothic arches, cloisters, and associated buildings, including the Chapter House, which retains the original shrine of the first abbot, William, by the entrance. The earl of Rutland owned Rievaulx after Henry VIII dissolved the monasteries in 1538, and he acted quickly to destroy the buildings. The abbey is a 1½-hour walk northwest from Helmsley by signposted footpath, or 2 mi by vehicle. ⊠ *Off B1257* ☎ *01439/798228* ⊕ *www.english-heritage. org.uk* ☜ *£3.80* ⊗ *Apr.–Sept., daily 10–6; Oct., daily 10–5; Nov.–Mar., daily 10–4.*

off the
beaten
path

RIEVAULX TERRACE AND TEMPLES – If you've wandered among the ruins of Rievaulx Abbey, you might like to drive up to the Rievaulx Terraces, a long, grassy walkway on the hillside above, terminating in the remains of several Tuscan- and Ionic-style classical temples. The views of the abbey from here are magnificent. ⊠ *Off B1257* ☎ *01439/798340* ⊕ *www.nationaltrust.org.uk* ☜ *£3.30* ⊗ *Late Mar.–Sept., daily 10:30–6; Oct., daily 10:30–5; last admission 1 hr before closing.*

Castle Howard

④ *14 mi southeast of Rievaulx Abbey, 12 mi southeast of Helmsley, 15 mi*
Fodor's Choice *northeast of York.*
★

Standing serene among the Howardian Hills to the west of Malton, Castle Howard is one of the grandest and most opulent stately homes in Britain, an imposing baroque building whose magnificent profile is punctuated by stone chimneys and a graceful central dome. Many people know it best as Brideshead, the home of the Flyte family in Evelyn Waugh's tale of aristocratic woe, *Brideshead Revisited,* because much of the 1981 TV series was filmed here. The house was designed for the Howard family (who still live here) by Sir John Vanbrugh (1664–1726). Considering its many theatrical, even flamboyant features, it seems fitting that Vanbrugh was praised more as a playwright than an architect (he also had careers as a soldier and adventurer). In 18th-century London, his plays were second in popularity only to Congreve's. Even more remarkably, this was Vanbrugh's first building design. His self-assurance knowing no bounds, he went on to create Blenheim Palace, the Versailles of England. For Castle Howard, however, Vanbrugh sought assistance, and turned to the brilliant but self-effacing Nicholas Hawksmoor (1661–1736), who at 18 had been under the tutelage of Christopher Wren. Hawksmoor encouraged adding bodies of water to the landscape, and he designed the imposing Mausoleum; many consider it a masterpiece equal to his churches in London.

The audacity of the great baroque house is startling, proclaiming the wealth and importance of the Howards and the self-assurance of Vanbrugh. It took 60 years to build (1699–1759), and it was worth every year. This was the first private residence in Britain built with a stone dome. A magnificent central hallway spanned by a hand-painted (in the 20th century) ceiling dwarfs all visitors, and there is no shortage of grandeur elsewhere: vast family portraits, delicate marble fireplaces, immense and fading tapestries, huge pieces of Victorian silver on polished tables, and a great many marble busts. Outside, the stately theme continues in one of the most stunning neoclassical landscapes in England; Horace Walpole, the 18th-century connoisseur, commented that a pheasant at Castle Howard lives better than most dukes elsewhere. Carefully arranged woods, lakes, bridges, and obelisks compose a scene far more like a painting than a natural English landscape. Make sure you see the Temple of the Four Winds and the Mausoleum, whose magnificence caused Walpole to comment that all who view it would wish to be buried alive. Costumed characters from the past are on hand to tell you about their contribution to the house, and hourly tours (included in the admission price) fill you in on more background and history. ⊠ *Off A64 and B1257, Coneysthorpe* ☎ *01653/648333* ⊕ *www.castlehoward. co.uk* ✍ *£9.50, gardens only £6.50* ⊙ *House mid-Feb.–Oct., daily 11–6, last admission 4. Grounds mid-Feb.–Dec., daily 10–6:30 or dusk, last admission 4:30.*

YORKSHIRE A TO Z

To research prices, get advice from other travelers, and book travel arrangements, visit www.fodors.com.

AIRPORTS

Leeds Bradford Airport, 8 mi northwest of Leeds, connects with domestic and European destinations. Manchester Airport, about 40 mi southwest of Leeds, is well served internationally.

🚹 **Leeds Bradford International Airport** ⊠ A658, Yeadon ☎ 0113/250-9696 ⊕ www. lbia.co.uk. **Manchester Airport** ⊠ Near Junctions 5 and 6 of M56 ☎ 0161/489-3000 ⊕ www.manairport.co.uk.

BIKE TRAVEL

Although the countryside is too hilly for extensive bicycle touring, except by experienced riders, you can rent bikes locally in several places. In York, where there are special bike paths, contact Europcar and pick up a cycling map from the tourist information center.

🚹 Bike Rentals **Europcar** ⊠ York Train Station, Station Rd., York ☎ 01904/656161.

BUS TRAVEL

National Express serves the region from London's Victoria Coach Station. Average travel times are 4¼ hours to Leeds, 6 hours to York, and 8 hours to Scarborough.

Each district has its own bus company; Traveline and local tourist information centers can help you discover the services. Timetable booklets for the Yorkshire Moors and Dales are widely available, and special summer services in both national parks provide useful bus connections. There are local Metro buses from Leeds and Bradford into the more remote parts of the Yorkshire Dales. Other companies are Harrogate & District for services to Ripon, Harrogate, and Leeds; Yorkshire Coastliner for Castle Howard, Scarborough, Whitby, Malton, and Leeds; and Arriva for Whitby, Scarborough, and Middlesbrough. In York, the main local bus operator is First.

CUTTING COSTS Many districts have Rover tickets; in York, the FirstWeek card (£10.50) gives a week's travel on all First bus services. With a West Yorkshire Day Rover you have a day's train and bus travel for £4.50; contact Metroline for details. The Moorsbus (information from any National Park office) runs every Sunday and bank-holiday Monday from April to the end of October, and daily from June to the end of September. It connects Danby, Hutton-le-Hole, Helmsley, Rievaulx Abbey, Rosedale Abbey, and Pickering and costs £3 for an all-day ticket.

FARES & SCHEDULES **Arriva** ☎ 0870/608-2608 ⊕ www.arriva.co.uk. **First** ☎ 01904/883000 ⊕ www. firstgroup.com. **Harrogate & District** ☎ 01423/566061. **Metroline** ☎ 0113/245-7676 ⊕ www.wymetro.com. **National Express** ☎ 0870/580-8080 ⊕ www.nationalexpress. com. **Traveline** ☎ 0870/608-2608 ⊕ www.traveline.org.uk. **Yorkshire Coastliner** ☎ 01653/692556 ⊕ www.yorkshirecoastliner.co.uk.

CAR RENTAL

Local Agencies Avis ✉ 81 Roseville Rd., Leeds ☎ 0113/243-9771 ✉ Leeds Bradford International Airport, A658, Yeadon ☎ 0113/250-3880. **Budget** ✉ 82-84 Clifton, York ☎ 01904/644919. **Europcar** ✉ Leeds Rd., Bradford ☎ 01274/733048. **Hertz** ✉ Unit 2, Emmanuel Trading Estate, Springwell Rd., Leeds ☎ 0113/242-9548 ✉ York Train Station, Station Rd., York ☎ 01904/612586.

CAR TRAVEL

The M1, the principal route north from London, gets you to the region in about two hours, with longer travel times up into North Yorkshire. For York (193 mi) and the Scarborough areas, stay on M1 to Leeds (189 mi), then take A64. For the Yorkshire Dales, take M1 to Leeds, then A660 to A65 north and west to Skipton. For the North York Moors, either take B1363 north from York to Helmsley, or leave A64 at Malton and follow the trans-moor A169 that runs to Whitby. The trans-Pennine motorway, the M62, between Liverpool and Hull, crosses the bottom of this region. North of Leeds, A1 is the major north–south road, although narrow stretches, roadwork, and heavy traffic make this slow going at times.

ROAD CONDITIONS Some of the steep, narrow roads in the countryside off the main routes are difficult drives and can be particularly perilous (or closed altogether) in winter. Main roads often closed by snowdrifts are the moorland A169 and the coast-and-moor A171. If you plan to drive in the dales or moors in winter, check the weather forecast in advance.

DISCOUNTS & DEALS

The Powerpass card, valid from late April through December, costs £2 and admits two adults for the price of one into 120 attractions in Yorkshire and Northumbria. Tourist offices in the area sell the card.

The York Pass offers unlimited free entry to more than 30 attractions in or near the city (including Castle Howard), plus free transportation on City Sightseeing bus tours. You also get discounts on restaurants and theaters. Adult passes cost £17 (1 day), £25 (2 days), and £32 (3 days), and can be purchased online, by phone, or at the York Tourist Information Centre.

🚩 **York Pass** ☎ 0870/242-9988 or 01904/621756 ⊕ www.yorkpass.com.

EMERGENCIES

🚩 **Ambulance, fire, police** ☎ 999. **Leeds General Infirmary** ⊠ Great George St. Leeds ☎0113/243-2799. **York District Hospital** ⊠Wiggington Rd., York ☎01904/631313. **Whitby Hospital** ⊠ Spring Hill, Whitby ☎ 01947/604851.

NATIONAL PARKS

For information about local visitor centers, walks, and guided tours, contact Yorkshire Dales National Park and North York Moors National Park.
🚩 **Yorkshire Dales National Park** ☎01756/752748 ⊕www.yorkshiredales.org.uk. **North York Moors National Park** ☎ 01439/770657 ⊕ www.northyorkmoors-npa.gov.uk.

TOURS

BUS TOURS City Sightseeing runs frequent tours of York (£8), including stops at the minster, the Castle Museum, the Shambles, and Jorvik that allow you to get on and off the bus as you please. Yorktour offers walking tours of the city of York and has an excursion bus to Castle Howard, June–September, Tuesday, Friday, and Sunday, departing around noon.
🚩 **City Sightseeing** ☎ 01904/655585 ⊕ www.citysightseeing.co.uk. **Yorktour** ☎ 01423/360222 ⊕ www.eddiebrowntours.com.

WALKING TOURS The York Association of Voluntary Guides arranges short walking tours around the city, which depart daily at 10:15; there are additional tours at 2:15 PM April through October, and at 6:45 PM July through August. The tours are free, but a gratuity is appreciated. Yorktour (⇨ Bus Tours) also schedules walks.
🚩 **York Association of Voluntary Guides** ⊠ De Grey Rooms, Exhibition Sq. ☎ 01904/640780.

TRAIN TRAVEL

Great Northeastern Railways serves the region from London's King's Cross and Euston stations. Average travel times from King's Cross are 2½ hours to Leeds and 2 hours to York. It is possible to reach the North Yorkshire coast by train; journey time from London to Scarborough (change at York) is four hours, to Whitby (change at Darlington and Middlesbrough) up to 6½ hours.

There is local service from Leeds to Skipton, and from York to Knaresborough and Harrogate and also to Scarborough (which has connections to the seaside towns of Filey and Bridlington). Whitby can be reached on the minor but attractive Esk Valley line from Middlesbrough. For train travel information in the region, call National Rail Enquiries.

CUTTING COSTS Two Regional Rover tickets for seven days' unlimited travel are available: North East and Coast and Peaks.

FARES & **Great Northeastern Railways** ☎ 0845/722-5225 booking line, 0845/748-4950 in-
SCHEDULES quiries ⊕ www.gner.co.uk. **National Rail Enquiries** ☎ 0845/748-4950 ⊕ www.
nationalrail.co.uk.

TRAVEL AGENCIES

Local Agent Referrals Thomas Cook ✉ 54 Kirkgate, Bradford ☎ 01274/332600 ✉ 83
Briggate, Leeds ☎ 0113/214-7700 ✉ 47 Westborough, Scarborough ☎ 01723/397200
✉ 4 Nessgate, York ☎ 01904/881400.

VISITOR INFORMATION

The Yorkshire Tourist Board has information about the area. Local tourist
information centers have varied opening hours. Many offices in the North
York Moors and Yorkshire Dales open only in summer.

Yorkshire Tourist Board ✉ 312 Tadcaster Rd., York, YO2 1GS ☎ 01904/707961
⊕ www.yorkshirevisitor.com. **Beverley** ✉ 34 Butcher Row, HU17 0AB ☎ 01482/867430
⊕ www.eastriding.gov.uk. **Bradford** ✉ City Hall, BD1 1HY ☎ 01274/433678 ⊕ www.
visitbradford.com. **Bridlington** ✉ 25 Prince St., Humberside, YO15 2NP ☎ 01262/
673474 ⊕ www.eastriding.gov.uk. **Harrogate** ✉ Royal Baths, Crescent Rd., HG1 2RR
☎ 01423/537300 ⊕ www.harrogate.gov.uk. **Haworth** ✉ 2-4 West La., BD22 8EF
☎ 01535/642329. **Helmsley** ✉ Town Hall, Market Pl., YO6 5BL ☎ 01439/770173 ⊕ www.
ryedale.gov.uk. **Knaresborough** ✉ 9 Castle Courtyard, Market Pl., HG5 8AE ☎ 01423/
866886 ⊕ www.harrogate.gov.uke. **Leeds** ✉ Leeds City Station, LS1 1PL ☎ 0113/242-
5242 ⊕ www.leeds.gov.uk. **Richmond** ✉ Friary Gardens, Victoria Rd., DL10 4AJ
☎ 01748/850252 ⊕ www.yorkshiredales.org. **Scarborough** ✉ Unit 3, Pavilion House,
Valley Bridge Rd., YO11 1UZ ☎ 01723/373333 ⊕ www.discoveryorkshirecoast.com. **Skipton** ✉ 35 Coach St., BD23 1LQ ☎ 01756/792809 ⊕ www.skiptononline.co.uk. **Whitby**
✉ Langbourne Rd., YO21 1YN ☎ 01947/602674. **York** ✉ De Grey Rooms, Exhibition Sq.,
YO1 2HB ☎ 01904/621756 ⊕ www.visityork.org ✉ York Train Station ☎ 01904/621756.

THE NORTHEAST

DURHAM, HADRIAN'S WALL, LINDISFARNE ISLAND

14

EXPLORE CASTLE COUNTRY
along the wild North Sea coast ⇨*p.657*

HIKE BY THE ROMANS' HANDIWORK
along Hadrian's Wall ⇨*671*

RELISH THE ROMANESQUE
at awesome Durham Cathedral ⇨*p.659*

SEEK INSPIRATION
from the *Angel of the North* ⇨*p.666*

EXPLORE VICTORIAN HIGH-TECH
in Tudor–style Cragside manor ⇨*p.677*

FOLLOW THE FOUNTAINS
at Alnwick Castle's gardens ⇨*p.678*

DON'T MISS THE KIPPERS
at Craster's Jolly Fisherman pub ⇨*p.680*

SAIL TO SEE BIRDS AND SEALS
on the wind-tossed Farne Islands ⇨*p.680*

Updated by
Kate Hughes

A DECIDED AIR OF REMOTENESS pervades much of England's northeast corner, although one village in this region—Allendale Town, southwest of Hexham—lays claim to being the geographical center of the British Isles. For many Britons the words "the Northeast" provoke a vision of somewhat bitter, near-Siberian isolation. The truth is a revelation. For although there are wind-hammered, wide-open spaces and empty roads that thread wild high moorland, the Northeast also has simple fishing towns, small villages of remarkable charm, and historic abbeys and castles that are all the more romantic for their often ruinous state. Even the remoteness can be relative. Suddenly, around the next bend of a country road, you may come across an imposing church, a tall monastery, or a gorgeous country house built by a Victorian-era millionaire. The value found in the shops and accommodations, the uncrowded beaches ideal for walking, and the friendliness of the people also add to the region's appeal.

Mainly composed of the two large counties of Durham and Northumberland, the Northeast includes English villages adjacent to the Scottish border area, renowned in ballads and romantic literature for feuds, raids, and battles. Hadrian's Wall, which marked the northern limit of the Roman Empire, stretches across prehistoric remains and moorland in this region. Much of it, remarkably, is still intact. Not far north of Hadrian's Wall are the 153,000-acre Kielder Forest; Kielder Water, the largest manmade lake in northern Europe; and some of the most interesting parts of Northumberland National Park. Steel, coal, railroads, and shipbuilding made prosperous towns such as Newcastle upon Tyne—now re-creating itself as a cultural center—Darlington, and Middlesbrough. Some sights reflect the area's industrial heritage, including the Beamish Open-Air Museum and the Darlington Railway Centre and Museum.

On the region's eastern side stretches a 100-mi-long line of largely undeveloped coast, one of the least-visited and most dramatic in all Europe. Several outstanding castles perch on headlands and promontories along here, including Bamburgh, which according to legend was the site of Joyous Garde, the castle of Sir Lancelot du Lac. The island of Lindisfarne is a landmark of early Christendom. Fittingly, Durham Cathedral, the greatest ecclesiastical structure of the region, has memorably been described as "half church of God, half castle 'gainst the Scot." For almost 800 years, this great cathedral was the seat of bishops who raised their own armies and ruled the turbulent northern diocese as prince-bishops with quasi-royal authority.

Exploring the Northeast

Many people travel from the south to arrive at the historic cathedral city of Durham, not far east of the wooded foothill valleys of the Pennines. Farther north, Newcastle, with Gateshead, straddles the region's main river, the Tyne. This reviving industrial city is making a bid for attention with new cultural facilities. Nearby, the still-impressive Roman fortifications of Hadrian's Wall snake through superb scenery to the west, and to the north lies the wilderness of Northumberland National Park. Huge castles and offshore gems such as the Farne Islands and Holy Island, also known as Lindisfarne, stud the stunning, final 40 mi of England's eastern coast, starting roughly an hour's drive north of Newcastle.

Although you can get a sense of the Northeast through an overnight stop en route to or from Scotland, spending four days to explore the region properly is well worth the time. One turn off the A1—the main north–south highway—and it becomes clear that driving along the meandering backcountry roads is often slow business, if only because the spectacular scenery encourages long stops.

Numbers in the text correspond to numbers in the margin and on the Northeast and Durham maps.

14

If you have 2 days

Base yourself in either ⊞ **Durham** ❶–❺ 🏳, with time to inspect the Norman cathedral and the castle to either side of the central Palace Green, or in smaller, quainter ⊞ **Alnwick** ㉕, with its cobbled square and its magnificent riverside castle and garden. Drive inland between the two for at least a brief glimpse of **Hadrian's Wall,** ideally at **Housesteads Roman Fort** ⑲, and wind up at the monastic settlement on **Lindisfarne** ㉛.

If you have 4 days

Having spent at least a half day exploring ⊞ **Durham** ❶–❺ 🏳, set aside a full day to follow the course of **Hadrian's Wall.** An overnight stop nearby in ⊞ **Hexham** ⑯ enables you to see the excellent museums of Roman finds at **Vindolanda** ⑱ and **Housesteads Roman Fort** ⑲. Then head east to overnight in ⊞ **Newcastle** ⑭, or drive northeast through the countryside to the little market town of ⊞ **Alnwick** ㉕ or ⊞ **Alnmouth** ㉖ on the coast. The next morning, walk from **Craster** ㉗ to the splendidly bleak ruin of **Dunstanburgh Castle** ㉘. Visit one or two of the huge beaches to the north as you head to ⊞ **Bamburgh** ㉚ for the night. Overlooking the windswept shore, its famous castle conjures up the days of chivalry as few others do. Whether you're heading back to Durham from there, or onward to Scotland, visit the wind-battered monastic outpost at **Lindisfarne** ㉛, a short distance north.

About the Restaurants

You can try fine local products here, but don't wait until 9:30 to have dinner or you can have a hard time getting a meal. Look for restaurants that serve game from the Kielder Forest, local lamb from the hillsides, salmon and trout from the rivers, and shellfish, crab and oysters from the coast. Oak-smoked kippers (herring) are a regional specialty, as are the lunchtime seafood sandwiches and the stotties (large bread buns) served for afternoon tea. You can sample Lindisfarne mead, a highly potent spirit produced on Holy Island and made of honey vatted with grape juice and mineral water. Less strong is Newcastle Brown ale, whose caramel overtones have found their way even into ice cream.

About the Hotels

The large hotel chains do not have much of a presence in the Northeast, outside the few large cities. Rather, you can expect to find country houses converted into welcoming hotels, old coaching inns that still greet guests after 300 years, and cozy bed-and-breakfasts convenient to hiking trails. Check ahead if you're contemplating budget accommodation in winter, as many such places will be closed.

	fffff	ffff	fff	ff	f
WHAT IT COSTS In pounds					
RESTAURANTS	over £22	£18–£22	£13–£17	£7–£12	under £7
HOTELS	over £160	£120–£160	£90–£120	£60–£90	under £50

Restaurant prices are for a main course at dinner. Hotel prices are for two people in a standard double room in high season, including VAT, with no meals or, if indicated, CP (with Continental breakfast), BP (Breakfast Plan, with full breakfast), or MAP (Modified American Plan, with breakfast and dinner).

Timing

Although Hadrian's Wall and the coastal castles are starkly impressive in a blanket of snow, the best time to see the Northeast is in summer. This ensures that the museums—and the roads—will be open, and you can take advantage of the countryside walks that are one of the region's greatest pleasures. Rough seas and inclement weather make it extremely difficult to swim at any of the beaches except in July and August. At the end of June, Alnwick hosts its annual fair, with a costumed reenactment of a medieval fair, a market, and concerts. The Durham Regatta, England's oldest rowing event, also takes place in June. The Northumberland Traditional Music Festival is scheduled in venues throughout the county over two weeks in October. The Berwick Military Tattoo, a more intimate version of its Edinburgh counterpart, is at the end of August.

DURHAM, NEWCASTLE & ENVIRONS

Durham—the first major northeastern town on the main road up from London—is by far the region's most interesting historic city. Newcastle, however, along with Gateshead across the River Tyne, is the region's biggest, liveliest, and most cosmopolitan city. Most other towns in the area made their fortunes during the Industrial Revolution and have since subsided into relative decline. Several, such as Darlington, birthplace of the modern railroad, do hold interesting relics of their 19th-century heyday. The land to the west, known as County Durham, toward the Pennine Hills, is far more scenic, and a daylong drive through the valleys of Teesdale and Weardale takes you past ruined castles, industrial heritage sites, isolated moorland villages, and tumbling waterfalls.

Durham

▶ *250 mi north of London, 15 mi south of Newcastle.*

The great medieval city of Durham, seat of County Durham, stands on a rocky spur, making it among the most dramatically sited cities in Britain. Despite the military advantages of its location, Durham was founded surprisingly late, probably in about the year 1000, growing up around a small Saxon church erected to house the remains of St. Cuthbert. It

14

Castle Country Fought over for centuries by the Scots and the English, and prey to Viking raiders from across the North Sea, the Northeast was one of the most heavily fortified regions in Britain. Cities such as Durham and Newcastle—where the "new castle" is 900 years old—still hold impressive relics, and exploring the stupendous fortresses along the exposed Northumbrian coastline is among the most memorable experiences the region has to offer. Alnwick Castle, the imposing inland seat of the dukes of Northumberland, is attracting attention because of its ambitious garden renovations. Perched on a cliff edge, ruined Dunstanburgh Castle near Craster is especially worth seeing, as is Bamburgh Castle, which overlooks miles of sandy beach.

Hiking & Biking Superb walking awaits you almost wherever you go in this region, but to gain an awe-inspiring sense of history with views of stunning scenery, nothing beats a hike along the route of ancient Hadrian's Wall. A national trail, the Hadrian's Wall Path, has made it easier to take short or long walks. Long-distance footpaths include the 90-mi Teesdale Way, which follows the course of the River Tees through Barnard Castle and Middleton-in-Teesdale, finishing at Dufton in Cumbria, and St. Cuthbert's Way, an ancient inland pilgrimage route running the 63 mi from the Scottish border to Lindisfarne. Otherwise, the russet hills and dales of Northumberland National Park, in the northwest corner of the area, will please any serious walker. Similarly, cyclists relish the wide vistas, quiet roads, and magnificently fresh air of the Northeast. Hadrian's Cycleway, which will follow the wall, will be fully open by 2005; other routes to explore—in whole or in part—are the 220-mi Northumbria's Cycling Kingdom loop and the 150-mi Pennine Cycleway North from Cumbria to Berwick-upon-Tweed. The 81-mi Coast and Castles cycle route follows minor roads from Tynemouth to Berwick-upon-Tweed and takes in Dunstanburgh and Bamburgh castles.

---

was the Normans, under William the Conqueror, who put Durham on the map, building the first defensive castle and beginning work on the cathedral. From here, Durham's prince-bishops, granted almost dictatorial local powers by William in 1072, kept a tight rein on the county, coining their own money, raising their own taxes, and maintaining their own laws and courts; not until 1836 were these rights finally restored to the English Crown.

Together, the cathedral and castle, a World Heritage Site, rise high on a wooded peninsula almost entirely encircled by the River Wear (rhymes with "beer"). For centuries these two ancient structures have dominated Durham—now a thriving university town, the Northeast's equivalent to Oxford or Cambridge—and the surrounding countryside. Durham is more than its cathedral and castle, however. It's a great place to explore, with steep, narrow streets overlooked by perilously angled medieval houses and 18th-century town houses. In the most attractive

The Northeast

GREAT BRITAIN

32 Berwick-upon-Tweed

31 Lindisfarne (Holy Island)

29 Farne Islands

30 Bamburgh

Seahouses
Beadnell

High-Newton-by-the-Sea

28 Dunstanburgh Castle

27 Craster

Littlehoughton

Belford

Wooler

Kelso

Jedburgh

SCOTLAND

CHEVIOT HILLS

Carter Bar

Alnwick 25

26 Alnmouth

North Sea

Rothbury 24

Longframlington

N O R T H U M B E R L A N D

Morpeth

Kielder Forest

22 Kielder Water

23 Wallington

Bellingham

North Tyne

Chesters Roman Fort

Housesteads Roman Fort

Chollerford

Hadrian's Wall

Vindolanda 19

South Tyne

20

17

Haltwhistle

18

Bardon Mill

Greenhead

Hexham 16

Corbridge 21

Wylam

Tyne

Newcastle upon Tyne 14

Wallsend

15 Jarrow

South Shields

Angel of the North 13

Sunderland

Beamish Open-Air Museum 12

11 Washington

Chester-le-Street

Seaham

Allendale Town

Blanchland

Durham
1 – 5
see detail map

Ireshopeburn

St. John's Chapel

D U R H A M

Wear

P E N N I N E S

High Force

Middleton-in-Teesdale

Frosterley

6 Bishop Auckland

Stockton

10 Middlesbrough

Raby Castle 7

Staindrop

Piercebridge

Darlington 9

Cotherstone

8 Barnard Castle

Tees

part of the city, near the Palace Green and along the river, people go boating, anglers cast their lines, and strollers walk along the shaded paths. Between 10 and 4 on Monday through Saturday, cars are charged £2 (on top of parking charges) to enter the Palace Green area. Bus 40 links parking lots and the train and bus stations with the cathedral.

❶ A Norman masterpiece, **Durham Cathedral,** in the heart of the city, is an
Fodor'sChoice   amazing vision of solidity and strength, a far cry from the airy lightness
★   of later, Gothic cathedrals. Construction began in about 1090, and the main body was finished in about 1150. Durham reveals the essence of an almost entirely Norman, or Romanesque, edifice: the round arches of the nave and the deep zigzag patterns carved into them typify the heavy, gaunt style of Norman building. The technology of Durham, however, was revolutionary. This was the first European cathedral to be given a stone, rather than a wooden, roof. When you consider the means of construction available to its builders—the stones that form the ribs of the roof had to be hoisted by hand and set on a wooden structure, which was then knocked away—the achievement seems staggering.

The origins of the cathedral go back to the 10th century. In 995, monks brought to this site the remains of St. Cuthbert, which had been removed from the monastery at Lindisfarne after a Viking raid in 875. Soon the wealth attracted by Cuthbert's shrine paid for the construction of a cathedral. The bishop's throne here was claimed to be the loftiest in medieval Christendom; the miter of the bishop is the only one to be encircled by a coronet, and his coat of arms is the only one to be crossed with a sword as well as a crosier. **Cuthbert's shrine** lies surrounded by columns of local marble, with the saint's remains buried below a simple slab. An unobtrusive tomb at the west end of the cathedral, in the handsome, Moorish-influenced **Galilee Chapel,** is the final resting place of the **Venerable Bede,** the 8th-century Northumbrian monk whose contemporary account of the English people made him the country's first reliable historian. He died in Jarrow in 735, and his remains were placed here in 1020.

Upon entering the cathedral, note the 12th-century bronze **Sanctuary Knocker,** shaped like the head of a ferocious mythological beast, mounted on the massive northwestern door. By grasping the ring clenched in the animal's mouth, medieval felons could claim sanctuary; cathedral records show that 331 criminals sought this protection between 1464 and 1524. The knocker is, in fact, a reproduction. The original is kept for security reasons in the cathedral **Treasury,** along with ancient illuminated manuscripts, fragments of St. Cuthbert's oak coffin, and more church treasures well worth a look. You can view a film and an exhibit about building the cathedral, and in good weather you can climb the **tower.** There's also a restaurant and a bookstore. ⊠ *Palace Green* ☎ *0191/ 386–4266* ⊕ *www.durhamcathedral.co.uk* ✎ *£3.50 donation requested; Treasury £2, tower £2, guided tours £3.50* ☉ *Cathedral mid-June–early Sept., daily 7:30 AM–8 PM; early Sept.–mid-June, Mon.–Sat. 7:30–6:15, Sun. 7:45–5. Treasury Mon.–Sat. 10–4:30, Sun. 2–4:30. Tower Apr.–Sept., Mon.–Sat. 9:30–4; Oct.–Mar, Mon.–Sat. 10–3. Choral evensong service Tues.–Sat. 5:15, Sun. 3:30. Guided tours mid-Apr.–Sept., Mon.–Sat. 11 and 2:30.*

Durham
Castle **2**

Durham
Cathedral **1**

Framwellgate
Bridge **4**

Prebends
Footbridge **3**

University
of Durham
Oriental
Museum **5**

❷ For almost 800 years Norman **Durham Castle** was the home of successive prince-bishops; from here, they ruled large tracts of northern England and kept the Scots at bay. Facing the cathedral across Palace Green, the castle commands a strategic position above the River Wear. It has required many renovations and repairs through the ages because of less-than-stable foundations, but it remains an impressive pile. Henry VIII first curtailed the bishops' independence, although it wasn't until the 19th century that the prince-bishops finally had their powers annulled. They abandoned the castle, turning it over to University College, one of several colleges of the University of Durham (founded 1832), the oldest in England after Oxford and Cambridge. You can visit the castle on a 45-minute guided tour. ⊠ *Palace Green* ☎ *0191/374–3800* ⊕ *www.durhamcastle.com* 🎫 *£3.50* ⊙ *Guided tours mid-Mar.–Sept., Mon.–Sat. 10–12:30 and 2–4, Sun. 10–noon and 2–4; Oct.–mid-Mar., Mon., Wed., and weekends 2–4.*

need a break? Drop into the **Almshouse Café** (⊠ Palace Green ☎ 0191/386–1054), in an ancient almshouse between the cathedral and castle, for fat brownies or tasty cheesecake. These sweet treats are the perfect accompaniment to your tea or coffee.

The **River Wear** winds through Durham, curving beneath the cathedral and castle, and playing host in mid-June each year to the Durham Regatta. Britain's oldest rowing event attracts 300 racing crews. Delightful views are the reward of a short stroll along the River Wear's leafy banks, especially as you cross **Prebends Footbridge,** reached from the southern end of Palace Green. J. M. W. Turner reveled in the view from here and painted a celebrated scene of Durham from the bridge. If you follow the far side of the Wear north from Prebends Footbridge, you can recross the river at **Framwellgate Bridge,** which dates from the 12th century. Many of the elegant town houses that line the narrow lanes back up to the cathedral now house departments of the University of Durham.

The **University of Durham Oriental Museum** displays fine art and craft work from all parts of Asia. The collection of Chinese ceramics is particularly noted, and don't miss the nearby 18-acre Botanic Gardens. ⊠ *Elvet Hill, off South Rd. (A1050)* ☎ *0191/374–7911* ⊕ *www.dur.ac.uk/oriental. museum* 🎫 *£1.50* ⊙ *Weekdays 10–5, weekends noon–5.*

Where to Stay & Eat

During college vacations (late March–April, July–September, and December), reasonably priced accommodations are available at the **University of Durham** (☎ 0191/374–3454 🖷 0191/374–3420 ⊕ www.dur.ac.uk/conference_tourism), in Durham Castle and in other buildings throughout the city.

££–£££ ✕ **Bistro 21.** Relaxed and cottagey, Durham's most fashionable restaurant lies a couple of miles northwest from the center, in a superbly restored farmhouse. The eclectic and seasonal menu lists brasserie classics, with plenty of fish choices as well as rich desserts. ⊠ *Aykley Heads* ☎ *0191/384–4354* 🖃 *AE, DC, MC, V* ⊙ *Closed Sun.*

£ ✕ **Vennel's Café.** You'll encounter a "vennel," a local word for the very narrowest of thoroughfares, as you squeeze up the alley to this welcoming café. Order at the counter and, in good weather, sit outside in the courtyard. Satisfying soups, salads, hot dishes, and cakes are the mainstays. ⊠ *Saddler's Yard, off Saddler St.* ☎ *0191/386–0484* 🖃 *No credit cards* ⊙ *No dinner.*

£ ✕🖻 **Seven Stars Inn.** Warm oranges and tartans in the public areas enhance the coziness of this good-value early-18th-century coaching inn. The simple bedrooms are done in creamy yellows and reds and have modern pine furniture. At the restaurant, tuck into such dishes as rib-eye steak with black pudding and bacon or monkfish on herb mashed potatoes with saffron sauce, and finish with apple crumble or sticky toffee pudding. The inn is 2 mi south of the city. ⊠ *High St. N, Shincliffe Village, DH1 2NU* ☎ *0191/384–8454* 🖷 *0191/386–0640* ⊕ *www.mortalman-inns.co.uk* ⇗ *8 rooms* ⚅ *Restaurant, some pets allowed; no a/c* 🖃 *AE, DC, MC, V* ⑩ *BP.*

££££ 🖻 **Swallow Three Tuns.** This cheery 16th-century inn has echoes of its solid country past. Some parts retain the old oak beams and fireplaces, and a colorful modern stained-glass ceiling illuminates other public rooms. The pastel modern bedrooms have a floral motif. Guests can use the indoor pool and health club at the nearby Swallow Royal County Hotel. Browns restaurant serves staples such as veal, steak, and salmon.

⊠ *New Elvet, DH1 3AQ* ☎ *0191/386–4326* 🖷 *0191/386–1406* ⊕ *www.swallowhotels.com* 🗷 *50 rooms* ♿ *Restaurant, cable TV, piano bar, meeting rooms, some pets allowed; no a/c* ➡ *AE, DC, MC, V* ⵏⵏ *BP.*

★ **££** 🏨 **Georgian Town House.** Exactly as the name suggests, this friendly, family-run hotel, at the top of a cobbled street overlooking the cathedral and castle, makes the best of its Georgian exterior and details. Stylish modern furnishings, paintings, and stencils, evidence of the owner's hand, give all rooms a colorful individuality. Rooms at the back have the best view. ⊠ *10 Crossgate, DH1 4PS* ☎☎ *0191/386–8070* ⊕ *www. thegeorgiantownhouse.co.uk* 🗷 *8 rooms* ♿ *No-smoking rooms; no a/c* ➡ *No credit cards* ⊘ *Closed last wk Dec.* ⵏⵏ *BP.*

Nightlife & the Arts

Durham's nightlife is geared to the university set. The **Coach-and-Eight** (⊠ Bridge House, Framwellgate Bridge ☎ 0191/386–3284) can get noisy with students, but outdoor seating makes it appealing. The **Hogshead** (⊠ 58 Saddler St. ☎ 0191/386–9550) pub is a true student haunt.

Durham's **Gala Theatre** (⊠ Millennium Pl. ☎ 0191/332–4041) presents plays, concerts, and opera year-round.

Sports & the Outdoors

Brown's Boat House (⊠ Elvet Bridge ☎ 0191/386–3779) rents rowboats April–early November and offers short cruises all year. **Cycleforce** (⊠ 87 Claypath ☎ 0191/3840319) has mountain bikes for rent at £12 per day.

Shopping

Bramwells Jewellers (⊠ 24 Elvet Bridge ☎ 0191/386–8006) has its own store specialty, a pendant copy of the gold-and-silver cross of St. Cuthbert. The food and bric-a-brac stalls in **Durham Indoor Market** (⊠ Market Pl. ☎ 0191/384–6153), a Victorian arcade, are open Monday–Saturday.

Bishop Auckland

❻ *10 mi southwest of Durham.*

For 700 years, between the 12th and 19th centuries, the prince-bishops of Durham had their country residence in Auckland Castle, in the town of Bishop Auckland. When finally deprived of their powers in 1836, the bishops left Durham and made Bishop Auckland their official home. The grand episcopal palace of **Auckland Castle** that you see today dates mainly from the 16th century, although the limestone and marble chapel, with its dazzling stained-glass windows, was built in 1665 from the ruins of a 12th-century banqueting hall. Among the palace's treasures are paintings by the 17th-century Spanish artist Zurbarán of Jacob and his 12 sons. (The Church of England intends to sell these, so check ahead.) The unusual 18th-century "deer house" of adjoining Bishops Park testifies to at least one of the bishops' extracurricular interests. ⊠ *Off Market Pl.* ☎ *01388/601627* ⊕ *www.auckland-castle.co.uk* 🎫 *£4* ⊘ *Apr.–July and Sept., Mon. and Sun. 2–5; Aug., Mon., Wed., and Sun. 2–5; park daily 7 AM–sunset.*

Raby Castle

7 *7 mi southwest of Bishop Auckland, 19 mi southwest of Durham.*

The stone battlements and turrets of moated Raby Castle, once the seat of the powerful Nevilles and currently the home of the 11th baron Barnard, stand amid a landscaped, 200-acre deer park and ornamental gardens. Charles Neville supported Mary, Queen of Scots in an uprising against Elizabeth I in 1569; when the uprising failed, the estate was confiscated. Dating mostly from the 14th century (using stone plundered from Barnard Castle) and renovated in the 18th and 19th centuries, the luxuriously furnished castle has displays of art and other treasures, including an important Meissen collection. Rooms in wonderfully elaborate Gothic Revival, Regency, and Victorian styles are open for viewing. Victorian domestic ware fills the well-preserved medieval kitchens. ⊠ *A688, 1 mi north of Staindrop* ☎ *01833/660202* ⊕ *www.rabycastle.com* ⌕ *Castle, park, and gardens £7, park and gardens £4* ⊙ *Castle May and Sept., Wed. and Sun. 1–5; June–Aug., Sun.–Fri. 1–5. Park and gardens May and Sept., Wed. and Sun. 11–5:30; July–Sept., Sun.–Fri. 11–5:30.*

Barnard Castle

8 *6 mi southwest of Raby Castle, 25 mi southwest of Durham.*

The handsome market town of Barnard Castle has sights of its own and can also serve as a base for venturing into the Teesdale Valley to the northwest. Its unusual butter-market hall (known locally as Market Cross), surmounted by a fire alarm bell, marks the junction of the streets Thorngate, Newgate, and Market Place. Stores, pubs, and cafés line these thoroughfares. In 1838 Charles Dickens stayed at the **King's Head Inn** here while doing research for his novel *Nicholas Nickleby,* which deals with the abuse of children in boarding schools. The local tourist office has a free *In the Footsteps of Charles Dickens* leaflet.

The substantial ruins of **Barnard Castle,** which gave its name to the town, cling to an aerie overlooking the River Tees. Inside you can see parts of the 14th-century Great Hall and the cylindrical, 13th-century tower, built by the castle's original owners, the Anglo-Scottish Balliol family. ⊠ *Off Galgate* ☎ *01833/638212* ⊕ *www.english-heritage.org. uk* ⌕ *£3* ⊙ *Apr.–Sept., daily 10–6; Oct., daily 10–5; Nov.–Mar., Thurs.–Mon. 10–4; call ahead in winter.*

★ The **Bowes Museum,** a vast French-inspired château a little more than a mile west of the town center, was built between 1869 and 1885 to house the outstanding art and artifacts gathered by philanthropists John and Josephine Bowes. Highlights include paintings by Canaletto, El Greco, Francisco Goya, and François Boucher, and one of the world's greatest collections of 18th-century French furniture. Ceramics, silver, and glass are also on view. Archaeological exhibits chart the history of County Durham from the Ice Age to the end of the Roman period, and another gallery displays 19th-century dollhouses and models. An extraordinary 18th-century life-size, mechanical silver swan, sitting on a stream of twisted glass rods, catches and swallows a silver fish at 12:30

and 3:30. ⊠ *Up Newgate, follow signs from town center* ☎ *01833/ 690606* ⊕ *www.bowesmuseum.org.uk* 🎟 *£6* ⊙ *Daily 11–5.*

off the beaten path

HIGH FORCE – The Upper Teesdale Valley's elemental nature shows its most volatile aspect in the sprays of England's highest waterfall, the 72-foot High Force. From the roadside parking lot it's a 10-minute walk through woodland to the massive rocks over which the water tumbles. A precarious viewpoint puts you right above the falls, at their best in springtime after a rain. The waterfall is 15 mi northwest of Barnard Castle. A welcome pub on the main road, the **High Force** (⊠ B6277 ☎ 01833/622222), serves bar meals and home-brewed beer, a boon in this isolated stretch of moorland road. ⊠ *Off B6277* ☎ *01833/640209* 🎟 *£1; parking £1.50* ⊙ *Mid-Apr.–Oct., daily 9:30–5; Nov.–mid-Apr., open but unattended.*

Where to Eat

£ ✕ **Market Place Teashop.** A nicely old-fashioned air pervades this 17th-century building on the main square. Uniformed waitresses serve such dishes as parsnip and bacon with Mornay sauce, or many vegetarian options, and afternoon tea comes in silver teapots. ⊠ *29 Market Pl.* ☎ *01833/690110* 🖃 *MC, V* ⊙ *Closed Sun. except afternoons Apr.–Oct. No dinner.*

Darlington

❾ *15 mi east of Barnard Castle, 21 mi south of Durham.*

Still visibly rooted in its 19th-century industrial past, the town of Darlington rocketed to fame in 1825, when George Stephenson piloted his steam-powered *Locomotion* along newly laid tracks the few miles to nearby Stockton, thus kick-starting the railway age. First envisaged as a means of transporting coal from the local pits to the dockside, Stephenson's invention soon attracted paying passengers, and even though it barely traveled faster than 15 mph, the *Locomotion* was a palpable hit. The story

★ ☾ of the coming of the railway is well told in the excellent **Darlington Railway Centre and Museum,** in the town's original train station, built in 1842 and now a (signposted) 20-minute walk outside the town center. The focus is on railroads in the Northeast, particularly around Darlington. You can inspect historic engines, including Stephenson's *Locomotion,* as well as photographs, documents, models, and paraphernalia associated with a 19th-century station. ⊠ *North Rd. Station, Station Rd.* ☎ *01325/460532* ⊕ *www.drcm.org.uk* 🎟 *£2.20* ⊙ *Daily 10–5.*

Where to Stay & Eat

££ ✕🖼 **George Hotel.** This sprawling 18th-century coaching inn, 4 mi west of Darlington in tiny Piercebridge, sits on the banks of the River Tees, with the road on the other side. Its claim to fame is the longcase clock, still in place, that was the inspiration for the song "My Grandfather's Clock" by Henry Clay Work. Rooms are plain and white with dark wood furniture, and the restaurant, whose windows overlook the river, serves traditional dishes such as roast pork with apple stuffing. ⊠ *B6275, Pierce-bridge-on-Tees, Darlington, DL2 3SW* ☎ *01325/374576* 🖷 *01325/*

374577 ⊕ www.thegeorgehotel.activehotels.com ➯ 35 rooms ⌂ Restaurant, 2 bars, some pets allowed; no a/c ⊟ AE, MC, V ⦿ BP.

Middlesbrough

⑩ *12 mi east of Darlington, 22 mi southeast of Durham.*

In 1802 a mere dozen people lived in Middlesbrough, near the mouth of the River Tees. With the discovery of iron ore, it became a boomtown, with steel mills and, later, chemical industries, doing much to boost the economy, although they blighted part of the town. The industrial heritage has created a few unique local attractions.

Middlesbrough's unusual **Transporter Bridge,** built in 1911, is the largest of its kind in the world, a vast structure like a giant's Erector-set model. The gantry system can carry up to 12 cars and 600 passengers across the river in two minutes, every 15 minutes. Upstream is Newport Bridge, the world's largest lift span bridge, another remarkable sight, but open only if weather permits. ☎ 01642/247563 ➣ *Pedestrians 30p, cars 80p* ☾ *Mon.–Sat. 5 AM–11 PM, Sun. 2–11.*

The **Captain Cook Birthplace Museum,** in the Middlesbrough suburb of Marton, vividly explores the life and times of Captain James Cook (1728–79), the celebrated circumnavigator and explorer. You can walk through Stewart Park to the modern museum building. Interactive displays, exhibits, and films cover Cook's remarkable voyages to Australia, New Zealand, Canada, Antarctica, and Hawaii, where he met an untimely death. ⊠ *Stewart Park, Marton, off A174, south of city center* ☎ *01642/311211* ➣ *£2.40* ☾ *Mar.–Oct., Tues.–Sun. 10–5:30; Nov.–Mar., Tues.–Sun. 9–4; last admission 45 mins before closing.*

Where to Eat

££–£££ ✕ **Purple Onion.** A treat as idiosyncratic as its name, this restaurant, lavishly decorated with antiques, serves a spirited modern menu. You can try creative sandwiches at lunch, and in the evening, char-grills with a choice of sauces, pastas, and seafood platters. There's jazz and funk in the cellar bar. ⊠ *80 Corporation Rd.* ☎ *01642/222250* ⊟ *MC, V* ☾ *Closed Sun. and Mon.*

Washington

⑪ *34 mi northwest of Middlesbrough, 12 mi north of Durham.*

Washington, a planned "new town" divided into numbered districts, holds a link to the history of the United States. **Washington Old Hall** is the ancestral home of the first U.S. president. George Washington's direct forebears, the de Wessyngtons, lived here between 1183 and 1288. Other family members resided in the house until 1613, when the property was rebuilt in its current form, using parts of the medieval manor. The stone house retains a Jacobean (17th-century) appearance, particularly in the fine wood paneling and the heavy furniture. Special celebrations take place on the Fourth of July. ✛ *From A1(M), 5 mi west of Sunderland, follow signs to Washington New Town, District 4, and on to Washington Village* ☎ *0191/416–6879* ⊕ *www.*

nationaltrust.org.uk ✉ *£3.50* ◷ *Apr.–Oct., Sun.–Wed. 11–5; last admission 4:30.*

Beamish Open-Air Museum

★ ⓬ *8 mi west of Washington, 3 mi west of Chester-le-Street.*

The buildings moved to this more-than-300-acre museum village from throughout the region interpret the history of the Northeast in the 1820s and early 1900s, the periods just before and at the peak of industralization. A streetcar takes you around the site and to the reconstructed 1920s High Street, with a dentist's operating room, a pub, and a grocery store. A stableman discusses the Clydesdale workhorses in his care, the kind that were used in the past to draw brewery wagons. On the farm are such local breeds as Durham Shorthorn cattle and Teeswater sheep. Other attractions include a small manor house, a railroad station, a coal mine, and a transportation collection; in summer a steam train makes a short run. The gift store specializes in period souvenirs and local crafts. Allow at least a half day if you come in summer; winter visits center on the reconstructed street, and admission prices are reduced. ✉ *Off A693, between Chester-le-Street and Stanley* ☎ *0191/370–4000* ⊕ *www.beamish.org.uk* ✉ *£14 Apr.–Oct., £5 Nov.–Mar.* ◷ *Apr.–Oct., daily 10–5; Nov.–mid-Dec. and Jan.–Mar., Tues.–Thurs. and weekends 10–4; last admission 3.*

Where to Stay & Eat

£££££ ✕🖾 **Lumley Castle Hotel.** This is a real Norman castle, right down to the
Fodor'sChoice dungeons and maze of dark flagstone corridors. Antiques, silks, and deep,
★ rich fabrics furnish all the sumptuous rooms, and the bedrooms are soothing and subtly lit; those in the courtyard annex are less expensive. You can join in the merriment of the Friday and Saturday night Elizabethan banquets or dine intimately in the Black Knight Restaurant on English fare such as sea bass with roasted fennel and onions. A full breakfast is included in the price on weekends. The hotel is just east of town via the B1284. ✉ *Chester-le-Street, DH3 4NX* ☎ *0191/389–1111* 🖷 *0191/387–1437* ⊕ *www.lumleycastle.com* 🛏 *59 rooms* ⚖ *Restaurant, in-room data ports, cable TV, bar, meeting rooms; no a/c* ▭ *AE, DC, MC, V.*

Angel of the North

★ ⓭ *6 mi north of Beamish Open-Air Museum.*

At the junction of A1(M) and A1 at Gateshead stands England's largest sculpture, the modern, rust-color steel *Angel of the North*, which has come to symbolize the region's renewal and cultural aspirations. Created by Antony Gormley in 1998, the sculpture is a figure with airplane-like wings rather than arms. It stands an impressive 65 feet tall and has a horizontal wingspan of 175 feet. There's parking nearby, signposted on A167.

Newcastle upon Tyne

⓮ *8 mi north of Beamish Open-Air Museum, 16 mi north of Durham.*

Durham may have the glories of its castle, cathedral, and university, but the main and liveliest city of the Northeast is Newcastle. Settled since

Roman times, this city on the Tyne River made its fortune twice, first by exporting coal in the Elizabethan age and then by building ships. As a 19th-century industrial center, Newcastle had few equals in Britain, showing off its wealth in grand Victorian buildings lining the sweeping, central, neoclassical streets. Many of these remain (particularly on Grey Street), and after years of industrial decline, the city has succeeded in reinventing itself as a cultural and architectural center; an efficient Metro system makes getting around quick and easy.

Much of the regeneration since the early 1990s has been because of the Gateshead Quays development on the historic quayside. Here the Baltic Centre for Contemporary Art and the pedestrian- and cyclist-only Millennium Bridge—the world's first tilting bridge, which opens and shuts like an eyelid—have risen from derelict wasteland. New housing and former warehouses converted into restaurants and bars stand alongside the surviving 17th-century houses. The tradition of commissioning public art, begun in the 1960s, is thriving, and figurative and more conceptual pieces are sited throughout the city. By the old quayside is the symbol of the city, the celebrated **Tyne Bridge** (1929), one of seven bridges spanning the river in the city. Its elegant proportions were reproduced by the architects responsible for Sydney's Harbour Bridge.

Overlooking the Tyne River, the remains of the **Norman castle** recall the city's earlier status as a defensive stronghold. This was the "new castle," built in 1080, that gave the city its name. ⊠ *St. Nicholas St.* ☎ *0191/232–7938* ⊕ *www.castlekeep-newcastle.org.uk* ⊠ *£1.50* ☉ *Apr.–Sept., daily 9:30–5:30; Oct.–Mar., daily 9:30–4:30; last admission 30 mins before closing.*

★ The finest art museum in the Northeast, the **Laing Art Gallery** merits at least an hour's visit for its selection of British art. Some of the most extraordinary paintings are those by 19th-century local artist John Martin, who produced dramatic biblical landscapes. The Pre-Raphaelites are on show, too, and the Art on Tyneside exhibition traces 400 years of local arts, highlighting glassware, pottery, and engraving. ⊠ *Higham Pl. near John Dobson St.* ☎ *0191/232–7734* ⊕ *www.twmuseums.org. uk* ⊠ *Free* ☉ *Mon.–Sat. 10–5, Sun. 2–5.*

need a break? The popular art deco **Tyneside Coffee Rooms** (⊠ 10 Pilgrim St. ☎ 0191/261–9291), on the second floor above the cinema, make an intriguing place to stop for teas, coffee, and a snack. It's closed Sunday.

The buildings of the **University of Newcastle upon Tyne** contain some of the city's best museums. The **Museum of Antiquities** (⊕ www.ncl.ac.uk/antiquities) shows finds from Hadrian's Wall and has a reconstruction of the 1st-century Temple of Mithras at Carrawburgh. The **Shefton Museum of Greek Art and Archaeology** (⊕ www.ncl.ac.uk/shefton-museum) of the Department of Classics contains ancient arms, decorative pottery, and figurines. ⊠ *The University* ☎ *0191/222–7849* ⊠ *Free* ☉ *Museum of Antiquities Mon.–Sat. 10–5; Shefton Museum weekdays 10–4.*

⟳ At the **Life Science Centre,** three high-tech shows and 60 exhibits bring science to life, from research on genes to the workings of the brain. There's also a virtual reality arcade, a Tunnel of Love, and a simulation ride that lets you jump off the Tyne Bridge without leaving your seat. In winter you can skate in the open-air ice rink. ⊠ *Times Sq.* ☎ *0191/243–8210* ⊕ *www.lifesciencecentre.org.uk* ⊠ *£6.95* ⊙ *Mon.–Sat. 10–6, Sun. 11–6; last admission 4.*

★ ⟳ The **Discovery Museum** remains the best place to take in the Newcastle story. Reconstructed streets and homes lead you from Roman times to the present day, and the Tyne galleries show off maritime and industrial achievements. *Turbinia* is a model of the 1897 ship that was the world's first to be powered by steam turbines. A lively exploration of the fashion industry rounds out the exhibits. ⊠ *Blandford Sq.* ☎ *0191/232–6789* ⊕ *www.twmuseums.org.uk* ⊠ *Free* ⊙ *Mon.–Sat. 10–5, Sun. 2–5.*

The **Segedunum Roman Fort, Baths and Museum** includes the remains of the substantial Roman fort of Segedunum, built around AD 125 as an eastern extension to Hadrian's Wall; part of the original wall as well as a reproduction section; and a reconstructed Roman bath complex (check ahead for days when it's heated up). A museum with interactive displays interprets finds from the area, and an observation tower provides views of the site and the adjoining busy, modern shipbuilding area. The Wallsend Metro stop is a two-minute walk away. ⊠ *Buddle St., Wallsend* ☎ *0191/236–9347* ⊕ *www.twmuseums.org.uk* ⊠ *£3.50* ⊙ *Apr.–Oct., daily 10–5; Nov.–Mar., daily 10–3:30.*

off the beaten path

GEORGE STEPHENSON'S BIRTHPLACE – In 1781 the Father of the Railroads was born in this tiny stone cottage. Four families shared the house; the Stephensons lived in just one room, and it's this room that is open to the public, a modest tribute to the engineer who invented the steam locomotive. You can park your car in the village by the war memorial, a 10-minute walk away. ⊠ *Wylam, 4 mi west of Newcastle, 1½ mi south of A69* ☎ *01661/853457* ⊕ *www.nationaltrust.org.uk* ⊠ *£1* ⊙ *Apr.–Oct., Thurs., weekends, and national holidays 1–5.*

Where to Stay & Eat

★ **£££££** ✕ **McCoy's Rooftop Restaurant.** You can choose between a Newcastle or Gateshead panorama when dining in this bright, airy restaurant at the top of the Baltic Centre. Choosing from the sophisticated fixed-price dinner menu, you might opt for the wild salmon with red wine and mushroom risotto and finish up with roast figs or chocolate and banana bread pudding. ⊠ *Baltic, Gateshead Quays* ☎ *0191/440–4949* ⌘ *Reservations essential* ⊟ *AE, DC, MC, V.*

£££–££££ ✕ **Treacle Moon.** Well-presented contemporary dishes with a Mediterranean touch are the specialty at this plush, modern, purple-painted restaurant centrally placed near the river. There's a good selection of unusual ice creams and sorbets, as well as house wines. The name comes from the poet Byron's description of his honeymoon at nearby Seaham; his words adorn the walls. ⊠ *5–7 The Side* ☎ *0191/232–5537* ⊟ *AE, DC, MC, V* ⊙ *Closed Sun. No lunch.*

★ **£££££** ✕🏨 **Seaham Hall.** Byron married Annabella Milbanke in this foursquare mansion in 1815; today the sumptuous, sensual contemporary interior filled with warm natural hues is a haven of luxury. Bedrooms have their own fireplaces, original artwork, large baths, and exotic flowers. At the equally elegant restaurant, indulge in dishes such as wild mushroom risotto and loin of lamb with sweetbreads and pea purée. Make some time for the Serenity Spa. Seaham is 15 mi south of the center of Newcastle, off A19. ✉ *Lord Byron's Walk, Seaham, SR7 7AG* ☎ *0191/516–1400* 📠 *0191/516–1410* ⊕ *www.seaham-hall.com* ⤳ *19 suites* ⚬ *Restaurant, in-room data ports, indoor pool, gym, spa, bar, meeting rooms* ⊟ *AE, DC, MC, V* ⊙❘ *CP.*

££££ ✕🏨 **Malmaison.** Converted from an old riverside warehouse, this member of a glamorous, design-conscious chain sits right beside the pedestrian Millennium Bridge. Bedrooms, done in soft colors, are spacious, the huge beds piled high with pillows. The discreet art deco Brasserie & Bar presents French fare, such as *moules marinière* (mussels cooked in butter with herbs) and grilled Toulouse sausage, in a room that overlooks the Tyne through arched windows. ✉ *Quayside, NE1 3DX* ☎ *0191/245–5000* 📠 *0191/245–4545* ⊕ *www.malmaison.com* ⤳ *116 rooms* ⚬ *Restaurant, in-room data ports, cable TV with movies, gym, spa, bar, meeting rooms, some pets allowed* ⊟ *AE, DC, MC, V.*

★ **££** 🏨 **Da Vinci's.** Italian flair prevails at this small hotel in the vibrant Jesmond district, a mile from the city center. Bedrooms are refreshingly simple and contemporary, with white walls and bed linen and blue carpets. Dine on Italian specialties in the popular restaurant. ✉ *73 Osborne Rd., NE2 2AN* ☎ *0191/281–5284* 📠 *0191/281–4103* ⊕ *www.davincis.co.uk* ⤳ *16 rooms* ⚬ *Restaurant, bar; no a/c* ⊟ *AE, MC, V* ⊙❘ *CP.*

Nightlife & the Arts

Nightlife centers around the Quayside, or you might head for the prettily lit, suburban Jesmond area, where lively bars and restaurants line Osborne Road. **Thirty 3i8ht** (✉ Exchange Building, Lombard St. ☎ 0191/261–6463), a classy, contemporary café-bar, has a no-smoking area, good food, and live music. The **Offshore** (✉ 40 Sandhill ☎ 0191/261–0921)
★ is an old pub with a nautical theme. The upstairs terrace of the **Pitcher and Piano** (✉ 108 Quayside ☎ 0191/232–4110), a popular pub, is the perfect viewing point for the Millennium Bridge and quayside.

The **Baltic Centre for Contemporary Art** (✉ Gateshead Quays ☎ 0191/477–1810), formerly a grain warehouse and now the country's largest national gallery for contemporary art outside London, schedules changing exhibitions (there's no permanent collection) and events.

The **Newcastle Opera House** (✉ 111 Westgate Rd. ☎ 0191/232–0899) presents dance and pop and rock music, as well as opera.

The **Sage Gateshead** (✉ Gateshead Quays ☎ 0191/443–4555), a curving, modern building designed by Norman Foster, will open on the north bank of the Tyne in winter 2004–2005 as the city's principal music venue.

Theatre Royal (✉ Grey St. ☎ 0191/232–2061), the region's most established theater, has high-quality productions and is also a venue for opera and dance.

CloseUp

THE JARROW CRUSADE

The most telling image of the impact of the Depression years in Britain was what became know as the Jarrow Crusade. In its heyday the shipyard at Jarrow on Tyneside, owned by the local Member of Parliament Charles Palmer, employed 10,000 workers and prided itself on the 80,000 ships it had built for the British empire. After World War I, when the demand for ships and steel declined, most of the workforce was gradually laid off; the yard closed in 1934. On October 5,

1936, 200 shipyard workers left Jarrow and marched to London to highlight the poverty of their "filthy, dirty, falling down, consumptive town." Twenty-five days and 300 mi later they petitioned the Houses of Parliament. This resulted in some financial assistance, but only with Britain's rearmament and the reopening of the shipyard before World War II did things really pick up.

Jarrow

⑮ *4 mi east of Newcastle.*

The name "Jarrow" is to British ears linked to the "Jarrow Crusade," a protest march to London led by unemployed former workers from the town's steelworks and shipyards in the depths of the 1930s. Travelers are attracted here, however, by its much more ancient history.

Bede's World holds substantial monastic ruins, a visitor center–museum, and the church of St. Paul, all reflecting the long tradition of religion and learning that began here in AD 681, when the first Saxon church was established on the site. The Venerable Bede, deemed to be England's earliest historian, was a scholar here and in AD 731 completed his *History of the English Church and People* while ensconced at the monastery. The museum explores the development of Northumbria, using excerpts from Bede's work as well as archaeological finds and reconstructions. You can gain a sense of medieval life from the reconstructed farm buildings and the rare breeds of pigs and cattle on the 11-acre Anglo-Saxon farm. St. Paul's contains the oldest dedicatory church inscription in Britain, a carved stone inscribed in AD 685. From the southern exit traffic circle at South Tyne tunnel, take A185 to South Shields and follow signs to St. Paul's Church and Jarrow Hall. ⊠ *Church Bank* ☎ *0191/489–2106* ⊕ *www.bedesworld.co.uk* ⊠ *£4.50* ⊙ *Apr.–Oct., Mon.–Sat. 10–5:30, Sun. noon–5:30; Nov.–Mar., Mon.–Sat. 10–4:30, Sun. noon–4:30; last admission 1 hr before closing.*

HADRIAN'S WALL COUNTRY

A formidable line of Roman fortifications, Hadrian's Wall was constructed in response to repeated barbarian invasions from Scotland. The land through which the wall marches is wild and inhospitable in places, but that seems only to add to the powerful sense of history the wall evokes. Sites, museums, and information centers along the wall make it possible to learn as much as you want about the Roman era, or you can simply reflect on the evidence of vanished power.

Hadrian's Wall

Fodor'sChoice ★ *73 mi from Wallsend, north of Newcastle, to Bowness-on-Solway, beyond Carlisle.*

Dedicated to the Roman god Terminus, the massive span of Hadrian's Wall once marked the northern frontier of the Roman Empire. The most significant reminder of the Roman presence in Britain extends 73 mi from Wallsend ("Wall's End") north of Newcastle, in the east, to Bowness-on-Solway beyond Carlisle, in the west. Its completion in just four years gives a good idea of Roman determination, and its construction bears all the hallmarks of Roman efficiency. The wall, a World Heritage Site, stretches across the narrowest part of the country and follows as straight a path as possible.

For more than 250 years the Roman army used the wall to control travel and trade and to fortify Roman Britain against the barbarians to the north. At Emperor Hadrian's command, three legions of soldiers began building the wall in AD 122. Around AD 200 Emperor Severus had the wall repaired and rebuilt. During the Roman era, the wall stood 15 feet high and 9 feet thick; behind it lay the vallum, a ditch about 20 feet wide and 10 feet deep. Spaced at 5-mi intervals along the wall were 3- to 5-acre forts (such as those at Housesteads and Chesters), which could hold 500 to 1,000 soldiers. Every mile was marked by a thick-walled milecastle (a smaller fort that housed about 30 soldiers), and between each milecastle were two smaller turrets, each lodging four men who kept watch from the tower's upper chamber.

During the Jacobite Rebellion of 1745, the English dismantled much of the Roman wall and used its stone to pave the Military Road, now B6318. The most substantial stretches of the remaining wall are between Housesteads and Birdoswald (west of Greenhead). Running through the southern edge of Northumberland National Park and along the sheer escarpment of Whin Sill, this section is also an area of dramatic natural beauty. The ancient ruins, rugged cliffs, dramatic vistas, and spreading pastures make it a good area for hiking.

Today, excavating, interpreting, repairing, and generally managing the Roman remains is a Northumbrian growth industry. At the forts, notably at Chesters, Housesteads (the best-preserved fort), and Vindolanda, and at the Roman Army Museum near Greenhead, you get a good introduction to the life led by Roman soldiers on the frontier. In summer most sites sponsor talks, Roman drama, and festivals; local tourist offices and the sites have details. A special Hadrian's Wall Bus runs daily between Hexham and Carlisle, stopping at major sites, from late May to mid-September. There is also one bus that runs daily from Wallsend to Bowness. For a memorable view, look east toward the fort of Housesteads from Cuddy's Crag, where the wall snakes up and down across the wild countryside.

Sports & the Outdoors

BIKING   You can follow the wall by bicycle on **Hadrian's Cycleway,** open between Newcastle and Haltwhistle; the whole route, which will extend to Silloth on the west coast, is due to be completed in spring 2005. **Eden's Lawn Cycle Hire** (☒ Eden's Lawn Garage, Haltwhistle ☎ 01434/320225) rents mountain bikes for £12 per day.

HIKING   **Hadrian's Wall Path** (☎ 01434/322022 ⊕ www.nationaltrail.co.uk/
★   hadrianswall), a national trail completed in 2003, extends the entire length of the wall. If you don't have time for it all, you can walk a section or take one of the less challenging circular routes, detailed in leaflets at tourist information offices along the way. One of the most scenic but also most rugged sections is the 12-mi western stretch between Sewingshields (east of Housesteads) and Greenhead.

HORSEBACK   Riding schools offer hour-long rides to full-day treks on horseback. For
RIDING   a full list, contact the Hexham tourist information office; advance booking is essential in summer.

Hexham

🔟   *22 mi west of Newcastle, 31 mi northwest of Durham.*

The historic market town of Hexham makes the best base for visiting Hadrian's Wall. Just a few miles from the most significant remains, it retains enough of interest in its medieval streets to warrant a stop in its own right. First settled in the 7th century, around a Benedictine monastery, Hexham later became a byword for monastic learning, famous for its book painting, sculpture, and liturgical singing.

★   Ancient **Hexham Abbey,** a place of Christian worship for more than 1,300 years, forms one side of the town's main square. Inside, you can climb the 35 worn stone "night stairs," which once led from the main part of the abbey to the canon's dormitory, to overlook the whole ensemble. Most of the current building dates from the 12th century, and much of the stone, including that of the Anglo-Saxon crypt, was taken from the Roman fort at Corbridge, a few miles northeast. The interior is alive with paintings; note the portraits on the 16th-century wooden rood screen and the four panels from a 15th-century Dance of Death in the sanctuary. ☒ *Beaumont St.* ☎ *01434/602031* ⊕ *www. hexhamabbey.org.uk* 🖃 *Requested donation £2* ☉ *May–Sept., daily 9:30–7; Oct.–Apr., daily 9:30–5. Crypt daily at 11:30 and 3. No tours during services.*

Hexham's central **Market Place** has been the site since 1239 of a weekly market, held each Tuesday. Crowded stalls are set out under the long slate roof of the Shambles; other stalls, protected only by bright awnings, take their chances with the weather.

Dating from 1330, Hexham's original jail, the Manor Office across Market Place from the abbey, houses the **Border History Museum.** Photographs, models, a Border house interior, armor, and weapons tell the story of the "Middle March," the medieval administrative area governed by a warden and centered on Hexham. ☒ *The Old Gaol, Hallgate* ☎ *01434/*

652351 ☎ £2 ⊙ Apr.–Oct., daily 10–4:30; Nov., Feb., and Mar., Mon., Tues., and Sat. 10–4:30.

Where to Stay & Eat

£££–£££££ ✕⌂ **Langley Castle Hotel.** Rescued from decline by a professor from the United States in the mid-1980s, this 14th-century castle with turrets and battlements is thoroughly lavish. Bedrooms within the castle, resplendent with tapestries and hangings, have deep window seats set in the 6-foot-thick walls; those in the Castle View annex are more modest. The baronial restaurant (fixed-price menu) showcases such dishes as cheese and apple tartlet and Kielder duckling with sweet-and-sour cabbage. The hotel is 6 mi west of Hexham. ⊠ Langley-on-Tyne, NE47 5LU ☎ 01434/688888 ⎙ 01434/684019 ⊕ www.langleycastle.com ↩ 18 rooms ⌂ Restaurant, in-room data ports, sauna, 2 bars, meeting rooms; no a/c ⊟ AE, DC, MC, V ⦾ CP.

££££ ✕⌂ **Lord Crewe Arms Hotel.** In a former role, this unusual hotel in a tiny stone village once provided guest accommodations for Blanchland Abbey. It has lots of medieval and Gothic corners, including a priest's hideout and a vault-roofed crypt with its own bar. Bedrooms are solidly furnished, some with antique wood pieces; a number have oak-beam ceilings. The fixed-price menu of the elegant, sequestered restaurant lists dishes such as roast partridge and rack of lamb in an herb and mustard crust. ⊠ Blanchland, DH8 9SP, off B6306, about 8 mi south of Hexham ☎ 01434/675251 ⎙ 01434/675337 ⊕ www.lordcrewehotel.com ↩ 19 rooms ⌂ Restaurant, bar, meeting rooms; no a/c ⊟ AE, DC, MC, V ⦾ BP.

£ ⌂ **Dene House.** This peaceful, stone-built farmhouse on 9 acres of farmland has beamed ceilings and cozy rooms with pine and antique pieces and colorful bed quilts. Breakfasts, taken in the homey kitchen, are cooked on the Aga range—save room for the homemade bread and preserves. The house is 4 mi south of Hexham; follow signs for Dye House. ⊠ B6303, Juniper, Hexham, NE46 1SJ ☎⎙ 01434/673413 ⊕ www.denehouse-hexham.co.uk ↩ 3 rooms ⌂ No a/c, no room phones, no room TVs, no smoking ⊟ AE, MC, V ⦾ BP.

Nightlife & the Arts

One of the Northeast's most adventurous arts venues, the **Queen's Hall Arts Centre** (⊠ Beaumont St. ☎ 01434/652477) presents drama, dance, and exhibitions by local artists. It sponsors events such as the annual jazz festival (June), which has dozens of concerts in one weekend.

Greenhead

⑰ 18 mi west of Hexham, 49 mi northwest of Durham.

Tiny Greenhead has an informative wall site. The **Roman Army Museum,** at the garrison fort of Carvoran, near the village, makes an excellent introduction to Hadrian's Wall. Full-size models and excavations bring to life this remote outpost of the empire; authentic Roman graffiti adorn the walls of an excavated barracks. The gift store stocks, among other unusual items, Roman rulers (1 foot = 11.6 inches) and Roman cookbooks. Opposite the museum, at Walltown Crags on the Pennine Way (a long-distance hiking route), are 400 yards of the best-preserved section of the wall. For a bird's-eye view of the wall, take the 15-minute Eagle's Eye simulated helicopter ride. ⊠ *Off B6318, 1 mi northeast of Greenhead* ☎ *016977/47485* ⊕ *www.vindolanda.com* ▧ *£3.50, joint ticket with Vindolanda £6.50* ☉ *Mid-Feb.–Mar., Oct., and Nov., daily 10–5; Apr.–Sept., daily 10–6.*

Where to Stay & Eat

£–££
Fodor's Choice
★

✕ **Milecastle Inn.** The snug traditional bars and restaurant of this remote and peaceful 17th-century pub make an excellent place to dine. Fine local meat goes into its famous pies; take your pick from rabbit, venison, wild boar, and duckling. The inn is on the north side of Haltwhistle on B6318. ⊠ *Military Rd., Haltwhistle* ☎ *01434/321372* ▤ *AE, MC, V.*

££–£££
✕🛏 **Centre of Britain Hotel.** In a building dating in part to the 15th century, this hotel skillfully blends Scandinavian style with original features. Room 3 has a sauna and whirlpool bath. The restaurant's fixed-price menu includes Norwegian dishes such as sweet cured herring on rye bread as well as local pork with apricot and sage sauce. ⊠ *Main St., Haltwhistle, NE49 0BH, 3 mi east of Greenhead* ☎ *01434/322422* 🖷 *01434/322655* ⊕ *www.centre-of-britain.org.uk* ⇝ *9 rooms* ♨ *Restaurant, bar, laundry facilities, meeting rooms; no a/c* ▤ *AE, DC, MC, V* ⏐◐⏐ *BP.*

££
🛏 **Holmhead Guest House.** This former farmhouse in open countryside is not only built *on* Hadrian's Wall but also *of* it. Stone arches and exposed beams add to the feeling of history. In addition to "the longest breakfast menu in the world," there's a set dinner (for guests only) with organic vegetables at the farmhouse table. On call is Pauline Staff, a qualified guide who can give talks and slide shows on Hadrian's Wall and the area. ⊠ *Off A69 about 18 mi west of Hexham, CA6 7HY* ☎🖷 *016977/47402* ⊕ *www.bandbhadrianswall.com* ⇝ *4 rooms* ♨ *Dining room; no a/c, no room TVs, no smoking* ▤ *MC, V* ⏐◐⏐ *BP.*

Vindolanda

❶⑧ *8 mi east of Greenhead, 41 mi northwest of Durham.*

The great garrison fort of Vindolanda holds the remains of eight successive Roman forts and civilian settlements, which have provided intriguing information about daily life in a military compound. Most of the visible remains date from the 2nd and 3rd centuries AD, and excavations are always under way. On view are a full-size reproduction of a section of the wall and a reconstructed temple, house, and shop. The museum displays many rare artifacts, including leather items, jewelry, glass, and writing tablets. ⊠ *Near Bardon Mill* ☎ *01434/344277* ⊕ *www.vindolanda.com* ▧ *£4.50, joint ticket with Roman Army Museum £6.50* ☉ *Mid-Nov.–mid-Jan., Wed.–Sun. 10–4; mid-Feb.–Mar., Oct., and Nov., daily 10–5; Apr.–Sept., daily 10–6; call to confirm times in winter.*

In Northumberland National Park, **Once Brewed National Park Visitor Centre,** ½ mi north of Vindolanda, has informative displays about the central section of Hadrian's Wall and can advise about local walks. It's also

a national tourist information center. ⊠ B6318 ☎ 01434/344396
⊕ *www.nnpa.org.uk* ⌨ *Free* ⊘ *Mid-Mar.–May, Sept., and Oct., daily*
9:30–5; June–Aug., daily 9–5:30; Nov.–mid-Mar., weekends 11–3.

Housesteads Roman Fort

★ ⑲ *3 mi east of Vindolanda, 38 mi northwest of Durham.*

If you have time to visit only one Hadrian's Wall site, Housesteads Roman
Fort, Britain's most complete example of a Roman fort, is your best bet.
It includes an interpretive center, views of long sections of the wall, the
excavated 5-acre fort itself, and a museum. The steep, 10-minute walk
up from the parking lot by B6318 to the site rewards the effort, especially for the sight of the wall disappearing over hills and crags into the
distance. Excavations have revealed granaries, gateways, barracks, and
the commandant's house. ⊠ *B6318, 3 mi northeast of Bardon Mill*
☎ *01434/344363* ⊕ *www.english-heritage.org.uk* ⌨ *£3.50* ⊘ *Apr.–Sept.,*
daily 10–6; Oct.–Mar., daily 10–4.

Chesters Roman Fort

⑳ *4 mi north of Hexham, 35 mi northwest of Durham.*

This cavalry fort in a wooded valley on the banks of the North Tyne
River was known as Cilurnum in Roman times, when it protected the
point where Hadrian's Wall crossed the river. You approach the fort directly from the parking lot, and, although the site cannot compete with
Housesteads in setting, the museum here holds a fascinating collection
of Roman artifacts, including statues of river and water gods, altars, mile-
stones, iron tools, weapons, and brooches. The military bathhouse is
the best-preserved example in Britain. ⊠ *B6318, ½ mi southwest of*
Chollerford ☎ *01434/681379* ⊕ *www.english-heritage.org.uk* ⌨ *£3.50*
⊘ *Apr.–Sept., daily 10–6; Oct.–Mar., daily 10–4.*

Corbridge

㉑ *8 mi southeast of Chesters Roman Fort, 19 mi west of Newcastle, 29*
mi northwest of Durham.

A small town of honey-color stone houses and riverside walks, Corbridge
is a prosperous-looking place with an abundance of welcoming pubs
and attractive shops. In the churchyard of St. Andrew's Church by
Market Place is the **Vicar's Pele,** built with stones taken from the Roman
fort at Corbridge. This nearly 700-year-old fortified tower served as a
refuge from Scottish raiders.

The ruins of the **Corbridge Roman Site,** occupied longer than any other
fort on Hadrian's Wall, actually predate the wall by 40 years. The fort
was strategically positioned at the junction of the east–west and
north–south Roman routes—Stanegate ran west to Carlisle, Dere Street
led north to Scotland and south to London. You can visit a museum rich
in artifacts and rent a headset and tape to explore the remains of two
giant granaries, as well as temples, houses, and garrison buildings.
⊹ *On a signposted back road ½ mi northwest of Corbridge* ☎ *01434/*

632349 ⊕ *www.english-heritage.org.uk* 🎫 *£3.50* ☉ *Apr.–Sept., daily 10–6; Oct., daily 10–4; Nov.–Mar., weekends 10–4.*

Where to Stay

£ 🏠 **Town Barns.** The stone-built former home of the novelist Catherine Cookson (1906–88) has three spacious rooms, approached from a double staircase and galleried landing and furnished with yew and mahogany pieces. Get set up for the day with a packed lunch and return to a cozy fire in the evening. It's best to call ahead for winter opening information. ⊠ *Off Trinity Terr., NE45 5HP* ☎ *01434/633345* 🛏 *3 rooms* ⌂ *No a/c, no smoking* ☰ *No credit cards* ⦿ *BP.*

Kielder Water

㉒ *24 mi northwest of Corbridge, 53 mi northwest of Durham.*

In the rugged hills on the western edge of Northumberland National Park, about 3 mi from the Scottish border, lies Kielder Water, northern Europe's largest man-made lake, surrounded by 153,000 acres of planted forest. It's a beautiful spot crisscrossed by hiking paths, a 10-mi riding trail, and mountain-bike trails, and with ample water-sports possibilities at **Leaplish Waterside Park.** Fishing is popular, and the upper part of the reservoir, designated a conservation area, attracts many bird-watchers. You can take a boat across to the stunning contemporary Belvedere shelter, constructed in mirrored stainless steel and warm yellow glass.

The **Tower Knowe Visitor Centre,** at the southeast corner of Kielder Water, is a springboard from which to explore not only the lake area but also the vast **Kielder Forest.** Exhibits and films illustrate the region's wildlife and natural history, and guided forest walks are offered in summer. A **cruise service** (☎ 01434/240398) operates from the center April–October; the 1-hour boat trip costs £5. ⊠ *Kielder Water* ☎ *01434/250294* ⊕ *www.kielder.org* ☉ *Apr.–June and Oct., daily 10–5; July and Aug., daily 9–6.*

Now a visitor center with exhibitions and a tearoom, 18th-century **Kielder Castle** was once a shooting lodge belonging to the duke of Northumberland. The center is at the northwest corner of Kielder Water, at the start of a 12-mi toll road that heads deep into the Kielder Forest to the north and meets A68 south of Carter Bar close to the Scottish border. Signposted footpaths provide good forest walks and there's an excellent sculpture trail. ⊠ *Kielder Water* ☎ *01434/250209* ⊕ *www.kielder.org* ☉ *Apr.–Oct., daily 10–5; Nov. and Dec., weekends 11–4.*

Sports & the Outdoors

You can rent mountain bikes at **Kielder Castle** (☎ 01434/250392). Water sports, including waterskiing and mountain biking are the focus at **Leaplish Waterside Park** (☎ 01434/250312), open all year; you can also use the indoor pool and sauna.

Wallington

㉓ *18 mi east of Kielder Water, 15 mi northeast of Hexham, 19 mi north-west of Newcastle.*

A striking 17th-century mansion with Victorian decoration, Wallington stands in the midst of a sparsely populated agricultural region. Besides the house, with its rococo plasterwork, Pre-Raphaelite murals, Asian porcelain, and dollhouse collection, the walled, terraced garden is a major attraction. In summer, productions of Shakespeare and concerts are held on the grounds, which include 100 acres of woodland and moor-land. ⊠ *B6342, Cambo* ☎ *01670/774283* ⊕ *www.nationaltrust.org. uk* ⊠ *House £7, grounds and garden £5* ⊙ *House Apr.–early Sept., daily 1–5:30; mid-Sept.–Oct., daily 1–4:30. Grounds daily 10–dusk. Garden Apr.–Sept., daily 10–7; Oct., daily 10–6.*

Rothbury

㉔ *10 mi north of Wallington (Cambo), 25 mi northeast of Hexham, 9 mi southwest of Alnwick.*

The small market town of Rothbury, in the heart of some stunning coun-tryside, developed as a Victorian resort, attracting the gentry who roamed its hills and glades. Buildings from the era survive in the hand-some center, although, as with many such towns, the sheer weight of modern traffic has blunted its appeal.

The helpful staff at the **Northumberland National Park Visitor Centre** can discuss walking routes through the Simonside Hills. It's also a national tourist information center and can advise you about accommodations and regional attractions. ⊠ *Church St.* ☎ *01669/620887* ⊕ *www. nnpa.org.uk* ⊙ *Mid-Mar.–May, Sept., and Oct., daily 10–5; June–Aug., daily 10–6; Nov.–mid-Mar., weekends 10–3.*

★ The extraordinary Tudor-style mansion of **Cragside** was built on a forested hillside between 1864 and 1895 by Lord Armstrong, an early electrical engineer. Designed by Richard Norman Shaw, a well-regarded late-Victorian architect, it epitomizes the heyday of the Victorian coun-try house. Besides having many modern conveniences (fire alarms, an elevator), this was the first house to be lit by hydroelectricity; the grounds also hold an energy center with restored mid-Victorian machinery. There are Pre-Raphaelite paintings and an elaborate mock-Renaissance marble chimneypiece. The gardens are as impressive as the house; in June rhododendrons bloom in the 660-acre park surrounding the mansion. ⊠ *Off A697 and B6341, 1 mi north of Rothbury* ☎ *01669/620333* ⊕ *www.nationaltrust.org.uk* ⊠ *House and grounds £8, grounds only £5.50* ⊙ *House Apr.–Sept., Tues.–Sun. 1–5:30; Oct., Tues.–Sun. 1–4:30; last admission 1 hr before closing. Grounds Apr.–Oct., Tues.–Sun. 10:30–7; Nov.–mid-Dec., Wed.–Sun. 11–4.*

Where to Stay & Eat

£££ ✕🏠 **Embleton Hall.** The 5 acres of beautiful grounds are reason enough to stay in this stone country mansion, parts of which date to 1730. Lovely antiques and paintings decorate the individually furnished guest rooms. The chintz draperies and cut-glass chandeliers in the restaurant (fixed-price menu only) make perfect accompaniments to traditional English dishes such as noisettes of lamb with mint and rosemary sauce. There are less expensive options in the bar. ⊠ *A697, Longframlington, NE65 8DT, 5 mi east of Rothbury* ☎ *01665/570249* 🖷 *01665/570056* ⊕ *www.embletonhall.com* ➷ *14 rooms* ⚲ *Restaurant, bar, meeting rooms, some pets allowed; no a/c* 🖃 *AE, DC, MC, V* ⫶◯⫶ *BP.*

£ 🏠 **Silverton Lodge.** The Hewisons rescued a derelict village school dating from 1902 and have transformed it into a peaceful, hospitable B&B with a fireplace in the guest lounge. Coordinating fabrics furnish the attractive bedrooms, and packed lunches and dinners are available. ⊠ *Silverton La., NE65 7RJ* ☎ *01669/620144* 🖷 *01669/621920* ⊕ *www. silvertonlodge.co.uk* ➷ *4 rooms* ⚲ *Dining room, bicycles; no a/c, no room TVs, no smoking* 🖃 *No credit cards* ⫶◯⫶ *BP.*

THE FAR NORTHEAST COAST

Before England gives way to Scotland, extraordinary medieval fortresses and monasteries line the final 40 mi of the Northeast coast, considered by many the best stretch anywhere on the North Sea. Northumbria was an enclave where the flame of learning was kept alive during Europe's so-called Dark Ages, most notably at Lindisfarne, home of saints and scholars. Castles abound, including the spectacularly sited Bamburgh and the desolate Dunstanburgh. The region also has some magnificent, broad beaches. Only on rare summer days is swimming advisable, but the walking is tremendous. The 3-mi walk from Seahouses to Bamburgh gives splendid views of the Farne Islands, and the 2-mi hike from Craster to Dunstanburgh Castle is unforgettable.

Alnwick

❷❺ *30 mi north of Newcastle, 46 mi north of Durham.*

Alnwick (pronounced *ann*-ick) is the best base from which to explore the dramatic coast and countryside of northern Northumberland. Its vast castle dominates the town, once a county seat, but there's more to see. A weekly open-air market (every Saturday) has been held in Alnwick's cobbled **Market Place** for more than 800 years. Note the market cross, built on the base of an older cross; the town crier once made his proclamations from here. Starting on the last Sunday in June, this site is host to the weeklong **Alnwick Fair,** a festival noteworthy for the enthusiastic participation of locals in medieval costume.

★ The grandly scaled **Alnwick Castle,** on the edge of the town center, is still the home of the dukes of Northumberland, whose family, the regal Percys, dominated the Northeast for centuries. Known as "the Windsor of the North," it has been remodeled several times since the first occupant, Henry de Percy, adapted the original Norman keep. Nowadays the castle is in favor as a set for films such as *Robin Hood: Prince of Thieves* and the first two Harry Potter movies (in the first, the castle grounds appear as the exterior of Hogwarts School in scenes such as the Quidditch match). In contrast with the cold, formidable exterior, the interior has all the opulence of the palatial home it still is. You see only six of the more than 150 rooms, but among the treasures on show are a galleried library, Meissen dinner services, ebony cabinets mounted on gilded wood, tables inlaid with intricate patterns, niches with larger-than-life-size marble statues, and Venetian-mosaic floors. The castle's gardens, undergoing a multiyear redevelopment, include a modern, 260-foot-long stepped water cascade with elaborate, computer-controlled fountain displays, as well as rose and ornamental gardens. ⊠ *Above the junction of Narrowgate and Bailiffgate* ☎ *01665/510777* ⊕ *www. alnwickcastle.com* ⊠ *Castle and garden £10, castle only £7.50, garden only £4* ⊙ *Castle Apr.–Oct., daily 11–5; last admission 4:15. Garden 10–dusk; last admission 45 mins before closing.*

Where to Stay & Eat

£££ ✕⌂ **White Swan Hotel.** The surprise feature of this comfortable, modernized, 18th-century coaching inn near the town square is that one lounge, the Olympic Suite, has been reconstructed with the paneling, stained glass, and mirrors of the *Olympic,* sister ship of the ill-fated *Titanic.* It's used as a function room, but guests can take a look. You can choose from the hearty dishes on the fixed-price menu in the Bondgate restaurant (dinner and Sunday lunch only); kipper pâté and steamed plum pudding help fill you up. ⊠ *Bondgate Within, NE66 1TD* ☎ *01665/602109* ⊟ *01665/510400* ⌖ *58 rooms* ⌂ *Restaurant, bar, meeting rooms, some pets allowed; no a/c* ⊟ *AE, MC, V* ⍟ *BP.*

Shopping

The **House of Hardy** (☎ 01665/602771), just outside Alnwick (from downtown, take A1 south to just beyond the traffic circle on the left, clearly marked), is one of Britain's finest stores for country sports. It has a worldwide reputation for handcrafted fishing tackle.

Alnmouth

㉖ *4 mi east of Alnwick.*

Beautifully sited on a steep spur of land between the estuary of the River Aln and the sea, Alnmouth has been a popular holiday spot since Victorian times. Beyond the cluster of seaside villas, the main street is an inviting mixture of solid 19th-century houses, pubs, and tearooms, interspersed with narrow alleyways.

Where to Stay

££ ⌂ **The Grange.** An elegant four-story 18th-century house in a walled garden overlooking the Aln estuary makes for a peaceful bed-and-breakfast stopover. Stylish modern furniture blends with antiques, and the subtly colored bedrooms are light and airy. ⊠ *Northumberland St., NE66 2RJ* ☎ *01665/830401* ⊕ *www.thegrange-alnmouth.com* ⌖ *5 rooms, 2 with bath* ⌂ *No a/c, no smoking* ⊟ *MC, V* ⍟ *Closed Nov.–Apr.* ⍟ *BP.*

Craster

27 *7 mi north of Alnmouth.*

The tiny fishing village of Craster is known for its footpath to Dunstanburgh Castle—and for that great English breakfast delicacy, kippers: herring salted and smoked over smoldering oak shavings. You can visit the tar-blackened smokehouses and see the fish hanging in ranks; then cross the road to the pub to taste for yourself.

Where to Eat

★ £ ✕ **Jolly Fisherman.** You can feast in this traditional pub on the famous fresh crab sandwiches or kipper pâté. The splendid picture window provides views of crashing waves; on sunny days, the garden beckons. ✉ *Haven Hill* ☎ *01665/576461* ▤ *MC, V.*

Shopping

L. Robson & Sons (✉ Haven Hill ☎ 01665/576223) has been smoking fish for four generations. The smokehouse is open Monday–Saturday all year for kippers, smoked cod, and salmon.

Dunstanburgh Castle

28 *1 mi north of Craster, 8 mi north of Alnmouth.*

Perched romantically on a cliff 100 feet above the shore, the ruins of Dunstanburgh Castle can be reached along a windy, mile-long coastal footpath from Craster. Built in 1316 by the earl of Lancaster as a defense against the Scots, and later enlarged by John of Gaunt (the powerful duke of Lancaster who virtually ruled England in the late 14th century), the castle is known to many from the popular paintings by 19th-century artist J. M. W. Turner. Several handsome sandy bays indent the coastline immediately to the north. ☎ *01665/576231* ⊕ *www.english-heritage.org.uk* ▣ *£2.50* ☉ *Apr.–Sept., daily 10–6; Oct., daily 10–4; Nov.–Mar., Thurs.–Mon. 10–4.*

Farne Islands

★ **29** *7 mi north of Craster, 13 mi northeast of Alnwick.*

Regular boat trips from the village of Seahouses provide access to two of the bleak, wind-tossed Farne Islands (owned by the National Trust), with their impressive colonies of seabirds, including puffins, kittiwakes, terns, shags, and guillemots. The islands also attract thriving gray-seal colonies. Inner Farne, where St. Cuthbert, the great abbot of Lindisfarne, died in AD 687, has a tiny chapel dedicated to his memory. All boat service leaves from Seahouses harbor. A 2½-hour cruise past the islands gives you a good view; during a 6-hour trip (May–July) you'll make landfall. Landing fees depend on the season, because more wildlife is visible in certain months. ☎ *01665/721099 National Trust information center, 01665/720308 boat trips, 01665/720884 Seahouses Tourist Information Centre (summer only)* ⊕ *www.nationaltrust.org.uk* ▣ *Boat trips £10–£20, landing fees £3.80–£4.80, payable to the wardens* ☉ *Boat trips daily, weather permitting; call in winter.*

Bamburgh

㉚ *14 mi north of Alnwick.*

Tiny Bamburgh has a splendid castle, and several beaches are a few minutes' walk away. Especially stunning when floodlighted at night, **Bamburgh Castle** dominates the coastal view for miles, set atop a great crag to the north of Seahouses and overlooking a magnificent sweep of sand backed by high dunes. Once regarded as the legendary Joyous Garde of Sir Lancelot du Lac, one of King Arthur's fabled knights, it's one of the most dramatically sited castles in Britain. The ramparts have sweeping views of Lindisfarne (Holy Island), the Farne Islands, the stormy coastline, and the Cheviot Hills inland. Much of the castle—the home of the Armstrong family since 1894—was restored during the 18th and 19th centuries, including the Victorian Great Hall, although the great Norman keep (central tower) remains intact. Exhibits include collections of armor, porcelain, jade, furniture, and paintings. ✉ *Bamburgh, 3 mi north of Seahouses* ☎ *01668/214515* ⊕ *www.bamburghcastle.com* ✈ *£5* ☉ *Mid-Mar.–Oct., daily 11–5; last admission 4:30.*

The **Grace Darling Museum** commemorates a local heroine as well as the Royal National Lifeboat Institute, an organization of volunteers who keep watch at the rescue stations on Britain's coasts. Grace Darling became a folk heroine in 1838, when she and her father saved the lives of nine shipwrecked sailors from the SS *Forfarshire*. ✉ *Radcliffe Rd., opposite church near village center* ☎ *01668/214465* ✈ *Donation requested* ☉ *Apr.–mid-Oct., Mon.–Sat. 10–5, Sun. noon–5.*

Where to Stay & Eat

££££–£££££   ╳ 🏨 **Waren House Hotel.** Six acres of woodland surround this Georgian hotel on a quiet bay between Bamburgh and Holy Island. Public areas are furnished comfortably in period style with an assortment of ornaments, and guest rooms have individual themes. The crisply elegant restaurant has romantic views of Holy Island when the leaves are not on the trees; three- to five-course dinners might include zucchini and apple soup, local game or salmon, and apple crumble. Smoking is permitted only in the library. ✉ *Waren Mill, Belford, NE70 7EE* ☎ *01668/214581* 🖨 *01668/214484* ⊕ *www.warenhousehotel.co.uk* ✈ *8 rooms, 2 suites* ♿ *Restaurant, some pets allowed; no a/c, no kids under 15* ▭ *AE, DC, MC, V* ¶◎¶ *BP.*

££–£££   ╳ 🏨 **Lord Crewe Arms.** This cozy, stone-walled inn with oak beams is in the heart of the village, close to Bamburgh Castle. It's an ideal spot for lunch while you're touring the area. Pine furnishings decorate the fairly simple guest rooms, but the food, especially the seafood, is excellent. ✉ *Front St., NE69 7BL* ☎ *01668/214243* 🖨 *01668/214273* ⊕ *www. lordcrewe.co.uk* ✈ *18 rooms* ♿ *Restaurant, bar, some pets allowed; no a/c, no kids under 5* ▭ *MC, V* ☉ *Closed Jan. and weekdays in Dec. and Feb.* ¶◎¶ *BP.*

Lindisfarne (Holy Island)

★ ㉛ *6 mi east of A1, north of Bamburgh; 22 mi north of Alnwick, 8 mi southeast of Berwick-upon-Tweed.*

Cradle of northern England's Christianity and home of St. Cuthbert, Lindisfarne (or Holy Island) has a religious history that dates from AD 635, when St. Aidan established a monastery here. Under its greatest abbot, the sainted Cuthbert, Lindisfarne became one of the foremost centers of learning in Christendom. The island is reached from the mainland by a long drive along a causeway that floods at high tide, so you *must* check to find out when crossing is safe. The times, which change daily, are displayed at the causeway and printed in local newspapers. Traffic can be heavy; allow at least a half hour for your return trip.

In the year 875, Vikings destroyed the Lindisfarne community; only a few monks managed to escape, carrying with them Cuthbert's bones, which they reburied in Durham. The sandstone Norman ruins of **Lindisfarne Priory,** reestablished in the 11th century by monks from Durham, remain both impressive and beautiful. A museum here displays Anglo-Saxon carvings. ⊠ *Lindisfarne* ☎ *01289/389200* ⊕ *www.english-heritage.org.uk* 🎟 *£3.50* ☺ *Apr.–Sept., daily 10–6; Feb., Mar., and Oct., daily 10–4; Nov.–Jan., weekends 10–4.*

Reached by a walk around the coast of the island, **Lindisfarne Castle** appears to grow out of the rocky pinnacle on which it was built 400 years ago, looking for all the world like a fairy-tale illustration. In 1903 architect Sir Edwin Lutyens converted the former Tudor fort into a private home that retains the original's ancient features. Across several fields from the castle is a walled garden designed by Gertrude Jekyll. ⊠ *Lindisfarne* ☎ *01289/389244* ⊕ *www.nationaltrust.org.uk* 🎟 *£5, garden only £1* ☺ *Apr.–Oct., Tues.–Sun. 10:30–3 or noon–4:30; call for hrs.*

Berwick-upon-Tweed

㉜ *10 mi northwest of Lindisfarne, 30 mi northwest of Alnwick, 77 mi north of Durham.*

Although Berwick-upon-Tweed now lies just inside the border of England, historians estimate that it has changed hands between the Scots and the English 14 times. The market on Wednesday and Saturday draws plenty of customers from both sides of the border. The town's thick 16th-century walls, among the best-preserved in Europe, completely encircle the old town; a path follows the ramparts, and the views are rewarding. The parish church, Holy Trinity, a mixture of Gothic and Renaissance styles, was built during Cromwell's Puritan Commonwealth with stone from a castle.

In the **Barracks,** built between 1717 and 1721, three accommodation wings surround a square, with the decorated gatehouse forming the fourth side. An exhibition called "By Beat of Drum" depicts the life of the common soldier from the 1660s to the 1880s. Other displays highlight the history of the local regiment, the King's Own Scottish Borderers, and that of the town itself. ⊠ *The Parade, off Church St. in town center* ☎ *01289/ 304493* ⊕ *www.english-heritage.org.uk* ⊠ *£3* ☉ *Apr.–Sept., daily 10–6; Oct.–Mar., Thurs.–Mon. 10–4.*

Where to Stay & Eat

£–££ ✕ **Town House.** Delicious fresh quiches, pastries, and other snacks are your reward for seeking out this tricky-to-find spot: cross Buttermarket under the Guildhall and go through the old jail. ⊠ *Marygate* ☎ *01289/307904* ▤ *MC, V* ☉ *Closed Thurs. afternoon and Sun. No dinner.*

£–£££ ⌂ **Coach House.** Part of a cluster of attractive, well-converted farm buildings, this friendly country guest house 10 mi southwest of Berwick-upon-Tweed includes a 17th-century cottage. Spacious bedrooms, some of which have rare chestnut beams, are done in traditional or modern style. You can relax by the fire in the lounge or try the books and games in the library at night. The breakfast menu is unending. ⊠ *A 697, Crookham, Cornhill-on-Tweed, TD12 4TD* ☎ *01890/ 820293* ⊕ *www.coachhousecrookham.com* ⇨ *9 rooms, 7 with bath* ⌂ *Dining room, bar, refrigerators, some pets allowed; no a/c* ▤ *MC, V* ⑩ *BP.*

££ ⌂ **No. 1 Sallyport.** In the heart of town, this treat of a bed-and-breakfast stands a mere 20 yards from the Elizabethan walls. Pleasantly furnished guest rooms hold pine furniture, books, paintings, and the odd antique; one has a fireplace. You have access to a kitchen with fresh coffee, which adds to the pampering. Breakfast is unbeatable, with choices from salmon fishcakes to kippers with eggs to a traditional full breakfast. Evening meals can be arranged. ⊠ *1 Sallyport, TD15 1EZ* ☎🖷 *01289/308827* ⊕ *www.1sallyport-bedandbreakfast.com* ⇨ *3 rooms* ⌂ *Dining room, some pets allowed; no a/c* ▤ *No credit cards* ⑩ *BP.*

THE NORTHEAST A TO Z

To research prices, get advice from other travelers, and book travel arrangements, visit www.fodors.com.

AIRPORTS

Newcastle Airport, 5 mi northwest of the city center, is well served for domestic destinations and major European cities. Metro trains connect the airport to the center of Newcastle, with service approximately every 8 minutes at peak times; cost is £2 one-way. The airport is about 15 minutes by car from the city center.

🛈 **Newcastle Airport** ⊠ Off A696 ☎ 0870/122-1488 ⊕ www.newcastleairport.com.

BUS TRAVEL

National Express serves the region from London's Victoria Coach Station. Average travel times are 6¾ hours to Durham, 7 hours to Newcastle, and 7½ hours to Berwick-upon-Tweed. Connecting services to other parts of the region leave from Durham and Newcastle. For all bus inquiries, call Traveline or National Express.

A special Hadrian's Wall Bus between Housesteads and Carlisle operates year-round (Monday–Saturday; also Sunday Apr.–Sept.), stopping at all the major sites. Local tourist offices have timetables; a Day Rover ticket costs £6.

CUTTING COSTS The Northeast Explorer Pass (£5.75, one day) allows unlimited travel on most local services and is available from the bus driver or local bus stations.

FARES & You can pick up free regional public transport guides from the tourist SCHEDULES information centers.

🚍 **National Express** ☎ 0870/580-8080 ⊕ www.nationalexpress.com. **Traveline** ☎ 0870/608-2608 ⊕ www.traveline.org.uk.

CAR RENTAL

🚍 **Local Agencies Avis** ✉ 7 George St., Newcastle upon Tyne ☎ 0191/232-5283. **Hertz** ✉ Newcastle Airport, off A696, Newcastle upon Tyne ☎ 0191/286-6748. **Jennings Ford** ✉ A1(M), High St., Carrville, Durham ☎ 0191/386-1155.

CAR TRAVEL

The most direct north–south route through the Northeast is A1, linking London and Edinburgh via Newcastle (274 mi from London; five to six hours) and Berwick-upon-Tweed (338 mi from London; two hours past Newcastle). A697, which branches west off A1 north of Morpeth, is a more attractive road, leading past the 16th-century battlefield of Flodden near the Scottish border. For Hexham and Hadrian's Wall, take the A69 west of Newcastle. For the coast, leave the A1 at Alnwick and follow the minor B1340 and B1339 for Craster, Seahouses, and Bamburgh. Holy Island is reached from a minor exit off the A1. A66 and A69 run east–west through the southern and middle parts of the region, respectively.

Many country roads provide quiet and scenic, if slower, alternatives to the main routes. Part of the Cheviot Hills, which run along the Northumbrian side of the Scottish border, is now a military firing range. Don't drive here when the warning flags are flying. The military, though, has restored the Roman road, Dere Street, which crosses this region. Try also B6318, a well-maintained road that runs alongside Hadrian's Wall on the south side.

EMERGENCIES

🚍 **Ambulance, fire, police** ☎ 999. **Berwick Infirmary** ✉ Well Close ☎ 01289/307484. **University Hospital of North Durham** ✉ North Rd., Durham ☎ 0191/333-2333. **Newcastle General Hospital** ✉ Westgate Rd. ☎ 0191/273-8811.

TOURS

North of England Tours specializes in general tours of northern England, and can help research family trees. Birdwatch Northumbria runs one-day and weekend tours in small groups throughout the year.

🚍 **Birdwatch Northumbria** ☎ 01670/783351 ⊕ www.birdwatchnorthumbria.co.uk. **North of England Tours** ☎ 01325/308094 🖷 01325/315940 ⊕ www.northofenglandtours.co.uk.

WALKING TOURS Durham County Council Environment Department organizes a year-round program of guided walks, both in the town and countryside, which cost

£2 per person. For the same price a daily guided walk at 2 PM (June–September) introduces you to the center of Newcastle. These walks are available through local tourist offices.

❼ Durham County Council Environment Department ☎ 0191/383-4144.

TRAIN TRAVEL

Great Northeastern Railways serves the region from London's King's Cross Station, en route to Scotland. Average travel times are 2¾ hours to Darlington, 3 hours to Durham, 3¼ hours to Newcastle, and 3¾ hours to Berwick-upon-Tweed. From Newcastle, there is local service north to Alnmouth (for Alnwick) and to Corbridge and Hexham on the east–west line to Carlisle.

FARES & SCHEDULES **❼ Great Northeastern Railways** ☎ 0845/722-5225 or 0845/748-4950 ⊕ www. gner.co.uk.

TRAVEL AGENCIES

❼ Local Agent Referrals Thomas Cook ⊠ 24-25 Market Pl., Durham ☎ 0191/382-6600 ⊠ 6 Northumberland St., Newcastle ☎ 0191/219-8000.

VISITOR INFORMATION

Northumbria Regional Tourist Board is open weekdays 8:30–5. Other tourist information centers are open Monday–Saturday 9:30–5:30, but times vary by season. The telephone for the Haltwhistle Tourist Information Centre serves as the Hadrian's Wall Information Line.

❼ Northumbria Regional Tourist Board ⊠ Aykley Heads, DH1 5UX ☎ 0191/375-3000 ⊕ www.visitnorthumbria.com. **Alnwick** ⊠ 2 the Shambles, NE66 1TN ☎ 01665/510665 ⊕ www.alnwick.gov.uk. **Barnard Castle** ⊠ Woodleigh, Flatts Rd., DL12 8AA ☎ 01833/690909 ⊕ www.teesdale.gov.uk. **Berwick-upon-Tweed** ⊠ 106 Marygate, TD15 1BN ☎ 01289/330733 ⊕ www.berwickonline.org.uk. **Bishop Auckland** ⊠ Town Hall, Market Pl., DL14 7NP ☎ 01388/604922 ⊕ www.durham.gov.uk. **Darlington** ⊠ 13 Horsemarket, DL1 5PW ☎ 01325/388666 ⊕ www.visitdarlington.net. **Durham** ⊠ Millennium Pl., DH1 1WA ☎ 0191/384-3720 ⊕ www.durhamtourism.co.uk. **Hadrian's Wall** ⊕ www.hadrians-wall.org. **Haltwhistle** ⊠ Railway Station, NE49 9HN ☎ 01434/322002. **Hexham** ⊠ Wentworth Car Park, NE46 1QE ☎ 01434/652220 ⊕ www.hadrianswallcountry.org. **Middlesbrough** ⊠ 99-101 Albert Rd., Cleveland, TS1 2PA ☎ 01642/358086 ⊕ www.middlesbrough.gov.uk. **Newcastle upon Tyne** ⊠ Central Arcade, 132 Grainger St., NE1 5AF ☎ 0191/277-8000 ⊠ Main Concourse, Central Station ☎ 0191/277-8000 ⊕ www.visitnewcastlegateshead.com.

SCOTLAND
EDINBURGH TO THE HIGHLANDS

15

STORM THE RAMPARTS
of mighty Edinburgh Castle ⇨*p.697*

TEE OFF BY THE SHINING SEA
at the St. Andrews Links ⇨*p.714*

SEE MACKINTOSH'S MASTERPIECE
on a Glasgow School of Art tour ⇨*p.718*

TELL MONSTERS FROM MIRAGES
on a tour around Loch Ness ⇨*p.742*

DRIVE TO THE QUEEN'S VIEW
for royally grand vistas ⇨*p.736*

GET LOST IN THE BORDERS
at enormous Floors Castle ⇨*p.729*

THRILL TO BALLET OR BAGPIPES
at festivals in Edinburgh ⇨*p.710*

Updated by
Nick Bruno,
James Gracie,
and Shona
Main

THE IDEA OF SCOTLAND IS WORLD-EMBRACING, although this small country is no bigger than the state of Maine and contains barely a tenth of the United Kingdom's population. Scotland has produced some of the world's stormiest history, some of its most romantic heroes and heroines, much of its most admired literature, and many of its most important inventions. Its local products, customs, music, and traditional dress—from tartans and bagpipes to tweeds—travel all over the globe. Scots throughout history, especially those who emigrated to the United States, Canada, Australia, and New Zealand, have been superb propagandists for the beloved land of their ancestors. Home-based national pride has been boosted with the reestablishment in 1999, after nearly 300 years, of Scotland's own Parliament, albeit one with restricted powers. Its responsibilities include health, education, transportation, housing, economic development, agriculture, and the environment; the national government in London is still responsible for foreign policy, defense, and economic policy.

There are really two Scotlands: the Lowlands (not low at all, but areas of flat land on the coast and between ranges of low hills), where populous cities such as Edinburgh and Glasgow are found; and the Highlands, which contain the highest mountains in the British Isles, the wildest lochs (lakes), and most of the islands. It is often assumed that as you travel north you proceed from Lowlands to Highlands. In fact, it is more of an east–west divide. Most travelers start out with Scotland's greatest cities, Edinburgh and Glasgow. After a while, however, those heather-clad mountain slopes and shining lochs exert their pull, as do the fast-flowing streams where salmon leap, and the great castles of baronial pride standing among the hills. There are many contrasts of landscape, building stone, and city size, and you don't have to travel too far to enjoy all of these.

Edinburgh (pronounced edin-burra) is very much a capital city, with all the dignity that implies. The Scottish Parliament is based here and, until its new building adjacent to the Palace of Holyroodhouse is complete in late 2004, has been meeting in the Assembly Hall of the Church of Scotland. Many elements make Edinburgh appealing: its outstanding geography (like Rome, it is built on seven hills); the Old Town district, with all the evidence of its colorful history; the New Town, with its elegant classical buildings conceived in a surge of artistic creativity during the second half of the 18th century.

Glasgow, Scotland's largest city, suffered gravely from the industrial decline of the 1960s and '70s, but efforts at commercial and cultural renewal have restored much of the style and grandeur it possessed in the 19th century, when it was at the height of its economic power. It is once again a vibrant metropolitan center with a thriving artistic life and an appetite for the visual and performing arts. Glasgow is a convenient touring center, too, with excellent transportation links to the rest of the country.

The Borders area comprises the great hills, moors, wooded river valleys, and farmland that stretch south from Lothian, the region crowned by Edinburgh, to England. Everything distinctive about Scotland, such as its paper currency, architecture, opening hours of pubs and stores, food and drink, and accent, starts right at the border; you won't find the Borders a diluted version of England. Northeast of Edinburgh, on the windswept east coast of Fife, stands the ancient town of St. Andrews, filled with historic sites and known the world over as the home of golf.

Beyond the central Lowlands, the pleasures and treasures of Aberdeen and northeast Scotland, Inverness, Loch Ness (with or without its "monster" Nessie), and the Highlands await. Aberdeen is Scotland's third-largest city, and a gateway to the splendor of Royal Deeside and the Grampian Mountains, a wealth of castles, and an unspoiled and, in places, spectacular coastline. Inverness, to the northwest, is the capital of the Highlands, with Loch Ness right on its doorstep. A map of Scotland gives a hint of the grandeur to be found here: fingers of inland lochs, craggy mountains, rugged promontories, and deep inlets. But the map does not give an inkling of the brilliant purple and emerald moorland, the forests, and the astonishingly varied wildlife: red deer, golden eagles, ospreys, seals, and dolphins. Nor can a map convey the courtesy of the soft-spoken inhabitants, and the depth of ancestral memory and clan mythology. All these delights await anyone who ventures out of the cities.

A car is essential for exploring well beyond the cities, in Scotland's wildest districts. For the short-term visitor, a bus excursion from Edinburgh or Aberdeen may give the best value. Whatever the mode of transport, try to spend a couple of days in a small Highland bed-and-breakfast, grand estate hotel, or fishing inn. Only then will you discover the spell of the Highlands, inexplicable magic that brings people back year after year.

Exploring Scotland

Edinburgh and Glasgow, Scotland's two major cities, are in the Lowlands, just 70 km (44 mi) apart by fast highway. Greatly different in style, they both divide easily into two: Edinburgh's Old and New Towns, and Glasgow's medieval-and-merchant heart and culture-rich West End. The Borders lie south of Edinburgh, with their green hillsides, river valleys, ruined abbeys, and stately homes; they can be discovered in one long day or taken in two bites, if you return to Edinburgh overnight. St. Andrews, along the east coast north of Edinburgh, beckons with golf and more. The Highlands take in many rugged landscapes, only a few of which are covered in this chapter: the remote islands of the western seaboard, the silvery granite city of Aberdeen on the east coast, the Grampian Mountains and "Castle Country" of Royal Deeside lying west of Aberdeen, the northern area toward Inverness and Loch Ness, and the Northern Highlands, with Scotland's tallest mountains and greatest lochs.

About the Restaurants

Edinburgh and Glasgow have an increasing number of sophisticated restaurants of all kinds, as does Aberdeen. At the best, reservations are essential. Many superior restaurants in the Borders and the Southwest are found within hotels; this is also true in the Northeast.

About the Hotels

Edinburgh, Glasgow, Aberdeen, and Inverness are served splendidly by accommodations from grand hotel suites done up in tartan fabrics to

15

To take in the diversity of sights and scenery in Scotland, you need at least a week. If you have less time, you may need to choose between city and countryside: the main attractions of Edinburgh or Glasgow could be seen in two or three days, or you could visit Aberdeen and Royal Deeside. With five or six days, you could base yourself at two centers, perhaps Edinburgh and Aberdeen, or Glasgow and Inverness. Alternatively, you could take day trips to St. Andrews and to the Borders from Edinburgh. To cover all the areas in this chapter, allow at least 10 days.

Numbers in the text correspond to numbers in the margin and on the Edinburgh, Borders, Glasgow, Aberdeen & Royal Deeside, and Inverness & Environs maps.

If you have 2–3 days

This will be long enough to see most of the major sights in one of these areas: ▣ **Edinburgh** ❶–㉗ ⚑, ▣ **Glasgow** ㉙–㊺ ⚑, ▣ **Aberdeen** ㊽ ⚑, or ▣ **Inverness** ㊿ ⚑ (and Loch Ness)—assuming that you select your own choices among the museums, galleries, or stately homes. You might want to break up your three-day visit to Edinburgh or Glasgow with an overnight excursion to the Borders, staying at ▣ **Melrose** ㊼ or ▣ **Peebles** ㊸ to enjoy a rural change of pace; or from Edinburgh, take a day trip to check out **St. Andrews** ㉘—there's actually much more to see in this town than the legendary Royal & Ancient Course.

If you have 5 days

At least two days and nights should be spent in ▣ **Edinburgh** ❶–㉗ ⚑ or ▣ **Glasgow** ㉙–㊺ ⚑ to allow for visits to the most important sights. (If you want to see both cities, you need the whole five days.) For your remaining nights, you have three options. The first is to head south for the Borders to explore Sir Walter Scott Country. Start out (and spend the night) in ▣ **Melrose** ㊼, visiting **Abbotsford House** ㊻, Scott's View, and **Dryburgh Abbey** ㊽ as well as sights farther afield, such as the abbey at **Jedburgh** ㊾. For those interested in grand Scottish residences, a visit to Floors Castle is a must. After enjoying the Scottish countryside on an afternoon walk, stay overnight in ▣ **Kelso** ㊿ before heading back to the capital.

Your second option, from Edinburgh or Glasgow, is to travel to ▣ **Aberdeen** ㊽, arriving in the evening. The next morning, follow in the footsteps of Queen Victoria and take a trip among the castles and glens of Royal Deeside. Set out for Crathes Castle and **Banchory** ㊱, with its largely unchanged Victorian High Street. After lunch, follow the river upstream to Aboyne, turning due north on B9094, then left onto B9119 and finally onto A93 to reach ▣ **Ballater** ㊲. The next morning, visit Her Majesty's **Balmoral Castle** ㊳ if royal residences are high on your list. (Note that Balmoral is open only April through July.) Treat yourself to a walk in nearby Glen Muick. Head for ▣ **Braemar** ㊴ for your next overnight stay. The next morning, set off for some serious castle-hopping—**Corgarff Castle** ㊵, **Kildrummy Castle** ㊶, **Craigievar Castle** ㊸, and **Castle Fraser** ㊹, stopping at **Alford** ㊷ to visit the Grampian Transport Museum. Return to Aberdeen, either stopping overnight or continuing south to Edinburgh or Glasgow.

Another option, after two days in Edinburgh or Glasgow, is to travel to the Highlands and ⊡ **Inverness** ⑥⑤ for two nights, aiming to arrive in the early evening. Spend the next morning exploring the city; in the afternoon pay a call on Nessie at Drumnadrochit on the banks of **Loch Ness** ⑥⑥. Return to Inverness for the night, then the next day follow signposts to **Culloden Moor** ⑥⑦, **Fort George** ⑥⑨, **Cawdor Castle** ⑦⓪, or **Brodie Castle** ⑦① for a finale in Macbeth Country. Spend the night at ⊡ **Nairn** ⑥⑧ before traveling south to Edinburgh or Glasgow.

If you have

10

days or

longer

If, having visited Edinburgh, Glasgow, the Borders, and Aberdeen and Royal Deeside (allowing two days for each), you wish to continue exploring the Highlands, turn west, after visiting one or two houses in Castle Country, at **Castle Fraser** ⑥④. Take A944 from Castle Fraser west, enjoying the valley of the River Don as far as Corgarff on A939. The A939 then climbs into the brown hills to Tomintoul, highest village in the Highlands. From there, continue west, dropping into Speyside via the A95 and A938 roads, to pick up the main A9 at Carrbridge and arrive by evening at ⊡ **Inverness** ⑥⑤. Spend your remaining time as described under the five-day option of Inverness and the surrounding area.

---

personal-touch bed-and-breakfasts. Some of the best lodgings are in lovely traditional Georgian or Victorian properties, but chic, ultramodern hotels are also finding favor. Because of the removal of much of its indigenous population by forced emigration in the 18th and 19th centuries, many parts of the Highlands became playgrounds for estate owners or Lowland industrialists, who built shooting lodges, grand mansions, and country estates. Many of these are now fine hotels or upscale B&B establishments. In rural areas, many farms also offer bed and breakfast.

WHAT IT COSTS In pounds				
££££	**££££**	**£££**	**££**	**£**
RESTAURANTS over £22	£18–£22	£13–£17	£7–£12	under £7
HOTELS over £160	£120–£160	£90–£120	£60–£90	under £60

Restaurant prices are for a main course at dinner. Hotel prices are for two people in a standard double room in high season, including VAT, with no meals or, if indicated, CP (with Continental breakfast), BP (Breakfast Plan, with full breakfast), or MAP (Modified American Plan, with breakfast and dinner).

Timing

August is the most exciting time to visit Edinburgh, largely because of the Edinburgh International Festival, when the city buzzes with cultural activity. However, this is also the busiest time, and anyone wishing to visit Edinburgh during August or the beginning of September should plan and book months in advance. Although the Borders are also busiest during summer festival time, its landscape can be fully appreciated in April and May as well. Scottish winters can be cold and wet, but the long summer evenings—with sunsets as late as 10:30 from June through September—are magical. The exuberant New Year celebrations known as Hogmanay draw crowds in Edinburgh and Glasgow.

15

Castles

If you love castles, you've come to the right place. Scotland has just about every type of castle imaginable—from brooding medieval ruins such as Kildrummy, complete with gory tales, to magnificent Georgian and Victorian piles, full of antiques and paintings and surrounded by parkland. History-rich Edinburgh Castle is splendid and not to be missed. The northeast of Scotland inland from Aberdeen, in particular, has a huge range of castles to admire, helpfully strung together along the Castle Trail. Whether still in private ownership and full of family atmosphere, like Cawdor or Floors, or under the care of the National Trust for Scotland or of Historic Scotland, or just a jumble of stones atop a hill, Scotland's castles and fortified houses vividly demonstrate the country's splendid if unsettled past and its historically uneasy relationship with its southern neighbor.

Festivals & Events

The annual Edinburgh International Festival in August or early September fills Edinburgh with cultural events in every art form, from traditional theater, big-name classical concerts, and jazz to experimental forms of dance and theater. Also held during this time is the Edinburgh Festival Fringe, the refreshingly irreverent, ever-growing, unruly child of the official festival. In the same time period, that stirring Scottish extravaganza—the Edinburgh Military Tattoo—is also performed. Tourist boards have information on the many other events that add breadth to Scotland's cultural year.

Caber tossing (the caber is a long pole) and other traditional events figure in the Highland Games, staged throughout the Highlands during summer. All tourist information centers have details. It is said that these games, a combination of music, dancing, and athletic prowess, grew out of the contests held by clan chiefs to find the strongest men for bodyguards, the fastest runners for messengers, and the best musicians and dancers to entertain guests and increase the chief's prestige.

Great Golf

Everyone wants to play just the big names in the British Open—St. Andrews, Turnberry, Royal Troon, and so on. This is a pity, because there are more golf courses in Scotland per capita than anywhere else in the world, and many are close to the major cities. The 400 or so courses include plenty of gems, from challenging coastal links to pinewood parkland delights. In the East Neuk of Fife, one of the prettiest Lowland areas of Scotland, the quiet town of St. Andrews beckons with its famous golf course, where the Royal & Ancient, the ruling body of the game worldwide, has its headquarters. Note that a round on a municipal course costs very little, and most clubs, apart from a few pretentious places modeled on the English fashion, demand only comparatively modest course fees.

Hiking & Walking

Walking is an unbeatable way to get to know Scotland's varied landscape of low-lying glens and major mountains. Walks in the Edinburgh area range from city walkways along the banks of the Water of Leith, to the Pentland Hills, whose breezy but not overdemanding slopes are popular with locals on weekends. Because the Borders are essentially rural and hilly, there are a number of walking options. Peebles, within easy reach of Edinburgh, has excellent, level walking along the banks of the River Tweed, and a visit to Melrose, with its abbey, can be enhanced by a climb to the top of the Eildon Hills, for wonderful views. The Southern Upland Way, a 212-mi official long-distance footpath from Cockburnspath in the east to Portpatrick in the west, also passes through the Borders. Official footpaths in the Highlands include the West Highland Way, running 98 mi from the outskirts of Glasgow to Fort William, by Loch Lomond, Rannoch Moor, and Glen Coe; and the Great Glen Way, which runs for 70 mi from Fort William to Inverness, via the Caledonian Canal and Lochs Lochy, Oich, and Ness. Slightly gentler is the Northeast's Spey-side Way, taking its name from one of Scotland's premier salmon rivers, which has excellent river-valley and some moorland walking for 47 mi, from the Moray Firth coast up to the foothills of the Cairngorms. All four long-distance paths are covered in official guides available from bookshops and tourist information centers. Keep in mind that Scottish weather is highly changeable: you may step out into a bright sunny morning but it could easily rain, blow a *gael* (a storm), or snow before lunchtime. If you are to venture out into the hills or glens, make sure you have warm, waterproof clothing, a map and compass, and that you have left word with your hotel regarding your planned route.

Shopping

Among the many traditional shopping favorites in Scotland are Shetland and Fair Isle woolens, tartan rugs and tweeds, Edinburgh crystal, and Caithness glass. Look for craft pottery and for unusual designs in Scottish jewelry, especially when they incorporate local stones. Glasgow has an excellent selection of designer clothing stores. Handmade chocolates, often with whisky or Drambuie fillings, and the traditional "petticoat tail" shortbread in tin boxes are popular, as is Scottish heather honey. Try some of the boiled sweets in jars from particular localities, such as Jethart snails, Edinburgh rock, and similar delights.

Spring in the Highlands can be glorious, when snow still lies on the highest peaks. Those exuberant Highland Games, with caber tossing and hammer throwing, are held during summer months: Braemar's games (September) are often attended by members of the Royal Family. Autumn in Royal Deeside is very colorful. If you wish to drop in on Balmoral, the royal residence in Deeside, keep in mind that it's open April through July only. If the royals are in residence, even the grounds are closed to visitors, so call to inquire. Most castles, whether in the Borders or Royal Deeside, are open April through October only; check in advance. Many accommodations and attractions in more isolated areas close from November through March.

EDINBURGH

▶ In a skyline of sheer drama, Edinburgh Castle watches over Scotland's capital city, and seems to frown down on Princes Street as if disapproving of its modern razzmatazz. Its ramparts still echo with gunfire when the one o'clock gun booms out each day. Nearly everywhere in the city, spectacular buildings with Doric, Ionic, and Corinthian columns add dignity to the landscape. To this largely Presbyterian-gray backdrop, numerous trees and gardens provide color. The top of Calton Hill, to the east, is cluttered with neoclassical monuments, like an abandoned set for a Greek drama. Also conspicuous from Princes Street is Arthur's Seat, an 800-foot-high mountain of bright green and yellow furze rearing up behind the spires of the Old Town. This child-size mountain has steep slopes and little crags, like a miniature Highlands in the middle of the busy city. These theatrical elements give a unique identity to downtown, but head to George Street (which runs parallel to Princes Street) and look north; the view is of blue sea and a patchwork of fields, not an endless cityscape. This is the county of Fife, beyond the wide inlet of the North Sea called the Firth of Forth; a reminder, like the misty mountains sometimes glimpsed on a clear day from Edinburgh's highest points, that the rest of Scotland lies within easy reach.

The Old Town

The brooding presence of the castle, the essence of Scotland's martial past, dominates Edinburgh. It is built on the hard, black volcanic plug of an extinct volcano, and during the last Ice Age an eastbound glacier scoured around this resistant core, creating steep cliffs on three sides. On the fourth side, a "tail" of rock was left, forming a ramp from the top that gradually runs away eastward. This became the street known as the Royal Mile, the backbone of the Old Town, leading from the castle down to the Palace of Holyroodhouse. "The Mile" is made up of one thoroughfare that bears, in consecutive sequence, different names: the Esplanade, Castlehill, Lawnmarket, Parliament Square, High Street, and Canongate. Adjacent to Holyroodhouse is the site of Scotland's Parliament building, under construction to a design by the late Barcelona architect Enric Miralles; until this is completed (scheduled for late 2004), the Parliament sits in the Assembly Hall of the Church of Scotland, overlooking the Mound (a street).

The narrow streets and passages (called "closes") leading off the Royal Mile and into the tenements or "lands" that lined the thoroughfare really *were* Edinburgh until the late 18th century saw expansions to the south and north. Everybody lived here, the richer folk on the ground floors of houses, the merchant classes on the middle floors, and the poor on the top floors. Time and redevelopment have swept away some of these closes and tenements, but enough survive for you to be able to imagine the original profile of Scotland's capital. Sir Walter Scott (1771–1832), Robert Louis Stevenson (1850–94), David Hume (1711–76), James Boswell (1740–95), the painter Allan Ramsay (1713–84), and many other well-known names are associated with the Old Town. But perhaps three are more famous than any others: John Knox (1513–72), Mary, Queen of Scots (1542–87), and Prince Charles Edward Stuart (1720–88).

a good walk

A perfect place to begin a tour of the Old Town is **Edinburgh Castle ❶** ▶. Having absorbed its attractions and taken in the city views, you can stroll eastward down the grand promenade that is the **Royal Mile ❷**. To the left of Castlehill, the Outlook Tower offers armchair views of the city with its **Camera Obscura ❸**. Opposite, the **Scotch Whisky Heritage Centre ❹** of-

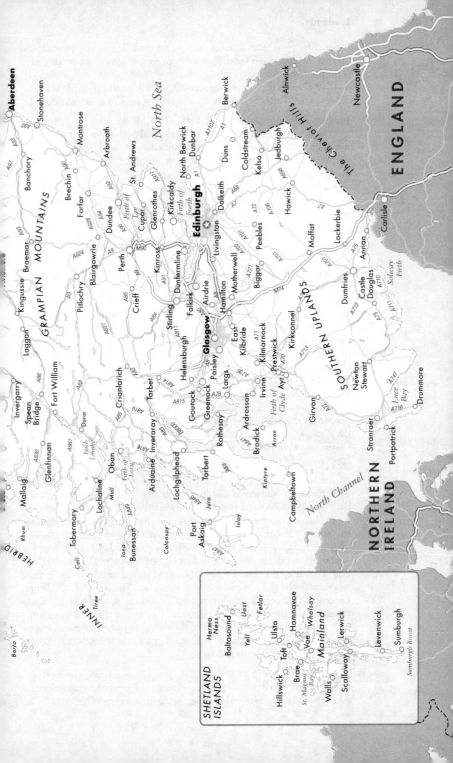

fers a chance to discover Scotland's liquid gold. The six-story tenement known as **Gladstone's Land ❺**, a survivor of 16th-century domestic life, is on the left as you walk down. Close by Gladstone's Land, down yet another close, is the **Writers' Museum ❻**, in a 17th-century house with exhibits on Sir Walter Scott, Robert Louis Stevenson, and Robert Burns.

Farther down on the right, the Tolbooth Kirk (kirk means "church") has the tallest spire in the city, 240 feet, and is the home of the Edinburgh International Festival offices. From Lawnmarket you can start your discovery of the Old Town closes. For a shopping diversion, turn right down George IV Bridge, then right down Victoria Street, a 19th-century addition to the Old Town. Its shops sell antiques, old prints, clothing, and high-quality giftware. Down in the **Grassmarket ❼**, which for centuries was an agricultural market, the shopping continues.

Walk from the Grassmarket back up Victoria Street to George IV Bridge, where you can see the **National Library of Scotland ❽**. Farther down George IV Bridge, on the right, is the **Kirk of the Greyfriars ❾**. Before returning to Lawnmarket, turn left down Chambers Street, which runs from the bottom of George IV Bridge toward South Bridge. Here, the **Royal Museum ❿** displays a collection of worldwide scope. Next door, in the magnificent Benson and Forsyth–designed Museum of Scotland, you can explore Scotland's history. Return to High Street and, near Parliament Square (site of the historic Parliament Building, not the current one), visit the **High Kirk of St. Giles ⓫**. Just east of St. Giles is another landmark, the **Mercat Cross ⓬**, which is still the site of royal proclamations. On the opposite side of High Street, below the City Chambers (the entrance is in Warriston's Court), lies the **Real Mary King's Close ⓭**, an Edinburgh street dating from the 16th century. When the bubonic plague hit the city in 1645, many of the street's inhabitants contracted the illness. They were removed and the street was sealed off. The City Chambers were built over it in the 18th century, preserving the houses. It is said to be one of Edinburgh's most haunted sites.

At the North Bridge and South Bridge junction with High Street is the Tron Kirk. The **Museum of Childhood ⓮** is nearby on High Street. Across the street lies **John Knox House ⓯**, associated with Scotland's 16th-century religious reformer. Down a close nearby is the **Brass Rubbing Centre,** where you can create an unusual souvenir. Beyond this point, you would once have passed beyond the safety provided by the town walls. A plaque outside the Netherbow Arts Centre depicts the former Netherbow Port (gate). Below is the Canongate area, named for the canons who once ran the abbey at Holyrood. Here you see the handsome **Canongate Tolbooth ⓰**, the graveyard of Canongate Kirk, and **Huntly House ⓱**, a museum of local history. Facing you at the end of Canongate are the wrought-iron gates of the **Palace of Holyroodhouse ⓲**, residence of the Queen when she is in Scotland. Under construction to the right is the Parliament Building.

TIMING   This walk contains a multitude of historical attractions, and its duration depends on your interests. Exploring the Royal Mile from the castle to the Palace of Holyroodhouse will easily take up to half a day. The

Grassmarket is a good lunch spot, with its pubs and small restaurants. The Museum of Scotland building can take up to half a day. Many sights have extended hours during the Edinburgh International Festival.

What to See

Arthur's Seat. For a grand bird's-eye view of Edinburgh, make your way up the 800 feet of the city's minimountain, Arthur's Seat, set in the park behind the **Palace of Holyroodhouse.** It's a steep walk but well worth it for the views from here and its neighboring eminence, Salisbury Crags.

Brass Rubbing Centre. A hands-on way to explore the past, brass rubbing attracts more serious fans every year. Fascinating reproduction brasses and inscribed stones are supplied with instructions and materials. ⊠ *Trinity Apse, Chalmers Close, Old Town* ☎ *0131/556–4364* ⊕ *www. cac.org.uk* ⊠ *Free, £1.20–£15 per rubbing* ☉ *Apr.–Oct., Mon.–Sat. 10–5, Sun. (during festival only) noon–5.*

Camera Obscura. Want to view Edinburgh as Victorian travelers did? The Outlook Tower holds this optical instrument, a sort of projecting telescope that creates a bird's-eye view of the whole city illuminated onto a concave table. Holograms and pinhole cameras are shown in other exhibits. ⊠ *Castlehill, Old Town* ☎ *0131/226–3709* ⊕ *www.camera-obscura.co.uk* ⊠ *£5.95* ☉ *Apr.–Oct., daily 9:30–6; Nov.–Mar., daily 10–5.*

16 Canongate Tolbooth. Canongate originally was an independent "burgh," or town, which explains the presence of the Canongate Tolbooth. Nearly every city and town in Scotland once had a tolbooth. Originally signifying a customhouse where tolls were gathered, the name came to mean the town hall and, later, a prison. Today, the Canongate Tolbooth contains **The People's Story,** an exhibition on the history of the people of Edinburgh. Next door is the graveyard of **Canongate Kirk,** where some notable Scots, including Adam Smith, the economist and author of *The Wealth of Nations,* are buried. ⊠ *Canongate, Old Town* ☎ *0131/529–4057* ⊠ *Free* ☉ *Mon.–Sat. 10–5, Sun. (during festival only) 12–5.*

1 Edinburgh Castle. The crowning glory of the Scottish capital, Edinburgh Castle is popular not only because it is the symbolic heart of Scotland but because of the views from its battlements: on a clear day the vistas, stretching to the "kingdom" of Fife, are breathtakingly lovely. Clear days are frequent now, as Edinburgh is officially smokeless and the nickname "Auld Reekie" ("Old Smokey") no longer applies.

Fodor's Choice

The castle encompasses much of Scottish history. Discover how Thomas Randolph, earl of Moray, nephew of freedom-fighter Robert Bruce, scaled the heights one dark night in 1313 with a small band of men, surprised the English guard, and recaptured the castle for the Scots. At the same time he destroyed every one of its buildings except for St. Margaret's Chapel, dating from around the 12th century, so that successive Stuart kings had to rebuild the place bit by bit. Scots and Englishmen, Catholics and Protestants, soldiers and royalty have held the castle. In the 16th century Mary, Queen of Scots, chose to give birth here to the future James VI of Scotland, who was also to rule England as James I.

Edinburgh

KEY

🛈 *Tourist information*

▶ *Start of walk*

Old Town

Camera Obscura **3**
Canongate Tolbooth ...**16**
Edinburgh Castle **1**
Gladstone's Land **5**
Grassmarket **7**
High Kirk of St. Giles ...**11**

Huntly House **17**
John Knox House **15**
Kirk of the Greyfriars ...**9**
Mercat Cross **12**
Museum of
Childhood **14**

National Library
of Scotland **8**
Palace of
Holyroodhouse **18**
Real Mary King's
Close **13**
Royal Mile **2**

Royal Museum and
Museum of Scotland ...**10**
Scotch Whisky
Heritage Centre **4**
Writers' Museum **6**

▶ New Town & Beyond

Calton Hill **23**
Georgian House **24**
Moray Place **26**
National Gallery
of Scotland **19**
Register House **22**

Royal Scottish
Academy **20**
Scott Monument **21**
Scottish National
Portrait Gallery **27**
West Register House ...**25**

In 1573 it was the last fortress to support Mary's claim as the rightful Catholic queen of Britain, only to be virtually destroyed by English artillery fire.

You enter across the **Esplanade,** the huge forecourt built in the 18th century as a parade ground; it now serves as the castle parking lot. It comes alive with color each August when it is used for the Tattoo, a magnificent military display, with the massed pipes and drums of the Scottish regiments beating retreat on the floodlit heights. Heading over the drawbridge and through the gatehouse, past the guards, you see the rough stone walls of the **Half Moon Battery,** where the one o'clock gun is fired every day in an impressively anachronistic ceremony. Climb up through a second gateway and you come to the oldest surviving building in the complex, tiny 12th-century **St. Margaret's Chapel.** Head up farther still to enter the heart of the mighty complex, the medieval fortress. Along the dimly lit, echoing corridors is the **Crown Room,** containing the "Honours of Scotland," the crown, scepter, and sword that once graced the Scottish monarch, and the Stone of Destiny, a sacred relic used in Scottish coronations. Here also is the **Great Hall,** under whose 16th-century hammer-beam roof official banquets are still held, and **Queen Mary's apartments,** where the queen gave birth to James. ☎ *0131/225–9846* ⊕ *www. historic-scotland.gov.uk* ▣ *£9.50* ⊙ *Apr.–Oct., daily 9:30–6; Nov.–Mar., daily 9:30–5; last entry 45 mins before closing.*

off the
beaten
path

EDINBURGH ZOO – In Edinburgh's western suburbs, this zoo includes more than 1,000 species, the majority of which are in conservation programs. It's one of the UK's leading zoological parks and is noted for its penguins and Penguin Parade, which takes place at 2:15 in summer and 12:45 in winter. However, the parade is voluntary on the part of the penguins and sometimes doesn't take place. ⊠ *Corstorphine Rd., Corstorphine* ☎ *0131/334–9171* ⊕ *www.edinburghzoo.org.uk* ▣ *£8.50* ⊙ *Apr.–Sept., daily 9–6; Oct. and Mar., daily 9–5; Nov.–Feb., daily 9–4:30.*

⑤ Gladstone's Land. A standout for those in search of authentic old Edinburgh, this six-story tenement dates from the 1550s, though what you see now is mainly from the 17th century. It includes an arcaded ground floor and intricately painted ceilings. The entire edifice is furnished in the style of a 17th-century merchant's house. ⊠ *477B Lawnmarket, Old Town* ☎ *0131/226–5856* ⊕ *www.nts.org.uk* ▣ *£5* ⊙ *Apr.–Oct., Mon.–Sat. 10–5, Sun. 2–5; last admission at 4:30.*

⑦ Grassmarket. As its name suggests, this was for centuries an agricultural market. Today, the shopping continues, but the goods are antiques, old prints, clothing, and quality giftware. More boutiques can be found in nearby Victoria Street and West Bow. ⊠ *Grassmarket, Old Town.*

⑪ High Kirk of St. Giles. Sometimes called St. Giles's Cathedral (it was briefly a cathedral in the mid-17th century), this is one of the city's principal churches, but it is more like a large parish church than a great European cathedral. The building is dominated by a stone crown, towering

161 feet above the ground. Inside the west end stands a life-size bronze statue of the Scot whose spirit still dominates the place, the great Protestant reformer and preacher John Knox, before whose zeal all Scotland once trembled. The most elaborate feature inside the church is the **Chapel of the Order of the Thistle,** which refers to Scotland's highest order of chivalry and the counterpart to England's Order of the Garter. St. Giles is about one-third of the way along the Royal Mile from Edinburgh Castle. ⊠ *High St., Old Town* ☎ *0131/225–9442* ⊕ *www.stgiles. net* ⊠ *£1 suggested donation* ⊙ *May–Sept., weekdays 9–7, Sat. 9–5, Sun. 1–5; Oct.–Apr., Mon.–Sat. 9–5, Sun. 1–5.*

⑰ Huntly House. This attractive building houses the fascinating Museum of Edinburgh, a must for those interested in the details of Old Town life. The collection includes Scottish pottery and Edinburgh glass and silver. ⊠ *142 Canongate, Old Town* ☎ *0131/529–4143* ⊕ *www.cac.org.uk* ⊠ *Free* ⊙ *Mon.–Sat. 10–5, Sun. (during festival only) 2–5.*

⑮ John Knox House. A typical 16th-century dwelling, this was not the home of Knox (1514–72), Scotland's fiery religious reformer, though he may have died here. It is full of mementos of his life and career. The house is closed for renovations until spring 2005. ⊠ *45 High St., Old Town* ☎ *0131/556–2647* ⊕ *www.scottishstorytellingcentre.co.uk* ⊠ *£2.25* ⊙ *Mon.–Sat. 10–5, Sun. in July 12–5, last admission ½ hr before closing.*

❾ Kirk of the Greyfriars. Here, in a 1620 church built on the site of a medieval monastery, the National Covenant was signed in 1638, declaring the Presbyterian Church in Scotland independent of the king. This triggered decades of civil war. After exploring the church, visit its ancient graveyard. Nearby, at the corner of George IV Bridge and Candlemaker Row, stands one of the most photographed sights in Scotland, the statue of **Greyfriars Bobby.** This famous Skye terrier kept vigil beside his master's grave in the churchyard for 14 years. ⊠ *Greyfriars Pl., Old Town* ☎ *0131/225–1900* ⊕ *www.greyfriarskirk.com* ⊠ *Free (donations box)* ⊙ *Easter–Oct., weekdays 10:30–4:30, Sat. 10:30–2:30; Nov.–Easter, Thurs. 1:30–3:30, Sun. church service 11–12:30.*

⑫ Mercat Cross. A great landmark of Old Town life, the Mercat Cross (mercat means "market") can be seen just east of the High Kirk of St. Giles. This area was a mercantile center, and in early days, it also saw executions. It is the spot where royal proclamations were—and are still—read. Most of the current cross dates from the time of Gladstone, the great Victorian prime minister and rival of Disraeli. ⊠ *High St., Old Town.*

☾ ⑭ Museum of Childhood. Even adults tend to enjoy this cheerful museum—a cacophony of childhood memorabilia, vintage toys, and dolls—the first in the world to be devoted solely to the history of childhood. ⊠ *42 High St., Old Town* ☎ *0131/529–4142* ⊕ *www.cac.org.uk* ⊠ *Free* ⊙ *Mon.–Sat. 10–5, Sun. (July and Aug.) 2–5.*

❽ National Library of Scotland. This leading research library is a special magnet for genealogists investigating family trees. Even amateur family sleuths will find the staff helpful. The library contains a superb collection of books on the history and culture of Scotland. ⊠ *George IV Bridge, Old Town* ☎ *0131/226–4531* ⊕ *www.nls.uk* ✉ *Free* ⊘ *Mon., Tues., Thurs., and Fri. 9:30–8:30, Wed. 10–8:30, Sat. 9:30–1; exhibitions Mon.–Sat. 10–5; festival hrs weekdays 10–8, Sat. 10–5, Sun. 2–5.*

★ ⑱ **Palace of Holyroodhouse.** Haunt of Mary, Queen of Scots, and the setting for high drama, including at least one notorious murder, a spectacular funeral, several major fires, and centuries of the colorful lifestyles of larger-than-life, power-hungry personalities, this is now the Queen's official residence in Scotland. The resolute and impressive palace, built around a graceful central court, stands at the foot of the Royal Mile in a hilly public park. Many monarchs, including Charles II, Queen Victoria, and George V, have left their mark on its rooms. Highlights include the **Great Picture Gallery**, 150 feet long and hung with the portraits of 111 Scottish monarchs. These portraits were commissioned by Charles II, eager to demonstrate his Scottish ancestry (some of the royal figures here are fictional, and the likenesses of others imaginary).

Also here is the little chamber in which, in 1566, David Rizzio, secretary to Mary, Queen of Scots, met an unhappy end. Partly because Rizzio was hated at court for his social-climbing ways, Mary's second husband, Lord Darnley, burst into the queen's rooms with his henchmen, dragged Rizzio into an antechamber, and stabbed him more than 50 times (a bronze plaque marks the spot). Darnley himself was murdered in Edinburgh the next year. When Charles II assumed the British throne in 1660, he ordered Holyrood rebuilt in the architectural style of French king Louis XIV, and that is the palace that you see today. When the Royal Family is not in residence, you are free to walk around the exterior and to go inside for an audio tour. At the main entrance to the palace grounds is the **Queen's Gallery**, which holds exhibitions of works from the Royal Collection. Behind the palace lie the open grounds of Holyrood Park, which enclose Edinburgh's own minimountain, **Arthur's Seat**; just west of the palace, Scotland's new **Parliament building** is under construction. ⊠ *Abbey Strand, Holyrood* ☎ *0131/556–7371, 0131/ 556–1096 recorded information* ⊕ *www.royal.gov.uk* ✉ *£6.50* ⊘ *Apr.–Oct., daily 9:30–5:15; Nov.–Mar., daily 9:30–3:45* ⊘ *Closed during royal visits.*

Parliament House. This was the seat of Scottish government until 1707, when the governments of Scotland and England were united, 104 years after the union of the two crowns. It is partially hidden by the bulk of the High Kirk of St. Giles and now houses the Supreme Law Courts of Scotland. ⊠ *Parliament Sq., Old Town* ☎ *0131/225–2595* ⊕ *www. scotcourts.gov.uk* ✉ *Free* ⊘ *Weekdays 10–4.*

⑬ **Real Mary King's Close.** This former street, now lying beneath the City Chambers (across from St. Giles), was closed off in 1645 when bubonic plague swept through Edinburgh. A few years later it was reopened, but the people who moved back in complained that it was haunted. In 1753 the Royal Exchange was built over the street, sealing it off and ensuring it wasn't destroyed. It is said to be one of the most haunted spots in the city, its most poignant ghost being that of a young girl (nicknamed "Annie"). People still leave offerings for her, such as candies and dolls. Children under five are not admitted, and due to its nature, the close is always semi-dark, with many stairs and steep slopes to negotiate. ⊠ *Warriston's Court, Old Town* ☎ *08702/430160 for enquiries, 08702/ 411415 for group reservations* ⊕ *www.realmarykingsclose.com* ✇ *£7.00.*

❷ Royal Mile. The most famous thoroughfare in Edinburgh begins immediately below the Esplanade. It runs roughly west to east from the castle to the Palace of Holyroodhouse, and progressively changes its name from Castlehill to Lawnmarket, High Street, and Canongate. Strolling downhill from the castle, it's easy to imagine and re-create the former life of the city, though you need sharp eyes to spot the numerous historic plaques and ornamental details.

★ ❿ Royal Museum and Museum of Scotland. In a lavish Victorian building, the **Royal Museum** displays extensive collections drawn from natural history, archaeology, the scientific and industrial past, and the history of mankind and civilization. The galleried Main Hall with its "birdcage" design is architecturally interesting in its own right. In an adjoining building, the **Museum of Scotland** concentrates on Scotland's heritage. This state-of-the-art museum is full of playful models, intricate reconstructions, and paraphernalia from the ancient Picts to modern Scottish culture. ⊠ *Chambers St., Old Town* ☎ *0131/225-7534* ⊕ *www.nms.ac. uk* ✇ *Free, both museums* ☉ *Mon. and Wed.–Sat. 10–5, Tues. 10–8, Sun. noon–5.*

❹ Scotch Whisky Heritage Centre. Here you can learn about the mysterious process that turns malted barley and spring water into one of Scotland's most important exports. ⊠ *354 Castlehill, Old Town* ☎ *0131/220-0441* ⊕ *www.whisky-heritage.co.uk* ✇ *£7.95* ☉ *May–Sept., daily 9:30–6:30, last tour 5:30; Oct.–Apr., daily 10–5, last tour 4:45.*

❻ Writers' Museum. This museum occupies a typical example of 17th-century urban architecture and evokes Scotland's literary past with exhibits on Sir Walter Scott, Robert Louis Stevenson, and Robert Burns. There are occasional exhibitions about other Scottish writers. ⊠ *Lady Stair's Close, off Lawnmarket, Old Town* ☎ *0131/529-4901* ⊕ *www.cac. org.uk* ✇ *Free* ☉ *Mon.–Sat. 10–5 (last admission 4:45), Sun. (during festival only) 2–5.*

The New Town & Beyond

It was not until the Scottish Enlightenment, a civilizing time of expansion in the late 1700s, that the city fathers decided to break away from the Royal Mile's rocky slope and create a fresh and uncluttered Edinburgh below the castle, a little to the north. This was to become the New Town, with elegant squares, classical facades, wide streets, and harmonious proportions. In 1767 a civic competition to design this revolutionary district was won by an unknown architect, James Craig (1744–95). His plan called for a grid of three main east–west streets, balanced at either end by two grand squares. These streets survive, though some buildings that line them have been altered by later development. Princes Street is the southernmost, with Queen Street to the north and George Street as the axis, punctuated by St. Andrew and Charlotte squares. A look at the map will reveal a symmetry unusual in Britain. Even Princes Street Gardens are balanced by Queen Street Gardens to the north. Princes Street was conceived as an exclusive residential address with an open vista facing the castle. It has been altered by the demands of business and shopping, but the vista remains.

a good walk

Start your walk on the Mound, the sloping street that joins the Old and New Towns. Two impressive buildings tucked immediately east of this great linking ramp are the work of W. H. Playfair (1789–1857), an architect whose neoclassical buildings contributed greatly to Edinburgh's earning the title "Athens of the North." The **National Gallery of Scotland** ⑲ ▶ has paintings from Renaissance art to postimpressionist works and one of the most impressive collections of Scottish art. The **Royal Scottish Academy** ⑳, with its columned facade overlooking Princes Street, hosts changing art exhibitions. Turn right on bustling **Princes Street,** the heart of the city. Walk east past the soaring Gothic spire of the 200-foot-high **Scott Monument** ㉑. **Register House** ㉒, farther down on the left, is an Adam-designed jewel of neoclassical architecture that marks the end of Princes Street. The monuments on **Calton Hill** ㉓ can be reached by continuing along Waterloo Place and either climbing steps to the hilltop or taking the road farther on that loops up at a more leisurely pace. On the opposite side of the road, in the Calton Old Burying Ground, is a monument to Abraham Lincoln and the Scottish-American dead of the Civil War. Cut through the St. James Centre shopping mall and find the branch of London's trendy Harvey Nichols department store and its associated fashion stores before heading west along George Street to Charlotte Square. Here behold the handsome **Georgian House** ㉔. Also in the square, the former St. George's Church now fulfills a different role as **West Register House** ㉕, a research facility.

To explore further in the New Town, choose your own route northward, down the elegant streets centering on **Moray Place** ㉖. A neo-Gothic building on Queen Street houses the **Scottish National Portrait Gallery** ㉗. Another attraction within reach of the New Town is the much-cherished **Royal Botanic Garden**. Walk down Dundas Street, the continuation of Hanover Street, onto Brandon Street and Brandon Terrace. Turn left and onto Inverleith Row and across the bridge over the Water of Leith, Edinburgh's small-scale river. This leads to the gardens.

TIMING Walking from the top of the Mound along the full length of Princes Street should take no more than an hour. It is well worth allocating a few hours for Calton Hill, which provides a 360° view of Edinburgh's magnificent skyline, as far as the Firth of Forth across to Fife. The grid system in the New Town provides easy navigation for a wander downhill to the Water of Leith. The Royal Botanic Garden is a 20-minute walk from Princes Street.

What to See

BRITANNIA – Moored on the waterfront at Leith, Edinburgh's port north of the city center, is the former Royal Yacht *Britannia*, launched in Scotland in 1953 and now retired to her home country. The Royal Apartments and the more functional engine room, bridge, galleys, and captain's cabin are all open to view. The land-based visitor center within the huge Ocean Terminal shopping mall has exhibits and photographs about the yacht's history. ⊠ *Ocean Terminal, Leith* ☎ *0131/555–5566* ⊕ *www.royalyachtbritannia.co. uk* 🖅 *£8.50* ☉ *Apr.–Sept., 9:30–4:30; Oct.–Mar., 10–3:30.*

㉓ Calton Hill. A vantage point from which to gain panoramic views, Calton Hill also has numerous historic monuments, including the incomplete Parthenon look-alike known as Edinburgh's Disgrace, intended to be a National War Memorial in 1822 (contributions fell short). You can climb the **Nelson Monument** (☎ 0131/556–2716 ⊕ www.cac.org.uk 🖅£2.00 ☉ Apr.–Sept., Mon. 1–6, Tues.–Sat. 10–6; Oct.–Mar., Mon.–Sat. 10–3) completed in 1815, for fine views. ⊠ *Off Regent Rd., Calton.*

FALKIRK WHEEL – In 2002 British Waterways opened the world's only rotating boat lift, which links two major waterways, the Forth and Clyde Canal and the Union Canal, between Edinburgh and Glasgow. Considered an engineering marvel, the wheel transports eight or more boats at a time from one canal to the other in about 45 minutes. The boats float into a cradlelike compartment full of water; as the wheel turns, they are transported up or down to meet the other canal. You can board tour boats at Falkirk to ride the wheel, though tickets should be booked by phone. Allow 30 minutes before your scheduled departure time to pick up your tickets and choose your boat. Falkirk is 25 mi west of Edinburgh. ⊠ *Lime Rd., Tamfourhill* ☎ *08700/ 500208* ⊕ *www.thefalkirkwheel.co.uk* 🖅 *Boat trips £8, visitor center free* ☉ *Boat trips Apr.–Oct., daily 9:30–5; Nov.–Mar., daily 10–3. Visitor center Apr.–Oct., daily 9–6:30; Nov.–Mar., daily 10–5.*

★ ㉔ Georgian House. Built in 1796, this house stands in Charlotte Square, the elegant urban set piece designed by Robert Adam at the west end of George Street. Graced by a palatial facade on its north side, the square is considered one of Britain's finest pieces of civic architecture. Thanks to the National Trust for Scotland, the Georgian House has been furnished in period style to show the domestic lifestyle of an affluent late-18th-century family. ⊠ *7 Charlotte Sq., New Town* ☎ *0131/225– 2160* ⊕ *www.nts.org.uk* 🖅 *£5* ☉ *Mar., Nov., and Dec., daily 11–3; Apr.–Oct., daily 11–5.*

㉖ Moray Place. With imposing porticoes and a central, secluded garden, this is an especially fine example of an 1820s development. The area remains primarily residential, in contrast to the area around Princes Street. The Moray Place gardens are still for residents only.

★ ▶ ⑲ National Gallery of Scotland. This honey-color neoclassical building, midway between the Old and the New Towns, contains just about the best collection of old masters in Britain outside the great London museums. It is relatively small, so you can easily tour the whole collection in a couple of hours. There are superb works by Caravaggio, Titian, Diego Velázquez, El Greco, Rembrandt, J. M. W. Turner, Edgar Degas, Claude Monet, and Vincent van Gogh, among many others. Scottish painters are also well represented, chief among them the portrait painter Sir Henry Raeburn (1756–1823). ⊠ *The Mound, Old Town* ☎ *0131/556–8921* ⊕ *www.nationalgalleries.org* ▱ *Free* ☉ *Mon.–Sat. 10–5 (extended during festival), Sun. noon–5; print room, weekdays 10–12:30 and 2–4:30 (by appointment only).*

Princes Street. In the humming center of Edinburgh, a ceaseless promenade of people patters along this street, with its mile or so of international chain stores and other retail establishments. The well-kept gardens on the other side of Princes Street act as the castle's wide green moat. The street is still a grand viewpoint for the dramatic grouping of the castle on its rocky outcrop and the long tail of Royal Mile tenements descending from it. ⊠ *New Town.*

㉒ Register House. Scotland's first custom-built archives depository was partly funded by the sale of estates forfeited by Jacobite landowners at the close of their last rebellion in Britain (1745–46). Work on the building, designed by Robert Adam, Scotland's most famous neoclassical architect, started in 1774. The statue in front is of the first duke of Wellington (1769–1852). Call ahead if you wish to carry out genealogical research. ⊠ *2 Princes St., New Town* ☎ *0131/535–1314* ⊕ *www.nas. gov.uk* ▱ *Free* ☉ *Weekdays 9–4:45.*

| need a break? | Immediately west of Register House is the **Café Royal** (⊠ 17 W. Register St., New Town ☎ 0131/557–4792), serving Scottish lagers and beers, and simple lunch items such as steak-and-ale pie and fish and chips. This pub, founded in 1862, is in an 18th-century building, and has plenty of character, with ornate tiles and stained-glass windows. |

Royal Botanic Garden. This garden ranks with the Royal Botanic Gardens at Kew in London in terms of the diversity of its plants and its lovely setting. The 70-acre site presents an immense display of specimens, from tropical to Nordic, including Britain's largest collection of rhododendrons and azaleas. There's also an impressive Chinese garden. You can stop in at the café, shop, and temporary exhibition area. The garden is north of the city center, a 10-minute bus ride from Princes Street. ⊠ *Inverleith Row, Inverleith* ☎ *0131/552–7171* ⊕ *www.rbge.org.uk* ▱ *Free* ☉ *Nov.–Feb., daily 10–4; Mar. and Oct., daily 10–6; Apr.–Sept., daily 10–7. Guided tours leave from the West Gate, Apr.–Sept., daily at 11 and 2.*

㉕ Royal Scottish Academy. The William Playfair–designed academy hosts temporary art exhibitions (Monet paintings, for example), but is also worth visiting for a look at the imposing, neoclassic architecture. ⊠ *Princes St., New Town* ☎ *0131/225–6671* ⊕ *www. royalscottishacademy.org* ▱ *£4–£8 (depending on exhibition)* ☉ *Mon.–Sat. 10–5, Sun. noon–5.*

㉑ **Scott Monument.** The great poems and novels (such as *Ivanhoe* and *Waverley*) of Sir Walter Scott (1771–1832) created a world frenzy for Scotland; the Scots were duly grateful and put up this great Gothic memorial to him in 1844. Under its graceful spire sits a statue of Scott himself, with his dog, Maida, at his feet. Behind the monument is pretty **Princes Street Gardens (East).** In the open-air theater, within **Princes Street Gardens (West),** and amid the park's trim flower beds and stately trees, brass bands, rock groups, and classical music ensembles occasionally perform in summer. ⊠ *Princes St., New Town* ☎ *0131/529–4068* ⊕ *www.cac. org.uk* 🎫 *£2.50* ☉ *Apr.–Sept., Mon.–Sat. 9–6, Sun. 10–6; Oct.–Mar., Mon.–Sat. 9–3, Sun. 10–3.*

㉗ **Scottish National Portrait Gallery.** Focusing on portraits of Scots, this museum contains a magnificent Thomas Gainsborough and portraits by the Scottish artists Allan Ramsay (1713–84) and Sir Henry Raeburn (1756–1823). Works by contemporary artists show sitters from sports stars to world leaders. The building itself is also of great interest, with richly colored murals in the main hall. ⊠ *Queen St., New Town* ☎ *0131/ 624–6200* ⊕ *www.nationalgalleries.org* 🎫 *Free, charge for special exhibitions* ☉ *Mon.–Wed. and Fri.–Sun. 10–5, Thurs. 10–7; extended hrs during the festival.*

㉕ **West Register House.** An extension of the original Register House, this research facility has records open for public examination, with helpful staff to assist you. It's best to check ahead if you wish to carry out genealogical research. ⊠ *17A Charlotte Sq., New Town* ☎ *0131/535–1413* ⊕ *www.nas.gov.uk* 🎫 *Free* ☉ *Weekdays 9–4:30 (last production of records 4:15).*

Where to Eat

The restaurants of this sophisticated city present a mix of Scottish and ethnic cuisine. Number One in the Balmoral Hotel and La Pompadour at the Caledonian Hilton are other choices for an elegant night out. Make reservations well in advance, especially at festival time.

££–£££££ ✕ **Oloroso.** In the heart of the New Town and close to the main shopping streets, this is the perfect place for a revitalizing lunch or dinner after exploring the city. Efficient service is allied to multicultural contemporary cooking that mixes influences from Europe and Asia. The bar is comfortable, and the dining room and roof terrace have stunning views across the Firth of Forth to the hills of Fife, and to the castle and city rooftops on the other side. ⊠ *33 Castle St., New Town* ☎ *0131/ 226–7614* 🖃 *AE, MC, V.*

★ ££££ ✕ **Martins.** Don't be put off by the forbidding facade of this fine contemporary restaurant tucked away in an alley between Frederick and Castle streets. All's well inside, and the food is light and delicious. Fish and game are specialties, and the cheese board is famous, using unpasteurized Scottish and Irish farmhouse cheeses. ⊠ *70 Rose St., North La., New Town* ☎ *0131/225–3106* 🍴 *Reservations essential* 🖃 *AE, DC, MC, V* ☉ *Closed Sun. and Mon. No lunch Sat. Closed 1 wk in May or June, 1 wk in Sept. or Oct., and 1 month over Christmas and New Year's.*

ON THE MENU

Culinary delights await: to sample genuine Scottish cuisine, look for the TASTE OF SCOTLAND sign in restaurant windows indicating the use of the best Scottish products, including marvelous salmon, beef, and venison. You might try spicy haggis, a sheep's stomach-lining filled with the animal's organ meats and then simmered; it is usually served with "neeps and tatties" (mashed turnip and potato). Look for nouvelle variations on old Scottish dishes such as Cullen skink (a rich smoked-fish soup) and Loch Fyne herring. Scotland is traditionally the "land o' cakes," so be sure to enjoy the delicious buns, scones, and biscuits. In the Highlands, game and seafood are often presented with great flair; many restaurants deal directly with local boats, so freshness is guaranteed. Oatmeal, local cheeses, and even malt whisky (turning up in any course) amplify the Scottish dimension. And speaking of whisky, try a "wee dram" of a single malt, the pale, unblended spirit, when you visit the Northeast, one of Scotland's major distilling areas.

££–££££ ✕ **Skippers Bistro.** Once a traditional pub, this superb seafood restaurant in the port of Leith remains cozy and cluttered, with dark wood, shining brass, and lots of pictures and ephemera. For a starter try Cullen skink, a traditional Scottish creamy fish soup. Main dishes change daily but might include halibut, salmon, or monkfish in delicious sauces. Reservations are essential on weekends. ⊠ 1A Dock Pl., Leith ☎ 0131/554–1018 ▱ AE, MC, V.

££–£££ ✕ **Beehive Inn.** The Beehive snuggles in the Grassmarket, under the castle's majestic shadow. Some 400 years ago it served the passengers of coaches, and outside the pub's doors once stood the main city gallows. Bar meals and snacks are served all day, downstairs or in the beer garden. Upstairs, Rafters Restaurant opens at 6 for dinner; try the grilled salmon or the prime Scottish steaks. Don't be put off by the noisy bar; there's usually a quieter spot to be found. You can book literary lunch and supper packages downstairs in conjunction with the Edinburgh Literary Pub Tour, which departs from here. ⊠ 18–20 Grassmarket, Old Town ☎ 0131/225–7171 ▱ AE, DC, MC, V.

££ ✕ **David Bann.** The excellent vegetarian food at this thriving restaurant off the Royal Mile is popular with students and young people. The light, airy dining room and wooden furniture make a pleasant setting for breakfast, sandwiches, or more substantial fare. Try the enchiladas or a phyllo parcel of cheeses and vegetables. ⊠ 56–58 St. Mary's St., Old Town ☎ 0131/556–5888 ▱ AE, MC, V.

££ ✕ **Howie's.** This neighborhood bistro has four branches and offers good modern Scottish fare. The steaks are tender Aberdeen beef, and the prime Scottish salmon is smoked to owner Howie Scott's own specification. All the branches are lively, but each has a personality all its own. ⊠ 29 Waterloo Pl., East End ☎ 0131/556–5766 ⊠ 10–14 Victoria St., Old Town ☎ 0131/225–1721 ⊠ 208 Bruntsfield Pl., Bruntsfield ☎ 0131/221–1777 ⊠ 4–6 Glanville Pl., New Town ☎ 0131/225–5553 ▱ AE, MC, V.

£–££ ✕ **Britannia Spice.** This restaurant, just a few hundred yards from the berth of the former royal yacht *Britannia*, offers a long menu of meat, fish, and vegetarian dishes from Europe, India, Bangladesh, Thailand, and Nepal. Try the Thai beef or the Nepalese trout with vegetables and green chilies. This is a good place to recover from the Ocean Terminal shopping experience. ☒ *150 Commercial St., Leith* ☎ *0131/555–2255* ▤ *AE, DC, MC, V.*

£–££ ✕ **Kalpna.** Don't be put off by the downmarket exterior or low-key in-
Fodor'sChoice terior of this vegetarian Indian restaurant. The food is excellent and al-
★ ways great value for money. *Dam aloo Kashmiri* is a medium-spicy potato dish with a sauce made from honey, pistachios, and almonds. *Bangan mirch masala* is spicier, with eggplant and red chili peppers. The lunchtime buffet is £5.50 and there is a Wednesday evening buffet for £10.00. ☒ *2–3 St. Patrick's Sq., South Side* ☎ *0131/667–9890* ▤ *MC, V* ☉ *Closed Sun. in Jan.–Mar.*

Where to Stay

★ **£££££** ▦ **Balmoral Hotel.** The attention to detail in the elegant rooms and the sheer élan that has re-created the Edwardian splendor of this grand, for-mer railroad hotel make staying at the Balmoral a special introduction to Edinburgh. Here, below the impressive clock tower marking the east end of Princes Street, you get a strong sense of being at the center of city life. The hotel's main restaurant is the plush and stylish Number One, serving the best of Scottish seafood and game. ☒ *1 Princes St., East End, EH2 2EQ* ☎ *0131/556–2414* ▤ *0131/557–3747* ⊕ *www.roccofortehotels.com* ➳ *188 rooms, 2 suites* ♧ *2 restaurants, in-room data ports, cable TV, indoor pool, health club, bar, meeting rooms, park-ing (fee)* ▤ *AE, DC, MC, V.*

£££££ ▦ **Channings.** Five Edwardian terraced houses have become an elegant boutique hotel in an upscale neighborhood minutes from Princes Street. Restrained colors, antiques, quiet rooms, and great views toward Fife (from the north-facing rooms) set the tone. Channings Restaurant of-fers excellent value, especially at lunchtime. ☒ *12–16 S. Learmonth Gar-dens, West End, EH4 1EZ* ☎ *0131/332–3232* ▤ *0131/332–9631* ⊕ *www.channings.co.uk* ➳ *46 rooms* ♧ *2 restaurants, lobby lounge, meeting rooms* ▤ *AE, DC, MC, V* ⦿ *BP.*

£££££ ▦ **The Scotsman.** When the *Scotsman* newspaper moved from these
Fodor'sChoice premises, it left behind a magnificent, turn-of-the-20th-century, gray sand-
★ stone building with a marble staircase and ornate fireplaces and mold-ings. A chic and luxurious modern hotel has been created within the shell of the old structure. Dark wood, earthy colors, and contemporary fur-nishings decorate the guest rooms and public spaces. ☒ *20 N. Bridge, Old Town, EH1 1YT* ☎ *0131/556–5565* ▤ *0131/652–3652* ⊕ *www.thescotsmanhotel.co.uk* ➳ *56 rooms, 12 suites* ♧ *2 restaurants, in-room data ports, cable TV, indoor pool, health club, spa, bar, Internet, busi-ness services, meeting rooms* ▤ *AE, DC, MC, V.*

★ ▦ **Caledonian Hilton Hotel.** "The Caley" recalls the days of the great rail-
££££–£££££ road hotels, although the nearby station is long gone. Its imposing Vic-torian decor has lost none of its dignity and elegance. Rooms are exceptionally large and well appointed. The main restaurant, La Pom-

padour, with elegant plasterwork and murals, would please even Louis XV. Its classic French cuisine uses top-quality Scottish foods; try the sea bass with crispy leeks and caviar-butter sauce. ✉ *Princes St., West End, EH1 2AB* ☎ *0131/222–8888* 🖷 *0131/222–8889* ⊕ *www.hilton.com* ➠ *249 rooms* ☐ *2 restaurants, cable TV, meeting rooms, parking (fee); no a/c* ▭ *AE, DC, MC, V* ⋈ *BP.*

££££–£££££ 🔟 **Malmaison.** A former seamen's hostel in the heart of Leith, Edinburgh's seaport, offers great value and stylish accommodation, with king-size beds and CD players in bedrooms that reflect a chic, bold, modern style. In the public areas a dramatic black, cream, and taupe color scheme prevails. The French theme of this boutique hotel (part of a small chain) is emphasized by its bar and brasserie. ✉ *1 Tower Pl., Leith, EH6 7DB* ☎ *0131/468–5000* 🖷 *0131/468–5002* ⊕ *www.malmaison.com* ➠ *101 rooms* ☐ *Restaurant, cable TV, bar, free parking* ▭ *AE, DC, MC, V* ⋈ *BP.*

£££ 🔟 **AmarAgua.** Deep-piled carpets, floral drapes with many swags, and well-designed furniture make for a feeling of restrained opulence in this Victorian town house, which is 10 minutes by bus from the city center. Rooms are themed around color combinations, and many look distinctly Asian, as the multilingual owners spent some time working in the Far East. "Carry out" breakfasts are available for guests leaving early to catch a bus or plane. ✉ *10 Kilmaurs Ter., South Side EH16 5DR* ☎ *0131/667–6775* 🖷 *0131/667–7687* ⊕ *www.amaragua.co.uk* ➠ *7 rooms* ☐ *Internet; no a/c, no pets, no smoking* ▭ *MC,V* ⊙ *Closed 2 wks in Oct.–Nov. and all of Jan.* ⋈ *BP.*

££–£££ 🔟 **Ardmor House.** A 15-minute walk from Princes Street, Ardmor is a Victorian house with a relaxed but elegant contemporary style. Bedrooms have the occasional carefully chosen antique. It is gay-owned but very straight-friendly, and co-owner Robin provides advice on what to see and do in Edinburgh. ✉ *74 Pilrig St., Pilrig, EH6 5AS* 🖷🖷 *0131/554–4944* ⊕ *www.ardmorhouse.com* ➠ *5 rooms* ☐ *Dining room, free parking, some pets allowed; no a/c, no smoking* ▭ *MC, V* ⋈ *BP.*

££–£££ 🔟 **Kew House and Apartments.** Inside this elegant house, dating from 1860, are tastefully modernized rooms with flowers, chocolates, and a complimentary decanter of sherry. The apartments, one of which is a five-minute walk from the house, have sitting rooms and full kitchens. The bar is for guests only. It's a 15-minute walk from the town center. ✉ *1 Kew Terr., New Town, EH12 5JE* ☎ *0131/313–0700* 🖷 *0131/313–0747* ⊕ *www.kewhouse.com* ➠ *6 rooms, 2 apartments* ☐ *Dining room, cable TV, bar, free parking; no a/c, no smoking* ▭ *AE, DC, MC, V* ⋈ *BP.*

★ ££–£££ 🔟 **Stuart House.** A Georgian/Victorian terraced house with some fine plasterwork operates as a classy B&B. The decoration suits the structure: bold colors, floral fabrics, and generously curtained windows combine with antique and traditional furniture to create a sense of opulence. Stuart House is a 15-minute walk from the city center. It is closed every year for two weeks, though times vary. ✉ *12 E. Claremont St., New Town, EH7 4JP* ☎ *0131/557–9030* 🖷 *0131/557–0563* ⊕ *www. stuartguesthouse.co.uk* ➠ *7 rooms, 2 apartments* ☐ *Some pets allowed; no a/c, no smoking* ▭ *AE, DC, MC, V* ⋈ *BP.*

££ 🔟 **The Conifers.** This trim B&B in a red-sandstone Victorian town house north of the New Town offers simple, traditionally decorated rooms.

Framed prints of old Edinburgh scenes adorn the walls. The owner, Liz Fulton, has a wealth of knowledge about what to see and do in Edinburgh. ⊠ *56 Pilrig St., Pilrig, EH6 5AS* ☎ *0131/554–5162* ⊕ *www.conifersguesthouse.com* ➿ *4 rooms, 3 with bath* ♿ *No a/c, no smoking* ⊟ *No credit cards* ¶◯¶ *BP.*

Nightlife & the Arts

Nightlife

COCKTAIL BARS   The **Opal Lounge** (⊠ 51A George St., New Town ☎ 0131/226–2275), a casual but stylish nightspot, evolves by a subtle change of mood and lighting from a restaurant to a club for drinks and dancing to soul or funk music. **Tonic** (⊠ 34A North Castle St., off George St., New Town ☎ 0131/225–6431) draws a mixed crowd in the 20–40 age group with lively music, snacks, and tapas. This stylish basement bar is done in pale wood and chrome, with bouncy bar stools and comfy sofas.

DISCOS/   **Club Massa** (⊠ 36–39 Market St., Old Town ☎ 0131/226–4224) has
NIGHTCLUBS   theme nights covering the full spectrum of musical sounds; this well-liked spot is open Wednesday through Sunday. **The Living Room** (⊠ 113–115 George St., New Town ☎ 0870/442–2718) has a bar/restaurant, with live blues and jazz except for Friday evenings, when a DJ takes over. **The Venue** (⊠ 15–21 Calton Rd., Old Town ☎ 0131/557–3073) is a three-floor venue that blares many forms of live and club music.

PUBS   **Deacon Brodie's Pub** (⊠ 435 Lawnmarket, Old Town ☎ 0131/225–6531), named for the infamous criminal who may have inspired Robert Louis Stevenson's *Strange Case of Dr. Jekyll and Mr. Hyde,* is an appealing spot for a traditional pub meal or a pint. **Guildford Arms** (⊠ 1 W. Register St., east end of Princes St., New Town ☎ 0131/556–4312) was established in 1896, and is still family-owned. It merits a visit for its interior alone: ornate plasterwork, cornices, friezes, and wood paneling form the backdrop for excellent draft ales. There's a small restaurant upstairs. **Milne's Bar** (⊠ 35 Hanover St., New Town ☎ 0131/225–6738) is known as the poets' pub because of its popularity with the Edinburgh literati, and photos of poets and writers going back to the 1960s adorn the walls. Pies and baked potatoes go well with its 10 real ales.

The Arts

FESTIVALS   The flagship arts event in the city, the **Edinburgh International Festival** (August 14–September 3, 2005) presents performing artists of international ★   caliber in a great celebration of music, opera, dance, and drama. Advance information, programs, tickets, and reservations are available from the Edinburgh Festival Centre, an impressive Victorian Gothic church building that was renovated and renamed the Hub. ⊠ *Castlehill, Old Town, EH1 2NE* ☎ *0131/473–2020 information, 0131/473–2000 tickets* 🖷 *0131/473–2003* ⊕ *www.eif.co.uk.*

The **Edinburgh Festival Fringe** (August 7–29, 2005) presents a huge assortment of theatrical and musical events, some by amateur groups (you have been warned), and it's much more of a grab bag than the official festival. The festival runs for three or four weeks in August and September during the Edinburgh International Festival. ⊠ *180 High St.,*

Old Town, EH1 1QS ☎ *0131/226–0026* 🖷 *0131/226–0016* ⊕ *www. edfringe.com.*

The **Edinburgh International Film Festival** (August 18–29, 2005) is part of the city's summer festival logjam. Advance information, tickets, and programs are available from the Film Festival Office. ✉ *88 Lothian Rd., West End, EH3 9BZ* ☎ *0131/228–4051* 🖷 *0131/229–5501* ⊕ *www. edfilmfest.org.uk.*

The **Edinburgh Military Tattoo** (August 5–27, 2005) might not be art, but it is entertainment. It's sometimes confused with the Edinburgh International Festival itself because their dates overlap. This great celebration of martial music (with plenty of bagpipes) and skills takes place on the castle esplanade, and the dramatic backdrop augments the spectacle. Dress warmly for the late-evening performances. Even if it rains, the show goes on. Tickets and information are available from Edinburgh Military Tattoo Office. ✉ *32 Market St., Old Town, EH1 1QB* ☎ *0131/225–1188 or 08707/555–1188* 🖷 *0131/225–8627* ⊕ *www. edintattoo.co.uk.*

PERFORMANCE HALLS
The **Festival Theatre** (✉ 13–29 Nicolson St., Old Town ☎ 0131/529–6000) hosts the Scottish Ballet and Scottish Opera, as well as large-scale musicals. The **Playhouse** (✉ Greenside Pl., East End ☎ 0870/606–3424) leans toward popular artists and musicals. The **Queen's Hall** (✉ Clerk St., Old Town ☎ 0131/668–2019) is intimate in scale and hosts smaller recitals. **Usher Hall** (✉ Lothian Rd., West End ☎ 0131/228–1155) is the city's grandest venue, and international artists and orchestras, including the Royal Scottish National Orchestra, perform here.

SCOTTISH ENTERTAINMENT
The Caledonian Brewery (✉ Festival Hall, 42 Slateford Rd., Dalry ☎ 0131/623–8066) is one place for traditional, foot-stomping Scottish musical evenings. The brewery organizes about three *ceilidhs* (a mix of country dancing, music, and song; pronounced *kay*-lees) per month, with loads of space and plenty of beer. The well-established **Jamie's Scottish Evening** (✉ Edinburgh Thistle Hotel, Leith St., New Town ☎ 0131/556–0111) is a popular night of traditional entertainment, held April–October.

THEATER
The **Festival Theatre** (✉ 13–29 Nicolson St., Old Town ☎ 0131/529–6000) stages operas, ballet, concerts, and occasional tours. The **King's Theatre** (✉ 2 Leven St., Tollcross ☎ 0131/529–6000) presents comedy, musicals, and drama, as well as Christmas pantomime. The **Royal Lyceum Theatre** (✉ Grindlay St., West End ☎ 0131/248–4848) offers contemporary and traditional drama, plus a yearly Christmas show. The **Traverse Theatre** (✉ 10 Cambridge St., West End ☎ 0131/228–1404) specializes in plays by contemporary Scottish writers.

Sports & the Outdoors

Golf

Edinburgh is well endowed with courses, with 20 or so near downtown (even before the nearby East Lothian courses are considered). **Braids** (✉ Braid Hills Approach ☎ 0131/447–6666), 3 mi south of the city, welcomes visitors to its two courses. The 18-hole course is 5345 yards, par 70; greens fees begin at £17. The 9-hole is 1,900 yards, par 30; greens fees start at £6 for nine holes. **Bruntsfield Links** (⊠ 32 Barnton Ave., David-son's Mains, ☎ 0131/336–1479), 2 mi northwest of the city, permits visitors to play on weekdays by appointment. The course is 6,407 yards, par 71; greens fees are £44 per round or £65 per day. **Duddingston** (⊠ Duddingston Rd. W, Duddingston ☎ 0131/661–7688) is a scenic golf club, with a creek acting as a hazard. It's 2 mi from the Edinburgh city center; visitors can play on weekdays by appointment. The course is 6,420 yards, par 72; greens fee is £35. The **Gullane Golf Club** (⊠ West Links Road, Gullane ☎ 01620/842255), about 20 mi east of Edin-burgh on A198, has three exceptional courses, all 18 holes. Number 1 is 6,075 yards, par 71; Number 2 is 6,244 yards, par 71; Number 3 course is 5,258 yards, par 58. Gullane has a 6-hole children's course. Greens fees are £19–£75; day tickets are also available. The excellent **Luffness New** (⊠ A198, Gullane ☎ 01620/843336) golf course is open to the pub-lic weekdays by advance booking. The course is 6,122 yards, par 69. Greens fees are £46 for a round or £66 per day.

Jogging

The most convenient spot downtown for joggers is **West Princes Street Gardens**, which is separated from traffic by a 30-foot embankment. It has a half-mile loop on asphalt paths. In **Holyrood Park**, stick to jogging on the road around the volcanic mountain for a 2¼-mi trip. For a real challenge, charge up to the summit of Arthur's Seat, or to the halfway point, the Cat's Nick.

Shopping

Edinburgh shops carry a cross section of Scottish specialties, such as tar-tans and tweeds. Antiques shops open and close rapidly, so concentrate on areas with many stores, such as Bruntsfield Place, Causewayside, or St. Stephen Street.

Princes Street in the New Town, despite its renown as a shopping street, may disappoint some visitors with its dull, anonymous, modern archi-tecture, average chain stores, and fast-food outlets. It is, however, one of the best spots to shop for tartans, tweeds, and knitwear, especially if your time is limited.

Edinburgh Crystal (⊠ Eastfield, Penicuik ☎ 01968/675128), south of the city, makes fine glassware stocked by many large stores in the city, but you can also visit its premises, which include shops with seconds and discontinued lines. At **Edinburgh Old Town Weaving Company** (⊠ 555 Castlehill, Old Town ☎ 0131/226–1555), you can chat with and buy from cloth and tapestry weavers as they work. **Geoffrey (Tailor) Highland Crafts** (⊠ 59 High St., Old Town ☎ 0131/557–0256), can clothe you in full Highland dress, with kilts made in its own workshops. **Jenners** (⊠ 48 Princes St., New Town ☎ 0131/225–2442) is Edinburgh's "mini-Harrods," an independent and top-quality department store.

George Street

George Waterston (⊠ 52 George St., New Town ☎ 0131/225–5690) car-ries stationery and Scottish gifts. **Hamilton and Inches** (⊠ 87 George St.,

New Town ☎ 0131/225–4898), established in 1866, is a silversmith and jeweler, noted for its fine and contemporary jewelry, luxury gift items, and the late-Georgian interior of its premises. **Joseph Bonnar** (✉ 72 Thistle St., Old Town ☎ 0131/226–2811), tucked behind George Street, specializes in antique jewelry. The bookstore **Waterstone's** (✉ 83 George St., New Town ☎ 0131/225–3436) carries a well-chosen selection of Scottish titles and has a café.

Victoria Street/West Bow/Grassmarket

Specialty stores abound where these three streets run together. **Bill Baber** (✉ 66 Grassmarket, Old Town ☎ 0131/225–3249) is one of the most imaginative of the many Scottish knitwear designers. **Clarksons** (✉ 87 West Bow, Old Town ☎ 0131/225–8141) sells handcrafted jewelry, including unique, contemporary Celtic designs.

Side Trip to St. Andrews

28 *42 mi northeast of Edinburgh.*

It may have a ruined cathedral, an ancient castle, and the grand St. Andrews University—the oldest in Scotland—but the modern fame of St. Andrews is mainly as the home of golf. Forget that John Knox preached here, or that Protestant martyrs were burned at the stake here. Thousands come to St. Andrews for one reason only—to play at the Old Course, home of the Royal & Ancient Club, and to follow in the footsteps of legendary linksmen such as Walter Hagen, Gene Sarazen, Bobby Jones, and Ben Hogan.

On the Royal & Ancient's course, golf was perhaps originally played with a piece of driftwood, a shore pebble, and a convenient rabbit hole on the sandy, coastal turf. It has been argued that golf came to Scotland from Holland, but the historical evidence points to Scotland being the cradle, if not the birthplace, of the game. Citizens of St. Andrews were playing golf on the town links (public land) as far back as the 15th century. Rich golfers, instead of gathering on the common links, formed themselves into clubs by the 18th century. Arguably, the world's first golf club was the Honourable Company of Edinburgh golfers (founded in Leith in 1744), which is now at Muirfield in East Lothian. The Society of St. Andrews Golfers, founded in 1754, became the Royal & Ancient Golf Club of St. Andrews in 1834.

The **British Golf Museum** traces the history of British golf from its origins to the golfing personalities of today. ✉ *Bruce Embankment* ☎ *01334/460046* ⊕ *www.britishgolfmuseum.co.uk* ✉ *£4* ☉ *Apr.–mid-Oct., daily 9:30–5:30; mid-Oct.–Easter, Thurs.–Mon. 11–3.*

St. Andrews Cathedral is a ruined fragment of what was the largest church in Scotland. Building began in 1160, and the cathedral fell into decay in the 16th century during the Reformation. Near it is St. Rule's tower, all that remains of an earlier, smaller cathedral. It's a stiff climb to the top, but the reward is a superb panoramic view of St. Andrews. The on-site museum helps you interpret the remains. ✉ *Off Pends Rd.* ☎ *01334/472563* ⊕ *www.historic-scotland.gov.uk* ✉ *£2.50, cathe-*

dral and St. Andrews Castle £4 ⊗ *Apr.–Sept., daily 9:30–6:30, last admission 5:45; Oct.–Mar., daily 9:30–4:30, last admission 3:45.*

Construction of **St. Andrews Castle,** once the home of the archbishops of St. Andrews, started at the end of the 13th century. The remains include a rare example of a gruesome bottle dungeon—a windowless, bottle-shape pit. The visitor center has a worthwhile audiovisual presentation on the castle's history. ⊠ *End of N. Castle St.* ☏ *01334/477196* ⊕ *www. historic-scotland.gov.uk* ✉ *£3.00, castle and St. Andrews Cathedral £4* ⊗ *Apr.–Sept., daily 9:30–6:30, last admission 5:45; Oct.–Mar., daily 9:30–4:30, last admission 3:45.*

Where to Stay & Eat

££ ✕ **Balaka.** At this Bangladeshi eatery with crisp white tablecloths and vases of roses, the Rouf family displays its exceptional cookery skills. Popular dishes include *Mas Bangla* (marinated Scottish salmon fried in mustard oil with garlic, spring onion, eggplant, and coriander) and chicken with green herbs, including fresh coriander from the restaurant's 1-acre herb garden. ⊠ *Alexandra Pl.* ☏ *01334/474825* ⊟ *AE, MC, V* ⊗ *No lunch Sun.*

£££££ ✕ ▦ **Rufflets Country House Hotel.** Ten acres of formal and informal gardens surround this luxurious, creeper-covered hotel just outside St. Andrews. Some rooms are modern in style, whereas others lean toward the traditional. The roomy Garden Restaurant (fixed-price menu) is famous for its use of local produce to create memorable dishes such as ravioli of smoked haddock in a tomato compote or pan-fried medallion of Scottish beef fillet spiked with prosciutto, roasted shallots and mushroom in a Madeira jus. ⊠ *Strathkinness Low Rd., KY16 7TX* ☏ *01334/ 472594* ⊟ *01334/478703* ⊕ *www.rufflets.co.uk* ⇦ *24 rooms* ⊘ *Restaurant, some in-room hot tubs, some minibars, cable TV, bar, no-smoking rooms; no a/c* ⊟ *AE, DC, MC, V* ◉⧵ *BP.*

££ ▦ **Aslar Guest House.** This Victorian terraced house stands close to shops, golf courses, and historic attractions such as the castle. All the rooms are large and individually decorated with striped or patterned wallpaper and quality furnishings. Four rooms have a fireplace and one has a four-poster bed. ⊠ *120 North St., KY16 9AF* ☏ *01334/473460* ⊟ *01334/477540* ⊕ *www.aslar.com* ⇦ *6 rooms* ⊘ *Cable TV, Internet; no a/c, no room phones* ⊟ *MC, V* ◉⧵ *BP.*

Sports

The **St. Andrews Links** (⊠ Reservations Department, St. Andrews Links Trust, Pilmour House, St. Andrews, Fife KY16 9SF ☏ 01334/466666 for reservations ⊕ www.standrews.org.uk) has six superb seaside courses, all of which welcome visitors and keep waiting lists as needed. The Old Course, New Course, Jubilee, Eden, and Strathtyrum have 18 holes; the Balgove Course has 9 holes. Greens fees range from £75 to £110 for a round on the Old Course and from £7 to £55 for a round on the other courses.

GLASGOW

▶ In 1727 Daniel Defoe, author of *Robinson Crusoe,* described Glasgow as the "cleanest and beautifullest and best-built of cities," but by 1980, many would not have recognized Scotland's largest city from that description. Stretching along both banks of the River Clyde, Glasgow was known as a depressed industrial city, and in the mid-20th century, its dockland and riverside slums were infamous. Since then Glasgow has undergone an urban renaissance: trendy downtown stores, a booming cultural life, stylish restaurants, and above all, a general air of confidence, have given grace and élan to Scotland's most exciting city and its major business destination. If Edinburgh is proud, age-of-elegance, and reserved, Glasgow is aggressive, industrial-revolution, and exuberant.

The city's development over the past two centuries has been unashamedly commercial, tied up with the wealth of its manufacturers and merchants, who constructed a vast number of civic buildings in the 19th century. Many of these have been preserved, and Glasgow claims, with some justification, to be Britain's greatest Victorian city. Among those who helped shape Glasgow's unique cityscape was the local-born architect Alexander "Greek" Thomson (1817–75). But Glasgow, always at the forefront of change, has, side by side with the overly Victorian, an architectural vision of the future in the work of Charles Rennie Mackintosh (1868–1928). The amazing Glasgow School of Art, the Willow Tearoom, and the churches and school buildings he designed for Glasgow point clearly to the clarity and simplicity of the best of 20th-century design. (You can purchase a Mackintosh Trail Ticket that admits you to many sites and includes transportation.) Glasgow is 44 mi west of Edinburgh; the journey takes an hour by car on the fast M8/A8 road, or 50 minutes by train.

Medieval Glasgow & the Merchant City

Alongside the relatively few surviving medieval buildings in this central part of the city are some of the best examples of the architectural confidence and exuberance that so characterized the burgeoning Glasgow of the late 19th century. Today this area is experiencing a renaissance.

a good walk

George Square ㉙ ▶, the center of Glasgow's business district, is the natural starting point for any walking tour. It's convenient to the Buchanan Street bus and underground stations and parking lot, as well as the two main railway stations, Queen Street and Glasgow Central. After viewing the **City Chambers** ㉚ on the east side of the square, leave George Square by the northeast corner and head eastward along George Street. Turn left at High Street, the spine of the downtown area before Glasgow expanded westward in the 18th century; then go up the hill to **Glasgow Cathedral** ㉛ and the **St. Mungo Museum of Religious Life and Art** ㉜. Opposite the cathedral, across Castle Street, is **Provand's Lordship** ㉝, Glasgow's oldest house. Retrace your steps down Castle Street and High Street, continuing on to reach the Tolbooth Steeple at **Glasgow Cross** ㉞. Continue southeast along London Road (under the bridge) about a quarter of a mile and you are at the Barras (barrows, or pushcarts), Scotland's largest and most colorful market (weekends only). Turn down Greendyke Street from London Road to reach Glasgow Green, Glasgow's oldest park, by the River Clyde, with the **People's Palace** ㉟ museum of social history as its centerpiece.

Take the walkway west through the Green to the towering McLennan Arch, then proceed via Saltmarket northward to Glasgow Cross. Continue westward along Trongate, where the powerful "tobacco lords" who traded with the Americas presided, then turn right into Hutcheson Street. This is Glasgow's Merchant City, with many handsome restored Georgian and Victorian buildings. At the end of the street, just south of George Square, look for **Hutchesons' Hall** ㊱, a visitor center and shop for the National Trust for Scotland. Turn west onto Ingram Street and left down Glassford Street to see the Trades House on the right, which has a facade built in 1791 to designs by Robert Adam. Turn right along Wilson Street to reach Virginia Street. Walk northward up Virginia Street back to Ingram Street. To the left is a view down to the elegant Royal Exchange Square and the former Royal Exchange building. Once a meeting place for merchants and traders, it is now the **Glasgow Gallery of Modern Art** ㊲. Royal Exchange Square leads, for pedestrians, westward to the pedestrian-zone shopping area of Buchanan Street. To the west of Buchanan Street is **The Lighthouse** ㊳, dedicated to the work of Charles Rennie Mackintosh. From Buchanan Street continue north across St. Vincent Street to reach Nelson Mandela Place. Here is the Scottish Stock Exchange, worthwhile for its ornate French Venetian–style exterior alone. Buchanan Galleries, a shopping mall, dominates the top of Buchanan Street beside the Glasgow Royal Concert Hall and Sauchiehall Street junction, anchored by a branch of John Lewis department store. For an art-filled finale, a short walk along Sauchiehall Street brings you to the **Willow Tearoom** ㊴, an art nouveau gem designed by Mackintosh; then head west one block to Renfrew Street to see Mackintosh's masterpiece, the **Glasgow School of Art** ㊵. A stop at the **Tenement House** ㊶, a few blocks to the north of Scott Street, shows the simpler side of city life.

TIMING   This walk can be accomplished comfortably in a day, which will allow time to browse in Glasgow Cathedral, the People's Palace, and the Glasgow Gallery of Modern Art. Aim to start after the end of the morning rush hour, say at 10, and to finish before the evening rush starts, at about 4. The Mackintosh sites—the Willow Tearoom and the Glasgow School of Art—are a coda to this walk. The Willow Tearoom closes at 4:30 PM, and the City Chambers is open only on weekdays.

What to See

★ ㉚ **City Chambers.** Dominating the east side of George Square, the home of the city government is a splendidly exuberant expression of Victorian confidence. Among the outstanding features of the late-19th-century interior are the vaulted ceiling of the entrance hall, the magnificent banqueting hall, the marble and alabaster staircases, and the Venetian mosaics. ✉ *George Sq., City Center* ☏ *0141/287–2000* ⊕ *www.glasgow. gov.uk* ⊙ *Weekdays 9–4:30; free guided tours weekdays at 10:30 and 2:30; may close for occasional civic functions.*

KEY

i Tourist information

▲ Start of walk

Glasgow

Medieval Glasgow & the Merchant City

City Chambers **30**
George Square **29**
Glasgow Cathedral ...**31**
Glasgow Cross **34**

Glasgow Gallery of Modern Art **37**
Glasgow School of Art **40**
Hutchesons' Hall **36**
The Lighthouse **38**
People's Palace **35**

Provand's Lordship ...**33**
St. Mungo Museum of Religious Life and Art ..**32**
Tenement House **41**
Willow Tearoom **39**

The West End
Hunterian Art Gallery **45**
Hunterian Museum ...**44**
Kelvingrove Park **42**
Museum of Transport **43**

0 330 yards
0 300 meters

► **㉙ George Square.** This is the focal point of Glasgow's business district; the area just south of the square is termed the Merchant City. An impressive collection of statues of worthies such as Queen Victoria and Sir Walter Scott fills the square. On the east side of the square stands the magnificent Italian Renaissance–style **City Chambers,** and the handsome **Merchants' House** of 1874 fills the northwest corner.

㉛ Glasgow Cathedral. On a site sacred since St. Mungo (later known as St. Kentigern) founded a church here in the 6th century, the cathedral is an unusual double church, one above the other. The lower church contains the splendid crypt of St. Mungo. ⊠ *Cathedral St., City Center* ☎ *0141/ 552–6891* ⊕ *www.glasgowcathedral.org.uk* ☞ *Free* ⊙ *Apr.–Sept., Mon.–Sat. 9:30–6, Sun. 1–5; Oct.–Mar., Mon.–Sat. 9:30–4, Sun. 1–4 and for services.*

㉞ Glasgow Cross. This was the historic commercial center of the medieval city. The market cross, topped by a unicorn, marks the spot where merchants met, where the market was held, and where criminals were executed. Here, too, was the *tron,* or weigh beam, installed in 1491 and used to check merchants' weights. The Tolbooth Steeple dates from 1626 and served as the civic center and place where travelers entering the city paid their tolls. ⊠ *Intersection of Saltmarket, Trongate, Gallowgate, and London Rd., City Center.*

> **need a break?** **Café Cossachok** (⊠ 10 King St., Glasgow Cross ☎ 0141/553– 0733), a colorful Russian café, serves excellent borscht and about 25 kinds of heartwarming vodka. The deep-red walls are peppered with artworks, and the low buzz of conversation keeps the place lively.

㉟ Glasgow Gallery of Modern Art. One of the city's boldest museums occupies the neoclassical Royal Exchange of 1827, originally a tobacco merchant's mansion. The modern art, craft, and design collections include Scottish figurative art, works by Scottish artists such as Peter Howson and John Bellany, and paintings and sculpture from elsewhere in the world, including Papua New Guinea, Ethiopia, and Mexico. The display scheme for each floor reflects the elements of air, fire, and water. ⊠ *Queen St., Merchant City* ☎ *0141/229–1996* ⊕ *www. glasgowmuseums.com* ☞ *Free* ⊙ *Mon.–Wed. and Sat. 10–5, Thurs. 10–8, Fri. and Sun. 11–5.*

★ **㊵ Glasgow School of Art.** Charles Rennie Mackintosh's masterpiece, this noted monument of 20th-century architecture and decorative arts was built between 1897 and 1909. The exterior and interior, structure, furnishings, and decoration form a unified whole, reflecting the genius of Mackintosh, who was 28 years old when he won the competition for its design. Because it's a working school of art, general access is sometimes limited. Guided tours are available; it's best to make reservations. A shop sells Mackintosh gifts (prints, postcards, and books) and contemporary art by students and alumni. ⊠ *167 Renfrew St., City Center* ☎ *0141/353–4526* ⊕ *www.gsa.ac.uk* ☞ *£5* ⊙ *Tours weekdays at 11 and 2, Sat. at 10:30 and 11:30.*

off the beaten path

GLASGOW SCIENCE CENTRE – This family attraction, on the former Glasgow Garden Festival site, consists of an IMAX theater, a fun-packed Science Mall, and the Glasgow Tower, an observation point closed because of structural problems. The Science Mall focuses its state-of-the-art displays on exploration, discovery, and the environment. Leave plenty of time to make the most of it. ⊠ *50 Pacific Quay, South Side* ☎ *0141/420–5000* ⊕ *www.gsc.org.uk* ▣ *IMAX films £5.95, Science Mall £6.95, both £9.95* ⊘ *Daily 10–6.*

36 **Hutchesons' Hall.** Now a visitor center and shop for the National Trust for Scotland, this elegant neoclassical building was designed by David Hamilton in 1802. It was originally a hospice founded by brothers George and Thomas Hutcheson. You can see their statues in niches in the facade. ⊠ *158 Ingram St., Merchant City* ☎ *0141/552–8391* ⊕ *www.nts.org.uk* ▣ *£2* ⊘ *Mon.–Sat. 10–5 (hall may be closed for occasional functions).*

38 **The Lighthouse.** This former newspaper office, designed by Charles Rennie Mackintosh, is Scotland's showcase for design and architecture. It houses the Mackintosh Interpretation Centre, focusing on some of the Glasgow-born designer's most important local buildings. ⊠ *11 Mitchell La., City Center* ☎ *0141/225–8414* ⊕ *www.thelighthouse.co.uk* ▣ *Interpretation Centre £3, changing exhibitions £1* ⊘ *Mon. and Wed.–Sat. 10:30–5, Tues. 11–5, Sun. noon–5.*

★ **35** **People's Palace.** An impressive Victorian red sandstone building houses an intriguing museum dedicated to the city's social history. Included among the exhibits is one devoted to the ordinary folk of Glasgow, called the People's Story. Behind the museum, the relatively sheltered Winter Gardens are favored by those who want to escape the often chilly winds whistling across the green. ⊠ *Glasgow Green, Glasgow Cross* ☎ *0141/554–0223* ⊕ *www.glasgowmuseums.com* ▣ *Free* ⊘ *Mon.–Thurs. and Sat. 10–5, Fri. and Sun. 11–5.*

33 **Provand's Lordship.** The oldest building in Glasgow is a 15th-century town house, built as a residence for churchmen. Mary, Queen of Scots is said to have stayed here. ⊠ *3 Castle St., City Center* ☎ *0141/552–8819* ⊕ *www.glasgowmuseums.com* ▣ *Free* ⊘ *Mon.–Thurs. and Sat. 10–5, Fri. and Sun. 11–5.*

off the beaten path

QUEEN'S CROSS CHURCH – To learn more about the innovative Glasgow-born designer Mackintosh, head for the Charles Rennie Mackintosh Society Headquarters, in a church designed by him. Although one of the leading lights in the art nouveau movement, Mackintosh died relatively unknown in 1928. You can view the church and gain further insight into Glasgow's other Mackintosh-designed buildings, which include Scotland Street School (on the South Side), the Glasgow School of Art, and reconstructed interiors in the Hunterian Art Gallery. A cab can get you here, or a bus heading toward Queen's Cross can be taken from stops along Hope Street. ⊠ *870 Garscube Rd., West End* ☎ *0141/946–6600* ▣ *£2* ⊘ *Weekdays 10.30–4.30, Sun. 2–5.*

32 **St. Mungo Museum of Religious Life and Art.** An outstanding collection of artifacts, including Celtic crosses and statuettes of Hindu gods, reflects the many religious groups that have settled throughout the centuries in Glasgow and the west of Scotland. The centerpiece is Salvador Dalí's magnificent painting *Christ of St. John of the Cross.* ✉ *2 Castle St., City Center* ☎ *0141/553–2557* ⊕ *www.glasgowmuseums.com* 💰 *Free* ⊘ *Mon.–Thurs. and Sat. 10–5, Fri. and Sun. 11–5.*

41 **Tenement House.** This ordinary, simple city-center apartment was occupied from 1911 to 1965 by Agnes Toward, who seems never to have thrown anything away. Her legacy is a fascinating time capsule, painstakingly preserved with her everyday furniture and belongings. The red-sandstone tenement building itself dates from 1892. ✉ *145 Buccleuch St., City Center* ☎ *0141/333–0183* ⊕ *www.nts.org.uk* 💰 *£3.50* ⊘ *Mar.–Oct., daily 2–5, last admission 4:30.*

39 **Willow Tearoom.** Now restored to its original art deco design by Mackintosh, this tearoom is a lovely place for a break. As you sip a cup of Earl Grey, drink in all of the marvelous details, right down to the decorated tables and chairs. The tree motifs reflect the street address, as *sauchie* is an old Scots word for "willow." A block away is Mackintosh's masterpiece, the Glasgow School of Art. ✉ *217 Sauchiehall St., City Center* ☎ *0141/332–0521* ⊘ *Mon.–Sat. 9–4:30, Sun. noon–3.30.*

The West End

Glasgow's West End has a stellar mix of education, culture, art, and parkland. The neighborhood is dominated by the University of Glasgow, founded in 1451, making it the third-oldest university in Scotland after St. Andrews and Aberdeen, and at least 130 years ahead of the University of Edinburgh. It has thrived as a center of educational excellence, particularly in the sciences. The university buildings are set in parkland, reminding you that Glasgow has more green space per citizen than any other city in Europe.

a good walk

Start in leafy **Kelvingrove Park** ㊷ ⌐, west of the M8 beltway, at the junction of Sauchiehall (pronounced *socky*-hall) and Argyle streets. The Glasgow Art Gallery and Museum here is closed for refurbishment until 2006, but the impressive red-sandstone building and its leafy surroundings still merit a visit. There are free parking facilities, and plenty of buses go to the park from downtown. Across Argyle Street next to the Kelvin Hall sports arena is the **Museum of Transport** ㊸. As you walk up tree-lined Kelvin Way, the skyline to your left is dominated by the Gilbert Scott building, the University of Glasgow's main edifice. Turn left up University Avenue. On each side of the road is an important gallery maintained by the university. On the south side of University Avenue, in the Victorian part of the university, is the **Hunterian Museum** ㊹. Even more interesting is the **Hunterian Art Gallery** ㊺, in an unremarkable 1970s building across the road.

TIMING 　The distance involved is not great, but a day might not be long enough for this walk, if you want to visit the park and all three museums.

What to See

★ **45** **Hunterian Art Gallery.** Part of the University of Glasgow, this museum contains 18th-century Glasgow doctor William Hunter's collection of paintings (his antiquarian collection is in the Hunterian Museum nearby), together with an outstanding collection of prints and drawings by Sir Joshua Reynolds, Auguste Rodin, Rembrandt, and Jacopo Robusti Tintoretto, and a major collection of paintings by James McNeill Whistler. Also in the gallery is a reproduction of Charles Rennie Mackintosh's town house (closed 12:30–1:30), which originally stood nearby. ☒ *Hillhead St., West End* ☎ *0141/330–5431* ⊕ *www.hunterian.gla.ac.uk* ☒ *Free* ⊙ *Mon.–Sat. 9:30–5.*

44 **Hunterian Museum.** The city's oldest museum (1807) and part of the University of Glasgow, the Hunterian contains part of the collections of William Hunter, an 18th-century Glasgow doctor who assembled a staggering quantity of extremely valuable material. (The doctor's art treasures are housed in the Hunterian Art Gallery nearby.) The museum displays Hunter's hoards of coins, manuscripts, scientific instruments, and archaeological artifacts in a striking Gothic building. ☒ *Off University Ave., West End* ☎ *0141/330–4221* ⊕ *www.hunterian.gla.ac.uk* ☒ *Free* ⊙ *Mon.–Sat. 9:30–5.*

▶ **42** **Kelvingrove Park.** A peaceful retreat, the park takes its name from the River Kelvin, which flows through it. A castlelike red-sandstone edifice here contains the Glasgow Art Gallery and Museum, closed for renovation until 2006; the McLellan Galleries in Sauchiehall Street in the City Center and the Burrell Collection on the South Side are exhibiting some of the gallery's artwork. Among the statues of prominent Glaswegians is one of Lord Kelvin (1824–1907), the Scottish mathematician and physicist who pioneered a great deal of work in electricity. The park also has a massive fountain, a duck pond, a play area, an open-air theater, and many exotic trees. ☒ *Northwest of city center, bounded roughly by Sauchiehall St., Woodlands Rd., and Kelvin Way, West End.*

McLellan Galleries. This museum displays a superior collection of 16th- and 17th-century paintings by Dutch and Italian masters, as well as contemporary work by both Scottish and international artists, such as David Hockney and David Mach. The galleries also house a portion of the Glasgow Art Gallery and Museum's collection—including paintings by Rembrandt, Monet, and van Gogh—while the museum is closed for renovation. ☒ *270 Sauchiehall St., City Center* ☎ *0141/565–4137* ⊕ *www.glasgowmuseums.com* ☒ *Free* ⊙ *Mon.–Thurs. and Sat. 10–5, Fri. and Sun. 11–5.*

★ **43** **Museum of Transport.** Here Glasgow's history of locomotive-building is dramatically displayed with full-size exhibits. The collection of Clyde-built ship models is world famous. Wallow in nostalgia at the re-created street scene from 1938, and study the many handsome Scottish automobiles, spanning the 20th century. ☒ *Kelvin Hall, 1 Bunhouse Rd., West End* ☎ *0141/287–2720* ⊕ *www.glasgowmuseums.com* ☒ *Free* ⊙ *Mon.–Thurs. and Sat. 10–5, Fri. and Sun. 11–5.*

off the
beaten
path

POLLOK PARK – A peaceful green oasis off Paisley Road, 3 mi southwest of the city center, this park includes two noted sights: the Burrell Collection, one of Scotland's finest art collections, and historic Pollok House. You can get there by taxi or car, by city bus, or by a train from Glasgow Central Station to Pollokshaws West Station.

The artistic treasures of the **Burrell Collection** (✉ 2060 Pollokshaws Rd., South Side ☎ 0141/287–2550 ⊕ www.glasgowmuseums.com ☑ Free ☉ Mon.–Thurs. and Sat. 10–5, Fri. and Sun. 11–5) are displayed in a modern, glass-wall building so that the holdings relate to their surroundings: art and nature in perfect harmony. Inside are Chinese ceramics, bronzes, and jade as well as medieval tapestries, stained glass, and 19th-century French paintings—the magpie collection of an eccentric millionaire, Sir William Burrell. The Burrell is also hosting works from the Glasgow Art Gallery and Museum while the latter is closed for renovations.

Dating from the mid-1700s, **Pollok House** (✉ Pollokshaws Rd., South Side ☎ 0141/616–6410 ⊕ www.nts.org.uk ☑ £5 Apr.–Oct., free Nov.–Mar. ☉ Daily 10–5) contains the Stirling Maxwell Collection of paintings, including works by El Greco, Murillo, Goya, Signorelli, and William Blake. Fine 18th- and early-19th-century furniture, silver, glass, and porcelain are also on display.

Where to Eat

Glasgow has been described as a "café society," which you can't get to know properly unless you spend time drinking coffee in as many cafés as possible. The city also has a sophisticated professional population that appreciates its many excellent restaurants.

££££–£££££
Fodor'sChoice
★
✕ **Rogano.** The striking black-and-gold art deco design of this restaurant is enough to recommend it. The bonus is that the food at the ground-floor main restaurant, at the lively Café Rogano, and in the oyster bar near the entrance is excellent. Specialties include seared scallops with elderflower dressing and loin of venison with a blackcurrant and liquorice jus. Café Rogano (£–££) is cheaper and more informal than the main restaurant. ✉ *11 Exchange Pl., City Center* ☎ *0141/248–4055* ▭ *AE, DC, MC, V.*

★ **£££–££££**
✕ **Yes.** This stylish restaurant belies its basement location with soigné lighting, grand mirrors, and piano accompaniment. Contemporary Scottish cuisine is the specialty, and the fresh fruit sushi is exquisite. Try the Surprise Menu, an eclectic four-course selection made with the day's fresh produce. The ground-floor café-bar serves Mediterranean-Italian specialties in flashy digs. ✉ *22 W. Nile St., City Center* ☎ *0141/221–8044* ▭ *AE, DC, MC, V ☉ Closed Sun.*

££–£££
✕ **Gordon Yuill and Company.** Bright, modern surroundings reinforce this busy restaurant's fresh approach to dishes based on the best of Scottish produce. You might try the excellent seafood options, such as a steamed mussels with lemongrass starter, or honey-glazed shank of lamb with

cinnamon and candied red cabbage. Imaginative Asian-influenced vegetarian dishes round out the less expensive choices. ⊠ *257 W. Campbell St., City Center* ☎ *0141/572–4052* ⌂ *Reservations essential* ⊟ *AE, DC, MC, V.*

££–£££ ✕ **Stravaigin.** One of a new breed of gastropubs, Stravaigin offers the liveliness of a Glasgow pub but with adventurous food and superior service. Scottish stalwarts, such as salmon and haggis, are given an international makeover. ⊠ *28 Gibson St., West End* ☎ *0141/334–2665* ⊟ *AE, DC, MC, V.*

£–£££ ✕ **Mussel Inn.** Shellfish farmers own this restaurant and feed their customers incredibly fresh, succulent oysters, scallops, and mussels. The kilo pots of mussels, beautifully steamed to order in any of a number of sauces, are revelatory. The surroundings and staff are unpretentious yet stylish. ⊠ *57 Hope St., City Center* ☎ *0141/572–1405* ⊟ *AE, MC, V* ⊗ *No lunch Sun.*

Where to Stay

££££–£££££ ▦ **One Devonshire Gardens.** A group of Victorian town houses on a sloping, tree-lined street make up this luxurious boutique hotel. Elegance is the keynote, from the sophisticated drawing room to the sumptuous guest rooms with their rich drapery and traditional furnishings, including four-poster beds (in 10 rooms). The hotel restaurant is equally stylish, with a different menu each month. Specialties include seared scallops with pink grapefruit salad and fillet of sole with chervil gnocchi. ⊠ *1–5 Devonshire Gardens, West End, G12 0UX* ☎ *0141/339–2001* ⎙ *0141/337–1663* ⊕ *www.onedevonshiregardens.com* ⇌ *40 rooms* ⌂ *Restaurant, room service, cable TV, lounge, meeting room, free parking; no a/c* ⊟ *AE, DC, MC, V* ⫶⊘⫶ *BP.*

★ **£££–££££** ▦ **Langs.** This hotel's sophisticated, ultramodern character fits perfectly with its proximity to the Glasgow Royal Concert Hall and the Buchanan Galleries shopping mall. The Japanese minimalist look extends from the wooden reception bar to the platform beds in the bright bedrooms. Mediterranean cuisine is the specialty of the Las Brisas restaurant, and Oshi serves excellent Japanese three-course pre- and post-theater menus for around £10. Japanese body treatments are available in the Oshi Spa. ⊠ *2 Port Dundas St., City Center, G2 3LD* ☎ *0141/333–1500* ⎙ *0141/333–5700* ⊕ *www.langshotels.co.uk* ⇌ *70 rooms, 30 suites* ⌂ *2 restaurants, cable TV, gym, spa, bar, meeting room, parking (fee); no a/c* ⊟ *AE, DC, MC, V* ⫶⊘⫶ *CP.*

★ **£££–££££** ▦ **Radisson SAS.** You can't miss this eye-catching edifice behind Central Station in Glasgow's up-and-coming financial quarter. Its glass front makes the interior, particularly the lounge, seem as though it were part of the street. Your room might be in Italian, Scandinavian, or Japanese style. Both restaurants—the pop art–inspired Collage, serving Continental cuisine, and Tapaell'Ya, the tapas bar—are popular with business and artist types, as is the sleek street-level bar. ⊠ *301 Argyle St., City Center, G2 8DL* ☎ *0141/203–3333* ⎙ *0141/204–3344* ⊕ *www.radissonsas.com* ⇌ *200 rooms, 4 suites* ⌂ *2 restaurants, minibars, cable TV, indoor pool, gym, bar, business services, parking (fee)* ⊟ *AE, DC, V* ⫶⊘⫶ *CP.*

££ ⊠ **Ambassador Hotel.** Opposite the West End's peaceful Botanic Gardens
Fodor'sChoice   and convenient for cab, bus, and underground travel to the city center,
★   the Ambassador forms part of an elegant terrace of town houses on the
banks of the River Kelvin. The interior echoes the peacefulness of the
location and the Victorian ethos of the spacious former family home.
Though largely traditional, the rooms have a contemporary edge, with
rich red-and-gold fabrics and beech furniture. ⊠ *7 Kelvin Dr., West End,
G20 8QG* ☎ *0141/946–1018* 🖷 *0141/945–5377* ⊕ *www.
glasgowhotelsandapartments.co.uk* 🛏 *17 rooms* ♿ *Bar, free parking,
no-smoking rooms; no a/c* ☰ *MC, V* ⏐⊙⏐ *BP.*

££ ⊠ **Kirklee Hotel.** Near the university and in the West End—a particularly quiet, leafy, and genteel district—this B&B in a cozy Edwardian
town house is replete with home-away-from-home comfort. A bay window overlooks the garden, and embroidered settees and silk-wash wallpaper adorn the Victorian morning room. Engravings and a large library
are appealing touches. ⊠ *11 Kensington Gate, West End, G12 9LG*
☎ *0141/334–5555* 🖷 *0141/339–3828* 📧 *kirklee@clara.net* 🛏 *9 rooms*
♿ *Library; no a/c* ☰ *AE, DC, MC, V* ⏐⊙⏐ *BP.*

£ ⊠ **Travel Inn Metro.** This may be part of a chain of budget hotels, but the
bright, metropolitan design and low prices appeal to savvy visitors. The
rooms are larger than most in the city, with up-to-date bathrooms and
coffeemakers. Rooms facing the street can be noisy at night, so ask for
one that overlooks the graveyard, where noisemakers are unlikely to be
found. ⊠ *187 George St., Merchant City, G1 1YU* ☎ *0870/238–3320*
🖷 *0141/553–2719* ⊕ *www.travelinn.co.uk* 🛏 *239 rooms* ♿ *Restaurant,
bar, parking (fee), no-smoking rooms; no a/c* ☰ *AE, MC, V.*

Nightlife & the Arts

Nightlife

If you visit only one pub in Glasgow, make it the **Horseshoe Bar** (⊠ 17–21
Drury St., City Center ☎ 0141/229–5711), which offers a sepia-tinted
glimpse of all the friendlier Glasgow myths. Refurbishment would be a
curse on its original tiling, stained glass, and deeply polished woodwork.
The clientele is a complete cross section of the city's populace. The best
★   Gaelic pub is **Uisge Beatha** (⊠ 232–246 Woodlands Rd., West End
☎ 0141/564–1596), pronounced *oos*-ki *bee*-ha, which means "water
of life" and is the origin of the word *whisky* (the term is a phonetic translit-
eration of the Gaelic word *uisge*). It serves *fraoch* (heather beer) in season and has live music on Wednesday and Sunday.

The Arts

Tickets for theatrical performances can be purchased at theater box offices or by telephone through the **Ticket Center** (☎ 0141/287–5511). **Citizens' Theatre** (⊠ 119 Gorbals St., South Side ☎ 0141/429–0022), one
of the most exciting theaters in Britain, stages productions of often
hair-raising originality. **Cottier's Arts Theatre** (⊠ 93 Hyndland St., West
End ☎ 0141/357–3868) presents contemporary works in a converted
church. The **King's Theatre** (⊠ Bath St., City Center ☎ 0141/240–1111)
focuses on light entertainment and musicals.

Glasgow Royal Concert Hall (✉ 2 Sauchiehall St., City Center ☎ 0141/ 353–8000) offers a calendar of classical concerts, pop concerts, jazz, and many international musical events. The Royal Scottish National Orchestra plays on many Thursdays and Saturdays throughout the year. The **Theatre Royal** (✉ Hope St., City Center ☎ 0141/332–9000) is the elegant home of Scottish Opera and Scottish Ballet. Both companies have developed a huge following and an international reputation for flamboyance and quality.

Held in January, **Celtic Connections** (☎ 0141/353–8000 ⊕ www. celticconnections.co.uk) is Scotland's biggest Celtic music festival.

Shopping

Glasgow, preferred by many to Edinburgh as a shopping center, supplies a lot more shopping fun than its staid rival. The main shopping districts occupy a Z-shape area that runs along Sauchiehall Street from Charing Cross to the Glasgow Royal Concert Hall and Buchanan Galleries, south down Buchanan Street to St. Enoch's Square, and east along Argyle Street. Many designer boutiques and shopping malls, complete with fountains and glass-wall elevators, can be found on Buchanan Street and along adjacent streets.

The **Argyll Arcade** (✉ Buchanan and Argyle Sts., City Center) is a handsome 19th-century shopping mall with a wide selection of jewelry shops (don't miss the mosaics over the Buchanan Street entrance). The **Buchanan Galleries mall** (✉ 220 Buchanan St., City Center ☎ 0141/333–9898) has major names such as John Lewis, Nike, and Virgin. **De Courcys** (✉ 5–21 Cresswell La., West End), an antiques and crafts arcade, has quite a few shops to visit, and lots of goods, including paintings and jewelry, are regularly auctioned here. It's on one of the cobblestone lanes to the rear of Byres Road.

Princes Square (✉ 48 Buchanan St., City Center ☎ 0141/204–1685) is a chic modern mall, with specialty shops on three levels and a café complex above, all under a glittering dome. Many top fashion names can be found here; visit the Scottish Craft Centre for unusual, high-quality items. **Borders Books, Music and Café** (✉ 98 Buchanan St., City Center ☎ 0141/222–7700), in a former bank, is particularly welcoming and carries many Scottish books. **MacDonald MacKay Ltd** (✉ 161 Hope St., City Center ☎ 0141/204–3930) makes, sells, and exports Highland dress, including kilts, and accessories for men and custom-made kilts and skirts for women. **Stockwell Bazaar** (✉ 67–77 Glassford St., Merchant City ☎ 0141/552–5781) specializes in fine china and giftware.

The **Barras,** Glasgow's weekend market, is just north of Glasgow Green and sells just about anything, in any condition, from very old model railroads to quality jewelry at bargain prices. Haggling is compulsory. Antiques-hunters might make a find, but don't be surprised if you come away empty-handed. ✉ *London Rd., Glasgow Cross* ☎ *0141/552– 4601* ☉ *Weekends 10–5.*

THE BORDERS
SIR WALTER SCOTT COUNTRY

The Borders region is the heartland of minstrelsy, ballad, and folklore, much of it arising from murky deeds of the past. This is the homeland of the tweed suit and cashmere sweater, of medieval abbeys, of the lordly River Tweed and its salmon, and of the descendants of the raiders and reivers (cattle thieves) who harried England. It's also the native soil of Sir Walter Scott, the early-19th-century poet, novelist, and creator of *Ivanhoe,* who helped transform Scotland's image from that of a land of brutal savages to one of romantic and stirring deeds and magnificent landscapes. One of the best ways to approach this district is to take as the theme of your visit the life and works of Scott. His novels are not read much nowadays, but the mystique that he created, the aura of historical romance, has outlasted his books and is much in evidence in the ruined abbeys, historical houses, and grand vistas of the Borders.

Abbotsford House

★ ㊻ *28 mi southeast of Edinburgh.*

The most visited of Scottish literary landmarks, Abbotsford House is the mansion that Sir Walter Scott made his home in the 1820s. It was a damp farmhouse called Cartleyhole when the novelist bought it in 1811 (the locals had nicknamed the spot *clarty* hole, *clarty* being an expressive Scots word meaning "muddy" or "dirty"), but soon it was transformed into what John Ruskin called "the most incongruous pile that gentlemanly modernism ever devised." The pseudo-baronial, pseudo-monastic castle is chock-full of Scottish curios, Ramsay portraits, and mounted deer heads, and seems an appropriate domicile for a man of such an extraordinarily romantic imagination. To Abbotsford came most of the famous poets and thinkers of Scott's day, including William Wordsworth and Washington Irving. Abbotsford is still owned by Scott's descendants. ⊠ *B6360, Galashiels* ☎ *01896/752043* ☎ *£4.20* ☉ *June–Sept., daily 9:30–5; Mar.–May and Oct., Mon.–Sat. 9:30–5, Sun. 2–5.*

Melrose

㊼ *3 mi east of Abbotsford, 30 mi south of Edinburgh.*

Melrose is small but bustling, the perfect example of a prosperous Scottish market town, set around a square lined with 18th- and 19th-century buildings. Just off the square are the ruins of the most famous of the great Borders abbeys. All the abbeys were burned in the 1540s in a calculated act of destruction by English invaders acting on the orders of Henry VIII. Sir Walter Scott supervised the partial reconstruction of
★ **Melrose Abbey,** one of the most beautiful ruins in Britain. "If thou would'st view fair Melrose aright/Go visit it in the pale moonlight," says Scott in his "Lay of the Last Minstrel," and so many of his fans took the advice literally that a sleepless custodian begged him to rewrite the lines. Today the abbey is still impressive: a red-sandstone shell with slen-

der windows in the Perpendicular Gothic style and some delicate tracery and carved capitals, carefully maintained. Among the carvings high on the roof is one of a bagpipe-playing pig. An audio tour is included in the admission price. ⊠ *Abbey St.* ☎ *01896/822562* ⊕ *www.historic-scotland.gov.uk* ⊠ *£3.50* ⊗ *Apr.–Sept., daily 9:30–6:30; Oct.–Mar., Mon.–Sat. 9:30–4:30, Sun. 2–4:30.*

The **Three Hills Roman Heritage Centre** displays artifacts from the largest Roman settlement in Scotland, which was at nearby Newstead. Tools and weapons, a blacksmith's shop, pottery, and scale models of the fort are on display. A guided 5-mi, four-hour walk to the site from Melrose takes place each Thursday afternoon from April to October (also on Tuesday in July and August). Phone for details. ⊠ *The Ormiston, Melrose Sq.* ☎ *01896/822651* ⊕ *www.trimontium.net* ⊠ *£1.50, walk £3.00* ⊗ *Apr.–Oct., weekdays 10:30–4:30, weekends 10:30–1 and 2–4:30.*

Where to Stay & Eat

£££ ✕🏨 **Burts Hotel.** This hostelry dating from the early 18th century offers period charm with modern comfort in the center of town. Bedrooms and public areas are individually decorated with reproduction antiques and floral pastels. The elegant dining room (fixed-price menu) focuses on Scottish dishes such as pheasant terrine and venison with a whisky-and-cranberry sauce. Bar food is also offered. ⊠ *Melrose Sq., TD6 9PL* ☎ *01896/822285* 🖷 *01896/822870* ⊕ *www.burtshotel.co.uk* 🛏 *20 rooms* ♨ *Restaurant, cable TV; no a/c* ☰ *AE, MC, V* ◎ *BP.*

Dryburgh Abbey

48 *5 mi southeast of Melrose, 38 mi south of Edinburgh.*

The final resting place of Sir Walter Scott and his wife, and of Field Marshal Douglas Haig, commander-in-chief of the British army during World War I, Dryburgh Abbey is the most secluded of the Borders abbeys, and sits on gentle parkland in a loop of the Tweed. It suffered, like Melrose, from English raids in 1544, and the damage was never repaired. However, the canons (clergy) continued to stay there, the last one dying in 1600, forty years after the Scottish Reformation. The style is transitional, a mingling of rounded Romanesque and pointed Early Gothic. The north transept, where members of the Haig and Scott families are buried, is lofty and pillared, and once formed part of the abbey church. ⊠ *B6404* ☎ *01835/822381* ⊕ *www.historic-scotland.gov.uk* ⊠ *£3* ⊗ *Apr.–Sept., daily 9:30–6:30; Oct.–Mar., Mon.–Sat. 9:30–4:30, Sun. 2–4:30.*

Where to Stay & Eat

£££££ ✕🏨 **Dryburgh Abbey Hotel.** Woodlands and verdant lawns surround this imposing 19th-century mansion, which stands next to the abbey ruins on a bend of the River Tweed. Guest rooms are large and sumptuous, with canopied beds and lace-trimmed curtains, and throughout the hotel is a sense of quiet and peace in keeping with the location. The restaurant specializes in traditional Scottish fare. ⊠ *Off B6404, St. Boswells, TD6 0RQ* ☎ *01835/822261* 🖷 *01835/823945* ⊕ *www.dryburgh.co.uk* 🛏 *36 rooms, 2 suites* ♨ *Restaurant, golf privileges, pool, fishing; no a/c* ☰ *AE, MC, V* ◎ *BP.*

---

en route   Combine a visit to Dryburgh Abbey with a stop at **Scott's View,** 3 mi north on B6356, which provides a magnificent panoramic view of the Tweed Valley and the Eildon Hills. Legend has it that the horses pulling Sir Walter Scott's hearse paused automatically at Scott's View, because Scott had so often halted them there.

Smailholm Tower

49 *5 mi east of St. Boswells, 6 mi west of Kelso.*

This characteristic Borders structure stands uncompromisingly on top of a barren, rocky ridge in the hills. Built solely for defense, the 15th-century peel tower offers memorable views. Sir Walter Scott's grandfather lived nearby, and the young Scott visited the tower often. The tower houses an exhibit of tapestries and costumed dolls relating to Scott's *Minstrelsy of the Scottish Borders.* ⊠ *Off B6404, Smailholm* ☎ *01573/ 460365* ⊕ *www.historic-scotland.gov.uk* ✉ *£2.20* ☉ *Apr.–Sept., daily 9:30–6:30; Oct., Sat.–Wed. 9:30–6:30; Nov.–March., Sat. 9:30–4:30 and Sun. 2:30–4:30.*

Kelso

⑤⓪ *8 mi east of Smailholm Tower, 46 mi southeast of Edinburgh.*

The Tweedside roads through Kelso and Coldstream sweep with the river through parkland and game preserve and past romantic red-stone gorges. Kelso has an unusual Continental air, with fine Georgian and early-Victorian buildings surrounding a spacious, cobbled marketplace. Not much of the once grand medieval Kelso Abbey remains.

Fodor'sChoice
★

On the bank of the River Tweed, just on the outskirts of Kelso, is palatial **Floors Castle,** the largest inhabited house in Scotland and the seat of the duke of Roxburghe. Designed by William Adam in 1721 and altered by William Playfair in the 1840s, Floors is an architectural extravagance bristling with pepper-mill turrets and towers that stand on the "floors" or flat terraces of the Tweed bank opposite the barely visible ruins of Roxburgh Castle. A holly tree in the magnificent deer park marks the place where King James II was killed in 1460 by a cannon that "brak in the shooting." ⊠ *A6089* ☎ *01573/223333* 🖶 *01573/226056* ⊕ *www. floorscastle.com* 💷 *£5.75, grounds only £3* ⊙ *Apr.–Oct., daily 10–4:30; last admission at 4.*

Where to Stay & Eat

££–£££ ✕🖫 **Edenwater House.** A handsome stone house, this antique-filled former manse overlooks the river Eden, 2 mi north of Kelso. Two of the luxurious guest rooms have beautiful views of the river and of the Cheviot Hills. Edenwater serves some of the best food in the Borders: roast saddle of hare with foie gras and fillet of monkfish crusted with basil and coriander in a beurre blanc typify the refined but simple menu. The dining room (£32.50 for a three-course dinner) is open to nonresidents on Friday and Saturday. ⊠ *Off B6461, Ednam, TD5 7QL* ☎ *01573/224070* 🖶 *01573/226615* ⊕ *www.edenwaterhouse.co.uk* 💭 *4 rooms* ⚘ *Restaurant, fishing, lounge, Internet; no a/c, no room phones* ▤ *MC, V* ⊙ *Closed 1st 2 wks of Jan.* ⅋ *BP.*

★ **£££–££££** 🖫 **Ednam House Hotel.** People return again and again to this large, stately hotel on the banks of the Tweed, close to Kelso's grand abbey and old Market Square. The main hall, part of the original 1761 home, welcomes you with deep-seated armchairs, paintings, and an open fire. The restaurant's three windowed walls overlook the garden and river. ⊠ *Bridge St., TD5 7HT* ☎ *01573/224168* 🖶 *01573/226319* ⊕ *www.ednamhouse. co.uk* 💭 *32 rooms* ⚘ *Restaurant, golf privileges, fishing, horseback riding; no a/c* ▤ *MC, V* ⊙ *Closed Christmas–early Jan.* ⅋ *BP.*

Jedburgh

⑤① *12 mi southwest of Kelso on A698, 50 mi south of Edinburgh.*

The town of Jedburgh (*-burgh* is always pronounced *burra* in Scots), 13 mi north of the border, was for centuries the first major Scottish target of invading English armies. The large landscaped area around the town's tourist information center was once a mill but now is a stamping ground for the armies of modern visitors. The past still clings to this little town, however.

★ **Jedburgh Abbey** was nearly destroyed in 1544–45, during the destructive time known as the Rough Wooing. This was English king Henry VIII's armed attempt to persuade the Scots to unite the kingdoms by the marriage of his young son to the infant Mary, Queen of Scots; the Scots sent Mary to France instead. The **Jedburgh Abbey Visitor Centre** has a video, interpretation boards, and displays about the ruins, as well as artifacts found within them. ⊠ *3–5 Abbey Bridgend* ☎ *01835/ 863925* ⊕ *www.historic-scotland.gov.uk* ⊠ *£3.50* ☉ *Apr.–Sept., daily 9:30–6:30; Oct.–Mar., Mon.–Sat. 9:30–4:30, Sun. 2–4:30; last admission 30 mins before closing.*

Mary, Queen of Scots House is a fortified dwelling characteristic of the 16th century; it may be contemporaneous with Mary herself. Though historians disagree on whether or not she actually visited here, the house has many displays commemorating Mary. ⊠ *Queen St.* ☎ *01835/ 863331* ⊠ *£3* ☉ *Easter–mid Nov., Mon.–Sat. 10–4:30, Sun. 11–4:30.*

Jedburgh Castle Jail was a Howard Reform Prison (John Howard was an 18th-century advocate for healthier prisons) established in 1820 on the site of Jedburgh Castle. Today you can inspect prison cells, rooms arranged with period furnishings, and costumed figures. Audiovisual displays recount the history of the Royal Burgh of Jedburgh. ⊠ *Castlegate* ☎ *01835/864750* ⊠ *£1.50* ☉ *Easter–Oct., Mon.–Sat. 10–4:30, Sun. 1–4:30.*

Where to Stay & Eat

★ **£–£££** ✕ **Cross Keys.** A national treasure, this traditional pub specializes in local produce, from fish to game. A splendid array of Scottish beers—real ale, as it is known here—is served. This is the quintessential village inn, right down to the green outside the front door. ⊠ *The Green, Ancrum, 3 mi north of Jedburgh, off A68* ☎ *01835/830344* ⊕ *www.ancrumcrosskeys. co.uk* ▤ *DC, MC, V.*

£–££ ▥ **Hundalee House.** Stunning views across to the English border at Carter Bar, and to the Cheviot Hills to the southeast, add appeal to this lodging. The tastefully furnished B&B is in a 300-year-old house with 14 acres of garden and woodland. Two bedrooms have four-posters. The house is 1 mi south of Jedburgh. ⊠ *Off A68, TD8 6PA* ☎ *01835/ 863011* ⊕ *www.accommodation-scotland.org* ➴ *4 rooms* ⚭ *No a/c, no room phones* ▤ *No credit cards* ☉ *Closed Nov.–Mar.* ⊺◎ *BP.*

£ ▥ **Spinney Guest House.** Made up of unpretentiously converted and modernized farm cottages, this B&B has high standards for the price. The log cabins have kitchenettes. ⊠ *Langlee, TD8 6PB* ☎ *01835/ 863525* 🖷 *01835/864883* ⊕ *www.thespinney-jedburgh.co.uk* ➴ *3 rooms, 3 cabins* ⚭ *Some kitchenettes, lounge; no a/c, no room phones* ▤ *MC, V* ⊺◎ *BP.*

Selkirk

❺❷ *14 mi northwest of Jedburgh, 40 mi south of Edinburgh.*

Selkirk is a hilly outpost with a smattering of antiques shops and an assortment of bakers selling the Selkirk Bannock (fruited sweet bread-cake) and other cakes. Sir Walter Scott was sheriff (judge) of Selkirkshire from

1800 until his death in 1832, and his statue stands in Market Place. To get here from Jedburgh, take A68 7 mi north to the A699 junction, turn left, and follow A699 7 mi through attractive river-valley scenery. **Sir Walter Scott's Courtroom,** where he presided, contains a display examining Scott's life, his writings, and his time as sheriff. ☒ *Market Pl.* ☎ *01750/20096* ☒ *Free* ☉ *Apr.–Sept., Mon.–Fri. 10–4, Sat., 10–2; May–Aug., Sun. 10–2; Oct., Mon.–Sat. 1–4.*

Halliwell's House Museum, tucked off the main square in Selkirk, was once an ironmonger's shop, now re-created downstairs. Upstairs is an art gallery and an exhibition that tells the story of the town. ☒ *Market Pl.* ☎ *01750/20096* ☒ *Free* ☉ *Apr.–Sept., Mon.–Sat. 10–5, Sun. 10–2; Oct., Mon.–Sat. 10–4.*

Innerleithen

53 *15 mi northwest of Selkirk, 29 mi south of Edinburgh.*

Innerleithen, in the pretty Tweed Valley, was once famous as a spa, and is the setting of Sir Walter Scott's novel *St. Ronan's Well.* **Robert Smail's Printing Works** is a fully restored Victorian print shop with its original machinery in working order and a printer in residence. ☒ *7–9 High St.* ☎ *01896/830206* ☒ *£3.50* ☉ *Easter weekend and June–Sept., Thurs.–Mon. noon–5, Sun. 1–5; last admission 45 mins before closing.*

★ **Traquair House** is said to be the oldest continually occupied house (since 1107) in Scotland. Secret stairs, intricate embroidery, more than 3,000 books, a maze, and a bed used by Mary, Queen of Scots, in 1566 are just a few of the discoveries. Ale is still brewed in the 18th-century brew house here, and it's worth a try. The house is 1 mi south of Innerleithen. ☒ *B709, Traquair* ☎ *01896/830323* ⎙ *01896/830639* ⊕ *www.traquair.co.uk* ☒ *£5.75* ☉ *Easter–May, daily 12:30–5; June–Aug., daily 10:30–5:30; Oct., daily 11–4; last admission 30 mins before closing.*

Where to Stay

££££ ⌂ **Traquair House.** Stay in the private quarters at Traquair to experience a slice of Scottish history. The sumptuously decorated rooms are furnished with antiques and chintz-hung canopy beds. In the 18th-century Lower Drawing Room, you can enjoy a glass of the house's own ale before going to dinner. ☒ *B709, Traquair, EH44 6PW* ☎ *01896/830323* ⎙ *01896/830639* ⊕ *www.traquair.co.uk* ⇄ *3 rooms* ♿ *No a/c* ⊟ *MC, V* ⎮❍⎮ *BP.*

Peebles

54 *7 mi west of Traquair on A72, 24 mi south of Edinburgh.*

This pleasant town on the banks of the Tweed lies in lush, green countryside, with hills deeply cleft by gorges and waterfalls. Thanks to its excellent though pricey shopping, the town gives the impression of catering primarily to country gentlefolk. Don't miss the splendid dolphins ornamenting the bridge crossing the River Tweed.

Neidpath Castle, a 15-minute walk upstream along the banks of the Tweed from Peebles, perches above a bend in the river. The castle is a medieval structure remodeled in the 17th century, with dungeons hewn from solid rock. You can return on the opposite riverbank after crossing an old railroad viaduct. ⊠ *Off A72* ☎ *01721/720333* 🖃 *£3* ⊙ *Easter weekend and May–Sept., Wed.–Sat. 10:30–5 (open some holiday weekends Mon.–Tues.), Sun. 12:30–5.*

Where to Stay & Eat

£££–£££££   ×🖻 **Cringletie House.** A Scottish baronial mansion amid 28 acres of gardens and woodland, Cringletie (pronounced "Cringle-tay") has a long tradition of pampering guests with friendly, personalized service. Public areas and guest rooms are done in British country-house style. The first-floor drawing room, with views extending up the Tweed Valley, is particularly restful. Fruit and vegetables from the hotel's kitchen garden accompany refined modern Scottish fare. Afternoon tea in the conservatory is a treat. ⊠ *Edinburgh Rd., off A703, EH45 8PL* ☎ *01721/725750* 🖷 *01721/725751* ⊕ *www.cringletie.com* ➴ *14 rooms* ⚘ *Restaurant, putting green, tennis court, fishing, croquet; no a/c* 🖃 *AE, MC, V* 🍽 *BP.*

ABERDEEN & ROYAL DEESIDE

Aberdeen, Scotland's third-largest city, is the gateway to a rural hinterland with a wealth of castles. Deeside, the valley running west from Aberdeen along which the River Dee flows, earned its "Royal" appellation when Queen Victoria and her consort, Albert, built their Scottish fantasy castle, Balmoral, here. To this day, where royalty goes, lesser aristocracy and millionaires from around the globe follow. Their yearning to possess an estate here is understandable, since birch woodland, purple moor, and blue river intermingle most tastefully.

Aberdeen

▶ 55 *131 mi north of Edinburgh.*

Local granite quarrying produced a durable silver stone that would be used to build the Aberdonian structures of the Victorian era. The granite was used boldly, and downtown Aberdeen remains one of the United Kingdom's most distinctive urban environments, although some would say it depends on the weather. The mica chips embedded in the rock act as a million mirrors in sunshine; in rain and heavy clouds, however, their sparkle is snuffed out.

The North Sea has always been important to Aberdeen: in the 1850s, the city was famed for its fast clippers, sleek sailing ships that raced to India for cargoes of tea. In the late 1960s, the course of Aberdeen's history was unequivocally altered when oil and gas were discovered in the North Sea. Aberdeen at first seemed destined to become a soulless boomtown, but some innate local caution has helped the now-wealthy city to retain a sense of perspective.

Aberdeen
& Royal Deeside

GREAT
BRITAIN

North Sea

KEY

▲ Start of itinerary

Newburgh
Oldmeldrum
Claft
Cabrach
Advie
Glenlivet
Mossat
Kemnay
Dunecht
Bucksburn
Aberdeen **55**
Stonehaven
Laurencekirk
Banchory
Crathes Castle **56**
Castle Fraser **54**
Grampian Transport Museum
Alford **62**
Craigievar Castle **63**
Kildrummy Castle **61**
Glenbuchat Castle
Strathdon
Corgarff Castle **60**
Kincardine O'Neill
Aboyne
Dinnet
The Queen's View
Ballater **57**
Balmoral Castle **58**
Glen Muick
Glen Gelder
Lochnagar
Braedownie
Clova
Spital of Glenshee
Braemar **59**
Inverey
Linn of Dee
Glen Clunie

GRAMPIAN MOUNTAINS

Don
Dee
Avon
Glen Avon
Glen Gairn

Ladder Hills
Howe of Alford

10 miles
15 km

A920
A96
A944
A93
A957
A90
A92
B966
B974
A93
B9119
A980
A97
B9094
A939
A976
A93
B955
A938
A939
A96

★ **Marischal College** was founded in 1593 by the earl Marischal as a Protestant alternative to the Catholic King's College in Old Aberdeen, though the two combined to form Aberdeen University in 1860. The current facade was built in 1891, and this is still the second-largest granite building in the world; only the Escorial in Madrid is larger. The fascinating main galleries of the **Marischal Museum** hold two exhibits: the Encyclopaedia of the North East displays artifacts and photographs relating to the region's heritage; Collecting the World explores what local collectors gathered on their world travels and displays Egyptian and 19th-century ethnographic material. ⊠ *Broad St.* ☎ *01224/274301* ⊕ *www. abdn.ac.uk* 🖃 *Free* ⊙ *Museum weekdays 10–5, Sun. 2–5.*

Provost Skene's House, now a museum portraying civic life, has restored, furnished period rooms and a painted chapel. Steeply gabled and rubble-built, it dates in part from 1545. The house was originally a mayor's domestic dwelling (provost is Scottish for "mayor"). ⊠ *Guestrow off Broad St.* ☎ *01224/641086* ⊕ *www.aagm.co.uk* 🖃 *Free* ⊙ *Mon.–Sat. 10–5, Sun. 1–4.*

Aberdeen Art Gallery houses a diverse collection of paintings, prints and drawings, sculpture, porcelain, costumes, and much else—from 18th-century art to major contemporary works by Lucien Freud and Henry Moore. Local marble has been used in interior walls, pillars, and the central fountain, designed by the acclaimed British sculptor Barbara Hepworth. ⊠ *Schoolhill* ☎ *01224/523700* ⊕ *www.aagm.co.uk* 🖃 *Free* ⊙ *Mon.–Sat. 10–5, Sun. 2–5.*

A library, church, and nearby theater on **Rosemount Viaduct** are collectively known by Aberdonians as Education, Salvation, and Damnation. Silvery and handsome, the **Central Library** and **St. Mark's Church** date from the last decade of the 19th century, and **His Majesty's Theatre** (1904–08) has been restored inside to its full Edwardian splendor.

★ ♔ **Provost Ross's House,** dating from 1593, with a striking modern extension, houses the excellent **Aberdeen Maritime Museum,** which tells the story of the city's involvement with the sea, from early inshore fisheries to tea clippers and the North Sea oil boom. It's a fascinating place for kids, with its ship models, paintings, and equipment associated with the fishing, shipbuilding, and oil and gas industries. ⊠ *Ship Row* ☎ *01224/ 337701* ⊕ *www.aagm.co.uk* 🖃 *Free* ⊙ *Mon.–Sat. 10–5, Sun. noon–3.*

Old Aberdeen, once an independent burgh, is north of the city, near the River Don. Although swallowed up by the expanding metropolis before the end of the 19th century, the area, which lies between **King's College** and **St. Machar's Cathedral,** retains a certain degree of character and integrity. Reach it by taking a bus north from a stop near Marischal College or up King Street, off Castlegate.

King's College (⊠ *High St.* ⊕ *www.abdn.ac.uk*), founded in 1494 and now part of the University of Aberdeen, has an unmistakable flying (or crown) spire to its **chapel,** which was built around 1500. The tall oak screen that separates nave from choir and the ribbed wooden ceiling and stalls constitute the finest medieval wood carvings in Scotland.

At the **King's College Centre** you can find out more about one of Britain's oldest universities. ⊠ *College Bounds* ☎ *01224/273702* ⊕ *www.abdn. ac.uk/kcc* 🖾 *Free* ⊙ *Weekdays 9:30–5, Sat. 11–4.*

Where to Stay & Eat

The Northeast is the land of Arbroath "smokies" (smoked haddock) and Cullen skink. With rich pastures supporting the famous Aberdeen-Angus beef cattle, high-quality viands are also guaranteed.

★ ££££ ✕ **Silver Darling.** This glass-fronted quayside restaurant is one of Aberdeen's most acclaimed. It specializes in fish, as the name suggests (a silver darling is a herring). The cooking style is French provincial, and the grilled fish and shellfish are particularly flavorful. ⊠ *Pocra Quay, Footdee* ☎ *01224/576229* ⚓ *Reservations essential* ▤ *AE, DC, MC, V* ⊙ *Closed Sun. No lunch Sat.*

£–££ ✕ **Lascala Ristorante.** Blue-and-red furnishings, sparkling chandeliers, and plants everywhere set the scene for classic Italian cuisine. Veal and fish are prominent on the menu, and daily specials make the most of fresh produce. ⊠ *51 Huntly St.* ☎ *01224/626566* ▤ *AE, DC, MC, V.*

£–££ ✕▥ **Atholl Hotel.** One of Aberdeen's many splendid silver-granite buildings, this turreted, gabled hotel is in a leafy residential area to the west of the city center. Rooms are done in rich, dark colors; if space is more important than a view, opt for a room on the first floor. The restaurant prepares simple seafood dishes and local cuts of meat. ⊠ *54 Kings Gate, AB15 4YN* ☎ *01224/323505* 🖨 *01224/321555* ⊕ *www.atholl-aberdeen.com* ⇥ *35 rooms* ⚴ *Restaurant, lounge, Internet; no a/c* ▤ *AE, DC, MC, V* ⦿❘ *BP.*

★ ▥ **Marcliffe at Pitfodels.** This spacious country-house hotel in the West
££££–£££££ End combines old and new in the individually decorated rooms to impressive effect. Some have reproduction antique furnishings; others are more modern. The conservatory dining area focuses on international fare with a Scottish flavor. The hotel can arrange activities such as fishing. ⊠ *N. Deeside Rd., AB15 9YA* ☎ *01224/861000* 🖨 *01224/868860* ⊕ *www.marcliffe.com* ⇥ *42 rooms* ⚴ *Restaurant, minibars, golf privileges, Internet, some pets allowed; no a/c* ▤ *AE, DC, MC, V* ⦿❘ *BP.*

Nightlife & the Arts

The **Prince of Wales** (⊠ 7 St. Nicholas La. ☎ 01224/640597) is one of the Granite City's oldest and busiest pubs. Unlike many of the bars in Aberdeen that have undergone constant renovations, the Prince of Wales refuses to be anything other than what it has always been: a no-frills place where friendliness and good banter are all that matter. **Aberdeen Arts Centre** (⊠ 33 King St. ☎ 01224/635208) presents all forms of theater, comedy shows, poetry readings, exhibitions, and other arts-based events. **His Majesty's Theatre** (⊠ Rosemount Viaduct ☎ 01224/637788) stages shows throughout the year. The **Lemon Tree** (⊠ 5 W. North St. ☎ 01224/642230) has an international program of dance, comedy, music (folk, jazz, rock and roll), and art exhibitions.

Shopping

Big, modern chain stores attract droves of countryfolk who do their major shopping here, but the city still has delightful specialty shops. At the **Ab-**

erdeen Family History Shop (✉ 158–164 King St. ☏ 01224/646323) you can browse through numerous publications related to local history and genealogical research. **Colin Wood** (✉ 25 Rose St. ☏ 01224/643019) specializes in antiques, and maps and prints of Scotland. **Nova** (✉ 20 Chapel St. ☏ 01224/641270) stocks gifts from Scottish silver jewelry to Neal's Yard toiletries.

Banchory

56 *19 mi west of Aberdeen.*

Banchory is an immaculate place with a pinkish tinge to its granite buildings. It's usually bustling with city strollers, out on a day trip from Aberdeen. If you visit Banchory in autumn, drive out to the **Brig o' Feuch** (pronounced fyooch, the *ch* as in loch), off the B974 south of town. In the area around this bridge, salmon leap in season, and the fall colors and foaming waters make for an attractive scene.

Crathes Castle, 3 mi east of Banchory, was once home of the Burnett family, keepers of the Forest of Drum for generations, and it retains some original family furnishings. The family acquired lands here by marriage and later built a castle, completed in 1596. The grand gardens are noted for their calculated symmetry and clipped yew hedges. ✉ *Off A93* ☏ *01330/844525* ⊕ *www.nts.org.uk* ☏ *£9, castle or walled garden only £7* ☉ *Castle Apr.–Sept., daily 10–5:30; Oct., daily 10–4:30; last admission 45 mins before closing. Tearoom and shop Apr.–Sept., daily 10–5:30; Oct., daily 10–4:30; Nov.–March., Wed.–Sun. 10–4. Garden and grounds daily 9–dusk.*

off the beaten path

QUEEN'S VIEW – From Banchory, follow the river upstream to Aboyne, turning north on B9094 and then left onto B9119 for 6 mi for a panoramic view (signposted), a bit north of Dinnet. This is one of the most spectacular vistas in northeast Scotland, stretching across the Howe of Cromar to Lochnagar.

Where to Stay & Eat

££££ ✕🏨 **Banchory Lodge.** With the River Dee running past at the bottom of the garden, this 17th-century house with modern additions is an ideal resting place for anglers. Rooms are individually decorated, though all have bold color schemes and tartan or floral fabrics. The restaurant (fixed-price menus) has high standards for its Scottish cuisine with French overtones; try the fillet of salmon, roast duckling, or guinea fowl with wild berries. ✉ *Dee St., off Bridge St., AB31 5HS* ☏ *01330/822625* 🖷 *01330/ 825019* ⊕ *www.banchorylodge.co.uk* 🛏 *22 rooms* ⚏ *Restaurant, fishing, bicycles, bar, playground; no a/c* 🖃 *AE, DC, MC, V* ⏺ *BP.*

Ballater

57 *25 mi west of Banchory, 43 mi west of Aberdeen.*

The quaint holiday resort of Ballater, once noted for the curative properties of its local well, has profited from the proximity of the royals at nearby Balmoral Castle. BY ROYAL APPOINTMENT signs proudly hang from many of its shops (even monarchs need bakers and butchers). If you get a chance, take time to stroll around this neat community, which is well laid out with groups of silver-gray buildings. Note that the railway station now houses the tourist information center as well as a display on the former glories of this Great North of Scotland branch line, closed in the 1960s, along with many others in this country.

Close to the town, you can explore the eastern Highlands in **Glen Muick** (Gaelic for "pig," pronounced mick). Cross the River Dee and turn upriver on the south side; shortly after, the road, which is signposted from B976, forks into this fine Highland valley. The native red deer are common throughout the Scottish Highlands, but Glen Muick is one of the best places to see them in abundance, with herds grazing the valley floor. Beyond the lower glen, the prospect opens to reveal fine views of the battlement of cliffs edging the famed mountain called Lochnagar.

Where to Stay & Eat

£££–££££ ✕▥ **Darroch Learg Hotel.** Standing amid tall trees on a hillside, this is everything a Victorian Scottish country-house hotel should be. Most guest rooms have a panoramic view south across Royal Deeside and are decorated with mahogany furniture and designer fabrics in rich colors. The Scottish cuisine in the conservatory restaurant (fixed-price menu) is sophisticated but substantial, with the rich flavors of local beef, venison, and fish. Less expensive rooms are in the neighboring Oak Hall, another Victorian house. ⊠ *Braemar Rd., AB35 5UX* ☎ *013397/ 55443* 🖷 *013397/55252* ✍ *nigel@darroch-learg.demon.co.uk* 🛏 *18 rooms* ⚭ *Restaurant, Internet; no a/c* ⊟ *AE, DC, MC, V* ☉ *Closed Jan.* ⦿❘ *BP.*

Balmoral Castle

㊳ *7 mi west of Ballater.*

Balmoral Castle, the Royal Family's Scottish summer residence, is a Victorian fantasy, designed by Prince Albert himself in 1855. "It seems like a dream to be here in our dear Highland Home again," Queen Victoria wrote. "Every year my heart becomes more fixed in this dear Paradise." In truth, there are more interesting and historic buildings to explore in the area, as the only part of the castle on view is the ballroom, with an exhibition of royal artifacts. The Carriage Hall has an exhibition of commemorative china, carriages, and a native wildlife display. Victoria loved Balmoral more for its setting than its house, so be sure to take in the pleasant gardens. Around and about Balmoral are some noted beauty spots: Cairn O'Mount, Cambus O'May, the Cairngorms from the Linn of Dee. Pony trekking is available on the Balmoral stalking-ponies around the grounds and estate. Note that if the royals are in residence, even the grounds are closed to visitors, so be sure to call before visiting. Cottages on the Balmoral estate can be rented by the week. ⊠ *A93, Crathie* ☎ *013397/42534* ⊕ *www.balmoralcastle.com* 🎟 *£5* ☉ *Apr.–July, daily 10–5; last admission at 4.*

Braemar

59 *10 mi west of Balmoral Castle, 17 mi west of Ballater.*

The village of Braemar, surrounded by the Grampian Mountains, is a useful base from which to explore the mountains and woodlands of Royal Deeside. **Braemar Castle** dates from the 17th century, with defensive walls later built in the outline of a pointed star. At Braemar (the braes, or slopes, of the district of Mar), the standard, or rebel flag, was first raised at the start of the unsuccessful Jacobite rebellion of 1715. Thirty years later, during the last rebellion, Braemar Castle was strengthened and garrisoned by Hanoverian (government) troops. ⊠ *A93* ☎ *013397/41219* ⊕ *www. braemarcastle.co.uk* ⌂ *£3.50* ⊙ *Apr.–June, Sept., and Oct., Mon.–Thurs. and weekends 10–6; July and Aug., daily 10–6.*

Braemar is associated with the **Braemar Highland Gathering** held every September, and distinguished by the presence of members of the Royal Family, owing to the proximity of their residence at Balmoral Castle.

Seven miles west of Braemar, on an unmarked road, is the **Linn of Dee** (*linn* is a Scots word meaning "rocky narrows"), where the river's rocky gash is deep and roaring. Park beyond the bridge and walk back to admire the river and woodland, with deep, tranquil pools with salmon glinting in them.

Where to Stay & Eat

££ ✕⊡ **Invercauld Arms.** This stone Victorian hotel in the center of Braemar has a bit of period style. The entrance lounge, with plush sofas and velvet chairs, leads to beautifully restored public rooms and to comfortable guest rooms with floral drapes and reproduction antique furniture. The restaurant serves a fixed-price dinner that might include venison with wild berries or salmon served with dill butter sauce. Note that a two-night stay is required unless you book close to the date and there's an opening. ⊠ *A93, AB35 5YR* ☎ *013397/41605* ⊟ *013397/41428* ⇌ *68 rooms* ⚬ *Restaurant, bar; no a/c* ⊟ *AE, DC, MC, V* ⊺⊙⊺ *BP.*

Sports

The **Braemar Golf Club** (⊠ Cluniebank Rd. ☎ 013397/41618) is a tricky 18-hole course with a yardage of 4916 and a par of 65. It is split in half by foaming waters, but erratic duffers, take note: the course managers have installed, near the water, poles with little nets on the end for those occasional shots that go awry.

Corgarff Castle

60 *23 mi northeast of Braemar, 14 mi northwest of Ballater.*

Eighteenth-century soldiers paved a military highway, now A939, north from Ballater to Corgarff Castle, a lonely tower house with a star-shape defensive wall, a curious reproduction of Braemar Castle. Corgarff was built as a hunting seat for the earls of Mar in the 16th century. After an eventful history that included the wife of a later laird being burned alive in a family dispute, the castle served as a garrison for Hanoverian troops. ⊠ *Off A939, Cock Bridge* ☎ *0131/668–8800* ⊕ *www.historic-*

scotland.gov.uk 🎫 *£3* 🕙 *Apr.–Sept., daily 9:30–6; Oct.–Mar., Sat. 9:30–4, Sun. 2–4.*

en route On A944, the castle signposting for the **Castle Trail** leads you to a few sites. The road meanders along the River Don to the village of Strathdon, where a mound by the roadside—on the left—turns out to be a motte, or the base of a wooden castle, built in the late 12th century. The A944 then joins A97 (go left) and just a few minutes later a sign points to Glenbuchat Castle, a plain Z-plan tower house.

Kildrummy Castle

★ ⑥ *18 mi northeast of Corgarff Castle, 23 mi north of Ballater.*

Its age (13th century) and its ties to the mainstream medieval traditions of European castle-building make this building significant. Kildrummy shares features with Harlech and Caernarfon in Wales, as well as with Continental sites, such as Château de Coucy near Laon, France. It underwent several expansions at the hands of England's king Edward I (1239–1307); the castle was back in Scottish hands in 1306, when Edward's son besieged it. The defenders were betrayed by Osbarn the Smith, who had been promised gold by the English. They gave it to him after the castle fell, pouring it molten down his throat, or so the story goes. Kildrummy's prominence ended after the collapse of the 1715 Jacobite uprising. It had been the rebel headquarters and was consequently dismantled. ✉ *A97, Kildrummy* ☎ *019755/71331* ⊕ *www.historic-scotland.gov.uk* 🎫 *£2.20* 🕙 *Apr.–Sept., daily 9:30–6.*

Where to Stay & Eat

★ ✕🏨 **Kildrummy Castle Hotel.** A grand, late-Victorian country house, this
££££–£££££ hotel offers a peaceful location, attentive service, and sports. Oak paneling, beautiful plasterwork, and gentle color schemes create a serene environment, enhanced by the views of Kildrummy Castle Gardens next door. The restaurant's traditional Scottish cuisine highlights local game and seafood. Fillet of beef Kildrummy Castle combines three quintessentially Scottish ingredients—beef, haggis, and Drambuie liqueur—in one dish. Golf, fishing, and horseback riding are available nearby. ✉ *Off A944, Kildrummy, AB33 8RA* ☎ *019755/71288* 🖨 *019755/71345* ⊕ *www.kildrummycastlehotel.co.uk* 🛏 *16 rooms* ⅄ *Restaurant, some pets allowed; no a/c* ▭ *MC, V* ⧛ *BP.*

Alford

⑥ *9 mi east of Kildrummy, 28 mi west of Aberdeen.*

A plain and sturdy settlement in the Howe (Hollow) of Alford, this village on the Castle Trail gives those who have grown weary of castle-hopping a break: it has a museum instead. The **Grampian Transport Museum,** in the center of town, specializes in road-based means of locomotion, including trams and Scottish-made cars, and has a library and archive facility. One of its more unusual exhibits is the *Craigievar Express,* a steam-driven creation invented by the local postman to deliver

mail more efficiently. ☎ *019755/62292* ⊕ *www.gtm.org.uk* 🎫 *£4.80*
🕐 *Apr.–Sept., daily 10–5; Oct., daily 10–4.*

Craigievar Castle

★ ⓺⓷ *5 mi south of Alford.*

A fine example of the Scottish baronial style, Craigievar Castle is much
as the stonemasons left it in 1626, with its pepper-pot turrets and towers, the whole slender shape covered in a pink-cream pastel. It was built
in relatively peaceful times by William Forbes, a merchant in trade with
the Baltic Sea ports. The well-preserved interior contains fine family portraits and 17th- and 18th-century furniture. ⊠ *A980* ☎ *013398/83635*
⊕ *www.nts.org.uk* 🎫 *£9 includes guided tour* 🕐 *Castle Apr.–Sept.,
Fri.–Tues. noon–5:30; grounds daily 9:30–sunset.*

Castle Fraser

⓺⓸ *13 mi east of Craigievar Castle, 8 mi southeast of Alford.*

Massive Castle Fraser, the largest of the castles of Mar (five castles built
by a family of masons named Bell), shows a variety of styles reflecting
the taste of its owners from the 15th through the 19th centuries. The
walled garden includes a re-creation of a 19th-century knot garden, with
box hedging, gravel paths, and splendid herbaceous borders. Have
lunch in the tearoom or the picnic area. ⊠ *Sauchen, off A944, near
Dunecht* ☎ *01330/833463* ⊕ *www.nts.org.uk* 🎫 *£7, gardens and
grounds only £2* 🕐 *Castle Apr.–June and Sept., Fri.–Tues. noon–5:30;
July and Aug., daily 11–5:30. Gardens daily 9:30–6. Grounds daily
9:30–dusk.*

INVERNESS & LOCH NESS

Inverness, the only sizable town in northern Scotland (though it is quite
small, nonetheless), is a compact place, built on both banks of the River
Ness, just northeast of Loch Ness. The loch itself, 24 mi long and very
deep (800 feet maximum), is surrounded by pretty scenery. Loch Ness
is the alleged home of "Nessie," world-famous monster and star of the
chamber of commerce. In 1933, during a quiet news week for the local
paper, the editor ran a story about a sighting of something in Loch Ness.
The story lives on, and the dubious Loch Ness phenomenon keeps cameras trained on the deep waters, which tend to create mirages in still conditions. The area sees plenty of tourist traffic, drawn by the well-marketed
hokum of the monster. But historic sites, castles, and mountain and lake
scenery give you much more to see.

Inverness

▶ ⓺⓹ *102 mi northwest of Aberdeen, 161 mi northwest of Edinburgh.*

Inverness makes a logical touring base, with excellent roads radiating
out from it to serve an extensive area. Although popularly called the
capital of the Highlands, the city is far from Highland in flavor. Part of

Inverness
& Environs

Cromarty Firth
Moray Firth

Black
Isle

Brodie
Castle

Elgin

Fort
George **69**

Nairn

68

71

TO
ABERDEEN

Auldern

Muir of Ord

70

Cawdor
Castle

Inverness **65**

67

Culloden
Moor

Urquhart
Castle

Drumnadrochit

66

Loch
Ness

STRATHSPEY

Spey

Boat of Garten

Nethy Bridge

Whitebridge

Aviemore

Fort
Augustus

Coylumbridge

KEY

Kincraig

GREAT
BRITAIN

▶ Start of itinerary

Kingussie
Newtonmore

CAIRNGORM MTS.

0   10 miles
0   15 km

its hinterland includes the farmlands of the Moray Firth coastal strip, as well as of the Black Isle. It is open to the sea winds off the Moray Firth, and the high hills, although close at hand, are mainly hidden. Few of Inverness's buildings are of great antiquity, thanks to the competing Highland clans' habit of burning towns to the ground. Even its castle is a Victorian-era replacement on the site of a fort blown up by Bonnie Prince Charlie. Now bypassed by A9, the town positively roars with visitors in summer. Be careful in its one-way traffic system, whether you are walking or driving.

The excellent, although small **Inverness Museum and Art Gallery** (⊠ Castle Wynd ☎ 01463/237114) covers archaeology, art, local history, and the natural environment in its lively displays.

Where to Stay & Eat

££££–£££££ ✕▥ **Dunain Park Hotel.** Individual attention is the key at this 18th-century mansion amid 6 acres of wooded gardens. An open fire awaits you in the living room, a relaxing place to sip a drink and browse through books and magazines. Antiques and traditional furnishings make the bedrooms equally cozy and attractive. The elegant restaurant serves French-influenced Scottish dishes such as Shetland salmon baked in sea salt and medallions of venison rolled in oatmeal with claret sauce. The hotel is

2½ mi southwest of Inverness. ⊠ *A82, Dunain, IV3 8JN* ☎ *01463/ 230512* 🖷 *01463/224532* ⊕ *www.dunainparkhotel.co.uk* ➥ *13 rooms* ⊘ *Restaurant, indoor pool, sauna, badminton, Internet, some pets allowed; no a/c* ⊟ *AE, MC, V* ⫶◯⫶ *BP.*

££ 🖼 **Ballifeary House Hotel.** The proprietors at this well-maintained Victorian B&B offer high standards of comfort and service. Rooms are individually decorated with modern furnishings, and the downstairs has reproduction antiques; there's a bar for guests. Ballifeary House is a 10-minute walk from downtown Inverness. ⊠ *10 Ballifeary Rd., IV3 5PJ* ☎ *01463/235572* 🖷 *01463/717583* ⊕ *www.ballifearyhousehotel.co. uk* ➥ *5 rooms* ⊘ *No a/c, no room phones, no kids under 15, no smoking* ⊟ *MC, V* ⫶◯⫶ *BP.*

★ **££** 🖼 **The Lodge at Daviot Mains.** This house, done in the style of a Highland shooting lodge, provides the perfect setting for home comforts and traditional Scottish cooking (guests only). Trout and lamb are cooked to perfection and there's a superior selection of Scottish malts. It is 5 mi south of Inverness. ⊠ *A9, IV2 5ER* ☎ *01463/772215* 🖷 *01463/ 772099* ⊕ *www.thelodgeatdaviotmains.co.uk* ➥ *6 rooms* ⊘ *Dining room, in-room data ports, some pets allowed; no a/c, no smoking* ⊟ *MC, V* ⫶◯⫶ *BP.*

Nightlife & the Arts

Eden Court (⊠ Bishops Rd. ☎ 01463/234234), a multipurpose 800-seat theater, cinema, restaurant, and art gallery, presents a varied program year-round, including performances by the excellent Scottish Ballet.

Shopping

Inverness has the usual indoor shopping malls with chain names and department stores, but the most interesting goods are in specialty shops. **Duncan Chisholm & Sons** (⊠47–51 Castle St. ☎01463/234599) specializes in Highland tartans, woolens, and crafts. Mail-order and made-to-measure services are available. **Hector Russell Kiltmakers** (⊠ 4–9 Huntly St. ☎ 01463/222781) carries a huge selection of kilts, or will create one for you made to measure. It can fulfill overseas mail orders. **James Pringle Weavers** (⊠ Holm Woollen Mills, Dores Rd. ☎ 01463/223311) offers self-guided mill tours, a weaving exhibition (where for £3 you can try a loom and receive a certificate), and a restaurant; it sells lovely tweeds, tartans, wool clothing, Caithness Glass items, and giftware. The indoor **Victorian Market** (⊠ Academy St.), built in 1870, houses more than 40 privately owned specialty shops.

Loch Ness

66 *9 mi southwest of Inverness.*

Inverness is the northern gateway to the Great Glen, a rift valley that is the result of an ancient earth movement that dislocated the top half of Scotland. Three lochs fill the fault line; the most well known, Loch Ness, can be seen from the main A82 road south, though leisurely drivers may prefer the east bank road, B862 and B852, to Fort Augustus, at the loch's southern end (a 32-mi drive). The scenery around Loch Ness is pleasant without being spectacular—heather-clad mountain slopes and birch woods closer to the water. In summer there are quite a few boats on the lake.

Midway between Inverness and Fort Augustus on the west bank road, **Loch Ness 2000** presents the facts and the fakes, the photographs, the unexplained sonar contacts, and the sincere testimony of eyewitnesses. Loch Ness's huge volume of water has a warming effect on the local weather, making the lake conducive to mirages in still, warm conditions; these are often the circumstances in which the "monster" appears. Whether or not the *bestia aquatilis* lurks in the depths—and in 1994, the man who took one of the most convincing photos of Nessie confessed that it was a fake—plenty of camera-toting, sonar-wielding, and submarine-traveling scientists and curiosity-seekers haunt the shores. ☒ *A82, Drumnadrochit* ☎ *01456/450573 or 01456/450218* ⊕ *www. loch-ness-scotland.com* ☞ *£5.95* ☉ *Easter–May, daily 9:30–5; June and Sept., daily 9–6; July and Aug., daily 9–8; Oct., daily 9:30–5:30; Nov.–Easter, daily 10–3:30; last admission 30 mins before closing.*

Two miles southeast of Drumnadrochit, right on the lakeshore, stands battered **Urquhart Castle,** which has been guarding Loch Ness since the 13th century. It was largely destroyed by the end of the 17th century, to prevent its use by Jacobite forces, but the ruins of what was one of the largest castles in Scotland are still impressive. Today swarms of bus tours pass through after investigating the Loch Ness phenomenon. Exhibits in the visitor center explore the castle's tumultuous history. ☒ *A82* ☎ *01456/ 450551* ⊕ *www.historic-scotland.gov.uk* ☞ *£6* ☉ *Apr.–Sept., daily 9:30–6; Oct.–Mar., daily 9:30–4; last admission 45 mins before closing.*

Where to Stay & Eat

★ **£££–££££** ✕🛏 **Polmaily House.** This country house amid lovely parkland is near the northern bank of Loch Ness. Books, log fires, and a helpful staff contribute to making the hotel warmer and more personal than many grander, more expensive places, and families are sincerely welcomed. The restaurant is noted for its British cuisine, which takes advantage of fresh Highland produce. Try salmon in pastry with dill sauce, roast rack of lamb with rosemary, or cold smoked venison with melon. ☒ *A831, Drumnadrochit, IV63 6XT* ☎ *01456/450343* 🖷 *01456/450813* ⊕ *www. polmaily.co.uk* ☞ *9 rooms, 5 suites* ⚹ *Restaurant, tennis court, indoor pool, boating, fishing, croquet, horseback riding, Internet, some pets allowed; no a/c* ⊟ *MC, V* ⦿ *BP.*

Culloden Moor

67 🌀 *5 mi east of Inverness.*

Culloden Moor was the scene of the last major battle fought on British soil—to this day considered one of the most infamous and tragic in all of warfare. Here, on a cold April day in 1746, the outnumbered Jacobite forces of Prince Charles Edward Stuart were destroyed by the superior firepower of George II's army. The victorious commander, the duke of Cumberland (George II's son), earned the name of "Butcher" Cumberland for the bloody reprisals carried out by his men on Highland families, Jacobite or not, caught in the vicinity. In the battle itself,

CloseUp

CLANS & TARTANS

WHATEVER THE ORIGINS of the clans—some with Norman roots, intermarried into Celtic society; some of Norse origin, the product of Viking raids on Scotland; others traceable to the monastic system; yet others possibly descended from Pictish tribes—by the 13th century the clan system was at the heart of Gaelic tribal culture. By the 15th century the clan chiefs of the Scottish Highlands were a threat even to the authority of the Stewart monarchs. The word clann means "family" or "children" in Gaelic, and it was the custom for clan chiefs to board out their sons among nearby families, a practice that helped bond the clan and create strong allegiances: the chief became "father" of the tribe and was owed loyalty by lesser chiefs and clansmen.

The clan chiefs' need for strong men-at-arms, fast-running messengers, and bards for entertainment and the preservation of clan genealogy was the probable origin of the Highland Games, still celebrated in many Highland communities each year, and which are an otherwise rather unusual mix of sports, music, and dance.

By the 18th century, increasing knowledge of Lowland agricultural improvements, and better roads into the Highlands that improved communication of ideas and "southern" ways, began to weaken the clan system: fine clothes, French wines, and even a Lowland education became more common in chiefly households. Even before the battle of Culloden in 1746, in which Prince Charles Edward Stuart, supported by some of the clans, was defeated by George II's army, the clan system had lost its tight grip on the Highlands. After Culloden, as more modern economic influences took hold, those on the "wrong" side lost all. Many chiefs lost their lands, tartan was banned, and clan culture withered.

Tartan's own origins as a part of the clan system are disputed; the Gaelic word for striped cloth is breacan—piebald or spotted—so even the word itself is not Highland. However, it is indisputable that in the days before mass manufacture, when cloth was locally spun, woven, and dyed using plant derivatives, each neighborhood would have different dyestuffs—bilberry, iris, bramble, water lily—and therefore different colors available. In this way, combinations of colors and favorite patterns could become associated with a particular area and therefore clan, but were not in any sense a clan's own.

Between 1746 and 1782 the wearing of tartan was generally prohibited. By the time the ban was lifted, many recipes for dyes and weaving patterns had been forgotten. In addition, some neighborhoods stopped making and coloring their own cloth because of the mechanization and use of chemical dyes in cloth production.

It took the influence of Sir Walter Scott, with his romantic (and fashionable) view of Highland history, to create the "modern myth" of clans and tartan. Sir Walter engineered George IV's visit to Scotland in 1822, which turned into a tartan extravaganza. The idea of one tartan or group of tartans "belonging" to a clan was created at this time, with new patterns and color ways dreamed up and "assigned" to particular clans. Queen Victoria and Prince Albert, with their passion for all things Scottish and for tartan in particular at Balmoral, reinforced the tartan culture later in the century, and it persists on and off to this day. You may be able to find a clan connection with the help of expertise such as that available at **Scotland's Clan Tartan Centre** (✉ 70–74 Bangor Rd., Leith ☎ 0131/553–5100), near Edinburgh.

the duke's army, greatly outnumbering the Scots, killed more than 1,000 soldiers. The National Trust for Scotland has, slightly eerily, re-created the battlefield as it looked in 1746. The uneasy silence of the open moor almost drowns out the merry clatter from the visitor center's coffee shop and the revs of the tour buses waiting in the parking lot. ⊠ *B9006* 🕾 *01463/790607* ⊕ *www.nts.org.uk* ▣ *Visitor center and audiovisual display £5* ☉ *Site, daily. Visitor center, restaurant, and shop Feb., Nov., and Dec., daily 11–4; Mar., daily 10–4; Apr.–June, Sept., and Oct., daily 9–6; July and Aug., daily 9–7; last entry 30 mins before closing.*

Nairn

68 *12 mi northeast of Culloden Moor, 17 mi northeast of Inverness, 92 mi northwest of Aberdeen.*

Once an unusual mixture of prosperous fishing port and farming community, Nairn still has a harmonious blend of old buildings in its busy shopping streets. The town is close to several historic sites.

★ **69** **Fort George,** started in 1748 and completed some 20 years later, is perhaps the best-preserved 18th-century military fortification in Europe. Because the fort is low-lying, its immense scale can be seen only from within. A visitor center and tableaux at the fort portray the 18th-century Scottish soldier's way of life, as does the **Regimental Museum of the Queen's Own Highlanders.** To reach the fort, take the B9092 north off A96 west of Nairn. ⊠ *Off B9092, Ardersier* 🕾 *01667/462777* ⊕ *www.historic-scotland.gov.uk* ▣ *Fort £6, museum free* ☉ *Apr.–Sept., daily 9:30–6:30; Oct.–Mar., daily 9:30–4:30; last admission 45 mins before closing.*

70 **Cawdor Castle,** south of Nairn, is the cheerfully idiosyncratic, mellow, **Fodor's**Choice and mossy seat of the Cawdor family, whose ancestors built it as a pri- ★ vate fortress and who continue to live here. Shakespeare's Macbeth was the Thane (or clan chief) of Cawdor, but the sense of history that exists is more than fictional. The castle's 15th-century central tower, family portraits, tapestries, and fine furniture reflect 600 years of history. The grounds include gardens and well-marked nature trails through woodlands with ancient oaks and beeches. ⊠ *Off B9090, Cawdor* 🕾 *01667/404401* ⊕ *www.cawdorcastle.com* ▣ *£6.50, garden and grounds only £3.50* ☉ *June–mid-Oct., daily 10–5.*

71 **Brodie Castle,** east of Nairn and in the care of the National Trust for Scotland, is of medieval origin, rebuilt and extended in the 17th and 19th centuries. Fine examples of late-17th-century plasterwork are preserved in the dining room and blue sitting room, and the good collection of paintings extends to works by 20th-century artists. ⊠ *Off A96* 🕾 *01309/641371* ⊕ *www.nts.org.uk* ▣ *£5, grounds only £1 (honesty box)* ☉ *Castle Apr., July, and Aug., daily noon–4; May, June–Sept., Sun.–Thurs. noon–4; grounds daily 9:30–sunset.*

Where to Stay & Eat

★ ✕🏠 **Boath House.** Two surprises await inside this stunning 1820s man-
££££–£££££ sion on 20 acres: an Aveda health and beauty spa in the basement, and

spacious rooms with 19th-century furniture, yet displaying contemporary Scottish art. The restaurant uses local produce, game in season, and seafood delivered fresh daily by local fishermen. For golfers, there are two courses nearby. ⊠ *Auldearn, IV12 5TE, near Nairn* ☎ *01667/454896* 🖷 *01667/455469* ⊕ *www.boath-house.com* 🛏 *5 rooms, 1 cottage* △ *Restaurant, spa, Internet, some pets allowed; no a/c* ⊟ AE, MC, V ❏❘BP.

Shopping

At **Auldearn Antiques** (⊠ Dalmore Manse, Lethen Rd., Auldearn ☎ 01667/453087) east of Nairn, it's easy to spend an hour or more wandering around the old church—filled with furniture, fireplaces, architectural antiques, and linens—and the converted farmsteads, with their tempting antique (or just old) chinaware and textiles. **Brodie Countryfare** (⊠ Brodie, east of Nairn ☎ 01309/641555) sells unusual knitwear, high-quality designer clothing and shoes, gifts, and toys, although they are *not* cheap. Also here are a food store, a delicatessen, and an excellent, inexpensive restaurant.

SCOTLAND A TO Z

To research prices, get advice from other travelers, and book travel arrangements, visit www.fodors.com.

AIR TRAVEL

CARRIERS Aberdeen is served by Air France, Atlantic Airways, Braathens, British Airways, British Midland/bmi, KLM UK, Coastair, EasyJet, Eastern Airways, Ryan Air, and Wideroe. Airlines serving Edinburgh (no transatlantic flights) include Aer Arran, Aer Lingus, Air France, British Airways, ScotAirways, British Midland/bmi, Czech Airlines, Eastern Airways, EasyJet, Flybe, KLM, Lufthansa, and Ryanair. Airlines serving Glasgow for transatlantic flights are Air Canada and American Airlines (both are summer only), and Continental and Icelandair (all year). Inverness is served by British Airways (including British Regional Airways/British Airways Express), bmi, EasyJet, Eastern Airways, and Loganair. Ryanair and EasyJet offer unbeatable no-frills fares between Edinburgh, Glasgow, Glasgow Prestwick, and London's four major airports.

AIRPORTS

Aberdeen Airport serves international and domestic flights and is in Dyce, 7 mi west of the city center on the A96. Edinburgh Airport, 7 mi west of the city center, has air links with all the major airports in Britain and many in Europe; the Airport Information Centre answers questions about schedules, tickets, and reservations. Glasgow Airport offers Scottish and British services, European and transatlantic services, and vacation-charter traffic. Inverness Airport, locally known as Dalcross Airport, is central for internal flights covering the Highlands and islands region. There are also flights to the Highlands and islands from London (Luton), Manchester, Edinburgh, and Glasgow.

Glasgow Prestwick Airport, on the Ayrshire coast about 30 mi southwest of Glasgow, is mainly concerned with package holidays and charter flights, but is also the base for Ryanair's good-value flights, and serves as the main diversion airport in Scotland in bad weather conditions, because it usually stays clear of the worst weather. It has excellent direct train service to Glasgow.

Aberdeen Airport ☎ 01224/722331 ⊕ www.baa.co.uk. **Edinburgh Airport Information Centre** ☎ 0131/333-1000 ⊕ www.baa.co.uk. **Glasgow Airport** ☎ 0141/887-1111 airport information desk ⊕ www.baa.co.uk. **Glasgow Prestwick Airport** ☎ 01292/511006 ⊕ www.gpia.co.uk. **Inverness Airport** ☎ 01667/464000 ⊕ www.hial.co.uk/inverness-airport.html.

BUS TRAVEL

Long-distance coach service operates to and from most parts of Scotland, England, and Wales. Edinburgh is approximately 8 hours by bus from London, Glasgow approximately 8½–9 hours. The main operator in Scotland is Scottish Citylink. From England and Wales, the main operator is National Express.

Lothian Buses, operating dark-red-and-white buses, is the main operator within Edinburgh. First Edinburgh provides much of the service into Edinburgh and also has day tours around and beyond the city and serves the Borders. Getting around the Inverness area and Royal Deeside is best done by car, but a number of post-bus services can help get you to the remote areas. For information contact Royal Mail. Note that if you head north of Aberdeen and Inverness, public transportation options can be limited on Sunday.

CUTTING COSTS   The Lothian Buses Edinburgh Day Saver ticket (£2.50) allows unlimited one-day travel on the city's buses, and the better-value Offpeak Day Saver (£1.80) allows unlimited travel after 9:30 AM weekdays and all day on weekends; both services can be purchased in advance, or on any LRT bus (exact fare will be required on a bus). Two travel passes are available from First Edinburgh for one day, seven days, or four weeks for unlimited travel in the Borders: the Reiver Rover for services within the Borders area, and the Waverley Wanderer for services within the Borders and to Edinburgh and Carlisle.

The many bus companies in Glasgow cooperate with the Underground and ScotRail to produce the Family Day Tripper Ticket (£14), an excellent way to get around the whole area from Loch Lomond to Ayrshire. Tickets are available from Strathclyde Passenger Transport (SPT) and at main railway and bus stations.

Scottish Citylink sells an Explorer Pass providing three, five, or eight days of unlimited travel on the entire Scottish Citylink network. Aberdeen and Inverness are well served from the central belt of Scotland.

FARES &   **First Edinburgh** ☎ 0870/872-7271 ⊕ www.firstgroup.com. **Lothian Buses** ☎ 0131/
SCHEDULES   555-6363 ⊕ www.lothianbuses.co.uk. **National Express** ☎ 0870/580-8080 ⊕ www.nationalexpress.com. **Scottish Citylink** ✉ Buchanan Street Bus Station, Glasgow ☎ 0870/550-5050 ⊕ www.citylink.co.uk. **Strathclyde Passenger Transport** ✉ Travel Centre, St. Enoch Sq., Glasgow ☎ 0870/608-2608 ⊕ www.spt.co.uk. **Royal Mail Post Buses** ✉ 7 Strothers La., Inverness ☎ 0845/774-0740 ⊕ www.royalmail.com/postbus.

CAR RENTAL
⁊ Local Agencies Alamo National Car Rental ⊠ 76 Lancefield Quay, Glasgow ☎ 0141/204-1051. **Avis** ⊠ Aberdeen Airport, Aberdeen ☎ 01224/722282 ⊠ 5 Westpark Pl., Dalry Rd., Edinburgh ☎ 0131/337-6363, 0131/344-3900 airport ⊠ 161 North St., Glasgow ☎ 0141/221-2827, 0141/842-7599 airport ⊠ Inverness Airport, Inverness ☎ 01667/464070. **Budget** ⊠ Wellshead Dr., Wellshead Industrial Estate, Dyce, Aberdeen ☎ 0800/181181 ⊠ Almond Rd., Edinburgh ☎ 0800/181181 ⊠ Glasgow Airport, Glasgow ☎ 0800/181181 ⊠ Burns Cottage, Railway Terr., Inverness ☎ 0800/181181. **Europcar** ⊠ 121 Causewayend, Aberdeen ☎ 01224/631199, 01224/770770 airport ⊠ 24 E. London St., Edinburgh ☎ 0131/557-3456, 0131/333-2588 airport ⊠ 38 Anderson Quay, Glasgow ☎ 0141/248-8788, 0141/887-0414 airport ⊠ Friars Bridge Service Station, Telford St., Inverness ☎ 01463/235337. **Hertz** ☎ 08705/996699 central reservations ⊠ Aberdeen Airport, Aberdeen ☎ 01224/722373 ⊠ 10 Picardy Pl., Edinburgh ☎ 0870/846-0013, 0870/846-0009 airport ⊠ 138 Hyde Park St., Glasgow ☎ 0141/248-7736 ⊠ Inverness Airport, Inverness ☎ 01667/462652 ⊠ Thistle Hotel, Millburn Rd., Inverness ☎ 01463/711479.

CAR TRAVEL
The center of downtown Edinburgh is Princes Street, which runs east–west. Entering from the east coast, drivers will come in on A1, with Meadowbank Stadium serving as a landmark. From the Borders, the approach to Princes Street is by A7 and A68 through Newington. Approaching from the southwest, drivers will join the west end of Princes Street, via A701 and A702, and those coming east from Glasgow or Stirling will meet Princes Street from A8 on the approach via M90/A90. From Forth Road Bridge, Perth, and the east coast, the key road for getting downtown is Queensferry Road.

Those who come to Glasgow from England and the south of Scotland will probably approach the city from M6, M74, and A74. The city center is clearly marked from these roads. From Edinburgh M8 leads to and cuts straight across the city center; all other roads feed into it.

It is possible to travel from Edinburgh to Aberdeen on a continuous stretch of M90, a fairly scenic route that runs up Strathmore. The coastal route, A92, is a more leisurely alternative. The most scenic route is probably A93 from Perth, north to Blairgowrie and into Glen Shee. The A93 then goes over the Cairnwell Pass, the highest main road in Scotland (not recommended in winter).

The direct Edinburgh–Inverness route is M9/A9. From Glasgow to Inverness, the route is M80, then A9. If you are coming from southern Scotland, allow a comfortable 3½ hours from Glasgow or Edinburgh to Inverness via A9, and two hours to Aberdeen via A90.

A car is essential if you want to explore Scotland's wildest and most beautiful districts. Roads are always well surfaced, though narrow in places. Although the area is large, road distances make it even larger: as the eagle flies, one town can be a certain distance from another, but it turns out to be three times that distance by the shortest road. Winter touring beyond the central Lowlands means you should check weather forecasts: minor roads are occasionally snowbound.

DISCOUNTS & DEALS

The Explorer Pass, available from any staffed Historic Scotland (HS) property, allows visits to HS properties over a 5-, 10-, or 21-day period. The Discovery Ticket issued by the National Trust for Scotland (NTS) is available for 3, 7, or 14 days and allows access to all NTS properties. It is available from the NTS, all NTS properties, or main tourist information centers. These tickets provide considerable savings if you intend to visit many historic sites.

🏛 **Historic Scotland** ☎ 0131/668-8600 ⊕ www.historic-scotland.gov.uk. **National Trust for Scotland** ☎ 0131/243-9300 ⊕ www.nts.org.uk.

EMERGENCIES

🏛 **Ambulance, fire, police** ☎ 999. **Aberdeen Royal Infirmary** ✉ Accident and Emergency Department, Foresterhill ☎ 01224/681818. **Edinburgh Royal Infirmary** ✉ Old Dalkeith Rd., Little France ☎ 0131/536-1000. **Glasgow Royal Infirmary** ✉ Castle St., City Center ☎ 0141/211-4000. **Raigmore Hospital** ✉ Old Perth Rd., Inverness ☎ 01463/704000.

TOURS

BUS TOURS Lothian Buses (⇨ Bus Travel) runs tours in and around Edinburgh departing from Waverley Bridge at regular intervals, from 9:30 to 5:30 daily. City Sightseeing also runs tours around Edinburgh in its open-top buses from Waverley Bridge. This company runs tours around Glasgow and Inverness as well. Prestige Tours runs luxury coach tours to most parts of Scotland. Discover Loch Ness schedules bus tours around the lake from Inverness; some tours include a cruise. Classique Tours has unusual vehicles: small touring coaches dating from the 1950s and restored to immaculate condition. Specialized tours of Scotland's gardens are operated by Brightwater Holidays.

🏛 **Brightwater Holidays** ☎ 01334/657155 ⊕ www.brightwaterholidays.com. **City Sightseeing** ☎ 0131/220-0770 ⊕ www.city-sightseeing.com. **Classique Tours** ☎ 0141/889-4050 ⊕ www.classiquetours.co.uk. **Discover Loch Ness** ☎ 0800/731-5564 ⊕ www.discoverlochness.com **Prestige Tours** ☎ 0141/886-1000 ⊕ www.prestigetours.com.

CHAUFFEURED TOURS Little's Chauffeur Drive offers personally tailored chauffeur-driven tours throughout Scotland.

🏛 **Little's Chauffeur Drive** ☎ 0141/883-2111 ⊕ www.littles.co.uk.

WALKING TOURS The Scottish Tourist Guides Association can recommend fully qualified guides who will arrange walking or driving excursions of varying lengths. The Cadies and Witchery Tours organizes tours of ghost-haunted Edinburgh all year. The Scottish Literary Tour Company takes you around Edinburgh's Old and New Town, with guides invoking Scottish literary characters; it also has regional tours around Scotland.

🏛 **Cadies and Witchery Tours** ✉ 84 West Bow, Edinburgh ☎ 0131/225-6745 ⊕ www.witcherytours.com. **Scottish Literary Tour Company** ✉ 97B West Bow, Suite 2, Edinburgh ☎ 0131/226-6657 ⊕ http://home.btconnect.com/sltc. **Scottish Tourist Guides Association** ✉ Old Town Jail, St. John's St., Stirling, FK8 1EA ☎☎ 01786/451953 ⊕ www.stga.co.uk.

TRAIN TRAVEL

Edinburgh's main train station, Waverley, is downtown, below Waverley Bridge. Travel time from Edinburgh to London by train is as little as four hours. Glasgow has two main rail stations: Central and Queen Street. Central is the arrival and departure point for trains from London Euston (journey time is approximately five hours), which come via Crewe and Carlisle in England, as well as via Edinburgh from Kings Cross. Travelers can reach Aberdeen directly from Edinburgh (three hours) and Inverness (2½ hours). There are sleeper connections from London to Inverness, as well as reliable links from Edinburgh. There is also a direct London–Aberdeen service that goes through Edinburgh. For those interested in train service to Aberdeen's airport, Dyce is on ScotRail's Inverness–Aberdeen route. The Borders has no rail service, and the nearest rail station to St. Andrews is Leuchars, on the Edinburgh–Aberdeen main line. For all inquiries, telephone National Rail Enquiries.

CUTTING COSTS The Go Roundabout Glasgow discount pass allows unlimited travel on the Underground and trains around Glasgow and out to surrounding towns for one day. Trains depart Edinburgh and Glasgow for Aberdeen, Inverness, and other towns in the north. ScotRail issues discount passes as well: the Central Scotland Rover ticket covers Edinburgh, Glasgow, and the Central Belt, whereas the Highland Rover ticket is for travel in the north and west Highlands. For details, contact ScotRail.

🚆 **National Rail Enquiries** ☎ 0845/748-4950 ⊕ www.nationalrail.co.uk. **ScotRail** ☎ 0845/755-0033 ⊕ www.scotrail.co.uk.

TRAVEL AGENCIES

🚩 Local Agent Referrals **American Express** ✉ 139 Princes St., West End, Edinburgh ☎ 0131/718-2501 or 0870/600-1060 ✉ 115 Hope St., City Center, Glasgow ☎ 0141/222-1405. **Thomas Cook** ✉ 26-28 Frederick St., Edinburgh ☎ 0131/465-7700 ✉ 15-17 Gordon St., City Center, Glasgow ☎ 0141/201-7200.

VISITOR INFORMATION

Edinburgh and Scotland Information Centre is adjacent to Waverley Station in Edinburgh (follow the tourist information center TIC signs in the station and throughout the city) and can book accommodations for you. Greater Glasgow and Clyde Valley Tourist Board offers an excellent tourist information service from its headquarters near Queen Street Station in Glasgow.

VisitScotland's Central Information Department, for telephone and written inquiries only, will answer questions on any aspect of your Scottish vacation and can supply literature by mail. It cannot book accommodations, although this may change. The Scottish Tourist Board in London, open Monday–Saturday (shorter Saturday hours mid-September–May) can supply information and also has an accommodation and travel booking agency for in-person visitors.

Within Scotland, area tourist boards run a network of more than 170 tourist information centers that offer comprehensive information and on-the-spot accommodation bookings. Many of these are listed below by town, after the national and regional tourist information offices.

🖪 **Edinburgh and Scotland Information Centre** ✉ 3 Princes St., East End, Edinburgh EH2 2QP ☎ 0131/473-3800 🖷 0131/473-3881 ⊕ www.edinburgh.org. **Greater Glasgow and Clyde Valley Tourist Board** ✉ 11 George Sq., City Center, Glasgow G2 1DY ☎ 0141/204-4400 🖷 0141/221-3524 ⊕ www.seeglasgow.com. **Scottish Tourist Board in London** ✉ 19 Cockspur St., near Trafalgar Sq. ✉ The Scotland Desk, Britain Visitor Centre, 1 Regent St., London SW1Y 4XT. **VisitScotland Central Information Department** ✉ 23 Ravelston Terr., Edinburgh EH4 3EU ☎ 0131/332-2433 🖷 0131/315-4545 ⊕ www.visitscotland.com.

Aberdeen and Grampian ✉ 27 Albyn Pl., Aberdeen ☎ 01224/288828, 01224/288825 reservations 🖷 01224/581367 ⊕ www.castlesandwhisky.com. **Ballater** ✉ Station Sq. ☎ 013397/55306. **Banchory** ✉ Bridge St. ☎ 01330/822000. **Inverness** ✉ Castle Wynd, IV2 3BJ ☎ 01463/234353 ⊕ www.highlandfreedom.com. **Jedburgh** ✉ Murrays Green ☎ 01835/863435. **St. Andrews** ✉ 70 Market St., KY16 9NU ☎ 01334/472021 ⊕ www.standrews.com/fife.

UNDERSTANDING
GREAT BRITAIN

GREAT BRITAIN AT A GLANCE

THE CURTAIN RISES ON THE PERFORMING ARTS

SPLENDID STONES & BRITISH ARCHITECTURE

BOOKS & MOVIES

CHRONOLOGY

GREAT BRITAIN AT A GLANCE

Fast Facts

Capital: London

London is a university with ten million graduates qualified to live and let live.
Oliver St. John Gogarty, 1937

National anthem: "God Save the Queen"
Type of government: Constitutional monarchy
Administrative divisions: 3 countries: England, Scotland, and Wales. Great Britain is the largest of the British Isles. The United Kingdom includes England, Scotland, Wales, and Northern Ireland.
Independence: England has existed as a unified entity since the 10th century. The union between England and Wales was enacted under the Statute of Rhuddlan in 1284, and England and Scotland agreed to permanent union as Great Britain in the Act of Union of 1707.
Constitution: The Constitution exists in no one document but is instead partly a centuries-old accumulation of statutes and partly common law and practice.

Legal system: English Common Law
Suffrage: 18 years of age
Legislature: Bicameral parliament
Population: 60,094,648
Population density: 248.75 persons per sq km (644.25 persons per sq mi)
Median age: Female 40, male 37
Life expectancy: Female 81, male 76
Infant mortality rate: 5.28 deaths per 1,000 live births
Literacy: 99%
Language: English (official), Welsh (about 26% of the population of Wales), Scottish form of Gaelic (about 60,000 in Scotland)
Ethnic groups: For the United Kingdom: English 81.5%; Scottish 9.6%; Irish 2.4%; Welsh 1.9%; Ulster 1.8%; West Indian, Indian, Pakistani, and other 2.8%
Religion: Anglican and Roman Catholic 67%; Muslim 2.5%; Presbyterian 1.3%; Methodist 1.3%; Sikh 0.8%; Hindu 0.8%; Jewish 0.6%

Geography & Environment

Land area: 241,590 sq km (93,278 sq mi)
Coastline: 12,429 km (7,723 mi)
Terrain: Rugged hills and low mountains, level to rolling plains in east and southeast

All places, all airs make unto me one country; I am in England, everywhere, and under any meridian.
Sir Thomas Browne, 1642

Natural resources: Clay, coal, limestone, iron ore, natural gas, petroleum, salt, tin
Natural hazards: Floods, winter windstorms

The English winter, ending in July To recommence in August.
Lord Byron, *Don Juan*, 1819

Environmental issues: Greenhouse gas emissions, industrial and commercial waste

Economy

Currency: British pound (GBP)
Exchange rate: 0.54 British pounds per U.S. dollar
GDP: £833.538 trillion ($1.528 trillion)
Per capita income: £13,909 ($25,500)
Inflation: 2.1%
Unemployment: 5.2%
Work force: 29.7 million (services 74%; agriculture 1%; industry 25%)
Debt: £434.544 billion ($785.4 billion)
Major industries: Aircraft, automation equipment, electric power equipment, machine tools, railroad equipment, shipbuilding
Agricultural products: Cattle, cereals, fish, oilseed, potatoes, poultry, sheep, vegetables

Exports: £156.2 billion ($286.3 billion)
Major export products: Beverages, chemicals, food, fuels, manufactured goods, tobacco
Export partners: U.S. 15.5%; Germany 11.2%; France 7.8%; Netherlands 6.3%; Belgium 5.2%; Italy 4.4%; Spain 4.3%
Imports: £180.05 billion ($330.1 billion)
Major import products: Foodstuffs, fuels, machinery, manufactured goods
Import partners: Germany 12.9%; U.S. 11.9%; France 7.8%; Netherlands 6.3%; Belgium 5%; Italy 4.4%

Did You Know?

• No location in Great Britain is more than 125 km from the coast.

• The United Kingdom is the only country that does not have its name on its stamps, but rather only the profile of the current monarch. The Universal Postal Union allows this because Britain was the first country to issue stamps.

• The shortest war on record, between Britain and Zanzibar in 1896, lasted a mere 38 minutes.

• After the Norman Conquest in 1066, French became the official language of England for over 300 years.

• The Shree Swaminarayan Mandir in London is the largest traditional Hindu temple outside of India. It covers an area of 6,071 sq m (65,347 sq ft) and was built using 26,300 pieces of stone.

• The number of applications to Scotland's University of St. Andrews went up by 44% after it was announced that Prince William intended to start studying there in 2001.

• The British appreciate tea, drinking a total of 165 million cups of the beverage each day.

THE CURTAIN RISES
ON THE PERFORMING ARTS

ONE OF THE MAIN REASONS people want to visit Britain is the country's enviable reputation in the performing arts, whether it's music or drama, opera or ballet. The country is exactly what Shakespeare described, an "isle full of noises, sounds and sweet airs that give delight and hurt not." Although government subsidies often fall short of spiraling costs, numerous National Lottery grants have kept many a show on the road, and the performing arts scene remains surprisingly healthy. There is a fluidity about the arts in Britain that helps build their strength and appeal. An actor playing Lear with the Royal Shakespeare Company one day could appear in a television farce the next; an opera that has played to the small, exclusive audience at Glyndebourne reappears the next week at the Albert Hall as part of the BBC's Promenade Concerts, delighting not only the 7,000 in attendance, but millions more by radio. The performing arts largely transcend the social barriers that bedevil many aspects of British life, providing cultural nourishment for the widest spectrum of people.

The Theater

An evening at a play is a vital element of any trip to Britain. Most people head first for London's West End, the city's fabled "Theatreland." Here, you might catch Judi Dench and Vanessa Redgrave doing star turns, fabulous musical revivals, more than one Andrew Lloyd Webber extravaganza, and Agatha Christie's apparently immortal *The Mousetrap,* which opened in 1955. Then there is that great mainstay, Shakespeare. At one time theater managers believed that "Shakespeare spelled ruin." Today he may spell big business; witness the movie *Shakespeare in Love,* plus other filmed versions of the Bard's classics coming out of Hollywood.

Shakespeare provides a touchstone by which actors can measure themselves, and

by which other people can measure them. Take *Hamlet,* for instance: occasionally a clutch of versions are staged at the same time. But that protracted procession of princes gives a fascinating lesson in the richness of talent available; indeed, Britain's actors are among the nation's greatest treasures. However poor the play, the talents of the performers rarely fail. In the end, all the Hamlets have something to offer that seems to shed fresh light on the weary text. Simply put, Spain has its bullfights, Italy its opera, Britain its theater.

The pinnacle of the dramatic scene consists of two great national companies, the Royal National Theatre and the Royal Shakespeare Company (generally known as the RSC). They do have separate identities, though it is not always easy to pin down the ways in which they differ. The RSC is more prolific, performing at theaters in the West End and touring the country. It also has three stages at Stratford-upon-Avon: the large Royal Shakespeare Theatre, the Swan, and the Other Place. The Swan, constructed on the lines of Shakespeare's Globe, is one of the most exciting acting spaces in the country. The Other Place is used for experimental staging. The National Theatre plays in the three auditoriums in its concrete fortress on London's South Bank: the Olivier, the Lyttelton, and the Cottesloe, in descending order of size, the Olivier being huge and the Cottesloe studio-size. Of the two companies, the RSC is the more cohesive, with an impressive volume of work and a steadily developing style. The great majority of its offerings are works of Shakespeare and other English classics, with occasional ventures into musicals. The National ransacks world drama and also mounts some of the best stagings of American musicals anywhere beyond Broadway. It attracts more star performers than the RSC; the RSC relies largely on teamwork and creates stars from its own ranks. Both companies suffer from financial problems, even though some of their best productions have extended runs and often grow into considerable hits.

As for the Bard of Bards, his fabled Globe Theatre, the most famous playhouse in the world, has risen again on the South Bank of the Thames in London, not 200 yards from where the original stood. England has always held special temptations for Shakespeare fans; the reconstructed Globe has added the thrill of seeing his plays performed in the neighborhood where he lived and on virtually the same kind of stage.

Beyond London, provincial theaters operate in most cities and large towns up and down the land, and many of them have developed national and international reputations. In Scarborough, a seaside town in Yorkshire, for example, the dramatist-director Alan Ayckbourn has run for years the Stephen Joseph Theatre, where he tries out his own plays. Most of these are transferred to London, appearing as often as not at the National Theatre. But the delight of British regional theaters lies in their great diversity and local panache. In the town of Richmond, in Yorkshire, the charming Georgian Theatre Royal seats about 200 in rows and balconies that still reflect 18th-century class divisions. Porthcurno, near Penzance in Cornwall, has the cliff-top Minack Theatre, which overlooks the sea. The National Trust runs the lovely, still fully functioning, 1819 Theatre Royal in Bury St. Edmunds. There are woodland theaters, theaters in barns, and several in grand old country houses.

If you're traveling around the country, it's worth your time to find out what is on in any spot you may hit, especially in summer. At that time Britain's acting fraternity takes to the open air and strives to outdo passing planes and nearby traffic. Notable venues include York, where a famous medieval cycle of mystery plays is performed every four years in surroundings that add incalculable richness; some of the quadrangles of Oxford and Cambridge, which come alive with Oliviers-in-the-bud; and London's Regent's Park, which offers the best performances of the open-air theaters. There you can watch Shakespeare, after having wandered in Queen Mary's rose garden. To sit in the dusk, as Puck and Oberon plot their magic, and the actors gradually create a world of fantasy, is to take part in an essentially British rite.

Opera

Dr. Samuel Johnson, who was a notable grouch, accused opera of being an exotic and irrational entertainment. Indeed, opera *is* irrational. It was born in the royal and ducal courts of Europe, where expense had no meaning. London's two main companies are poles apart. The Royal Opera at Covent Garden is socially the most prestigious. This is the place for spectacles and productions to equal those presented anywhere. The English National Opera (ENO) at the Coliseum, beside Trafalgar Square, has a wider appeal, with classic operas sung in English, produced by an innovative directorial team that has established its reputation as the leader of opera fashion. Seat prices for the ENO are generally much gentler than those at the Royal Opera, and the company consists mostly of British singers. The one drawback is that the auditorium sometimes dwarfs the voices.

Britain has two other national opera companies: the Welsh National at Cardiff, and the Scottish National in Glasgow. They both embrace adventuresome artistic policies, attacking such blockbusters as Wagner's *Ring* and *The Trojans* by Berlioz. They also tour, the Welsh National especially, appearing in small towns around the country, even performing in movie houses. Opera North, a spin-off of the English National, is based in Leeds and is as venturesome as its begetter. Sadler's Wells, in north London, is a regular venue for regional opera as well as touring national and international dance companies.

Opera has always been an extravagant art form from a financial standpoint, but one company managed to build its own home in 1994. Glyndebourne, in deepest Sussex, relies entirely on sponsors and ticket sales, having no state subsidy. A visit there will cost you an arm and a leg, but you may feel like a guest at a superior house party.

Ballet

Ballet is a surprising art to flourish in Britain, and it does so only with a struggle. The Royal Ballet, the premier company, has one of its own veteran dancers, Monica Mason, in the hot seat as director. Few other companies present the classics with such seemingly effortless style and accomplishment.

The sibling Birmingham Royal Ballet is a dynamic company to watch, with its zesty director-choreographer David Bintley. The English National Ballet (ENB) goes from strength to strength in its mission to give ballet more mass appeal. You can catch the ENB performing its winter season at the London Coliseum, with summer shows at the Royal Albert Hall. Between times, it tours countrywide with a repertoire of classics. The Scottish Ballet is making waves with ex–Royal Ballet principal dancer and choreographer Ashley Page at the helm. The Northern Ballet Theatre, based in Leeds, has popular appeal with its romantic take on such productions as *Wuthering Heights* and *Madame Butterfly*. If you want to catch some of these companies on tour in London, check out the performance schedules at Sadler's Wells and the Peacock Theatre.

Music

Britain's amazingly vibrant musical life fills halls and theaters, churches and chapels throughout the land. In London, the three concert halls of the South Bank Centre, together with the Barbican, the Albert Hall, and the Wigmore Hall, provide the capital with venues for rich and varied musical fare. For example, every night for six weeks in summer, the Albert Hall is host of the BBC-sponsored "Proms," the biggest series of concerts in the world, involving 10 or more orchestras and dozens of other artists. Outside London, cities with fine resident orchestras include Birmingham (home to the noted City of Birmingham Symphony Orchestra), Liverpool, Manchester, and even the seaside town of Bournemouth.

Every week of the year you can attend performances of great choral works in concert halls, recitals of lieder in stately homes by candlelight, modern pieces on remote Scottish islands in the rich Celtic twilight of ancient buildings, and lively madrigals from boats on moonlit rivers. It's not just the Welsh who can say, in Dylan Thomas's words, "Thank God we are a musical nation."

Arts Festivals

Britain is a land of festivals, mostly, though not exclusively, in summer. Whatever the size of the town, it will have a festival at some time. Some are of international scope, whereas others are small local wingdings. London may be the focus for annual film, dance, and music festivals in locations from its grand halls to its parks, but the capital doesn't steal the whole show. A leading light is the Edinburgh Festival, mid-August–early September, born in the dark days after World War II, when people needed cheering up. It keeps going strong, with opera, drama, recitals, and ballet by artists from all over the world. The festival has the added attraction of the Fringe, a concurrent event, with as many as 800 performances crammed into three weeks: small-scale productions from the classic to the bizarre.

Smaller than Edinburgh's event, but still notable, are the dozens of festivals around the country. In Bath the International Festival, late May–mid-June, wins praise for its music especially. In Aldeburgh, a windswept East Anglian seaside town, the Festival of Music and the Arts, mid–late June, honors the memory of Benjamin Britten and is mainly a music festival.

Cheltenham has a musical celebration in July and an early–mid-October festival dedicated to literature, with readings, seminars, and lectures. York holds an early music festival in summer and a Viking-related festival in February. Llandrindod Wells, in Wales, goes Victorian and dresses up in late August. Worcester, Hereford, and Gloucester take turns mounting the annual Three Choirs Festival in mid-August, the oldest in the world; this event has seen premieres of some notable music. Truro stages the Three Spires Festival in June in imitation. Wales has an annual feast of song and poetry late July–early August, called the National Eisteddfod. At Chichester in Sussex a summer drama festival has proved so popular that the town has built a theater especially for it. At Ludlow, Shakespeare is performed in summer in the open air, with the dramatic castle as backdrop.

All these festivals have the advantage of focusing a visit to a town and helping you to meet the locals, but be sure to book well in advance, because they are extremely popular. Once the worst of the winter chill seeps out of everyone's bones, festival fever sets in. Year-round, however, Britain's performing arts offer one of the grandest and most unforgettable pageants in the world.

SPLENDID STONES & BRITISH ARCHITECTURE

N BRITAIN YOU CAN SEE STRUCTURES that go back to the dawn of history, in the hauntingly mysterious circles of monoliths at Stonehenge or Avebury, or view the resurrected remains of Roman empire-builders preserved in towns such as Bath and Cirencester. On the other hand, you can startle your eyes with the very current, very controversial designs of contemporary architects in areas such as London's Docklands. Appreciating the wealth of Britain's architectural heritage does not require a degree in art history, but knowing a few hallmarks of particular styles can enhance your enjoyment of what you see. Here, then, is a primer of a millennium of architectural styles.

Norman

Duke William of Normandy brought the solid Norman style to Britain when he invaded and conquered England in 1066, although William's predecessor, King Edward (the Confessor) used the style in the building of Westminster Abbey a little earlier, in 1042. Until around 1200, it was favored for buildings of any importance, and William's castles and churches soon dominated the countryside. Norman towers tended to be hefty and square, arches always round-topped, and the vaulting barrel-shaped. Decoration was mostly geometrical, but within those limits, ornate. Norman motte and bailey castles had two connecting stockaded mounds, with the keep on the higher mound and other buildings on the lower mound. *Best seen in the Tower of London and in the cathedrals of St. Albans, Ely, Gloucester, Durham, and Norwich, and at Tewkesbury Abbey.*

Gothic Early English

From 1130 to 1300, pointed arches began to supplant rounded ones, buttresses became heavier than the Norman variety, and windows lost their rounded tops to become more pointed and lancet shaped. Buildings climbed skyward, less squat and heavy, with the soaring effect accentuated by steep roofs and spires. *Best seen in the cathedrals of York, Salisbury, Ely, Worcester, Wells (interior), and Canterbury (east end), and Westminster Abbey's Chapter House.*

Decorated. From the late 1100s until around 1400, elegance and ornament became fully integrated into architectural design, rather than applied to the surface of a solid, basic form. Windows filled more of the walls and were divided into sections by carved mullions. Vaulting grew increasingly complex, with ribs and ornamented bosses proliferating; spires became even more pointed; arches took on the ogee shape, with its unique double curve. This style was one of England's greatest gifts to world architecture. *Best seen at the cathedrals of Wells, Lincoln, Durham (east transept), and Ely (Lady Chapel and Octagon).*

Perpendicular. In later Gothic architecture, the emphasis on the vertical grew even more pronounced, as shown in features such as slender pillars, huge expanses of glass, and superb fan vaulting resembling the formalized branches of frozen trees. Walls were divided by panels. One of the chief areas in which to see Perpendicular architecture is East Anglia, where towns that grew rich from the wool trade built magnificent churches in the style. Houses, too, began to reflect prevailing taste. Perpendicular Gothic lasted for well over two centuries from its advent around 1330. *Best seen at St. George's Chapel in Windsor, the cathedrals of Gloucester (cloister) and Hereford (chapter house), Henry VII's Chapel in Westminster Abbey, Bath Abbey, and King's College Chapel in Cambridge.*

Tudor

With the great period of cathedral building over, from 1500 to 1560 the nation's attention turned to the construction of spacious homes characterized by this latest fashionable architectural style. The rapidly expanding, newly rich middle class, created by the two Tudor Henrys (VII and VIII) to challenge the power of the aristocracy, built spacious manor houses, often on the foundations of pillaged monasteries. Thus began the era of the great stately homes. Brick replaced stone as the most popular medium, and plasterwork and carved wood were used to display the elaborate motifs of the age. Timber-frame and plaster buildings were also popular in this period for domestic and commercial use. Many "black-and-white" structures, as they are called, are copies made in later eras, but notable originals survive. (The Victorians are responsible for the fashion of painting half-timber buildings, of whatever era, black and white.) Wealthier individuals could afford to have the exposed wood beams carved or shaped; Little Moreton Hall, in Congleton near the Peak District, has wonderfully intricate patterns. Harvard House in Stratford-upon-Avon is another notable example of the style. Another way the social climbers could make their mark, and ensure their place in the next world, was by building churches. Money earned in the wool trade funded splendid parish churches. Some of the most magnificent are in Suffolk, Norfolk, and the Cotswolds. *Domestic architecture is best seen at Hampton Court and St. James's Palace, London; for wool churches, Lavenham and Long Melford (though its tower is much later) in Suffolk, and Cirencester, Chipping Campden, Northleach, and Winchcombe in the Cotswolds.*

Renaissance Elizabethan

For a short period under Elizabeth I, 1560–1600, this development of Tudor style flourished as Italian influences began to seep into England, seen especially in symmetrical facades. The most notable example was Hardwick Hall in Derbyshire, built in the 1590s by Bess of Hardwick; the jingle that describes it goes "Hardwick Hall, more glass than wall." However grand the houses were, they were still on a human scale, warm and livable, built of a mellow amalgam of brick and stone. *Other great Elizabethan houses are Montacute in Somerset, Longleat in Wiltshire, and Burghley House in Cambridgeshire.*

Jacobean

At the beginning of the 17th century, for the first 15 years of the reign of James I (the name Jacobean is taken from the Latin word for James, Jacobus), architecture did not change noticeably. Windows were still large in proportion to the wall surfaces. Gables, in the style of the Netherlands, were popular. Carved decoration in wood and plaster (especially the geometrical patterning called "strapwork," another element of Dutch origin, which resembled intertwined leather belts) remained exuberant, now even more so. A change was on the way, though. Inigo Jones (1573–1652), the first great modern British architect, attempted to synthesize the architectural heritage of England with current Italian theories. Two of his finest remaining buildings—the Banqueting House, Whitehall, and the Queen's House at Greenwich—epitomize his genius, which was to introduce to England the Italian-created Palladian style that would dominate British architecture for centuries. It uses the classical Greek orders: Doric, Ionic, and Corinthian. This was grandeur. But the classical style that proved so monumentally effective under a hot Mediterranean sun was somehow transformed in Britain, domesticated and tamed. Columns and pediments decorated the facades, and huge frescoes provided acres of color to interior walls and ceilings, all in the Italian manner. These architectural elements had not yet been totally naturalized, however. There were in fact two quite distinct styles running concurrently: the comfortably domestic and the purer classical in public buildings. They were finally fused by the talent of Christopher Wren. *Jacobean is best seen at the Bodleian Library, Oxford; Chastleton House, near Stow-on-the Wold; Audley End, Essex; and Clare College, Cambridge.*

Wren & the English Baroque

The work of Sir Christopher Wren (1632–1723) constituted an architectural era all by itself. Not only was he one of the world's greatest architects, but he was also given an unparalleled opportunity in 1666 when the disastrous Great Fire of London wiped out the center of the capital, destroying no fewer than 89 churches and 13,200 houses. Although Wren's great scheme for a modern city center was rejected, he did build 51 churches in London, the greatest of which was St. Paul's, completed in just 35 years. The range of Wren's designs is extremely wide, from simple classical shapes to the extravagantly dramatic baroque. He was also at home with domestic architecture, where his combinations of brick and stone produced a warm, homey effect. The influence of the Italian baroque can be seen in Sir John Vanbrugh's Blenheim Palace, where the facade echoes the piazza of St. Peter's in Rome, and at Vanbrugh's exuberant Castle Howard in Yorkshire. Nicholas Hawksmoor, Wren's pupil, designed some notable London churches and also the baroque Mausoleum at Castle Howard. The baroque had only a brief heyday in England; by 1725 the Palladian style was firmly in favor and the vast pile of Blenheim was being mocked by trendsetters. *Wren's ecclesiastical architecture is best seen at St. Paul's Cathedral (baroque with classical touches) and his other remaining London churches, his domestic style at Hampton Court Palace, Kensington Palace, the Royal Hospital in Chelsea, and the former Royal Naval College in Greenwich. English baroque is best seen at Blenheim Palace (Oxfordshire) and Castle Howard (Yorkshire).*

Palladian

In Britain, this style is often referred to as Georgian, so-called from the Hanoverian kings George I through IV, although it was introduced as early as Inigo Jones's time. During the 18th century, classical inspiration was thoroughly acclimatized in Britain. Though they looked completely at home among the hills, lakes, and trees of the British countryside, Palladian buildings were derived from the Roman-inspired designs of the Italian architectural theorist Andrea Palladio (1508–80), with pillared porticoes, triangular pediments, and strictly balanced windows. In domestic architecture, this large-scale classicism was usually modified to quiet simplicity, preserving mathematical proportions of windows, doors, and the exactly calculated volume of room space, to create a feeling of balance and harmony. The occasional departures from the classical manner at this time included the over-the-top Indian-style Royal Pavilion in Brighton, built for the prince regent (later George IV) by John Nash. The Regency style comes under the Palladian heading, though strictly speaking it lasted only for the few years of the actual Regency (1811–20). Architects in Britain, such as the brilliant Robert Adam, handled the Palladian style with more freedom than their counterparts elsewhere in Europe, and the United States took its cue from the British. *Among the best Palladian examples are Regent's Park Terraces (London), the library at Kenwood (London), the Royal Crescent and other streets in Bath, and Holkham Hall (Norfolk).*

Victorian

Elements of imaginative fantasy, already seen in the Palladian era, came to the fore during the long reign of Victoria (1837–1901). The country's vast profits made from the Industrial Revolution were spent lavishly. Civic building accelerated in all the major cities, with town halls modeled after medieval castles or French châteaux. The Victorians plundered the past for styles, with Gothic, about which the scholarly Victorians were very knowledgeable, leading the field. The supreme examples here are the Houses of Parliament by Charles Barry and Augustus Pugin, and the Albert Memorial by George Gilbert Scott, both in London. (To distinguish between the Victorian variety and a version of the style that flourished in the late 1700s, the earlier one is commonly spelled "Gothick.") But there were other styles in the running, including the attractively named, and self-explanatory, "Wrenaissance." *Other striking examples of Victorian architecture are Truro Cathedral, Manchester Town Hall, Ironbridge, and Cragside (Northumberland).*

Edwardian

Toward the end of the Victorian era, in the late 1800s, architecture calmed down considerably, with a return to a solid sort of classicism, and even to a muted baroque. The Arts and Crafts movement, especially the work of William Morris and work inspired by Morris, produced simpler designs, sometimes returning to medieval models. In an age of increasing mechanization, craftsmanship was emphasized. Architectural elements incorporated stylized natural motifs. *Best seen in Buckingham Palace and the Admiralty Arch in London. Kelmscott Manor (the interior of William Morris's Tudor home in the Thames Valley), Standen in East Grinstead (West Sussex), Rodmarton Manor near Tetbury (the Cotswolds), and Blackwell in Windermere (Cumbria) are notable Arts and Crafts houses.*

Modern

A furious public debate has raged in Britain for years between traditionalists and the adherents of modernistic architecture. Britons tend to be strongly conservative when it comes to their environment. These arguments have been highlighted by the intervention of such notable figures as Prince Charles, who derides excessive modernism and who said, for instance, that the design for the Sainsbury Wing of the National Gallery in Trafalgar Square would be like "a carbuncle on a much-loved face." One reason for the strength of the British attitude is that the country suffered from much ill-conceived development after World War II, when large areas of city centers had to be rebuilt after the devastation caused by German bombs. Town planners and architects encumbered the country with badly built and worse-designed towers and shopping areas. Today, however, there appears to be an increased readiness to embrace the new, as designers draw people into user-friendly, fun buildings such as City Hall in London and the Baltic Centre for Contemporary Art in Newcastle.

The situation created in the '50s and '60s is slowly being reversed. High-rise apartment blocks are being taken down and replaced by more humanly scaled housing. Commercial areas in a number of cities are being rethought and slowly rebuilt. The emphasis has gradually moved to planning, design, and construction that pays more attention to the needs of inhabitants. A healthier attitude also exists toward the conservation of old buildings. As part of the postwar building splurge, older houses that should have been treasured were torn down wholesale. Happily, many of those that survived the wreckers' ball are now being restored and put back to use.

Nowadays, a number of architectural styles prevail in Britain. A predominant one draws largely on the past, with nostalgic echoes of the country cottage, and leans heavily on variegated brickwork and close attention to decorative detail. Urban centers have buildings in the most innovative styles, which are exciting and ecologically sensitive, too, using light to more thoughtful effect. These new designs have turned many fatigued or declining areas into destinations to see and be seen in.

In London, the Lloyd's of London tower in the City, by Sir Richard Rogers, designer of the Pompidou Center in Paris, began the trend toward modernism in the 1980s, but it took the millennium year to focus institutional minds on the creation of forward-looking images. The now-closed Millennium Dome, Rogers's tour de force, transformed the industrial blot of Greenwich peninsula. Sir Norman Foster's graceful Millennium Bridge has made equal headlines. Foster's glassy masterpiece, City Hall, near Tower Bridge, has been knocked as looking like a "glass testicle," but it is one of the boldest designs in London. Skyscrapers in the City of London are the exception rather than the rule, although the regenerated space of the old Docklands has allowed more room for imagination, as at Canary Wharf. Other buildings, such as Barclays Bank with its jukebox dome, and Swiss Re's "erotic gherkin" at 30 St. Mary Axe, the latter by Foster and looking akin to a glittering carousel pole, have begun to push height limitations established because of the proximity of historic buildings.

Other centers of modern architectural excellence include Manchester, with the Imperial War Museum North by Daniel Libeskind. Since the city center was bombed by the IRA in 1996, Manchester has received an impressive face-lift. Also in the north, Gateshead Quays is the spectacularly renovated industrial area around the River Tyne and Newcastle. The tilting Millennium Bridge in Newcastle is as dramatic as London's, and the city has opened the largest arts space in Europe, the Baltic Centre for Contemporary Art, with a vista that could rival Sydney Harbor's. Cornwall has the Eden Project, the world's largest conservatories, which are set in a former china clay pit and massed to make a giant glass crater.

Elsewhere, on a more sober scale, smaller public buildings are being built; schools and libraries, designed in a muted modernism, use traditional, natural materials, such as wood, stone, and brick. Numerous cultural institutions, particularly in London, have undergone innovative renovations, in part to add visitor-friendly, interactive technology. The Royal Opera House, Tate Modern and Tate Britain, the Great Court at the British Museum, the Queen's Gallery, and the Wellcome Wing at the Science Museum are among the most noteworthy projects that have embraced the new, with a subtle emphasis on complementing the old. Anyone with an interest in architecture should visit the headquarters of the Royal Institute of British Architects (RIBA) in Portland Place, London, for exhibits on buildings great and small, new and old. *Among other buildings to see are Richmond House and the Clore Building at Tate Britain (in London), the campus of Sussex University (outside Brighton), the Royal Regatta Building (Henley), the Sainsbury Centre for the Visual Arts (Norwich), the Lowry Centre (Manchester), and the Burrell Collection (Glasgow).*

BOOKS & MOVIES

Books

Many writers' names have become inextricably linked with the regions in which they set their books or plays. Hardy's Wessex, Daphne Du Maurier's Cornwall, Wordsworth's Lake District, Shakespeare's Arden, and Brontë Country are now evocative catchphrases, treasured by local tourist boards. However hackneyed the tags may be, you *can* still get a heightened insight about an area through the eyes of authors of genius, even though they may have written a century or more ago. Here are a few works that may provide you with an understanding of their authors' loved territory.

Thomas Hardy's novels *The Mayor of Casterbridge, Tess of the d'Urbervilles,* and *Far from the Madding Crowd* (and indeed almost everything he wrote) are solidly based on his Wessex (Dorset) homeland. Daphne Du Maurier had a deep love of Cornwall from her childhood; *Frenchman's Creek, Jamaica Inn,* and *The King's General* all capture the county's Celtic mood. The wildness of Exmoor in Devon is captured in the historical novel *Lorna Doone* by R. D. Blackmore. The Brontë sisters' *Wuthering Heights, The Tenant of Wildfell Hall,* and *Jane Eyre* breathe the sharp air of the moors around the writers' Haworth home. William Wordsworth, who was born at Cockermouth in the Lake District, depicts the area's rugged beauty in many of his poems, especially the *Lyrical Ballads.*

Virginia Woolf's visits to Vita Sackville-West at her ancestral home of Knole, in Sevenoaks, inspired the novel *Orlando.* The stately home is now a National Trust property. The country around Bateman's, near Burwash in East Sussex, the home where Rudyard Kipling lived for more than 30 years, was the inspiration for *Puck of Pook's Hill* and *Rewards and Fairies.* American writer Henry James lived at Lamb House in Rye, also in East Sussex, as did E. F. Benson, whose delicious Lucia novels take place in a thinly disguised version of the town. Bateman's and Lamb House are National Trust buildings.

A highly irreverent and very funny version of academic life, *Porterhouse Blue,* by Tom Sharpe, will guarantee that you look at Oxford and Cambridge with a totally different eye. John Fowles's *The French Lieutenant's Woman,* largely set in Lyme Regis, is full of local color about Dorset.

The late James Herriot's veterinary surgeon books, among them *All Creatures Great and Small,* give evocative accounts of life in the Yorkshire dales during much of the 20th century; the books were made into popular television shows. For a perceptive account of life in the English countryside, try Ronald Blythe's well-regarded *Akenfield: Portrait of an English Village.*

Mysteries are almost a way of life in Britain, partly because many of the best English mystery writers set their plots in their home territories. Modern whodunits by P. D. James and Ruth Rendell convey a fine sense of place, and Ellis Peters's Brother Cadfael stories re-create life in medieval Shrewsbury with a wealth of telling detail. Colin Dexter's Inspector Morse mysteries capture the flavor of Oxford's town and gown. There are also always the villages, vicarages, and scandals of Agatha Christie's "Miss Marple" books.

The fans of Arthurian legends can turn to some excellent, imaginative novels that not only tell the stories but also give fine descriptions of the British countryside. Among them are *Sword at Sunset,* by Rosemary Sutcliffe, *The Once and Future King,* by T. H. White, and the four Merlin novels by Mary Stewart; *The Crystal Cave, The Hollow Hills, The Last Enchantment,* and *The Wicked Day.* Edward Rutherfurd's historical novels *Sarum, London,* and *The Forest* deal with British history with a grand sweep from the prehistoric past to the present.

An animal's close-to-the-earth viewpoint can reveal all kinds of countryside insights about Britain. *Watership Down,* a runaway best-seller about rabbits, was written by Richard Adam in the early '70s. *The Wind in the Willows,* by Kenneth Grahame, gives a vivid impression of the Thames Valley almost 100 years ago, which still holds largely true today. Devon, the northern part in particular, is the setting of Henry Williamson's *Tarka the Otter,* a beloved nature story published in the 1920s; many paths in the region are signposted as part of the Tarka Trail.

Those interested in writers and the surroundings that influenced their works should look at *A Literary Guide to London,* by Ed Glinert, and *The Oxford Literary Guide to the British Isles,* edited by Dorothy Eagle and Hilary Carnell (now out of print). One author currently in vogue is Jane Austen: Janeites will want to read Maggie Lane's *Jane Austen's World* and Nigel Nicolson's wonderful *World of Jane Austen.* For a vast portrait of everyone's favorite English author, dig into Peter Ackroyd's *Dickens.*

Good background books on English history are *The Oxford Illustrated History of Britain,* edited by Kenneth O. Morgan, and *The Story of England,* by Christopher Hibbert. *The Isles,* a history by Norman Davies, challenges conventional Anglocentric assumptions. *The English: A Portrait of a People,* by Jeremy Paxman, examines the concept of Englishness in a changing world. *The London Encyclopaedia,* by Ben Weinreb and Christopher Hibbert, now out of print, is invaluable as a source of information on the capital. Simon Schama's three-volume *History of Britain,* with handsome color illustrations, was written to accompany the BBC–History Channel television series. Peter Ackroyd's illustrated nonfiction *London: A Biography* captures the city's energy and its quirks from prehistory to the present. Jan Morris's *The Matter of Wales*

is a notable introduction to the country.

The finest book on the country's stately homes is Nigel Nicolson's *Great Houses of Britain,* written for the National Trust (now out of print). Also spectacular are the picture books *Great Houses of Britain and Wales* and *Great Houses of Scotland,* by Hugh Montgomery-Massingberd. *The Buildings of England* and *The Buildings of Scotland,* written by Nikolaus Pevsner but much updated since his death, are part of a multivolume series, organized by county, which sets out to chronicle in detail every building of any importance. Pevsner's *Best Buildings of Britain* is a grand anthology with lush photographs. New Pevsner Architectural Guides continue to be published. For the golden era of Georgian architecture, check out John Summerson's definitive *Architecture in Britain 1530–1830.* Simon Jenkins's *England's Thousand Best Churches,* with photographs, describes parish churches (not cathedrals) large and small. Mark Girouard has written several books that are incomparable for their behind-the-scenes perspective on art and architecture: *Life in the English Country House* focuses on houses over the centuries, and *The Victorian Country House* addresses the lifestyles of the rich and famous of the 19th century. For the ultimate look at English villages, see *The Most Beautiful Villages of England,* by James Bentley, with ravishing photographs by Hugh Palmer.

There are many delightful travel books about Britain, including Susan Allen Toth's *England for All Seasons* and *My Love Affair with England.* Bill Bryson's *Notes from a Small Island* is perennially popular. Few of today's authors have managed to top the wit and perception of Henry James's magisterial *English Hours.* As for "the flower of cities all," *London Perceived* is a classic text by the noted literary critic V. S. Pritchett, and John Russell's *London* is a superlative text written by a particularly eloquent art historian.

Movies

From *Wuthering Heights* to *Jane Eyre,* great classics of British literature have been rendered into great classics of film. It's surprising to learn, however, how many of them were creations of Hollywood and not the British film industry (which had its heyday from the 1940s to the 1960s). From Laurence Olivier to Kenneth Branagh, noted director-actors have cross-pollinated the cinema in Britain and the United States. A survey can begin with the dramas of Shakespeare: Olivier gave the world a memorable *Othello* and *Hamlet,* Orson Welles a moody *Macbeth,* Branagh gave up mod versions of *Hamlet* and *Much Ado About Nothing.* Leonardo DiCaprio graced Australian Baz Luhrmann's contemporary version of *Romeo and Juliet.* Going behind the scenes, so to speak, Tom Stoppard created the Oscar winner *Shakespeare in Love.* Charles Dickens has also provided the foundation for film favorites: David Lean's immortal *Great Expectations,* George Cukor's *David Copperfield,* and *A Christmas Carol,* with Alastair Sim as Scrooge, top this list, which continues to grow with additions such as Douglas McGrath's *Nicholas Nickleby.*

McGrath's *Emma,* starring Gwyneth Paltrow, and Ang Lee's *Sense and Sensibility,* starring Emma Thompson and Kate Winslet, are just two of the recent film versions of Jane Austen's works. *Pandaemonium,* about the youthful Wordsworth and Coleridge, is fanciful but has great Lake District scenery and some insight into the poets' early work.

Harry Potter and the Sorcerer's Stone (in Britain, *Harry Potter and the Philosopher's Stone*), based on the wildly popular children's books by J. K. Rowling, was filmed in many British locations, including London, Gloucester, the Cotswolds, Northumbria, and Yorkshire. The film attracted such attention that the British Tourist Authority created a Harry Potter map, "Discovering the Magic of Britain," as a guide to the film sites and places of related interest. The second movie, *Harry Potter and the Chamber of Secrets,* used some of the same settings as the first. *Harry Potter and the Prisoner of Azkaban* hit theaters in summer 2004, and *Harry Potter and the Goblet of Fire* is scheduled for release late in 2005.

Of the film versions of Agatha Christie's books, one is especially treasured: *Murder, She Said,* which starred the inimitable Margaret Rutherford. With its quiet English village setting, harpsichord score, and the dotty Miss Marple as portrayed by Rutherford, this must be the most English of all Christie films.

Lovers of opulence, spectacle, and history have many choices—in particular, Robert Bolt's version of Sir Thomas More's life and death, *A Man for All Seasons.* His *Lady Caroline Lamb* is surely the most beautiful historical film ever made. Richard Harris made a stirring Lord Protector in *Cromwell,* and the miniseries on Queen Elizabeth I, starring Glenda Jackson, is a great BBC addition to videos. Elizabeth's adversary came to breathless life in Vanessa Redgrave's rendition of *Mary, Queen of Scots,* certainly one of her finest performances. The 2004 movie *Arthur,* with Clive Owen and Keira Knightley, gives a new spin to Arthurian tales.

Musicals? Near the top of anyone's list are four films set in England—three of them in Hollywood's England—that rank among the greatest musicals of all time: Walt Disney's *Mary Poppins,* George Cukor's *My Fair Lady,* Sir Carol Reed's Oscar-winner *Oliver!,* and—yeah, yeah, yeah!—the Beatles' *A Hard Day's Night,* a British production.

If you're seeking a look at contemporary Britain, you might view *My Beautiful Laundrette,* about Asians in London; *Secrets and Lies,* about a dysfunctional London family; or *Trainspotting,* about Edinburgh's dark side. Manchester's rocking music scene from the 1970s to early 1990s is the subject of the well-named *24*

Hour Party People. You might lighten up with *The Full Monty,* about six former steelworkers in Sheffield who become strippers, or one of numerous romantic comedies: *Notting Hill,* with Julia Roberts and Hugh Grant; Hugh Grant again in *Four Weddings and a Funeral;* Gwyneth Paltrow in *Sliding Doors;* and Renée Zellweger (and Hugh Grant, again) in *Bridget Jones's Diary* and *Bridget Jones: The Edge of Reason.* Grant is also good in *About a Boy,* the film version of Nick Hornby's book about a cynical Londoner who learns about commitment. *Calendar Girls,* filmed in rural Yorkshire, follows the true story of a group of middle-aged women who raise money for charity with an (almost) bare-all calendar.

Quintessentially British are some comedies of the 1950s and 1960s: Alec Guinness's *Kind Hearts and Coronets,* Peter Sellers's *The Mouse That Roared,* and Tony Richardson's Oscar-winner and cinematic style-setter, *Tom Jones,* starring Albert Finney, are best bets. In 2001 American director Robert Altman took a biting look at the British class system in *Gosford Park,* a country-house murder mystery set in the 1930s that stars mostly British actors, including Jeremy Northam and Maggie Smith. A more staid, upstairs-downstairs look at the class system is the film of the novel *The Remains of the Day,* featuring Anthony Hopkins as the stalwart butler, with Emma Thompson. Today many people's visions of turn-of-the-last-century England have been captured by the Merchant and Ivory films, notably their *Howard's End,* which won many awards.

CHRONOLOGY

3000 BC   First building of Stonehenge (later building 2100–1900 BC)

54 BC–AD 43   Julius Caesar's exploratory invasion of England. Romans conquer England, led by Emperor Claudius

60   Boudicca, a native British queen, razes the first Roman London (Londinium)

122–27   Emperor Hadrian completes the Roman conquest and builds a wall across the north to keep back the Scottish Picts

300–50   Height of Roman colonization, administered from such towns as Verulamium (St. Albans), Colchester, Lincoln, and York

410   Roman rule of Britain ends, after waves of invasion by Jutes, Angles, and Saxons

ca. 490   Possible period for the legendary King Arthur, who may have led resistance to Anglo-Saxon invaders; in 500 the Battle of Badon is fought

550–700   Seven Anglo-Saxon kingdoms emerge—Essex, Wessex, Sussex, Kent, Anglia, Mercia, and Northumbria—to become the core of English social and political organization for centuries

563   St. Columba, an Irish monk, founds monastery on the Scottish island of Iona; begins to convert Picts and Scots to Christianity

597   St. Augustine arrives in Canterbury to Christianize Britain

871–99   Alfred the Great, king of Wessex, unifies the English against Viking invaders, who are then confined to the northeast

1040   Edward the Confessor moves his court to Westminster and founds Westminster Abbey

1066   William, duke of Normandy, invades, defeats King Harold at the Battle of Hastings, and is crowned William I at Westminster in December

1086   Domesday Book completed, a survey of all taxpayers in England, drawn up to assist administration of the realm

1167   Oxford University founded

1170   Thomas à Becket murdered in Canterbury; his shrine becomes center for international pilgrimage

1189   Richard the Lionhearted embarks on the Third Crusade

1209   Cambridge University founded

1215   King John forced to sign Magna Carta at Runnymede. It promulgates basic principles of English law: no taxation except through Parliament, trial by jury, and property guarantees

1272–1307   Edward I, a great legislator; in 1282–83 he conquers Wales and reinforces his rule with a chain of massive castles

1337–1453 Edward III claims the French throne, starting the Hundred Years War. In spite of dramatic English victories—1346 at Crécy, 1356 at Poitiers, 1415 at Agincourt—the long war of attrition ends with the French driving the English out from everywhere but Calais, which finally falls in 1558

1348–49 The Black Death (bubonic plague) reduces the population of Britain from around 4,250,000 to around 2½ million; decades of social unrest follow

1399 Henry Bolingbroke (Henry IV) deposes and murders his cousin Richard II; beginning of the rivalry between houses of York and Lancaster

1402–10 The Welsh, led by Owain Glendwr̂, rebel against English rule

1455–85 The Wars of the Roses; the York-Lancaster struggle erupts into civil war

1477 William Caxton prints first book in England

1485 Henry Tudor (Henry VII) defeats Richard III at the Battle of Bosworth and founds the Tudor dynasty; he suppresses private armies, develops administrative efficiency and royal absolutism

1530s Under Henry VIII the Reformation takes hold; he dissolves the monasteries and finally demolishes medieval England, replacing it with a restructured society. The land goes to wealthy merchant families, creating new gentry

1555 During the reign of papal supporter Mary I (reigned 1553–58), Protestant bishops Ridley and Latimer are burned in Oxford; in 1556 Archbishop Cranmer is burned

1558–1603 Reign of Elizabeth I: Protestantism reestablished; Drake, Raleigh, and other freebooters establish English claims in the West Indies and North America

1568 Mary, Queen of Scots, flees to England; in 1587 she is executed

1588 Spanish Armada fails to invade England

1603 James VI of Scotland, son of Mary, Queen of Scots and Lord Darnley, becomes James I of England

1605 Guy Fawkes and friends plot to blow up Parliament

1611 King James Authorized Version of the Bible published

1620 Pilgrims sail from Plymouth on the *Mayflower* and settle in what becomes New England

1629 Charles I dissolves Parliament, decides to rule alone

1642–49 Civil War between the Royalists and Parliamentarians (Cavaliers and Roundheads); the Parliamentarians win

1649 Charles I executed; England is a republic

1653   Oliver Cromwell becomes Lord Protector, establishing England's only dictatorship

1660   The Restoration: Charles II restored to the throne; accepts limits to royal power

1666   The Great Fire: London burns for three days; its medieval center is destroyed

1689   Accession of William III (of Orange) and his wife, Mary II, as joint monarchs; royal power further limited

1707   Union of English and Scots parliaments under Queen Anne

1714   The German Hanoverians succeed to the throne; George I's deficiency in English leads to the establishment of a council of ministers, the beginning of the cabinet system of government

1700s   Under the first four Georges, the Industrial Revolution develops and with it Britain's domination of world trade

1715, 1745–46   Two Jacobite rebellions fail to restore the House of Stuart to the throne; in 1746 Charles Edward Stuart (Bonnie Prince Charlie) is decisively defeated at Culloden Moor in Scotland

1756–63   Seven Years' War; Britain wins colonial supremacy from the French in Canada and India

1775–83   Britain loses the American colonies that become the United States

1795–1815   Britain and its allies defeat France in the Napoleonic Wars; in 1805, Admiral Lord Nelson is killed at Trafalgar; in 1815, Battle of Waterloo is fought

1801   Union with Ireland

1811–20   Prince Regent rules during his father's (George III) madness, the Regency period

1825   The Stockton to Darlington railway, the world's first passenger line with regular service, is established

1832   The Reform Bill extends the franchise, limiting the power of the great landowners

1834   Parliament outlaws slavery

1837–1901   During the long reign of Victoria, Britain becomes the world's richest country, and the British Empire reaches its height; railways, canals, and telegraph lines draw Britain into one vast manufacturing net

1851   The Great Exhibition, Prince Albert's brainchild, is held in the Crystal Palace, Hyde Park

1861   Prince Albert dies from typhoid fever at 42

1887   Victoria celebrates her Golden Jubilee; in 1901 she dies, marking the end of an era

1914–18 World War I: fighting against Germany, Britain loses a whole generation, with 750,000 men killed in trench warfare alone; enormous debts and inept diplomacy in the postwar years undermine Britain's position as a world power

1919 Ireland declares independence from England; bloody Black-and-Tan struggle is one result

1936 Edward VIII abdicates to marry American divorcée Wallis Simpson

1939–45 World War II: Britain faces Hitler alone until the bombing of Pearl Harbor; London badly damaged during the Blitz, September '40–May '41; Britain's economy shattered

1945 Labour wins a landslide victory; stays in power for six years, transforming Britain into a welfare state

1952 Queen Elizabeth II accedes to the throne

1973 Britain joins the European Economic Community after referendum

1975 Britain begins to pump North Sea oil

1981 Marriage of Prince Charles and Lady Diana Spencer

1982 Falklands regained in war with Argentina

1987 Conservatives under Margaret Thatcher win a third term in office

1990 John Major takes over as prime minister, ending Margaret Thatcher's illustrious, if controversial, term

1991 The Persian Gulf War

1992 Great Britain and the European countries join to form one European Community (EC), whose name was officially changed to European Union in 1993

1994 The Channel Tunnel opens a direct rail link between Britain and Europe

1996 The Prince and Princess of Wales receive a divorce.

1997 "New Labour" comes to power, with Tony Blair as prime minister. Diana, Princess of Wales, dies at 36 in a car crash in Paris. She is buried at Althorp in Northamptonshire

1999 London welcomes the new century on December 31, with the gala opening of the Millennium Dome in Greenwich

2001 The Millennium Dome closes, its future uncertain. Prime Minister Tony Blair is elected to a second term

2002 Queen Elizabeth celebrates her Golden Jubilee. Queen Elizabeth (the Queen Mother) and Princess Margaret die. Euro coins and notes enter circulation as the currency of 12 European Union nations, but Britain continues to ponder adopting the euro

2003 Britain joins U.S. and coalition forces in invading Iraq; Saddam Hussein is overthrown, and he is captured before the end of the year

INDEX

A

@Bristol, *215*
A la Ronde, *260*
Abbey Hotel and Restuarant ✕⌺, *237–238*
Abbey Road Studios, *42*
Abbey Ruins and Botanical Gardens, *573–574*
Abbot Hall, *516*
Abbotsbury, *204*
Abbotsbury Swannery, *204*
Abbotsford House, *726*
Aberconwy House, *442*
Aberdeen, *732, 734–736*
Aberdeen Art Gallery, *736*
Abergavenny, *459–461*
Abergavenny Castle, *460*
Abergavenny Food Festival, *459*
Aberystwyth, *448–450*
Aberystwyth Cliff Railway, *449*
Adlard's Restaurant ✕, *586*
Admiral Benbow Inn ✕, *237*
Afternoon tea, *67*
Aintree Racecourse, *497*
Air travel, *F37–F40*
with children, *F47*
luggage, *F63*
Aira Force, *535*
Airports, *F40*
Albert Dock, *490*
Albert Memorial, *43*
Alcester, *328–329*
Aldeburgh, *580–582*
Aldeburgh Festival, *582*
Alderminster, *327–328*
Alexander Kieller Museum and Barn Gallery, *191*
Alford, *739–740*
Alice in Wonderland Centre, *443*
All Saints Church (Hereford), *408*
All Saints Church (Royal Tunbridge Wells), *148*
Allhallows Museum, *260*
Almeida (theater), *89*
Almshouses, *313*
Alnmouth, *679*
Alnwick, *678–679*
Alnwick Castle, *678–679*
Althorp, *301–302*
Alum Bay & the Needles, *181*
Ambassador Hotels ⌺, *F31, 724*

Amberley Castle ⌺, *141*
Ambleside, *525–526*
American Bar (bar), *82*
American Museum and Gardens, *338*
Angel Hill, *573*
Angel Hotel, *573*
Angel of the North (sculpture), **666**
Angel Posting House and Livery ✕⌺, *1145*
Anglican Cathedral, *490*
Anne Hathaway's Cottage, *313*
Anne of Cleves House, *132*
Apartment and villa rentals, *F57*
Apsley House (Wellington Museum), *43*
Aquarium of the Lakes, *522*
Arlington Mill, *368*
Arlington Row, *368*
Armitt Museum, *525*
Arncliffe, *622*
Arthur, King, *231*
Arthurian Centre, *231*
Arthur's Seat, *697*
Arundel, *140–141*
Arundel Castle, *140*
Ascot, *277–278*
Ascot Racecourse, *277*
Ashmolean Museum, *286*
Askrigg, *623*
Aston Cantlow, *322*
Athelhampton House and Gardens, *201*
Athenaeum, *573*
ATMs, *F61–F62*
Attingham Park, *414–415*
Auckland Castle, *662*
Audley End House and Gardens, *569*
Austen, Jane, *171–173, 341–342*
Avebury, *190–191*
Avebury Stone Circles, *190–191*
Avoncroft Museum of Historic Buildings, *393*
Aylesbury, *297–299*

B

Baddesley Clinton, *322–323*
Bakewell, *501–502*
Bala, *433–434*
Bala Lake Railway, *433*
Ballater, *736–737*

Ballet, *87, 399, 757*
Balliol College, *286*
Balmoral Castle, *737*
Balmoral Hotel ⌺, *708*
Baltic ✕, *64*
Bamburgh, *681*
Bamburgh Castle, *681*
Banchory, *736*
Bancroft Gardens, *313*
Bank of England, *28*
Banqueting House, *9*
Bar Norman, *613*
Barbara Hepworth Museum and Sculpture Garden, *234*
Barber Institute of Fine Arts, *393*
Barbican (Plymouth), *246*
Barbican Centre (London), *28–29*
Barmouth, *452–453*
Barnard Castle, *663–664*
Barnstaple, *228*
Barracks (Berwick-upon-Tweed), *682–683*
Bassenthwaite, *532*
Bateman's, *156*
Bath, *336–338, 340–348*
Bath Abbey, *338*
Bath and the Cotswolds, *333–340, 342–351, 353–384*
Bath and environs, 336–338, 340–341, 343–350
children, attractions for, 350, 356, 358, 365, 372, 379
Cotswolds, 350–351, 353–374
essential information, 381–384
Gloucester to the Forest of Dean, 374–381
hotels, 346–347, 349, 354–355, 356, 358–359, 360–361, 362–363, 364, 365, 366, 367, 368, 369–370, 371–372, 374, 377, 378, 379, 380, 381
itinerary recommendations, 335–336
nightlife and the arts, 348, 355, 370
outdoor activities and sports, 348, 355, 370–371, 377, 382–383
pleasures and pastimes, 339
price categories, 334
restaurants, 345–346, 349, 353–354, 356, 358–359, 360–361, 362–363, 364, 366, 367, 368, 369–370, 371,

372, 374, 377, 378, 379, 380, 381
shopping, 348, 355, 361, 364, 365, 371, 374, 377, 382
Bath Intenational Music Festival, 348
Battle, 129–130
Battle Abbey, 129–130
Beaches, 640–641
Beamish Open-Air Museum, 666
Beatles, the, 42, 475, 490–491
Beatles Shop, The, 497
Beatles Story, 423
Beatrix Potter Gallery, 532
Beaulieu, 194
Beaumaris, 440–441
Beaumaris Castle, 440
Bed-and-Breakfasts (B&Bs), F57
Bede's World, 670
Beech Tree Guest House ⬚, 531
Beer, 260
Beer Quarry Caves, 260
Belgrave Place (London), 43
Bempton Cliffs, 638
Berkeley Castle, 380–381
Berwick-upon-Tweed, 682–683
Betty's ✕, 631
Betws-y-Coed, 437–438
Beverley, 638
Beverley Minster, 638
Bewdley, 409
Bibury, 368
Bicycling, F41, F66
East Anglia, 551, 566, 599
Lake District, 526, 532, 539
Lancashire and the Peaks, 507
the Northeast, 672
Thames Valley, 292
West Country, 233
Yorkshire, 649
Bideford, 228–229
Big Pit Mining Museum, 460
Birmingham, 388–390, 393–400
Birmingham Cathedral, 393
Birmingham Museum and Art Gallery, 393
Birmingham Repertory Theatre, 393
Bishop Auckland, 662
Bishop's Palace (Wells), 221
Bishopstrow House ✕⬚, 190
Black Country Living Museum, 410

Blackgang Chine, 180
Blackwell, 521–522
Bladon, 295
Blaenavon Ironworks, 460
Blaenau Ffestiniog, 434
Blakeney, 589
Blakeney Point, 589
Blakes ⬚, 75
Blanch House ✕⬚, 138
Blandford Forum, 198
Bleak House, 124
Blenheim Palace, F35, 294–295
Blickling Hall, 588–589
Boath House ⬚, 745–746
Boating and boat travel, F41–F42, F66
Bath and the Cotswolds, 348, 377
East Anglia, 589
Lake District, 524, 531, 537–538, 543
Lancashire and the Peaks, 509
the Northeast, 662
Shakespeare Country, 320, 330
the South, 206
Thames Valley, 303
Welsh Borders, 399, 402
West Country, 262
Bodelwyddan Castle, 444
Bodiam Castle, 155
Bodleian Library, 287–288
Bodmin, 244
Bodnant Garden, F33, 442–443
Bodysgallen Hall ✕⬚, 444
Bolton Priory, 619
Books and movies, 764–767
Border History Museum, 672–673
Borrowdale, F34, 540–541
Borrowdale Fells, 540
Boscastle, 230
Boston, 599
Bournemouth, 195–197
Bournemouth International Centre, 196
Bourton-on-the-Water, 364–365
Bowes Museum, 663–664
Bowness-on-Windermere, 521–524
Bowood House and Gardens, 350
Box Hill, 146
Bradford, 614–616
Brading, 180
Brading Roman Villa, 180
Braemar, 735

Braemar Castle, 735
Braemar Highland Gathering, 735
Brantwood, 530–531
Brass Rubbing Centre (Edinburgh), 697
Braunton Burrows National Nature Reserve, 228
Brecknock Museum, 461–462
Brecon, 461–463
Brecon Beacons National Park Visitor Centre, 462
Brecon Cathedral, 461–462
Brendon hills, 225
Bridge Cottage, 578
Bridge House, 525
Bridgnorth, 417
Bridlington, 637–638
Bridgewater Hall, 486
Brighton, 134–140
Brighton Festival, 139
Brighton Museum and Art Gallery, 136
Brighton Pier, 132
Brig o'Feuch, 736
Bristol, 212, 214–217, 220
Bristol Zoo Gardens, 215
Britannia (royal yacht), 704
Britannia Inn ✕⬚, 529
British Airways London Eye, 36
British Empire and Commonwealth Museum, 214–215
British Engineerium, 137
British Golf Museum, 713
British Library, 24–25
British Museum, 25–26
Britons Protection, The (pub), 485
Brixham, 245
Broadlands, 177
Broadstairs, 124
Broadway, 358–359
Broadway Dolls and Bears, 358
Broadway Tower Country Park, 358
Brodie Castle, 745
Brontë Parsonage Museum, 617
Brontë Waterfall, 617
Broughton Castle, 327
Brown's ✕, 401
Buckden, 623
Buckingham Palace, 9
Buckland Abbey, 249
Buckland Manor ✕⬚, 358
Buckler's Hard, 195

Building of Bath Museum, *338*
Builth Wells, *446–447*
Burford, *367*
Burghley House, *595–596*
Burrell Collection, *722*
Burwash, *156*
Bury St. Edmunds, *573–575*
busabe eathai ✕ , *F32, 64*
Bus travel, *F41–F43*
Business hours, *F42*
Butchers Row, *228*
Butler & Wilson (jewelry store), *100*
Butler's Wharf, *36*
Butterfly Farm, *313*
Buttermarket, *115*
Buxton, *499–501*
Buxton Museum, *499–500*
Buxton Opera House, *500, 501*
Buxton's Victorian Guesthouse 🏨 , *500*
Bwlch y Groes, *433*

C

Cabinet War Rooms, *13*
Cadbury Castle, *262*
Cadbury World, *394*
Cadair Idris, *452*
Caernarfon, *438–440*
Caernarfon Castle, *438–439*
Caerphilly Castle, *457*
Café @ All Saints ✕ , *408*
Caledonian Hilton Hotel 🏨 , *708–709*
Calendar of events, *F23–F26*
Calls, The, *611*
Calton Hill, *704*
Cambridge, *551, 554, 556–567*
Camera Obscura, *449, 697*
Cameras and photography, *F43*
Camping, *F57–F58*
Canal wharf, *432*
Canoeing, *244*
Canongate Tolbooth, *697*
Canterbury, *114–117, 120–122*
Canterbury Cathedral, *115–116*
Canterbury Roman Museum, *115*
Canterbury Tales (exhibition), *116*
Capers ✕ , *255*
Captain Cook and Staithes Heritage Centre, *645*

Captain Cook Birthplace Museum, *665*
Captain Cook Memorial Museum, *643*
Car rental, *F43–F44*
Car travel, *F44–F46*
Cardiff, *454–459*
Cardiff Bay, *456*
Cardiff Castle, *454–455*
Cardigan, *466–467*
Cardynham House 🏨 , *F31, 372*
Carfax Tower, *286*
Carisbrooke Castle, *181*
Carlton House Terrace, *13*
Carnaby Street (London), *21–22*
Castell Coch, *457*
Casterbridge Hotel 🏨 , *202*
Castle, The ✕🏨 , *224–225*
Castle Combe, *F36, 348–349*
Castle Cottage ✕🏨 , *436*
Castle Drago, *252*
Castle Fraser, *740*
Castle Howard, *F35, 648–649*
Castle Museum, *626*
Castle Rising, *592*
Castle Trail, *739*
Castlefield Urban Heritage Park, *479*
Castlegate House Gallery, *541*
Castlerigg Stone Circle, *538*
Castles, *117*
  Bath and the Cotswolds, 356–357, 380–381
  East Anglia, 569, 576, 579, 580, 584–585, 592, 597
  Lake District, 517, 533
  Lancashire and the Peaks, 505
  the Northeast, 660, 662, 663, 667, 676, 678–679, 680, 681, 682
  Scotland, 691, 697, 699, 714, 729, 732, 736, 737, 738, 739, 740, 743, 745
  Shakespeare Country, 323–324, 325, 327
  the South, 165, 173, 181, 188, 198
  the Southeast, 125–126, 127, 128, 130, 131, 140, 150, 152, 154–155
  Thames Valley, 269, 272–273
  Wales, 428–429, 435, 438–439, 440, 441–442, 444, 445, 449, 453, 454–455, 457, 460, 465, 467
  Welsh Borders, 405, 406, 413, 417, 420

  West Country, 226 230–231, 240, 241, 245, 252, 253, 258, 262
  Yorkshire, 620, 624, 639, 648–649
Castleton, *505–506*
Cathedral Church of St. Andrew, *221*
Cathedral Church of St. Mary, *242*
Cathedral Close, *184*
Cathedral of St. David, *465–466*
Cathedral of St. Mary, *596–597*
Cathedral of St. Peter, *256*
Caverns, *222, 260, 379, 434, 500, 503, 505–506*
Cawdor Castle, *F35, 745*
Celtica, *451*
Centenary Square (Birmingham), *394*
Central Library (Manchester), *479*
Centre for Alternative Technology, *451*
Ceredigion Museum, *449*
Cerne Abbas, *202*
Cerne Abbey, *202*
Chagford, *251–252*
Changing of the Guard, *F34, 9*
Channel Tunnel, *F46*
Chapel Street, *207*
Charlecote Park, *326*
Charles Dickens Centre, *153*
Charleston, *132*
Charlestown, *242–243*
Chartwell, *152*
Chastleton House, *363–364*
Chatsworth House, *504–505*
Chavenage, *373*
Chawton, *171, 173*
Chedworth Roman Villa, *368*
Cheltenham, *351, 353–355*
Cheltenham Art Gallery and Museum, *353*
Cherhill Down, *190*
Chesil Beach, *203–204*
Chester, *419–421*
Chester Castle, *420*
Chester Cathedral, *420*
Chester Crabwall Manor ✕🏨 , *421*
Chester Zoo, *420*
Chesters Roman Fort, *675*
Chewton Glen ✕🏨 , *196–197*
Chichester, *141–143*
Chichester Cathedral, *142*
Children, attractions for, *F48*

Bath and the Cotswolds, 350, 356, 358, 365, 372, 379
East Anglia, 570–571, 576, 584–585, 597
Lake District, 521, 522, 533–534, 537, 541
Lancashire and the Peaks, 480–481, 491–492, 503, 504–505
London, 13, 17, 22, 23, 25–26, 30, 32–33, 36, 37, 38, 40, 43–44, 46, 47, 49, 50, 51, 92
the Northeast, 664, 668
Scotland, 697, 700, 731, 734
Shakespeare Country, 313, 316, 321, 323–324
the South, 171, 174–175, 180, 189–190, 194, 201, 205
the Southeast, 117, 120, 125–126, 129, 131, 136, 137, 155
Thames Valley, 272–273, 287, 299, 301
Wales, 432–433, 435, 438, 439, 440, 443, 449–450, 451, 456–457
Welsh Borders, 395, 396, 409, 410, 415–416, 420
West Country, 214–215, 223, 239, 240, 246, 253, 261–262
Yorkshire, 611, 615, 617, 628–629, 636–637, 639
Children,traveling with, F46–F48
Chilford Hall, 557
Chilham, 123
Chipping Campden, 359–361
Chirk, 428–429, 432
Chirk Castle, 428–429
Christ Church, 286
Christ Church Picture Gallery, 286–287
Christchurch Gate, 115
Christ's College, 557
Church of King Charles the Martyr, 148
Church of St. Botolph, 599
Church of St. Mary, 373
Church of St. Mary and St. Nicholas, 440
Church of St. Mary Redcliffe, 212, 214
Church of St. Peter and St. Paul, 572
Churches
Bath and the Cotswolds, 356, 359, 366, 367, 369, 373, 375–376
East Anglia, 558, 559,

567–568, 570, 572, 573, 577, 584, 586, 594–595, 596–597, 599
Lancashire and the Peaks, 480, 481, 490, 492
London, 17–18, 19–20, 31–32, 40
the Northeast, 659
Scotland, 699, 700, 713–714, 718, 734
Shakespeare Country, 313, 314–315, 323, 326
the South, 164, 165, 182–184, 188, 196, 197
the Southeast, 115–116, 142, 144, 148, 153–154
Thames Valley, 280, 286, 288, 296, 299
Wales, 440, 456, 461–462, 465–466
Welsh Borders, 393, 395, 396, 400–401, 406, 407, 408, 411, 412–413, 420
West Country, 212, 214, 221, 242, 256
Yorkshire, 629–630, 636, 638, 639, 642–643, 647–648
Churchyard at Lyndhurst, 193
Cider Museum, 408
Cilgerran Castle, 467
Cinderford, 379
Circus, the (Bath), 340
Cirencester, 369–371
City Art Gallery (Leeds), 611
City Chambers (Glasgow), 716
City Fish Bar ✕, F31, 121
City Hall (Norwich), 586
City Mill (Winchester), 165–166
City Museum (Winchester), 165
City of Birmingham Symphony Orchestra, 399
City walls (York), 626, 628
Civic Centre, 455
Clandon Park, 145
Clans, 744
Clarence House, 14
Claridge's ⌂, 78
Clearwell Caves, 379
Clifford's Tower, 628
Clifton Suspension Bridge, 215
Climate, F22
Clink (prison), 36–37
Cliveden, 278–279
Cliveden ✕⌂, F30, 278
Close, 164
Clouds Hill, 198–199

Clovelly, F36, 229
Club Gascon ✕, 56
Cobb, The, 205
Cockermouth, 541–542
Cockington, 254–255
Colchester, 576–577
Colchester Castle Museum, 576
Coleford, 379–380
Collegiate Church of St. Mary, 323
Commandery, 401
Community Heritage and Cordell Museum, 460
Compton Verney, 326
Compton Wynyates, 327
Computers on the road, F48
Coniston, 530–531
Coniston Water, 530
Constitution Hill, 449
Consumer protection, F48
Conwy, 441–443
Conwy Castle, F34, 441–442
Corbridge, 675–676
Corbridge Roman Site, 675–676
Corfe Castle, 198–199
Corgarff Castle, 738
Corinium Museum, 369
Cotehele House and Quay, 249–250
Cotswold Motor Museum and Toy Collection, 365
Cottages, F58
Coughton Court, 329
County Hall Travel Inn Capital ⌂, F31, 81
Courtauld Institute Gallery, 22
Courthouse, 440
Covent Garden Hotel ⌂, F30, 72
Covent Garden Piazza, 22
Coventry, 325–326
Coventry Cathederal, 326
Covered Market, 463
Cow, The ✕, 61
Cowes, 178–179
Cragside, 677
Craigievar Castle, 740
Craster, 680
Crathes Castle, 736
Credit cards, F62
Crescent, 499
Criccieth, 435
Cricket, 91, 292, 399
Crickhowell, 461
Cross Keys ✕, 730
Crown and Castle ✕⌂, 580
Cruise travel, F48

Culloden Moor, *743, 745*
Cumberland Hotel, *196*
Cumberland Pencil Museum, *537*
Cumberland Toy and Model Museum, *541*
Currency, *F62*
Custom House, *257*
Customs and duties, *F48–F50*
Cutty Sark (historic ship), *49*

D

Da Vinci's ⊡, *669*
Dalemain, *535*
Dales Countryside Museum, *623–624*
Dairy Guest House ⊡, *F31, 632–633*
Danby, *646*
Dane John Mound, *120*
Darlington, *664–665*
Darlington Railway Centre and Museum, *665*
Dartington Hall (arts center), *253–254*
Dartmoor National Park, *248–249*
Dartmouth, *252–253*
D-Day Museum, *174*
Deal, *125*
Deal Castle, *125*
Dean Heritage Centre, *379*
Dedham, *F36, 577–578*
Denbigh, *444–445*
Denbigh Castle, *445*
Derwentwater, *537–538*
Design Museum, *37*
Devil's Bridge, *448, 449–450*
Devonshire Arms ✕⊡, *619*
Devonshire Royal Hospital, *499*
Dickens House, *26*
Dickens House Museum, *124*
Dimbola Lodge, *181*
Dining, *F52–F54, 57*
Dinosaur Museum, *201*
Dinosaurland Fossil Museum, *205*
Disabilities & accessibility, *F50–F51*
Discounts and deals, *F51–F52*
air travel, F38–F39
bus travel, F43
car rental, F44
lodging, F60
in London, 105
in Scotland, 749
train travel, F70–F71

in Yorkshire, 650–651
in Wales, 469
Discovery Museum, *668*
Dr. Johnson's House, *29*
Dolgellau, *452*
Donmar Warehouse (theater), *90*
Dora's Field, *527*
Dorchester, The ⊡, *F30, 78–79*
Dorchester, *199–202*
Dorchester Abbey, *296*
Dorchester-on-Thames, *296–297*
Dorking, *146*
Dormy House Hotel ✕⊡, *358–359*
Dorset County Museum, *200*
Dove, The ⊡, *139*
Dove Cottage, *528*
Dover, *125–126*
Dover Castle, *125–126*
Dozmary Pool, *244–245*
Drunken Duck Inn ✕⊡, *F32, 532*
Drusilla's Park, *131*
Dryburgh Abbey, *727*
Dudley, *410*
Dunstanburgh Castle, *680*
Dunster, *225*
Dunster Castle, *225*
Durham, *656–657, 659–662*
Durham Castle, *660*
Durham Cathedral, *F34, 659*
Dutch Quarter, *577*
Dylan Thomas Center, *463*

E

E & O ✕, *62*
Eagle, The ✕, *F33, 57*
East Anglia, *548, 550–551, 554, 556–602*
children, attractions for, 570–571, 576, 584–585, 597
Colchester & the Aldeburgh Coast, 575–583
essential information, 599–602
From Ely to Bury St. Edmunds, 567–575
hotels, 563–565, 568, 569, 570, 571, 572, 574–575, 577, 578, 579, 580, 581–582, 583, 587, 589, 590–591, 592–593, 598
itinerary recommendations, 549
Lincoln, Boston & Stamford, 593–599

nightlife & the arts, 565–566, 575, 582, 587, 593, 598
Norwich to North Norfolk, 583–593
outdoor activities and sports, 566, 587–588, 591
pleasures and pastimes, 551
price categories, 550
restaurants, 562–563, 568, 570, 571, 572, 574–575, 577, 578, 579, 580, 581, 583, 586–587, 589, 590–591, 592–593, 598
shopping, 566–567, 588, 598
East Bergholt, *577*
East Grinstead, *147*
Eastbridge Hospital of St. Thomas, *116*
Eastnor Castle, *405*
Eating and drinking, *F52–F54, 57, 225*
Edale, *506–507*
Eden Project, *F33, 243*
Edinburgh, *692–693, 696–697, 699–713*
Edinburgh Castle, *697, 699*
Edinburgh Zoo, *699*
Ednam House Hotel, *729*
Egypt Centre, *463*
Elan Valley, *448*
Electric Brasserie ✕, *61–62*
Electricity, *F54*
Elgar Birthplace Museum, *403*
Elizabethan Moot Hall, *581*
Elm Hill, *586*
Elterwater, *529–530*
Ely, *567–568*
Ely Cathedral, *567–568*
Embassies, *F54*
Emergencies, *F55*
Bath and the Cotswolds, 382
and car travel, F45
East Anglia, 600
Lake District, 544
Lancashire and the Peaks, 509
London, 105
the Northeast, 684
Scotland, 749
Shakespeare Country, 330
the South, 207
the Southeast, 157
Thames Valley, 303
Wales, 469
Welsh Borders, 422
West Country, 263
Yorkshire, 651
Emmanuel College, *557*
Endeavour ✕⊡, *645*
Etiquette & behavior, *F54–F55*

Eton, *275–276*
Eton College, *276*
Ettington Park Hotel ✕⌂, *327–328*
Ewelme, *283*
Exeter, *255–259*
Exmoor National Park, *225*
Explosion!, *175*
Express by Holiday Inn ⌂, *F31, 495–496*

F

Fabric (dance club), *83*
Fairfax House, *628*
Fairyhill ✕⌂, *464*
Falcon, *622*
Falkirk Wheel, *704*
Falkland Arms ✕⌂, *362–363*
Falmouth, *239–240*
Farmhouses, *F58*
Farne Islands, *680–681*
Fat Duck ✕, *273*
Faversham, *123–124*
Feather's, The ✕⌂, *294*
Ferries, *F41–F42, 49.* ⇨ *Also* Boating and boat travel
Festival of Literature, *355*
Festivals and seasonal events, *F23–F26, 757–758*
 Bath and the Cotswolds, 348, 355
 East Anglia, 566, 582, 593
 Lake District, 515, 539
 Lancashire and the Peaks, 501
 Scotland, 691, 710–711, 725
 Shakespeare Country, 320
 the South, 186
 Thames Valley, 279, 291
 Wales, 441, 446, 447
 Welsh Borders, 402, 403, 404, 414, 417, 419
 West Country, 224, 259
 Yorkshire, 633, 635, 644
Ffestiniog Railway, *435*
Figure of a giant, *202*
Film, *87–88, 486, 539*
Fischer's ✕⌂, *502*
Fishbourne Roman Palace, *143*
Fishguard, *466*
fish! ✕, *65*
Fishing, *539*
Fitzwilliam Museum, *557–558*
Flambards Theme Park, *239*
Flamborough Head, *638*
Flatford Mill, *578*
Fleet Air Arm Museum, *261–262*
Floors Castle, *F35, 729*

Florence Nightingale Museum, *37*
Floris (gift shop), *100*
Fodor's Choice, *F30–F36*
Folk Museum, *558*
Football, *91, 486–487, 496–497*
Fordwich, *122*
Forest of Dean, *378*
Fort George, *745*
Fortnum & Mason (gift shop), *100*
Fountains Abbey, *635–636*
Fowey, *243–244*
Fox, The ✕, *100*
Framlingham Castle, *579*
Framwellgate Bridge, *661*
Frogshole Oast ⌂, *155*
Fydell House, *599*

G

G. R. Pratley (shop), *402*
Gainsborough's House, *569–570*
Gaol, *440*
Gardens, *F27*
 Bath and the Cotswolds, 338, 339, 350, 361, 371, 374
 East Anglia, 562, 569, 573–574
 London, 44, 51–52
 Scotland, 705
 Shakespeare Country, 313
 the South, 180, 201
 the Southeast, 144–145, 147, 154–155, 156
 Thames Valley, 288, 293, 298, 300
 Wales, 442–443, 464
 West Country, 249, 256
 Yorkshire, 634
Gardens of the Rose, *300*
Gay and lesbian travel, *F55*
Geevor Tin Mine, *235*
George Square (Glasgow), *718*
George Stephenson's Birthplace, *668*
Georgian House, *704*
Georgian Town House ⌂, *662*
Gerrard Street (London), *22*
Gidleigh Park ✕⌂, *252*
Gladstone's Land, *699*
Glasgow, *715–716, 718–725*
Glasgow Cathedral, *718*
Glasgow Cross, *718*
Glasgow Gallery of Modern Art, *718*
Glasgow School of Art, *718*

Glasgow Science Center, *719*
Glass House ✕, *526*
Glastonbury, *222–224*
Glastonbury Abbey, *223*
Glastonbury Tor, *223*
Glen Muick, *737*
Gloucester, *375–377*
Gloucester Cathedral, *375–376*
Gloucester Folk Museum, *376*
Gloucester and Warwickshire Railway, *356*
Goathland, *643*
God's House Tower, *176*
Gold Hill, *187–188*
 Golden Hinde (galleon), *34*
Golf, *F66–F67*
 Bath and the Cotswolds, 348, 355
 Scotland, 691, 711–712, 714, 738
 the South, 194
 Thames Valley, 282
Goodrich, *406*
Goodrich Castle, *406*
Goods Shed, The ✕, *120–121*
Gordale Scar, *622*
Gordon Ramsay ✕, *53, 56*
Gordon Ramsay at Claridge's ✕, *F31, 61*
Gower Peninsula, *463–464*
Grace Darling Museum, *681*
Grampian Transport Museum, *739–740*
Granary Wharf, *611*
Grand Café ✕, *F33, 289*
Grand Theatre, *613*
Grange, *540*
Grantchester, *558*
Grasmere, *527–529*
Grassington, *620–621*
Grassmarket, *699*
Gravetye Manor ✕⌂, *147*
Great Aberystwyth Camera Obscura, *449*
Great Bookham, *146*
Great Dixter House and Gardens, *156*
Great Hall, *165*
Great Malvern, *403–404*
Great Milton, *297*
Great Orme Mines, *443*
Great St. Mary's, *558*
Greenhead, *673–674*
Greenwich, *49–51*
Greyfriars, *401*
Guild Chapel, *313–314*
Guildford, *144–145*
Guildford Cathedral, *144*

Guildford Museum, *144*
Guildhall (Exeter), *256*
Guildhall (London), *29*
Guildhall (Stratford-upon-Avon), *314*
Guildhall (Worcester), *401*
Guildhall (York), *628*
Guildhall Museum, *599*
Guildhall of Corpus Christi, *571*
Gyms, *91*

H

Haddon Hall, *F35, 502–503*
Hadrian's Wall, *F35, 671*
Hall of Memory, *394*
Halliwell's House Museum, *731*
Hall's Croft, *314*
Hampton Court Palace, *51*
Handel House Museum, *43*
Harbledown, *122–123*
Hardwick Hall, *503–504*
Hardy, Thomas, *200*
Hardy Monument, *204*
Hardy's Cottage, *200*
Harewood House, *614*
Harlech Castle, *435*
Harrods, *43–44, 93*
Harrogate, *634–635*
Harry Potter sites, *F29*
  Alnwick Castle, *678–679*
  Bodleian Library, *287*
  Christ Church, *286*
  Gloucester Cathedral, *375–376*
  King's Cross Station, *26*
  Lacock Abbey, *349*
  London Zoo, *46*
Harvard House, *314*
Hastings, *128–129*
Hastings Castle, *129*
Hatchards (book store), *96*
Hatfield House, *299–300*
Hawes, *623–624*
Hawkshead, *531–532*
Haworth, *616–618*
Hay Festival, *446*
Hay-on-Wye, *446*
Hay's Galleria, *37*
Hayward Gallery, *37–38*
Hazlitt's 🔟, *73*
Health, *F55*
Hedinham Castle, *569*
Heights of Abraham Country Park and Caverns, *503*
Hellens, *405–406*
Helmsley, *647*
Helston, *239*
Helvellyn, *535*

Henley-on-Thames, *280–282*
Henley-in-Arden, *322*
Henley Royal Regatta, *269*
Herbie's ✕, *258*
Hereford, *407–408*
Hereford Cathedral, *407*
Heron Lodge 🔟, *319–320*
Herstmonceux Castle, *130*
Hever Castle, *150, 152*
Hexham, *672–673*
Hexham Abbey, *672*
Hibiscus ✕, *F31, 418*
Hidcote Bartrim, *361–362*
Hidcote Manor Gardens, *F33, 361–362*
High Force, *664*
High Kirk of St. Giles, *699–700*
High Street Gate (Salisbury), *184*
Highlands. ⇨ *See* Scotland: Edinburgh to the Highlands
Hiking. ⇨ *See* Walking
Hill Top, *532*
Himalayan Gurkha Restaurant ✕, *149*
Historic buildings, accommodations in, *F58*
Historic Dockyard, *154*
HMS Belfast (historic ship), *38*
HMS Victory (historic ship), *174*
HMS Warrior (historic ship), *174*
Hoe, *246*
Holburne Museum, *340*
Holidays, *F56*
Holkham Hall, *F35, 590*
Hollytrees Museum, *576*
Holy Trinity Church (Long Melford), *570*
Holy Trinity Church (Straford-upon-Avon), *314–315*
Home exchanges, *F58*
Honister Pass, *541*
Honiton, *260–261*
Horn of Plenty ✕🔟, *250*
Horse Guards Parade, *14*
Horse racing, *355, 402, 497*
Horseback riding, *251, 672*
Horsted Place ✕🔟, *132*
Hoste Arms ✕🔟, *590*
Hostels, *F59*
House in the Clouds, *581*
Hotel Maes-y-Neuadd ✕🔟, *436*
Hotel Portmeirion ✕🔟, *436*

Hotels, *F59.* ⇨ *Also under specific areas and regions*
  grading system, F59
  price categories, F57
Houghton Hall, *591*
Houses of Parliament (London), *14–15, F34*
Housesteads Roman Fort, *675*
Howard's House ✕🔟, *185–186*
Howe Keld 🔟, *539*
Humblebee Wood, *356*
Hungerford Bridge, *38*
Hunterian Art Gallery, *721*
Hunterian Museum, *721*
Huntly House, *700*
Hutcheson's Hall, *719*
Hutton-le-Hole, *647*
Hyde Park, *44*

I

Ice-skating, *91–92*
Ickworth Hotel ✕🔟, *574–575*
Ickworth House, *574*
Ightham Mote, *F35, 153*
Ikon Gallery, *394–395*
Imperial, The 🔟, *255*
Imperial War Museum, *38*
Imperial War Museum Duxford, *558*
Imperial War Museum North, *479*
Industrial Museum and Horses at Work, *615*
Innerleithen, *731*
Institute of Contemporary Arts, *15*
Insurance, *F56*
International Convention Centre, *395*
International Festival, *635*
International Musical Eisteddfod, *433*
Inverness, *740–742*
Inverness Museum and Art Gallery, *741*
Ireland's Mansion, *411*
Ironbridge Gorge, *415–417*
Ironbridge Gorge Museum, *415–416*
Isle of Portland, *203–204*
Isles of Scilly, *237*
Ivy, The ✕, *58*

J

Jack the Ripper's London, *29*
Jane Austen Centre, *341–342*

Jane Austen's House, *171, 173*
Jarrow, *670*
Jazz Café (jazz club), *84*
Jedburgh, *729–730*
Jedburgh Abbey, *730*
Jedburgh Castle Jail, *730*
Jesus College, *559*
Jewellery Quarter (Birmingam), *395, 399–400*
Jogging, *712*
John Knox House, *700*
John Rylands Library, *479–480*
Jolly Fisherman ✕, *680*
Jorvik, *628–629*
Juniper ✕, *482*

K

Kalpna ✕, *F33, 708*
Keighley & Worth Valley Railway, *617*
Keith Harding's World of Mechanical Music, *366–367*
Kelmscott Manor, *295*
Kelso, *729*
Kelvingrove Park, *721*
Kendal, *516–517, 520–521*
Kendal Museum, *517*
Kenilworth Castle, *325*
Kennett Stone Avenue, *191*
Kensington Gardens, *44*
Kensington Palace, *44–45*
Kensington Palace Gardens, *45*
Kentwell Hall, *570–571*
Keswick, *537–540*
Keswick Museum and Art Gallery, *537*
Keswick-on-Derwentwater Launch, *537–538*
Kettle's Yard, *559*
Kettlewell, *622–623*
Kew Gardens, *F33, 51–52*
Kielder Castle, *676*
Kielder Water, *676*
Kildrummy Castle, *739*
Kildrummy Castle Hotel ✕⌂, *739*
Kilpeck, *406–407*
Kilpeck Church, *406–407*
King Harry Ferry, *240–241*
King's Arms Hotel, *623*
King's College, *734*
King's College Centre, *735*
King's College Chapel, *559*
King's Cross Station, *26*
King's Gate, *164–165*

King's Lynn, *591–592*
King's Lynn Arts Centre, *592*
Kingston Lacy, *197–198*
Kirk of the Greyfriars, *700*
Knaresborough, *635*
Knole, *F35, 152*
Kynance Cove, *239*

L

La Poule au Pot ✕, *60*
Lacock, *F36, 349–350*
Lacock Abbey, *349–350*
Laing Gallery, *667*
Lake Country House ✕⌂, *447*
Lake District, *511–517, 520–546*
children, attractions for, 521, 522, 533–534, 537, 541
essential information, 542–546
hotels, 520, 523–524, 526, 528,529, 530, 531, 532, 534, 535–536, 538–539, 540, 541, 542
itinerary recommendations, 513
nightlife and the arts, 520, 539
outdoor activities and sports, 524, 526, 529, 530, 531, 532, 539
Penrith and the North Lakes, 533–542
pleasures and pastimes, 515
price categories, 514
restaurants, 517, 520, 522–524, 526, 528–529, 531, 532, 534, 535–536, 538–539, 540, 541, 542
shopping, 520–521, 524, 529, 534, 539–540
Southern Lakes, 516–517, 520–532
Lake District National Park Information Centre, *540*
Lake District National Park Visitor Centre at Brockhole, *525*
Lakeside & Haverthwaite Railway Company, *522*
Lake Vyrnwy Hoel ✕⌂, *434*
Lamb House, *127*
Lambeth Palace, *38*
Lamperts Cottage ⌂, *F31, 202*
Lancashire and the Peaks, *472–478, 479–510*
children, attractions for, 480–481, 491–492, 503, 504–505
essential information, 507–510

hotels, 483–485, 494–496, 500–501, 502, 503, 506
itinerary recommendations, 473
nightlife and the arts, 485–486, 496, 501
outdoor activities and sports, 486–487, 496–497, 503
Peak District, 497, 499–507
pleasures and pastimes, 475
price categories, 474
restaurants, 482–483, 493–494, 500, 502, 503, 505
shopping, 487, 497, 501
Landgate Bistro ✕, *127*
Land's End, *235–236*
Land's End Experience (theme park), *236*
Lanes, the, *136*
Langs ⌂, *723*
Lanhydrock, *F35–F36, 244*
Launceston, *245*
Launceston Castle, *245*
Lavenham, *F36, 571–572*
Lavenham Priory ⌂, *572*
Le Champignon Sauvage ✕, *353*
Le Gallois ✕, *457*
Le Gavroche ✕, *61*
Le Manoir aux Quat' Saisons ✕, *F32, 297*
Le Petit Blanc (Oxford) ✕, *289*
Le Petit Blanc ✕, *396–397*
Le Pont de al Tour ✕, *65*
Le Poussin at Parkhill ✕⌂, *193–194*
Le Talbooth ✕, *578*
Ledbury, *405*
Leeds, *610–614*
Leeds Castle, *154*
Legoland, *273*
Leicester Square, *22*
Leighton House, *45*
Levens Hall, *517*
Lewes, *131–133*
Lewes Castle, *131*
Liberty (department store), *96*
Libraries
Lancashire and the Peaks, 479–480
London, 24–25
Scotland, 700–701
Thames Valley, 287–288
Wales, 448–449
Welsh Borders, 407
Library House ⌂, *416*
Lichfield Cathedral, *395*
Life Science Centre, *668*

Lighthouse (Glasgow), *719*
Lime Street Station, *491*
Lincoln, *596–598*
Lincoln Castle, *597*
Lincoln's Inn, *26*
Lindisfarne (Holy Island), *682*
Lindisfarne Castle, *682*
Lindisfarne Priory, *682*
Linley Sambourne House, *45–46*
Linn of Dee, *738*
Little Hall, *571*
Little Moreton Hall, *499*
Liverpool, *487–497*
Liverpool's Historic Waterfront, *491*
Lizard Peninsula, *239*
Llanberis, *438*
Llanberis Pass, *438*
Llandaff, *456*
Llandrindod Wells, *447–448*
Llandudno, *443–444*
Llanerchaeron, *450*
Llangollen, *432–433*
Llangollen Railway, *432–433*
Llechwedd Slate Caverns, *434*
Lloyds ✕ , *120*
Lloyd's of London, *30*
Locanda Locatelli ✕ , *F32, 61*
Loch Ness, *742–743*
Loch Ness 2000, *743*
Lodge at Daviot Mains, The 🏨 , *742*
Lodging, *F56–F60.* ⇨ *Also* Hotels
London, *2–9, 13–53, 56–69, 72–93, 96–109*
afternoon tea, 67
Bloomsbury and Legal London, 23–27
children, attractions for, 13, 17, 22, 23, 25–26, 30, 32–33, 36, 37, 38, 43–44, 46, 47, 49, 50, 51, 92
the City, 27–34
essential information, 102–109
hotels, 67–69, 72–81
Hyde Park, 44
itinerary recommendations, 3–4
Kensington, Knightsbridge and Mayfair, 41–48
nightlife and the arts, 82–90
outdoor activities and sports, 90–92
parks, 17, 44, 47
pleasures and pastimes, 7–8
price categories, 52, 68
pubs, 7, 65–67

restaurants, 52–53, 56–65
shopping, 43–44, 92–93, 96–102
Soho and Covent Garden, 20–23
South Bank, 34–41
Thames River, 48–52
Westminster & Royal London, 6, 8–9, 13–20
London Aquarium, *38*
London Dungeon, *38–39*
London Zoo, *46*
London's Transport Museum, *23*
Long Bridge, *184–185*
Long Man of Wilmington, *131*
Long Melford, *570–571*
Longleat House, *189–190*
Lord Leycester Hospital, *323*
Lord's (cricket), *91*
Lower Broadheath, *403*
Lower Slaughter, *F36, 365–366*
Lowry, The, *480*
Lowry Hotel, The 🏨 , *F30, 483*
Lucy's on a Plate ✕ , *526*
Ludlow, *F36, 417–419*
Ludlow and the Marches Food Festival, *417*
Ludlow Castle, *417*
Luggage, *F63*
Lumley Castle Hotel 🏨 , *F30, 666*
Lydford Gorge, *250–251*
Lyme Regis, *204–206*
Lyndhurst, *193–194*
Lynton & Lynmouth, *227–228*
Lypiatt House 🏨 , *355*

M

Machynlleth, *451*
Madame Tussaud's, *46*
Magdalen College (Oxford), *287*
Magdalene College (Cambridge), *559–560*
Magna, *612*
Magpie Café ✕ , *F32, 643–644*
Maiden Castle, *202–203*
Mail and shipping, *F60*
Main Street (Haworth), *616–617*
Malham, *621–622*
Malmaison ✕🏨 , *612–613*
Manchester, *474–477, 479–487*
Manchester Art Gallery, *480*

Manchester Cathedral, *480*
Mandarin Oriental Hyde Park 🏨 , *77*
Manor House Hotel 🏨 , *349*
Manor House Museum, *574*
Manor houses. ⇨ *See* Stately homes
Mapledurham House, *282–283*
Mappa Mundi and Chained Library Exhibition, *407*
Marcliffe at Pitfodels 🏨 , *735*
Marischal College, *734*
Maritime museums
Lancashire and the Peaks, 491–492
London, 49–50
Scotland, 734
the South, 174–175, 176, 195
West Country, 240
Maritime Quarter, *463*
Market Hall, *359*
Market House, *373*
Market Place (Alnwick), *678*
Market Place (Hexham), *672*
Market Place (Norwich), *586*
Market Square (Salisbury), *184*
Market Square (Dorchester), *199–200*
Marlborough, *191–192*
Marlow, *279–280*
Martins ✕ , *706–707*
Mary Arden's House, *321–322*
Mary, Queen of Scots House, *730*
Mary Rose (historic ship), *174*
Mathew Street, *491*
Matlock, *503*
Matlock River Illuminations, *503*
Maumbury Rings, *200*
Max Gate, *200*
Mayflower Park and the Pilgrim Fathers' Memorial, *176*
Mayflower Steps, *246*
McCoy's Rooftop Restaurant ✕ , *668*
McLellan Galleries, *721*
Meal plans, *F56–F57*
Media, *F60–F61*
Medieval Bishop's Palace, *597*
Medieval city walls (Canterbury), *117*
Melford Hall, *570*
Melrose, *726–727*
Melrose Abbey, *726–727*

Melton's ✕, 631
Mendips, 491
Mercat Cross, 700
Merchant Adventurers' Hall, 629
Merchant House, The ✕, F32, 418
Merchant's House, 246
Mermaid, The ✕, 127
Merseyside Maritime Museum, 491–492
Metropolitan, The 🖾, 79
Metropolitan Cathedral of Christ the King, 492
Middlesbrough, 665
Middlethorpe Hall 🖾, F30, 631
Midsummer House ✕, 562
Milecastle Inn ✕, F33, 674
Millennium Bridge, 30
Millennium Stadium, 456
Miller's Residence 🖾, 69
Minack Theatre, 236
Minster Yard, 597
Mr. Underhill's ✕🖾, 418
Model Railway Exhibition, 365
Model Village, 365
Mol's Coffee House, 256
Momo ✕, 63
Mompesson House, 184
Money matters, F61–F62
Monk's House, 132
Montacute House, 261
Monument, 30
Moors Centre, 646
Moot Hall, 540
Moray Place, 704
Moreton-in-Marsh, 362–363
Morwellham Quay, 250
Mother Shipton's Cave, 635
Mousehole, 236
Movies and books, 764–767
Moyse's Hall, 574
Much Marcle, 405–406
Much Wenlock, 415
Mulberry Hall (shop), 633
Museum in Docklands, 30
Museum in the Park, 372
Museum of Archaeology and Anthropology, 560
Museum of Bath at Work, 342
Museum of Canterbury, 116–117
Museum of Childhood, 700
Museum of Childhood Memories, 440
Museum of Costume and Assembly Rooms, 342
Museum of Dartmoor Life, 251

Museum of East Asian Art, 342
Museum of Lakeland Life, 516–517
Museum of Liverpool Life, 492
Museum of London, 28, 30
Museum of Science and Industry, 480
Museum of the History of Science, 287
Museum of the Jewellery Quarter, 395
Museum of the Quakers, 452
Museum of Transport, 721
Museum of Welsh Life, 456–457
Museum of the Welsh Woolen Industry, 467
Museums
  Bath and the Cotswolds, 338, 340, 341, 344–345, 349, 353, 365, 372, 376
  East Anglia, 557–558, 560, 568, 571, 574, 576, 577, 578, 582, 584–585, 586, 590, 592, 595, 597–598, 599
  Lake District, 516–517, 525, 528, 530, 533, 537, 541
  Lancashire and the Peaks, 479, 480–481, 482, 490, 492, 493, 499–500
  London,15–17, 18, 19, 20, 23, 25–26, 29, 30, 37, 38, 40–41, 43, 46, 47–48
  the Northeast, 661, 663, 664, 665, 666, 667, 668, 670, 672–673, 681
  Scotland, 700, 702, 704–705, 706, 713, 718, 719, 720, 721, 731, 734, 739–740, 741, 745
  Shakespeare Country, 316, 324
  the South, 165, 171, 173, 174, 176, 184, 191, 194, 195, 196, 197, 200, 201, 205
  the Southeast, 115, 116–117, 124, 126–127, 131, 136, 137, 142, 143, 144, 148
  Thames Valley, 281, 286–287, 299
  Wales, 438, 439, 440, 447, 449, 451, 452, 453, 455–456, 457, 460, 462, 463, 464
  Welsh Borders, 393, 395, 401, 403, 408, 409, 410, 412, 413, 415–416, 420
  West Country, 214–215, 223, 234, 237, 240, 242, 246, 251, 256, 259, 260, 261–262

  Yorkshire, 611–612, 615, 617, 623–624, 626, 628–629, 630, 634, 639, 643, 645, 647
Music, F27, 757. ➪ Also Festivals and seasonal events
  Lancashire and the Peaks, 485–486
  London, 85–86
  the Northeast, 669
  Scotland, 711, 725
  the South, 197
  Thames Valley, 291
  Wales, 433
  Welsh Borders, 396, 399
  Yorkshire, 633, 644
Myddleton Arms, 445
myhotel bloomsbury 🖾, 74

N

Nairn, 745–746
Nant Gwetheyrn, 435–436
Nash's House and New Place, 315
National Botanic Garden of Wales, 464
National Film Theatre, 39
National Gallery, 15–16
National Gallery of Scotland, 704–705
National Library of Scotland, 700–701
National Library of Wales, 448–449
National Marine Aquarium, 246
National Maritime Museum (London), 49–50
National Maritime Museum Cornwall, 240
National Museum and Gallery, 455–456
National Museum of Photography, Film, and Television, 615
National Park Centre (Grassington), 621
National Park Information Centre (Edale), 507
National parks, 225, 248–249, 263, 428, 462, 469, 507, 509, 544, 621, 651
National Portrait Gallery, 16
National Railway Museum, 629
National Sea Life Centre, 395

National Trust properties and historic houses. ⇨ See Stately homes
Natural History Museum, 46–47
Natural Waterways Museum, 376
Nature in Art, 376
Needles, the, 181
Neidpath Castle, 732
Nelson's Column, 16
Net shops, 128
New Alresford, 171
New College, 286
New Forest, 193
New Hall 🖾, 397–398
New Room, 214
New Royal Brierley Experience, 410
Newby Hall, 636–637
Newcastle upon Tyne, 666–669
Newlyn, 236
Newquay, 233
Norman castle (Newcastle-upon-Tyne), 667
North Sea Fish Restaurant ✕, 53
North Yorkshire Moors Railway, 643
the Northeast, 654–656, 659–685
children, attractions for, 664, 668
Durham, Newcastle, and environs, 656–657, 659–670
essential information, 683–685
Far Northeast Coast, 678–683
Hadrian's Wall Country, 670–678
hotels, 661–662, 664–665, 666, 669, 673, 674, 676, 677–678, 679, 681, 683
itinerary recommendations, 655
nightlife and the arts, 662, 669, 673
outdoor activities and sports, 657, 662, 672, 676
pleasures and pastimes, 657
price categories, 656
restaurants, 661, 664, 665, 666, 668–669, 673, 674, 677–678, 679, 680, 681, 683
shopping, 662, 679, 680
Northleach, 366–367
Northumberland National Park Visitor Centre, 677
Norwich, 583–588
Norwich Castle, 584–585

Norwich Cathedral, 584
Notting Hill, 47
Number One Guest House 🖾, 126
Number One Royal Crescent, 341, 343
Number 3 🖾, 223
Nutshell, The (pub), 574
Nymans Garden, 147

O

Ocean House 🖾, F31, 582
Offshore (pub), 669
Okehampton, 251
Okehampton Castle, 251
Old Aberdeen, 734
Old Bailey, 30–31
Old Dungeon Ghyll Hotel 🖾, 530
Old Grammar School, 405
Old House, 407
Old Mill, 185
Old Nag's Head, 506–507
Old Parsonage 🖾, 290
Old Post Office, 230
Old Rectory, The 🖾, F31, 230
Old Royal Observatory, 50
Old Sarum, 185
Old Town Gaol, 126
Old Vicarage, The 🖾, 526
Oliver Cromwell's House, 568
Once Brewed National Park Visitor Centre, 674–675
One Aldwych 🖾, F30, 72–73
Opera, 756–757
Bath and the Cotswolds, 355
Lancashire and the Peaks, 501
London, 88
the Northeast, 669
Thames Valley, 291
Yorkshire, 613–614
Orford, 579–580
Orford Castle, 580
Orford Ness, 580
Origins, 585
Orrest Head, 522
Osborne House, 178–179
Outdoor activities and sports, F28–F29, F66–F67. ⇨ Also specific activities
Owain Glyndŵr Centre, 451
Owlpen, 372–373
Owlpen Manor, 373
Oxford Story Exhibition, 287
Oxford University Museum of Natural History, 287
OXO Tower, 39

P

Package deals, F52
Packing, F62–F63
Packwood House, 322
Padstow, 232–233
Painswick, 371–372
Painswick Rococo Garden, 371
Palace of Holyroodhouse, 701
Pallant House, 142
Pannier Market, 228
Pantiles, 148
Paris ✕, 396
Parliament House, 701
Passports, F63–F64
Pavilion, 500
Peak Cavern, 505
Pear Tree Cottage ✕🖾, 321–322
Peebles, 731–732
Pelirocco 🖾, 138–139
Pembroke, 465
Pembroke Castle, 465
Pembroke College, 560
Pendennis Castle, 240
Penlee House Gallery and Museum, 237
Penrith, 533–534
Penrith Castle, 533
Penrith Museum, 533
Penshurst Place, 150
Penzance, 236–238
People's Palace, 719
Perranporth, 233
Pershore, 402–403
Pershore Abbey, 403
Peter Pan (statue), 41
Peterborough, 594–595
Peterborough Cathedral, 594–595
Peterborough Museum and Art Gallery, 595
Peterhouse College, 560
Petersfield, 173
Petworth House, F36, 143–144
Peveril Castle, 505
Pheasant, The ✕🖾, 532
Philharmonic (pub), 496
Philharmonic Hall, 496
Philpot Museum, 205
Pier Head (Liverpool), 492
Pistyll Rhaeadr, 432
Pittville Pump Room, 353
Plas Mawr, 442
Plas Newydd (Llangollen), 432
Plas Newydd (Beaumaris), 441

Plymouth, *246–248*
Plymouth Dome, *246*
Polesden Lacey, *146*
Pollok House, *722*
Pollok Park, *722*
Polmaily House ✕🖾 , *743*
Poole's Cavern, *500*
Porlock, *226–227*
Porlock Hill, *227*
Porlock Weir, *226*
Port Isaac, *231–232*
Porthole Eating House ✕ , *522*
Portchester Castle, *173*
Porthmadog, *434–437*
Portmeirion, *F36, 435*
Portobello Gold 🖾 , *F31, 72*
Portobello Market, *101*
Portsmouth, *173–175*
Portsmouth Historic Dockyard, *174*
Potter, Beatrix, *521, 532*
Potter, Harry, *F29.* ⇨ *Also* Harry Potter sites
Poultry Cross, *184*
Powderham Castle, *248*
Powis Castle, *453*
Powysland Museum, *453*
Prebends Footbridge, *661*
Price categories, *F53, F57*
Bath and the Cotswolds, 334
East Anglia, 550
Lake District, 514
Lancashire and the Peaks, 474
London, 52, 68
the Northeast, 656
Scotland, 690
Shakespeare Country, 308
the South, 162
the Southeast, 112
Thames Valley, 268
Wales, 426
Welsh Borders, 388
West Country, 211
Yorkshire, 606
Priest's House Museum, *197*
Princes Street, *705*
Prior Park, *343*
Priory, *404*
Provand's Lordship, *719*
Providores ✕ , *60*
Provost Ross's House, *734*
Provost Skene's House, *734*
Pubs, *F27–F28*
Pulls Ferry, *584*
Pulteney Bridge, *343*
PumpHouse: People's History Museum, *480–481*
Pump Room, *447*

Punting, *292, 566*
Punting on the river, *F34, 566*

Q

Quantock hills, *225*
Quarry Park, *412*
Quay House, *257*
Queen Elizabeth Country Park, *173*
Queen Mary's Doll's House, *272–273*
Queen Square, *343*
Queens' College, *560–561*
Queen's Cross Church, *719*
Queen's Gallery, *16–17*
Queen's Head Inn ✕🖾 , *534*
Queen's House, *50*
Queen's View, *736*
Queensberry Hotel 🖾 , *F30, 346*
Quince & Medlar ✕ , *541*

R

Raby Castle, *663*
Racine ✕ , *56*
Radcliffe Camera, *287–288*
Radisson SAS 🖾 , *723*
Radnorshire Museum, *447*
Ragley Hall, *329*
Railroads
Bath and the Cotswolds, 356
Lake District, 522
London, 108
the South, 171
the Southeast, 136
Wales, 429, 432–433, 435, 438, 439, 449–450
Welsh Borders, 409
West Country, 253
Yorkshire, 617, 619, 643
Ralph Cross, *646*
Ranger's House, *50*
Ray's Jazz (shop), *97*
Read's ✕ , *123*
Regent's Park, *47*
Real Mary King's Close, *701–702*
Register House, *705*
Restaurant Margaux ✕ , *316*
Restaurants. ⇨ *Also under specific areas and regions*
price categories, F53
Rest rooms, *F64*
Rheged, *533–534*
Riber Hall ✕🖾 , *503*
Richmond, *624–625*
Richmond Castle, *624*

Rievaulx Abbey, *647–648*
Rievaulx Terraces and Temples, *648*
Ripon, *636*
Ripon Cathedral, *636*
River & Rowing Museum, *281*
River Wear, *661*
Robert Smail's Printing Works, *731*
Robin Hood's Bay, *640–641*
Rochester, *153–154*
Rochester Castle, *153*
Rochester Cathedral, *153–154*
Rodmarton Manor, *373*
Rogano ✕ , *F32, 722*
Rollright Stones, *362*
Roman amphitheater, *576*
Roman Army Museum, *673–674*
Roman artifacts
Bath and the Cotswolds, 368
the Northeast, 668, 673–674, 675–676
the South, 180, 200
the Southeast, 125, 143
Thames Valley, 299
Roman Baths, *343–344*
Roman Painted House, *125*
Roman Theater, *299*
Roman Walls, *576*
Romsey, *177–178*
Rosamund the Fair ✕ , *289*
Rosemount Viaduct, *734*
Ross-on-Wye, *406*
Rothbury, *677–678*
Rotunda Museum, *639*
Rougemont Gardens, *256*
Rousham Park House & Garden, *293*
Rowing, *282*
Rowling, J.K., *F29.* ⇨ *Also* Harry Potter sites
Rows (Chester), *419*
Royal Albert Hall, *47, 85*
Royal Albert Memorial Museum, *256*
Royal Armouries (Leeds), *611*
Royal Botanic Garden, *705*
Royal Citadel, *246*
Royal Clarence Hotel, *256, 258*
Royal Cornwall Museum, *242*
Royal Crescent Hotel ✕🖾 , *346*
Royal Exchange, *481*
Royal Family, *13*
Royal Festival Hall, *39*
Royal Liver Building, *492*
Royal Mews, *17*

Royal Mile, 702
Royal Museum of Scotland, 702
Royal National Theatre, 39
Royal Naval College, 50–51
Royal Naval Museum, 174
Royal Opera House, 23, 88
Royal Pavilion, 134–135
Royal Pump Room Museum, 634
Royal Scottish Academy, 705
Royal Shakespeare Theatre, F34, 315, 320
Royal Tunbridge Wells, 148–150
Royal Welsh Agricultural Show, 447
Royal Worcester Porcelain Factory, 401
Rumwong ✕, 145
Runnymede, 276–277
Ruskin Museum, 530
Russell-Cotes Art Gallery and Museum, 196
Ruthin, 445
Ruthin Gaol, 445
Rydal, 527
Rydal Mount, 527
Ryde, 179–180
Rye, 126–128
Rye Castle Museum, 126–127
Rye Treasury of Mechanical Music, 127
Ryedale Folk Museum, 647

S

Saatchi Gallery, 39–40
Sadler's Wells (dance venue, 87
Safety, F64–F65
Saffron Walden, 568–569
Safety, F64–F65
Sainsbury Centre for the Visual Arts, 586
St. Albans, 299–301
St. Albans Cathedral, 299
St. Alkmund's, 411
St. Andrews, 713–714
St. Andrews Castle, 714
St. Andrew's Cathedral, 713–714
St. Anne's Chapel, 228
St. Ann's Church, 481
St. Augustine's Abbey, 117, 120
St. Bride's, 31
St. Chad (Shrewsbury), 412–413

St. Chad's Roman Catholic Cathedral (Birmingham), 396
St. David's, 465–466
St. David's Cathedral, 465–466
St. David's Centre, 456
St. David's Hotel and Spa 🏨, 458
St. Edmundsbury Cathedral, 573
St. George's Church, 115
St. George's Hall, 492
St. Giles's Hill, 166
St. Ives, 233–235
St. Ives Society of Artists Gallery, 234
St. James (church), 359
St. James's Palace, 17
St. James's Park, 17
St. John ✕, F32, 56
St. John Church, 367
St. John the Baptist, 369
St. John's College (Cambridge), 561
St. John's College (Oxford), 288
St. John's House, 324
St. Just in Roseland, 241
St. Margaret's 🏨, F31, 74
St. Martin-in-the-Fields, 17–18
St. Mary (Scarborough), 639
St. Mary (Whitby), 642
St. Mary-le-Bow, 31
St. Mary's (Bury St. Edmunds), 573
St. Mary's (Shrewsbury), 411
St. Mary's Church (Henley-on-Thames), 280
St. Mawes, 241–242
St. Mawes Castle, 241
St. Michael's Mount, 238
St. Mungo Museum of Religious Life and Art, 720
St. Olaves ✕, 258
St. Paul's Cathedral, 31–32
St. Peter and St. Paul, 366
St. Peter Hungate, 586
St. Peter Mancroft, 586
St. Peter's Church (Bournemouth), 196
St. Peter's Church (Winchcombe), 356
St. Thomas's Church, 184
Salisbury, 182–187
Salisbury and South Wiltshire Museum, 184
Salisbury Cathedral, 182–184
view of, F35

Salisbury Festival, 186
Saltaire, 615
Saltram, 248
Samling, The ✕🏨, 523
Sandringham House, 591
Sandwich, 124–125
Savoy, The 🏨, 73
Scafell Pike, 540
Scarborough, 638–640
Scarborough Castle, 639
Scarborough Sea Life Centre, 639
Science Museum, 47
Scotch Whisky Heritage Centre, 702
Scotland: Edinburgh to the Highlands, 687–693, 696–697, 699–716, 718–732, 734–751
Aberdeen and Royal Deeside, 732, 734–629–636
the Borders, 726–629
children, attractions for, 697, 700, 731, 734
essential information, 746–751
hotels, 708–710, 714, 723–724, 727, 729, 730, 731, 732, 735, 736, 737, 738, 739, 741–742, 743, 745–7461
Inverness and Loch Ness, 740–746
itinerary recommendations, 689–690
nightlife and the arts, 710–711, 724–725, 735, 742
outdoor activities and sports, 711–712, 738
pleasures and pastimes, 691–692
price categories, 690
restaurants, 706–708, 714, 722–723, 727, 729, 730, 732, 735, 736, 737, 738, 739, 741–742, 743, 745–746
shopping, 692, 712–713, 725, 735–736, 742, 746
Scotsman, The 🏨, F30, 708
Scott, Sir Walter, 706, 726
Scott Monument, 706
Scottish National Portrait Gallery, 706
Scott's View, 728
Sculpture at Goodwood, 143
Sea Life Centre, 136
Seafood Bar ✕, 240
Seafood Restaurant, The ✕, F32, 232
Seckford Hall 🏨, 579
Sedgemoor, 224

Segedunum Archaeological
Park and Museum, 668
Segontium Roman Museum,
439
Selkirk, 730–731
Senior-citizen travel, F65
Severn Valley Railway, 409
Sezincote, 362
Shaftesbury, 187–188
Shakespeare Country,
305–311, 313–331
Around Shakespeare Country,
321–329
children, attractions for, 313,
316, 321, 323–324
essential information, 329–331
hotels, 317–320, 321–322, 324,
325, 327, 328–329
itinerary recommendations, 307
nightlife and the arts, 320
outdoor activities and sports,
320
pleasures and pastimes, 309
price categories, 308
restaurants, 316–317, 324, 325,
327, 328–329
shopping, 320–321
Stratford-upon-Avon, 308–321
Shakespeare Hotel ☒, 318
Shakespeare's Birthplace, 316
Shakespeare's Birthplace
Trust, 311
Shakespeare's Globe Theatre,
40, 90
Shambles (museum;
Bewdley), 409
Shambles (street; York), 629
Shakespeare Hotel ☒, 318
Sharrow Bay ✕☒, 535–536
Sheldonian Theatre, 288
Shelley's Hotel ☒, 227–228
Sheppy's, 224
Sherborne, 188
Sherborne Abbey, 188
Sherborne Castle, 188
Shopping, F66–F66
Shrewsbury, 411–414
Shrewsbury Abbey, 413
Shrewsbury Castle, 413
Shrewsbury Museum and Art
Gallery, 412
Sidney Sussex College, 561
Silbury Hill, 191
Silk Mill, 360
Silver Darling ✕, 735
Simply Heathcote's ✕, 483
Singleton, 143
Sir John Soane's Museum,
26–27

Sir Walter Scott's Courtroom,
731
Sissinghurst Castle Garden,
F33, 154–155
Sizergh Castle, 517
Sketch ✕, 63
Skipton, 619–620
Skipton Castle, 620
Slimbridge Wildfowl and
Wetlands Trust, 380
Smailholm Tower, 728
Smallest house in Britain, 442
Smeaton's Tower, 246
Smuggler's Adventure, 129
Snowdon Mountain Railway,
438
Snowdonia National Park,
428
Snowshill Manor, 357
Soldiers of Gloucestershire
Museum, 376
Somerset House, 23, 91
Somerset Rural Life Museum,
223
Sonning-on-Thames, 282
Soudley, 378–379
the South, 160–167,
170–171, 173–208
Bournemouth to Lyme Regis,
195–206
children, attractions for, 171,
174–175, 180, 189–190, 194,
201, 205
essential information, 206–208
hotels, 166–167, 170–171, 175,
176–177, 179–180, 181,
185–186, 188, 189, 190,
192, 193–194, 196–197, 198,
199, 201, 202, 203, 204, 205
Isle of Wight, 178–181
itinerary recommendations,
163–164
nightlife & the arts, 177, 186,
197
outdoor activities & sports,
180, 181, 186, 192, 194,
202, 206
pleasures & pastimes, 167
price categories, 162
restaurants, 166–167, 170, 175,
176, 179, 185–186, 189,
190, 191, 193–194, 196–197,
198, 199, 201, 203, 204, 205
Salisbury to the New Forest,
182–195
shopping, 171, 187
Winchester to Southhampton,
162, 164–167, 170–171,
173–178

South Devon Railway, 253
South Wales Borderers'
Museum, 462
the Southeast, 111–117,
120–150, 152–158
Brighton to East Grinstead,
133–147
Canterbury to Dover, 114–117,
120–126
children, attractions for, 117,
120, 125–126, 129, 131,
136, 137, 155
essential information, 156–158
hotels, 121–122, 123–124, 126,
127–128, 129, 130, 131,
132–133, 138–139, 141, 142,
145, 147, 149, 150, 154, 155
itinerary recommendations,
113–114
Masterpieces & Moats,
147–150, 152–156
nightlife & the arts, 122, 124,
124, 133, 139–140, 141,
142–143, 145, 154
price categories, 112
restaurants, 120–121, 123–124,
127, 128, 129, 130,
132–133, 141, 137, 138,
142, 145, 146, 147, 149,
150, 155
Rye to Glyndebourne, 126–133
shopping, 122, 128, 140
sports and the outdoors, 156
Southampton, 175–177
Southampton Maritime
Museum, 176
Southwark Cathedral, 40
Southwold, 582–583
Southwold Museum, 582
Speedwell Cavern, 505–506
Speke Hall and Gardens,
492–493
Spencer House, 18
Spinnaker Tower, 174
Square Orange Cafe ✕,
538
SS Great Britain (historic
ship), 215
Staithes, 644–645
Stamford, 595–596
Standen, 147
Stanton Drew Circles, 220
Stanway House, 357
Stately homes, F35–F36, 117,
151
Bath and the Cotswolds,
341–342, 350, 357, 362,
363–364, 373
East Anglia, 569, 570–571,

574, 581, 588–589, 590, 591, 595–596
Lake District, 517, 521–522, 530–531, 535
Lancashire and the Peaks, 491, 492–493, 499, 502–503, 504–505
London, 13, 18, 23, 26–27, 45–46
the Northeast, 677
Scotland, 700, 701, 726, 731
Shakespeare Country, 314, 315, 322–323, 326, 327, 329
the South, 177, 178–179, 181, 184, 187, 188–190, 194, 197–198, 201
the Southeast, 127, 132, 134–136, 142, 143–144, 145, 146, 147, 150, 152, 153, 156
Thames Valley, 278, 282–283, 293, 295, 297–298, 299–300, 301–302
Wales, 432, 440, 441, 442, 450, 464–465
Welsh Borders, 405–406, 407, 411, 414–415
West Country, 244, 249–250, 254, 261
Yorkshire, 614, 628, 629, 636–637, 639
Statue of Gainsborough, 569
Steine, 134
Stephen Joseph Theatre, 640
Stephenson, George, 668
Stoke-on-Trent: The Potteries, 498
Stokesay Castle, 417
Stonegate, 629
Stonehenge, 192–193
early morning, F34
Stourbridge, 409–410
Stourhead, F33, 188–189
Stourport Steamer Co., 409–410
Stowe Landscape Garden, F34, 298
Stow-on-the-Wold, 315–316
Stranton Derw Circles, 220
Stray, the, 634
Stroud, 372
Stuart Crystal Visitor Centre and Factory Shop, 410
Stuart House 🏠 , 709
Students, F67
Studley Royal, 635–636
Submarine World, 174–175
Sudbury, 569–570
Sudeley Castle, 356–357
Sun Hotel ✕🏠 , 531

Surfing, 233
Sutton Hoo, 579
Swaledale, 624
Swallow Falls, 437
Swan Hotel, 571
Swan-Upping, 279
Swansea, 463–464
Swansea Museum, 463
Swimming, 92
Symbols and icons, F9
Symond's Yat, 406
Symphony Hall, 396

T

Tarn Hows, 532
Tartans, 744
Tate Britain (London), 18
Tate Liverpool, 493
Tate Modern (London), 40–41, 87
Tate St. Ives, 234
Taunton, 224–225
Taxes, F67–F68
Taxis, 106
Techniquest, 456
Teddy Bear Museum (Stratford-upon-Avon), 320
Teifi Valley, 466–467
Telephones, F68–F69
Temple, 27
Temple of Mithras, 32
Temple Newsam, 611–612
Ten Downing Street, 18
Tenby, 464–465
Tenby Museum, 464
Tenement House, 720
Tennis, 92
Terre à Terre ✕ , 137
Tetbury, 373–374
Tewkesbury, 378
Tewkesbury Abbey, 378
T'Gallants 🏠 , F31, 243
Thackray Medical Museum, 611
Thackray's House ✕ , 149
Thames Valley, 266–269, 272–283, 285–304
Blenheim Palace to Althorp, 293–302
children, attractions for, 272–273, 287, 299, 301
essential information, 302–304
hotels, 274–275, 276, 277–278, 280, 281, 282, 289–291, 294, 296–297, 298–299, 300–301
itinerary recommendations, 267

nightlife & the arts, 275, 282, 291–292
outdoor activities & sports, 275, 279, 282, 292
Oxford, 283, 285–293
pleasures and pastimes, 269
price categories, 268
restaurants, 273–274, 276, 278, 279–280, 281, 282, 289, 294, 297, 298, 300–301
shopping, 275, 292–293
Windsor & Environs, 268–269, 272–279
Theater
Bath and the Cotswolds, 344, 348, 355
Lake District, 539
Lancashire and the Peaks, 486
London, 40, 88–90
the Northeast, 662, 669
Scotland, 711, 725, 735, 742
Shakespeare Country, 309, 315, 320
Thames Valley, 292
Welsh Borders, 393, 399
West Country, 220, 236, 248
Yorkshire, 633, 640
Theatre Royal (Bath), 344
Theatre Royal (Richmond), 624
Thermae Bath Spa, 344
Thinktank, 396
Thirsk, 637
Thomas, Dylan, 463
Thornbury Castle ✕🏠 , 381
Thorpeness, 581
Three Hills Roman Heritage Centre 727
Time, F69
Timing the trip, F22
Tintagel, 230–231
Tintagel Castle, F34, 230–231
Tintern Abbey, 457
Tipping, F69
Tombland, 586
Topsham, 259–260
Topsham Museum, 260
Top Withins, 617
Torbay, 254–255
Torre Abbey Mansion, 254
Totnes, 253–254
Totnes Castle, 253
Tours and packages, F69–F70
Tower Bridge, 32
Tower Knowe Visitor Centre, 676
Tower of London, 32–34
Town Hall (Birmingham), 396

Town Hall (Colchester), 576–577
Town Hall (Leeds), 610
Town Hall (Manchester), 481
Trafalgar Square, 18–19
Train travel, F70–F71.
⇨ *Also* Railroads
Transportation around Great Britain, F71–F72
Transporter Bridge, 665
Traquair House, 731
Travel agencies, F72
disabilities and accessibility, F51
Traveler's checks, F62
Treasurer's House, 629
Trelissick, 240–241
Tremadog, 435
Tresanton Hotel 🛏, 241
Tretower Court, 461
Trinity College, 561
Trinity Guildhall, 592
Trinity Hall College, 561
Trouble House ✕,374
Truro, 241
Tudor Merchant's House, 464–465
Tudor Rose, 440
Tunbridge Wells Museum and Art Gallery, 148
Turkish Baths, 634
Tutankhamun Exhibition, 201
20 Forthlin Road (Paul McCartney's house), 493
Tymperley's Clock Museum, 577
Tyne Bridge, 667
Tyntesfield, 216

U

Uffington, 295–296
Ullswater, 535–536
Underground Passages, 256–257
Union Chapel music (club), 84
University Botanic Gardens, 562
University Church of St. Mary the Virgin, 288
University housing, F60
University of Durham Oriental Museum, 661
University of Newcastle upon Tyne, 667
University of Oxford Botanic Garden, 288
Upper Slaughter, 365–366
Urbis, 481
Urquhart Castle, 743
Usher Gallery, 597–598

V

Vale of Ceiriog, 428–429, 432
Vale of Rheidol Railway, 449–450
Vale of the White Horse, 295–296
Valley Gardens, 634
Ventnor, 180
Ventnor Botanic Gardens, 180
Verulamium Museum, 299
Verulamium Park, 299
Vicar's Close, 221
Vicar's Pele, 675
Victoria and Albert Museum, 47–48
Victoria at Holkham ✕🛏, F30, 590
Victoria Quarter, 614
Victorian Festival, 447
Vindolanda, 674–675
Visas, F63–F64
Visitor information, F72–F73
Volk's Electric Railway, 136

W

Waddesdon Manor, 297–298
Walberswick, 582–583
Wales, 425–429, 432–470
children, attractions for, 432–433, 435, 438, 439, 440, 443, 449–450, 451, 456–457
essential information, 467–470
hotels, 432, 433, 434, 436–437, 438, 439, 441, 443, 444, 445, 446, 447–448, 450, 451–452, 453, 458, 460–461, 462, 464, 465, 466, 467
itinerary recommendations, 427
nightlife and the arts, 433, 441, 458–459, 462–463
Mid-Wales, 445–453
North Wales, 428–429, 432–445
outdoor activities and sports, 433, 437, 440, 452, 459, 469
pleasures and pastimes, 429
price categories, 426
restaurants, 432, 434, 436–437, 439, 441, 443, 444, 446, 447, 450, 451–452, 457–458, 460–461, 462, 464, 466
shopping, 446, 459, 463
South Wales, 454–467
Walker Art Gallery, 493
Walking, F67
Bath and the Cotswolds, 339
East Anglia, 551

Lake District, 515, 526, 529, 530, 531
Lancashire and the Peaks, 507, 509
London, 107
the Northeast, 657
Scotland, 691–692
Shakespeare Country, 309
the South, 194
the Southeast, 117
Thames Valley, 269, 304
Wales, 429
Welsh Borders, 389, 415
West Country, 217, 233, 263
Yorkshire, 607
Wallace Collection, 48
Wallington, 677
Walls (Chester), 419
Walmer Castle, 125
Warwick, 323–325
Warwick Castle, 323–324
Warwickshire Doll Museum, 323–324
Washington, 665–666
Washington Old Hall, 665–666
Water sports, 217, 370, 539
Watercress Line, 171
Waterfalls, 432, 535, 617
Weald and Downland Open Air Museum, 143
Weavers' Houses, 116
Web sites, F73
Welford-on-Avon, 328
Wellington Arch, 48
Wellington Barracks, 19
Wells, 221–222
Wells-next-the-Sea, 589–591
Welsh Borders, 386–390, 393–423
children, attractions for, 395, 396, 409, 410, 415–416, 420
essential information, 421–423
hotels, 397–398, 402, 403, 404, 405, 406, 408, 409, 414, 416, 418–419, 420–421
itinerary recommendations, 387
nightlife and the arts, 399, 402, 404, 414, 419
outdoor activities and sports, 399, 402, 415, 422
pleasures and pastimes, 389
price categories, 388
restaurants, 396–397, 401–402, 404, 405, 408, 409, 413–414, 416, 418, 420–421
shopping, 399–400, 402, 408, 410, 414, 421

Shrewsbury to Chester,
410–421
Worcester to Dudley, 400–410
Welsh Highland Railway/
Rheilffordd Eryri, *439*
Welsh Slate Museum, *438*
Welshpool, *453*
Wenlock Priory, *415*
Wensleydale Creamery Visitor
Centre, *623*
West Country, *210–217,*
220–264
Bristol to North Devon,
212–217, 220–229
children, attractions for,
214–215, 223, 239, 240,
246, 253, 261
Cornwall (Coast and Moor),
229–245
essential information, 262–264
hotels, 216–217, 220, 222, 223,
224–225, 227, 228, 229,
230, 232–233, 234–235,
237–238, 239, 240, 241,
242, 243, 244, 245, 248,
250, 251, 252, 253, 255,
258–259, 260, 261
itinerary recommendations,
213–214
nightlife and the arts, 220, 224,
236, 248, 253–254, 259
outdoor activities and sports,
220, 233, 238, 244, 251, 263
pleasures and pastimes, 217
price categories, 211
restaurants, 216–217, 222,
224–225, 227, 228, 229,
230, 232–233, 234–235,
237–238, 239, 240, 241,
242, 243, 245, 247–248,
250, 251, 252, 253, 255,
258–259, 260, 261
shopping, 254, 259, 261
South Devon to Cadbury
Castle, 245–262
West Gate Museum, *117*
West Kennett Long Barrow, *191*
West Register House, *706*
Westminster Abbey, *F35,*
19–20
Westonbirt Arboretum, *374*
Weymouth, *203*
When to travel, *F22*
Whitby, *F36, 641–644*
Whitby Abbey, *642–643*

Whitby Folk Week, *644*
Whitby Museum, *643*
Whiechapel Art Gallery, *87*
White Hart ☒ , *598*
White Horse and Griffon ✕☒,
644
White Horse Inn ✕☒,
123–124
White Moss House ✕☒,
528–529
Whitworth Art Gallery,
481–482
Wigmore Hall (music hall), *86*
William Herschel Museum,
344–345
Willow Tearoom, *720*
Willy Lott's House, *578*
Wilmington, *131*
Wilton, *187*
Wilton House, *187*
Wimborne Minster, *197–198*
Winchcombe, *356*
Winchelsea, *128*
Winchester, *162, 164–167,*
170–171
Winchester Cathedral, *164*
Winchester College, *165*
Windermere, *521–524*
Windermere Steamboat
Centre, *521*
Windsor, *268–269, 272–275*
Windsor Castle, *269,*
272–273
Windsor Great Park, *273*
Winnats Pass, *506*
Wisley, *F34, 144–145*
Witley Court, *408–409*
Woburn Abbey, *301*
Wolseley, The ✕ , *F32, 62–63*
Woodbridge, *578–579*
Wood End, *639*
Woodstock, *293–294*
Wookey Hole Caves, *222*
Worcester, *400–402*
Worcester Cathedral,
400–401
Wordsworth, William, *527,*
528, 536, 541
Wordsworth House, *541*
World of Beatrix Potter, *521*
World of James Herriot, *637*
Wrekin, *415*
Writers' Museum, *702*
Wykeham Arms ✕ , *167, 170*

Y

Y Tabernacl Museum of
Modern Art, *451*
Yalbury Cottage ✕☒ , *201*
Yeovilton, *261–262*
Yes ✕ , *722*
Ynyshir Hall ✕☒ , *451*
York, *625–626, 628–633*
York Minster, *629–630*
Yorkshire, *604–607,*
610–626, 628–652
children, attractions for, 611,
615, 617, 628–629, 636–637,
639
essential information, 649–652
hotels, 612–613, 616, 617–618,
619, 620, 621, 622, 623,
625, 631–633, 634–635, 636,
640, 641, 644, 645, 646,
647
itinerary recommendations, 605
nightlife and the arts, 613–614,
633, 635, 640, 644, 645
North York Moors, 645–649
North Yorkshire Coast,
637–645
outdoor activities and sports,
622, 641, 647
pleasures and pastimes, 607
price categories, 606
restaurants, 612–613, 615–616,
617–618, 619, 620, 621,
622–623, 624, 630–631,
634–635, 638, 639–640, 641,
643–644
shopping, 614, 633
West Yorkshire & Brontë
Country, 607, 610–618
York Environs, 633–637
Yorkshire Dales, 618–625
Yorkshire Museum, *630*
Yang Sing ✕ , *483*
Young Vic (theater), *90*
Ypres Tower, *127*

Z

Zoos
London, 46
Scotland, 699
the Southeast, 131
Welsh Borders, 420
West Country, 215